Making Great

SAUSAGE

LARK BOOKS

ASHEVILLE, NORTH CAROLINA

Making Great

SAUSAGE

30 SAVORY LINKS
FROM AROUND THE WORLD

PLUS DOZENS
OF DELICIOUS
SAUSAGE DISHES

**Chris
Kobler**

JANE LAFERLA
Editor

CHRIS BRYANT
Book and cover design
and production, food styling,
and photostyling

EVAN BRACKEN
Photography

HEATHER SMITH
Editorial assistance

HANNES CHAREN
Production assistance

VAL ANDERSON
Proofreader

Library of Congress Cataloging-in-Publication Data

Kobler, Chris, 1946–
    Making great sausage : 30 savory links from around the world
plus dozens of delicious sausage dishes / by Chris Kobler.—1st ed.
        p. cm.
    Includes bibliographical references and index.
    ISBN 1-57990-131-X (hardcover)
    1. Cookery (Sausages)   2. Sausages.   I. Title
TX749.5.S28K63   1999
    641.6'6—dc21   99-25466
                                                                    CIP

10 9 8 7 6 5 4 3 2 1

First Edition

Published by Lark Books
50 College Street
Asheville, North Carolina 28801
USA

© 1999, Chris Kobler

For information about distribution in the U.S., Canada, the U.K.,
Europe, and Asia, call Lark Books at 828-253-0467.

Distributed in Australia by Capricorn Link (Australia) Pty. Ltd.,
P.O. Box 6651, Baulkham Hills Business Centre, NSW 2153, Australia

Distributed in New Zealand by Southern Publishers Group,
22 Burleigh St., Grafton, Aukland, New Zealand

Printed in China by L. Rex Printing Company, Ltd.

ISBN 1-57990-131-x

acknowledgements

I happily dedicate this book to my daughters, Nora and Emily.

I WISH TO THANK the staff of Lark Books for the vote of confidence in allowing me to write this book. To owner, dance partner, and Capo di tutti Capo, Rob Pulleyn; publisher Carol Taylor; senior editor (and friend) Deborah Morgenthal; editor Jane LaFerla; art director Chris Bryant; and photographer Evan Bracken. Actually, they've all become friends. My tasters-in- waiting (including all of the above) earned my thanks and a guest pass to the gymnasium— you know who you are. I cooked it and you all came. Hand holders and encouragers include Brigid, Bob, Doug and Angela, Pam and Paul, Hank and Marita, and the gang at Gold Hill. Special thanks to Victor Giancola. Thanks also to the Vienna Sausage Company, Neto Sausage Company, Panizzera Meat Company, The National Hot Dog and Sausage Council, the Sheboygan, Wisconsin, Chamber of Commerce and their Bratwurst Days celebration and the New Braunfels, Texas, Chamber of Commerce, and their Best of the Wurst festival.

preface

"ONE CANNOT THINK WELL, LOVE WELL, SLEEP WELL, IF ONE HAS NOT DINED WELL."—Virginia Woolf

Somewhere, in an all-but-forgotten text, I once read that, when what you are doing is what you are, what you are doing is art. I believe that feeding people can be fine art, ephemeral perhaps, but art nonetheless. I have found that I express myself best in this lovely melding of nurture and craft.

"EATING IS NOT MERELY A MATERIAL PLEASURE. EATING WELL GIVES A SPECTACULAR JOY TO LIFE AND CONTRIBUTES IMMENSELY TO GOODWILL AND HAPPY COMPANIONSHIP. IT IS OF GREAT IMPORTANCE TO THE MORALE."— Elsa Schiaparelli

That said, I need also tell you that nothing pleases me quite so much as to find myself well regarded by my fellows. My way of sticking to the ribs of your regard is to feed you meals that you will remember. To correct a superstition of the food-frightened who believe food is merely a substitute for love, I believe that feeding is loving. Thus in feeding you, I offer you intimacy by providing your most basic need—and I wish to do so beautifully.

"AFTER A GOOD DINNER ONE CAN FORGIVE ANYBODY, EVEN ONE'S OWN RELATIONS."—Oscar Wilde

We can, all of us, produce in our own homes all but the most pyrotechnic of dishes. I have discovered in a lifetime of feeding people that wonderful food can be produced by virtually anyone, anywhere, anytime, with easily found ingredients and common tools. I have been able to create wonderful unplanned dinner parties when trapped in dormitories, stranded in beach houses, exiled on camping trips, jungles, deserts, and islands. No matter the locale, we (whoever it was that made the other portion of we) were able to delight ourselves with delicious improvised meals that were precisely rendered.

"ONE HALF OF THE WORLD CANNOT UNDERSTAND THE PLEASURES OF THE OTHER."—Jane Austen, *Emma*, ch. 9 (1816).

It is true that there are people who are food blind (bless their hearts); those unable, or unwilling, to open themselves to new combinations of flavor and texture. There are also finicky eaters, food fanatics, and food police constantly on the prowl for violations against their personal food codes. There are many who claim they are unable to cook. While all of the above may be unlikely to read this book, they are all welcome at my table.

contents

introduction

Myron Floren (left), longtime Lawrence Welk band member, celebrates with friends at The Best of The Wurst Festival held annually in New Braunfels, Texas. Photograph courtesy of the New Braunfels Chamber of Commerce

During Sheboyagn, Wisconsin's Bratwurst Day, cooks turn a large rack of bratwurst that will feed revelers at this annual celebration. Photograph courtesy of the Sheboygan County Chamber of Commerce

sausages are a celebration!

IF YOU DOUBT THIS SIMPLE ACCOLADE, ALLOW YOUR SENSE MEMORY TO ROAM. Picture an Italian street festival. (Little Italy in New York or the North End of Boston immediately come to mind.) Smell the miles of Italian sausage sizzling on the grills in the booths that line the streets. A vendor beckons, places a done-to-perfection beauty in a sliced length of crusty bread, then tops the whole thing off with a blanket of peppers cooked in olive oil.

Conjure up the remembrance of the best hot dog you've ever eaten. Was it at a ball park—a house special smothered in relish and mustard, and washed down with a cold beer and a winning home run? Was it at the beach—a natural accompaniment to sunburn, salt air, and a leisurely stroll on the boardwalk? Or was it the first one you impaled on a stick and roasted over a smoky campfire—which rendered it slightly charred but still delicious beyond belief?

Whether it's bratwurst cooked outside and shared on a steamy summer night with friends and neighbors, Polish sausage so juicy and luscious that you could almost hear the skin crack at first bite, or a simple salami sandwich on white in your lunch box, the remembrances of sausages past are as personal and numerous as the varied experiences of life. But you'll soon find that it's the pleasure of sausage present and future that await you when you learn to make your own.

Today's savvy cooks are rediscovering the craft of sausage making as an important way to sample the best of the world's culinary heritage. Mention home-made sausage and inevitably someone tells how their mother or grandmother made the weekly sausage for the family, or of a cousin who still makes incredible venison sausage once a year, or that they've heard of a family who gathers together to make traditional sausage as a part of their holiday ritual. If these stories have ever inspired you to someday try making your own sausage, now is the time.

A HISTORY

Sausages can be considered an almost perfect food. They combine wonderful herbs and spices, flavorful meats, vegetables, and grains in a natural casing. They can be poached, boiled, steamed, baked, roasted, or grilled. In their charmingly odd package, the ingredients meld when cooked, basted in their own savory juices. Then, when eaten, the contained goodness bursts upon your palate in the most festive way possible. Is it any wonder that many cultures through the centuries have created innumerable local festivals to celebrate, honor, and consume this incredible food?

Sausages have been with us for a very long time. The word comes from Latin, *salsicius*, meaning prepared by salting, which is a simple method of preserving meats. Sausage making is one of the oldest methods of food preparation. Virtually every culture has developed sausage to preserve meats that could not all be consumed at the time of slaughter. What began as safe and economical food storage, over time became cuisine.

The earliest mention of sausage was in the *Odyssey* by Homer in the 9th century B.C. People in this era and earlier knew that without preservation, meats would rapidly become unfit for consumption. They learned to cut or grind meat into small pieces, season it with salt and spices, and then to dry it.

The sausage was paid early tribute by the Greek playwright Epicharmus, who wrote Orya (The Sausage) in about 500 B.C. Sausages have been favored by plain folk and royalty alike over the centuries; Nebuchadnezzar, the Babylonian king, may have been the first royal fan of this food.

The preservation process used by ancient cultures, including Chinese, Greek, Roman, and Babylonian, produced meat that was essentially fermented and dried. You can only wonder how many

Panizzera Meat Company of Occidental, California, was founded in 1914 by Constante and Margaret (photo left), Italian immigrants from the Lake Como region. Today their grandson, Bob Panizzera, uses the family recipes to carry on the company's famous sausage making traditions. Photographs courtesy of Panizzera Meat Company

Since 1948 The Neto Sausage Company of Santa Clara, California, has been producing linguiça, a Portuguese sausage, from a generations-old family recipe. They also produce andouille, chorizo, and Spanish longaniza. Photographs courtesy of Neto Sausage Company

people perished in the attempt to achieve safety? The larger dried sausages that we are familiar with today, such as salami, probably most closely resemble these earliest sausages.

A favorite recipe of butchers in Ancient Rome included cutting pork and beef into small pieces, adding salt, pine nuts, cumin seed, bay leaves, and black pepper. They would stuff the mixture into animal skins and hang them to dry in special rooms. They knew the meat was safe to consume many months later. These Roman sausage makers formed guilds and guarded their secrets closely. Furthermore, if you believe that we are overinspected and regulated today, Roman shops were inspected and licensed by their government.

Sausage has a political history as well. In 320 A.D., the Roman Emperor Constantine the Great banned certain pagan festivals, and, as sausage was a featured food at the festivals, he banned those also! Sausage production at that time never quite dried up, it merely went underground until the ban was later repealed in response to popular opinion.

Through the ages sausage has become a universal food; it is easily recognizable throughout the world as sausage no matter what the locals call it. The unique and interesting combinations of the different flavors from each culture provide for almost endless variation to this simple food—and perhaps that is sausage's enduring charm.

Even when family sausage recipes have crossed the oceans and taken up residence in other lands, sausage continues to ignite fierce loyalties. Be it British bangers, Cajun boudin, andouille and chaurice, French saucisson a l'ail, Chinese sweet sausage, Swedish potato sausage, Italian fennel sausage and salami, Mexican chorizo, Portuguese linguiça, Pennsylvania Dutch scrapple, Southern liver mush, Scottish black pudding, bratwurst, braunschweiger, wienerwurst, bologna, genoa, cotto, mortadella, cottechino, or kielbasa, everyone seems to have a favorite sausage inspired by the traditions of a national or cultural cuisine.

GETTING STARTED

Now on to the meat of the matter (or, the matter of the meat). Let me confess that I came to this project uninformed but eager and curious. That is to say, I was recruited to write this book not because I was known as a great charcuterier but because I am a writer who likes to cook. So I researched and stuffed, cooked and served, and I received immediate accolades.

To judge response to the recipes featured in this book, I prepared many sausage-centered meals and hosted sausage tastings for family and friends. While my guests thought the sausages wonderful, they seemed more impressed by the fact that they were homemade. Many people regard some cooking as beyond the home pale, considering it either too technical or difficult. With this attitude, they automatically exclude, to their own detriment, great recipes from their menus as being beyond their range of culinary skills.

In fact, I have found sausage making to be both easy and fun. Since it requires very little equipment, it is also economical. In addition, when you make your own sausage, you know exactly what's in it, and can be assured that the ingredients are as fresh as possible. I would even recommend to you to gather a group of friends for an evening of fun, frivolity, and sausage making. For now, forget fondue, pack away the pasta machine, and bring out the grinder. Aside from the lighthearted companionship of a unique shared cooking experience, you will be producing a product that is indisputably delicious.

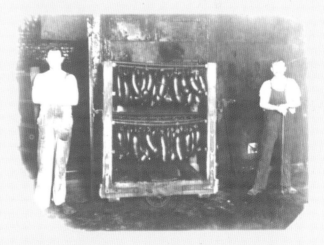

Two young immigrants from Austria-Hungary started the Vienna Sausage Company in 1893 when they first sold their sausage at the Chicago Columbia Exposition. While known for their exceptional hot dogs, Vienna Sausage of Chicago, Illinois, also produces bratwurst, polish sausage, and a variety of deli meats and products.
Photographs courtesy of the Vienna Sausage Company

During the 1950s, movie actress Jayne Mansfield reigned for one year as the National Hot Dog Queen. She is seen here dispensing her duties.
Photograph courtesy of the National Hot Dog and Sausage Council

HOW TO USE THIS BOOK

The basics section will take you through the rudiments of sausage making. You will learn about the equipment you need and how to use it, as well as ingredients, fat ratios, and the different sausage casings. Pay special attention to the section on sanitation for the proper handling and storage of meat.

The first recipe will be for a bulk breakfast sausage. Try it to get a general feel for sausage making, and then prepare it as a wonderful part of a country breakfast accompanied by fresh biscuits and gravy. You'll find a section with sausage recipes grouped according to their countries or cultures of origin. The last section of the book features recipes from around the world that use sausage as the main ingredient, plus extra recipes for complements to your sausage such as mustard, spreads, and relishes.

If squeamish feelings about handling the ingredients have held you back from attempting this craft, I encourage you to set aside your preconceived notions and to try one recipe. Once you do, you won't think twice about the ingredients or the process as being much different from other from-scratch cooking projects. Besides, you'll find homemade sausage so superior to store-bought, that the process will ultimately become an enjoyable means of procuring the product.

It's also my hope (and duty to inform you as an adventurous, inquisitive cook), that once you feel comfortable with the process of sausage making, you will experiment with your own recipes. That secret ingredient you stumble upon may be the beginning of a guarded family recipe.

So, lets get started—and remember to smile—since sausages are the ultimate cartoon food. The hot dog squirts out of the bun. The dog runs out of the butcher shop with a string of brats waving in the breeze. Somewhere, not far from where you're sitting, some joker is driving down a highway in a car built and painted to look like a wiener. And I say that there is much more fun to be had.

first steps of making sausage

sau·sage (sô'sĭj), *n.* finely chopped and seasoned meat, especially pork, usually stuffed into a prepared animal intestine or other casing, and cooked or cured.

...SO SAYS THE DICTIONARY. Of course there are no limitations to ingredients and styles. In *The Great Book of Sausages*, by Antony and Araminta Hippesley Coxe, the undisputed encyclopedia of this cuisine, 600 types of sausage are listed and described from Armadillo sausage to Zwyczajna. (I hope you can surmise by the spelling of the last sausage that it is of Polish origin.) As you study the topic further, you'll find that the principle ingredient of any one sausage recipe may not even be meat—the spectrum ranges from blood to tofu, and can even include beans and fruit. I know of recipes for chocolate salami.

While sausage casing comes traditionally from the intestines of pigs, sheep, or cows, any spare animal part or edible material may be recruited to serve the simple function of holding the filling together in a neat package. Some alternative animal-based casings can include a boned pig's foot, chicken necks, sheep's stomachs, beef bladders, and caul fat (the fat on the membrane that extends from the stomach to the large intestine).

A common commercial casing is made from collagen, the protein found in connective tissue, which is derived entirely from animal products, then processed and formed into a continuous hollow tube. If you buy Polish or smoked sausage at the grocery store, it is most likely stuffed in collagen casings. Artificial casings are made from cellulose and plastic. Technically you could use hollowed-out vegetables and edible leaves as casings.

Of course the sausage need not be stuffed. Fresh, bulk sausage is chopped meat mixed together with herbs, spices, and flavorings, and often some form of binder or extender, such as egg or bread crumbs, which helps hold the seasoned meat together for cooking. You can make the breakfast sausage below using only a mixing bowl and a frying pan. Once you make this recipe, you will know the essential procedure that universally extends through all the recipes about seasoning and mixing the meat.

BULK BREAKFAST SAUSAGE

INGREDIENTS

- ½ lb (224 g) ground pork
- ½ lb (224 g) ground lamb
- 1 egg
- ½ cup (70 g) seasoned bread crumbs
- ½ teaspoon rubbed sage
- ½ teaspoon salt
- Black pepper and red pepper flakes to taste
- ½ cup (120 mL) milk
- 1 tablespoon all-purpose flour

METHOD

Thoroughly clean a large mixing bowl in soapy water and rinse, then scald the bowl with boiling water. (I prefer stainless steel bowls, but ceramic or heavy plastic will do.) Your only other tool will be your hands—so wash and rinse them well. Put all the ingredients, except for the milk and flour, into the bowl. Using your hands, reach across the ingredients, grasp a handful, and push it down through the center of the mass. Turn the bowl a quarter turn and repeat. Continue turning and pushing down until well mixed.

Refrigerate the mixture for 1 hour to allow the flavors to meld and strengthen. Remove from the refrigerator and form the mixture into balls, then flatten into patties, each approximately 2 to 3 inches (5 to 7.5 cm) across. In the frying pan, brown the patties over medium-high heat, then lower the temperature to medium and cook through. You want the juices of the patties to run clear without a trace of pink. When the patties are cooked, keep them warm before serving by placing the sausages on a heated platter in a warm oven.

To make the gravy, pour off all but 1 to 2 tablespoons of fat. With the pan at a medium temperature, gradually sprinkle the flour into the pan and cook to remove the flour taste, stirring and scraping to get all of the browned bits into the gravy. After about 3 minutes, gradually pour in the milk, stirring all the while. Continue until the gravy thickens, approximately 4 to 5 minutes.

Serve the sausages with a side dish of prepared eggs, and pour the gravy over hot, fresh biscuits. (You'll find another recipe for bulk breakfast sausage on page 93.)

MAKING A COUNTRY BREAKFAST

1. Form the patties.

2. Fry them until well browned on both sides, then drain them on a paper towel.

3. Make the gravy by first browning the flour in the hot grease.

4. Add the milk and blend into the flour until thickened.

5. To make the eggs, pour the beaten eggs into a clean pan.

6. Season eggs with salt and pepper.

TYPES OF SAUSAGE

Fresh Sausage

The preceding recipe for breakfast sausage is an example of fresh, bulk sausage made of minced raw meat and spices. Fresh sausage, made this way, is formed and fried or grilled soon after it is made, just as you would a hamburger, or the uncooked mixture is frozen for future use. Fresh sausage may be broken up and cooked before using it as an ingredient in other dishes such as casseroles or sauces. Bulk sausage left raw should be wrapped and can be refrigerated for three days or frozen for three months.

Fresh sausage is also the *forcemeat*, defined as chopped up, seasoned meat or fish, that you stuff into casings. Once encased, fresh sausage may be fried, grilled, poached, baked, or simmered. The recipes in this book focus on fresh sausage that is to be prepared and eaten soon after you make it or frozen for future use.

Smoked Sausage

Sausages can be either cold- or hot-smoked. I find the flavor that results (particularly with aromatic woods such as hickory, mesquite, and apple woods) from smoking is delicious. Since you are smoking the sausages to both impart flavor and to retard spoilage, it is important that you follow the instructions on your smoker when you are trying this "old fashioned" method.

Cold-smoked sausages are smoked over a low heat for a long time. Depending on the recipe, this can mean many hours or even days. Cold smoking dries the sausages somewhat but does not fully cook them, so that any cold-smoked meats must be cooked before eating. They are, however, dried enough to extend their refrigerated life beyond that of fresh sausage, and can be kept, wrapped and refrigerated, for up to two weeks.

Hot-smoked sausages (such as bologna and mortadella) are smoked over a higher heat. The heat makes them ready to eat and they need no further cooking. Like cold-smoked sausages, hot-smoked sausages may be refrigerated for up to two weeks. You may freeze both cold- and hot-smoked sausages, and can keep them in the freezer for up to six months. For more information about hot-smoking see page 000.

You can approximate the smoky flavor (rather well, actually) by using liquid smoke, a bottled flavoring made from condensed smoke. A very small amount, approximately ¼ teaspoon per pound of meat, is effective. Remember, of course, that this meat is only flavored, not treated, and is still raw, so you will need to prepare it just as you would fresh meat.

Cured Sausage

Cured sausage (such as salami and pepperoni) is firmer and keeps much longer than fresh or smoked sausage. Curing meats retards spoilage by removing most of the moisture. In order to keep the meat from spoiling as it dries, it is necessary to treat the meat with small amounts of chemical curing agents.

There are two basic substances used in curing meats, *nitrates* and *nitrites*. The use of these agents has become controversial, with claims that these substances may be carcinogenic. I can recommend *Great Sausage Recipes and Meat Curing*, by Rytek Kutas for a thorough discussion of the process, and an argument for its safety.

Whatever your belief about the various additives used in curing meats, there is one issue that every layperson can agree on; the diseases that can result from uncured or improperly cured meat are well known and severe. Like many of the substances we all consume in one form or another, the additives used for curing meats can be toxic to some of us in any amount and to all of us in large amounts. I will allow that I occasionally eat commercially cured meats, such as bacon, Genoa salami, and cured Kielbasa, believing that moderation is the key to enjoyment.

To conclude this discussion, I am neither a chemist nor a physician, and my approach is to eschew home curing of meats. My concern is that I have no way of knowing (at least in advance of consuming the product) if I have used the correct amount of chemicals to protect me and my guests from both the disease and the cure (pun intended). For the purposes of this book, I do not offer recipes for home curing sausage. Each of the recipes may be smoked if you like and, as I indicated earlier, for safety's sake, always refer to your smoker's operating manual for temperatures, smoking times, and the kinds of wood to use.

CASINGS

There is no delicate way to introduce this topic. Simply stated, many sausages are encased, and the casings are, more often than not, of animal origin. If you are a true sausage lover, this should not faze you in the least. You must admit, natural casings are the ultimate example of waste-not-want-not, recycling, and using what you have at hand. If you have any misgivings, perhaps the follow-ing information will demystify the concept, and you can view casings as just one more efficiently convenient natural ingredient used in the world's cuisine.

Up until the 20th century, all sausages were stuffed in natural casings made primarily from animal intestines. The portion of the intestine that is used is the submucosa, a layer of connective tissue that has several properties. The submucosa is a thin and flexible tissue made of a natural protein called collagen. It is strong, almost transparent, and semi-permeable, which allows flavors such as smoke to penetrate at the same time that it protects and concentrates the flavors within. Commercially processed natural casings do not impart conflicting flavors to the finished sausage.

Collagen, a constituent of bone, cartilage, and tendons, may be reduced by boiling to form gelatin. In this century, manufacturers have developed techniques to process collagen to make artificial edible casings of convenient sizes and shapes. Entirely artificial casings are made of plastic, cloth, and paper, and are, of course, not intended to be eaten. It stretches the point somewhat, but one could create a loose casing substitute using vegetable leaves that can enfold a forcemeat; obvious examples include grape leaves and corn husks.

Natural casings are derived from domesticated hogs, sheep, and cows. The intestines (or stomach in some cases) are stripped of fat and other membranes and thoroughly cleaned. They are often gathered together in hanks (much like yarn) and salted. Once cleaned and salted, the casings may be kept indefinitely under refrigeration.

Hog casings are easiest to work with, being quite strong and large enough to easily manipulate. Sheep casings are smaller, thinner-walled, and require delicate handling and the use of a smaller funnel when filling the casings. What are called beef middles are larger casings that come from beef but are much tougher in consistency than casings from pigs or sheep. Because hog casings are far easier to find than sheep or cow casings, all of the recipes in this book assume that you will be using hog casings.

In addition to the intestine, stomachs, bladders, and a portion of the intestine that seems equivalent to the human appendix, called the bung, are also used. These large pieces work best for bologna, salamis, liverwurst, and other large types of sausage. The best known use of the stomach is the dubious Scottish delicacy haggis (see page 56).

Of all the various types of casings, I prefer, by far, natural casings for flavor, texture, and tradition. Hog casings are inexpensive, easy to find, and versatile to use. I have been able to purchase a 60-foot (55 m) hank at a local meat-rendering plant for less than I would pay for a pound of commercially prepared sausage. Sheep casings are available through mail-order butchers and sausage suppliers. Unfortunately, it is difficult to find sheep casings in less than large commercial quantities, giving you many more casings than you would ever need for small homemade

Hog casings being rinsed with water

batches. If you would like to try sheep casings, perhaps you could network with other local sausage makers and split a large quantity between yourselves. Again, all of the recipes in this book assume that you will use hog casings, and I find them always acceptable.

MEAT AND FAT

One of the great advantages to making and cooking items that most people get at the store is that you have complete control over all the ingredients. It is commonplace to not want to know what goes into hot dogs. In fact, the phrase "meat and meat by-products," always gives me a chill when I read the labels. However, if you make it yourself, you will always know what goes into your recipe, and will no longer need to second-guess someone else's definition of what constitutes meat.

When you begin to make these sausages (or prepare any recipe) you might be tempted to create your own variations. This tendency is particularly strong with regard to reducing fat content. I recommend that you absolutely follow this impulse. However, you will find as have I, that low fat means dry and high fat means juicy. I will not begin to advise anyone about diet (I myself am happily ungoverned, which means I pay the price in working it off at the gym).

As you begin this culinary adventure, you might consider making the sausage with the standard amount of fat in ratio to lean which is 25 to 30 percent fat. If this traditional quantity sounds too steep for your personal fat consumption, perhaps you can compensate by eating less than traditional quantities of the finished product. As in any recipe, you can only substitute ingredients so far until it becomes a totally separate entity, rather than an authentic derivative.

That said, there are two basic approaches to the meats you will use. The first, and simplest, is to choose a cut of meat that naturally contains the approximate traditional balance of fat to lean. Boston butt pork roast, which comes from the shoulder of the pig, contains about 20 percent fat which I find almost ideal. When preparing this cut of meat, it is only necessary to remove any bone, obvious tendons, and sinew. Occasionally a roast will need more trimming or even the addition of extra fat. The best way to learn about the fat content of various cuts is to speak to your butcher.

Secondly, you can purchase a lean meat, such as tenderloin, and add minced fat in the quantities you

This well-marbled Boston butt pork roast contains approximately 20 percent fat.

wish. This is an excellent approach from the perspective of fat control, although it pushes the grocery bill to the high end, since tenderloin is one of the choicest of cuts. Furthermore, unless you wish to use a flavored fat like bacon, be sure to avoid salted fats.

When making beef, lamb, poultry, and seafood sausages, you will need to look at different requirements for preparation before grinding, including providing different fat resources. Commonly, less expensive cuts of red meats (beef and lamb) contain more connective tissue and fat throughout. For many purposes, including sausage, this is an advantage since the connective tissue produces richer flavors. The drawback is that the tougher tissues need to be laboriously cut out.

As you will see, the poultry recipes rely on available fat primarily in the form of skin. You can also collect poultry fat from roasting birds, then strain it and store it for later use. Since seafood sausages tend to have little fat, which often comes in the form of butter or oil, they need moist and brief cooking methods to help prevent them from drying out; poaching is ideal. In summary, when making sausage, don't be too timid when talking about fat. What makes sausage such a special dish in my opinion results from packing together, within the casing, not only the meats and spices, but also the fat which becomes the cooking medium. Remember, the fat bastes and flavors the meat as the sausage cooks, bathing it with the herbs and spices that infuse the taste.

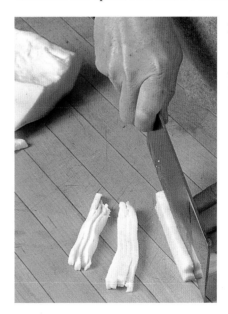

Adding additional fat may be necessary when making sausage with leaner cuts of meat.

sausage
making
basics

Following are the basic concepts and techniques for home sausage making:

EQUIPMENT

PREPARATION

GRINDING, EMULSIFYING, AND HAND CUTTING

MIXING

STUFFING

SANITATION

STORAGE AND COOKING

THIS CHAPTER WILL DISCUSS the equipment you will need for making sausage and introduce you to the general how-to steps. You'll find that the processes involved are very simple. Let me begin by very briefly describing the basic procedures: Grind or chop the meat; mix it with herbs, spices, and other ingredients until it becomes, by definition, forcemeat; then stuff the force-meat into a package. At this point the sausage is either cooked and eaten, or is preserved by one of several methods.

While all this sounds relatively easy, and it is for the most part, there are some skills involved in sausage making that elevate it to a craft, and I will cover these as we go along.

EQUIPMENT

Sausage making does not require a large investment in new tools. In theory, if you have a good knife, a cutting board, and a funnel, you can make sausage. However, unless you value doing things the hard way, I recommend that you add some inexpensive pieces.

Kitchen Tools

The basic, all-purpose kitchen tools listed below are ones that I assume you already have at hand. Understand that each item should be prefaced with the word "good," as in "a good, sharp knife." Good does not necessarily mean professional-grade; the tools you use should be those with which you are most comfortable and that effectively get the job done. (I'm not advocating that you run out and purchase new tools for the purposes of this book; however, if you were looking for an excuse to up grade, feel free to do so!).

Make sure the tools you use are easy to clean: A well-used plastic or wood cutting board are acceptable; chipped and pitted ones are not recommended.

BONING KNIFE optional—but you will be grateful to have one

CHEF'S KNIFE with a heavy blade, at least 8 inches (20 cm) long

CUTTING BOARDS—either wood or non-porous plastic or acrylic

FUNNEL—with a tube that you can push your thumb through (I have found that most standard funnels have spouts that are too narrow to be of use for hand stuffing sausage. The spout must be narrow enough for sliding the casing over it, and wide enough to allow the forcemeat to pass through. There are funnels made especially for making sausage; you may be lucky enough to find one—try looking in an old-fashioned hardware store.

KITCHEN SCALE—if you don't own one, buy one please! (I recommend a digital scale that is sensitive to a tenth of an ounce. There is simply no better way to portion ingredients such as meats and fats than by weight. Without a scale, it is almost impossible to guess how much meat is left after you've boned and trimmed a roast. While very experienced chefs are good at estimating weights, they still use scales.)

KITCHEN TWINE—undyed, unbleached cotton thread for tying ends and links

PARING KNIFE

PLASTIC STORAGE CONTAINERS

STAINLESS STEEL MIXING BOWLS—large enough to accommodate 4 to 5 pounds (1.8 to 2.3 kg) of meat and both of your hands

Grinders

The basic process of making the forcemeat involves either reducing the meat to a paste, or at least to small chunks. While this can be done (laboriously) with knives, effort, and patience, I recommend a grinder. You can find grinders in cookware and hardware stores.

HAND GRINDER

One of the most common and versatile grinders, or meat mincers, clamps on the edge of a worktable or kitchen counter. My grinder is imported from Poland (where sausage forms a religion), and is sold as a kit including a stuffing funnel and two round mincing plates (one coarse, one fine). To grind, you put the meat in the hopper, then turn the handle to push the ingredients via a large internal screw through the mincing plate.

You can also use the hand grinder to stuff the sausage. Once the meat is ground and the other

Hand grinder

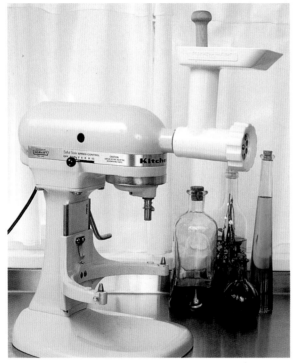

Electric mixer with grinder attachment

Grinder attachment

ingredients mixed in to make the forcemeat, you remove the mincing plate and attach the sausage funnel. You then put the forcemeat in the hopper, and turn the handle to push it through the funnel and into the casing. I find it extremely awkward to turn the handle while manipulating the casing and much prefer using either a separate hand stuffer (see next page), or the attachment for an electric mixer.

GRINDER ATTACHMENT

The device I use most often for making sausage is the food grinder attachment for my electric mixer. Like the hand grinder, it comes with an assortment of mincer plates for grinding and a sausage funnel for stuffing. I prefer this device for three reasons: First, it is powered. Since you do not need to turn the handle to force the meat through the plates or into the funnel, both hands are free for manipulating the ingredients. Secondly, the mixer sits higher above the work surface than the hand grinder, allowing the ground extrusion or finished sausage to trail into a waiting bowl or container. And finally, of all the devices I have tried, this particular one allows the easiest and most controlled stuffing process.

Stuffing tube for grinder attachment

TO POWER OR NOT TO POWER

As with many traditional crafts, arguments can be made both ways when it comes to choosing whether to use hand- or electric- powered tools. Whatever your preference or reasons for choosing one over the other, either the hand grinder or the attachment for the electric mixer provide excellent results. Both of these devices are easy to master, disassemble easily for cleaning, can be used for both grinding and stuffing, and are almost the same price. (The attachment for the electric mixer costs a little more. However, if you don't already have an electric mixer, the cost will be substantially higher!)

Food Processor

I recommend a food processor to achieve the very fine-grained, smooth paste needed when making emulsified forcemeat, such as in hot dogs, bologna, and liver sausage. While you can continue to pass the forcemeat through the fine mincer plate on a hand grinder or grinder attachment to partially emulsify the mixture, a food processor will do the work much quicker and with much better results.

Be aware that some food authors suggest that a food processor may substitute for a grinder. I find, however, that using a food processor in this way makes it all but impossible to get an even, coarse cut when needed; some portions of the meat will become paste while others will be left too large.

Sausage stuffer

Stuffers

The most elemental sausage stuffer is your thumb and a funnel. This works extremely well and should not be discounted if you are eager to get to the recipes. You may also want to try hand stuffing to see if you like the process of making fresh sausage enough (and the delicious end product) to invest in basic equipment.

As discussed above, both a hand grinder and grinding attachment for an electric mixer include the needed components for stuffing. If you prefer using a hand grinder for making your forcemeat, I believe it's much easier to use a device designed exclusively for stuffing rather than using the grinder for stuffing. You can purchase a separate stuffer that consists of a bent tube with an arm/lever that pushes the forcemeat through a stuffing tube and into the casing. This device allows you to fill the casings with uniform pressure that you control.

Stuffing the sausage by hand

An example of everything in its place (*mise en place*), showing the ingredients for chorizo.

Cut the par-frozen meat into finger-sized pieces.

PREPARATION

Mise en place is the important culinary principle that means everything in place; it plays an important role in all cooking procedures. When you practice this principle, you will save yourself not only time and trouble, but the ultimate frustration of not having the crucial ingredient in your kitchen or the proper utensil within reach.

The most basic advice is to always read a recipe through before you begin. Determine everything you will need—and purchase enough! Individual recipes will indicate whether you need to chop vegetables, grind spices, etc., beforehand. All of this preparation should be completed by the time you begin to make the sausage.

Always be certain to follow the rules of sanitation (see page 35). Clean and dry all utensils, bowls, plastic containers, equipment, cutting boards, and work surfaces before you begin.

Preparing the Meat

Unless otherwise indicated in an individual recipe, you will need to grind the meat before mixing it with the other ingredients.In order for the meat to easily fit into the hopper of the grinder or grinder attachment, you need to first bone the meat if necessary, then cut it into manageable pieces.

Boning entails removing any obvious large bones as well as checking for and eliminating any smaller pieces of bone or bone fragments that may remain. Inspect the meat and remove as much tendon and sinew as possible. If you judge the meat to be too fatty to maintain the proper 20 to 25 percent fat to lean ratio, remove extra fat at your discretion.

I've found, and highly recommend, that boned, par-frozen (semifrozen) meat is much easier to cut. After boning, you can wrap the meat and place it in the freezer until ice crystals begin to form; or, you can thaw boned and frozen meat to the stage where you are just able to cut it easily. You want to cut the meat into finger-sized pieces. To do this, first slice the meat into slabs that are approximately 1-inch (2.5 cm) thick. Next, stack the slabs and cut them into strips. Refrigerate until ready.

Preparing the Casings

Straight from their package, casings look like wet string and feel slippery like cooked spaghetti. The recipe (and your experience) will indicate how much casing you will need. Using a knife or scissors, cut a little more than the required length. In the sink, with the water running, open one end of the casing and rinse through thoroughly several times. You may discover holes in the casing when rinsing. If you find that there are too many holes in one section, cut another length. If the portion with the leak is toward the front or back of the length, cut it off. While it isn't absolutely necessary, I like to soak the casings in fresh water for about an hour before use; simply leave the casing covered with clean water in a bowl until you need it. I find that this hydrates the casing and makes it slightly easier to handle.

Cut the length of casing you need.

Open the end of the casing.

Begin to run water through the casing.

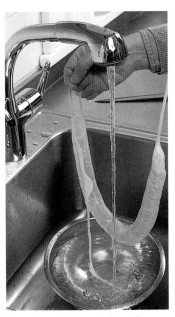

Move the water through the casing.

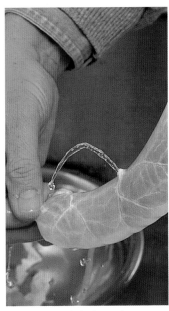

Look for any leaks in the casing.

Coarse grind using the hand grinder

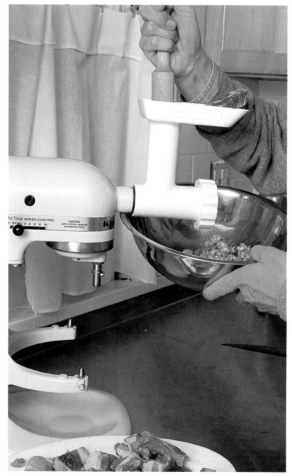

Grinding meat using the grinder attachment

GRINDING, EMULSIFYING, AND HAND CUTTING

Each individual recipe will indicate whether the ingredients need to be ground either coarse or fine, emulsified, or hand-cut. (The Chinese sausage on page 84 calls for the meat and fat to be separately hand diced, and requires no grinding.) If you have followed my advice under Preparing the Meat, and the meat is semifrozen, you should have little difficulty with any of these processes.

Grinding

There are no particular tricks to using a hand grinder or grinder attachment for an electric mixer. Each (see Grinders on page 21) comes with detailed instructions that will explain assembly and how to mount the device.

If the grinder is the sort that clamps onto your counter or worktable, secure it as tightly as you can. Be aware that the jaws of the clamp are often hard enough to damage wood, so I recommend that you place two or three thicknesses of shirt cardboard between the clamp's jaws and your table.

The recipe will tell you whether you need to grind the ingredients coarse or fine and will determine which mincer plate you will use in the grinder. As you become experienced with making sausage, you will develop and understand your own preferences for texture and consistency. I enjoy a chunky consistency in most sausage and will occasionally modify traditional forms to suit myself. Always, please yourself.

You will need to place a receiving bowl beneath the mouth of the grinder. I prefer stainless steel, but ceramic or heavy plastic will do. Be aware that the most important element to consider when choosing utensils is to find those that can be thoroughly cleaned.

Once you've assembled your grinder, either begin turning the handle (clockwise), or start the machine at a slow speed. With your free hand, begin feeding the prepared meat pieces into the hopper on top of your device. Since I've neglected to include any recipes for finger sausage, please be cautious when working any machine, no matter how safe you think it might be.

If you have a stomper, a wooden pestle-like device for pushing meat into the grinding mechanism, use it! Otherwise, be extremely careful when putting meat into the grinder. If the meat or ingredients get stuck when you are using an electric appliance, unplug the machine before beginning your investigation.

Ground meat. **LEFT TO RIGHT**: coarse and fine

Emulsifying

If the recipe requires the filling to be emulsified, you will need to use a food processor, as discussed under Grinders on page 21. Emulsification means that the fat is broken up very finely and distributed evenly throughout the forcemeat. As a point of reference, shaking a bottle of salad dressing to mix the oil with the vinegar emulsifies the solution.

To prepare the meat for emulsification, you will need to cut it into pieces that are small enough to fit in your processor. This means cutting them into pieces smaller than the finger-size pieces suitable for grinding. To emulsify, place the ingredients in the food processor and process the mixture until it resembles a fine-grained paste. As you process, stop occasionally and use a rubber spatula to scrape the sides of the container to ensure that the ingredients process evenly.

Emulsified meat compared to ground meat

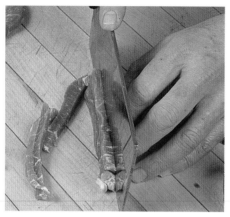

Cut the par-frozen ¼-inch (.6 cm) slabs of meat into ¼-inch strips.

Cut the meat into ¼-inch (.6 cm) dice.

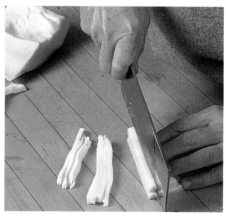

Cut the par-frozen ¼-inch (.6 cm) slabs of fat into ¼-inch strips.

Hand Cutting

The texture of some sausages requires cutting the meat and fat by hand rather than grinding or emulsifying them. When this is the case, the recipe will indicate the size of the dice. If you fancy Italian mortadella, you know that the pieces of fat in the sausage is generally a larger dice. The Chinese sausage on page 84 calls for the meat and fat to be diced fine or small.

When you are hand cutting the meat, it must be semifrozen. When making a small dice you will need to slice the meat into slabs, stack it, cut it into strips, then reorient it, and dice. You will dice the meat and fat separately. Although this process is somewhat tedious compared to grinding, the result is appropriate and wonderful to the style of sausage you are making.

MIXING

Nothing adequately substitutes for using your bare hands for many cooking procedures, and this is one. Aside from providing a guilt-free experience for playing with your food, mixing with your hands provides a second line of defense for finding bone shards and sinew. Make sure you wash your hands well before and after mixing.

As you did for the bulk breakfast sausage on page 14, put all ingredients in a large mixing bowl. Reach across the ingredients, grasp a handful, and push it down through the center of the mass. Turn the bowl a quarter turn and repeat. Continue in this way until all the ingredients are well mixed.

STUFFING

Getting the forcemeat into the casing is the only tricky aspect of sausage making. At first, you may wonder if sausage makers possess a special coordination that you lack. Until you get the feel of it, stuffing sausage is akin to learning how to pat your head and rub your tummy at the same time—it takes the same amount of concentration, and may provide you with the same amount of laughs.

The three phases of stuffing sausage are opening the casing, loading the casing onto the funnel, and packing. With some perseverance, you should have the process perfected after your first batch. Once you have stuffed a sausage, you will know why it is considered a craft.

Opening the Casing

Casings are slippery and need to stay that way if the process is to work. As I mentioned in Preparing the Casings on page 25, I like to keep the casing covered with clean water in a bowl until I need it.

The hardest part of working with casings is finding the opening at the end of the tube. To do this, work in the sink under running water. Let the casing slip through your fingers until you grasp one end. Run water into the end of the casing. You should be able to see and grasp the edge of the tube. This may take several attempts; you can console yourself with the thought that you are developing a useful, though not marketable, skill.

Mix the ingredients by hand.

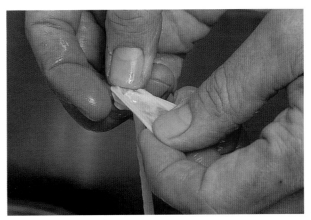

Open the end of the casing.

Loading the Funnel

Now you are ready to *load the funnel*, the term for running the casing onto the outside of the funnel. Your grinder or stuffer should allow you to remove the funnel attachment. Set the funnel on a clean surface with the pointed end facing up. Having opened one end of the casing, gently slide it over the end of the funnel. Hold the trailing portion of the casing in one hand while massaging the casing down over the funnel with the thumb and forefinger of the free hand. This is just like pushing your shirt sleeves up your arm without rolling them (assuming that you were underwater wearing a shirt made out of tissue paper). With practice you will learn how much pressure to use and how tightly to slide the casing on the funnel. To prevent the forcemeat from coming out of the end of the casing as you stuff, tie a simple overhand knot in the casing's end, or use a small piece of kitchen twine to tie off the end.

Loaded stuffing tube on the grinder attachment

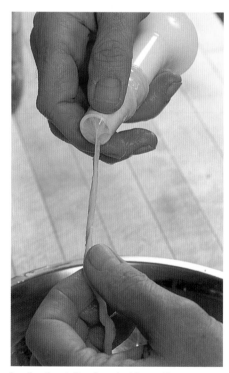

Loading the stuffing funnel with the casing while the funnel is on a flat surface

Loading the stuffing funnel while working away from a surface

Packing

The last stage of stuffing is packing the forcemeat into the casing. Begin by placing the loaded funnel securely on either the hand grinder, the sausage stuffer, or the grinder attachment for your electric mixer.

If you are using a hand grinder, you may want to consider calling in another pair of hands. Since the hand you use for turning the handle is also the hand you need for placing the forcemeat into the hopper, working alone necessitates that you stop turning the handle while you add more forcemeat. A helper will greatly streamline the process.

A sausage stuffer is designed to hold a substantial volume of forcemeat. Once you load the stuffer's tube, you can concentrate on working the lever with one hand, while guiding the forcemeat into the casing with the other hand.

Tie the end of the casing using an overhand knot or piece of kitchen twine.

Stuffing the sausage with a sausage stuffer

Hold the loaded stuffing tube in your hand to guide the casing off of the tube.

Working with the grinder attachment for an electric mixer allows the most ease in packing, since you use one hand for placing the forcemeat into the hopper while the power pushes it into the funnel. You can then easily use the other hand for guiding the forcemeat into the casing.

As the forcemeat is pushed out of whichever device you are using, the pressure will open the casing. As the forcemeat enters the casing, hold the sausage loosely in your hand while gently pulling the casing back toward the funnel; this will give you the control you need to pack the casing firmly or loosely as the recipe recommends (or as you prefer). The casing will burst if the forcemeat is too tightly packed. You will discover how tightly you can pack the casing only by going too far. With practice, you will know exactly how much forcemeat you can pack in.

As the forcemeat enters the casing, hold the sausage loosly in your hand while gently pulling the casing back toward the funnel.

Stuffing the sausage by hand

Hold the stuffing tube firmly as you push the forcemeat with your thumb.

If you want to make links, it's crucial to *not* overfill the casing at this stage. Keep in mind that in order to twist the sausage every few inches after it is made, you will need to leave some slack in the casing—the only way to do this is to slightly underfill the casing (see Making Links below).

ELIMINATING AIR BUBBLES

It is important to eliminate air bubbles while packing. You will see any large air pockets and bubbles as the forcemeat is being pushed into the casing. You can easily correct this by using your hand to manipulate and rearrange the forcemeat in the casing. In my experience, it is almost impossible to completely eliminate bubbles during the filling stage. The solution is to finish the sausage, then examine it closely. Using a clean needle, prick the bubbles and massage the air out. The small hole made by the needle will not cause the casing to split open when you cook the sausage.

Remove any air pockets by piercing them with a clean needle.

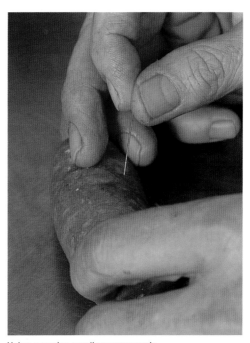

Using a sewing needle to remove air pockets from a chorizo sausage

Lay the sausage on a flat surface and twist into links.

Making Links

Some butchers use elaborate methods (many passed down through the generations) for tying off links. I found that a few twists between links will effectively hold them together while giving you enough casing to cut when you want to separate the links. To make links, first lay the stuffed sausage on a work surface. Starting at one end of the sausage, begin to measure, then twist the sausage to make the size links you want. Do not attempt to twist the links as the sausage is coming off the funnel. By placing the sausage flat on a surface before twisting, the links will not unroll. If you are going to poach the sausages immediately after they are made, you may want to tie short lengths of kitchen twine between each link. This provides a little extra security to prevent the links from unrolling as you place them in the pot for poaching.

Do not make the links this way—they will come untwisted. It's always better to work on a flat surface.

Use short lengths of kitchen twine to tie off the twists between links.

SANITATION

You cannot overstress the importance of proper sanitation when making sausage. Most cooking involves risks of contamination, and meats in particular provide potential for food poisoning and a vector for serious (and very highly publicized though actually quite rare) diseases such as Escherichia coli (*e. coli*), trichinosis, and botulism. My response to the risks is to be scrupulous with the following rules:

• Thoroughly wash all utensils and work surfaces that come in contact with meats with hot, soapy water. Try to avoid cross contamination by always rinsing your cloth or sponge in the hot soapy water *after* cleaning a surface or utensil, *before* you wipe another surface or utensil with the same cloth or sponge.

• If equipment can be disassembled, always take it apart and separately clean those piece that have come in contact with the food. It's always best to rinse or immerse implements in boiling water after they have been thoroughly cleaned.

• Never reuse work surfaces without washing after each process.

• A cursory wiping is not sufficient to clean and sanitize the surface. Again, use hot soapy water and a well-rinsed cloth or sponge.

• Never store meats in the vessels in which they have been prepared. Small particles of unseasoned meat left in vessels after preparation could be a breeding ground for bacteria when left at room temperature. When you reintroduce your prepared mixture, these small particles could contaminate the entire batch.

• Keep all ingredients as cold as possible. If you need to do further preparation or need to leave the kitchen for any length of time, place the ingredients or the meat mixture into the refrigerator.

• Always cook sausage thoroughly. This, in itself, is a skill often learned by trial and error involving one too many overly done sausages. While you don't want to undercook the sausages, you don't want to overcook them either (see below).

Cleaning supplies

Sterilizing utensils with boiling water

Sausages ready to dry in the refrigerator. Note the bowl under the rack to catch the liquid. You may also use a colander placed over a pan.

Some recipes call for sautéed crumbled sausage. (See recipe on page 97.)

STORAGE AND COOKING

Link sausages benefit from a bit of drying which allows them to brown nicely during frying or grilling. Once you've made your fresh sausage, arrange the links so they do not touch each other. Some recipes call for you to cover them, others do not. You may want to place them on a rack in a shallow pan to allow the pan to catch any drippings from the sausage. Store them overnight in the refrigerator.

Having dried them, you can then cook them in any one of several ways (see below), or wrap them in butcher paper or wax paper and refrigerate the sausages for up to three days. To freeze, dry the sausage overnight as above, then place the sausage in a freezer bag (removing as much air as you can before sealing) and freeze for up to three months. To thaw, place them in the refrigerator for a day.

The method you choose for cooking depends on your own pleasure. I love the texture of fried or grilled sausage—they are beautifully brown, crack out loud when you bite into them, and the juices burst in your mouth. Unless I plan to serve sausages cold (there is no better reason to make a sandwich than cold sausage), I always try to serve them immediately off the grill or stove; the longer they sit, the more the juices will soften the crisp skins. For some meals I prefer poached sausage for the moist result and the way the texture complements other ingredients and sauces. When sausage is to be added to a soup, such as the earthy Caldo Verde on page 96, I prefer the poaching method.

When you are ready to cook your sausages, try the following approaches. The directions assume you are cooking sausages stuffed into hog casings that are approximately 1 to 1½ inches (2.5 to 4 cm) wide. You will need to adjust your cooking time for any sausages that are less than 1 inch (2.5 cm) or more than 2 inches (5 cm) in diameter. Enjoy each of the methods, remembering that variety is not the hobgoblin of great cooking.

Baking

I generally prefer other methods of cooking sausage; however, baking is a great solution for cooking for a large gathering. Furthermore, baking sausage for a long time over very low heat is an alternate method of making a sausage that approximates the texture and flavors of dried sausages such as salami.

Should you wish to bake sausage for a meal, preheat your oven to 300°F (150°C). Arrange the sausages on a rack over a pan to catch the drippings. Using a fork or needle, prick each link several times. Bake for 45 minutes; the juices should be quite clear when done.

Crumbled Sausage

Many dishes call for crumbled sausage, which is fried first and then added to the remaining ingredients—or even assembled at the table, such as make-your-own tacos. To prepare sausage this way, remove the casing from the sausage before cooking. I find it easiest to cook the sausage using a wooden spoon that breaks up the meat into small pieces as they fry. During cooking, the fat melts out from the meat and forms the ideal cooking medium for these morsels. Some dishes ask you to remove and reserve the meat, allowing you to use some of the sausage fat for cooking (and seasoning) other ingredients.

Frying

Place the sausage links in a pan that is large enough to hold them in a single layer without them touching each other. Use a fork or needle to prick each sausage four or five times. Just barely cover the links with cold water and bring to a boil. Lower the heat immediately and simmer for 10 minutes. If foam forms, skim it. If the sausage floats, turn them halfway through the simmering. After the 10 minutes are up, pour off the remaining water. Again, prick each sausage two or

easy cleaning

A lick-and-a-promise cleaning is no longer suitable for today's discriminating cooks who are fearful of e. coli and salmonella contamination. While proper use of hot soapy water is sufficient for cleaning home food preparation areas, you can provide an extra measure of cleanliness by making your own inexpensive spray from bleach and water. Simply mix one teaspoon of bleach with 32 ounces (.95 L) of water. Once you've cleaned with hot soapy water, spray the bleach solution on desired surfaces and let stand for a few minutes. Then rinse the surface and air dry, or use paper towels to pat the surface dry. You will smell the bleach when it is wet; however, since so little bleach is used, it will dissipate over time and will not affect future food preparation.

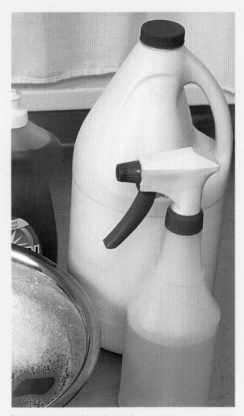

Spray bottle with bleach solution

Split and grilled merguez sausage (recipe on page 86)

To poach, place the sausage in enough water to cover by at least 1 inch (2.5 cm).

three times to release some of the fat. Be careful at this point because the fat is under some pressure and may shoot out. If you do not get enough sausage fat from piercing the sausages to coat the pan with a thin film of fat, add a little olive or vegetable oil to prevent the sausage from sticking. Raise the heat to medium and brown the sausages on all sides—this should take approximately three minutes.

Grilling

There are no tricks to grilling sausage except satisfying each guest's particular preference for level of burn. I like to poach mine lightly so they hold together during the initial cooking stage, and to ensure that the links are cooked through before they are blackened on the outside. The casing tends to stick to the grill and tear. If this bothers you, I recommend one of those hinged grilling frames used for delicate foods. When one side is properly crisp, you invert the whole device to grill the other side. Alternatively, you can brush the links with a bit of vegetable oil to keep them from sticking.

Poaching

Using a fork or needle, prick each sausage link a few times. If you have a steamer or pasta insert, place it in a pot large enough to hold all of the sausage you wish to poach. Add enough cold water to cover the sausage by at least 1 inch (2.5 cm).

Over high heat, bring the liquid just to the point where the first bubbles appear—you never want to let the liquid come to a boil, since this will toughen the sausage. Immediately reduce the heat to the lowest setting, add the sausage, cover the pot, and let simmer for 20 minutes. If the sausage begins to float, place a plate on it while it simmers to keep the sausage in the water. After 20 minutes you can serve or chill.

NOTE: Over the years I have developed some cooking habits that form my personal kitchen style. For example, if ever a recipe requires boiling or poaching (in any liquid, including wine, stock, water, or beer), I always throw in some aromatic vegetables, such as carrots, onions, garlic, celery, a piece of ginger, a slice of lemon peel, a bay leaf—or all of the above. This not only gently flavors the sausage, but makes an easy and delicious stock. Because of the fat content of the sausage, remember to thoroughly degrease this stock before use.

Smoking

There are a wide variety of smokers on the market, and you may already own one. We referred earlier to hot smoking (see page 76) as a method of extending the shelf life of sausage. Here, we are looking at the smoker as a method of cooking. Each type of smoker will have its own slight variations in the smoking process, but one main issue remains the same. That is, you need a temperature hot enough to cook the sausage thoroughly and low enough to keep them from charring before they are smoked.

SMOKING GUIDELINES

The links should be dry. Build and light the charcoal fire, and let it burn down to a smooth gray ash. It should reach a temperature of about 275°F (135°C). Place soaked wood chips on the prepared charcoal. Install the filled water bowl and, above that, the grids with the sausage. Close the smoker, and monitor the temperature to control the speed of cooking. With a chef's thermometer (one that will register the temperature instantly) check for an internal temperature of 170°F (78°C). This should take approximately three to five hours. Always refer to your smoker's manual and the recipes.

While poaching, never let water boil, but simmer for specified time.

You may need to weight down the poaching sausages with a plate to keep them submerged in the water as they cook.

recipes for great sausages

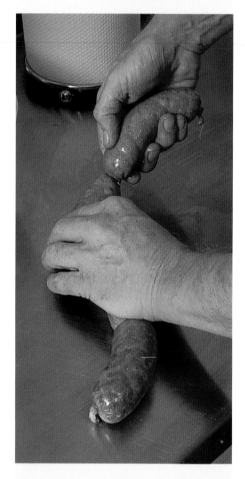

an international experience

MANY OF US REFER TO SAUSAGES BY THE COUNTRY FROM WHICH THEY CAME. I was raised by a pair of otherwise sophisticated cooks who talked broadly of Polish, Italian, Portuguese, or German sausage, rather than of the astounding variety within these cuisines. I have finally discovered what some of you may already know, that kielbasa is not actually a type of sausage, as in Polish kielbasa, but merely a Polish word for all sausage.

The more I learn of international cuisine the greater the richness and variety becomes apparent to me. I mentioned earlier the 600 sausage varieties described in *The Great Book of Sausages*. Within this survey is listed 118 varieties of French, 108 German, 65 English, and 40 Italian sausages.

I have organized the following sausage recipes by country. I have chosen many of my favorite sausages and have also introduced myself to varieties that I had never tried, such as Chinese and Swedish potato sausage. All have been winners.

For the purposes of this book I have limited my recipes to those that can be made with commonly available ingredients. I have always found it frustrating to be told of a transcendent dish only to discover that the ingredient that elevates the food heavenward is unavailable in my hemisphere.

Keep in mind that the goal of this (and I believe any) cookbook is to provide you with two things that should lead you to a third. First, I have tried to give you a decent background in the concept and general theory. Second, I want to provide you with experience in making your own sausage through these recipes. Finally, having obtained the theory and practice of home sausage making, I hope you will branch out and develop your own variations. You'll soon find what textures please you most, how intensely you like your sausage spiced and flavored, and how much fat you need to reach the balance you prefer.

Allow your imagination to be limited only by the seasons and the availability of great ingredients. Take advantage of your own garden, your cousin who hunts, the farmer's market in your town. Shop for the most beautiful produce in its season.

Try something you've never tasted. If you never had quite enough garlic in your sausage, push the limits. Try ostrich meat or add raisins and dried mango to a curried lamb mixture. I'm not a great fan of tofu, however, it offers fun possibilities for meatless sausage with olive oil as the fat. I say, cry havoc and let loose the hot dogs of boar (or soy).

the sausages

ITALY
salsiccie
luganega
cotechino
mortadella

FRANCE
saucisson a l'ail
boudin blanc
boudin blanc aux pommes
cervelas aux pistache

GREAT BRITAIN
bangers
oyster sausage

IBERIA AND MEXICO
linguiça
butifarra
chorizo

SCANDINAVIA
julkorv
ingefarapolse
medvurst
kaalikaaryleet
riismakkara

GERMANY
bockwurst
bratwurst
liverwurst
vienna sausage

ASIA, THE MIDDLE EAST, AND GREECE
lop cheong
si klok
merguez
keftedakia

UNITED STATES
hot dogs
cajun boudin
southern country sausage

italy

EVERY CUISINE OFFERS AT LEAST A FEW SUPREME ACCOMPLISHMENTS.
Italy has, of course, retired the trophy. I require the fruit of all cuisines for my happiness to be complete; however, if I *had to choose* one and only one culinary source, I would not hesitate to choose Italy.

Italy is the one country that, I believe, best understands the principles of feeding—whether it involves feeding themselves, feeding their guests, or feeding their identities. It is characteristic of Italian life that each village and city believes that it, and it alone, truly understands rice, or fish, or fungi… or sausage (even though there are perhaps fewer named types of sausage in Italy than in France or Germany).

If ever a war was fought over sausage, it would be in this country. Often the only difference between the garlic sausage in one village and that of the next is the lineage of the pig. Those of us who are not of Italy born can only travel through the country and reap the bounty of the argument.

I once spent a Bohemian summer in Hamburg (this is not an oxymoron…I simply mean I was poor and artistic) working in a kitchen as a *plongeur* (French for pearl diver…you know, a dishwasher). I was part of a wonderfully motley society of others, auslandern, who spoke no common language except a very rudimentary German. In order to communicate we created a patois such that any given sentence included German, French, Italian, English, and Spanish words strung together in a vaguely Teutonic syntax.

The two most vocal of our group were Giuseppe and Luighi, both Roman. They gave me the reverence I have held ever since for the food of Italy. They actually wept in misery over the food we were given twice daily as part of our pay. It would not have been considered bad by most of America in the 1950s mind you, being a little bland and a little too efficient. Once a week we were served a large mound of boiled rice with boiled chicken necks in white sauce. It was definitely fuel, not food—enough to keep us going until we were freed at midnight.

Throughout the summer, Giuseppe would lecture us on the Italian attitude toward food, while Luighi would supply the sound effects— moaning, slurping, and various other noises connoting ecstasy and disdain. We learned that as important as punctuality was to the German, so was food to the Italian. They claimed that, in Italy, the poorest people ate well.

From these impromptu and entertaining (thanks to Luighi) talks, I gleaned two bits of information that continue to guide me when I cook Italian (or otherwise). First, it is important that each ingredient be of high quality. And second, that the integrity of those ingredients is a hallmark; flavors must never be buried underneath other flavors but each allowed to sing its own essential note.

Grilled Italian
salsiccie (recipe next
page), served with
peppers in olive oil
(recipe page 123)

SALSICCIE

Salsiccie is a basic Italian sausage, and is closest to what we in the U.S. think of as Italian sausage. Stewed with green peppers in a red sauce, this defines the "Little Italy" in many American cities.

This recipe is very satisfying to me, and I've produced it in a larger than normal quantity. I believe that it is one of the great basic sausages, and you *need* to always keep some in your freezer. Various regional differences can be approximated by substituting coriander or anise for the fennel seed, adding thyme, vermouth, or cayenne.

INGREDIENTS

5 pounds (2.27 kg) pork butt, boned and trimmed of sinew

OR,

4 pounds (1.8 kg) lean pork loin and 1 pound (448 g) unsalted pork fat

2½ teaspoons sea salt

1 tablespoon (heaping) of black pepper, or a generous grinding

1 tablespoon whole fennel seed

Crushed red pepper to taste (use for hot sausage, omit for sweet sausage)

5 feet (1.8 m) of prepared hog casing

METHOD

Par freeze the meat and fat. You will need to work quickly to keep the ingredients chilled. Have the grinder and stuffing attachments sterile and assembled. Load the casing onto the stuffing horn and set aside. Have all ingredients ready and arrayed adjacent to your work surface.

Slice the meat and fat into 1-inch (2.5 cm) slabs. Stack the slabs, then cut again into finger-size pieces. Grind the meat and fat together using the coarse disk for your grinder or grinder attachment.

In a large mixing bowl that has been thoroughly cleaned in soapy water and scalded with boiling water, mix the meat and fat with all remaining ingredients. Using your hands to mix, reach across the ingredients, grasp a handful, and push it down through the center of the mass. Turn bowl a quarter turn and repeat. Continue until well mixed.

Stuff the completed forcemeat firmly into the casings. You may leave the sausage in coils or twist the finished sausage into 3- to 6-inch (7.5 to 15 cm) links. If you will be making links, remember to leave some slack in the casing by understuffing slightly to prevent the casing from bursting when you twist the sausage.

If you will be cooking the sausage within three days, arrange on sheet pans and refrigerate, uncovered, overnight to dry the skins. Then cook, or wrap and store the sausages in the refrigerator until ready to cook. Freeze the remainder of the sausage in meal-sized portions by first wrapping the portions in butcher or wax paper, then placing the wrapped portion in freezer bags from which you remove as much air as possible.

This sausage keeps in the freezer for three months. They will be perfectly safe if you leave them in the freezer longer, but their flavor may begin to fade. When you wish to defrost sausage, place the package in the refrigerator overnight before unwrapping.

YIELD: Approximatley 5 pounds (2.27 kg) of sausage

LUGANEGA

This delicious northern Italian sausage is made without the ubiquitous fennel seed. The parmesan cheese and white wine give this sausage a subtle bite with mellow overtones. If you've only eaten Italian sausage with fennel seed, make this sausage!

INGREDIENTS

2½ pounds (1.12 kg) pork butt, boned and trimmed of sinew

OR,

2 pounds (896 g) lean pork loin and ½ pound (224 g) unsalted pork fat

½ cup (60 g) grated Parmesan cheese

½ teaspoon sea salt

½ tablespoon of white pepper

¼ cup (60 mL) dry white wine

1 tablespoon minced fresh oregano (if using dry oregano, use 1½ teaspoons)

2 cloves fresh garlic, finely minced

4 feet (1.2 m) of prepared hog casing

METHOD

Par freeze the meat and fat. You will need to work quickly to keep the ingredients chilled. Have the grinder and stuffing attachments sterile and assembled. Load the casing onto the stuffing horn and set aside. Have all ingredients ready and arrayed adjacent to your work surface.

Slice the meat and fat into 1-inch (2.5 cm) slabs. Stack the slabs, then cut again into finger-size pieces. Grind the meat and fat together using the coarse disk for your grinder or grinder attachment.

In a large mixing bowl that has been thoroughly cleaned in soapy water and scalded with boiling water, mix the meat and fat with all remaining ingredients. Using your hands, reach across the ingredients, grasp a handful, and push it down through the center of the mass. Turn bowl a quarter turn and repeat. Continue until well mixed.

Stuff the completed forcemeat firmly into the casings. You may leave the sausage in coils or twist the finished sausage into 3- to 6-inch (7.5 to 15 cm) links. If you will be making links, remember to leave some slack in the casing by understuffing slightly to prevent the casing from bursting when you twist the sausage.

If you will be cooking the sausage within three days, arrange on sheet pans and refrigerate, uncovered, overnight to dry the skins. Then cook, or wrap and store the sausages in the refrigerator until ready to cook. Freeze the remainder of the sausage in meal-sized portions by first wrapping the portions in butcher or wax paper, then placing the wrapped portion in freezer bags from which you remove as much air as possible.

This sausage keeps in the freezer for three months. They will be perfectly safe if you leave them in the freezer longer, but their flavor may begin to fade. When you wish to defrost sausage, place the package in the refrigerator overnight before unwrapping.

YIELD: Approximately 3 pounds (1.35 kg) of sausage

COTECHINO

Cotechino has always been a rare treat for me (like sweetbreads, I will always order it when I find it on a menu). The combination of nutmeg, cinnamon, and cloves gives it a distinct spicy flavor. Served with a light lemon sauce and stewed lentils, it is simply wonderful. This is an important New Year's dish in Rome, where the lentils symbolize coins to portend a prosperous year, and the large, fresh, garlic sausage is often stuffed and tied in a boned pig's foot (in which case, it is called Zampone). Barring that, cotechino are typically large sausages stuffed into bungs. This recipe calls for the more easily available hog casings.

INGREDIENTS

- 5 pounds (2.27 kg) of fresh ham, boned and trimmed of sinew
- 1 pound (448 g) of the skin and fat from the ham
- ¼ cup (30 g) of grated Parmesan cheese
- 3 teaspoons sea salt
- 4 teaspoons ground pepper
- ¼ cup (60 mL) dry white wine
- 1 teaspoon cayenne
- 2 teaspoons ground nutmeg
- 2 teaspoons ground cinnamon
- 1 teaspoon ground cloves
- 5 cloves fresh garlic, finely minced
- 5 feet (1.5 m) of prepared hog casing

METHOD

Par freeze the meat and fat. You will need to work quickly to keep the ingredients chilled. Have the grinder and stuffing attachments sterile and assembled. Load the casing onto the stuffing horn and set aside. Have all ingredients ready and arrayed adjacent to your work surface.

Slice the meat and fat into 1-inch (2.5 cm) slabs. Stack the slabs, then cut again into finger-size pieces. Grind the meat and fat together using the coarse disk for your grinder or grinder attachment.

Mix the meat and fat with all remaining ingredients. Grind this mixture a second time, using the fine disk for your grinder or grinder attachment.

Stuff the completed forcemeat firmly into the casings. You may leave the sausage in coils or twist the finished sausage into 3- to 6-inch (7.5 to 15 cm) links. If you will be making links, remember to leave some slack in the casing by understuffing slightly to prevent the casing from bursting when you twist the sausage.

If you will be cooking the sausage within three days, arrange on sheet pans and refrigerate, uncovered, overnight to dry the skins. Then cook, or wrap and store the sausages in the refrigerator until ready to cook. Freeze the remainder of the sausage in meal-sized portions by first wrapping the portions in butcher or wax paper, then placing the wrapped portion in freezer bags from which you remove as much air as possible.

TIP: You may also store these sausages by making a kind of confit, which is meat preserved in solidified fat. To do this, poach the links for 45 minutes, then cool them thoroughly. Place them in a canning jar, and cover them with hot melted fat. You can keep them in the refrigerator for up to two weeks. To serve, reheat the sausages, draining off the fat.

YIELD: Approximatley 6 pounds (2.72 kg) of sausage

cotechino's cousin

Zampone is cotechino stuffed into a boned pig's foot—the word zampa being Italian for pig's foot. Legend has it that this delicacy came about in the 16th century when Modena, its city of origin, was besieged, and the residents could only find pigs' hooves to use as casings for their sausage.

MORTADELLA

In my search for great food with which to feed my friends and family, there are several cooks on whom I know that I can rely. One of these is Marcella Hazan. Although she seems to doubt very much that I will ever be able to find edible ingredients outside of Italy, I have been unfailingly successful with her recipes. One such recipe has become an autumn favorite of mine, Capellacci del Nuovo Mundo, or, pasta stuffed with sweet potatoes. This surprising dish calls for mortadella, the aristocrat of bolognas, which is a large, smooth, pink, pre-cooked sausage unctuous with little islands of snowy fat and studded with peppercorns.

For this mortadella to be authentic, you will need a food processor to emulsify most of the fat and to create a forcemeat that is very fine grained. Also, to be strictly correct, you will need hog bungs or muslin bags (see page 80) to make the sausage as wide as you can, at least 3 inches (7.5 cm). However, you can make it in hog casings. Finally, to achieve the pinkness that we associate with all bolognas, they should be smoked. As an alternative, you can bake them as described below. Enjoy!

INGREDIENTS

- 3 pounds (1.36 kg) of lean pork
- ¾ pound (336 g) of pork fat
- 3 garlic cloves
- 1 teaspoon ground mace
- ¼ teaspoon ground cloves
- ¼ cup (60 mL) dry white wine (such as vermouth)
- 2 tablespoons sea salt
- 1 teaspoon liquid smoke (omit if you will be smoking these)
- 1 teaspoon coriander seeds
- ½ cup (56 g) unsalted, shelled pistachios
- 1½ teaspoons whole peppercorns (or more, I like to mix black and green peppercorns in a ratio of 2 to 1)
- 5 feet (1.5 m) of prepared hog casings, or hog bungs or muslin bags

METHOD

Set aside one-third of the fat and cut it into ¼-inch (.6 cm) cubes. Prepare the remainder of the fat and the meat by cutting them into pieces that are small enough to fit in your food processor. Working in manageable batches, put the remainder of the fat and the meat into your food processor that is fitted with a steel blade, and process until completely smooth. When finished, the mixture should be a fine-grained paste.

Add the garlic, mace, cloves, wine, salt, and liquid smoke (if not smoking the sausage in a smoker) to the emulsified meat and fat mixture, and reprocess in the food processor until all the ingredients are well blended. Place the forcemeat in a mixing bowl, and carefully add all remaining ingredients and the fat that has been cut into ¼-inch (.6 cm) cubes. Mix gently but thoroughly.

Stuff the completed forcemeat firmly into the casings. You may leave the sausage in coils or twist into 3- to 6-inch (7.5 to 15 cm) links. Remember, if you are preparing the sausage for links, leave enough slack in the casing by slightly understuffing to prevent the casing from bursting as you twist.

If you are leaving the sausage in a coil, and before you make links, search for air pockets, prick them with a clean needle, and massage the air out. If you are using a muslin bag, follow the stuffing instructions for Liverwurst on page 80.

If you are using a smoker, cook the mortadella at 275°F (135°C) until it reaches an internal temperature of 170°F (77°C). If you are not using a smoker, place the sausage on a baking sheet and cook the sausage by baking at 200°F (95°C) for 5 hours. Once the mortadella is either smoked or baked, wrap and refrigerate it, where it will keep for two weeks.

YIELD: Approximately 4 pounds (1.8 kg) of sausage

making poultry sausage

Over the past several years, poultry sausage has become very popular in the U.S. Wide varieties are offered in gourmet shops and markets. These products can be excellent, and are typically much lower in fat than those produced from their hoofed brethren. However, when thinking of making poultry sausage, keep in mind this rule of thumb: Low fat can mean dry sausage.

While you can add some pork fat to moisten poultry sausage, it is better (and more common) to use poultry fat and the skin, which you grind into your mixture, as the fat source. Furthermore, dark meat is much more flavorful than white meat. I prefer a mixture of chicken and turkey thighs, which I bone in advance and freeze for future use in 1-pound (.45 kg) portions. Until you have boned poultry a few times, you may find this a little tedious. If you are starting out, you may want to work with a small quantity at first, then build up a reserve over time.

A particularly tasty sausage can be made from free-range chickens, turkeys, ducks, geese, or game birds. Free-range birds exercise all of their muscles, which bathes the flesh in blood and enriches its flavor. Since free-range birds are leaner, you won't get as much fat from the thighs as you would from commercially raised birds, so feel free to include the breast meat if you like. As a side note: Duck and goose fat is extraordinarily unctuous and will produce very moist sausage. Also, as a cooking medium, I prefer it to butter since it burns at a much higher temperature—so even if you don't use it in sausage, save it (or send it to me!).

Remove the bottom of the bone.

Slice the inside length of the leg and thigh.

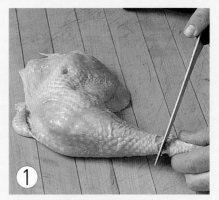
Scrape the meat away from both sides of the bones, then remove the bones.

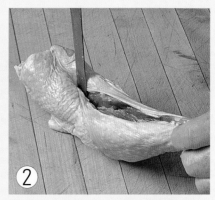
Cut the meat away from the tendons.

Remove the tendons.

Remove the sheet tendons.

PURE POULTRY SAUSAGE
WITH YUCATAN SEASONING

The Yucatan Peninsula is one of my favorite spots on earth. The sun, ancient stone ruins, the ocean—all conspire to put me in a hammock. Sooner or later, I find myself nibbling on appetizers called botanas (spicy pickled onions, carrots, and garlic cloves) waiting for something with cilantro, chilies, and lime juice. Sounds good? Then try these.

INGREDIENTS

- 2 pounds (896 g) boned chicken or turkey thighs with skin
- 1 cup (180 g) onion, minced
- 2 tablespoons vegetable oil
- 2 cloves fresh garlic, minced
- ½ bunch fresh cilantro, leaves only, roughly chopped
- 1 serrano pepper, minced and seeded
- 1 teaspoon salt
- ½ teaspoon allspice, ground
- ½ teaspoon cumin, ground
- ¼ teaspoon cinnamon, ground
- 1 tablespoons sundried tomatoes, soaked in water and minced
  Juice of 1 lime
- 4 feet (1.2 m) of prepared hog casing

METHOD

If not already done, bone the chicken or turkey thighs (see page 48). Par freeze the meat with skin. Have the grinder and stuffing attachments sterile and assembled. Load the casing onto the stuffing horn and set aside. Have all ingredients ready and arrayed adjacent to your work surface.

Slice the meat with skin into 1-inch (2.5 cm) slabs. Stack the slabs, then cut again into finger-size pieces. Grind the meat and skin using the coarse disk for your grinder or grinder attachment.

In a large mixing bowl that has been thoroughly cleaned in soapy water and scalded with boiling water, use your hands to mix the ground meat with all remaining ingredients.

Stuff the completed forcemeat firmly into the casings. Twist the sausage into 4- to 6-inch (10 to 15 cm) links. Since you will be making links, remember to leave some slack in the casing by understuffing slightly to prevent the casing from bursting when you twist the sausage. Remove any air pockets by piercing with a clean needle.

Poach the sausage for 30 minutes (see the directions for poaching on page 38). Prepare and eat immediately, or cool, wrap, and store in the refrigerator for five days, or in the freezer for three months.

YIELD: Approximately 2½ pounds (1.12 kg) of sausage

france

THE NOTION OF FRENCH FOOD IS TOO OFTEN TAKEN EXCLUSIVELY TO INDICATE HIGH SOPHISTICATION. Yet haute cuisine does not even come close to telling the story of this rich tradition. Peasant food, cooked and eaten by those who grow it—*that* forms the spine of the great foods of France. These include intense, rich stews, pot-au-feu or cassoulet (white beans cooked with garlic sausage and preserved duck), and choucroute garnie, the autumn glory of Alsace with braised sweet sauerkraut served with a variety of meats and sausage.

Sausage is peasant food, the richly flavored and ingenious use of "the rest of the beast" left after the farmer has sold the expensive cuts—the tenderloins and rib roasts of beef and pork, and the loin lamb and veal chops. France is known for having more different cheeses than the days of the year, and they could be equally renowned for their variety of sausage.

There are basic types of French sausage: Andouille, andouilletes, boudins noir and blanc, gallantines, crepinettes, saucisson, saucisette, and on and on. Of each type, there are many regional variations. I won't go into all of them, but I will share some history and sausiculture (to coin a word).

One of the signature French sausages, andouillette, consists primarily of one section of pigs' intestines stuffed into another. In a treatise on the French language (written by Henry VIII's Chaplain) the 16th century French word for the section to be stuffed is *endoile*. It comes as a shock for many Americans to learn that the word's early English equivalent was *chyterling*. If you know about cuisine in the southern United States, this should start to sound familiar. To further trace this sausage's lineage, Louisiana's wonderful, spicy Cajun sausage that is a requirement for red beans and rice and many gumbos is called *andouille*.

Back in France it seems that finding the andouille's lineage is not as straightforward. The authors of the survey volume, *The Great Book of Sausages*, found themselves as judges at the annual festival of the society of andouille lovers, known as *La Confrérie des Chevaliers du Goûte-Andouille*. (In France, there are at least two other national associations of friends, or actually knights, of the andouille.) During this festival the Coxes were asked to judge among 80 examples of these delicacies. They report that they were defeated by the task, having made it through only 44 samples of every imaginable permutation of basic ingredients. Just contemplating so many different varieties of one sausage, you must admit, is an indication that France takes its sausage seriously.

One more factoid before we can make some French sausage. The enormous volume, *Larousse Gastronimique, Encyclopedia of Food, Wines and Cookery* by Prosper Montagné has several pages referring to boudins (which also have a Cajun variation). Montagné tells us that boudin noir (a blood sausage) comes to us as a dish very little altered from that produced by the Assyrian pork butchers of Tyre. Among several recipes, one is reproduced in verse as it was written by the French cook/poet Achille Ozanne. This recipe is, unfortunately, neither useful instruction nor good poetry. Merely, that it was written and is preserved speaks volumes. And so, on to the good stuff…

French cassoulet provides a hearty, tasty one-dish meal. (recipe on page 111)

SAUCISSON A L'AIL
GARLIC SAUSAGE

I consider this a quintessentially Gallic sausage. My approach calls for twice the amount of garlic that you might find in other cookbooks, but still less than you might find in a French charcuterie.

During the 1970s and `80s, I lived in Washington, D.C., where the French community was large enough to support a terrific shop called "The French Market." They made the most redolently garlic sausages I had ever tasted. While my culinary courage has occasionally taken me places I will not return, in this case I became a convert. These sausages stood up to the stewing process and partnered with the white beans and preserved duck in the most warming cassoulet I had eaten. Magnificent!

INGREDIENTS

5½ pounds (2.48 kg) of pork butt, boned and trimmed of sinew

OR,

4 pounds (1.8 kg) lean pork loin and 1½ pounds (672 g) unsalted pork fat

1 tablespoon sea salt

1 teaspoon white pepper

1 teaspoon thyme

1 cup (240 mL) cognac

1 bay leaf, minced

5 cloves fresh garlic, finely minced

7 feet (2.3 m) of prepared hog casing

METHOD

Par freeze the meat and fat. You will need to work quickly to keep the ingredients chilled. Have the grinder and stuffing attachments sterile and assembled. Load the casing onto the stuffing horn and set aside. Have all ingredients ready and arrayed adjacent to your work surface.

Slice the meat and fat into 1-inch (2.5 cm) slabs. Stack the slabs, then cut again into finger-size pieces. Grind the meat and fat together using the coarse disk for your grinder or grinder attachment.

In a large mixing bowl that has been thoroughly cleaned in soapy water and scalded with boiling water, mix the meat and fat with all remaining ingredients. Using your hands, reach across the ingredients, grasp a handful, and push it down through the center of the mass. Turn bowl a quarter turn and repeat. Continue until well mixed.

Stuff the completed forcemeat firmly into the casings. You may leave the sausage in coils or twist the finished sausage into 3- to 6-inch (7.5–15 cm) links. If you will be making links, remember to leave some slack in the casing by understuffing slightly to prevent the casing from bursting when you twist the sausage.

If you will be cooking the sausage within three days, arrange on sheet pans and refrigerate, uncovered, overnight to dry the skins. Then cook, or wrap and store the sausages in the refrigerator until ready to cook. Freeze the remainder of the sausage in meal-sized portions by first wrapping the portions in butcher or wax paper, then placing the wrapped portion in freezer bags from which you remove as much air as possible.

This sausage keeps in the freezer for three months. They will be perfectly safe if you leave them in the freezer longer, but their flavor may begin to fade. When you wish to defrost sausage, place the package in the refrigerator overnight before unwrapping.

YIELD: Approximately 5½ pounds (2.48 kg) of sausage

BOUDIN BLANC

Boudin blanc is perhaps the most common sausage in France. Many of them, like this recipe, mix poultry with pork. Where rabbits are plentiful, they are used as well. It is a Christmas and New Year's tradition to serve a version of these very delicate sausages flecked with truffles. If you are feeling flush, buy a small jar or can of black truffles, mince them finely and add them, with their juice, to the sausage mixture.

INGREDIENTS

- ½ pound (224 g) lean pork
- ½ pound (224 g) skinless and boneless chicken breast
- ½ pound (224 g) unsalted pork fat
- 1 small onion, roughly chopped
- 1 tablespoon butter
- 1 cup (240 mL) heavy cream
- ½ cup (115 g) tightly packed, good, white French bread torn into small pieces
- ½ teaspoon of an equal mixture of ground cloves, coriander, and nutmeg
- 1½ teaspoons sea salt
- ¼ teaspoon white pepper
- 1 large whole egg
- 1 egg white
- 3 feet (.9 m) of prepared hog casing

METHOD

Par freeze the meats and fat. Have the grinder and stuffing attachments sterile and assembled. Load the casing onto the stuffing horn and set aside. Have all ingredients ready and arrayed adjacent to your work surface.

Cook the onion in butter until translucent (do not brown), and set aside to cool. Scald (but do not boil) the cream. Pour the cream over the bread that is in a small bowl, and stir in spices, salt, and pepper.

Slice the meats and fat into 1-inch (2.5 cm) slabs. Stack the slabs, then cut again into finger-size pieces. Grind the meats and fat together using the coarse disk for your grinder or grinder attachment.

In a large mixing bowl that has been thoroughly cleaned in soapy water and scalded with boiling water, mix the meat and fat with all remaining ingredients, including the onion and the cream-soaked bread. Using you hands,

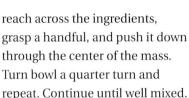

reach across the ingredients, grasp a handful, and push it down through the center of the mass. Turn bowl a quarter turn and repeat. Continue until well mixed.

Stuff the completed forcemeat firmly into the casings. Twist the finished sausage into 3- to 6-inch (7.5 to 15 cm) links. Since you will be making links, remember to leave some slack in the casing by understuffing slightly to prevent the casing from bursting when you twist the sausage. Remove any air bubbles by pricking them with a clean needle.

NOTE: Since this sausage is so delicate, it is best cooked and eaten soon after making it. I suggest that you simply grill it, then serve them with mashed potatoes and a green salad.

YIELD: Approximately 2 pounds (896 g) of sausage

BOUDIN BLANC AUX POMMES
APPLE SAUSAGE

These are among my favorites. If you like to offer tastings with varieties of sausage (as do I), this is one you must include. It is a Norman specialty made with apples, butter, and Calvados, an apple brandy. It is made with half pork and half chicken, and can be made with all chicken if you like. Poach these sausages after stuffing, then heat them through to serve. Another method of serving is to skin them carefully after poaching, roll them in bread crumbs, then fry them in butter until browned.

INGREDIENTS

½ pound (224 g) lean pork

½ pound (224 g) skinless and boneless chicken breast

¼ pound (112 g) unsalted pork fat

2 tablespoons butter

1 small onion, peeled and minced

½ cup (75 g) finely chopped, tart apples, such as Granny Smith

1½ teaspoons sea salt

White pepper, generous grind to taste

½ teaspoon of an equal mixture of ground cloves, ginger, coriander, and cinnamon

2 tablespoons Calvados or cognac

3 feet (.9 m) of prepared hog casing

METHOD

Par freeze the meats and fat. You will need to work quickly to keep the ingredients chilled. Have the grinder and stuffing attachments sterile and assembled. Load the casing onto the stuffing horn and set aside. Have all ingredients ready and arrayed adjacent to your work surface.

In a small sauté pan, melt the butter and cook the onion slowly until translucent. Add the apple to the pan and continue to cook for five minutes. Set aside to cool.

Slice the meats and fat into 1-inch (2.5 cm) slabs. Stack the slabs, then cut again into finger-size pieces. Grind the meat and fat together using the coarse disk for your grinder or grinder attachment.

In a large mixing bowl that has been thoroughly cleaned in soapy water and scalded with boiling water, mix the meat and fat with all remaining ingredients. Using you hands, reach across the ingredients, grasp a handful, and push it down through the center of the mass. Turn bowl a quarter turn and repeat. Continue until well mixed.

Stuff the completed forcemeat firmly into the casings. Twist the finished sausage into 3- to 6-inch (7.5 to 15 cm) links. Since you will be making links, remember to leave some slack in the casing by understuffing slightly to prevent the casing from bursting when you twist the sausage. Remove any bubbles by pricking them with a clean needle.

Since these are to be poached, it is unnecessary to dry them. Poach them for 20 minutes following the directions for poaching on page 38. The sausages are cooked after poaching. You may keep them in the refrigerator for up to three days—simply reheat to serve.

YIELD: Approximately 1½ pounds (672 g) of sausage

CERVELAS AUX PISTACHE
PISTACHIO SAUSAGE

These delicately flavored sausages are excellent breakfast food to serve with omelets. I have suggested that you poach these after stuffing them. Poaching will increase their life in the refrigerator, and they can be easily reheated. They are excellent cold with some French mustard, and look lovely sliced diagonally and arranged on a platter. The meat may be left in bulk to use as a stuffing for Cornish game hens or to make a wonderful sausage roll baked in a short crust, saucisse en croute.

INGREDIENTS

1¼ pounds (560 g) pork butt, boned and trimmed of sinew

OR,

1 pound (448 g) lean pork loin and ¼ pound (112 g) unsalted pork fat

3 ounces (85 g) shelled, unsalted pistachios, roughly chopped

1 teaspoon sea salt

Black pepper, generous grind to taste

⅛ teaspoon nutmeg

¼ teaspoon fresh thyme, or ⅛ teaspoon if using dried thyme

1 clove fresh garlic, finely minced

2 tablespoons cognac

3 feet (.9 m) of prepared hog casing

METHOD

Par freeze the meat and fat. You will need to work quickly to keep the ingredients chilled. Have the grinder and stuffing attachments sterile and assembled. Load the casing onto the stuffing horn and set aside. Have all ingredients ready and arrayed adjacent to your work surface.

Slice the meat and fat into 1-inch (2.5 cm) slabs. Stack the slabs, then cut again into finger-size pieces. Grind the meat and fat together using the coarse disk for your grinder or grinder attachment.

In a large mixing bowl that has been thoroughly cleaned in soapy water and scalded with boiling water, mix the meat and fat with all remaining ingredients. Using your hands, reach across the ingredients, grasp a handful, and push it down through the center of the mass. Turn bowl a quarter turn and repeat. Continue until well mixed.

Stuff the completed forcemeat firmly into the casings. You may leave the sausage in coils or twist the finished sausage into 3- to 4-inch (7.5 to 10 cm) links. If you will be making links, remember to leave some slack in the casing by understuffing slightly to prevent the casing from bursting when you twist the sausage. Remove any bubbles by pricking them with a clean needle.

Since these are to be poached, it is unnecessary to dry them. Poach them for 20 minutes following the directions for Poaching on page 38. The sausages are cooked after poaching. You may keep them in the refrigerator for up to three days—simply reheat to serve. Or, you can freeze the poached sausage for future use. Note: I recommend that you do not freeze these sausages, since the delicate flavor is best enjoyed soon after it is made.

YIELD:
Approximately
1½ half pounds
(672 g) of sausage

THE FRENCH WORD BOUDIN PROVIDES THE ROOT FOR THE ENGLISH WORD PUDDING. Though there is an affinity between the two words, allow me to share with you an example of how concepts often get lost in translation. I will do so by passing on a recipe for white pudding, a dish that is made throughout Great Britain in different versions. The one I share with you below has been blamed on the Scots.

WHITE PUDDING

INGREDIENTS

2 pounds (896 g) oatmeal, toasted lightly in the oven

1 pound (448 g) beef suet, finely minced

2 onions, finely minced

Salt, pepper, and sugar

METHOD

Mix all ingredients and stuff loosely in casings, tying the ends with cotton string. Boil the puddings for an hour, dry them thoroughly, and hang them in a dry ventilated space. These will keep for several months.

Or, you may throw them away immediately. Yes, I understand that these may be appealing to some, just not to me.

I suppose that I should apologize for this cultural slur. I actually have an abiding love for Scotland. Having completed my military obligation in the late 1960s almost unscathed but with a small pension, I scooted across the pond and fetched up on the Scottish Isle of Arran. I intended to spend a month there finding myself; instead, I stayed for two years among the sweetest people I have ever known.

Still, as much as I love Scotland, I ate more turnips with cheese sauce than a man should. It is true that my budget forced me into a diet even more bland than was customary. I still shudder when I think of the Burns' Night Supper I attended. These yearly feasts revolve around a meal that is possible only in a land that has produced single malt whiskey. The whiskey, you see, is so ambrosial and powerful, that when you are under its influence you can eat anything.

The traditional menu on these evenings included Haggis, boiled turnips, boiled potatoes, and boiled suet pudding. Haggis, if you don't already know, is a dish consisting of a mixture of the minced heart, lungs, and liver of a sheep or calf mixed with suet, onions, oatmeal, and seasonings, and boiled in the stomach of the slaughtered animal. In order to convince us to eat the Haggis, we were not only plied with malt whiskey but serenaded with Burns' poetry, climaxing with his immortal *Address to a Haggis*.

While I have not been kidding about the previous British dishes, I will continue by saying that Great Britain has a more conventional, and quite delicious, sausage larder. The British idiosyncrasy is to rely on grain and bread extenders, providing results that are actually very good. The bangers and oyster sausage that follow are two that I have enjoyed.

British bangers and mash (mashed potatoes) are pub food staples.

ADDRESS TO A HAGGIS

– I –

Fair fa' your honest, sonsie face,
Great chieftain o' the puddin-race!
Aboon them a' ye tak your place,
    Painch, tripe, or thairm;
Weel are ye wordy of a grace
    As lang's my arm

– II –

The groaning trencher there ye fill,
Your hurdies like a distant hill,
Your pin wad help to mend a mill
    In time o' need,
While thro' your pores the dews distil
    Like amber bead...

– V –

Os there that owre his French ragout
or olio that wad staw a sow
Or fricasse wad mak her spew
    Wi perfect sconner,
Looks down, wi sneering, scoenful view
    On sic a dinner?...

– VII –

But mark the Rustic, haggis-fed,
The trembling earth resounds his tread,
Clap in his wailie nieve a blade,
    He'll make it whissle;
An' legs, an' arms, an heads will sned
    Like taps of' thrissle.

– VIII –

Ye Pow'rs wha make mankind your care,
And dish them out their bill o' fare,
Auld Scotland wants nae skinking ware,
    That jaups in luggies;
But, if ye wish her gratefu' prayer
    Gie her a Haggis!

BANGERS

Bangers (or Oxford sausages) are perhaps the best known and most common of British sausage. I have maintained the traditional percentage of fat for these versatile treats, although you may wish to reduce it somewhat. Be mindful that the bread will tend to dry out the sausages if you use too little fat.

INGREDIENTS

½ pound (224 g) of lean pork

½ pound (224 g) of lean veal

½ pound (224 g) unsalted pork fat

3 slices white bread with crust, finely chopped

1 cup (240 mL) heavy cream

1 teaspoon sea salt

¼ teaspoon black pepper

¼ teaspoon cayenne

⅛ teaspoon of an equal mixture of ground nutmeg and mace

⅛ teaspoon each of crumbled thyme and marjoram

1 teaspoon crumbled sage

1 teaspoon finely grated lemon peel

1 large whole egg

3 feet (.9 m) of prepared hog casing

METHOD

Par freeze the meats and fat. Have the grinder and stuffing attachments sterile and assembled. Load the casing onto the stuffing horn and set aside. Have all ingredients ready and arrayed adjacent to your work surface.

Slice the meats and fat into 1-inch (2.5 cm) slabs. Stack the slabs, then cut again into finger-size pieces. Grind the meat and fat together using the coarse disk for your grinder or grinder attachment.

In a large mixing bowl that has been thoroughly cleaned in soapy water and scalded with boiling water, knead the meats, fat, and bread together until well mixed. Add the remaining ingredients and mix. Using your hands, reach across the ingredients to grasp a handful, and push it down through the center of the mass. Turn bowl a quarter turn and repeat. Continue until well mixed.

Stuff the completed forcemeat firmly into the casings. Twist the finished sausage into 4- to 6-inch (10 to 15 cm) links. Since you will be making links, remember to leave some slack in the casing by understuffing slightly to prevent the casing from bursting when you twist the sausage. Remove any bubbles by pricking them with a clean needle.

If you will be cooking the sausage within three days, arrange on sheet pans and refrigerate, uncovered, overnight to dry the skins. Then cook, or wrap and store the sausages in the refrigerator until ready to cook. Freeze the remainder of the sausage in meal-sized portions by first wrapping the portions in butcher or wax paper, then placing the wrapped portion in freezer bags from which you remove as much air as possible.

When you wish to defrost sausage, place the package in the refrigerator overnight before unwrapping.

YIELD: Approximately 2 pounds (896 g) of sausage

OYSTER SAUSAGE

These are very simple bulk sausages, coming from a time when oysters were far cheaper than meat in both England and America. Today they make an exotic main course. You can also cook and drain the sausage patties, then break them up into a cornbread stuffing or add the crumbled sausage to a soup.

INGREDIENTS

2 cups (448 g) chopped raw oysters

1 pound (448 g) lean veal

1 slice bacon

½ cup (70 g) bread crumbs

2 teaspoons sea salt

1 teaspoon white pepper

¼ teaspoon nutmeg

Butter, enough for frying the sausage

METHOD

Using a food processor with the steel blade, emulsify the oysters, veal, and bacon.

Place the emulsified ingredients in a bowl. Add the bread crumbs, salt, pepper, and nutmeg. Using a spoon, mix the ingredients together. The mixture will be sticky, so moisten your hands and form them into four to six patties, each approximately ½ inch (1.3 cm) thick.

To cook, heat the butter in a skillet and brown the patties all over. When browned, add enough water to the pan to come halfway up the sides of the sausages. Reduce the heat to medium low, cover and simmer for 8 minutes until the patties are cooked through.

YIELD: 4–6 patties

stocks and broths: *pot-au-feu*

Recognizing that I tend to the extreme in the world of cooking and food, I still believe there are some traditional procedures that clearly make all the difference. If I were reduced to espousing one principle alone, it would be that food benefits more from decent stocks than any other single element. Most people avoid making their own stocks because they view it as a labor of intensive drudgery. Not so.

The liquid by-product of poaching a chicken, fish, or vegetables will make an easy, mild, but serviceable stock. For a full-bodied stock, get in the habit of saving the liquid whenever you poach, then freeze it, and use it the next time you poach something. Continue this process as many times as desired. In this way, you gradually achieve the enriching broth of a pot-au-feu, or fire pot, meaning pot on the stove. In the ideal French farmhouse, this wonderful dish is simply the accumulation of scraps of meat and herbs that is kept bubbling on the back of the stove.

Over time, you'll find that you have created a true, rich stock that will fill the house with warm, delectable aromas—enough to fool anyone who walks in. Only you will know how simple the process is, and how little stove time it actually involves.

THOUGH THERE IS A DARKNESS AND MYSTERY TO THE FOODS OF ALL SPANISH-SPEAKING COUNTRIES, THOSE OF US WHO HAVE SAMPLED THE AUTHENTIC CUISINES HAVE BEEN WON OVER. However, with the exception of a hybrid Mexican cuisine, restaurants that represent the savory and spicy spectrum of these cooking traditions are rare in the United States. Fortunately this is changing, particularly in large cities.

There have always been many wonderful Hispanic/Portuguese restaurants in those cities fortunate to have strong expatriate communities. In Miami, one can eat Cuban foods; in Providence, Rhode Island, Portuguese; in Honolulu, Hawaii, Philippine; and in Washington, D.C., Salvadoran, Colombian, and Brazilian delicacies. (Note that I group the cuisine under the heading Hispanic/Portuguese as a convenience only; the variety of foods from Spain, Portugal, Mexico, the many countries of Latin America and the Caribbean, parts of Africa, and the Philippines is wildly disparate.)

Until recently, a fast-food chain was the only connection most of us have had to the foods of the Iberian peninsula and its former colonies around the world. While the hybrids Tex-Mex, New Mex-Mex, and California-Mex are each interesting and often very satisfying cuisines, they are, frankly, very different from the authentic (and multiple) cuisines of Mexico. I said earlier in the section on Italy, "…if I *had to choose* one and only one culinary source, I would not hesitate to choose Italy." Let me add that the cuisine I might miss most if I did make such a choice would be Mexican.

Very much like the Italian approach to foods, fresh ingredients at the peak of their flavor are crucial to Mexican food. I recommend that you travel within Mexico to sample the enormous fiesta that is celebrated at their national dining table. One reason that I make this suggestion is the labor-intensiveness of Mexican cooking. A close friend who traveled widely in Latin America, and who shared my love for these foods, once said to me as we happily waded through elaborate dishes, "The secret to Mexican cooking is to begin with servants."

The fact that this book interests you, however, suggests that you, like me and my friends, are willing to go the extra mile in the kitchen. Therefore, I recommend for further study all of the wonderful books written by the doyen (for the English-speaking world) of Mexican cuisines, Diana Kennedy.

My concentration on Mexico (and the Mexican approach to chorizo sausage that follows) is simply because of my personal experience and infatuation with that country's food. Equal rhapsody is due to Spain, Portugal, and, in fact, each of those Latin countries blessed with rich soil or waters to create and sustain the traditions of great food. Following you will find three recipes for wonderful sausage—one each from Mexico, Spain, and Portugal.

Caldo verde, flavored with kale, potatoes, and chorizo, is quick and easy to make. (recipe on page 96)

LINGUIÇA

Linguiça is an important component of Portuguese cuisine and is most often smoked. The Spanish equivalent, longaniza, is most often made and used fresh. This version is a compromise and suggests liquid smoke (unless you have access to a smoker). Either way, this sausage benefits from a two- to three-day refrigeration period before cooking (or smoking) to develop the flavors.

INGREDIENTS

1¼ pounds (560 g) pork butt
OR,
1 pound (448 g) lean pork and ¼ pound (112 g) unsalted pork fat

1½ teaspoons sea salt

2 teaspoons sweet paprika

1 teaspoon fresh rosemary, finely minced

2 cloves of fresh garlic, finely minced

2 tablespoons of white vinegar

½ teaspoon liquid smoke (omit if you will be smoking these)

3 feet (.9 m) of prepared hog casing

METHOD

Par freeze the meat and fat. Have the grinder and stuffing attachments sterile and assembled. Load the casing onto the stuffing horn and set aside. Have all ingredients ready and arrayed adjacent to your work surface.

Slice the meat and fat into 1-inch (2.5 cm) slabs. Stack the slabs, then cut again into finger-size pieces. Grind the meat and fat together using the coarse disk for your grinder or grinder attachment.

In a large mixing bowl that has been thoroughly cleaned in soapy water and scalded with boiling water, mix the meat and fat with all remaining ingredients. Using your hands, reach across the ingredients, grasp a handful, and push it down through the center of the mass. Turn bowl a quarter turn and repeat. Continue until well mixed.

Stuff the completed forcemeat firmly into the casings. You may leave the sausage in coils or twist the finished sausage into 3- to 6-inch (7.5 to 15 cm) links. If you will be making links, remember to leave some slack in the casing by understuffing slightly to prevent the casing from bursting when you twist the sausage. Pierce any air pockets with a clean needle.

To develop the flavor before cooking, place the sausage in a colander, loosely covering (not wrapping) the sausage with wax paper or plastic wrap. Place the colander over a pan that is large enough to catch the drippings and place in the refrigerator for two to three days. Discard the drippings daily. Then cook, or wrap and store the sausages in the refrigerator until ready to cook. Use within three days. You may also smoke the sausages after developing the flavor. (See page 39 for general directions for smoking, or follow the manufacturer's instructions for your smoker.)

YIELD: Approximately 1½ pounds (672 kg) of sausage

BUTIFARRA

This delicious sausage comes from Catalonia in northeast Spain. The spicing is complex, and while it is excellent in casseroles or stews, it shines in clear soups. The Spanish institution of tapas, or light meals composed of small portions of several appetizers, features omelets cut into small pieces and served with toast. The Spanish omelet is called a tortilla, and the tortilla Gallego features sausage and potato—butifarra serves this dish superbly.

INGREDIENTS

2 pounds (896 g) pork butt

OR,

1½ pounds (672 g) lean pork and ½ pound (224 g) unsalted pork fat

2 tablespoons white wine

⅛ teaspoon each, cinnamon, nutmeg, cloves, and thyme

2 teaspoons sea salt

⅛ teaspoon sweet paprika

¼ teaspoon black pepper, ground

3 feet (.9 m) of prepared hog casing

METHOD

Par freeze the meat and fat. Have the grinder and stuffing attachments sterile and assembled. Load the casing onto the stuffing horn and set aside. Have all ingredients ready and arrayed adjacent to your work surface.

Slice the meat and fat into 1-inch (2.5 cm) slabs. Stack the slabs, then cut again into finger-size pieces. Grind the meat and fat together using the coarse disk for your grinder or grinder attachment.

Mix the wine with the herbs and spices before mixing with the meat and fat. Put all ingredients in a large mixing bowl that has been thoroughly cleaned in soapy water and scalded with boiling water. Using your hands, reach across the ingredients, grasp a handful, and push it down through the center of the mass. Turn bowl a quarter turn and repeat. Continue until well mixed.

Stuff the completed forcemeat firmly into the casings to form two 30-inch (75 cm) links. Remove any air pockets by piercing them with a clean needle.

Arrange the sausages on a sheet pan and refrigerate, uncovered, for two days to dry the skins. After two days, poach the sausages (see page 38) for 40 minutes. To serve, reheat, or cool and wrap the sausages to store in the refrigerator or freeze.

YIELD: Approximately 2 pounds (896 g) of sausage

round-and-round

Ring bologna and other sausages with ring-like or round shapes that you find in the grocery store are most likely encased in beef rounds. They are the part of the intestine that naturally forms a spiral, making them the perfect choice for encasing recipes that call for this traditional shaping.

CHORIZO

It is probable that every Spanish-speaking country has multiple versions of this sausage. They all contain pork, spices, and vinegar, but beyond that, the variations are many. I am particularly fond of this version to which I have added chipotle peppers—the smoked and dried jalapeños with a very special kick. This recipe is quite spicy, and you may wish to substitute a mild chile powder for the chile mixture.

INGREDIENTS

2½ pounds (1.12 kg) pork butt

OR,

2 pounds (896 g) of lean pork and ½ pound (224 g) unsalted pork fat

5 chiles anchos, minced

2 dried chiles chipotle (or 2 chiles in adobo sauce), minced

½ teaspoon ground coriander

3 whole cloves, ground fresh

½ teaspoon peppercorns

½ teaspoon oregano

¼ teaspoon cumin seed

2 tablespoons sweet paprika

4 cloves fresh garlic, minced

2½ teaspoons sea salt

⅓ cup (80 mL) white vinegar

4 feet (1.2 m) of prepared hog casing

NOTE: Chorizo are often skinned, crumbled, fried, and drained before being added to dishes.

YIELD: Approximately 2½ pounds (1.12 kg) of sausage

METHOD

Par freeze the meat and fat. Have the grinder and stuffing attachments sterile and assembled. Load the casing onto the stuffing horn and set aside. Have all ingredients ready and arrayed adjacent to your work surface.

Place all the dried spices, including chiles, in a dry frying pan and heat until ingredients are pungent and toasted but not smoking. Place them in a coffee grinder, spice mill, or mortar and grind. Set aside.

Slice the meat and fat into 1-inch (2.5 cm) slabs. Stack the slabs, then cut again into finger-size pieces. Grind the meat and fat together using the coarse disk for your grinder or grinder attachment.

In a large mixing bowl that has been thoroughly cleaned in soapy water and scalded with boiling water, mix the meat and fat with all remaining ingredients. Using your hands, reach across the ingredients, grasp a handful, and push it down through the center of the mass. Turn bowl a quarter turn and repeat. Continue until well mixed.

Stuff the completed forcemeat firmly into the casings. You may leave the sausage in coils or twist the finished sausage into 3- to 6-inch (7.5 to 15 cm) links. If you will be making links, remember to leave some slack in the casing by understuffing slightly to prevent the casing from bursting when you twist the sausage. Pierce any air pockets with a clean needle.

These sausages taste better and will keep longer in the refrigerator or freezer if they are slightly dried. To do this, place the fresh sausages in a colander, loosely covering (not wrapping) the sausage with wax paper or plastic wrap. Place the colander over a pan that is large enough to catch the drippings, and place in the refrigerator. The sausages will drain liquid for up to three days. Discard the liquid daily. After three days, arrange the sausage on a sheet pan, making sure you separate them from each other. Bake at 200°F (95°C) for 5 hours. Allow to cool, then wrap and store them in the refrigerator for up to two weeks, or you can store them for many months in the freezer

making seafood sausage

In my experimentation with seafood sausage, I have made some with great success. From my experience, I want to encourage an adventurous spirit—with some warnings. First, keep in mind that most seafood flavors and textures are ephemeral, requiring that seafood be cooked to just the right degree. If you overcook, you bleach the flavor and toughen the texture. If you over-spice, you overwhelm the delicate flavor.

Confusingly, there are exceptions to both rules. Shrimp, crab, and clams can withstand high spice and still exert their flavors. Octopus and squid need lengthy cooking, except when small young specimens are available.

Unlike red meats and poultry, seafood, when ground, can-not be easily formed into shapes. Seafood has a very high moisture content and relatively low viscosity (a kind of well-behaved stickiness) which make it hard to work with. Furthermore, seafood tends to be very low in fat content.

To give seafood sausage some body, grind the seafood with some bread, cooked rice, or potato, then mix with beaten egg. You can also emulsify the seafood in the food processor, adding the binding ingredients toward the end of the process. Another approach is to leave some of the seafood in pieces to mix with ground or emulsified ingredients, providing a visual and textural mosaic to the finished sausage.

The preferred (and my recommended) method for cook-ing seafood sausage is to poach it gently and briefly until warm. This allows the juices to remain in the seafood both to enhance the flavor and keep the delicate texture. Once the sausages are poached you can eat them imme-diately. Or, as the French do, let them cool, cut the cas-ings away, roll the sausages gently in fine bread crumbs, then sauté lightly in butter and serve. Bon appétit!

ABOVE: You can handstuff the emulsified seafood forcemeat.

BELOW: To poach, place sausage in the hot water.

SEAFOOD SAUSAGE

I was raised in a seagoing family. My parents both joined the Coast Guard at the outbreak of World War II. Mother was one of the original SPARS, and the two of them became the first American military officer couple to be married. Dad made a career of it, so for the first 18 years of my life, I was never further than a few miles from the sea.

As a 13 year old, I spent nine months on the Basswood, a buoy tender out of Honolulu. We sailed from our home port to Yokusuka, Japan. I ate some of almost everything that came from the ocean, raw and cooked, from giant clam chowder at an island called Falalop in the Ulithi atoll of Micronesia, to sashimi of tuna belly in Tokyo. If I was ever indifferent to seafood, I cannot remember it.

When it came to this book, I looked forward to making seafood sausage—and I have not been disappointed! Here is a base recipe for which you can substitute any fresh fish or shellfish. Look for clear-eyed fish and sweet-smelling bivalves. The good stuff should not smell fishy at all. While I recognize the contradiction, I do find frozen seafood to be acceptable *if and only if* I can't get fresh. I think of frozen seafood almost as a different food to which I bring different expectations.

I like to poach my seafood sausage in a fish or mixed fish and shellfish fumet, which is a concentrated stock. If I don't have available stock, I will, in a pinch, use bottled clam juice and water in a ratio of 1 to 1. For this recipe (and any that contain raw egg) stuff loosely, since the egg will expand as it cooks.

Even out the seafood forcemeat in the casing by running your hand over the sausage two or three times.

Twist the sausage into links

Use short lengths of kitchen twine to tie off the twists.

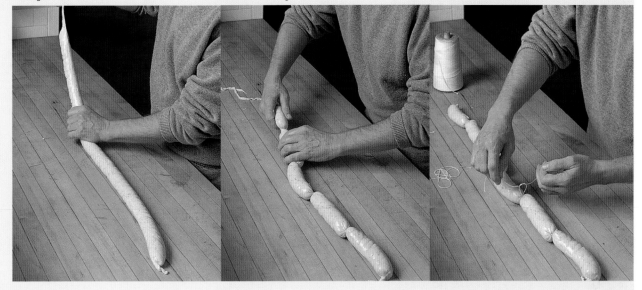

INGREDIENTS

- 1 pound (448 g) fish fillet (choose a mild, non-oily ocean fish such as flounder, cod, or salmon), cubed
- ¼ pound (112 g) bay scallops
- ¼ pound (112 g) crab meat, picked over to remove cartilage
- ¼ pound (112 g) shucked oysters (optional)
- ½ pound (224 g) small shrimp, peeled and deveined
- ½ teaspoon sea salt
- ¼ cup (45 g) onion, minced
- 2 eggs, lightly beaten
- 1 teaspoon fresh dill, minced (½ teaspoon if using dried)
- 2 cloves fresh garlic, minced
- ¼ cup (60 mL) heavy cream
- ½ cup (65 g) unseasoned bread crumbs (optional)
- 3 feet (.9 m) of prepared hog casing.

METHOD

Have the stuffing equipment sterile and assembled. Load the casing onto the stuffing horn and set aside. Have the food processor assembled. Have all ingredients ready and arrayed adjacent to your work surface.

Using the food processor with the steel blade, process all ingredients until emulsified. The forcemeat will resemble a fine, moist paste. If the mixture is too moist, you may wish to add some or all of the bread crumbs to stiffen the mixture before stuffing.

Stuff the forcemeat loosely (since the egg will expand) into the prepared casings. Since the forcemeat is so moist, run your hand over the sausage once or twice after it is stuffed to smooth and even out the forcemeat in the casing. Twist into 7-inch (17.5 cm) links, using kitchen twine to tie off between the links. Remove any air pockets by piercing them with a clean needle.

Poach the sausage for 20 minutes (see the directions for Poaching on page 38). Serve immediately or within 24 hours. You may also wrap and freeze them, where they will keep for three months. To serve, gently reheat by poaching in a flavored broth or dry white wine and water in a ratio of 1 to 1. Or, remove the casings by gently cutting them away, dip the sausage in beaten egg, roll in bread crumbs, and fry in butter until golden.

YIELD: Approximately 3 pounds (1.36 kg) of sausage

scandinavia

THERE ARE IDIOSYNCRATIC APPROACHES TO MEALS THAT OFTEN MAKE IT EASY TO IDENTIFY THE COUNTRY BY THE TABLE. As you might expect, the preservation of foods would be an important consideration for countries with limited growing and hunting seasons. While the requirements of the land shape a cuisine, the foods and food traditions that are subsequently produced define the country. The countries of Scandinavia are renowned (at least in Europe) for their preserved meats. While there are very interesting differences between each country's approach, one of the shared characteristics is unusual spicing such as ginger and cardamom. Norwegian sausages, called pølse (as they are also known in Denmark), tend to rely on herbs for flavoring, while the others tend toward spices.

While lamb is rare in Denmark and in Sweden, it is prized in Norway. Danish sausages benefit from the extremely high standards that the country assigns to its beef and pork. Blood sausages in many forms have always been popular and continue so in Norway. Reindeer meat, all but unheard of in the rest of the world, is exported from Lapland to all of Scandinavia.

The sausage (as well as the entire cuisine) of Finland is influenced by its disparate neighbors, Sweden and Russia. Finnish sausage, makkara, and other meats were once grilled on the stones that provide the heat in saunas. Today, it is common for sauna dressing rooms to have fireplaces for this purpose. Scandinavians prefer a thick yellow pea soup with chunks of smoked sausage, while further south in Belgium, the same dish is served with green split peas.

I have included a recipe for Swedish potato sausage julkorv (*korv* is the Swedish word for sausage) that is central to their Christmas table. These treats are part of the elaborate set of customs and rituals that revolve around this important holiday. I once enjoyed a Christmas with a Swedish-American family that seemed to share dozens of events and meals that were clearly annual expectations. I particularly enjoyed a wonderful braided bread flavored with dill weed. After the holiday, I asked the hostess to make it again. She was astounded that I might even consider eating this Christmas dish out of its season!

To extend the life of the meats, the Swedes often store them in a sugar and salt brine. This instinct to store and preserve for the winter is carried by the Swedes throughout the world. I had a shipmate on an ocean-going towboat where I cooked for a summer who traveled everywhere with an oak cask and pickling spices. He often put up herring, but it could have easily been värmlandskorv, a variation on the following recipe for Christmas sausage.

Split pea soup and julkorv, a potatoe sausage, is classic Scandinavian fare. (recipe for soup is on page 110)

MEDVURST

This is a traditional smoked beef and pork sausage that is delicious in vegetable or pea soups. In Denmark, beautiful open-faced sandwiches called smorrebrød are often topped with poached slices of this sausage. If you come from the northern Midwest of the United States and remember smorgasbord, you may have tasted this sausage.

INGREDIENTS

- 1 pound (448 g) lean pork, finely ground
- 1 pound (448 g) lean beef, finely ground
- ¼ pound (112 g) unsalted pork fat, finely ground
- ¼ cup (60 mL) lager beer
- 2 teaspoons sea salt
- 1 teaspoon sugar
- ½ teaspoon ground black pepper
- ⅛ teaspoon ground cloves
- ⅛ teaspoon nutmeg
- ¼ teaspoon caraway seeds
- ¼ teaspoon ground coriander
- ⅜ teaspoon dried mustard
- ½ teaspoon liquid smoke (omit if you will be smoking these)
- 4 teaspoons coarse salt
- 2 teaspoons sugar
- 4 feet (1.2 m) of prepared hog casing

METHOD

Par freeze the meats and fat. Have the grinder and stuffing attachments sterile and assembled. Load the casing onto the stuffing horn and set aside. Have all ingredients ready and arrayed adjacent to your work surface.

Slice the meats and fat into 1-inch (2.5 cm) slabs. Stack the slabs, then cut again into finger-size pieces. Grind the meats and fat together using the fine disk for your grinder or grinder attachment.

Add all but the 4 teaspoons of coarse salt and 2 teaspoons of sugar to the beer. In a large mixing bowl that has been thoroughly cleaned in soapy water and scalded with boiling water, use your hands to mix the ground beef, pork, and fat together. When well mixed, add the beer mixture to the meat.

Stuff the completed forcemeat firmly into the casings. Twist into 4-inch (10 cm) links. Since you will be making links, remember to leave some slack in the casing by understuffing slightly to prevent the casing from bursting when you twist the sausage. Remove any air pockets by piercing them with a clean needle. Mix the remaining sugar with the coarse salt and rub over the sausages.

Place the sausages in a colander, loosely covering (not wrapping) the sausage with wax paper or plastic wrap. Place the colander over a pan that is large enough to catch the drippings, and place in the refrigerator. Keep in this way until the sausages no longer release liquid. This can take up to two days. Rinse the sausages.

Poach the sausages for 20 minutes (see the directions for Poaching on page 38). Alternatively if you have a smoker, rinse and wipe the sausages after they have finished releasing liquid. Smoke them at 275°F (135°C) until they reach an internal temperature of 170°F (77°C). This should take approximately 4 hours. (See the basic directions for smoking on page 39.)

YIELD: Approximately 2½ pounds (1.12 kg) of sausage

KAALIKAARYLEET

Have you considered that stuffed cabbage meets most of the definition of sausage? You can also use grape leaves, onions, or lettuce leaves as your casing. Some historians have speculated that the Vikings, who traded with Constantinople in the 10th century, might have brought back from the Middle East the notion of forcemeat stuffed into vegetables. Here is a Finnish version that contains barley.

INGREDIENTS

- ⅓ cup (67 g) pearl barley, soaked in water to cover for 1 to 4 hours
- 1 cup (240 mL) water
- 1 large head of cabbage
- 1 pound (448 g) beef with approximately 20% fat, coarsely ground ¼ pound (112 g) veal, coarsely ground
- 1 teaspoon sea salt
- ¼ teaspoon black pepper
- ½ teaspoon allspice
- ¼ cup (60 mL) heavy cream
- 3 tablespoons unsalted butter
- 4 teaspoons molasses
- 1 tablespoon white flour

YIELD: Approximately 12 rolls

METHOD

Drain the barley and cook in the water for 30 minutes. Strain and cool. Boil the cabbage in a large pot of water for 10 minutes, or until the leaves are pliable.

If you are grinding your own meat, par freeze the meat, then slice into 1-inch (2.5 cm) slabs. Stack the slabs, then cut again into finger-size pieces. Grind the meats together using the coarse disk for your grinder or grinder attachment.

Put the barley, meats, salt, pepper, allspice, and cream in a large mixing bowl that has been thoroughly cleaned in soapy water and scalded with boiling water. Mix by hand until well mixed.

Carefully detach 12 large cabbage leaves and cut out the hard rib of the stem, allowing the leaves to fold without breaking.

Place a generous tablespoonful of the filling on the leaf, leaving a 1-inch (2.5 cm) border on each side of the leaf, and a ½-inch (1.5 cm) border on the end nearest to you. Fold the sides over the meat toward the center, then roll the package up away from you. Repeat until the filling is gone.

Preheat the oven to 350˚F (175˚C). Melt the butter in an ovenproof skillet large enough to contain all of the cabbage rolls. Place the rolls in the skillet, seam side down, and brown on all sides, turning as needed. Carefully pour in enough water to not quite cover the rolls, and place in the oven for 1 hour. Drizzle the molasses over the rolls, and bake an additional 30 minutes.

Remove the rolls from the skillet, keeping them covered and warm. Place the skillet on the stove top. Over medium heat, gradually stir in the flour and cook, stirring until the sauce is smooth and thickend. Pour over the rolls and serve.

RIISMAKKARA

This Finnish sausage provides a lovely contrast in flavors and textures between rice, raisins, and the richness of liver. These can be served as chilled slices for an appetizer, or skinned and mixed with cream cheese as a spread. When making the sausage, try to avoid breaking up the rice and raisins; maintaining the contrast in textures is an important part of this recipe.

INGREDIENTS

2¼ cups (540 mL) milk

½ cup (112 g) rice

½ pound (224 g) beef or pork liver, finely ground

1 small onion, minced

3 tablespoons unsalted butter (or beef suet)

3 tablespoons corn syrup

½ teaspoon ginger

6 tablespoons raisins

1 teaspoon salt

¼ teaspoon black pepper

2 feet (.6 m) of prepared hog casing

METHOD

Have the grinder and stuffing attachments sterile and assembled. Load the casing onto the stuffing horn and set aside. Have all ingredients ready and arrayed adjacent to your work surface.

Bring 1½ cups (360 mL) of the milk to a boil. Add the rice, and lower the heat to a low simmer. Cover and cook for 15 minutes or until the milk has been absorbed. Be careful that the rice does not burn. Cool.

If you are grinding your own liver, par freeze the liver, then slice into 1-inch (2.5 cm) slabs. Stack the slabs, then cut again into finger-size pieces. Grind the liver using the fine disk for your grinder or grinder attachment.

Melt the butter or suet slowly in a skillet, then cook the onion in it until it is translucent. Add the liver and break it up as small as you can while it cooks. Remove from the heat, and cool slightly.

In a large bowl, add the contents of the skillet, the rice, and the remaining ingredients, including the rest of the milk. Stuff the completed forcemeat loosely into the casings. Twist the sausage into 4-inch (10 cm) links, using kitchen twine to tie off between the links. Remove any air pockets by piercing them with a clean needle.

Poach the sausage for 45 minutes. (See the directions for Poaching on page 38.) If the sausage floats during poaching, prick them a few times with a fork. After poaching, the sausages are ready to eat. Or, wrap and refrigerate for use within five days. These sausages do not freeze well.

YIELD: Approximately 1¼ pounds (560 g) of sausage

making game sausage

If you hunt, or know someone who does, you'll find that making (and eating) sausage from game will provide you with one of the world's tastiest offerings. Handling game meat when making sausage follows the basic procedures of grinding, mixing, and stuffing. However, since game meat tends to be lean, be aware that you may need to add additional fat in the form of suet or fatback to reach the ideal 20 to 25 percent fat to lean ratio. You can judge this by examining the cut of meat for the amount of marbling running through the flesh. Also be aware that game may need more attention when trimming tendons and sinew from the meat. Some traditional seasonings you may want to try in your game sausage are sage and garlic. If you want to experiment further, try dried mushrooms (that have been soaked) and walnuts in the recipe for an earthy complement.

GAME SAUSAGE

As discussed, the original purpose of sausage was to make the best use of meats when slaughtering took place. It is rare for us today to need to preserve a full carcass except, of course, when hunting season is on. Venison, rabbit, duck, boar... all wild game, is excellent for sausage. The following recipe comes from a restaurant in San Antonio, Texas, that specializes in southwestern cuisine. If you do not have a good source for fresh rattlesnake meat, venison will do.

INGREDIENTS

½   pound (224 g) rattlesnake meat

¼   pound (112 g) lean pork

¼   pound (112 g) fatback, blanched and drained

1   tablespoon brandy

2   teaspoons cumin, ground

1   teaspoon salt

1   teaspoon white pepper, ground

½   teaspoon smoked venison (you can substitute Canadian bacon), diced

1   tablespoon fresh tarragon (or 1 teaspoon if using dried)

2   tablespoons red pepper, diced

2   feet (.6 m) of prepared hog casing

METHOD

Bone and skin the rattlesnake.

Par freeze the meat and fat. Have the grinder and stuffing attachments sterile and assembled. Load the casing onto the stuffing horn and set aside. Have all ingredients ready and arrayed adjacent to your work surface.

Slice the meat and fat into 1-inch (2.5 cm) slabs. Stack the slabs, then cut again into finger-size pieces. Grind the meat and fat together using the coarse disk for your grinder or grinder attachment.

In a food processor with a steel blade, mix the spices and brandy with the ground meat and fat. Process until the mixture resembles a fine paste. In a large mixing bowl that has been thoroughly cleaned in soapy water and scalded with boiling water, mix the meat mixture with the diced smoked meat, tarragon, and red pepper.

Stuff the completed forcemeat firmly into the casings. Twist the sausage into 4- to 6- inch (10 to 15 cm) links. Since you will be making links, remember to leave some slack in the casing by understuffing slightly to prevent the casing from bursting when you twist the sausage. Remove any air pockets by piercing them with a sterile needle.

Poach the sausage for 30 minutes (see the directions for Poaching on page 38). Eat immediately by preparing as desired (they are also very good smoked). Or cool, wrap, and store in the refrigerator for five days or in the freezer for three months.

YIELD: Approximately 1 pound (448 g) of sausage

germany

AS I MENTIONED EARLIER, PART OF MY FORMATION AS A COOK INCLUDED MY SUMMER IN A GERMAN KITCHEN. While living in that country, I quickly learned that there is much to celebrate in German food, and chief among these celebrations are the vast array of sausages or wursts. Say what you will about German cuisine, but much of what the world knows about sausages is owed to our Teutonic cousins.

Germany and Austria, from which half of my ancestors come, are best known for their white sausages and liver sausages. Liverwurst may be the best known product, although the Midwest of the United States might collapse without the mighty bratwurst. The chauvinism of my Italian friends prevented them from admitting it, but some of the finest street food in the world can be picked up from vendors of wurstchen.

Most of the sausage producers of the world make varieties of head-cheese. While I am unable to get my daughters to try it, I am very fond of this most economic of dishes. When I worked in the kitchen in Hamburg, we were fed twice each shift (a work schedule spanning 3 P.M. to midnight). The second of these meals was called abendbrot (evening bread) and consisted of a mild butterkäse, or butter cheese; volkornbrot, a dense, sour bread full of nutty kernels of grain; and a rich slice of headcheese.

This rich mosaic of bits of meat in its own jelly was a secret vice. It's simple to make. Irma Rombauer (whose *Joy of Cooking* is the one indispensable cookbook I know of) says (as if we all have cooperative butchers), "Have the butcher skin and quarter a calf head. Clean the teeth with a stiff brush and remove ears, brains, eyes, snout and most of the fat..." I won't go any further, except to explain that one cooks the head with some vegetables until the meat falls off the bones. You then gather the meat, strain the stock, concentrate it further, season it, pour it over the meat bits in a mold, and chill until set. Slice and serve. Trust me or try it, it is delicious.

Here, I present some more conventional sausages, including a recipe that may revive the soiled concept of Vienna sausage (although they solved my hunger as a young Boy Scout unable to actually live off the land without a can or two). You'll find that these are far better than the pale versions found in your grocery store.

A German slachtplatte, or butcher's plate, is a perfect way to serve a variety of sausages.

BOCKWURST

Like many of the great German white sausages, bockwurst is composed of veal with some milk. This one is best when very finely ground, and I recommend emulsifying the forcemeat with a food processor. If you do not have a food processor, you can put all of the ingredients through the fine disk of your grinder two or three times.

INGREDIENTS

- 1¾ pounds (784 g) veal
- ¼ pound (112 g) unsalted pork fat
- ¼ cup (45 g) onion, minced
- ¾ teaspoon ground cloves
- ½ teaspoon white pepper
- 2 teaspoons fresh parsley, minced
- ½ teaspoon sea salt
- 1 egg, beaten
- 1 cup (240 mL) milk
- 4 feet (1.2 m) of prepared hog casing

METHOD

Par freeze the meat and fat. Have the grinder and stuffing attachments sterile and assembled. Load the casing onto the stuffing horn and set aside. Have all ingredients ready and arrayed adjacent to your work surface.

Slice the meat and fat into 1-inch (2.5 cm) slabs. Stack the slabs, then cut again into finger-size pieces. Grind the meat and fat together using the fine disk for your grinder or grinder attachment.

In a large mixing bowl that has been thoroughly cleaned in soapy water and scalded with boiling water, mix the ground meat and fat with all remaining ingredients. Using your hands, reach across the ingredients, grasp a handful, and push it down through the center of the mass. Turn bowl a quarter turn and repeat. Continue until well mixed.

Place the mixed forcemeat into your food processor with a steel blade. Process the forcemeat until it is emulsified and resembles a fine-grained paste. If you do not have a food processor, regrind the forcemeat two or three times through the fine disk of your grinder.

Stuff the completed forcemeat firmly into the casings. Twist the sausage into 4-inch (10 cm) links. Since you will be making links, remember to leave some slack in the casing by understuffing slightly to prevent the casing from bursting when you twist the sausage. Remove any air pockets by piercing with a clean needle.

To cook, boil for 30 minutes. If you are not eating these immediately after cooking, wrap and store the sausages in the refrigerator for up to five days, then reheat when ready to serve.

YIELD: Approximately 2 pounds (896 g) of sausage

BRATWURST

For a summer meal, grilled brats accompanied by potato salad, sauerkraut, mustard, and beer are unbeatable. Come to think of it, this meal may be necessary to the full enjoyment of football tailgate parties as well.

INGREDIENTS

1½ pounds (672 g) pork butt

⅔ pound (297 g) veal

¼ cup (58 g) white bread, no crust

¾ cups (180 mL) milk

1 teaspoon salt

¼ teaspoon white pepper

¼ teaspoon mace

¼ teaspoon crumbled marjoram

4 feet (1.2 m) of prepared hog casing

METHOD

Par freeze the meats. Soak the bread in the milk until the bread is soft. Drain the bread, reserving the milk, and set aside.

Have the grinder and stuffing attachments sterile and assembled. Load the casing onto the stuffing horn and set aside. Have all ingredients ready and arrayed adjacent to your work surface.

Slice the meats into 1-inch (2.5 cm) slabs. Stack the slabs, then cut again into finger-size pieces. Grind the meats together using the coarse disk for your grinder or grinder attachment. You can emulsify the meat in a food processor with a steel blade if you wish, processing until the meats resemble a fine-grained paste. However, I prefer to grind the meats coarse for a chunky consistency.

Place the meat and all remaining ingredients in a large mixing bowl that has been thoroughly cleaned in soapy water and scalded with boiling water. Using your hands, reach across the ingredients, grasp a handful, and push it down through the center of the mass. Turn bowl a quarter turn and repeat. Continue until well mixed.

Stuff the completed forcemeat firmly into the casings. Twist the sausage into 4-inch (10 cm) links. Since you will be making links, remember to leave some slack in the casing by understuffing slightly to prevent the casing from bursting when you twist the sausage. Remove any air pockets by piercing them with a clean needle.

You may poach the sausage for 20 minutes (see the directions for Poaching on page 38), then fry the brats just before eating. However, I prefer and highly recommend them grilled fresh. You can wrap and store the cooled poached sausage in the refrigerator for up to five days, and in the freezer for three months.

YIELD: Approximately 2½ pounds (1.2 kg) of sausage

LIVERWURST

No discussion of German sausage is complete without this delicatessen standby. As a college student in New York City, I often ate a bagel covered with a thick slice of liverwurst that was slathered in mustard and topped with Bermuda onion for breakfast. As well as satisfying my hunger, it helped get me a seat on the subway.

For this sausage, you really need a casing larger than hog casings. If you are unable to find hog bungs, make a muslin casing as follows: Obtain unbleached muslin and cut a piece 8 by 12 inches (20 x 30 cm). Fold it lengthwise and, leaving an ⅛-inch (.3 cm) border, stitch the open side and one end to form a sleeve. Turn the sleeve inside out so that the stitching is on the inside. If you suspect that the muslin has been sized with glue, soak the casing in plain water and wring it out, letting it dry thoroughly before stuffing.

INGREDIENTS

1 pound (448 g) pork butt

OR,

¾ pound (336 g) lean pork loin and ¼ pound (112 g) unsalted pork fat

1 pound (448 g) fresh pork liver

1 large yellow onion, minced

1½ teaspoons sea salt

¼ cup (35 g) powdered milk

1 teaspoon white pepper

2 teaspoons paprika

1 teaspoon sugar

½ teaspoon crumbled marjoram

½ teaspoon ground coriander

¼ teaspoon mace

¼ teaspoon allspice

¼ teaspoon cardamom

Muslin casing or hog bung

YIELD: Approximately 2 pounds (896 g) of sausage

METHOD

Par freeze the meats and fat. At all times keep the ingredients quite cold, refrigerating when necessary. Have the grinder and stuffing attachments sterile and assembled. Load the casing onto the stuffing horn and set aside. Have all ingredients ready and arrayed adjacent to your work surface.

Slice the meats and fat into 1-inch (2.5 cm) slabs. Stack the slabs, then cut again into finger-size pieces. Grind the meats and fat together using the fine disk for your grinder or grinder attachment.

Place the ground meat, fat, and remaining ingredients in a large mixing bowl that has been thoroughly cleaned in soapy water and scalded with boiling water. Using your hands, reach across the ingredients, grasp a handful, and push it down through the center of the mass. Turn bowl a quarter turn and repeat. Continue until well mixed.

Place the mixed forcemeat into a food processor with a steel blade. Process the forcemeat until it is emulsified and resembles fine-grained paste. If you do not have a food processor, regrind the forcemeat through the fine disk of your grinder two or three times. Refrigerate the emulsified mixture for 30 minutes. Since the mixture is sticky, it is easier to pack it into the muslin casing if it is chilled.

To stuff, fold back the open end of the muslin casing and pack the forcemeat into it as firmly as you can, leaving approximately a ½-inch (1.3 cm) seam allowance at the top of the bag. Either sew the top end shut or, using pliers and strong wire, wrap the wire around the end. Whether you sew the end or wrap with wire, make sure the end is tied off very tightly to prevent any forcemeat from seeping out as the sausage cooks.

In a large pot, boil enough water to cover the sausage by 2 or 3 inches (5 or 7.5 cm). Immerse the sausage and weight it down with a plate to keep it submerged. When the water returns to a boil, reduce the heat to barely a simmer and cook for 3 hours. When finished, drain the water and cover the sausage with ice water until cool. Refrigerate overnight and remove casing. Wrap and store the liverwurst in the refrigerator, where it will keep for up to 10 days.

VIENNA SAUSAGE

You may poach and refrigerate these sausages once they are made as I suggest below. Or you can preserve them as a confit which is one way to extend the shelf life of the sausage while adding extra flavor. To make a confit, poach the links for 45 minutes, then cool them thoroughly. Place them in a canning jar and cover them with hot melted fat, cover the jar and store in the refrigerator, where the sausages will keep for eight weeks. To serve, reheat them and drain off the fat.

INGREDIENTS

1½ pound (672 g) pork butt

OR,

1 pound (448 g) lean pork loin and ½ pound (224 g) unsalted pork fat

1 pound (448 g) lean beef

½ pound (224 g) veal

2 tablespoons onion, minced

1½ teaspoons sea salt

½ teaspoon cayenne

1 teaspoon paprika

1 teaspoon sugar

1½ teaspoons ground coriander

½ teaspoon mace

½ cup (70 g) powdered milk

½ cup (120 mL) cold water

4 feet (1.2 m) of prepared hog casing

YIELD: Approximately 3 pounds (1.36 kg) of sausage

METHOD

Par freeze the meats and fat. Have the grinder and stuffing attachments sterile and assembled. Load the casing onto the stuffing horn and set aside. Have all ingredients ready and arrayed adjacent to your work surface.

Slice the meats and fat into 1-inch (2.5 cm) slabs. Stack the slabs, then cut again into finger-size pieces. Grind the meats and fat together using the fine disk for your grinder or grinder attachment.

Place the ground meat, fat, and remaining ingredients in a large mixing bowl that has been thoroughly cleaned in soapy water and scalded with boiling water. Using your hands, reach across the ingredients, grasp a handful, and push it down through the center of the mass. Turn bowl a quarter turn and repeat. Continue until well mixed.

Place the mixed forcemeat into a food processor with a steel blade. Process the forcemeat until it is emulsified and resembles fine-grained paste. If you do not have a food processor, regrind the forcemeat through the fine disk of your grinder two or three times. Refrigerate the emulsified mixture for 30 minutes.

Stuff the emulsified forcemeat into the casings. Twist the sausage into 4-inch (10 cm) links. Using kitchen twine, tie off the links between twists. Since you will be making links, remember to leave some slack in the casing by understuffing slightly to prevent the casing from bursting when you twist the sausage. Remove any air pockets by piercing them with a clean needle.

Poach the sausage for 30 minutes (see poaching directions on page 38). After poaching, cool the sausages. Make sure they are dry before wrapping them to store in the refrigerator. They will keep for one week. You may also make a confit as suggested above.

asia, the middle east, and greece

BEFORE I RETURN TO THE UNITED STATES IN THE NEXT SECTION, I WANT TO VISIT THE REST OF THE WORLD. It may be an injustice to the enormous variety of cultures and cuisines outside of Europe to relegate such small space to them. However, this is due in part to my own limited experience, combined with the fact that there are not as many sausages to present. To summarize this chapter, let me quote Spencer Tracy as he regarded the slender Katharine Hepburn, "There's not much there. But what's there is choice."

One limitation in the world of Asian sausage may result from the restricted amount of meat in the overall diet. This can be better understood when you realize that beef was only introduced in the 16th century by European traders. Finally, although there are several indigenous types of sausage throughout Asia, China seems to have gotten it right the first time. I refer to the fact that one sausage, lop cheong, is used throughout Asia, and used far more often than any other variety. It is wonderful and unlike any European sausage.

These Chinese sausages (as they are referred to everywhere) are extremely versatile, and show up sliced along with bowls of rice or noodles, baked or steamed in dough, and in exotic Thai salads. If you've never had them, the recipe for them may alone justify the purchase of this book. I have included the Thai crab and pork si klok as a very good example of a mixed meat and seafood sausage. Be careful— Thai food can burn out your taste buds if you are unaccustomed to highly spiced foods.

The recipe for lamb sausage, merguez, is Tunisian and Algerian, although I first tasted it in a Lebanese restaurant. This style of skinless sausage from North Africa and the Middle East has influenced European cooking. Much of Southern Africa has adopted variations on British and Dutch sausage. Although the bulk of North Africa and the Middle East is Moslem, and therefore they eat no pork, they more than compensate with inventive spicing and lamb.

Greece, which has given us some of the earliest references to sausages, still loves them. The example I have included, keftedakia, is available grilled in the Acropolis in Athens. There are shops in Greece, known as *allantopoleion*, that are devoted to sausages.

This Thai salad, featuring the Asian sausage lop cheong, is a perfect balance of sweet, sour, and spicy flavors. (recipe on page 101)

LOP CHEONG

These sausages are used throughout Asia as we might use ham—in salads, diced in noodle or rice dishes, or sliced into soups. They are unusual in their sweetness, making them quite exotic, savory, and wonderful. I have made them both by grinding the meat and fat and by cubing them. While it is a bit tedious to cube the meat and fat into small uniform bits, the result is much more interesting. When you are finished making these, they will be thoroughly baked and will keep for two weeks in the refrigerator or six months in the freezer. If you buy them at an Asian market, they are cured and dried, and will keep in the refrigerator for two months.

INGREDIENTS

2 pounds (896 g) lean pork

¾ pound (336 g) unsalted pork fat

3 tablespoons sugar

2 tablespoons soy sauce

2 tablespoons sweet rice wine

2 tablespoons sake

2 teaspoons salt

¼ teaspoon 5-spice powder

4 feet (1.2 m) of prepared hog casing

YIELD: Approximately 2¾ pounds (1.2 kg) of sausage

METHOD

Par freeze the meat and fat. Preheat your oven to 200°F (95°C). Work quickly and keep ingredients chilled. Have grinder and stuffing attachments sterile and assembled. Load casing onto stuffing horn and set aside. Have all ingredients ready and arrayed adjacent to your work surface.

Beginning with the meat, slice it into ¼-inch (.6 cm) slabs. Stack the slabs, then cut again into ¼-inch (.6 cm) sticks pieces. Align the sticks and cut into cubes. You want to aim for a ¼-inch (.6 cm) dice. Repeat this process with the fat. (See page 28 for the how-to photos illustrating this process.)

In a large mixing bowl that has been thoroughly cleaned in soapy water and scalded with boiling water, combine the diced meat and fat with all remaining ingredients. Use your hands to mix until well mixed.

Stuff the completed forcemeat firmly into the casings. Because the forcemeat is diced rather than ground or emulsified, you want to stuff the sausage firmly, but will need to allow a little slack for making the links to accommodate the chunkier texture. Twist into three-inch (7.5 cm) links. Pierce any air pockets with a clean needle.

Place a baking rack on top of a sheet pan. Arrange the sausages on the rack so they do not touch each other. Place the sausages in the oven and bake at 200°F (95°C) for 5 hours. After 5 hours, turn off the oven and, without opening the oven door, leave the sausages in the oven for another 2 hours. When you remove the sausages from the oven, wipe off any excess fat.

The sausages are ready to eat, or can be kept in the refrigerator or freezer as noted above. These sausages are particularly nice when sliced for stir-fry or steamed.

SI KLOK

These are from Thailand and are meant to be very spicy—you may need to adjust the level of heat to suit your taste. You can make them using all pork or, as presented here, with half pork meat and half pure crabmeat. Although the sausages are normally eaten poached in Thailand, they are delicious sliced and stir-fried or grilled.

INGREDIENTS

- ½ pound (224 g) pork butt, finely ground
- ½ pound (224 g) crabmeat, cooked and shredded
- 2 teaspoons fish sauce
- 2 tablespoons unsweetened coconut milk
- ¼ teaspoon salt
- ¼ teaspoon chili paste
- ⅛ teaspoon black pepper
- 2 tablespoons fresh coriander, minced (never substitute with dried coriander)
- 3 tablespoons regular chunky peanut butter, avoid extra chunky
- 1 clove fresh garlic, minced
- 2 feet (.6 m) of prepared hog casing

METHOD

Par freeze the meat and fat. Have the grinder and stuffing attachments sterile and assembled. Load the casing onto the stuffing horn and set aside. Have all ingredients ready and arrayed adjacent to your work surface.

Slice the meat and fat into 1-inch (2.5 cm) slabs. Stack the slabs, then cut again into finger-size pieces. Grind the meat using the fine disk for your grinder or grinder attachment.

In a large mixing bowl that has been thoroughly cleaned in soapy water and scalded with boiling water, mix the liquids and spices together first. Then add the ground meat, crabmeat, peanut butter, and garlic. Using your hands, reach across the ingredients, grasp a handful, and push it down through the center of the mass. Turn bowl a quarter turn and repeat. Continue until well mixed.

Stuff the completed forcemeat firmly into the casing to form a single link. Tie off the end by making an overhand knot in the casing or by using a short length of kitchen twine. Remove any air pockets by pricking them with a clean needle.

Poach for 30 minutes (see the directions for poaching on page 38). Eat immediately, or cool before wrapping and storing in the refrigerator, where they will keep for one to one and one-half weeks, or in the freezer for three months.

YIELD: Approximately 1 pound (448 g) of sausage

MERGUEZ

One of my favorite restaurants in Washington, D.C.'s polyglot community was a wonderful Lebanese place south of Dupont Circle. Out of the tourists' path, down a flight of stairs in a warm room, it was always full of groups arguing over the politics of the world, while sharing mezze or appetizers Middle Eastern-style.

One of the most delicious dishes was a lamb sausage that was split open and broiled. It was spicy with harissa, a chili condiment popular throughout the Arabic world (and in my house). With a squeeze of lemon juice and a basket of toasted pita bread wedges I was in my element—solving the world's problems over heated discussions and great food.

The sausages may be made with goat or beef, but I far prefer lamb. You can prepare this as a bulk sausage rather than stuffing the forcemeat in a casing.

INGREDIENTS

1 pound (448 g) lamb, coarsely ground

¾ teaspoon harissa

OR, if you can't find harissa, a reasonable substitute can be made by mixing ¼ teaspoon ground cumin, ½ teaspoon minced garlic, and ¼ teaspoon cayenne (or more if you dare!)

¼ teaspoon black pepper

¼ teaspoon salt

2 feet (.6 m) of prepared hog casing

METHOD

If grinding your own, par freeze the meat. If stuffing, have the grinder and stuffing attachments sterile and assembled. Load the casing onto the stuffing horn and set aside. Have all ingredients ready and arrayed adjacent to your work surface.

Slice the meat into 1-inch (2.5 cm) slabs. Stack the slabs, then cut again into finger-size pieces. Grind the meat using the coarse disk for your grinder or grinder attachment.

In a large mixing bowl that has been thoroughly cleaned in soapy water and scalded with boiling water, use your hands to mix all the ingredients together.

If stuffing, stuff the completed forcemeat firmly into the casing. Twist the sausage into 3-inch (7.5 cm) links. Since you will be making links, remember to leave some slack in the casing by understuffing slightly to prevent the casing from bursting when you twist the sausage. Remove any air pockets by piercing them with a clean needle.

Poach the sausages lightly for approximately 10 minutes (see the directions for Poaching on page 38), then split and grill. If you are making bulk sausage, form the forcemeat into small patties, and broil or grill until brown and crisp all over.

YIELD: Approximately 1 pound (448 g) of sausage

KEFTEDAKIA

This delicious lamb sausage comes from Greece and may have been the source of inspiration for Epicharmus in 500 B.C., prompting him to write the play I mentioned in the introduction. Try these bulk sausages in souvlaki sandwiches—they are a welcome succulent change from the dried out, overcooked lamb that is most often the standard fare.

INGREDIENTS

- 1 pound (448 g) lamb, coarsely ground (you may also use ground beef)
- 1 small yellow onion, minced
- ¾ teaspoon sea salt
- ¼ teaspoon black pepper
- ¼ teaspoon cinnamon
- ¼ teaspoon allspice
- ½ teaspoon whole anise seed
- 2 teaspoons fresh parsley, minced
- 2 teaspoons fresh mint, chopped (or 1 teaspoon if using dried mint)
- 1 tablespoon freshly grated kefalotiri, or Parmesan cheese
- 1 tablespoon red wine (or better yet, ouzo!)
- 1 large egg, beaten
- Flour for dusting your hands
- Vegetable oil

METHOD

If grinding your own, par freeze the meat. Have the grinder attachments sterile and assembled. Have all ingredients ready and arrayed adjacent to your work surface.

Slice the meat into 1-inch (2.5 cm) slabs. Stack the slabs, then cut again into finger-size pieces. Grind the meat using the coarse disk for your grinder or grinder attachment.

In a large mixing bowl that has been thoroughly cleaned in soapy water and scalded with boiling water, use your hands to mix all but the final two ingredients.

Dust your hands lightly with flour before forming the forcemeat into eight sausage shapes, each approximately 5 inches (12.5 cm) long. Fry the sausages in hot oil until browned all over, then drain on paper towels.

YIELD: Approximately 1 pound (448 g) of sausage

plastic or wood?

The debate continues as to which material is better for use as cutting boards. Non-porous plastic or acrylic boards have an advantage when it comes to cleaning. They can be washed in the dishwasher that will clean them with water that is set at a much higher temperature than water from the tap. Wood, when properly cleaned with hot soapy water, will provide a safe cutting surface. If you prefer using wood boards, you should consider keeping two separate boards; one used only for raw meats and poultry, the other for breads and produce. Whether you use plastic or wood boards, you should discard them once they develop deep nicks or grooves that are hard to clean.

AS A NATIONAL CULTURE, THE UNITED STATES IS OFTEN ACCUSED OF TRYING TO DOMINATE AND REPLACE CULTURES AROUND THE GLOBE. The fact of the matter, apparent in our founding, is that a large part of our existence is an excuse to blend. We are a cultural fusion—and that is supremely apparent in our foods.

Our country grew up with pockets of homesick cooks who would try new and often strange ingredients, in hopes of reproducing the flavors and smells of their own cultures. The result? The hot dog. Our pizza. Biscuits. Sweet potato pie.

Now we are struggling to identify ourselves as having developed a distinctive cuisine, unique to the U.S. And we have produced a recognizable (if not always wonderful) style of cooking and dining. We each have an idea of what we mean when we talk of California cuisine or southern cooking, or a clam bake or New England boiled dinner.

It is true that much of what distinguishes our regional dishes is owed to the attempt to recapture old world flavors with new world exigencies, but what does it matter? If our foods please us and if they help us to celebrate our identity, then they are right. One of the great ways to be who we are happens when we eat what we are. For example, we are never more American than at Thanksgiving or at a ball game.

I'm no statistician but I read with enough avidity to be intrigued by questions like: "How many hot dogs, placed end to end, would it take to circle the globe or take us to the moon and back?" And, do we Americans eat that many in a year?

Well, if the average hot dog is 8 inches (20 cm) long and the earth is 25,000 miles (40,000 km) in circumference, we need to eat far less than one per citizen, or 198 million wieners, to circle the globe. To get to the moon and back, we will need to consume between 14 and 15 hot dogs each—considerably more than needed to surround our planet, but judging by my own personal consumption this past year, it's a reasonable quantity.

Of course, there is a place in our collective sausage cuisine beyond the hot dog. It's estimated that Americans eat over five billion pounds of sausage annually. That is not a misprint. Billion.

Fresh
sausage
patties are
a highlight of
this Southern
country
breakfast.
(recipe on
page 93)

recipes for great sausages **89**

HOT DOGS

Americans have been eating hot dogs since before the Civil War, though they didn't get their famous nickname until the early 20th century. They are claimed to be descendants from Czechoslovakian parkys, Austrian wieners or German frankfurters (depending on who you talk to). They are offered to us in a selection so broad they almost merit their own section in the supermarket. Originally made from pork, they can now be found made from beef, turkey, and textured vegetable protein (you may have my portion of the latter).

Unless you are very lucky, you eat hot dogs that are skinned before they are packed, giving them little succulence and no snap when you bite into them. If you are lucky (typically in big cities) you can get the old fashioned sort that are a very lowbrow delicacy. I find the good ones to be the greatest street food anywhere.

The ones you can make here will have snap, juice, and texture, while seducing you with the flavor of mace backed with complex spicing. They will not be pink, since I omit food coloring and preservatives—you won't miss them. However, if you *must* have a pink hot dog, try adding a little beet powder for a natural colorant that won't alter the taste. I am including both pork and beef versions, although you may substitute chicken or turkey or a mixture of both.

PORK HOT DOGS

INGREDIENTS

2¼ pounds (1 kg) pork butt
OR,
  2 pounds (896 g) lean pork loin and ¼ pound (112 g) unsalted pork fat

½ cup (120 mL) milk

2 teaspoons light corn syrup

½ teaspoon liquid smoke (omit if you are smoking these)

½ cup (90 g) onion, minced

1 tablespoon sea salt

1 tablespoon dry mustard

2 teaspoons ground coriander

1 teaspoon mace

½ teaspoon white pepper

¼ teaspoon celery seeds, ground

4 feet (1.2 kg) of prepared hog casing

YIELD: Approximately 2½ pounds (1.12 kg) of sausage

BEEF HOT DOGS

INGREDIENTS

These satisfy Kosher requirements

1½ pounds (672 g) beef

½ pound (224 g) veal

½ pound (224 g) beef suet

½ cup (120 mL) cold water

1 teaspoon light corn syrup

½ teaspoon liquid smoke (omit if you are smoking these)

½ cup (90 g) onion, minced

2 cloves fresh garlic, minced

1 tablespoon sea salt

1 teaspoon dry mustard

1 teaspoon prepared coarse mustard

2 teaspoons ground coriander

1 teaspoon mace

1 teaspoon paprika

½ teaspoon black pepper

4 feet (1.2 m) of prepared lamb casing

YIELD: Approximately 3 pounds (1.36 kg) of sausage

METHOD

Par freeze the meats and fat. At all times keep the ingredients quite cold, refrigerating when necessary. Have the grinder and stuffing attachments sterile and assembled. Load the casing onto the stuffing horn and set aside. Have all ingredients ready and arrayed adjacent to your work surface.

Slice the meats and fat into 1-inch (2.5 cm) slabs. Stack the slabs, then cut again into finger-size pieces. Grind the meats and fat together using the fine disk for your grinder or grinder attachment.

Mix the liquids with the remaining ingredients before mixing them with the meat and fat. Place the ground meat and fat and remaining ingredients in a large mixing bowl that has been thoroughly cleaned in soapy water and scalded with boiling water. Using your hands, reach across the ingredients, grasp a handful, and push it down through the center of the mass. Turn bowl a quarter turn and repeat. Continue until well mixed.

Place the mixed forcemeat into a food processor with a steel blade. Process the forcemeat until it is emulsified and resembles fine-grained paste. If you do not have a food processor, regrind the forcemeat through the fine disk of your grinder two or three times. Refrigerate the emulsified mixture for 30 minutes.

Stuff the completed forcemeat firmly into the casings. Twist the finished sausage into 7-inch (17.5 cm) links. Since you will be making links, remember to leave some slack in the casing by understuffing slightly to prevent the casing from bursting when you twist the sausage. Remove any air pockets by piercing them with a clean needle.

Poach the sausage for 15 minutes (see the directions for Poaching on page 38). Eat immediately as is, or cook as desired. (I will not presume to tell an American how to cook their hot dogs.) To store, cool, dry, wrap, and refrigerate. They will keep one week in the refrigerator and three months in the freezer. If you have a smoker, smoke at 275°F (135°C) until the sausages reach an internal temperature of 170°F (77°C).

hot dog!

Once known as dachshund sausage or little-dog sausage, hot dogs got their name in 1901 at the New York Polo Grounds. A vendor placed the sausages in buns and called out, "They're red hot," to entice potential customers. A cartoonist heard the phrase, and drew a picture of barking dachshund sausages snuggled in buns. He wasn't sure how to spell dachshund, and penned the caption "Hot Dog!"

happy birthday

Frankfurt-am-Main, Germany, claims to be the birthplace of the hot dog. In 1987 they celebrated its 500th anniversary.

billions!!!

Americans consume approximately 20 billion hot dogs per year. One hundred and fifty million of these are eaten in major league ballparks

CAJUN BOUDIN

I love this sausage which is in a category all its own. My first introduction to this boudin (which in no way resembles the French boudins) was in print. I finally bit into one at a small, informal Cajun restaurant in Bethesda, Maryland, which remains one of my favorite eateries anywhere. No, I'm not giving out the name—it's already too hard to get a seat. Find your own paradise.

Although these need nothing other than beer as an accompaniment, I love a remoulade sauce (see page 121 or a spicy creole mustard. As always, please yourself. (But don't stint on the cayenne!)

INGREDIENTS

- 1 pound (448 g) lean pork and ½ pound (224 g) unsalted pork fat
- ¾ cup (150 g) uncooked rice
- 1 tablespoon sea salt
- ¼ cup (28 g) fresh parsley, minced
- ¾ cup (112 g) scallions, chopped
- 1 teaspoon cayenne
- ½ teaspoon ground black pepper
- ¼ teaspoon allspice
- 3 feet (.9 m) of prepared hog casing

METHOD

Par freeze the meat and fat. Have the grinder and stuffing attachments sterile and assembled. Load the casing onto the stuffing horn and set aside. Have all ingredients ready and arrayed adjacent to your work surface. Cook the rice and allow to cool slightly.

Slice the meat and fat into 1-inch (2.5 cm) slabs. Stack the slabs, then cut again into finger-size pieces. Grind the meat and fat together using the coarse disk for your grinder or grinder attachment.

In a large mixing bowl that has been thoroughly cleaned in soapy water and scalded with boiling water, use your hands to mix the meat and fat with all remaining ingredients.

Stuff the completed forcemeat firmly into the casings. Twist the sausage into 7-inch (18 cm) links. Since you will be making links, remember to leave some slack in the casing by understuffing slightly to prevent the casing from bursting when you twist the sausage. Remove any air pockets by piercing them with a clean needle.

Poach the sausage for 25 minutes (see the directions for Poaching on page 38). Eat immediately, preparing the sausages as you like. To store, rinse, cool, wrap, and refrigerate. The sausages will keep for three to five days. Do not freeze these sausages; the rice will become unpleasantly soft and ruin the texture.

YIELD: Approximately 2 pounds (896 kg) of sausage

SOUTHERN COUNTRY SAUSAGE

I once operated a very sophisticated French bakery in Knoxville, Tennessee, in the old city. The buildings dated back to the mid-19th century, and were layered with history and atmosphere. The crusty, golden baguettes were a hit—except on Saturday morning. As if possessed by the ghosts of their ancestors, anyone not cooking their own breakfast headed out for sausages, biscuits, and gravy. Here is why. This is a spicier version of the bulk breakfast sausage found at the beginning of the book.

INGREDIENTS

2¾ pounds (1.2 kg) pork butt, boned and trimmed of sinew

OR,

2 pounds (896 g) lean pork loin and ¾ pound (336 g) unsalted pork fat

2 teaspoons sea salt

½ teaspoon black pepper

1 tablespoon fresh sage, minced (½ tablespoon if using dried) ½ teaspoon fresh thyme (¼ teaspoon if using dried)

½ teaspoon fresh rosemary (¼ teaspoon if using dried)

½ teaspoon nutmeg

½ teaspoon cloves

½ teaspoon cayenne

1 tablespoon brown sugar

4 feet (1.2 m) of prepared hog casing, if stuffing

METHOD

Par freeze the meat and fat. Have the grinder and stuffing attachments sterile and assembled. If stuffing the sausage, load the casing onto the stuffing horn and set aside. Have all ingredients ready and arrayed adjacent to your work surface.

Slice the meat and fat into 1-inch (2.5 cm) slabs. Stack the slabs, then cut again into finger-size pieces. Grind the meat and fat together using the coarse disk for your grinder or grinder attachment.

In a large mixing bowl that has been thoroughly cleaned in soapy water and scalded with boiling water, mix the meat and fat with all remaining ingredients. Using your hands, reach across the ingredients, grasp a handful, and push it down through the center of the mass. Turn bowl a quarter turn and repeat. Continue until well mixed.

If using as a bulk sausage, cook immediately by forming the forcemeat into patties and frying in a skillet until brown and crisp. (You'll find a milk gravy recipe on page 14 and a recipe for redeye gravy below.) You can also store the forcemeat, wrapping it and keeping in the refrigerator for three days. Or wrap and store in the freezer for three months.

If you are stuffing the forcemeat, stuff firmly into the casings. Twist the sausage into 4-inch (10 cm) links. Since you will be making links, remember to leave some slack in the casing by understuffing slightly to prevent the casing from bursting when you twist the sausage. Remove any air pockets by piercing them with a clean needle. To store, follow the directions above for storing the bulk sausage.

YIELD: Approximately 2¾ pounds (1.2 kg) of sausage

REDEYE GRAVY

You'll find that this variant of the traditional milk-and-flour sausage gravy is kinder to your waistline. When you have fried up a "mess" of breakfast or southern country sausage, pour off all but a small bit of fat and immediately deglaze the pan with two or three tablespoons of strong black coffee. Salt to taste.

sausage cuisine

THERE ARE MANY GLORIOUS MEALS BASED ON SAUSAGE—and the cultures of the world show little limitation in what they have done to serve this staple. You would have to be marooned on a desert island to not have experienced many of these recipes.

Some cultural signatures are simply arrays of a variety of sausage and other meats served seasonally. These include, from Alsace Lorraine, choucroute garnie served with sauerkraut and flavored with juniper berries, and the hearty German slachtplatte, or butcher's plate (*schlacten*—to butcher). These dishes are a source of great pride.

Other sausage dishes are rich and complex stews, such as cassoulet from France; gumbo, a Cajun interpretation of an African okra stew; bigos which is a Polish game stew with sausages and mushrooms—and many others. Sausage often is best served simply—grilled or poached—and shines with great side dishes and relishes. At a Christmas dinner once, a patriotic Swede confessed that the julkorv (Christmas potato sausage) was "only so-so until served with a great mustard." Sometimes the meeting of condiment and sausage are unexpected (try a dab of bitter orange marmalade with a juicy garlic sausage) and ultimately delightful.

I have included several main dishes and accompaniments in this recipe section. But keep in mind the purpose of books like this is to launch you into your own creative uses of seasonal provender. Once you've learned the fundamentals of sausage making and the methods of cooking them, apply the techniques on your shopping trips to search for ingredients that will help you invent new combinations.

In many ways sausage is a blank canvas, and we are like young art students. We begin by copying and trying to reproduce the classics and, if we wish (and I wish you to do so), we then begin to find our own style, subtle and tender or bold and exciting. Enjoy your favorites, but stretch occasionally. Remember to follow the underlying theme of this book to please yourself (and your fortunate guest!). Here are some dishes that I love.

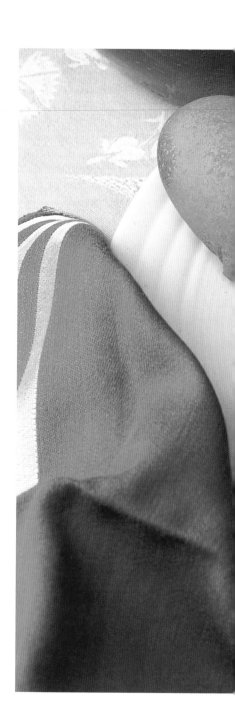

delicious
sausage dishes

Caldo verde
(recipe on page 96)

CALDO VERDE
KALE AND POTATO SOUP

Hearty, healthy, and quick to prepare, this soup is a way to enjoy your vegetables with a spicy kick—even if you're running late. Served with crusty bread, it becomes a satisfying one-dish meal.

INGREDIENTS

1	pound (448 g) kale
1	pound (448 g) potatoes
1½	quarts (1.4 L) water
2	tablespoons olive oil
½	pound (224 g) garlic sausage or chorizo, sliced, browned, and drained of fat
	Salt and pepper to taste

METHOD

Tear the kale leaves into bite-sized pieces and mince the stalks. Peel the potatoes if you like (I do not), and slice them into chunks. Place the minced kale stalks in salted water and bring to a boil.

Add the potatoes and lower to a simmer for 20 minutes or until tender. Using a slotted spoon, remove the potatoes, mash them, then return them to the pot. Add the kale leaves and sausage, and cook until the kale is tender. This takes approximately 5 to 10 minutes, although it may take a little longer.

YIELD: Four servings

STUFFED ONIONS

We don't often think about onions taking a starring role in a dish—most often they are a featured player. I prefer the stronger taste of yellow onion to complement the spicy chorizo. Some of you may prefer using one of the varieties of milder, sweet onions that are readily available in the early summer.

INGREDIENTS

12 large onions
    Cooking oil

1 pound (448 g) chorizo, skinned

½ cup (90 g) carrot, minced

½ cup (90 g) celery, minced

1 cup (70 g) bread crumbs

METHOD

Preheat the oven to 450˚F (230˚C). Carefully peel the onions, leaving them whole. In a large pot of boiling water, parboil the onions for 10 minutes, drain, and cool. Cut a slice off the root end and scoop out approximately three-quarters of each onion.

Place the onions, hollowed side up, in a baking dish while you prepare the filling.

In a skillet, heat a small amount of cooking oil and fry the chorizo, breaking it apart with a wooden spoon as it cooks. When the sausage is an even color through-out, cooked but not brown, add the vegetables and cook on low heat until the vegetables are soft, approx-imately 10 minutes.

Using a slotted spoon to allow as much fat as possible to drain out, scoop out portions of the sausage and vegetable mixture, and fill each hollowed-out onion just to the rim. Top each onion with bread crumbs.

Pour enough water in a baking pan to come up to just ½ inch (1.5 cm) around the filled onions and bake for 20 minutes.

YIELD: 12 servings

JAMBALAYA

The origins of this dish are draped in Spanish moss. Chef Paul Prudhomme credits the French and Yoruba languages for giving this dish its name—*jambon* (ham) *a la ya* (Yoruba for rice)—hence *Jamb-a-la-ya*. For the rest of us, it is simply a highly spiced rice dish with ham and almost any meat and, often, tomatoes. I say eat it all up.

INGREDIENTS

¼ cup (60 mL) cooking oil

¼ pound (112 g) ham, diced

1 pound (448 g) sausage, sliced

1½ cups (270 g) onions, chopped

1½ cups (270 g) celery, chopped

1 cup (180 g) green pepper, chopped

4 cloves fresh garlic, minced

2 bay leaves

1 teaspoon cayenne

1 teaspoon white pepper

1 teaspoon black pepper

1 teaspoon thyme

1 teaspoon cumin, ground

1 teaspoon salt

2 cups (448 g) uncooked rice

1 quart (.95 L) stock, beef or chicken

1 pound (448 g) large shrimp, peeled and deveined

METHOD

Heat the oil in a large skillet or heavy pot, and cook the ham and sausage until they begin to crisp at the edges. Add all the vegetables and seasonings, and cook, stirring frequently, for 10 minutes.

Stir in the rice and add the stock. Bring to a boil, reduce heat to low, cover, and cook for 20 minutes, until rice is done. Jambalaya is often served while the rice is still a little underdone and slightly crunchy.

Please yourself—but please, add the shrimp at the last minute, adding a little water or stock if the rice is too dry, and cook just until the shrimp colors all the way through.

YIELD: 8 servings

sausage feast

A RECIPE FOR CELEBRATION

WHILE THIS IS NOT A STANDARD COOKING RECIPE—one that provides the means for making a prepared dish—it is a recipe nonetheless. Consider the following as a guideline for assembling the ingredients of your life and shaping them into a feast for the soul.

One irresistible impulse that often overtakes the home chef (a cook with pretensions) is to fill the table to groaning under the weight of one's culinary wizardry. With a little help, sausage can be the star to which you can hitch your wagon. First, let's find an excuse.

Think of the four days each year during which the perfection of the season causes us (wherever we live) to exclaim (whether we are extroverts or alone), "This is why we live here!" At these moments, in our respective perfect worlds, we need a feast. A winter/summer solstice bacchanal, Bastille Day, Guy Faulk's day, the Fourth, the Ides of whatever, the Nones of October, the Day of the Dead, the author's birthday.

What is it that characterizes a feast? They are most often gatherings designed to remember and honor people and events that have great meaning for a community. One encyclopedia suggests that feasts often are celebrations of cherished folkways. They are part of what expresses the whole concept of community. Feasts have always (though no longer exclusively) been associated with harvests or plantings to celebrate the bounty or bless the undertaking.

Surely, you can think of something worth celebrating. When you've seen the first fireflies in summer, or you can calculate the day when the leaves will be their most colorful, Bloomsday, D-day, April 15th, Juneteenth, the day you stopped smoking... come on over. I'll do the food.

Nowhere is the admonishment to please yourself more useful than in the structure of your own personal feast day. I will give you some ideas. Think in terms of critical mass. How many guests are necessary to ignite a festive day? I personally believe children are required (at least two in strollers, up to five in the running around, ungoverned stage, and a pinch of teens to be publicly aloof while privately pleased to be here). It helps if at least two supervising parents are present, one to tell the stories and the other to edit and correct. The grown children will have to drive a long way or, better still, fly in to get there. And don't forget institutional memory, you need an elder or two, the crustier the better.

Now, where were we? Food. Sausage. At least three varieties cooked in three different methods. Three salads or cold dishes. One soup (three in Winter). Three breads (crusty French, homemade biscuits, and either cornbread or pita). Three hot vegetable dishes and one or two starches. Something with pasta and something with potatoes. Rice is good, too. Dips and spreads and sauces in abundance.

If it is at all possible, have everyone bring something. Some dish will not turn out well, but there will be plenty for everyone. Resist, if you can, the temptation to sculpt something out of sausage meat. Never permit guests to make costumes that include sausage as an element. Be certain to have storage containers and sturdy freezer bags, because guests should never depart a feast without extras.

Finally, arrange as much of the cooking to be done in advance as possible—except the sausage. Casseroles and stews are one thing, but don't grill or poach sausage in advance. While sausage makes fine leftovers, the fresh-off-the-grill juice and snap are the acme only you, the home sausage maker, can provide.

THAI SAUSAGE SALAD

The seductive combinations of sweet, hot, and sour with crisp and yielding textures and exotic herbiness make this salad an adventure.

DRESSING INGREDIENTS

- 1 cup (240 mL) lime juice
- ½ cup (100 g) sugar
- ¾ cup (180 mL) fish sauce
- 1 jalapeno or serrano chile, minced
- 4 cloves of fresh garlic, minced
- 2 bulbs lemongrass, minced

SALAD INGREDIENTS

- 3 heads Romaine lettuce, torn into small pieces
- 3 large cucumbers, peeled and sliced
- 1 red onion, peeled and thinly sliced
- 6 carrots, shredded
- 1 cup (180 g) radishes, sliced
- 1 cup (50 g) fresh coriander leaves
- ¼ cup (12 g) fresh mint, chopped
- ¼ cup (12 g) fresh basil, chopped
- 1 pound (448 g) sliced, browned, and drained lop cheong sausage

METHOD

Mix the dressing ingredients and set aside. Slice the sausage diagonally and place them in a medium-sized frying pan. Add approximately ¼ inch (.6) of water to the pan. Cook the sausages, allowing the water to evaporate. Continue cooking the sausages until they are lightly and evenly browned, then drain. Toss the salad, add sausage and dressing, and serve immediately.

YIELD: 6–8 servings

SHU MAI—POT STICKERS

These are called pot stickers because that is what they do. These filled dumplings are cooked in a small amount of water and oil. First they steam, which cooks the filling and makes the dough wrapper silken and supple. Then, when the water has cooked off, their bases fry in the oil to form a crust on the bottom.

Shu Mai are one form of *dim sum*, which are among the great delights of Chinese cooking. Whole meals can be composed of these packaged fillings which are fried, deep fried, steamed, poached, boiled, or baked. They are the source of such Italian delights as tortellini and ravioli. I offer you a more classic recipe for which I have substituted a mild sausage for the traditional ground or chopped pork. My advice is to assemble a crew around the kitchen table and make a variety of these dumplings.

For the dough wrapper, you may buy wonton skins or egg roll wrappers typically offered in the grocery store where Asian vegetables are displayed. I am including a recipe for the dough because I think the result is better.

DOUGH

INGREDIENTS

- 2 cups (280 g) all-purpose flour
- 1 cup (240 mL) boiling water

METHOD

In a large bowl, combine the flour and boiling water, mixing as well as you can. Let the mixture rest for 20 minutes, then knead it until it is smooth and soft (use as much flour as you need to work the dough).

Roll it into a sausage, and cut it into 16 equal pieces. Pat each piece into rounds, and roll them into 4-inch (10 cm) circles. Flour each piece and stack them, covering them with a damp towel until you need them.

POT STICKERS

INGREDIENTS

- 1 recipe of the dough described above, or enough wonton skins to make 24 dumplings
- ½ pound (224 g) pork, or chicken and pork sausage
- 2 cloves fresh garlic (unless the sausage has lots of garlic already), minced
- 2 slices fresh ginger, peeled and minced
- 1 scallion, finely chopped
- 1 cup (180 g) bok choy or any variety Chinese cabbage, finely chopped
- 1 tablespoon cornstarch dissolved in ¼ cup (60 mL) of water
- 1 tablespoon sesame oil

  Salt and black pepper to taste
- 2 tablespoons vegetable oil, plus, 1 cup (240 mL) boiling water mixed with 2 tablespoons of oil

POT STICKERS METHOD

Mix meat with the garlic, ginger, and scallion. Sprinkle approximately ¼ teaspoon salt on the chopped bok choy, and let it sit for 5 minutes. Squeeze out excess moisture and add to the meat mixture. Add cornstarch and sesame oil, and mix thoroughly, adding salt and pepper to taste.

When you have made the hot water dough, cut it into 24 pieces, rolling them into 3-inch (7.5 cm) circles. Shaping pot stickers can be as simple or as complex as you want. The traditional shape is made as follows: Lay a circle of dough in the palm of your hand. On one edge pinch the dough together to form little pleats so that the dough forms a kind of shell-shaped cup. Place a teaspoonful of filling in the cup and seal the unpleated edge to the pleated edge (you may need to moisten the dough so it will adhere). Gently, hold the dumplings seam side up and tamp them on the counter to form a flat bottom so that they stand up easily. Set the finished dumplings on a flour-dusted surface spaced to not touch each other. When all the dumplings are finished, they can be frozen on a cookie sheet and then bagged until needed.

When you are ready to cook them, first prepare a dipping sauce. I like them with the traditional sauce that combines Chinese black vinegar and minced garlic. They are also delicious with a sushi dip of soy sauce and a little prepared wasabi. All of these items are available in oriental groceries and, increasingly, at most supermarkets.

To cook, heat 2 tablespoons oil in a heavy skillet or a wok, and place all of the dumplings upright in the oil. Pour in the oil and boiling water mixture, and reduce the heat to medium. Loosen any dumplings that have stuck to the pan, then cover the pan and cook for 10 minutes to steam them. Remove the cover and boil off the remaining water to fry the bottoms golden brown.

YIELD: 24 dumplings

HUEVOS RANCHEROS

This is the real thing. Making your own salsa ranchera seals the authenticity. If you want to go even further, try making your own corn tortillas! Serve this egg, sausage, and cheese dish anytime—it's too good to save only for weekend brunch.

INGREDIENTS

- 1 large ripe tomato
- 1 chile serrano
- 1 clove fresh garlic, minced
- 1 tablespoon peanut oil
- 1 thick slice of onion, minced
  Salt to taste
- 2 tablespoons peanut oil
- 2 corn tortillas per serving
- 4 inches (10 cm) of chorizo, skinned, per serving
- 2 eggs per serving
- 2 tablespoons crumbled queso fresca or feta cheese per serving

METHOD

First make the salsa ranchera. Line a broiling pan with tin foil. Broil the tomato until slightly blackened. Be careful to avoid placing the broiler too close to the flame (or element) or it will burn the tomato before it is warmed through. In a hot, dry pan, toast the serrano for about one minute. Blend the tomato, serrano, and garlic in a blender until smooth.

In a skillet, heat 1 tablespoon of peanut oil and cook the onion until translucent. Add the blended ingredients and heat through, cooking until just slightly thickened. Salt to your taste and set aside. This is enough for four servings.

Heat the 2 tablespoons of oil until hot. Fry the tortillas briefly so that they heat through and soften but not until they become crisp. In the same oil, fry the chorizo, breaking it apart as it browns. Remove the sausage from the pan with a slotted spoon to drain the fat.

In the same pan, fry the eggs until set. (Cook them to your preference; I like formed whites with crisp edges and a still runny yolk.)

On a single serving gratin (or any plate that you can stick under the broiler flame or element) place the tortillas, cover them with the chorizo, the eggs, and a generous portion of the salsa ranchera. Sprinkle some of the cheese on top and place under broiler just until the cheese begins to melt.

YIELD: 1 serving is 2 eggs and 2 tortillas

GRATIN DE POMMES DE TERRE ET SAUCISSON
POTATOES AU GRATIN WITH SAUSAGE

On an ordinary night, your family might just refer to these as cheesy potatoes. But dress them up with sausage, a little white wine, a fresh salad, and candlelight, and they become a French delight.

INGREDIENTS

> 3 cups (448 g) sliced, cooked potatoes
>
> 1 cup (90 g) onions, minced
>
> 1 pound (448 g) sliced, browned, and drained mild sausage (such as boudins blancs)
>
> 3 eggs
>
> 1½ cup (360 mL) cream
>
> Salt and pepper to taste
>
> ¼ cup (30 g) grated Gruyere (or Swiss cheese)
>
> Butter

METHOD

Preheat oven to 375°F (190°C). In an ovenproof dish or pie pan, arrange layers of potatoes, onions, and sausage, ending with a layer of potatoes.

Mix the eggs and cream with the salt and pepper, and pour into the dish. Sprinkle the top with cheese and dot with butter. Bake for 30 minutes or until the cheese begins to brown.

YIELD: 4 servings

PEA SOUP AND JULKORV

I am told that the Swedes prefer their pea soup, which they love, very thick. Whatever the particular preference, the combination of pea soup, julkorv (Christmas potato sausage), and cold weather offers warmth and security— the very essence of comfort food. I prefer the sausage poached and served separately (rather than cooked in the soup) with a good mustard or mustard thinned with a little sour cream (fresh dill wouldn't hurt).

I believe that making soup at any time is a healing experience. If you have no current emotional wounds or soft sadnesses to heal, make a soup anyway, and find someone who needs comforting. If you can arrange to do this in the winter on a long twilit afternoon, you will probably have the beginnings of a short story (to para-phrase the usual) about man's humanity to man. At the worst, you'll have a lovely, comforting meal.

INGREDIENTS

2 cups (400 g) split peas

1 meaty ham bone

½ cup (90 g) onions, minced

½ cup (90 g) carrots, minced

1 cup (180 g) celery, minced

1 bay leaf

Julkorv, enough to serve at least one link to each guest

METHOD

Wash and soak the peas for several hours or over-night. Do not discard the soaking liquid. Place the peas and the soaking liquid in a heavy pot, along with the ham bone and enough extra water to make about 2½ quarts (2.4 L). Cover and simmer for 3 hours.

Add the remaining ingredients and cook for an additional ½ hour. Just before you add the vegetables, bring a pot of water to a simmer and poach the sausage for 20 minutes. Sköl!

YIELD: 8 servings

LENTILS COOKED WITH SAUSAGE

Lentils are peasant food that kings love. I am, depending on the day, either or both. I particularly like to use tiny, French Dupuy lentils which work well with this dish that I call a stewp—that is to say a soup that is thick enough to serve on a plate, but not quite a stew. Use smoked sausage, or sausage flavored with liquid smoke, to add a hearty note.

INGREDIENTS

1 tablespoon olive oil

¼ pound (112 g) sausage, diced small

1 cup (180 g) each, carrots, onions, and celery, chopped

1 pound (448 g) lentils, washed and drained (they do not need a preliminary soak)

1 bay leaf

½ teaspoon thyme

Salt and pepper to taste

2½ quarts (2.4 L) water (or half water, half chicken or beef stock)

½ pound (224 g) sausage (particularly those that are smoked or flavored with liquid smoke), sliced

METHOD

Heat the oil in a heavy pot and brown the diced sausage. Add the vegetables and cook until softened, about 10 minutes. Add the lentils, herbs, and water/stock, and simmer for 3 hours or until lentils are softened but not mushy. When the lentils are done, brown the remaining sausage and add it to the soup before serving.

YIELD: 4 servings

CASSOULET

First invite a dozen friends, select a favorite wine, and purchase a few loaves of crusty bread. This elegant peasant dish is bound to inspire convivial conversation and camaraderie.

INGREDIENTS

- 1½ pounds (672 g) dry white beans, picked over and soaked in water overnight
- 1 yellow onion, peeled
- 4 whole cloves
- 2 sprigs each, fresh parsley, rosemary, and thyme
- 1 bay leaf
- 2 carrots, peeled and thinly sliced
- 1½ quarts (1.4 L) homemade or low-salt chicken stock
- 6 tablespoons duck fat or lard
- 6 cloves of fresh garlic, smashed with a knife blade
- ¾ pound (340 g) salt pork, rinsed several times in clean water and cubed
- 1 pound (448 g) lamb, cubed
- 1 pound (448 g) pork loin, cubed
- 1 pound (448 g) garlic sausage (saussison a l'ail, salsiccie or luganega)
- 1 pound (448 g) duck confit, fat reserved, or, 1 duck cut into serving pieces
- 2 large onions, chopped
- 1 can of tomatoes, 20 ounces (560 g)
- Breadcrumbs (optional)

METHOD

First, drain and rinse the soaked beans and place in a large casserole or ovenproof pot. (All of the ingredients will eventually be in this one pot.) Stick the 4 whole cloves into the peeled onion and add to the pot along with the fresh herbs, bay leaf, carrots, and stock. Bring to a boil, lower heat, and simmer during the next step, which will take approximately 45 minutes.

Preheat the oven to 350°F (175°C). In a large skillet, heat the fat and sauté the garlic until soft, and add to pot. Then, successively brown the salt pork, lamb, pork, sausages, duck, and onions. Drain the fat after browning each of these and before adding to the pot.

Add tomatoes to the pot, push the meats below the beans, and place in oven. Bake for 1½ hours. During this period, stir occasionally, pushing the meats below surface. If you like, for the last 20 minutes, top the mixture with bread crumbs.

YIELD: 12 servings

CHOUCROUTE BRAISÉE A L'ALSACIENNE GARNIE

BRAISED SAUERKRAUT WITH MEATS, ALSATIAN STYLE

Discover the delicious blending of French and German cooking traditions with this Alsatian dish. The slow cooking of the sauerkraut with the other ingredients renders it sweet and savory—a perfect companion to the sausage and meat.

INGREDIENTS

- 2 pounds (896 g) sauerkraut
- ½ pound (224 g) thick sliced bacon, cut into 2-inch (5 cm) pieces
- ¼ cup (60 mL) vegetable oil
- ½ cup (90 g) sliced carrots
- 1 cup (180 g) sliced onions
- 4 sprigs fresh parsley

- 6 whole peppercorns
- 10 juniper berries
- 1 cup (240 mL) dry white wine
- 1 quart (.95 L) chicken stock
- 6 pork chops, thick-cut
- 1 pound (448 g) garlic sausage
- 6 slices cooked ham, thinly sliced

METHOD

Soak and drain the sauerkraut in three changes of water—soak for 20 minutes, drain, then soak again, repeat. Preheat oven to 325°F (165°C). Blanch the bacon by simmering in water for 10 minutes, then drain.

Heat the oil in a large lidded ovenproof pot, and cook the bacon, carrots, and onions for 10 minutes (do not brown). Stir in the sauerkraut, and cook, covered, for 10 more minutes. Add herbs and liquids to the pot, restore to a simmer, and put in the oven for 3 hours.

Brown the pork and sausage in a sauté pan, add to the pot, and return to the oven for ½ hour. Remove the pot from the oven. Arrange the sauerkraut over the meats and cover with the thinly sliced ham for a final ½ hour of cooking.

YIELD: 6–8 servings

RISOTTO WITH SAUSAGE

Of all the gifts of Italy, I am most grateful for risotto (aside from its sausages, of course). There are many shortcuts around for making risotto including baking and the use of microwave ovens. While these methods produce nice rice dishes, they don't produce risotto. Nothing compares with standing and stirring and a first-rate stock.

INGREDIENTS

- 5 cups (1.2 L) rich stock, either chicken or veal
- 3 tablespoons butter
- 2 teaspoons olive oil
- 2 tablespoons shallot, minced
- 2 cups (448 g) Arborio rice, no substitutes!
- ¾ pound (340 g) luganega sausage, cut into 2-inch (5 cm) pieces
- ¼ cup (60 mL) dry white wine
- Salt and pepper to taste
- 3 tablespoons Parmesan cheese, freshly grated
- 2 tablespoons water

METHOD

In a small pot bring the stock to a simmer. In a heavy pot, heat 2 tablespoons of the butter and the olive oil, add the shallot and cook until it is translucent. Add the rice and stir until each grain is coated in the oil and butter.

Add a ladleful of the hot stock to the rice, stirring constantly until the stock is visibly absorbed by the rice. As one ladle is absorbed add the next, stirring frequently. As the last of the stock is cooked into the rice, the rice starch and the stock will form a creamy sauce that will hold the dish together. The rice is done when it is no longer crunchy but only just chewy.

In the meantime, place the cut sausage and the wine in a skillet. Cook until the wine evaporates, then continue to cook the sausage in its fat until brown. When brown, remove the sausage and set aside. Keep the juices in the pan and set aside.

When the rice is risotto, mix in, very gently, the last tablespoon of butter and the Parmesan cheese. Mound the risotto on a platter, creating a hollow in the center of the mound.

Turn the heat on under the skillet containing the juice from the sausage. Pour off all but 1 tablespoon of fat and deglaze the pan with 2 tablespoons of water. Return the sausages to the pan and heat through.

To serve, place the sausages and their sauce in the hollow in the center of the risotto mound.

YIELD: 6 servings

SAUSAGE DUMPLINGS FOR SOUPS

These are useful to perk up a bland soup or to make it more filling. Since they are essentially little meatballs, they can be cooked as such. It is most efficient to make these with the forcemeat meat that's left over from stuffing normal links, then you can freeze them for future use.

INGREDIENTS

¼ cup (45 g) onion, minced

1 tablespoon butter

½ pound (224 g) sausage forcemeat

2 slices white bread, dipped in milk and mashed

2 egg yolks

¼ teaspoon nutmeg, grated

2 tablespoons Parmesan cheese, grated

1 quart (.95 L) chicken, beef, or vegetable stock

METHOD

Sauté the onion in butter until translucent. Cool slightly and mix with the sausage and all remaining ingredients, except for the stock. Mix thoroughly and form walnut-sized balls.

To cook, bring a quart of stock to a boil and drop in the dumplings. Reduce heat immediately to a simmer, and cook for 20 minutes. Add them either by themselves or with the broth, to a soup.

YIELD: Approximately 12 dumplings

CROSTINI WITH SAUSAGE AND CHEESE

These slices of toast, topped with the prepared sausage mixture, can serve as an hors d'oeuvre or as a luncheon dish.

INGREDIENTS

½ cup (224 g) ricotta cheese

3 tablespoons water (optional)

5 tablespoons Parmesan cheese, grated

½ teaspoon salt

3 links of Luganega or other mild garlic sausage

¼ cup (60 mL) water

¼ cup (56 g) butter

¼ cup (60 mL) olive oil

12 slices good white bread, you may remove the crusts

12 slices of Fontina or Gruyäre cheese, trimmed to fit the bread slices

METHOD

If the ricotta is dry, moisten it with the water, otherwise omit. Beat the Parmesan cheese and salt into the ricotta until creamy.

Preheat oven to 325˚F (165˚C). Cook sausages, using the poach and fry method—boil the sausages in a skillet with ¼ cup (60 mL) water until the water evaporates, then continue cooking until brown. Cool the sausage, chop fine, and mix into the cheese mixture.

In a clean skillet, heat the butter and olive oil and fry the bread until one side is golden brown. Spread a portion of the cheese mixture on the toasted side and place on a cookie sheet. Bake for 5 minutes, remove from the oven, and top each piece with a slice of cheese. Return the bread to the oven just long enough to melt the cheese.

YIELD: 12 servings

FAGIOLI DALL'OCCHIO CON SALSICCE
BLACK-EYED PEAS AND SAUSAGES IN TOMATO SAUCE

Combining these "beans with eyes" and garlic sausage creates a filling and tasty dish. The olive oil and tomatoes contribute to make this a sophisticated peasant stew.

INGREDIENTS

¼ cup (60 mL) olive oil

½ yellow onion, minced

1 clove fresh garlic, minced

½ cup (90 g) carrots, minced

½ cup (90 g) celery, minced

1 cup (224 g) canned tomatoes with their juice, roughly chopped

1 pound (448 g) Luganega (or other garlic sausage)

1 cup (224 g) dried black-eyed peas soaked in warm water for at least one hour

METHOD

Heat olive oil in the bottom of a heavy, ovenproof pot. Over medium heat, cook onions until translucent and yellowed from the olive oil. Add garlic until it colors slightly. Add carrots and celery and cook for five minutes, stirring occasionally. Finally, add tomatoes, turn heat to low, and simmer for 20 minutes.

Preheat oven to 350°F (150°C). Prick sausage four or five times each and add to pot, cooking slowly for 15 minutes. Drain the soaked peas and add to the pot. Add water to the stew, covering the ingredients by ½ inch (1.5 cm). Cover the pot, and bring to a simmer.

Place the covered pot in the oven and cook until peas are tender, approximately 1½ hours. Check occasionally and add water if necessary. If the peas are done and the stew is still soupy, return the pot to the top of the stove and cook over medium high heat until the liquid is reduced to a stew consistency. Before serving, tilt pot and ladle off excess fat.

YIELD: 4 servings

CLOCKWISE FROM TOP: Horseradish sauce, Remoulade, and Mustard.

The sausage is grilled merguez served with pita bread and lemon wedges. (recipe on page 86)

sauces and condiments

Use the following recipes as complements to your prepared sausage when looking for compliments for your new sausage making skills. Invite friends over for a sausage tasting, lay out the condiments and accompaniments, chill the wine, frost the beer mugs, and have a celebration. Use the following sparingly or slather them on, but most of all enjoy them as the perfect grace notes to your great homemade sausages!

REMOULADE

This recipe is complex, although it is essentially a flavored mayonnaise. You can, if you like, substitute store-bought mayonnaise for the egg yolks and oil, and continue as below. Wait, on second thought, don't...it's better if you make your own. Trust me—a lot better!

INGREDIENTS

2 egg yolks

¼ cup (60 mL) vegetable oil

½ cup (90 g) celery, minced

½ cup (90 g) green onions, minced

¼ cup (12 g) fresh parsley, minced

¼ cup (90 g) fresh grated horseradish, or use ½ cup (180 g) prepared

¼ lemon, seeds removed then finely chopped—rind included

1 bay leaf

2 tablespoons Creole mustard (I like Zaterain's)

2 tablespoons catsup

1 tablespoon hot mustard

1 tablespoon white vinegar

1 tablespoon tabasco sauce

1 tablespoon fresh garlic, minced

2 teaspoons paprika

1 teaspoon salt

METHOD

Use a blender or food processor. First add the eggs yolks and beat for approximately 2 minutes until they are thick and pale yellow.

With the machine running, add the oil in a thin stream. (Voila, you have made mayonnaise—wasn't that easy?). Add each successive ingredient, one at a time, until well blended. Remember to use the entire lemon piece, being certain that it and its rind is finely chopped before placing in the machine.

YIELD: Approximately 2 cups (.55 L)

MUSTARD

If ever wars have been fought over sausages, battles also have been waged over mustard. I cannot claim to present the definitive recipe—nor am I divulging any family secrets. This mustard delivers a sweet-sour, spicy tang with just a faint hint of brewed hops and barley.

INGREDIENTS

6 tablespoons mustard seeds

½ cup (56 g) dry mustard

¼ cup (60 mL) cider vinegar

¼ cup (40 g) brown sugar

1 teaspoon salt

2 cloves fresh garlic, minced

¼ teaspoon allspice

¼ teaspoon cloves

¼ teaspoon fresh tarragon

1 tablespoon honey

¾ cup (180 mL) pale, dry beer

METHOD

Using a blender or food processor, place the mustard seeds and dry mustard in the machine. Place the other ingredients, except for the honey and beer, in a saucepan. Bring to a boil, then pour into the machine with the dry mustard and seeds. Process until smooth.

Leave the mixture in your machine for three hours, add the honey and beer, and reprocess. Keep refrigerated in a tightly closed jar for several months.

YIELD: 2 cups (.55 L)

SALSA VERDE

This sauce is excellent with all poached sausages, hot or cold. It is equally good served with all cold meats as well as with fish dishes.

INGREDIENTS

4 anchovies, mashed, or 1 tablespoon of anchovy paste

1 medium potato, boiled and mashed

2 tablespoons onion, finely minced

1 clove fresh garlic, minced

½ cup (25 g) parsley, chopped

6 small sour gherkins, minced, preferably French cornichon or Italian cetriolini sott'aceto

6 tablespoons olive oil

2 tablespoons lemon juice

2 tablespoons white wine vinegar

METHOD

I find it is easiest to mix the ingredients in a jar that holds more than a pint (480 mL) and has a tight-fitting lid. As you add each ingredient, shake thoroughly.

Otherwise, assemble the ingredients, and in a stainless steel bowl, whisk everything but the olive oil, lemon juice, and vinegar. When the ingredients are combined, add, 1 tablespoon at a time, all of the olive oil, shaking or beating after each addition. Finally, stir in the lemon juice and vinegar.

YIELD: Approximately 2 cups (.55 mL)

HORSERADISH SAUCE

This sauce is excellent to serve with any boiled meat and many vegetable dishes. Dip browned sausage "coins" pierced with cocktail picks into this or any of the previous sauces at a buffet or pass them around at a party.

INGREDIENTS

2 tablespoons butter

1½ tablespoons flour

1 cup (240 mL) milk

3 tablespoons prepared horseradish, or 1½ tablespoons fresh grated

2 tablespoons whipping cream

1 teaspoon sugar

1 teaspoon dry mustard

1 tablespoon vinegar

METHOD

This is best served right after making it. First, make a white roux. Heat the butter over a low heat, then, using a wire whisk, gradually add the flour. Cook for 3 to 4 minutes to cook off the raw flavor of flour. Very gradually, stir in the milk until thoroughly blended and the sauce begins to thicken. Remove from the heat and add remaining ingredients. Reheat without boiling, and serve.

YIELD: Approximately 1½ cups (360 mL)

PEPPERS IN OLIVE OIL

Easy to make and wonderful to eat, serve these peppers with grilled sausages, particularly salsiccie or luganega. Add a few hot peppers and serve with spicy chorizo or merguez. For a classic sandwich, start with grilled sausage and crusty bread. Lay the peppers and oil on top, allowing the flavored olive oil to soak into the bread.

INGREDIENTS

3 bell peppers, for added color use one each of green, red, and yellow

Olive oil

Oregano, dried

Salt to taste

METHOD

Cut the peppers in half lengthwise, removing the cores and seeds. Cut the peppers into strips and place in a pot. Add olive oil to half the depth of the peppers. Add approximately 3 tablespoons (more if desired) of dried oregano, and stir. Place over medium high heat. Get the oil hot but not boiling. At this point, reduce the heat to low and cover. Allow the peppers to stew until soft. As they cook, occasionally shake the pot with the cover on to blend the oil and herb through the peppers. Salt to taste. Serve immediately or keep in the refrigerator for five days. Reheat to serve.

YIELD: 4–6 servings

what to drink?

According to an informal online survey by the National Hot Dog and Sausage Council, most people prefer Italian sausage and Polish kielbasa. Their number one beverage of choice to accompany them? Beer.

glossary

BULK SAUSAGE Forcemeat that is not stuffed into a casing but usually formed into patties before cooking. It may also be cooked until it crumbles before being added to recipes.

CASING Any wrapper that surrounds the forcemeat. Most commonly a pork, beef, or sheep intestine, it can also be a vegetable leaf, paper, or a muslin bag.

CURING A method of preserving meat by removing most of the moisture. Chemical curing agents, most commonly nitrates and nitrites, are added to prevent the meat from spoiling as it dries.

DEGLAZE The use of liquid to lift any residue remaining in a pan from the frying process (the bits that are "glazed" to the pan) for the purpose of making a sauce or gravy.

EMULSIFY To grind meat into a very fine, paste-like mixture for the purpose of evenly distributing the fat.

FORCEMEAT The ground or emulsified meat that has been mixed with other ingredients such as herbs, spices, and vegetables.

NATURAL CASING Casings made from the submucosa, which is a largely collagen layer of the intestine.

PACKING To stuff a sausage casing with forcemeat.

PAR FREEZE Partially frozen.

POACHING To cook or semi-cook in water that is near the boiling point for a short amount of time.

SAUSAGE Finely chopped and seasoned meat that is usually stuffed into a casing before being cooked or cured.

SMOKING Using a smoky fire to impart flavor to, or to preserve meat. Cold smoking imparts flavor but does not cook the meat. Hot smoking imparts flavor and cooks the meat.

bibliography

Aidells, Bruce and Dennis Kelly. *Flying Sausages.* San Francisco: Chronicle Books, 1995.

Armstrong, Alison. *The Joyce of Cooking: Food and Drink from James Joyce's Dublin.* Barrytown, NY: Station Hill Press, 1986.

Child, Julia. *The French Chef Cookbook.* New York: Alfred A. Knopf, 1968.

Glen, Camille. *The Heritage of Southern Cooking.* New York: Workman Publishing, 1986.

Hazan, Marcella. *The Classic Italian Cook Book.* New York: Harper's Magazine Press, 1973.

Hippsley Coxe, Antony and Araminta Hippsley Coxe. *The Great Book of Sausages.* Woodstock, NY: The Overlook Press, 1996.

Kennedy, Diana. *The Cuisines of Mexico.* New York: Harper and Rowe, 1972.

Kuo, Irene. *The Key to Chinese Cooking.* New York: Alfred A. Knopf, 1981.

Kutas, Rytek. *Great Sausage Recipes and Meat Curing.* Buffalo, NY: MacMillan, 1987.

Lobel, Leon and Stanley Lobel. *All About Meat.* New York: Harcourt Brace Jovanovitch, 1975.

Merinoff, Linda. *The Savory Sausage: A Culinary Tour Around the World.* New York: Poseidon Press, Simon and Schuster, Inc., 1987.

Montagné, Prosper. *Larousse Gastronomique The Encyclopedia of Food, Wine, and Cookery.* 1st American ed. New York: Crown Publishers, Inc., 1961.

Neal, Bill. *Biscuits, Spoon Bread, and Sweet Potato Pie.* New York: Alfred A. Knopf, 1990.

Prudhomme, Paul. *Chef Paul Prudhomme's Louisiana Kitchen.* New York: William Morrow, 1984.

Reavis, Charles G. *Home Sausage Making.* Rev. ed. Pownal, VT: Garden Way Publishing, Storey Communications, Inc., 1987.

Thorne, John. *Simple Cooking.* New York: Viking, 1987.

metric equivalents

SOLID MEASUREMENT
in grams (g) and kilograms (kg)

U.S.	Metric
¼ pound	112 g
⅓ pound	148 g
½ pound	224 g
⅔ pound	297 g
¾ pound	336 g
1 pound	448 g
1¼ pounds	560 g
1½ pounds	672 g
2 pounds	896 g
2¼ pounds	1 kg
2½ pounds	1.1 kg
3 pounds	1.4 kg
3½ pounds	1.6 kg
4 pounds	1.8 kg
4½ pounds	2 kg
5 pounds	2.2 kg

FLUID MEASUREMENT
in milliliters (mL) and liters (L)

U.S.	Metric
1 teaspoon	5 mL
1 tablespoon (3 teaspoons)	15 mL
2 tablespoons (1 ounce)	30 mL
¼ cup	60 mL
⅓ cup	90 mL
½ cup	120 mL
¾ cup	180 mL
1 cup	240 mL
2 cups	.47 L
1 quart	.95 L
1½ quart	1.4 L
2 quarts	1.9 L

¼ cup = 2 fluid ounces
½ cup = 4 fluid ounces)
1 cup = 8 fluid ounces
2 cups = 1 pint
2 pints = 1 quart

LENGTH

U.S.	Metric
1 inch	2.5 cm

TEMPERATURE EQUIVALENTS

170°F = 78°C
180°F = 82°C
190°F = 88°C
200°–205°F = 95°C
220°–225°F = 120°C
245°–250°F = 120°C
275°F = 135°C
300°–305°F = 150°C
325°–330°F = 165°C
345°–350°F = 175°C
370°–375°F = 190°C
400°–405°F = 205°C
425°–430°F = 220°C
445°–450°F = 230°C
470°–475°F = 245°C
500°F = 260°C

TO CONVERT FAHRENHEIT TO CELSIUS:
subtract 32, multiply by 5, and divide by 9

OVEN TEMPERATURES

U.S.	Metric
32° F (water freezes)	0° C
212° F	100° C
300° F (slow oven)	150° C
350° F (moderate oven)	175° C
400° F (hot oven)	205° C

sausage-makers'
sources for Equipment, Supplies, and Information

ALLIED KENCO SALES

26 Lyerly St.
Houston, TX 77022

PHONE: 713-691-2935

TOLL FREE: 800-356-5189

FAX: 713-691-3250

E-MAIL: aks@alliedkenco.com

"Everything but the meat"
*Equipment, casings, spices,
seasoning kits, starter kits*

MICHLITCH CO., INC.

210 W. Pacific Avenue
Spokane, WA 99201-0124

PHONE: 509-624-1490

FAX: 509-624-0822

WEBSITE: www.mitlitch.com

*Equipment, casings, spices,
books*

NETO SASAUGE CO.

3499 The Alameda
Santa Clara, CA 95050

MAILING ADDRESS:
PO Box 578
Santa Clara, CA 95052

PHONE: 408-296-0818

TOLL FREE: 888-482-NETO (6386)

FAX: 408-296-0538

WEB SITE: www.netosausage.com

Sheep casings

STUFFERS SUPPLY COMPANY

2298 Fraser Highway
Langly BC V2Z 2T9
Canada

PHONE: 604-534-7374

FAX: 604-534-3089

Equipment, casings, seasonings

index

Related Titles From Lark Books

Making Great Cheese
30 Simple Recipes from Cheddar to Chèvre
BY BARBARA CILETI

Hardcover
includes photos and recipes
ISBN 1-57990-109-3

The Food Lover's Guide to Canning
Contemporary Recipies & Techniques
BY CHRIS RICH & LUCY CLARK CRAWFORD

Hardcover
128 pages, 100 color plates
ISBN 1-887374-46-9

Candy!
A Sweet Selection of Fun & Easy Recipes
BY LAURA DOVER DORAN

Hardcover with concealed wire binding
128 pages, 130 color photos
ISBN 1-57990-055-0

In Praise of Apples
A Harvest of History, Horticulture & Recipes
BY MARK ROSENSTEIN

Hardcover
176 pages, 185 color photos, 15 b/w photos
ISBN 1-887374-04-3

LARK
BOOKS

List of the Elements with Their Atomic Symbols and Atomic Weights

Name	Symbol	Atomic Number	Atomic Weight	Name	Symbol	Atomic Number	Atomic Weight
Actinium	Ac	89	227.028	Mendelevium	Md	101	(258)
Aluminum	Al	13	26.9815	Mercury	Hg	80	200.59
Americium	Am	95	(243)	Molybdenum	Mo	42	95.94
Antimony	Sb	51	121.76	Neodymium	Nd	60	144.24
Argon	Ar	18	39.948	Neon	Ne	10	20.1797
Arsenic	As	33	74.9216	Neptunium	Np	93	237.048
Astatine	At	85	(210)	Nickel	Ni	28	58.693
Barium	Ba	56	137.327	Niobium	Nb	41	92.9064
Berkelium	Bk	97	(247)	Nitrogen	N	7	14.0067
Beryllium	Be	4	9.01218	Nobelium	No	102	(259)
Bismuth	Bi	83	208.980	Osmium	Os	76	190.23
Bohrium	Bh	107	(264)	Oxygen	O	8	15.9994
Boron	B	5	10.811	Palladium	Pd	46	106.42
Bromine	Br	35	79.904	Phosphorus	P	15	30.9738
Cadmium	Cd	48	112.411	Platinum	Pt	78	195.08
Calcium	Ca	20	40.078	Plutonium	Pu	94	(244)
Californium	Cf	98	(251)	Polonium	Po	84	(209)
Carbon	C	6	12.011	Potassium	K	19	39.0983
Cerium	Ce	58	140.115	Praseodymium	Pr	59	140.908
Cesium	Cs	55	132.905	Promethium	Pm	61	(145)
Chlorine	Cl	17	35.4527	Protactinium	Pa	91	231.036
Chromium	Cr	24	51.9961	Radium	Ra	88	226.025
Cobalt	Co	27	58.9332	Radon	Rn	86	(222)
Copper	Cu	29	63.546	Rhenium	Re	75	186.207
Curium	Cm	96	(247)	Rhodium	Rh	45	102.906
Darmstadtium	Ds	110	(271)	Roentgenium	Rg	111	(272)
Dubnium	Db	105	(262)	Rubidium	Rb	37	85.4678
Dysprosium	Dy	66	162.50	Ruthenium	Ru	44	101.07
Einsteinium	Es	99	(252)	Rutherfordium	Rf	104	(261)
Erbium	Er	68	167.26	Samarium	Sm	62	150.36
Europium	Eu	63	151.965	Scandium	Sc	21	44.9559
Fermium	Fm	100	(257)	Seaborgium	Sg	106	(266)
Fluorine	F	9	18.9984	Selenium	Se	34	78.96
Francium	Fr	87	(223)	Silicon	Si	14	28.0855
Gadolinium	Gd	64	157.25	Silver	Ag	47	107.868
Gallium	Ga	31	69.723	Sodium	Na	11	22.9898
Germanium	Ge	32	72.61	Strontium	Sr	38	87.62
Gold	Au	79	196.967	Sulfur	S	16	32.066
Hafnium	Hf	72	178.49	Tantalum	Ta	73	180.948
Hassium	Hs	108	(269)	Technetium	Tc	43	(98)
Helium	He	2	4.00260	Tellurium	Te	52	127.60
Holmium	Ho	67	164.930	Terbium	Tb	65	158.925
Hydrogen	H	1	1.00794	Thallium	Tl	81	204.383
Indium	In	49	114.818	Thorium	Th	90	232.038
Iodine	I	53	126.904	Thulium	Tm	69	168.934
Iridium	Ir	77	192.22	Tin	Sn	50	118.710
Iron	Fe	26	55.847	Titanium	Ti	22	47.88
Krypton	Kr	36	83.80	Tungsten	W	74	183.84
Lanthanum	La	57	138.906	Uranium	U	92	238.029
Lawrencium	Lr	103	(260)	Vanadium	V	23	50.9415
Lead	Pb	82	207.2	Xenon	Xe	54	131.29
Lithium	Li	3	6.941	Ytterbium	Yb	70	173.04
Lutetium	Lu	71	174.967	Yttrium	Y	39	88.9059
Magnesium	Mg	12	24.3050	Zinc	Zn	30	65.39
Manganese	Mn	25	54.9381	Zirconium	Zr	40	91.224
Meitnerium	Mt	109	(268)				

PEARSON

ALWAYS LEARNING

Fundamentals of General, Organic, and Biological Chemistry

Custom Edition for the University of Oregon

Taken from:
Fundamentals of General, Organic, and Biological Chemistry, Sixth Edition
by John McMurry, Mary Castellion, David S. Ballantine,
Carl A. Hoeger, Virginia E. Peterson

Pearson Learning Solutions, 501 Boylston Street, Suite 900, Boston, MA 02116
A Pearson Education Company
www.pearsoned.com

Printed in the United States of America

1 2 3 4 5 6 7 8 9 10 V0ZN 16 15 14 13 12 11

000200010270790481

MT

ISBN 10: 1-256-33886-9
ISBN 13: 978-1-256-33886-4

Dear Student:

In this course you will be using MasteringChemistry®, an online tutorial and homework program that accompanies your textbook. *If you have joined a MasteringChemistry course before and can still log in*: Save time by following the guide for joining another course (available from www.masteringchemistry.com > Tours & Training > Getting Started) instead of this page.

What You Need:

- ✓ **A valid email address**
- ✓ **A student access code**
  (Comes in the Student Access Code Card/Kit that may have been packaged with your new textbook or that may be available separately in your school's bookstore. Otherwise, you can purchase access online at www.masteringchemistry.com.)
- ✓ **The ZIP or other postal code for your school:** _____
- ✓ **A Course ID:** _____ (Provided by your instructor)

1. Register

- Go to www.masteringchemistry.com and click **Students** under **Register**.
- To register using the student access code inside the MasteringChemistry Student Access Code Card/Kit, select **Yes, I have an access code**. Click **Continue**.

  –OR– *Purchase access online*: Select **No, I need to purchase access online now**. Select your textbook, whether you want access to the eText, and click **Continue**. Follow the on-screen instructions to purchase access using a credit card. The purchase path includes registration, but the process is a bit different from the steps printed here.

- **License Agreement and Privacy Policy:** Click **I Accept** to indicate that you have read and agree to the license agreement and privacy policy.
- Select the appropriate option under "Do you have a Pearson Education account?" Continue to give the requested information until you complete the process. The **Confirmation & Summary** page confirms your registration. This information will also be emailed to you for your records. You can either click **Log In Now** or return to www.masteringchemistry.com later.

2. Log In

- Go to www.masteringchemistry.com.
- Enter your Login Name and Password that you specified during registration and click **Log In**.

3. Join Your Instructor's Online Course and/or Open Self-Study Resources

Upon first login, you'll be asked to do one or more of the following:

- **Join a Course** by entering the **MasteringChemistry Course ID** provided by your instructor. If you don't have a Course ID now, you can return to join the MasteringChemistry course later. When you join a course, you may also be asked for a Student ID (follow on-screen instructions).
- **Explore the Study Area** or **Launch Your eText**, if these resources are available for your textbook.

To Access MasteringChemistry Again Later

Simply go to www.masteringchemistry.com, enter your Login Name and Password, and click **Log In**.

After you have joined a course: You can open any assignments from the **Assignments Due Soon** area or from the **Assignments** page. For self-study, click **eText** or **Study Area**, if these options are available.

Support

Access Customer Support at http://www.masteringchemistry.com/support, where you will find:

- System Requirements
- Answers to Frequently Asked Questions
- Registration Tips & Tricks video
- Additional contact information for Customer Support, including Live Chat

ALWAYS LEARNING   **PEARSON**

About the Authors

John McMurry, educated at Harvard and Columbia, has taught approximately 17,000 students in general and organic chemistry over a 30-year period. A Professor of Chemistry at Cornell University since 1980, Dr. McMurry previously spent 13 years on the faculty at the University of California at Santa Cruz. He has received numerous awards, including the Alfred P. Sloan Fellowship (1969–71), the National Institute of Health Career Development Award (1975–80), the Alexander von Humboldt Senior Scientist Award (1986–87), and the Max Planck Research Award (1991).

David S. Ballantine received his B.S. in Chemistry in 1977 from the College of William and Mary in Williamsburg, VA, and his Ph.D. in Chemistry in 1983 from the University of Maryland at College Park. After several years as a researcher at the Naval Research Labs in Washington, DC, he joined the faculty in the Department of Chemistry and Biochemistry of Northern Illinois University, where he has been a professor for the past twenty years. He was awarded the Excellence in Undergraduate Teaching Award in 1998 and was recently named the departmental Director of Undergraduate Studies. In addition, he is the faculty advisor to the NIU Chemistry Club, an American Chemical Society Student Affiliate program.

Carl A. Hoeger received his B.S. in Chemistry from San Diego State University and his Ph.D. in Organic Chemistry from the University of Wisconsin, Madison in 1983. After a postdoctoral stint at the University of California, Riverside, he joined the Peptide Biology Laboratory at the Salk Institute in 1985 where he ran the NIH Peptide Facility while doing basic research in the development of peptide agonists and antagonists. During this time he also taught general, organic, and biochemistry at San Diego City College, Palomar College, and Miramar College. He joined the teaching faculty at University of Califiornia, San Diego in 1998. Dr. Hoeger has been teaching chemistry to undergraduates for over 20 years, where he continues to explore the use of technology in the classroom. In 2004 he won the Paul and Barbara Saltman Distinguished Teaching Award from UCSD. He is currently the General Chemistry coordinator at UCSD, where he is also responsible for the training and guidance of over 100 teaching assistants in the Chemistry and Biochemistry departments.

Virginia E. Peterson received her B.S. in Chemistry in 1967 from the University of Washington in Seattle, and her Ph.D. in Biochemistry in 1980 from the University of Maryland at College Park. Between her undergraduate and graduate years she worked in lipid, diabetes, and heart disease research at Stanford University. Following her Ph.D. she took a position in the Biochemistry Department at the University of Missouri in Columbia and is now an Associate Professor. Currently she is the Director of Undergraduate Advising for the department and teaches both senior capstone classes and biochemistry classes for nonscience majors. Awards include both the college level and the university-wide Excellence in Teaching Award and, in 2006, the University's Outstanding Advisor Award and the State of Missouri Outstanding University Advisor Award. Dr. Peterson believes in public service and in 2003 received the Silver Beaver Award for service from the Boy Scouts of America.

Brief Contents

Contents

Applications

Preface

This textbook is primarily designed to provide students in the allied health sciences with an appropriate background in chemistry and biochemistry. But it also provides a general context for many of the chemical concepts so that students in other disciplines will gain a better appreciation of the importance of chemistry in everyday life. The coverage in this sixth edition includes sufficient breadth and depth to ensure adequate context and to provide students with opportunities to expand their knowledge.

To teach chemistry all the way from "What is an atom?" to "How do we get energy from glucose?" is a challenge. Throughout our general chemistry and organic chemistry coverage, the focus is on concepts fundamental to the chemistry of living things and everyday life. In our biochemistry coverage we strive to meet the further challenge of providing a context for the application of those concepts in biological systems. Our goal is to provide enough detail for thorough understanding while avoiding so much detail that students are overwhelmed. Many practical and relevant examples are included to illustrate the concepts and enhance student learning.

The material covered is ample for a two-term introduction to general, organic, and biological chemistry. While the general and early organic chapters contain concepts that are fundamental to understanding the material in biochemistry, the later chapters can be covered individually and in an order that can be adjusted to meet the needs of the students and the duration of the course.

The writing style is clear and concise and punctuated with practical and familiar examples from students' personal experience. Art work, diagrams, and molecular models are used extensively to provide graphical illustration of concepts to enhance student understanding. Since the true test of knowledge is the ability to apply that knowledge appropriately, we include numerous worked examples that incorporate consistent problem-solving strategies.

Regardless of their career paths, all students will be citizens in an increasingly technological society. When they recognize the principles of chemistry at work not just in their careers but in their daily lives, they are prepared to make informed decisions on scientific issues based on a firm understanding of the underlying concepts.

Organization

GENERAL CHEMISTRY: CHAPTERS 1–11   The introduction to elements, atoms, the periodic table, and the quantitative nature of chemistry (Chapters 1–3) is followed by chapters that individually highlight the nature of ionic and molecular compounds (Chapters 4 and 5). The next two chapters discuss chemical reactions and their stoichiometry, energies, rates, and equilibria (Chapters 6 and 7). Topics relevant to the chemistry of life follow: Gases, Liquids, and Solids (Chapter 8); Solutions (Chapter 9); and Acids and Bases (Chapter 10). Nuclear Chemistry (Chapter 11) closes the general chemistry sequence.

ORGANIC CHEMISTRY: CHAPTERS 12–17   These chapters concisely focus on what students must know in order to understand biochemistry. The introduction to hydrocarbons (Chapters 12 and 13) includes the basics of nomenclature, which is thereafter kept to a minimum. Discussion of functional groups with single bonds to oxygen, sulfur, or a halogen (Chapter 14) is followed by a short chapter on amines, which are so important to the chemistry of living things and drugs (Chapter 15). After introducing aldehydes and ketones (Chapter 16), the chemistry of carboxylic acids and their derivatives (including amides) is covered (Chapter 17), with a focus on similarities among the derivatives.

BIOLOGICAL CHEMISTRY: CHAPTERS 18–29 Rather than proceed through the complexities of protein, carbohydrate, lipid, and nucleic acid structure before getting to the roles of these compounds in the body, structure and function are integrated in this text. Protein structure (Chapter 18) is followed by enzyme and coenzyme chemistry (Chapter 19). After that we cover the function of hormones and neurotransmitters, and the action of drugs (Chapter 20). With enzymes introduced, the central pathways and themes of biochemical energy production can be described (Chapter 21). If the time you have available to cover biochemistry is limited, stop with Chapter 21 and your students will have an excellent preparation in the essentials of metabolism. The following chapters cover carbohydrate chemistry (Chapters 22 and 23), then lipid chemistry (Chapters 24 and 25). Next we discuss nucleic acids and protein synthesis (Chapter 26) and genomics (Chapter 27). The last two chapters cover protein and amino acid metabolism (Chapter 28) and provide an overview of the chemistry of body fluids (Chapter 29).

Changes to This Edition

COVERAGE OF GENERAL CHEMISTRY

Once again, there is a major emphasis in this edition on problem-solving strategies. This is reflected in expanded solutions in the Worked Example problems and the addition of more Key Concept Problems that focus on conceptual understanding. The most significant change in the Worked Example problems is the addition of a Ballpark Estimate at the beginning of many problems. The Ballpark Estimate provides an opportunity for students to evaluate the relationships involved in the problem and allows them to use an intuitive approach to arrive at a first approximation of the final answer. The ability to think through a problem before attempting a mathematical solution is a skill that will be particularly useful on exams, or when solving "real world" problems.

Other specific changes to chapters are provided below:

Chapter 1

- The Scientific Method is introduced in the text and reinforced in Applications presented in the chapter.

Chapter 3

- Discussion of the critical experiments of Thomson, Millikan, and Rutherford are included in the Application "Are Atoms Real" to provide historical perspective on the development of our understanding of atomic structure.
- Electron dot structures are introduced in Chapter 3 to emphasize the importance of the valence shell electronic configurations with respect to chemical behavior of the elements.

Chapter 4

- Electron dot structures are used to reinforce the role of valence shell electronic configurations in explaining periodic behavior and the formation of ions.

Chapter 5

- The two methods for drawing Lewis dot structures (the "general" method and the streamlined method for molecules containing C, N, O, X, and H) are discussed back-to-back to highlight the underlying principle of the octet rule common to both methods.

Chapter 6

- The concept of limiting reagents is incorporated in Section 6.7 in the discussion of reaction stoichiometry and percent yields.

Chapter 7

- The discussion of free energy and entropy in Section 7.4 has been revised to help students develop a more intuitive understanding of the role of entropy in spontaneous processes.
- Section 7.8 includes more discussion of how the equilibrium constant is calculated and what it tells us about the extent of reaction.

Chapter 8

- Sections 8.3–8.10 include more emphasis on use of the kinetic molecular theory to understand the behavior of gases described by the gas laws.
- Section 8.15 includes more discussion on the energetics of phase changes to help students understand the difference between heat transfer associated with a temperature change and heat transfer associated with the phase change of a substance.

Chapter 9

- Discussion of equivalents in Section 9.10 has been revised to emphasize the relationship between ionic charge and equivalents of ionic compounds.
- Discussion of osmotic pressure (Section 9.12) now includes the osmotic pressure equation and emphasizes the similarity with the ideal gas law.

Chapter 10

- Both the algebraic and logarithmic forms of K_w are presented in Section 10.8 to give students another approach to solving pH problems.
- The discussion of buffer systems now introduces the Henderson-Hasselbalch equation. This relationship makes it easier to identify the factors that affect the pH of a buffer system and is particularly useful in biochemical applications in later chapters.
- Discussion of common acid-base reactions has been moved back in the chapter to provide a more logical segue into titrations in Section 10.15.

Chapter 11

- Treatment of half-life in Section 11.5 now includes a generic equation to allow students to determine the fraction of isotope remaining after an integral or non-integral number of half-lives, which is more consistent with "real world" applications.
- The Applications in this chapter have been expanded to include discussion of new technologies such as Boron Neutron-Capture Therapy (BNCT), or to clear up misconceptions about current methods such as MRI.

COVERAGE OF ORGANIC CHEMISTRY

A major emphasis in this edition was placed on making the fundamental reactions organic molecules undergo much clearer to the reader, with particular vision toward those reactions encountered again in biochemical transformations. Also new to this edition is the expanded use and evaluation of line-angle structure for organic molecules, which are so important when discussing biomolecules. Most of the Applications have been updated to reflect current understanding and research.

Other specific changes to chapters are provided below:

Chapter 12

- This chapter has been significantly rewritten to provide the student with a stronger foundation for the organic chemistry chapters that follow.
- A clearer description of what a functional group is, as well as a more systematic approach to drawing alkane isomers have been made.

- The topic of how to draw and interpret line structures for organic molecules has been added, along with worked examples of such.
- The discussion of conformations has been expanded.

Chapter 13

- A more general discussion of cis and trans isomers has been added.
- The discussion of organic reaction types, particularly rearrangement reactions, have been simplified.

Chapter 14

- The topic of oxidation in organic molecules has been clarified.

Chapter 15

- The role of NO in human biology has been updated to reflect current research.

Chapter 16

- A more detailed discussion of what is meant by toxic or poisonous has been added.

Chapter 17

- A discussion of ibuprofen has been added.

COVERAGE OF BIOLOGICAL CHEMISTRY

New topics, such as the use of anabolic steroids in sports, have been added to many of these chapters to highlight the relevance of biochemistry in modern society. In this text, nutrition is not treated as a separate subject but is integrated with the discussion of each type of biomolecule.

Chapter 18

- The discussion of sickle cell anemia has been expanded and the role of an amino acid substitution on hemoglobin structure clarified.
- The Application *Prions—Proteins That Cause Disease* has been updated to reflect current research.

Chapter 19

- Incorporated the information about lead poisoning into the discussion of enzyme inhibition.

Chapter 20

- The discussion of anabolic steroids has been updated.
- The discussion of drugs and their interaction with the neurotransmitter acetylcholine has been expanded.

Chapter 21

- The discussion of ATP energy production has been revised.

Chapter 22

- An explanation of the chair conformation of glucose has been included to enhance understanding of the shape of cyclic sugars.
- The Application *Chirality and Drugs* has been updated.
- The Application *Cell Surface Carbohydrates and Blood Type* has been revised.

Chapter 23

- The explanation of substrate level phosphorylation has been expanded for clarity.
- The emerging medical condition referred to as Metabolic Syndrome has been added to the text discussion of diabetes.
- The Application *Diagnosis and Monitoring of Diabetes* has been updated to include metabolic syndrome.
- Section 23.11 now contains an expanded discussion of gluconeogenesis.
- The discussion of polysaccharides has been updated.

Chapter 24

- The description of the cell membrane has been expanded.
- A discussion of some inhibitors of Cox 1 and Cox 2 enzymes, important in inflammation, has been added.

Chapter 25

- The discussion of triacylglycerol synthesis has been expanded.
- The discussion of ketone body formation has been expanded.
- A thorough explanation of the biosynthesis of fatty acids has been added.

Chapter 26

- The Application *Viruses and AIDS* has been updated.
- Information about the 1918 influenza pandemic was included in the Application *"Bird Flu": The Next Epidemic?*

Chapter 27

- A discussion of the problems associated with using recombinant DNA for commercial protein manufacture has been added.
- In Section 27.5, new bioethical issues are pointed out to reflect modern concerns.
- The discussion of recombinant DNA and polymerase chain reactions has been moved to this chapter from Chapter 26.

Focus on Learning

WORKED EXAMPLES   Most Worked Examples, both quantitative and not quantitative, include an Analysis section that precedes the Solution. The Analysis lays out the approach to solving a problem of the given type. When appropriate, a "Ballpark Estimate" gives students an overview of the relationships needed to solve the problem, and provides an intuitive approach to arrive at a rough estimate of the answer. The Solution presents the worked-out example using the strategy laid out in the Analysis and, in many cases, includes expanded discussion to enhance student understanding. The use of the two-column format introduced in the fifth edition for quantitative problems has been applied to more Worked Examples throughout the text. Following the Solution there is a Ballpark Check that compares the calculated answer to the Ballpark Estimate, when appropriate, and verifies that the answer makes chemical and physical sense.

KEY CONCEPT PROBLEMS are integrated throughout the chapters to focus attention on the use of essential concepts, as do the ***Understanding Key Concepts*** problems at the end of each chapter. Understanding Key Concepts problems are designed to test students' mastery of the core principles developed in the chapter. Students thus have an opportunity to ask "Did I get it?" before they proceed. Most of these Key Concept Problems use graphics or molecular-level art to illustrate the core principles and will be particularly useful to visual learners.

PROBLEMS The problems within the chapters, for which brief answers are given in an appendix, cover every skill and topic to be understood. One or more problems, many of which are *new* to this edition, follow each Worked Example and others stand alone at the ends of sections.

MORE COLOR-KEYED, LABELED EQUATIONS It is entirely too easy to skip looking at a chemical equation while reading. We have extensively used color to call attention to the aspects of chemical equations and structures under discussion, a continuing feature of this book that has been judged very helpful.

MOLECULAR MODELS Additional computer-generated molecular models have been introduced, including the use of *electrostatic-potential maps for molecular models*.

KEY WORDS Every key term is boldfaced on its first use, fully defined in the margin adjacent to that use, and listed at the end of the chapter. These are the terms students must understand to get on with the subject at hand. Definitions of all Key Words are collected in the Glossary.

END-OF-CHAPTER SUMMARIES Here, the answers to the questions posed at the beginning of the chapter provide a summary of what is covered in that chapter. Where appropriate, the types of chemical reactions in a chapter are also summarized.

Focus on Relevancy

Chemistry is often considered to be a difficult and tedious subject. But when students make a connection between a concept in class and an application in their daily lives the chemistry comes alive, and they get excited about the subject. The applications in this book strive to capture student interest and emphasize the relevance of the scientific concepts. The use of relevant applications makes the concepts more accessible and increases understanding.

- **Applications** are both integrated into the discussions in the text and set off from the text in Application boxes. Each boxed application provides sufficient information for reasonable understanding and, in many cases, extends the concepts discussed in the text in new ways. The boxes end with a cross-reference to end-of-chapter problems that can be assigned by the instructor. Some well-received Applications from previous editions that have been retained include *Breathing and Oxygen Transport, Buffers in the Body, Prions, Protein Analysis by Electrophoresis, The Biochemistry of Running,* and *DNA Fingerprinting.*

- **New Applications in this edition** include *Aspirin—A Case Study, Temperature-Sensitive Materials, Anemia—A Limiting Reagent Problem, GERD: Too Much Acid or Not Enough,* and *It's a Ribozyme!*

FOCUS ON MAKING CONNECTIONS AMONG GENERAL, ORGANIC, AND BIOLOGICAL CHEMISTRY This can be a difficult course to teach. Much of what students are interested in lies in the last part of the course, but the material they need to understand the biochemistry is found in the first two-thirds. It is easy to lose sight of the connections among general, organic, and biological chemistry so we use a feature, **Concepts to Review**, to call attention to these connections. From Chapter 4 on, the Concepts to Review section at the beginning of the chapter lists topics covered in earlier chapters that form the basis for what is discussed in the current chapter.

We have also retained the successful concept link icons and Looking Ahead notes.

- **Concept link icons** ⊂◯⊃ are used extensively to indicate places where previously covered material is relevant to the discussion at hand. These links provide for cross-references and also serve to highlight important chemical themes as they are revisited.

- **Looking Ahead notes** call attention to connections between just-covered material and discussions in forthcoming chapters. These notes are designed to illustrate to the students why what they are learning will be useful in what lies ahead.

Making It Easier to Teach: Supplements for Instructors

MasteringChemistry™ **(www.masteringchemistry.com)** MasteringChemistry is the first adaptive-learning online homework system. It provides selected end-of-chapter problems from the text, as well as hundreds of tutorials with automatic grading, immediate answer-specific feedback, and simpler questions on request. Based on extensive research of precise concepts students struggle with, MasteringChemistry uniquely responds to your immediate needs, thereby optimizing your study time.

Instructor Resource Manual (0-32-161241-8) Features lecture outlines with presentation suggestions, teaching tips, suggested in-class demonstrations, and topics for classroom discussion.

Test Item File (0-32-161514-X) Updated to reflect the revisions in this text and contains questions in a bank of more than 2,000 multiple-choice questions.

Transparency Pack (0-32-161513-1) More than 225 full-color transparencies chosen from the text put principles into visual perspective and save you time while you are preparing for your lectures.

Instructor Resource Center on CD/DVD (0-32-161242-6) This CD/DVD provides an intergrated collection of resources designed to help you make efficient and effective use of your time. This CD/DVD features most art from the text, including figures and tables in PDF format for high-resolution printing, as well as four pre-built PowerPoint™ presentations. The first presentation contains the images/figures/tables embedded within the PowerPoint slides, while the second includes a complete modifiable lecture outline. The final two presentations contain worked "in chapter" sample exercises and questions to be used with Classroom Response Systems. This CD/DVD also contains movies and animations, as well as the TestGen version of the Test Item File, which allows you to create and tailor exams to your needs.

BlackBoard® and WebCT®—Practice and assessment materials are available upon request in these course management platforms.

Making It Easier to Learn: Supplements for Students

Study Guide and Full Solutions Manual (0-32-161238-8) and **Study Guide and Selected Solutions Manual (0-32-161239-6)**, both by Susan McMurry. The selected version provides solutions only to those problems that have a short answer in the text's Selected Answer Appendix (problems numbered in blue in the text). Both versions explain in detail how the answers to the in-text and end-of-chapter problems are obtained. They also contain chapter summaries, study hints, and self-tests for each chapter.

For the Laboratory

Exploring Chemistry: Laboratory Experiments in General, Organic and Biological Chemistry, 2nd Edition (0-13-047714-1) by Julie R. Peller of Indiana University. Written specifically to accompany Fundamentals of General, Organic and Biological Chemistry, this manual contains 34 fresh and accessible experiments specifically for GOB students.

Catalyst: The Prentice Hall Custom Laboratory Program for Chemistry. This program allows you to custom-build a chemistry lab manual that matches your content needs and course organization. You can either write your own labs using the Lab Authoring Kit tool, or select from the hundreds of labs available at www.prenhall.com/catalyst. This program also allows you to add your own course notes, syllabi, or other materials.

Acknowledgments

From conception to completion, the development of a modern textbook requires both a focused attention on the goals and the coordinated efforts of a diverse team. We have been most fortunate to have had the services of many talented and dedicated individuals whose efforts have contributed greatly to the overall quality of this text.

First and foremost, we are grateful to Kent Porter Hamann who, as senior editor of this text through many past revisions, provided exemplary leadership and encouragement to the team in the early stages of this project. Very special appreciation goes to Ray Mullaney, editor in chief of book development, who mentored the new team members and managed to coordinate the many and varied details. Irene Nunes, our developmental editor, worked closely with the authors to ensure accuracy and consistency. We also are grateful for the services of Wendy Perez, project manager; Laurie Varites, assistant editor; Lia Tarabokjia, and Jill Traut and Robert Walters, production project managers. Finally, special thanks also to Susan McMurry and Margaret Trombley, whose efforts on the Solutions Manuals and MasteringChemistry tutorial software, respectively, have added value to the overall package.

Finally, many instructors and students who have used the fifth edition have provided valuable insights and feedback and improved the accuracy of the current edition. We gratefully acknowledge the following reviewers for their contributions to the sixth edition:

Sheikh Ahmed, *West Virginia University*
Stanley Bajue, *CUNY-Medgar Evers College*
Daniel Bender, *Sacramento City College*
Dianne A. Bennett, *Sacramento City College*
Alfredo Castro, *Felician College*
Gezahegn Chaka, *Louisiana State University, Alexandria*
Michael Columbia, *Indiana University-Purdue University, Fort Wayne*
Rajeev B. Dabke, *Columbus State University*
Danae R. Quirk-Dorr, *Minnesota State University, Mankato*
Pamela S. Doyle, *Essex County College*
Marie E. Dunstan, *York College of Pennsylvania*

Karen L. Ericson, *Indiana University-Purdue University, Fort Wayne*
Charles P. Gibson, *University of Wisconsin, Oshkosh*
Clifford Gottlieb, *Shasta College*
Mildred V. Hall, *Clark State Community College*
Meg Hausman, *University of Southern Maine*
Ronald Hirko, *South Dakota State University*
L. Jaye Hopkins, *Spokane Community College*
Margaret Isbell, *Sacramento City College*
James T. Johnson, *Sinclair Community College*
Margaret G. Kimble, *Indiana University-Purdue University Fort Wayne*

Grace Lasker, *Lake Washington Technical College*

Ashley Mahoney, *Bethel University*

Matthew G. Marmorino, *Indiana University, South Bend*

Diann Marten, *South Central College, Mankato*

Barbara D. Mowery, *York College of Pennsylvania*

Tracey Arnold Murray, *Capital University*

Andrew M. Napper, *Shawnee State University*

Lisa Nichols, *Butte Community College*

Glenn S. Nomura, *Georgia Perimeter College*

Douglas E. Raynie, *South Dakota State University*

Paul D. Root, *Henry Ford Community College*

Victor V. Ryzhov, *Northern Illinois University*

Karen Sanchez, *Florida Community College, Jacksonville-South*

Mir Shamsuddin, *Loyola University, Chicago*

Jeanne A. Stuckey, *University of Michigan*

John Sullivan, *Highland Community College*

Deborah E. Swain, *North Carolina Central University*

Susan T. Thomas, *University of Texas, San Antonio*

Yakov Woldman, *Valdosta State University*

The authors are committed to maintaining the highest quality and accuracy and look forward to comments from students and instructors regarding any aspect of this text and supporting materials. Questions or comments should be directed to the lead co-author.

David S. Ballantine
dballant@niu.edu

Concise, Accessible, and Unique

QUANTITATIVE AND CONCEPTUAL

Worked Examples
These examples have been modified to emphasize both problem-solving strategies and conceptual understanding.

Analysis
Most Worked Examples include an Analysis section that precedes the solution. The Analysis lays out the approach to solving a problem of the given type.

NEW! Ballpark Estimates
Ballpark Estimates help students arrive at a rough estimate of the final answer based on an intuitive approach to the problem.

Solution
The Solution shows students how to apply the appropriate problem-solving strategy and guides them through the steps to follow in obtaining the answer.

Ballpark Check
Many of the Worked Examples culminate with a Ballpark Check that helps students quickly check whether the answer they have calculated in numerical Worked Examples is reasonable.

WORKED EXAMPLE 8.4 Using Boyle's Law: Finding Volume at a Given Pressure

In a typical automobile engine, the fuel/air mixture in a cylinder is compressed from 1.0 atm to 9.5 atm. If the uncompressed volume of the cylinder is 750 mL, what is the volume when fully compressed?

ANALYSIS This is a Boyle's law problem because the volume and pressure in the cylinder change but the amount of gas and the temperature remain constant. According to Boyle's law, the pressure of the gas times its volume is constant:

$$P_1V_1 = P_2V_2$$

Knowing three of the four variables in this equation, we can solve for the unknown.

◀ A cut-away diagram of internal combustion engine shows movement of pistons during expansion and compression cycles.

BALLPARK ESTIMATE Since the pressure *increases* approximately tenfold (from 1.0 atm to 9.5 atm), the volume must *decrease* to approximately one-tenth, from 750 mL to about 75 mL.

SOLUTION

STEP 1: **Identify known information.** Of the four variables in Boyle's law, we know P_1, V_1, and P_2.

$P_1 = 1.0$ atm
$V_1 = 750$ mL
$P_2 = 9.5$ atm

STEP 2: **Identify answer and units.**

$V_2 = ??$ mL

STEP 3: **Identify equation.** In this case, we simply substitute the known variables into Boyle's law and rearrange to isolate the unknown.

$$P_1V_1 = P_2V_2 \implies V_2 = \frac{P_1V_1}{P_2}$$

STEP 4: **Solve. Substitute the known information into the equation.** Make sure units cancel so that the answer is given in the units of the unknown variable.

$$V_2 = \frac{P_1V_1}{P_2} = \frac{(1.0 \text{ atm})(750 \text{ mL})}{(9.5 \text{ atm})} = 79 \text{ mL}$$

BALLPARK CHECK Our estimate was 75 mL.

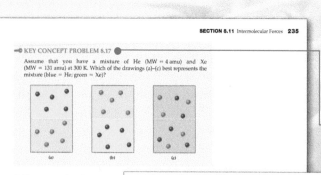

Key Concept Problems
These problems are integrated within the chapter, appearing at the end of a Worked Example or after the discussion of an important concept. These problems immediately focus students' attention on essential concepts and help them to test their understanding.

Looking Ahead
Looking Ahead Notes provide students with a preview of how the material being presented connects to the discussion in forthcoming chapters.

Concept Links
These links indicate where concepts in the text build on material from earlier chapters. This chain link icon provides a quick visual reminder that new material being discussed relates to a concept introduced previously.

VISUALIZATION

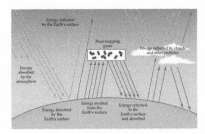

APPLICATION ▶ Greenhouse Gases and Global Warming

The mantle of gases surrounding the earth is far from the uniform mixture you might expect, consisting of layers that vary in composition and properties at different altitudes. The ability of the gases in these layers to absorb radiation is responsible for life on earth as we know it.

The *stratosphere*—the layer extending from about 12 km up to 50 km altitude—contains the ozone layer that is responsible for absorbing harmful UV radiation. The *troposphere* is the layer extending from the surface up to about 12 km altitude. It should not surprise you to learn that the troposphere is the layer most easily disturbed by human activities and that this layer has the greatest impact on the earth's surface conditions. Among those impacts, a process called the *greenhouse effect* is much in the news today.

The greenhouse effect refers to the warming that occurs in the troposphere as gases absorb radiant energy. Much of the radiant energy reaching the earth's surface from the sun is reflected back into space, but some is absorbed by atmospheric gases—particularly those referred to as—*greenhouse gases* (GHGs)—water vapor, carbon dioxide, and methane. This absorbed radiation warms the atmosphere and acts to maintain a relatively stable temperature of 15 °C (59 °F) at the earth's surface. Without the greenhouse effect, the average surface temperature would be about −18 °C (0 °F)—a temperature so low that Earth would be frozen and unable to sustain life.

The basis for concern about the greenhouse effect is the fear that human activities over the past century have disturbed the earth's delicate thermal balance. Should increasing amounts of radiation be absorbed, increased atmospheric heating will result, and global temperatures will continue to rise.

Measurements show that the concentration of atmospheric CO_2 has been rising in the last 150 years, largely because of the increased use of fossil fuels, from an estimated 290 parts per million (ppm) in 1850 to current levels approaching 380 ppm. The increase in CO_2 levels correlates with a concurrent increase in average global temperatures, with the 11 years between 1995 and 2006 ranking among the 12-highest since recording of global temperatures began in 1850. The latest report of the Intergovernmental Panel on Climate Change published in November 2007 concluded that "Warming of the climate system is unequivocal, as is now evident from observations of increases in global average air and ocean temperatures, widespread melting of snow and ice and rising global average sea level. . . . Continued GHG emissions at or above current rates would cause further warming and induce many changes in the global climate system during the 21st century that would *very likely* be larger than those observed during the 20th century."

See Additional Problems 8.101 and 8.102 at the end of the chapter.

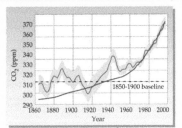

▲ Concentrations of atmospheric (age temperatures have increased d 150 years because of increased fo serious changes in earth's climate s
© Crown copyright 2006 data provided by t

Applications

These boxed Application essays connect the chemical concepts within each chapter to topics that are drawn from everyday life, clinical practice, health and nutrition, ecology, biotechnology, and chemical research.

Molecular Models

These computer-generated molecular models promote students' understanding of chemistry on a molecular level with electrostatic potential maps.

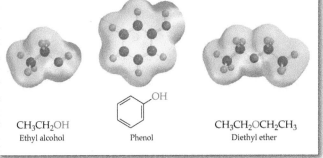

CH_3CH_2OH — Ethyl alcohol

OH — Phenol

$CH_3CH_2OCH_2CH_3$ — Diethyl ether

6.5 Mole Relationships and Chemical Equations

In a typical recipe, the amount of ingredients needed are specified using a variety of units: The amount of flour, for example, is usually specified in cups, whereas the amount of salt or vanilla flavoring might be indicated in teaspoons. In chemical reactions, the appropriate unit to specify the relationship between reactants and products is the mole.

The coefficients in a balanced chemical equation tell how many *molecules*, and thus how many *moles*, of each reactant are needed and how many molecules, and thus moles, of each product are formed. You can then use molar mass to calculate reactant and product masses. If, for example, you saw the following balanced equation for the industrial synthesis of ammonia, you would know that 3 mol of H_2 (3 mol × 2.0 g/mol = 6.0 g) are required for reaction with 1 mol of N_2 (28.0 g) to yield 2 mol of NH_3 (2 mol × 17.0 g/mol = 34.0 g).

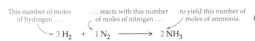

This number of moles of hydrogen . . .   . . . reacts with this number of moles of nitrogen . . .   to yield this number of moles of ammonia.

$$3 H_2 + 1 N_2 \longrightarrow 2 NH_3$$

The coefficients can be put in the form of *mole ratios*, which act as conversion factors when setting up factor-label calculations. In the ammonia synthesis, for example, the mole ratio of H_2 to N_2 is 3:1, the mole ratio of H_2 to NH_3 is 3:2, and the mole ratio of N_2 to NH_3 is 1:2:

$$\frac{3 \text{ mol } H_2}{1 \text{ mol } N_2} \quad \frac{3 \text{ mol } H_2}{2 \text{ mol } NH_3} \quad \frac{1 \text{ mol } N_2}{2 \text{ mol } NH_3}$$

Worked Example 6.9 shows how to set up and use mole ratios.

Color and Labeling Equations

Color has been extensively used to call attention to the aspects of chemical equations and structures under discussion. The number of explanatory labels set in balloons that focus on the important details in chemical equations and structures have also been increased.

A Balanced Approach to General, Organic, and Biological Chemistry

UNDERSTANDING CORE PRINCIPLES

Summary: Revisiting the Chapter Goals

The chapter summary revisits the chapter goals that open the chapter. Each of the questions posed at the start of the chapter is answered by a summary of the essential information needed to attain the corresponding goal.

Key Words

All of the chapter's boldface terms are listed in alphabetical order and are cross-referenced to the page where it appears in the text.

PROBLEM 5.25

A white crystalline solid has a melting point of 128 °C. It is soluble in water, but the resulting solution does not conduct electricity. Is the substance ionic or molecular? Explain.

PROBLEM 5.26

Aluminum chloride ($AlCl_3$) has a melting point of 190 °C, whereas aluminum oxide (Al_2O_3) has a melting point of 2070 °C. Explain.

● KEY WORDS

Binary compound, *p. 90*

Bond angle, *p. 91*

Bond length, *p. 92*

Condensed structure, *p. 102*

Coordinate covalent bond, *p. 103*

Covalent bond, *p. 105*

Double bond, *p. 109*

Electronegativity, *p. 110*

Lewis structure, *p. 110*

Lone pair, *p. 114*

Molecular compound, *p. 120*

Molecular formula, *p. 120*

Molecule, *p. 122*

Polar covalent bond, *p. 125*

Regular tetrahedron, *p. 126*

Single bond, *p. 130*

Structural formula, *p. 131*

Triple bond, *p. 132*

Valence-shell electron-pair repulsion (VSEPR) model, *p. 132*

● SUMMARY: REVISITING THE CHAPTER GOALS

1. **What is a covalent bond?** A *covalent bond* is formed by the sharing of electrons between atoms rather than by the complete transfer of electrons from one atom to another. Atoms that share two electrons are joined by a *single bond* (such as C—C), atoms that share four electrons are joined by a *double bond* (such as C=C), and atoms that share six electrons are joined by a *triple bond* (such as C≡C). The group of atoms held together by covalent bonds is called a *molecule*.

   Electron sharing typically occurs when a singly occupied valence orbital on one atom *overlaps* a singly occupied valence orbital on another atom. The two electrons occupy both overlapping orbitals and belong to both atoms, thereby bonding the atoms together. Alternatively, electron sharing can occur when a filled orbital containing an unshared, *lone pair* of electrons on one atom overlaps a vacant orbital on another atom to form a *coordinate covalent bond*.

2. **How does the octet rule apply to covalent bond formation?** Depending on the number of valence electrons, different atoms form different numbers of covalent bonds. In general, an atom shares enough electrons to reach a noble gas configuration. Hydrogen, for instance, forms one covalent bond because it needs to share one more electron to achieve the helium configuration ($1s^2$). Carbon and other group 4A elements form four covalent bonds because they need to share four more electrons to reach an octet. In the same way, nitrogen and other group 5A elements form three covalent bonds, oxygen and other group 6A elements form two covalent bonds, and halogens (group 7A elements) form one covalent bond.

3. **How are molecular compounds represented?** Formulas such as H_2O, NH_3, and CH_4, which show the numbers and kinds of atoms in a molecule, are called *molecular formulas*. More useful are *Lewis structures*, which show how atoms are connected in molecules. Covalent bonds are indicated as lines between atoms, and valence electron lone pairs are shown as dots. Lewis structures are drawn by counting the total number of valence electrons in a molecule or polyatomic ion and then placing shared pairs (bonding) and lone pairs (nonbonding) so that all electrons are accounted for.

4. **What is the influence of valence-shell electrons on molecular shape?** Molecules have specific shapes that depend on the number of electron charge clouds (bonds and lone pairs) surrounding the various atoms. These shapes can often be predicted using the *valence-shell electron-pair repulsion* (*VSEPR*) model. Atoms with two electron charge clouds adopt linear geometry, atoms with three charge clouds adopt planar triangular geometry, and atoms with four charge clouds adopt tetrahedral geometry.

5. **When are bonds and molecules polar?** Bonds between atoms are *polar covalent* if the bonding electrons are not shared equally between the atoms. The ability of an atom to attract electrons in a covalent bond is the atom's *electronegativity* and is highest for reactive nonmetal elements on the upper right of the periodic table and lowest for metals on the lower left. Comparing electronegativities allows a prediction of whether a given bond is covalent, polar covalent, or ionic. Just as individual bonds can be polar, entire molecules can be polar if electrons are attracted more strongly to one part of the molecule than to another. Molecular polarity is due to the sum of all individual bond polarities and lone-pair contributions in the molecule.

6. **What are the major differences between ionic and molecular compounds?** *Molecular compounds* can be gases, liquids, or low-melting solids. They usually have lower melting points and boiling points than ionic compounds, many are water insoluble, and they do not conduct electricity when melted or dissolved.

Demanding, yet logical, this text sets itself apart by requiring students to master problem-solving strategies and conceptual understanding before moving on to the next concept.

Understanding Key Concepts

These problems at the end of each chapter allow students to test their mastery of the core principles developed in the chapter. Students have an opportunity to ask "Did I get it?" before they proceed.

UNDERSTANDING KEY CONCEPTS

5.27 Which of the drawings shown here is more likely to represent an ionic compound and which a covalent compound?

(a) (b) (c) (d)

5.28 If yellow spheres represent sulfur atoms and red spheres represent oxygen atoms, which of the following drawings depicts a collection of sulfur dioxide molecules?

(a) (b)

(c) (d)

5.29 What is the geometry around the central atom in the following molecular models? (There are no "hidden" atoms; all atoms in each model are visible.)

(a) (b)

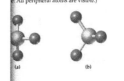

(c)

5.31 The ball-and-stick molecular model shown here is a representation of acetaminophen, the active ingredient in such over-the-counter headache remedies as Tylenol. The lines indicate only the connections between atoms, not whether the bonds are single, double, or triple (red = O, gray = C, blue = N, ivory = H).
(a) What is the molecular formula of acetaminophen?
(b) Indicate the positions of the multiple bonds in acetaminophen.
(c) What is the geometry around each carbon and each nitrogen?

Acetaminophen

5.32 The atom-to-atom connections in vitamin C (ascorbic acid) are as shown here. Convert this skeletal drawing to a Lewis electron-dot structure for vitamin C by showing the positions of any multiple bonds and lone pairs of electrons.

Vitamin C

5.33 The ball-and-stick molecular model shown here is a representation of thalidomide, a drug that causes terrible birth defects when taken by expectant mothers but has been approved for treating leprosy. The lines indicate only the connections between atoms, not whether the bonds are single, double, or triple (red = O, gray = C, blue = N, ivory = H).
(a) What is the molecular formula of thalidomide?
(b) Indicate the positions of the multiple bonds in thalidomide.

...e following molecular models have a tetrahe...al atom, and one does not. Which is the odd ...: All peripheral atoms are visible.)

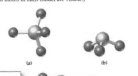

(a) (b)

5.72 Predict the three-dimensional shape of the following molecules:
(a) SiF_4
(b) CF_2Cl_2
(c) SO_3
(d) BBr_3
(e) NF_3

5.73 Predict the geometry around each carbon atom in the amino acid alanine.

$$CH_3CHCOH$$
$$NH_2$$
Alanine

5.74 Predict the geometry around each carbon atom in vinyl acetate, a precursor of the poly(vinyl alcohol) polymer used in automobile safety glass.

$$H_2C=CH-O-C-CH_3$$
Vinyl acetate

POLARITY OF BONDS AND MOLECULES

5.75 Where in the periodic table are the most electronegative elements found, and where are the least electronegative elements found?

5.76 Predict the electronegativity of the yet undiscovered element with Z = 119.

5.77 Look at the periodic table, and then order the following elements according to increasing electronegativity: Li, K, Br, C, Cl.

5.78 Look at the periodic table, and then order the following elements according to decreasing electronegativity: C, Ca, Cs, Cl, Cu.

5.79 Which of the following bonds are polar? Identify the negative and positive ends of each bond by using $\delta-$ and $\delta+$.
(a) I—Br (b) O—H
(c) C—F (d) N—C
(e) C—C

5.80 Which of the following bonds are polar? Identify the negative and positive ends of each bond by using $\delta-$ and $\delta+$.
(a) O—Br (b) N—H
(c) P—O (d) C—S
(e) C—Li

5.81 Based on electronegativity differences, would you expect bonds between the following pairs of atoms to be largely ionic or largely covalent?
(a) Be and F (b) Ca and Cl
(c) O and H (d) Be and Br

5.82 Arrange the following molecules in order of the increasing polarity of their bonds:
(a) HCl (b) PH_3
(c) H_2O (d) CF_4

5.83 Ammonia, NH_3, and phosphorus trihydride, PH_3, both have a trigonal pyramid geometry. Which one is more polar? Explain.

5.84 Decide whether each of the compounds listed in Problem 5.82 is polar, and show the direction of polarity.

5.85 Carbon dioxide is a nonpolar molecule, whereas sulfur dioxide is polar. Draw Lewis structures for each of these molecules to explain this observation.

5.86 Water (H_2O) is more polar than hydrogen sulfide (H_2S). Explain.

NAMES AND FORMULAS OF MOLECULAR COMPOUNDS

5.87 Name the following binary compounds:
(a) NO_2 (b) SF_6
(c) BrI_3 (d) N_2O_3
(e) NI_3 (f) IF_7

5.88 Name the following compounds:
(a) $SiCl_4$ (b) NaH
(c) SbF_5 (d) OsO_4

5.89 Write formulas for the following compounds:
(a) Phosphorus triiodide
(b) Arsenic trichloride
(c) Tetraphosphorus trisulfide
(d) Dialuminum hexafluoride
(e) Dinitrogen tetroxide
(f) Arsenic pentachloride

5.90 Write formulas for the following compounds:
(a) Selenium dioxide
(b) Xenon tetroxide
(c) Dinitrogen pentasulfide
(d) Triphosphorus tetraselenide

Applications

5.91 Draw electron-dot structures for CO and NO. Why are these molecules so reactive? [*CO and NO: Pollutants or Miracle Molecules?*, p. 116]

5.92 What is a vasodilator, and why would it be useful in treating hypertension (high blood pressure)? [*CO and NO: Pollutants or Miracle Molecules?*, p. 116]

5.93 How is a polymer formed? [*VERY Big Molecules*, p. 127]

5.94 Do any polymers exist in nature? Explain. [*VERY Big Molecules*, p. 127]

5.95 Why are many chemical names so complex? [*Damascenone by Any Other Name, p. 135*]

5.96 Can you tell from the name whether a chemical is natural or synthetic? [*Damascenone by Any Other Name, p. 135*]

General Questions and Problems

5.97 The discovery in the 1960s that xenon and fluorine react to form a molecular compound was a surprise to most chemists, because it had been thought that noble gases could not form bonds.
(a) Why was it thought that noble gases could not form bonds?
(b) Draw a Lewis structure of XeF_4.

Application Problems

Each boxed application essay throughout the text ends with a cross-reference to end-of-chapter problems. These problems help students test their understanding of the material and, more importantly, help students see the connection between chemistry and the world around them.

General Questions and Problems

These problems are cumulative, pulling together topics from various parts of the chapter and previous chapters. These help students synthesize the material just learned while helping them review topics from previous chapters.

Three Steps to Make Learning
Part of the Grade

MasteringChemistry™ emulates the instructor's office-hour environment, coaching students on problem-solving techniques by asking questions that reveal gaps in understanding, giving them the power to answer questions on their own. It tutors them individually—with feedback specific to their errors, offering optional simpler steps.

1. Submit an answer and receive immediate, error-specific feedback.

MasteringChemistry is the only system to provide instantaneous feedback specific to the most-common wrong answers, accumulated over eight years of capturing and researching student errors.

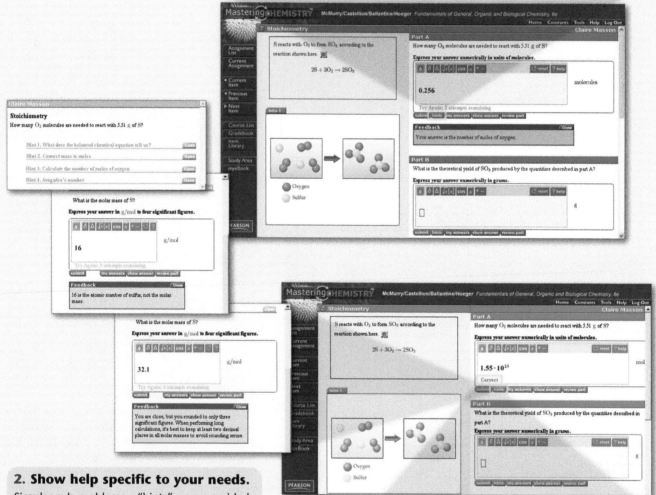

2. Show help specific to your needs.

Simpler sub-problems—"hints"—are provided upon request. From these, students can pick and choose only the help they need. These hints are built on data of key steps and concepts that students are found to struggle with nationally.

3. Partial credit means motivation for method.

MasteringChemistry is uniquely able to provide partial credit for the student's method (based on the simpler subproblems requested and errors made). Credit is at the heart of student motivation and so MasteringChemistry encourages students to focus on their method as well as their final answer.

Mastering CHEMISTRY™

www.masteringchemistry.com

Incorporate Dynamic Homework into Your Course with Automatic Grading

Homework Assignments of Ideal Difficulty and Duration

MasteringChemistry™ is unique in providing instructors with national data on difficulty and duration of every problem and tutorial. This allows you to quickly build homework assignments uniquely tailored to the ability of your students and goals of your course. Alternately, you can customize or choose pre-built weekly assignments to your needs.

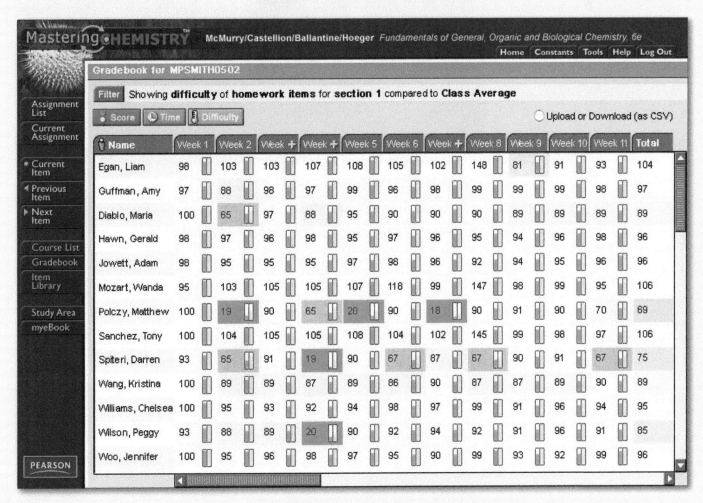

Unmatched Gradebook Capability

By capturing more detailed work of every student than any other homework system, MasteringChemistry provides the most powerful gradebook and diagnostics available. Spot students in trouble at a glance with the color-coded gradebook, effortlessly identify the most difficult Problem (and step within that problem) in your last assignment, or critique the detailed work of any one student who needs more help. Compare results on any problem and any step with a previous class, or the national average.

CHAPTER 1

Matter and Life

▲ The variety of exotic colors and aromas featured in this marketplace is due to the chemical and physical properties of chemicals.

CONTENTS

We will begin in this chapter by looking at the following topics:

1. What is matter?

THE GOAL: Be able to discuss the properties of matter and describe the three states of matter.

2. How is matter classified?

THE GOAL: Be able to distinguish between mixtures and pure substances, and between elements and compounds.

3. What kinds of properties does matter have?

THE GOAL: Be able to distinguish between chemical and physical properties.

4. How are chemical elements represented?

THE GOAL: Be able to name and give the symbols of common elements.

Look around you. Everything you see, touch, taste, and smell is made of chemicals. Many of these chemicals—those in rocks, trees, and your own body—occur naturally, but others are synthetic. Many of the plastics, fibers, and medicines that are so important a part of modern life do not occur in nature but have been created in the chemical laboratory.

Just as everything you see is made of chemicals, many of the natural changes you see taking place around you are the result of *chemical reactions*—the change of one chemical into another. The crackling fire of a log burning in the fireplace, the color change of a leaf in the fall, and the changes that a human body undergoes as it grows and ages are all the results of chemical reactions. To understand these and all other natural processes, you must have a basic understanding of chemistry.

As you might expect, the chemistry of living organisms is complex and it is not possible to jump right into it. Thus, the general plan of this book is to increase gradually in complexity, beginning in the first eleven chapters with a grounding in the scientific fundamentals that govern all of chemistry. In the next six chapters we look at the nature of the carbon-containing substances, or *organic chemicals*, that compose all living things. In the final twelve chapters we apply what we have learned to biological chemistry.

1.1 Chemistry: The Central Science

Chemistry is often referred to as "the central science" because it is crucial to all other sciences. In fact, as more and more is learned, the historical dividing lines between chemistry, biology, and physics are fading and current research is becoming more interdisciplinary. Figure 1.1 diagrams the relationship of chemistry and biological chemistry to some other fields of scientific study. Whatever the discipline in which you are most interested, the study of chemistry builds the necessary foundation.

Chemistry is the study of matter—its nature, properties, and transformations. **Matter**, in turn, is a catchall word used to describe anything physically real—anything you can see, touch, taste, or smell. In more scientific terms, matter is anything that has mass and volume. As with our knowledge of all the other sciences, our knowledge of chemistry has developed by application of a process called the **scientific method**. Starting with observations of the physical world, we form hypotheses to explain what we have observed. These hypotheses can then be tested by experiments to improve our understanding.

How might we describe different kinds of matter more specifically? Any characteristic that can be used to describe or identify something is called a **property**; size, color, and temperature are all familiar examples. Less familiar properties include *chemical composition*, which describes what matter is made of, and *chemical reactivity*, which describes how matter behaves. Rather than focus on the properties themselves, however, it is often more useful to think about *changes* in properties. Changes are of two types: *physical* and *chemical*. A **physical change** is one that does not alter the chemical makeup of a substance, whereas a **chemical change** is one that *does* alter a substance's chemical makeup. The melting of solid ice to give liquid water, for instance, is a physical change because the water changes only in form but not in chemical makeup. The rusting of an iron bicycle left in the rain, however, is

Chemistry The study of the nature, properties, and transformations of matter.

Matter The physical material that makes up the universe; anything that has mass and occupies space.

Scientific Method The systematic process of observation, hypothesis, and experimentation used to expand and refine a body of knowledge.

Property A characteristic useful for identifying a substance or object.

Physical change A change that does not affect the chemical makeup of a substance or object.

Chemical change A change in the chemical makeup of a substance.

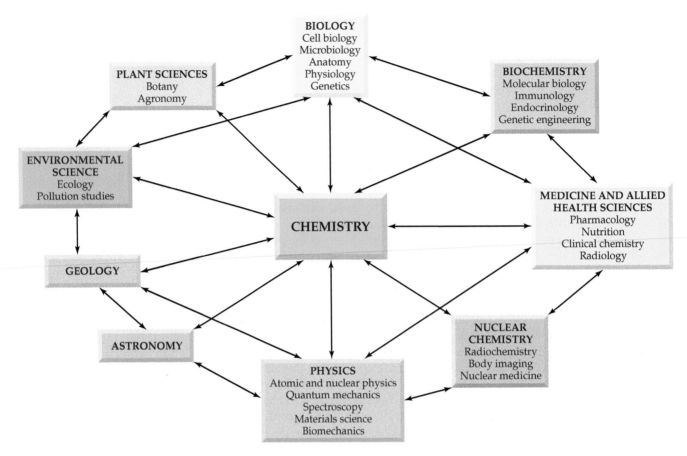

▲ **FIGURE 1.1** Some relationships between chemistry, the central science, and other scientific and health-related disciplines.

▲ **FIGURE 1.2** Samples of the pure substances water, sugar, and baking soda.

a chemical change because iron combines with oxygen and moisture from the air to give a new substance, rust.

Figure 1.2 shows several familiar substances—water, table sugar (sucrose), and baking soda (sodium bicarbonate)—and Table 1.1 lists their composition and some

TABLE 1.1   Some Properties of Water, Sugar, and Baking Soda

WATER	SUGAR (SUCROSE)	BAKING SODA (SODIUM BICARBONATE)
Physical properties		
Colorless liquid	White crystals	White powder
Odorless	Odorless	Odorless
Melting point: 0 °C	Begins to decompose at 160 °C, turning black and giving off water.	Decomposes at 270 °C, Giving off water and carbon dioxide.
Boiling point: 100 °C	—	—
Chemical properties		
Composition:*	Composition:*	Composition:*
11.2% hydrogen	6.4% hydrogen	27.4% sodium
88.8% oxygen	42.1% carbon	1.2% hydrogen
	51.5% oxygen	14.3% carbon
		57.1% oxygen
Does not burn.	Burns in air.	Does not burn.

Compositions are given by mass percent.

properties. Note in Table 1.1 that the changes occurring when sugar and baking soda are heated are chemical changes because new substances are produced.

PROBLEM 1.1

Which of the following are made of chemicals? Which might consist of "natural" chemicals and which of "synthetic" chemicals?

(a) Apple juice   (b) Laundry bleach

(c) Glass   (d) Coffee beans

PROBLEM 1.2

Identify each of the following as a physical change or a chemical change:

(a) A metal surface being ground   (b) Fruit ripening

(c) Wood burning   (d) A rain puddle evaporating

▲ Burning of potassium in water is an example of a chemical change.

1.2 States of Matter

Matter exists in three forms: solid, liquid, and gas. A **solid** has a definite volume and a definite shape that does not change regardless of the container in which it is placed; for example, a wooden block, marbles, or a cube of ice. A **liquid**, by contrast, has a definite volume but an indefinite shape. The volume of a liquid, such as water, does not change when it is poured into a different container, but its shape does. A **gas** is different still, having neither a definite volume nor a definite shape. A gas expands to fill the volume and take the shape of any container it is placed in, such as the helium in a balloon, or steam formed by boiling water (Figure 1.3).

Solid A substance that has a definite shape and volume.

Liquid A substance that has a definite volume but assumes the shape of its container.

Gas A substance that has neither a definite volume nor a definite shape.

(a) Ice: A solid has a definite volume and a definite shape independent of its container.

(b) Water: A liquid has a definite volume but a variable shape that depends on its container.

(c) Steam: A gas has both variable volume and shape that depend on its container.

◄ **FIGURE 1.3 The three states of matter—solid, liquid, and gas.**

Many substances, such as water, can exist in all three phases, or **states of matter**—the solid state, the liquid state, and the gaseous state—depending on the temperature. The conversion of a substance from one state to another is known as a **change of state** and is a common occurrence. The melting of a solid, the freezing or boiling of a liquid, and the condensing of a gas to a liquid are familiar to everyone.

State of matter The physical state of a substance as a solid, liquid, or gas.

Change of state The conversion of a substance from one state to another—for example, from liquid to gas.

WORKED EXAMPLE **1.1**

Formaldehyde is a disinfectant, a preservative, and a raw material for plastics manufacture. Its melting point is −92 °C, and its boiling point is −19.5 °C. Is formaldehyde a gas, a liquid, or a solid at room temperature (25 °C)? (The symbol °C means degrees Celsius.)

ANALYSIS The state of matter of any substance depends on its temperature. How do the melting point and boiling point of formaldehyde compare with room temperature?

SOLUTION
At room temperature (25 °C), the formaldehyde temperature is above the boiling point and so the formaldehyde is a gas.

PROBLEM 1.3

Acetic acid, which gives the sour taste to vinegar, has a melting point of 16.7 °C and a boiling point of 118 °C. Does a bottle of acetic acid contain a solid or a liquid on a chilly morning with the window open and the laboratory at 10 °C?

Pure substance A substance that has a uniform chemical composition throughout.

Mixture A blend of two or more substances, each of which retains its chemical identity.

Element A fundamental substance that cannot be broken down chemically into any simpler substance.

Chemical compound A pure substance that can be broken down into simpler substances by chemical reactions.

Reactant A starting substance that undergoes change during a chemical reaction.

Product A substance formed as the result of a chemical reaction.

Chemical reaction A process in which the identity and composition of one or more substances are changed.

1.3 Classification of Matter

The first question a chemist asks about an unknown substance is whether it is a pure substance or a mixture. Every sample of matter is one or the other. Water and sugar alone are pure substances, but stirring some sugar into a glass of water creates a *mixture*.

What is the difference between a pure substance and a mixture? One difference is that a **pure substance** is uniform in its chemical composition and its properties all the way down to the microscopic level. Every sample of water, sugar, or baking soda, regardless of source, has the composition and properties listed in Table 1.1. A **mixture**, however, can vary in both composition and properties, depending on how it is made (⊂⊃ , Section 9.1). The amount of sugar dissolved in a glass of water will determine the sweetness, boiling point, and other properties of the mixture. Note that you often cannot distinguish between a pure substance and a mixture just by looking. The sugar–water mixture *looks* just like pure water but differs on a molecular level.

Another difference between a pure substance and a mixture is that the components of a mixture can be separated without changing their chemical identities. Water can be separated from a sugar–water mixture, for example, by boiling the mixture to drive off the steam and then condensing the steam to recover the pure water. Pure sugar is left behind in the container.

Pure substances are themselves classified into two groups: those that can undergo a chemical breakdown to yield simpler substances and those that cannot. A pure substance that cannot be broken down chemically into simpler substances is called an **element** (⊂⊃ , Section 1.5). Examples include hydrogen, oxygen, aluminum, gold, and sulfur. At the time this book was printed, 117 elements had been identified, and all the millions of other substances in the universe are derived from them.

Any pure material that *can* be broken down into simpler substances by a chemical change is called a **chemical compound**. The term *compound* implies "more than one" (think "compound fracture"). A chemical compound, therefore, is formed by combining two or more elements to make a new substance. Water, sugar, baking soda, and millions of other substances are examples. Water, for example, can be chemically changed by passing an electric current through it to produce hydrogen and oxygen. In writing this chemical change, the **reactant** (water) is written on the left, the **products** (hydrogen and oxygen) are written on the right, and an arrow connects the two parts to indicate a chemical change, or **chemical reaction**. The conditions necessary to bring about the reaction are written above and below the arrow.

▲ Individually, sugar and water are pure substances. Honey, however, is a mixture composed mostly of sugar and water.

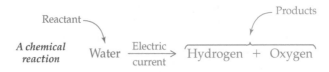

The classification of matter into mixtures, pure compounds, and elements is summarized in Figure 1.4.

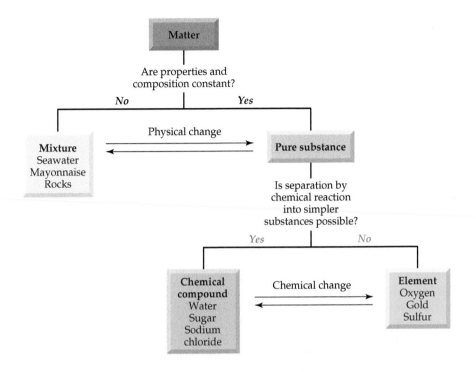

◄ **FIGURE 1.4   A scheme for the classification of matter.**

WORKED EXAMPLE   **1.2** Classifying Matter

Classify each of the following as a mixture or a pure substance:

　(a) Vanilla ice cream　　　　**(b)** Sugar

ANALYSIS Refer to the definitions of pure substances and mixtures. Is the substance composed of more than one kind of matter?

SOLUTION

　(a) Vanilla ice cream is composed of more than one substance—cream, sugar, and vanilla flavoring. This is a mixture.

　(b) Sugar is composed of only one kind of matter—pure sugar. This is a pure substance.

PROBLEM 1.4

Classify each of the following as a mixture or a pure substance:

(a) Concrete　　　　　　　　**(b)** The helium in a balloon

(c) A lead weight　　　　　　**(d)** Wood

PROBLEM 1.5

Classify each of the following as a physical change or a chemical change:

(a) Dissolving sugar in water.

(b) Producing carbon dioxide gas and solid lime by heating limestone

(c) Frying an egg

▲ The reactants. The flat dish contains pieces of nickel, an element that is a typical, lustrous metal. The bottle contains hydrochloric acid, a solution of the chemical compound hydrogen chloride in water. These reactants are about to be combined in the test tube.

▲ The reaction As the chemical reaction occurs, the colorless solution turns green when water-insoluble nickel metal slowly changes into the water-soluble chemical compound nickel chloride. Gas bubbles of the element hydrogen are produced and rise slowly through the green solution.

▶ The product Hydrogen gas can be collected as it bubbles from the solution. Removal of water from the solution leaves behind the other product, a solid green chemical compound known as nickel chloride.

◄● KEY CONCEPT PROBLEM 1.6

Identify the process illustrated in the figure below as a chemical change or a physical change. Explain.

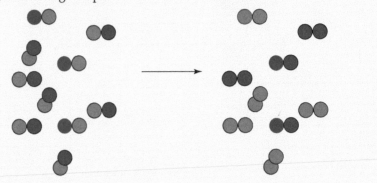

1.4 An Example of a Chemical Reaction

If we take a quick look at an example of a chemical reaction, we can reinforce some of the ideas discussed in the previous section. The element *nickel* is a hard, shiny metal, and the compound *hydrogen chloride* is a colorless gas that dissolves in water to give a solution called *hydrochloric acid*. When pieces of nickel are added to hydrochloric acid in a test tube, the nickel is slowly eaten away, the colorless solution turns green, and a gas bubbles out of the test tube. The change in color, the dissolving of the nickel, and the appearance of gas bubbles are indications that a chemical reaction is taking place.

Overall, the reaction of nickel with hydrochloric acid can be either written in words or represented in a shorthand notation using symbols, as shown below in brackets. We will explain the meaning of these symbols in the next section.

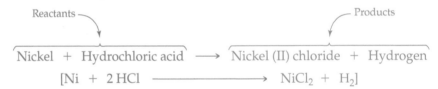

Reactants ⌐   ⌐ Products

$$\text{Nickel} + \text{Hydrochloric acid} \longrightarrow \text{Nickel (II) chloride} + \text{Hydrogen}$$

$$[\text{Ni} + 2\,\text{HCl} \longrightarrow \text{NiCl}_2 + \text{H}_2]$$

1.5 Chemical Elements and Symbols

As of the date this book was printed, 117 chemical elements had been identified. Some are certainly familiar to you—oxygen, helium, iron, aluminum, copper, and gold, for example—but many others are probably unfamiliar—rhenium, niobium, thulium, and promethium. Rather than write out the full names of elements, chemists use a shorthand notation in which elements are referred to by one- or two-letter symbols. The names and symbols of some common elements are listed in Table 1.2, and a complete alphabetical list is given inside the front cover of this book.

Note that all two-letter symbols have only their first letter capitalized, whereas the second letter is always lowercase. The symbols of most common elements are the first one or two letters of the elements' commonly used names, such as

APPLICATION ▶ Aspirin—A Case Study

Acetylsalicylic acid, more commonly known as aspirin, is perhaps the first true wonder drug. It is used as an analgesic to reduce fevers and to relieve headaches and body pains. It possesses anticoagulant properties, which in low doses can help prevent heart attacks and minimize the damage caused by strokes. But how was it discovered, and how does it work? The "discovery" of aspirin is a combination of serendipity and the scientific method.

The origins of aspirin can be traced back to the ancient Greek physician Hippocrates in 400 B.C., who prescribed the bark and leaves of the willow tree to relieve pain and fever. In 1828 scientists isolated from willow bark a bitter-tasting yellow extract, called salicin, that was identified as the active ingredient responsible for the observed medical effects. Salicin could be easily converted to salicylic acid (SA), which by the late 1800s was being mass-produced and marketed. SA had an unpleasant taste, however, and often caused stomach irritation and indigestion.

The discovery of acetylsalicylic acid (ASA) has often been attributed to Felix Hoffman, a chemist working for the Bayer pharmaceutical labs, but the first synthesis of ASA was reported by a French chemist, Charles Gerhardt, in 1853. Nevertheless, Hoffman obtained a patent for ASA in 1900, and Bayer marketed the new drug, now called aspirin, in water-soluble tablets.

How does aspirin work? In 1971 the British pharmacologist John Vane discovered that aspirin suppresses the body's production of prostaglandins (⊂⊃, Section 24.9), which are

▲ **Hippocrates.** The ancient Greek physician, prescribed a precursor of aspirin found in willowbark to relieve pain.

responsible for the pain and swelling that accompany inflammation. This discovery of this mechanism led to the development of new analgesic drugs.

Research continues to explore aspirin's potential for preventing colon cancer, cancer of the esophagus, and other diseases.

See Additional Problem 1.52 at the end of the chapter.

H (hydrogen) and Al (aluminum). Pay special attention, however, to the elements grouped in the last column to the right in Table 1.2. The symbols for these elements are derived from their original Latin names, such as Na for sodium, once known as *natrium*. The only way to learn these symbols is to memorize them; fortunately they are few in number.

Only 90 of the elements occur naturally; the remaining elements have been produced artificially by chemists and physicists. Each element has its own distinctive

TABLE 1.2 Names and Symbols for Some Common Elements

ELEMENTS WITH SYMBOLS BASED ON MODERN NAMES						ELEMENTS WITH SYMBOLS BASED ON LATIN NAMES	
Al	Aluminum	**Co**	Cobalt	**N**	Nitrogen	**Cu**	Copper (*cuprum*)
Ar	Argon	**F**	Fluorine	**O**	Oxygen	**Au**	Gold (*aurum*)
Ba	Barium	**He**	Helium	**P**	Phosphorus	**Fe**	Iron (*ferrum*)
Bi	Bismuth	**H**	Hydrogen	**Pt**	Platinum	**Pb**	Lead (*plumbum*)
B	Boron	**I**	Iodine	**Rn**	Radon	**Hg**	Mercury (*hydrargyrum*)
Br	Bromine	**Li**	Lithium	**Si**	Silicon	**K**	Potassium (*kalium*)
Ca	Calcium	**Mg**	Magnesium	**S**	Sulfur	**Ag**	Silver (*argentum*)
C	Carbon	**Mn**	Manganese	**Ti**	Titanium	**Na**	Sodium (*natrium*)
Cl	Chlorine	**Ni**	Nickel	**Zn**	Zinc	**Sn**	Tin (*stannum*)

TABLE 1.3 Elemental Composition of the Earth's Crust and the Human Body*

EARTH'S CRUST		HUMAN BODY	
Oxygen	46.1%	Oxygen	61%
Silicon	28.2%	Carbon	23%
Aluminum	8.2%	Hydrogen	10%
Iron	5.6%	Nitrogen	2.6%
Calcium	4.1%	Calcium	1.4%
Sodium	2.4%	Phosphorus	1.1%
Magnesium	2.3%	Sulfur	0.20%
Potassium	2.1%	Potassium	0.20%
Titanium	0.57%	Sodium	0.14%
Hydrogen	0.14%	Chlorine	0.12%

*Mass percent values are given.

Chemical formula A notation for a chemical compound using element symbols and subscripts to show how many atoms of each element are present.

properties, and just about all of the first 95 elements have been put to use in some way that takes advantage of those properties. As indicated in Table 1.3, which shows the approximate elemental composition of the earth's crust and the human body, the naturally occurring elements are not equally abundant. Oxygen and silicon together account for nearly 75% of the mass in the earth's crust; oxygen, carbon, and hydrogen account for nearly all the mass of a human body.

Just as elements combine to form chemical compounds, symbols are combined to produce **chemical formulas**, which show by subscripts how many *atoms* (the smallest fundamental units) of different elements are in a given chemical compound. For example, the formula H_2O represents water, which contains 2 hydrogen atoms combined with 1 oxygen atom. Similarly, the formula CH_4 represents methane (natural gas), and the formula $C_{12}H_{22}O_{11}$ represents table sugar (sucrose). When no subscript is given for an element, as for carbon in the formula CH_4, a subscript of "1" is understood.

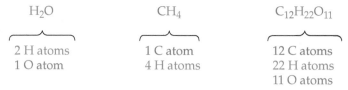

$$H_2O \qquad\qquad CH_4 \qquad\qquad C_{12}H_{22}O_{11}$$

2 H atoms	1 C atom	12 C atoms
1 O atom	4 H atoms	22 H atoms
		11 O atoms

PROBLEM 1.7

Look at the alphabetical list inside the front cover of this book and find the symbols for the following elements:

(a) Sodium, a major component in table salt

(b) Titanium, used in artificial hip and knee replacement joints

(c) Strontium, used to produce brilliant red colors in fireworks

(d) Yttrium, used in many lasers

(e) Fluorine, added to municipal water supplies to strengthen tooth enamel

(f) Hydrogen, used in fuel cells

PROBLEM 1.8

What elements do the following symbols represent?

(a) U **(b)** Ca **(c)** Nd

(d) K **(e)** W **(f)** Sn

PROBLEM 1.9

Identify the elements represented in each of the following chemical formulas, and tell the number of atoms of each element:

(a) NH_3 (ammonia)

(b) $NaHCO_3$ (sodium bicarbonate)

(c) C_8H_{18} (octane, a component of gasoline)

(d) $C_6H_8O_6$ (vitamin C)

1.6 Elements and the Periodic Table

The symbols of the known elements are normally presented in a tabular format called the **periodic table**, as shown in Figure 1.5 and the inside front cover of this book. We will have much more to say about the periodic table and how it is numbered in Sections 3.4–3.8 but will note for now that it is the most important organizing principle in chemistry. An enormous amount of information is embedded in the periodic table, information that gives chemists the ability to explain known chemical behavior of elements and to predict new behavior. The elements can be roughly divided into three groups: *metals*, *nonmetals*, and *metalloids* (sometimes called *semimetals*).

Periodic table A tabular format listing all known elements.

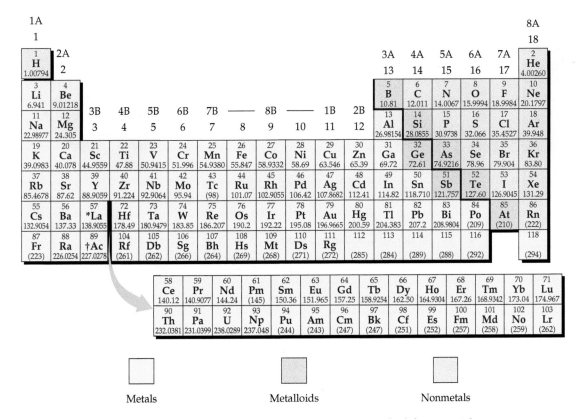

FIGURE 1.5 The periodic table of the elements. Metals appear on the left, nonmetals on the right, and metalloids in a zigzag band between metals and nonmetals. The numbering system is explained in Section 3.4.

Ninety of the currently known elements are metals—aluminum, gold, copper, and zinc, for example. **Metals** are solid at room temperature (except for mercury), usually have a lustrous appearance when freshly cut, are good conductors of heat and electricity, and are malleable rather than brittle. That is, a metal can be pounded into a different shape rather than shattering when struck. Note that metals occur on the left side of the periodic table.

Metal A malleable element with a lustrous appearance that is a good conductor of heat and electricity.

(a)

(b)

(c)

▲ **Metals: Gold, zinc, and copper.** (a) Known for its beauty, gold is very unreactive and is used primarily in jewelry and in electronic components. (b) Zinc, an essential trace element in our diets, has industrial uses ranging from the manufacture of brass, to roofing materials, to batteries. (c) Copper is widely used in electrical wiring, in water pipes, and in coins.

Nonmetal An element that is a poor conductor of heat and electricity.

Seventeen elements are **nonmetals**. All are poor conductors of heat and electricity, eleven are gases at room temperature, five are brittle solids, and one is a liquid. Oxygen and nitrogen, for example, are gases present in air; sulfur is a solid found in large underground deposits. Bromine is the only liquid nonmetal. Note that nonmetals occur on the right side of the periodic table.

(a)

(b)

(c)

▲ **Nonmetals: Nitrogen, sulfur, and iodine.** (a) Nitrogen, (b) sulfur, and (c) iodine are essential to all living things. Pure nitrogen, which constitutes almost 80% of air, is a gas at room temperature and does not condense to a liquid until it is cooled to −328 °F. Sulfur, a yellow solid, is found in large underground deposits in Texas and Louisiana. Iodine is a dark violet, crystalline solid first isolated from seaweed.

Metalloid An element whose properties are intermediate between those of a metal and a nonmetal.

Only seven elements are **metalloids**, so-named because their properties are intermediate between those of metals and nonmetals. Boron, silicon, and arsenic are examples. Pure silicon has a lustrous or shiny surface, like a metal. But it is brittle, like a nonmetal, and its electrical conductivity lies between that of metals and nonmetals. Note that metalloids occur in a zigzag band between metals on the left and nonmetals on the right side of the periodic table.

Those elements essential for human life are listed in Table 1.4. In addition to the well-known elements carbon, hydrogen, oxygen, and nitrogen, less familiar elements such as molybdenum and selenium are also important.

⊂⚪⚪⊃ Looking Ahead

The elements listed in Table 1.4 are not present in our bodies in their free forms, of course. Instead, they are combined into many thousands of different chemical compounds. We will talk about some compounds formed by metals in Chapter 4 and compounds formed by nonmetals in Chapter 5. ⊂⚪⚪⊃

TABLE 1.4 Elements Essential for Human Life*

ELEMENT	SYMBOL	FUNCTION
Carbon	C	These four elements are present in all living organisms
Hydrogen	H	
Oxygen	O	
Nitrogen	N	
Arsenic	As	May affect cell growth and heart function
Boron	B	Aids in the use of Ca, P, and Mg
Calcium*	Ca	Necessary for growth of teeth and bones
Chlorine*	Cl	Necessary for maintaining salt balance in body fluids
Chromium	Cr	Aids in carbohydrate metabolism
Cobalt	Co	Component of vitamin B_{12}
Copper	Cu	Necessary to maintain blood chemistry
Fluorine	F	Aids in the development of teeth and bones
Iodine	I	Necessary for thyroid function
Iron	Fe	Necessary for oxygen-carrying ability of blood
Magnesium*	Mg	Necessary for bones, teeth, and muscle and nerve action
Manganese	Mn	Necessary for carbohydrate metabolism and bone formation
Molybdenum	Mo	Component of enzymes necessary for metabolism
Nickel	Ni	Aids in the use of Fe and Cu
Phosphorus*	P	Necessary for growth of bones and teeth; present in DNA/RNA
Potassium*	K	Component of body fluids; necessary for nerve action
Selenium	Se	Aids vitamin E action and fat metabolism
Silicon	Si	Helps form connective tissue and bone
Sodium*	Na	Component of body fluids; necessary for nerve and muscle action
Sulfur*	S	Component of proteins; necessary for blood clotting
Zinc	Zn	Necessary for growth, healing, and overall health

*C, H, O, and N are present in all foods. Other elements listed vary in their distribution in different foods. Those marked with an asterisk are macronutrients, essential in the diet at more than 100 mg/day; the rest, other than C, H, O, and N, are micronutrients, essential at 15 mg or less per day.

(a)

(b)

◀ **Metalloids: Boron and silicon.** (a) Boron is a strong, hard metalloid used in making the composite materials found in military aircraft. (b) Silicon is well known for its use in making computer chips.

PROBLEM 1.10

Look at the periodic table inside the front cover, locate the following elements and identify them as metals or nonmetals:

(a) Cr, chromium

(b) K, potassium

(c) S, sulfur

(d) Rn, radon

PROBLEM 1.11

The seven metalloids are boron (B), silicon (Si), germanium (Ge), arsenic (As), antimony (Sb), tellurium (Te), and astatine (At). Locate them in the periodic table, and tell where they appear with respect to metals and nonmetals.

APPLICATION ▶ Mercury and Mercury Poisoning

Mercury, the only metallic element that is liquid at room temperature, has fascinated people for millennia. Egyptian kings were buried in their pyramids along with containers of mercury, alchemists during the Middle Ages used mercury to dissolve gold, and Spanish galleons carried loads of mercury to the New World in the 1600s for use in gold and silver mining. Even its symbol, Hg, from the Latin *hydrargyrum,* meaning "liquid silver," hints at mercury's uniqueness.

Much of the recent interest in mercury has concerned its toxicity, but there are some surprises. For example, the mercury compound Hg_2Cl_2 (called *calomel*) is nontoxic and has a long history of medical use as a laxative, yet it is also used as a fungicide and rat poison. Dental amalgam, a solid alloy of approximately 50% elemental mercury, 35% silver, 13% tin, 1% copper, and trace amounts of zinc, has been used by dentists for many years to fill tooth cavities. Yet exposure to elemental mercury *vapor* for long periods leads to mood swings, headaches, tremors, and loss of hair and teeth. The widespread use of mercuric nitrate, a mercury compound to make the felt used in hats, exposed many hatters of the eighteenth and nineteenth centuries to toxic levels of mercury. The eccentric behavior displayed by hatters suffering from mercury poisoning led to the phrase "mad as a hatter"—the Mad Hatter from Lewis Carroll's *Alice in Wonderland* is a parody of this stereotype.

Why is mercury toxic in some forms but not in others? It turns out that the toxicity of mercury and its compounds is related to solubility. Only soluble mercury compounds are toxic, because they can be transported through the bloodstream to all parts of the body where they react with different enzymes and interfere with various biological processes. Elemental mercury and insoluble mercury compounds become toxic only when converted into soluble compounds, reactions that are extremely slow in the body. Calomel, for example, is an insoluble mercury compound that passes

▲ The Mad Hatter's erratic behavior was a parody of the symptoms commonly associated with mercury poisoning.

through the body long before it is converted into any soluble compounds. Mercury alloys were considered safe for dental use because mercury does not evaporate readily from the alloys and it neither reacts with nor dissolves in saliva. Mercury vapor, however, remains in the lungs when breathed, until it is slowly converted into soluble compounds.

Of particular concern with regard to mercury toxicity is the environmental danger posed by pollution from both natural and industrial sources. Microorganisms present in lakes and streams are able to convert many mercury-containing wastes into a soluble and highly toxic compound called *methylmercury*. Methylmercury is concentrated to high levels in fish, particularly in shark and swordfish, which are then hazardous when eaten. Although the commercial fishing catch is now monitored carefully, more than 50 deaths from eating contaminated fish were recorded in Minimata, Japan, during the 1950s before the cause of the problem was realized.

See Additional Problem 1.53 at the end of the chapter.

SUMMARY: REVISITING THE CHAPTER GOALS

1. *What is matter?* *Matter* is anything that has mass and occupies volume—that is, anything physically real. Matter can be classified by its physical state as *solid*, *liquid*, or *gas*. A solid has a definite volume and shape, a liquid has a definite volume but indefinite shape, and a gas has neither a definite volume nor shape.

2. *How is matter classified?* A substance can be characterized as being either *pure* or a *mixture*. A pure substance is uniform in its composition and properties, but a mixture can vary in both composition and properties, depending on how it was made. Every pure substance is either an *element* or a *chemical compound*. Elements are fundamental substances that cannot be chemically changed into anything simpler. A chemical compound, by contrast, can be broken down by chemical change into simpler substances.

3. *What kinds of properties does matter have?* A *property* is any characteristic that can be used to describe or identify something. A *physical property* can be seen or measured without changing the chemical identity of the substance, (that is, color, melting point). A *chemical property* can only be seen or measured when the substance undergoes a *chemical change*, such as a chemical reaction.

4. *How are chemical elements represented?* Elements are represented by one- or two-letter symbols, such as H for hydrogen, Ca for calcium, Al for aluminum, and so on. Most symbols are the first one or two letters of the element name, but some symbols are derived from Latin names—Na (sodium), for example. All the known elements are commonly organized into a form called the *periodic table*. Most elements are *metals*, 17 are *nonmetals*, and 7 are *metalloids*.

KEY WORDS

Change of state, *p. 5*

Chemical change, *p. 3*

Chemical compound, *p. 6*

Chemical formula, *p. 10*

Chemical reaction, *p. 6*

Chemistry, *p. 3*

Element, *p. 6*

Gas, *p. 5*

Liquid, *p. 5*

Matter, *p. 3*

Metal, *p. 11*

Metalloid, *p. 12*

Mixture, *p. 6*

Nonmetal, *p. 12*

Periodic table, *p. 11*

Physical change, *p. 3*

Pure substance, *p. 6*

Product, *p. 6*

Property, *p. 3*

Reactant, *p. 6*

Scientific Method, *p. 3*

Solid, *p. 5*

State of matter, *p. 5*

UNDERSTANDING KEY CONCEPTS

The problems in this section are intended as a bridge between the Chapter Summary and the Additional Problems that follow. Primarily visual in nature, they are designed to help you test your grasp of the chapter's most important principles before attempting to solve quantitative problems. Answers to all Key Concept problems are at the end of the book following the appendixes.

1.12 Six of the elements at the far right of the periodic table are gases at room temperature. Identify them using the periodic table inside the front cover of this book.

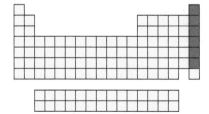

1.13 The so-called "coinage metals" are located near the middle of the periodic table. Identify them using the periodic table inside the front cover of this book.

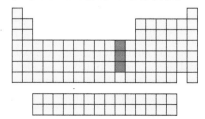

1.14 Identify the three elements indicated on the following periodic table and tell which is a metal, which is a nonmetal, and which is a metalloid.

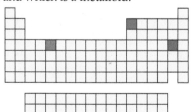

1.15 The radioactive element indicated on the following periodic table is used in smoke detectors. Identify it, and tell whether it is a metal, a nonmetal, or a metalloid.

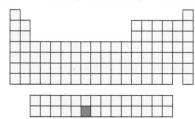

ADDITIONAL PROBLEMS

These exercises are divided into sections by topic. Each section begins with review and conceptual questions, followed by numerical problems of varying levels of difficulty. The problems are presented in pairs, with each even-numbered problem followed by an odd-numbered one requiring similar skills. The final section consists of unpaired General Questions and Problems that draw on various parts of the chapter and, in future chapters, may even require the use of concepts from previous chapters. Answers to all even-numbered problems are given at the end of the book following the appendixes.

CHEMISTRY AND THE PROPERTIES OF MATTER

1.16 What is chemistry?

1.17 Identify the following chemicals as natural or synthetic.

(a) The nylon used in stockings
(b) The substances that give roses their fragrance
(c) The yeast used in bread dough

1.18 Which of the following is a physical change and which is a chemical change?

(a) Boiling water
(b) Decomposing water by passing an electric current through it
(c) Dissolving sugar in water
(d) Exploding of potassium metal when placed in water
(e) Breaking of glass

1.19 Which of the following is a physical change and which is a chemical change?

(a) Steam condensing
(b) Milk souring
(c) Ignition of matches
(d) Breaking of a dinner plate
(e) Nickel sticking to a magnet
(f) Exploding of nitroglycerin

STATES AND CLASSIFICATION OF MATTER

1.20 Name and describe the three states of matter.

1.21 Name two changes of state, and describe what causes each to occur.

1.22 Sulfur dioxide is a compound produced when sulfur burns in air. It has a melting point of $-72.7\ ^\circ C$ and a boiling point of $-10\ ^\circ C$. In what state does it exist at room temperature ($25\ ^\circ C$)? (The symbol $^\circ C$ means degrees Celsius.)

1.23 Menthol, a chemical compound obtained from peppermint or other mint oils, melts at $45\ ^\circ C$ and boils at $212\ ^\circ C$. In what state is it found at:

(a) Room temperature ($25\ ^\circ C$)? (b) $60\ ^\circ C$? (c) $260\ ^\circ C$?

1.24 Classify each of the following as a mixture or a pure substance:

(a) Pea soup   (b) Seawater
(c) The contents of a propane tank
(d) Urine   (e) Lead
(f) A multivitamin tablet

1.25 Classify each of the following as a mixture or a pure substance. If it is a pure substance, classify it as an element or a compound:

(a) Blood   (b) Silicon
(c) Dishwashing liquid (d) Toothpaste
(e) Gold   (f) Gaseous ammonia

1.26 Classify each of the following as an element, a compound, or a mixture:

(a) Aluminum foil (b) Table salt   (c) Water
(d) Air   (e) A banana   (f) Notebook paper

1.27 Which of these terms, (i) mixture, (ii) solid, (iii) liquid, (iv) gas, (v) chemical element, (vi) chemical compound, applies to the following substances at room temperature?

(a) Gasoline   (b) Iodine   (c) Water
(d) Air   (e) Sodium bicarbonate

1.28 Hydrogen peroxide, often used in solutions to cleanse cuts and scrapes, breaks down to yield water and oxygen:

$$\text{Hydrogen peroxide} \longrightarrow \text{Water} + \text{Oxygen}$$

(a) Identify the reactants and products.
(b) Which of the substances are chemical compounds, and which are elements?

1.29 When sodium metal is placed in water, the following change occurs:

$$\text{Sodium} + \text{Water} \longrightarrow \text{Hydrogen} + \text{Sodium hydroxide}$$

(a) Identify the reactants and products.
(b) Which of the substances are elements, and which are chemical compounds?

ELEMENTS AND THEIR SYMBOLS

1.30 How many elements are presently known? About how many occur naturally?

1.31 Where in the periodic table are the metallic elements found? The nonmetallic elements? The metalloid elements?

1.32 Describe the general properties of metals, nonmetals, and metalloids.

1.33 What is the most abundant element in the earth's crust? In the human body? List the name and symbol for each.

1.34 What are the symbols for the following elements?

(a) Gadolinium (used in color TV screens)
(b) Germanium (used in semiconductors)
(c) Technetium (used in biomedical imaging)
(d) Arsenic (used in pesticides)
(e) Cadmium (used in rechargeable batteries)

1.35 What are the symbols for the following elements?

(a) Tungsten   (b) Mercury   (c) Boron
(d) Gold   (e) Silicon   (f) Argon
(g) Silver   (h) Magnesium

1.36 Give the names corresponding to the following symbols:

(a) N   (b) K   (c) Cl
(d) Ca   (e) P   (f) Mn

1.37 Give the names corresponding to the following symbols:

(a) Te   (b) Re   (c) Be
(d) Cr   (e) Pu   (f) Mn

1.38 The symbol CO stands for carbon monoxide, a chemical compound, but the symbol Co stands for cobalt, an element. Explain how you can tell them apart.

1.39 Explain why the symbol for sulfur is S, but the symbol for sodium is Na.

1.40 What is wrong with the following statements? Correct them.

(a) The symbol for bromine is BR.
(b) The symbol for manganese is Mg.
(c) The symbol for carbon is Ca.
(d) The symbol for potassium is Po.

1.41 What is wrong with the following statements? Correct them.

(a) Carbon dioxide has the formula CO2.
(b) Carbon dioxide has the formula Co_2.
(c) Table salt, NaCl, is composed of nitrogen and chlorine.

1.42 What is wrong with the following statements? Correct them.

(a) "Fool's gold" is a mixture of iron and sulfur with the formula IrS_2.
(b) "Laughing gas" is a compound of nitrogen and oxygen with the formula NiO.

1.43 What is wrong with the following statements? Correct them.

(a) Soldering compound is an alloy of tin and lead with the formula TiPb.
(b) White gold is an alloy of gold and nickel with the formula GdNI.

1.44 Name the elements combined in the chemical compounds represented by the following formulas:

(a) $MgSO_4$ (b) $FeBr_2$ (c) CoP
(d) AsH_3 (e) $CaCr_2O_7$

1.45 How many atoms of what elements are represented by the following formulas?

(a) Propane (LP gas), C_3H_8
(b) Sulfuric acid, H_2SO_4
(c) Aspirin, $C_9H_8O_4$
(d) Rubbing alcohol, C_3H_8O

1.46 The amino acid glycine has the formula $C_2H_5NO_2$. What elements are present in glycine? What is the total number of atoms represented by the formula?

1.47 Benzyl salicylate, a chemical compound sometimes used as a sunscreen, has the formula $C_{14}H_{12}O_3$. What is the total number of atoms represented by the formula? How many are carbon?

1.48 What is the formula for ibuprofen: 13 carbons, 18 hydrogens, and 2 oxygens.

1.49 What is the formula for penicillin V: 16 carbons, 18 hydrogens, 2 nitrogens, 5 oxygens, and 1 sulfur.

1.50 Which of the following two elements is a metal, and which is a nonmetal?

(a) Osmium, a hard, shiny, very dense solid that conducts electricity
(b) Xenon, a colorless, odorless gas

1.51 Which of the following elements is likely to be a metal and which a metalloid?

(a) Tantalum, a hard, shiny solid that conducts electricity
(b) Germanium, a brittle, gray solid that conducts electricity poorly

Applications

1.52 The active ingredient in aspirin, acetylsalicylic acid (ASA), has the formula $C_9H_8O_4$ and melts at 140 °C.

Identify the elements and how many atoms of each are present in ASA. Is it a solid or a liquid at room temperature? [*Aspirin—A Case Study, p. 9*]

1.53 Why is Hg_2Cl_2 harmless when swallowed, yet elemental mercury is toxic when breathed? [*Mercury and Mercury Poisoning, p. 14*]

General Questions and Problems

1.54 Distinguish between the following:

(a) Physical changes and chemical changes
(b) Melting point and boiling point
(c) Elements, compounds, and mixtures
(d) Chemical symbols and chemical formulas
(e) Reactants and products
(f) Metals and nonmetals

1.55 Are the following statements true or false? If false, explain why.

(a) The combination of sodium and chlorine to produce sodium chloride is a chemical reaction.
(b) The addition of heat to solid sodium chloride until it melts is a chemical reaction.
(c) The formula for a chemical compound that contains lead and oxygen is LiO.
(d) By stirring together salt and pepper we can create a new chemical compound to be used for seasoning food.
(e) Heating sugar to make caramel is a physical change.

1.56 Which of the following are chemical compounds, and which are elements?

(a) H_2O_2 (b) Al   (c) CO
(d) N_2 (e) $NaHCO_3$

1.57 A white solid with a melting point of 730 °C is melted. When electricity is passed through the resultant liquid, a brown gas and a molten metal are produced. Neither the metal nor the gas can be broken down into anything simpler by chemical means. Classify each—the white solid, the molten metal, and the brown gas—as a mixture, a compound, or an element.

1.58 As a clear red liquid sits at room temperature, evaporation occurs until only a red solid remains. Was the original liquid an element, a compound, or a mixture?

1.59 Describe how you could physically separate a mixture of iron filings, table salt, and white sand.

1.60 Small amounts of the following elements in our diets are essential for good health. What is the chemical symbol for each?

(a) Iron   (b) Copper   (c) Cobalt
(d) Molybdenum   (e) Chromium   (f) Fluorine
(g) Sulfur

1.61 Obtain a bottle of multivitamins from your local drug store or pharmacy and identify as many of the essential elements from Table 1.4 as you can. How many of them are listed as elements, and how many are included as part of chemical compounds?

1.62 Consider the recently discovered or as yet undiscovered elements with atomic numbers 115, 117, and 119. Is element 115 likely to be a metal or a nonmetal? What about element 117? Element 119?

1.63 How high would the atomic number of a new element need to be to appear under uranium in the periodic table?

CHAPTER 2

Measurements in Chemistry

▲ The success of many endeavors, such as NASA's Deep Impact comet probe, depends on both the accuracy and the precision of measurements.

CONTENTS

CHAPTER GOALS

In this chapter we will deal with the following questions about measurement:

1. **How are measurements made, and what units are used?**

   THE GOAL: Be able to name and use the metric and SI units of measure for mass, length, volume, and temperature.

2. **How good are the reported measurements?**

   THE GOAL: Be able to interpret the number of significant figures in a measurement and round off numbers in calculations involving measurements.

3. **How are large and small numbers best represented?**

   THE GOAL: Be able to interpret prefixes for units of measure and express numbers in scientific notation.

4. **How can a quantity be converted from one unit of measure to another?**

   THE GOAL: Be able to convert quantities from one unit to another using conversion factors.

5. **What techniques are used to solve problems?**

   THE GOAL: Be able to analyze a problem, use the factor-label method to solve the problem, and check the result to ensure that it makes sense chemically and physically.

6. **What are temperature, specific heat, density, and specific gravity?**

   THE GOAL: Be able to define these quantities and use them in calculations.

How often do you make an observation or perform an action that involves measurement? Whenever you check the temperature outside, make a pitcher of lemonade, or add detergent to the laundry, you are making a measurement. Likewise, whenever you use chemical compounds—whether you are adding salt to your cooking, putting antifreeze in your car radiator, or choosing a dosage of medicine—quantities of substances must be measured. A mistake in measuring the quantities could ruin the dinner, damage the engine, or harm the patient.

2.1 Physical Quantities

Height, volume, temperature, and other physical properties that can be measured are called **physical quantities** and are described by both a number and a **unit** of defined size:

Number   Unit

61.2 kilograms

Physical quantity A physical property that can be measured.

Unit A defined quantity used as a standard of measurement.

The number alone is not much good without a unit. If you asked how much blood an accident victim had lost, the answer "three" would not tell you much. Three drops? Three milliliters? Three pints? Three liters? (By the way, an adult human has only 5–6 liters of blood.)

Any physical quantity can be measured in many different units. For example, a person's height might be measured in inches, feet, yards, centimeters, or many other units. To avoid confusion, scientists from around the world have agreed on a system of standard units, called by the French name *Système International d'Unites* (International System of Units), abbreviated *SI*. **SI units** for some common physical quantities are given in Table 2.1. Mass is measured in *kilograms* (kg), length is measured in *meters* (m), volume is measured in *cubic meters* (m^3), temperature is measured in *kelvins* (K), and time is measured in *seconds* (s, not sec).

SI units are closely related to the more familiar *metric units* used in all industrialized nations of the world except the United States. If you compare the SI and metric units shown in Table 2.1, you will find that the basic metric unit of mass is the *gram* (g) rather than the kilogram (1 g = 1/1000 kg), the metric unit of volume is the *liter* (L) rather than the cubic meter (1 L = 1/1000 m^3), and the metric unit of temperature is the *Celsius degree* (°C) rather than the kelvin. The meter is the unit of

SI units Units of measurement defined by the International System of Units.

TABLE 2.1   Some SI and Metric Units and Their Equivalents

QUANTITY	SI UNIT (SYMBOL)	METRIC UNIT (SYMBOL)	EQUIVALENTS
Mass	Kilogram (kg)	Gram (g)	1 kg = 1000 g = 2.205 lb
Length	Meter (m)	Meter (m)	1 m = 3.280 ft
Volume	Cubic meter (m³)	Liter (L)	1 m³ = 1000 L = 264.2 gal
Temperature	Kelvin (K)	Celsius degree (°C)	See Section 2.9
Time	Second (s)	Second (s)	—

length and the second is the unit of time in both systems. Although SI units are now preferred in scientific research, metric units are still used in some fields. You will probably find yourself working with both.

In addition to the units listed in Table 2.1, many other widely used units are derived from them. For instance, units of *meters per second* (m/s) are often used for *speed*—the distance covered in a given time. Similarly, units of *grams per cubic centimeter* (g/cm³) are often used for *density*—the mass of substance in a given volume. We will see other such derived units in future chapters.

One problem with any system of measurement is that the sizes of the units often turn out to be inconveniently large or small for the problem at hand. A biologist describing the diameter of a red blood cell (0.000 006 m) would find the meter to be an inconveniently large unit, but an astronomer measuring the average distance from the earth to the sun (150,000,000,000 m) would find the meter to be inconveniently small. For this reason, metric and SI units can be modified by prefixes to refer to either smaller or larger quantities. For instance, the SI unit for mass—the kilogram—differs by the prefix *kilo-* from the metric unit gram. *Kilo-* indicates that a kilogram is 1000 times as large as a gram:

$$1 \text{ kg} = (1000)(1 \text{ g}) = 1000 \text{ g}$$

Small quantities of active ingredients in medications are often reported in *milligrams* (mg). The prefix *milli-* shows that the unit gram has been divided by 1000, which is the same as multiplying by 0.001:

$$1 \text{ mg} = \left(\frac{1}{1000}\right)(1 \text{ g}) = (0.001)(1 \text{ g}) = 0.001 \text{ g}$$

A list of prefixes is given in Table 2.2, with the most common ones displayed in color. Note that the exponents are multiples of 3 for *mega-* (10^6), *kilo-* (10^3), *milli-* (10^{-3}), *micro-* (10^{-6}), *nano-* (10^{-9}), and *pico-* (10^{-12}). (The use of exponents is reviewed in Section 2.5.) The prefixes *centi-*, meaning 1/100, and *deci-*, meaning 1/10, indicate exponents that are not multiples of 3. *Centi-* is seen most often in the length unit *centimeter* (1 cm = 0.01 m), and *deci-* is used most often in clinical chemistry, where the concentrations of blood components are given in milligrams per deciliter (1 dL = 0.1 L). These prefixes allow us to compare the magnitudes of different numbers by noting how the prefixes modify a common unit. For example,

$$1 \text{ meter} = 10 \text{ dm} = 100 \text{ cm} = 1000 \text{ mm} = 1{,}000{,}000 \ \mu m$$

Such comparisons will be useful when we start performing calculations involving units in Section 2.7. Note also in Table 2.2 that numbers having five or more digits to the right of the decimal point are shown with thin spaces every three digits for convenience—0.000 001, for example. This manner of writing numbers is becoming more common and will be used throughout this book.

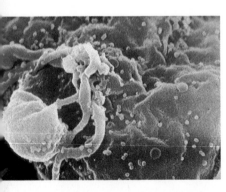

▲ The HIV-1 virus particles (in green) budding from the surface of a lymphocyte have an approximate diameter of 0.000 000 120 m.

TABLE 2.2   Some Prefixes for Multiples of Metric and SI Units

PREFIX	SYMBOL	BASE UNIT MULTIPLIED BY*	EXAMPLE
mega	M	$1{,}000{,}000 = 10^6$	1 megameter (Mm) $= 10^6$ m
kilo	k	$1000 = 10^3$	1 kilogram (kg) $= 10^3$ g
hecto	h	$100 = 10^2$	1 hectogram (hg) $= 100$ g
deka	da	$10 = 10^1$	1 dekaliter (daL) $= 10$ L
deci	d	$0.1 = 10^{-1}$	1 deciliter (dL) $= 0.1$ L
centi	c	$0.01 = 10^{-2}$	1 centimeter (cm) $= 0.01$ m
milli	m	$0.001 = 10^{-3}$	1 milligram (mg) $= 0.001$ g
micro	μ	$0.000\,001 = 10^{-6}$	1 micrometer (μm) $= 10^{-6}$ m
nano	n	$0.000\,000\,001 = 10^{-9}$	1 nanogram (ng) $= 10^{-9}$ g
pico	p	$0.000\,000\,000\,001 = 10^{-12}$	1 picogram (pg) $= 10^{-12}$ g
femto	f	$0.000\,000\,000\,000\,001 = 10^{-15}$	1 femtogram $= 10^{-15}$ g

*The scientific notation method of writing large and small numbers (for example, 10^6 for 1,000,000) is explained in Section 2.5.

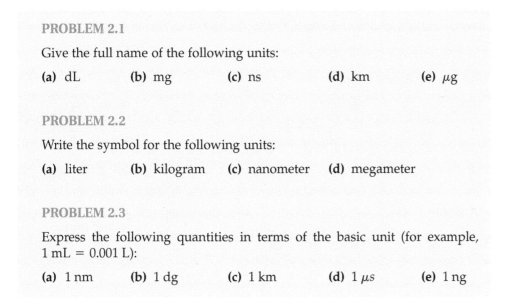

PROBLEM 2.1

Give the full name of the following units:

(a) dL   **(b)** mg   **(c)** ns   **(d)** km   **(e)** μg

PROBLEM 2.2

Write the symbol for the following units:

(a) liter   **(b)** kilogram   **(c)** nanometer   **(d)** megameter

PROBLEM 2.3

Express the following quantities in terms of the basic unit (for example, 1 mL = 0.001 L):

(a) 1 nm   **(b)** 1 dg   **(c)** 1 km   **(d)** 1 μs   **(e)** 1 ng

2.2 Measuring Mass

The terms *mass* and *weight*, though often used interchangeably, really have quite different meanings. **Mass** is a measure of the amount of matter in an object, whereas **weight** is a measure of the gravitational pull that the earth, moon, or other large body exerts on an object. Clearly, the amount of matter in an object does not depend on location. Whether you are standing on the earth or standing on the moon, the mass of your body is the same. On the other hand, the weight of an object *does* depend on location. Your weight on earth might be 140 lb, but it would only be 23 lb on the moon because the pull of gravity there is only about one-sixth as great.

At the same location, two objects with identical masses have identical weights; that is, gravity pulls equally on both. Thus, the *mass* of an object can be determined by comparing the *weight* of the object to the weight of a known reference standard. Much of the confusion between mass and weight is simply due to a language problem: We speak of "weighing" when we really mean that we are measuring mass by

Mass A measure of the amount of matter in an object.

Weight A measure of the gravitational force that the earth or other large body exerts on an object.

(a) (b)

▶ **FIGURE 2.1** (a) The single-pan balance has a sliding counterweight that is adjusted until the weight of the object on the pan is just balanced. (b) A modern electronic balance.

▲ This pile of 400 pennies has a mass of about 1 kg.

comparing two weights. Figure 2.1 shows two types of balances used for measuring mass in the laboratory.

One kilogram, the SI unit for mass, is equal to 2.205 lb—too large a quantity for many purposes in chemistry and medicine. Thus, smaller units of mass such as the gram, milligram (mg), and microgram (μg), are more commonly used. Table 2.3 shows the relationships between metric and common units for mass.

TABLE 2.3   **Units of Mass**

UNIT	EQUIVALENT	UNIT	EQUIVALENT
1 kilogram (kg)	= 1000 grams = 2.205 pounds	1 ton	= 2000 pounds = 907.03 kilograms
1 gram (g)	= 0.001 kilogram = 1000 milligrams = 0.035 27 ounce	1 pound (lb)	= 16 ounces = 0.454 kilogram = 454 grams
1 milligram (mg)	= 0.001 gram = 1000 micrograms	1 ounce (oz)	= 0.028 35 kilogram = 28.35 grams
1 microgram (μg)	= 0.000 001 gram = 0.001 milligram		= 28,350 milligrams

2.3 Measuring Length and Volume

The meter is the standard measure of length, or distance, in both the SI and metric systems. One meter is 39.37 inches (about 10% longer than a yard), a length that is much too large for most measurements in chemistry and medicine. Other, more commonly used measures of length are the *centimeter* (cm; 1/100 m) and the *millimeter* (mm; 1/1000 m). One centimeter is a bit less than half an inch—0.3937 inch to be exact. A millimeter, in turn, is 0.03937 inch, or about the thickness of a dime. Table 2.4 lists the relationships of these units.

Volume is the amount of space occupied by an object. The SI unit for volume—the cubic meter, m^3—is so large that the liter (1 L = 0.001 m^3 = 1 dm^3) is much more commonly used in chemistry and medicine. One liter has the volume of a cube 10 cm (1 dm) on edge and is a bit larger than one U.S. quart. Each liter is further divided into 1000 *milliliters* (mL), with 1 mL being the size of a cube 1 cm on edge, or 1 cm^3. In fact, the milliliter is often called a *cubic centimeter* (cm^3, or cc) in medical work. Figure 2.2 shows the divisions of a cubic meter, and Table 2.5 shows the relationships among units of volume.

TABLE 2.4   Units of Length

UNIT	EQUIVALENT	UNIT	EQUIVALENT
1 kilometer (km)	= 1000 meters = 0.6214 mile	1 mile (mi)	= 1.609 kilometers = 1609 meters
1 meter (m)	= 100 centimeters = 1000 millimeters = 1.0936 yards = 39.37 inches	1 yard (yd)	= 0.9144 meter = 91.44 centimeters
		1 foot (ft)	= 0.3048 meter = 30.48 centimeters
1 centimeter (cm)	= 0.01 meter = 10 millimeters = 0.3937 inch	1 inch (in.)	= 2.54 centimeters = 25.4 millimeters
1 millimeter (mm)	= 0.001 meter = 0.1 centimeter		

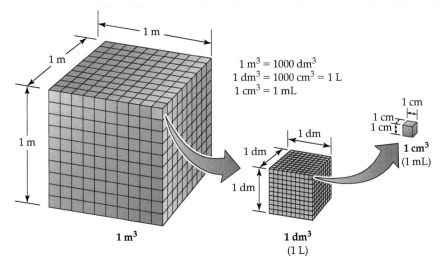

$1\ m^3 = 1000\ dm^3$
$1\ dm^3 = 1000\ cm^3 = 1\ L$
$1\ cm^3 = 1\ mL$

▲ FIGURE 2.2   A cubic meter is the volume of a cube 1 m on edge. Each cubic meter contains 1000 cubic decimeters (liters), and each cubic decimeter contains 1000 cubic centimeters (milliliters). Thus, there are 1000 mL in a liter and 1000 L in a cubic meter.

TABLE 2.5   Units of Volume

UNIT	EQUIVALENT
1 cubic meter (m^3)	= 1000 liters = 264.2 gallons
1 liter (L)	= 0.001 cubic meter = 1000 milliliters = 1.057 quarts
1 deciliter (dL)	= 0.1 liter = 100 milliliters
1 milliliter (mL)	= 0.001 liter = 1000 microliters
1 microliter (μL)	= 0.001 milliliter
1 gallon (gal)	= 3.7854 liters
1 quart (qt)	= 0.9464 liter = 946.4 milliliters
1 fluid ounce (fl oz)	= 29.57 milliliters

▲ The tennis ball weighs 54.07 g on this common laboratory balance, which is capable of determining mass to about 0.01 g.

Significant figures The number of meaningful digits used to express a value.

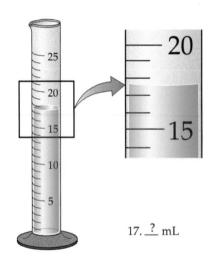

17. _?_ mL

▲ **FIGURE 2.3** What is the volume of liquid in this graduated cylinder?

2.4 Measurement and Significant Figures

How much does a tennis ball weigh? If you put a tennis ball on an ordinary bathroom scale, the scale would probably register 0 lb (or 0 kg if you have a metric scale). If you placed the same tennis ball on a common laboratory balance, however, you might get a reading of 54.07 g. Trying again by placing the ball on an expensive analytical balance like those found in clinical and research laboratories, you might find a weight of 54.071 38 g. Clearly, the precision of your answer depends on the equipment used for the measurement.

Every experimental measurement, no matter how precise, has a degree of uncertainty to it because there is always a limit to the number of digits that can be determined. An analytical balance, for example, might reach its limit in measuring mass to the fifth decimal place, and weighing the tennis ball several times might produce slightly different readings, such as 54.071 39 g, 54.071 38 g, and 54.071 37 g. Also, different people making the same measurement might come up with slightly different answers. How, for instance, would you record the volume of the liquid shown in Figure 2.3? It is clear that the volume of liquid lies between 17.0 and 18.0 mL, but the exact value of the last digit must be estimated.

To indicate the precision of a measurement, the value recorded should use all the digits known with certainty, plus one additional estimated digit that is usually considered uncertain by plus or minus 1 (written as ±1). The total number of digits used to express such a measurement is called the number of **significant figures**. Thus, the quantity 54.07 g has four significant figures (5, 4, 0, and 7), and the quantity 54.071 38 g has seven significant figures. *Remember*: All but one of the significant figures are known with certainty; the last significant figure is only an estimate accurate to ±1.

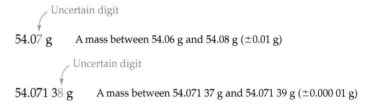

Uncertain digit

54.07 g   A mass between 54.06 g and 54.08 g (±0.01 g)

Uncertain digit

54.071 38 g   A mass between 54.071 37 g and 54.071 39 g (±0.000 01 g)

Deciding the number of significant figures in a given measurement is usually simple, but can be troublesome when zeros are involved. Depending on the circumstances, a zero might be significant or might be just a space-filler to locate the decimal point. For example, how many significant figures does each of the following measurements have?

94.072 g	Five significant figures (9, 4, 0, 7, 2)
0.0834 cm	Three significant figures (8, 3, 4)
0.029 07 mL	Four significant figures (2, 9, 0, 7)
138.200 m	Six significant figures (1, 3, 8, 2, 0, 0)
23,000 kg	*Anywhere* from two (2, 3) to five (2, 3, 0, 0, 0) significant figures

The following rules are helpful for determining the number of significant figures when zeros are present:

RULE 1. Zeros in the middle of a number are like any other digit; they are always significant. Thus, 94.072 g has five significant figures.

RULE 2. Zeros at the beginning of a number are not significant; they act only to locate the decimal point. Thus, 0.0834 cm has three significant figures, and 0.029 07 mL has four.

RULE 3. Zeros at the end of a number and *after* the decimal point are significant. It is assumed that these zeros would not be shown unless they were significant. Thus, 138.200 m has six significant figures. If the value were known to only four significant figures, we would write 138.2 m.

RULE 4. Zeros at the end of a number and *before* an implied decimal point may or may not be significant. We cannot tell whether they are part of the measurement or whether they act only to locate the unwritten but implied decimal point. Thus, 23,000 kg may have two, three, four, or five significant figures. Adding a decimal point at the end would indicate that all five numbers are significant.

Often, however, a little common sense is useful. A temperature reading of 20 °C probably has two significant figures rather than one, because one significant figure would imply a temperature anywhere from 10 °C to 30 °C and would be of little use. Similarly, a volume given as 300 mL probably has three significant figures. On the other hand, a figure of 150,000,000 km for the distance between the earth and the sun has only two or three significant figures because the distance is variable. We will see a better way to deal with this problem in the next section.

One final point about significant figures: Some numbers, such as those obtained when counting objects and those that are part of a definition, are *exact* and effectively have an unlimited number of significant figures. Thus, a class might have *exactly* 32 students (not 31.9, 32.0, or 32.1), and 1 foot is defined to have *exactly* 12 inches.

▲ How many CDs are in this stack? (Answer: *exactly* 29.)

WORKED EXAMPLE **2.1** Significant Figures of Measurements

How many significant figures do the following measurements have?

   (a) 2730.78 m   **(b)** 0.0076 mL   **(c)** 3400 kg   **(d)** 3400.0 m^2

ANALYSIS All nonzero numbers are significant; the number of significant figures will then depend on the status of the zeros in each case. (Hint: which rule applies in each case?)

SOLUTION

   (a) Six (rule 1)   **(b)** Two (rule 2)
   (c) Two, three, or four (rule 4)   **(d)** Five (rule 3)

PROBLEM 2.4

How many significant figures do the following measurements have?

   (a) 3.45 m   **(b)** 0.1400 kg
   (c) 10.003 L   **(d)** 35 cents

KEY CONCEPT PROBLEM 2.5

What is the temperature reading on the following Celsius thermometer? How many significant figures do you have in your answer?

2.5 Scientific Notation

Scientific notation A number expressed as the product of a number between 1 and 10, times the number 10 raised to a power.

Rather than write very large or very small numbers in their entirety, it is more convenient to express them using *scientific notation*. A number is written in **scientific notation** as the product of a number between 1 and 10, times the number 10 raised to a power. Thus, 215 is written in scientific notation as 2.15×10^2:

$$215 = 2.15 \times 100 = 2.15 \times (10 \times 10) = 2.15 \times 10^2$$

Notice that in this case, where the number is *larger* than 1, the decimal point has been moved *to the left* until it follows the first digit. The exponent on the 10 tells how many places we had to move the decimal point to position it just after the first digit:

$$215. = 2.15 \times 10^2$$

Decimal point is moved two places to the left, so exponent is 2.

To express a number *smaller* than 1 in scientific notation, we have to move the decimal point *to the right* until it follows the first digit. The number of places moved is the negative exponent of 10. For example, the number 0.002 15 can be rewritten as 2.15×10^{-3}:

$$0.002\ 15 = 2.15 \times \frac{1}{1000} = 2.15 \times \frac{1}{10 \times 10 \times 10} = 2.15 \times \frac{1}{10^3} = 2.15 \times 10^{-3}$$

$$0.002\ 15 = 2.15 \times 10^{-3}$$

Decimal point is moved three places to the right, so exponent is −3.

To convert a number written in scientific notation to standard notation, the process is reversed. For a number with a *positive* exponent, the decimal point is moved to the *right* a number of places equal to the exponent:

$$3.7962 \times 10^4 = 37,962$$

Positive exponent of 4, so decimal point is moved to the right four places.

For a number with a *negative* exponent, the decimal point is moved to the *left* a number of places equal to the exponent:

$$1.56 \times 10^{-8} = 0.000\ 000\ 015\ 6$$

Negative exponent of −8, so decimal point is moved to the left eight places.

Scientific notation is particularly helpful for indicating how many significant figures are present in a number that has zeros at the end but to the left of a decimal point. If we read, for instance, that the distance from the earth to the sun is 150,000,000 km, we do not really know how many significant figures are indicated. Some of the zeros might be significant, or they might merely act to locate the decimal point. Using scientific notation, however, we can indicate how many of the zeros are significant. Rewriting 150,000,000 as 1.5×10^8 indicates two significant figures, whereas writing it as 1.500×10^8 indicates four significant figures.

Scientific notation is not ordinarily used for numbers that are easily written, such as 10 or 175, although it is sometimes helpful in doing arithmetic. Rules for doing arithmetic with numbers written in scientific notation are reviewed in Appendix A.

WORKED EXAMPLE   **2.2** Significant Figures and Scientific Notation

There are 1,760,000,000,000,000,000,000 molecules of sucrose (table sugar) in 1 g. Use scientific notation to express this number with four significant figures.

ANALYSIS Because the number is larger than 1, the exponent will be positive. You will have to move the decimal point 21 places to the left.

SOLUTION

The first four digits—1, 7, 6, and 0—are significant, meaning that only the first of the 19 zeros is significant. Because we have to move the decimal point 21 places to the left to put it after the first significant digit, the answer is 1.760×10^{21}.

▲ How many molecules are in this 1 g pile of table sugar?

WORKED EXAMPLE **2.3** Scientific Notation

The rhinovirus responsible for the common cold has a diameter of 20 nm, or 0.000 000 020 m (See Application on p. 28). Express this number in scientific notation.

ANALYSIS The number is smaller than 1, and so the exponent will be negative. You will have to move the decimal point eight places to the right.

SOLUTION

There are only two significant figures, because zeros at the beginning of a number are not significant. We have to move the decimal point 8 places to the right to place it after the first digit, so the answer is 2.0×10^{-8} m.

WORKED EXAMPLE **2.4** Scientific Notation and Unit Conversions

A clinical laboratory found that a blood sample contained 0.0026 g of phosphorus and 0.000 101 g of iron.

(a) Give these quantities in scientific notation.

(b) Give these quantities in the units normally used to report them—milligrams for phosphorus and micrograms for iron.

ANALYSIS Is the number larger or smaller than 1? How many places do you have to move the decimal point?

SOLUTION

(a) 0.0026 g phosphorus $= 2.6 \times 10^{-3}$ g phosphorus

0.000 101 g iron $= 1.01 \times 10^{-4}$ g iron

(b) We know that 1 mg $= 1 \times 10^{-3}$ g, where the exponent is -3. Expressing the amount of phosphorus in milligrams is straightforward because the amount in grams (2.6×10^{-3} g) already has an exponent of -3. Thus, 2.6×10^{-3} g $= 2.6$ mg of phosphorus.

$$(2.6 \times 10^{-3}\ \cancel{g})\left(\frac{1\ \text{mg}}{1 \times 10^{-3}\ \cancel{g}}\right) = 2.6\ \text{mg}$$

We know that 1 μg $= 1 \times 10^{-6}$ g, where the exponent is -6. Expressing the amount of iron in micrograms thus requires that we restate the amount in grams so that the exponent is -6. We can do this by moving the decimal point six places to the right:

0.000 101 g iron $= 101 \times 10^{-6}$ g iron $= 101\ \mu$g iron

APPLICATION ▶ Powers of 10

It is not easy to grasp the enormous differences in size represented by powers of 10 (scientific notation). A sodium atom has a diameter of 388 pm (3.88×10^{-10} m), a typical rhinovirus may have a diameter of 20 nm (2.0×10^{-8} m), and a single bacteria cell may be 3 μm long (3×10^{-6} m). Even though none of these objects can be seen with the naked eye, scientists know that the size of an atom relative to the size of a bacterium would be like comparing the size of a bowling ball with that of a baseball stadium. So how do scientists know the relative sizes of these items if we can not see them?

To study the miniature world of bacteria and viruses requires special tools. Optical light microscopes, for example, can magnify an object up to 1500 (1.5×10^3) times,

enabling us to study objects as small as 0.2 μm, such as bacteria. To study smaller objects, such as viruses, requires even higher magnification. Electron microscopy, which uses a beam of electrons instead of light, can achieve magnifications of 1×10^5 for scanning electron microscopy (SEM), and the ability to distinguish features on the order of 0.1 nm in length are possible with scanning tunneling microscopes (STM).

The change in magnification needed to distinguish features from 1 mm to 1 nm may not seem great, but it represents a million-fold (10^6) increase—enough to open a whole new world. Powers of 10 are powerful indeed.

See Additional Problems 2.78 and 2.79 at the end of the chapter.

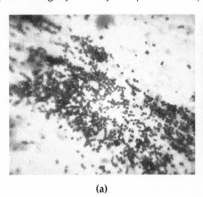 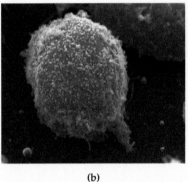 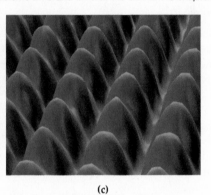

(a)　　　　　　　　　(b)　　　　　　　　　(c)

▲ (a) A light microscope image of bacteria; (b) a color-enhanced SEM image showing a T-lymphocyte white blood cell (in orange) with HIV particles (in blue) budding on the surface of the cell membrane; (c) an STM image of a "blue nickel" surface showing the orientation of individual metal atoms.

PROBLEM 2.6

Convert the following values to scientific notation:

(a) 0.058 g　　　　**(b)** 46,792 m　　　　**(c)** 0.006 072 cm　　　　**(d)** 345.3 kg

PROBLEM 2.7

Convert the following values from scientific notation to standard notation:

(a) 4.885×10^4 mg　　　　**(b)** 8.3×10^{-6} m　　　　**(c)** 4.00×10^{-2} m

PROBLEM 2.8

Rewrite the following numbers in scientific notation as indicated:

(a) 630,000 with five significant figures

(b) 1300 with three significant figures

(c) 794,200,000,000 with four significant figures

PROBLEM 2.9

Ordinary table salt, or sodium chloride, is made up of small particles called *ions*, which we will discuss in Chapter 4. If the distance between a sodium ion and a chloride ion is 0.000 000 000 278 m, what is the distance in scientific notation? How many picometers is this?

2.6 Rounding Off Numbers

It often happens, particularly when doing arithmetic on a pocket calculator, that a quantity appears to have more significant figures than are really justified. For example, you might calculate the gas mileage of your car by finding that it takes 11.70 gallons of gasoline to drive 278 miles:

$$\text{Mileage} = \frac{\text{Miles}}{\text{Gallons}} = \frac{278 \text{ mi}}{11.70 \text{ gal}} = 23.760\,684 \text{ mi/gal (mpg)}$$

Although the answer on a pocket calculator has eight digits, your measurement is really not as precise as it appears. In fact, as we will see below, your answer is good to only three significant figures and should be **rounded off** to 23.8 mi/gal.

How do you decide how many digits to keep? The full answer to this question is a bit complex and involves a mathematical treatment called *error analysis*, but for many purposes, a simplified procedure using just two rules is sufficient:

Rounding off A procedure used for deleting nonsignificant figures.

RULE 1. In carrying out a multiplication or division, the answer cannot have more significant figures than either of the original numbers. This is just a common-sense rule if you think about it. After all, if you do not know the number of miles you drove to better than three significant figures (278 could mean 277, 278, or 279), you certainly cannot calculate your mileage to more than the same number of significant figures.

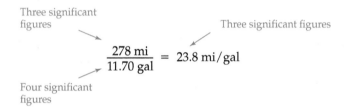

Three significant figures

Three significant figures

$$\frac{278 \text{ mi}}{11.70 \text{ gal}} = 23.8 \text{ mi/gal}$$

Four significant figures

▲ Calculators often display more digits than are justified by the precision of the data.

RULE 2. In carrying out an addition or subtraction, the answer cannot have more digits after the decimal point than either of the original numbers. For example, if you have 3.18 L of water and you add 0.013 15 L more, you now have 3.19 L. Again, this rule is just common sense. If you do not know the volume you started with past the second decimal place (it could be 3.17, 3.18, or 3.19), you cannot know the total of the combined volumes past the same decimal place.

Volume of water at start ⟶ 3.18? ?? L ⟵ Two digits after decimal point
Volume of water added ⟶ + 0.013 15 L ⟵ Five digits after decimal point
Total volume of water ⟶ 3.19? ?? L ⟵ Two digits after decimal point

If a calculation has several steps, it is generally best to round off at the end after all the steps have been carried out, keeping the number of significant figures determined by the least precise number in your calculations. Once you decide how many digits to retain for your answer, the rules for rounding off numbers are straightforward:

RULE 1. If the first digit you remove is 4 or less, drop it and all following digits. Thus, 2.4271 becomes 2.4 when rounded off to two significant figures because the first of the dropped digits (a 2) is 4 or less.

RULE 2. If the first digit you remove is 5 or greater, round the number up by adding a 1 to the digit to the left of the one you drop. Thus, 4.5832 becomes 4.6 when rounded off to two significant figures because the first of the dropped digits (an 8) is 5 or greater.

WORKED EXAMPLE **2.5** Significant Figures and Calculations: Addition/Subtraction

Suppose that you weigh 124 lb before dinner. How much will you weigh after dinner if you eat 1.884 lb of food?

ANALYSIS When performing addition or subtraction, the number of significant figures you report in the final answer is determined by the number of digits in the least precise number in the calculation.

SOLUTION
Your after-dinner weight is found by adding your original weight to the weight of the food consumed:

$$
\begin{array}{r}
124 \quad \text{lb} \\
\underline{1.884 \text{ lb}} \\
125.884 \text{ lb} \quad \text{(Unrounded)}
\end{array}
$$

Because the value of your original weight has no significant figures after the decimal point, your after-dinner weight also must have no significant figures after the decimal point. Thus, 125.884 lb must be rounded off to 126 lb.

WORKED EXAMPLE **2.6** Significant Figures and Calculations: Multiplication/Division

To make currant jelly, 13.75 cups of sugar was added to 18 cups of currant juice. How much sugar was added per cup of juice?

ANALYSIS For calculations involving multiplication or division, the final answer cannot have more significant figures than either of the original numbers.

SOLUTION
The quantity of sugar must be divided by the quantity of juice:

$$
\frac{13.75 \text{ cups sugar}}{18 \text{ cups juice}} = 0.763\,888\,89 \frac{\text{cup sugar}}{\text{cup juice}} \text{(Unrounded)}
$$

The number of significant figures in the answer is limited to two by the quantity 18 cups in the calculation and must be rounded to 0.76 cup of sugar per cup of juice.

PROBLEM 2.10

Round off the following quantities to the indicated number of significant figures:

(a) 2.304 g (three significant figures)
(b) 188.3784 mL (five significant figures)
(c) 0.008 87 L (one significant figure)
(d) 1.000 39 kg (four significant figures)

PROBLEM 2.11

Carry out the following calculations, rounding each result to the correct number of significant figures:

(a) 4.87 mL + 46.0 mL   (b) 3.4 × 0.023 g
(c) 19.333 m − 7.4 m   (d) 55 mg − 4.671 mg + 0.894 mg
(e) 62,911 ÷ 611

2.7 Problem Solving: Converting a Quantity from One Unit to Another

Many activities in the laboratory and in medicine—measuring, weighing, preparing solutions, and so forth—require converting a quantity from one unit to another. For example: "These pills contain 1.3 grains of aspirin, but I need 200 mg. Is one pill enough?" Converting between units is not mysterious; we all do it every day. If you run 9 laps around a 400 meter track, for instance, you have to convert between the distance unit "lap" and the distance unit "meter" to find that you have run 3600 m (9 laps times 400 m/lap). If you want to find how many miles that is, you have to convert again to find that 3600 m = 2.237 mi.

The simplest way to carry out calculations involving different units is to use the **factor-label method**. In this method, a quantity in one unit is converted into an equivalent quantity in a different unit by using a **conversion factor** that expresses the relationship between units:

$$\text{Starting quantity} \times \text{Conversion factor} = \text{Equivalent quantity}$$

As an example, we said in Section 2.3 that 1 km = 0.6214 mi. Writing this relationship as a fraction restates it in the form of a conversion factor, either kilometers per mile or miles per kilometer.

Since 1 km = 0.6214 mi, then:

Conversion factors between kilometers and miles
$$\frac{1 \text{ km}}{0.6214 \text{ mi}} = 1 \quad \text{or} \quad \frac{0.6214 \text{ mi}}{1 \text{ km}} = 1$$

Note that this and all other conversion factors are numerically equal to 1 because the value of the quantity above the division line (the numerator) is equal in value to the quantity below the division line (the denominator). Thus, multiplying by a conversion factor is equivalent to multiplying by 1 and so does not change the value of the quantity being multiplied:

These two quantities are the same.
$$\frac{1 \text{ km}}{0.6214 \text{ mi}} \quad \text{or} \quad \frac{0.6214 \text{ mi}}{1 \text{ km}}$$
These two quantities are the same.

The key to the factor-label method of problem solving is that units are treated like numbers and can thus be multiplied and divided (though not added or subtracted) just as numbers can. When solving a problem, the idea is to set up an equation so that all unwanted units cancel, leaving only the desired units. Usually, it is best to start by writing what you know and then manipulating that known quantity. For example, if you know there are 26.22 mi in a marathon and want to find how many kilometers that is, you could write the distance in miles and multiply by the conversion factor in kilometers per mile. The unit "mi" cancels because it appears both above and below the division line, leaving "km" as the only remaining unit.

$$26.22 \; \cancel{\text{mi}} \times \frac{1 \text{ km}}{0.6214 \; \cancel{\text{mi}}} = 42.20 \text{ km}$$

Starting quantity   Conversion factor   Equivalent quantity

The factor-label method gives the right answer only if the equation is set up so that the unwanted unit (or units) cancel. If the equation is set up in any other way, the units will not cancel and you will not get the right answer. Thus, if you selected the incorrect conversion factor (miles per kilometer) for the above problem,

▲ These runners have to convert from laps to meters to find out how far they have run.

Factor-label method A problem-solving procedure in which equations are set up so that unwanted units cancel and only the desired units remain.

Conversion factor An expression of the numerical relationship between two units.

you would end up with an incorrect answer expressed in meaningless units:

$$\text{Incorrect } 26.22 \text{ mi} \times \frac{0.6214 \text{ mi}}{1 \text{ km}} = 16.29 \frac{\text{mi}^2}{\text{km}} \text{ Incorrect}$$

WORKED EXAMPLE **2.7** Factor Labels: Unit Conversions

Write conversion factors for the following pairs of units (use Tables 2.3–2.5):

(a) Deciliters and milliliters

(b) Pounds and grams

ANALYSIS Start with the appropriate equivalency relationship and rearrange to form conversion factors.

SOLUTION

(a) Since 1 dL = 0.1 L and 1 mL = 0.001L, then

$$1 \text{ dL} = (0.1 \text{ L}) \left(\frac{1 \text{ mL}}{0.001\text{L}} \right) = 100 \text{ mL. The conversion factors are}$$

$$\frac{1 \text{ dL}}{100 \text{ mL}} \quad \text{and} \quad \frac{100 \text{ mL}}{1 \text{ dL}}$$

(b) $\dfrac{1 \text{ lb}}{454 \text{ g}}$ and $\dfrac{454 \text{ g}}{1 \text{ lb}}$

WORKED EXAMPLE **2.8** Factor Labels: Unit Conversions

(a) Convert 0.75 lb to grams.

(b) Convert 0.50 qt to deciliters.

ANALYSIS Start with conversion factors and set up equations so that units cancel appropriately.

SOLUTION

(a) Select the conversion factor from Worked Example 2.7(b) so that the "lb" units cancel and "g" remains:

$$0.75 \text{ lb} \times \frac{454 \text{ g}}{1 \text{ lb}} = 340 \text{ g}$$

(b) In this, as in many problems, it is convenient to use more than one conversion factor. As long as the unwanted units cancel correctly, two or more conversion factors can be strung together in the same calculation. In this case, we can convert first between quarts and milliliters, and then between milliliters and deciliters:

$$0.50 \text{ qt} \times \frac{946.4 \text{ mL}}{1 \text{ qt}} \times \frac{1 \text{ dL}}{100 \text{ mL}} = 4.7 \text{ dL}$$

PROBLEM 2.12

Write conversion factors for the following pairs of units:

(a) liters and milliliters   (b) grams and ounces

(c) liters and quarts

PROBLEM 2.13

Carry out the following conversions:

(a) 16.0 oz = ? g   **(b)** 2500 mL = ? L   **(c)** 99.0 L = ? qt

PROBLEM 2.14

Convert 0.840 qt to milliliters in a single calculation using more than one conversion factor.

PROBLEM 2.15

One international nautical mile is defined as exactly 6076.1155 ft, and a speed of 1 knot is defined as one international nautical mile per hour. What is the speed in meters per second of a boat traveling at a speed of 14.3 knots?

2.8 Problem Solving: Estimating Answers

The main drawback to using the factor-label method is that it is possible to get an answer without really understanding what you are doing. It is therefore best when solving a problem to first think through a rough estimate, or *ballpark estimate*, as a check on your work. If your ballpark estimate is not close to the final calculated solution, there is a misunderstanding somewhere and you should think the problem through again. If, for example, you came up with the answer 5.3 cm^3 when calculating the volume of a human cell, you should realize that such an answer could not possibly be right. Cells are too tiny to be distinguished with the naked eye, but a volume of 5.3 cm^3 is about the size of a walnut. The Worked Examples at the end of this section show how to estimate the answers to simple unit-conversion problems.

The factor-label method and the use of ballpark estimates are techniques that will help you solve problems of many kinds, not just unit conversions. Problems sometimes seem complicated, but you can usually sort out the complications by analyzing the problem properly:

STEP 1: Identify the information given, including units.

STEP 2: Identify the information needed in the answer, including units.

STEP 3: Find the relationship(s) between the known information and unknown answer, and plan a series of steps, including conversion factors, for getting from one to the other.

STEP 4: Solve the problem.

BALLPARK CHECK: Make a ballpark estimate at the beginning and check it against your final answer to be sure the value and the units of your calculated answer are reasonable.

Worked Examples 2.9, 2.10 and 2.11 illustrate how to use the analysis steps and ballpark checks as an aid in dosage calculations.

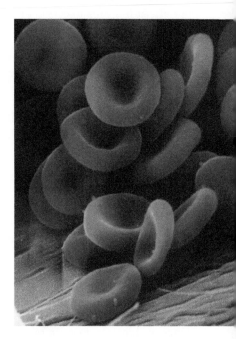

▲ What is the volume of a red blood cell?

WORKED EXAMPLE   **2.9** Factor Labels: Unit Conversions

A child is 21.5 in. long at birth. How long is this in centimeters?

ANALYSIS This problem calls for converting from inches to centimeters, so we will need to know how many cm are in an inch, and how to use this information as a conversion factor.

BALLPARK ESTIMATE It takes about 2.5 cm to make 1 in., and so it should take 2.5 times as many centimeters to make a distance equal to approximately 20 in., or about 20 in. × 2.5 = 50 cm.

SOLUTION

STEP 1: Identify given information.

STEP 2: Identify answer and units.

STEP 3: Identify conversion factor.

STEP 4: Solve Multiply the known length (in inches) by the conversion factor so that units cancel, providing the answer (in cm).

Length = 21.5 in.

Length = ?? cm

$1 \text{ in.} = 2.54 \text{ cm} \rightarrow \dfrac{2.54 \text{ cm}}{1 \text{ in.}}$

$21.5 \text{ in.} \times \dfrac{2.54 \text{ cm}}{1 \text{ in.}} = 54.6 \text{ cm}$ (Rounded off from 54.61)

BALLPARK CHECK How does this value compare with the ballpark estimate we made at the beginning? Are the final units correct?

WORKED EXAMPLE **2.10** Factor Labels: Concentration to Mass

A patient requires injection of 0.012 g of a pain killer available as a 15 mg/mL solution. How many milliliters should be administered?

ANALYSIS Knowing the amount of pain killer in 1 mL allows us to use the concentration as a conversion factor to determine the volume of solution that would contain the desired amount.

BALLPARK ESTIMATE One milliliter contains 15 mg of the pain killer, or 0.015 g. Since only 0.012 g is needed, a little less than 1.0 mL should be administered.

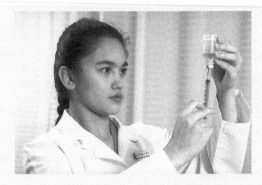

▲ How many milliliters should be injected?

SOLUTION

STEP 1: Identify known information.

STEP 2: Identify answer and units.

STEP 3: Identify conversion factors. Two conversion factors are needed. First, g must be converted to mg. Once we have the mass in mg, then we can calculate mL using the conversion factor of mL/mg.

STEP 4: Solve. Starting from the desired dosage, we use the conversion factors to cancel units, obtaining the final answer in mL.

Dosage = 0.012 g
Concentration = 15 mg/mL

Volume to administer = ?? mL

$1 \text{ mg} = .001 \text{ g} \Rightarrow \dfrac{1 \text{ mg}}{0.001 \text{ g}}$

$15 \text{ mg/mL} \Rightarrow \dfrac{1 \text{ mL}}{15 \text{ mg}}$

$(0.012 \text{ g})\left(\dfrac{1 \text{ mg}}{0.001 \text{ g}}\right)\left(\dfrac{1 \text{ mL}}{15 \text{ mg}}\right) = 0.80 \text{ mL}$

BALLPARK CHECK Consistent with our initial estimate of a little less than 1 mL.

WORKED EXAMPLE **2.11** Factor Labels: Multiple Conversion Calculations

Administration of digitalis to control atrial fibrillation in heart patients must be carefully regulated because even a modest overdose can be fatal. To take differences between patients into account, dosages are sometimes prescribed in micrograms per kilogram of body weight (μg/kg). Thus, two people may differ greatly in weight, but both will receive the proper dosage. At a dosage of 20 μg/kg body weight, how many milligrams of digitalis should a 160 lb patient receive?

ANALYSIS Knowing the patient's body weight (in kg) and the recommended dosage (in μg/kg), we can calculate the appropriate amount of digitalis.

BALLPARK ESTIMATE Since a kilogram is roughly equal to 2 lb, a 160 lb patient has a mass of about 80 kg. At a dosage of 20 μg/kg, an 80 kg patient should receive 80 × 20 μg, or about 1600 μg of digitalis, or 1.6 mg.

SOLUTION

STEP 1: **Identify known information.**

Patient weight = 160 lb
Prescribed dosage = 20 μg digitalis/kg body weight
Delivered dosage = ?? mg digitalis

STEP 2: **Identify answer and units.**

STEP 3: **Identify conversion factors.** Two conversions are needed. First, convert the patient's weight in pounds to weight in kg. The correct dose can then be determined based on μg digitalis/kg of body weight. Finally the dosage in μg is converted to mg.

$$1 \text{ kg} = 2.205 \text{ lb} \rightarrow \frac{1 \text{ kg}}{2.205 \text{ lb}}$$

$$1 \text{ mg} = (0.001 \text{ g})\left(\frac{1 \mu g}{10^{-6} \text{ g}}\right) = 1000 \mu g$$

STEP 4: **Solve.** Use the known information and the conversion factors so that units cancel, obtaining the answer in mg.

$$160 \text{ lb} \times \frac{1 \text{ kg}}{2.205 \text{ lb}} \times \frac{20 \mu g \text{ digitalis}}{1 \text{ kg}} \times \frac{1 \text{ mg}}{1000 \mu g}$$

$$= 1.5 \text{ mg digitalis (Rounded off)}$$

BALLPARK CHECK Close to our estimate of 1.6 mg.

PROBLEM 2.16

(a) How many kilograms does a 7.5 lb infant weigh?
(b) How many milliliters are in a 4.0 fl oz bottle of cough medicine?

PROBLEM 2.17

Calculate the dosage in milligrams per kilogram body weight for a 135 lb adult who takes two aspirin tablets containing 0.324 g of aspirin each. Calculate the dosage for a 40 lb child who also takes two aspirin tablets.

2.9 Measuring Temperature

Temperature, the measure of how hot or cold an object is, is commonly reported either in Fahrenheit (°F) or Celsius (°C) units. The SI unit for reporting temperature, however, is the *kelvin* (K). (Note that we say only "kelvin," not "kelvin degree.")

The kelvin and the Celsius degree are the same size—both are 1/100 of the interval between the freezing point of water and the boiling point of water at atmospheric pressure. Thus, a change in temperature of 1 °C is equal to a change of 1 K. The only difference between the Kelvin and Celsius temperature scales is that they have different zero points. The Celsius scale assigns a value of 0 °C to the freezing point of water, but the Kelvin scale assigns a value of 0 K to the coldest possible temperature, sometimes called *absolute zero*, which is equal to −273.15 °C. Thus, 0 K = −273.15 °C, and +273.15 K = 0 °C. For example, a warm spring day with a temperature of 25 °C has a Kelvin temperature of 25 + 273.15 = 298 K (for most purposes, rounding off to 273 is sufficient):

Temperature in K = Temperature in °C + 273.15
Temperature in °C = Temperature in K − 273.15

For practical applications in medicine and clinical chemistry, the Fahrenheit and Celsius scales are used almost exclusively. The Fahrenheit scale defines the freezing point of water as 32 °F and the boiling point of water as 212 °F, whereas 0 °C and 100 °C are the freezing and boiling points of water on the Celsius scale. Thus, it takes 180 Fahrenheit degrees to cover the same range encompassed by only 100 Celsius degrees, and a Celsius degree is therefore exactly 180/100 = 9/5 = 1.8

Temperature The measure of how hot or cold an object is.

▲ Gold metal is a liquid at temperatures above 1064.4 °C?

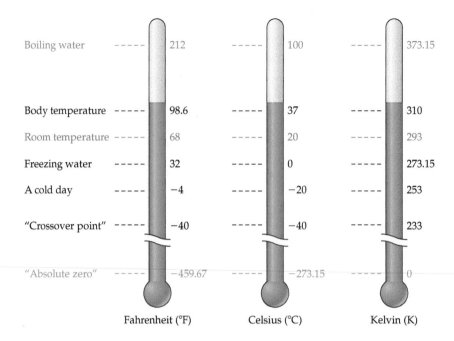

	Fahrenheit (°F)	Celsius (°C)	Kelvin (K)
Boiling water	212	100	373.15
Body temperature	98.6	37	310
Room temperature	68	20	293
Freezing water	32	0	273.15
A cold day	−4	−20	253
"Crossover point"	−40	−40	233
"Absolute zero"	−459.67	−273.15	0

▶ **FIGURE 2.4 A comparison of the Fahrenheit, Celsius, and Kelvin temperature scales.** One Fahrenheit degree is 5/9 the size of a kelvin or a Celsius degree.

times as large as a Fahrenheit degree. In other words, a change in temperature of 1.0 °C is equal to a change of 1.8 °F. Figure 2.4 gives a comparison of all three scales.

Converting between the Fahrenheit and Celsius scales is similar to converting between different units of length or volume, but is a bit more complex because two corrections need to be made—one to adjust for the difference in degree size and one to adjust for the different zero points. The size correction is made by using the relationship 1 °C = (9/5) °F and 1 °F = (5/9) °C. The zero-point correction is made by

APPLICATION ▶ Temperature–Sensitive Materials

Wouldn't it be nice to be able to tell if the baby's formula bottle is too hot? Or if the package of chicken you are buying for dinner has been stored appropriately? Temperature-sensitive materials are being used in these and other applications.

A class of materials called thermochromic materials change color as their temperature increases and they change from the liquid phase to a semicrystalline ordered state. These "liquid crystals" can be incorporated into plastics or paints, and can be used to monitor the temperature of the products or packages in which they are incorporated. For example, some meat packaging now includes a temperature strip that darkens when the meat is stored above a certain temperature, making the meat unsafe to eat. Hospitals and other medical facilities now routinely use temperature strips that, when placed under the tongue or applied to the forehead, change color to indicate the patient's body temperature. There are even clothes that change color based on the air temperature.

Can't decide what color bathing suit to wear to the beach? Pick one that will change color to fit your mood!

See Additional Problems 2.80 and 2.81 at the end of the chapter.

remembering that the freezing point is higher by 32 on the Fahrenheit scale than on the Celsius scale. Thus, if you want to convert from Celsius to Fahrenheit, you do a size adjustment (multiply °C by 9/5) and then a zero-point adjustment (add 32); if you want to convert from Fahrenheit to Celsius, you find out how many Fahrenheit degrees there are above freezing (by subtracting 32) and then do a size adjustment (multiply °C by 5/9). The following formulas show the conversion methods:

Celsius to Fahrenheit:

$$°F = \left(\frac{9\,°F}{5\,°C} \times °C \right) + 32\,°F$$

Fahrenheit to Celsius:

$$°C = \frac{5\,°C}{9\,°F} \times (°F - 32\,°F)$$

WORKED EXAMPLE **2.12** Temperature Conversions: Fahrenheit to Celsius

A body temperature above 107 °F can be fatal. What does 107 °F correspond to on the Celsius scale?

ANALYSIS Using the temperature (in °F) and the appropriate temperature conversion equation we can convert from the Fahrenheit scale to the Celsius scale.

BALLPARK ESTIMATE Note in Figure 2.4 that normal body temperature is 98.6 °F or 37 °C. A temperature of 107 °F is approximately 8 °F above normal; since 1 °C is nearly 2 °F, then 8 °F is about 4 °C. Thus, the 107 °F body temperature is 41 °C.

SOLUTION

STEP 1: **Identify known information.**	Temperature = 107 °F
STEP 2: **Identify answer and units.**	Temperature = ?? °C
STEP 3: **Identify conversion factors.** We can convert from °F to °C using this equation.	$°C = \dfrac{5\,°C}{9\,°F} \times (°F - 32\,°F)$
STEP 4: **Solve.** Substitute the known temperature (in °F) into the equation.	$°C = \dfrac{5\,°C}{9\,°F} \times (107\,°F - 32\,°F) = 42\,°C^*$

BALLPARK CHECK Close to our estimate of 41 °C.
(Rounded off from 41.666 667 °C)

*It is worth noting that the 5/9 conversion factor in the equation is an exact conversion, and so does not impact the number of significant figures in the final answer.

PROBLEM 2.18

The highest land temperature ever recorded was 136 °F in Al Aziziyah, Libya, on September 13, 1922. What is this temperature on the Celsius scale?

PROBLEM 2.19

The use of mercury thermometers is limited by the fact that mercury freezes at –38.9 °C. To what temperature does this correspond on the Fahrenheit scale? On the Kelvin scale?

2.10 Energy and Heat

All chemical reactions are accompanied by a change in **energy**, which is defined in scientific terms as *the capacity to do work or supply heat* (Figure 2.5). Detailed discussion of the various kinds of energy will be included in Chapter 7, but for now we will look at the various units used to describe energy, and the way heat energy can be gained or lost by matter.

Energy is measured in SI units by the unit *joule* (J; pronounced "jool"), but the metric unit *calorie* (cal) is still widely used in medicine. One calorie is the amount of heat necessary to raise the temperature of 1 g of water by 1 °C. A *kilocalorie* (kcal), often called a *large calorie (Cal)* or *food calorie* by nutritionists, equals 1000 cal:

$$1000 \text{ cal} = 1 \text{ kcal} \qquad 1000 \text{ J} = 1 \text{ kJ}$$
$$1 \text{ cal} = 4.184 \text{ J} \qquad 1 \text{ kcal} = 4.184 \text{ kJ}$$

Not all substances have their temperatures raised to the same extent when equal amounts of heat energy are added. One calorie raises the temperature of 1 g of water by 1 °C but raises the temperature of 1 g of iron by 10 °C. The amount of heat needed to raise the temperature of 1 g of a substance by 1 °C is called the **specific heat** of the substance. It is measured in units of cal/(g · °C).

$$\text{Specific heat} = \frac{\text{Calories}}{\text{Grams} \times °C}$$

Specific heats vary greatly from one substance to another, as shown in Table 2.6. The specific heat of water, 1.00 cal/(g · °C), is higher than that of most other substances, which means that a large transfer of heat is required to change the temperature of a given amount of water by a given number of degrees. One consequence is that the human body, which is about 60% water, is able to withstand changing outside conditions.

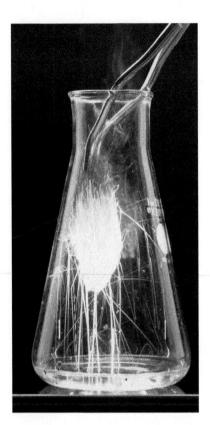

▲ **FIGURE 2.5 The reaction of aluminum with bromine releases energy in the form of heat.** When the reaction is complete, the products undergo no further change.

Energy The capacity to do work or supply heat.

Specific heat The amount of heat that will raise the temperature of 1 g of a substance by 1 °C.

TABLE 2.6 Specific Heats of Some Common Substances

SUBSTANCE	SPECIFIC HEAT [cal/(g · °C)]
Ethanol	0.59
Gold	0.031
Iron	0.106
Mercury	0.033
Sodium	0.293
Water	1.00

Knowing the mass and specific heat of a substance makes it possible to calculate how much heat must be added or removed to accomplish a given temperature change, as shown in Worked Example 2.13.

$$\text{Heat (cal)} = \text{Mass (g)} \times \text{Temperature change (°C)} \times \text{Specific heat}\left(\frac{\text{cal}}{\text{g} \cdot °C}\right)$$

WORKED EXAMPLE **2.13** Specific Heat: Mass, Temperature, and Energy

Taking a bath might use about 95 kg of water. How much energy (in calories) is needed to heat the water from a cold 15 °C to a warm 40 °C?

ANALYSIS From the amount of water being heated (95 kg) and the amount of the temperature change (40 °C − 15 °C = 25 °C), the total amount of energy needed can be calculated by using specific heat [1.00 cal/(g · °C)] as a conversion factor.

BALLPARK ESTIMATE The water is being heated 25 °C (from 15 °C to 40 °C), and it therefore takes 25 cal to heat each gram. The tub contains nearly 100,000 g (95 kg is 95,000 g), and so it takes about 25 × 100,000 cal, or 2,500,000 cal, to heat all the water in the tub.

SOLUTION

STEP 1: **Identify known information.**

STEP 2: **Identify answer and units.**

STEP 3: **Identify conversion factors.** The amount of energy (in cal) can be calculated using the specific heat of water (cal/g·°C), and will depend on both the mass of water (in g) to be heated and the total temperature change (in °C). In order for the units in specific heat to cancel correctly, the mass of water must first be converted from kg to g.

STEP 4: **Solve.** Starting with the known information, use the conversion factors to cancel unwanted units.

Mass of water = 95 kg

Temperature change = 40 °C − 15 °C = 25 °C

Heat = ?? cal

$$\text{Specific heat} = \frac{1.0\ \text{cal}}{\text{g} \cdot {}^\circ\text{C}}$$

$$1\ \text{kg} = 1000\ \text{g} \rightarrow \frac{1000\ \text{g}}{1\ \text{kg}}$$

$$95\ \cancel{\text{kg}} \times \frac{1000\ \cancel{\text{g}}}{\cancel{\text{kg}}} \times \frac{1.00\ \text{cal}}{\cancel{\text{g}} \cdot \cancel{{}^\circ\text{C}}} \times 25\ \cancel{{}^\circ\text{C}} = 2,400,000\ \text{cal}$$

$$= 2.4 \times 10^6\ \text{cal}$$

BALLPARK CHECK Close to our estimate of 2.5 × 10⁶ cal.

PROBLEM 2.20

Assuming that Coca-Cola has the same specific heat as water, how much energy in calories is removed when 350 g of Coke (about the contents of one 12 oz can) is cooled from room temperature (25 °C) to refrigerator temperature (3 °C)?

PROBLEM 2.21

What is the specific heat of aluminum if it takes 161 cal to raise the temperature of a 75 g aluminum bar by 10.0 °C?

Density The physical property that relates the mass of an object to its volume; mass per unit volume.

2.11 Density

One further physical quantity that we will take up in this chapter is **density**, which relates the mass of an object to its volume. Density is usually expressed in units of grams per cubic centimeter (g/cm³) for solids and grams per milliliter (g/mL) for liquids. Thus, if we know the density of a substance, we know both the mass of a given volume and the volume of a given mass. The densities of some common materials are listed in Table 2.7.

$$\text{Density} = \frac{\text{Mass (g)}}{\text{Volume (mL or cm}^3)}$$

Most substances change their volume by expanding or contracting when heated or cooled, and densities are therefore temperature-dependent. For example, at 3.98 °C a 1 mL container holds exactly 1.0000 g of water (density = 1.0000 g/mL). As the temperature rises, however, the volume occupied by the water expands so that only 0.9584 g fits in the 1 mL container at 100 °C (density = 0.9584 g/mL). When reporting a density, the temperature must also be specified.

Although most substances contract when cooled and expand when heated, water behaves differently. Water contracts when cooled from 100 °C to 3.98 °C, but

▲ Which has the greater mass, the pillow or the brass cylinder? In fact, they have similar masses, but the brass cylinder has a higher *density* because of its smaller volume.

TABLE 2.7   Densities of Some Common Materials at 25 °C

SUBSTANCE	DENSITY*	SUBSTANCE	DENSITY*
Gases		Solids	
Helium	0.000 194	Ice (0 °C)	0.917
Air	0.001 185	Gold	19.3
Liquids		Human fat	0.94
Water (3.98 °C)	1.0000	Cork	0.22–0.26
Urine	1.003–1.030	Table sugar	1.59
Blood plasma	1.027	Balsa wood	0.12
		Earth	5.54

*Densities are in g/cm^3 for solids and g/mL for liquids and gases.

▲ Ice floats because its density is less than that of water.

below this temperature it begins to *expand* again. The density of liquid water is at its maximum of 1.0000 g/mL at 3.98 °C but decreases to 0.999 87 g/mL at 0 °C. When freezing occurs, the density drops still further to a value of 0.917 g/cm^3 for ice at 0 °C. Since a less dense substance will float on top of a more dense fluid, ice and any other substance with a density less than that of water will float. Conversely, any substance with a density greater than that of water will sink.

Knowing the density of a liquid is useful because it is often easier to measure a liquid's volume rather than its mass. Suppose, for example, that you need 1.50 g of ethanol. Rather than use a dropper to weigh out exactly the right amount, it would be much easier to look up the density of ethanol (0.7893 g/mL at 20 °C) and measure the correct volume (1.90 mL) with a syringe or graduated cylinder. Thus, density acts as a conversion factor between mass (g) and volume (mL).

$$1.50 \text{ g ethanol} \times \frac{1 \text{ mL ethanol}}{0.7893 \text{ g ethanol}} = 1.90 \text{ mL ethanol}$$

WORKED EXAMPLE   **2.14** Density: Mass-to-Volume Conversion.

What volume of isopropyl alcohol (rubbing alcohol) would you use if you needed 25.0 g? The density of isopropyl alcohol is 0.7855 g/mL at 20 °C.

ANALYSIS   The known information is the mass of isopropyl alcohol needed (25.0 g). The density (0.7855 g/mL) acts as a conversion factor between mass and the unknown volume of isopropyl alcohol.

BALLPARK ESTIMATE   Because 1 mL of isopropyl alcohol contains only 0.7885 g of the alcohol, obtaining 1 g of alcohol would require almost 20% more than 1 mL, or about 1.2 mL. Therefore, a volume of about 25 × 1.2 mL = 30 mL is needed to obtain 25 g of alcohol.

SOLUTION

STEP 1: **Identify known information.**

Mass of rubbing alcohol = 25.0 g
Density of rubbing alcohol = 0.7855 g/mL

STEP 2: **Identify answer and units.**

Volume of rubbing alcohol = ?? mL

STEP 3: **Identify conversion factors.** Starting with the mass of isopropyl alcohol (in g), the corresponding volume (in mL) can be calculated using density (g/mL) as the conversion factor.

Density = g/mL → 1/density = mL/g

STEP 4: **Solve.** Starting with the known information, set up the equation with conversion factors so that unwanted units cancel.

$$25.0 \text{ g alcohol} \times \frac{1 \text{ mL alcohol}}{0.7855 \text{ g alcohol}} = 31.8 \text{ mL alcohol}$$

BALLPARK CHECK   Our estimate was 30 mL.

APPLICATION ▶ Obesity and Body Fat

According to the U.S. Center for Disease Control, the U.S. population is suffering from a fat epidemic. Over the last 25 years, the percentage of adults (20 years or older) identified as obese increased from 15% in the late 1970s to nearly 33% in 2004. Even children and adolescents are gaining too much weight: the number of overweight children in all age groups increased by nearly a factor of 3, with the biggest increase seen among teenagers (from 5% to 17.4%). How do we define obesity, however, and how is it measured?

Obesity is defined by reference to *body mass index* (BMI), which is equal to a person's mass in kilograms divided by the square of his or her height in meters. Alternatively, a person's weight in pounds divided by the square of her or his height in inches is multiplied by 703 to give the BMI. For instance, someone 5 ft 7 in. (67 inches; 1.70 m) tall weighing 147 lb (66.7 kg) has a BMI of 23:

$$BMI = \frac{weight\ (kg)}{[height\ (m)]^2}, \quad or \quad \frac{weight\ (lb)}{[height\ (in.)]^2} \times 703$$

A BMI of 25 or above is considered overweight, and a BMI of 30 or above is obese. By these standards, approximately 61% of the U.S. population is overweight.

Health professionals are concerned by the rapid rise in obesity in the United States because of the link between BMI and health problems. Many reports have documented the correlation between health and BMI, including a recent study on more than one million adults. The lowest death risk from any cause, including cancer and heart disease, is associated with a BMI between 22 and 24. Risk increases steadily as BMI increases, more than doubling for a BMI above 29.

Fat is not the enemy, however, because having some body fat is not just good, it is necessary! The layer of adipose tissue (body fat) lying just beneath our skin acts as a shock absorber and as a thermal insulator to maintain body temperature. It also serves as a long-term energy storehouse (see Section 25.6). A typical adult body contains about 50% muscles and other cellular material, 24% blood and other fluids, 7% bone, and 19% body fat. Overweight sedentary individuals

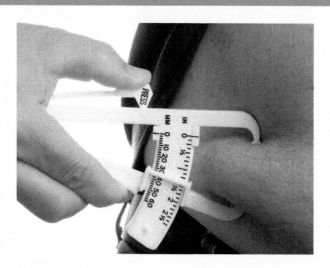

▲ A person's percentage body fat can be estimated by measuring the thickness of the fat layer under the skin.

have a higher fat percentage, whereas some world-class athletes have as little as 3% body fat. The problem occurs when the percentage of body fat is excessive.

An individual's percentage of body fat is most easily measured by the skinfold thickness method. The skin at several locations on the arm, shoulder, and waist is pinched, and the thickness of the fat layer beneath the skin is measured with calipers. Comparing the measured results to those in a standard table gives an estimation of percentage body fat.

As an alternative to skinfold measurement, a more accurate assessment of body fat can be made by underwater immersion. The person's underwater body weight is less than her weight on land because water gives the body buoyancy. The higher the percentage of body fat, the more buoyant the person and the greater the difference between land weight and underwater body weight. Checking the observed buoyancy on a standard table then gives an estimation of body fat.

See Additional Problems 2.82 and 2.83 at the end of the chapter.

Weight (lb)

Height	110	115	120	125	130	135	140	145	150	155	160	165	170	175	180	185	190	195	200
5′0″	21	22	23	24	25	26	27	28	29	30	31	32	33	34	35	36	37	38	39
5′2″	20	21	22	23	24	25	26	27	27	28	29	30	31	32	33	34	35	36	37
5′4″	19	20	21	21	22	23	24	25	26	27	27	28	29	30	31	32	33	33	34
5′6″	18	19	19	20	21	22	23	23	24	25	26	27	27	28	29	30	31	31	32
5′8″	17	17	18	19	20	21	21	22	23	24	24	25	26	27	27	28	29	30	30
5′10″	16	17	17	18	19	19	20	21	22	22	23	24	24	25	26	27	27	28	29
6′0″	15	16	16	17	18	18	19	20	20	21	22	22	23	24	24	25	26	26	27
6′2″	14	15	15	16	17	17	18	19	19	20	21	21	22	22	23	24	24	25	26
6′4″	13	14	15	15	16	16	17	18	18	19	19	20	21	21	22	23	23	24	24

Body Mass Index (numbers in boxes)

2.12 Specific Gravity

Specific gravity The density of a substance divided by the density of water at the same temperature.

For many purposes, ranging from winemaking to medicine, it is more convenient to use *specific gravity* than density. The **specific gravity** (sp gr) of a substance (usually a liquid) is simply the density of the substance divided by the density of water at the same temperature. Because all units cancel, specific gravity is unitless:

$$\text{Specific gravity} = \frac{\text{Density of substance (g/mL)}}{\text{Density of water at the same temperature (g/mL)}}$$

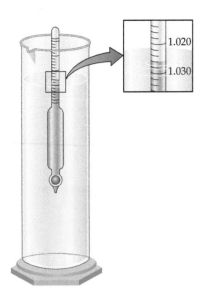

At normal temperatures, the density of water is very close to 1 g/mL. Thus, the specific gravity of a substance is numerically equal to its density and is used in the same way.

The specific gravity of a liquid can be measured using an instrument called a *hydrometer*, which consists of a weighted bulb on the end of a calibrated glass tube, as shown in Figure 2.6. The depth to which the hydrometer sinks when placed in a fluid indicates the fluid's specific gravity: The lower the bulb sinks, the lower the specific gravity of the fluid.

Water that contains dissolved substances can have a specific gravity either higher or lower than 1.00. In winemaking, for instance, the amount of fermentation taking place is gauged by observing the change in specific gravity on going from grape juice, which contains 20% dissolved sugar and has a specific gravity of 1.082, to dry wine, which contains 12% alcohol and has a specific gravity of 0.984. (Pure alcohol has a specific gravity of 0.789.)

▲ **FIGURE 2.6 A hydrometer for measuring specific gravity.** The instrument has a weighted bulb at the end of a calibrated glass tube. The depth to which the hydrometer sinks in a liquid indicates the liquid's specific gravity.

In medicine, a hydrometer called a *urinometer* is used to indicate the amount of solids dissolved in urine. Although the specific gravity of normal urine is about 1.003–1.030, conditions such as diabetes mellitus or a high fever cause an abnormally high urine specific gravity, indicating either excessive elimination of solids or decreased elimination of water. Abnormally low specific gravity is found in individuals using diuretics—drugs that increase water elimination.

▲ The amount of fermentation that has taken place in the wine can be measured with a hydrometer.

SUMMARY: REVISITING THE CHAPTER GOALS

1. **How are measurements made, and what units are used?** A property that can be measured is called a *physical quantity* and is described by both a number and a label, or *unit*. The preferred units are either those of the International System of Units (*SI units*) or the *metric system*. Mass, the amount of matter an object contains, is measured in *kilograms* (kg) or *grams* (g). Length is measured in *meters* (m). Volume is measured in *cubic meters* (m^3) in the SI system and in *liters* (L) or *milliliters* (mL) in the metric system. Temperature is measured in *kelvins* (K) in the SI system and in *degrees Celsius* (°C) in the metric system.

2. **How good are the reported measurements?** When measuring physical quantities or using them in calculations, it is important to indicate the exactness of the measurement by *rounding off* the final answer using the correct number of *significant figures*. All but one of the significant figures in a number is known with certainty; the final digit is estimated to ±1.

3. **How are large and small numbers best represented?** Measurements of small and large quantities are usually written in *scientific notation* as the product of a number between 1 and 10, times a power of 10. Numbers greater than 10 have a positive exponent, and numbers less than 1 have a negative exponent. For example, $3562 = 3.562 \times 10^3$, and $0.003\ 91 = 3.91 \times 10^{-3}$.

4. **How can a quantity be converted from one unit of measure to another?** A measurement in one unit can be converted to another unit by multiplying by a *conversion factor* that expresses the exact relationship between the units.

5. **What techniques are used to solve problems?** Problems are best solved by applying the *factor-label method*, in which units can be multiplied and divided just as numbers can. The idea is to set up an equation so that all unwanted units cancel, leaving only the desired units. Usually it is best to start by identifying the known and needed information, then

KEY WORDS

Conversion factor, *p. 31*

Density, *p. 39*

Energy, *p. 38*

Factor-label method, *p. 31*

Mass, *p. 21*

Physical quantity, *p. 19*

Rounding off, *p. 29*

Scientific notation, *p. 26*

SI units, *p. 19*

Significant figures, *p. 24*

Specific gravity, *p. 42*

Specific heat, *p. 38*

Temperature, *p. 35*

Unit, *p. 19*

Weight, *p. 21*

decide how to convert the known information to the answer, and finally check to make sure the answer is reasonable both chemically and physically.

6. What are temperature, specific heat, density, and specific gravity? *Temperature* is a measure of how hot or cold an object is. The *specific heat* of a substance is the amount of heat necessary to raise the temperature of 1 g of the substance by 1 °C. Water has an unusually high specific heat, which helps our bodies to maintain an even temperature. *Density*, the physical property that relates mass to volume, is expressed in units of grams per milliliter (g/mL) for a liquid or grams per cubic centimeter (g/cm^3) for a solid. The *specific gravity* of a liquid is the density of the liquid divided by the density of water at the same temperature. Because the density of water is approximately 1 g/mL, specific gravity and density have the same numerical value.

UNDERSTANDING KEY CONCEPTS

2.26 How many milliliters of water does the graduated cylinder in (a) contain, and how tall in centimeters is the paper clip in (b)? How many significant figures do you have in each answer?

(a)   (b)

2.27 Using a metric ruler, measure the following objects:

(a) Length of your calculator
(b) Width of a page in this text book
(c) Height and diameter of a 12 ounce can

2.28 (a) What is the specific gravity of the following solution?
(b) How many significant figures does your answer have?
(c) Is the solution more dense or less dense than water?

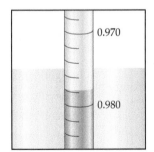

2.29 Assume that you have two graduated cylinders, one with a capacity of 5 mL (a) and the other with a capacity of 50 mL (b). Draw a line in each showing how much liquid you would add if you needed to measure 2.64 mL of water. Which cylinder do you think is more precise? Explain.

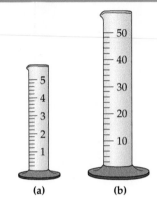

(a)   (b)

2.30 State the length of the pencil depicted in the accompanying figure in both inches and cm.

2.31 Assume that you are delivering a solution sample from a pipette. Figures (a) and (b) show the volume level before and after dispensing the sample, respectively. State the liquid level (in mL) before and after dispensing the sample, and calculate the volume of the sample.

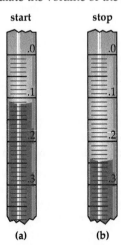

(a)   (b)

2.32 **(a)** Pour the contents of a 12 ounce can into a measuring cup. Record the volume in both fluid ounces and in cups. Which measurement is more precise?

(b) Pour the contents of a 12 ounce can into a 400 mL beaker. What is the volume in mL?

2.33 Assume that identical hydrometers are placed in ethanol (sp gr 0.7893) and in chloroform (sp gr 1.4832). In which liquid will the hydrometer float higher? Explain.

ADDITIONAL PROBLEMS

DEFINITIONS AND UNITS

2.34 What is the difference between a physical quantity and a number?

2.35 What is the difference between mass and weight?

2.36 What are the units used in the SI system to measure mass, volume, length, and temperature?

2.37 What are the units used in the metric system to measure mass, volume, length, and temperature?

2.38 What is the difference between a cubic decimeter (SI) and a liter (metric)?

2.39 What is the difference between a kelvin (SI) and a Celsius degree (metric)?

2.40 Give the full name of the following units:

(a) cL   **(b)** dm   **(c)** mm
(d) nL   **(e)** mg   **(f)** m^3
(g) cc

2.41 Write the symbol for the following units:

(a) nanogram   **(b)** centimeter   **(c)** microliter
(d) micrometer   **(e)** milligram

2.42 How many picograms are in 1 mg? In 35 ng?

2.43 How many microliters are in 1 L? In 20 mL?

SCIENTIFIC NOTATION AND SIGNIFICANT FIGURES

2.44 Express the following numbers in scientific notation:

(a) 9457   **(b)** 0.000 07
(c) 20,000,000,000 (four significant figures)
(d) 0.012 345   **(e)** 652.38

2.45 Convert the following numbers from scientific notation to standard notation:

(a) 5.28×10^3 **(b)** 8.205×10^{-2}
(c) 1.84×10^{-5} **(d)** 6.37×10^4

2.46 How many significant figures does each of the following numbers have?

(a) 237,401   **(b)** 0.300   **(c)** 3.01
(d) 244.4   **(e)** 50,000   **(f)** 660

2.47 How many significant figures are there in each of the following quantities?

(a) Distance from New York City to Wellington, New Zealand, 14,397 km
(b) Average body temperature of a crocodile, 25.6 °C
(c) Melting point of gold, 1064 °C
(d) Diameter of an influenza virus, 0.000 01 mm
(e) Radius of a phosphorus atom, 0.110 nm

2.48 The diameter of the earth at the equator is 7926.381 mi.

(a) Round off the earth's diameter to four significant figures, to two significant figures, and to six significant figures.
(b) Express the earth's diameter in scientific notation.

2.49 Round off each of the numbers in Problem 2.46 to two significant figures, and express them in scientific notation.

2.50 Carry out the following calculations, express each answer to the correct number of significant figures, and include units in the answers.

(a) 9.02 g + 3.1 g
(b) 88.80 cm + 7.391 cm
(c) 362 mL − 99.5 mL
(d) 12.4 mg + 6.378 mg + 2.089 mg

2.51 Carry out the following calculations, express the answers to the correct numbers of significant figures, and include units in the answers.

(a) $5{,}280\ \dfrac{\text{ft}}{\text{mi}} \times 6.2\ \text{mi}$

(b) 4.5 m × 3.25 m

(c) $2.50\ \text{g} \div 8.3\ \dfrac{\text{g}}{\text{cm}^3}$

(d) 4.70 cm × 6.8 cm × 2.54 cm

UNIT CONVERSIONS AND PROBLEM SOLVING

2.52 Carry out the following conversions:

(a) 3.614 mg to centigrams
(b) 12.0 kL to megaliters
(c) 14.4 μm to millimeters
(d) 6.03×10^{-6} cg to nanograms
(e) 174.5 mL to deciliters
(f) 1.5×10^{-2} km to centimeters

2.53 Carry out the following conversions. Consult Tables 2.3–2.5 as needed.

(a) 56.4 mi to kilometers and to megameters
(b) 2.0 L to to quarts and to fluid ounces
(c) 7 ft 2.0 in. to centimeters and to meters
(d) 1.35 lb to kilograms and to decigrams

2.54 Express the following quantities in more convenient units by using SI unit prefixes:

(a) 9.78×10^4 g   **(b)** 1.33×10^{-4} L
(c) 0.000 000 000 46 g   **(d)** 2.99×10^8 cm

2.55 Which SI unit prefix corresponds to each of the following multipliers?

(a) 10^3 **(b)** 10^{-3}
(c) 10^6 **(d)** 10^{-6}

2.56 The speed limit in Canada is 100 km/h.

(a) How many miles per hour is this?
(b) How many feet per second?

2.57 The muzzle velocity of a projectile fired from a 9 mm handgun is 1200 ft/s.

(a) How many miles per hour is this?
(b) How many meters per second?

2.58 The diameter of a red blood cell is 6×10^{-6} m. How many red blood cells are needed to make a line 1 in. long?

2.59 The Sears Tower in Chicago has an approximate floor area of 418,000 m^2. How many square feet of floor is this?

2.60 A normal value for blood cholesterol is 200 mg/dL of blood. If a normal adult has a total blood volume of 5 L, how much total cholesterol is present?

2.61 One bottle of aspirin holds 50 tablets, each containing 250 mg of aspirin, and sells for $1.95. Another bottle holds 100 tablets, each containing 200 mg of aspirin, and sells for $3.75. For each bottle, calculate the value in milligrams of aspirin per dollar. Which bottle is the better bargain?

2.62 The white blood cell concentration in normal blood is approximately 12,000 cells/mm^3 of blood. How many white blood cells does a normal adult with 5 L of blood have? Express the answer in scientific notation.

2.63 The recommended daily dose of calcium for an 18-year-old male is 1200 mg. If 1.0 cup of whole milk contains 290 mg of calcium and milk is his only calcium source, how much milk should an 18-year-old male drink each day?

ENERGY, HEAT, AND TEMPERATURE

2.64 What is the normal temperature of the human body (98.6 °F) in degrees Celsius? In kelvins?

2.65 The boiling point of liquid nitrogen, used in the removal of warts and in other surgical applications, is −195.8 °C. What is this temperature in kelvins and in degrees Fahrenheit?

2.66 Diethyl ether, a substance once used as a general anesthetic, has a specific heat of 0.895 cal/(g · °C). How many calories and how many kilocalories of heat are needed to raise the temperature of 30.0 g of diethyl ether from 10.0 °C to 30.0 °C?

2.67 Copper has a specific heat of 0.092 cal/(g · °C). When 52.7 cal of heat is added to a piece of copper, the temperature increases from 22.4 °C to 38.6 °C. What is the mass of the piece of copper?

2.68 Calculate the specific heat of copper if it takes 23 cal to heat a 5.0 g sample from 25 °C to 75 °C.

2.69 The specific heat of fat is 0.45 cal/(g · °C), and the density of fat is 0.94 g/cm^3. How much energy (in calories) is needed to heat 10 cm^3 of fat from room temperature (25 °C) to its melting point (35 °C)?

2.70 A 150 g sample of mercury and a 150 g sample of iron are at an initial temperature of 25.0 °C. If 250 cal of heat is applied to each sample, what is the final temperature of each? (See Table 2.6.)

2.71 When 100 cal of heat is applied to a 125 g sample, the temperature increases by 28 °C. Calculate the specific heat of the sample and compare your answer to the values in Table 2.6. What is the identity of the sample?

DENSITY AND SPECIFIC GRAVITY

2.72 Aspirin has a density of 1.40 g/cm^3. What is the volume in cubic centimeters of a tablet weighing 250 mg?

2.73 Gaseous hydrogen has a density of 0.0899 g/L at 0 °C. How many liters would you need if you wanted 1.0078 g of hydrogen?

2.74 What is the density of lead (in g/cm^3) if a rectangular bar measuring 0.500 cm in height, 1.55 cm in width, and 25.00 cm in length has a mass of 220.9 g?

2.75 What is the density of lithium metal (in g/cm^3) if a cube measuring 0.82 cm × 1.45 cm × 1.25 cm has a mass of 0.794 g?

2.76 What is the density of isopropyl alcohol (rubbing alcohol) in grams per milliliter if a 5.000 mL sample has a mass of 3.928 g at room temperature? What is the specific gravity of isopropyl alcohol?

2.77 Ethylene glycol, commonly used as automobile antifreeze, has a specific gravity of 1.1088 at room temperature. What is the volume of 1.00 kg of ethylene glycol? What is the volume of 2.00 lb of ethylene glycol?

Applications

2.78 The typical rhinovirus has a diameter of 20 nm, or 2.0×10^{-8} m

(a) What is the length in centimeters?

(b) How many rhinoviruses would need to be laid end to end to make a chain 1 in. long? [*Powers of 10, p. 28*]

2.79 Blood cells have a mean cell volume of 90 fL, or 9.0×10^{-14} L

(a) Convert this volume to cubic centimeters.

(b) The formula for the volume of a sphere is $V = 4\pi r^2/3$. Assuming a spherical shape, calculate the mean diameter of a blood cell in centimeters. [*Powers of 10, p. 28*]

2.80 A thermochromic plastic chip included in a shipping container for beef undergoes an irreversible color change if the storage temperature exceeds 28 °F. What is this temperature on the Celsius and Kelvin scales? [*Temperature-Sensitive Materials, p. 36*]

2.81 A temperature-sensitive bath toy undergoes several color changes in the temperature range from 37 °C to 47 °C. What is the corresponding temperature range on the Fahrenheit scale? [*Temperature-Sensitive Materials, p. 36*]

2.82 Calculate the BMI for an individual who is:

(a) 5 ft 1 in. tall and weighs 155 lb

(b) 5 ft 11 in. tall and weigh 170 lb

(c) 6 ft 3 in. tall and weigh 195 lb

Which of these individuals is likely to have increased health risks? [*Obesity and Body Fat, p. 41*]

2.83 Liposuction is a technique for removing fat deposits from various areas of the body. How many liters of fat would have to be removed to result in a 5.0 lb weight loss? The density of human fat is 0.94 g/mL. [*Measuring Body Fat, p.41*]

General Questions and Problems

2.84 Refer to the pencil in Problem 2.30. Using the equivalent values in Table 2.4 as conversion factors, convert the length measured in inches to centimeters. Compare the calculated length in centimeters to the length in centimeters measured using the metric ruler. How do the two values compare? Explain any differences.

2.85 Gemstones are weighed in carats, where 1 carat = 200 mg exactly. What is the mass in grams of the Hope diamond, the world's largest blue diamond, at 44.4 carats?

2.86 If you were cooking in an oven calibrated in Celsius degrees, what temperature would you use if the recipe called for 350 °F?

2.87 What dosage in grams per kilogram of body weight does a 130 lb woman receive if she takes two 250 mg tablets of penicillin? How many 125 mg tablets should a 40 lb child take to receive the same dosage?

2.88 A clinical report gave the following data from a blood analysis: iron, 39 mg/dL; calcium, 8.3 mg/dL; cholesterol, 224 mg/dL. Express each of these quantities in grams per deciliter, writing the answers in scientific notation.

2.89 The density of air at room temperature is 1.3 g/L. What is the mass of the air **(a)** in grams and **(b)** in pounds in a room that is 4.0 m long, 3.0 m wide, and 2.5 m high?

2.90 Approximately 75 mL of blood is pumped by a normal human heart at each beat. Assuming an average pulse of 72 beats per minute, how many milliliters of blood are pumped in one day?

2.91 A doctor has ordered that a patient be given 15 g of glucose, which is available in a concentration of 50.00 g glucose/1000.0 mL of solution. What volume of solution should be given to the patient?

2.92 Reconsider the volume of the sample dispensed by pipette in Problem 2.31. Assuming that the solution in the pipette has a density of 0.963 g/mL, calculate the mass of solution dispensed in the problem to the correct number of significant figures.

2.93 Today thermometers containing mercury are used less frequently than in the past because of concerns regarding the toxicity of mercury and because of its relatively high melting point (−39 °C), which means that mercury thermometers cannot be used in very cold environments because the mercury is a solid under such conditions. Alcohol thermometers, however, can be used over a temperature range from −115 °C (the melting point of alcohol) to 78.5 °C (the boiling point of alcohol).

(a) What is the effective temperature range of the alcohol thermometer in °F?

(b) The densities of alcohol and mercury are 0.79 g/mL and 13.6 g/mL, respectively. If the volume of liquid in a typical laboratory thermometer is 1.0 mL, what mass of alcohol is contained in the thermometer? What mass of mercury?

2.94 In a typical person, the level of glucose (also known as blood sugar) is about 85 mg/100 mL of blood. If an average body contains about 11 pints of blood, how many grams and how many pounds of glucose are present in the blood?

2.95 A patient is receiving 3000 mL/day of a solution that contains 5 g of dextrose (glucose) per 100 mL of solution. If glucose provides 4 kcal/g of energy, how many kilocalories per day is the patient receiving from the glucose?

2.96 A rough guide to fluid requirements based on body weight is 100 mL/kg for the first 10 kg of body weight, 50 mL/kg for the next 10 kg, and 20 mL/kg for weight over 20 kg. What volume of fluid per day is needed by a 55 kg woman? Give the answer with two significant figures.

2.97 Chloral hydrate, a sedative and sleep-inducing drug, is available as a solution labeled 10.0 gr/fluidram. What volume in milliliters should be administered to a patient who is meant to receive 7.5 gr per dose? (1 gr = 64.8 mg; 1 fluidram = 3.72 mL)

2.98 When 1.0 tablespoon of butter is burned or used by our body, it releases 100 kcal (100 food calories) of energy. If we could use all the energy provided, how many tablespoons of butter would have to be burned to raise the temperature of 3.00 L of water from 18.0 °C to 90.0 °C?

2.99 An archeologist finds a 1.62 kg goblet that she believes to be made of pure gold. When 1350 cal of heat is added to the goblet, its temperature increases by 7.8 °C. Calculate the specific heat of the goblet. Is it made of gold? Explain.

2.100 In another test, the archeologist in Problem 2.99 determines that the volume of the goblet is 205 mL. Calculate the density of the goblet and compare it with the density of gold (19.3 g/mL), lead (11.4 g/mL), and iron (7.86 g/mL). What is the goblet probably made of?

2.101 The density of sulfuric acid, H_2SO_4, is 1.83 g/mL. What volume of sulfuric acid is needed to obtain 98.0 g of H_2SO_4?

2.102 Sulfuric acid (Problem 2.101) is produced in larger amounts than any other chemical: 2.01×10^{11} lb worldwide in 2004. What is the volume of this amount in liters?

2.103 The caliber of a gun is expressed by measuring the diameter of the gun barrel in hundredths of an inch. A "22" rifle, for example, has a barrel diameter of 0.22 in. What is the barrel diameter of a .22 rifle in millimeters?

2.104 Amounts of substances dissolved in solution are often expressed as mass per unit volume. For example, normal human blood has a cholesterol concentration of about 200 mg of cholesterol/100 mL of blood. Express this concentration in the following units:

(a) milligrams per liter **(b)** micrograms per liter
(c) grams per liter **(d)** nanograms per microliter

2.105 The element gallium (Ga) has the second largest liquid range of any element, melting at 29.8 °C and boiling at 2204 °C at atmospheric pressure.

(a) Is gallium a metal, a nonmetal, or a metalloid?
(b) What is the density of gallium in grams per cubic centimeter at 25 °C if a 1.00 in. cube has a mass of 0.2133 lb?

2.106 A sample of water at 293.2 K was heated for 8 min and 25 s, and the heating was carried out so that the temperature increased at a constant rate of 3.0 °F/min. What is the final temperature of the water in degrees Celsius?

2.107 At a certain point, the Celsius and Fahrenheit scales "cross," and at this point the numerical value of the Celsius temperature is the same as the numerical value of the Fahrenheit temperature. At what temperature does this crossover occur?

2.108 Imagine that you place a piece of cork measuring 1.30 cm × 5.50 cm × 3.00 cm in a pan of water and that on top of the cork you place a small cube of lead measuring 1.15 cm on each edge. The density of cork is 0.235 g/cm³, and the density of lead is 11.35 g/cm³. Will the combination of cork plus lead float or sink?

CHAPTER 3

Atoms and the Periodic Table

▲ The mineral formations of the Giant's Causeway in Northern Ireland are an example of periodicity—the presence of regularly repeating patterns—found throughout nature.

CONTENTS

CHAPTER GOALS

We will take up the following questions about atoms and atomic theory:

1. What is the modern theory of atomic structure?

THE GOAL: Be able to explain the major assumptions of atomic theory.

2. How do atoms of different elements differ?

THE GOAL: Be able to explain the composition of different atoms according to the number of protons, neutrons, and electrons they contain.

3. What are isotopes, and what is atomic weight?

THE GOAL: Be able to explain what isotopes are and how they affect an element's atomic weight.

4. How is the periodic table arranged?

THE GOAL: Be able to describe how elements are arranged in the periodic table, name the subdivisions of the periodic table, and relate the position of an element in the periodic table to its electronic structure.

5. How are electrons arranged in atoms?

THE GOAL: Be able to explain how electrons are distributed in shells and subshells around the nucleus of an atom, how valence electrons can be represented as electron-dot symbols, and how the electron configurations can help explain the chemical properties of the elements.

C hemistry must be studied on two levels. In the past two chapters we have dealt with chemistry on the large-scale, or *macroscopic*, level, looking at the properties and transformations of matter that we can see and measure. Now we are ready to look at the sub-microscopic, or atomic level, studying the behavior and properties of individual atoms. Although scientists have long been convinced of their existence, only within the past twenty years have powerful new instruments made it possible to see individual atoms themselves. In this chapter we will look at modern atomic theory and at how the structure of atoms influences macroscopic properties.

3.1 Atomic Theory

Take a piece of aluminum foil and cut it in two. Then take one of the pieces and cut *it* in two, and so on. Assuming that you have extremely small scissors and extraordinary dexterity, how long can you keep dividing the foil? Is there a limit, or is matter infinitely divisible into ever smaller and smaller pieces? Historically, this argument can be traced as far back as the ancient Greek philosophers. Aristotle believed that matter could be divided infinitely, while Democritus argued (correctly) that there is a limit. The smallest and simplest bit that aluminum (or any other element) can be divided into and still be identifiable as aluminum is called an **atom**, a word derived from the Greek *atomos*, meaning "indivisible."

Chemistry is founded on four fundamental assumptions about atoms and matter, which together make up modern **atomic theory**:

- All matter is composed of atoms.
- The atoms of a given element differ from the atoms of all other elements.
- Chemical compounds consist of atoms combined in specific ratios. That is, only whole atoms can combine—one A atom with one B atom, or one A atom with two B atoms, and so on. The enormous diversity in the substances we see around us is based on the vast number of ways that atoms can combine with one another.
- Chemical reactions change only the way that atoms are combined in compounds. The atoms themselves are unchanged.

Atoms are extremely small, ranging from about 7.4×10^{-11} m in diameter for a hydrogen atom to 5.24×10^{-10} m for a cesium atom. In mass, atoms vary from 1.67×10^{-24} g for hydrogen to 3.95×10^{-22} g for uranium, one of the heaviest naturally occurring atoms. It is difficult to appreciate just how small atoms are, although it might help if you realize that a fine pencil line is about 3 *million* atoms across, and that even the smallest speck of dust contains about 10^{16} atoms.

Atom The smallest and simplest particle of an element.

Atomic theory A set of assumptions proposed by the English scientist John Dalton to explain the chemical behavior of matter.

▲ How small can a piece of aluminum foil be cut?

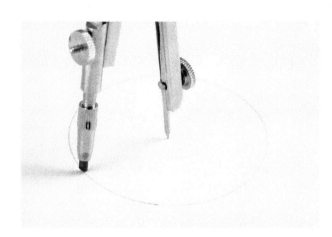

▶ Atoms are so small that the radius of this circle is about three million atoms wide.

Subatomic particles Three kinds of fundamental particles from which atoms are made: protons, neutrons, and electrons.

Proton A positively charged subatomic particle.

Neutron An electrically neutral subatomic particle.

Electron A negatively charged subatomic particle.

Atomic mass unit (amu) A convenient unit for describing the mass of an atom; 1 amu = $\frac{1}{12}$ the mass of a carbon-12 atom.

Nucleus The dense, central core of an atom that contains protons and neutrons.

Atoms are composed of tiny **subatomic particles** called *protons, neutrons,* and *electrons*. A **proton** has a mass of $1.672\ 622 \times 10^{-24}$ g and carries a positive (+) electrical charge; a **neutron** has a mass similar to that of a proton ($1.674\ 927 \times 10^{-24}$ g) but is electrically neutral; and an **electron** has a mass that is only 1/1836 that of a proton ($9.109\ 328 \times 10^{-28}$ g) and carries a negative (−) electrical charge. In fact, electrons are so much lighter than protons and neutrons that their mass is usually ignored. Table 3.1 compares the properties of the three fundamental subatomic particles.

TABLE 3.1   A Comparison of Subatomic Particles

NAME	SYMBOL	MASS		CHARGE (CHARGE UNITS)
		(GRAMS)	(AMU)	
Proton	p	$1.672\ 622 \times 10^{-24}$	1.007 276	+1
Neutron	n	$1.674\ 927 \times 10^{-24}$	1.008 665	0
Electron	e^-	$9.109\ 328 \times 10^{-28}$	$5.485\ 799 \times 10^{-4}$	−1

The masses of atoms and their constituent subatomic particles are so small when measured in grams that it is more convenient to express them on a *relative* mass scale. That is, one atom is assigned a mass, and all others are measured relative to it. The process is like deciding that a golf ball (46.0 g) will be assigned a mass of 1. A baseball (149 g), which is 149/46.0 = 3.24 times heavier than a golf ball, would then have a mass of about 3.24, a volleyball (270 g) would have a mass of 270/46.0 = 5.87, and so on.

The basis for the relative atomic mass scale is an atom of carbon that contains 6 protons and 6 neutrons. Such an atom is assigned a mass of exactly 12 **atomic mass units (amu;** also called a *dalton* in honor of the English scientist John Dalton, who proposed most of atomic theory as we know it), where 1 amu = $1.660\ 539 \times 10^{-24}$ g. Thus, for all practical purposes, both a proton and a neutron have a mass of 1 amu (Table 3.1). Hydrogen atoms are only about one-twelfth as heavy as carbon atoms and have a mass close to 1 amu, magnesium atoms are about twice as heavy as carbon atoms and have a mass close to 24 amu, and so forth.

Subatomic particles are not distributed at random throughout an atom. Rather, the protons and neutrons are packed closely together in a dense core called the **nucleus.** Surrounding the nucleus, the electrons move about rapidly through a large, mostly empty volume of space (Figure 3.1). Measurements show that the diameter of a nucleus is only about 10^{-15} m, whereas that of the atom itself is about 10^{-10} m. For comparison, if an atom were the size of a large domed stadium, the nucleus would be approximately the size of a small pea in the center of the playing field.

▲ The relative size of a nucleus in an atom is the same as that of a pea in the middle of this stadium.

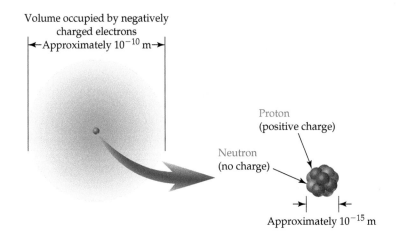

◀ **FIGURE 3.1 The structure of an atom.** Protons and neutrons are packed together in the nucleus, whereas electrons move about in the large surrounding volume. Virtually all the mass of an atom is concentrated in the nucleus.

The structure of the atom is determined by an interplay of different attractive and repulsive forces. Because unlike charges attract one another, the negatively charged electrons are held near the positively charged nucleus. But because like charges repel one another, the negatively charged electrons try to get as far away from one another as possible, accounting for the relatively large volume they occupy. The positively charged protons in the nucleus also repel one another, but are nevertheless held together by a unique attraction called the *nuclear strong force*, which is beyond the scope of this text.

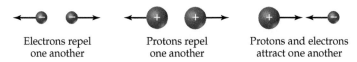

Electrons repel one another   Protons repel one another   Protons and electrons attract one another

WORKED EXAMPLE   **3.1** Atomic Mass Units: Gram-to-Atom Conversions

How many atoms are in a small piece of aluminum foil with a mass of 0.100 g? The mass of an atom of aluminum is 27.0 amu.

ANALYSIS We know the sample mass in grams and the mass of one atom in atomic mass units. To find the number of atoms in the sample, two conversions are needed, the first between grams and atomic mass units and the second between atomic mass units and the number of atoms. The conversion factor between atomic mass units and grams is $1 \text{ amu} = 1.660\,539 \times 10^{-24}$ g.

BALLPARK ESTIMATE An atom of aluminum has a mass of 27.0 amu; since $1 \text{ amu} \sim 10^{-24}$ g, the mass of a single aluminum atom is very small ($\approx 10^{-23}$ g). A very *large* number of atoms, therefore (10^{22} ?), is needed to obtain a mass of 0.100 g.

SOLUTION

STEP 1: Identify known information.

Mass of aluminum foil = 0.100 g

1 Al atom = 27.0 amu

STEP 2: Identify unknown answer and units.

Number of Al atoms = ?

STEP 3: Identify needed conversion factors.
Knowing the mass of foil (in g) and the mass of individual atoms (in amu) we need to convert from amu/atom to g/atom.

$1 \text{ amu} = 1.660\,539 \times 10^{-24}$ g

$$\rightarrow \frac{1 \text{ amu}}{1.660539 \times 10^{-24} \text{ g}}$$

STEP 4: Solve. Set up an equation using known information and conversion factors so that unwanted units cancel.

$$(0.100 \text{ g})\left(\frac{1 \text{ amu}}{1.660\,539 \times 10^{-24} \text{ g}}\right)\left(\frac{1 \text{ Al atom}}{27.0 \text{ amu}}\right)$$

$$= 2.23 \times 10^{21} \text{ Al atoms}$$

BALLPARK CHECK: Our estimate was 10^{22}, which is within a factor of 10.

PROBLEM 3.1

What is the mass in atomic mass units of a nitrogen atom weighing 2.33×10^{-23} g?

PROBLEM 3.2

What is the mass in grams of 150×10^{12} iron atoms, each having a mass of 56 amu?

PROBLEM 3.3

How many atoms are in each of the following?

(a) 1.0 g of hydrogen atoms, each of mass 1.0 amu

(b) 12.0 g of carbon atoms, each of mass 12.0 amu

(c) 23.0 g of sodium atoms, each of mass 23.0 amu

PROBLEM 3.4

What pattern do you see in your answers to Problem 3.3? (We will return to this very important pattern in Chapter 6.)

APPLICATION ▶ Are Atoms Real?

Chemistry rests on the premise that matter is composed of the tiny particles we call atoms. Every chemical reaction and every physical law that governs the behavior of matter are explained by chemists in terms of atomic theory. But how do we know that atoms are real and not just an imaginary concept? And how do we know the structure of the atom? Our understanding of atomic structure is another example of the scientific method at work.

Dalton's atomic theory was originally published in 1808, but many prominent scientists dismissed it. Over the next century, however, several unrelated experiments provided insight into the nature of matter and the structure of the atom. Nineteenth-century investigations into electricity, for example, demonstrated that matter was composed of charged particles—rubbing a glass rod with a silk cloth would generate "static electricity," the same phenomenon that shocks you when you walk across a carpet and then touch a metal surface. It was also known that passing electricity through certain substances, such as water, decomposed the compounds into their constituent elements.

In 1897, J. J. Thomson used magnetic fields to deflect a beam of particles emitted from a cathode ray tube, demonstrating that these particles had a negative charge and were 1000 times lighter than the lightest charged particles found in aqueous solution (H^+). (⊂⊐⊃ Section 6.10 and Chapter 10) This result implied that atoms were *not* the smallest particles of matter but could be divided into even smaller particles. In 1909, Robert Millikan studied the behavior of oil droplets in a

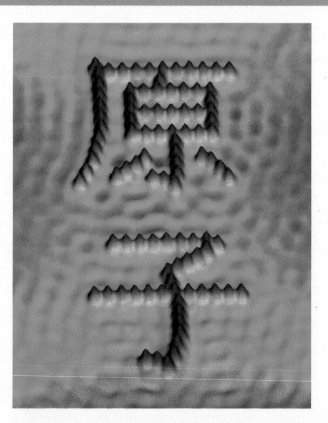

▲ Colored scanning tunneling micrograph of the surface of graphite, a form of the element carbon. The hexagonal pattern is related to an identical arrangement of the carbon atoms.

chamber containing electrically charged plates. When Millikan bombarded the atmosphere in the chamber with x-rays, the droplets acquired a negative charge. Millikan observed that by varying the strength of the electric field associated with the charged plates he could alter the rate of descent of the droplets or even suspend them in midair! From these results he was able to calculate the charge associated with the electron (16×10^{-19} coulombs). Finally, in 1910 Ernest Rutherford bombarded a gold foil with positively charged "alpha" particles emitted from radium during radioactive decay. The majority of these particles passed straight through the foil, but a small fraction of them were deflected, and a few even bounced backward. From these results Rutherford deduced that an atom consists mostly of empty space (occupied by the negatively charged electrons) and that most of the mass and all of the positive charge are contained in a relatively small, dense region that he called the nucleus.

We can now actually "see" and manipulate individual atoms through the use of a device called a *scanning tunneling microscope*, or STM (⬭⬭ see Application on p. 28). With the STM, invented in 1981 by a research team at the IBM Corporation, magnifications of up to ten million have been achieved, allowing chemists to look directly at atoms. The accompanying photograph shows a computer-enhanced representation of carbon atoms in graphite that have been deposited on a copper surface.

Most present uses of the STM involve studies of surface chemistry, such as the events accompanying the corrosion of metals and the ordering of large molecules in polymers. Work is also under way using the STM to determine the structures of complex biological molecules.

See Additional Problems 3.90 and 3.91 at the end of the chapter.

3.2 Elements and Atomic Number

Atoms of different elements differ from one another according to how many protons they contain, a value called the element's **atomic number (Z)**. Thus, if we know the number of protons in an atom, we can identify the element. Any atom with 6 protons, for example, is a carbon atom because carbon has $Z = 6$.

Atoms are neutral overall and have no net charge because the number of positively charged protons in an atom is the same as the number of negatively charged electrons. Thus, the atomic number also equals the number of electrons in every atom of a given element. Hydrogen, $Z = 1$, has only 1 proton and 1 electron; carbon, $Z = 6$, has 6 protons and 6 electrons; sodium, $Z = 11$, has 11 protons and 11 electrons; and so on up to the newly discovered element with $Z = 118$. In a periodic table, elements are listed in order of increasing atomic number, beginning at the upper left and ending at the lower right.

Atomic number (Z) The number of protons in atoms of a given element; the number of electrons in atoms of a given element

The sum of the protons and neutrons in an atom is called the atom's **mass number (A)**. Hydrogen atoms with 1 proton and no neutrons have mass number 1; carbon atoms with 6 protons and 6 neutrons have mass number 12; sodium atoms with 11 protons and 12 neutrons have mass number 23; and so on. Except for hydrogen, atoms generally contain at least as many neutrons as protons, and frequently contain more. There is no simple way to predict how many neutrons a given atom will have.

Mass number (A) The total number of protons and neutrons in an atom

WORKED EXAMPLE **3.2** Atomic Structure: Protons, Neutrons, and Electrons

Phosphorus has atomic number $Z = 15$. How many protons, electrons, and neutrons are there in phosphorus atoms, which have mass number $A = 31$?

ANALYSIS The atomic number gives the number of protons, which is the same as the number of electrons, and the mass number gives the total number of protons plus neutrons.

SOLUTION

Phosphorus atoms, with $Z = 15$, have 15 protons and 15 electrons. To find the number of neutrons, subtract the atomic number from the mass number:

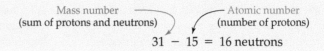

Mass number   Atomic number
(sum of protons and neutrons)   (number of protons)

$$31 - 15 = 16 \text{ neutrons}$$

WORKED EXAMPLE **3.3** Atomic Structure: Atomic Number and Atomic Mass

An atom contains 28 protons and has $A = 60$. Give the number of electrons and neutrons in the atom, and identify the element.

ANALYSIS The number of protons and the number of electrons are the same and are equal to the atomic number Z, 28 in this case. Subtracting the number of protons (28) from the total number of protons plus neutrons (60) gives the number of neutrons.

SOLUTION

The atom has 28 electrons and $60 - 28 = 32$ neutrons. Looking at the list of elements inside the front cover shows that the element with atomic number 28 is nickel (Ni).

PROBLEM 3.5

Use the list inside the front cover to identify elements with the following atomic numbers:

(a) $Z = 75$

(b) $Z = 20$

(c) $Z = 52$

PROBLEM 3.6

The cobalt used in cancer treatments has $Z = 27$ and $A = 60$. How many protons, neutrons, and electrons are in these cobalt atoms?

PROBLEM 3.7

A certain atom has $A = 98$ and contains 55 neutrons. Identify the element.

3.3 Isotopes and Atomic Weight

All atoms of a given element have the same number of protons—the atomic number Z characteristic of that element—but different atoms of an element can have different numbers of neutrons and therefore different mass numbers. Atoms with identical atomic numbers but different mass numbers are called **isotopes**. Hydrogen, for example, has three isotopes. The most abundant hydrogen isotope, called *protium*, has no neutrons and thus has a mass number of 1. A second hydrogen isotope, called *deuterium*, has one neutron and a mass number of 2; and a third isotope, called *tritium*, has two neutrons and a mass number of 3. Tritium is unstable and does not occur naturally in significant amounts, although it can be made in nuclear reactors (⊂▭⊃, see Section 11.11).

Isotopes Atoms with identical atomic numbers but different mass numbers.

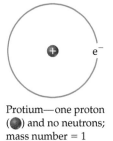

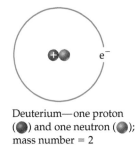

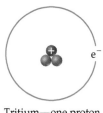

Protium—one proton
(●) and no neutrons;
mass number = 1

Deuterium—one proton
(●) and one neutron (●);
mass number = 2

Tritium—one proton
(●) and two neutrons (●);
mass number = 3

A specific isotope is represented by showing its mass number (A) as a superscript and its atomic number (Z) as a subscript in front of the atomic symbol, for example, $^A_Z X$, where X represents the symbol for the element. Thus, protium is $^1_1 H$, deuterium is $^2_1 H$, and tritium is $^3_1 H$.

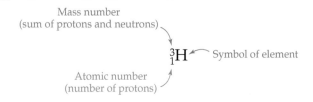

Mass number
(sum of protons and neutrons)

$^3_1 H$ ← Symbol of element

Atomic number
(number of protons)

Unlike the three isotopes of hydrogen, the isotopes of most elements do not have distinctive names. Instead, the mass number of the isotope is given after the name of the element. The $^{235}_{92} U$ isotope used in nuclear reactors, for example, is usually referred to as uranium-235, or U-235.

Most naturally occurring elements are mixtures of isotopes. In a large sample of naturally occurring hydrogen atoms, for example, 99.985% have mass number $A = 1$ (protium) and 0.015% have mass number $A = 2$ (deuterium). It is therefore useful to know the *average* mass of the atoms in a large sample, a value called the element's **atomic weight**. For hydrogen, the atomic weight is 1.008 amu. Atomic weights for all elements are given inside the front cover of this book.

To calculate the atomic weight of an element, the individual masses of the naturally occurring isotopes and the percentage of each must be known. The atomic weight can then be calculated as the sum of the masses of the individual isotopes for that element, or

$$\text{Atomic weight} = \Sigma(\text{isotopic abundance}) \times (\text{isotopic mass})$$

where the Greek symbol Σ indicates the mathematical summing of terms.

Chlorine, for example, occurs on earth as a mixture of 75.77% Cl-35 atoms (mass = 34.97 amu) and 24.23% Cl-37 atoms (mass = 36.97 amu). The atomic weight is found by calculating the percentage of the mass contributed by each isotope. For chlorine, the calculation is done in the following way (to four significant figures), giving an atomic weight of 35.45 amu:

Contribution from ^{35}Cl: (0.7577)(34.97 amu) = 26.4968 amu

Contribution from ^{37}Cl: (0.2423)(36.97 amu) = 8.9578 amu

Atomic weight = 35.4546 = 35.45 amu
(rounded to four significant figures)

The final number of significant figures in this case (four) was determined by the atomic masses. Note that the final rounding to four significant figures was not done until *after* the final answer was obtained.

Atomic weight The weighted average mass of an element's atoms.

WORKED EXAMPLE **3.4** Average Atomic Mass: Weighted-Average Calculation

Gallium is a metal with a very low melting point—it will melt in the palm of your hand. It has two naturally occurring isotopes: 60.4% is Ga-69, (mass = 68.9257 amu), and 39.6% is Ga-71, (mass = 70.9248 amu). Calculate the average atomic weight for gallium.

ANALYSIS We can calculate the average atomic mass for the element by summing up the contributions from each of the naturally occurring isotopes.

BALLPARK ESTIMATE The masses of the two naturally occurring isotopes of gallium differ by 2 amu (68.9 and 70.9 amu). Since slightly more than half of the Ga atoms are the lighter isotope (Ga-69), the average mass will be slightly less than halfway between the two isotopic masses; estimate = 69.8 amu.

SOLUTION

STEP 1: **Identify known information.**	Ga-69 (60.4% at 68.9257 amu)
	Ga-71 (39.6% at 70.9248 amu)
STEP 2: **Identify the unknown answer and units.**	Average atomic weight for Ga (in amu) = ?
STEP 3: **Identify conversion factors or equations.** This equation calculates the average atomic weight as a weighted average of all naturally occurring isotopes.	Atomic weight = Σ(isotopic abundance) $\times$ (isotopic mass)
STEP 4: **Solve.** Substitute known information and solve.	Atomic weight = (0.604) $\times$ (68.9257 amu) = 41.6311 amu
	+ (0.396) $\times$ (70.9248 amu) = 28.0862 amu
	Atomic weight = 69.7 amu
	(3 significant figures)

BALLPARK CHECK: Our estimate (69.8 amu) is close!

WORKED EXAMPLE **3.5** Identifying Isotopes from Atomic Mass and Atomic Number

Identify element X in the symbol $^{194}_{78}$X and give its atomic number, mass number, number of protons, number of electrons, and number of neutrons.

ANALYSIS The identity of the atom corresponds to the atomic number—78.

SOLUTION
Element X has Z = 78, which shows that it is platinum. (Look inside the front cover for the list of elements.) The isotope $^{194}_{78}$Pt has a mass number of 194, and we can subtract the atomic number from the mass number to get the number of neutrons. This platinum isotope therefore has 78 protons, 78 electrons, and 194 − 78 = 116 neutrons.

PROBLEM 3.8

Potassium (K) has two naturally occurring isotopes: K-39 (93.12%; mass = 38.9637 amu), and K-41 (6.88%; 40.9618 amu). Calculate the atomic weight for potassium. How does your answer compare with the atomic mass given in the list inside the front cover of this book?

PROBLEM 3.9

Bromine, an element present in compounds used as sanitizers and fumigants (for example, ethylene bromide), has two naturally occurring isotopes, with mass numbers 79 and 81. Write the symbols for both, including their atomic numbers and mass numbers.

Complete the following isotope symbols:

(a) $^{11}_{5}?$ (b) $^{56}_{?}Fe$ (c) $^{37}_{17}?$

3.4 The Periodic Table

Ten elements have been known since the beginning of recorded history: antimony (Sb), carbon (C), copper (Cu), gold (Au), iron (Fe), lead (Pb), mercury (Hg), silver (Ag), sulfur (S), and tin (Sn). It is worth noting that the symbols for many of these elements are derived from their Latin names, a reminder that they have been known since the time when Latin was the language used for all scholarly work. The first "new" element to be found in several thousand years was arsenic (As), discovered in about 1250. In fact, only 24 elements were known up to the time of the American Revolution in 1776.

As the pace of discovery quickened in the late 1700s and early 1800s, chemists began to look for similarities among elements that might make it possible to draw general conclusions. Particularly important was Johann Döbereiner's observation in 1829 that there were several *triads*, or groups of three elements, that appeared to have similar chemical and physical properties. For example, lithium, sodium, and potassium were all known to be silvery metals that react violently with water; chlorine, bromine, and iodine were all known to be colored nonmetals with pungent odors.

Numerous attempts were made in the mid-1800s to account for the similarities among groups of elements, but the great breakthrough came in 1869 when the Russian chemist Dmitri Mendeleev organized the elements into a forerunner of the modern periodic table, introduced previously in Section 1.6 and shown again in Figure 3.2. The table has boxes for each element that give the symbol, atomic number, and atomic weight of the element:

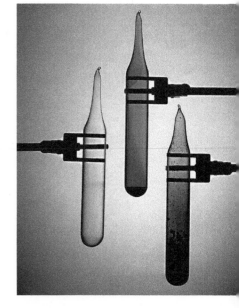

▲ Samples of chlorine, bromine, and iodine, one of Döbereiner's triads of elements with similar chemical properties.

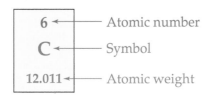

Beginning at the upper left corner of the periodic table, elements are arranged by increasing atomic number into seven horizontal rows, called **periods**, and 18 vertical columns, called **groups**. When organized in this way, *the elements in a given group have similar chemical properties.* Lithium, sodium, potassium, and the other elements in group 1A behave similarly. Chlorine, bromine, iodine, and the other elements in group 7A behave similarly, and so on throughout the table.

Note that different periods (rows) contain different numbers of elements. The first period contains only 2 elements, hydrogen and helium; the second and third periods each contain 8 elements; the fourth and fifth periods each contain 18; the sixth period contains 32; and the seventh period (incomplete as yet) contains 31 elements. Note also that the 14 elements following lanthanum (the *lanthanides*) and the 14 following actinium (the *actinides*) are pulled out and shown below the others.

Groups are numbered in two ways, both shown in Figure 3.2. The two large groups on the far left and the six on the far right are called the **main group elements** and are numbered 1A through 8A. The ten smaller groups in the middle of the table are called the **transition metal elements** and are numbered 1B through 8B. Alternatively, all 18 groups are numbered sequentially from 1 to 18. The 14 groups shown separately at the bottom of the table are called the **inner transition metal elements** and are not numbered.

Period One of the 7 horizontal rows of elements in the periodic table.

Group One of the 18 vertical columns of elements in the periodic table.

Main group element An element in one of the two groups on the left or the six groups on the right of the periodic table.

Transition metal element An element in one of the 10 smaller groups near the middle of the periodic table.

Inner transition metal element An element in one of the 14 groups shown separately at the bottom of the periodic table.

Main groups

Main groups

	1A																		8A
Period	1	2A												3A	4A	5A	6A	7A	18

Transition metal groups

Period 1

1																			2
H	2																		He
1.00794																			4.00260

Period 2

3	4													5	6	7	8	9	10
Li	Be	3B	4B	5B	6B	7B	—	8B	—	1B	2B		13	B	C	N	O	F	Ne
6.941	9.01218	3	4	5	6	7	8	9	10	11	12			10.81	12.011	14.0067	15.9994	18.9984	20.1797

Period 3

11	12												13	14	15	16	17	18
Na	Mg												Al	Si	P	S	Cl	Ar
22.98977	24.305												26.98154	28.0855	30.9738	32.066	35.4527	39.948

Period 4

19	20	21	22	23	24	25	26	27	28	29	30	31	32	33	34	35	36
K	Ca	Sc	Ti	V	Cr	Mn	Fe	Co	Ni	Cu	Zn	Ga	Ge	As	Se	Br	Kr
39.0983	40.078	44.9559	47.88	50.9415	51.996	54.9380	55.847	58.9332	58.69	63.546	65.39	69.72	72.61	74.9216	78.96	79.904	83.80

Period 5

37	38	39	40	41	42	43	44	45	46	47	48	49	50	51	52	53	54
Rb	Sr	Y	Zr	Nb	Mo	Tc	Ru	Rh	Pd	Ag	Cd	In	Sn	Sb	Te	I	Xe
85.4678	87.62	88.9059	91.224	92.9064	95.94	(98)	101.07	102.9055	106.42	107.8682	112.41	114.82	118.710	121.757	127.60	126.9045	131.29

Period 6

55	56	57	72	73	74	75	76	77	78	79	80	81	82	83	84	85	86
Cs	Ba	*La	Hf	Ta	W	Re	Os	Ir	Pt	Au	Hg	Tl	Pb	Bi	Po	At	Rn
132.9054	137.33	138.9055	178.49	180.9479	183.85	186.207	190.2	192.22	195.08	196.9665	200.59	204.383	207.2	208.9804	(209)	(210)	(222)

Period 7

87	88	89	104	105	106	107	108	109	110	111	112	113	114	115	116		118
Fr	Ra	†Ac	Rf	Db	Sg	Bh	Hs	Mt	Ds	Rg							
(223)	226.0254	227.0278	(261)	(262)	(266)	(264)	(269)	(268)	(271)	(272)	(285)	(284)	(289)	(288)	(292)		(294)

Lanthanides

58	59	60	61	62	63	64	65	66	67	68	69	70	71
Ce	Pr	Nd	Pm	Sm	Eu	Gd	Tb	Dy	Ho	Er	Tm	Yb	Lu
140.12	140.9077	144.24	(145)	150.36	151.965	157.25	158.9254	162.50	164.9304	167.26	168.9342	173.04	174.967

Actinides

90	91	92	93	94	95	96	97	98	99	100	101	102	103
Th	Pa	U	Np	Pu	Am	Cm	Bk	Cf	Es	Fm	Md	No	Lr
232.0381	231.0399	238.0289	237.048	(244)	(243)	(247)	(247)	(251)	(252)	(257)	(258)	(259)	(262)

Metals   Metalloids   Nonmetals

▲ **FIGURE 3.2   The periodic table of the elements.**   Each element is identified by a one- or two-letter symbol and is characterized by an *atomic number*. The table begins with hydrogen (H, atomic number 1) in the upper left-hand corner and continues to the yet unnamed element with atomic number 118. The 14 elements following lanthanum (La, atomic number 57) and the 14 elements following actinium (Ac, atomic number 89) are pulled out and shown below the others.

Elements are organized into 18 vertical columns, or *groups*, and 7 horizontal rows, or *periods*. The two groups on the left and the six on the right are the *main groups*; the ten in the middle are the *transition metal groups*. The 14 elements following lanthanum are the *lanthanides*, and the 14 elements following actinium are the *actinides*; together these are known as the *inner transition metals*. Two systems for numbering the groups are explained in the text.

Those elements (except hydrogen) on the left-hand side of the zigzag line running from boron (B) to astatine (At) are *metals*, those elements to the right of the line are *nonmetals*, and most elements abutting the line are *metalloids*.

▲ Sodium, an alkali metal, reacts violently with water to yield hydrogen gas and an alkaline (basic) solution.

PROBLEM 3.11

Locate aluminum in the periodic table, and give its group number and period number.

PROBLEM 3.12

Identify the group 1B element in period 5 and the group 2A element in period 4.

PROBLEM 3.13

There are five elements in group 5A of the periodic table. Identify them, and give the period of each.

3.5 Some Characteristics of Different Groups

To see why the periodic table has the name it does, look at the graph of atomic radius versus atomic number in Figure 3.3. The graph shows an obvious *periodicity*—a repeating, rise-and-fall pattern. Beginning on the left with atomic number 1 (hydrogen), the sizes of the atoms increase to a maximum at atomic number 3 (lithium), then decrease to a minimum, then increase again to a maximum at atomic number 11 (sodium), then decrease, and so on. It turns out that the maxima occur for atoms of group 1A elements—Li, Na, K, Rb, Cs, and Fr—and the minima occur for atoms of the group 7A elements.

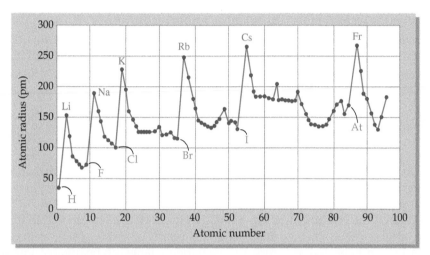

▲ **FIGURE 3.3** **A graph of atomic radius in picometers (pm) versus atomic number shows a periodic rise-and-fall pattern.** The maxima occur for atoms of the group 1A elements (Li, Na, K, Rb, Cs, Fr); the minima occur for atoms of the group 7A elements. Accurate data are not available for the group 8A elements.

There is nothing unique about the periodicity of atomic radii shown in Figure 3.3. The melting points of the first 100 elements, for example, exhibit similar periodic behavior, as shown in Figure 3.4. Many other physical and chemical properties can be plotted in a similar way with similar results. In fact, the various elements in a given group of the periodic table usually show remarkable similarities

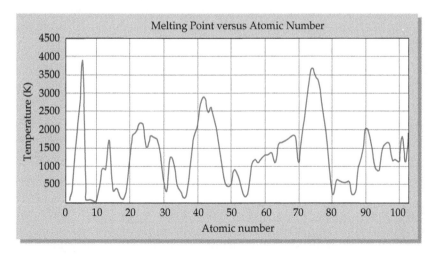

▲ **FIGURE 3.4** **A graph of melting point versus atomic number shows periodic properties similar to the trend in Figure 3.3.** While the maxima and minima are not as sharp as in Figure 3.3, the change in melting points of the elements still shows the same periodic trend.

Alkali metal An element in group 1A of the periodic table.

Alkaline earth metal An element in group 2A of the periodic table.

Halogen An element in group 7A of the periodic table.

Noble gas An element in group 8A of the periodic table.

▲ Magnesium, an alkaline earth metal, burns in air. Magnesium alloys are often used in welding rods.

▲ Chlorine, a halogen, is a toxic, corrosive green gas.

▲ Neon and other noble gases are used in neon lights, signs, and works of art.

in many of their chemical and physical properties. Look at the following four groups, for example:

- **Group 1A—Alkali metals:** Lithium (Li), sodium (Na), potassium (K), rubidium (Rb), cesium (Cs), and francium (Fr) are shiny, soft metals with low melting points. All react rapidly (often violently) with water to form products that are highly alkaline, or basic—hence the name *alkali metals*. Because of their high reactivity, the alkali metals are never found in nature in the pure state but only in combination with other elements.

- **Group 2A—Alkaline earth metals:** Beryllium (Be), magnesium (Mg), calcium (Ca), strontium (Sr), barium (Ba), and radium (Ra) are also lustrous, silvery metals, but are less reactive than their neighbors in group 1A. Like the alkali metals, the alkaline earths are never found in nature in the pure state.

- **Group 7A—Halogens:** Fluorine (F), chlorine (Cl), bromine (Br), iodine (I), and astatine (At) are colorful and corrosive nonmetals. All are found in nature only in combination with other elements, such as with sodium in table salt (sodium chloride, NaCl). In fact, the group name *halogen* is taken from the Greek word *hals*, meaning salt.

- **Group 8A—Noble gases:** Helium (He), neon (Ne), argon (Ar), krypton (Kr), xenon (Xe), and radon (Rn) are colorless gases. The elements in this group were labeled the "noble" gases because of their lack of chemical reactivity—helium, neon, and argon don't combine with any other elements, whereas krypton and xenon combine with very few.

Although the resemblances are not as pronounced as they are within a single group, *neighboring* elements often behave similarly as well. Thus, as noted in Section 1.6 and indicated in Figure 3.2, the periodic table can be divided into three major classes of elements—*metals*, *nonmetals*, and *metalloids* (metal-like). Metals, the largest category of elements, are found on the left side of the periodic table, bounded on the right by a zigzag line running from boron (B) at the top to astatine (At) at the bottom. Nonmetals are found on the right side of the periodic table, and seven of the elements adjacent to the zigzag boundary between metals and nonmetals are metalloids.

⊂⊃ Looking Ahead

Carbon, the element on which life is based, is a group 4A nonmetal near the top right of the periodic table. Clustered near carbon are other elements often found in living organisms, including oxygen, nitrogen, phosphorus, and sulfur. We will look at the subject of *organic chemistry*—the chemistry of carbon compounds—in Chapters 12–17, and move on to *biochemistry*—the chemistry of living things—in Chapters 18–29. ⊂⊃

PROBLEM 3.14

Identify the following elements as metals, nonmetals, or metalloids:

(a) Ti   **(b)** Te   **(c)** Se
(d) Sc   **(e)** At   **(f)** Ar

PROBLEM 3.15

Locate **(a)** krypton, **(b)** strontium, **(c)** nitrogen, and **(d)** cobalt in the periodic table. Indicate which categories apply to each: (i) metal, (ii) nonmetal, (iii) transition element, (iv) main group element, (v) noble gas.

APPLICATION ▶ The Origin of Chemical Elements

Astronomers believe that the universe began some 15 billion years ago in an extraordinary moment they call the "big bang." Initially, the temperature must have been inconceivably high, but after 1 second, it had dropped to about 10^{10} K and subatomic particles began to form: protons, neutrons, and electrons. After 3 minutes, the temperature had dropped to 10^9 K, and protons began fusing with neutrons to form helium nuclei, $^4_2$He.

Matter remained in this form for many millions of years until the expanding universe had cooled to about 10,000 K and electrons were then able to bind to protons and to helium nuclei, forming stable hydrogen and helium atoms.

The attractive force of gravity acting on regions of higher-than-average density slowly produced massive local concentrations of matter and ultimately formed billions of galaxies, each with many billions of stars. As the gas clouds of hydrogen and helium condensed under gravitational attraction and stars formed, their temperatures reached 10^7 K, and their densities reached 100 g/cm^3. Protons and neutrons again fused to yield helium nuclei, generating vast amounts of heat and light.

Most of these early stars probably burned out after a few billion years, but a few were so massive that, as their nuclear fuel diminished, gravitational attraction caused a rapid contraction leading to still higher core temperatures and higher densities—up to 5×10^8 K and 5×10^5 g/cm^3. Under such extreme conditions, larger nuclei were formed, including carbon, oxygen, silicon, magnesium, and iron. Ultimately, the

▲ The stars in the Milky Way galaxy condensed from gas clouds under gravitational attraction.

stars underwent a gravitational collapse resulting in the synthesis of still heavier elements and an explosion visible throughout the universe as a *supernova.*

Matter from exploding supernovas was blown throughout the galaxy, forming a new generation of stars and planets. Our own sun and solar system formed about 4.5 billion years ago from matter released by former supernovas. Except for hydrogen and helium, all the atoms in our bodies and our entire solar system were created more than five billion years ago in exploding stars. We and our world are made from the ashes of dying stars.

See Additional Problems 3.92 and 3.93 at the end of this chapter.

⌐◉ KEY CONCEPT PROBLEM 3.16

Identify the elements shown in red and in blue on the following periodic table. For each, tell its group number, its period number, and whether it is a metal, nonmetal, or metalloid.

3.6 Electronic Structure of Atoms

Why does the periodic table have the shape it does, with periods of different length? Why are periodic variations observed in atomic radii and in so many other characteristics of the elements? And why do elements in a given group of the periodic table show similar chemical behavior? These questions occupied the thoughts of chemists for more than 50 years after Mendeleev, and it was not until well into the 1920s that the answers were established. Today, we know that *the properties of the elements are determined by the arrangement of electrons in their atoms.*

Our current understanding of the electronic structure of atoms is based on the now accepted *quantum mechanical model*, developed by Austrian physicist Erwin Schrödinger in 1926. Although a detailed discussion of the model is beyond the scope of this text, one of the fundamental assumptions of the model is that electrons have both particle-like and wave-like properties, and that the behavior of electrons can be described using a mathematical equation called a wave function. One consequence of this assumption is that electrons are not perfectly free to move about in an atom. Instead, each electron is restricted to moving about in only a certain region of space within the atom, depending on the energy level of the electron. Different electrons have different amounts of energy and thus occupy different regions within the atom. Furthermore, the energies of electrons are *quantized*, or restricted to having only certain values.

To understand the idea of quantization, think about the difference between stairs and a ramp. A ramp is *not* quantized because it changes height continuously. Stairs, by contrast, *are* quantized because they change height only by a fixed amount. You can climb one stair or two stairs, but you cannot climb 1.5 stairs. In the same way, the energy values available to electrons in an atom change only in steps rather than continuously.

The wave functions derived from the quantum mechanical model also provide important information about the location of electrons in an atom. Just as a person can be found by giving his or her address within a state, an electron can be found by giving its "address" within an atom. Furthermore, just as a person's address is composed of several successively narrower categories—city, street, and house number—an electron's address is also composed of successively narrower categories—*shell, subshell,* and *orbital,* which are defined by the quantum mechanical model.

The electrons in an atom are grouped around the nucleus into **shells**, roughly like the layers in an onion, according to the energy of the electrons. The farther a shell is from the nucleus, the larger it is, the more electrons it can hold, and the higher the energies of those electrons. The first shell (the one nearest the nucleus) can hold only 2 electrons, the second shell can hold 8, the third shell can hold 18, and the fourth shell can hold 32 electrons.

▲ Stairs are *quantized* because they change height in discrete amounts. A ramp, by contrast, is not quantized because it changes height continuously.

Shell (electron) A grouping of electrons in an atom according to energy.

Shell number:	1	2	3	4
Electron capacity:	2	8	18	32

Subshell (electron) A grouping of electrons in a shell according to the shape of the region of space they occupy.

Within shells, electrons are further grouped into **subshells** of four different types, identified in order of increasing energy by the letters *s, p, d,* and *f.* The first shell has only an *s* subshell; the second shell has an *s* and a *p* subshell; the third shell has an *s,* a *p,* and a *d* subshell; and the fourth shell has an *s,* a *p,* a *d,* and an *f* subshell. Of the four types, we will be concerned mainly with *s* and *p* subshells because most of the elements found in living organisms use only these. A specific subshell is symbolized by writing the number of the shell, followed by the letter for the subshell. For example, the designation 3*p* refers to the *p* subshell in the third shell.

Shell number:	1	2	3	4
Subshell designation:	*s*	*s , p*	*s , p , d*	*s , p , d , f*

Note that the number of subshells in a given shell is equal to the shell number. For example, shell number 3 has 3 subshells.

Orbital A region of space within an atom where an electron in a given subshell can be found.

Finally, within each subshell, electrons are grouped into **orbitals**, regions of space within an atom where the specific electrons are most likely to be found. There are different numbers of orbitals within the different kinds of subshells. A given *s* subshell has only 1 orbital, a *p* subshell has 3 orbitals, a *d* subshell has 5 orbitals, and an *f* subshell has 7 orbitals. Each orbital can hold only two electrons, which differ in a property known as *spin*. If one electron in an orbital has a clockwise spin, the other electron in the same orbital must have a counterclockwise spin.

Shell number:	1	2	3	4
Subshell designation:	s	s , p	s , p , d	s , p , d , f
Number of orbitals:	1	1 , 3	1 , 3 , 5	1 , 3 , 5 , 7

Different orbitals have different shapes and orientations, which are described by the quantum mechanical model. Orbitals in *s* subshells are spherical regions centered about the nucleus, whereas orbitals in *p* subshells are roughly dumbbell-shaped regions (Figure 3.5). As shown in Figure 3.5(b), the three *p* orbitals in a given subshell are oriented at right angles to one another.

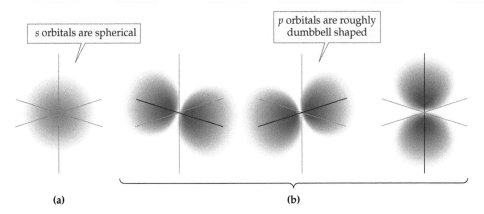

s orbitals are spherical

p orbitals are roughly dumbbell shaped

(a) (b)

▲ **FIGURE 3.5 The shapes of s and p orbitals.** (a) The *s* orbitals and (b) the *p* orbitals. The three *p* orbitals in a given subshell are oriented at right angles to one another. Each orbital can hold only two electrons.

The overall electron distribution within an atom is summarized in Table 3.2 and in the following list:

- The first shell holds only 2 electrons. The 2 electrons have different spins and are in a single 1*s* orbital.
- The second shell holds 8 electrons. Two are in a 2*s* orbital, and 6 are in the three different 2*p* orbitals (two per 2*p* orbital).
- The third shell holds 18 electrons. Two are in a 3*s* orbital, 6 are in three 3*p* orbitals, and 10 are in five 3*d* orbitals.
- The fourth shell holds 32 electrons. Two are in a 4*s* orbital, 6 are in three 4*p* orbitals, 10 are in five 4*d* orbitals, and 14 are in seven 4*f* orbitals.

TABLE 3.2 Electron Distribution in Atoms

SHELL NUMBER:	1	2	3	4
Subshell designation:	s	s , p	s , p , d	s , p , d , f
Number of orbitals:	1	1 , 3	1 , 3 , 5	1 , 3 , 5 , 7
Number of electrons:	2	2 , 6	2 , 6 , 10	2 , 6 , 10 , 14
Total electron capacity:	2	8	18	32

WORKED EXAMPLE **3.6** Atomic Structure: Electron Shells

How many electrons are present in an atom that has its first and second shells filled and has 4 electrons in its third shell? Name the element.

ANALYSIS The number of electrons in the atom is calculated by adding the total electrons in each shell. We can identify the element from the number of protons in the nucleus, which is equal to the number of electrons in the atom.

SOLUTION

The first shell of an atom holds 2 electrons in its $1s$ orbital, and the second shell holds 8 electrons (2 in a $2s$ orbital and 6 in three $2p$ orbitals). Thus, the atom has a total of $2 + 8 + 4 = 14$ electrons and must be silicon (Si).

PROBLEM 3.17

What is the maximum number of electrons that can occupy the following subshells?

(a) $3p$ subshell

(b) $2s$ subshell

(c) $2p$ subshell

PROBLEM 3.18

How many electrons are present in an atom in which the $1s$, $2s$, and $2p$ subshells are filled? Name the element.

PROBLEM 3.19

How many electrons are present in an atom in which the first and second shells and the $3s$ subshell are filled? Name the element.

▲ Following the energy level diagram for the electronic orbitals, the orbital filling order can be predicted as indicated in this figure.

Electron configuration The specific arrangement of electrons in an atom's shells and subshells.

▲ **FIGURE 3.6 Order of orbital energy levels.** Above the $3p$ level, there is some crossover of energies among orbitals in different shells.

3.7 Electron Configurations

The exact arrangement of electrons in an atom's shells and subshells is called the atom's **electron configuration** and can be predicted by applying three rules:

RULE 1. **Electrons occupy the lowest-energy orbitals available, beginning with $1s$ and continuing in the order shown in Figure 3.6.** Within each shell, the orbital energies increase in the order s, p, d, f. The overall ordering is complicated, however, by the fact that some "crossover" of energies occurs between orbitals in different shells above the $3p$ level. The $4s$ orbital is lower in energy than the $3d$ orbitals, for example, and is therefore filled first.

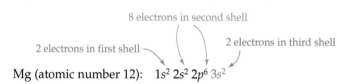

8 electrons in second shell

2 electrons in first shell

2 electrons in third shell

Mg (atomic number 12): $1s^2\ 2s^2\ 2p^6\ 3s^2$

RULE 2. **Each orbital can hold only two electrons, which must be of opposite spin.**

RULE 3. **Two or more orbitals with the same energy—the three p orbitals or the five d orbitals in a given shell, for example—are each half filled by one electron before any one orbital is completely filled by addition of the second electron.**

TABLE 3.3   Electron Configurations of the First 20 Elements

	ELEMENT	ATOMIC NUMBER	ELECTRON CONFIGURATION
H	Hydrogen	1	$1s^1$
He	Helium	2	$1s^2$
Li	Lithium	3	$1s^2\ 2s^1$
Be	Beryllium	4	$1s^2\ 2s^2$
B	Boron	5	$1s^2\ 2s^2\ 2p^1$
C	Carbon	6	$1s^2\ 2s^2\ 2p^2$
N	Nitrogen	7	$1s^2\ 2s^2\ 2p^3$
O	Oxygen	8	$1s^2\ 2s^2\ 2p^4$
F	Fluorine	9	$1s^2\ 2s^2\ 2p^5$
Ne	Neon	10	$1s^2\ 2s^2\ 2p^6$
Na	Sodium	11	$1s^2\ 2s^2\ 2p^6\ 3s^1$
Mg	Magnesium	12	$1s^2\ 2s^2\ 2p^6\ 3s^2$
Al	Aluminum	13	$1s^2\ 2s^2\ 2p^6\ 3s^2\ 3p^1$
Si	Silicon	14	$1s^2\ 2s^2\ 2p^6\ 3s^2\ 3p^2$
P	Phosphorus	15	$1s^2\ 2s^2\ 2p^6\ 3s^2\ 3p^3$
S	Sulfur	16	$1s^2\ 2s^2\ 2p^6\ 3s^2\ 3p^4$
Cl	Chlorine	17	$1s^2\ 2s^2\ 2p^6\ 3s^2\ 3p^5$
Ar	Argon	18	$1s^2\ 2s^2\ 2p^6\ 3s^2\ 3p^6$
K	Potassium	19	$1s^2\ 2s^2\ 2p^6\ 3s^2\ 3p^6\ 4s^1$
Ca	Calcium	20	$1s^2\ 2s^2\ 2p^6\ 3s^2\ 3p^6\ 4s^2$

Electron configurations of the first 20 elements are shown in Table 3.3. Notice that the number of electrons in each subshell is indicated by a superscript. For example, the notation $1s^2\ 2s^2\ 2p^6\ 3s^2$ for magnesium means that magnesium atoms have 2 electrons in the first shell, 8 electrons in the second shell, and 2 electrons in the third shell.

As you read through the following electron configurations, check the atomic number and the location of each element in the periodic table (Figure 3.2). See if you can detect the relationship between electron configuration and position in the table.

- **Hydrogen (Z = 1):** The single electron in a hydrogen atom is in the lowest-energy, $1s$ level. The configuration can be represented in either of two ways:

$$\text{H}\qquad 1s^1\quad\text{or}\quad \frac{\uparrow}{1s^1}$$

In the written representation, the superscript in the notation $1s^1$ means that the $1s$ orbital is occupied by one electron. In the graphic representation, the $1s$ orbital is indicated by a line and the single electron in this orbital is shown by an up arrow ($\uparrow$). A single electron in an orbital is often referred to as being *unpaired*.

- **Helium (Z = 2):** The two electrons in helium are both in the lowest-energy, $1s$ orbital, and their spins are *paired*, as represented by up and down arrows ($\uparrow\downarrow$):

$$\text{He}\qquad 1s^2\quad\text{or}\quad \frac{\uparrow\downarrow}{1s^2}$$

- **Lithium (Z = 3):** With the first shell full, the second shell begins to fill. The third electron goes into the $2s$ orbital:

$$\text{Li}\qquad 1s^2\ 2s^1\quad\text{or}\quad \frac{\uparrow\downarrow}{1s^2}\ \frac{\uparrow}{2s^1}$$

Because [He] has the configuration of a filled $1s^2$ orbital, it is sometimes substituted for the $1s^2$ orbital in depictions of electron pairing. Using this alternative shorthand notation, the electron configuration for Li is written [He] $2s^1$.

- **Beryllium (Z = 4):** An electron next pairs up to fill the $2s$ orbital:

$$\text{Be} \quad 1s^2\, 2s^2 \quad \text{or} \quad \underset{1s^2}{\uparrow\downarrow} \quad \underset{2s^2}{\uparrow\downarrow} \quad \text{or} \quad [\text{He}]\, 2s^2$$

- **Boron (Z = 5), Carbon (Z = 6), Nitrogen (Z = 7):** The next three electrons enter the three $2p$ orbitals, one at a time. Note that representing the configurations with lines and arrows gives more information than the alternative written notation because the filling and pairing of electrons in individual orbitals within the p subshell is shown.

$$\text{B} \quad 1s^2\, 2s^2\, 2p^1 \quad \text{or} \quad \underset{1s^2}{\uparrow\downarrow} \quad \underset{2s^2}{\uparrow\downarrow} \quad \underset{2p^1}{\underbrace{\uparrow \;\; \_\;\; \_}} \quad \text{or} \quad [\text{He}]\, 2s^2\, 2p^1$$

$$\text{C} \quad 1s^2\, 2s^2\, 2p^2 \quad \text{or} \quad \underset{1s^2}{\uparrow\downarrow} \quad \underset{2s^2}{\uparrow\downarrow} \quad \underset{2p^2}{\underbrace{\uparrow \;\; \uparrow\;\; \_}} \quad \text{or} \quad [\text{He}]\, 2s^2\, 2p^2$$

$$\text{N} \quad 1s^2\, 2s^2\, 2p^3 \quad \text{or} \quad \underset{1s^2}{\uparrow\downarrow} \quad \underset{2s^2}{\uparrow\downarrow} \quad \underset{2p^3}{\underbrace{\uparrow \;\; \uparrow\;\; \uparrow}} \quad \text{or} \quad [\text{He}]\, 2s^2\, 2p^3$$

- **Oxygen (Z = 8), Fluorine (Z = 9), Neon (Z = 10):** Electrons now pair up one by one to fill the three $2p$ orbitals and fully occupy the second shell:

$$\text{O} \quad 1s^2\, 2s^2\, 2p^4 \quad \text{or} \quad \underset{1s^2}{\uparrow\downarrow} \quad \underset{2s^2}{\uparrow\downarrow} \quad \underset{2p^4}{\underbrace{\uparrow\downarrow \;\; \uparrow\;\; \uparrow}} \quad \text{or} \quad [\text{He}]\, 2s^2\, 2p^4$$

$$\text{F} \quad 1s^2\, 2s^2\, 2p^5 \quad \text{or} \quad \underset{1s^2}{\uparrow\downarrow} \quad \underset{2s^2}{\uparrow\downarrow} \quad \underset{2p^5}{\underbrace{\uparrow\downarrow \;\; \uparrow\downarrow\;\; \uparrow}} \quad \text{or} \quad [\text{He}]\, 2s^2\, 2p^5$$

$$\text{Ne} \quad 1s^2\, 2s^2\, 2p^6 \quad \text{or} \quad \underset{1s^2}{\uparrow\downarrow} \quad \underset{2s^2}{\uparrow\downarrow} \quad \underset{2p^6}{\underbrace{\uparrow\downarrow \;\; \uparrow\downarrow\;\; \uparrow\downarrow}}$$

At this point we may use the shorthand notation [Ne] to represent the electron configuration for a completely filled set of orbitals in the second shell.

- **Sodium to Calcium (Z = 11 − 20):** The pattern seen for lithium through neon is seen again for sodium (Z = 11) through argon (Z = 18) as the $3s$ and $3p$ subshells fill up. For elements having a third filled shell, we may use [Ar] to represent a completely filled third shell. After argon, however, the first crossover in subshell energies occurs. As indicated in Figure 3.6, the $4s$ subshell is lower in energy than the $3d$ subshell and is filled first. Potassium (Z = 19) and calcium (Z = 20) therefore have the following electron configurations:

$$\text{K} \quad 1s^2\, 2s^2\, 2p^6\, 3s^2\, 3p^6\, 4s^1 \;\; \text{or} \;\; [\text{Ar}]\, 4s^1 \quad\quad \text{Ca} \quad 1s^2\, 2s^2\, 2p^6\, 3s^2\, 3p^6\, 4s^2 \;\; \text{or} \;\; [\text{Ar}]\, 4s^2$$

WORKED EXAMPLE **3.7** Atomic Structure: Electron Configurations

Show how the electron configuration of magnesium can be assigned.

ANALYSIS Magnesium, $Z = 12$, has 12 electrons to be placed in specific orbitals. Assignments are made by putting 2 electrons in each orbital, according to the order shown in Figure 3.6.

- The first 2 electrons are placed in the 1s orbital ($1s^2$).
- The next 2 electrons are placed in the 2s orbital ($2s^2$).
- The next 6 electrons are placed in the three available 2p orbitals ($2p^6$).
- The remaining 2 electrons are both put in the 3s orbital ($3s^2$).

SOLUTION

Magnesium has the configuration $1s^2\ 2s^2\ 2p^6\ 3s^2$ or [Ne] $3s^2$.

WORKED EXAMPLE **3.8** Electron Configurations: Orbital-Filling Diagrams

Write the electron configuration of phosphorus, Z = 15, using up and down arrows to show how the electrons in each orbital are paired.

ANALYSIS Phosphorus has 15 electrons, which occupy orbitals according to the order shown in Figure 3.6.

- The first 2 are paired and fill the first shell ($1s^2$).
- The next 8 fill the second shell ($2s^2\ 2p^6$). All electrons are paired.
- The remaining 5 electrons enter the third shell, where 2 fill the 3s orbital ($3s^2$) and 3 occupy the 3p subshell, one in each of the three p orbitals.

SOLUTION

$$P \quad \underset{1s^2}{\uparrow\downarrow} \quad \underset{2s^2}{\uparrow\downarrow} \quad \underbrace{\uparrow\downarrow \;\; \uparrow\downarrow \;\; \uparrow\downarrow}_{2p^6} \quad \underset{3s^2}{\uparrow\downarrow} \quad \underbrace{\uparrow \;\; \uparrow \;\; \uparrow}_{3p^3}$$

PROBLEM 3.20

Write electron configurations for the following elements. (You can check your answers in Table 3.3.)

(a) C   (b) P   (c) Cl   (d) K

PROBLEM 3.21

Write electron configurations for the elements with atomic numbers 14 and 36.

PROBLEM 3.22

For an atom containing 33 electrons, identify the incompletely filled subshell, and show the paired and/or unpaired electrons in this subshell using up and down arrows.

◖● KEY CONCEPT PROBLEM 3.23

Identify the atom with the following orbital-filling diagram.

$$1s^2\ 2s^2\ 2p^6\ 3s^2\ 3p^6 \quad \underset{4s}{\updownarrow} \quad \underset{}{\updownarrow} \;\; \updownarrow \;\; \underset{3d}{\updownarrow} \;\; \updownarrow \;\; \updownarrow \quad \underset{4p}{\uparrow} \;\; \_\_ \;\; \_\_$$

3.8 Electron Configurations and the Periodic Table

How is an atom's electron configuration related to its chemical behavior, and why do elements with similar behavior occur in the same group of the periodic table? As shown in Figure 3.7, the periodic table can be divided into four regions, or *blocks*, of elements according to the electron shells and subshells occupied by *the subshell filled last*.

s-Block element A main group element that results from the filling of an *s* orbital.

p-Block element A main group element that results from the filling of *p* orbitals.

d-Block element A transition metal element that results from the filling of *d* orbitals.

f-Block element An inner transition metal element that results from the filling of *f* orbitals.

- The main group 1A and 2A elements on the left side of the table (plus He) are called the **s-block elements** because an *s* subshell is filled last in these elements.
- The main group 3A–8A elements on the right side of the table (except He) are the **p-block elements** because a *p* subshell is filled last in these elements.
- The transition metals in the middle of the table are the **d-block elements** because a *d* subshell is filled last in these elements.
- The inner transition metals detached at the bottom of the table are the **f-block elements** because an *f* subshell is filled last in these elements.

Thinking of the periodic table as outlined in Figure 3.7 provides a simple way to remember the order of orbital filling shown previously in Figure 3.6. Beginning at the top left corner of the periodic table, the first row contains only two elements (H and He) because only two electrons are required to fill the *s* orbital in the first shell, $1s^2$. The second row begins with two s-block elements (Li and Be) and continues with six p-block elements (B through Ne), so electrons fill the next available *s* orbital (2*s*) and then the first available *p* orbitals (2*p*). The third row is similar to the second row, so the 3*s* and 3*p* orbitals are filled next. The fourth row again starts with two s-block elements (K and Ca) but is then followed by ten d-block elements (Sc through Zn) and six p-block elements (Ga through Kr). Thus, the order of orbital filling is 4*s* followed by the first available *d* orbitals (3*d*) followed by 4*p*. Continuing through successive rows of the periodic table gives the entire filling order, identical to that shown in Figure 3.6.

$$1s \rightarrow 2s \rightarrow 2p \rightarrow 3s \rightarrow 3p \rightarrow 4s \rightarrow 3d \rightarrow 4p \rightarrow 5s \rightarrow$$
$$4d \rightarrow 5p \rightarrow 6s \rightarrow 4f \rightarrow 5d \rightarrow 6p \rightarrow 7s \rightarrow 5f \rightarrow 6d$$

But why do the elements in a given group of the periodic table have similar properties? The answer emerges when you look at Table 3.4, which gives electron

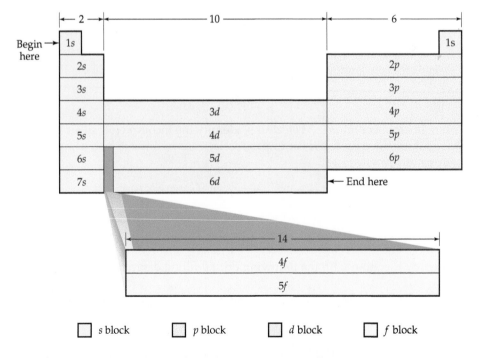

▶ **FIGURE 3.7 The blocks of elements in the periodic table correspond to filling the different types of subshells.** Beginning at the top left and going across successive rows of the periodic table provides a method for remembering the order of orbital filling: $1s \rightarrow 2s \rightarrow 2p \rightarrow 3s \rightarrow 3p \rightarrow 4s \rightarrow 3d \rightarrow 4p$, and so on.

TABLE 3.4   Valence-Shell Electron Configurations for Group 1A, 2A, 7A, and 8A Elements

GROUP	ELEMENT	ATOMIC NUMBER	VALENCE-SHELL ELECTRON CONFIGURATION
1A	Li (lithium)	3	$2s^1$
	Na (sodium)	11	$3s^1$
	K (potassium)	19	$4s^1$
	Rb (rubidium)	37	$5s^1$
	Cs (cesium)	55	$6s^1$
2A	Be (beryllium)	4	$2s^2$
	Mg (magnesium)	12	$3s^2$
	Ca (calcium)	20	$4s^2$
	Sr (strontium)	38	$5s^2$
	Ba (barium)	56	$6s^2$
7A	F (fluorine)	9	$2s^2\,2p^5$
	Cl (chlorine)	17	$3s^2\,3p^5$
	Br (bromine)	35	$4s^2\,4p^5$
	I (iodine)	53	$5s^2\,5p^5$
8A	He (helium)	2	$1s^2$
	Ne (neon)	10	$2s^2\,2p^6$
	Ar (argon)	18	$3s^2\,3p^6$
	Kr (krypton)	36	$4s^2\,4p^6$
	Xe (xenon)	54	$5s^2\,5p^6$

configurations for elements in the main groups 1A, 2A, 7A, and 8A. Focusing only on the electrons in the outermost shell, or **valence shell**, *elements in the same group of the periodic table have similar electron configurations in their valence shells.* The group 1A elements, for example, all have one **valence electron**, ns^1 (where n represents the number of the valence shell: $n = 2$ for Li; $n = 3$ for Na; $n = 4$ for K; and so on). The group 2A elements have two valence electrons (ns^2); the group 7A elements have seven valence electrons ($ns^2\,np^5$); and the group 8A elements (except He) have eight valence electrons ($ns^2\,np^6$). You might also notice that the group numbers from 1A through 8A give the numbers of valence electrons for the elements in each main group.

What is true for the main group elements is also true for the other groups in the periodic table: Atoms within a given group have the same number of valence electrons and have similar electron configurations. *Because the valence electrons are the most loosely held, they are the most important in determining an element's properties.* Similar electron configurations thus explain why the elements in a given group of the periodic table have similar chemical behavior.

⊂⊃⊂ Looking Ahead

We have seen that elements in a given group have similar chemical behavior because they have similar valence electron configurations, and that many chemical properties exhibit periodic trends across the periodic table. The *chemical* behavior of nearly all the elements can be predicted based on their position in the periodic table, and will be examined in more detail in Chapters 4–6. Similarly, the *nuclear* behavior of the different isotopes of a given element is related to the configuration of the nucleus (that is, the number of neutrons and protons), and will be examined in Chapter 11.

Valence shell   The outermost electron shell of an atom.

Valence electron   An electron in the valence shell of an atom.

WORKED EXAMPLE **3.9** Electron Configurations: Valence Electrons

Write the electron configuration for the following elements, using both the complete and the shorthand notations. Indicate which electrons are the valence electrons.

    (a) Na   **(b)** Cl   **(c)** Zr

ANALYSIS Locate the row and the block in which each of the elements is found in Figure 3.7. The location can be used to determine the complete electron configuration and to identify the valence electrons.

SOLUTION

    (a) Na (sodium) is located in the third row, and in the first column of the s-block. Therefore, all orbitals up to the $3s$ are completely filled, and there is one electron in the $3s$ orbital.

        Na: $1s^2\ 2s^2\ 2p^6\ \underline{3s^1}$ or $[\text{Ne}]\ \underline{3s^1}$ (valence electrons are underlined)

    (b) Cl (chlorine) is located in the third row, and in the fifth column of the p-block.

        Cl: $1s^2\ 2s^2\ 2p^6\ \underline{3s^2\ 3p^5}$ or $[\text{Ne}]\ \underline{3s^2\ 3p^5}$

    (c) Zr (zirconium) is located in the fifth row, and in the second column of the d-block. All orbitals up to the $4d$ are completely filled, and there are 2 electrons in the $4d$ orbitals. Note that the $4d$ orbitals are filled after the $5s$ orbitals in both Figures 3.6 and 3.7.

        Zr: $1s^2\ 2s^2\ 2p^6\ 3s^1\ 3p^6\ 4s^2\ 3d^{10}\ 4p^6\ \underline{5s^2\ 4d^2}$ or $[\text{Kr}]\ \underline{5s^2\ 4d^2}$

WORKED EXAMPLE **3.10** Electron Configurations: Valence-Shell
                          Configurations

Using n to represent the number of the valence shell, write a general valence-shell configuration for the elements in group 6A.

ANALYSIS The elements in group 6A have 6 valence electrons. In each element, the first two of these electrons are in the valence s subshell, giving ns^2, and the next four electrons are in the valence p subshell, giving np^4.

SOLUTION
For group 6A, the general valence-shell configuration is $ns^2\ np^4$.

WORKED EXAMPLE **3.11** Electron Configurations: Inner Shells
                          versus Valence Shell

How many electrons are in a tin atom? Give the number of electrons in each shell. How many valence electrons are there in a tin atom? Write the valence-shell configuration for tin.

ANALYSIS The total number of electrons will be the same as the atomic number for tin ($Z = 50$). The number of valence electrons will equal the number of electrons in the valence shell.

SOLUTION

Checking the periodic table shows that tin has atomic number 50 and is in group 4A. The number of electrons in each shell is

Shell number:	1	2	3	4	5
Number of electrons:	2	8	18	18	4

As expected from the group number, tin has 4 valence electrons. They are in the $5s$ and $5p$ subshells and have the configuration $5s^2\,5p^2$.

PROBLEM 3.24

Write the electron configuration for the following elements, using both the complete and the shorthand notations. Indicate which electrons are the valence electrons.

(a) F   **(b)** Al   **(c)** As

PROBLEM 3.25

Identify the group in which all elements have the valence-shell configuration ns^2.

PROBLEM 3.26

For chlorine, identify the group number, give the number of electrons in each occupied shell, and write its valence-shell configuration.

KEY CONCEPT PROBLEM 3.27

Identify the group number, and write the general valence-shell configuration (for example, ns^1 for group 1A elements) for the elements indicated in red in the following periodic table.

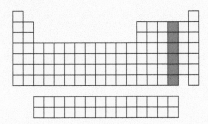

3.9 Electron-Dot Symbols

Valence electrons play such an important role in the behavior of atoms that it is useful to have a method for including them with atomic symbols. In an **electron-dot symbol**, dots are placed around the atomic symbol to indicate the number of valence electrons present. A group 1A atom, such as sodium, has a single dot; a group 2A atom, such as magnesium, has two dots; a group 3A atom, such as boron, has three dots; and so on.

Table 3.5 gives electron-dot symbols for atoms of the first few elements in each main group. As shown, the dots are distributed around the four sides of the element symbol, singly at first until each of the four sides has one dot. As more electron dots

Electron-dot symbol An atomic symbol with dots placed around it to indicate the number of valence electrons.

TABLE 3.5 Electron-Dot Symbols for Some Main Group Elements

1A	2A	3A	4A	5A	6A	7A	NOBLE GASES
H·							He:
Li·	·Be·	·Ḃ·	·Ċ·	·N̈·	·Ö·	·F̈:	:N̈e:
Na·	·Mg·	·Äl·	·S̈i·	·P̈:	·S̈:	·C̈l:	:Är:
K·	·Ca·	·Ga·	·Ge·	·Äs:	·S̈e:	·B̈r:	:K̈r:

are added they will form pairs, with no more than two dots on a side. Note that helium differs from other noble gases in having only two valence electrons rather than eight. Nevertheless, helium is considered a member of group 8A because its properties resemble those of the other noble gases and because its highest occupied subshell is filled ($1s^2$).

WORKED EXAMPLE **3.12** Electron Configurations: Electron-Dot Symbols

Write the electron-dot symbol for any element X in group 5A.

ANALYSIS The group number, 5A, indicates 5 valence electrons. The first four are distributed singly around the four sides of the element symbol, and any additional are placed to form electron pairs.

SOLUTION

 ·Ẍ: (5 electrons)

PROBLEM 3.28

Write the electron-dot symbol for any element X in group 3A.

PROBLEM 3.29

Write electron-dot symbols for radon, lead, xenon, and radium.

APPLICATION ▶ Atoms and Light

What we see as *light* is really a wave of energy moving through space. The shorter the length of the wave (the *wavelength*), the higher the energy; the longer the wavelength, the lower the energy.

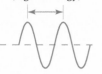

Shorter wavelength (higher energy)   Longer wavelength (lower energy)

Visible light has wavelengths in the range 400–800 nm, but that is just one small part of the overall *electromagnetic spectrum*, shown in the accompanying figure. Although we cannot see the other wavelengths of electromagnetic energy, we use them for many purposes and their names may be familiar to you: gamma rays, X rays, ultraviolet (UV) rays, infrared (IR) rays, microwaves, and radio waves, for example.

What happens when a beam of electromagnetic energy collides with an atom? Remember that electrons are located in orbitals based on their energy levels. An atom with its electrons in their usual, lowest-energy locations is said to be in its *ground state.* If the amount of electromagnetic energy is just right, an electron can be kicked up from its usual energy level to a higher one. Energy from an electrical discharge or in the form of heat can have the same effect. With one of its electrons promoted to a higher energy, an atom is said to be *excited.* The excited state does not last long, though, because the electron quickly drops back to its more stable, ground-state energy level, releasing its extra energy in the process. If the released energy falls in the range of visible light, we can see the result. Many practical applications, from neon lights to fireworks, are the result of this phenomenon.

In "neon" lights, noble gas atoms are excited by an electric discharge, giving rise to a variety of colors that depend on the gas—red from neon, white from krypton, and blue from argon. Similarly, mercury or sodium atoms excited by electrical energy are responsible for the intense bluish or yellowish light, respectively, provided by some street lamps. In the same manner, metal atoms excited by heat are responsible for the spectacular colors of fireworks—red from strontium, green from barium, and blue from copper, for example.

The concentration of certain metals in body fluids is measured by sensitive instruments relying on the same principle of electron excitation that we see in fireworks. These instruments determine the intensity of the flame color produced by lithium (red), sodium (yellow), and potassium (violet),

▲ The brilliant colors of fireworks are due to the release of energy from excited atoms as electrons fall from higher to lower energy levels.

yielding the concentrations of these metals given in most clinical lab reports. Calcium, magnesium, copper, and zinc concentrations are also found by measuring the energies of excited atoms.

See Additional Problems 3.94 and 3.95 at the end of the chapter.

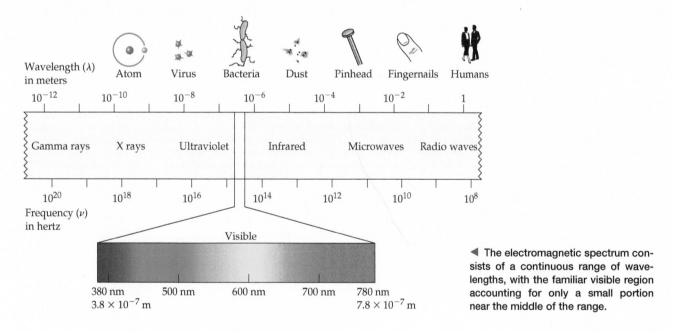

◀ The electromagnetic spectrum consists of a continuous range of wavelengths, with the familiar visible region accounting for only a small portion near the middle of the range.

SUMMARY: REVISITING THE CHAPTER GOALS

1. What is the modern theory of atomic structure? All matter is composed of *atoms.* An atom is the smallest and simplest unit into which a sample of an element can be divided while maintaining the properties of the element. Atoms are made up of subatomic particles called *protons, neutrons,* and *electrons.* Protons have a positive electrical charge, neutrons are electrically neutral, and electrons have a negative electrical charge. The protons and neutrons in an atom are present in a dense, positively charged central region called

KEY WORDS

Alkali metal, *p. 60*

Alkaline earth metal, *p. 60*

Atom, *p. 49*

Atomic mass unit (amu), *p. 50*

the *nucleus*. Electrons are situated a relatively large distance away from the nucleus, leaving most of the atom as empty space.

2. **How do atoms of different elements differ?** Elements differ according to the number of protons their atoms contain, a value called the element's *atomic number* (Z). All atoms of a given element have the same number of protons and an equal number of electrons. The number of neutrons in an atom is not predictable but is generally as great or greater than the number of protons. The total number of protons plus neutrons in an atom is called the atom's *mass number* (A).

3. **What are isotopes, and what is atomic weight?** Atoms with identical numbers of protons and electrons but different numbers of neutrons are called *isotopes*. The atomic weight of an element is the weighted average mass of atoms of the element's naturally occurring isotopes measured in *atomic mass units* (amu).

4. **How is the periodic table arranged?** Elements are organized into the *periodic table*, consisting of 7 rows, or *periods*, and 18 columns, or *groups*. The two groups on the left side of the table and the six groups on the right are called the *main group elements*. The ten groups in the middle are the *transition metal groups*, and the 14 groups pulled out and displayed below the main part of the table are called the *inner transition metal groups*. Within a given group in the table, elements have the same number of valence electrons in their valence shell and similar electron configurations.

5. **How are electrons arranged in atoms?** The electrons surrounding an atom are grouped into layers, or *shells*. Within each shell, electrons are grouped into *subshells*, and within each subshell into *orbitals*—regions of space in which electrons are most likely to be found. The s orbitals are spherical, and the p orbitals are dumbbell-shaped.

Each shell can hold a specific number of electrons. The first shell can hold 2 electrons in an s orbital ($1s^2$); the second shell can hold 8 electrons in one s and three p orbitals ($2s^2\ 2p^6$); the third shell can hold 18 electrons in one s, three p, and five d orbitals ($3s^2\ 3p^6\ 3d^{10}$); and so on. The *electron configuration* of an element is predicted by assigning the element's electrons into orbitals, beginning with the lowest-energy orbital. The electrons in the outermost shell, or *valence shell*, can be represented using electron-dot symbols.

UNDERSTANDING KEY CONCEPTS

3.30 Which of the following drawings represents an s orbital, and which represents a p orbital?

     (a)   **(b)**

3.31 Where on the following outline of a periodic table do the indicated elements or groups of elements appear?

   (a) Alkali metals   **(b)** Halogens
   (c) Alkaline earth metals **(d)** Transition metals
   (e) Hydrogen   **(f)** Helium   **(g)** Metalloids

3.32 Is the element marked in red on the following periodic table likely to be a gas, a liquid, or a solid? What is the atomic number of the element in blue? Name at least one other element that is likely to be chemically similar to the element in green.

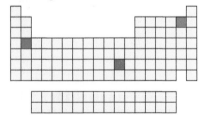

3.33 Use the blank periodic table at the top of the next page to show where elements matching the following descriptions appear.

(a) Elements with the valence-shell electron configuration $ns^2\,np^5$

(b) An element whose third shell contains two p electrons

(c) Elements with a completely filled valence shell

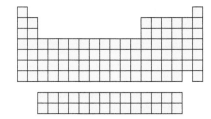

3.34 What atom has the following orbital-filling diagram?

$1s^2\,2s^2\,2p^6\,3s^2\,3p^6$ $\underline{\uparrow\downarrow}$ $\underline{\uparrow\downarrow}\ \underline{\uparrow\downarrow}\ \underline{\uparrow\downarrow}\ \underline{\uparrow\downarrow}\ \underline{\uparrow\downarrow}$ $\underline{\uparrow\downarrow}\ \underline{\uparrow}\ \underline{\uparrow}$

$\qquad\qquad\quad 4s\qquad\qquad\quad 3d\qquad\qquad\qquad 4p$

3.35 Use the orbital-filling diagram below to show the electron configuration for As:

$1s^2\,2s^2\,2p^6\,3s^2\,3p^6$ $\underline{\quad}$ $\underline{\quad}\ \underline{\quad}\ \underline{\quad}\ \underline{\quad}\ \underline{\quad}$ $\underline{\quad}\ \underline{\quad}\ \underline{\quad}$

$\qquad\qquad\quad 4s\qquad\qquad\quad 3d\qquad\qquad\qquad 4p$

ADDITIONAL PROBLEMS

ATOMIC THEORY AND THE COMPOSITION OF ATOMS

3.36 What four fundamental assumptions about atoms and matter make up modern atomic theory?

3.37 How do atoms of different elements differ?

3.38 Find the mass in grams of one atom of the following elements:

(a) Bi, atomic weight 208.9804 amu
(b) Xe, atomic weight 131.29 amu
(c) He, atomic weight 4.0026 amu

3.39 Find the mass in atomic mass units of the following:

(a) 1 O atom, with a mass of 2.66×10^{-23} g
(b) 1 Br atom, with a mass of 1.31×10^{-22} g

3.40 What is the mass in grams of 6.022×10^{23} N atoms of mass 14.01 amu?

3.41 What is the mass in grams of 6.022×10^{23} O atoms of mass 16.00 amu?

3.42 How many O atoms of mass 15.99 amu are in 15.99 g of oxygen?

3.43 How many C atoms of mass 12.00 amu are in 12.00 g of carbon?

3.44 What are the names of the three subatomic particles? What are their approximate masses in atomic mass units, and what electrical charge does each have?

3.45 Where within an atom are the three types of subatomic particles located?

3.46 Identify the following atoms:

(a) Contains 19 protons
(b) Contains 50 protons
(c) Has $Z = 30$

3.47 Identify the following atoms:

(a) Contains 15 electrons
(b) Contains 41 protons
(c) Has $Z = 27$

3.48 Give the number of neutrons in each naturally occurring isotope of argon: argon-36, argon-38, argon-40.

3.49 Give the number of protons, neutrons, and electrons in the following isotopes:

(a) Al-27
(b) $^{28}_{14}\text{Si}$
(c) B-11
(d) $^{115}_{47}\text{Ag}$

3.50 Which of the following symbols represent isotopes of the same element?

(a) $^{19}_{9}\text{X}$ **(b)** $^{19}_{10}\text{X}$
(c) $^{21}_{9}\text{X}$ **(d)** $^{21}_{12}\text{X}$

3.51 Complete the following isotope symbols:

(a) $^{206}_{?}\text{Po}$ **(b)** $^{224}_{88}\text{?}$
(c) $^{197}_{79}\text{?}$ **(d)** $^{84}_{?}\text{Kr}$

3.52 Name the isotope represented by each symbol in Problem 3.50.

3.53 Give the number of neutrons in each isotope listed in Problem 3.51.

3.54 Write the symbols for the following isotopes:

(a) Its atoms contain 6 protons and 8 neutrons.
(b) Its atoms have mass number 39 and contain 19 protons.
(c) Its atoms have mass number 20 and contain 10 electrons.

3.55 Write the symbols for the following isotopes:

(a) Its atoms contain 9 electrons and 10 neutrons.
(b) Its atoms have $A = 79$ and $Z = 35$.
(c) Its atoms have $A = 51$ and contain 23 electrons.

3.56 There are three naturally occurring isotopes of carbon, with mass numbers of 12, 13, and 14. How many neutrons does each have? Write the symbol for each isotope, indicating its atomic number and mass number.

3.57 The isotope of iodine with mass number 131 is often used in medicine as a radioactive tracer. Write the symbol for this isotope, indicating both mass number and atomic number.

3.58 Naturally occurring copper is a mixture of 69.17% ^{63}Cu with a mass of 62.93 amu and 30.83% ^{65}Cu with a mass of 64.93 amu. What is the atomic weight of copper?

3.59 Naturally occurring lithium is a mixture of 92.58% ^{7}Li with a mass of 7.016 amu and 7.42% ^{6}Li with a mass of 6.015 amu. What is the atomic weight of lithium?

THE PERIODIC TABLE

3.60 Why does the third period in the periodic table contain eight elements?

3.61 Why does the fourth period in the periodic table contain 18 elements?

3.62 Americium, atomic number 95, is used in household smoke detectors. What is the symbol for americium? Is americium a metal, a nonmetal, or a metalloid?

3.63 Antimony, Z = 51, is alloyed with lead for use in automobile batteries. What is the symbol for antimony? Is antimony a metal, a nonmetal, or a metalloid?

3.64 Answer the following questions for the elements from scandium through zinc:

(a) Are they metals or nonmetals?
(b) To what general class of elements do they belong?
(c) What subshell is being filled by electrons in these elements?

3.65 Answer the following questions for the elements from cerium through lutetium:

(a) Are they metals or nonmetals?
(b) To what general class of elements do they belong?
(c) What subshell is being filled by electrons in these elements?

3.66 For (a) rubidium (b) tungsten, (c) germanium, and (d) krypton, which of the following terms apply? (i) metal, (ii) nonmetal, (iii) metalloid (iv) transition element, (v) main group element, (vi) noble gas, (vii) alkali metal, (viii) alkaline earth metal

3.67 For (a) calcium, (b) palladium, (c) carbon, and (d) radon, which of the following terms apply? (i) metal, (ii) nonmetal, (iii) metalloid (iv) transition element, (v) main group element, (vi) noble gas, (vii) alkali metal, (viii) alkaline earth metal

3.68 Name an element in the periodic table that you would expect to be chemically similar to sulfur.

3.69 Name an element in the periodic table that you would expect to be chemically similar to magnesium

3.70 What elements in addition to lithium make up the alkali metal family?

3.71 What elements in addition to fluorine make up the halogen family?

ELECTRON CONFIGURATIONS

3.72 What is the maximum number of electrons that can go into an orbital?

3.73 What are the shapes and locations within an atom of s and p orbitals?

3.74 What is the maximum number of electrons that can go into the first shell? The second shell? The third shell?

3.75 What is the total number of orbitals in the third shell? The fourth shell?

3.76 How many subshells are there in the third shell? The fourth shell? The fifth shell?

3.77 How many orbitals would you expect to find in the last subshell of the fifth shell? How many electrons would you need to fill this subshell?

3.78 How many electrons are present in an atom with its $1s$, $2s$, and $2p$ subshells filled? What is this element?

3.79 How many electrons are present in an atom with its $1s$, $2s$, $2p$, and $3s$ subshells filled and with two electrons in the $3p$ subshell? What is this element?

3.80 Use arrows to show electron pairing in the valence p subshell of:

(a) Sulfur
(b) Bromine
(c) Silicon

3.81 Use arrows to show electron pairing in the $5s$ and $4d$ orbitals of:

(a) Strontium
(b) Technetium
(c) Palladium

3.82 Determine the number of unpaired electrons for each of the atoms in Problems 3.80 and 3.81.

3.83 Without looking back in the text, write the electron configurations for the following:

(a) Calcium, Z = 20
(b) Sulfur, Z = 16
(c) Fluorine, Z = 9
(d) Cadmium, Z = 48

3.84 How many electrons does the element with Z = 12 have in its valence shell? Write the electron-dot symbol for this element.

3.85 How many valence electrons do group 4A elements have? Explain. Write a generic electron-dot symbol for elements in this group.

3.86 Identify the valence subshell occupied by electrons in beryllium and arsenic atoms.

3.87 What group in the periodic table has the valence-shell configuration $ns^2\,np^3$?

3.88 Give the number of valence electrons and draw electron-dot symbols for atoms of the following elements:

(a) Kr   (b) C
(c) Ca   (d) K
(e) B   (f) Cl

3.89 Using n for the number of the valence shell, write a general valence-shell configuration for the elements in group 7A and in group 1A.

Applications

3.90 What is the advantage of using a scanning tunneling microscope rather than a normal light microscope? [*Are Atoms Real? p. 52*]

3.91 Before Rutherford's experiments, atomic structure was represented using a *"plum pudding" model* proposed by Thomson, in which negatively charged electrons were embedded in diffuse, positively charged matter like raisins in plum pudding. How might Rutherford's experimental results have been different if this model were correct? [*Are Atoms Real? p. 52*]

3.92 What are the first two elements that are made in stars? [*The Origin of Chemical Elements, p. 61*]

3.93 How are elements heavier than iron made? [*The Origin of Chemical Elements, p. 61*]

3.94 Which type of electromagnetic energy in the following pairs is of higher energy? [*Atoms and Light, p. 72*]

(a) Infrared, ultraviolet
(b) Gamma waves, microwaves
(c) Visible light, X rays

3.95 Why do you suppose ultraviolet rays from the sun are more damaging to the skin than visible light? [*Atoms and Light, p. 72*]

General Questions and Problems

3.96 What elements in addition to helium make up the noble gas family?

3.97 Hydrogen is placed in group 1A on many periodic charts, even though it is not an alkali metal. On other periodic charts, however, hydrogen is included with group 7A even though it is not a halogen. Explain. (Hint: draw electron-dot symbols for H and for the 1A and 7A elements.)

3.98 Tellurium ($Z = 52$) has a *lower* atomic number than iodine ($Z = 53$), yet it has a *higher* atomic weight (127.60 amu for Te versus 126.90 amu for I). How is this possible?

3.99 What is the atomic number of the yet undiscovered element directly below francium (Fr) in the periodic table?

3.100 Give the number of electrons in each shell for lead.

3.101 Identify the highest-energy occupied subshell in atoms of the following elements:

(a) Argon
(b) Magnesium
(c) Technetium
(d) Iron

3.102 What is the atomic weight of naturally occurring bromine, which contains 50.69% Br-79 of mass 78.92 amu and 49.31% Br-81 of mass 80.91 amu?

3.103 Naturally occurring magnesium consists of three isotopes: 78.99% ^{24}Mg with a mass of 23.99 amu, 10.00% ^{25}Mg with a mass of 24.99 amu, and 11.01% ^{26}Mg with a mass of 25.98 amu. Calculate the atomic weight of magnesium.

3.104 If you had one atom of hydrogen and one atom of carbon, which would weigh more? Explain.

3.105 If you had a pile of 10^{23} hydrogen atoms and another pile of 10^{23} carbon atoms, which of the two piles would weigh more? (See Problem 3.104.)

3.106 If your pile of hydrogen atoms in Problem 3.105 weighed about 1 gram, how much would your pile of carbon atoms weigh?

3.107 Based on your answer to Problem 3.106, how much would you expect a pile of 10^{23} sodium atoms to weigh?

3.108 An unidentified element is found to have an electron configuration by shell of 2 8 18 8 2. To what group and period does this element belong? Is the element a metal or a nonmetal? How many protons does an atom of the element have? What is the name of the element? Write its electron-dot symbol.

3.109 Germanium, atomic number 32, is used in building semiconductors for microelectronic devices. If germanium, has an electron configuration by shell of 2 8 18 4, in what orbital are the valence electrons?

3.110 Tin, atomic number 50, is directly beneath germanium (Problem 3.109) in the periodic table. What electron configuration by shell would you expect tin to have? Is tin a metal or a nonmetal?

3.111 A blood sample is found to contain 8.6 mg/dL of Ca. How many atoms of Ca are present in 8.6 mg? The atomic weight of Ca is 40.08 amu.

3.112 What is wrong with the following electron configurations?

(a) Ni $1s^2\, 2s^2\, 2p^6\, 3s^2\, 3p^6\, 3d^{10}$
(b) N $1s^2\, 2p^5$
(c) Si $1s^2\, 2s^2\, 2p$ ↑↓ __ __
(d) Mg $1s^2\, 2s^2\, 2p^6\, 3s$ ↑↑

3.113 Not all elements follow exactly the electron-filling order described in Figure 3.7. Atoms of which elements are represented by the following electron configurations? (Hint: count the total number of electrons!)

(a) $1s^2\, 2s^2\, 2p^6\, 3s^2\, 3p^6\, 3d^5\, 4s^1$
(b) $1s^2\, 2s^2\, 2p^6\, 3s^2\, 3p^6\, 3d^{10}\, 4s^1$
(c) $1s^2\, 2s^2\, 2p^6\, 3s^2\, 3p^6\, 3d^{10}\, 4s^2\, 4p^6\, 4d^5\, 5s^1$
(d) $1s^2\, 2s^2\, 2p^6\, 3s^2\, 3p^6\, 3d^{10}\, 4s^2\, 4p^6\, 4d^{10}\, 5s^1$

3.114 What similarities do you see in the electron configurations for the atoms in Problem 3.113? How might these similarities explain their anomalous electron configurations?

3.115 What orbital is filled last in the yet undiscovered element 117?

CHAPTER 4

Ionic Compounds

CONCEPTS TO REVIEW

The Periodic Table
(Sections 3.4 and 3.5)

Electron Configurations
(Sections 3.7 and 3.8)

▲ Stalagmites and stalactites, such as these in a cave in the Nangu Stone Forest in China, are composed of the ionic compounds calcium carbonate, $CaCO_3$, and magnesium carbonate, $MgCO_3$.

CONTENTS

CHAPTER GOALS

We will answer the following questions in this chapter:

1. **What is an ion, what is an ionic bond, and what are the general characteristics of ionic compounds?**

   THE GOAL: Be able to describe ions and ionic bonds, and give the general properties of compounds that contain ionic bonds.

2. **What is the octet rule, and how does it apply to ions?**

   THE GOAL: Be able to state the octet rule and use it to predict the electron configurations of ions of main group elements.

3. **What is the relationship between an element's position in the periodic table and the formation of its ion?**

   THE GOAL: Be able to predict what ions are likely to be formed by atoms of a given element.

4. **What determines the chemical formula of an ionic compound?**

   THE GOAL: Be able to write formulas for ionic compounds, given the identities of the ions.

5. **How are ionic compounds named?**

   THE GOAL: Be able to name an ionic compound from its formula or give the formula of a compound from its name.

6. **What are acids and bases?**

   THE GOAL: Be able to recognize common acids and bases.

There are more than 19 million known chemical compounds, ranging in size from small *diatomic* (two-atom) substances like carbon monoxide, CO, to deoxyribonucleic acid (DNA), which can contain several *billion* atoms linked together in a precise way. Clearly, there must be some force that holds atoms together in compounds; otherwise, the atoms would simply drift apart and no compounds could exist. The forces that hold atoms together are called *chemical bonds* and are of two major types: *ionic bonds* and *covalent bonds*. In this chapter, we look at ionic bonds and at the substances formed by them. In the next chapter, we will look at covalent bonds.

All chemical bonds result from the electrical attraction between opposite charges—between positively charged nuclei and negatively charged electrons. As a result, the way in which different elements form bonds is related to their different electron configurations.

4.1 Ions

A general rule noted by early chemists is that metals, on the left side of the periodic table, tend to form compounds with nonmetals, on the right side of the table. The alkali metals of group 1A, for instance, react with the halogens of group 7A to form a variety of compounds. Sodium chloride (table salt), formed by the reaction of sodium with chlorine, is a familiar example. The names and chemical formulas of some other compounds containing elements from groups 1A and 7A include:

Potassium iodide, KI   Added to table salt to provide iodide ion needed by the thyroid gland

Sodium fluoride, NaF   Added to many municipal water supplies to provide fluoride ion for the prevention of tooth decay

Sodium iodide, NaI   Used in laboratory scintillation counters to detect radiation (See Section 11.8)

Both the compositions and the properties of these alkali metal–halogen compounds are similar. For instance, the two elements always combine in a 1:1 ratio: one alkali metal atom for every halogen atom. Each compound has a high melting point (all are over 500 °C); each is a stable, white, crystalline solid; and each is soluble in water. Furthermore, the water solution of each compound conducts electricity, a property that gives a clue to the kind of chemical bond holding the atoms together.

Electricity can flow only through a medium containing charged particles that are free to move. The electrical conductivity of metals, for example, results from the

▲ A solution of sodium chloride in water conducts electricity, allowing the bulb to light.

movement of negatively charged electrons through the metal. But what charged particles might be present in the water solutions of alkali metal–halogen compounds? To answer this question, think about the composition of atoms. Atoms are electrically neutral because they contain equal numbers of protons and electrons. By gaining or losing one or more electrons, however, an atom can be converted into a charged particle called an **ion**.

Ion   An electrically charged atom or group of atoms.

The *loss* of one or more electrons from a neutral atom gives a *positively* charged ion called a **cation** (cat-ion). As we saw in Section 3.8, sodium and other alkali metal atoms have a single electron in their valence shell and an electron configuration symbolized as ns^1, where n represents the shell number. By losing this electron, an alkali metal is converted to a cation.

Cation   A positively charged ion.

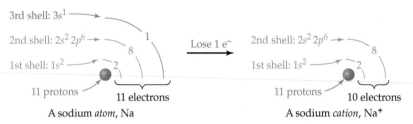

Anion   A negatively charged ion.

Conversely, the *gain* of one or more electrons by a neutral atom gives a *negatively* charged ion called an **anion** (an-ion). Chlorine and other halogen atoms have $ns^2 np^5$ valence electrons and can easily gain an additional electron to fill out their valence subshell, thereby forming anions.

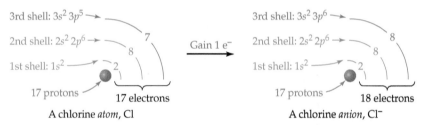

The symbol for a cation is written by adding the positive charge as a superscript to the symbol for the element; an anion symbol is written by adding the negative charge as a superscript. If one electron is lost or gained, the charge is +1 or −1 but the number 1 is omitted in the notation, as in Na^+ and Cl^-. If two or more electrons are lost or gained, however, the charge is ±2 or greater and the number *is* used, as in Ca^{2+} and N^{3-}.

PROBLEM 4.1

Magnesium atoms lose two electrons when they react. Write the symbol of the ion that results. Is it a cation or an anion?

PROBLEM 4.2

Sulfur atoms gain two electrons when they react. Write the symbol of the ion that results. Is it a cation or an anion?

➥ KEY CONCEPT PROBLEM 4.3

Write the symbol for the ion depicted here. Is it a cation or an anion?

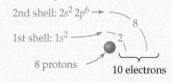

4.2 Periodic Properties and Ion Formation

The ease with which an atom loses an electron to form a positively charged cation is measured by a property called the atom's **ionization energy**, defined as the energy required to remove one electron from a single atom in the gaseous state. Conversely, the ease with which an atom *gains* an electron to form a negatively charged anion is measured by a property called **electron affinity**, defined as the energy released on adding an electron to a single atom in the gaseous state.

Ionization energy The energy required to remove one electron from a single atom in the gaseous state.

Electron affinity The energy released on adding an electron to a single atom in the gaseous state.

Ionization energy
(energy is added)
$$\text{Atom} + \text{Energy} \longrightarrow \text{Cation} + \text{Electron}$$

Electron affinity
(energy is released)
$$\text{Atom} + \text{Electron} \longrightarrow \text{Anion} + \text{Energy}$$

The relative magnitudes of ionization energies and electron affinities for elements in the first four rows of the periodic table are shown in Figure 4.1. Because ionization energy measures the amount of energy that must be *added* to pull an electron away from a neutral atom, the small values shown in Figure 4.1 for alkali metals (Li, Na, K) and other elements on the left side of the periodic table mean that these elements lose an electron easily. Conversely, the large values shown for halogens (F, Cl, Br) and noble gases (He, Ne, Ar, Kr) on the right side of the periodic table mean that these elements do not lose an electron easily. Electron affinities, however, measure the amount of energy *released* when an atom gains an electron. Although electron affinities are small compared to ionization energies, the halogens nevertheless have the largest values and therefore gain an electron most easily, whereas metals have the smallest values and do not gain an electron easily:

Alkali metal
{
Small ionization energy—electron easily lost
Small electron affinity—electron not easily gained
Net result: Cation formation is favored.
}

Halogen
{
Large ionization energy—electron not easily lost
Large electron affinity—electron easily gained
Net result: Anion formation is favored.
}

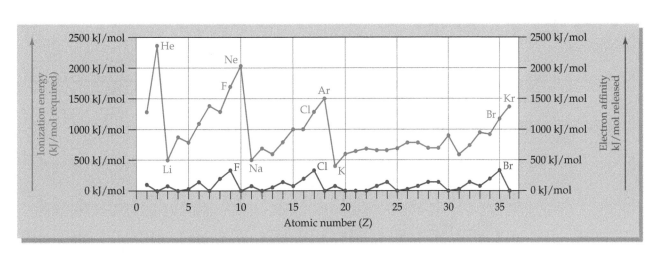

▲ **FIGURE 4.1 Relative ionization energies (red) and electron affinities (blue) for elements in the first four rows of the periodic table.** Those elements having a value of zero for electron affinity do not accept an electron. Note that the alkali metals (Li, Na, K) have the lowest ionization energies and lose an electron most easily, whereas the halogens (F, Cl, Br) have the highest electron affinities and gain an electron most easily. The noble gases (He, Ne, Ar, Kr) neither gain nor lose an electron easily.

You might also note in Figure 4.1 that main group elements near the *middle* of the periodic table—boron (Z = 5), carbon (Z = 6, group 4A), and nitrogen (Z = 7, group 5A)—neither lose nor gain electrons easily and thus do not form ions easily. In the next chapter, we will see that these elements tend not to form ionic bonds but form covalent bonds instead.

Because alkali metals such as sodium tend to lose an electron, and halogens such as chlorine tend to gain an electron, these two elements (sodium and chlorine) will react with each other by transfer of an electron from the metal to the halogen (Figure 4.2). The product that results—sodium chloride (NaCl)—is electrically neutral because the positive charge of each Na^+ ion is balanced by the negative charge of each Cl^- ion.

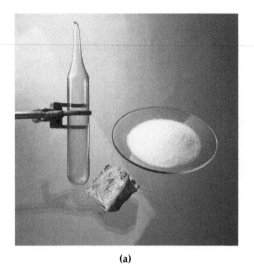

(a)   **(b)**

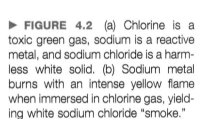

▶ **FIGURE 4.2** (a) Chlorine is a toxic green gas, sodium is a reactive metal, and sodium chloride is a harmless white solid. (b) Sodium metal burns with an intense yellow flame when immersed in chlorine gas, yielding white sodium chloride "smoke."

WORKED EXAMPLE   **4.1** Periodic Trends: Ionization Energy

Look at the periodic trends in Figure 4.1, and predict where the ionization energy of rubidium is likely to fall on the chart.

ANALYSIS Identify the group number of rubidium (group 1A), and find where other members of the group appear in Figure 4.1.

SOLUTION
Rubidium (Rb) is the alkali metal below potassium (K) in the periodic table. Since the alkali metals Li, Na, and K all have ionization energies near the bottom of the chart, the ionization energy of rubidium is probably similar.

WORKED EXAMPLE   **4.2** Periodic Trends: Formation of Anions and Cations

Which element is likely to lose an electron more easily, Mg or S?

ANALYSIS Identify the group numbers of the elements, and find where members of those groups appear in Figure 4.1.

SOLUTION
Magnesium, a group 2A element on the left side of the periodic table, has a relatively low ionization energy, and loses an electron easily. Sulfur, a group 6A element on the right side of the table, has a higher ionization energy, and loses an electron less easily.

PROBLEM 4.4

Look at the periodic trends in Figure 4.1, and predict approximately where the ionization energy of xenon is likely to fall.

PROBLEM 4.5

Which element in the following pairs is likely to lose an electron more easily?

(a) Be or B   **(b)** Ca or Co   **(c)** Sc or Se

PROBLEM 4.6

Which element in the following pairs is likely to gain an electron more easily?

(a) H or He   **(b)** S or Si   **(c)** Cr or Mn

4.3 Ionic Bonds

When sodium reacts with chlorine, the product is sodium chloride, a compound completely unlike either of the elements from which it is formed. Sodium is a soft, silvery metal that reacts violently with water, and chlorine is a corrosive, poisonous, green gas (Figure 4.2a). When chemically combined, however, they produce our familiar table salt containing Na^+ ions and Cl^- ions. Because opposite electrical charges attract each other, the positive Na^+ ion and negative Cl^- ion are said to be held together by an **ionic bond.**

When a vast number of sodium atoms transfer electrons to an equally vast number of chlorine atoms, a visible crystal of sodium chloride results. In this crystal, equal numbers of Na^+ and Cl^- ions are packed together in a regular arrangement. Each positively charged Na^+ ion is surrounded by six negatively charged Cl^- ions, and each Cl^- ion is surrounded by six Na^+ ions (Figure 4.3). This packing arrangement allows each ion to be stabilized by the attraction of unlike charges on its six nearest-neighbor ions, while being as far as possible from ions of like charge.

Because of the three-dimensional arrangement of ions in a sodium chloride crystal, we cannot speak of specific ionic bonds between specific pairs of ions. Rather, there are many ions attracted by ionic bonds to their nearest neighbors. We therefore speak of the whole NaCl crystal as being an **ionic solid** and of such compounds as being **ionic compounds.** The same is true of all compounds composed of ions.

Ionic bond The electrical attractions between ions of opposite charge in a crystal.

Ionic solid A crystalline solid held together by ionic bonds.

Ionic compound A compound that contains ionic bonds.

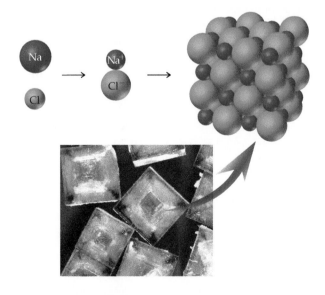

◀ **FIGURE 4.3 The arrangement of Na^+ and Cl^- ions in a sodium chloride crystal.** Each positively charged Na^+ ion is surrounded by six negatively charged Cl^- ions, and each Cl^- ion is surrounded by six Na^+ ions. The crystal is held together by ionic bonds—the attraction between oppositely charged ions.

▲ The melting point of sodium chloride is 801 °C.

4.4 Some Properties of Ionic Compounds

Like sodium chloride, ionic compounds are usually crystalline solids. Different ions vary in size and charge, however, and therefore are packed together in crystals in different ways. The ions in each compound settle into a pattern that efficiently fills space and maximizes ionic bonding.

Because the ions in an ionic solid are held rigidly in place by attraction to their neighbors, they cannot move about. Once an ionic solid is dissolved in water, however, the ions can move freely, thereby accounting for the electrical conductivity of these compounds in solution.

The high melting points and boiling points observed for ionic compounds are also accounted for by ionic bonding. The attractive force between oppositely charged particles is extremely strong, and the ions need to gain a large amount of energy by being heated to high temperatures for them to loosen their grip on one another. Sodium chloride, for example, melts at 801 °C and boils at 1413 °C; potassium iodide melts at 681 °C and boils at 1330 °C.

Despite the strength of ionic bonds, ionic solids shatter if struck sharply. A blow disrupts the orderly arrangement of cations and anions, and the electrical repulsion between ions of like charge that have been pushed together helps to split apart the crystal.

Ionic compounds dissolve in water if the attraction between water and the ions overcomes the attraction of the ions for one another. Compounds like sodium chloride are very soluble and can be dissolved to make solutions of high concentration. Do not be misled, however, by the ease with which sodium chloride and other familiar ionic compounds dissolve in water. Many other ionic compounds are not water-soluble, because water is unable to overcome the ionic forces in many crystals.

4.5 Ions and the Octet Rule

We have seen that alkali metal atoms have a single valence-shell electron, ns^1. The electron-dot symbol $X \cdot$ is consistent with this valence electron configuration. Halogens, having seven valence electrons, ns^2np^5, can be represented using $:\ddot{X}\cdot$ as the electron-dot symbol. Noble gases can be represented as $:\ddot{X}:$, since they have eight valence electrons, ns^2np^6. Both the alkali metals and the halogens are extremely reactive, undergoing many chemical reactions and forming many compounds. The noble gases, however, are quite different. They are the least reactive of all elements.

Now look at sodium chloride and similar ionic compounds. When sodium or any other alkali metal reacts with chlorine or any other halogen, the metal transfers an electron from its valence shell to the valence shell of the halogen. Sodium thereby changes its valence-shell electron configuration from $2s^22p^63s^1$ in the atom to $2s^22p^6(3s^0)$ in the Na^+ ion, and chlorine changes from $3s^23p^5$ in the atom to $3s^23p^6$ in the Cl^- ion. *In so doing, both sodium and chlorine gain noble gas electron configurations, with 8 valence electrons.* The Na^+ ion has 8 electrons in the $n = 2$ shell, matching the electron configuration of neon. The Cl^- ion has 8 electrons in the $n = 3$ shell, matching the electron configuration of argon.

$$\underset{1s^2\,2s^2\,2p^6\,3s^1}{Na} \;+\; \underset{1s^2\,2s^2\,2p^6\,3s^2\,3p^5}{Cl} \;\longrightarrow\; \underset{\underbrace{1s^2\,2s^2\,2p^63s^0}_{\substack{\text{Neon}\\\text{configuration}}}}{Na^+} \;+\; \underset{\underbrace{1s^2\,2s^2\,2p^6\,3s^2\,3p^6}_{\substack{\text{Argon}\\\text{configuration}}}}{Cl^-}$$

$$Na\cdot \;+\; \cdot\ddot{\underset{\cdot\cdot}{Cl}}: \;\longrightarrow\; Na \;+\; :\ddot{\underset{\cdot\cdot}{Cl}}:$$

Evidently there is something special about having 8 valence electrons (filled *s* and *p* subshells) that leads to stability and lack of chemical reactivity. In fact,

APPLICATION ▶ Minerals and Gems

If you are wearing a sapphire, ruby, emerald, or zircon ring, you have a crystalline ionic compound on your finger. The gem came from the earth's crust, the source of most of our chemical raw materials. These gemstones are *minerals*, which to a geologist means that they are naturally occurring, crystalline chemical compounds. (To a nutritionist, by contrast, a "mineral" is one of the metal ions essential to human health.)

Sapphire and ruby are forms of the mineral *corundum*, or aluminum oxide (Al_2O_3). The blue of sapphire is due to traces of iron and titanium ions also present in the crystal, and the red of ruby is due to traces of chromium ions. Many minerals are *silicates*, meaning that their anions contain silicon and oxygen combined in a variety of ways. Zircon is zirconium silicate ($ZrSiO_4$), and emerald is a form of the mineral beryl, $Be_3Al_2(Si_6O_{18})$, which is composed of Al^{3+}, Be^{2+}, and silicate rings.

Many minerals not sufficiently beautiful for use in jewelry are valuable as sources for the exotic metals so essential to our industrial civilization. Extraction of the metals from these minerals requires energy and a series of chemical reactions to convert the metal ions into free elements—the reverse of ion formation from atoms.

See Additional Problem 4.82 at the end of the chapter.

(a)

(b)

(c)

▲ Many minerals are silicates, which are compounds made up of polyatomic anions of silicon and oxygen. Their colors are determined largely by the cations they contain. (a) A crystal of tourmaline, a complex silicate of boron, aluminum, and other elements. (b) Dioptase from Namibia and (c) epidote from Pakistan.

observations of a great many chemical compounds have shown that main group elements frequently combine in such a way that each winds up with 8 valence electrons, a so-called *electron octet*. This conclusion is summarized in a statement called the **octet rule**:

Octet rule   Main group elements tend to undergo reactions that leave them with 8 valence electrons.

Put another way, main group *metals* tend to lose electrons when they react so that they attain an electron configuration like that of the noble gas just *before* them in the periodic table, and reactive main group *nonmetals* tend to gain electrons when they react so that they attain an electron configuration like that of the noble gas just *after* them in the periodic table. In both cases, the product ions have filled *s* and *p* subshells in their valence electron shell.

WORKED EXAMPLE **4.3** Electron Configurations: Octet Rule for Cations

Write the electron configuration of magnesium ($Z = 12$). Show how many electrons a magnesium atom must lose to form an ion with a valence octet, and write the configuration of the ion. Explain the reason for the ion's charge, and write the ion's symbol.

ANALYSIS Write the electron configuration of magnesium as described in Section 3.7 and count the number of electrons in the valence shell.

SOLUTION

Magnesium has the electron configuration $1s^2 2s^2 2p^6 3s^2$. Since the second shell contains an octet of electrons ($2s^2 2p^6$) whereas the third shell is only partially filled ($3s^2$), magnesium can achieve a valence-shell octet by losing the two electrons in the $3s$ subshell. The result is formation of a doubly charged cation, Mg^{2+} with the neon configuration:

$$Mg^{2+} \quad 1s^2 2s^2 2p^6 \quad \text{(Neon configuration)(or [Ne])}$$

A neutral magnesium atom has 12 protons and 12 electrons. With the loss of 2 electrons, there is an excess of 2 protons, accounting for the +2 charge of the ion, Mg^{2+}.

WORKED EXAMPLE **4.4** Electron Configurations: Octet Rule for Anions

How many electrons must a nitrogen atom, $Z = 7$, gain to attain a noble gas configuration? Write the electron-dot and ion symbols for the ion formed.

ANALYSIS Write the electron configuration of nitrogen, and see how many more electrons are needed to reach a noble gas configuration.

SOLUTION

Nitrogen, a group 5A element, has the electron configuration $1s^2 2s^2 2p^3$. The second shell contains 5 electrons ($2s^2 2p^3$) and needs 3 more to reach an octet. The result is formation of a triply charged anion, N^{3-}, with 8 valence electrons, matching the neon configuration:

$$N^{3-} \quad 1s^2 2s^2 2p^6 \quad \text{(Neon configuration)} \quad :\ddot{N}:^{3-}$$

PROBLEM 4.7

Write the electron configuration of potassium, $Z = 19$, and show how a potassium atom can attain a noble gas configuration.

PROBLEM 4.8

How many electrons must an aluminum atom, $Z = 13$, lose to attain a noble gas configuration? Write the symbol for the ion formed.

➥ KEY CONCEPT PROBLEM 4.9

Which atom in the reaction depicted here gains electrons, and which loses electrons? Draw the electron-dot symbols for the resulting ions.

$$X: + \cdot\ddot{Y}\cdot \longrightarrow ?$$

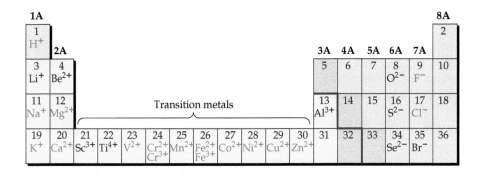

4.6 Ions of Some Common Elements

The periodic table is the key to understanding and remembering which elements form ions and which do not. As shown in Figure 4.4, atoms of elements in the same group tend to form ions of the same charge. The metals of groups 1A and 2A, for example, form only +1 and +2 ions, respectively. The ions of these elements all have noble gas configurations as a result of electron loss from their valence s subshells. (Note in the following equations that the electrons being lost are shown as products.)

Group 1A: $M\cdot \rightarrow M^+ + e^-$
           (M = Li, Na, K, Rb, or Cs)

Group 2A: $M: \rightarrow M^{2+} + 2e^-$
           (M = Be, Mg, Ca, Sr, Ba, or Ra)

Four of these ions, Na^+, K^+, Mg^{2+}, and Ca^{2+}, are present in body fluids, where they play extremely important roles in biochemical processes.

The only group 3A element commonly encountered in ionic compounds is aluminum, which forms Al^{3+} by loss of three electrons from its valence s and p subshells. Aluminum is not thought to be an essential element in the human diet, although it is known to be present in some organisms.

The first three elements in groups 4A (C, Si, Ge) and 5A (N, P, As) do not ordinarily form cations or anions, because either too much energy is required to remove an electron or not enough energy is released by adding an electron to make the process energetically favorable. The bonding of these elements is largely covalent and will be described in the next chapter. Carbon, in particular, is the key element on which life is based. Together with hydrogen, nitrogen, phosphorus, and oxygen, carbon is present in all the essential biological compounds that we will be describing throughout the latter half of this book.

The group 6A elements oxygen and sulfur form large numbers of compounds, some of which are ionic and some of which are covalent. Their ions have noble gas configurations, achieved by gaining two electrons:

Group 6A: $\cdot\ddot{O}\cdot \; + \; 2\,e^- \; \longrightarrow \; :\ddot{O}:^{2-}$

           $\cdot\ddot{S}\cdot \; + \; 2\,e^- \; \longrightarrow \; :\ddot{S}:^{2-}$

The halogens are present in many compounds as −1 ions, formed by gaining one electron:

Group 7A: $\cdot\ddot{X}: \; + \; e^- \; \longrightarrow \; :\ddot{X}:^-$
           (X = F, Cl, Br, I)

Transition metals lose electrons to form cations, some of which are present in the human body. The charges of transition metal cations are not as predictable as those of main group elements, however, because many transition metal atoms can lose one or more d electrons in addition to losing valence s electrons. For example, iron ($\ldots 3s^2 3p^6 3d^6 4s^2$) forms Fe^{2+} by losing two electrons from the $4s$ subshell and also forms Fe^{3+} by losing an additional electron from the $3d$ subshell. Looking at the iron configuration shows why the octet rule is limited to main group elements: Transition metal cations generally do not have noble gas configurations because they would have to lose *all* their d electrons.

Important Points about Ion Formation and the Periodic Table:

*   Metals form cations by losing one or more electrons.
    *   Group 1A and 2A metals form +1 and +2 ions, respectively (for example, Li^+ and Mg^{2+}) to achieve a noble gas configuration.
    *   Transition metals can form cations of more than one charge (for example, Fe^{2+} and Fe^{3+}) by losing a combination of valence-shell s electrons and inner-shell d electrons.
*   Reactive nonmetals form anions by gaining one or more electrons to achieve a noble gas configuration.
    *   Group 6A nonmetals oxygen and sulfur form the anions O^{2-} and S^{2-}.
    *   Group 7A elements (the halogens) form -1 ions; for example, F^- and Cl^-.
*   Group 8A elements (the noble gases) are unreactive.
*   Ionic charges of main group elements can be predicted using the group number and the octet rule.
    *   For 1A and 2A metals, cation charge = group number
    *   For nonmetals in groups 5A, 6A, and 7A, anion charge = 8 − (group number)

WORKED EXAMPLE **4.5** Formation of Ions: Gain/Loss of Valence Electrons

Which of the following ions is likely to form?

    (a) S^{3-} **(b)** Si^{2+} **(c)** Sr^{2+}

ANALYSIS Count the number of valence electrons in each ion. For main group elements, only ions with a valence octet of electrons are likely to form.

SOLUTION

    (a) Sulfur is in group 6A, has 6 valence electrons, and needs only two more to reach an octet. Gaining two electrons gives an S^{2-} ion with a noble gas configuration, but gaining three electrons does not. The S^{3-} ion is therefore unlikely to form.

    (b) Silicon is a nonmetal in group 4A. Like carbon, it does not form ions because it would have to gain or lose too many (4) electrons to reach a noble gas electron configuration. The Si^{2+} ion does not have an octet and will not form.

    (c) Strontium is a metal in group 2A, has only 2 outer-shell electrons, and can lose both to reach a noble gas configuration. The Sr^{2+} ion has an octet and therefore forms easily.

PROBLEM 4.10

Is molybdenum more likely to form a cation or an anion? Why?

PROBLEM 4.11

Which of the following elements can form more than one cation?

    (a) Strontium   **(b)** Chromium   **(c)** Bromine

PROBLEM 4.12

Write symbols, both with and without electron dots, for the ions formed by the following processes:

(a) Gain of two electrons by selenium

(b) Loss of two electrons by barium

(c) Gain of one electron by bromine

APPLICATION ▶ Salt

I f you are like most people, you feel a little guilty about reaching for the salt shaker at mealtime. The notion that high salt intake and high blood pressure go hand in hand is surely among the most highly publicized pieces of nutritional lore ever to appear.

Salt has not always been held in such disrepute. Historically, salt has been prized since the earliest recorded times as a seasoning and a food preservative. Words and phrases in many languages reflect the importance of salt as a life-giving and life-sustaining substance. We refer to a kind and generous person as "the salt of the earth," for instance, and we speak of being "worth one's salt." In Roman times, soldiers were paid in salt; the English word "salary" is derived from the Latin word for paying salt wages (*salarium*).

Salt is perhaps the easiest of all minerals to obtain and purify. The simplest method, used for thousands of years throughout the world in coastal climates where sunshine is abundant and rainfall is scarce, is to evaporate seawater. Though the exact amount varies depending on the source, seawater contains an average of about 3.5% by mass of dissolved substances, most of which is sodium chloride. It has been estimated that evaporation of all the world's oceans would yield approximately *4.5 million cubic miles* of NaCl.

Only about 10% of current world salt production comes from evaporation of seawater. Most salt is obtained by mining the vast deposits of *halite*, or *rock salt*, formed by evaporation of ancient inland seas. These salt beds vary in thickness up to hundreds of meters and vary in depth from a few meters to thousands of meters below the earth's surface. Salt mining has gone on for at least 3400 years, and the Wieliczka mine in Galicia, Poland, has been worked continuously from A.D. 1000 to the present.

Now, back to the dinner table. What about the link between dietary salt intake and high blood pressure? There is no doubt that most people in industrialized nations have a relatively high salt intake, and also that high blood pressure among industrialized populations is on the rise. How closely, though, are the two observations related?

In a study called the DASH-Sodium study published in 2001, a strong correlation was found between a change in salt intake and a change in blood pressure. When volunteers cut back their salt intake from 8.3 g per day—roughly what Americans typically consume—to 3.8 g per day, significant

▲ In many areas of the world salt is still harvested by evaporation of ocean or tidal waters.

drops in blood pressure were found. The largest reduction in blood pressure was seen in people already diagnosed with hypertension, but subjects with normal blood pressure also lowered their readings by several percent.

What should an individual do? The best answer, as in so many things, is to use moderation and common sense. People with hypertension should make a strong effort to lower their sodium intake; others might be well advised to choose unsalted snacks, use less salt in preparing food, and read nutrition labels for sodium content.

See Additional Problems 4.83 and 4.84 at the end of this chapter.

4.7 Naming Ions

Main group metal cations in groups 1A, 2A, and 3A are named by identifying the metal, followed by the word "ion," as in the following examples:

$$K^+ \qquad\qquad Mg^{2+} \qquad\qquad Al^{3+}$$

Potassium ion   Magnesium ion   Aluminum ion

It is sometimes a little confusing to use the same name for both a metal and its ion, and you may occasionally have to stop and think about what is meant. For example, it is common practice in nutrition and health-related fields to talk about sodium or potassium in the bloodstream. Because both sodium and potassium *metals* react violently with water, however, they cannot possibly be present in blood. The references are to dissolved sodium and potassium *ions*.

For transition metals, such as iron or chromium, which can form more than one type of cation, a method is needed to differentiate these ions. Two systems are used. The first is an old system that gives the ion with the smaller charge the word ending -*ous* and the ion with the larger charge the ending -*ic*.

The second is a newer system in which the charge on the ion is given as a Roman numeral in parentheses right after the metal name. For example:

$$Cr^{2+} \qquad\qquad Cr^{3+}$$

Old name: Chrom*ous* ion   Chrom*ic* ion

New name: Chromium(II) ion   Chromium(III) ion

We will generally emphasize the new system in this book, but it is important to understand both because the old system is often found on labels of commercially supplied chemicals. The small differences between the names in either system illustrate the importance of reading a name very carefully before using a chemical. There are significant differences between compounds consisting of the same two elements but having different charges on the cation. In treating iron-deficiency anemia, for example, iron(II) compounds are preferable because the body absorbs them considerably better than iron(III) compounds.

The names of some common transition metal cations are listed in Table 4.1. Notice that the old names of the copper, iron, and tin ions are derived from their Latin names (*cuprum, ferrum,* and *stannum*).

Anions are named by replacing the ending of the element name with -*ide*, followed by the word "ion" (Table 4.2). For example, the anion formed by fluor*ine* is the fluor*ide* ion, and the anion formed by sulf*ur* is the sulf*ide* ion.

TABLE 4.1   Names of Some Transition Metal Cations

ELEMENT	SYMBOL	OLD NAME	NEW NAME
Chromium	Cr^{2+}	Chromous	Chromium(II)
	Cr^{3+}	Chromic	Chromium(III)
Copper	Cu^+	Cuprous	Copper(I)
	Cu^{2+}	Cupric	Copper(II)
Iron	Fe^{2+}	Ferrous	Iron(II)
	Fe^{3+}	Ferric	Iron(III)
Mercury	$^*Hg_2^{2+}$	Mercurous	Mercury(I)
	Hg^{2+}	Mercuric	Mercury(II)
Tin	Sn^{2+}	Stannous	Tin(II)
	Sn^{4+}	Stannic	Tin(IV)

*This cation is composed of two mercury atoms, each of which has an average charge of +1.

TABLE 4.2   Names of Some Common Anions

ELEMENT	SYMBOL	NAME
Bromine	Br^-	Bromide ion
Chlorine	Cl^-	Chloride ion
Fluorine	F^-	Fluoride ion
Iodine	I^-	Iodide ion
Oxygen	O^{2-}	Oxide ion
Sulfur	S^{2-}	Sulfide ion

PROBLEM 4.13

Name the following ions:

(a) Cu^{2+} (b) F^- (c) Mg^{2+} (d) S^{2-}

PROBLEM 4.14

Write the symbols for the following ions:

(a) Silver(I) ion   (b) Iron(II) ion   (c) Cuprous ion   (d) Telluride ion

PROBLEM 4.15

Ringer's solution, which is used intravenously to adjust ion concentrations in body fluids, contains the ions of sodium, potassium, calcium, and chlorine. Give the names and symbols of these ions.

4.8 Polyatomic Ions

Ions that are composed of more than one atom are called **polyatomic ions**. Most polyatomic ions contain oxygen and another element, and their chemical formulas show by subscripts how many of each type of atom are combined. Sulfate ion, for example, is composed of one sulfur atom and four oxygen atoms, and has a -2 charge: SO_4^{2-}. The atoms in a polyatomic ion are held together by covalent bonds, of the sort discussed in the next chapter, and the entire group of atoms acts as a single unit. A polyatomic ion is charged because it contains a total number of electrons different from the total number of protons in the combined atoms.

The most common polyatomic ions are listed in Table 4.3. Note that the ammonium ion, NH_4^+, and the hydronium ion, H_3O^+, are the only cations; all the others

Polyatomic ion An ion that is composed of more than one atom.

▲ The brilliant blue mineral chalcanthite consists of the hydrated ionic compound copper sulfate, $CuSO_4$ $5H_2O$.

TABLE 4.3   Some Common Polyatomic Ions

NAME	FORMULA	NAME	FORMULA
Hydronium ion	H_3O^+	Nitrate ion	NO_3^-
Ammonium ion	NH_4^+	Nitrite ion	NO_2^-
Acetate ion	$CH_3CO_2^-$	Oxalate ion	$C_2O_4^{2-}$
Carbonate ion	CO_3^{2-}	Permanganate ion	MnO_4^-
Hydrogen carbonate ion (bicarbonate ion)	HCO_3^-	Phosphate ion	PO_4^{3-}
		Hydrogen phosphate ion	HPO_4^{2-}
Chromate ion	CrO_4^{2-}	Dihydrogen phosphate ion	$H_2PO_4^-$
Dichromate ion	$Cr_2O_7^{2-}$	Sulfate ion	SO_4^{2-}
Cyanide ion	CN^-	Hydrogen sulfate ion (bisulfate ion)	HSO_4^-
Hydroxide ion	OH^-		
Hypochlorite ion	OCl^-	Sulfite ion	SO_3^{2-}

APPLICATION ▶ Biologically Important Ions

The human body requires many different ions for proper functioning. Several of these ions, such as Ca^{2+}, Mg^{2+}, and HPO_4^{2-}, are used as structural materials in bones and teeth in addition to having other essential functions. Although 99% of Ca^{2+} is contained in bones and teeth, small amounts in body fluids play a vital role in transmission of nerve impulses. Other ions, including essential transition metal ions such as Fe^{2+}, are required for specific chemical reactions in the body. And still others, such as K^+, Na^+, and Cl^-, are present in fluids throughout the body.

Solutions containing ions must have overall neutrality, and several polyatomic anions, especially HCO_3^- and HPO_4^{2-}, are present in body fluids where they help balance the cation charges. Some of the most important ions and their functions are shown in the accompanying table.

See Additional Problems 4.85, 4.86, and 4.87 at the end of the chapter.

Some Biologically Important Ions

ION	LOCATION	FUNCTION	DIETARY SOURCE
Ca^{2+}	Outside cell; 99% of Ca^{2+} is in bones and teeth as $Ca_3(PO_4)_2$ and $CaCO_3$	Bone and tooth structure; necessary for blood clotting, muscle contraction, and transmission of nerve impulses	Milk, whole grains, leafy vegetables
Fe^{2+}	Blood hemoglobin	Transports oxygen from lungs to cells	Liver, red meat, leafy green vegetables
K^+	Fluids inside cells	Maintain ion concentrations in cells; regulate insulin release and heartbeat	Milk, oranges, bananas, meat
Na^+	Fluids outside cells	Protect against fluid loss; necessary for muscle contraction and transmission of nerve impulses	Table salt, seafood
Mg^{2+}	Fluids inside cells; bone	Present in many enzymes; needed for energy generation and muscle contraction	Leafy green plants, seafood, nuts
Cl^-	Fluids outside cells; gastric juice	Maintain fluid balance in cells; help transfer CO_2 from blood to lungs	Table salt, seafood
HCO_3^-	Fluids outside cells	Control acid–base balance in blood	By-product of food metabolism
HPO_4^{2-}	Fluids inside cells; bones and teeth	Control acid–base balance in cells	Fish, poultry, milk

are anions. These ions are encountered so frequently in chemistry, biology, and medicine that there is no alternative but to memorize their names and formulas. Fortunately, there are only a few of them.

Note in Table 4.3 that several pairs of ions— CO_3^{2-} and HCO_3^-, for example— are related by the presence or absence of a hydrogen ion, H^+. In such instances, the ion with the hydrogen is sometimes named using the prefix *bi-*. Thus, CO_3^{2-} is the carbonate ion and HCO_3^- is the bicarbonate ion; similarly, SO_4^{2-} is the sulfate ion and HSO_4^- is the bisulfate ion.

PROBLEM 4.16

Name the following ions:

(a) NO_3^- (b) CN^- (c) OH^- (d) HPO_4^{2-}

PROBLEM 4.17

Write the formulas of the following ions:

(a) Bicarbonate ion   **(b)** Ammonium ion

(c) Phosphate ion   **(d)** Permanganate ion

4.9 Formulas of Ionic Compounds

Since all chemical compounds are neutral, it is relatively easy to figure out the formulas of ionic compounds. Once the ions are identified, all we need to do is decide how many ions of each type give a total charge of zero. Thus, the chemical formula of an ionic compound tells the ratio of anions and cations.

If the ions have the same charge, only one of each ion is needed:

$$K^+ \quad \text{and} \quad F^- \quad \text{form} \quad KF$$
$$Ca^{2+} \quad \text{and} \quad O^{2-} \quad \text{form} \quad CaO$$

This makes sense when we look at how many electrons must be gained or lost by each atom in order to satisfy the octet rule:

$$K\cdot \ + \ \cdot \ddot{F}\!: \ \rightarrow \ K^+ \ + \ :\ddot{F}\!:^-$$
$$Ca\!: \ + \ \cdot \ddot{O}\cdot \ \rightarrow \ Ca^{2+} \ + \ :\ddot{O}\!:^{2-}$$

If the ions have different charges, however, unequal numbers of anions and cations must combine in order to have a net charge of zero. When potassium and oxygen combine, for example, it takes two K^+ ions to balance the -2 charge of the O^{2-} ion. Put another way, it takes two K atoms to provide the two electrons needed in order to complete the octet for the O atom:

$$2\,K\cdot \ + \ \cdot \ddot{O}\cdot \ \rightarrow \ 2\,K^+ \ + \ :\ddot{O}\!:^{2-}$$
$$2\,K^+ \quad \text{and} \quad O^{2-} \quad \text{form} \quad K_2O$$

The situation is reversed when a Ca^{2+} ion reacts with a Cl^- ion. One Ca atom can provide two electrons; each Cl atom requires only one electron to achieve a complete octet. Thus, there is one Ca^{2+} cation for every two Cl^- anions:

$$Ca\!: \ + \ 2\cdot\ddot{Cl}\!: \ \rightarrow \ Ca^{2+} \ + \ 2 :\ddot{Cl}\!:^-$$
$$Ca^{2+} \quad \text{and} \quad 2\,Cl^- \quad \text{form} \quad CaCl_2$$

It sometimes helps when writing the formulas for an ionic compound to remember that, when the two ions have different charges, the number of one ion is equal to the charge on the other ion. In magnesium phosphate, for example, the charge on the magnesium ion is $+2$ and the charge on the polyatomic phosphate ion is -3. Thus, there must be 3 magnesium ions with a total charge of $3 \times (+2) = +6$ and 2 phosphate ions with a total charge of $2 \times (-3) = -6$ for overall neutrality:

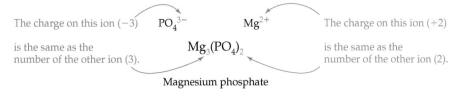

The charge on this ion (-3) $PO_4{}^{3-}$ Mg^{2+} The charge on this ion $(+2)$

is the same as the $Mg_3(PO_4)_2$ is the same as the
number of the other ion (3).   number of the other ion (2).

Magnesium phosphate

The formula of an ionic compound shows the lowest possible ratio of atoms in the compound and is thus known as a *simplest formula*. Because there is no such

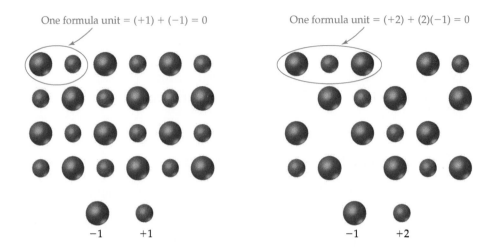

One formula unit = $(+1) + (-1) = 0$ One formula unit = $(+2) + (2)(-1) = 0$

-1 $+1$ -1 $+2$

▶ **FIGURE 4.5 Formula units of ionic compounds.** The sum of charges on the ions in a formula unit equals zero.

Formula unit The formula that identifies the smallest neutral unit of an ionic compound.

thing as a single neutral *particle* of an ionic compound, however, we use the term **formula unit** to identify the smallest possible neutral *unit* (Figure 4.5). For NaCl, the formula unit is one Na^+ ion and one Cl^- ion; for K_2SO_4, the formula unit is two K^+ ions and one SO_4^{2-} ion; for CaF_2, the formula unit is one Ca^{2+} ion and two F^- ions; and so on.

Once the numbers and kinds of ions in a compound are known, the formula is written using the following rules:

- List the cation first and the anion second; for example, NaCl rather than ClNa.
- Do not write the charges of the ions; for example, KF rather than K^+F^-.
- Use parentheses around a polyatomic ion formula if it has a subscript; for example, $Al_2(SO_4)_3$ rather than Al_2SO_{43}.

WORKED EXAMPLE   **4.6** Ionic Compounds: Writing Formulas

Write the formula for the compound formed by calcium ions and nitrate ions.

ANALYSIS Knowing the formula and charges on the cation and anion (Table 4.4), we determine how many of each are needed to yield a neutral formula for the ionic compound.

SOLUTION
The two ions are Ca^{2+} and NO_3^-. Two nitrate ions, each with a -1 charge, will balance the $+2$ charge of the calcium ion.

Ca^{2+} Charge = $1 \times (+2) = +2$
$2\,NO_3^-$ Charge = $2 \times (-1) = -2$

Since there are two nitrate ions, the nitrate formula must be enclosed in parentheses:

$Ca(NO_3)_2$ Calcium nitrate

PROBLEM 4.18

Write the formulas for the ionic compounds that silver(I) forms with each of the following:

(a) Iodide ion

(b) Oxide ion

(c) Phosphate ion

PROBLEM 4.19

Write the formulas for the ionic compounds that sulfate ion forms with the following:

(a) Sodium ion   **(b)** Iron(II) ion   **(c)** Chromium(III) ion

PROBLEM 4.20

The ionic compound containing ammonium ion and carbonate ion gives off the odor of ammonia, a property put to use in smelling salts for reviving someone who has fainted. Write the formula for this compound.

PROBLEM 4.21

An *astringent* is a compound that causes proteins in blood, sweat, and other body fluids to coagulate, a property put to use in deodorants. Two safe and effective astringents are the ionic compounds of aluminum with sulfate ion and with acetate ion. Write the formulas of both.

KEY CONCEPT PROBLEM 4.22

Three ionic compounds are represented on this periodic table—red cation with red anion, blue cation with blue anion, and green cation with green anion. Give a likely formula for each compound.

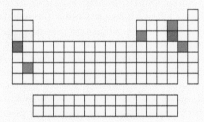

KEY CONCEPT PROBLEM 4.23

The ionic compound calcium nitride is represented here. What is the formula for calcium nitride, and what are the charges on the calcium and nitride ions?

Ca ion

N ion

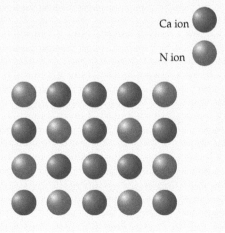

4.10 Naming Ionic Compounds

Just as in writing formulas for ionic compounds, these compounds are named by citing first the cation and then the anion, with a space between words. There are two kinds of ionic compounds, and the rules for naming them are slightly different.

Type I: Ionic compounds containing cations of main group elements (1A, 2A, aluminum). Since the charges on these cations do not vary, we do not need to specify the charge on the cation as discussed in Section 4.7.

Type II: Ionic compounds containing metals that can exhibit more than one charge. Since some metals, including the transition metals, often form more than one ion, we need to specify the charge on the cation in these compounds. Either the old (-ous, -ic) or the new (Roman numerals) system described in Section 4.7 can be used. Thus, $FeCl_2$ is called iron(II) chloride (or ferrous chloride), and $FeCl_3$ is called iron(III) chloride (or ferric chloride). Note that we do *not* name these compounds iron *di*chloride or iron *tri*chloride—once the charge on the metal is known, the number of anions needed to yield a neutral compound is also known and does not need to be included as part of the compound name. Ions of elements that form only one type of ion, such as Na^+ and Ca^{2+}, do not need Roman numerals. Table 4.4 lists some common ionic compounds and their uses.

⊂⊃⊃ Looking Ahead

Because the formula unit for an ionic compound must be neutral, we can unambiguously write the formula from the name of the compound, and vice versa. As we shall see in Chapter 5, covalent bonding between atoms can produce a much greater variety of compounds. The rules for naming covalent compounds must be able to accommodate multiple combinations of elements (for example, CO and CO_2).   ⊂⊃⊃

TABLE 4.4   Some Common Ionic Compounds and Their Applications

CHEMICAL NAME (COMMON NAME)	FORMULA	APPLICATIONS
Ammonium carbonate	$(NH_4)_2CO_3$	Smelling salts
Calcium hydroxide (hydrated lime)	$Ca(OH)_2$	Mortar, plaster, whitewash
Calcium oxide (lime)	CaO	Lawn treatment, industrial chemical
Lithium carbonate ("lithium")	Li_2CO_3	Treatment of manic depression
Magnesium hydroxide (milk of magnesia)	$Mg(OH)_2$	Antacid
Magnesium sulfate (Epsom salts)	$MgSO_4$	Laxative, anticonvulsant
Potassium permanganate	$KMnO_4$	Antiseptic, disinfectant*
Potassium nitrate (saltpeter)	KNO_3	Fireworks, matches, and desensitizer for teeth
Silver nitrate	$AgNO_3$	Antiseptic, germicide
Sodium bicarbonate (baking soda)	$NaHCO_3$	Baking powder, antacid, mouthwash, deodorizer
Sodium hypochlorite	NaOCl	Disinfectant; active ingredient in household bleach
Zinc oxide	ZnO	Skin protection, in calamine lotion

An antiseptic kills or inhibits growth of harmful microorganisms on the skin or in the body; a disinfectant kills harmful microorganisms but is generally not used on living tissue.

WORKED EXAMPLE   **4.7** Ionic Compounds: Formulas Involving Polyatomic Ions

Magnesium carbonate is used as an ingredient in Bufferin tablets. Write its formula.

ANALYSIS Since magnesium is a main group metal, we can determine its ionic compound formula by identifying the charges and formulas for the anion and the cation, remembering that the overall formula must be neutral.

SOLUTION
Look at the cation and the anion parts of the name separately. Magnesium, a group 2A element, forms the doubly positive Mg^{2+} cation; carbonate anion is doubly negative, CO_3^{2-}. Because the charges on the anion and cation are equal, a formula of $MgCO_3$ will be neutral.

WORKED EXAMPLE **4.8** Ionic Compounds: Formulas and Ionic Charges

Sodium and calcium both form a wide variety of ionic compounds. Write formulas for the following compounds:

   (a) Sodium bromide and calcium bromide

   (b) Sodium sulfide and calcium sulfide

   (c) Sodium phosphate and calcium phosphate

ANALYSIS Using the formulas and charges for the cations and the anions (from Tables 4.2 and 4.3) we determine how many of each cation and anion are needed to yield a formula that is neutral.

SOLUTION

   (a) Cations = Na^+ and Ca^{2+}; anion = Br^-: NaBr and $CaBr_2$

   (b) Cations = Na^+ and Ca^{2+}; anion = S^{2-}: Na_2S and CaS

   (c) Cations = Na^+ and Ca^{2+}; anion = PO_4^{3-}: Na_3PO_4 and $Ca_3(PO_4)_2$

WORKED EXAMPLE **4.9** Naming Ionic Compounds

Name the following compounds, using Roman numerals to indicate the charges on the cations where necessary:

   (a) KF   **(b)** $MgCl_2$ **(c)** $AuCl_3$ **(d)** Fe_2O_3

ANALYSIS For main group metals, the charge is determined from the group number and no Roman numerals are necessary. For transition metals, the charge on the metal can be determined from the total charge(s) on the anion(s).

SOLUTION

   (a) Potassium fluoride. No Roman numeral is necessary because a group 1A metal forms only one cation.

   (b) Magnesium chloride. No Roman numeral is necessary because magnesium (group 2A) forms only Mg^{2+}.

   (c) Gold(III) chloride. The three Cl^- ions require a +3 charge on the gold for a neutral formula. Since gold is a transition metal that can form other ions, the Roman numeral is necessary to specify the +3 charge.

   (d) Iron(III) oxide. Because the three oxide anions (O^{2-}) have a total negative charge of −6, the two iron cations must have a total charge of +6. Thus, each is Fe^{3+}, and the charge on each is indicated by the Roman numeral (III).

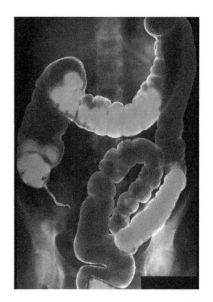

PROBLEM 4.24

Barium sulfate is an ionic compound swallowed by patients before having an X-ray of their gastrointestinal tract. Write its formula.

PROBLEM 4.25

The compound Ag_2S is responsible for much of the tarnish found on silverware. Name this compound, and give the charge on the silver ion.

▲ A barium sulfate "cocktail" is given to patients prior to an X-ray to help make the gastrointestinal tract visible on the film.

PROBLEM 4.26

Name the following compounds:

(a) SnO_2 (b) $Ca(CN)_2$ (c) Na_2CO_3

(d) Cu_2SO_4 (e) $Ba(OH)_2$ (f) $Fe(NO_3)_2$

PROBLEM 4.27

Write formulas for the following compounds:

(a) Lithium phosphate

(b) Copper(II) carbonate

(c) Aluminum sulfite

(d) Cuprous fluoride

(e) Ferric sulfate

(f) Ammonium chloride

KEY CONCEPT PROBLEM 4.28

The ionic compound formed between chromium and oxygen is shown here. Name the compound and write its formula.

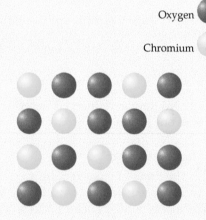

Oxygen

Chromium

4.11 H^+ and OH^- Ions: An Introduction to Acids and Bases

Two of the most important ions we will be discussing in the remainder of this book are the hydrogen cation (H^+) and the hydroxide anion (OH^-). Since a hydrogen *atom* contains one proton and one electron, a hydrogen *cation* is simply a proton. When an acid dissolves in water, the proton typically attaches to a molecule of water to form the hydronium ion (H_3O^+), but chemists routinely use the H^+ and H_3O^+ ions interchangeably. A hydroxide anion, by contrast, is a polyatomic ion in which an oxygen atom is covalently bonded to a hydrogen atom. Although much of Chapter 10 is devoted to the chemistry of H^+ and OH^- ions, it is worth taking a preliminary look now.

The importance of the H^+ cation and the OH^- anion is that they are fundamental to the concepts of *acids* and *bases*. In fact, one definition of an **acid** is a substance that provides H^+ ions when dissolved in water, and one definition of a **base** is a substance that provides OH^- ions when dissolved in water.

Acid   A substance that provides H^+ ions in water; for example, HCl, HNO_3, H_2SO_4, H_3PO_4

Base   A substance that provides OH^- ions in water; for example, NaOH, KOH, $Ba(OH)_2$

Hydrochloric acid (HCl), nitric acid (HNO_3), sulfuric acid (H_2SO_4), and phosphoric acid (H_3PO_4) are among the most common acids. When any of these substances is dissolved in water, H^+ ions are formed along with the corresponding anion (Table 4.5).

TABLE 4.5   Some Common Acids and Ions Derived from Them

ACIDS		IONS	
Acetic acid	CH_3COOH	Acetate ion	*CH_3COO^-
Carbonic acid	H_2CO_3	Hydrogen carbonate ion (bicarbonate ion)	HCO_3^-
		Carbonate ion	CO_3^{2-}
Hydrochloric acid	HCl	Chloride ion	Cl^-
Nitric acid	HNO_3	Nitrate ion	NO_3^-
Nitrous acid	HNO_2	Nitrite ion	NO_2^-
Phosphoric acid	H_3PO_4	Dihydrogen phosphate ion	$H_2PO_4^-$
		Hydrogen phosphate ion	HPO_4^{2-}
		Phosphate ion	PO_4^{3-}
Sulfuric acid	H_2SO_4	Hydrogen sulfate ion	HSO_4^-
		Sulfate ion	SO_4^{2-}

*Sometimes written $C_2H_3O_2^-$ or as $CH_3CO_2^-$.

Different acids can provide different numbers of H^+ ions per acid molecule. Hydrochloric acid, for instance, provides one H^+ ion per acid molecule; sulfuric acid can provide two H^+ ions per acid molecule; and phosphoric acid can provide three H^+ ions per acid molecule.

Sodium hydroxide (NaOH; also known as *lye* or *caustic soda*), potassium hydroxide (KOH; also known as *caustic potash*), and barium hydroxide $[Ba(OH)_2]$ are examples of bases. When any of these compounds dissolves in water, OH^- anions go into solution along with the corresponding metal cation. Sodium hydroxide and potassium hydroxide provide one OH^- ion per formula unit; barium hydroxide provides two OH^- ions per formula unit, as indicated by its formula, $Ba(OH)_2$.

PROBLEM 4.29

Which of the following compounds are acids, and which are bases? Explain.

(a) HF

(b) $Ca(OH)_2$

(c) LiOH

(d) HCN

KEY CONCEPT PROBLEM 4.30

One of these pictures represents a solution of HCl, and one represents a solution of H_2SO_4. Which is which?

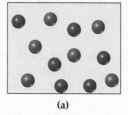
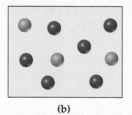

(a)   (b)

APPLICATION ▶ Osteoporosis

Bone consists primarily of two components, one mineral and one organic. About 70% of bone is the ionic compound *hydroxyapatite*, $Ca_{10}(PO_4)_6(OH)_2$, called the *trabecular*, or spongy, bone. This mineral component is intermingled in a complex matrix with about 30% by mass of fibers of the protein *collagen*, called the *cortical*, or compact, bone. Hydroxyapatite gives bone its hardness and strength, whereas collagen fibers add flexibility and resistance to breaking.

Total bone mass in the body increases from birth until reaching a maximum in the mid 30s. By the early 40s, however, an age-related decline in bone mass begins to occur in both sexes. Should this thinning of bones become too great and the bones become too porous and brittle, a clinical condition called *osteoporosis* can result. Osteoporosis is, in fact, the most common of all bone diseases, affecting approximately 25 million people in the United States. Approximately 1.5 million bone fractures each year are caused by osteoporosis at an estimated health-care cost of $14 billion.

Although both sexes are affected by osteoporosis, the condition is particularly common in postmenopausal women, who undergo cortical bone loss at a rate of 2–3% per year

over and above that of the normal age-related loss. The cumulative lifetime bone loss, in fact, may approach 40–50% in women versus 20–30% in men. It has been estimated that half of all women over age 50 will have an osteoporosis-related bone fracture at some point in their life. Other risk factors in addition to sex include being thin, being sedentary, having a family history of osteoporosis, smoking, and having a diet low in calcium.

No cure yet exists for osteoporosis, but treatment for its prevention and management includes estrogen replacement therapy for postmenopausal women as well as several approved medications called *bisphosphonates* to prevent further bone loss. Calcium supplements are also recommended, as is appropriate weight-bearing exercise. In addition, treatment with sodium fluoride is under active investigation and shows considerable promise. Fluoride ion reacts with hydroxyapatite to give *fluorapatite*, in which OH^- ions are replaced by F^-, increasing both bone strength and density.

$$Ca_{10}(PO_4)_6(OH)_2 + 2\ F^- \longrightarrow Ca_{10}(PO_4)_6F_2$$

Hydroxyapatite   Fluorapatite

See Additional Problems 4.88 and 4.89 at the end of the chapter.

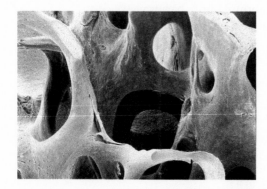
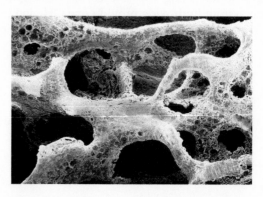

▲ Normal bone is strong and dense; a bone affected by osteoporosis is weak and spongy in appearance.

SUMMARY: REVISITING THE CHAPTER GOALS

1. **What is an ion, what is an ionic bond, and what are the general characteristics of ionic compounds?** Atoms are converted into *cations* by the loss of one or more electrons and into *anions* by the gain of one or more electrons. Ionic compounds are composed of cations and anions held together by *ionic bonds*, which result from the attraction between opposite electrical charges. Ionic compounds conduct electricity when dissolved in water, and they are generally crystalline solids with high melting points and high boiling points.

2. **What is the octet rule, and how does it apply to ions?** A valence-shell electron configuration of 8 electrons in filled *s* and *p* subshells leads to stability and lack of reactivity, as typified by the noble gases in group 8A. According to the *octet rule*, atoms of main group elements tend to form ions in which they have gained or lost the appropriate number of electrons to reach a noble gas configuration.

3. **What is the relationship between an element's position in the periodic table and the formation of its ion?** Periodic variations in *ionization energy*, the amount of energy that must be supplied to remove an electron from an atom, show that metals lose electrons more easily than nonmetals. As a result, metals usually form cations. Similar periodic variations in *electron affinity*, the amount of energy released on adding an electron to an atom, show that reactive nonmetals gain electrons more easily than metals. As a result, reactive nonmetals usually form anions. The ionic charge can be predicted from the group number and the octet rule. For main group metals, the charge on the cation is equal to the group number. For nonmetals, the charge on the anion is equal to 8 − (group number).

4. **What determines the chemical formula of an ionic compound?** Ionic compounds contain appropriate numbers of anions and cations to maintain overall neutrality, thereby providing a means of determining their chemical formulas.

5. **How are ionic compounds named?** Cations have the same name as the metal from which they are derived. Monatomic anions have the name ending *-ide*. For metals that form more than one ion, a Roman numeral equal to the charge on the ion is added to the name of the cation. Alternatively, the ending *-ous* is added to the name of the cation with the lesser charge and the ending *-ic* is added to the name of the cation with the greater charge. To name an ionic compound, the cation name is given first, with the charge of the metal ion indicated if necessary, and the anion name is given second.

6. **What are acids and bases?** The hydrogen ion (H^+) and the hydroxide ion (OH^-) are among the most important ions in chemistry because they are fundamental to the idea of acids and bases. According to one common definition, an *acid* is a substance that yields H^+ ions when dissolved in water, and a *base* is a substance that yields OH^- ions when dissolved in water.

KEY WORDS

Acid, *p. 99*

Anion, *p. 80*

Base, *p. 99*

Cation, *p. 80*

Electron affinity, *p. 81*

Formula unit, *p. 94*

Ion, *p. 80*

Ionic bond, *p. 83*

Ionic compound, *p. 83*

Ionic solid, *p. 83*

Ionization energy, *p. 81*

Octet rule, *p. 85*

Polyatomic ion, *p. 91*

UNDERSTANDING KEY CONCEPTS

4.31 Where on the blank outline of the periodic table are the following elements found?

(a) Elements that commonly form only one type of cation

(b) Elements that commonly form anions

(c) Elements that can form more than one type of cation

(d) Elements that do not readily form either anions or cations

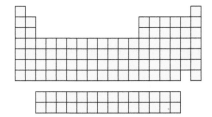

4.32 Where on the blank outline of the periodic table are the following elements found?

(a) Elements that commonly form +2 ions

(b) Elements that commonly form −2 ions

(c) An element that forms a +3 ion

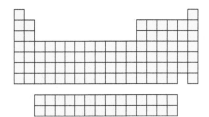

4.33 Which of these drawings represents a Ca atom, which an Na^+ ion, and which an O^{2-} ion?

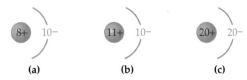

4.34 One of these drawings represents an Na atom, and one represents an Na^+ ion. Tell which is which, and explain why there is a difference in size.

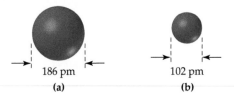

4.35 One of these drawings represents a Cl atom, and one represents a Cl^- ion. Tell which is which, and explain why there is a difference in size.

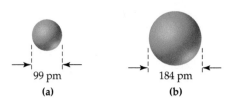

4.36 Three ionic compounds are represented in this outline of the periodic table—red cation with red anion, blue cation with blue anion, and green cation with green anion. Give a likely formula for each compound, and tell the name of each.

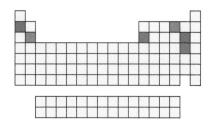

4.37 Each of these drawings (a)–(d) represents one of the following ionic compounds: $PbBr_2$, ZnS, CrF_3, Al_2O_3. Which is which?

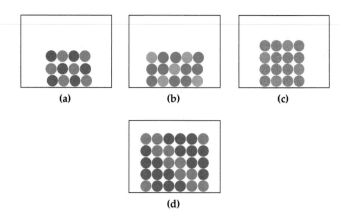

ADDITIONAL PROBLEMS

IONS AND IONIC BONDING

4.38 Write electron-dot symbols for the following atoms:
 (a) Beryllium
 (b) Neon
 (c) Strontium
 (d) Aluminum

4.39 Write electron-dot symbols for the following atoms:
 (a) Nitrogen
 (b) Selenium
 (c) Iodine
 (d) Strontium

4.40 Write equations for loss or gain of electrons by atoms that result in formation of the following ions from the corresponding atoms:
 (a) Ca^{2+}
 (b) Au^+
 (c) F^-
 (d) Cr^{3+}

4.41 Write symbols for the ions formed by the following:
 (a) Gain of 3 electrons by phosphorus
 (b) Loss of 1 electron by lithium
 (c) Loss of 2 electrons by cobalt
 (d) Loss of 3 electrons by thallium

4.42 Tell whether each statement about ions is true or false:
 (a) A cation is formed by addition of one or more electrons to an atom.
 (b) Group 4A elements tend to lose 4 electrons to yield ions with a +4 charge.
 (c) Group 4A elements tend to gain 4 electrons to yield ions with a −4 charge.
 (d) The individual atoms in a polyatomic ion are held together by covalent bonds.

4.43 Tell whether each statement about ionic solids is true or false:
 (a) Ions are randomly arranged in ionic solids.
 (b) All ions are the same size in ionic solids.
 (c) Ionic solids can often be shattered by a sharp blow.
 (d) Ionic solids have low boiling points.

IONS AND THE OCTET RULE

4.44 What is the *octet rule*?

4.45 Why do H and He not obey the octet rule?

4.46 What is the charge of an ion that contains 34 protons and 36 electrons?

4.47 What is the charge of an ion that contains 20 protons and 18 electrons?

4.48 Identify the element X in the following ions, and tell which noble gas has the same electron configuration.

(a) X^{2+}, a cation with 36 electrons
(b) X^-, an anion with 36 electrons

4.49 Element Z forms an ion Z^{3+}, which contains 31 protons. What is the identity of Z, and how many electrons does Z^{3+} have?

4.50 Write the electron configuration for the following ions:

(a) Rb^+
(b) Br^-
(c) S^{2-}
(d) Ba^{2+}
(e) Al^{3+}

4.51 The following ions have a noble gas configuration. Identify the noble gas.

(a) Ca^{2+}
(b) Li^+
(c) O^{2-}
(d) F^-
(e) Mg^{2+}

PERIODIC PROPERTIES AND ION FORMATION

4.52 Looking only at the periodic table, tell which member of each pair of atoms has the larger ionization energy and thus loses an electron less easily:

(a) Li and O
(b) Li and Cs
(c) K and Zn
(d) Mg and N

4.53 Looking only at the periodic table, tell which member of each pair of atoms has the larger electron affinity and thus gains an electron more easily:

(a) Li and S
(b) Ba and I
(c) Ca and Br

4.54 Which of the following ions are likely to form? Explain.

(a) Li^{2+}
(b) K^-
(c) Mn^{3+}
(d) Zn^{4+}
(e) Ne^+

4.55 Which of the following elements are likely to form more than one cation?

(a) Magnesium
(b) Silicon
(c) Manganese

4.56 Write the electron configurations of Cr^{2+} and Cr^{3+}.

4.57 Write the electron configurations of Co, Co^{2+}, and Co^{3+}.

4.58 Would you expect the ionization energy of Li^+ to be less than, greater than, or the same as the ionization energy of Li? Explain.

4.59 (a) Write equations for the loss of an electron by a K atom and the gain of an electron by a K^+ ion.
(b) What is the relationship between the equations?
(c) What is the relationship between the ionization energy of a K atom and the electron affinity of a K^+ ion?

SYMBOLS, FORMULAS, AND NAMES FOR IONS

4.60 Name the following ions:

(a) S^{2-}
(b) Sn^{2+}
(c) Sr^{2+}
(d) Mg^{2+}
(e) Au^+

4.61 Name the following ions in both the old and the new systems:

(a) Cu^{2+}
(b) Fe^{2+}
(c) Hg_2^{2+}

4.62 Write symbols for the following ions:

(a) Selenide ion
(b) Oxide ion
(c) Silver(I) ion

4.63 Write symbols for the following ions:

(a) Ferric ion
(b) Cobalt(II) ion
(c) Lead (IV) ion

4.64 Write formulas for the following ions:

(a) Hydroxide ion
(b) Bisulfate ion
(c) Acetate ion
(d) Permanganate ion
(e) Hypochlorite ion
(f) Nitrate ion
(g) Carbonate ion
(h) Dichromate ion

4.65 Name the following ions:

(a) SO_3^{2-}
(b) CN^-
(c) H_3O^+
(d) PO_4^{3-}

NAMES AND FORMULAS FOR IONIC COMPOUNDS

4.66 Write formulas for the compounds formed by the sulfate ion with the following cations:

(a) Aluminum
(b) Silver(I)
(c) Zinc
(d) Barium

4.67 Write formulas for the compounds formed by the carbonate ion with the following cations:

(a) Strontium
(b) Fe(III)
(c) Ammonium
(d) Sn(IV)

4.68 Write the formula for the following substances:

(a) Sodium bicarbonate (baking soda)
(b) Potassium nitrate (a backache remedy)
(c) Calcium carbonate (an antacid)
(d) Ammonium nitrate (first aid cold packs)

4.69 Write the formula for the following compounds:

(a) Calcium hypochlorite, used as a swimming pool disinfectant

(b) Copper(II) sulfate, used to kill algae in swimming pools

(c) Sodium phosphate, used in detergents to enhance cleaning action

4.70 Complete the table by writing in the formula of the compound formed by each pair of ions:

	S^{2-}	Cl^-	$PO_4{}^{3-}$	$CO_3{}^{2-}$
Copper(II)	CuS			
Ca^{2+}				
$NH_4{}^+$				
Ferric ion				

4.71 Complete the table by writing in the formula of the compound formed by each pair of ions:

	O^{2-}	$HSO_4{}^-$	$HPO_4{}^{2-}$	$C_2O_4{}^{2-}$
Na^+	Na_2O			
Zn^{2+}				
$NH_4{}^+$				
Ferrous ion				

4.72 Write the name of each compound in the table for Problem 4.70.

4.73 Write the name of each compound in the table for Problem 4.71.

4.74 Name the following substances:

(a) $MgCO_3$
(b) $Ca(CH_3CO_2)_2$
(c) $AgCN$
(d) $Na_2Cr_2O_7$

4.75 Name the following substances:

(a) $Fe(OH)_2$
(b) $KMnO_4$
(c) Na_2CrO_4
(d) $Ba_3(PO_4)_2$

4.76 Which of the following formulas is most likely to be correct for calcium phosphate?

(a) Ca_2PO_4
(b) $CaPO_4$
(c) $Ca_2(PO_4)_3$
(d) $Ca_3(PO_4)_2$

4.77 Fill in the missing information to give the correct formula for each compound:

(a) $Na_?SO_4$
(b) $Ba_?(PO_4)_?$
(c) $Ga_?(SO_4)_?$

ACIDS AND BASES

4.78 What is the difference between an acid and a base?

4.79 Identify the following substances as either an acid or a base:

(a) H_2CO_3
(b) HCN

(c) $Mg(OH)_2$
(d) KOH

4.80 Write equations to show how the substances listed in Problem 4.79 give ions when dissolved in water.

4.81 Name the anions that result when the acids in Problem 4.79 are dissolved in water.

Applications

4.82 What is the difference between a geologist's and a nutritionist's definition of a mineral? [*Minerals and Gems, p. 85*]

4.83 How is salt obtained? [*Salt, p. 89*]

4.84 What is the effect of normal dietary salt on most people? [*Salt, p. 89*]

4.85 Where are most of the calcium ions found in the body? [*Biologically Important Ions, p. 92*]

4.86 Excess sodium ion is considered hazardous, but a certain amount is necessary for normal body functions. What is the purpose of sodium in the body? [*Biologically Important Ions, p. 92*]

4.87 Before a person is allowed to donate blood, a drop of the blood is tested to be sure that it contains a sufficient amount of iron (men, 41 $\mu g/dL$; women, 38 $\mu g/dL$). Why is this required? [*Biologically Important Ions, p. 92*]

4.88 Name each ion in hydroxyapatite, $Ca_{10}(PO_4)_6(OH)_2$; give its charge; and show that the formula represents a neutral compound. [*Osteoporosis, p. 100*]

4.89 Sodium fluoride reacts with hydroxyapatite to give fluorapatite. What is the formula of fluorapatite? [*Osteoporosis, p. 100*]

General Questions and Problems

4.90 Explain why the hydride ion, H^-, has a noble gas configuration.

4.91 The H^- ion (Problem 4.90) is stable, but the Li^- ion is not. Explain.

4.92 Many compounds containing a metal and a nonmetal are not ionic, yet they are named using the Roman numeral system for ionic compounds described in Section 4.7. Write the chemical formulas for the following such compounds.

(a) Chromium(VI) oxide
(b) Vanadium(V) chloride
(c) Manganese(IV) oxide
(d) Molybdenum(IV) sulfide

4.93 The arsenate ion has the formula $AsO_4{}^{3-}$. Write the formula of lead(II) arsenate, used as an insecticide.

4.94 One commercially available calcium supplement contains calcium gluconate, a compound that is also used as an anticaking agent in instant coffee.

(a) If this compound contains one calcium ion for every two gluconate ions, what is the charge on a gluconate ion?

(b) What is the ratio of iron ions to gluconate ions in iron(III) gluconate, a commercial iron supplement?

4.95 The names given for the following compounds are incorrect. Write the correct name for each compound.

(a) Cu_3PO_4, copper(III) phosphate
(b) Na_2SO_4, sodium sulfide
(c) MnO_2, manganese(II) oxide
(d) $AuCl_3$, gold chloride
(e) $Pb(CO_3)_2$, lead(II) acetate
(f) Ni_2S_3, nickel(II) sulfide

4.96 The formulas given for the following compounds are incorrect. Write the correct formula for each compound.

(a) Cobalt(II) cyanide, $CoCN_2$
(b) Uranium(VI) oxide, UO_6
(c) Tin(II) sulfate, $Ti(SO_4)_2$
(d) Manganese(IV) oxide; MnO_4
(e) Potassium phosphate, K_2PO_4
(f) Calcium phosphide, CaP
(g) Lithium bisulfate, $Li(SO_4)_2$
(h) Aluminum hydroxide; $Al_2(OH)_3$

4.97 How many protons, electrons, and neutrons are in each of these following ions?

(a) $^{16}O^{2-}$
(b) $^{89}Y^{3+}$
(c) $^{133}Cs^+$
(d) $^{81}Br^-$

4.98 Element X reacts with element Y to give a product containing X^{3+} ions and Y^{2-} ions.

(a) Is element X likely to be a metal or a nonmetal?
(b) Is element Y likely to be a metal or a nonmetal?
(c) What is the formula of the product?
(d) What groups of the periodic table are elements X and Y likely to be in?

4.99 Identify each of the ions having the following charges and electron configurations:

(a) X^{3+}; $[Ar]\ 4s^0 3d^5$
(b) X^{2+}; $[Ar]\ 4s^0 3d^8$
(c) X^{6+}; $[Ar]\ 4s^0 3d^0$

CHAPTER 5

Molecular Compounds

▲ In living systems, as in this print by the Dutch artist M. C. Escher (1898–1972), the shapes of the component parts determine their contribution to the whole.

CONTENTS

CHAPTER GOALS

In this chapter, we will explore the following questions about molecules and covalent bonds:

1. What is a covalent bond?

THE GOAL: Be able to describe the nature of covalent bonds and how they are formed.

2. How does the octet rule apply to covalent bond formation?

THE GOAL: Be able to use the octet rule to predict the numbers of covalent bonds formed by common main group elements.

3. How are molecular compounds represented?

THE GOAL: Be able to interpret molecular formulas and draw Lewis structures for molecules.

4. What is the influence of valence-shell electrons on molecular shape?

THE GOAL: Be able to use Lewis structures to predict molecular geometry.

5. When are bonds and molecules polar?

THE GOAL: Be able to use electronegativity and molecular geometry to predict bond and molecular polarity.

6. What are the major differences between ionic and molecular compounds?

THE GOAL: Be able to compare the structures, compositions, and properties of ionic and molecular compounds.

We saw in the preceding chapter that ionic compounds are crystalline solids composed of positively and negatively charged ions. Not all substances, however, are ionic. In fact, with the exception of table salt (NaCl), baking soda ($NaHCO_3$), lime for the garden (CaO), and a few others, most of the compounds around us are *not* crystalline, brittle, high-melting ionic solids. We are much more likely to encounter gases (like those in air), liquids (such as water), low-melting solids (such as butter), and flexible solids like plastics. All these materials are composed of *molecules* rather than ions, all contain *covalent* bonds rather than ionic bonds, and all consist primarily of nonmetal atoms rather than metals.

5.1 Covalent Bonds

How do we describe the bonding in carbon dioxide, water, polyethylene, and the many millions of nonionic compounds that make up our bodies and much of the world around us? Simply put, the bonds in such compounds are formed by the *sharing* of electrons between atoms (in contrast to ionic bonds, which involve the complete transfer of electrons from one atom to another). The bond formed when atoms share electrons is called a **covalent bond**, and the group of atoms held together by covalent bonds is called a **molecule**. A single molecule of water, for example, contains two hydrogen atoms and one oxygen atom covalently bonded to one another. We might visualize a water molecule using a space-filling model as shown here:

Covalent bond   A bond formed by sharing electrons between atoms.

Molecule   A group of atoms held together by covalent bonds.

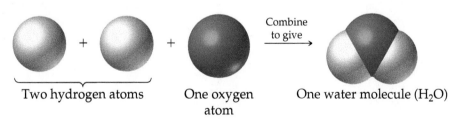

Two hydrogen atoms   +   One oxygen atom   Combine to give→   One water molecule (H_2O)

Recall that according to the *octet rule* (Section 4.5), main group elements tend to undergo reactions that leave them with completed outer subshells with eight valence electrons (or two for hydrogen), so that they have a noble gas electron configuration. (⊂⊃, p. 85) Although metals and reactive nonmetals can achieve an electron octet by gaining or losing an appropriate number of electrons to form ions, the nonmetals can also achieve an electron octet by *sharing* an appropriate number of electrons in covalent bonds.

As an example of how covalent bond formation occurs, let us look first at the bond between two hydrogen atoms in a hydrogen molecule, H_2. Recall that a hydrogen *atom* consists of a positively charged nucleus and a single, negatively charged $1s$ valence electron, which we represent as H· using the electron-dot symbols. When two hydrogen atoms come together, electrical interactions occur. Some of these interactions are repulsive—the two positively charged nuclei repel each other and the two negatively charged electrons repel each other. Other interactions, however, are attractive—each nucleus attracts both electrons and each electron attracts both nuclei (Figure 5.1). Because the attractive forces are stronger than the repulsive forces, a covalent bond is formed and the hydrogen atoms stay together.

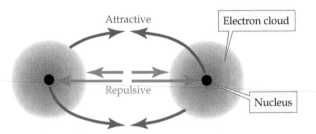

Attractive

Electron cloud

Repulsive

Nucleus

▲ **FIGURE 5.1** **A covalent H—H bond is the net result of attractive and repulsive forces.** The nucleus–electron attractions (blue arrows) are greater than the nucleus–nucleus and electron–electron repulsions (red arrows), resulting in a net attractive force that holds the atoms together to form an H_2 molecule.

In essence, the electrons act as a kind of "glue" to bind the two nuclei together into an H_2 molecule. Both nuclei are simultaneously attracted to the same electrons and are therefore held together, much as two tug-of-war teams pulling on the same rope are held together.

▶ The two teams are joined together because both are holding onto the same rope. In a similar way, two atoms are bonded together when both hold onto the same electrons.

Covalent bond formation in the H—H molecule can be visualized by imagining that the spherical $1s$ orbitals from the two individual atoms blend together and *overlap* to give an egg-shaped region in the H_2 molecule. The two electrons in the H—H covalent bond occupy the central region between the nuclei, giving both atoms a share in two valence electrons and the $1s^2$ electron configuration of the noble gas helium. For simplicity, the shared pair of electrons in a covalent bond is often represented as a line between atoms. Thus, the symbols H—H, H:H, and H_2 all represent a hydrogen molecule.

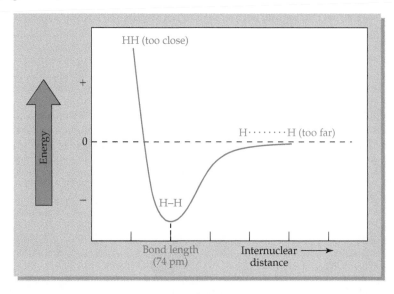

As you might imagine, the magnitudes of the various attractive and repulsive forces between nuclei and electrons in a covalent bond depend on how close the atoms are to each other. If the atoms are too far apart, the attractive forces are small and no bond exists. If the atoms are too close, the repulsive interaction between nuclei is so strong that it pushes the atoms apart. Thus, there is an optimum point where net attractive forces are maximized and where the H_2 molecule is most stable. This optimum distance between nuclei is called the **bond length** and is 74 pm (7.4×10^{-11} m) in the H_2 molecule. On a graph of energy versus internuclear distance, the bond length corresponds to the minimum-energy, most stable arrangement (Figure 5.2).

Bond length The optimum distance between nuclei in a covalent bond.

◀ **FIGURE 5.2 A graph of potential energy versus internuclear distance for the H_2 molecule.** If the hydrogen atoms are too far apart, attractions are weak and no bonding occurs. If the atoms are too close, strong repulsions occur. When the atoms are optimally separated, the energy is at a minimum. The distance between nuclei at this minimum-energy point is called the *bond length*.

As another example of covalent bond formation, look at the chlorine molecule, Cl_2. An individual chlorine atom has seven valence electrons and the valence-shell electron configuration $3s^2 3p^5$. Using the electron-dot symbols for the valence electrons, each Cl atom can be represented as :C̈l·. The 3s orbital and two of the three 3p orbitals are filled by two electrons each, but the third 3p orbital holds only one electron. When two chlorine atoms approach each other, the unpaired 3p electrons are shared by both atoms in a covalent bond. Each chlorine atom in the resultant Cl_2 molecule now "owns" six outer-shell electrons and "shares" two more, giving each a valence-shell octet like that of the noble gas argon. We can represent the formation of a covalent bond between chlorine atoms as

$$:\ddot{\text{C}}\text{l}\cdot + \cdot\ddot{\text{C}}\text{l}: \longrightarrow :\ddot{\text{C}}\text{l}:\ddot{\text{C}}\text{l}:$$

Such bond formation can also be pictured as the overlap of the 3p orbitals containing the single electrons, with resultant formation of a region of high electron density between the nuclei:

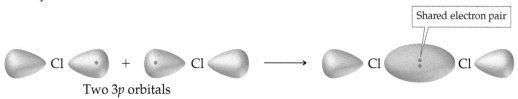

Two 3p orbitals

In addition to H_2 and Cl_2, five other elements always exist as *diatomic* (two-atom) molecules (Figure 5.3): Nitrogen (N_2) and oxygen (O_2) are colorless, odorless, nontoxic gases

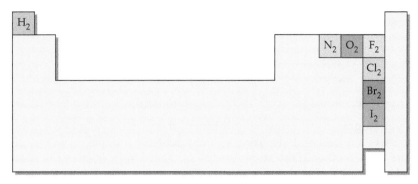

▶ **FIGURE 5.3 Diatomic elements in the periodic table.**

present in air; fluorine (F_2) is a pale yellow, highly reactive gas; bromine (Br_2) is a dark red, toxic liquid; and iodine (I_2) is a violet, crystalline solid.

PROBLEM 5.1

Draw the iodine molecule using electron-dot symbols, and indicate the shared electron pair. What noble gas configuration do the iodine atoms have in an I_2 molecule?

5.2 Covalent Bonds and the Periodic Table

Molecular compound A compound that consists of molecules rather than ions.

Covalent bonds can form between unlike atoms as well as between like atoms, making possible a vast number of **molecular compounds**. Water molecules, for example, consist of two hydrogen atoms joined by covalent bonds to an oxygen atom, H_2O; ammonia molecules consist of three hydrogen atoms covalently bonded to a nitrogen atom, NH_3; and methane molecules consist of four hydrogen atoms covalently bonded to a carbon atom, CH_4.

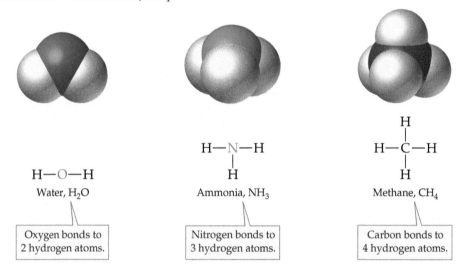

Note that in all these examples, each atom shares enough electrons to achieve a noble gas configuration: two electrons for hydrogen, and octets for oxygen, nitrogen, and carbon. Hydrogen, with one valence electron ($H\cdot$), needs one more electron to achieve a noble gas configuration (that of helium, $1s^2$) and thus forms one covalent bond. Oxygen, with six valence electrons ($\cdot\ddot{O}\cdot$), needs two more electrons to have an octet; this happens when oxygen forms two covalent bonds. Nitrogen, with five valence electrons ($\cdot\ddot{N}\cdot$), needs three more electrons to achieve an octet and thus forms three covalent bonds. Carbon, with four valence electrons ($\cdot\dot{C}\cdot$), needs four more electrons and thus forms four covalent bonds. Figure 5.4 summarizes the number of covalent bonds typically formed by common main group elements.

The octet rule is a useful guideline, but it has numerous exceptions. Boron, for example, has only three valence electrons it can share ($\cdot\dot{B}\cdot$) and thus forms

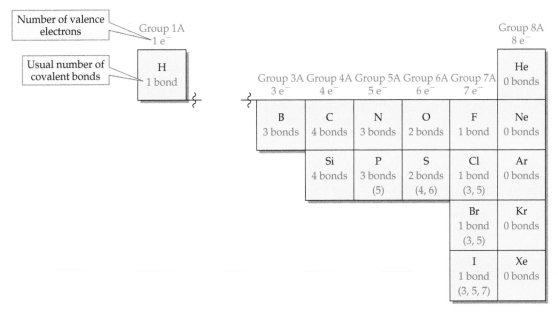

▲ **FIGURE 5.4 Numbers of covalent bonds typically formed by main group elements to achieve octet configurations.** For P, S, Cl, and other elements in the third period and below, the number of covalent bonds may vary. Numbers in parentheses indicate other possible numbers of bonds that result in exceptions to the octet rule as explained in the text.

compounds in which it has only 3 covalent bonds and 6 electrons, such as BF_3. Exceptions to the octet rule are also seen with elements in the third row and below in the periodic table because these elements have vacant *d* orbitals that can be used for bonding. Phosphorus, for example, sometimes forms 5 covalent bonds (using 10 bonding electrons); sulfur sometimes forms 4 or 6 covalent bonds (using 8 and 12 bonding electrons, respectively); and chlorine, bromine, and iodine sometimes form 3, 5, or 7 covalent bonds. Phosphorus and sulfur, for example, form molecules such as PCl_5, SF_4, and SF_6.

BF₃
Boron trifluoride
(6 valence electrons on B)

PCl₅
Phosphorus pentachloride
(10 valence electrons on P)

SF₆
Sulfur hexafluoride
(12 valence electrons on S)

WORKED EXAMPLE | **5.1** Molecular Compounds: Octet Rule and Covalent Bonds

Look at Figure 5.4 and tell whether the following molecules are likely to exist.

(a)
$$Br-\overset{\displaystyle Br}{\underset{\displaystyle Br}{C}}-Br$$
CBr₃

(b) I—Cl
ICl

(c)
$$H-\overset{\displaystyle H}{\underset{\displaystyle H}{F}}-H$$
FH₄

(d) H—S—H
H₂S

ANALYSIS Count the number of covalent bonds formed by each element and see if the numbers correspond to those shown in Figure 5.4.

SOLUTION

(a) No. Carbon needs four covalent bonds but has only three in CBr_3.

(b) Yes. Both iodine and chlorine have one covalent bond in ICl.

(c) No. Fluorine only needs one covalent bond to achieve an octet. It cannot form more than one covalent bond because it is in the second period and does not have valence d orbitals to use for bonding.

(d) Yes. Sulfur, which is in group 6A like oxygen, often forms two covalent bonds.

WORKED EXAMPLE   **5.2** Molecular Compounds: Electron-Dot Symbols

Using electron-dot symbols, show the reaction between a hydrogen atom and a fluorine atom.

ANALYSIS The electron-dot symbols show the valence electrons for the hydrogen and fluorine atoms. A covalent bond is formed by the sharing of unpaired valence electrons between the two atoms.

SOLUTION
Draw the electron-dot symbols for the H and F atoms, showing the covalent bond as a shared electron pair.

$$\text{H} \cdot \ + \ \cdot \ddot{\underset{..}{\text{F}}}: \ \longrightarrow \ \text{H} \colon \ddot{\underset{..}{\text{F}}}:$$

WORKED EXAMPLE   **5.3** Molecular Compounds: Predicting Number of Bonds

What are likely formulas for the following molecules?

(a) $SiH_2Cl_?$ (b) $HBr_?$ (c) $PBr_?$

ANALYSIS The numbers of covalent bonds formed by each element should be those shown in Figure 5.4.

SOLUTION

(a) Silicon typically forms 4 bonds: SiH_2Cl_2

(b) Hydrogen forms only 1 bond: HBr

(c) Phosphorus typically forms 3 bonds: PBr_3

PROBLEM 5.2

How many covalent bonds are formed by each atom in the following molecules? Draw molecules using the electron-dot symbols and lines to show the covalent bonds.

(a) PH_3 (b) H_2Se (c) HCl   (d) SiF_4

PROBLEM 5.3

Lead forms both ionic and molecular compounds. Using Figure 5.4 and the periodic table, predict whether a molecular compound containing lead and chlorine is more likely to be $PbCl_4$ or $PbCl_5$.

PROBLEM 5.4

What are likely formulas for the following molecules?

(a) $CH_2Cl_?$ (b) $BH_?$ (c) $NI_?$ (d) $SiCl_?$

5.3 Multiple Covalent Bonds

The bonding in some molecules cannot be explained by the sharing of only two electrons between atoms. For example, the carbon and oxygen atoms in carbon dioxide (CO_2) and the nitrogen atoms in the N_2 molecule cannot have electron octets if only two electrons are shared:

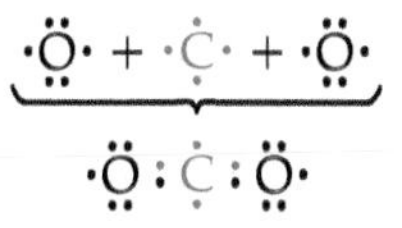

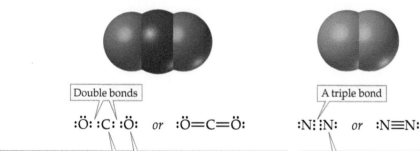

UNSTABLE—Carbon has only 6 electrons; each oxygen has only 7.   UNSTABLE—Each nitrogen has only 6 electrons.

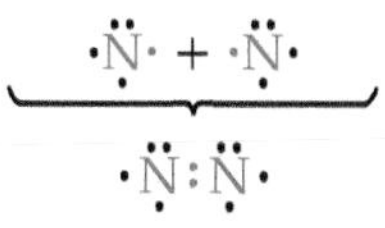

The only way the atoms in CO_2 and N_2 can have outer-shell electron octets is by sharing *more* than two electrons, resulting in the formation of *multiple* covalent bonds. Only if the carbon atom shares four electrons with each oxygen atom do all atoms in CO_2 have electron octets, and only if the two nitrogen atoms share six electrons do both have electron octets. A bond formed by sharing two electrons (one pair) is a **single bond**, a bond formed by sharing four electrons (two pairs) is a **double bond**, and a bond formed by sharing six electrons (three pairs) is a **triple bond**. Just as a single bond is represented by a single line between atoms, a double bond is represented by two lines between atoms and a triple bond by three lines:

Single bond A covalent bond formed by sharing one electron pair.

Double bond A covalent bond formed by sharing two electron pairs.

Triple bond A covalent bond formed by sharing three electron pairs.

Double bonds   A triple bond

:Ö::C::Ö: *or* :Ö=C=Ö: :N⋮⋮N: *or* :N≡N:

Each atom has 8 electrons:
    C: 2 double bonds (4 e⁻ each) = 8 e⁻
    Each O: 1 double bond (4 e⁻) + 4 lone pair e⁻ = 8 e⁻

Each N: triple bond (6 e⁻) + 2 lone pair e⁻ = 8 e⁻

Carbon, nitrogen, and oxygen are the elements most often present in multiple bonds. Carbon and nitrogen form both double and triple bonds; oxygen forms double bonds. Multiple covalent bonding is particularly common in *organic* molecules, which consist predominantly of the element carbon. For example, ethylene, a simple compound used commercially to induce ripening in fruit, has the formula C_2H_4. The only way for the two carbon atoms to have octets is for them to share four electrons in a carbon—carbon double bond:

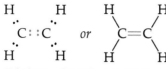

Ethylene—the carbon atoms share 4 electrons in a double bond.

As another example, acetylene, the gas used in welding, has the formula C_2H_2. To achieve octets, the two acetylene carbons share six electrons in a carbon—carbon triple bond:

H : C⫶⫶C : H   *or*   H—C≡C—H

Acetylene—the carbon atoms share
6 electrons in a triple bond.

Note that in compounds with multiple bonds like ethylene and acetylene, each carbon atom still forms a total of 4 covalent bonds.

▲ Acetylene is frequently used for welding metal because it burns with such a hot flame.

WORKED EXAMPLE **5.4** Molecular Compounds: Multiple Bonds

The compound 1-butene contains a multiple bond. In the following representation, however, only the connections between atoms are shown; the multiple bond is not specifically indicated. Identify the position of the multiple bond.

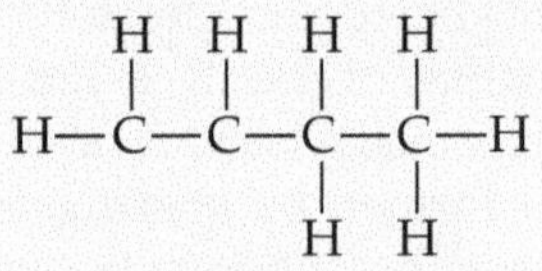

```
    H   H   H   H
    |   |   |   |
H — C — C — C — C — H
    |       |   |
    H       H   H
```

1-Butene

ANALYSIS Look for two adjacent atoms that appear to have fewer than the typical number of covalent bonds, and connect those atoms by a double or triple bond. Refer to Figure 5.4 to see how many bonds will typically be formed by hydrogen and carbon atoms.

SOLUTION

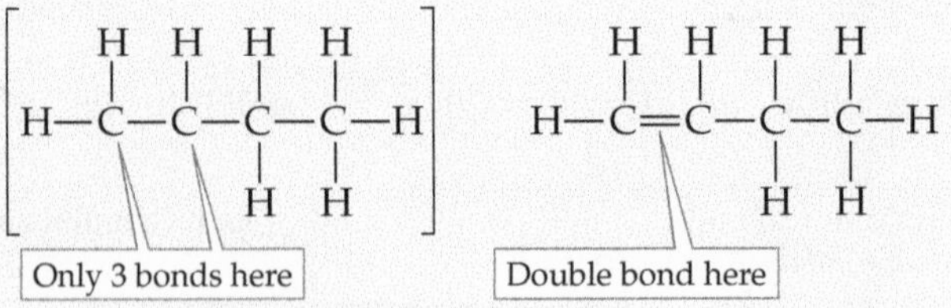

```
[    H   H   H   H  ]        H   H   H   H
[    |   |   |   |  ]        |   |   |   |
[H — C — C — C — C — H]  H — C = C — C — C — H
[    |   |   |   |  ]            |   |   |
[    H   H   H   H  ]            H   H   H
```

Only 3 bonds here   Double bond here

WORKED EXAMPLE **5.5** Multiple Bonds: Electron-Dot and Line Structures

Draw the oxygen molecule (a) using the electron-dot symbols, and (b) using lines rather than dots to indicate covalent bonds.

ANALYSIS Each oxygen atom has six valence electrons, and will tend to form two covalent bonds to reach an octet. Thus, each oxygen will need to share four electrons to form a double bond.

SOLUTION

:Ö⫶⫶Ö: or   :Ö=Ö:

PROBLEM 5.5

Acetic acid, the organic constituent of vinegar, can be drawn using electron-dot symbols as shown below. How many outer-shell electrons are associated with each atom? Draw the structure using lines rather than dots to indicate covalent bonds.

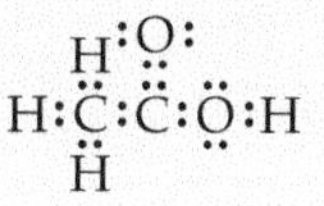

$$
\begin{array}{c}
\quad\quad H\ \ddot{\text{:}O\text{:}} \\
H\text{:}\ddot{C}\text{:}\ddot{C}\text{:}\ddot{O}\text{:}H \\
\quad\quad \ddot{H}
\end{array}
$$

PROBLEM 5.6

Identify the position of the double bond in methyl ethyl ketone, a common industrial solvent with the following connections among atoms.

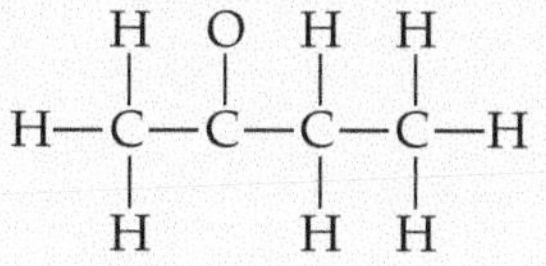

$$
\begin{array}{ccccc}
H & O & H & H \\
| & | & | & | \\
H-C-C-C-C-H \\
| & & | & | \\
H & & H & H
\end{array}
$$

Methyl ethyl ketone

5.4 Coordinate Covalent Bonds

In the covalent bonds we have seen thus far, the shared electrons have come from different atoms. That is, the bonds result from the overlap of two singly occupied valence orbitals, one from each atom. Sometimes, though, a bond is formed by the overlap of a filled orbital on one atom with a vacant orbital on another atom so that both electrons come from the *same* atom. The bond that results in this case is called a **coordinate covalent bond**.

Coordinate covalent bond The covalent bond that forms when both electrons are donated by the same atom.

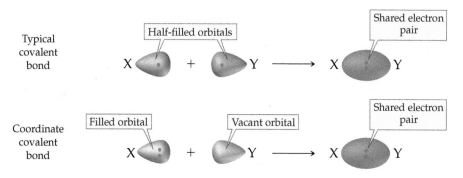

The ammonium ion, NH_4^+, is an example of a species with a coordinate covalent bond. When ammonia reacts in water solution with a hydrogen ion, H^+, the nitrogen atom donates two electrons from a filled valence orbital to form a coordinate covalent bond to the hydrogen ion, which has a vacant $1s$ orbital.

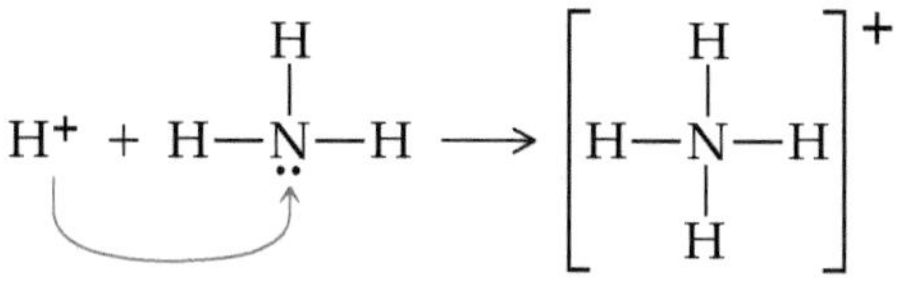

$$
H^+ + H-\underset{\underset{\displaystyle H}{|}}{\overset{\overset{\displaystyle H}{|}}{\ddot{N}}}-H \longrightarrow \left[H-\underset{\underset{\displaystyle H}{|}}{\overset{\overset{\displaystyle H}{|}}{N}}-H \right]^+
$$

Once formed, a coordinate covalent bond contains two shared electrons and is no different from any other covalent bond. All four covalent bonds in NH_4^+ are identical, for example. Note, however, that formation of a coordinate covalent bond results in unusual bonding patterns, such as an N atom with four covalent bonds rather than the usual three.

APPLICATION ▶ CO and NO: Pollutants or Miracle Molecules?

Carbon monoxide (CO) is a killer; everyone knows that. It is to blame for an estimated 3500 accidental deaths and suicides each year in the United States and is the number one cause of all deaths by poisoning. Nitric oxide (NO) is formed in combustion engines and reacts with oxygen to form nitrogen dioxide (NO_2), the reddish-brown gas associated with urban smog. What most people do not know, however, is that our bodies cannot function *without* these molecules. A startling discovery made in 1992 showed that CO and NO are key chemical messengers in the body, used by cells to regulate critical metabolic processes.

The toxicity of CO in moderate concentration is due to its ability to bind to hemoglobin molecules in the blood, thereby preventing the hemoglobin from carrying oxygen to tissues. The high reactivity of NO leads to the formation of compounds that are toxic irritants. At the same time, though, low concentrations of CO and NO are produced in cells throughout the body. Both CO and NO are highly soluble in water and can diffuse from one cell to another, where they stimulate production of a substance called *guanylyl cyclase*. Guanylyl cyclase, in turn, controls the production of another substance called *cyclic GMP*, which regulates many cellular functions.

Levels of CO production are particularly high in certain regions of the brain, including those associated with long-term memory. Evidence from experiments with rat brains suggests that a special kind of cell in the brain's hippocampus is signaled by transfer of a molecular messenger from a neighboring cell. The receiving cell responds back to the signaling cell by releasing CO, which causes still more messenger molecules to be sent. After several rounds of this back-and-forth communication, the receiving cell undergoes some sort of change that serves as a memory. When CO production is blocked, long-term memories are no longer stored, and those memories that previously existed are erased. When CO production is stimulated, however, memories are again laid down.

NO controls a seemingly limitless range of functions in the body. The immune system uses NO to fight infections and tumors. It also is used to transmit messages between nerve cells and is associated with the processes involved in learning and memory, sleeping, and depression. Its most advertised role, however, is as a *vasodilator*, a substance that allows blood vessels to relax and dilate. This discovery led to

▲ Los Angeles at sunset. Carbon monoxide is a major component of photochemical smog, but it also functions as an essential chemical messenger in our bodies.

the development of a new class of drugs that stimulate production of enzymes called nitric oxide synthases (NOS). These drugs can be used to treat conditions from erectile dysfunction (Viagra) to hypertension. Given the importance of NO in the fields of neuroscience, physiology, and immunology, it is not surprising that it was named "Molecule of the Year" in 1992.

See Additional Problems 5.91 and 5.92 at the end of the chapter.

⬭ Looking Ahead

An entire class of substances is based on the ability of transition metals to form coordinate covalent bonds with nonmetals. Called *coordination compounds*, many of these substances have important roles in living organisms. For example, toxic metals can be removed from the bloodstream by forming water-soluble coordination compounds. As another example, we will see in Chapter 19 that essential metal ions are held in enzyme molecules by coordinate covalent bonds. ⬭

5.5 Molecular Formulas and Lewis Structures

Formulas such as H_2O, NH_3, and CH_4, which show the numbers and kinds of atoms in one molecule of a compound, are called **molecular formulas**. Though important, molecular formulas are limited in their use because they do not provide information about how the atoms in a given molecule are connected.

Much more useful are **structural formulas**, which use lines to show how atoms are connected, and **Lewis structures**, which show both the connections among atoms and the placement of unshared valence electrons. In a water molecule, for instance, the oxygen atom shares two electron pairs in covalent bonds with two hydrogen atoms and has two other pairs of valence electrons that are not shared in bonds. Such unshared pairs of valence electrons are called **lone pairs**. In an ammonia molecule, three electron pairs are used in bonding and there is one lone pair. In methane, all four electron pairs are bonding.

Molecular formula A formula that shows the numbers and kinds of atoms in one molecule of a compound.

Structural formula A molecular representation that shows the connections among atoms by using lines to represent covalent bonds.

Lewis structure A molecular representation that shows both the connections among atoms and the locations of lone-pair valence electrons.

Lone pair A pair of electrons that is not used for bonding.

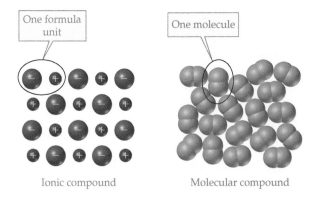

Lewis structures

Electron lone pairs

H—Ö—H   H—N̈—H   H—C—H
Water | |
           H   H
        Ammonia   Methane

▲ Ammonia is used as a fertilizer to supply nitrogen to growing plants.

Note how a molecular formula differs from an ionic formula, described previously in Section 4.10. A *molecular* formula gives the number of atoms that are combined in one molecule of a compound, whereas an *ionic* formula gives only a ratio of ions (Figure 5.5). The formula C_2H_4 for ethylene, for example, says that every ethylene molecule consists of two carbon atoms and four hydrogen atoms. The formula NaCl for sodium chloride, however, says only that there are equal numbers of Na^+ and Cl^- ions in the crystal; the formula says nothing about how the ions interact with one another.

One formula
unit

One molecule

Ionic compound   Molecular compound

◄ **FIGURE 5.5 The distinction between ionic and molecular compounds.** In ionic compounds, the smallest particle is an ion. In molecular compounds, the smallest particle is a molecule.

5.6 Drawing Lewis Structures

To draw a Lewis structure, you first need to know the connections among atoms. Sometimes the connections are obvious. Water, for example, can only be H—O—H because only oxygen can be in the middle and form two covalent bonds. Other times, you will have to be told how the atoms are connected.

Two approaches are used for drawing Lewis structures once the connections are known. The first is particularly useful for organic molecules like those found in living organisms because common bonding patterns are followed by the atoms. The second approach is a more general, stepwise procedure that works for all molecules.

Lewis Structures for Molecules Containing C, N, O, X (Halogen), and H

As summarized in Figure 5.4, carbon, nitrogen, oxygen, halogen, and hydrogen atoms usually maintain consistent bonding patterns:

- H forms one covalent bond.
- C forms four covalent bonds and often bonds to other carbon atoms.
- N forms three covalent bonds and has one lone pair of electrons.
- O forms two covalent bonds and has two lone pairs of electrons.
- Halogens (X = F, Cl, Br, I) form one covalent bond and have three lone pairs of electrons.

$-\overset{\displaystyle |}{\underset{\displaystyle |}{C}}-$	$-\overset{\displaystyle \cdot\cdot}{\underset{\displaystyle |}{N}}-$	$-\overset{\displaystyle \cdot\cdot}{\underset{\displaystyle \cdot\cdot}{O}}-$	$:\overset{\displaystyle \cdot\cdot}{\underset{\displaystyle \cdot\cdot}{X}}-$	$H-$
Carbon 4 bonds	Nitrogen 3 bonds	Oxygen 2 bonds	Halogen 1 bond	Hydrogen 1 bond

Relying on these common bonding patterns simplifies writing Lewis structures. In ethane (C_2H_6), a constituent of natural gas, for example, three of the four covalent bonds of each carbon atom are used in bonds to hydrogen, and the fourth is a carbon—carbon bond. There is no other arrangement in which all eight atoms can have their usual bonding patterns. In acetaldehyde (C_2H_4O), a substance used in manufacturing perfumes, dyes, and plastics, one carbon has three bonds to hydrogen, while the other has one bond to hydrogen and a double bond to oxygen.

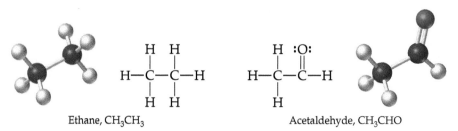

Ethane, CH_3CH_3 Acetaldehyde, CH_3CHO

Condensed structure A molecular representation in which bonds are understood by the order in which they are written rather than specifically shown.

Because Lewis structures are awkward for larger organic molecules, ethane is more frequently written as a **condensed structure** in which the bonds are not specifically shown. In its condensed form, ethane is CH_3CH_3, meaning that each carbon atom has three hydrogen atoms bonded to it (CH_3) and the two CH_3 units are bonded to each other. In the same way, acetaldehyde can be written as CH_3CHO. Note that neither the lone-pair electrons nor the C=O double bond in acetaldehyde are shown explicitly. You will get a lot more practice with such condensed structures in later chapters.

Many of the computer-generated pictures we will be using from now on will be *ball-and-stick models* rather than the space-filling models used previously. Space-filling models are more realistic, but ball-and-stick models do a better job of showing connections and molecular geometry. All models, regardless of type, use a consistent color code in which C is dark gray or black, H is white or ivory, O is red, N is blue, S is yellow, P is dark blue, F is light green, Cl is greenish yellow, Br is brownish red, and I is purple.

Space-filling

Ball-and-stick

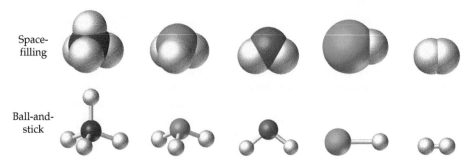

A General Method for Drawing Lewis Structures

A Lewis structure can be drawn for any molecule or polyatomic ion by following a five-step procedure. Take PCl_3, for example, a substance in which three chlorine atoms surround the central phosphorus atom.

STEP 1: Find the total number of valence electrons of all atoms in the molecule or ion. For a polyatomic ion, add one electron for each negative charge or subtract one for each positive charge. In PCl_3, for example, phosphorus (group 5A) has 5 valence electrons and chlorine (group 7A) has 7 valence electrons, giving a total of 26:

$$P + (3 \times Cl) = PCl_3$$
$$5\,e^- + (3 \times 7\,e^-) = 26\,e^-$$

In OH^-, the total is 8 electrons (6 from oxygen, 1 from hydrogen, plus 1 for the negative charge). In NH_4^+, the total is 8 (5 from nitrogen, 1 from each of 4 hydrogens, minus 1 for the positive charge).

STEP 2: Draw a line between each pair of connected atoms to represent the two electrons in a covalent bond. Remember that elements in the second row of the periodic table form the number of bonds discussed earlier in this section, whereas elements in the third row or lower can use more than 8 electrons and form more than the "usual" number of bonds (Figure 5.4). A particularly common pattern is that an atom in the third row or lower occurs as the central atom in a cluster. In PCl_3, for example, the phosphorus atom is in the center with the three chlorine atoms bonded to it:

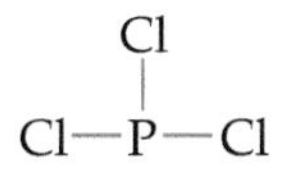

$$
\begin{array}{c}
Cl \\
| \\
Cl - P - Cl
\end{array}
$$

STEP 3: Add lone pairs so that each atom connected to the central atom (except H) gets an octet. In PCl_3, each Cl atom needs three lone pairs:

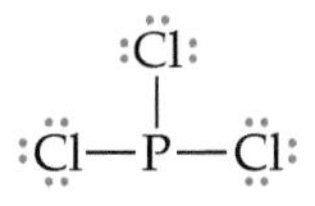

$$
\begin{array}{c}
:\ddot{C}l: \\
| \\
:\ddot{C}l - P - \ddot{C}l:
\end{array}
$$

STEP 4: Place all remaining electrons in lone pairs on the central atom. In PCl_3, we have used 24 of the 26 available electrons—6 in three single bonds and 18 in the three lone pairs on each chlorine atom. This leaves 2 electrons for one lone pair on phosphorus:

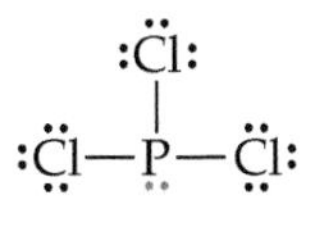

$$
\begin{array}{c}
:\ddot{C}l: \\
| \\
:\ddot{C}l - \ddot{P} - \ddot{C}l:
\end{array}
$$

STEP 5: If the central atom does not yet have an octet after all electrons have been assigned, take a lone pair from a neighboring atom and form a multiple bond to the central atom. In PCl_3, each atom has an octet, all 26 available electrons have been used, and the Lewis structure is finished.

Worked Examples 5.6–5.8 shows how to deal with cases where this fifth step is needed.

WORKED EXAMPLE 5.6 Multiple Bonds: Electron Dots and Valence Electrons

Draw a Lewis structure for the toxic gas hydrogen cyanide, HCN. The atoms are connected in the order shown in the preceding sentence.

ANALYSIS Follow the procedure outlined in the text.

SOLUTION

STEP 1: Find the total number of valence electrons:

$$H = 1, C = 4, N = 5 \quad \text{Total number of valence electrons} = 10$$

STEP 2: Draw a line between each pair of connected atoms to represent bonding electron pairs:

$$H\!-\!C\!-\!N \quad \text{two bonds} = 4 \text{ electrons; 6 electrons remaining}$$

STEP 3: Add lone pairs so that each atom (except H) has a complete octet:

$$H\!-\!C\!-\!\ddot{N}\!:$$

STEP 4: All valence electrons have been used, and so step 4 is not needed. H and N have filled valence shells, but C does not.

STEP 5: If central atom (C in this case) does not yet have an octet, use lone pairs from a neighboring atom (N) to form multiple bonds. This results in a triple bond between the C and N atoms, as shown n the electron dot and ball-and stick representations below:

We can check the structure by noting that all 10 valence electrons have been used (in four covalent bonds and one lone pair) and that each atom has the expected number of bonds (one bond for H, three for N, and four for C).

WORKED EXAMPLE 5.7 Lewis Structures: Location of Multiple Bonds

Draw a Lewis structure for vinyl chloride, C_2H_3Cl, a substance used in making poly(vinyl chloride), or PVC, plastic.

ANALYSIS Since H and Cl form only one bond each, the carbon atoms must be bonded to each other, with the remaining atoms bonded to the carbons. With only four atoms available to bond with them, the carbon atoms cannot have four covalent bonds each unless they are joined by a double bond.

SOLUTION

STEP 1: The total number of valence electrons is 18; 4 from each of the two C atoms, 1 from each of the three H atoms, and 7 from the Cl atom.

STEP 2: Place the two C atoms in the center and divide the other four other atoms between them:

$$
\begin{array}{ccc}
H & & Cl \\
\backslash & & / \\
& C\!-\!C & \\
/ & & \backslash \\
H & & H
\end{array}
$$

The five bonds account for 10 valence electrons, with 8 remaining.

STEP 3: Place 6 of the remaining valence electrons around the Cl atom so that it has a complete octet, and the remaining 2 valence electrons on one of the C atoms (either C, it does not matter):

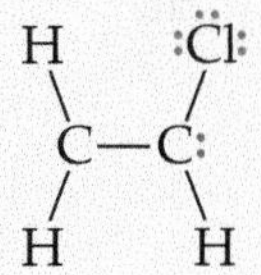

$$\text{H} \quad :\ddot{\text{C}}\text{l}:$$
$$\text{C}-\text{C}:$$
$$\text{H} \quad\quad \text{H}$$

When all the valence electrons are distributed, the C atoms still do not have a complete octet; they each need 4 bonds but have only 3.

STEP 5: The lone pair of electrons on the C atom can be used to form a double bond between the C atoms, giving each a total of four bonds (8 electrons). Placement of the double bond yields the Lewis structure and ball-an-stick model for vinyl chloride shown below:

All 18 valence electrons are accounted for in six covalent bonds and three lone pairs, and each atom has the expected number of bonds.

WORKED EXAMPLE **5.8** Lewis Structures: Octet Rule and Multiple Bonds

Draw a Lewis structure for sulfur dioxide, SO_2. The connections are O—S—O.

ANALYSIS Follow the procedure outlined in the text.

SOLUTION

STEP 1: The total number of valence electrons is 18, 6 from each atom:

$$S + (2 \times O) = SO_2$$
$$6e^- + (2 \times 6e^-) = 18e^-$$

STEP 2: O—S—O Two covalent bonds use 4 valence electrons.

STEP 3: $:\ddot{O}-S-\ddot{O}:$ Adding three lone pairs to each oxygen to give each an octet uses 12 additional valence electrons.

STEP 4: $:\ddot{O}-\underset{..}{\overset{..}{S}}-\ddot{O}:$ The remaining 2 valence electrons are placed on sulfur, but sulfur still does not have an octet.

STEP 5: Moving one lone pair from a neighboring oxygen to form a double bond with the central sulfur gives sulfur an octet (it does not matter on which side the S=O bond is written):

$$:\ddot{O}-\underset{..}{S}=\ddot{O}:$$

PROBLEM 5.7

Methylamine, CH_5N, is responsible for the characteristic odor of decaying fish. Draw a Lewis structure of methylamine.

PROBLEM 5.8

Add lone pairs where appropriate to the following structures:

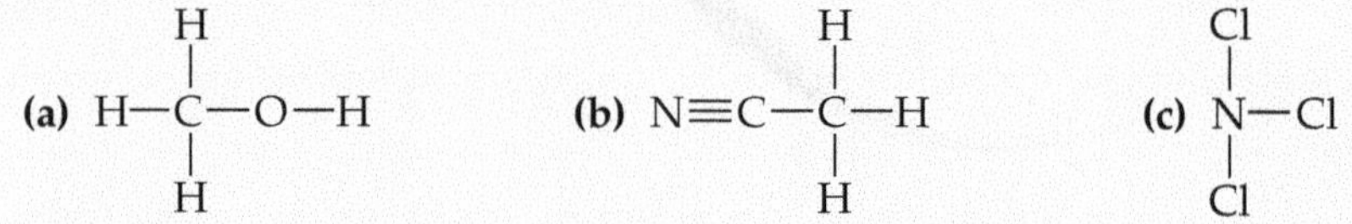

(a) $H-\overset{\displaystyle H}{\underset{\displaystyle H}{C}}-O-H$ (b) $N\equiv C-\overset{\displaystyle H}{\underset{\displaystyle H}{C}}-H$ (c) $\overset{\displaystyle Cl}{\underset{\displaystyle Cl}{N}}-Cl$

PROBLEM 5.9

Draw Lewis structures for the following:

(a) Phosgene, $COCl_2$, a poisonous gas
(b) Hypochlorite ion, OCl^-, present in many swimming pool chemicals
(c) Hydrogen peroxide, H_2O_2
(d) Sulfur dichloride, SCl_2

PROBLEM 5.10

Draw a Lewis structure for nitric acid, HNO_3. The nitrogen atom is in the center, and the hydrogen atom is bonded to an oxygen atom.

KEY CONCEPT PROBLEM 5.11

The molecular model shown here is a representation of methyl methacrylate, a starting material used to prepare Lucite plastic. Only the connections between atoms are shown; multiple bonds are not indicated.

(a) What is the molecular formula of methyl methacrylate?

(b) Indicate the positions of the multiple bonds and lone pairs in methyl methacrylate.

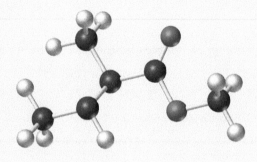

5.7 The Shapes of Molecules

Look back at the computer-generated drawings of molecules in the preceding section and you will find that the molecules are shown with specific shapes. Acetylene is *linear*, water is *bent*, ammonia is *pyramid-shaped*, methane is *tetrahedral*, and ethylene is flat, or *planar*. What determines such shapes? Why, for example, are the three atoms in water connected at an angle of 104.5° rather than in a straight line? Like so many properties, molecular shapes are related to the numbers and locations of the valence electrons around atoms.

Molecular shapes can be predicted by noting how many bonds and electron pairs surround individual atoms and applying what is called the **valence-shell electron-pair repulsion (VSEPR) model**. The basic idea of the VSEPR model is that the constantly moving valence electrons in bonds and lone pairs make up negatively

Valence-shell electron-pair repulsion (VSEPR) model A method for predicting molecular shape by noting how many electron charge clouds surround atoms and assuming that the clouds orient as far away from one another as possible.

charged clouds of electrons, which electrically repel one another. The clouds therefore tend to keep as far apart as possible, causing molecules to assume specific shapes. There are three steps to applying the VSEPR model:

STEP 1: **Draw a Lewis structure of the molecule, and identify the atom whose geometry is of interest.** In a simple molecule like PCl_3 or CO_2, this is usually the central atom.

STEP 2: **Count the number of electron charge clouds surrounding the atom of interest.** The number of charge clouds is simply the total number of lone pairs plus connections to other atoms. It does not matter whether a connection is a single bond or a multiple bond because we are interested only in the *number* of charge clouds, not in how many electrons each cloud contains. The carbon atom in carbon dioxide, for instance, has two double bonds to oxygen ($O{=}C{=}O$), and thus has two charge clouds.

STEP 3: **Predict molecular shape by assuming that the charge clouds orient in space so that they are as far away from one another as possible.** How they achieve this favorable orientation depends on their number, as summarized in Table 5.1.

TABLE 5.1 Molecular Geometry Around Atoms with 2, 3, and 4 Charge Clouds

NUMBER OF BONDS	NUMBER OF LONE PAIRS	TOTAL NUMBER OF CHARGE CLOUDS	MOLECULAR GEOMETRY		EXAMPLE
2	0	2		 Linear	$O{=}C{=}O$
3	0	3		 Planar triangular	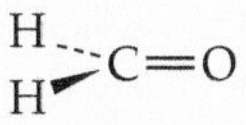
2	1			 Bent	
4	0	4		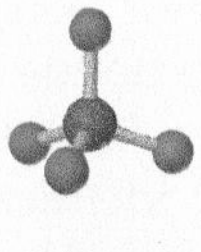 Tetrahedral	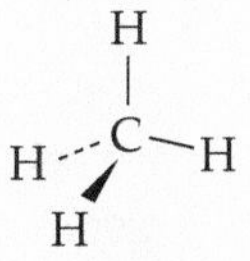
3	1			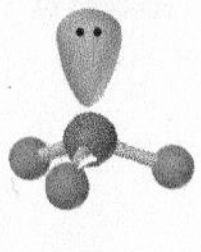 Pyramidal	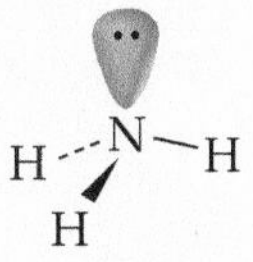
2	2			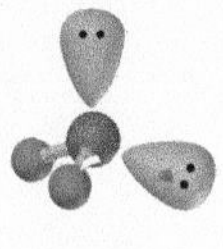 Bent	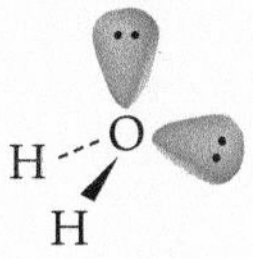

If there are only two charge clouds, as occurs on the central atom of CO_2 (two double bonds) and HCN (one single bond and one triple bond), the clouds are farthest apart when they point in opposite directions. Thus, both HCN and CO_2 are linear molecules, with **bond angles** of 180°:

Bond angle The angle formed by three adjacent atoms in a molecule.

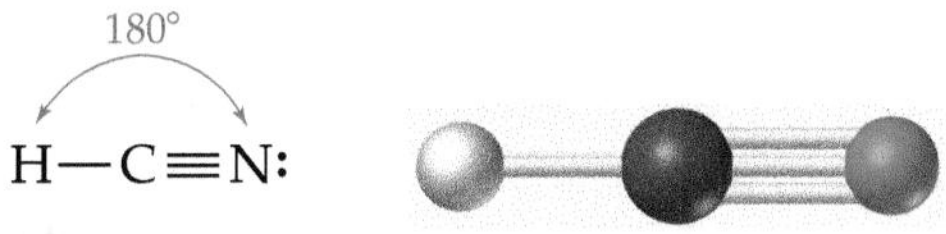

180°

$$H{-}C{\equiv}N{:}$$

These molecules are linear, with bond angles of 180°.

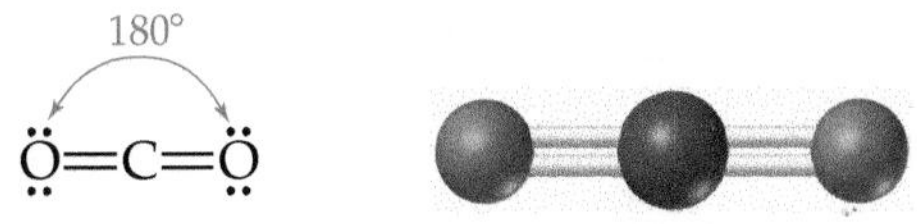

180°

$$\ddot{O}{=}C{=}\ddot{O}$$

When there are three charge clouds, as occurs on the central atom in formaldehyde (two single bonds and one double bond) and SO_2 (one single bond, one double bond, and one lone pair), the clouds will be farthest apart if they lie in a plane and point to the corners of an equilateral triangle. Thus, a formaldehyde molecule is planar triangular, with all bond angles near 120°. In the same way, an SO_2 molecule has a planar triangular arrangement of its three electron clouds, but one point of the triangle is occupied by a lone pair. The relationship of the three atoms themselves is therefore bent rather than linear, with an O—S—O bond angle of approximately 120°:

A formaldehyde molecule is planar triangular, with bond angles of roughly 120°. Note: solid wedges and dashed lines indicate bonds projecting out from and into the plane of the page, respectively.

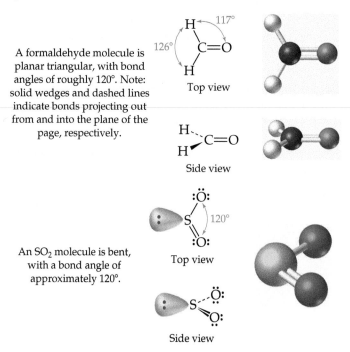

An SO_2 molecule is bent, with a bond angle of approximately 120°.

When there are four charge clouds, as occurs on the central atom in CH_4 (four single bonds), NH_3 (three single bonds and one lone pair), and H_2O (two single bonds and two lone pairs), the clouds can be farthest apart when they extend to the corners of a *regular tetrahedron*. As illustrated in Figure 5.6, a **regular tetrahedron** is a geometric solid whose four identical faces are equilateral triangles. The central atom is at the center of the tetrahedron, the charge clouds point to the corners, and the angle between lines drawn from the center to any two corners is 109.5°.

Regular tetrahedron A geometric figure with four identical triangular faces.

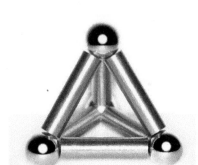

▲ The tetrahedral arrangement of atoms at the corners of a trigonal pyramid is clearly seen in this model.

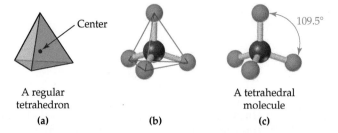

A regular tetrahedron

(a)

A tetrahedral molecule

(c)

▲ **FIGURE 5.6   The tetrahedral geometry of an atom surrounded by four charge clouds.** The atom is located at the center of the regular tetrahedron, and the four charge clouds point toward the corners. The bond angle between the center and any two corners is 109.5°.

Because valence-shell electron octets are so common, a great many molecules have geometries based on the tetrahedron. In methane (CH_4), for example, the carbon atom has tetrahedral geometry with H—C—H bond angles of exactly 109.5°. In ammonia (NH_3), the nitrogen atom has a tetrahedral arrangement of its four charge clouds, but one corner of the tetrahedron is occupied by a lone pair, resulting in an overall pyramidal shape for the molecule. Similarly, water, which has two corners of the tetrahedron occupied by lone pairs, has an overall bent shape.

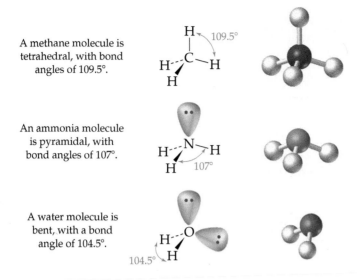

A methane molecule is tetrahedral, with bond angles of 109.5°.

An ammonia molecule is pyramidal, with bond angles of 107°.

A water molecule is bent, with a bond angle of 104.5°.

Note how the three-dimensional shapes of molecules like methane, ammonia, and water are shown. Solid lines are assumed to be in the plane of the paper; a dashed line recedes behind the plane of the paper away from the viewer; and a dark wedged line protrudes out of the paper toward the viewer. This standard method for showing three-dimensionality will be used throughout the rest of the book. Note also that the H—N—H bond angle in ammonia (107°) and the H—O—H bond angle in water (104.5°) are close to, but not exactly equal to, the ideal 109.5° tetrahedral value. The angles are diminished somewhat from their ideal value because the lone-pair charge clouds repel other electron clouds strongly and compress the rest of the molecule.

The geometry around atoms in larger molecules also derives from the shapes shown in Table 5.1. For example, each of the two carbon atoms in ethylene (H_2C=CH_2) has three charge clouds, giving rise to planar triangular geometry. It turns out that the molecule as a whole is also planar, with H—C—C and H—C—H bond angles of approximately 120°:

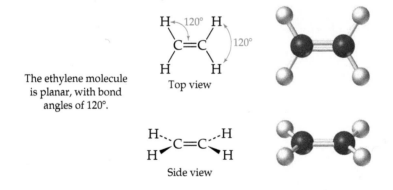

The ethylene molecule is planar, with bond angles of 120°.

Top view

Side view

Carbon atoms bonded to four other atoms are each at the center of a tetrahedron, as shown here for ethane, H_3C—CH_3:

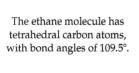

The ethane molecule has tetrahedral carbon atoms, with bond angles of 109.5°.

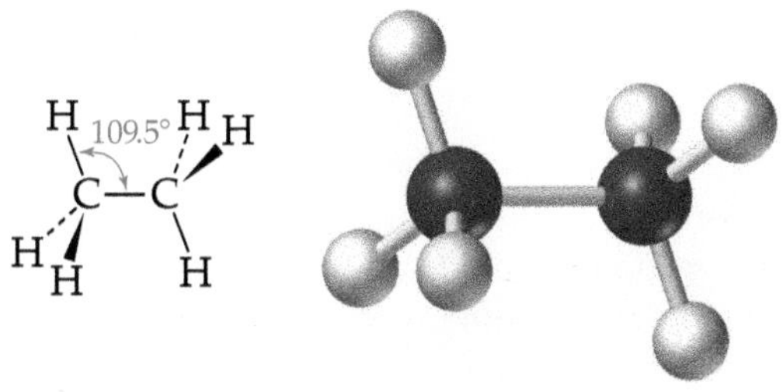

WORKED EXAMPLE 5.9 Lewis Structures: Molecular Shape

What shape do you expect for the hydronium ion, H_3O^+?

ANALYSIS Draw the Lewis structure for the molecular ion and count the number of charge clouds around the central oxygen atom; imagine the clouds orienting as far away from one another as possible.

SOLUTION
The Lewis structure for the hydronium ion shows that the oxygen atom has four charge clouds (three single bonds and one lone pair). The hydronium ion is therefore pyramidal with bond angles of approximately 109.5°:

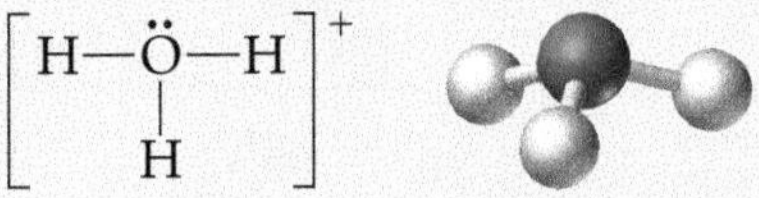

$$\left[\begin{array}{c} H-\overset{\displaystyle ..}{O}-H \\ | \\ H \end{array} \right]^+$$

WORKED EXAMPLE 5.10 Lewis Structures: Charge Cloud Geometry

Predict the geometry around each of the carbon atoms in an acetaldehyde molecule, CH_3CHO.

ANALYSIS Draw the Lewis structure and identify the number of charge clouds around each of the central carbon atoms.

SOLUTION
The Lewis structure of acetaldehyde shows that the CH_3 carbon has four charge clouds (four single bonds) and the CHO carbon atom has three charge clouds (two single bonds, one double bond). Table 5.1 indicates that the CH_3 carbon is tetrahedral, but the CHO carbon is planar triangular.

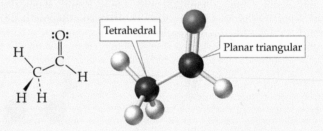

PROBLEM 5.12

Boron typically only forms three covalent bonds because it only has three valence electrons, but can form coordinate covalent bonds. Draw the Lewis structure for BF_4^- and predict the molecular shape of the ion.

PROBLEM 5.13

Predict shapes for the organic molecules chloroform, $CHCl_3$, and dichloroethylene, $Cl_2C{=}CH_2$.

PROBLEM 5.14

Electron-pair repulsion influences the shapes of polyatomic *ions* in the same way it influences neutral molecules. Draw electron-dot symbols and predict the shape of the ammonium ion, NH_4^+, and the sulfate ion, SO_4^{2-}.

APPLICATION ▶ | VERY Big Molecules

How big can a molecule be? The answer is very, *very* big. The really big molecules in our bodies and in many items we buy are all *polymers*. Like a string of beads, a polymer is formed of many repeating units connected in a long chain. Each "bead" in the chain comes from a simple molecule that has formed chemical bonds at both ends, linking it to other molecules. The repeating units can be the same:

$$-a-a-a-a-a-a-a-a-a-a-a-$$

or they can be different. If different, they can be connected in an ordered pattern:

$$-a-b-a-b-a-b-a-b-a-b-a-b-$$

or in a random pattern:

$$-a-b-b-a-b-a-a-a-b-a-b-b-$$

Furthermore, the polymer chains can have branches, and the branches can have either the same repeating unit as the main chain or a different one:

```
        a
        |
        a-a-a-a-
        |
        a
        |
        a
        |
        a-a-a-a-
        |
        a
        |
        a-a-a-a-
        |
        a
```

or

```
        a
        |
        a-b-b-b-
        |
        a
        |
        a
        |
        a-b-b-b-
        |
        a
        |
        a-b-b-b-
        |
        a
```

Still other possible variations include complex, three-dimensional networks of "cross-linked" chains. The rubber used in tires, for example, contains polymer chains connected by cross-linking atoms of sulfur to impart greater rigidity.

We all use synthetic polymers every day—we usually call them "plastics." Common synthetic polymers are made by connecting up to several hundred thousand smaller molecules together, producing giant polymer molecules with masses up to several million atomic mass units. Polyethylene, for example, is made by combining as many as 50,000 ethylene molecules ($H_2C=CH_2$) to give a polymer with repeating $-CH_2CH_2-$ units:

$$\text{Many } H_2C=CH_2 \longrightarrow -CH_2CH_2CH_2CH_2CH_2CH_2-$$

Ethylene   Polyethlene

The product is used in such items as chairs, toys, drain pipes, milk bottles, and packaging films.

Nature began to exploit the extraordinary variety of polymer properties long before humans did. In fact, despite great progress in recent years, there is still much to be learned about the polymers in living things. Carbohydrates and proteins are polymers, as are the giant molecules of deoxyribonucleic acid (DNA) that govern the reproduction of viruses, bacteria, plants, and all living creatures. Nature's polymer molecules, though, are larger and more complex than any that chemists have yet created. We will see the structures of these natural polymers in later chapters.

▲ The protective gear used by these firefighters is composed of advanced materials based on polymers.

See Additional Problems 5.93 and 5.94 at the end of the chapter.

PROBLEM 5.15

Hydrogen selenide (H_2Se) resembles hydrogen sulfide (H_2S) in that both compounds have terrible odors and are poisonous. What are their shapes?

━○ KEY CONCEPT PROBLEM 5.16

Draw a structure corresponding to the molecular model of the amino acid methionine shown here and describe the geometry around the indicated atoms. (Remember the color key discussed in Section 5.6: black = carbon; white = hydrogen; red = oxygen; blue = nitrogen; yellow = sulfur.)

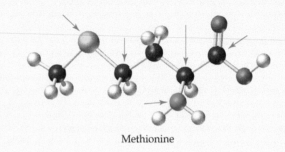

Methionine

5.8 Polar Covalent Bonds and Electronegativity

Electrons in a covalent bond occupy the region between the bonded atoms. If the atoms are identical, as in H_2 and Cl_2, the electrons are attracted equally to both atoms and are shared equally. If the atoms are *not* identical, however, as in HCl, the bonding electrons may be attracted more strongly by one atom than by the other and may thus be shared unequally. Such bonds are said to be **polar covalent bonds**. In hydrogen chloride, for example, electrons spend more time near the chlorine atom than near the hydrogen atom. Although the molecule as a whole is neutral, the chlorine is more negative than the hydrogen, resulting in *partial* charges on the atoms. These partial charges are represented by placing a $\delta-$ (Greek lowercase *delta*) on the more negative atom and a $\delta+$ on the more positive atom.

A particularly helpful way of visualizing this unequal distribution of bonding electrons is to look at what is called an *electrostatic potential map*, which uses color to portray the calculated electron distribution in a molecule. In HCl, for example, the electron-poor hydrogen is blue, and the electron-rich chlorine is reddish-yellow:

Polar covalent bond A bond in which the electrons are attracted more strongly by one atom than by the other.

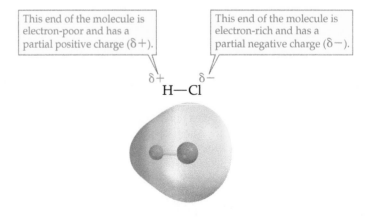

This end of the molecule is electron-poor and has a partial positive charge ($\delta+$).

This end of the molecule is electron-rich and has a partial negative charge ($\delta-$).

$$\overset{\delta+}{H}-\overset{\delta-}{Cl}$$

The ability of an atom to attract electrons in a covalent bond is called the atom's **electronegativity**. Fluorine, the most electronegative element, is assigned a value of 4, and less electronegative atoms are assigned lower values, as shown in Figure 5.7. Metallic elements on the left side of the periodic table attract electrons only weakly and have lower electronegativities, whereas the halogens and other reactive nonmetal elements on the upper right side of the table attract electrons strongly and have higher electronegativities. Note also in Figure 5.7 that electronegativity generally decreases going down the periodic table within a group.

Electronegativity The ability of an atom to attract electrons in a covalent bond.

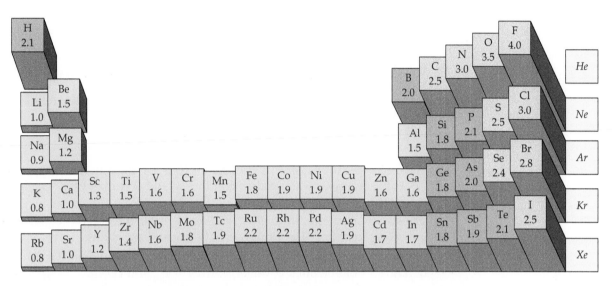

▲ **FIGURE 5.7** **Electronegativities of several main-group and transition-metal elements.** Reactive nonmetals at the top right of the periodic table are most electronegative, and metals at the lower left are least electronegative. The noble gases are not assigned values.

Comparing the electronegativities of bonded atoms makes it possible to compare the polarities of bonds and to predict the occurrence of ionic bonding. Both oxygen (electronegativity 3.5) and nitrogen (3.0), for instance, are more electronegative than carbon (2.5). As a result, both C—O and C—N bonds are polar, with carbon at the positive end. The larger difference in electronegativity values shows that the C—O bond is the more polar of the two:

Less polar $\delta+C{\uparrow}N^{\delta-}$

Electronegativity difference: $3.0 - 2.5 = 0.5$

More polar $\delta+C{\uparrow}O^{\delta-}$

Electronegativity difference: $3.5 - 2.5 = 1.0$

As a rule of thumb, electronegativity differences of less than 0.5 result in nonpolar covalent bonds, differences up to 1.9 indicate increasingly polar covalent bonds, and differences of 2 or more indicate substantially ionic bonds. The electronegativity differences show, for example, that the bond between carbon and fluorine is highly polar covalent, the bond between sodium and chlorine is largely ionic, and the bond between rubidium and fluorine is almost completely ionic:

E.N difference		Type of bond
0 — 0.4	~	Covalent
0.5 — 1.9	~	Polar covalent
2.0 and above	~	Ionic

$$\delta+C—F^{\delta-} \quad Na^+Cl^- \quad Rb^+F^-$$

Electronegativity difference: 1.5   2.1   3.2

Note, though, that there is no sharp dividing line between covalent and ionic bonds; most bonds fall somewhere between two extremes.

CXD **Looking Ahead**

The values given in Figure 5.7 indicate that carbon and hydrogen have similar electronegativities. As a result, C—H bonds are nonpolar. We will see in Chapters 12–25 how this fact helps explain the properties of organic and biological compounds, all of which have carbon and hydrogen as their principal constituents. CXD

WORKED EXAMPLE **5.11** Electronegativity: Ionic, Nonpolar, and Polar Covalent Bonds

Predict whether each of the bonds between the following atoms would be ionic, polar covalent, or nonpolar covalent. If polar covalent, which atom would carry the partial positive and negative charges?

(a) C and Br   (b) Li and Cl   (c) N and H   (d) Si and I

ANALYSIS Compare the electronegativity values for the atoms and classify the nature of the bonding based on the electronegativity difference.

SOLUTION

(a) The electronegativity for C is 2.5, and for Br is 2.8; the difference is 0.3, indicating nonpolar covalent bonding would occur between these atoms.

(b) The electronegativity for Li is 1.0, and for Cl is 3.0; the difference is 2.0, indicating ionic bonding would occur between these atoms.

(c) The electronegativity for N is 3.0, and for H is 2.5; the difference is 0.5. Bonding would be polar covalent, with $N = \delta^-$, and $H = \delta^+$.

(d) The electronegativity for Si is 1.8, and for I is 2.5; the difference is 0.7. Bonding would be polar covalent, with $I = \delta^-$, and $Si = \delta^+$.

PROBLEM 5.17

Arrange the elements commonly bonded to carbon in organic compounds, H, N, O, P, and S, in order of increasing electronegativity.

PROBLEM 5.18

Use electronegativity differences to classify bonds between the following pairs of atoms as ionic, nonpolar covalent, or polar covalent:

(a) I and Cl   (b) Li and O   (c) Br and Br   (d) P and Br

PROBLEM 5.19

Use the symbols $\delta+$ and $\delta-$ to identify the location of the partial charges on the polar covalent bonds formed between the following:

(a) Fluorine and sulfur

(b) Phosphorus and oxygen

(c) Arsenic and chlorine

5.9 Polar Molecules

Just as individual bonds can be polar, entire *molecules* can be polar if electrons are attracted more strongly to one part of the molecule than to another. Molecular polarity is due to the sum of all individual bond polarities and lone-pair contributions in the molecule and is often represented by an arrow pointing in the direction that electrons are displaced. The arrow is pointed at the negative end and is crossed at the positive end to resemble a plus sign, $(\delta+) \longmapsto (\delta-)$.

Molecular polarity depends on the shape of the molecule as well as the presence of polar covalent bonds and lone pairs. In water, for example, electrons are displaced away from the less electronegative hydrogen atoms toward the more electronegative oxygen atom so that the net polarity points between the two O—H bonds. In chloromethane, CH_3Cl, electrons are attracted from the carbon/hydrogen part of the molecule toward the electronegative chlorine atom so that the net polarity points along the C—Cl bond. Electrostatic potential maps show these polarities clearly, with electron-poor regions in blue and electron-rich regions in red.

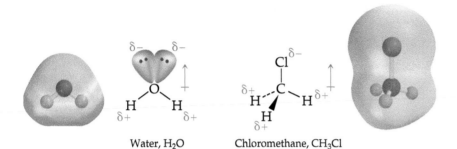

Water, H_2O Chloromethane, CH_3Cl

Furthermore, just because a molecule has polar covalent bonds does not mean that the molecule is necessarily polar overall. Carbon dioxide (CO_2) and tetra-chloromethane (CCl_4) molecules, for instance, have no net polarity because their symmetrical shapes cause the individual C=O and C—Cl bond polarities to cancel.

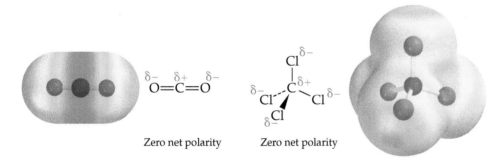

Zero net polarity   Zero net polarity

Polarity has a dramatic effect on the physical properties of molecules, particularly on melting points, boiling points, and solubilities. We will see numerous examples of such effects in subsequent chapters.

WORKED EXAMPLE **5.12** Electronegativity: Polar Bonds and Polar Molecules

Look at the structures of (a) hydrogen cyanide (HCN) and (b) vinyl chloride (H_2C=CHCl) described in Worked Examples 5.6 and 5.7, decide whether the molecules are polar, and show the direction of net polarity in each.

ANALYSIS Draw a Lewis structure for each molecule to find its shape, and identify any polar bonds using the electronegativity values in Figure 5.7. Then decide on net polarity by adding the individual contributions.

SOLUTION

(a) The carbon atom in hydrogen cyanide has two charge clouds, making HCN a linear molecule. The C—H bond is relatively nonpolar, but the C≡N bonding electrons are pulled toward the electronegative nitrogen atom. In addition, a lone pair protrudes from nitrogen. Thus, the molecule has a net polarity:

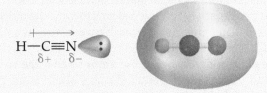

(b) Vinyl chloride, like ethylene, is a planar molecule. The C—H and C=C bonds are nonpolar, but the C—Cl bonding electrons are displaced toward the electronegative chlorine. Thus, the molecule has a net polarity:

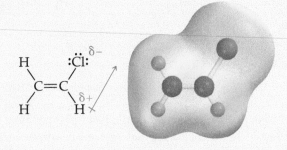

PROBLEM 5.20

Look at the molecular shape of formaldehyde (CH_2O) described on page 124, decide whether the molecule is polar, and show the direction of net polarity.

PROBLEM 5.21

Draw a Lewis structure for dimethyl ether (CH_3OCH_3), predict its shape, and tell whether the molecule is polar.

KEY CONCEPT PROBLEM 5.22

From this electrostatic potential map of methyllithium, identify the direction of net polarity in the molecule. Explain this polarity based on electronegativity values.

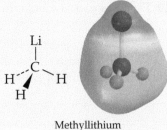

Methyllithium

5.10 Naming Binary Molecular Compounds

Binary compound A compound formed by combination of two different elements.

When two different elements combine, they form what is called a **binary compound**. The formulas of binary molecular compounds are usually written with the less electronegative element first. Thus, metals are always written before nonmetals, and a nonmetal farther left on the periodic table generally comes before a nonmetal farther right. For example,

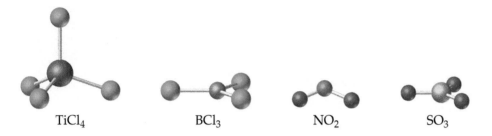

| TiCl₄ | BCl₃ | NO₂ | SO₃ |

As we learned in Section 4.10, the formulas of ionic compounds indicate the number of anions and cations necessary for a neutral formula unit, which depends on the charge on each of the ions. With molecular compounds, however, many combinations of atoms are possible since nonmetals are capable of forming multiple covalent bonds. When naming binary molecular compounds, therefore, we must identify exactly how many atoms of each element are included in the molecular formula. The names of binary molecular compounds are assigned in two steps, using the prefixes listed in Table 5.2 to indicate the number of atoms of each element combined.

TABLE 5.2 Numerical Prefixes Used in Chemical Names

NUMBER	PREFIX
1	mono-
2	di-
3	tri-
4	tetra-
5	penta-
6	hexa-
7	hepta-
8	octa-
9	nona-
10	deca-

STEP 1: Name the first element in the formula, using a prefix if needed to indicate the number of atoms.

STEP 2: Name the second element in the formula, using an -*ide* ending as for anions (Section 4.8), along with a prefix if needed.

The prefix *mono-*, meaning one, is omitted except where needed to distinguish between two different compounds with the same elements. For example, the two oxides of carbon are named carbon *mon*oxide for CO and carbon *di*oxide for CO₂. (Note that we say *mon*oxide rather than *mono*oxide.) Some other examples are

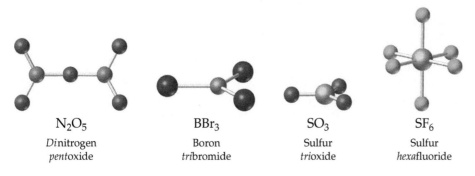

| N₂O₅ | BBr₃ | SO₃ | SF₆ |
| *Di*nitrogen *pent*oxide | Boron *tri*bromide | Sulfur *tri*oxide | Sulfur *hexa*fluoride |

WORKED EXAMPLE **5.13** Naming Molecular Compounds

Name the following compounds:

(a) N_2O_3 (b) $GeCl_4$ (c) PCl_5

SOLUTION

(a) Dinitrogen trioxide
(b) Germanium tetrachloride
(c) Phosphorus pentachloride

WORKED EXAMPLE **5.14** Writing Formulas for Molecular Compounds

Write molecular formulas for the following compounds:

(a) Nitrogen triiodide
(b) Silicon tetrachloride
(c) Carbon disulfide

SOLUTION

(a) NI_3 (b) $SiCl_4$ (c) CS_2

PROBLEM 5.23

Name the following compounds:

(a) S_2Cl_2 (b) ICl (c) ICl_3

PROBLEM 5.24

Write formulas for the following compounds:

(a) Selenium tetrafluoride
(b) Diphosphorus pentoxide
(c) Bromine trifluoride

5.11 Characteristics of Molecular Compounds

We saw in Section 4.4 that ionic compounds have high melting and boiling points because the attractive forces between oppositely charged ions are so strong that the ions are held tightly together. *Molecules*, however, are neutral, so there is no strong electrical attraction between different molecules to hold them together. There are, however, several weaker forces between molecules, called *intermolecular forces*, that we will look at in more detail in Chapter 8.

When intermolecular forces are very weak, molecules of a substance are so weakly attracted to one another that the substance is a gas at ordinary temperatures. If the forces are somewhat stronger, the molecules are pulled together into a liquid; and if the forces are still stronger, the substance becomes a molecular solid. Even so, the melting points and boiling points of molecular solids are usually lower than those of ionic solids.

In addition to having lower melting points and boiling points, molecular compounds differ from ionic compounds in other ways. Most molecular compounds are insoluble in water, for instance, because they have little attraction to strongly polar water molecules. In addition, they do not conduct electricity when melted because they have no charged particles. Table 5.3 provides a comparison of the properties of ionic and molecular compounds.

APPLICATION ▶ Damascenone by Any Other Name Would Smell as Sweet

What's in a name? According to Shakespeare's *Romeo and Juliet*, a rose by any other name would smell as sweet. Chemical names, however, often provoke less favorable responses: "It's unpronounceable." "It's too complicated." "It must be something bad."

Regarding pronunciation, chemical names are usually pronounced using every possible syllable. *Phenylpropanolamine*, for instance, a substance used in over-the-counter decongestants, is spoken with seven syllables: phen-yl-pro-pa-**nol**-a-mine.

Regarding complexity, the reason is obvious once you realize that there are more than 19 *million* known chemical compounds: The full name of a chemical compound has to include enough information to tell chemists the composition and structure of the compound. It is as if every person on earth had to have his or her own unique name that described height, hair color, and other identifying characteristics.

But does it really follow that a chemical with a really complicated name must be bad? These days, it seems that a different chemical gets into the news every week, often in a story describing some threat to health or the environment. The unfortunate result is that people sometimes conclude that everything with a chemical name is unnatural and dangerous. Neither is true, though. Acetaldehyde, for instance, is present naturally in most tart, ripe fruits and is often added in small amounts to artificial flavorings. When *pure*, however, acetaldehyde is also a flammable gas that is toxic and explosive in high concentrations.

Similar comparisons of desirable and harmful properties can be made for almost all chemicals, including water, sugar, and salt. The properties of a substance and the conditions surrounding its use must be evaluated before judgments are made. And damascenone, by the way, is the chemical largely responsible for the wonderful odor of roses.

▲ The scent of these roses contains the following: β-damascenone, β-ionone, citronellol, geraniol, nerol, eugenol, methyl eugenol, β-phenylethyl, alcohol, farnesol, linalool, terpineol, rose oxide, carvone, and many other natural substances.

See Additional Problems 5.95 and 5.96 at the end of the chapter.

TABLE 5.3 A Comparison of Ionic and Molecular Compounds

IONIC COMPOUNDS	MOLECULAR COMPOUNDS
Smallest components are ions (e.g., Na^+, Cl^-)	Smallest components are molecules (e.g., CO_2, H_2O)
Usually composed of metals combined with nonmetals	Usually composed of nonmetals with nonmetals
Crystalline solids	Gases, liquids, or low-melting solids
High melting points (e.g., NaCl = 801 °C)	Low melting points (H_2O = 0.0 °C)
High boiling points (above 700 °C) (e.g., NaCl = 1413 °C)	Low boiling points (e.g. H_2O = 100 °C; CH_3CH_2OH = 76 °C)
Conduct electricity when molten or dissolved in water	Do not conduct electricity
Many are water-soluble	Relatively few are water-soluble
Not soluble in organic liquids	Many are soluble in organic liquids

PROBLEM 5.25

A white crystalline solid has a melting point of 128 °C. It is soluble in water, but the resulting solution does not conduct electricity. Is the substance ionic or molecular? Explain.

PROBLEM 5.26

Aluminum chloride ($AlCl_3$) has a melting point of 190 °C, whereas aluminum oxide (Al_2O_3) has a melting point of 2070 °C. Explain.

KEY WORDS

Binary compound, *p. 132*

Bond angle, *p. 123*

Bond length, *p. 109*

Condensed structure, *p. 118*

Coordinate covalent bond, *p. 115*

Covalent bond, *p. 107*

Double bond, *p. 113*

Electronegativity, *p. 129*

Lewis structure, *p. 117*

Lone pair, *p. 117*

Molecular compound, *p. 110*

Molecular formula, *p. 117*

Molecule, *p. 107*

Polar covalent bond, *p. 128*

Regular tetrahedron, *p. 124*

Single bond, *p. 113*

Structural formula, *p. 117*

Triple bond, *p. 113*

Valence-shell electron-pair repulsion (VSEPR) model, *p. 122*

SUMMARY: REVISITING THE CHAPTER GOALS

1. **What is a covalent bond?** A *covalent bond* is formed by the sharing of electrons between atoms rather than by the complete transfer of electrons from one atom to another. Atoms that share two electrons are joined by a *single bond* (such as C—C), atoms that share four electrons are joined by a *double bond* (such as C=C), and atoms that share six electrons are joined by a *triple bond* (such as C≡C). The group of atoms held together by covalent bonds is called a *molecule*.

   Electron sharing typically occurs when a singly occupied valence orbital on one atom *overlaps* a singly occupied valence orbital on another atom. The two electrons occupy both overlapping orbitals and belong to both atoms, thereby bonding the atoms together. Alternatively, electron sharing can occur when a filled orbital containing an unshared, *lone pair* of electrons on one atom overlaps a vacant orbital on another atom to form a *coordinate covalent bond*.

2. **How does the octet rule apply to covalent bond formation?** Depending on the number of valence electrons, different atoms form different numbers of covalent bonds. In general, an atom shares enough electrons to reach a noble gas configuration. Hydrogen, for instance, forms one covalent bond because it needs to share one more electron to achieve the helium configuration ($1s^2$). Carbon and other group 4A elements form four covalent bonds because they need to share four more electrons to reach an octet. In the same way, nitrogen and other group 5A elements form three covalent bonds, oxygen and other group 6A elements form two covalent bonds, and halogens (group 7A elements) form one covalent bond.

3. **How are molecular compounds represented?** Formulas such as H_2O, NH_3, and CH_4, which show the numbers and kinds of atoms in a molecule, are called *molecular formulas*. More useful are *Lewis structures*, which show how atoms are connected in molecules. Covalent bonds are indicated as lines between atoms, and valence electron lone pairs are shown as dots. Lewis structures are drawn by counting the total number of valence electrons in a molecule or polyatomic ion and then placing shared pairs (bonding) and lone pairs (nonbonding) so that all electrons are accounted for.

4. **What is the influence of valence-shell electrons on molecular shape?** Molecules have specific shapes that depend on the number of electron charge clouds (bonds and lone pairs) surrounding the various atoms. These shapes can often be predicted using the *valence-shell electron-pair repulsion (VSEPR)* model. Atoms with two electron charge clouds adopt linear geometry, atoms with three charge clouds adopt planar triangular geometry, and atoms with four charge clouds adopt tetrahedral geometry.

5. **When are bonds and molecules polar?** Bonds between atoms are *polar covalent* if the bonding electrons are not shared equally between the atoms. The ability of an atom to attract electrons in a covalent bond is the atom's *electronegativity* and is highest for reactive nonmetal elements on the upper right of the periodic table and lowest for metals on the lower left. Comparing electronegativities allows a prediction of whether a given bond is covalent, polar covalent, or ionic. Just as individual bonds can be polar, entire molecules can be polar if electrons are attracted more strongly to one part of the molecule than to another. Molecular polarity is due to the sum of all individual bond polarities and lone-pair contributions in the molecule.

6. **What are the major differences between ionic and molecular compounds?** *Molecular compounds* can be gases, liquids, or low-melting solids. They usually have lower melting points and boiling points than ionic compounds, many are water insoluble, and they do not conduct electricity when melted or dissolved.

5.27 Which of the drawings shown here is more likely to represent an ionic compound and which a covalent compound?

(a)   (b)

5.28 If yellow spheres represent sulfur atoms and red spheres represent oxygen atoms, which of the following drawings depicts a collection of sulfur dioxide molecules?

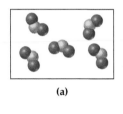
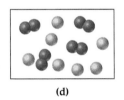

(a)   (b)

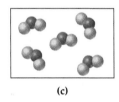
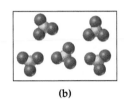

(c)   (d)

5.29 What is the geometry around the central atom in the following molecular models? (There are no "hidden" atoms; all atoms in each model are visible.)

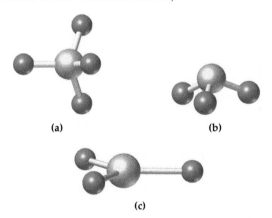

(a)   (b)

(c)

5.30 Three of the following molecular models have a tetrahedral central atom, and one does not. Which is the odd one?

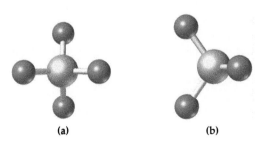

(a)   (b)

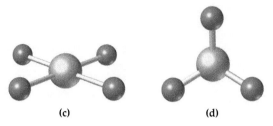

(c)   (d)

5.31 The ball-and-stick molecular model shown here is a representation of acetaminophen, the active ingredient in such over-the-counter headache remedies as Tylenol. The lines indicate only the connections between atoms, not whether the bonds are single, double, or triple (red = O, gray = C, blue = N, ivory = H).

(a) What is the molecular formula of acetaminophen?
(b) Indicate the positions of the multiple bonds in acetaminophen.
(c) What is the geometry around each carbon and each nitrogen?

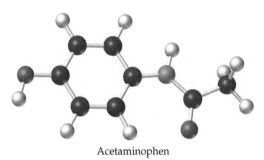

Acetaminophen

5.32 The atom-to-atom connections in vitamin C (ascorbic acid) are as shown here. Convert this skeletal drawing to a Lewis electron-dot structure for vitamin C by showing the positions of any multiple bonds and lone pairs of electrons.

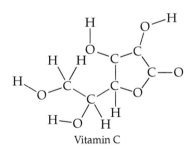

Vitamin C

5.33 The ball-and-stick molecular model shown here is a representation of thalidomide, a drug that causes terrible birth defects when taken by expectant mothers but has been approved for treating leprosy. The lines indicate only the connections between atoms, not whether the bonds are single, double, or triple (red = O, gray = C, blue = N, ivory = H).

(a) What is the molecular formula of thalidomide?
(b) Indicate the positions of the multiple bonds in thalidomide.

(c) What is the geometry around each carbon and each nitrogen?

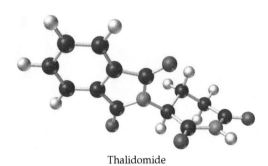

Thalidomide

5.34 Show the position of any electron lone pairs in this structure of acetamide, and indicate the electron-rich and electron-poor regions.

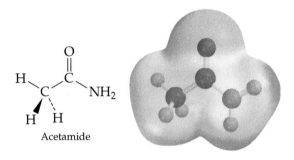

Acetamide

ADDITIONAL PROBLEMS

COVALENT BONDS

5.35 What is a covalent bond, and how does it differ from an ionic bond?

5.36 What is a coordinate covalent bond and how does it differ from a covalent bond?

5.37 Which of the following elements would you expect to form (i) diatomic molecules, (ii) mainly covalent bonds, (iii) mainly ionic bonds, (iv) both covalent and ionic bonds? (More than one answer may apply.)

(a) Oxygen
(b) Potassium
(c) Phosphorus
(d) Iodine
(e) Hydrogen
(f) Cesium

5.38 Identify the bonds formed between the following pairs of atoms as either covalent or ionic.

(a) Aluminum and bromine
(b) Carbon and fluorine
(c) Cesium and iodine
(d) Zinc and fluorine
(e) Lithium and chlorine

5.39 Write electron-dot symbols to show the number of covalent bonds in the molecules that are formed by reactions between the atoms in Problem 5.38.

5.40 Look up tellurium ($Z = 52$) in the periodic table and predict how many covalent bonds it is likely to form. Explain.

5.41 Germanium (atomic number 32) is an element used in the manufacture of transistors. Judging from its position in the periodic table, how many covalent bonds does it usually form?

5.42 Which of the following contains a coordinate covalent bond?

(a) $PbCl_2$ (b) $Cu(NH_3)_4{}^{2+}$ (c) $NH_4{}^+$

5.43 Which of the following contain a coordinate covalent bond?

(a) H_2O (b) $BF_4{}^-$ (c) H_3O^+

5.44 Tin forms both an ionic compound and a covalent compound with chlorine. The ionic compound is $SnCl_2$. Is the covalent compound more likely to be $SnCl_3$, $SnCl_4$, or $SnCl_5$? Explain.

5.45 A compound of gallium with chlorine has a melting point of 77 °C and a boiling point of 201 °C. Is the compound ionic or covalent? What is a likely formula?

5.46 Nitrous oxide, N_2O, has the following structure. Which bond in N_2O is a coordinate covalent bond?

$$:N\equiv N-\ddot{O}:$$

Nitrous oxide

5.47 Thionyl chloride, $SOCl_2$, has the following structure. Which bond in $SOCl_2$ is a coordinate covalent bond?

$$\ddot{O}:$$
$$|$$
$$S$$
$$:\ddot{C}l \qquad \ddot{C}l:$$

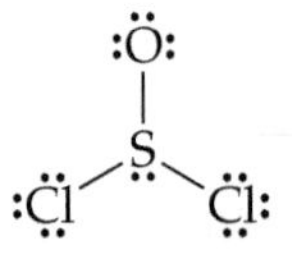

Thionyl chloride

STRUCTURAL FORMULAS

5.48 Distinguish between the following:

(a) A molecular formula and a structural formula
(b) A structural formula and a condensed structure
(c) A lone pair and a shared pair of electrons

5.49 Assume that you are given samples of two white, crystalline compounds, one of them ionic and one covalent. Describe how you might tell which is which.

5.50 Give the total number of valence electrons in the following molecules:

(a) N_2 (b) CO
(c) CH_3CH_2CHO (d) OF_2

5.51 Add lone pairs where appropriate to the following structures:

(a) $C\equiv O$ (b) CH_3SH

(c) 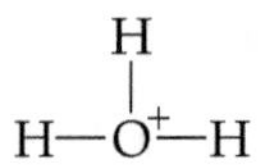 $H-\overset{H}{\underset{|}{\overset{|}{O^+}}}-H$ (d) 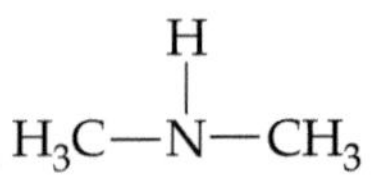 $H_3C-\overset{H}{\underset{|}{N}}-CH_3$

5.52 If a research paper appeared reporting the structure of a new molecule with formula C_2H_8, most chemists would be highly skeptical. Why?

5.53 Which of these possible structural formulas for $C_3H_6O_2$ is correct? Explain.

(a)
```
      H   H   O
      |   |   ||
  H — C — C — C — OH
      |   |
      H   H
```

(b)
```
      H       OH
      |       |
  H — C — C — C — H
      |   |
      H   OH
```

(c)
```
      H       H
      |       |
  H — C — O — C — C = O
      |       |
      H       H
```

5.54 Convert the following Lewis structures into structural formulas in which lines replace the bonding electrons. Include the lone pairs.

(a) $H\!:\!\overset{..}{\underset{..}{O}}\!:\!\overset{..}{N}\!:\!:\!\overset{..}{\underset{..}{O}}\!:$ (b) $H\!:\!\overset{H}{\underset{..}{C}}\!:\!C\!:\!:\!:\!N\!:$ (c) $H\!:\!\overset{..}{\underset{..}{F}}\!:$

5.55 Convert the following Lewis structure for the nitrate ion into a line structure that includes the lone pairs. Why does the nitrate ion have a −1 charge?

$$\left[\begin{array}{c} :\overset{..}{O}: \\ \overset{..}{O}\!:\!\overset{..}{N}\!:\!\overset{..}{O}\!: \end{array} \right]^{-}$$

5.56 Convert the following structural formulas into condensed structures.

(a)
```
      H   H   H
      |   |   |
  H — C — C — C — H
      |   |   |
      H   H   H
```

(b)
```
      H             H   H
       \           /
        C = C
       /           \
      H             H
```

(c)
```
      H   H
      |   |
  H — C — C — Cl
      |   |
      H   H
```

5.57 Expand the following condensed structures into the correct structural formulas.

(a) $CH_3COCH_2CH_3$
(b) CH_3CH_2COOH
(c) $CH_3CH_2OCH_3$

5.58 Acetic acid is the major organic constituent of vinegar. Convert the following structural formula of acetic acid into a condensed structure.

```
      H   O
      |   ||
  H — C — C — O — H
      |
      H
```

DRAWING LEWIS STRUCTURES

5.59 Draw a Lewis structure for the following molecules:

(a) SiF_4
(b) $AlCl_3$
(c) CH_2O
(d) SO_2
(e) BBr_3
(f) NF_3

5.60 Draw a Lewis structure for the following molecules:

(a) Nitrous acid, HNO_2 (H is bonded to an O atom)
(b) Ozone, O_3
(c) Acetaldehyde, CH_3CHO

5.61 Ethanol, or "grain alcohol," has the formula C_2H_6O and contains an O—H bond. Propose a structure for ethanol that is consistent with common bonding patterns.

5.62 Dimethyl ether has the same molecular formula as ethanol (Problem 5.61) but very different properties. Propose a structure for dimethyl ether in which the oxygen is bonded to two carbons.

5.63 Hydrazine, a substance used to make rocket fuel, has the formula N_2H_4. Propose a structure for hydrazine.

5.64 Tetrachloroethylene, C_2Cl_4, is used commercially as a dry cleaning solvent. Propose a structure for tetrachloroethylene based on the common bonding patterns expected in organic molecules. What kind of carbon–carbon bond is present?

5.65 Draw a Lewis structure for carbon disulfide, CS_2, a foul-smelling liquid used as a solvent for fats. What kind of carbon–sulfur bonds are present?

5.66 Draw a Lewis structure for hydroxylamine, NH_2OH.

5.67 The nitrate ion, NO_3^-, contains a double bond. Draw a Lewis structure for the ion and show why it has a negative charge.

5.68 Draw a Lewis structure for the following polyatomic ions:

(a) Formate, HCO_2^-
(b) Carbonate, CO_3^{2-}
(c) Sulfite, SO_3^{2-}
(d) Thiocyanate, SCN^-
(e) Phosphate, PO_4^{3-}
(f) Chlorite, ClO_2^- (chloride is the central atom)

MOLECULAR GEOMETRY

5.69 Predict the geometry and bond angles around atom A for molecules with the general formulas AB_3 and AB_2E, where B represents another atom and E represents an electron pair.

5.70 Predict the geometry and bond angles around atom A for molecules with the general formulas AB_4, AB_3E, and AB_2E_2, where B represents another atom and E represents an electron pair.

5.71 Sketch the three-dimensional shape of the following molecules:

(a) Chloroform, $CHCl_3$
(b) Hydrogen sulfide, H_2S
(c) Ozone, O_3
(d) Nitrogen triiodide, NI_3
(e) Chlorous acid, $HClO_2$

5.72 Predict the three-dimensional shape of the following molecules:

(a) SiF_4
(b) CF_2Cl_2
(c) SO_3
(d) BBr_3
(e) NF_3

5.73 Predict the geometry around each carbon atom in the amino acid alanine.

$$CH_3CHCOH$$

with O double-bonded above the C and NH_2 below

Alanine

5.74 Predict the geometry around each carbon atom in vinyl acetate, a precursor of the poly(vinyl alcohol) polymer used in automobile safety glass.

$$H_2C=CH-O-C-CH_3$$

with O double-bonded above the C

Vinyl acetate

POLARITY OF BONDS AND MOLECULES

5.75 Where in the periodic table are the most electronegative elements found, and where are the least electronegative elements found?

5.76 Predict the electronegativity of the yet undiscovered element with $Z = 119$.

5.77 Look at the periodic table, and then order the following elements according to increasing electronegativity: Li, K, Br, C, Cl.

5.78 Look at the periodic table, and then order the following elements according to decreasing electronegativity: C, Ca, Cs, Cl, Cu.

5.79 Which of the following bonds are polar? Identify the negative and positive ends of each bond by using $\delta-$ and $\delta+$.

(a) I—Br
(b) O—H
(c) C—F
(d) N—C
(e) C—C

5.80 Which of the following bonds are polar? Identify the negative and positive ends of each bond by using $\delta-$ and $\delta+$.

(a) O—Br
(b) N—H
(c) P—O
(d) C—S
(e) C—Li

5.81 Based on electronegativity differences, would you expect bonds between the following pairs of atoms to be largely ionic or largely covalent?

(a) Be and F
(b) Ca and Cl
(c) O and H
(d) Be and Br

5.82 Arrange the following molecules in order of the increasing polarity of their bonds:

(a) HCl
(b) PH_3
(c) H_2O
(d) CF_4

5.83 Ammonia, NH_3, and phosphorus trihydride, PH_3, both have a trigonal pyramid geometry. Which one is more polar? Explain.

5.84 Decide whether each of the compounds listed in Problem 5.82 is polar, and show the direction of polarity.

5.85 Carbon dioxide is a nonpolar molecule, whereas sulfur dioxide is polar. Draw Lewis structures for each of these molecules to explain this observation.

5.86 Water (H_2O) is more polar than hydrogen sulfide (H_2S). Explain.

NAMES AND FORMULAS OF MOLECULAR COMPOUNDS

5.87 Name the following binary compounds:

(a) NO_2
(b) SF_6
(c) BrI_5
(d) N_2O_3
(e) NI_3
(f) IF_7

5.88 Name the following compounds:

(a) $SiCl_4$
(b) NaH
(c) SbF_5
(d) OsO_4

5.89 Write formulas for the following compounds:

(a) Phosphorus triiodide
(b) Arsenic trichloride
(c) Tetraphosphorus trisulfide
(d) Dialuminum hexafluoride
(e) Dinitrogen tetroxide
(f) Arsenic pentachloride

5.90 Write formulas for the following compounds:

(a) Selenium dioxide
(b) Xenon tetroxide
(c) Dinitrogen pentasulfide
(d) Triphosphorus tetraselenide

Applications

5.91 Draw electron-dot structures for CO and NO. Why are these molecules so reactive? [*CO and NO: Pollutants or Miracle Molecules?, p. 116*]

5.92 What is a vasodilator, and why would it be useful in treating hypertension (high blood pressure)? [*CO and NO: Pollutants or Miracle Molecules?, p. 116*]

5.93 How is a polymer formed? [*VERY Big Molecules, p. 127*]

5.94 Do any polymers exist in nature? Explain. [*VERY Big Molecules, p. 127*]

5.95 Why are many chemical names so complex? [*Damascenone by Any Other Name, p. 135*]

5.96 Can you tell from the name whether a chemical is natural or synthetic? [*Damascenone by Any Other Name, p. 135*]

General Questions and Problems

5.97 The discovery in the 1960s that xenon and fluorine react to form a molecular compound was a surprise to most chemists, because it had been thought that noble gases could not form bonds.

(a) Why was it thought that noble gases could not form bonds?

(b) Draw a Lewis structure of XeF_4.

5.98 Acetone, a common solvent used in some nail polish removers, has the molecular formula C_3H_6O and contains a carbon—oxygen double bond.

    (a) Propose two Lewis structures for acetone.

    (b) What is the geometry around the carbon atoms in each of the structures?

    (c) Which of the bonds in each structure are polar?

5.99 Draw the structural formulas for two compounds having the molecular formula C_2H_4O. What is the molecular geometry around the carbon atoms in each of these molecules? Would these molecules be polar or nonpolar? (Hint: there is one double bond.)

5.100 The following formulas are unlikely to be correct. What is wrong with each?

    (a) CCl_3 **(b)** N_2H_5

    (c) H_3S **(d)** C_2OS

5.101 Which of the compounds (a) through (d) contain one or more of the following: (i) ionic bonds, (ii) covalent bonds, (iii) coordinate covalent bonds?

    (a) $BaCl_2$ **(b)** $Ca(NO_3)_2$

    (c) BCl_4^- **(d)** $TiBr_4$

5.102 The phosphonium ion, PH_4^+, is formed by reaction of phosphine, PH_3, with an acid.

    (a) Draw the Lewis structure of the phosphonium ion.

    (b) Predict its molecular geometry.

    (c) Describe how a fourth hydrogen can be added to PH_3.

    (d) Explain why the ion has a +1 charge.

5.103 Compare the trend in electronegativity seen in Figure 5.7 (p. 129) with the trend in electron affinity shown in Figure 4.1 (p. 81). What similarities do you see? What differences? Explain.

5.104 Name the following compounds. Be sure to determine whether the compound is ionic or covalent so that you use the proper rules.

    (a) $CaCl_2$ **(b)** $TeCl_2$ **(c)** BF_3

    (d) $MgSO_4$ **(e)** K_2O **(f)** FeF_3

    (g) PF_3

5.105 Titanium forms both molecular and ionic compounds with nonmetals, as, for example, $TiBr_4$ and TiO_2. One of these compounds has a melting point of 39 °C, and the other has a melting point of 1825 °C. Which is ionic and which is molecular? Explain your answer in terms of electronegativities of the atoms involved in each compound.

5.106 Draw a Lewis structure for chloral hydrate, known in detective novels as "knockout drops." Indicate all lone pairs.

$$\begin{array}{ccc} Cl & O-H & \\ | & | & \\ Cl-C-&C-O-H & \text{Chloral hydrate} \\ | & | & \\ Cl & H & \end{array}$$

5.107 The dichromate ion, $Cr_2O_7{}^{2-}$, has neither Cr—Cr nor O—O bonds. Write a Lewis structure.

5.108 Oxalic acid, $H_2C_2O_4$, is a poisonous substance found in uncooked spinach leaves. If oxalic acid has a C—C single bond, draw its Lewis structure.

5.109 Identify the elements in the fourth row of the periodic table that form the following compounds.

    (a) $\ddot{O}{=}\ddot{X}{=}\ddot{O}$ **(b)** $:\!\ddot{F}\diagdown\,\diagup\ddot{F}:$ $:\ddot{X}:$

5.110 Write Lewis structures for molecules with the following connections, showing the positions of any multiple bonds and lone pairs of electrons.

$$\text{(a)} \quad \begin{array}{cc} O & H \\ \| & | \\ Cl-C-O-&C-H \\ & | \\ & H \end{array} \qquad \text{(b)} \quad \begin{array}{c} H \\ | \\ H-C-C-C-H \\ | \\ H \end{array}$$

CHAPTER 6

Chemical Reactions: Classification and Mass Relationships

CONCEPTS TO REVIEW

Problem Solving: Converting a Quantity from One Unit to Another
(Section 2.7)

Periodic Properties and Ion Formation
(Section 4.2)

H^+ and OH^- Ions: An Introduction to Acids and Bases
(Section 4.11)

▲ The A320 Airbus shown on the assembly line in Toulouse, France. Commercial air transport relies on oxidation-reduction reactions, from the production of lightweight materials used for construction to the generation of energy required for flight.

CONTENTS

CHAPTER GOALS

Among the questions we will answer are the following:

1. How are chemical reactions written?

THE GOAL: Given the identities of reactants and products, be able to write a balanced chemical equation or net ionic equation.

2. What is the mole, and why is it useful in chemistry?

THE GOAL: Be able to explain the meaning and uses of the mole and Avogadro's number.

3. How are molar quantities and mass quantities related?

THE GOAL: Be able to convert between molar and mass quantities of an element or compound.

4. What are the limiting reagent, theoretical yield, and percent yield of a reaction?

THE GOAL: Be able to take the amount of product actually formed in a reaction, calculate the amount that could

form theoretically, and express the results as a percent yield.

5. How are chemical reactions of ionic compounds classified?

THE GOAL: Be able to recognize precipitation, acid–base neutralization, and redox reactions.

6. What are oxidation numbers, and how are they used?

THE GOAL: Be able to assign oxidation numbers to atoms in compounds and identify the substances oxidized and reduced in a given reaction.

A log burns in the fireplace, an oyster makes a pearl, a seed grows into a plant—these and almost all other changes you see taking place around you are the result of *chemical reactions*. The study of how and why chemical reactions happen is a major part of chemistry, providing information that is both fascinating and practical. In this chapter, we will begin to look at chemical reactions, starting with a discussion of how to represent them in writing. Next we will describe the mass relationships among substances involved in chemical reactions, and then introduce a few easily recognized classes of chemical reactions.

6.1 Chemical Equations

One way to view chemical reactions is to think of them as "recipes." Like recipes, all the "ingredients" in a chemical equation and their relative amounts are given, as well as the amount of product that would be obtained. Take, for example, a recipe for making s'mores, a concoction of chocolate, marshmallows, and graham crackers, which could be written as

Graham crackers + Roasted marshmallows + Chocolate bars $\longrightarrow$ S'mores

This recipe, however, is simply a list of ingredients and gives no indication of the relative amounts of each ingredient, or how many s'mores we would obtain. A more detailed recipe would be

2 Graham crackers + 1 Roasted marshmallow + $\frac{1}{4}$ Chocolate bar $\longrightarrow$ 1 S'more

In this case, the relative amounts of each ingredient are given, as well as the amount of the final product.

Let us extend this analogy to a typical chemical reaction. When sodium bicarbonate is heated in the range 50–100 °C, sodium carbonate, water, and carbon dioxide are produced. In words, we might write the reaction as

Sodium bicarbonate $\xrightarrow{\text{Heat}}$ Sodium carbonate + Water + Carbon dioxide

Just as in the recipe, the starting materials and final products are listed. Replacing the chemical names with formulas converts the word description of this reaction into a **chemical equation**:

$$2 \underbrace{NaHCO_3}_{\text{Reactant}} \xrightarrow{\text{Heat}} \underbrace{Na_2CO_3 + H_2O + CO_2}_{\text{Products}}$$

Chemical equation An expression in which symbols and formulas are used to represent a chemical reaction.

Reactant A substance that undergoes change in a chemical reaction and is written on the left side of the reaction arrow in a chemical equation.

Product A substance that is formed in a chemical reaction and is written on the right side of the reaction arrow in a chemical equation.

Balanced equation A chemical equation in which the numbers and kinds of atoms are the same on both sides of the reaction arrow.

Coefficient A number placed in front of a formula to balance a chemical equation.

Look at how this equation is written. The **reactants** are written on the left, the **products** are written on the right, and an arrow is placed between them to indicate a chemical change. Conditions necessary for the reaction to occur—heat in this particular instance—are often specified above the arrow.

Why is the number 2 placed before $NaHCO_3$ in the equation? The 2 is necessary because of a fundamental law of nature called the *law of conservation of mass*:

Law of conservation of mass Matter is neither created nor destroyed in chemical reactions.

The bonds between atoms in the reactants are rearranged to form new compounds in chemical reactions, but none of the atoms disappear and no new ones are formed. As a consequence, chemical equations must be **balanced**, meaning that *the numbers and kinds of atoms must be the same on both sides of the reaction arrow.*

The numbers placed in front of formulas to balance equations are called **coefficients**, and they multiply all the atoms in a formula. Thus, the symbol "$2\,NaHCO_3$" indicates two units of sodium bicarbonate, which contain 2 Na atoms, 2 H atoms, 2 C atoms, and 6 O atoms ($2 \times 3 = 6$, the coefficient times the subscript for O). Count the numbers of atoms on the right side of the equation to convince yourself that it is indeed balanced.

The substances that take part in chemical reactions may be solids, liquids, or gases, or they may be dissolved in a solvent. Ionic compounds, in particular, frequently undergo reaction in *aqueous solution*— that is, dissolved in water. Sometimes this information is added to an equation by placing the appropriate symbols after the formulas:

$$\begin{array}{cccc}(s) & (l) & (g) & (aq)\\ \text{Solid} & \text{Liquid} & \text{Gas} & \text{Aqueous solution}\end{array}$$

Thus, the decomposition of solid sodium bicarbonate can be written as

$$2\,NaHCO_3(s) \xrightarrow{\text{Heat}} Na_2CO_3(s) + H_2O(l) + CO_2(g)$$

WORKED EXAMPLE **6.1** Balancing Chemical Reactions

Interpret in words the following equation for the reaction used in extracting lead metal from its ores. Show that the equation is balanced.

$$2\,PbS(s) + 3\,O_2(g) \longrightarrow 2\,PbO(s) + 2\,SO_2(g)$$

SOLUTION

The equation can be read as, "Solid lead(II) sulfide plus gaseous oxygen yields solid lead(II) oxide plus gaseous sulfur dioxide."

To show that the equation is balanced, count the atoms of each element on each side of the arrow:

On the left:	2 Pb	2 S	$(3 \times 2)\,O = 6\,O$
On the right:	2 Pb	2 S	$2\,O + (2 \times 2)\,O = 6\,O$

From 2 PbO   From 2 SO_2

The numbers of atoms of each element are the same in the reactants and products, so the equation is balanced.

PROBLEM 6.1

Interpret the following equations in words:

(a) $CoCl_2(s) + 2\,HF(g) \longrightarrow CoF_2(s) + 2\,HCl(g)$

(b) $Pb(NO_3)_2(aq) + 2\,KI(aq) \longrightarrow PbI_2(s) + 2\,KNO_3(aq)$

PROBLEM 6.2

Which of the following equations are balanced?

(a) $HCl + KOH \longrightarrow H_2O + KCl$

(b) $CH_4 + Cl_2 \longrightarrow CH_2Cl_2 + HCl$

(c) $H_2O + MgO \longrightarrow Mg(OH)_2$

(d) $Al(OH)_3 + H_3PO_4 \longrightarrow AlPO_4 + 2\, H_2O$

6.2 Balancing Chemical Equations

Just as a recipe indicates the appropriate amounts of each ingredient needed to make a given product, a balanced chemical equation indicates the appropriate amounts of reactants needed to generate a given amount of product. Balancing chemical equations can often be done using a mixture of common sense and trial-and-error. There are four steps:

STEP 1: Write an unbalanced equation, using the correct formulas for all reactants and products. For example, hydrogen and oxygen must be written as H_2 and O_2, rather than as H and O, since we know that both elements exist as diatomic molecules. Remember that *the subscripts in chemical formulas cannot be changed in balancing an equation because doing so would change the identity of the substances in the reaction.*

STEP 2: Add appropriate coefficients to balance the numbers of atoms of each element. It helps to begin with elements that appear in only one formula on each side of the equation, which usually means leaving oxygen and hydrogen until last. For example, in the reaction of sulfuric acid with sodium hydroxide to give sodium sulfate and water, we might balance first for sodium. We could do this by adding a coefficient of 2 for NaOH:

$$H_2SO_4 + NaOH \longrightarrow Na_2SO_4 + H_2O \quad \text{(Unbalanced)}$$

$$H_2SO_4 + 2\,NaOH \longrightarrow Na_2SO_4 + H_2O \quad \text{(Balanced for Na)}$$

Add this coefficient . . .   . . . to balance these 2 Na.

If a polyatomic ion appears on both sides of an equation, it is treated as a single unit. For example, the sulfate ion ($SO_4{}^{2-}$) in our example is balanced because there is one on the left and one on the right:

$$H_2SO_4 + 2\,NaOH \longrightarrow Na_2SO_4 + H_2O \quad \text{(Balanced for Na and sulfate)}$$

One sulfate here . . .   . . . and one here.

At this point, the equation can be balanced for H and O by adding a coefficient of 2 for H_2O

$$H_2SO_4 + 2\,NaOH \longrightarrow Na_2SO_4 + 2\,H_2O \quad \text{(Completely balanced)}$$

4 H and 2 O here.   4 H and 2 O here.

STEP 3: Check the equation to make sure the numbers and kinds of atoms on both sides of the equation are the same.

STEP 4: Make sure the coefficients are reduced to their lowest whole-number values. For example, the equation

$$2\,H_2SO_4 + 4\,NaOH \longrightarrow 2\,Na_2SO_4 + 4\,H_2O$$

is balanced but can be simplified by dividing all coefficients by 2:

$$H_2SO_4 + 2\,NaOH \longrightarrow Na_2SO_4 + 2\,H_2O$$

WORKED EXAMPLE 6.2 Balancing Chemical Equations

Write a balanced chemical equation for the Haber process, an important industrial reaction in which elemental nitrogen and hydrogen combine to form ammonia according to the following unbalanced reaction:

$$N_2(g) + H_2(g) \longrightarrow NH_3(g)$$

SOLUTION

STEP 1: Write an unbalanced equation, using the correct formulas for all reactants and products. The unbalanced equation is provided above. By examination, we see that only two elements, N and H, need to be balanced. Both these elements exist in nature as diatomic gases, as indicated on the reactant side of the unbalanced equation.

STEP 2: Add appropriate coefficients to balance the numbers of atoms of each element. Remember that the subscript 2 in N_2 and H_2 indicates that these are diatomic molecules (that is, two N atoms or two H atoms per molecule). Since there are two nitrogen atoms on the left, we must add a coefficient of 2 in front of the NH_3 on the right side of the equation to balance the equation with respect to N:

$$N_2(g) + H_2(g) \longrightarrow 2\,NH_3(g)$$

Now we see that there are two H atoms on the left, but six H atoms on the right. We can balance the equation with respect to hydrogen by adding a coefficient of 3 in front of the $H_2(g)$ on the left side:

$$N_2(g) + 3\,H_2(g) \longrightarrow 2\,NH_3(g)$$

STEP 3: Check the equation to make sure the numbers and kinds of atoms on both sides of the equation are the same.

On the left: $(1 \times 2)\,N = 2\,N$ $\quad (3 \times 2)\,H = 6\,H$

On the right: $(2 \times 1)\,N = 2\,N$ $\quad (2 \times 3)\,H = 6\,H$

STEP 4: Make sure the coefficients are reduced to their lowest whole-number values. In this case, the coefficients already represent the lowest whole-number ratios.

WORKED EXAMPLE 6.3 Balancing Chemical Equations

Natural gas (methane, CH_4) burns in oxygen to yield water and carbon dioxide (CO_2). Write a balanced equation for the reaction.

SOLUTION

STEP 1: Write the unbalanced equation, using correct formulas for all substances:

$$CH_4 + O_2 \longrightarrow CO_2 + H_2O \text{ (Unbalanced)}$$

STEP 2: Since carbon appears in one formula on each side of the arrow, let us begin with that element. In fact, there is only one carbon atom in each formula, so the equation is already balanced for that element. Next, note that there are four hydrogen atoms on the left (in CH_4) and only two on the right (in H_2O). Placing a coefficient of 2 before H_2O gives the same number of hydrogen atoms on both sides:

$$CH_4 + O_2 \longrightarrow CO_2 + 2\,H_2O \text{ (Balanced for C and H)}$$

Finally, look at the number of oxygen atoms. There are two on the left (in O_2) but four on the right (two in CO_2 and one in each H_2O). If we place a 2 before the O_2, the number of oxygen atoms will be the same on both sides, but the numbers of other elements will not change:

$$CH_4 + 2\,O_2 \longrightarrow CO_2 + 2\,H_2O \text{ (Balanced for C, H, and O)}$$

STEP 3: Check to be sure the numbers of atoms on both sides are the same.

On the left: 1 C 4 H (2×2) O $= 4$ O

On the right: 1 C (2×2) H $= 4$ H 2 O $+$ 2 O $= 4$ O

From CO_2 From 2 H_2O

STEP 4: Make sure the coefficients are reduced to their lowest whole-number values. In this case, the answer is already correct.

WORKED EXAMPLE   **6.4** Balancing Chemical Equations

Sodium chlorate ($NaClO_3$) decomposes when heated to yield sodium chloride and oxygen, a reaction used to provide oxygen for the emergency breathing masks in airliners. Write a balanced equation for this reaction.

SOLUTION

STEP 1: The unbalanced equation is

$$NaClO_3 \longrightarrow NaCl + O_2$$

STEP 2: Both the Na and the Cl are already balanced, with only one atom of each on the left and right sides of the equation. There are three O atoms on the left, but only two on the right. The O atoms can be balanced by placing a coefficient of 1½ in front of O_2 on the right side of the equation:

$$NaClO_3 \longrightarrow NaCl + 1^1/_2 O_2$$

STEP 3: Checking to make sure the same number of atoms of each type occurs on both sides of the equation, we see one atom of Na and Cl on both sides, and three O atoms on both sides.

STEP 4: In this case, obtaining all coefficients in their smallest whole-number values requires that we multiply all coefficients by 2 to obtain

$$2\,NaClO_3 \longrightarrow 2\,NaCl + 3\,O_2$$

Checking gives

On the left: 2 Na 2 Cl (2×3) O $= 6$ O

On the right: 2 Na 2 Cl (3×2) O $= 6$ O

▲ The oxygen in emergency breathing masks comes from heating sodium chlorate.

PROBLEM 6.3

Ozone (O_3) is formed in the earth's upper atmosphere by the action of solar radiation on oxygen molecules (O_2). Write a balanced equation for the formation of ozone from oxygen.

PROBLEM 6.4

Balance the following equations:

(a) $Ca(OH)_2 + HCl \longrightarrow CaCl_2 + H_2O$

(b) $Al + O_2 \longrightarrow Al_2O_3$

(c) $CH_3CH_3 + O_2 \longrightarrow CO_2 + H_2O$

(d) $AgNO_3 + MgCl_2 \longrightarrow AgCl + Mg(NO_3)_2$

KEY CONCEPT PROBLEM 6.5

The following diagram represents the reaction of A (red spheres) with B₂ (blue spheres). Write a balanced equation for the reaction.

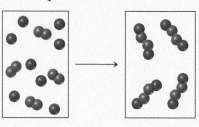

6.3 Avogadro's Number and the Mole

The balanced chemical equation indicates what is happening at the molecular level. Now let us imagine a laboratory experiment: the reaction of ethylene (C_2H_4) with hydrogen chloride (HCl) to prepare ethyl chloride (C_2H_5Cl), a colorless, low-boiling liquid used by doctors and athletic trainers as a spray-on anesthetic. The reaction is represented as

$$C_2H_4(g) + HCl(g) \rightarrow C_2H_5Cl(g)$$

In this reaction, one molecule of ethylene reacts with one molecule of hydrogen chloride to produce one molecule of ethyl chloride.

How, though, can you be sure you have a 1 to 1 ratio of reactant molecules in your reaction flask? Since it is impossible to hand-count the number of molecules correctly, you must weigh them instead. (This is a common method for dealing with all kinds of small objects: Nails, nuts, and grains of rice are all weighed rather than counted.) But the weighing approach leads to another problem. How many molecules are there in one gram of ethylene, hydrogen chloride, or any other substance? The answer depends on the identity of the substance because different molecules have different masses.

To determine how many molecules of a given substance are in a certain mass, it is helpful to define a quantity called *molecular weight*. Just as the *atomic* weight of an element is the average mass of the element's *atoms* (Section 3.3), the **molecular weight (MW)** of a molecule is the average mass of a substance's *molecules*. (⚬▭▭⚬, p. 55) Numerically, a substance's molecular weight (or **formula weight** for an ionic compound) is equal to the sum of the atomic weights for all the atoms in the molecule or formula unit.

▲ Ethyl chloride is often used as a spray-on anesthetic for athletic injuries.

Molecular weight	The sum of atomic weights of all atoms in a molecule
Formula weight	The sum of atomic weights of all atoms in one formula unit of any compound, whether molecular or ionic

For example, the molecular weight of ethylene (C_2H_4) is 28.0 amu, the molecular weight of HCl is 36.5 amu, and the molecular weight of ethyl chloride (C_2H_5Cl) is 64.5 amu. (The actual values are known more precisely but are rounded off here for convenience.)

For ethylene, C_2H_4:

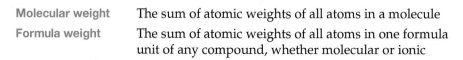

Atomic weight of 2 C = 2 × 12.0 amu = 24.0 amu

Atomic weight of 4 H = 4 × 1.0 amu = 4.0 amu

MW of C_2H_4 = 28.0 amu

For hydrogen chloride, HCl:

$$\text{Atomic weight of H} = 1.0 \text{ amu}$$

$$\underline{\text{Atomic weight of Cl} = 35.5 \text{ amu}}$$

$$\text{MW of HCl} \qquad = 36.5 \text{ amu}$$

For ethyl chloride, C_2H_5Cl:

$$\text{Atomic weight of 2 C} = 2 \times 12.0 \text{ amu} = 24.0 \text{ amu}$$

$$\text{Atomic weight of 5 H} = 5 \times 1.0 \text{ amu} = 5.0 \text{ amu}$$

$$\underline{\text{Atomic weight of Cl} \qquad\qquad\qquad = 35.5 \text{ amu}}$$

$$\text{MW of } C_2H_5Cl \qquad\qquad\qquad = 64.5 \text{ amu}$$

How are molecular weights used? Since the mass ratio of *one* ethylene molecule to *one* HCl molecule is 28.0 to 36.5, the mass ratio of *any* given number of ethylene molecules to the same number of HCl molecules is also 28.0 to 36.5. In other words, a 28.0 to 36.5 *mass* ratio of ethylene and HCl always guarantees a 1 to 1 *number* ratio. *Samples of different substances always contain the same number of molecules or formula units whenever their mass ratio is the same as their molecular or formula weight ratio* (Figure 6.1).

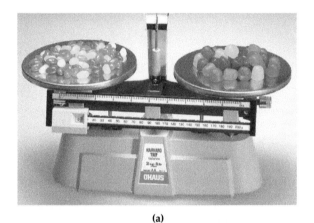

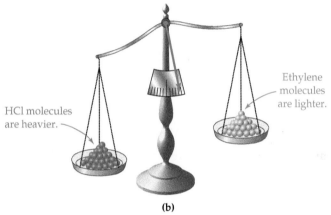

HCl molecules are heavier.

Ethylene molecules are lighter.

(a)

(b)

▲ **FIGURE 6.1** (a) Because one gumdrop weighs more than one jellybean, you cannot get equal numbers by taking equal weights. The same is true for atoms or molecules of different substances. (b) Equal numbers of ethylene and HCL molecules always have a mass ratio equal to the ratio of their molecular weights, 28.0 to 36.5.

A particularly convenient way to use this mass/number relationship for molecules is to measure amounts in grams that are numerically equal to molecular weights. If, for instance, you were to carry out your experiment with 28.0 g of ethylene and 36.5 g of HCl, you could be certain that you would have a 1 to 1 ratio of reactant molecules.

◄ These samples of water, sulfur, table sugar, mercury, and copper each contain 1 mol. Do they all weigh the same?

When referring to the vast numbers of molecules or formula units that take part in a visible chemical reaction, it is convenient to use a counting unit called a **mole**, abbreviated *mol*. One mole of any substance is the amount whose mass in grams—its *molar mass*—is numerically equal to its molecular or formula weight. One mole of ethylene has a mass of 28.0 g, one mole of HCl has a mass of 36.5 g, and one mole of ethyl chloride has a mass of 64.5 g.

> **Mole**   The amount of a substance whose mass in grams is numerically equal to its molecular or formula weight.

Avogadro's number (N_A) The number of units in 1 mol of anything; 6.022×10^{23}.

Just how many molecules are there in a mole? Experiments show that one mole of any substance contains 6.022×10^{23} formula units, a value called **Avogadro's number** (abbreviated N_A) after the Italian scientist who first recognized the importance of the mass/number relationship in molecules. Avogadro's number of formula units of any substance—that is, one mole—has a mass in grams numerically equal to the molecular weight of the substance.

$$1 \text{ mol HCl} = 6.022 \times 10^{23} \text{ HCl molecules} = 36.5 \text{ g HCl}$$

$$1 \text{ mol C}_2\text{H}_4 = 6.022 \times 10^{23} \text{ C}_2\text{H}_4 \text{ molecules} = 28.0 \text{ g C}_2\text{H}_4$$

$$1 \text{ mol C}_2\text{H}_5\text{Cl} = 6.022 \times 10^{23} \text{ C}_2\text{H}_5\text{Cl molecules} = 64.5 \text{ g C}_2\text{H}_5\text{Cl}$$

How big is Avogadro's number? Our minds cannot really conceive of the magnitude of a number like 6.022×10^{23}, but the following comparisons will give you a sense of the scale:

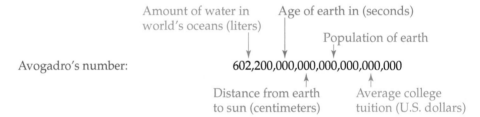

WORKED EXAMPLE   **6.5** Molar Mass and Avogadro's Number: Number of Molecules

Pseudoephedrine hydrochloride ($C_{10}H_{16}ClNO$) is a nasal decongestant commonly found in cold medication. (a) What is the molar mass of pseudoephedrine hydrochloride? (b) How many molecules of pseudoephedrine hydrochloride are in a tablet that contains 30.0 mg of this decongestant ?

ANALYSIS We are given a mass and need to convert to a number of molecules. This is most easily accomplished by using the molecular weight of pseudoephedrine hydrochloride calculated in part (a) as the conversion factor from mass to moles and realizing that this mass (in grams) contains Avogadro's number of molecules (6.022×10^{23}).

BALLPARK ESTIMATE The formula for pseudoephedrine contains ten carbon atoms (each one of atomic weight 12.0 amu), so the molecular weight is greater than 120 amu, probably near 200 amu. Thus the molar mass should be near 200 g/mol. The mass of 30 mg of pseudoepinephrine HCl is less than the mass of 1 mol of this compound by a factor of roughly 10^4 (0.03 g versus 200 g), which means the number of molecules should also be smaller by a factor of 10^4 (on the order of 10^{19} in the tablet versus 10^{23} in 1 mol).

SOLUTION

(a) The molecular weight of pseudoephedrine is found by summing the atomic weights of all atoms in the molecule:

Atomic Weight of 10 atoms of C:	10×12.011 amu	$= 120.11$ amu
16 atoms of H:	16×1.00794 amu $=$	16.127 amu
1 atom of Cl:	1×35.4527 amu $=$	35.4527 amu
1 atom of N:	1×14.0067 amu $=$	14.0067 amu
1 atom of O:	1×15.9994 amu $=$	15.9994 amu

MW of $C_{10}H_{16}ClNO$	$= 201.6958$ amu $\rightarrow 201.70$ g/mol

Remember that atomic mass in amu converts directly to molecular weight in g/mol. Also, following the rules for significant figures from Section 2.6, our final answer is rounded to the second decimal place.

(b) Since this problem involves unit conversions, we can use the step-wise solution introduced in Chapter 2.

STEP 1: Identify known information. We are given the mass of pseudoephedrine hydrochloride (in mg).	30.0 mg pseudoephedrine hydrochloride
STEP 2: Identify answer and units. We are looking for the number of molecules of pseudoephedrine hydrochloride in a 30 mg tablet.	?? = molecules
STEP 3: Identify conversion factors. Since the molecular weight of pseudoephedrine hydrochloride is 201.70 amu, 201.70 g contains 6.022×10^{23} molecules. We can use this ratio as a conversion factor to convert from mass to molecules. We will also need to convert from mg to g.	$\dfrac{6.022 \times 10^{23} \text{ molecules}}{201.70 \text{ g}}$ $\dfrac{.001 \text{ g}}{1 \text{ mg}}$
STEP 4: Solve. Set up an equation so that unwanted units cancel.	$(30.0 \text{ mg pseudoephedrine hydrochloride}) \times \left(\dfrac{.001 \text{ g}}{1 \text{ mg}} \right) \times$ $\left(\dfrac{6.022 \times 10^{23} \text{ molecules}}{201.70 \text{ g}} \right)$ $= 8.96 \times 10^{19} \text{ molecules of pseudoephedrine hydrochloride}$

BALLPARK CHECK: Our estimate for the number of molecules was on the order of 10^{19}, which is consistent with the calculated answer.

WORKED EXAMPLE **6.6** Avogadro's Number: Atom to Mass Conversions

A tiny pencil mark just visible to the naked eye contains about 3×10^{17} atoms of carbon. What is the mass of this pencil mark in grams?

ANALYSIS We are given a number of atoms and need to convert to mass. The conversion factor can be obtained by realizing that the atomic weight of carbon in grams contains Avogadro's number of atoms (6.022×10^{23}).

BALLPARK ESTIMATE Since we are given a number of atoms that is six orders of magnitude less than Avogadro's number, we should get a corresponding mass that is six orders of magnitude less than the molar mass of carbon, which means a mass for the pencil mark of about 10^{-6} g.

SOLUTION

STEP 1: Identify known information. We know the number of carbon atoms in the pencil mark.	3×10^{17} atoms of carbon
STEP 2: Identify answer and units.	Mass of carbon = ?? g
STEP 3: Identify conversion factors. The atomic weight of carbon is 12.01 amu, so 12.01 g of carbon contains 6.022×10^{23} atoms.	$\dfrac{12.01 \text{ g carbon}}{6.022 \times 10^{23} \text{ atoms}}$
STEP 4: Solve. Set up an equation using the conversion factors so that unwanted units cancel.	$(3 \times 10^{17} \text{ atoms}) \left(\dfrac{12.01 \text{ g carbon}}{6.022 \times 10^{23} \text{ atoms}} \right) = 6 \times 10^{-6} \text{ g carbon}$

BALLPARK CHECK: The answer is of the same magnitude as our estimate and makes physical sense.

PROBLEM 6.6

Calculate the molecular weight of the following substances:

(a) Ibuprofen, $C_{13}H_{18}O_2$
(b) Phenobarbital, $C_{12}H_{12}N_2O_3$

PROBLEM 6.7

How many molecules of ascorbic acid (vitamin C, $C_6H_8O_6$) are in a 500 mg tablet?

PROBLEM 6.8

What is the mass in grams of 5.0×10^{20} molecules of aspirin ($C_9H_8O_4$)?

KEY CONCEPT PROBLEM 6.9

What is the molecular weight of cytosine, a component of DNA (deoxyribonucleic acid)? (Gray = C, blue = N, red = O, ivory = H.)

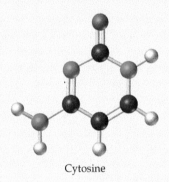

Cytosine

6.4 Gram–Mole Conversions

To ensure that we have the correct molecule to molecule (or mole to mole) relationship between reactants as specified by the balanced chemical equation, we can take advantage of the constant mass ratio between reactants, as indicated previously. The mass in grams of 1 mol of any substance (that is, Avogadro's number of molecules or formula units) is called the **molar mass** of the substance.

Molar mass   The mass in grams of 1 mol of a substance, numerically equal to molecular weight.

Molar mass = Mass of 1 mol of substance

= Mass of 6.022×10^{23} molecules (formula units) of substance

= Molecular (formula) weight of substance in grams

In effect, molar mass serves as a conversion factor between numbers of moles and mass. If you know how many moles you have, you can calculate their mass; if you know the mass of a sample, you can calculate the number of moles. Suppose, for example, we need to know how much 0.25 mol of water weighs. The molecular weight of H_2O is $(2 \times 1.0 \text{ amu}) + 16.0 \text{ amu} = 18.0 \text{ amu}$, so the molar mass of water is 18.0 g. Thus, the conversion factor between moles of water and mass of water is 18.0 g/mol:

Molar mass used as conversion factor

$$0.25 \text{ mol } H_2O \times \frac{18.0 \text{ g } H_2O}{1 \text{ mol } H_2O} = 4.5 \text{ g } H_2O$$

APPLICATION ▶ Did Ben Franklin Have Avogadro's Number? A Ballpark Calculation

At length being at Clapham, where there is on the common a large pond . . . I fetched out a cruet of oil and dropped a little of it on the water. I saw it spread itself with surprising swiftness upon the surface. The oil, though not more than a teaspoonful, produced an instant calm over a space several yards square which spread amazingly and extended itself gradually . . . making all that quarter of the pond, perhaps half an acre, as smooth as a looking glass. *Excerpt from a letter of Benjamin Franklin to William Brownrigg, 1773.*

▲ **What did these two have in common? [Benjamin Franklin (left), Amedeo Avogadro (right)]**

Benjamin Franklin, author and renowned statesman, was also an inventor and a scientist. Every schoolchild knows of Franklin's experiment with a kite and a key, demonstrating that lightning is electricity. Less well known is that his measurement of the extent to which oil spreads on water makes possible a simple estimate of molecular size and Avogadro's number.

The calculation goes like this: Avogadro's number is the number of molecules in 1 mol of any substance. So if we can estimate both the number of molecules and the number of moles in Franklin's teaspoon of oil, we can calculate Avogadro's number. Let us start by calculating the number of molecules in the oil.

1. The volume (V) of oil Franklin used was 1 tsp = 4.9 cm^3, and the area (A) covered by the oil was 1/2 acre = 2.0×10^7 cm^2. We will assume that the oil molecules are tiny cubes that pack closely together and form a layer only one molecule thick. As shown in the accompanying figure, the volume of the oil is equal to the surface area of the layer times the length (l) of the side of one molecule: $V = A \times l$. Rearranging this equation to find the length then gives us an estimate of molecular size:

$$l = \frac{V}{A} = \frac{4.9 \text{ cm}^3}{2.0 \times 10^7 \text{ cm}^2} = 2.5 \times 10^{-7} \text{ cm}$$

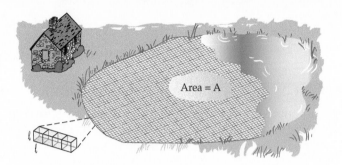

Area = A

2. The area of the oil layer is the area of the side of one molecule (l^2) times the number of molecules (N) of oil: $A = l^2 \times N$. Rearranging this equation gives us the number of molecules:

$$N = \frac{A}{l^2} = \frac{2 \times 10^7 \text{ cm}^2}{(2.5 \times 10^{-7} \text{ cm})^2} = 3.2 \times 10^{20} \text{ molecules}$$

3. To calculate the number of moles, we first need to know the mass (M) of the oil. This could have been determined by weighing the oil, but Franklin neglected to do so. Let us therefore estimate the mass by multiplying the volume (V) of the oil by the density (D) of a typical oil, 0.95 g/cm^3. (Since oil floats on water, it is not surprising that the density of oil is a bit less than the density of water, which is 1.00 g/cm^3.)

$$M = V \times D = 4.9 \text{ cm}^3 \times 0.95 \frac{\text{g}}{\text{cm}^3} = 4.7 \text{ g}$$

4. We now have to make one final assumption about the molecular weight of the oil before we complete the calculation. Assuming that a typical oil has MW = 200, then the mass of 1 mol of oil is 200 g. Dividing the mass of the oil (M) by the mass of 1 mol gives the number of moles of oil:

$$\text{Moles of oil} = \frac{4.7 \text{ g}}{200 \text{ g/mol}} = 0.024 \text{ mol}$$

5. Finally, the number of molecules per mole—Avogadro's number—can be obtained:

$$\text{Avogadro's number} = \frac{3.2 \times 10^{20} \text{ molecules}}{0.024 \text{ mol}} = 1.3 \times 10^{22}$$

The calculation is not very accurate, of course, but Ben was not really intending for us to calculate Avogadro's number when he made a rough estimate of how much his oil spread out. Nevertheless, the result is not too bad for such a simple experiment.

See Additional Problem 6.93 at the end of the chapter.

Alternatively, suppose we need to know how many moles of water are in 27 g of water. The conversion factor is 1 mol/18.0 g:

Molar mass used as conversion factor

$$27 \text{ g } H_2O \times \frac{1 \text{ mol } H_2O}{18.0 \text{ g } H_2O} = 1.5 \text{ mol } H_2O$$

Worked Examples 6.7 and 6.8 give more practice in gram–mole conversions.

WORKED EXAMPLE **6.7** Molar Mass: Mole to Gram Conversion

The nonprescription pain relievers Advil and Nuprin contain ibuprofen ($C_{13}H_{18}O_2$), whose molecular weight is 206.3 amu (Problem 6.6a). If all the tablets in a bottle of pain reliever together contain 0.082 mol of ibuprofen, what is the number of grams of ibuprofen in the bottle?

ANALYSIS We are given a number of moles and asked to find the mass. Molar mass is the conversion factor between the two.

BALLPARK ESTIMATE Since 1 mol of ibuprofen has a mass of about 200 g, 0.08 mol has a mass of about $0.08 \times 200 \text{ g} = 16 \text{ g}$.

SOLUTION

STEP 1: **Identify known information.**

0.082 mol ibuprofen in bottle

STEP 2: **Identify answer and units.**

mass ibuprofen in bottle = ?? g

STEP 3: **Identify conversion factor.** We use the molecular weight of ibuprofen to convert from moles to grams.

1 mol ibuprofen = 206.3 g

$$\frac{206.3 \text{ g ibuprofen}}{1 \text{ mol ibuprofen}}$$

STEP 4: **Solve.** Set up an equation using the known information and conversion factor so that unwanted units cancel.

$$0.082 \text{ mol } C_{13}H_{18}O_2 \times \frac{206.3 \text{ g ibuprofen}}{1 \text{ mol ibuprofen}} = 17 \text{ g } C_{13}H_{18}O_2$$

BALLPARK CHECK: The calculated answer is consistent with our estimate of 16 g.

WORKED EXAMPLE **6.8** Molar Mass: Gram to Mole Conversion

The maximum dose of sodium hydrogen phosphate (Na_2HPO_4, MW = 142.0 g/mol) that should be taken in one day for use as a laxative is 3.8 g. How many moles of sodium hydrogen phosphate, how many moles of Na^+ ions, and how many total moles of ions are in this dose?

ANALYSIS Molar mass is the conversion factor between mass and number of moles. The chemical formula Na_2HPO_4 shows that each formula unit contains 2 Na^+ ions and 1 HPO_4^{2-} ion.

BALLPARK ESTIMATE The maximum dose is about two orders of magnitude smaller than the molecular weight (approximately 4 g compared to 142 g). Thus, the number of moles of sodium hydrogen phosphate in 3.8 g should be about two orders of magnitude less than one mole. The number of moles of $NaHPO_4$ and total moles of ions, then, should be on the order of 10^{-2}.

SOLUTION

STEP 1: **Identify known information.** We are given the mass and molecular weight of Na_2HPO_4.

3.8 g Na_2HPO_4; MW = 142.0 amu

STEP 2: **Identify answer and units.** We need to find the number of moles of Na_2HPO_4, and the total number of moles of ions.

Moles of Na_2HPO_4 = ?? mol

Moles of Na^+ ions = ?? mol

Total moles of ions = ?? mol

STEP 3: **Identify conversion factor.** We can use the molecular weight of Na_2HPO_4 to convert from grams to moles.

$$\frac{1 \text{ mol } Na_2HPO_4}{142.0 \text{ g } Na_2HPO_4}$$

STEP 4: **Solve.** We use the known information and conversion factor to obtain moles of Na_2HPO_4; since 1 mol of Na_2HPO_4 contains 2 mol of Na^+ ions and 1 mol of HPO_4^{2-} ions, we multiply these values by the number of moles in the sample.

$$3.8 \text{ g } Na_2HPO_4 \times \frac{1 \text{ mol } Na_2HPO_4}{142.0 \text{ g } Na_2HPO_4} = 0.027 \text{ mol } Na_2HPO_4$$

$$\frac{2 \text{ mol } Na^+}{1 \text{ mol } Na_2HPO_4} \times 0.027 \text{ mol } Na_2HPO_4 = 0.054 \text{ mol } Na^+$$

$$\frac{3 \text{ mol ions}}{1 \text{ mol } Na_2HPO_4} \times 0.027 \text{ mol } Na_2HPO_4 = 0.081 \text{ mol ions}$$

BALLPARK CHECK: The calculated answers (0.027 mol Na_2HPO_4, 0.081 mol ions) are on the order of 10^{-2}, consistent with our estimate.

PROBLEM 6.10

How many moles of ethyl alcohol, C_2H_6O, are in a 10.0 g sample? How many grams are in a 0.10 mol sample of ethyl alcohol?

PROBLEM 6.11

Which weighs more, 5.00 g or 0.0225 mol of acetaminophen ($C_8H_9NO_2$)?

6.5 Mole Relationships and Chemical Equations

In a typical recipe, the amount of ingredients needed are specified using a variety of units: The amount of flour, for example, is usually specified in cups, whereas the amount of salt or vanilla flavoring might be indicated in teaspoons. In chemical reactions, the appropriate unit to specify the relationship between reactants and products is the mole.

The coefficients in a balanced chemical equation tell how many *molecules*, and thus how many *moles*, of each reactant are needed and how many molecules, and thus moles, of each product are formed. You can then use molar mass to calculate reactant and product masses. If, for example, you saw the following balanced equation for the industrial synthesis of ammonia, you would know that 3 mol of H_2 (3 mol $\times$ 2.0 g/mol = 6.0 g) are required for reaction with 1 mol of N_2 (28.0 g) to yield 2 mol of NH_3 (2 mol $\times$ 17.0 g/mol = 34.0 g).

This number of moles of hydrogen . . .   . . . reacts with this number of moles of nitrogen . . .   to yield this number of moles of ammonia.

$$3 \, H_2 \; + \; 1 \, N_2 \longrightarrow 2 \, NH_3$$

The coefficients can be put in the form of *mole ratios*, which act as conversion factors when setting up factor-label calculations. In the ammonia synthesis, for example, the mole ratio of H_2 to N_2 is 3:1, the mole ratio of H_2 to NH_3 is 3:2, and the mole ratio of N_2 to NH_3 is 1:2:

$$\frac{3 \text{ mol } H_2}{1 \text{ mol } N_2} \qquad \frac{3 \text{ mol } H_2}{2 \text{ mol } NH_3} \qquad \frac{1 \text{ mol } N_2}{2 \text{ mol } NH_3}$$

Worked Example 6.9 shows how to set up and use mole ratios.

> **WORKED EXAMPLE** 6.9 Balanced Chemical Equations: Mole Ratios
>
> Rusting involves the reaction of iron with oxygen to form iron(III) oxide, Fe_2O_3:
>
> $$4 \, Fe(s) + 3 \, O_2(g) \longrightarrow 2 \, Fe_2O_3(s)$$
>
> **(a)** What are the mole ratios of the product to each reactant and of the reactants to each other?
>
> **(b)** How many moles of iron(III) oxide are formed by the complete oxidation of 6.2 mol of iron?
>
> ANALYSIS AND SOLUTION
>
> **(a)** The coefficients of a balanced equation represent the mole ratios:
>
> $$\frac{2 \, mol \, Fe_2O_3}{4 \, mol \, Fe} \quad \frac{2 \, mol \, Fe_2O_3}{3 \, mol \, O_2} \quad \frac{4 \, mol \, Fe}{3 \, mol \, O_2}$$
>
> **(b)** To find how many moles of Fe_2O_3 are formed, write down the known information—6.2 mol of iron—and select the mole ratio that allows the quantities to cancel, leaving the desired quantity:
>
> $$6.2 \, \cancel{mol \, Fe} \times \frac{2 \, mol \, Fe_2O_3}{4 \, \cancel{mol \, Fe}} = 3.1 \, mol \, Fe_2O_3$$
>
> Note that mole ratios are exact numbers and therefore do not limit the number of significant figures in the result of a calculation.

> PROBLEM 6.12
>
> **(a)** Balance the following equation, and tell how many moles of nickel will react with 9.81 mol of hydrochloric acid.
>
> $$Ni(s) + HCl(aq) \longrightarrow NiCl_2(aq) + H_2(g)$$
>
> **(b)** How many moles of $NiCl_2$ can be formed in the reaction of 6.00 mol of Ni and 12.0 mol of HCl?

> PROBLEM 6.13
>
> Plants convert carbon dioxide and water to glucose ($C_6H_{12}O_6$) and oxygen in the process of photosynthesis. Write a balanced equation for this reaction, and determine how many moles of CO_2 are required to produce 15.0 mol of glucose.

6.6 Mass Relationships and Chemical Equations

It is important to remember that the coefficients in a balanced chemical equation represent molecule to molecule (or mole to mole) relationships between reactants and products. Mole ratios make it possible to calculate the molar amounts of reactants and products, but actual amounts of substances used in the laboratory are weighed out in grams. Regardless of what units we use to specify the amount of reactants and/or products (mass, volume, number of molecules, and so on), the reaction always takes place on a mole to mole basis. Thus, we need to be able to carry out three kinds of conversions when doing chemical arithmetic:

- **Mole to mole conversions** are carried out using *mole ratios* as conversion factors. Worked Example 6.9 at the end of the preceding section is an example of this kind of calculation.

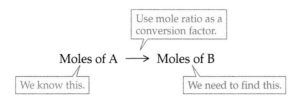

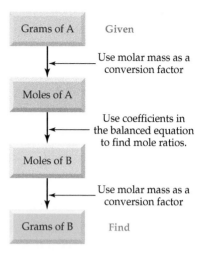

- **Mole to mass and mass to mole conversions** are carried out using *molar mass* as a conversion factor. Worked Examples 6.7 and 6.8 at the end of Section 6.4 are examples of this kind of calculation.

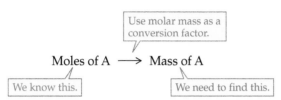

- **Mass to mass conversions** are frequently needed but cannot be carried out directly. If you know the mass of substance A and need to find the mass of substance B, you must first convert the mass of A into moles of A, then carry out a mole to mole conversion to find moles of B, and then convert moles of B into the mass of B (Figure 6.2).

Overall, there are four steps for determining mass relationships among reactants and products:

STEP 1: Write the balanced chemical equation.

STEP 2: Choose molar masses and mole ratios to convert the known information into the needed information.

STEP 3: Set up the factor-label expression and calculate the answer.

STEP 4: Check the answer against the ballpark estimate you made before you began your calculations.

▲ **FIGURE 6.2 A summary of conversions between moles and grams for substances in a chemical reaction.** The numbers of moles tell how many molecules of each substance are needed, as given by the coefficients in the balanced equation; the numbers of grams tell what mass of each substance is needed.

WORKED EXAMPLE **6.10** Mole Ratios: Mole to Mass Conversions

In the atmosphere, nitrogen dioxide reacts with water to produce NO and nitric acid, which contributes to pollution by acid rain:

$$3\,NO_2(g) + H_2O(l) \longrightarrow 2\,HNO_3(aq) + NO(g)$$

How many grams of HNO_3 are produced for every 1.0 mol of NO_2 that reacts? The molecular weight of HNO_3 is 63.0 amu.

ANALYSIS We are given the number of moles of a reactant and are asked to find the mass of a product. Problems of this sort always require working in moles and then converting to mass, as outlined in Figure 6.2.

BALLPARK ESTIMATE The molar mass of nitric acid is approximately 60 g/mol, and the coefficients in the balanced equation say that 2 mol of HNO_3 are formed for each 3 mol of NO_2 that undergo reaction. Thus, 1 mol of NO_2 should give about 2/3 mol HNO_3, or 2/3 mol × 60 g/mol = 40 g.

SOLUTION

STEP 1: **Write balanced equation.**

$$3\,NO_2(g) + H_2O(l) \longrightarrow 2\,HNO_3(aq) + NO(g)$$

STEP 2: **Identify conversion factors.** We need a mole to mole conversion to find the number of moles of product, and then a mole to mass conversion to find the mass of product. For the first conversion we use the mole ratio of NO_2 to HNO_3 as a conversion factor, and for the mole to mass calculation we use the molar mass of HNO_3 (63.0 g) as a conversion factor.

$$\frac{2\,mol\,HNO_3}{3\,mol\,NO_2}$$

$$\frac{63.0\,g\,HNO_3}{1\,mol\,HNO_3}$$

STEP 3: **Set up factor labels.** Identify appropriate mole-ratio factor labels to convert moles NO_2 to moles HNO_3, and moles HNO_3 to grams.

$$1.0 \; \cancel{mol \; NO_2} \times \frac{2 \; \cancel{mol \; HNO_3}}{3 \; \cancel{mol \; NO_2}} \times \frac{63.0 \; g \; HNO_3}{1 \; \cancel{mol \; HNO_3}} = 42 \; g \; HNO_3$$

STEP 4: BALLPARK CHECK

Our estimate was 40 g!

WORKED EXAMPLE **6.11** Mole Ratios: Mass to Mole/Mole to Mass Conversions

The following reaction produced 0.022 g of calcium oxalate (CaC_2O_4). What mass of calcium chloride was used as reactant? (The molar mass of CaC_2O_4 is 128.1 g, and the molar mass of $CaCl_2$ is 111.0 g.)

$$CaCl_2(aq) + Na_2C_2O_4(aq) \longrightarrow CaC_2O_4(s) + 2\,NaCl(aq)$$

ANALYSIS Both the known information and that to be found are masses, so this is a mass to mass conversion problem. The mass of CaC_2O_4 is first converted into moles, a mole ratio is used to find moles of $CaCl_2$, and the number of moles of $CaCl_2$ is converted into mass.

BALLPARK ESTIMATE The balanced equation says that 1 mol of CaC_2O_4 is formed for each mole of $CaCl_2$ that reacts. Because the formula weights of the two substances are similar, it should take about 0.02 g of $CaCl_2$ to form 0.02 g of CaC_2O_4.

SOLUTION

STEP 1: **Write the balanced equation.**

$$CaCl_2(aq) + Na_2C_2O_4(aq) \longrightarrow CaC_2O_4(s) + 2\,NaCl(aq)$$

STEP 2: **Identify conversion factors.** Convert the mass of CaC_2O_4 into moles, use a mole ratio to find moles of $CaCl_2$, and convert the number of moles of $CaCl_2$ to mass. We will need three conversion factors.

mass CaC_2O_4 to moles: $\dfrac{1 \; mol \; CaC_2O_4}{128.1 \; g}$

moles Ca C_2O_4 to moles $CaCl_2$: $\dfrac{1 \; mol \; CaCl_2}{1 \; mol \; CaC_2O_4}$

moles $CaCl_2$ to mass: $\dfrac{111.0 \; CaCl_2}{1 \; mol \; CaCl_2}$

STEP 3: **Set up factor-labels.** We will need to perform gram to mole and mole to mole conversions to get from grams CaC_2O_4 to grams $CaCl_2$.

$$0.022 \; g \; \cancel{CaC_2O_4} \times \frac{1 \; \cancel{mol \; CaC_2O_4}}{128.1 \; g \; \cancel{CaC_2O_4}} \times$$

$$\frac{1 \; \cancel{mol \; CaCl_2}}{1 \; \cancel{mol \; CaC_2O_4}} \times \frac{111.0 \; g \; CaCl_2}{1 \; \cancel{mol \; CaCl_2}} = 0.019 \; g \; CaCl_2$$

STEP 4: BALLPARK CHECK

The calculated answer (0.019 g) is consistent with our estimate (0.02 g).

▲ The floral pattern on this glass was created by *etching*, a process based on the reaction of HF with glass.

PROBLEM 6.14

Hydrogen fluoride is one of the few substances that react with glass (which is made of silicon dioxide, SiO_2).

$$4\,HF(g) + SiO_2(s) \longrightarrow SiF_4(g) + 2\,H_2O(l)$$

(a) How many moles of HF will react completely with 9.90 mol of SiO_2?

(b) What mass of water (in grams) is produced by the reaction of 23.0 g of SiO_2?

PROBLEM 6.15

The tungsten metal used for filaments in light bulbs is made by reaction of tungsten trioxide with hydrogen:

$$WO_3(s) + 3\,H_2(g) \longrightarrow W(s) + 3\,H_2O(g)$$

How many grams of tungsten trioxide and how many grams of hydrogen must you start with to prepare 5.00 g of tungsten? (For WO_3, MW = 231.8 amu.)

6.7 Limiting Reagent and Percent Yield

All the calculations we have done in the last several sections have assumed that 100% of the reactants are converted to products. Only rarely is this the case in practice, though. Let us return to the recipe for s'mores presented previously:

2 Graham crackers + 1 Roasted marshmallow + $\frac{1}{4}$ Chocolate bar ⟶ 1 S'more

When you check your supplies, you find that you have 20 graham crackers, 8 marshmallows, and 3 chocolate bars. How many s'mores can you make? (Answer = 8!) You have enough graham crackers and chocolate bars to make more, but you will run out of marshmallows after you have made eight s'mores. In a similar way, when running a chemical reaction we don't always have the exact amounts of reagents to allow all of them to react completely. The reactant that is exhausted first in such a reaction is called the **limiting reagent.** The amount of product you obtain if the limiting reagent is completely consumed is called the **theoretical yield** of the reaction.

Suppose that, while you are making s'mores, one of your eight marshmallows gets burned to a crisp. If this happens, the actual number of s'mores produced will be less than what you predicted based on the amount of starting materials. Similarly, chemical reactions do not always yield the exact amount of product predicted by the initial amount of reactants. More frequently, a majority of the reactant molecules behave as written but other processes, called *side reactions*, also occur. In addition, some of the product may be lost in handling. As a result, the amount of product actually formed—the reaction's **actual yield**—is somewhat less than the theoretical yield. The amount of product actually obtained in a reaction is usually expressed as a **percent yield:**

$$\text{Percent yield} = \frac{\text{Actual yield}}{\text{Theoretical yield}} \times 100\%$$

A reaction's actual yield is found by weighing the amount of product obtained. The theoretical yield is found by using the amount of limiting reagent in a mass to mass calculation like those illustrated in the preceding section (see Worked Example 6.11). Worked Examples 6.12–6.14 involve limiting reagent, percent yield, actual yield, and theoretical yield calculations.

Limiting reagent The reactant that runs out first.

Theoretical yield The amount of product formed assuming complete reaction of the limiting reagent.

Actual yield The amount of product actually formed in a reaction.

Percent yield The percent of the theoretical yield actually obtained from a chemical reaction.

WORKED EXAMPLE **6.12** Percent Yield

The combustion of acetylene gas (C_2H_2) produces carbon dioxide and water as indicated in the following reaction:

$$2\,C_2H_2(g) + 5\,O_2(g) \longrightarrow 4\,CO_2(g) + 2\,H_2O(g)$$

When 26.0 g of acetylene is burned in sufficient oxygen for complete reaction, the theoretical yield of CO_2 is 88.0 g. Calculate the percent yield for this reaction if the actual yield is only 72.4 g CO_2.

ANALYSIS The percent yield is calculated by dividing the actual yield by the theoretical yield and multiplying by 100.

BALLPARK ESTIMATE The theoretical yield (88.0 g) is close to 100 g. The actual yield (72.4 g) is about 15 g less than the theoretical yield. The actual yield is thus about 15% less than the theoretical yield, so the percent yield is about 85%.

SOLUTION

$$\text{Percent yield} = \frac{\text{Actual yield}}{\text{Theoretical yield}} \times 100 = \frac{72.4\text{ g }CO_2}{88.0\text{ g }CO_2} \times 100 = 82.3\%$$

BALLPARK CHECK The calculated percent yield agrees very well with our estimate of 85%.

WORKED EXAMPLE 6.13 Mass to Mole Conversions: Limiting Reagent and Theoretical Yield

The element boron is produced commercially by the reaction of boric oxide with magnesium at high temperature:

$$B_2O_3(l) + 3\,Mg(s) \longrightarrow 2\,B(s) + 3\,MgO(s)$$

What is the theoretical yield of boron when 2350 g of boric oxide is reacted with 3580 g of magnesium? The molar masses of boric oxide and magnesium are 69.6 g/mol and 24.3 g/mol, respectively.

ANALYSIS To calculate theoretical yield, we first have to identify the limiting reagent. The theoretical yield in grams is then calculated from the amount of limiting reagent used in the reaction. The calculation involves the mass to mole and mole to mass conversions discussed in the preceding section.

SOLUTION

STEP 1: Identify known information. We have the masses and molar masses of the reagents.

2350 g B_2O_3, molar mass 69.6 g/mol
3580 g Mg, molar mass 24.3 g/mol

STEP 2: Identify answer and units. We are solving for the theoretical yield of boron.

Theoretical mass of B = ?? g

STEP 3: Identify conversion factors. We can use the molar masses to convert from masses to moles of reactants (B_2O_3, Mg). From moles of reactants, we can use mole ratios from the balanced chemical equation to find the number of moles of B produced. B_2O_3 is the limiting reagent, since complete reaction of this reagent yields less product (B).

$$(2350 \text{ g } B_2O_3) \times \frac{1 \text{ mol } B_2O_3}{69.6 \text{ g } B_2O_3} = 33.8 \text{ mol } B_2O_3$$

$$(3580 \text{ g Mg}) \times \frac{1 \text{ mol Mg}}{24.3 \text{ g Mg}} = 147 \text{ mol Mg}$$

$$33.8 \text{ mol } B_2O_3 \times \frac{2 \text{ mol B}}{1 \text{ mol } B_2O_3} = 67.6 \text{ mol B*}$$

$$147 \text{ mol Mg} \times \frac{2 \text{ mol B}}{3 \text{ mol Mg}} = 98.0 \text{ mol B}$$

(*limiting reagent!)

STEP 4: Solve. Once the limiting reagent has been identified (B_2O_3), the theoretical amount of B that should be formed can be calculated using a mole to mass conversion.

$$67.6 \text{ mol B} \times \frac{10.8 \text{ g B}}{1 \text{ mol B}} = 730 \text{ g B}$$

WORKED EXAMPLE 6.14 Mass to Mole Conversion: Percent Yield

The reaction of ethylene with water to give ethyl alcohol (CH_3CH_2OH) occurs in 78.5% actual yield. How many grams of ethyl alcohol are formed by reaction of 25.0 g of ethylene? (For ethylene, MW = 28.0 amu; for ethyl alcohol, MW = 46.0 amu.)

$$H_2C{=}CH_2 + H_2O \longrightarrow CH_3CH_2OH$$

ANALYSIS Treat this as a typical mass relationship problem to find the amount of ethyl alcohol that can theoretically be formed from 25.0 g of ethylene, and then multiply the answer by 78.5% to find the amount actually formed.

BALLPARK ESTIMATE The 25.0 g of ethylene is a bit less than 1 mol; since the percent yield is about 78%, a bit less than 0.78 mol of ethyl alcohol will form—perhaps about 3/4 mol, or 3/4 × 46 g = 34 g.

SOLUTION
The theoretical yield of ethyl alcohol is

$$25.0 \text{ g ethylene} \times \frac{1 \text{ mol ethylene}}{28.0 \text{ g ethylene}} \times \frac{1 \text{ mol ethyl alc.}}{1 \text{ mol ethylene}} \times \frac{46.0 \text{ g ethyl alc.}}{1 \text{ mol ethyl alc.}} = 41.1 \text{ g ethyl alcohol}$$

and so the actual yield is

$$41.1 \text{ g ethyl alc.} \times 0.785 = 32.3 \text{ g ethyl alcohol}$$

BALLPARK CHECK The calculated result (32.3 g) is close to our estimate (34 g).

PROBLEM 6.16

What is the theoretical yield of ethyl chloride in the reaction of 19.4 g of ethylene with 50 g of hydrogen chloride? What is the percent yield if 25.5 g of ethyl chloride is actually formed? (For ethylene, MW = 28.0 amu; for hydrogen chloride, MW = 36.5 amu; for ethyl chloride, MW = 64.5 amu.)

$$H_2C{=}CH_2 + HCl \longrightarrow CH_3CH_2Cl$$

PROBLEM 6.17

The reaction of ethylene oxide with water to give ethylene glycol (automobile antifreeze) occurs in 96.0% actual yield. How many grams of ethylene glycol are formed by reaction of 35.0 g of ethylene oxide? (For ethylene oxide, MW = 44.0 amu; for ethylene glycol, MW = 62.0 amu.)

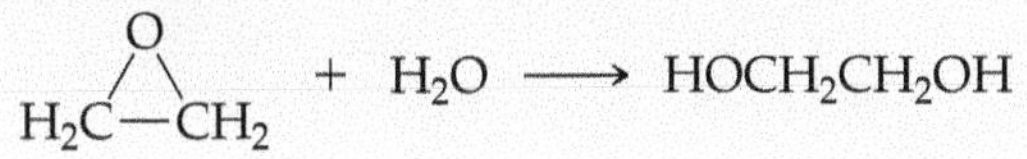

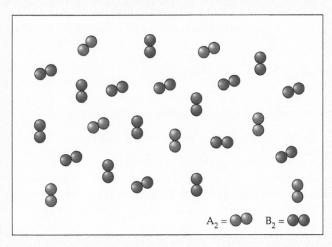

Ethylene oxide   Ethylene glycol

KEY CONCEPT PROBLEM 6.18

Identify the limiting reagent in the reaction mixture shown below (red = A_2, blue = B_2). The balanced reaction is

$$A_2 + 2\,B_2 \longrightarrow 2\,AB_2$$

$A_2 =$ ◯◯ $B_2 =$ ●●

6.8 Classes of Chemical Reactions

One of the best ways to understand any subject is to look for patterns that help us categorize large amounts of information. When learning about chemical reactions, for instance, it is helpful to group the reactions of ionic compounds into three general classes: *precipitation reactions, acid–base neutralization reactions,* and *oxidation–reduction reactions.* This is not the only possible way of categorizing reactions nor does the list include all possibilities, but it is useful nonetheless. Let us look briefly at examples of each of these three reaction classes before studying them in more detail in subsequent sections.

- **Precipitation reactions** are processes in which an insoluble solid called a **precipitate** forms when reactants are combined in aqueous solution. Most precipitations take place when the anions and cations of two ionic compounds change

Precipitate An insoluble solid that forms in solution during a chemical reaction.

APPLICATION ▶ Anemia – A Limiting Reagent Problem?

Anemia is the most commonly diagnosed blood disorder, with symptoms typically including lethargy, fatigue, poor concentration, and sensitivity to cold. While anemia has many causes, including genetic factors, the most common cause is insufficient dietary intake or absorption of iron.

Hemoglobin (abbreviated Hb), the iron-containing protein found in red blood cells, is responsible for oxygen transport throughout the body (⬭, p. 266) Low iron levels in the body result in decreased production and incorporation of Hb in red blood cells. In addition, blood loss due to injury or to menstruation in women increases the body's demand for iron in order to replace lost Hb. In the United States, nearly 20% of women of child-bearing age suffer from iron-deficiency anemia compared to only 2% of adult men.

The recommended minimum daily iron intake is 8 mg for adult men and 18 mg for pre-menopausal women. One way to ensure sufficient iron intake is a well-balanced diet that includes iron-fortified grains and cereals, red meat, egg yolks, leafy green vegetables, tomatoes, and raisins. Vegetarians should pay extra attention to their diet since the iron in fruits and vegetables is not as readily absorbed by the body as the iron in meat, poultry, and fish. Vitamin supplements containing folic acid and either ferrous sulfate or ferrous glutonate can decrease iron deficiencies, and vitamin C increases the absorption of iron by the body.

▲ Can cooking in cast iron pots decrease anemia?

However, the simplest way to increase dietary iron may be to use cast iron cookware. Studies have demonstrated that the iron content of many foods increases when cooked in an iron pot. Other studies involving Ethiopian children showed that those who ate food cooked in iron cookware were less likely to suffer from iron-deficiency anemia than their playmates who ate similar foods prepared in aluminum cookware.

See Additional Problem 6.94 at the end of the chapter.

Salt An ionic compound formed from reaction of an acid with a base.

Oxidation–reduction (redox) reaction A reaction in which electrons are transferred from one atom to another.

▲ Reaction of aqueous $Pb(NO_3)_2$ with aqueous KI gives a yellow precipitate of PbI_2.

partners. For example, an aqueous solution of lead(II) nitrate reacts with an aqueous solution of potassium iodide to yield an aqueous solution of potassium nitrate plus an insoluble yellow precipitate of lead iodide:

$$Pb(NO_3)_2(aq) + 2\,KI(aq) \longrightarrow 2\,KNO_3(aq) + PbI_2(s)$$

- **Acid–base neutralization reactions** are processes in which an acid reacts with a base to yield water plus an ionic compound called a **salt**. We will look at both acids and bases in more detail in Chapter 10, but you might recall for the moment that we previously defined acids as compounds that produce H^+ ions and bases as compounds that produce OH^- ions when dissolved in water (Section 4.11). (⬭, p. 99) Thus, a neutralization reaction removes H^+ and OH^- ions from solution and yields neutral H_2O. The reaction between hydrochloric acid and sodium hydroxide is a typical example:

$$HCl(aq) + NaOH(aq) \longrightarrow H_2O(l) + NaCl(aq)$$

Note that in this reaction, the "salt" produced is sodium chloride, or common table salt. In a general sense, however, *any* ionic compound produced in an acid–base reaction is also called a salt.

- **Oxidation–reduction reactions**, or **redox reactions**, are processes in which one or more electrons are transferred between reaction partners (atoms, molecules, or ions). As a result of this transfer, the number of electrons assigned to individual atoms in the various reactants change. When metallic magnesium reacts with iodine vapor, for instance, a magnesium atom gives an electron to each of two iodine atoms, forming an Mg^{2+} ion and two I^- ions. The charge on the magnesium changes from 0 to +2, and the charge on each iodine changes from 0 to −1:

$$Mg(s) + I_2(g) \longrightarrow MgI_2(s)$$

WORKED EXAMPLE **6.15** Classifying Chemical Reactions

Classify the following processes as a precipitation, acid–base neutralization, or redox reaction.

(a) $Ca(OH)_2(aq) + 2\,HBr(aq) \longrightarrow 2\,H_2O(l) + CaBr_2(aq)$

(b) $Pb(ClO_4)_2(aq) + 2\,NaCl(aq) \longrightarrow PbCl_2(s) + 2\,NaClO_4(aq)$

(c) $2\,AgNO_3(aq) + Cu(s) \longrightarrow 2\,Ag(s) + Cu(NO_3)_2(aq)$

ANALYSIS One way to identify the class of reaction is to examine the products that form and match them with the descriptions for the types of reactions provided in this section. By process of elimination, we can readily identify the appropriate reaction classification.

SOLUTION

(a) The products of this reaction are water and an ionic compound, or salt ($CaBr_2$). This is consistent with the description of an acid–base neutralization reaction.

(b) This reaction involves two aqueous reactants, $Pb(ClO_4)_2$ and $NaCl$, which combine to form a solid product, $PbCl_2$. This is consistent with a precipitation reaction.

(c) The products of this reaction are a solid, $Ag(s)$, and an aqueous ionic compound, $Cu(NO_3)_2$. This does not match the description of a neutralization reaction, which would form *water* and an ionic compound. One of the products *is* a solid, but the reactants are not both aqueous compound; one of the reactants is *also* a solid (Cu). Therefore, this reaction would not be classified as a precipitation reaction. By process of elimination, then, it must be a redox reaction.

PROBLEM 6.19

Classify each of the following processes as a precipitation, acid–base neutralization, or redox reaction.

(a) $AgNO_3(aq) + KCl(aq) \longrightarrow AgCl(s) + KNO_3(aq)$

(b) $2\,Al(s) + 3\,Br_2(l) \longrightarrow 2\,AlBr_3(s)$

(c) $Ca(OH)_2(aq) + 2\,HNO_3(aq) \longrightarrow 2\,H_2O(l) + Ca(NO_3)_2(aq)$

6.9 Precipitation Reactions and Solubility Guidelines

Now let us look at precipitation reactions in more detail. To predict whether a precipitation reaction will occur on mixing aqueous solutions of two ionic compounds, you must know the **solubilities** of the potential products—how much of each compound will dissolve in a given amount of solvent at a given temperature. If a substance has a low solubility in water, then it is likely to precipitate from an aqueous solution. If a substance has a high solubility in water, then no precipitate will form.

Solubility is a complex matter, and it is not always possible to make correct predictions. As a rule of thumb, though, the following solubility guidelines for ionic compounds are useful.

Solubility The amount of a compound that will dissolve in a given amount of solvent at a given temperature.

General Rules on Solubility

RULE 1. **A compound is probably soluble if it contains one of the following** *cations*:

- Group 1A cation: Li^+, Na^+, K^+, Rb^+, Cs^+
- Ammonium ion: NH_4^+

▲ Azurite (blue) and malachite (green) are mineral forms of the insoluble copper (II) carbonate.

RULE 2. A compound is probably soluble if it contains one of the following *anions*:

- Halide: Cl^-, Br^-, I^- *except Ag^+, Hg_2^{2+}, and Pb^{2+} compounds*
- Nitrate (NO_3^-), perchlorate (ClO_4^-), acetate ($CH_3CO_2^-$), sulfate (SO_4^{2-}) *except Ba^{2+}, Hg_2^{2+}, and Pb^{2+} sulfates*

If a compound does *not* contain at least one of the ions listed above, it is probably *not* soluble. Thus, Na_2CO_3 is soluble because it contains a group 1A cation, and $CaCl_2$ is soluble because it contains a halide anion. The compound $CaCO_3$, however, is *insoluble* because it contains none of the ions listed above. The guidelines are given in a different form in Table 6.1.

TABLE 6.1 General Solubility Guidelines for Ionic Compounds in Water

SOLUBLE	EXCEPTIONS
Ammonium compounds (NH_4^+)	None
Lithium compounds (Li^+)	None
Sodium compounds (Na^+)	None
Potassium compounds (K^+)	None
Nitrates (NO_3^-)	None
Perchlorates (ClO_4^-)	None
Acetates ($CH_3CO_2^-$)	None
Chlorides (Cl^-)	
Bromides (Br^-)	Ag^+, Hg_2^{2+}, and Pb^{2+} compounds
Iodides (I^-)	
Sulfates (SO_4^{2-})	Ba^{2+}, Hg_2^{2+}, and Pb^{2+} compounds

Let us try a problem. What will happen if aqueous solutions of sodium nitrate ($NaNO_3$) and potassium sulfate (K_2SO_4) are mixed? To answer this question, look at the guidelines to find the solubilities of the two possible products, Na_2SO_4 and KNO_3. Because both have group 1A cations (Na^+ and K^+), both are water-soluble and no precipitation will occur. If aqueous solutions of silver nitrate ($AgNO_3$) and sodium carbonate (Na_2CO_3) are mixed, however, the guidelines predict that a precipitate of insoluble silver carbonate (Ag_2CO_3) will form.

$$2\ AgNO_3(aq) + Na_2CO_3(aq) \longrightarrow Ag_2CO_3(s) + 2\ NaNO_3(aq)$$

WORKED EXAMPLE **6.16** Chemical Reactions: Solubility Rules

Will a precipitation reaction occur when aqueous solutions of $CdCl_2$ and $(NH_4)_2S$ are mixed?

SOLUTION
Identify the two potential products, and predict the solubility of each using the guidelines in the text. In this instance, $CdCl_2$ and $(NH_4)_2S$ might give CdS and NH_4Cl. Since the guidelines predict that CdS is insoluble, a precipitation reaction will occur:

$$CdCl_2(aq) + (NH_4)_2S(aq) \longrightarrow CdS(s) + 2\ NH_4Cl(aq)$$

PROBLEM 6.20

Predict the solubility of the following compounds:

(a) $CdCO_3$ (b) Na_2S (c) $PbSO_4$

(d) $(NH_4)_3PO_4$ (e) Hg_2Cl_2

APPLICATION ▶ Gout and Kidney Stones: Problems in Solubility

One of the major pathways in the body for the breakdown of the nucleic acids DNA and RNA is by conversion to a substance called *uric acid*, $C_5H_4N_4O_3$, so named because it was first isolated in 1776 from urine. Most people excrete about 0.5 g of uric acid every day in the form of sodium urate, the salt that results from an acid–base reaction of uric acid. Unfortunately, the amount of sodium urate that dissolves in water (or urine) is fairly low—only about 0.07 mg/mL at the normal body temperature of 37 °C. When too much sodium urate is produced or mechanisms for its elimination fail, its concentration in blood and urine rises, and the excess sometimes precipitates in the joints and kidneys.

Gout is a disorder of nucleic acid metabolism that primarily affects middle-aged men (only 5% of gout patients are women). It is characterized by an increased sodium urate concentration in blood, leading to the deposit of sodium urate crystals in soft tissue around the joints, particularly in the hands and at the base of the big toe. Deposits of the sharp, needle-like crystals cause an extremely painful inflammation that can lead ultimately to arthritis and even to bone destruction.

Just as increased sodium urate concentration in blood can lead to gout, increased concentration in urine can result in the formation of one kind of *kidney stones*, small crystals that precipitate in the kidney. Although often quite small, kidney stones cause excruciating pain when they pass through the ureter, the duct that carries urine from the kidney to the bladder. In some cases, complete blockage of the ureter occurs.

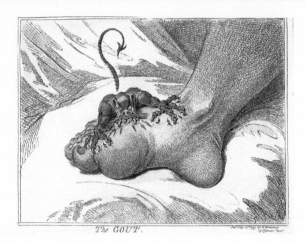

▲ This old cartoon leaves little doubt about how painful gout can be.

Treatment of excessive sodium urate production involves both dietary modification and drug therapy. Foods such as liver, sardines, and asparagus should be avoided, and drugs such as allopurinol can be taken to lower production of sodium urate. Allopurinol functions by inhibiting the action of an enzyme called *xanthine oxidase*, thereby blocking a step in nucleic acid metabolism.

See Additional Problem 6.95 at the end of the chapter.

PROBLEM 6.21

Predict whether a precipitation reaction will occur in the following situations:

(a) $NiCl_2(aq) + (NH_4)_2S(aq) \longrightarrow$

(b) $AgNO_3(aq) + CaBr_2(aq) \longrightarrow$

6.10 Acids, Bases, and Neutralization Reactions

When acids and bases are mixed in the correct proportion, both acidic and basic properties disappear because of a **neutralization reaction**. The most common kind of neutralization reaction occurs between an acid (generalized as HA), and a metal hydroxide (generalized as MOH), to yield water and a salt. The H^+ ion from the acid combines with the OH^- ion from the base to give neutral H_2O, whereas the anion from the acid (A^-) combines with the cation from the base (M^+) to give the salt:

Neutralization reaction The reaction of an acid with a base.

A neutralization reaction: $HA(aq) + MOH(aq) \longrightarrow H_2O(l) + MA(aq)$
Acid   Base   Water   A salt

The reaction of hydrochloric acid with potassium hydroxide to produce potassium chloride is an example:

$$HCl(aq) + KOH(aq) \longrightarrow H_2O(l) + KCl(aq)$$

Another kind of neutralization reaction occurs between an acid and a carbonate (or bicarbonate) to yield water, a salt, and carbon dioxide. Hydrochloric acid reacts with potassium carbonate, for example, to give H_2O, KCl, and CO_2:

$$2\,HCl(aq) + K_2CO_3(aq) \longrightarrow H_2O(l) + 2\,KCl(aq) + CO_2(g)$$

The reaction occurs because the carbonate ion ($CO_3{}^{2-}$) reacts initially with H^+ to yield H_2CO_3, which is unstable and immediately decomposes to give CO_2 plus H_2O.

We will defer a more complete discussion of carbonates as bases until Chapter 10, but note for now that they yield OH^- ions when dissolved in water just as KOH and other bases do.

$$K_2CO_3(s) + H_2O(l) \xrightarrow{\text{Dissolve in water}} 2K^+(aq) + HCO_3{}^-(aq) + OH^-(aq)$$

Looking Ahead

Acids and bases are enormously important in biological chemistry. We will see in Chapter 18, for instance, how acids and bases affect the structure and properties of proteins.

WORKED EXAMPLE **6.17** Chemical Reactions: Acid–Base Neutralization

Write an equation for the neutralization reaction of aqueous HBr and aqueous $Ba(OH)_2$.

SOLUTION

The reaction of HBr with $Ba(OH)_2$ involves the combination of a proton (H^+) from the acid with OH^- from the base to yield water and a salt ($BaBr_2$).

$$2\,HBr(aq) + Ba(OH)_2(aq) \longrightarrow 2\,H_2O(l) + BaBr_2(aq)$$

PROBLEM 6.22

Write and balance equations for the following acid–base neutralization reactions:

(a) $CsOH(aq) + H_2SO_4(aq) \longrightarrow$
(b) $Ca(OH)_2(aq) + CH_3CO_2H(aq) \longrightarrow$
(c) $NaHCO_3(aq) + HBr(aq) \longrightarrow$

6.11 Redox Reactions

Oxidation-reduction (redox) reactions, the third and final category of reactions that we will discuss, are more complex than precipitation and neutralization reactions. Look, for instance, at the following examples and see if you can tell what they have in common. Copper metal reacts with aqueous silver nitrate to form silver metal and aqueous copper(II) nitrate; iron rusts in air to form iron(III) oxide; the zinc metal container on the outside of a battery reacts with manganese dioxide and ammonium chloride inside the battery to generate electricity and give aqueous zinc chloride plus manganese(III) oxide. Although these and many thousands of other reactions appear unrelated, all are examples of redox reactions.

$$Cu(s) + 2\,AgNO_3(aq) \longrightarrow 2\,Ag(s) + Cu(NO_3)_2(aq)$$
$$2\,Fe(s) + 3\,O_2(g) \longrightarrow Fe_2O_3(s)$$
$$Zn(s) + 2\,MnO_2(s) + 2\,NH_4Cl(s) \longrightarrow$$
$$ZnCl_2(aq) + Mn_2O_3(s) + 2\,NH_3(aq) + H_2O(l)$$

Historically, the word *oxidation* referred to the combination of an element with oxygen to yield an oxide, and the word *reduction* referred to the removal of oxygen from an oxide to yield the element. Today, though, the words have taken on a much broader meaning. An **oxidation** is now defined as the loss of one or more electrons by an atom, and a **reduction** is the gain of one or more electrons. Thus, an oxidation–reduction reaction, or redox reaction, is one in which *electrons are transferred from one atom to another.*

Oxidation The loss of one or more electrons by an atom.

Reduction The gain of one or more electrons by an atom.

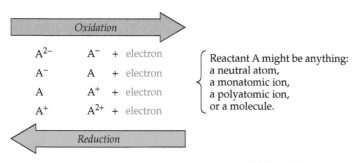

▲ The copper wire reacts with aqueous Ag^+ ion and becomes coated with metallic silver. At the same time, copper(II) ions go into solutions, producing the blue color.

Take the reaction of copper with aqueous Ag^+ as an example. Copper metal gives an electron to each of two Ag^+ ions, forming Cu^{2+} and silver metal. Copper is oxidized in the process, and Ag^+ is reduced. You can follow the transfer of the electrons by noting that the charge on the copper increases from 0 to +2 when it loses two electrons, whereas the charge on Ag^+ decreases from +1 to 0 when it gains an electron.

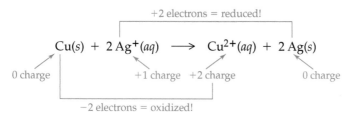

Similarly, in the reaction of aqueous iodide ion with bromine, iodide ion gives an electron to bromine, forming iodine and bromide ion. Iodide ion is oxidized as its charge increases from −1 to 0, and bromine is reduced as its charge decreases from 0 to −1.

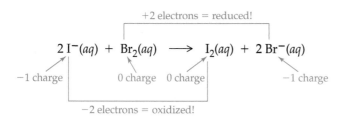

As these examples show, oxidation and reduction always occur together. Whenever one substance loses an electron (is oxidized), another substance must gain that electron (be reduced). The substance that gives up an electron and causes the reduction—the copper atom in the reaction of Cu with Ag^+ and the iodide ion in the reaction of I^- with Br_2—is called a **reducing agent**. The substance that gains an electron and causes the oxidation—the silver ion in the reaction of Cu with Ag^+ and the bromine molecule in the reaction of I^- with Br_2—is called an **oxidizing agent**. The charge on the reducing agent increases during the reaction, and the charge on the oxidizing agent decreases.

Reducing agent A reactant that causes a reduction by giving up electrons to another reactant.

Oxidizing agent A reactant that causes an oxidation by taking electrons from another reactant.

Reducing agent
Loses one or more electrons
Causes reduction
Undergoes oxidation
Becomes more positive (or less negative)

Oxidizing agent   Gains one or more electrons
Causes oxidation
Undergoes reduction
Becomes more negative (or less positive)

Among the simplest of redox processes is the reaction of an element, usually a metal, with an aqueous cation to yield a different element and a different ion. Iron metal reacts with aqueous copper(II) ion, for example, to give iron(II) ion and copper metal. Similarly, magnesium metal reacts with aqueous acid to yield magnesium ion and hydrogen gas. In both cases, the reactant element (Fe or Mg) is oxidized, and the reactant ion (Cu^{2+} or H^+) is reduced.

$$Fe(s) + Cu^{2+}(aq) \longrightarrow Fe^{2+}(aq) + Cu(s)$$
$$Mg(s) + 2\,H^+(aq) \longrightarrow Mg^{2+}(aq) + H_2(g)$$

The reaction of a metal with water or aqueous acid (H^+) to release H_2 gas is a particularly important process. As you might expect based on the periodic properties discussed in Section 4.2, the alkali metals and alkaline earth metals (on the left side of the periodic table) are the most powerful reducing agents (electron donors), so powerful that they even react with pure water, in which the concentration of H^+ is very low. Ionization energy, which is a measure of how easily an element will lose an electron, tends to decrease as we move to the left and down in the periodic table. In contrast, metals toward the middle of the periodic table, such as iron and chromium, do not lose electrons as readily; they react only with aqueous acids but not with water. Those metals near the bottom right of the periodic table, such as platinum and gold, react with neither aqueous acid nor water. At the other extreme, the reactive nonmetals at the top right of the periodic table are extremely weak reducing agents and instead are powerful oxidizing agents (electron acceptors). This is, again, predictable based on the periodic property of electron affinity (⬭⬭, Section 4.2) which becomes more energetically favored as we move up and to the right in the periodic table.

We can make a few generalizations about the redox behavior of metals and nonmetals.

1. In reactions involving metals and nonmetals, metals tend to lose electrons while nonmetals tend to gain electrons. The number of electrons lost or gained can often be predicted based on the position of the element in the periodic table. (⬭⬭, Section 4.5)

2. In reactions involving nonmetals, the "more metallic" element (farther down and/or to the left in the periodic table) tends to lose electrons, and the "less metallic" element (up and/or to the right) tends to gain electrons.

   Redox reactions involve almost every element in the periodic table, and they occur in a vast number of processes throughout nature, biology, and industry. Here are just a few examples:

- **Corrosion** is the deterioration of a metal by oxidation, such as the rusting of iron in moist air. The economic consequences of rusting are enormous: It has been estimated that up to one-fourth of the iron produced in the United States is used to replace bridges, buildings, and other structures that have been destroyed by corrosion. (The raised dot in the formula $Fe_2O_3 \cdot H_2O$ for rust indicates that one water molecule is associated with each Fe_2O_3 in an undefined way.)

- **Combustion** is the burning of a fuel by rapid oxidation with oxygen in air. Gasoline, fuel oil, natural gas, wood, paper, and other organic substances of carbon and hydrogen are the most common fuels that burn in air. Even some metals, though, will burn in air. Magnesium and calcium are examples.

$$CH_4(g) + 2\,O_2(g) \longrightarrow CO_2(g) + 2\,H_2O(l)$$
Methane
(natural gas)
$$2\,Mg(s) + O_2(g) \longrightarrow 2\,MgO(s)$$

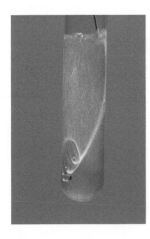

▲ Magnesium metal reacts with aqueous acid to give hydrogen gas and Mg^{2+} ion.

- **Respiration** is the process of breathing and using oxygen for the many biological redox reactions that provide the energy that living organisms need. We will see in Chapters 21–22 that energy is released from food molecules slowly and in complex, multistep pathways, but the overall result of respiration is similar to that of combustion reactions. For example, the simple sugar glucose ($C_6H_{12}O_6$) reacts with O_2 to give CO_2 and H_2O according to the following equation:

$$C_6H_{12}O_6 + 6\,O_2 \longrightarrow 6\,CO_2 + 6\,H_2O + \text{Energy}$$
Glucose
(a carbohydrate)

- **Bleaching** makes use of redox reactions to decolorize or lighten colored materials. Dark hair is bleached to turn it blond, clothes are bleached to remove stains, wood pulp is bleached to make white paper, and so on. The oxidizing agent used depends on the situation: hydrogen peroxide (H_2O_2) is used for hair, sodium hypochlorite (NaOCl) for clothes, and elemental chlorine for wood pulp, but the principle is always the same. In all cases, colored organic materials are destroyed by reaction with strong oxidizing agents.

- **Metallurgy,** the science of extracting and purifying metals from their ores, makes use of numerous redox processes. Worldwide, approximately 800 million tons of iron is produced each year by reduction of the mineral hematite, Fe_2O_3, with carbon monoxide.

$$Fe_2O_3(s) + 3\,CO(g) \longrightarrow 2\,Fe(s) + 3\,CO_2(g)$$

WORKED EXAMPLE **6.18** Chemical Reactions: Redox Reactions

For the following reactions, indicate which atom is oxidized and which is reduced, based on the definitions provided in this section. Identify the oxidizing and reducing agents.

(a) $Cu(s) + Pt^{2+}(aq) \rightarrow Cu^{2+}(aq) + 2\,Pt(s)$
(b) $2\,Mg(s) + CO_2(g) \rightarrow 2\,MgO(s) + C(s)$

ANALYSIS The definitions for oxidation include a loss of electrons, an increase in charge, and a gain of oxygen atoms; reduction is defined as a gain of electrons, a decrease in charge, or a loss of oxygen atoms.

SOLUTION

(a) In this reaction, the charge on the Cu atom increases from 0 to 2+. This corresponds to a loss of 2 electrons. The Cu is therefore oxidized, and acts as the reducing agent. Conversely, each Pt^{2+} ion undergoes a decrease in charge from 2+ to 0, corresponding to a gain of 2 electrons per Pt^{2+} ion. The Pt^{2+} is reduced, and acts as the oxidizing agent.

(b) In this case, the gain or loss of oxygen atoms is the easiest way to identify which atoms are oxidized and reduced. The Mg atom is gaining oxygen to form MgO; therefore, the Mg is being oxidized and acts as the reducing agent. The C atom in CO_2 is losing oxygen. Therefore, the C atom is being reduced and acts as the oxidizing agent.

WORKED EXAMPLE **6.19** Chemical Reactions: Identifying Oxidizing/ Reducing Agents

For the respiration and metallurgy examples discussed above, identify the atoms being oxidized and reduced, and label the oxidizing and reducing agents.

ANALYSIS Again, using the definitions of oxidation and reduction provided in this section, we can determine which atom(s) are gaining/losing electrons or gaining/losing oxygen atoms.

SOLUTION

$$\text{Respiration:} \quad C_6H_{12}O_6 + 6\,O_2 \longrightarrow 6\,CO_2 + 6\,H_2O$$

Since the charge associated with the individual atoms is not evident, we will use the definition of oxidation/reduction as the gaining/losing of oxygen atoms. In this reaction, there is only one reactant besides oxygen ($C_6H_{12}O_6$), so we must determine *which* atom in the compound is changing. The ratio of carbon to oxygen in $C_6H_{12}O_6$ is 1:1, while the ratio in CO_2 is 1:2. Therefore, the C atoms are gaining oxygen and are oxidized; the C is the reducing agent. The O_2 is the oxidizing agent. Note that the ratio of hydrogen to oxygen in $C_6H_{12}O_6$ and in H_2O is 2:1. The H atoms are neither oxidized nor reduced.

$$\text{Metallurgy:} \quad Fe_2O_3(s) + 3\,CO(g) \longrightarrow 2\,Fe(s) + 3\,CO_2(g)$$

The Fe_2O_3 is losing oxygen to form Fe(s); it is being reduced, and acts as the oxidizing agent. In contrast, the CO is gaining oxygen to form CO_2; it is being oxidized and acts as the reducing agent.

WORKED EXAMPLE **6.20** Chemical Reactions: Identifying Redox Reactions

For the following reactions, identify the atom(s) being oxidized and reduced:

(a) $2\,Al(s) + 3\,Cl_2(g) \longrightarrow 2\,AlCl_3(s)$

(b) $C(s) + 2\,Cl_2(g) \longrightarrow CCl_4(l)$

ANALYSIS Again, there is no obvious increase or decrease in charge to indicate a gain or loss of electrons. Also, the reactions do not involve a gain or loss of oxygen. We can, however, evaluate the reactions in terms of the typical behavior of metals and nonmetals in reactions.

SOLUTION

(a) In this case, we have the reaction of a metal (Al) with a nonmetal (Cl_2). Since metals tend to lose electrons and nonmetals tend to gain electrons, we can assume that the Al atom is oxidized (loss of electrons), and the Cl_2 is reduced (gains electrons).

(b) In this case, we have a reaction involving two nonmetals. The carbon is the more metallic element (farther to the left) and is more likely to lose electrons (oxidized). The less metallic element (Cl) will tend to gain electrons and be reduced.

PROBLEM 6.23

Identify the oxidized reactant, the reduced reactant, the oxidizing agent, and the reducing agent in the following reactions:

(a) $Fe(s) + Cu^{2+}(aq) \longrightarrow Fe^{2+}(aq) + Cu(s)$

(b) $Mg(s) + Cl_2(g) \longrightarrow MgCl_2(s)$

(c) $2\,Al(s) + Cr_2O_3(s) \longrightarrow 2\,Cr(s) + Al_2O_3(s)$

PROBLEM 6.24

Potassium, a silvery metal, reacts with bromine, a corrosive, reddish liquid, to yield potassium bromide, a white solid. Write the balanced equation, and identify the oxidizing and reducing agents.

APPLICATION ▶ Batteries

Imagine life without batteries: no cars (they do not start very easily without their batteries!), no heart pacemakers, no flashlights, no hearing aids, no portable computers, radios, cellular phones, or thousands of other things. Modern society cannot exist without batteries.

Although they come in many types and sizes, all batteries are based on redox reactions. In a typical redox reaction carried out in the laboratory—say, the reaction of zinc metal with Ag^+ to yield Zn^{2+} and silver metal—the reactants are simply mixed in a flask and electrons are transferred by direct contact between the reactants. In a battery, however, the two reactants are kept in separate compartments and the electrons are transferred through a wire running between them.

▲ Think of all the devices we use every day–laptop computers, cell phones, iPods—that depend on batteries.

The common household battery used for flashlights and radios is the *dry-cell*, developed in 1866. One reactant is a can of zinc metal, and the other is a paste of solid manganese dioxide. A graphite rod sticks into the MnO_2 paste to provide electrical contact, and a moist paste of ammonium chloride separates the two reactants. When the zinc can and the graphite rod are connected by a wire, zinc sends electrons flowing through the wire toward the MnO_2 in a redox reaction. The resultant electrical current can then be used to light a bulb or power a radio. The accompanying figure shows a cutaway view of a dry-cell battery.

$$Zn(s) + 2\ MnO_2(s) + 2\ NH_4Cl(s) \longrightarrow$$
$$ZnCl_2(aq) + Mn_2O_3(s) + 2\ NH_3(aq) + H_2O(l)$$

Closely related to the dry-cell battery is the familiar *alkaline* battery, in which the ammonium chloride paste is replaced by an alkaline, or basic, paste of NaOH or KOH. The alkaline battery has a longer life than the standard dry-cell battery because the zinc container corrodes less easily under basic conditions. The redox reaction is

$$Zn(s) + 2\ MnO_2(s) \longrightarrow ZnO(aq) + Mn_2O_3(s)$$

The batteries used in implanted medical devices such as pacemakers must be small, corrosion-resistant, reliable, and able to last up to 10 years. Nearly all pacemakers being implanted today—about 750,000 each year—use titanium-encased, lithium-iodine batteries, whose redox reaction is

$$2\ Li(s) + I_2(s) \longrightarrow 2\ LiI(aq)$$

See Additional Problem 6.96 at the end of the chapter.

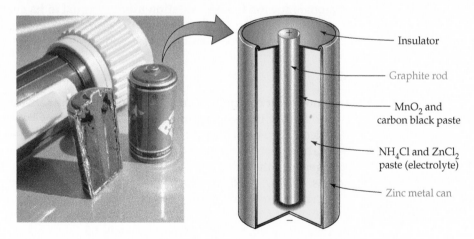

▲ A dry-cell battery. The cutaway view shows the two reactants that make up the redox reaction.

- Insulator
- Graphite rod
- MnO_2 and carbon black paste
- NH_4Cl and $ZnCl_2$ paste (electrolyte)
- Zinc metal can

▲ Sulfur burns in air to yield SO_2. Is this a redox reaction?

Oxidation number A number that indicates whether an atom is neutral, electron-rich, or electron-poor.

6.12 Recognizing Redox Reactions

How can you tell when a redox reaction is taking place? When ions are involved, it is simply a matter of determining whether there is a change in the charges. For reactions involving metals and nonmetals, we can predict gain or loss of electrons as discussed previously. When molecular substances are involved, though, it is not as obvious. Is the combining of sulfur with oxygen a redox reaction? If so, which partner is the oxidizing agent and which is the reducing agent?

$$S(s) + O_2(g) \longrightarrow SO_2(g)$$

One way to evaluate this reaction is in terms of the oxygen gain by sulfur, indicating that S atoms are oxidized and O atoms are reduced. But can we also look at this reaction in terms of the gain or loss of electrons by the S and O atoms? Because oxygen is more electronegative than sulfur (Section 5.8), the oxygen atoms in SO_2 attract the electrons in the S—O bonds more strongly than sulfur does, giving the oxygen atoms a larger share of the electrons than sulfur. (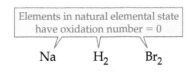, p. 129) By extending the ideas of oxidation and reduction to an increase or decrease in electron *sharing* instead of complete electron *transfer*, we can say that the sulfur atom is oxidized in its reaction with oxygen because it loses a share in some electrons, whereas the oxygen atoms are reduced because they gain a share in some electrons.

A formal system has been devised for keeping track of changes in electron sharing, and thus for determining whether atoms are oxidized or reduced in reactions. To each atom in a substance, we assign a value called an **oxidation number** (or *oxidation state*), which indicates whether the atom is neutral, electron-rich, or electron-poor. By comparing the oxidation number of an atom before and after reaction, we can tell whether the atom has gained or lost shares in electrons. Note that *oxidation numbers do not necessarily imply ionic charges*. They are simply a convenient device for keeping track of electrons in redox reactions.

The rules for assigning oxidation numbers are straightforward:

- **An atom in its elemental state has an oxidation number of 0.**

Elements in natural elemental state have oxidation number = 0

Na H_2 Br_2

- **A monatomic ion has an oxidation number equal to its charge.**

Oxidation number
+1
Na^+

Oxidation number
+2
Ca^{2+}

Oxidation number
−1
Cl^-

Oxidation number
−2
O^{2-}

- **In a molecular compound, an atom usually has the same oxidation number it would have if it were a monatomic ion.** Recall from Chapters 4 and 5 that the less electronegative elements (hydrogen and metals) on the left side of the periodic table tend to form cations, and the more electronegative elements (oxygen, nitrogen, and the halogens) near the top right of the periodic table tend to form anions. (, p. 88) Hydrogen and metals therefore have positive oxidation numbers in most compounds, whereas reactive nonmetals generally have negative oxidation numbers. Hydrogen is usually +1, oxygen is usually −2, nitrogen is usually −3, and halogens are usually −1:

+1   −1   +1   −2   +1   +1   −3   +1

H—Cl   H—O—H   H—N—H

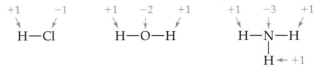

H ← +1

For compounds with more than one nonmetal element, such as SO_2, NO, or CO_2, the more electronegative element—oxygen in these examples—has a negative oxidation number and the less electronegative element has a positive oxidation number. Thus, in answer to the question posed at the beginning of this section, combining sulfur with oxygen to form SO_2 is a redox reaction because the oxidation number of sulfur increases from 0 to +4 and that of oxygen decreases from 0 to −2.

$$\overset{-2}{O}-\overset{+4}{S}=\overset{-2}{O} \qquad \overset{+2}{N}=\overset{-2}{O} \qquad \overset{-2}{O}=\overset{+4}{C}=\overset{-2}{O}$$

- **The sum of the oxidation numbers in a neutral compound is 0.** Using this rule, the oxidation number of any atom in a compound can be found if the oxidation numbers of the other atoms are known. In the SO_2 example just mentioned, each of the two O atoms has an oxidation number of −2, so the S atom must have an oxidation number of +4. In HNO_3, the H atom has an oxidation number of +1 and the strongly electronegative O atom has an oxidation number of −2, so the N atom must have an oxidation number of +5. In a polyatomic ion, the sum of the oxidation numbers equals the charge on the ion.

$$\overset{+1}{H}-\overset{-2}{O}-\overset{+5}{N}=\overset{-2}{O} \qquad \text{Total} = 1 + 5 + 3(-2) = 0$$
$$\underset{\overset{|}{O}}{}\overset{-2}{}$$

Worked Examples 6.21 and 6.22 show further instances of assigning and using oxidation numbers.

WORKED EXAMPLE **6.21** Redox Reactions: Oxidation Numbers

What is the oxidation number of the titanium atom in $TiCl_4$? Name the compound using a Roman numeral (Section 4.11).

SOLUTION
Chlorine, a reactive nonmetal, is more electronegative than titanium and has an oxidation number of −1. Because there are four chlorine atoms in $TiCl_4$, the oxidation number of titanium must be +4. The compound is named titanium(IV) chloride. Note that the Roman numeral IV in the name of this molecular compound refers to the oxidation number +4 rather than to a true ionic charge.

WORKED EXAMPLE **6.22** Redox Reactions: Identifying Redox Reactions

Use oxidation numbers to show that the production of iron metal from its ore (Fe_2O_3) by reaction with charcoal (C) is a redox reaction. Which reactant has been oxidized, and which has been reduced? Which reactant is the oxidizing agent, and which is the reducing agent?

$$2\,Fe_2O_3(s) + 3\,C(s) \longrightarrow 4\,Fe(s) + 3\,CO_2(g)$$

SOLUTION
The idea is to assign oxidation numbers to both reactants and products, and see if there has been a change. In the production of iron from Fe_2O_3, the oxidation number of Fe changes from +3 to 0, and the oxidation number of C changes from 0 to +4. Iron has thus been reduced (decrease in oxidation number), and carbon has been oxidized (increase in oxidation number). Oxygen is neither oxidized nor reduced because its oxidation number does not change. Carbon is the reducing agent and Fe_2O_3 is the oxidizing agent.

$$2\,\overset{+3}{Fe_2}\overset{-2}{O_3} + 3\,\overset{0}{C} \longrightarrow 4\,\overset{0}{Fe} + 3\,\overset{+4}{C}\overset{-2}{O_2}$$

PROBLEM 6.25

What are the oxidation numbers of the metal atoms in the following compounds? Name each, using the oxidation number as a Roman numeral.

(a) VCl_3 **(b)** $SnCl_4$ **(c)** CrO_3 **(d)** $Cu(NO_3)_2$ **(e)** $NiSO_4$

PROBLEM 6.26

Assign an oxidation number to each atom in the reactants and products shown here to determine which of the following reactions are redox reactions:

(a) $Na_2S(aq) + NiCl_2(aq) \longrightarrow 2\,NaCl(aq) + NiS(s)$

(b) $2\,Na(s) + 2\,H_2O(l) \longrightarrow 2\,NaOH(aq) + H_2(g)$

(c) $C(s) + O_2(g) \longrightarrow CO_2(g)$

(d) $CuO(s) + 2\,HCl(aq) \longrightarrow CuCl_2(aq) + H_2O(l)$

(e) $2\,MnO_4^-(aq) + 5\,SO_2(g) + 2\,H_2O(l) \longrightarrow 2\,Mn^{2+}(aq) + 5\,SO_4^{2-}(aq) + 4\,H^+(aq)$

6.13 Net Ionic Equations

In the equations we have been writing up to this point, all the substances involved in reactions have been written using their full formulas. In the precipitation reaction of lead(II) nitrate with potassium iodide mentioned in Section 6.8, for example, only the parenthetical (*aq*) indicated that the reaction actually takes place in aqueous solution, and nowhere was it explicitly indicated that ions are involved:

$$Pb(NO_3)_2(aq) + 2\,KI(aq) \longrightarrow 2\,KNO_3(aq) + PbI_2(s)$$

In fact, lead(II) nitrate, potassium iodide, and potassium nitrate dissolve in water to yield solutions of ions. Thus, it is more accurate to write the reaction as an **ionic equation**, in which all the ions are explicitly shown:

Ionic equation An equation in which ions are explicitly shown.

An ionic equation: $Pb^{2+}(aq) + 2\,NO_3^-(aq) + 2\,K^+(aq) + 2\,I^-(aq) \longrightarrow$
$$2\,K^+(aq) + 2\,NO_3^-(aq) + PbI_2(s)$$

A look at this ionic equation shows that the NO_3^- and K^+ ions undergo no change during the reaction. They appear on both sides of the reaction arrow and act merely as **spectator ions**, that is, they are present but play no role. The actual reaction, when stripped to its essentials, can be described more simply by writing a **net ionic equation**, which includes only the ions that undergo change and ignores all spectator ions:

Spectator ion An ion that appears unchanged on both sides of a reaction arrow.

Net ionic equation An equation that does not include spectator ions.

Ionic equation: $Pb^{2+}(aq) + 2\,\cancel{NO_3^-}(aq) + 2\,\cancel{K^+}(aq) + 2\,I^-(aq) \longrightarrow$
$$2\,\cancel{K^+}(aq) + 2\,\cancel{NO_3^-}(aq) + PbI_2(s)$$

Net Ionic equation: $Pb^{2+}(aq) + 2\,I^-(aq) \rightarrow PbI_2(s)$

Note that a net ionic equation, like all chemical equations, must be balanced both for atoms and for charge, with all coefficients reduced to their lowest whole numbers. Note also that all compounds that do *not* give ions in solution—all insoluble compounds and all molecular compounds—are represented by their full formulas.

We can apply the concept of ionic equations to acid–base neutralization reactions and redox reactions as well. Consider the neutralization reaction between KOH and HNO_3:

$$KOH(aq) + HNO_3(aq) \longrightarrow H_2O(l) + KNO_3(aq)$$

Since acids and bases are identified based on the ions they form when dissolved in aqueous solutions, we can write an ionic equation for this reaction:

Ionic equation: $\quad K^+(aq) + OH^-(aq) + H^+(aq) + NO_3^-(aq) \longrightarrow$

$$H_2O(l) + K^+(aq) + NO_3^-(aq)$$

Eliminating the spectator ions (K^+ and NO_3^-) we obtain the net ionic equation for the neutralization reaction:

Net ionic equation: $\quad OH^-(aq) + H^+(aq) \longrightarrow H_2O(l)$

The net ionic equation confirms the basis of the acid–base neutralization; the OH^- from the base and the H^+ from the acid neutralize each other to form water.

Similarly, many redox reactions can be viewed in terms of ionic equations. Consider the reaction between $Cu(s)$ and $AgNO_3$ from Section 6.11:

$$Cu(s) + 2\, AgNO_3(aq) \longrightarrow 2\, Ag^+(aq) + Cu(NO_3)_2(aq)$$

The aqueous products and reactants can be written as dissolved ions:

Ionic equation: $\quad Cu(s) + 2\, Ag^+(aq) + 2\, NO_3^-(aq) \longrightarrow$

$$2\, Ag(s) + Cu^{2+}(aq) + 2\, NO_3^-(aq)$$

Again, eliminating the spectator ions (NO_3^-), we obtain the net ionic equation for this redox reaction:

Net ionic equation: $\quad Cu(s) + 2\, Ag^+(aq) \longrightarrow 2\, Ag(s) + Cu^{2+}(aq)$

It is now clear that the $Cu(s)$ loses two electrons and is oxidized, whereas each Ag^+ ion gains an electron and is reduced.

WORKED EXAMPLE   **6.23** Chemical Reactions: Net Ionic Reactions

Write balanced net ionic equations for the following reactions:

(a) $AgNO_3(aq) + ZnCl_2(aq) \longrightarrow$
(b) $HCl(aq) + Ca(OH)_2(aq) \longrightarrow$
(c) $6\, HCl(aq) + 2\, Al(s) \longrightarrow 2\, AlCl_3(aq) + 3\, H_2(g)$

SOLUTION

(a) The solubility guidelines discussed in Section 6.9 predict that a precipitate of insoluble $AgCl$ forms when aqueous solutions of Ag^+ and Cl^- are mixed. Writing all the ions separately gives an ionic equation, and eliminating spectator ions Zn^{2+} and NO_3^- gives the net ionic equation.

Ionic equation: $\quad 2\, Ag^+(aq) + 2\, NO_3^-(aq) + Zn^{2+}(aq) + 2\, Cl^-(aq) \longrightarrow$

$$2\, AgCl(s) + Zn^{2+}(aq) + 2\, NO_3^-(aq)$$

Net ionic equation: $\quad 2\, Ag^+(aq) + 2\, Cl^-(aq) \longrightarrow 2\, AgCl(s)$

The coefficients can all be divided by 2 to give

Net ionic equation: $\quad Ag^+(aq) + Cl^-(aq) \longrightarrow AgCl(s)$

A check shows that the equation is balanced for atoms and charge (zero on each side).

(b) Allowing the acid HCl to react with the base $Ca(OH)_2$ leads to a neutralization reaction. Writing the ions separately, and remembering to write a complete formula for water, gives an ionic equation. Then eliminating the spectator ions and dividing the coefficients by 2 gives the net ionic equation.

Ionic equation: $2\,H^+(aq) + \cancel{2\,Cl^-(aq)} + \cancel{Ca^{2+}(aq)} + 2\,OH^-(aq) \longrightarrow$
$$2\,H_2O(l) + \cancel{Ca^{2+}(aq)} + \cancel{2\,Cl^-(aq)}$$

Net ionic equation: $H^+(aq) + OH^-(aq) \longrightarrow H_2O(l)$

A check shows that atoms and charges are the same on both sides of the equation.

(c) The reaction of Al metal with acid (HCl) is a redox reaction. The Al is oxidized, since the oxidation number increases from $0 \rightarrow +3$, whereas the H in HCl is reduced from $+1 \rightarrow 0$. We write the ionic equation by showing the ions that are formed for each aqueous ionic species. Eliminating the spectator ions yields the net ionic equation.

Ionic equation: $6\,H^+(aq) + \cancel{6\,Cl^-(aq)} + 2\,Al(s) \longrightarrow$
$$2\,Al^{3+}(aq) + \cancel{6\,Cl^-(aq)} + 3\,H_2(g)$$

Net ionic equation: $6\,H^+(aq) + 2\,Al(s) \longrightarrow 2\,Al^{3+}(aq) + 3\,H_2(g)$

A check shows that atoms and charges are the same on both sides of the equation.

PROBLEM 6.27

Write net ionic equations for the following reactions:

(a) $Zn(s) + Pb(NO_3)_2(aq) \longrightarrow Zn(NO_3)_2(aq) + Pb(s)$

(b) $2\,KOH(aq) + H_2SO_4(aq) \longrightarrow K_2SO_4(aq) + 2\,H_2O(l)$

(c) $2\,FeCl_3(aq) + SnCl_2(aq) \longrightarrow 2\,FeCl_2(aq) + SnCl_4(aq)$

KEY WORDS

Actual yield, *p. 159*

Avogadro's number (N_A), *p. 150*

Balanced equation, *p. 144*

Chemical equation, *p. 143*

Coefficient, *p. 144*

Formula weight, *p. 148*

Ionic equation, *p. 174*

Law of conservation of mass, *p. 144*

Limiting reagent, *p. 159*

Molar mass, *p. 152*

Mole, *p. 150*

Molecular weight (MW), *p. 148*

Net ionic equation, *p. 174*

Neutralization reaction, *p. 165*

SUMMARY: REVISITING THE CHAPTER GOALS

1. **How are chemical reactions written?** Chemical equations must be *balanced*; that is, the numbers and kinds of atoms must be the same in both the reactants and the products. To balance an equation, *coefficients* are placed before formulas but the formulas themselves cannot be changed.

2. **What is the mole, and why is it useful in chemistry?** A *mole* refers to *Avogadro's number* (6.022×10^{23}) of formula units of a substance. One mole of any substance has a mass (a *molar mass*) equal to the molecular or formula weight of the substance in grams. Because equal numbers of moles contain equal numbers of formula units, molar masses act as conversion factors between numbers of molecules and masses in grams.

3. **How are molar quantities and mass quantities related?** The coefficients in a balanced chemical equation represent the numbers of moles of reactants and products in a reaction. Thus, the ratios of coefficients act as *mole ratios* that relate amounts of reactants and/or products. By using molar masses and mole ratios in factor-label calculations, unknown masses or molar amounts can be found from known masses or molar amounts.

4. **What are the limiting reagent, theoretical yield, and percent yield of a reaction?** The *limiting reagent* is the reactant that runs out first. The *theoretical yield* is the amount of product that would be formed based on the amount of the limiting reagent. The *actual yield* of a reaction is the amount of product obtained. The *percent yield* is the amount of product obtained divided by the amount theoretically possible and multiplied by 100%.

5. **How are chemical reactions of ionic compounds classified?** There are three common types of reactions of ionic compounds: *Precipitation reactions* are processes in which an insoluble solid called a *precipitate* is formed. Most precipitations take place when the anions and cations of two ionic compounds change partners. Solubility guidelines for ionic compounds are used to predict when precipitation will occur.

Acid–base neutralization reactions are processes in which an acid reacts with a base to yield water plus an ionic compound called a *salt*. Since acids produce H^+ ions and bases produce OH^- ions when dissolved in water, a neutralization reaction removes H^+ and OH^- ions from solution and yields neutral H_2O.

Oxidation–reduction (redox) reactions are processes in which one or more electrons are transferred between reaction partners. An *oxidation* is defined as the loss of one or more electrons by an atom, and a *reduction* is the gain of one or more electrons. An *oxidizing agent* causes the oxidation of another reactant by accepting electrons, and a *reducing agent* causes the reduction of another reactant by donating electrons.

6. **What are oxidation numbers, and how are they used?** *Oxidation numbers* are assigned to atoms in reactants and products to provide a measure of whether an atom is neutral, electron-rich, or electron-poor. By comparing the oxidation number of an atom before and after reaction, we can tell whether the atom has gained or lost shares in electrons and thus whether a redox reaction has occurred.

Oxidation, *p. 167*

Oxidation number, *p. 172*

Oxidation–reduction (redox) reaction, *p. 162*

Oxidizing agent, *p. 167*

Percent yield, *p. 159*

Precipitate, *p. 161*

Product, *p. 144*

Reactant, *p. 144*

Reducing agent, *p. 167*

Reduction, *p. 167*

Salt, *p. 162*

Solubility, *p. 163*

Spectator ion, *p. 174*

Theoretical yield, *p. 159*

UNDERSTANDING KEY CONCEPTS

6.28 Assume that the mixture of substances in drawing (a) undergoes a reaction. Which of the drawings (b)–(d) represents a product mixture consistent with the law of conservation of mass?

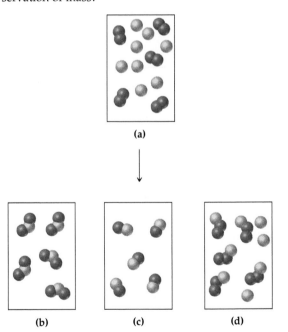

(a)

(b) (c) (d)

6.29 Reaction of A (green spheres) with B (blue spheres) is shown in the following diagram:

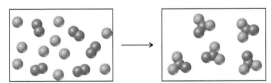

Which equation best describes the reaction?

(a) $A_2 + 2\,B \longrightarrow A_2B_2$ (b) $10\,A + 5\,B_2 \longrightarrow 5\,A_2B_2$
(c) $2\,A + B_2 \longrightarrow A_2B_2$ (d) $5\,A + 5\,B_2 \longrightarrow 5\,A_2B_2$

6.30 If blue spheres represent nitrogen atoms and red spheres represent oxygen atoms in the following diagrams, which box represents reactants and which represents products for the reaction $2\,NO(g) + O_2(g) \longrightarrow 2\,NO_2(g)$?

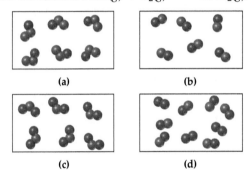

(a) (b)

(c) (d)

6.31 Methionine, an amino acid used by organisms to make proteins, can be represented by the following ball-and-stick molecular model. Write the formula for methionine, and give its molecular weight (red = O, gray = C, blue = N, yellow = S, ivory = H).

Methionine

6.32 The following diagram represents the reaction of A_2 (red spheres) with B_2 (blue spheres):

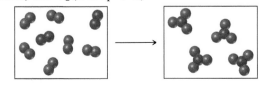

(a) Write a balanced equation for the reaction.

(b) How many moles of product can be made from 1.0 mol of A_2? From 1.0 mol of B_2?

6.33 Assume that an aqueous solution of a cation (represented as red spheres in the diagram) is allowed to mix with a solution of an anion (represented as yellow spheres). Three possible outcomes are represented by boxes (1)–(3):

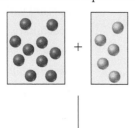

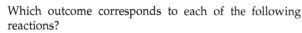

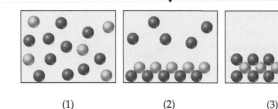

(1)   (2)   (3)

Which outcome corresponds to each of the following reactions?

(a) $2\,Na^+(aq) + CO_3{}^{2-}(aq) \longrightarrow$

(b) $Ba^{2+}(aq) + CrO_4{}^{2-}(aq) \longrightarrow$

(c) $2\,Ag^+(aq) + SO_3{}^{2-}(aq) \longrightarrow$

6.34 An aqueous solution of a cation (represented as blue spheres in the diagram) is allowed to mix with a solution of an anion (represented as green spheres) and the following result is obtained:

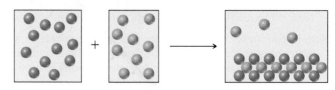

Which combinations of cation and anion, chosen from the following lists, are compatible with the observed results? Explain.

Cations: Na^+, Ca^{2+}, Ag^+, Ni^{2+}

Anions: Cl^-, $CO_3{}^{2-}$, $CrO_4{}^{2-}$, $NO_3{}^-$

6.35 The following drawing represents the reaction of ethylene oxide with water to give ethylene glycol, a compound used as automobile antifreeze. What mass in grams of ethylene oxide is needed to react with 9.0 g of water, and what mass in grams of ethylene glycol is formed?

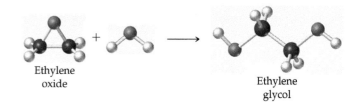

Ethylene oxide   Ethylene glycol

ADDITIONAL PROBLEMS

BALANCING CHEMICAL EQUATIONS

6.36 What is meant by the term "balanced equation"?

6.37 Why is it not possible to balance an equation by changing the subscript on a substance, say from H_2O to H_2O_2?

6.38 Write balanced equations for the following reactions:

(a) Gaseous sulfur dioxide reacts with water to form aqueous sulfurous acid (H_2SO_3).

(b) Liquid bromine reacts with solid potassium metal to form solid potassium bromide.

(c) Gaseous propane (C_3H_8) burns in oxygen to form gaseous carbon dioxide and water vapor.

6.39 Balance the following equation for the synthesis of hydrazine, N_2H_4, a substance used as rocket fuel.

$$NH_3(g) + Cl_2(g) \longrightarrow N_2H_4(l) + NH_4Cl(s)$$

6.40 Which of the following equations are balanced? Balance those that need it.

(a) $2\,C_2H_6(g) + 5\,O_2(g) \longrightarrow 2\,CO_2(g) + 6\,H_2O(l)$

(b) $3\,Ca(OH)_2(aq) + 2\,H_3PO_4(aq) \longrightarrow$
$$Ca_3(PO_4)_2(aq) + 6\,H_2O(l)$$

(c) $Mg(s) + O_2(g) \longrightarrow 2\,MgO(s)$

(d) $K(s) + H_2O(l) \longrightarrow KOH(aq) + H_2(g)$

6.41 Which of the following equations are balanced? Balance those that need it.

(a) $CaC_2 + 2\,H_2O \longrightarrow Ca(OH)_2 + C_2H_2$

(b) $C_2H_8N_2 + 2\,N_2O_4 \longrightarrow 2\,N_2 + 2\,CO_2 + 4\,H_2O$

(c) $3\,MgO + 2\,Fe \longrightarrow Fe_2O_3 + 3\,Mg$

(d) $N_2O \longrightarrow N_2 + O_2$

6.42 Balance the following equations:

(a) $Hg(NO_3)_2(aq) + LiI(aq) \longrightarrow LiNO_3(aq) + HgI_2(s)$

(b) $I_2(s) + Cl_2(g) \longrightarrow ICl_5(s)$

(c) $Al(s) + O_2(g) \longrightarrow Al_2O_3(s)$

(d) $CuSO_4(aq) + AgNO_3(aq) \longrightarrow$
$$Ag_2SO_4(s) + Cu(NO_3)_2(aq)$$

(e) $Mn(NO_3)_3(aq) + Na_2S(aq) \longrightarrow$
$$Mn_2S_3(s) + NaNO_3(aq)$$

(f) $NO_2(g) + O_2(g) \longrightarrow N_2O_5(g)$

(g) $P_4O_{10}(s) + H_2O(l) \longrightarrow H_3PO_4(aq)$

6.43 Write a balanced equation for the reaction of aqueous sodium carbonate (Na_2CO_3) with aqueous nitric acid (HNO_3) to yield CO_2, $NaNO_3$, and H_2O.

6.44 When organic compounds are burned, they react with oxygen to form CO_2 and H_2O. Write balanced equations for the combustion of the following:

(a) C_4H_{10} (butane, used in lighters)

(b) C_2H_6O (ethyl alcohol, used in gasohol and as race car fuel)

(c) C_8H_{18} (octane, a component of gasoline)

MOLAR MASSES AND MOLES

6.45 What is a mole of a substance? How many molecules are in 1 mol of a molecular compound?

6.46 What is the difference between molecular weight and formula weight? Between molecular weight and molar mass?

6.47 How many Na^+ ions are in a mole of Na_2SO_4? How many SO_4^{2-} ions?

6.48 How many moles of ions are in 1.75 mol of K_2SO_4?

6.49 How many calcium atoms are in 16.2 g of calcium?

6.50 What is the mass in grams of 2.68×10^{22} atoms of uranium?

6.51 Calculate the molar mass of each of the following compounds:

(a) Calcium carbonate, $CaCO_3$
(b) Urea, $CO(NH_2)_2$
(c) Ethylene glycol, $C_2H_6O_2$

6.52 How many moles of carbon atoms are there in 1 mol of each compound in Problem 6.51?

6.53 How many atoms of carbon and how many grams of carbon are there in 1 mol of each compound in Problem 6.51?

6.54 Caffeine has the formula $C_8H_{10}N_4O_2$. If an average cup of coffee contains approximately 125 mg of caffeine, how many moles of caffeine are in one cup?

6.55 How many moles of aspirin, $C_9H_8O_4$, are in a 500 mg tablet?

6.56 What is the molar mass of diazepam (Valium), $C_{16}H_{13}ClN_2O$?

6.57 Calculate the molar masses of the following substances:

(a) Aluminum sulfate, $Al_2(SO_4)_3$
(b) Sodium bicarbonate, $NaHCO_3$
(c) Diethyl ether, $(C_2H_5)_2O$
(d) Penicillin V, $C_{16}H_{18}N_2O_5S$

6.58 How many moles are present in a 4.50 g sample of each compound listed in Problem 6.57?

6.59 The recommended daily dietary intake of calcium for adult men and pre-menopausal women is 1000 mg/day. Calcium citrate , $Ca_3(C_6H_5O_7)_2$ (MW = 498.5 g/mol), is a common dietary supplement. What mass of calcium citrate would be needed to provide the recommended daily intake of calcium?

6.60 What is the mass in grams of 0.0015 mol of aspirin, $C_9H_8O_4$? How many aspirin molecules are there in this 0.0015 mol sample?

6.61 How many grams are present in a 0.075 mol sample of each compound listed in Problem 6.57?

6.62 The principal component of many kidney stones is calcium oxalate, CaC_2O_4. A kidney stone recovered from a typical patient contains 8.5×10^{20} formula units of calcium oxalate. How many moles of CaC_2O_4 are present in this kidney stone? What is the mass of the kidney stone in grams?

MOLE AND MASS RELATIONSHIPS FROM CHEMICAL EQUATIONS

6.63 At elevated temperatures in an automobile engine, N_2 and O_2 can react to yield NO, an important cause of air pollution.

(a) Write a balanced equation for the reaction.
(b) How many moles of N_2 are needed to react with 7.50 mol of O_2?
(c) How many moles of NO can be formed when 3.81 mol of N_2 reacts?

(d) How many moles of O_2 must react to produce 0.250 mol of NO?

6.64 Ethyl acetate reacts with H_2 in the presence of a catalyst to yield ethyl alcohol:

$$C_4H_8O_2(l) + H_2(g) \longrightarrow C_2H_6O(l)$$

(a) Write a balanced equation for the reaction.
(b) How many moles of ethyl alcohol are produced by reaction of 1.5 mol of ethyl acetate?
(c) How many grams of ethyl alcohol are produced by reaction of 1.5 mol of ethyl acetate with H_2?
(d) How many grams of ethyl alcohol are produced by reaction of 12.0 g of ethyl acetate with H_2?
(e) How many grams of H_2 are needed to react with 12.0 g of ethyl acetate?

6.65 The active ingredient in Milk of Magnesia (an antacid) is magnesium hydroxide, $Mg(OH)_2$. A typical dose (one tablespoon) contains 1.2 g of $Mg(OH)_2$. Calculate (a) the molar mass of magnesium hydroxide, and (b) the amount of magnesium hydroxide (in moles) in one teaspoon.

6.66 Ammonia, NH_3, is prepared for use as a fertilizer by reacting N_2 with H_2.

(a) Write a balanced equation for the reaction.
(b) How many moles of N_2 are needed for reaction to make 16.0 g of NH_3?
(c) How many grams of H_2 are needed to react with 75.0 g of N_2?

6.67 Hydrazine, N_2H_4, a substance used as rocket fuel, reacts with oxygen as follows:

$$N_2H_4(l) + O_2(g) \longrightarrow NO_2(g) + H_2O(g)$$

(a) Balance the equation.
(b) How many moles of oxygen are needed to react with 165 g of hydrazine?
(c) How many grams of oxygen are needed to react with 165 g of hydrazine?

6.68 One method for preparing pure iron from Fe_2O_3 is by reaction with carbon monoxide:

$$Fe_2O_3(s) + CO(g) \longrightarrow Fe(s) + CO_2(g)$$

(a) Balance the equation.
(b) How many grams of CO are needed to react with 3.02 g of Fe_2O_3?
(c) How many grams of CO are needed to react with 1.68 mol of Fe_2O_3?

6.69 Magnesium metal burns in oxygen to form magnesium oxide, MgO.

(a) Write a balanced equation for the reaction.
(b) How many grams of oxygen are needed to react with 25.0 g of Mg? How many grams of MgO will result?
(c) How many grams of Mg are needed to react with 25.0 g of O_2? How many grams of MgO will result?

6.70 Titanium metal is obtained from the mineral rutile, TiO_2. How many kilograms of rutile are needed to produce 95 kg of Ti?

6.71 In the preparation of iron from hematite (Problem 6.68) how many moles of carbon monoxide are needed to react completely with 105 kg of Fe_2O_3.

LIMITING REAGENT AND PERCENT YIELD

6.72 Once made by heating wood in the absence of air, methanol (CH_3OH) is now made by reacting carbon monoxide and hydrogen at high pressure:

$$CO(g) + 2\,H_2(g) \longrightarrow CH_3OH(l)$$

(a) If 25.0 g of CO is reacted with 6.00 g of H_2, which is the limiting reagent?

(b) How many grams of CH_3OH can be made from 10.0 g of CO if it all reacts?

(c) If 9.55 g of CH_3OH is recovered when the amounts in part (b) are used, what is the percent yield?

6.73 In Problem 6.67 hydrazine reacted with oxygen according to the (unbalanced) equation:

$$N_2H_4(l) + O_2(g) \longrightarrow NO_2(g) + H_2O(g)$$

(a) If 75.0 kg of hydrazine are reacted with 75.0 kg of oxygen, which is the limiting reagent?

(b) How many kilograms of NO_2 are produced from the reaction of 75.0 kg of the limiting reagent?

(c) If 59.3 kg of NO_2 are obtained from the reaction in part (a), what is the percent yield?

6.74 Dichloromethane, CH_2Cl_2, the solvent used to decaffeinate coffee beans, is prepared by reaction of CH_4 with Cl_2.

(a) Write the balanced equation. (HCl is also formed.)

(b) How many grams of Cl_2 are needed to react with 50.0 g of CH_4?

(c) How many grams of dichloromethane are formed from 50.0 g of CH_4 if the percent yield for the reaction is 76%?

6.75 Cisplatin [$Pt(NH_3)_2Cl_2$], a compound used in cancer treatment, is prepared by reaction of ammonia with potassium tetrachloroplatinate:

$$K_2PtCl_4 + 2\,NH_3 \longrightarrow 2\,KCl + Pt(NH_3)_2Cl_2$$

(a) How many grams of NH_3 are needed to react with 55.8 g of K_2PtCl_4?

(b) How many grams of cisplatin are formed from 55.8 g of K_2PtCl_4 if the percent yield for the reaction is 95%?

TYPES OF CHEMICAL REACTIONS

6.76 Identify the following reactions as a precipitation, neutralization, or redox reaction:

(a) $Mg(s) + 2\,HCl(aq) \longrightarrow MgCl_2(aq) + H_2(g)$

(b) $KOH(aq) + HNO_3(aq) \longrightarrow KNO_3(aq) + H_2O(l)$

(c) $Pb(NO_3)_2(aq) + 2\,HBr(aq) \longrightarrow$ $PbBr_2(s) + 2\,HNO_3(aq)$

(d) $Ca(OH)_2(aq) + 2\,HCl(aq) \longrightarrow 2\,H_2O(l) + CaCl_2(aq)$

6.77 Write balanced ionic equations and net ionic equations for the following reactions:

(a) Aqueous sulfuric acid is neutralized by aqueous potassium hydroxide.

(b) Aqueous magnesium hydroxide is neutralized by aqueous hydrochloric acid.

6.78 Write balanced ionic equations and net ionic equations for the following reactions:

(a) A precipitate of barium sulfate forms when aqueous solutions of barium nitrate and potassium sulfate are mixed.

(b) Zinc ion and hydrogen gas form when zinc metal reacts with aqueous sulfuric acid.

6.79 Which of the following substances are likely to be soluble in water?

(a) $ZnSO_4$ **(b)** $NiCO_3$
(c) $PbCl_2$ **(d)** $Ca_3(PO_4)_2$

6.80 Which of the following substances are likely to be soluble in water?

(a) Ag_2O **(b)** $Ba(NO_3)_2$
(c) $SnCO_3$ **(d)** Al_2S_3

6.81 Use the solubility guidelines in Section 6.9 to predict whether a precipitation reaction will occur when aqueous solutions of the following substances are mixed.

(a) $NaOH + HClO_4$ **(b)** $FeCl_2 + KOH$
(c) $(NH_4)_2SO_4 + NiCl_2$

6.82 Use the solubility guidelines in Section 6.9 to predict whether precipitation reactions will occur between the listed pairs of reactants. Write balanced equations for those reactions that should occur.

(a) $NaBr$ and $Hg_2(NO_3)_2$ **(b)** $CuCl_2$ and K_2SO_4
(c) $LiNO_3$ and $Ca(CH_3CO_2)_2$ **(d)** $(NH_4)_2CO_3$ and $CaCl_2$
(e) KOH and $MnBr_2$ **(f)** Na_2S and $Al(NO_3)_3$

6.83 Write net ionic equations for the following reactions:

(a) $Mg(s) + CuCl_2(aq) \longrightarrow MgCl_2(aq) + Cu(s)$

(b) $2\,KCl(aq) + Pb(NO_3)_2(aq) \longrightarrow$ $PbCl_2(s) + 2\,KNO_3(aq)$

(c) $2\,Cr(NO_3)_3(aq) + 3\,Na_2S(aq) \longrightarrow$ $Cr_2S_3(s) + 6\,NaNO_3(aq)$

6.84 Write net ionic equations for the following reactions:

(a) $2\,AuCl_3(aq) + 3\,Sn(s) \longrightarrow 3\,SnCl_2(aq) + 2\,Au(s)$

(b) $2\,NaI(aq) + Br_2(l) \longrightarrow 2\,NaBr(aq) + I_2(s)$

(c) $2\,AgNO_3(aq) + Fe(s) \longrightarrow Fe(NO_3)_2(aq) + 2\,Ag(s)$

REDOX REACTIONS AND OXIDATION NUMBERS

6.85 Where in the periodic table are the best reducing agents found? The best oxidizing agents?

6.86 Where in the periodic table are the most easily reduced elements found? The most easily oxidized?

6.87 In each of the following, tell whether the substance gains electrons or loses electrons in a redox reaction:

(a) An oxidizing agent
(b) A reducing agent
(c) A substance undergoing oxidation
(d) A substance undergoing reduction

6.88 For the following substances, tell whether the oxidation number increases or decreases in a redox reaction:

(a) An oxidizing agent
(b) A reducing agent
(c) A substance undergoing oxidation
(d) A substance undergoing reduction

6.89 Assign an oxidation number to each element in the following compounds or ions:

(a) N_2O_5 **(b)** SO_3^{2-}
(c) CH_2O **(d)** $HClO_3$

6.90 Assign an oxidation number to the metal in the following compounds:

(a) $CoCl_3$ **(b)** $FeSO_4$ **(c)** UO_3
(d) CuF_2 **(e)** TiO_2 **(f)** SnS

6.91 Which element is oxidized and which is reduced in the following reactions?

(a) $Si(s) + 2 Cl_2(g) \longrightarrow SiCl_4(l)$
(b) $Cl_2(g) + 2 NaBr(aq) \longrightarrow Br_2(aq) + 2 NaCl(aq)$
(c) $SbCl_3(s) + Cl_2(g) \longrightarrow SbCl_5(s)$

6.92 Which element is oxidized and which is reduced in the following reactions?

(a) $2 SO_2(g) + O_2(g) \longrightarrow 2 SO_3(g)$
(b) $2 Na(s) + Cl_2(g) \longrightarrow 2 NaCl(s)$
(c) $CuCl_2(aq) + Zn(s) \longrightarrow ZnCl_2(aq) + Cu(s)$
(d) $2 NaCl(aq) + F_2(g) \longrightarrow 2 NaF(aq) + Cl_2(g)$

Applications

6.93 What do you think are some of the errors involved in calculating Avogadro's number by spreading oil on a pond? [*Did Ben Franklin Have Avogadro's Number?, p. 153*]

6.94 Ferrous sulfate is one dietary supplement used to treat iron-deficiency anemia. What are the molecular formula and molecular weight of this compound? How many milligrams of iron are in 250 mg of ferrous sulfate? [*Anemia— A Limiting Reagent Problem?, p. 162*]

6.95 Sodium urate, the principal constituent of some kidney stones, has the formula $NaC_5H_3N_4O_3$. In aqueous solution, the solubility of sodium urate is only 0.067 g/L. How many moles of sodium urate dissolve in 1.00 L of water? [*Gout and Kidney Stones, p. 165*]

6.96 Identify the oxidizing and reducing agents in a typical dry-cell battery. [*Batteries, p. 171*]

General Questions and Problems

6.97 Zinc metal reacts with hydrochloric acid (HCl) according to the equation:

$$Zn(s) + 2 HCl(aq) \longrightarrow ZnCl_2(aq) + H_2(g)$$

(a) How many grams of hydrogen are produced if 15.0 g of zinc reacts?
(b) Is this a redox reaction? If so, tell what is reduced, what is oxidized, and reducing and oxidizing agents.

6.98 Lithium oxide is used aboard the space shuttle to remove water from the atmosphere according to the equation

$$Li_2O(s) + H_2O(g) \longrightarrow 2 LiOH(s)$$

(a) How many grams of Li_2O must be carried on board to remove 80.0 kg of water?
(b) Is this a redox reaction? Why or why not?

6.99 Balance the following equations.

(a) The thermite reaction, used in welding:

$$Al(s) + Fe_2O_3(s) \longrightarrow Al_2O_3(l) + Fe(l)$$

(b) The explosion of ammonium nitrate:

$$NH_4NO_3(s) \longrightarrow N_2(g) + O_2(g) + H_2O(g)$$

6.100 Batrachotoxin, $C_{31}H_{42}N_2O_6$, an active component of South American arrow poison, is so toxic that 0.05 μg can kill a person. How many molecules is this?

6.101 Look at the solubility guidelines in Section 6.9 and predict whether a precipitate forms when $CuCl_2(aq)$ and $Na_2CO_3(aq)$ are mixed. If so, write both the balanced equation and the net ionic equation for the process.

6.102 When table sugar (sucrose, $C_{12}H_{22}O_{11}$) is heated, it decomposes to form C and H_2O.

(a) Write a balanced equation for the process.
(b) How many grams of carbon are formed by the breakdown of 60.0 g of sucrose?
(c) How many grams of water are formed when 6.50 g of carbon are formed?

6.103 Although Cu is not sufficiently active to react with acids, it can be dissolved by concentrated nitric acid, which functions as an oxidizing agent according to the following equation:

$$Cu(s) + 4 HNO_3(aq) \longrightarrow$$
$$Cu(NO_3)_2(aq) + 2 NO_2(g) + 2 H_2O(l)$$

(a) Write the net ionic equation for this process.
(b) Is 35.0 g of HNO_3 sufficient to dissolve 5.00 g of copper?

6.104 The net ionic equation for the Breathalyzer test used to indicate alcohol concentration in the body is

$$16 H^+(aq) + 2 Cr_2O_7{}^{2-}(aq) + 3 C_2H_6O(aq) \longrightarrow$$
$$3 C_2H_4O_2(aq) + 4 Cr^{3+}(aq) + 11 H_2O(l)$$

(a) How many grams of $K_2Cr_2O_7$ must be used to consume 1.50 g of C_2H_6O?
(b) How many grams of $C_2H_4O_2$ can be produced from 80.0 g of C_2H_6O?

6.105 Ethyl alcohol is formed by enzyme action on sugars and starches during fermentation:

$$C_6H_{12}O_6 \longrightarrow 2 CO_2 + 2 C_2H_6O$$

If the density of ethyl alcohol is 0.789 g/mL, how many quarts can be produced by the fermentation of 100.0 lb of sugar?

6.106 Balance the following equations:

(a) $Al(OH)_3(aq) + HNO_3(aq) \longrightarrow$
   $Al(NO_3)_3(aq) + H_2O(l)$
(b) $AgNO_3(aq) + FeCl_3(aq) \longrightarrow$
   $AgCl(s) + Fe(NO_3)_3(aq)$
(c) $(NH_4)_2Cr_2O_7(s) \longrightarrow Cr_2O_3(s) + H_2O(g) + N_2(g)$
(d) $Mn_2(CO_3)_3(s) \longrightarrow Mn_2O_3(s) + CO_2(g)$

6.107 White phosphorus (P_4) is a highly reactive form of elemental phosphorus that reacts with oxygen to form a variety of molecular compounds, including diphosphorus pentoxide.

(a) Write the balanced chemical equation for this reaction.
(b) Calculate the oxidation number for P and O on both sides of the reaction, and identify the oxidizing and reducing agents.

6.108 The combustion of fossil fuels containing sulfur contributes to the phenomenon known as acid rain. The combustion process releases sulfur in the form of sulfur dioxide, which is converted to sulfuric acid in a process involving two reactions.

(a) In the first reaction, sulfur dioxide reacts with molecular oxygen to form sulfur trioxide. Write the balanced chemical equation for this reaction.
(b) In the second reaction, sulfur trioxide reacts with water in the atmosphere to form sulfuric acid. Write the balanced chemical equation for this reaction.
(c) Calculate the oxidation number for the S atom in each compound in these reactions.

CHAPTER 7

Chemical Reactions: Energy, Rates, and Equilibrium

CONCEPTS TO REVIEW

Energy and Heat
(Section 2.10)

Ionic Bonds
(Section 4.3)

Covalent Bonds
(Section 5.1)

Chemical Equations
(Section 6.1)

▲ Many spontaneous chemical reactions are accompanied by the release of energy, in some cases explosively.

CONTENTS

CHAPTER GOALS

In this chapter, we will look more closely at chemical reactions and answer the following questions:

1. **What energy changes take place during reactions?**

THE GOAL: Be able to explain the factors that influence energy changes in chemical reactions.

2. **What is "free energy," and what is the criterion for spontaneity in chemistry?**

THE GOAL: Be able to define enthalpy, entropy, and free-energy changes, and explain how the values of these quantities affect chemical reactions.

3. **What determines the rate of a chemical reaction?**

THE GOAL: Be able to explain activation energy and other factors that determine reaction rate.

4. **What is chemical equilibrium?**

THE GOAL: Be able to describe what occurs in a reaction at equilibrium and write the equilibrium equation for a given reaction.

5. **What is Le Châtelier's principle?**

THE GOAL: Be able to state Le Châtelier's principle and use it to predict the effect of changes in temperature, pressure, and concentration on reactions.

We have yet to answer many questions about reactions. Why, for instance, do reactions occur? Just because a balanced equation can be written does not mean it will take place. We can write a balanced equation for the reaction of gold with water, for example, but the reaction does not occur in practice, so your gold jewelry is safe in the shower.

Balanced, but does not occur $2\,Au(s) + 3\,H_2O(l) \longrightarrow Au_2O_3(s) + 3\,H_2(g)$

To describe reactions more completely, several fundamental questions are commonly asked: Is energy released or absorbed when a reaction occurs? Is a given reaction fast or slow? Does a reaction continue until all reactants are converted to products or is there a point beyond which no additional product forms?

7.1 Energy and Chemical Bonds

There are two fundamental and interconvertible kinds of energy: *potential* and *kinetic*. **Potential energy** is stored energy. The water in a reservoir behind a dam, an automobile poised to coast downhill, and a coiled spring have potential energy waiting to be released. **Kinetic energy**, by contrast, is the energy of motion. When the water falls over the dam and turns a turbine, when the car rolls downhill, or when the spring uncoils and makes the hands on a clock move, the potential energy in each is converted to kinetic energy. Of course, once all the potential energy is converted, nothing further occurs. The water at the bottom of the dam, the car at the bottom of the hill, and the uncoiled spring no longer have potential energy and thus undergo no further change.

In chemical compounds, the attractive forces between ions (ionic bonds) or atoms (covalent bonds) are a form of potential energy. In many chemical reactions, this potential energy is often converted into **heat**—the kinetic energy of the moving particles that make up the compound. Because the reaction products have less potential energy than the reactants, we say that the products are *more stable* than the reactants. The term "stable" is used in chemistry to describe a substance that has little remaining potential energy and consequently little tendency to undergo further change. Whether a reaction occurs, and how much energy or heat is associated with the reaction, depends on the amount of potential energy contained in the reactants and products.

Potential energy   Stored energy.

Kinetic energy   The energy of an object in motion.

Heat   A measure of the transfer of thermal energy.

7.2 Heat Changes during Chemical Reactions

Why does chlorine react so easily with many elements and compounds but nitrogen does not? What difference between Cl_2 molecules and N_2 molecules accounts for their different reactivities? The answer is that the nitrogen–nitrogen triple bond is much *stronger* than the chlorine–chlorine single bond and cannot be broken as easily in chemical reactions.

The strength of a covalent bond is measured by its **bond dissociation energy**, defined as the amount of energy that must be supplied to break the bond and separate the atoms in an isolated gaseous molecule. The triple bond in N_2, for example, has a bond dissociation energy of 226 kcal/mol, whereas the single bond in chlorine has a bond dissociation energy of only 58 kcal/mol:

Bond dissociation energy The amount of energy that must be supplied to break a bond and separate the atoms in an isolated gaseous molecule.

$$:N:::N: \xrightarrow{\text{226 kcal/mol}} :\overset{.}{\underset{.}{N}}\cdot \; + \; \cdot\overset{.}{\underset{.}{N}}: \qquad N_2 \text{ bond dissociation energy} = 226 \text{ kcal/mol}$$

$$:\overset{..}{\underset{..}{Cl}}:\overset{..}{\underset{..}{Cl}}: \xrightarrow{\text{58 kcal/mol}} :\overset{..}{\underset{..}{Cl}}\cdot \; + \; \cdot\overset{..}{\underset{..}{Cl}}: \qquad Cl_2 \text{ bond dissociation energy} = 58 \text{ kcal/mol}$$

A chemical change like bond breaking that absorbs heat is said to be **endothermic**, from the Greek words *endon* (within) and *therme* (heat), meaning that *heat is put in*. The reverse of bond breaking is bond formation, a process that *releases* heat and is described as **exothermic**, from the Greek *exo* (outside), meaning that heat goes *out*. The amount of energy released in forming a bond is numerically the same as that absorbed in breaking it. When nitrogen atoms combine to give N_2, 226 kcal/mol of heat is released. Similarly, when Cl_2 molecules are pulled apart into atoms, 58 kcal/mol of heat is absorbed; when chlorine atoms combine to give Cl_2, 58 kcal/mol of heat is released.

Endothermic A process or reaction that absorbs heat and has a positive ΔH.

Exothermic A process or reaction that releases heat and has a negative ΔH.

$$:\overset{.}{\underset{.}{N}}\cdot \; + \; \cdot\overset{.}{\underset{.}{N}}: \longrightarrow :N:::N: \; + \; 226 \text{ kcal/mol heat released}$$

$$:\overset{..}{\underset{..}{Cl}}\cdot \; + \; \cdot\overset{..}{\underset{..}{Cl}}: \longrightarrow :\overset{..}{\underset{..}{Cl}}:\overset{..}{\underset{..}{Cl}}: \; + \; 58 \text{ kcal/mol heat released}$$

The same energy relationships that govern bond breaking and bond formation apply to every physical or chemical change. That is, the amount of heat transferred during a change in one direction is numerically equal to the amount of heat transferred during the change in the opposite direction. Only the *direction* of the heat transfer is different. This relationship reflects a fundamental law of nature called the *law of conservation of energy*:

Law of conservation of energy   Energy can be neither created nor destroyed in any physical or chemical change.

If more energy could be released by an exothermic reaction than was consumed in its reverse, the law would be violated and we could "manufacture" energy out of nowhere by cycling back and forth between forward and reverse reactions—a clear impossibility.

In every chemical reaction, some bonds in the reactants are broken and new bonds are formed in the products. The difference between the energy absorbed in breaking bonds and the energy released in forming bonds is called the **heat of reaction** and is a quantity that we can measure. Heats of reaction that are measured when a reaction is held at constant pressure are represented by the abbreviation ΔH, where Δ (the Greek capital letter delta) is a general symbol used to indicate "a change in" and *H* is a quantity called **enthalpy**. Thus, the value of ΔH represents the **enthalpy change** that occurs during a reaction. The terms *enthalpy change* and *heat of reaction* are often used interchangeably, but we will generally use the latter term in this book.

Enthalpy (H) A measure of the amount of energy associated with substances involved in a reaction.

Heat of reaction ΔH = Energy of bonds formed in products minus
(Enthalpy change)   energy of bonds broken in reactants

7.3 Exothermic and Endothermic Reactions

When the total strength of the bonds formed in the products is *greater* than the total strength of the bonds broken in the reactants, energy is released and a reaction is exothermic. All combustion reactions are exothermic; for example, burning 1 mol of methane releases 213 kcal of energy in the form of heat. The heat released in an exothermic reaction can be thought of as a reaction product, and ΔH is assigned a *negative* value because heat *leaves*.

An exothermic reaction—negative ΔH

Heat is a product.

$$CH_4(g) + 2\,O_2(g) \longrightarrow CO_2(g) + 2\,H_2O(l) + 213\,kcal$$

or

$$CH_4(g) + 2\,O_2(g) \longrightarrow CO_2(g) + 2\,H_2O(l) \qquad \Delta H = -213\,kcal/mol$$

Note that ΔH is given in units of kilocalories per mole, where "per mole" means the reaction of *molar amounts of products and reactants as represented by the coefficients of the balanced equation*. Thus, the value $\Delta H = -213\,kcal/mol$ refers to the amount of heat released when 1 mol (16.0 g) of methane reacts with O_2 to give 1 mol of CO_2 gas and 2 mol of liquid H_2O. If we were to double the amount of methane from 1 mol to 2 mol, the amount of heat released would also double.

The quantities of heat released in the combustion of several fuels, including natural gas (which is primarily methane), are compared in Table 7.1. The values are given in kilocalories per gram to make comparisons easier. You can see from the table why there is interest in the potential of hydrogen as a fuel.

TABLE 7.1   Energy Values of Some Common Fuels

FUEL	ENERGY VALUE (kcal/g)
Wood (pine)	4.3
Ethyl alcohol	7.1
Coal (anthracite)	7.4
Crude oil (Texas)	10.5
Gasoline	11.5
Natural gas	11.7
Hydrogen	34.0

▲ The reaction between aluminum metal and iron(III) oxide, called the *thermite reaction*, is so strongly exothermic that it melts iron.

When the total energy of the bonds formed in the products is *less* than the total energy of the bonds broken in the reactants, energy is absorbed and a reaction is endothermic. The combination of nitrogen and oxygen to give nitrogen oxide (also known as nitric oxide), a gas present in automobile exhaust, is such a reaction. The heat added in an endothermic reaction is like a reactant, and ΔH is assigned a *positive* value because heat is *added*.

An endothermic reaction—positive ΔH

Heat is a reactant.

$$N_2(g) + O_2(g) + 43\,kcal \longrightarrow 2\,NO(g)$$

or

$$N_2(g) + O_2(g) \longrightarrow 2\,NO(g) \qquad \Delta H = +43\,kcal/mol$$

Important points about heat transfers and chemical reactions

- An exothermic reaction releases heat to the surroundings; ΔH is negative.
- An endothermic reaction absorbs heat from the surroundings; ΔH is positive.

- The reverse of an exothermic reaction is endothermic.
- The reverse of an endothermic reaction is exothermic.
- The amount of heat absorbed or released in the reverse of a reaction is equal to that released or absorbed in the forward reaction, but ΔH has the opposite sign.

Worked Examples 7.1-7.3 show how to calculate the amount of heat absorbed or released for reaction of a given amount of reactant. All that is needed is the balanced equation and its accompanying ΔH. Mole ratios and molar masses are used to convert between masses and moles of reactants or products, as discussed in Sections 6.5 and 6.6.

▲ Methane produced from rotting refuse is trapped and used for energy production to ease the energy crisis in California.

WORKED EXAMPLE   **7.1** Heat of Reaction

Methane undergoes combustion with O_2 according to the following equation:

$$CH_4(g) + 2\,O_2(g) \longrightarrow CO_2(g) + 2\,H_2O(l) \quad \Delta H = -213\frac{kcal}{mol\ CH_4}$$

How much heat is released during the combustion of 0.35 mol of methane?

ANALYSIS Since the value of ΔH for the reaction (213 kcal/mol) is negative, it indicates the amount of heat released when 1 mol of methane reacts with O_2. We need to find the amount of heat released when an amount other than 1 mol reacts, using appropriate factor-label calculations to convert from our known or given units to kilocalories.

BALLPARK ESTIMATE Since 213 kcal is released for each mole of methane that reacts, 0.35 mol of methane should release about one-third of 213 kcal, or about 70 kcal.

SOLUTION
To find the amount of heat released (in kilocalories) by combustion of 0.35 mol of methane, we use a conversion factor of kcal/mol:

$$0.35 \text{ mol } CH_4 \times \frac{-213 \text{ kcal}}{1 \text{ mol } CH_4} = -75 \text{ kcal}$$

The negative sign indicates that the 75 kcal of heat is released.

BALLPARK CHECK The calculated answer is consistent with our estimate (70 kcal).

WORKED EXAMPLE   **7.2** Heat of Reaction: Mass to Mole Conversion

How much heat is released during the combustion of 7.50 g of methane (MW = 16.0 g/mol)?

$$CH_4(g) + 2\,O_2(g) \longrightarrow CO_2(g) + 2\,H_2O(l) \quad \Delta H = -213\frac{kcal}{mol\ CH_4}$$

ANALYSIS We can find the moles of methane involved in the reaction by using the molecular weight in a mass to mole conversion, and then use ΔH to find the heat released.

BALLPARK ESTIMATE Since 1 mol of methane (MW = 16.0 g/mol) has a mass of 16.0 g, 7.50 g of methane is a little less than 0.5 mol. Thus, less than half of 213 kcal, or about 100 kcal, is released from combustion of 7.50 g.

SOLUTION
Going from a given mass of methane to the amount of heat released in a reaction requires that we first find the number of moles of methane by including

molar mass (in mol/g) in the calculation and then converting moles to kilocalories:

$$7.50 \text{ g } \cancel{CH_4} \times \frac{1 \text{ mol } \cancel{CH_4}}{16.0 \text{ g } \cancel{CH_4}} \times \frac{-213 \text{ kcal}}{1 \text{ mol } \cancel{CH_4}} = -99.8 \text{ kcal}$$

The negative sign indicates that the 99.8 kcal of heat is released.

BALLPARK CHECK Our estimate was −100 kcal!

> **WORKED EXAMPLE** **7.3** Heat of Reaction: Mole Ratio Calculations
>
> How much heat is released when 2.50 mol of O_2 reacts completely with methane?
>
> $$CH_4(g) + 2 O_2(g) \longrightarrow CO_2(g) + 2 H_2O(l) \quad \Delta H = -213 \frac{\text{kcal}}{\text{mol } CH_4}$$
>
> ANALYSIS Since the ΔH for the reaction is based on the combustion of 1 mol of methane, we will need to perform a mole ratio calculation.
>
> BALLPARK ESTIMATE The balanced equation shows that 213 kcal is released for each 2 mol of oxygen that reacts. Thus, 2.50 mol of oxygen should release a bit more than 213 kcal, perhaps about 250 kcal.
>
> SOLUTION
> To find the amount of heat released by combustion of 2.50 mol of oxygen, we include in our calculation a mole ratio based on the balanced chemical equation:
>
> $$2.50 \text{ mol } \cancel{O_2} \times \frac{1 \text{ mol } \cancel{CH_4}}{2 \text{ mol } \cancel{O_2}} \times \frac{-213 \text{ kcal}}{1 \text{ mol } \cancel{CH_4}} = -266 \text{ kcal}$$
>
> The negative sign indicates that the 266 kcal of heat is released.
>
> BALLPARK CHECK The calculated answer is close to our estimate (250 kcal).

PROBLEM 7.1

In photosynthesis, green plants convert carbon dioxide and water into glucose ($C_6H_{12}O_6$) according to the following equation:

$$6 CO_2(g) + 6 H_2O(l) + 678 \text{ kcal} \longrightarrow C_6H_{12}O_6(aq) + 6 O_2(g)$$

(a) Is the reaction exothermic or endothermic?
(b) What is the value of ΔH for the reaction?
(c) Write the equation for the reverse of the reaction, including heat as a reactant or product.

PROBLEM 7.2

The following equation shows the conversion of aluminum oxide (from the ore bauxite) to aluminum:

$$2 Al_2O_3(s) \longrightarrow 4 Al(s) + 3 O_2(g) \quad \Delta H = +801 \text{ kcal/mol}$$

(a) Is the reaction exothermic or endothermic?
(b) How many kilocalories are required to produce 1.00 mol of aluminum?
(c) How many kilocalories are required to produce 10.0 g of aluminum?

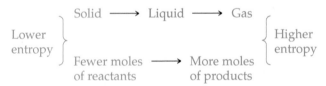

▲ Events that lead to lower energy tend to occur spontaneously. Thus, water always flows *down* a waterfall, not up.

Spontaneous process A process or reaction that, once started, proceeds on its own without any external influence.

Entropy (S) A measure of the amount of molecular disorder in a system.

PROBLEM 7.3

How much heat is absorbed during production of 127 g of NO by the combination of nitrogen and oxygen?

$$N_2(g) + O_2(g) \longrightarrow 2\,NO(g) \quad \Delta H = +43\,kcal/mol$$

7.4 Why Do Chemical Reactions Occur? Free Energy

Events that lead to lower energy tend to occur spontaneously. Water falls downhill, for instance, releasing its stored (potential) energy and reaching a lower-energy, more stable position. Similarly, a wound-up spring uncoils when set free. Applying this lesson to chemistry, the obvious conclusion is that exothermic processes—those that release heat energy—should be spontaneous. A log burning in a fireplace is just one example of a spontaneous reaction that releases heat. At the same time, endothermic processes, which absorb heat energy, should not be spontaneous. Often, these conclusions are correct, but not always. Many, but not all, exothermic processes take place spontaneously, and many, but not all, endothermic processes are nonspontaneous.

Before exploring the situation further, it is important to understand what the word "spontaneous" means in chemistry, which is not quite the same as in everyday language. A **spontaneous process** is one that, once started, proceeds on its own without any external influence. The change does not necessarily happen quickly, like a spring suddenly uncoiling or a car coasting downhill. It can also happen slowly, like the gradual rusting away of an abandoned bicycle. A *nonspontaneous process*, by contrast, takes place only in the presence of a continuous external influence: Energy must be continually expended to rewind a spring or push a car uphill. The reverse of a spontaneous process is always nonspontaneous.

As an example of a process that takes place spontaneously yet absorbs heat, think about what happens when you take an ice cube out of the refrigerator. The ice spontaneously melts to give liquid water above 0 °C, even though it *absorbs* heat energy from the surroundings. What this and other spontaneous processes that absorb heat energy have in common is *an increase in molecular disorder, or randomness*. When the solid ice melts, the H_2O molecules are no longer locked in position but are now free to move around randomly in the liquid water.

The amount of disorder in a system is called the system's **entropy**, symbolized S and expressed in units of calories per mole-kelvin [cal/(mol·K)]. The greater the disorder, or randomness, of the particles in a substance or mixture, the larger the value of S (Figure 7.1). Gases have more disorder and therefore higher entropy than liquids because particles in the gas move around more freely than particles in the liquid. Similarly, liquids have higher entropy than solids. In chemical reactions, entropy increases when, for example, a gas is produced from a solid or when 2 mol of reactants split into 4 mol of products.

Lower entropy

Solid ⟶ Liquid ⟶ Gas

Fewer moles of reactants ⟶ More moles of products

Higher entropy

The entropy *change* for a process, ΔS, has a *positive* value if disorder increases because the process adds disorder to the system. The melting of ice to give water is an example. Conversely, ΔS has a *negative* value if the disorder of a system decreases. The freezing of water to give ice is an example.

It thus appears that two factors determine the spontaneity of a chemical or physical change: the release or absorption of heat, ΔH, and the increase or decrease in entropy, ΔS. *To decide whether a process is spontaneous, both the enthalpy change and*

APPLICATION ▶ Energy from Food

Any serious effort to lose weight usually leads to studying the caloric values of foods. Have you ever wondered how the numbers quoted on food labels are obtained?

Food is "burned" in the body to yield H_2O, CO_2, and energy, just as natural gas is burned in furnaces to yield the same products. In fact, the "caloric value" of a food is just the heat of reaction for complete combustion of the food (minus a small correction factor). The value is the same whether the food is burned in the body or in the laboratory. One gram of protein releases 4 kcal, 1 g of table sugar (a carbohydrate) releases 4 kcal, and 1 g of fat releases 9 kcal (see Table).

The caloric value of a food is usually given in "Calories" (note the capital C), where 1 Cal = 1000 cal = 1 kcal. To determine these values experimentally, a carefully dried and weighed food sample is placed together with oxygen into an instrument called a *calorimeter*, the food is ignited, the temperature change is measured, and the amount of heat given off is calculated from the temperature change. In the calorimeter, the heat from the food is released very quickly and the temperature rises dramatically. Clearly, though, something a bit different goes on when food is burned in the body, otherwise we would burst into flames after a meal!

It is a fundamental principle of chemistry that the total heat released or absorbed in going from reactants to products is the same, no matter how many reactions are involved.

Caloric Values of Some Foods

SUBSTANCE, SAMPLE SIZE	CALORIC VALUE (kcal)
Protein, 1 g	4
Carbohydrate, 1 g	4
Fat, 1 g	9
Alcohol, 1 g	7.1
Cola drink, 12 fl oz (369 g)	160
Apple, one medium (138 g)	80
Iceberg lettuce, 1 cup shredded (55 g)	5
White bread, 1 slice (25 g)	65
Hamburger patty, 3 oz (85 g)	245
Pizza, 1 slice (120 g)	290
Vanilla ice cream, 1 cup (133 g)	270

The body applies this principle by withdrawing energy from food a bit at a time in a long series of interconnected reactions rather than all at once in a single reaction. These and other reactions continually taking place in the body—called the body's *metabolism*—will be examined in later chapters.

See Additional Problems 7.70 and 7.71 at the end of the chapter.

▲ Eating this dessert gives your body 550 Calories. Burning the dessert in a calorimeter releases 550 kcal as heat.

▶ **FIGURE 7.1 Entropy and values of S.** The mixture on the right has more disorder and a higher entropy than the mixture on the left, and has a higher value of S. The value of the entropy change, ΔS, for converting the mixture on the left to that on the right is positive because entropy increases.

the entropy change must be taken into account. We have already seen that a negative ΔH favors spontaneity, but what about ΔS? The answer is that an increase in molecular disorder (ΔS positive) favors spontaneity. A good analogy is the bedroom or office that seems to spontaneously become more messy over time (increase in disorder means increase in entropy, ΔS positive); to clean it up (a decrease in disorder, ΔS negative) requires an input of energy, a nonspontaneous process. Using our chemical example, the combustion of a log spontaneously converts large, complex molecules like lignin and cellulose (high molecular order, low entropy) into CO_2 and H_2O (smaller molecules with less molecular order and higher entropy). For this process, the level of disorder increases, and so ΔS is positive. The reverse process—turning CO_2 and H_2O back into cellulose—does occur in photosynthesis, but it requires a significant input of energy in the form of sunlight.

When enthalpy and entropy are both favorable (ΔH negative, ΔS positive), a process is spontaneous; when both are unfavorable, a process is nonspontaneous. Clearly, however, the two factors do not have to operate in the same direction. It is possible for a process to be *unfavored* by enthalpy (the process absorbs heat and so has a positive ΔH) and yet be *favored* by entropy (there is an increase in disorder and so ΔS is positive). The melting of an ice cube above 0 °C, for which ΔH = +1.44 kcal/mol and ΔS = +5.26 cal/(mol·K) is just such a process. To take both heat of reaction (ΔH) and change in disorder (ΔS) into account when determining the spontaneity of a process, a quantity called the **free-energy change (ΔG)** is needed:

Free-energy change

| Heat of reaction | Temperature (in kelvins) | Entropy change |

$$\Delta G = \Delta H - T\Delta S$$

Exergonic A spontaneous reaction or process that releases free energy and has a negative ΔG.

Endergonic A nonspontaneous reaction or process that absorbs free energy and has a positive ΔG.

The value of the free-energy change ΔG determines spontaneity. A negative value for ΔG means that free energy is released and the reaction or process is spontaneous. Such events are said to be **exergonic**. A positive value for ΔG means that free energy must be added and the process is nonspontaneous. Such events are said to be **endergonic**.

Spontaneous process   ΔG is negative; free energy is released; process is exergonic.

Nonspontaneous process   ΔG is positive; free energy is added; process is endergonic.

The equation for the free-energy change shows that spontaneity also depends on temperature (T). At low temperatures, the value of $T\Delta S$ is often small so that ΔH is the dominant factor. At a high enough temperature, however, the value of $T\Delta S$ can become larger than ΔH. Thus, an endothermic process that is nonspontaneous at low temperature can become spontaneous at a higher temperature. An example is the industrial synthesis of hydrogen by reaction of carbon with water:

$$C(s) + H_2O(l) \longrightarrow CO(g) + H_2(g) \qquad \begin{array}{ll} \Delta H = +31.3\,\text{kcal/mol} & \text{(Unfavorable)} \\ \Delta S = +32\,\text{cal/(mol} \cdot \text{K)} & \text{(Favorable)} \end{array}$$

The reaction has an unfavorable (positive) ΔH term but a favorable (positive) ΔS term because disorder increases when a solid and a liquid are converted into two gases. No reaction occurs if carbon and water are mixed together at 25 °C (298 K) because the unfavorable ΔH is larger than the favorable $T\,\Delta S$. Above about 700 °C (973 K), however, the favorable $T\,\Delta S$ becomes larger than the unfavorable ΔH, so the reaction becomes spontaneous.

Important points about spontaneity and free energy

- A spontaneous process, once begun, proceeds without any external assistance and is exergonic; that is, it has a negative value of ΔG.
- A nonspontaneous process requires continuous external influence and is endergonic; that is, it has a positive value of ΔG.
- The value of ΔG for the reverse of a reaction is numerically equal to the value of ΔG for the forward reaction, but has the opposite sign.
- Some nonspontaneous processes become spontaneous with a change in temperature.

⬤⬤ Looking Ahead

In later chapters, we will see that a knowledge of free-energy changes is especially important for understanding how metabolic reactions work. Living organisms cannot raise their temperatures to convert nonspontaneous reactions into spontaneous reactions, so they must resort to other strategies, which we will explore in Chapter 21. ⬤⬤

WORKED EXAMPLE **7.4** Entropy Change of Processes

Does entropy increase or decrease in the following processes?

    (a) Smoke from a cigarette disperses throughout a room rather than remaining in a cloud over the smoker's head.

    (b) Water boils, changing from liquid to vapor.

    (c) A chemical reaction occurs: $3\,H_2(g) + N_2(g) \longrightarrow 2\,NH_3(g)$

ANALYSIS Entropy is a measure of molecular disorder. Entropy increases when the products are more disordered than the reactants; entropy decreases when the products are less disordered than the reactants.

SOLUTION

    (a) Entropy increases because smoke particles are more disordered when they are randomly distributed in the larger volume.

    (b) Entropy increases because H_2O molecules have more freedom and disorder in the gas phase than in the liquid phase.

    (c) Entropy decreases because 4 mol of reactant gas particles become 2 mol of product gas particles, with a consequent decrease in freedom and disorder.

WORKED EXAMPLE **7.5** Spontaneity of Reactions: Enthalpy, Entropy, and Free Energy

The industrial method for synthesizing hydrogen by reaction of carbon with water has ΔH = +31.3 kcal/mol and ΔS = +32 cal/(mol·K). What is the value of ΔG for the reaction at 27 °C (300 K)? Is the reaction spontaneous or nonspontaneous at this temperature?

$$C(s) + H_2O(l) \longrightarrow CO(g) + H_2(g)$$

ANALYSIS The reaction is endothermic (ΔH positive) and does not favor spontaneity, whereas the ΔS indicates an increase in disorder (ΔS positive), which *does* favor spontaneity. Calculate ΔG to determine spontaneity.

BALLPARK ESTIMATE The unfavorable ΔH (+31.3 kcal/mol) is 1000 times greater than the favorable ΔS (+32 cal/mol·K), so the reaction will be spontaneous (ΔG negative) only when the temperature is high enough to make the $T\Delta S$ term in the equation for ΔG larger than the ΔH term. This happens at $T \geq 1000$ K. Since $T = 300$ K, expect ΔG to be positive and the reaction to be nonspontaneous.

SOLUTION
Use the free-energy equation to determine the value of ΔG at this temperature. (Remember that ΔS has units of *calories* per mole-kelvin, not kilocalories per mole-kelvin.)

$$\Delta G = \Delta H - T\,\Delta S$$

$$= +31.3\frac{\text{kcal}}{\text{mol}} - (300\text{ K})\left(+32\frac{\text{cal}}{\text{mol}\cdot\text{K}}\right)\left(\frac{1\text{ kcal}}{1000\text{ cal}}\right)$$

$$= +21.7\frac{\text{kcal}}{\text{mol}}$$

BALLPARK CHECK Because ΔG is positive, the reaction is nonspontaneous at 300 K, consistent with our estimate.

PROBLEM 7.4

Does entropy increase or decrease in the following processes?

(a) After raking your leaves into a neat pile, a breeze blows them all over your lawn.

(b) Gasoline fumes escape as the fuel is pumped into your car.

(c) $Mg(s) + Cl_2(g) \longrightarrow MgCl_2(s)$

PROBLEM 7.5

Lime (CaO) is prepared by the decomposition of limestone ($CaCO_3$).

$$CaCO_3(s) \longrightarrow CaO(s) + CO_2(g) \quad \Delta G = +31 \text{ kcal/mol at 25 °C}$$

(a) Does the reaction occur spontaneously at 25 °C?

(b) Does entropy increase or decrease in this reaction?

(c) Would you expect the reaction to be spontaneous at higher temperatures?

PROBLEM 7.6

The melting of solid ice to give liquid water has ΔH = 1.44 kcal/mol and ΔS = +5.26 cal/(mol·K). What is the value of ΔG for the melting process at the following temperatures? Is the melting spontaneous or nonspontaneous at these temperatures?

(a) −10 °C (263 K)

(b) 0 °C (273 K)

(c) +10 °C (283 K)

KEY CONCEPT PROBLEM 7.7

The following diagram portrays a reaction of the type A(s) ⟶ B(s) + C(g), where the different colored spheres represent different molecular structures. Assume that the reaction has $\Delta H = -23.5$ kcal/mol.

(a) What is the sign of ΔS for the reaction?

(b) Is the reaction likely to be spontaneous at all temperatures, nonspontaneous at all temperatures, or spontaneous at some but nonspontaneous at others?

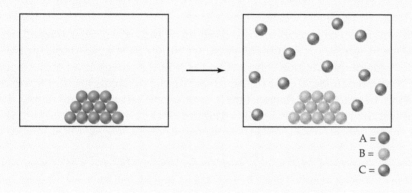

A =
B =
C =

7.5 How Do Chemical Reactions Occur? Reaction Rates

Just because a chemical reaction has a favorable free-energy change does not mean that it occurs rapidly. The value of ΔG tells us only whether a reaction *can* occur; it says nothing about how *fast* the reaction will occur or about the details of the molecular changes that take place during the reaction. It is now time to look into these other matters.

For a chemical reaction to occur, reactant particles must collide, some chemical bonds have to break, and new bonds have to form. Not all collisions lead to products, however. One requirement for a productive collision is that the colliding molecules must approach with the correct orientation so that the atoms about to form new bonds can connect. In the reaction of ozone (O_3) with nitric oxide (NO) to give oxygen (O_2) and nitrogen dioxide (NO_2), for example, the two reactants must collide so that the nitrogen atom of NO strikes a terminal oxygen atom of O_3 (Figure 7.2).

Another requirement for a reaction to occur is that the collision must take place with enough energy to break the appropriate bonds in the reactant. If the reactant particles are moving slowly, collisions might be too gentle to overcome the repulsion between electrons in the different reactants, and the particles will simply bounce apart. Only if the collisions are sufficiently energetic will a reaction ensue.

For this reason, many reactions with a favorable free-energy change do not occur at room temperature. To get such a reaction started, energy (heat) must be

▲ Matches are unreactive at room temperature but burst into flames when struck. The frictional heat produced on striking provides enough energy to start the combustion.

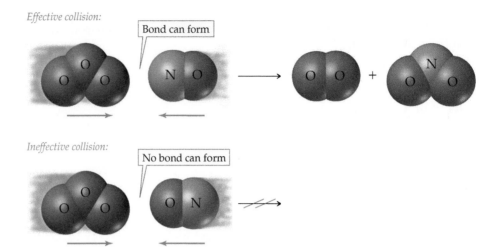

Effective collision:

Bond can form

Ineffective collision:

No bond can form

▶ **FIGURE 7.2 How do chemical reactions occur?** For a collision between NO and O_3 molecules to give O_2 and NO_2, the molecules must collide so that the correct atoms come into contact. No bond forms if the molecules collide with the wrong orientation.

added. The heat causes the reactant particles to move faster, thereby increasing both the frequency and the force of the collisions. We all know that matches burn, for instance, but we also know that they do not burst into flame until struck. The heat of friction provides enough energy for a few molecules to react. Once started, the reaction sustains itself as the energy released by reacting molecules gives other molecules enough energy to react.

The energy change that occurs during the course of a chemical reaction can be visualized in an energy diagram like that in Figure 7.3. At the beginning of the reaction (left side of the diagram), the reactants are at the energy level indicated. At the end of the reaction (right side of the diagram), the products are at a lower energy level than the reactants if the reaction is exergonic (Figure 7.3a) but higher than the reactants if the reaction is endergonic (Figure 7.3b).

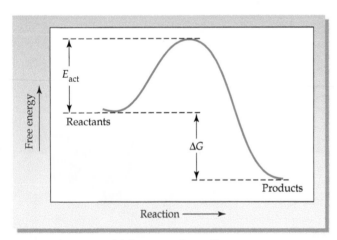

(a) An exergonic reaction

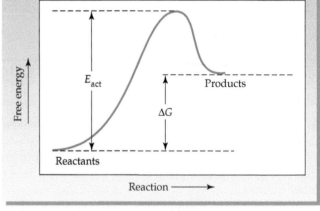

(b) An endergonic reaction

▲ **FIGURE 7.3 Reaction energy diagrams show energy changes during a chemical reaction.** A reaction begins on the left and proceeds to the right. (a) In an exergonic reaction, the product energy level is lower than that of reactants. (b) In an endergonic reaction, the situation is reversed. The height of the barrier between reactant and product energy levels is the activation energy, E_{act}. The difference between reactant and product energy levels is the free-energy change, ΔG.

Activation energy (E_{act}) The amount of energy necessary for reactants to surmount the energy barrier to reaction; determines reaction rate.

Reaction rate A measure of how rapidly a reaction occurs; determined by E_{act}.

Lying between the reactants and the products is an energy "barrier" that must be surmounted. The height of this barrier represents the amount of energy the colliding particles must have for productive collisions to occur, an amount called the **activation energy (E_{act})** of the reaction. The size of the activation energy determines the **reaction rate**, or how fast the reaction occurs. The lower the activation energy, the greater the number of productive collisions in a given amount of time, and the faster the reaction. Conversely, the higher the activation energy, the lower the number of productive collisions, and the slower the reaction.

Note that the size of the activation energy and the size of the free-energy change are unrelated. A reaction with a large E_{act} takes place very slowly even if it has a large negative ΔG. Every reaction is different; each has its own characteristic activation energy and free-energy change.

WORKED EXAMPLE   **7.6** Energy of Reactions: Energy Diagrams

Draw an energy diagram for a reaction that is very fast but has a small negative free-energy change.

ANALYSIS   A very fast reaction has a small E_{act}. A reaction with a small negative free-energy change is a favorable reaction with a small energy difference between starting materials and products.

SOLUTION

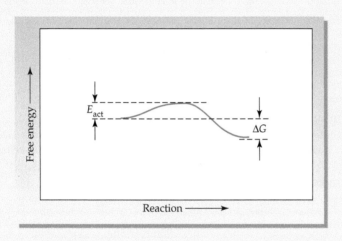

PROBLEM 7.8

Draw an energy diagram for a reaction that is very slow but highly favorable.

PROBLEM 7.9

Draw an energy diagram for a reaction that is slightly unfavorable.

7.6 Effects of Temperature, Concentration, and Catalysts on Reaction Rates

Several things can be done to help reactants over an activation energy barrier and thereby speed up a reaction. Let us look at some possibilities.

Temperature

One way to increase reaction rate is to add energy to the reactants by raising the temperature. With more energy in the system, the reactants move faster, so the frequency of collisions increases. Furthermore, the force with which collisions occur increases, making them more likely to overcome the activation barrier. As a rule of thumb, a 10 °C rise in temperature causes a reaction rate to double.

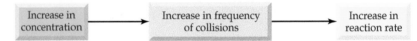

Concentration

Concentration A measure of the amount of a given substance in a mixture.

A second way to speed up a reaction is to increase the **concentrations** of the reactants. As the concentration increases reactants are crowded together, and collisions between reactant molecules become more frequent. As the frequency of collisions increases, reactions between molecules become more likely. Flammable materials burn more rapidly in pure oxygen than in air, for instance, because the concentration of O_2 molecules is higher (air is approximately 21% oxygen). Hospitals must therefore take extraordinary precautions to ensure that no flames are used near patients receiving oxygen. Although different reactions respond differently to concentration changes, doubling or tripling a reactant concentration often doubles or triples the reaction rate.

| Increase in concentration | → | Increase in frequency of collisions | → | Increase in reaction rate |

Catalysts

Catalyst A substance that speeds up the rate of a chemical reaction but is itself unchanged.

A third way to speed up a reaction is to add a **catalyst**—a substance that accelerates a chemical reaction but is itself unchanged in the process. For example, such metals as nickel, palladium, and platinum catalyze the addition of hydrogen to the carbon–carbon double bonds in vegetable oils to yield semisolid margarine. Without the metal catalyst, the reaction does not occur.

A catalyst does not affect the energy level of either reactants or products. Rather, it increases reaction rate either by letting a reaction take place through an alternative pathway with a lower energy barrier, or by orienting the reacting molecules appropriately. In a reaction energy diagram, the catalyzed reaction has a lower activation energy (Figure 7.4). It is worth noting that the free-energy change

▶ **FIGURE 7.4 A reaction energy diagram for a reaction in the presence (green curve) and absence (red curve) of a catalyst.** The catalyzed reaction has a lower (E_{act}) because it uses an alternative pathway with a lower energy barrier. The free-energy change ΔG is unaffected by the presence of a catalyst.

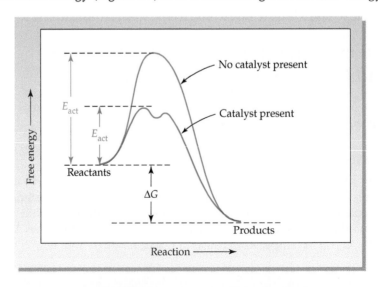

for a reaction depends *only* on the difference in the energy levels of the reactants and products, and *not* on the pathway of the reaction. Therefore, a catalyzed reaction releases (or absorbs) the same amount of energy as an uncatalyzed reaction. It simply occurs more rapidly.

In addition to their widespread use in industry, we also rely on catalysts to reduce the air pollution created by exhaust from automobile engines. The catalytic converters in most automobiles are tubes packed with catalysts of two types (Figure 7.5). One catalyst accelerates the complete combustion of hydrocarbons and CO in the exhaust to give CO_2 and H_2O, and the other decomposes NO to N_2 and O_2.

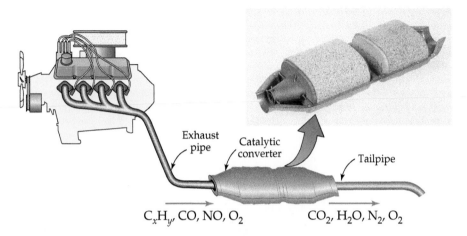

Exhaust pipe   Catalytic converter   Tailpipe

C_xH_y, CO, NO, O_2 CO_2, H_2O, N_2, O_2

◀ **FIGURE 7.5 A catalytic converter.** The exhaust gases from an automobile pass through a two-stage catalytic converter. In one stage, carbon monoxide and unburned hydrocarbons are converted to CO_2 and H_2O. In the second stage, NO is converted to N_2 and O_2.

Table 7.2 summarizes the effects of changing conditions on reaction rates.

TABLE 7.2   Effects of Changes in Reaction Conditions on Reaction Rate

CHANGE	EFFECT
Concentration	Increase in reactant concentration increases rate.
	Decrease in reactant concentration decreases rate.
Temperature	Increase in temperature increases rate.
	Decrease in temperature decreases rate.
Catalyst added	Increases reaction rate.

⊂⊙⊃ Looking Ahead

The thousands of biochemical reactions continually taking place in our bodies are catalyzed by large protein molecules called *enzymes*, which promote reaction by controlling the orientation of the reacting molecules. Since almost every reaction is catalyzed by its own specific enzyme, the study of enzyme structure, activity, and control is a central part of biochemistry. We will look more closely at enzymes and how they work in Chapters 19 and 20.   ⊂⊙⊃

PROBLEM 7.10

Ammonia is synthesized industrially by reaction of nitrogen and hydrogen in the presence of an iron catalyst according to the equation $3\,H_2(g) + N_2(g) \longrightarrow 2\,NH_3(g)$.

What effect will the following changes have on the reaction rate?

(a) The temperature is raised from 600 K to 700 K.

(b) The iron catalyst is removed.

(c) The concentration of H_2 gas is halved.

7.7 Reversible Reactions and Chemical Equilibrium

Many chemical reactions result in the virtually complete conversion of reactants into products. When sodium metal reacts with chlorine gas, for example, both are entirely consumed. The sodium chloride product is so much more stable than the reactants that, once started, the reaction keeps going until it is complete.

What happens, though, when the reactants and products are of approximately equal stability? This is the case, for example, in the reaction of acetic acid (the main organic constituent of vinegar) with ethyl alcohol to yield ethyl acetate, a solvent used in nail-polish remover and glue.

$$\underset{\text{Acetic acid}}{CH_3\overset{\overset{\displaystyle O}{\|}}{C}OH} + \underset{\text{Ethyl alcohol}}{HOCH_2CH_3} \underset{\text{Or this direction?}}{\overset{\text{This direction?}}{\rightleftharpoons}} \underset{\text{Ethyl acetate}}{CH_3\overset{\overset{\displaystyle O}{\|}}{C}OCH_2CH_3} + \underset{\text{Water}}{H_2O}$$

APPLICATION ▶   Regulation of Body Temperature

Maintaining normal body temperature is crucial. If the body's thermostat is unable to maintain a temperature of 37 °C, the rates of the many thousands of chemical reactions that take place constantly in the body will change accordingly, with potentially disastrous consequences.

If, for example, a skater fell through the ice of a frozen lake, *hypothermia* could soon result. Hypothermia is a dangerous state that occurs when the body is unable to generate enough heat to maintain normal temperature. All chemical reactions in the body slow down because of the lower temperature, energy production drops, and death can result. Slowing the body's reactions can also be used to advantage, however. During open-heart surgery, the heart is stopped and maintained at about 15 °C, while the body, which receives oxygenated blood from an external pump, is cooled to 25–32 °C.

Conversely, a marathon runner on a hot, humid day might become overheated, and *hyperthermia* could result. Hyperthermia, also called *heat stroke*, is an uncontrolled rise in temperature as the result of the body's inability to lose sufficient heat. Chemical reactions in the body are accelerated at higher temperatures, the heart struggles to pump blood faster to supply increased oxygen, and brain damage can result if the body temperature rises above 41 °C.

Body temperature is maintained both by the thyroid gland and by the hypothalamus region of the brain, which act together to regulate metabolic rate. When the body's environment changes, temperature receptors in the skin, spinal cord, and abdomen send signals to the hypothalamus, which contains both heat-sensitive and cold-sensitive neurons.

Stimulation of the heat-sensitive neurons on a hot day causes a variety of effects: Impulses are sent to stimulate the sweat glands, dilate the blood vessels of the skin, decrease muscular activity, and reduce metabolic rate. Sweating cools the body through evaporation; approximately 540 cal is removed by evaporation of 1.0 g of sweat. Dilated blood vessels cool the body by allowing more blood to flow close to

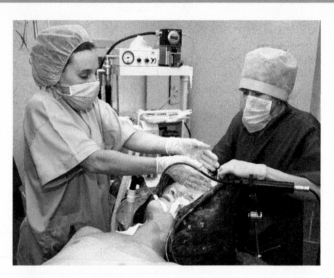

▲ The body is cooled to 25–32 °C by immersion in ice prior to open-heart surgery to slow down metabolism.

the surface of the skin where heat is removed by contact with air. Decreased muscular activity and a reduced metabolic rate cool the body by lowering internal heat production.

Stimulation of the cold-sensitive neurons on a cold day also causes a variety of effects: The hormone epinephrine is released to stimulate metabolic rate; peripheral blood vessels contract to decrease blood flow to the skin and prevent heat loss; and muscular contractions increase to produce more heat, resulting in shivering and "goosebumps."

One further comment: Drinking alcohol to warm up on a cold day actually has the opposite effect. Alcohol causes blood vessels to dilate, resulting in a warm feeling as blood flow to the skin increases. Although the warmth feels good temporarily, body temperature ultimately drops as heat is lost through the skin at an increased rate.

See Problems 7.72 and 7.73 at the end of the chapter.

Imagine the situation if you mix acetic acid and ethyl alcohol. The two begin to form ethyl acetate and water. But as soon as ethyl acetate and water form, they begin to go back to acetic acid and ethyl alcohol. Such a reaction, which easily goes in either direction, is said to be **reversible** and is indicated by a double arrow ($\rightleftharpoons$) in equations. The reaction read from left to right as written is referred to as the *forward reaction*, and the reaction from right to left is referred to as the *reverse reaction*.

Now suppose you mix some ethyl acetate and water. The same thing occurs: As soon as small quantities of acetic acid and ethyl alcohol form, the reaction in the other direction begins to take place. No matter which pair of reactants is mixed together, both reactions occur until ultimately the concentrations of reactants and products reach constant values and undergo no further change. At this point, the reaction vessel contains all four substances—acetic acid, ethyl acetate, ethyl alcohol, and water—and the reaction is said to be in a state of **chemical equilibrium**.

Since the reactant and product concentrations undergo no further change once equilibrium is reached, you might conclude that the forward and reverse reactions have stopped. That is not the case, however. The forward reaction takes place rapidly at the beginning of the reaction but then slows down as reactant concentrations decrease. At the same time, the reverse reaction takes place slowly at the beginning but then speeds up as product concentrations increase (Figure 7.6). Ultimately, the forward and reverse rates become equal and change no further.

Reversible reaction A reaction that can go in either direction, from products to reactants or reactants to products.

Chemical equilibrium A state in which the rates of forward and reverse reactions are the same.

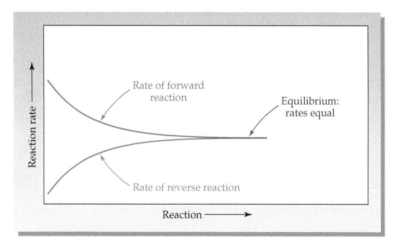

▲ **FIGURE 7.6 Reaction rates in an equilibrium reaction.** The forward rate is large initially but decreases as the concentrations of reactants drop. The reverse rate is small initially but increases as the concentrations of products increase. At equilibrium, the forward and reverse reaction rates are equal.

Chemical equilibrium is an active, dynamic condition. All substances present are continuously being made and unmade at the same rate, so their concentrations are constant at equilibrium. As an analogy, think of two floors of a building connected by up and down escalators. If the number of people moving up is the same as the number of people moving down, the numbers of people on each floor remain constant. *Individual people* are continuously changing from one floor to the other, but the *total populations* of the two floors are in equilibrium.

Note that it is not necessary for the concentrations of reactants and products at equilibrium to be equal (just as it is not necessary for the numbers of people on two floors connected by escalators to be equal). Equilibrium can be reached at any point between pure products and pure reactants. The extent to which the forward or reverse reaction is favored over the other is a characteristic property of a given reaction under given conditions.

▲ When the number of people moving up is the same as the number of people moving down, the number of people on each floor remains constant, and the two populations are in equilibrium.

7.8 Equilibrium Equations and Equilibrium Constants

Remember that the rate of a reaction depends on the number of collisions between molecules (Section 7.5), and that the number of collisions in turn depends on concentration, i.e., the number of molecules in a given volume (Section 7.6). For a reversible reaction, then, the rates of both the forward *and* the reverse reactions must depend on the concentration of reactants and products, respectively. When a reaction reaches equilibrium the rates of the forward and reverse reactions are equal, and the concentration of reactants and products remain constant. We can use this fact to obtain useful information about a reaction.

Let us look at the details of a specific equilibrium reaction. Suppose that you allow various mixtures of sulfur dioxide and oxygen to come to equilibrium with sulfur trioxide at a temperature of 727 °C and then measure the concentrations of all three gases in the mixtures.

$$2\,SO_2(g) + O_2(g) \rightleftharpoons 2\,SO_3(g)$$

In one experiment, we start with only 1.00 mol of SO_2 and 1.00 mol of O_2 in a 1.00 L container. In other words, the initial concentrations of reactants are 1.00 mol/L. When the reaction reaches equilibrium, we have 0.0620 mol/L of SO_2, 0.538 mol/L of O_2, and 0.938 mol/L of SO_3. In another experiment, we start with only 1.00 mol/L of SO_3. When this reaction reaches equilibrium, we have 0.150 mol/L of SO_2, 0.0751 mol/L of O_2, and 0.850 mol/L of SO_3. In both cases, we see that there is substantially more product than reactants when the reaction reaches equilibrium, regardless of the starting conditions. Is it possible to predict what the equilibrium conditions will be for any given reaction?

As it turns out, the answer is YES! No matter what the original concentrations, and no matter what concentrations remain at equilibrium, we find that a constant numerical value is obtained if the equilibrium concentrations are substituted into the expression

$$\frac{[SO_3]^2}{[SO_2]^2[O_2]} = 429 \quad \text{(at a constant temperature of 72 °C)}$$

The square brackets in this expression indicate the concentration of each substance expressed as moles per liter. Using the equilibrium concentrations for each of the experiments described above, we can verify that this is true:

Experiment 1. $\dfrac{[SO_3]^2}{[SO_2]^2[O_2]} = \dfrac{(0.938 \text{ mol/L})^2}{(0.0620 \text{ mol/L})^2(0.538 \text{ mol/L})} = 425$

Experiment 2. $\dfrac{[SO_3]^2}{[SO_2]^2[O_2]} = \dfrac{(0.850 \text{ mol/L})^2}{(0.150 \text{ mol/L})^2(0.0751 \text{ mol/L})} = 428$

Within experimental error, the ratios of product and reactant concentrations at equilibrium yield the same result. Numerous experiments like those just described have led to a general equation that is valid for any reaction. Consider a general reversible reaction:

$$aA + bB + \cdots \rightleftharpoons mM + nN + \cdots$$

where A, B, . . . are reactants; M, N, . . . are products; and $a, b, \ldots, m, n, \ldots$ are coefficients in the balanced equation. At equilibrium, the composition of the reaction mixture obeys the following *equilibrium equation*, where K is the **equilibrium constant**.

Equilibrium equation $K = \dfrac{[M]^m[N]^n \cdots}{[A]^a[B]^b \cdots}$ Product concentrations / Reactant concentrations

Equilibrium constant

The equilibrium constant K is the number obtained by multiplying the equilibrium concentrations of the products and dividing by the equilibrium concentrations of the reactants, with the concentration of each substance raised to a power equal to its coefficient in the balanced equation. If we take another look at the reaction between sulfur dioxide and oxygen, we can now see how the equilibrium constant was obtained:

$$2\,SO_2\,(g) + O_2\,(g) \rightleftharpoons 2\,SO_3\,(g)$$

$$K = \frac{[SO_3]^2}{[SO_2]^2\,[O_2]}$$

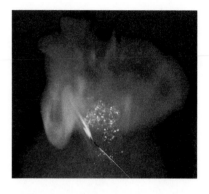

▲ The hydrogen gas in these soap bubbles reacts completely with oxygen when ignited to form water.

Note that if there is no coefficient for a reactant or product in the reaction equation it is assumed to be 1. The value of K varies with temperature—25 °C is assumed unless otherwise specified—and units are usually omitted.

The value of the equilibrium constant indicates the position of a reaction at equilibrium. If the forward reaction is favored, the product term $[M]^m[N]^n$ is larger than the reactant term $[A]^a[B]^b$, and the value of K is larger than 1. If instead the reverse reaction is favored, $[M]^m[N]^n$ is smaller than $[A]^a[B]^b$ at equilibrium, and the value of K is smaller than 1.

For a reaction such as the combination of hydrogen and oxygen to form water vapor, the equilibrium constant is enormous (3.1×10^{81}), showing how greatly the formation of water is favored. Equilibrium is effectively nonexistent for such reactions, and the reaction is described as *going to completion*.

On the other hand, the equilibrium constant is very small for a reaction such as the combination of nitrogen and oxygen at 25 °C to give NO (4.7×10^{-31}), showing what we know from observation—that N_2 and O_2 in the air do not combine noticeably at room temperature:

$$N_2(g) + O_2(g) \rightleftharpoons 2\,NO(g) \quad K = \frac{[NO]^2}{[N_2][O_2]} = 4.7 \times 10^{-31}$$

When K is close to 1, say between 10^3 and 10^{-3}, significant amounts of both reactants and products are present at equilibrium. An example is the reaction of acetic acid with ethyl alcohol to give ethyl acetate (Section 7.7). For this reaction, $K = 3.4$.

$$CH_3CO_2H + CH_3CH_2OH \rightleftharpoons CH_3CO_2CH_2CH_3 + H_2O$$

$$K = \frac{[CH_3CO_2CH_2CH_3][H_2O]}{[CH_3CO_2H][CH_3CH_2OH]} = 3.4$$

We can summarize the meaning of equilibrium constants in the following way:

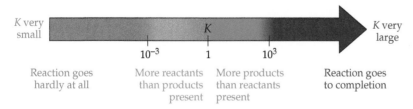

K much smaller than 0.001   Only reactants are present at equilibrium; essentially no reaction occurs.

K between 0.001 and 1   More reactants than products are present at equilibrium.

| K between 1 and 1000 | More products than reactants are present at equilibrium. |
| K much larger than 1000 | Only products are present at equilibrium; reaction goes essentially to completion. |

WORKED EXAMPLE **7.7** Writing Equilibrium Equations

The first step in the industrial synthesis of hydrogen is the reaction of steam with methane to give carbon monoxide and hydrogen. Write the equilibrium equation for the reaction.

$$H_2O(g) + CH_4(g) \rightleftharpoons CO(g) + 3\,H_2(g)$$

ANALYSIS The equilibrium constant K is the number obtained by multiplying the equilibrium concentrations of the products (CO and H_2) and dividing by the equilibrium concentrations of the reactants (H_2O and CH_4), with the concentration of each substance raised to the power of its coefficient in the balanced equation.

SOLUTION

$$K = \frac{[CO][H_2]^3}{[H_2O][CH_4]}$$

WORKED EXAMPLE **7.8** Equilibrium Equations: Calculating K

In the reaction of Cl_2 with PCl_3, the concentrations of reactants and products were determined experimentally at equilibrium and found to be 7.2 mol/L for PCl_3, 7.2 mol/L for Cl_2, and 0.050 mol/L for PCl_5.

$$PCl_3(g) + Cl_2(g) \rightleftharpoons PCl_5(g)$$

Write the equilibrium equation, and calculate the equilibrium constant for the reaction. Which reaction is favored, the forward one or the reverse one?

ANALYSIS All the coefficients in the balanced equation are 1, so the equilibrium constant equals the concentration of the product, PCl_5, divided by the product of the concentrations of the two reactants, PCl_3 and Cl_2. Insert the values given for each concentration, and calculate the value of K.

BALLPARK ESTIMATE At equilibrium, the concentration of the reactants (7.2 mol/L for each reactant) is higher than the concentration of the product (0.05 mol/L), so we expect a value of K less than 1.

SOLUTION

$$K = \frac{[PCl_5]}{[PCl_3][Cl_2]} = \frac{0.050 \text{ mol/L}}{(7.2 \text{ mol/L})(7.2 \text{ mol/L})} = 9.6 \times 10^{-4}$$

The value of K is less than 1, so the reverse reaction is favored. Note that units for K are omitted.

BALLPARK CHECK Our calculated value of K is just as we predicted: $K < 1$.

PROBLEM 7.11

Write equilibrium equations for the following reactions:

(a) $N_2O_4(g) \rightleftharpoons 2\,NO_2(g)$

(b) $CH_4(g) + Cl_2(g) \rightleftharpoons CH_3Cl(g) + HCl(g)$

(c) $2\,BrF_5(g) \rightleftharpoons Br_2(g) + 5\,F_2(g)$

PROBLEM 7.12

Do the following reactions favor reactants or products at equilibrium?

(a) Sucrose(aq) + H_2O(l) $\rightleftharpoons$ Glucose(aq) + Fructose(aq) $K = 1.4 \times 10^5$
(b) NH_3(aq) + H_2O(l) $\rightleftharpoons$ NH_4^+(aq) + OH^-(aq) $K = 1.6 \times 10^{-5}$
(c) Fe_2O_3(s) + 3 CO(g) $\rightleftharpoons$ 2 Fe(s) + 3 CO_2(g)   K(at 727°C) = 24.2

PROBLEM 7.13

For the reaction H_2(g) + I_2(g) $\rightleftharpoons$ 2 HI(g), equilibrium concentrations at 25 °C are $[H_2]$ = 0.0510 mol/L, $[I_2]$ = 0.174 mol/L, and $[HI]$ = 0.507 mol/L. What is the value of K at 25 °C?

KEY CONCEPT PROBLEM 7.14

The following diagrams represent two similar reactions that have achieved equilibrium:

   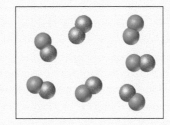

$A_2 + B_2 \longrightarrow 2\,AB$ $C_2 + D_2 \longrightarrow 2\,CD$

Which reaction has the larger equilibrium constant, and which has the smaller equilibrium constant?

7.9 Le Châtelier's Principle: The Effect of Changing Conditions on Equilibria

The effect of a change in reaction conditions on chemical equilibrium is predicted by a general rule called *Le Châtelier's principle:*

Le Châtelier's principle   When a stress is applied to a system at equilibrium, the equilibrium shifts to relieve the stress.

The word "stress" in this context means any change in concentration, pressure, volume, or temperature that disturbs the original equilibrium and causes the rates of the forward and reverse reactions to become temporarily unequal.

We saw in Section 7.6 that reaction rates are affected by changes in temperature and concentration, and by addition of a catalyst. But what about equilibria? Are they similarly affected? The answer is that changes in concentration, temperature, and pressure *do* affect equilibria, but that addition of a catalyst does not (except to reduce the time it takes to reach equilibrium). The change caused by a catalyst affects forward and reverse reactions equally so that equilibrium concentrations are the same in both the presence and the absence of the catalyst.

Effect of Changes in Concentration

Let us look at the effect of a concentration change by considering the reaction of CO with H_2 to form CH_3OH (methanol). Once equilibrium is reached, the concentrations of the reactants and product are constant, and the forward and reverse reaction rates are equal.

$$CO(g) + 2\,H_2(g) \rightleftharpoons CH_3OH(g)$$

What happens if the concentration of CO is increased? To relieve the "stress" of added CO, according to Le Châtelier's principle, the extra CO must be used up. In other words, the rate of the forward reaction must increase to consume CO. Think of the CO added on the left as "pushing" the equilibrium to the right:

$$[CO \longrightarrow]$$
$$CO(g) + 2\,H_2(g) \rightleftharpoons CH_3OH(g)$$

Of course, as soon as more CH_3OH forms, the reverse reaction also speeds up, and so some CH_3OH converts back to CO and H_2. Ultimately, the forward and reverse reaction rates adjust until they are again equal, and equilibrium is reestablished. At this new equilibrium state, the value of $[H_2]$ is lower because some of the H_2 reacted with the added CO and the value of $[CH_3OH]$ is higher because CH_3OH formed as the reaction was driven to the right by the addition of CO. The changes offset each other, however, so that the value of the equilibrium constant K remains constant.

$$CO(g) + 2\,H_2(g) \rightleftharpoons CH_3OH(g)$$

If this increases . . .   . . . then this decreases . . .   . . . and this increases . . .

. . . but this remains constant. $K = \dfrac{[CH_3OH]}{[CO]\,[H_2]^2}$

What happens if CH_3OH is added to the reaction at equilibrium? Some of the methanol reacts to yield CO and H_2, making the values of $[CO], [H_2]$, and $[CH_3OH]$ higher when equilibrium is reestablished. As before, the value of K does not change.

If this increases . . .

$$CO(g) + 2\,H_2(g) \rightleftharpoons CH_3OH(g)$$

. . . then this increases . . .   . . . and this increases . . .

. . . but this remains constant. $K = \dfrac{[CH_3OH]}{[CO]\,[H_2]^2}$

Alternatively, we can view chemical equilibrium as a *balance* between the energy of the reactants (on the left) and the products (on the right). Adding more reactants tips the balance in favor of the reactants. In order to restore the balance, reactants must be converted to products, or the reaction must shift to the right. If, instead, we remove reactants, then the balance is too heavy on the products side and the reaction must shift left, generating more reactants to restore balance.

Finally, what happens if a reactant is continuously supplied or a product is continuously removed? Because the concentrations are continuously changing, equilibrium can never be reached. As a result, it is sometimes possible to force a reaction to produce large quantities of a desirable product even when the equilibrium constant is unfavorable. Take the reaction of acetic acid with ethanol to yield ethyl

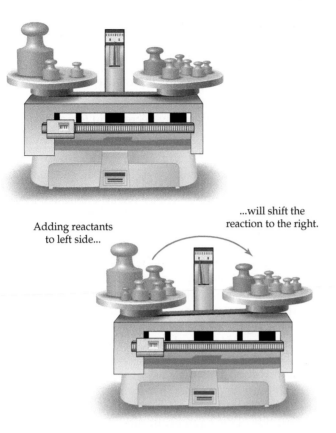

▲ Equilibrium represents a balance between the energy of reactants and products. Adding reactants (or products) to one side upsets the balance, and the reaction will proceed in a direction to restore the balance.

acetate, for example. As discussed in the preceding section, the equilibrium constant K for this reaction is 3.4, meaning that substantial amounts of reactants and products are both present at equilibrium. If, however, the ethyl acetate is removed as soon as it is formed, the production of more and more product is forced to occur, in accord with Le Châtelier's principle.

> Continuously removing this product from the reaction forces more of it to be produced.

$$CH_3\overset{\displaystyle O}{\overset{\|}{C}}OH \ + \ CH_3CH_2OH \ \rightleftharpoons \ CH_3\overset{\displaystyle O}{\overset{\|}{C}}OCH_2CH_3 \ + \ H_2O$$

Acetic acid   Ethyl alcohol   Ethyl acetate

Metabolic reactions sometimes take advantage of this effect, with one reaction prevented from reaching equilibrium by the continuous consumption of its product in a further reaction.

Effect of Changes in Temperature and Pressure

We noted in Section 7.2 that the reverse of an exothermic reaction is always endothermic. Equilibrium reactions are therefore exothermic in one direction and endothermic in the other. Le Châtelier's principle predicts that an increase in temperature will cause an equilibrium to shift in favor of the endothermic reaction so the additional heat is absorbed. Conversely, a decrease in temperature will cause an equilibrium to shift in favor of the exothermic reaction so additional heat is released. In other words, you can think of heat as a reactant or product whose increase or decrease stresses an equilibrium just as a change in reactant or product concentration does.

Endothermic reaction (Heat is absorbed)	Favored by increase in temperature
Exothermic reaction (Heat is released)	Favored by decrease in temperature

In the exothermic reaction of N_2 with H_2 to form NH_3, for example, raising the temperature favors the reverse reaction, which absorbs the heat:

$$[\longleftarrow \text{Heat}]$$
$$N_2(g) + 3 H_2(g) \rightleftarrows 2 NH_3(g) + \text{Heat}$$

We can also use the balance analogy to predict the effect of temperature on an equilibrium mixture; this time we think of heat as a reactant or product. Increasing the temperature of the reaction is the same as adding heat to the left side (for an endothermic reaction) or to the right side (for an exothermic reaction). The reaction then proceeds in the appropriate direction to restore "balance" to the system.

What about changing the pressure? Pressure influences an equilibrium only if one or more of the substances involved is a gas. As predicted by Le Châtelier's principle, decreasing the volume to increase the pressure in such a reaction shifts the equilibrium in the direction that decreases the number of molecules in the gas phase and thus decreases the pressure. For the ammonia synthesis, decreasing the volume *increases* the concentration of reactants and products, but has a greater effect on the reactant side of the equilibrium since there are more moles of gas phase reactants. Increasing the pressure, therefore, favors the forward reaction because 4 mol of gas is converted to 2 mol of gas.

$$[\text{Pressure} \longrightarrow]$$
$$\underbrace{N_2(g) + 3 H_2(g)}_{\text{4 mol of gas}} \rightleftarrows \underbrace{2 NH_3(g)}_{\text{2 mol of gas}}$$

The effects of changing reaction conditions on equilibria are summarized in Table 7.3.

TABLE 7.3 Effects of Changes in Reaction Conditions on Equilibria

CHANGE	EFFECT
Concentration	Increase in reactant concentration or decrease in product concentration favors forward reaction.
	Increase in product concentration or decrease in reactant concentration favors reverse reaction.
Temperature	Increase in temperature favors endothermic reaction.
	Decrease in temperature favors exothermic reaction.
Pressure	Increase in pressure favors side with fewer moles of gas.
	Decrease in pressure favors side with more moles of gas.
Catalyst added	Equilibrium reached more quickly; value of K unchanged.

◁▢▷ **Looking Ahead**

In Chapter 21, we will see how Le Châtelier's principle is exploited to keep chemical "traffic" moving through the body's metabolic pathways. It often happens that one reaction in a series is prevented from reaching equilibrium because its product is continuously consumed in another reaction. ◁▢▷

APPLICATION ▶ Nitrogen Fixation

All plants and animals need nitrogen—it is present in all proteins and nucleic acids, and is the fourth most abundant element in the human body. Because the triple bond in the N_2 molecule is so strong, however, plants and animals cannot use the free element directly. It is up to nature and the fertilizer industry to convert N_2, which makes up 78% of the atmosphere, into usable nitrogen compounds in a process called *nitrogen fixation*. Plants use ammonia (NH_3), nitrates (NO_3^-), urea (H_2NCONH_2), and other simple, water-soluble compounds as their sources of nitrogen. Animals then get their nitrogen by eating plants or other plant-eating animals. All these processes contribute to the global *nitrogen cycle* (see figure).

Natural Nitrogen Fixation

Because of the very strong triple bond in the N_2 molecule, the rate of conversion of nitrogen to ammonia or nitrate is very slow under normal conditions. However, lightning in the atmosphere supplies sufficient energy to overcome the large activation energy and drive the endothermic reaction between N_2 and O_2 to form NO. Further reactions with O_2 or O_3 ultimately produce water-soluble nitrates that can be used by plants. Lightning produces small amounts of ammonia as well.

Nitrogen fixation also occurs as a result of bacterial activity in the soil. These bacteria are either free-living, such as *cyanobacteria*, or are associated symbiotically with plants, such as the *Rhizobium* found in the root nodules of legumes (peas, beans, and clover). The biological fixation of nitrogen is represented by the following equation:

$$N_2 + 8\,H^+ + 8\,e^- + 16\,ATP \longrightarrow 2\,NH_3 + H_2 + 16\,ADP$$

where ATP and ADP are adenosine triphosphate and adenosine diphosphate respectively, in the reaction that serves as the major source of energy in many organisms (Chapter 21). This reaction is made possible by an enzyme complex called *nitrogenase*, which acts as a catalyst to lower the energy barrier.

Industrial Nitrogen Fixation

Most industrial nitrogen fixation results from fertilizer production utilizing the *Haber process*, the reaction between nitrogen and hydrogen to give ammonia:

The Haber process

$$N_2(g) + 3\,H_2(g) \longrightarrow 2\,NH_3(g)$$

This reaction is performed at high temperatures and pressures in the presence of an iron-based catalyst to increase the rate of reaction and shift the equilibrium in favor of ammonia. Since the reaction is reversible, an equilibrium would quickly be established between products and reactants; by removing ammonia as it forms, the reaction is continuously shifted to the right according to Le Châtelier's principle to maximize ammonia production.

See Additional Problems 7.74 and 7.75 at the end of the chapter.

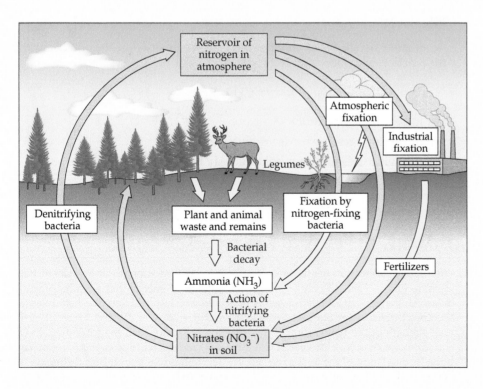

◀ The nitrogen cycle, showing how N_2 in the atmosphere is fixed, used by plants and animals, and then returned to the atmosphere.

WORKED EXAMPLE **7.9** Le Châtelier's Principle and Equilibrium Mixtures

Nitrogen reacts with oxygen to give NO:

$$N_2(g) + O_2(g) \rightleftharpoons 2\,NO(g) \quad \Delta H = +43\,\text{kcal/mol}$$

Explain the effects of the following changes on reactant and product concentrations:

(a) Increasing temperature

(b) Increasing the concentration of NO

(c) Adding a catalyst

SOLUTION

(a) The reaction is endothermic (positive ΔH), so increasing the temperature favors the forward reaction. The concentration of NO will be higher at equilibrium.

(b) Increasing the concentration of NO, a product, favors the reverse reaction. At equilibrium, the concentrations of both N_2 and O_2, as well as that of NO, will be higher.

(c) A catalyst accelerates the rate at which equilibrium is reached, but the concentrations at equilibrium do not change.

PROBLEM 7.15

Is the yield of SO_3 at equilibrium favored by a higher or lower pressure? By a higher or lower temperature?

$$2\,SO_2(g) + O_2(g) \rightleftharpoons 2\,SO_3(g) \quad \Delta H = -47\,\text{kcal/mol}$$

PROBLEM 7.16

What effect do the listed changes have on the position of the equilibrium in the reaction of carbon with hydrogen?

$$C(s) + 2\,H_2(g) \rightleftharpoons CH_4(g) \quad \Delta H = -18\,\text{kcal/mol}$$

(a) Increasing temperature

(b) Increasing pressure by decreasing volume

(c) Allowing CH_4 to escape continuously from the reaction vessel

---

KEY WORDS

Activation energy (E_{act}) p. 194

Bond dissociation energy, p. 184

Catalyst, p. 196

Chemical equilibrium, p. 199

Concentration, p. 196

SUMMARY: REVISITING THE CHAPTER GOALS

1. **What energy changes take place during reactions?** The strength of a covalent bond is measured by its *bond dissociation energy*, the amount of energy that must be supplied to break the bond in an isolated gaseous molecule. For any reaction, the heat released or absorbed by changes in bonding is called the *heat of reaction*, or *enthalpy change* (ΔH). If the total strength of the bonds formed in a reaction is greater than the total strength of the bonds broken, then heat is released (negative ΔH) and the reaction is said to be *exothermic*. If the total strength of the bonds formed in a reaction is less than the total strength of the bonds broken, then heat is absorbed (positive ΔH) and the reaction is said to be *endothermic*.

2. **What is "free energy," and what is the criterion for spontaneity in chemistry?** *Spontaneous reactions* are those that, once started, continue without external influence; nonspontaneous reactions require a continuous external influence. Spontaneity depends on two factors, the amount of heat absorbed or released in a reaction (ΔH) and the *entropy change* (ΔS), which measures the change in molecular disorder in a reaction. Spontaneous reactions are favored by a release of heat (negative ΔH) and an increase in disorder (positive ΔS). The *free-energy change* (ΔG) takes both factors into account, according to the equation $\Delta G = \Delta H - T\Delta S$. A negative value for ΔG indicates spontaneity, and a positive value for ΔG indicates nonspontaneity.

3. **What determines the rate of a chemical reaction?** A chemical reaction occurs when reactant particles collide with proper orientation and sufficient energy. The exact amount of collision energy necessary is called the *activation energy* (E_{act}). A high activation energy results in a slow reaction because few collisions occur with sufficient force, whereas a low activation energy results in a fast reaction. Reaction rates can be increased by raising the temperature, by raising the concentrations of reactants, or by adding a *catalyst*, which accelerates a reaction without itself undergoing any change.

4. **What is chemical equilibrium?** A reaction that can occur in either the forward or reverse direction is *reversible* and will ultimately reach a state of *chemical equilibrium*. At equilibrium, the forward and reverse reactions occur at the same rate, and the concentrations of reactants and products are constant. Every reversible reaction has a characteristic *equilibrium constant* (K), given by an *equilibrium equation*.

For the reaction: $aA + bB + \cdots \rightleftharpoons mM + nN + \cdots$

Product concentrations raised to powers equal to coefficients

$$K = \frac{[M]^m[N]^n \cdots}{[A]^a[B]^b \cdots}$$ Reactant concentrations raised to powers equal to coefficients

If K is larger than 1, the forward reaction is favored; if K is less than 1, the reverse reaction is favored.

5. **What is Le Châtelier's principle?** *Le Châtelier's principle* states that when a stress is applied to a system in equilibrium, the equilibrium shifts so that the stress is relieved. Applying this principle allows prediction of the effects of changes in temperature, pressure, and concentration.

UNDERSTANDING KEY CONCEPTS

7.17 What are the signs of ΔH, ΔS, and ΔG for the spontaneous conversion of a crystalline solid into a gas? Explain.

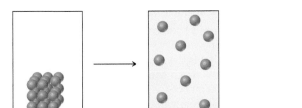

7.18 What are the signs of ΔH, ΔS, and ΔG for the spontaneous condensation of a vapor to a liquid? Explain.

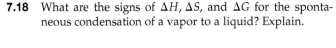
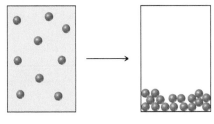

7.19 Consider the following spontaneous reaction of A_2 molecules (red) and B_2 molecules (blue):

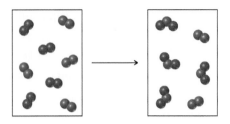

(a) Write a balanced equation for the reaction.
(b) What are the signs of ΔH, ΔS, and ΔG for the reaction? Explain.

7.20 Two curves are shown in the following energy diagram:

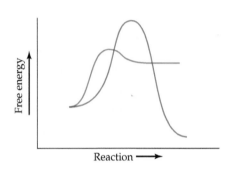

(a) Which curve represents the faster reaction, and which the slower?
(b) Which curve represents the spontaneous reaction, and which the nonspontaneous?

7.21 Two curves are shown in the following energy diagram. Which curve represents the catalyzed reaction, and which the uncatalyzed?

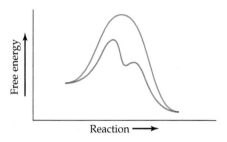

7.22 Draw energy diagrams for the following situations:

(a) A slow reaction with a large negative ΔG
(b) A fast reaction with a small positive ΔG

7.23 The following diagram portrays a reaction of the type $A(s) \longrightarrow B(g) + C(g)$, where the different colored spheres represent different molecular structures. Assume that the reaction has $\Delta H = +9.1$ kcal/mol.

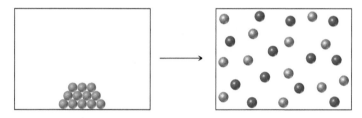

(a) What is the sign of ΔS for the reaction?
(b) Is the reaction likely to be spontaneous at all temperatures, nonspontaneous at all temperatures, or spontaneous at some but nonspontaneous at others?

ADDITIONAL PROBLEMS

ENTHALPY AND HEAT OF REACTION

7.24 Is the total enthalpy (H) of the reactants for an endothermic reaction greater than or less than the total enthalpy of the products?

7.25 What is meant by the term *heat of reaction*? What other name is a synonym for this term?

7.26 The vaporization of Br_2 from the liquid to the gas state requires 7.4 kcal/mol.

(a) What is the sign of ΔH for this process?
(b) How many kilocalories are needed to vaporize 5.8 mol of Br_2?
(c) How many kilocalories are needed to evaporate 82 g of Br_2?

7.27 Converting liquid water to solid ice releases 1.44 kcal/mol.

(a) What is the sign of ΔH for this process?
(b) How many kilocalories are released by freezing 2.5 mol of H_2O?
(c) How many kilocalories are released by freezing 32 g of H_2O?
(d) How many kilocalories are absorbed by melting 1 mol of ice?

7.28 Glucose, also known as "blood sugar," has the formula $C_6H_{12}O_6$.

(a) Write the equation for the combustion of glucose with O_2 to give CO_2 and H_2O.
(b) If 3.8 kcal is released by combustion of each gram of glucose, how many kilocalories are released by the combustion of 1.50 mol of glucose?
(c) What is the minimum amount of energy a plant must absorb to produce 15.0 g of glucose?

7.29 During the combustion of 5.00 g of octane, C_8H_{18}, 239.5 kcal is released.

(a) Write a balanced equation for the combustion reaction.
(b) What is the sign of ΔH for this reaction?
(c) How much energy is released by the combustion of 1.00 mol of C_8H_{18}?
(d) How many grams and how many moles of octane must be burned to release 450.0 kcal?
(e) How many kilocalories are released by the combustion of 17.0 g of C_8H_{18}?

ENTROPY AND FREE ENERGY

7.30 Which of the following processes results in an increase in entropy of the system?

(a) A drop of ink spreading out when it is placed in water

(b) Steam condensing into drops on windows

(c) Constructing a building from loose bricks

7.31 For each of the following processes, specify whether entropy increases or decreases. Explain each of your answers.

(a) Assembling a jigsaw puzzle

(b) $I_2(s) + 3 F_2(g) \longrightarrow 2 IF_3(g)$

(c) A precipitate forming when two solutions are mixed

(d) $C_6H_{12}O_6(aq) + 6 O_2(g) \longrightarrow 6 CO_2(g) + 6 H_2O(g)$

(e) $CaCO_3(s) \longrightarrow CaO(s) + CO_2(g)$

(f) $Pb(NO_3)_2(aq) + 2 NaCl(aq) \longrightarrow$ $PbCl_2(s) + 2 NaNO_3(aq)$

7.32 What is meant by a *spontaneous* process?

7.33 How is the sign of the free-energy change related to the spontaneity of a process?

7.34 What two factors affect the spontaneity of a reaction?

7.35 What is the difference between an exothermic reaction and an exergonic reaction?

7.36 Why are most spontaneous reactions exothermic?

7.37 Is it possible for a reaction to be nonspontaneous yet exothermic? Explain.

7.38 For the reaction

$$NaCl(s) \xrightarrow{\text{Water}} Na^+(aq) + Cl^-(aq), \quad \Delta H = +1.00 \text{ kcal/mol}$$

(a) Is this process endothermic or exothermic?

(b) Does entropy increase or decrease in this process?

(c) Table salt (NaCl) readily dissolves in water. Explain, based on your answers to parts (a) and (b).

7.39 For the reaction $2 Hg(l) + O_2(g) \longrightarrow 2 HgO(s)$, $\Delta H = -43$ kcal/mol.

(a) Does entropy increase or decrease in this process? Explain.

(b) Under what conditions would you expect this process to be spontaneous?

7.40 The reaction of gaseous H_2 and liquid Br_2 to give gaseous HBr has $\Delta H = -17.4$ kcal/mol and $\Delta S = 27.2$ cal/(mol·K).

(a) Write the balanced equation for this reaction.

(b) Does entropy increase or decrease in this process?

(c) Is this process spontaneous at all temperatures? Explain.

(d) What is the value of ΔG for the reaction at 300 K?

7.41 The following reaction is used in the industrial synthesis of PVC polymer:

$$Cl_2(g) + H_2C{=}CH_2(g) \longrightarrow$$
$$ClCH_2CH_2Cl(l) \quad \Delta H = -52 \text{ kcal/mol}$$

(a) Is ΔS positive or negative for this process?

(b) Is this process spontaneous at all temperatures? Explain.

RATES OF CHEMICAL REACTIONS

7.42 What is the activation energy of a reaction?

7.43 Which reaction is faster, one with $E_{act} = +10$ kcal/mol or one with $E_{act} = +5$ kcal/mol? Explain.

7.44 Draw energy diagrams for exergonic reactions that meet the following descriptions:

(a) A slow reaction that has a small free-energy change

(b) A fast reaction that has a large free-energy change

7.45 Draw an energy diagram for a reaction whose products have the same free energies as its reactants. What is free-energy change in this case?

7.46 Give two reasons why increasing temperature increases the rate of a reaction.

7.47 Why does increasing concentration generally increase the rate of a reaction?

7.48 What is a catalyst, and what effect does it have on the activation energy of a reaction?

7.49 If a catalyst changes the activation energy of a forward reaction from 28.0 kcal/mol to 23.0 kcal/mol, what effect does it have on the reverse reaction?

7.50 For the reaction $C(s, \text{diamond}) \longrightarrow C(s, \text{graphite})$, $\Delta G = -0.693$ kcal/mol at 25 °C.

(a) According to this information, do diamonds spontaneously turn into graphite?

(b) In light of your answer to part (a), why can diamonds be kept unchanged for thousands of years?

7.51 The reaction between hydrogen gas and carbon to produce the gas known as ethylene is $2 H_2(g) + 2 C(s) \longrightarrow H_2C{=}CH_2(g)$, $\Delta G = +16.3$ kcal/mol at 25 °C.

(a) Is this reaction spontaneous at 25 °C?

(b) Would it be reasonable to try to develop a catalyst for the reaction run at 25 °C? Explain.

CHEMICAL EQUILIBRIA

7.52 What is meant by the term "chemical equilibrium"? Must amounts of reactants and products be equal at equilibrium?

7.53 Why do catalysts not alter the amounts of reactants and products present at equilibrium?

7.54 Write the equilibrium equations for the following reactions:

(a) $2 CO(g) + O_2(g) \rightleftharpoons 2 CO_2(g)$

(b) $C_2H_6(g) + 2 Cl_2(g) \rightleftharpoons C_2H_4Cl_2(g) + 2 HCl(g)$

(c) $HF(aq) + H_2O(l) \rightleftharpoons H_3O^+(aq) + F^-(aq)$

(d) $3 O_2(g) \rightleftharpoons 2 O_3(g)$

7.55 Write the equilibrium equations for the following reactions, and tell whether reactants or products are favored in each case.

(a) $S_2(g) + 2 H_2(g) \rightleftharpoons 2 H_2S(g)$ $K = 2.8 \times 10^{-21}$

(b) $CO(g) + 2 H_2(g) \rightleftharpoons CH_3OH(g)$ $K = 10.5$

(c) $Br_2(g) + Cl_2(g) \rightleftharpoons 2 BrCl(g)$ $K = 58.0$

(d) $I_2(g) \rightleftharpoons 2I(g)$ $K = 6.8 \times 10^{-3}$

7.56 For the reaction $N_2O_4(g) \rightleftharpoons 2 NO_2(g)$, the equilibrium concentrations at 25 °C are $[NO_2] = 0.0325$ mol/L and $[N_2O_4] = 0.147$ mol/L. What is the value of K at 25 °C?

7.57 For the reaction $2 CO(g) + O_2(g) \rightleftharpoons 2 CO_2(g)$, the equilibrium concentrations at a certain temperature are $[CO_2] = 0.11$ mol/L, $[O_2] = 0.015$ mol/L, $[CO] = 0.025$ mol/L.

What is the value of K at this temperature?

7.58 Use your answer from Problem 7.56 to calculate the following:

(a) $[N_2O_4]$ at equilibrium when $[NO_2]$ = 0.0250 mol/L

(b) $[NO_2]$ at equilibrium when $[N_2O_4]$ = 0.0750 mol/L

7.59 Use your answer from Problem 7.57 to calculate the following:

(a) $[O_2]$ at equilibrium when $[CO_2]$ = 0.18 mol/L and $[CO]$ = 0.0200 mol/L

(b) $[CO_2]$ at equilibrium when $[CO]$ = 0.080 mol/L and $[O_2]$ = 0.520 mol/L

7.60 Would you expect to find relatively more reactants or more products for the reaction in Problem 7.56 if the pressure is raised? Explain.

7.61 Would you expect to find relatively more reactants or more products for the reaction in Problem 7.57 if the pressure is lowered?

LE CHÂTELIER'S PRINCIPLE

7.62 Oxygen can be converted into ozone by the action of lightning or electric sparks:

$$3\,O_2(g) \rightleftharpoons 2\,O_3(g)$$

For this reaction, ΔH = +68 kcal/mol and $K = 2.68 \times 10^{-29}$ at 25 °C.

(a) Is the reaction exothermic or endothermic?

(b) Are the reactants or the products favored at equilibrium?

(c) Explain the effect on the equilibrium of:

  (1) Increasing pressure by decreasing volume

  (2) Increasing the concentration of $O_2(g)$

  (3) Increasing the concentration of $O_3(g)$

  (4) Adding a catalyst

  (5) Increasing the temperature

7.63 Hydrogen chloride can be made from the reaction of chlorine and hydrogen:

$$Cl_2(g) + H_2(g) \longrightarrow 2\,HCl(g)$$

For this reaction, $K = 26 \times 10^{33}$ and ΔH = −44 kcal/mol at 25 °C.

(a) Is the reaction endothermic or exothermic?

(b) Are the reactants or the products favored at equilibrium?

(c) Explain the effect on the equilibrium of:

  (1) Increasing pressure by decreasing volume

  (2) Increasing the concentration of $HCl(g)$

  (3) Decreasing the concentration of $Cl_2(g)$

  (4) Increasing the concentration of $H_2(g)$

  (5) Adding a catalyst

7.64 When the following equilibria are disturbed by increasing the pressure, does the concentration of reaction products increase, decrease, or remain the same?

(a) $2\,CO_2(g) \rightleftharpoons 2\,CO(g) + O_2(g)$

(b) $N_2(g) + O_2(g) \rightleftharpoons 2\,NO(g)$

(c) $Si(s) + 2\,Cl_2(g) \rightleftharpoons SiCl_4(g)$

7.65 For the following equilibria, use Le Châtelier's principle to predict the direction of the reaction when the pressure is increased by decreasing the volume of the equilibrium mixture.

(a) $C(s) + H_2O(g) \rightleftharpoons CO(g) + H_2(g)$

(b) $2\,H_2(g) + O_2(g) \rightleftharpoons 2\,H_2O(g)$

(c) $2\,Fe(s) + 3\,H_2O(g) \rightleftharpoons Fe_2O_3(s) + 3\,H_2(g)$

7.66 The reaction $CO(g) + H_2O(g) \rightleftharpoons CO_2(g) + H_2(g)$ has ΔH = −9.8 kcal/mol. Does the amount of H_2 in an equilibrium mixture increase or decrease when the temperature is decreased?

7.67 The reaction $3\,O_2(g) \rightleftharpoons 2\,O_3(g)$ has ΔH = +68 kcal/mol. Does the equilibrium constant for the reaction increase or decrease when the temperature increases?

7.68 The reaction $H_2(g) + I_2(g) \rightleftharpoons 2\,HI(g)$ has ΔH = −2.2 kcal/mol. Will the equilibrium concentration of HI increase or decrease when:

(a) I_2 is added?

(b) H_2 is removed?

(c) A catalyst is added?

(d) The temperature is increased?

7.69 The reaction $Fe^{3+}(aq) + Cl^-(aq) \rightleftharpoons FeCl^{2+}(aq)$ is endothermic. How will the equilibrium concentration of $FeCl^{2+}$ change when:

(a) $Fe(NO_3)_3$ is added?

(b) Cl^- is precipitated by addition of $AgNO_3$?

(c) The temperature is increased?

(d) A catalyst is added?

Applications

7.70 Which provides more energy, 1 g of carbohydrate or 1 g of fat? [*Energy from Food, p. 189*]

7.71 How many Calories (that is, kilocalories) are in a 45.0 g serving of potato chips if we assume that they are essentially 50% carbohydrate, and 50% fats? [*Energy from Food, p. 189*]

7.72 Which body organs help to regulate body temperature? [*Regulation of Body Temperature, p. 198*]

7.73 What is the purpose of blood vessel dilation? [*Regulation of Body Temperature, p. 198*]

7.74 What does it mean to "fix" nitrogen, and what natural processes accomplish nitrogen fixation? [*Nitrogen Fixation, p. 207*]

7.75 The enthalpy change for the production of ammonia from its elements is ΔH = −22 kcal/mol, yet this reaction does not readily occur at room temperature. Give two reasons why this is so. [*Nitrogen Fixation, p. 207*]

General Questions and Problems

7.76 For the unbalanced combustion reaction shown below, 1 mol of ethanol, C_2H_5OH, releases 327 kcal.

$$C_2H_5OH + O_2 \longrightarrow CO_2 + H_2O$$

(a) Write a balanced equation for the combustion reaction.

(b) What is the sign of ΔH for this reaction?

(c) How much heat (in kilocalories) is released from the combustion of 5.00 g of ethanol?

(d) How many grams of C_2H_5OH must be burned to raise the temperature of 500.0 mL of water from 20.0 °C to 100.0 °C? (The specific heat of water is 1.00 cal/g · °C. See Section 2.10)

(e) If the density of ethanol is 0.789 g/mL, calculate the combustion energy of ethanol in kilocalories/milliliter

7.77 For the production of ammonia from its elements, $\Delta H = -22$ kcal/mol.

(a) Is this process endothermic or exothermic?
(b) How many kilocalories are involved in the production of 0.700 mol of NH_3?

7.78 Magnetite, an iron ore with formula Fe_3O_4, can be reduced by treatment with hydrogen to yield iron metal and water vapor.

(a) Write the balanced equation.
(b) This process requires 36 kcal for every 1.00 mol of Fe_3O_4 reduced. How much energy (in kilocalories) is required to produce 55 g of iron?
(c) How many grams of hydrogen are needed to produce 75 g of iron?
(d) This reaction has $K = 2.3 \times 10^{-18}$. Are the reactants or the products favored?

7.79 Hemoglobin (Hb) reacts reversibly with O_2 to form HbO_2, a substance that transfers oxygen to tissues:

$$Hb(aq) + O_2(aq) \rightleftharpoons HbO_2(aq)$$

Carbon monoxide (CO) is attracted to Hb 140 times more strongly than O_2 and establishes another equilibrium.

(a) Explain, using Le Châtelier's principle, why inhalation of CO can cause weakening and eventual death.
(b) Still another equilibrium is established when both O_2 and CO are present:

$$Hb(CO)(aq) + O_2(aq) \rightleftharpoons HbO_2(aq) + CO(aq)$$

Explain, using Le Châtelier's principle, why pure oxygen is often administered to victims of CO poisoning.

7.80 Many hospitals administer glucose intravenously to patients. If 3.8 kcal is provided by each gram of glucose, how many grams must be administered to maintain a person's normal basal metabolic needs of about 1700 kcal/day?

7.81 For the evaporation of water, $H_2O(l) \longrightarrow H_2O(g)$, at 100 °C, $\Delta H = +9.72$ kcal/mol.

(a) How many kilocalories are needed to vaporize 10.0 g of $H_2O(l)$?
(b) How many kilocalories are released when 10.0 g of $H_2O(g)$ is condensed?

7.82 Ammonia reacts slowly in air to produce nitrogen monoxide and water vapor:

$$NH_3(g) + O_2(g) \rightleftharpoons NO(g) + H_2O(g) + Heat$$

(a) Balance the equation.
(b) Write the equilibrium equation.
(c) Explain the effect on the equilibrium of:
(1) Raising the pressure
(2) Adding NO(g)
(3) Decreasing the concentration of NH_3
(4) Lowering the temperature

7.83 Methanol, CH_3OH, is used as race car fuel.

(a) Write the balanced equation for the combustion of methanol.
(b) $\Delta H = -174$ kcal/mol methanol for the process. How many kilocalories are released by burning 50.0 g of methanol?

7.84 Sketch an energy diagram for a system in which the forward reaction has $E_{act} = +25$ kcal/mol and the reverse reaction has $E_{act} = +35$ kcal/mol.

(a) Is the forward process endergonic or exergonic?
(b) What is the value of ΔG for the reaction?

7.85 The thermite reaction (photograph, p. 185), in which aluminum metal reacts with iron(III) oxide to produce a spectacular display of sparks, is so exothermic that the product (iron) is in the molten state:

$$2\,Al(s) + Fe_2O_3(s) \longrightarrow 2\,Al_2O_3(s) + 2\,Fe(l)$$
$$\Delta H = -202.9 \text{ kcal/mol}$$

How much heat (in kilocalories) is released when 5.00 g of Al is used in the reaction?

7.86 How much heat (in kilocalories) is evolved or absorbed in the reaction of 1.00 g of Na with H_2O? Is the reaction exothermic or endothermic?

$$2\,Na(s) + 2\,H_2O(l) \longrightarrow 2\,NaOH(aq) + H_2(g)$$
$$\Delta H = -88.0 \text{ kcal/mol}$$

CHAPTER 8

Gases, Liquids, and Solids

CONCEPTS TO REVIEW

Ionic Bonds
(Section 4.3)

Polar Covalent Bonds
and Polar Molecules
(Sections 5.8 and 5.9)

Enthalpy, Entropy, and
Free Energy
(Sections 7.2–7.4)

▲ The three states of matter—solid (rock), liquid (lava, water), and gas (steam)—all come together as this lava stream flows into the ocean.

CONTENTS

CHAPTER GOALS

In this chapter, we will answer the following questions:

1. How do scientists explain the behavior of gases?

THE GOAL: Be able to state the assumptions of the kinetic–molecular theory and use these assumptions to explain the behavior of gases.

2. How do gases respond to changes in temperature, pressure, and volume?

THE GOAL: Be able to use Boyle's law, Charles's law, Gay-Lussac's law, and Avogadro's law to explain the effect on gases of a change in pressure, volume, or temperature.

3. What is the ideal gas law?

THE GOAL: Be able to use the ideal gas law to find the pressure, volume, temperature, or molar amount of a gas sample.

4. What is partial pressure?

THE GOAL: Be able to define partial pressure and use Dalton's law of partial pressures.

5. What are the major intermolecular forces, and how do they affect the states of matter?

THE GOAL: Be able to explain dipole–dipole forces, London dispersion forces, and hydrogen bonding, and recognize which of these forces affect a given molecule.

6. What are the various kinds of solids, and how do they differ?

THE GOAL: Be able to recognize the different kinds of solids and describe their characteristics.

7. What factors affect a change of state?

THE GOAL: Be able to apply the concepts of heat change, equilibrium, and vapor pressure to changes of state.

The previous seven chapters dealt with matter at the atomic level. We have seen that all matter is composed of atoms, ions, or molecules; that these particles are in constant motion; that atoms combine to make compounds using chemical bonds; and that physical and chemical changes are accompanied by the release or absorption of energy. Now it is time to look at a different aspect of matter, concentrating not on the properties and small-scale behavior of individual atoms but on the properties and large-scale behavior of visible amounts of matter.

8.1 States of Matter and Their Changes

Matter exists in any of three phases, or *states*—solid, liquid, and gas. The state in which a compound exists under a given set of conditions depends on the relative strength of the attractive forces between particles compared to the kinetic energy of the particles. Kinetic energy (Section 7.1) is energy associated with motion, and is related to the temperature of the substance. In gases, the attractive forces between particles are very weak compared to their kinetic energy, so the particles move about freely, are far apart, and have almost no influence on one another. In liquids, the attractive forces between particles are stronger, pulling the particles close together but still allowing them considerable freedom to move about. In solids, the attractive forces are much stronger than the kinetic energy of the particles, so the atoms, molecules, or ions are held in a specific arrangement and can only wiggle around in place (Figure 8.1).

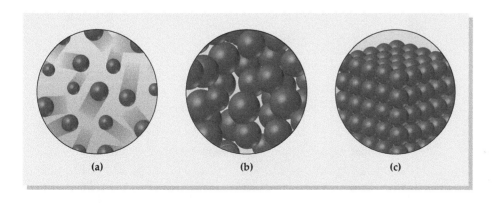

(a) (b) (c)

◀ FIGURE 8.1 **A molecular comparison of gases, liquids, and solids.** (a) In gases, the particles feel little attraction for one another and are free to move about randomly. (b) In liquids, the particles are held close together by attractive forces but are free to slide over one another. (c) In solids, the particles still move slightly, but are held in a specific arrangement with respect to one another.

Change of state The change of a substance from one state of matter (gas, liquid, or solid) to another.

The transformation of a substance from one state to another is called a *phase change*, or a **change of state**. Every change of state is reversible and, like all chemical and physical processes, is characterized by a free-energy change, ΔG. A change of state that is spontaneous in one direction (exergonic, negative ΔG) is nonspontaneous in the other direction (endergonic, positive ΔG). As always, the free-energy change ΔG has both an enthalpy term ΔH and a temperature-dependent entropy term ΔS, according to the equation $\Delta G = \Delta H - T\Delta S$. (You might want to reread Section 7.4 to brush up on these ideas.)(⬤⬤ , p. 188)

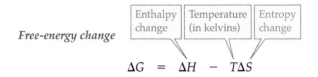

Free-energy change

$$\Delta G = \Delta H - T\Delta S$$

The enthalpy change ΔH is a measure of the heat absorbed or released during a given change of state. In the melting of a solid to a liquid, for example, heat is absorbed and ΔH is positive (endothermic). In the reverse process—the freezing of a liquid to a solid—heat is released and ΔH is negative (exothermic). Look at the change between ice and water for instance:

Melting: $H_2O(s) \longrightarrow H_2O(l)$ $\Delta H = +1.44$ kcal/mol

Freezing: $H_2O(l) \longrightarrow H_2O(s)$ $\Delta H = -1.44$ kcal/mol

The entropy change ΔS is a measure of the change in molecular disorder or freedom that occurs during a process. In the melting of a solid to a liquid, for example, disorder increases because particles gain freedom of motion, so ΔS is positive. In the reverse process—the freezing of a liquid to a solid—disorder decreases as particles are locked into position, so ΔS is negative. Look at the change between ice and water:

Melting: $H_2O(s) \longrightarrow H_2O(l)$ $\Delta S = +5.26$ cal/(mol·K)

Freezing: $H_2O(l) \longrightarrow H_2O(s)$ $\Delta S = -5.26$ cal/(mol·K)

As with all processes that are unfavored by one term in the free-energy equation but favored by the other, the sign of ΔG depends on the temperature (Section 7.4). The melting of ice, for instance, is unfavored by a positive ΔH but favored by a positive ΔS. Thus, at a low temperature, the unfavorable ΔH is larger than the favorable

▶ **FIGURE 8.2 Changes of state.** The changes are endothermic from bottom to top and exothermic from top to bottom. Solid and liquid states are in equilibrium at the melting point; liquid and gas states are in equilibrium at the boiling point.

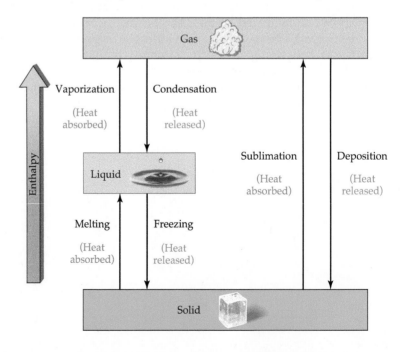

$T\Delta S$ so ΔG is positive and no melting occurs. At a higher temperature, however, $T\Delta S$ becomes larger than ΔH, so ΔG is negative and melting *does* occur. The exact temperature at which the changeover in behavior occurs is called the **melting point (mp)** and represents the temperature at which solid and liquid coexist in equilibrium. In the corresponding change from a liquid to a gas, the two states are in equilibrium at the **boiling point (bp)**.

The names and enthalpy changes associated with the different changes of state are summarized in Figure 8.2. Note a solid can change directly to a gas without going through the liquid state—a process called *sublimation*. Dry ice (solid CO_2) at atmospheric pressure, for example, changes directly to a gas without melting.

Melting point (mp) The temperature at which solid and liquid are in equilibrium.

Boiling point (bp) The temperature at which liquid and gas are in equilibrium.

WORKED EXAMPLE **8.1** Change of State: Enthalpy, Entropy, and Free Energy

The change of state from liquid to gas for chloroform, formerly used as an anesthetic, has $\Delta H = +6.98$ kcal/mol and a $\Delta S = +20.9$ cal/(mol·K).

(a) Is the change of state from liquid to gas favored or unfavored by ΔH? by ΔS?

(b) Is the change of state from liquid to gas favored or unfavored at 35 °C?

(c) Is this change of state spontaneous at 65 °C?

ANALYSIS A process will be favored if energy is released (ΔH = negative) and if there is a decrease in disorder (ΔS = positive). In cases in which one factor is favorable and the other is unfavorable, then we can calculate the free energy change to determine if the process is favored:

$$\Delta G = \Delta H - T\Delta S$$

When ΔG is negative, the process is favored.

SOLUTION

(a) The ΔH does NOT favor this change of state (ΔH = positive), but the ΔS does favor the process. Since the two factors are not in agreement, we must use the equation for free-energy change to determine if the process is favored at a given temperature.

(b) Substituting the values for ΔH and ΔS into the equation for free energy change we can determine if ΔG is positive or negative at 35 °C (308 K). Note that we must first convert degrees Celsius to kelvins and convert the ΔS from cal to kcal so the units can be added together.

$$\Delta G = \Delta H - T\Delta S = \left(\frac{6.98 \text{ kcal}}{\text{mol}}\right) - (308 \text{ K})\left(\frac{20.9 \text{ cal}}{\text{mol·K}}\right)\left(\frac{1 \text{ kcal}}{1000 \text{ cal}}\right)$$

$$= 6.98\frac{\text{kcal}}{\text{mol}} - 6.44\frac{\text{kcal}}{\text{mol}} = +0.54\frac{\text{kcal}}{\text{mol}}$$

Since the ΔG = positive, this change of state is not favored at 35 °C.

(c) Repeating the calculation using the equation for free-energy change at 65 °C (338 K):

$$\Delta G = \Delta H - T\Delta S = \left(\frac{6.98 \text{ kcal}}{\text{mol}}\right) - (338 \text{ K})\left(\frac{20.9 \text{ cal}}{\text{mol·K}}\right)\left(\frac{1 \text{ kcal}}{1000 \text{ cal}}\right)$$

$$= 6.98\frac{\text{kcal}}{\text{mol}} - 7.06\frac{\text{kcal}}{\text{mol}} = -0.08\frac{\text{kcal}}{\text{mol}}$$

Because ΔG is negative in this case, the change of state is favored at this temperature.

8.2 Gases and the Kinetic–Molecular Theory

Gases behave quite differently from liquids and solids. Gases, for instance, have low densities and are easily compressed to a smaller volume when placed under pressure, a property that allows them to be stored in large tanks. Liquids and solids, by contrast, are much more dense and much less compressible. Furthermore, gases undergo a far larger expansion or contraction when their temperature is changed than do liquids and solids.

Kinetic–molecular theory of gases A group of assumptions that explain the behavior of gases.

The behavior of gases can be explained by a group of assumptions known as the **kinetic–molecular theory of gases**. We will see in the next several sections how the following assumptions account for the observable properties of gases:

- **A gas consists of many particles, either atoms or molecules, moving about at random with no attractive forces between them.** Because of this random motion, different gases mix together quickly.

- **The amount of space occupied by the gas particles themselves is much smaller than the amount of space between particles.** Most of the volume taken up by gases is empty space, accounting for the ease of compression and low densities of gases.

- **The average kinetic energy of gas particles is proportional to the Kelvin temperature.** Thus, gas particles have more kinetic energy and move faster as the temperature increases. (In fact, gas particles move much faster than you might suspect. The average speed of a helium atom at room temperature and atmospheric pressure is approximately 1.36 km/s, or 3000 mi/hr, nearly that of a rifle bullet.)

- **Collisions of gas particles, either with other particles or with the wall of their container, are elastic; that is, the total kinetic energy of the particles is constant.** The pressure of a gas against the walls of its container is the result of collisions of the gas particles with the walls. The more collisions and the more forceful each collision, the higher the pressure.

Ideal gas A gas that obeys all the assumptions of the kinetic–molecular theory.

A gas that obeys all the assumptions of the kinetic–molecular theory is called an **ideal gas**. In practice, though, there is no such thing as a perfectly ideal gas. All gases behave somewhat differently than predicted when, at very high pressures or very low temperatures, their particles get closer together and interactions between particles become significant. As a rule, however, most real gases display nearly ideal behavior under normal conditions.

8.3 Pressure

We are all familiar with the effects of air pressure. When you fly in an airplane, the change in air pressure against your eardrums as the plane climbs or descends can cause a painful "popping." When you pump up a bicycle tire, you increase the pressure of air against the inside walls of the tire until the tire feels hard.

Pressure (P) The force per unit area pushing against a surface.

In scientific terms, **pressure (P)** is defined as a force (F) per unit area (A) pushing against a surface; that is, $P = F/A$. In the bicycle tire, for example, the pressure you feel is the force of air molecules colliding with the inside walls of the tire. The units you probably use for tire pressure are pounds per square inch (psi), where 1 psi is equal to the pressure exerted by a 1 pound object resting on a 1 square inch surface.

We on earth are under pressure from the atmosphere, the blanket of air pressing down on us (Figure 8.3). Atmospheric pressure is not constant, however; it varies slightly from day to day depending on the weather, and it also varies with altitude. Due to gravitational forces, the density of air is greatest at the earth's surface and decreases with increasing altitude. As a result, air pressure is greatest at the surface: about 14.7 psi at sea level but only about 4.7 psi on the summit of Mt. Everest.

One of the most commonly used units of pressure is the *millimeter of mercury*, abbreviated *mmHg* and often called a *torr* (after the Italian physicist Evangelista Torricelli). This unusual unit dates back to the early 1600s when Torricelli made the first mercury *barometer*. As shown in Figure 8.4, a barometer consists of a long, thin tube that is sealed at one end, filled with mercury, and then inverted into a dish of mercury. Some mercury runs from the tube into the dish until the downward pressure of the mercury in the column is exactly balanced by the outside atmospheric pressure, which presses down on the mercury in the dish and pushes it up into the column. The height of the mercury column varies depending on the altitude and weather conditions, but standard atmospheric pressure at sea level is defined to be exactly 760 mm.

Gas pressure inside a container is often measured using an open-end *manometer*, a simple instrument similar in principle to the mercury barometer. As shown in Figure 8.5, an open-end manometer consists of a U-tube filled with mercury, with one end connected to a gas-filled container and the other end open to the atmosphere. The difference between the heights of the mercury levels in the two arms of the U-tube indicates the difference between the pressure of the gas in the container and the pressure of the atmosphere. If the gas pressure inside the container is less than atmospheric, the mercury level is higher in the arm connected to the container (Figure 8.5a). If the gas pressure inside the container is greater than atmospheric, the mercury level is higher in the arm open to the atmosphere (Figure 8.5b).

Pressure is given in the SI system (Section 2.1) by a unit named the *pascal* (Pa), where 1 Pa = 0.007500 mmHg (or 1 mmHg = 133.32 Pa). Measurements in pascals are becoming more common, and many clinical laboratories have made the

▲ **FIGURE 8.3 Atmospheric pressure.** A column of air weighing 14.7 lb presses down on each square inch of the earth's surface at sea level, resulting in what we call atmospheric pressure.

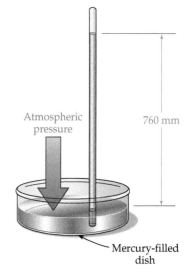

▲ **FIGURE 8.4 Measuring atmospheric pressure.** A mercury barometer measures atmospheric pressure by determining the height of a mercury column in a sealed glass tube. The downward pressure of the mercury in the column is exactly balanced by the outside atmospheric pressure, which presses down on the mercury in the dish and pushes it up into the column.

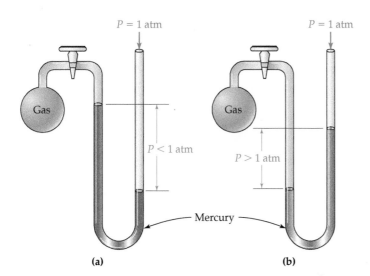

▲ **FIGURE 8.5 Open-end manometers for measuring pressure in a gas-filled bulb.** (a) When the pressure in the gas-filled container is lower than atmospheric, the mercury level is higher in the arm open to the container. (b) When the pressure in the container is higher than atmospheric, the mercury level is higher in the arm open to the atmosphere.

switchover. Higher pressures are often still given in *atmospheres* (atm), where 1 atm = 760 mmHg exactly.

Pressure units: 1 atm = 760 mmHg = 14.7 psi = 101,325 Pa
1 mmHg = 1 torr = 133.32 Pa

WORKED EXAMPLE 8.2 Unit Conversions (Pressure): psi, Atmospheres, and Pascals

A typical bicycle tire is inflated with air to a pressure of 55 psi. How many atmospheres is this? How many pascals?

ANALYSIS Using the starting pressure in psi, the pressure in atm and pascals can be calculated using the equivalent values in as conversion factors.

SOLUTION

STEP 1: **Identify known information.**	Pressure = 55 psi
STEP 2: **Identify answer and units.**	Pressure = ?? atm = ?? pascals

STEP 3: **Identify conversion factors.** Using equivalent values in appropriate units, we can obtain conversion factors to convert to atm and pascals.

$$14.7 \text{ psi} = 1 \text{ atm} \rightarrow \frac{1 \text{ atm}}{14.7 \text{ psi}}$$

$$14.7 \text{ psi} = 101,325 \text{ Pa} \rightarrow \frac{101,325 \text{ Pa}}{14.7 \text{ psi}}$$

STEP 4: **Solve.** Use the appropriate conversion factors to set up an equation in which unwanted units cancel.

$$(55 \text{ psi}) \times \left(\frac{1 \text{ atm}}{14.7 \text{ psi}} \right) = 3.7 \text{ atm}$$

$$(55 \text{ psi}) \times \left(\frac{101,325 \text{ Pa}}{14.7 \text{ psi}} \right) = 3.8 \times 10^5 \text{ Pa}$$

WORKED EXAMPLE 8.3 Unit Conversions (Pressure): mmHg to Atmospheres

The pressure in a closed flask is measured using a manometer. If the mercury level in the arm open to the sealed vessel is 23.6 cm higher than the level of mercury in the arm open to the atmosphere, what is the gas pressure (in atm) in the closed flask?

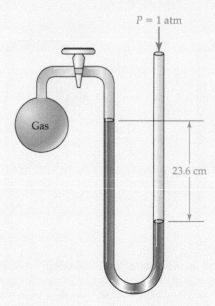

ANALYSIS Since the mercury level is higher in the arm open to the flask, the gas pressure in the flask is lower than atmospheric pressure (1 atm = 760 mmHg). We can convert the difference in the level of mercury in the two arms of the manometer from mmHg to atmospheres to determine the difference in pressure.

BALLPARK ESTIMATE The height difference (23.6 cm) is about one-third the height of a column of Hg that is equal to 1 atm (or 76 cm Hg). Therefore, the pressure in the flask should be about 0.33 atm lower than atmospheric pressure, or about 0.67 atm.

SOLUTION
Since the height difference is given in cm Hg, we must first convert to mmHg, and then to atm. The result is the difference in gas pressure between the flask and the open atmosphere (1 atm).

$$(23.6 \text{ cm Hg})\left(\frac{10 \text{ mmHg}}{\text{cm Hg}}\right)\left(\frac{1 \text{ atm}}{760 \text{ mmHg}}\right) = 0.311 \text{ atm}$$

The pressure in the flask is calculated by subtracting this difference from 1 atm:

$$1 \text{ atm} - 0.311 \text{ atm} = 0.689 \text{ atm}$$

BALLPARK CHECK: This result agrees well with our estimate, 0.67 atm.

PROBLEM 8.2

The air pressure outside a jet airliner flying at 35,000 ft is about 220 mmHg. How many atmospheres is this? How many pounds per square inch? How many pascals?

◀● KEY CONCEPT PROBLEM 8.3

What is the pressure of the gas inside the following manometer (in mmHg) if outside pressure is 750 mmHg?

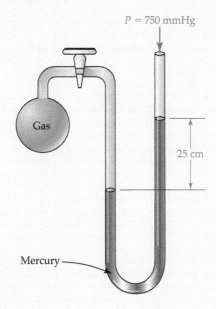

$P = 750 \text{ mmHg}$

Gas

25 cm

Mercury

8.4 Boyle's Law: The Relation between Volume and Pressure

The physical behavior of all gases is much the same, regardless of identity. Helium and chlorine, for example, are completely different in their *chemical* behavior, but are very similar in many of their physical properties. Observations of many different gases by scientists in the 1700s led to the formulation of what are now called the **gas laws**, which make it possible to predict the influence of pressure (P), volume (V), temperature (T), and molar amount (n) on any gas or mixture of gases. We will begin by looking at *Boyle's law*, which describes the relation between volume and pressure.

Imagine that you have a sample of gas inside a cylinder that has a movable plunger at one end (Figure 8.6). What happens if you double the pressure on the gas by pushing the plunger down, while keeping the temperature constant? Since the gas particles are forced closer together, the volume of the sample decreases.

Gas laws A series of laws that predict the influence of pressure (P), volume (V), and temperature (T) on any gas or mixture of gases.

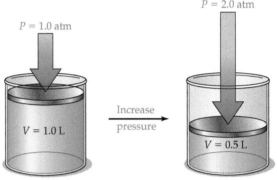

▶ **FIGURE 8.6 Boyle's law.** The volume of a gas decreases proportionately as its pressure increases. If the pressure of a gas sample is doubled, the volume is halved.

According to **Boyle's law**, the volume of a fixed amount of gas at a constant temperature is inversely proportional to its pressure, meaning that volume and pressure change in opposite directions. As pressure goes up, volume goes down; as pressure goes down, volume goes up (Figure 8.7). This observation is consistent with the kinetic–molecular theory. Since most of the volume occupied by gases is empty space, gases are easily compressed into smaller volumes. Since the average kinetic energy remains constant, the number of collisions must increase as the interior surface area of the container decreases, leading to an increase in pressure.

Boyle's law The volume of a gas is inversely proportional to its pressure for a fixed amount of gas at a constant temperature. That is, P times V is constant when the amount of gas n and the temperature T are kept constant. (The symbol $\propto$ means "is proportional to," and k denotes a constant value.)

$$\text{Volume } (V) \propto \frac{1}{\text{Pressure } (P)}$$

$$\text{or} \quad PV = k \quad \text{(A constant value)}$$

▶ **FIGURE 8.7 Boyle's law.** Pressure and volume are inversely related. Graph (a) demonstrates the decrease in volume as pressure increases, whereas graph (b) shows the linear relationship between V and $1/P$.

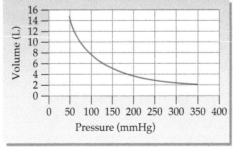

(a)

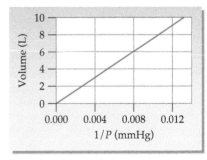

(b)

APPLICATION ▶ Blood Pressure

Having your blood pressure measured is a quick and easy way to get an indication of the state of your circulatory system. Although blood pressure varies with age, a normal adult male has a reading near 120/80 mmHg, and a normal adult female has a reading near 110/70 mmHg. Abnormally high values signal an increased risk of heart attack and stroke.

Pressure varies greatly in different types of blood vessels. Usually, though, measurements are carried out on arteries in the upper arm as the heart goes through a full cardiac cycle. *Systolic pressure* is the maximum pressure developed in the artery just after contraction, as the heart forces the maximum amount of blood into the artery. *Diastolic pressure* is the minimum pressure that occurs at the end of the heart cycle.

Blood pressure is most often measured by a *sphygmomanometer*, a device consisting of a squeeze bulb, a flexible cuff, and a mercury manometer. The cuff is placed around the upper arm over the brachial artery and inflated by the squeeze bulb to about 200 mmHg pressure, an amount great enough to squeeze the artery shut and prevent blood flow. Air is then slowly released from the cuff, and pressure drops. As cuff pressure reaches the systolic pressure, blood spurts through the artery, creating a turbulent tapping sound that can be heard through a stethoscope. The pressure registered on the manometer at the moment the first sounds are heard is the systolic blood pressure.

Sounds continue until the pressure in the cuff becomes low enough to allow diastolic blood flow. At this point, blood flow becomes smooth, no sounds are heard, and a diastolic

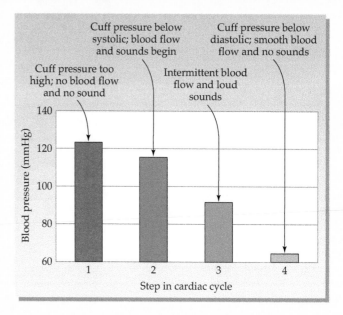

▲ The sequence of events during blood pressure measurement, including the sounds heard.

blood pressure reading is recorded on the manometer. Readings are usually recorded as systolic/diastolic, for example, 120/80. The accompanying Figure shows the sequence of events during measurement.

See Additional Problem 8.100 at the end of the chapter.

Because $P \times V$ is a constant value for a fixed amount of gas at a constant temperature, the starting pressure (P_1) times the starting volume (V_1) must equal the final pressure (P_2) times the final volume (V_2). Thus, Boyle's law can be used to find the final pressure or volume when the starting pressure or volume is changed.

Since $\quad P_1V_1 = k \quad$ and $\quad P_2V_2 = k$

then $\quad P_1V_1 = P_2V_2$

so $\quad P_2 = \dfrac{P_1V_1}{V_2} \quad$ and $\quad V_2 = \dfrac{P_1V_1}{P_2}$

As an example of Boyle's law behavior, think about what happens every time you breathe. Between breaths, the pressure inside your lungs is equal to atmospheric pressure. When inhalation takes place, your diaphragm lowers and the rib cage expands, increasing the volume of the lungs and thereby decreasing the pressure inside them (Figure 8.8). Air must then move into the lungs to equalize their pressure with that of the atmosphere. When exhalation takes place, the diaphragm rises and the rib cage contracts decreasing the volume of the lungs and increasing pressure inside them. Now gases move out of the lungs until pressure is again equalized with the atmosphere.

▲ Air pressure in tires, typically reported in units of pounds per square inch (psi), is another example of Boyle's Law.

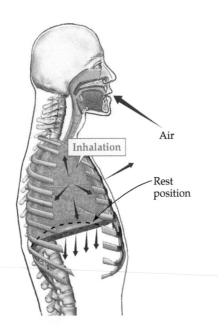

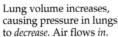

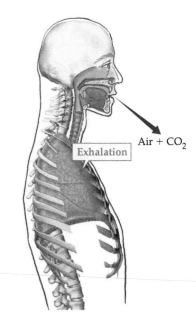

▶ **FIGURE 8.8 Boyle's law in breathing.** During inhalation, the diaphragm moves down and the rib cage moves up and out, thus increasing lung volume, decreasing pressure, and drawing in air. During exhalation, lung volume decreases, pressure increases, and air moves out.

Lung volume increases, causing pressure in lungs to *decrease*. Air flows *in*.

Lung volume decreases, causing pressure in lungs to *increase*. Air flows *out*.

WORKED EXAMPLE 8.4 Using Boyle's Law: Finding Volume at a Given Pressure

In a typical automobile engine, the fuel/air mixture in a cylinder is compressed from 1.0 atm to 9.5 atm. If the uncompressed volume of the cylinder is 750 mL, what is the volume when fully compressed?

ANALYSIS This is a Boyle's law problem because the volume and pressure in the cylinder change but the amount of gas and the temperature remain constant. According to Boyle's law, the pressure of the gas times its volume is constant:

$$P_1V_1 = P_2V_2$$

Knowing three of the four variables in this equation, we can solve for the unknown.

◀ A cut-away diagram of internal combustion engine shows movement of pistons during expansion and compression cycles.

BALLPARK ESTIMATE Since the pressure *increases* approximately tenfold (from 1.0 atm to 9.5 atm), the volume must *decrease* to approximately one-tenth, from 750 mL to about 75 mL.

SOLUTION

STEP 1: **Identify known information.** Of the four variables in Boyle's law, we know P_1, V_1, and P_2.

$P_1 = 1.0$ atm
$V_1 = 750$ mL
$P_2 = 9.5$ atm

STEP 2: **Identify answer and units.**

$V_2 = ??$ mL

STEP 3: **Identify equation.** In this case, we simply substitute the known variables into Boyle's law and rearrange to isolate the unknown.

$$P_1V_1 = P_2V_2 \implies V_2 = \frac{P_1V_1}{P_2}$$

STEP 4: **Solve. Substitute the known information into the equation.** Make sure units cancel so that the answer is given in the units of the unknown variable.

$$V_2 = \frac{P_1V_1}{P_2} = \frac{(1.0 \text{ atm})(750 \text{ mL})}{(9.5 \text{ atm})} = 79 \text{ mL}$$

BALLPARK CHECK Our estimate was 75 mL.

8.5 Charles's Law: The Relation between Volume and Temperature

Imagine that you again have a sample of gas inside a cylinder with a plunger at one end. What happens if you double the sample's Kelvin temperature while letting the plunger move freely to keep the pressure constant? The gas particles move with twice as much energy and collide twice as forcefully with the walls. To maintain a constant pressure, the volume of the gas in the cylinder must double (Figure 8.9).

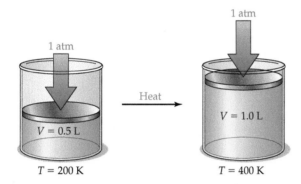

▲ **FIGURE 8.9 Charles's law.** The volume of a gas is directly proportionately to its Kelvin temperature at constant n and P. If the Kelvin temperature of the gas is doubled, its volume doubles.

According to **Charles's law**, the volume of a fixed amount of gas at constant pressure is directly proportional to its Kelvin temperature. Note the difference between *directly* proportional in Charles's law and *inversely* proportional in Boyle's law. Directly proportional quantities change in the same direction: As temperature goes up or down, volume also goes up or down (Figure 8.10).

Charles's law The volume of a gas is directly proportional to its Kelvin temperature for a fixed amount of gas at a constant pressure. That is, V divided by T is constant when n and P are held constant.

$$V \propto T \quad \text{(In kelvins)}$$

$$\text{or} \quad \frac{V}{T} = k \quad \text{(A constant value)}$$

$$\text{or} \quad \frac{V_1}{T_1} = \frac{V_2}{T_2}$$

This observation is consistent with the kinetic–molecular theory. As temperature increases, the average kinetic energy of the gas molecules increases, as does the

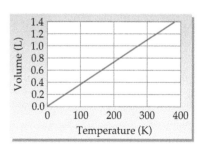

▲ The volume of the gas in the balloon increases as it is heated, causing a decrease in density and allowing the balloon to rise.

▲ **FIGURE 8.10 Charles's law.** Volume is directly proportional to the Kelvin temperature for a fixed amount of gas at a constant pressure. As the temperature goes up, the volume also goes up.

energy of molecular collisions with the interior surface of the container. The volume of the container must increase to maintain a constant pressure. As an example of Charles's law, think about what happens when a hot-air balloon is inflated. Heating causes the air inside to expand and fill the balloon. The air inside the balloon is less dense than the air outside the balloon, creating the buoyancy effect.

WORKED EXAMPLE **8.5** Using Charles's Law: Finding Volume at a Given Temperature

An average adult inhales a volume of 0.50 L of air with each breath. If the air is warmed from room temperature (20 °C = 293 K) to body temperature (37 °C = 310 K) while in the lungs, what is the volume of the air exhaled?

ANALYSIS This is a Charles's law problem because the volume and temperature of the air change while the amount and pressure remain constant. Knowing three of the four variables, we can rearrange Charles's law to solve for the unknown.

BALLPARK ESTIMATE Charles's Law predicts an increase in volume directly proportional to the increase in temperature from 273 K to 310 K. The increase of less than 20 K represents a relatively small change compared to the initial temperature of 273 K. A 10% increase, for example, would be equal to a temperature change of 27 K; so a 20 K change would be less than 10%. We would therefore expect the volume to increase by less than 10%, from 0.50 L to a little less than 0.55 L.

SOLUTION

STEP 1: **Identify known information.** Of the four variables in Charles's law, we know T_1, V_1, and T_2.

$T_1 = 293$ K
$V_1 = 0.50$ L
$T_2 = 310$ K

STEP 2: **Identify answer and units.**

$V_2 = ??$ L

STEP 3: **Identify equation.** Substitute the known variables into Charles's law and rearrange to isolate the unknown.

$$\frac{V_1}{T_1} = \frac{V_2}{T_2} \Rightarrow V_2 = \frac{V_1 T_2}{T_1}$$

STEP 4: **Solve.** Substitute the known information into Charles's law; check to make sure units cancel.

$$V_2 = \frac{V_1 T_2}{T_1} = \frac{(0.50 \text{ L})(310 \text{ K})}{293 \text{ K}} = 0.53 \text{ L}$$

BALLPARK CHECK This is consistent with our estimate!

PROBLEM 8.6

A sample of chlorine gas has a volume of 0.30 L at 273 K and 1 atm pressure. What is its volume at 250 K and 1 atm pressure? At 525 °C and 1 atm?

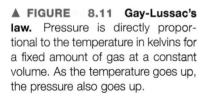

▲ **FIGURE 8.11 Gay-Lussac's law.** Pressure is directly proportional to the temperature in kelvins for a fixed amount of gas at a constant volume. As the temperature goes up, the pressure also goes up.

8.6 Gay-Lussac's Law: The Relation between Pressure and Temperature

Imagine next that you have a fixed amount of gas in a sealed container whose volume remains constant. What happens if you double the temperature (in kelvins)? The gas particles move with twice as much energy and collide with the walls of the container with twice as much force. Thus, the pressure in the container doubles. According to **Gay-Lussac's law**, the pressure of a fixed amount of gas at constant volume is directly proportional to its Kelvin temperature. As temperature goes up or down, pressure also goes up or down (Figure 8.11).

Gay-Lussac's law The pressure of a gas is directly proportional to its Kelvin temperature for a fixed amount of gas at a constant volume. That is, P divided by T is constant when n and V are held constant.

$$P \propto T \quad \text{(In kelvins)}$$

$$\text{or } \frac{P}{T} = k \quad \text{(A constant value)}$$

$$\text{or } \frac{P_1}{T_1} = \frac{P_2}{T_2}$$

▲ Because of the possibility of explosion (see warning label), aerosol containers cannot be incinerated, requiring disposal in landfills.

According to the kinetic–molecular theory, the kinetic energy of molecules is directly proportional to absolute temperature. As the average kinetic energy of the molecules increases, the energy of collisions with the interior surface of the container increases, causing an increase in pressure. As an example of Gay-Lussac's law, think of what happens when an aerosol can is thrown into an incinerator. As the can gets hotter, pressure builds up inside and the can explodes (hence the warning statement on aerosol cans).

WORKED EXAMPLE **8.6** Using Gay-Lussac's Law: Finding Pressure at a Given Temperature

What does the inside pressure become if an aerosol can with an initial pressure of 4.5 atm is heated in a fire from room temperature (20 °C) to 600 °C?

ANALYSIS This is a Gay-Lussac's law problem because the pressure and temperature of the gas inside the can change while its amount and volume remain constant. We know three of the four variables in the equation for Gay-Lussac's law, and can find the unknown by substitution and rearrangement.

BALLPARK ESTIMATE Gay-Lussac's law states that pressure is directly proportional to temperature. Since the Kelvin temperature increases approximately threefold (from about 300 K to about 900 K), we expect the pressure to also increase by approximately threefold, from 4.5 atm to about 14 atm.

SOLUTION

STEP 1: **Identify known information.** Of the four variables in Gay-Lussac's law, we know P_1, T_1 and T_2. (Note that T must be in kelvins.)

$P_1 = 4.5$ atm
$T_1 = 20\,°C = 293$ K
$T_2 = 600\,°C = 873$ K

STEP 2: **Identify answer and units.**

$P_2 = ??$ atm

STEP 3: **Identify equation.** Substituting the known variables into Gay-Lussac's law, we rearrange to isolate the unknown.

$$\frac{P_1}{T_1} = \frac{P_2}{T_2} \implies P_2 = \frac{P_1 T_2}{T_1}$$

STEP 4: **Solve.** Substitute the known information into Gay-Lussac's law, check to make sure units cancel.

$$P_2 = \frac{P_1 T_2}{T_1} = \frac{(4.5 \text{ atm})(873 \text{ K})}{293 \text{ K}} = 13 \text{ atm}$$

BALLPARK CHECK Our estimate was 14 atm.

PROBLEM 8.7

Driving on a hot day causes tire temperature to rise. What is the pressure inside an automobile tire at 45 °C if the tire has a pressure of 30 psi at 15 °C? Assume that the volume and amount of air in the tire remain constant.

8.7 The Combined Gas Law

Since PV, V/T, and P/T all have constant values for a fixed amount of gas, these relationships can be merged into a **combined gas law**, which holds true whenever the amount of gas is fixed.

COMBINED GAS LAW $\dfrac{PV}{T} = k$ (A constant value)

or $\dfrac{P_1V_1}{T_1} = \dfrac{P_2V_2}{T_2}$

If any five of the six quantities in this equation are known, the sixth quantity can be calculated. Furthermore, if any of the three variables T, P, or V is constant, that variable drops out of the equation, leaving behind Boyle's law, Charles's law, or Gay-Lussac's law. As a result, *the combined gas law is the only equation you need to remember for a fixed amount of gas*. Worked Example 8.7 gives a sample calculation.

Since $\qquad\qquad \dfrac{P_1V_1}{T_1} = \dfrac{P_2V_2}{T_2}$

At constant T: $\dfrac{P_1V_1}{T} = \dfrac{P_2V_2}{T}$ gives $P_1V_1 = P_2V_2$ (Boyle's law)

At constant P: $\dfrac{PV_1}{T_1} = \dfrac{PV_2}{T_2}$ gives $\dfrac{V_1}{T_1} = \dfrac{V_2}{T_2}$ (Charles's law)

At constant V: $\dfrac{P_1V}{T_1} = \dfrac{P_2V}{T_2}$ gives $\dfrac{P_1}{T_1} = \dfrac{P_2}{T_2}$ (Gay-Lussac's law)

WORKED EXAMPLE   **8.7** Using the Combined Gas Law: Finding Temperature

A 6.3 L sample of helium gas stored at 25 °C and 1.0 atm pressure is transferred to a 2.0 L tank and maintained at a pressure of 2.8 atm. What temperature is needed to maintain this pressure?

ANALYSIS This is a combined gas law problem because pressure, volume, and temperature change while the amount of helium remains constant. Of the six variables in this equation, we know P_1, V_1, T_1, P_2, and V_2, and we need to find T_2.

BALLPARK ESTIMATE Since the volume goes down by a little more than a factor of about 3 (from 6.3 L to 2.0 L) and the pressure goes up by a little less than a factor of about 3 (from 1.0 atm to 2.8 atm), the two changes roughly offset each other, and so the temperature should not change much. Since the volume-decrease factor (3.2) is slightly greater than the pressure-increase factor (2.8), the temperature will drop slightly ($T \propto V$).

SOLUTION

STEP 1: Identify known information. Of the six variables in combined-gas-law we know P_1, V_1, T_1, P_2, and V_2. (As always, T must be converted from Celsius degrees to kelvins.)

$P_1 = 1.0$ atm, $P_2 = 2.8$ atm
$V_1 = 6.3$ L, $V_2 = 2.0$ L
$T_1 = 25$ °C $= 298$ K

STEP 2: Identify answer and units.

$T_2 = ??$ kelvin

STEP 3: Identify the equation. Substituting the known variables into the equation for the combined gas law and rearrange to isolate the unknown.

$\dfrac{P_1V_1}{T_1} = \dfrac{P_2V_2}{T_2} \Rightarrow T_2 = \dfrac{P_2V_2T_1}{P_1V_1}$

STEP 4: Solve. Solve the combined gas law equation for T_2; check to make sure units cancel.

$T_2 = \dfrac{P_2V_2T_1}{P_1V_1} = \dfrac{(2.8\ \text{atm})(2.0\ \text{L})(298\ \text{K})}{(1.0\ \text{atm})(6.3\ \text{L})} = 260\ \text{K}(\Delta T = -38\ °\text{C})$

BALLPARK CHECK The relatively small decrease in temperature (38 °C, or 13% compared to the original temperature) is consistent with our prediction.

PROBLEM 8.8

A weather balloon is filled with helium to a volume of 275 L at 22 °C and 752 mmHg. The balloon ascends to an altitude where the pressure is 480 mmHg, and the temperature is −32 °C. What is the volume of the balloon at this altitude?

KEY CONCEPT PROBLEM 8.9

A balloon is filled under the initial conditions indicated below. If the pressure is then increased to 2 atm while the temperature is increased to 50 °C, which balloon on the right, (a) or (b), represents the new volume of the balloon?

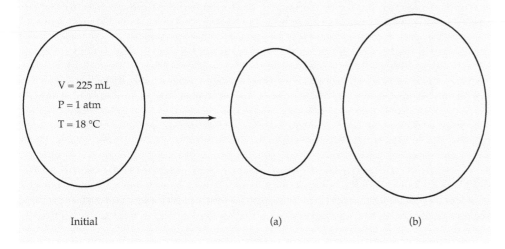

V = 225 mL

P = 1 atm

T = 18 °C

Initial   (a)   (b)

8.8 Avogadro's Law: The Relation between Volume and Molar Amount

Here we look at one final gas law, which takes changes in amount of gas into account. Imagine that you have two different volumes of a gas at the same temperature and pressure. How many moles does each sample contain? According to **Avogadro's law**, the volume of a gas is directly proportional to its molar amount at a constant pressure and temperature (Figure 8.12). A sample that contains twice the molar amount has twice the volume.

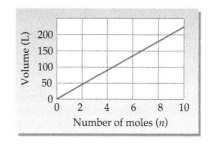

Avogadro's law   The volume of a gas is directly proportional to its molar amount at a constant pressure and temperature. That is, V divided by n is constant when P and T are held constant.

Volume $(V) \propto$ Number of moles (n)

or $\dfrac{V}{n} = k$ (A constant value; the same for all gases)

or $\dfrac{V_1}{n_1} = \dfrac{V_2}{n_2}$

▲ **FIGURE 8.12 Avogadro's law.** Volume is directly proportional to the molar amount, n, at a constant temperature and pressure. As the number of moles goes up, the volume also goes up.

Because the particles in a gas are so tiny compared to the empty space surrounding them, there is no interaction among gas particles as proposed by the kinetic–molecular theory. As a result, the chemical identity of the particles does not matter and the value of the constant k in the equation $V/n = k$ is the same for all gases. It is therefore possible to compare the molar amounts of *any* two gases simply by comparing their volumes at the same temperature and pressure.

Notice that the *values* of temperature and pressure do not matter; it is only necessary that T and P be the same for both gases. To simplify comparisons of gas samples, however, it is convenient to define a set of conditions called **standard temperature and pressure (STP)**:

Standard temperature and pressure (STP)   0 °C (273.15 K); 1 atm (760 mmHg)

At standard temperature and pressure, 1 mol of any gas (6.02×10^{23} particles) has a volume of 22.4 L, a quantity called the **standard molar volume** (Figure 8.13).

Standard molar volume of any ideal gas at STP   22.4 L/mol

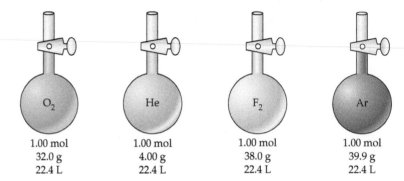

▶ **FIGURE 8.13 Avogadro's law.** Each of these 22.4 L bulbs contains 1.00 mol of gas at 0 °C and 1 atm pressure. Note that the volume occupied by 1 mol of gas is the same even though the mass of 1 mol of each gas is different.

O_2	He	F_2	Ar
1.00 mol	1.00 mol	1.00 mol	1.00 mol
32.0 g	4.00 g	38.0 g	39.9 g
22.4 L	22.4 L	22.4 L	22.4 L

WORKED EXAMPLE   **8.8** Using Avogadro's Law: Finding Moles in a Given Volume at STP

Use the standard molar volume of a gas at STP (22.4 L) to find how many moles of air at STP are in a room measuring 4.11 m wide by 5.36 m long by 2.58 m high.

ANALYSIS We first find the volume of the room and then use standard molar volume as a conversion factor to find the number of moles.

SOLUTION

STEP 1: Identify known information. We are given the room dimensions.

Length = 5.36 m
Width = 4.11 m
Height = 2.58 m

STEP 2: Identify answer and units.

Moles of air = ?? mol

STEP 3: Identify the equation. The volume of the room is the product of its three dimensions. Once we have the volume (in m³), we can convert to liters and use the molar volume at STP as a conversion factor to obtain moles of air.

$$\text{Volume} = (4.11\ \text{m})(5.36\ \text{m})(2.58\ \text{m}) = 56.8\ \text{m}^3$$

$$= 56.8\ \text{m}^3 \times \frac{1000\ \text{L}}{1\ \text{m}^3} = 5.68 \times 10^4\ \text{L}$$

$$1\ \text{mol} = 22.4\ \text{L} \rightarrow \frac{1\ \text{mol}}{22.4\ \text{L}}$$

STEP 4: Solve. Use the room volume and the molar volume at STP to set up an equation, making sure unwanted units cancel.

$$5.68 \times 10^4\ \cancel{\text{L}} \times \frac{1\ \text{mol}}{22.4\ \cancel{\text{L}}} = 2.54 \times 10^3\ \text{mol}$$

PROBLEM 8.10

How many moles of methane gas, CH_4, are in a 1.00×10^5 L storage tank at STP? How many grams of methane is this? How many grams of carbon dioxide gas could the same tank hold?

8.9 The Ideal Gas Law

The relationships among the four variables P, V, T, and n for gases can be combined into a single expression called the **ideal gas law**. If you know the values of any three of the four quantities, you can calculate the value of the fourth.

Ideal gas law $\dfrac{PV}{nT} = R$ (A constant value)

or $PV = nRT$

The constant R in the ideal gas law (instead of the usual k) is called the **gas constant**. Its value depends on the units chosen for pressure, with the two most common values

Gas constant (R) The constant R in the ideal gas law, $PV = nRT$.

For P in atmospheres: $R = 0.0821 \dfrac{\text{L} \cdot \text{atm}}{\text{mol} \cdot \text{K}}$

For P in millimeters Hg: $R = 62.4 \dfrac{\text{L} \cdot \text{mmHg}}{\text{mol} \cdot \text{K}}$

In using the ideal gas law, it is important to choose the value of R having pressure units that are consistent with the problem and, if necessary, to convert volume into liters and temperature into kelvins.

Table 8.1 summarizes the various gas laws, and Worked Example 8.9 shows how to use the ideal gas law.

TABLE 8.1   A Summary of the Gas Laws

	GAS LAW	VARIABLES	CONSTANT
Boyle's law	$P_1V_1 = P_2V_2$	P, V	n, T
Charles's law	$V_1/T_1 = V_2/T_2$	V, T	n, P
Gay-Lussac's law	$P_1/T_1 = P_2/T_2$	P, T	n, V
Combined gas law	$P_1V_1/T_1 = P_2V_2/T_2$	P, V, T	n
Avogadro's law	$V_1/n_1 = V_2/n_2$	V, n	P, T
Ideal gas law	$PV = nRT$	P, V, T, n	R

WORKED EXAMPLE   **8.9** Using Ideal Gas Law: Finding Moles

How many moles of air are in the lungs of an average person with a total lung capacity of 3.8 L? Assume that the person is at 1.0 atm pressure and has a normal body temperature of 37 °C.

ANALYSIS This is an ideal gas law problem because it asks for a value of n when P, V, and T are known: $n = PV/RT$. The volume is given in the correct unit of liters, but temperature must be converted to kelvins.

SOLUTION

STEP 1: **Identify known information.**
We know three of the four variables in the ideal gas law.

$P = 1.0 \text{ atm}$

$V = 3.8 \text{ L}$

$T = 37 \,°\text{C} = 310 \text{ K}$

STEP 2: **Identify answer and units.**

Moles of air, $n = $?? mol

STEP 3: **Identify the equation.** Knowing three of the four variables in the ideal gas law, we can rearrange and solve for the unknown variable, n. (Note: because pressure is given in atm, we use the value of R that is expressed in atm:

$$PV = nRT \implies n = \frac{PV}{RT}$$

$$R = 0.0821 \frac{L \cdot atm}{mol \cdot K}$$

STEP 4: **Solve.** Substitute the known information and the appropriate value of R into the ideal gas law equation and solve for n.

$$n = \frac{PV}{RT} = \frac{(1.0 \text{ atm})(3.8 \text{ L})}{\left(0.0821\dfrac{L \cdot atm}{mol \cdot K}\right)(310 \text{ K})} = 0.15 \text{ mol}$$

WORKED EXAMPLE 8.10 Using the Ideal Gas Law: Finding Pressure

Methane gas is sold in steel cylinders with a volume of 43.8 L containing 5.54 kg. What is the pressure in atmospheres inside the cylinder at a temperature of 20.0 °C (293.15 K)? The molar mass of methane (CH_4) is 16.0 g/mol.

ANALYSIS This is an ideal gas law problem because it asks for a value of P when V, T, and n are given. Although not provided directly, enough information is given so that we can calculate the value of n ($n = g/MW$).

SOLUTION

STEP 1: **Identify known information.** We know two of the four variables in the ideal gas law; V, T, and can calculate the third, n, from the information provided.

$V = 43.8 \text{ L}$
$T = 37 \degree C = 310 \text{ K}$

STEP 2: **Identify answer and units.**

Pressure, $P = ??$ atm

STEP 3: **Identify equation.** First, calculate the number of moles n of methane in the cylinder by using molar mass (16.0 g/mol) as a conversion factor. Then use the ideal gas law to calculate the pressure.

$$n = (5.54 \text{ kg methane})\left(\frac{1000 \text{ g}}{1 \text{ kg}}\right)\left(\frac{1 \text{ mol}}{16.0 \text{ g}}\right) = 346 \text{ mol methane}$$

$$PV = nRT \implies P = \frac{nRT}{V}$$

STEP 4: **Solve.** Substitute the known information and the appropriate value of R into the ideal gas law equation and solve for P.

$$P = \frac{nRT}{V} = \frac{(346 \text{ mol})\left(0.0821\dfrac{L \cdot atm}{mol \cdot K}\right)(293 \text{ K})}{43.8 \text{ L}} = 190 \text{ atm}$$

PROBLEM 8.11

An aerosol spray can of deodorant with a volume of 350 mL contains 3.2 g of propane gas (C_3H_8) as propellant. What is the pressure in the can at 20 °C?

PROBLEM 8.12

A helium gas cylinder of the sort used to fill balloons has a volume of 180 L and a pressure of 2200 psi (150 atm) at 25 °C. How many moles of helium are in the tank? How many grams?

●━ KEY CONCEPT PROBLEM 8.13

Show the approximate level of the movable piston in drawings (a) and (b) after the indicated changes have been made to the initial gas sample.

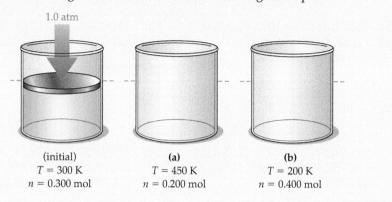

(initial)	(a)	(b)
$T = 300$ K	$T = 450$ K	$T = 200$ K
$n = 0.300$ mol	$n = 0.200$ mol	$n = 0.400$ mol

8.10 Partial Pressure and Dalton's Law

According to the kinetic–molecular theory, each particle in a gas acts independently of all others because there are no attractive forces between them and they are so far apart. To any individual particle, the chemical identity of its neighbors is irrelevant. Thus, *mixtures* of gases behave the same as pure gases and obey the same laws.

Dry air, for example, is a mixture of about 21% oxygen, 78% nitrogen, and 1% argon by volume, which means that 21% of atmospheric air pressure is caused by O_2 molecules, 78% by N_2 molecules, and 1% by Ar atoms. The contribution of each gas in a mixture to the total pressure of the mixture is called the **partial pressure**. of that gas. According to **Dalton's law**, the total pressure exerted by a gas mixture (P_{total}) is the sum of the partial pressures of the components in the mixture:

> **Partial pressure** The contribution of a given gas in a mixture to the total pressure.

Dalton's law $P_{total} = P_{gas\ 1} + P_{gas\ 2} + \cdots$

In dry air at a total air pressure of 760 mmHg, the partial pressure caused by the contribution of O_2 is 0.21×760 mmHg = 160 mmHg, the partial pressure of N_2 is 0.78×760 mmHg = 593 mmHg, and that of argon is 7 mmHg. *The partial pressure exerted by each gas in a mixture is the same pressure that the gas would exert if it were alone.* Put another way, the pressure exerted by each gas depends on the frequency of collisions of its molecules with the walls of the container. But this frequency does not change when other gases are present because the different molecules have no influence on one another.

To represent the partial pressure of a specific gas, we add the formula of the gas as a subscript to P, the symbol for pressure. You might see the partial pressure of oxygen represented as P_{O_2}, for instance. Moist air inside the lungs at 37 °C and atmospheric pressure has the following average composition at sea level. Note that P_{total} is equal to atmospheric pressure, 760 mmHg.

$$P_{total} = \quad P_{N_2} \quad + \quad P_{O_2} \quad + \quad P_{CO_2} \quad + \quad P_{H_2O}$$
$$= 573 \text{ mmHg} + 100 \text{ mmHg} + 40 \text{ mmHg} + 47 \text{ mmHg}$$
$$= 760 \text{ mmHg}$$

The composition of air does not change appreciably with altitude, but the total pressure decreases rapidly. The partial pressure of oxygen in air therefore decreases with increasing altitude, and it is this change that leads to difficulty in breathing at high elevations.

| WORKED EXAMPLE | **8.11** Using Dalton's Law: Finding Partial Pressures |

Humid air on a warm summer day is approximately 20% oxygen, 75% nitrogen, 4% water vapor, and 1% argon. What is the partial pressure of each component if the atmospheric pressure is 750 mmHg?

ANALYSIS According to Dalton's law, the partial pressure of any gas in a mixture is equal to the percent concentration of the gas times the total gas pressure (750 mmHg). In this case,

$$P_{total} = P_{O_2} + P_{N_2} + P_{H_2O} + P_{Ar}$$

SOLUTION

Oxygen partial pressure (P_{O_2}): $0.20 \times 750 \text{ mmHg} = 150 \text{ mmHg}$
Nitrogen partial pressure (P_{N_2}): $0.75 \times 750 \text{ mmHg} = 560 \text{ mmHg}$
Water vapor partial pressure (P_{H_2O}): $0.04 \times 750 \text{ mmHg} = 30 \text{ mmHg}$
Argon partial pressure (P_{Ar}): $0.01 \times 750 \text{ mmHg} = 8 \text{ mmHg}$

Total pressure = 748 mmHg → 750 mmHg (rounding to 2 significant figures!)

Note that the sum of the partial pressures must equal the total pressure (within rounding error).

▲ Because of the lack of sufficient oxygen at the top of Mt. Everest, most climbers rely on bottled oxygen supplies.

PROBLEM 8.14

Assuming a total pressure of 9.5 atm, what is the partial pressure of each component in the mixture of 98% helium and 2.0% oxygen breathed by deep-sea divers? How does the partial pressure of oxygen in diving gas compare with its partial pressure in normal air?

PROBLEM 8.15

Determine the percent composition of air in the lungs from the following composition in partial pressures: $P_{N_2} = 573 \text{ mmHg}$, $P_{O_2} = 100 \text{ mmHg}$, $P_{CO_2} = 40 \text{ mmHg}$, $P_{H_2O} = 47 \text{ mmHg}$; all at 37 °C and 1 atm pressure.

PROBLEM 8.16

The atmospheric pressure on the top of Mt. Everest, an altitude of 29,035 ft, is only 265 mmHg. What is the partial pressure of oxygen in the lungs at this altitude?

KEY CONCEPT PROBLEM 8.17

Assume that you have a mixture of He (MW = 4 amu) and Xe (MW = 131 amu) at 300 K. Which of the drawings (a)–(c) best represents the mixture (blue = He; green = Xe)?

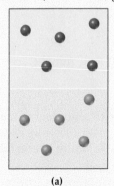

(a)

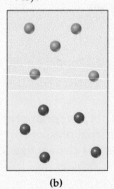

(b)

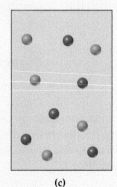

(c)

8.11 Intermolecular Forces

What determines whether a substance is a gas, a liquid, or a solid at a given temperature? Why does rubbing alcohol evaporate much more readily than water? Why do molecular compounds have lower melting points than ionic compounds? To answer these and a great many other such questions, we need to look into the nature of **intermolecular forces**—the forces that act *between different molecules* rather than within an individual molecule.

In gases, the intermolecular forces are negligible, so the gas molecules act independently of one another. In liquids and solids, however, intermolecular forces are strong enough to hold the molecules in close contact. As a general rule, the stronger the intermolecular forces in a substance, the more difficult it is to separate the molecules, and the higher the melting and boiling points of the substance.

There are three major types of intermolecular forces: *dipole–dipole, London dispersion*, and *hydrogen bonding*. We will discuss each in turn.

> **Intermolecular force** A force that acts between molecules and holds molecules close to one another.

Dipole–Dipole Forces

Recall from Sections 5.8 and 5.9 that many molecules contain polar covalent bonds and may therefore have a net molecular polarity. (, pp. 128, 130) In such cases, the positive and negative ends of different molecules are attracted to one another by what is called a **dipole–dipole force**. (Figure 8.14).

> **Dipole–dipole force** The attractive force between positive and negative ends of polar molecules.

▲ **FIGURE 8.14 Dipole–dipole forces.** The positive and negative ends of polar molecules are attracted to one another by dipole–dipole forces. As a result, polar molecules have higher boiling points than nonpolar molecules of similar size.

Dipole–dipole forces are weak, with strengths on the order of 1 kcal/mol compared to the 70–100 kcal/mol typically found for the strength of a covalent bond. Nevertheless, the effects of dipole–dipole forces are important, as can be seen by looking at the difference in boiling points between polar and nonpolar molecules. Butane, for instance, is a nonpolar molecule with a molecular weight of 58 amu and a boiling point of −0.5 °C, whereas acetone has the same molecular weight yet boils 57 °C higher because it is polar. (Recall from Section 5.8 how molecular polarities can be visualized using electrostatic potential maps. (, p. 128)

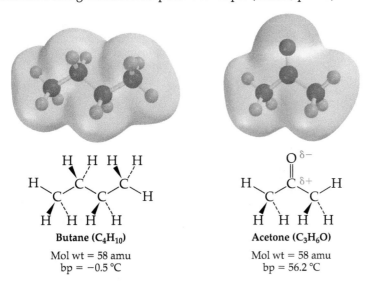

Butane (C_4H_{10})
Mol wt = 58 amu
bp = −0.5 °C

Acetone (C_3H_6O)
Mol wt = 58 amu
bp = 56.2 °C

APPLICATION ▶ Greenhouse Gases and Global Warming

The mantle of gases surrounding the earth is far from the uniform mixture you might expect, consisting of layers that vary in composition and properties at different altitudes. The ability of the gases in these layers to absorb radiation is responsible for life on earth as we know it.

The *stratosphere*—the layer extending from about 12 km up to 50 km altitude—contains the ozone layer that is responsible for absorbing harmful UV radiation. The *troposphere* is the layer extending from the surface up to about 12 km altitude. It should not surprise you to learn that the troposphere is the layer most easily disturbed by human activities and that this layer has the greatest impact on the earth's surface conditions. Among those impacts, a process called the *greenhouse effect* is much in the news today.

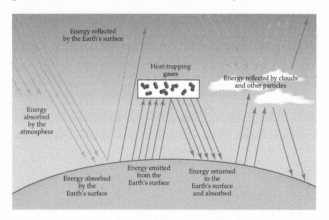

▲ Greenhouse gases (GHG) trap heat reflected from the earth's surface, resulting in the increase in surface temperatures known as global warming.

The greenhouse effect refers to the warming that occurs in the troposphere as gases absorb radiant energy. Much of the radiant energy reaching the earth's surface from the sun is reflected back into space, but some is absorbed by atmospheric gases—particularly those referred to as—*greenhouse gases* (GHGs)—water vapor, carbon dioxide, and methane. This absorbed radiation warms the atmosphere and acts to maintain a relatively stable temperature of 15 °C (59 °F) at the earth's surface. Without the greenhouse effect, the average surface temperature would be about −18 °C (0 °F)—a temperature so low that Earth would be frozen and unable to sustain life.

The basis for concern about the greenhouse effect is the fear that human activities over the past century have disturbed the earth's delicate thermal balance. Should increasing amounts of radiation be absorbed, increased atmospheric heating will result, and global temperatures will continue to rise.

Measurements show that the concentration of atmospheric CO_2 has been rising in the last 150 years, largely because of the increased use of fossil fuels, from an estimated 290 parts per million (ppm) in 1850 to current levels approaching 380 ppm. The increase in CO_2 levels correlates with a concurrent increase in average global temperatures, with the 11 years between 1995 and 2006 ranking among the 12-highest since recording of global temperatures began in 1850. The latest report of the Intergovernmental Panel on Climate Change published in November 2007 concluded that "Warming of the climate system is unequivocal, as is now evident from observations of increases in global average air and ocean temperatures, widespread melting of snow and ice and rising global average sea level. . . . Continued GHG emissions at or above current rates would cause further warming and induce many changes in the global climate system during the 21st century that would *very likely* be larger than those observed during the 20th century."

See Additional Problems 8.101 and 8.102 at the end of the chapter.

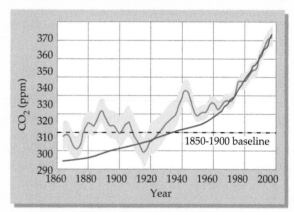

▲ Concentrations of atmospheric CO_2 and global average temperatures have increased dramatically in the last 150 years because of increased fossil fuel use, causing serious changes in earth's climate system.

© Crown copyright 2006 data provided by the Met office

London Dispersion Forces

London dispersion force The short-lived attractive force due to the constant motion of electrons within molecules.

Only polar molecules experience dipole–dipole forces, but all molecules, regardless of structure, experience *London dispersion forces*. **London dispersion forces** are caused by the constant motion of electrons within molecules. Take even a simple nonpolar molecule like Br_2, for example. Averaged over time, the distribution of electrons throughout the molecule is uniform, but at any given *instant* there may be more electrons at one end of the molecule than at the other (Figure 8.15). At that instant, the

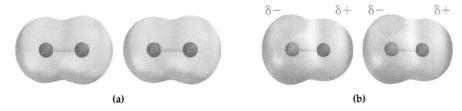

▲ **FIGURE 8.15** (a) Averaged over time, the electron distribution in a Br_2 molecule is symmetrical. (b) At any given instant, however, the electron distribution may be unsymmetrical, resulting in a temporary polarity that induces a complementary polarity in neighboring molecules.

molecule has a short-lived polarity. Electrons in neighboring molecules are attracted to the positive end of the polarized molecule, resulting in a polarization of the neighbor and creation of an attractive London dispersion force that holds the molecules together. As a result, Br_2 is a liquid at room temperature rather than a gas.

London dispersion forces are weak—in the range 0.5–2.5 kcal/mol—but they increase with molecular weight and amount of surface contact between molecules. The larger the molecular weight, the more electrons there are moving about and the greater the temporary polarization of a molecule. The larger the amount of surface contact, the greater the close interaction between different molecules.

The effect of surface contact on the magnitude of London dispersion forces can be seen by comparing a roughly spherical molecule with a flatter, more linear one having the same molecular weight. Both 2,2-dimethylpropane and pentane, for instance, have the same formula (C_5H_{12}), but the nearly spherical shape of 2,2-dimethylpropane allows for less surface contact with neighboring molecules than does the more linear shape of pentane (Figure 8.16). As a result, London dispersion forces are smaller for 2,2-dimethylpropane, molecules are held together less tightly, and the boiling point is correspondingly lower: 9.5 °C for 2,2-dimethylpropane versus 36 °C for pentane.

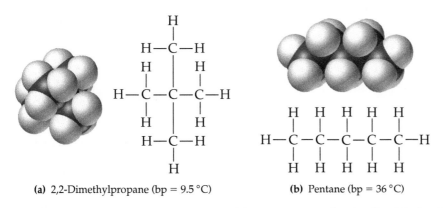

(a) 2,2-Dimethylpropane (bp = 9.5 °C)   (b) Pentane (bp = 36 °C)

▲ **FIGURE 8.16 London dispersion forces.** More compact molecules like 2,2-dimethylpropane have smaller surface areas, weaker London dispersion forces, and lower boiling points. By comparison, flatter, less compact molecules like pentane have larger surface areas, stronger London dispersion forces, and higher boiling points.

Hydrogen Bonds

In many ways, hydrogen bonding is responsible for life on earth. It causes water to be a liquid rather than a gas at ordinary temperatures, and it is the primary intermolecular force that holds huge biomolecules in the shapes needed to play their essential roles in biochemistry. Deoxyribonucleic acid (DNA) and keratin (Figure 8.17), for instance, are long molecular chains that form a coiled structure called an α-helix.

A **hydrogen bond** is an attractive interaction between an unshared electron pair on an electronegative O, N, or F atom and a positively polarized hydrogen atom

Hydrogen bond The attraction between a hydrogen atom bonded to an electronegative O, N, or F atom and another nearby electronegative O, N, or F atom.

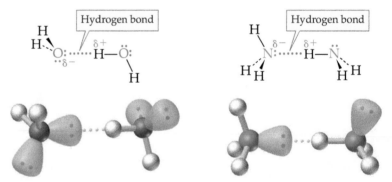

▶ **FIGURE 8.17** The α-helical structure of keratin results from hydrogen bonding along the amino acid backbone of the molecule.

bonded to another electronegative O, N, or F. For example, hydrogen bonds occur in both water and ammonia:

Hydrogen bonding is really just a special kind of dipole–dipole interaction. The O—H, N—H, and F—H bonds are highly polar, with a partial positive charge on the hydrogen and a partial negative charge on the electronegative atom. In addition, the hydrogen atom has no inner-shell electrons to act as a shield around its nucleus, and it is small so it can be approached closely. As a result, the dipole–dipole attractions involving positively polarized hydrogens are unusually strong, and hydrogen bonds result. Water, in particular, is able to form a vast three-dimensional network of hydrogen bonds because each H_2O molecule has two hydrogens and two electron pairs (Figure 8.18).

▶ **FIGURE 8.18 Hydrogen bonding in water.** The intermolecular attraction in water is especially strong because each oxygen atom has two lone pairs and two hydrogen atoms, allowing the formation of as many as four hydrogen bonds per molecule. Individual hydrogen bonds are constantly being formed and broken.

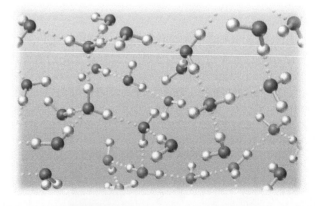

Hydrogen bonds can be quite strong, with energies up to 10 kcal/mol. To see the effect of hydrogen bonding, look at Table 8.2, which compares the boiling points of binary hydrogen compounds of second-row elements with their third-row counterparts. Because NH_3, H_2O, and HF molecules are held tightly together by hydrogen bonds, an unusually large amount of energy must be added to separate them in the boiling process. As a result, the boiling points of NH_3, H_2O, and HF are much higher than the boiling points of their second-row neighbor CH_4 and of related third-row compounds.

TABLE 8.2   Boiling Points for Binary Hydrogen Compounds of Some Second-row and Third-row Elements

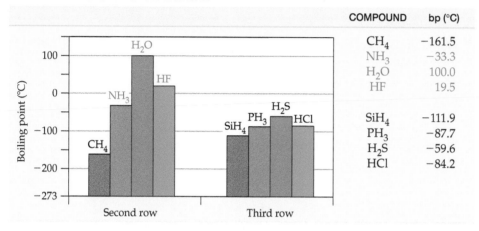

COMPOUND	bp (°C)
CH_4	−161.5
NH_3	−33.3
H_2O	100.0
HF	19.5
SiH_4	−111.9
PH_3	−87.7
H_2S	−59.6
HCl	−84.2

A summary and comparison of the various kinds of intermolecular forces is shown in Table 8.3.

TABLE 8.3   A Comparison of Intermolecular Forces

FORCE	STRENGTH	CHARACTERISTICS
Dipole–dipole	Weak (1 kcal/mol)	Occurs between polar molecules
London dispersion	Weak (0.5–2.5 kcal/mol)	Occurs between all molecules; strength depends on size
Hydrogen bond	Moderate (2–10 kcal/mol)	Occurs between molecules with O—H, N—H, and F—H bonds

Looking Ahead

Dipole–dipole forces, London dispersion forces, and hydrogen bonds are traditionally called "intermolecular forces" because of their influence on the properties of molecular compounds. But these same forces can also operate between different parts of a very large molecule. In this context, they are often referred to as "noncovalent interactions." In later chapters, we will see how noncovalent interactions determine the shapes of biologically important molecules such as proteins and nucleic acids.

WORKED EXAMPLE   **8.12** Identifying Intermolecular Forces: Polar versus Nonpolar

Identify the intermolecular forces that influence the properties of the following compounds:

    (a) Methane, CH_4 **(b)** HCl   **(c)** Acetic acid, CH_3CO_2H

ANALYSIS The intermolecular forces will depend on the molecular structure; what type of bonds are in the molecule (polar or non-polar) and how are they arranged.

SOLUTION

(a) Since methane contains only C—H bonds, it is a nonpolar molecule; it has only London dispersion forces.

(b) The H—Cl bond is polar, so this is a polar molecule; it has both dipole–dipole forces and London dispersion forces.

(c) Acetic acid is a polar molecule with an O—H bond. Thus, it has dipole–dipole forces, London dispersion forces, and hydrogen bonds.

PROBLEM 8.18

Would you expect the boiling points to increase or decrease in the following series? Explain.

(a) Kr, Ar, Ne   (b) Cl_2, Br_2, I_2

PROBLEM 8.19

Which of the following compounds form hydrogen bonds?

Methyl alcohol   Ethylene   Methylamine
        (a)   (b)   (c)

PROBLEM 8.20

Identify the intermolecular forces (dipole–dipole, London dispersion, hydrogen bonding) that influence the properties of the following compounds:

(a) Ethane, CH_3CH_3 (b) Ethyl alcohol, CH_3CH_2OH

(c) Ethyl chloride, CH_3CH_2Cl

8.12 Liquids

Vapor The gas molecules in equilibrium with a liquid.

Molecules are in constant motion in the liquid state, just as they are in gases. If a molecule happens to be near the surface of a liquid, and if it has enough energy, it can break free of the liquid and escape into the gas state, called **vapor**. In an open container, the now gaseous molecule will wander away from the liquid, and the process will continue until all the molecules escape from the container (Figure 8.19a). This, of course, is what happens during *evaporation*. We are all familiar with puddles of water evaporating after a rainstorm.

▶ **FIGURE 8.19 The transfer of molecules between liquid and gas states.** (a) Molecules escape from an open container and drift away until the liquid has entirely evaporated. (b) Molecules in a closed container cannot escape. Instead, they reach an equilibrium in which the rates of molecules leaving the liquid and returning to the liquid are equal, and the concentration of molecules in the gas state is constant.

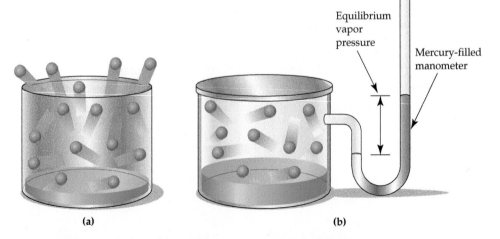

If the liquid is in a closed container, the situation is different because the gaseous molecules cannot escape. Thus, the random motion of the molecules occasionally brings them back into the liquid. After the concentration of molecules in the gas state has increased sufficiently, the number of molecules reentering the liquid becomes equal to the number escaping from the liquid (Figure 8.19b). At this point, a dynamic equilibrium exists, exactly as in a chemical reaction at equilibrium. Evaporation and condensation take place at the same rate, and the concentration of vapor in the container is constant as long as the temperature does not change.

Once molecules have escaped from the liquid into the gas state, they are subject to all the gas laws previously discussed. In a closed container at equilibrium, for example, the gas molecules make their own contribution to the total pressure of the gas above the liquid according to Dalton's law (Section 8.10). We call this contribution the **vapor pressure** of the liquid.

Vapor pressure depends on both temperature and the chemical identity of a liquid. As the temperature rises, molecules become more energetic and more likely to escape into the gas state. Thus, vapor pressure rises with increasing temperature until ultimately it becomes equal to the pressure of the atmosphere (Figure 8.20). At this point, bubbles of vapor form under the surface and force their way to the top, giving rise to the violent action observed during a vigorous boil. At an atmospheric pressure of exactly 760 mmHg, boiling occurs at what is called the **normal boiling point.**

▲ Because bromine is colored, it is possible to see its gaseous reddish vapor above the liquid.

Vapor pressure The partial pressure of gas molecules in equilibrium with a liquid.

Normal boiling point The boiling point at a pressure of exactly 1 atmosphere.

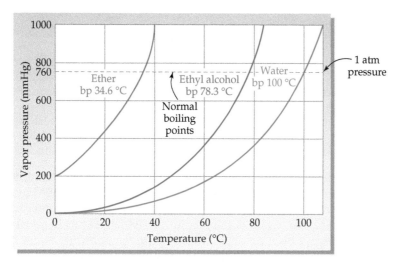

▲ **FIGURE 8.20** **A plot of the change of vapor pressure with temperature for ethyl ether, ethyl alcohol, and water.** At a liquid's boiling point, its vapor pressure is equal to atmospheric pressure. Commonly reported boiling points are those at 760 mmHg.

If atmospheric pressure is higher or lower than normal, the boiling point of a liquid changes accordingly. At high altitudes, for example, atmospheric pressure is lower than at sea level, and boiling points are also lower. On top of Mt. Everest (29,035 ft; 8850 m), atmospheric pressure is about 245 mmHg and the boiling temperature of water is only 71 °C. If the atmospheric pressure is higher than normal, the boiling point is also higher. This principle is used in strong vessels known as *autoclaves*, in which water at high pressure is heated to the temperatures needed for sterilizing medical and dental instruments (170 °C).

Many familiar properties of liquids can be explained by the intermolecular forces just discussed. We all know, for instance, that some liquids, such as water or gasoline, flow easily when poured, whereas others, such as motor oil or maple syrup, flow sluggishly.

The measure of a liquid's resistance to flow is called its *viscosity*. Not surprisingly, viscosity is related to the ease with which individual molecules move around in the liquid and thus to the intermolecular forces present. Substances such as gasoline, which have small, nonpolar molecules, experience only weak intermolecular

▲ Medical instruments are sterilized in this autoclave by heating them with water at high pressure.

▲ Surface tension allows a water strider to walk on water without penetrating the surface.

forces and have relatively low viscosities, whereas more polar substances such as glycerin [$C_3H_5(OH)_3$] experience stronger intermolecular forces and so have higher viscosities.

Another familiar property of liquids is *surface tension*, the resistance of a liquid to spread out and increase its surface area. The beading-up of water on a newly waxed car and the ability of a water strider to walk on water are both due to surface tension.

Surface tension is caused by the difference between the intermolecular forces experienced by molecules at the surface of the liquid and those experienced by molecules in the interior. Molecules in the interior of a liquid are surrounded and experience maximum intermolecular forces, whereas molecules at the surface have fewer neighbors and feel weaker forces. Surface molecules are therefore less stable, and the liquid acts to minimize their number by minimizing the surface area (Figure 8.21).

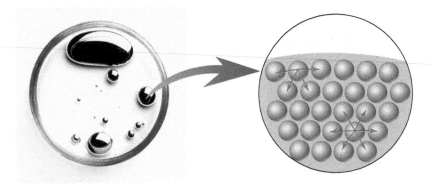

▲ **FIGURE 8.21 Surface tension.** Surface tension is caused by the different forces experienced by molecules in the interior of a liquid and those on the surface. Molecules on the surface are less stable because they feel fewer attractive forces, so the liquid acts to minimize their number by minimizing surface area.

8.13 Water: A Unique Liquid

Ours is a world based on water. Water covers nearly 71% of the earth's surface, it accounts for 66% of the mass of an adult human body, and it is needed by all living things. The water in our blood forms the transport system that circulates substances throughout our body, and water is the medium in which all biochemical reactions are carried out. Largely because of its strong hydrogen bonding, water has many properties that are quite different from those of other compounds.

▲ The moderate year-round temperatures in San Francisco are due to the large heat capacity of the surrounding waters.

Water has the highest specific heat of any liquid (Section 2.10), giving it the capacity to absorb a large quantity of heat while changing only slightly in temperature. (⊂⊃, p. 38) As a result, large lakes and other bodies of water tend to moderate the air temperature and climate of surrounding areas. Another consequence of the high specific heat of water is that the human body is better able to maintain a steady internal temperature under changing outside conditions.

In addition to a high specific heat, water has an unusually high *heat of vaporization* (540 cal/g), meaning that it carries away a large amount of heat when it evaporates. You can feel the effect of water evaporation on your wet skin when the wind blows. Even when comfortable, your body is still relying for cooling on the heat carried away from the skin and lungs by evaporating water. The heat generated by the chemical reactions of metabolism is carried by blood to the skin, where water moves through cell walls to the surface and evaporates. When metabolism, and therefore heat generation, speeds up, blood flow increases and capillaries dilate so that heat is brought to the surface faster.

Water is also unique in what happens as it changes from a liquid to a solid. Most substances are more dense as solids than as liquids because molecules are more closely packed in the solid than in the liquid. Water, however, is different. Liquid water has a maximum density of 1.000 g/mL at 3.98 °C but then becomes *less* dense as it cools. When it freezes, its density decreases still further to 0.917 g/mL.

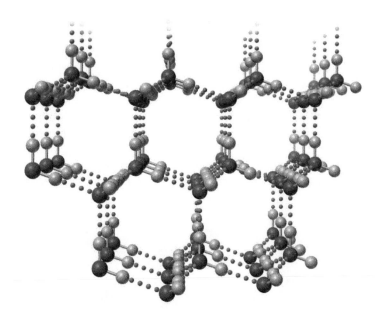

◀ FIGURE 8.22 **Ice.** Ice consists of individual H_2O molecules held rigidly together in an ordered manner by hydrogen bonds. The open cage-like crystal structure shows why ice is less dense than liquid water.

As water freezes, each molecule is locked into position by hydrogen bonding to four other water molecules (Figure 8.22). The resulting structure has more open space than does liquid water, accounting for its lower density. As a result, ice floats on liquid water, and lakes and rivers freeze from the top down. If the reverse were true, fish would be killed in winter as they became trapped in ice at the bottom.

8.14 Solids

A brief look around us reveals that most substances are solids rather than liquids or gases. It is also obvious that there are many different kinds of solids. Some, such as iron and aluminum, are hard and metallic; others, such as sugar and table salt, are crystalline and easily broken; and still others, such as rubber and many plastics, are soft and amorphous.

The most fundamental distinction between solids is that some are crystalline and some are amorphous. A **crystalline solid** is one whose particles—whether atoms, ions, or molecules—have an ordered arrangement extending over a long range. This order on the atomic level is also seen on the visible level, because crystalline solids usually have flat faces and distinct angles.

Crystalline solid A solid whose atoms, molecules, or ions are rigidly held in an ordered arrangement.

◀ Crystalline solids, such as the gypsum (left) and fluorite (right) shown here, have flat faces and distinct angles. These regular macroscopic features reflect a similarly ordered arrangement of particles at the atomic level.

▲ The sand on this beach is silica, SiO_2, a covalent network solid. Each grain of sand is essentially one large molecule.

Crystalline solids can be further categorized as ionic, molecular, covalent network, or metallic. *Ionic solids* are those like sodium chloride, whose constituent particles are ions. A crystal of sodium chloride is composed of alternating Na^+ and Cl^- ions ordered in a regular three-dimensional arrangement and held together by ionic bonds, as discussed in Section 4.3. (⊂⊃, p. 83) *Molecular solids* are those like sucrose or ice, whose constituent particles are molecules held together by the intermolecular forces discussed in Sections 8.11 and 8.12. A crystal of ice, for example, is composed of H_2O molecules held together in a regular way by hydrogen bonding (Figure 8.22). *Covalent network solids* are those like diamond (Figure 8.23) or quartz (SiO_2), whose atoms are linked together by covalent bonds into a giant three-dimensional array. In effect, a covalent network solid is one *very* large molecule.

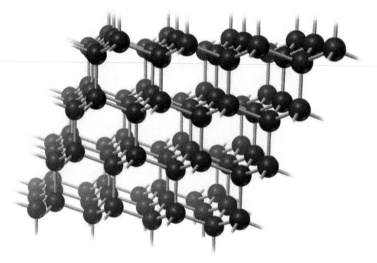

▲ **FIGURE 8.23 Diamond.** Diamond is a covalent network solid—one very large molecule of carbon atoms linked by covalent bonds.

Metallic solids, such as silver or iron, can be viewed as vast three-dimensional arrays of metal cations immersed in a sea of electrons that are free to move about. This continuous electron sea acts both as a glue to hold the cations together and as a mobile carrier of charge to conduct electricity. Furthermore, the fact that bonding attractions extend uniformly in all directions explains why metals are malleable rather than brittle. When a metal crystal receives a sharp blow, no spatially oriented bonds are broken; instead, the electron sea simply adjusts to the new distribution of cations.

Amorphous solid A solid whose particles do not have an orderly arrangement.

An **amorphous solid**, by contrast with a crystalline solid, is one whose constituent particles are randomly arranged and have no ordered long-range structure. Amorphous solids often result when liquids cool before they can achieve internal order, or when their molecules are large and tangled together, as happens in many polymers. Glass is an amorphous solid, as are tar, the gemstone opal, and some hard candies. Amorphous solids differ from crystalline solids by softening over a wide temperature range rather than having sharp melting points, and by shattering to give pieces with curved rather than planar faces.

A summary of the different types of solids and their characteristics is given in Table 8.4.

8.15 Changes of State

What happens when a solid is heated? As more and more energy is added, molecules begin to stretch, bend, and vibrate more vigorously, and atoms or ions wiggle about with more energy. Finally, if enough energy is added and the motions become vigorous enough, particles start to break free from one another and the substance starts to melt. Addition of more heat continues the melting process until all particles have broken free and are in the liquid phase. The quantity of heat required to completely melt a substance once it reaches its melting point is called

TABLE 8.4   Types of Solids

SUBSTANCE	SMALLEST UNIT	INTERPARTICLE FORCES	PROPERTIES	EXAMPLES
Ionic solid	Ions	Attraction between positive and negative ions	Brittle and hard; high mp; crystalline	NaCl, KI, $Ca_3(PO_4)_2$
Molecular solid	Molecules	Intermolecular forces	Soft; low to moderate mp; crystalline	Ice, wax, frozen CO_2, all solid organic compounds
Covalent network	Atoms	Covalent bonds	Very hard; very high mp; crystalline	Diamond, quartz (SiO_2), tungsten carbide (WC)
Metal or alloy	Metal atoms	Metallic bonding (attraction between metal ions and surrounding mobile electrons)	Lustrous; soft (Na) to hard (Ti); high melting; crystalline	Elements (Fe, Cu, Sn, . . .), bronze (CuSn alloy), amalgams (Hg + other metals)
Amorphous solid	Atoms, ions, or molecules (including polymer molecules)	Any of the above	Noncrystalline; no sharp mp; able to flow (may be very slow); curved edges when shattered	Glasses, tar, some plastics

its **heat of fusion**. After melting is complete, further addition of heat causes the temperature of the liquid to rise.

The change of a liquid into a vapor proceeds in the same way as the change of a solid into a liquid. When you first put a pan of water on the stove, all the added heat goes into raising the temperature of the water. Once the boiling point is reached, further absorbed heat goes into freeing molecules from their neighbors as they escape into the gas state. The quantity of heat needed to completely vaporize a liquid once it reaches its boiling point is called its **heat of vaporization**. A liquid with a low heat of vaporization, like rubbing alcohol (isopropyl alcohol), evaporates rapidly and is said to be *volatile*. If you spill a volatile liquid on your skin, you will feel a cooling effect as it evaporates because it is absorbing heat from your body.

It is important to know the difference between heat that is added or removed to change the *temperature* of a substance and heat that is added or removed to change the *phase* of a substance. Remember that temperature is a measure of the kinetic energy in a substance (Section 7.1, p. 183). When a substance is above or below its phase change temperature (i.e., melting point or boiling point) adding or removing heat will simply change the kinetic energy and, hence, the temperature of the substance. The amount of heat needed to produce a given temperature change was presented previously (Section 2.10), but is worth presenting again here:

$$\text{Heat (cal)} = \text{Mass (g)} \times \text{Temperature change (°C)} \times \text{Specific heat} \left(\frac{\text{cal}}{\text{g} \times \text{°C}} \right)$$

In contrast, when a substance is at its phase change temperature, heat that is added is being used to overcome the intermolecular forces holding particles in that phase. The temperature remains constant until *all* particles have been converted to the next phase. The energy needed to complete the phase change depends only on the amount of the substance, and the heat of fusion (for melting) or the heat of vaporization (for boiling).

$$\text{Heat (cal)} = \text{Mass (g)} \times \text{Heat of fusion} \left(\frac{\text{cal}}{\text{g}} \right)$$

$$\text{Heat (cal)} = \text{Mass (g)} \times \text{Heat of vaporization} \left(\frac{\text{cal}}{\text{g}} \right)$$

If the intermolecular forces are strong then large amounts of heat must be added to overcome these forces, and the heats of fusion and vaporization will be large. A list of heats of fusion and heats of vaporization for some common substances is given in Table 8.5. Butane, for example, has a small heat of vaporization since the

Heat of fusion   The quantity of heat required to completely melt one gram of a substance once it has reached its melting point.

Heat of vaporization   The quantity of heat needed to completely vaporize one gram of a liquid once it has reached its boiling point.

TABLE 8.5   Melting Points, Boiling Points, Heats of Fusion, and Heats of Vaporization of Some Common Substances

SUBSTANCE	MELTING POINT (°C)	BOILING POINT (°C)	HEAT OF FUSION (cal/g)	HEAT OF VAPORIZATION (cal/g)
Ammonia	−77.7	−33.4	84.0	327
Butane	−138.4	−0.5	19.2	92.5
Ether	−116	34.6	23.5	85.6
Ethyl alcohol	−117.3	78.5	26.1	200
Isopropyl alcohol	−89.5	82.4	21.4	159
Sodium	97.8	883	14.3	492
Water	0.0	100.0	79.7	540

APPLICATION ▶ Biomaterials for Joint Replacement

Freely movable joints in the body, such as those in the shoulder, knee, or hip, are formed by the meeting of two bones. The bony surfaces are not in direct contact, of course; rather, they are covered by cartilage for nearly frictionless motion and are surrounded by a fluid-containing capsule for lubrication. The hip, for instance, is a ball-and-socket joint, formed where the rounded upper end of the femur meets a cup-shaped part of the pelvic bone called the acetabulum.

Unfortunately, joints can wear out or fail, particularly when the cartilage is damaged by injury or diseased by degenerative arthritis. At some point, it may even be necessary to replace the failing joint—an estimated 500,000 joint-replacement surgeries are performed each year in the United States (170,000 hips, 325,000 knees). Although total joint replacement is not without problems, the lifetime of an artificial joint is nearly 20 years in 80% of the cases.

The first joint-replacement material, used in 1962, was stainless steel, but slow corrosion in the body led to its abandonment in favor of more resistant titanium or cobalt–chromium alloys. A typical modern hip-replacement joint consists of three parts: a polished metal ball to replace the head of the femur, a titanium alloy stem that is cemented into the shaft of the femur for stability, and a polyethylene cup to replace the hip socket.

Even with these materials, though, abrasion at the ball/cup contact can lead to joint wear. Over time, the constant repetitive movement of the polyethylene socket over the metal ball results in billions of microscopic polyethylene particles being sloughed off into the surrounding fluid. In addition, the cement holding the metal stem to the femur can slowly degrade, releasing other particles. The foreign particles are attacked by the body's immune system, resulting in the release of enzymes that cause the death of adjacent bone cells, loosening of the metal stem, and ultimate failure of the joint.

A potential solution to the problem involves the use of *biomaterials*—new materials that are created specifically for use in biological systems and do not provoke an immune response. It has been found, for instance, that the titanium

▲ This artificial hip joint is bonded to a thin layer of calcium phosphate to stimulate attachment of natural bone.

stem of the artificial joint can be bonded to an extremely thin layer of calcium phosphate, $Ca_3(PO_4)_2$, a close relative of hydroxyapatite $Ca_{10}(PO_4)_6(OH)_2$, the primary mineral constituent of bone (see the Chapter 4 Application, *Osteoporosis*). Natural bone then grows into the calcium phosphate, forming a strong natural bond to the stem, and making cement unnecessary. Other biomaterials are being designed to replace the polyethylene socket.

See Additional Problem 8.103 at the end of the chapter.

predominant intermolecular forces in butane (dispersion) are relatively weak. Water, on the other hand, has a particularly high heat of vaporization because of its unusually strong hydrogen bonding interactions. Thus, water evaporates more slowly than many other liquids, takes a long time to boil away, and absorbs more heat in the process. A so-called *heating curve*, which indicates the temperature and state changes as heat is added, is shown in Figure 8.24.

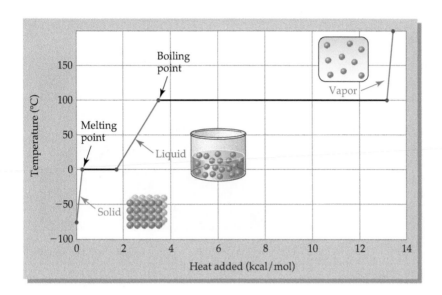

◀ **FIGURE 8.24 A heating curve for water, showing the temperature and state changes that occur when heat is added.** The horizontal lines at 0 °C and 100 °C represent the heat of fusion and heat of vaporization, respectively.

WORKED EXAMPLE **8.13** Heat of Fusion: Calculating Total Heat of Melting

Naphthalene, an organic substance often used in mothballs, has a heat of fusion of 35.7 cal/g and a molar mass of 128.0 g/mol. How much heat in kilocalories is required to melt 0.300 mol of naphthalene?

ANALYSIS The heat of fusion tells how much heat is required to melt 1 g. To find the amount of heat needed to melt 0.300 mol, we need a mole to mass conversion.

BALLPARK ESTIMATE Naphthalene has a molar mass of 128.0 g/mol, so 0.300 mol has a mass of about one-third this amount, or about 40 g. Approximately 35 cal is required to melt 1 g, so we need about 40 times this amount of heat, or (35 × 40 = 1400 cal = 1.4 kcal).

SOLUTION

STEP 1: Identify known information. We know heat of fusion (cal/g), and the number of moles of naphthalene.	Heat of fusion = 35.7 cal/g Moles of naphthalene = 0.300 mol
STEP 2: Identify answer and units.	Heat = ?? cal
STEP 3: Identify conversion factors. First convert moles of naphthalene to grams using the molar mass (128 g/mol) as a conversion factor. Then use the heat of fusion as a conversion factor to calculate the total heat necessary to melt the mass of naphthalene.	$(0.300 \text{ mol naphthalene})\left(\dfrac{128.0 \text{ g}}{1 \text{ mol}}\right) = 38.4 \text{ g naphthalene}$ Heat of fusion = 35.7 cal/g
STEP 4: Solve. Multiplying the mass of naphthalene by the heat of fusion then gives the answer.	$(38.4 \text{ g naphthalene})\left(\dfrac{35.7 \text{ cal}}{1 \text{ g naphthalene}}\right) = 1370 \text{ cal} = 1.37 \text{ kcal}$

BALLPARK CHECK The calculated result agrees with our estimate (1.4 kcal).

PROBLEM 8.21

How much heat in kilocalories is required to melt and boil 1.50 mol of isopropyl alcohol (rubbing alcohol; molar mass = 60.0 g/mol)? The heat of fusion and heat of vaporization of isopropyl alcohol are given in Table 8.5.

APPLICATION ▶ CO₂ as an Environmentally Friendly Solvent

▲ The caffeine in these coffee beans can be removed by extraction with supercritical CO_2.

How can CO_2 be a solvent? After all, carbon dioxide is a gas, not a liquid, at room temperature. Furthermore, CO_2 at atmospheric pressure does not become liquid even when cooled. When the temperature drops to −78 °C at 1 atm pressure, CO_2 goes directly from gas to solid (dry ice) without first becoming liquid. Only when the pressure is raised does liquid CO_2 exist. At a room temperature of 22.4 °C, a pressure of 60 atm is needed to force gaseous CO_2 molecules close enough together so they condense to a liquid. Even as a liquid, though, CO_2 is not a particularly good solvent. Only when it enters an unusual and rarely seen state of matter called the *supercritical state* does CO_2 become a remarkable solvent.

To understand the supercritical state of matter, think about the liquid and gas states at the molecular level. In the liquid state, molecules are packed closely together, and most of the available volume is taken up by the molecules themselves. In the gas state, molecules are far apart, and most of the available volume is empty space. In the supercritical state, however, the situation is intermediate between liquid and gas. There is *some* space between molecules, but not much. The molecules are too far apart to be truly a liquid, yet they are too close together to be truly a gas. Supercritical CO_2 exists when the pressure is above 72.8 atm and the temperature is above 31.2 °C. This pressure is high enough to force molecules close together and prevent them from expanding into the gas state. Above this temperature, however, the molecules have too much kinetic energy to condense into the liquid state.

Because open spaces already exist between CO_2 molecules, it is energetically easy for dissolved molecules to slip in, and supercritical CO_2 is therefore an extraordinarily good solvent. Among its many applications, supercritical CO_2 is used in the beverage and food processing industries to decaffeinate coffee beans and to obtain spice extracts from vanilla, pepper, cloves, nutmeg, and other seeds. In the cosmetics and perfume industry, fragrant oils are extracted from flowers using supercritical CO_2. Perhaps the most important future application is the use of carbon dioxide for dry-cleaning clothes, thereby replacing environmentally harmful chlorinated solvents.

The use of supercritical CO_2 as a solvent has many benefits, including the fact that it is nontoxic and nonflammable. Most important, though, is that the technology is environmentally friendly. Industrial processes using CO_2 are designed as closed systems so that CO_2 is recaptured after use and continually recycled. No organic solvent vapors are released into the atmosphere and no toxic liquids seep into groundwater supplies, as can occur with current procedures using chlorinated organic solvents. The future looks bright for this new technology.

See Additional Problems 8.104 and 8.105 at the end of the chapter.

KEY WORDS

SUMMARY: REVISITING THE CHAPTER GOALS

1. **How do scientists explain the behavior of gases?** According to the *kinetic–molecular theory of gases*, the physical behavior of gases can be explained by assuming that they consist of particles moving rapidly at random, separated from other particles by great distances, and colliding without loss of energy. Gas *pressure* is the result of molecular collisions with a surface.

2. **How do gases respond to changes in temperature, pressure, and volume?** *Boyle's law* says that the volume of a fixed amount of gas at constant temperature is inversely proportional to its pressure ($P_1V_1 = P_2V_2$). *Charles's law* says that the volume of a fixed amount of gas at constant pressure is directly proportional to its Kelvin temperature ($V_1/T_1 = V_2/T_2$). *Gay-Lussac's law* says that the pressure of a fixed amount of gas at

constant volume is directly proportional to its Kelvin temperature ($P_1/T_1 = P_2/T_2$). Boyle's law, Charles's law, and Gay-Lussac's law together give the *combined gas law* ($P_1V_1/T_1 = P_2V_2/T_2$), which applies to changing conditions for a fixed quantity of gas. *Avogadro's law* says that equal volumes of gases at the same temperature and pressure contain the same number of moles ($V_1/n_1 = V_2/n_2$).

3. **What is the ideal gas law?** The four gas laws together give the *ideal gas law*, $PV = nRT$, which relates the effects of temperature, pressure, volume, and molar amount. At 0 °C and 1 atm pressure, called *standard temperature and pressure (STP)*, 1 mol of any gas (6.02×10^{23} molecules) occupies a volume of 22.4 L.

4. **What is partial pressure?** The amount of pressure exerted by an individual gas in a mixture is called the *partial pressure* of the gas. According to *Dalton's law*, the total pressure exerted by the mixture is equal to the sum of the partial pressures of the individual gases.

5. **What are the major intermolecular forces, and how do they affect the states of matter?** There are three major types of *intermolecular forces*, which act to hold molecules near one another in solids and liquids. *Dipole–dipole forces* are the electrical attractions that occur between polar molecules. *London dispersion forces* occur between all molecules as a result of temporary molecular polarities due to unsymmetrical electron distribution. These forces increase in strength with molecular weight and with the surface area of molecules. *Hydrogen bonding*, the strongest of the three intermolecular forces, occurs between a hydrogen atom bonded to O, N, or F and a nearby O, N, or F atom.

6. **What are the various kinds of solids, and how do they differ?** Solids are either crystalline or amorphous. *Crystalline solids* are those whose constituent particles have an ordered arrangement; *amorphous solids* lack internal order and do not have sharp melting points. There are several kinds of crystalline solids: *Ionic solids* are those like sodium chloride, whose constituent particles are ions. *Molecular solids* are those like ice, whose constituent particles are molecules held together by intermolecular forces. *Covalent network solids* are those like diamond, whose atoms are linked together by covalent bonds into a giant three-dimensional array. *Metallic solids*, such as silver or iron, also consist of large arrays of atoms, but their crystals have metallic properties such as electrical conductivity.

7. **What factors affect a change of state?** When a solid is heated, particles begin to move around freely at the *melting point*, and the substance becomes liquid. The amount of heat necessary to melt a given amount of solid at its melting point is its *heat of fusion*. As a liquid is heated, molecules escape from the surface of a liquid until an equilibrium is reached between liquid and gas, resulting in a *vapor pressure* of the liquid. At a liquid's *boiling point*, its vapor pressure equals atmospheric pressure, and the entire liquid is converted into gas. The amount of heat necessary to vaporize a given amount of liquid at its boiling point is called its *heat of vaporization*.

Combined gas law, *p. 228*

Crystalline solid, *p. 243*

Dalton's law, *p. 233*

Dipole–dipole force, *p. 235*

Gas constant (*R*), *p. 231*

Gas laws, *p. 222*

Gay-Lussac's law, *p. 227*

Heat of fusion, *p. 245*

Heat of vaporization, *p. 245*

Hydrogen bond, *p. 237*

Ideal gas, *p. 218*

Ideal gas law, *p. 231*

Intermolecular force, *p. 235*

Kinetic–molecular theory of gases, *p. 218*

London dispersion force, *p. 236*

Melting point (mp), *p. 217*

Normal boiling point, *p. 241*

Partial pressure, *p. 233*

Pressure (*P*), *p. 218*

Standard temperature and pressure (STP), *p. 230*

Standard molar volume, *p. 230*

Vapor, *p. 240*

Vapor pressure, *p. 241*

UNDERSTANDING KEY CONCEPTS

8.22 Assume that you have a sample of gas in a cylinder with a movable piston, as shown in the following drawing:

Redraw the apparatus to show what the sample will look like after the following changes:

(a) The temperature is increased from 300 K to 450 K at constant pressure.

(b) The pressure is increased from 1 atm to 2 atm at constant temperature.

(c) The temperature is decreased from 300 K to 200 K and the pressure is decreased from 3 atm to 2 atm.

8.23 Assume that you have a sample of gas at 350 K in a sealed container, as represented in part (a). Which of the drawings (b)–(d) represents the gas after the temperature is lowered from 350 K to 150 K?

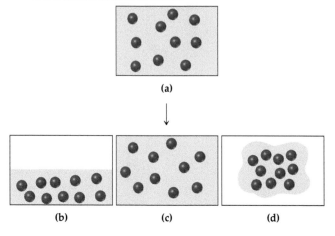

8.24 Assume that drawing (a) represents a sample of H_2O at 200 K. Which of the drawings (b)–(d) represents what the sample will look like when the temperature is raised to 300 K?

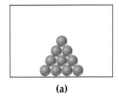

(a)

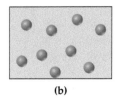

(b)

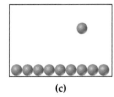

(c)

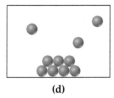

(d)

8.25 Three bulbs, two of which contain different gases and one of which is empty, are connected as shown in the following drawing:

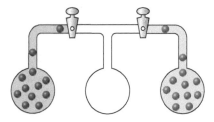

Redraw the apparatus to represent the gases after the stopcocks are opened and the system is allowed to come to equilibrium.

8.26 Redraw the following open-end manometer to show what it would look like when stopcock A is opened.

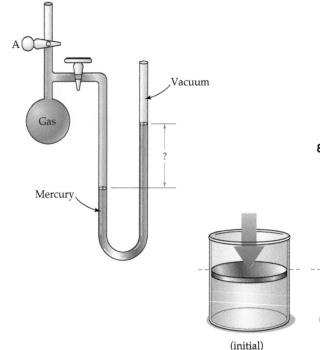

8.27 The following graph represents the heating curve of a hypothetical substance:

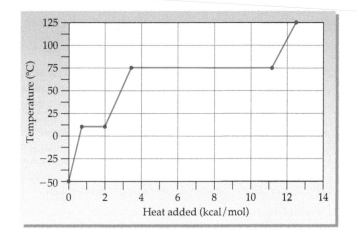

(a) What is the melting point of the substance?
(b) What is the boiling point of the substance?
(c) Approximately what is the heat of fusion for the substance in kcal/mol?
(d) Approximately what is the heat of vaporization for the substance in kcal/mol?

8.28 Show the approximate level of the movable piston in drawings (a)–(c) after the indicated changes have been made to the gas.

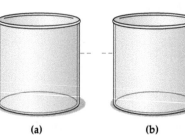

(initial)
$T = 25\ °C$
$n = 0.075$ mol
$P = 0.92$ atm

(a)
$T = 50\ °C$
$n = 0.075$ mol
$P = 0.92$ atm

(b)
$T = 175\ °C$
$n = 0.075$ mol
$P = 2.7$ atm

(c)
$T = 25\ °C$
$n = 0.22$ mol
$P = 2.7$ atm

8.29 What is the partial pressure of each gas—red, yellow, and green—if the total pressure inside the following container is 600 mmHg?

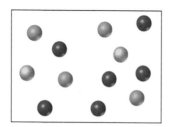

ADDITIONAL PROBLEMS

GASES AND PRESSURE

8.30 How is 1 atm of pressure defined?

8.31 List four common units for measuring pressure.

8.32 What are the four assumptions of the kinetic–molecular theory of gases?

8.33 How does the kinetic–molecular theory of gases explain gas pressure?

8.34 Convert the following values into mmHg:

  (a) Standard pressure **(b)** 25.3 psi
  (c) 7.5 atm **(d)** 28.0 in. Hg
  (e) 41.8 Pa

8.35 Atmospheric pressure at the top of Mt. Whitney in California is 440 mmHg.

  (a) How many atmospheres is this?
  (b) How many pascals is this?

8.36 What is the pressure (in mmHg) inside a container of gas connected to a mercury-filled, open-end manometer of the sort shown in Figure 8.5 when the level in the arm connected to the container is 17.6 cm lower than the level in the arm open to the atmosphere, and the atmospheric pressure reading outside the apparatus is 754.3 mmHg?

8.37 What is the pressure (in atmospheres) inside a container of gas connected to a mercury-filled, open-end manometer of the sort shown in Figure 8.5 when the level in the arm connected to the container is 28.3 cm higher than the level in the arm open to the atmosphere, and the atmospheric pressure reading outside the apparatus is 1.021 atm?

BOYLE'S LAW

8.38 What is Boyle's law, and what variables must be kept constant for the law to hold?

8.39 Which assumption(s) of the kinetic–molecular theory explain the behavior of gases described by Boyle's Law? Explain your answer.

8.40 The pressure of gas in a 600.0 mL cylinder is 65.0 mmHg. To what volume must it be compressed to increase the pressure to 385 mmHg?

8.41 The volume of a balloon is 2.85 L at 1.00 atm. What pressure is required to compress the balloon to a volume of 1.70 L?

8.42 The use of chlorofluorocarbons (CFCs) as refrigerants and propellants in aerosol cans has been discontinued as a result of concerns about the ozone layer. If an aerosol can contained 350 mL of CFC gas at a pressure of 5.0 atm, what volume would this gas occupy at 1.0 atm?

8.43 A sample of neon gas used in a neon sign occupies a volume of 1.50 L at a pressure of 630 torr. Calculate the volume of the gas if the pressure in the glass tube of the sign is 793 torr.

CHARLES'S LAW

8.44 What is Charles's law, and what variables must be kept constant for the law to hold?

8.45 Which assumption(s) of the kinetic–molecular theory explain the behavior of gases described by Charles's Law? Explain your answer.

8.46 A hot-air balloon has a volume of 960 L at 18 °C. To what temperature must it be heated to raise its volume to 1200 L, assuming the pressure remains constant?

8.47 A hot-air balloon has a volume of 875 L. What is the original temperature of the balloon if its volume changes to 955 L when heated to 56 °C?

8.48 A gas sample has a volume of 185 mL at 38 °C. What is its volume at 97 °C?

8.49 A balloon has a volume of 43.0 L at 25 °C. What is its volume at −8 °C?

GAY-LUSSAC'S LAW

8.50 What is Gay-Lussac's law, and what variables must be kept constant for the law to hold?

8.51 Which assumption(s) of the kinetic–molecular theory explain the behavior of gases described by Gay-Lussac's Law? Explain your answer.

8.52 A glass laboratory flask is filled with gas at 25 °C and 0.95 atm pressure, sealed, and then heated to 117 °C. What is the pressure inside the flask?

8.53 An aerosol can has an internal pressure of 3.85 atm at 25 °C. What temperature is required to raise the pressure to 18.0 atm?

COMBINED GAS LAW

8.54 A gas has a volume of 2.84 L at 1.00 atm and 0 °C. At what temperature does it have a volume of 7.50 L at 520 mmHg?

8.55 A helium balloon has a volume of 3.50 L at 22.0 °C and 1.14 atm. What is its volume if the temperature is increased to 30.0 °C and the pressure is increased to 1.20 atm?

8.56 When H_2 gas was released by the reaction of HCl with Zn, the volume of H_2 collected was 75.4 mL at 23 °C and 748 mmHg. What is the volume of the H_2 at 0 °C and 1.00 atm pressure (STP)?

8.57 A compressed-air tank carried by scuba divers has a volume of 6.80 L and a pressure of 120 atm at 20 °C. What is the volume of air in the tank at 0 °C and 1.00 atm pressure (STP)?

8.58 What is the effect on the pressure of a gas if you simultaneously:

(a) Halve its volume and double its Kelvin temperature?
(b) Double its volume and halve its Kelvin temperature?

8.59 What is the effect on the volume of a gas if you simultaneously:

(a) Halve its pressure and double its Kelvin temperature?
(b) Double its pressure and double its Kelvin temperature?

8.60 A sample of oxygen produced in a laboratory experiment had a volume of 590 mL at a pressure of 775 mmHg and a temperature of 352 K. What is the volume of this sample at 25 °C and 800.0 mmHg pressure?

8.61 A small cylinder of helium gas used for filling balloons has a volume of 2.30 L and a pressure of 1850 atm at 25 °C. How many balloons can you fill if each one has a volume of 1.5 L and a pressure of 1.25 atm at 25 °C?

AVOGADRO'S LAW AND STANDARD MOLAR VOLUME

8.62 Explain Avogadro's law using the kinetic–molecular theory of gases.

8.63 What conditions are defined as standard temperature and pressure (STP)?

8.64 How many liters does 1 mol of gas occupy at STP?

8.65 How many moles of gas are in a volume of 48.6 L at STP?

8.66 Which sample contains more molecules: 1.0 L of O_2 at STP or 1.0 L of H_2 at STP? Which sample has the larger mass?

8.67 How many milliliters of Cl_2 gas must you have to obtain 0.20 g at STP?

8.68 What is the mass of CH_4 in a sample that occupies a volume of 16.5 L at STP?

8.69 Assume that you have 1.75 g of the deadly gas hydrogen cyanide, HCN. What is the volume of the gas at STP?

8.70 A typical room is 4.0 m long, 5.0 m wide, and 2.5 m high. What is the total mass of the oxygen in the room assuming that the gas in the room is at STP and that air contains 21% oxygen and 79% nitrogen?

8.71 What is the total mass of nitrogen in the room described in Problem 8.70?

IDEAL GAS LAW

8.72 What is the ideal gas law?

8.73 How does the ideal gas law differ from the combined gas law?

8.74 Which sample contains more molecules: 2.0 L of Cl_2 at STP, or 3.0 L of CH_4 at 300 K and 1.5 atm? Which sample weighs more?

8.75 Which sample contains more molecules: 2.0 L of CO_2 at 300 K and 500 mmHg, or 1.5 L of N_2 at 57 °C and 760 mmHg? Which sample weighs more?

8.76 If 2.3 mol of He has a volume of 0.15 L at 294 K, what is the pressure in atm?

8.77 If 3.5 mol of O_2 has a volume of 27.0 L at a pressure of 1.6 atm, what is its temperature in kelvins?

8.78 If 15.0 g of CO_2 gas has a volume of 0.30 L at 310 K, what is its pressure in mmHg?

8.79 If 20.0 g of N_2 gas has a volume of 4.00 L and a pressure of 6.0 atm, what is its temperature in degrees Celsius?

8.80 If 18.0 g of O_2 gas has a temperature of 350 K and a pressure of 550 mmHg, what is its volume?

8.81 How many moles of a gas will occupy a volume of 0.55 L at a temperature of 347 K and a pressure of 2.5 atm?

DALTON'S LAW AND PARTIAL PRESSURE

8.82 What is meant by *partial pressure*?

8.83 What is Dalton's law?

8.84 If the partial pressure of oxygen in air at 1.0 atm is 160 mmHg, what is the partial pressure on the summit of Mt. Whitney, where atmospheric pressure is 440 mmHg? Assume that the percent oxygen is the same.

8.85 Patients suffering from respiratory disorders are often treated in oxygen tents in which the atmosphere is enriched in oxygen. What is the partial pressure of O_2 in an oxygen tent consisting of 45% O_2 for an atmospheric pressure of 753 mmHg?

LIQUIDS AND INTERMOLECULAR FORCES

8.86 What is the vapor pressure of a liquid?

8.87 What is the value of a liquid's vapor pressure at its normal boiling point?

8.88 What is the effect of pressure on a liquid's boiling point?

8.89 What is a liquid's heat of vaporization?

8.90 What characteristic must a compound have to experience the following intermolecular forces?

(a) London dispersion forces
(b) Dipole–dipole forces
(c) Hydrogen bonding

8.91 In which of the following compounds are dipole–dipole attractions the most important intermolecular force?

(a) N_2 (b) HCN   (c) CCl_4
(d) $MgBr_2$ (e) CH_3Cl (f) CH_3CO_2H

8.92 Dimethyl ether (CH_3OCH_3) and ethanol (C_2H_5OH) have the same formula (C_2H_6O), but the boiling point of dimethyl ether is −25 °C while that of ethanol is 78 °C. Explain.

8.93 Iodine is a solid at room temperature (mp = 113.5 °C) while bromine is a liquid (mp = −7 °C). Explain in terms of intermolecular forces.

8.94 The heat of vaporization of water is 9.72 kcal/mol.

(a) How much heat (in kilocalories) is required to vaporize 3.00 mol of H_2O?
(b) How much heat (in kilocalories) is released when 320 g of steam condenses?

8.95 Patients with a high body temperature are often given "alcohol baths." The heat of vaporization of isopropyl alcohol (rubbing alcohol) is 159 cal/g. How much heat is removed from the skin by the evaporation of 190 g (about ½ cup) of isopropyl alcohol?

SOLIDS

8.96 What is the difference between an amorphous and a crystalline solid?

8.97 List three kinds of crystalline solids, and give an example of each.

8.98 The heat of fusion of acetic acid, the principal organic component of vinegar, is 45.9 cal/g. How much heat (in kilocalories) is required to melt 1.75 mol of solid acetic acid?

8.99 The heat of fusion of sodium metal is 630 cal/mol. How much heat (in kilocalories) is required to melt 262 g of sodium?

Applications

8.100 What is the difference between a systolic and a diastolic pressure reading? Is a blood pressure of 180/110 within the normal range? [*Blood Pressure, p. 223*]

8.101 What are the three most important greenhouse gases? [*Greenhouse Gases and Global Warming, p. 236*]

8.102 What evidence is there that global warming is occurring? [*Greenhouse Gases and Global Warming, p. 236*]

8.103 What is the mass ratio of calcium to phosphate in calcium phosphate, $Ca_3(PO_4)_2$? In hydroxyapatite, $Ca_{10}(PO_4)_6(OH)_2$? [*Biomaterials for Joint Replacement, p. 246*]

8.104 What is a supercritical fluid? [*CO_2 as an Environmentally Friendly Solvent, p. 248*]

8.105 What are the environmental advantages of using supercritical CO_2 in place of chlorinated organic solvents? [*CO_2 as an Environmentally Friendly Solvent, p. 248*]

General Questions and Problems

8.106 Use the kinetic–molecular theory to explain why gas pressure increases if the temperature is raised and the volume is kept constant.

8.107 Hydrogen and oxygen react according to the equation $2 H_2 + O_2 \longrightarrow 2 H_2O$. According to Avogadro's law, how many liters of hydrogen are required to react with 2.5 L of oxygen at STP?

8.108 If 3.0 L of hydrogen and 1.5 L of oxygen at STP react to yield water, how many moles of water are formed? What gas volume does the water have at a temperature of 100 °C and 1 atm pressure?

8.109 Approximately 240 mL/min of CO_2 is exhaled by an average adult at rest. Assuming a temperature of 37 °C and 1 atm pressure, how many moles of CO_2 is this?

8.110 How many grams of CO_2 are exhaled by an average resting adult in 24 hours? (See Problem 8.109.)

8.111 Imagine that you have two identical containers, one containing hydrogen at STP and the other containing oxygen at STP. How can you tell which is which without opening them?

8.112 When fully inflated, a hot-air balloon has a volume of 1.6×10^5 L at an average temperature of 375 K and 0.975 atm. Assuming that air has an average molar mass of 29 g/mol, what is the density of the air in the hot-air balloon? How does this compare with the density of air at STP?

8.113 A 10.0 g sample of an unknown gas occupies 14.7 L at a temperature of 25 °C and a pressure of 745 mmHg. What is the molar mass of the gas?

8.114 One mole of any gas has a volume of 22.4 L at STP. What are the molecular weights of the following gases, and what are their densities in grams per liter at STP?

(a) CH_4 (b) CO_2 (c) O_2

8.115 Gas pressure outside the space shuttle is approximately 1×10^{-14} mm Hg at a temperature of approximately 1 K. If the gas is almost entirely hydrogen atoms (H, not H_2), what volume of space is occupied by 1 mol of atoms? What is the density of H gas in atoms per liter?

8.116 Ethylene glycol, $C_2H_6O_2$, has one OH bonded to each carbon.

(a) Draw the Lewis dot structure of ethylene glycol.
(b) Draw the Lewis dot structure of chloroethane, C_2H_5Cl.
(c) Chloroethane has a slightly higher molar mass than ethylene glycol, but a much lower boiling point (3 °C versus 198 °C). Explain.

8.117 A rule of thumb for scuba diving is that the external pressure increases by 1 atm for every 10 m of depth. A diver using a compressed air tank is planning to descend to a depth of 25 m.

(a) What is the external pressure at this depth? (Remember that the pressure at sea level is 1 atm.)
(b) Assuming that the tank contains 20% oxygen and 80% nitrogen, what is the partial pressure of each gas in the diver's lungs at this depth?

8.118 The *Rankine* temperature scale used in engineering is to the Fahrenheit scale as the Kelvin scale is to the Celsius scale. That is, 1 Rankine degree is the same size as 1 Fahrenheit degree, and 0 °R = absolute zero .

(a) What temperature corresponds to the freezing point of water on the Rankine scale?
(b) What is the value of the gas constant R on the Rankine scale in $(L \cdot atm)/(°R \cdot mol)$?

8.119 Isooctane, C_8H_{18}, is the component of gasoline from which the term *octane rating* derives.

(a) Write a balanced equation for the combustion of isooctane to yield CO_2 and H_2O.
(b) Assuming that gasoline is 100% isooctane and that the density of isooctane is 0.792 g/mL, what mass of CO_2 (in kilograms) is produced each year by the annual U.S. gasoline consumption of 4.6×10^{10} L?
(c) What is the volume (in liters) of this CO_2 at STP?

CHAPTER 9

Solutions

▲ The giant sequoia relies on osmotic pressure—a colligative property of solutions—to transport water and nutrients from the roots to the treetops 300 ft up.

CONTENTS

1. What are solutions, and what factors affect solubility?

THE GOAL: Be able to define the different kinds of mixtures and explain the influence on solubility of solvent and solute structure, temperature, and pressure.

2. How is the concentration of a solution expressed?

THE GOAL: Be able to define, use, and convert between the most common ways of expressing solution concentrations.

3. How are dilutions carried out?

THE GOAL: Be able to calculate the concentration of a solution prepared by dilution and explain how to make a desired dilution.

4. What is an electrolyte?

THE GOAL: Be able to recognize strong and weak electrolytes and nonelectrolytes, and express electrolyte concentrations.

5. How do solutions differ from pure solvents in their behavior?

THE GOAL: Be able to explain vapor pressure lowering, boiling point elevation, and freezing point depression for solutions.

6. What is osmosis?

THE GOAL: Be able to describe osmosis and some of its applications.

U p to this point, we have been concerned primarily with pure substances, both elements and compounds. In day-to-day life, however, most of the materials we come in contact with are mixtures. Air, for example, is a gaseous mixture of primarily oxygen and nitrogen; blood is a liquid mixture of many different components; and many rocks are solid mixtures of different minerals. In this chapter, we look closely at the characteristics and properties of mixtures, with particular attention to the uniform mixtures we call *solutions*.

9.1 Mixtures and Solutions

As we saw in Section 1.3, a *mixture* is an intimate combination of two or more substances, both of which retain their chemical identities. (⬤▭, p. 6) Mixtures can be classified as either *heterogeneous* or *homogeneous* as indicated in Figure 9.1, depending on their appearance. **Heterogeneous mixtures** are those in which the mixing is

Heterogeneous mixture A nonuniform mixture that has regions of different composition.

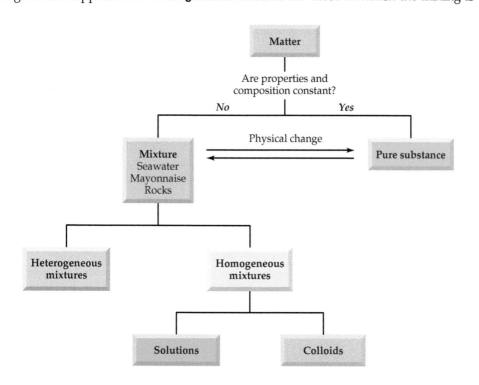

◄ **FIGURE 9.1 Classification of mixtures.** The components in heterogeneous mixtures are not uniformly mixed, and the composition varies with location. In homogeneous mixtures, the components are uniformly mixed at the molecular level.

not uniform and which therefore have regions of different composition. Rocky Road ice cream, for example, is a heterogeneous mixture, with something different in every spoonful. Granite and many other rocks are also heterogeneous, having a grainy character due to the heterogeneous mixing of different minerals. **Homogeneous mixtures** are those in which the mixing *is* uniform and that therefore have the same composition throughout. Seawater, a homogeneous mixture of soluble ionic compounds in water, is an example.

Homogeneous mixtures can be further classified as either *solutions* or *colloids* according to the size of their particles. **Solutions**, the most important class of homogeneous mixtures, contain particles the size of a typical ion or small molecule—roughly 0.1–2 nm in diameter. **Colloids**, such as milk and fog, are also homogeneous in appearance but contain larger particles than solutions—in the range 2–500 nm diameter.

Homogeneous mixture A uniform mixture that has the same composition throughout.

Solution A homogeneous mixture that contains particles the size of a typical ion or small molecule.

Colloid A homogeneous mixture that contains particles that range in diameter from 2 to 500 nm.

(a)

(b)

(c)

▲ (a) Wine is a solution of dissolved molecules, and (b) milk is a colloid with fine particles that do not separate out on standing. (c) An aerosol spray, by contrast, is a heterogeneous mixture of small particles visible to the naked eye.

Liquid solutions, colloids, and heterogeneous mixtures can be distinguished in several ways. For example, liquid solutions are transparent (although they may be colored). Colloids may appear transparent if the particle size is small, but they have a murky or opaque appearance if the particle size is larger. Neither solutions nor small-particle colloids separate on standing, and the particles in both are too small to be removed by filtration. Heterogeneous mixtures and large-particle colloids, also known as "suspensions," are murky and opaque and their particles will slowly settle on prolonged standing. House paint is an example.

Table 9.1 gives some examples of solutions, colloids, and heterogeneous mixtures. It is interesting to note that blood has characteristics of all three. About 45%

TABLE 9.1 Some Characteristics of Solutions, Colloids, and Heterogeneous Mixtures

TYPE OF MIXTURE	PARTICLE SIZE	EXAMPLES	CHARACTERISTICS
Solution	<2.0 nm	Air, seawater, gasoline, wine	Transparent to light; does not separate on standing; nonfilterable
Colloid	2.0–500 nm	Butter, milk, fog, pearl	Often murky or opaque to light; does not separate on standing; nonfilterable
Heterogeneous	>500 nm	Blood, paint, aerosol sprays	Murky or opaque to light; separates on standing; filterable

by volume of blood consists of suspended red and white cells, which settle slowly on standing; the remaining 55% is *plasma*, which contains ions in solution and colloidal protein molecules.

Although we usually think of solids dissolved in liquids when we talk about solutions, solutions actually occur in all three phases of matter (Table 9.2). Metal alloys like 14-karat gold (58% gold with silver and copper) and brass (10–40% zinc with copper), for instance, are solutions of one solid with another. For solutions in which a gas or solid is dissolved in a liquid, the dissolved substance is called the **solute** and the liquid is called the **solvent**. When one liquid is dissolved in another, the minor component is usually considered the solute and the major component is the solvent.

Solute A substance dissolved in a liquid.

Solvent The liquid in which another substance is dissolved.

TABLE 9.2 **Some Different Types of Solutions**

TYPE OF SOLUTION	EXAMPLE
Gas in gas	Air (O_2, N_2, Ar, and other gases)
Gas in liquid	Seltzer water (CO_2 in water)
Gas in solid	H_2 in palladium metal
Liquid in liquid	Gasoline (mixture of hydrocarbons)
Liquid in solid	Dental amalgam (mercury in silver)
Solid in liquid	Seawater (NaCl and other salts in water)
Solid in solid	Metal alloys such as 14-karat gold (Au, Ag, and Cu)

PROBLEM 9.1

Classify the following liquid mixtures as heterogeneous or homogeneous. Further classify each homogeneous mixture as a solution or colloid.

(a) Orange juice   (b) Apple juice

(c) Hand lotion   (d) Tea

9.2 The Solution Process

What determines whether a substance is soluble in a given liquid? Solubility depends primarily on the strength of the attractions between solute and solvent particles relative to the strengths of the attractions within the pure substances. Ethyl alcohol is soluble in water, for example, because hydrogen bonding (Section 8.11) is nearly as strong between water and ethyl alcohol molecules as it is between water molecules alone or ethyl alcohol molecules alone. (⊂⊃, p. 238)

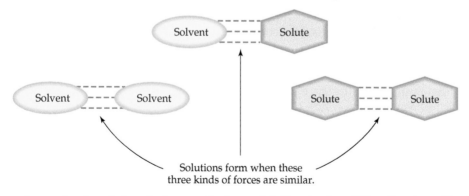

Solutions form when these
three kinds of forces are similar.

A good rule of thumb for predicting solubility is that "like dissolves like," meaning that substances with similar intermolecular forces form solutions with one another, whereas substances with different intermolecular forces do not (Section 8.11). (⊂⊃, p. 235)

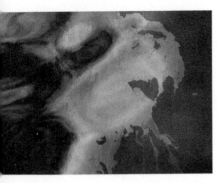

▲ Oil and water do not mix because they have different intermolecular forces, resulting in the formation of oil slicks.

Solvation The clustering of solvent molecules around a dissolved solute molecule or ion.

Polar solvents dissolve polar and ionic solutes; nonpolar solvents dissolve nonpolar solutes. Thus, a polar, hydrogen-bonding compound like water dissolves ethyl alcohol and sodium chloride, whereas a nonpolar organic compound like hexane (C_6H_{14}) dissolves other nonpolar organic compounds like fats and oils. Water and oil, however, do not dissolve one another, as summed up by the old saying, "Oil and water don't mix." The intermolecular forces between water molecules are so strong that after an oil–water mixture is shaken, the water layer re-forms, squeezing out the oil molecules.

Water solubility is not limited to ionic compounds and ethyl alcohol. Many polar organic substances, such as sugars, amino acids, and even some proteins, dissolve in water. In addition, small, moderately polar organic molecules such as chloroform ($CHCl_3$) are soluble in water to a limited extent. When mixed with water, a small amount of the organic compound dissolves, but the remainder forms a separate liquid layer. As the number of carbon atoms in organic molecules increases, though, water solubility decreases.

The process of dissolving an ionic solid in a polar liquid can be visualized as shown in Figure 9.2 for sodium chloride. When NaCl crystals are put in water, ions at the crystal surface come into contact with polar water molecules. Positively charged Na^+ ions are attracted to the negatively polarized oxygen of water, and negatively charged Cl^- ions are attracted to the positively polarized hydrogens. The combined forces of attraction between an ion and several water molecules pull the ion away from the crystal, exposing a fresh surface, until ultimately the crystal dissolves. Once in solution, Na^+ and Cl^- ions are completely surrounded by solvent molecules, a phenomenon called **solvation** (or, specifically for water, *hydration*). The water molecules form a loose shell around the ions, stabilizing them by electrical attraction.

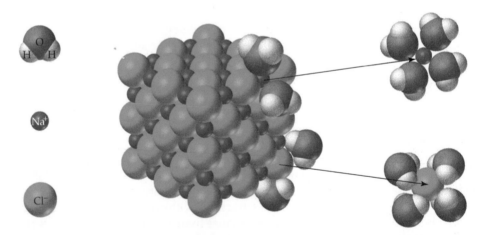

▲ **FIGURE 9.2 Dissolution of an NaCl crystal in water.** Polar water molecules surround the individual Na^+ and Cl^- ions at an exposed edge or corner, pulling them from the crystal surface into solution and surrounding them. Note how the negatively polarized oxygens of water molecules cluster around Na^+ ions and the positively polarized hydrogens cluster around Cl^- ions.

The dissolution of a solute in a solvent is a physical change since the solution components retain their chemical identities. Like all chemical and physical changes, the dissolution of a substance in a solvent has associated with it a heat change, or *enthalpy* change (Section 7.2). (◁◯◯▷, p. 184) Some substances dissolve exothermically, releasing heat and warming the resultant solution, whereas other substances dissolve endothermically, absorbing heat and cooling the resultant solution. Calcium chloride, for example, *releases* 19.4 kcal/mol of heat energy when it dissolves in water, but ammonium nitrate (NH_4NO_3) *absorbs* 6.1 kcal/mol of heat energy. Athletes and others take advantage of both situations when they use instant hot packs or cold packs to treat injuries. Both hot and cold packs consist of a pouch of water and a dry chemical, such as $CaCl_2$ or $MgSO_4$ for hot packs and NH_4NO_3 for cold packs. Squeezing the pack breaks the pouch and the solid dissolves, either raising or lowering the temperature.

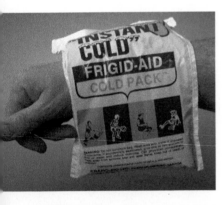

▲ Instant cold packs used to treat muscle strains and sprains often take advantage of the endothermic enthalpy of a solution of salts such as ammonium nitrate.

WORKED EXAMPLE **9.1** Formation of Solutions

Which of the following pairs of substances would you expect to form solutions?

    (a) Carbon tetrachloride (CCl_4) and hexane (C_6H_{14}).

    (b) Octane (C_8H_{18}) and methyl alcohol (CH_3OH).

ANALYSIS Identify the kinds of intermolecular forces in each substance (Section 8.11). Substances with similar intermolecular forces tend to form solutions.

SOLUTION

    (a) Hexane contains only C—H and C—C bonds, which are nonpolar. Carbon tetrachloride contains polar C—Cl bonds, but they are distributed symmetrically in the tetrahedral molecule so that it too is nonpolar. The major intermolecular force for both compounds is London dispersion forces, so they will form a solution.

    (b) Octane contains only C—H and C—C bonds and so is nonpolar; the major intermolecular force is dispersion. Methyl alcohol contains polar C—O and O—H bonds; it is polar and forms hydrogen bonds. The intermolecular forces for the two substances are so dissimilar that they do not form a solution.

PROBLEM 9.2

Which of the following pairs of substances would you expect to form solutions?

(a) CCl_4 and water

(b) Benzene (C_6H_6) and $MgSO_4$

(c) Hexane (C_6H_{14}) and heptane (C_7H_{16})

(d) Ethyl alcohol (C_2H_5OH) and heptanol ($C_7H_{15}OH$)

Hygroscopic Having the ability to pull water molecules from the surrounding atmosphere.

9.3 Solid Hydrates

Some ionic compounds attract water strongly enough to hold onto water molecules even when crystalline, forming what are called *solid hydrates*. For example, the plaster of Paris used to make decorative objects and casts for broken limbs is calcium sulfate hemihydrate, $CaSO_4 \cdot \frac{1}{2}H_2O$. The dot between $CaSO_4$ and $\frac{1}{2}H_2O$ in the formula indicates that for every two $CaSO_4$ formula units in the crystal there is also one water molecule present.

$$CaSO_4 \cdot \tfrac{1}{2}H_2O \quad \text{A solid hydrate}$$

After being ground up and mixed with water to make plaster, $CaSO_4 \cdot \frac{1}{2}H_2O$ gradually changes into the crystalline dihydrate $CaSO_4 \cdot 2\,H_2O$, known as *gypsum*. During the change, the plaster hardens and expands in volume, causing it to fill a mold or shape itself closely around a broken limb. Table 9.3 lists some other ionic compounds that are handled primarily as hydrates.

Still other ionic compounds attract water so strongly that they pull water vapor from humid air to become hydrated. Compounds that show this behavior, such as calcium chloride ($CaCl_2$), are called **hygroscopic** and are often used as drying agents. You might have noticed a small bag of a hygroscopic compound (probably silica gel, SiO_2) included in the packing material of a new MP3 player, camera, or other electronic device to keep humidity low during shipping.

▲ Plaster of Paris ($CaSO_4 \cdot \frac{1}{2}H_2O$) slowly turns into gypsum ($CaSO_4 \cdot 2\,H_2O$) when added to water. In so doing, the plaster hardens and expands, causing it to fill a mold.

TABLE 9.3   Some Common Solid Hydrates

FORMULA	NAME	USES
$AlCl_3 \cdot 6\,H_2O$	Aluminum chloride hexahydrate	Antiperspirant
$CaSO_4 \cdot 2\,H_2O$	Calcium sulfate dihydrate (gypsum)	Cements, wallboard molds
$CaSO_4 \cdot \frac{1}{2}H_2O$	Calcium sulfate hemihydrate (plaster of Paris)	Casts, molds
$CuSO_4 \cdot 5\,H_2O$	Copper(II) sulfate pentahydrate (blue vitriol)	Pesticide, germicide, topical fungicide
$MgSO_4 \cdot 7\,H_2O$	Magnesium sulfate heptahydrate (epsom salts)	Laxative, anticonvulsant
$Na_2B_4O_7 \cdot 10\,H_2O$	Sodium tetraborate decahydrate (borax)	Cleaning compounds, fireproofing agent
$Na_2S_2O_3 \cdot 5\,H_2O$	Sodium thiosulfate pentahydrate (hypo)	Photographic fixer

PROBLEM 9.3

Write the formula of sodium sulfate decahydrate, known as Glauber's salt and used as a laxative.

PROBLEM 9.4

What masses of Glauber's salt must be used to provide 1.00 mol of sodium sulfate?

9.4 Solubility

We saw in Section 9.2 that ethyl alcohol is soluble in water because hydrogen bonding is nearly as strong between water and ethyl alcohol molecules as it is between water molecules alone or ethyl alcohol molecules alone. So similar are the forces in this particular case, in fact, that the two liquids are **miscible**, or mutually soluble in all proportions. Ethyl alcohol will continue to dissolve in water no matter how much is added.

Miscible   Mutually soluble in all proportions.

Most substances, however, reach a solubility limit beyond which no more will dissolve in solution. Imagine, for instance that you are asked to prepare a saline solution (aqueous NaCl). You might measure out some water, add solid NaCl, and stir the mixture. Dissolution occurs rapidly at first but then slows down as more and more NaCl is added. Eventually the dissolution stops because an equilibrium is reached when the numbers of Na^+ and Cl^- ions leaving a crystal and going into solution are equal to the numbers of ions returning from solution to the crystal. At this point, the solution is said to be **saturated**. A maximum of 35.8 g of NaCl will dissolve in 100 mL of water at 20 °C. Any amount above this limit simply sinks to the bottom of the container and sits there.

Saturated solution   A solution that contains the maximum amount of dissolved solute at equilibrium.

The equilibrium reached by a saturated solution is like the equilibrium reached by a reversible reaction (Section 7.7). (, p. 198) Both are dynamic situations in which no *apparent* change occurs because the rates of forward and backward processes are equal. Solute particles leave the solid surface and reenter the solid from solution at the same rate.

$$\text{Solid solute} \underset{\text{Crystallize}}{\overset{\text{Dissolve}}{\rightleftharpoons}} \text{Solution}$$

Solubility   The maximum amount of a substance that will dissolve in a given amount of solvent at a specified temperature.

The maximum amount of a substance that will dissolve in a given amount of solvent at a given temperature, usually expressed in grams per 100 mL (g/100 mL), is called the substance's **solubility**. Solubility is a characteristic property of a specific solute–solvent combination, and different substances have greatly differing solubilities. Only 9.6 g of sodium hydrogen carbonate will dissolve in 100 mL of water at 20 °C, for instance, but 204 g of sucrose will dissolve under the same conditions.

9.5 The Effect of Temperature on Solubility

As anyone who has ever made tea or coffee knows, temperature often has a dramatic effect on solubility. The compounds in tea leaves or coffee beans, for instance, dissolve easily in hot water but not in cold water. The effect of temperature is different for every substance, however, and is usually unpredictable. As shown in Figure 9.3(a), the solubilities of most molecular and ionic solids increase with increasing temperature, but the solubilities of others (NaCl) are almost unchanged, and the solubilities of still others $[Ce_2(SO_4)_3]$ decrease with increasing temperature.

Solids that are more soluble at high temperature than at low temperature can sometimes form what are called **supersaturated solutions**, which contain even more solute than a saturated solution. Suppose, for instance, that a large amount of a substance is dissolved at a high temperature. As the solution cools, the solubility decreases and the excess solute should precipitate to maintain equilibrium. But if

Supersaturated solution A solution that contains more than the maximum amount of dissolved solute; a nonequilibrium situation.

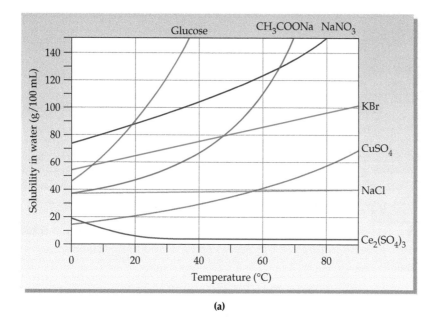

(a)

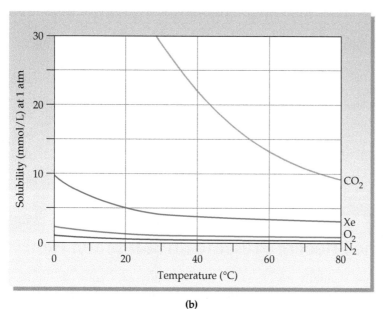

(b)

◀ **FIGURE 9.3 Solubilities of some (a) solids and (b) gases, in water as a function of temperature.** Most solid substances become more soluble as temperature rises (although the exact relationship is usually complex), while the solubility of gases decreases.

▲ **FIGURE 9.4 A supersaturated solution of sodium acetate in water.** When a tiny seed crystal is added, larger crystals rapidly grow and precipitate from the solution until equilibrium is reached.

the cooling is done very slowly, and if the container stands quietly, crystallization might not occur immediately and a supersaturated solution might result. Such a solution is unstable, however, and precipitation can occur dramatically when a tiny seed crystal is added to initiate crystallization (Figure 9.4).

Unlike solids, the influence of temperature on the solubility of gases *is* predictable: Addition of heat decreases the solubility of most gases, as seen in Figure 9.3(b) (helium is the only common exception). One result of this temperature-dependent decrease in gas solubility can sometimes be noted in a stream or lake near the outflow of warm water from an industrial operation. As water temperature increases, the concentration of dissolved oxygen in the water decreases, killing fish that cannot tolerate the lower oxygen levels.

WORKED EXAMPLE **9.2** Solubility of Gases: Effect of Temperature

From the following graph of solubility versus temperature for O_2, estimate the concentration of dissolved oxygen in water at 25 °C and at 35 °C. By what percentage does the concentration of O_2 change?

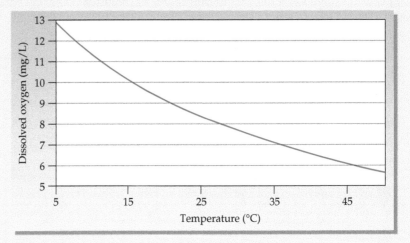

ANALYSIS The solubility of O_2 (on the *y*-axis) can be determined by finding the appropriate temperature (on the *x*-axis) and extrapolating. The percent change is calculated as

$$\frac{(\text{Solubility at 25 °C}) - (\text{Solubility at 35 °C})}{(\text{Solubility at 25 °C})} \times 100$$

SOLUTION

From the graph we estimate that the solubility of O_2 at 25 °C is approximately 8.3 mg/L and at 35 °C is 7.0 mg/L. The percent change in solubility is

$$\frac{8.3 - 7.0}{8.3} \times 100 = 16\%$$

PROBLEM 9.5

Look at the graph of solubility versus temperature in Figure 9.3, and estimate the solubility of KBr in water at 50 °C in g/100 mL.

9.6 The Effect of Pressure on Solubility: Henry's Law

Pressure has virtually no effect on the solubility of a solid or liquid, but it has a strong effect on the solubility of a gas. According to **Henry's law**, the solubility (or concentration) of a gas in a liquid is directly proportional to the partial pressure

(a) Equilibrium   (b) Pressure increase   (c) Equilibrium restored

◀ **FIGURE 9.5 Henry's law.** The solubility of a gas is directly proportional to its partial pressure. An increase in pressure causes more gas molecules to enter solution until equilibrium is restored between the dissolved and undissolved gas.

of the gas over the liquid. (Recall from Section 8.10 that each gas in a mixture exerts a partial pressure independent of other gases present (⬤⬤, p. 233). If the partial pressure of the gas doubles, solubility doubles; if the gas pressure is halved, solubility is halved (Figure 9.5).

Henry's law The solubility (or concentration) of a gas is directly proportional to the partial pressure of the gas if the temperature is constant. That is, concentration (C) divided by pressure (P) is constant when T is constant,

or $\dfrac{C}{P_{gas}} = k$ (At a constant temperature)

Henry's law can be explained using Le Châtelier's principle (Section 7.9), which states that when a system at equilibrium is placed under stress, the equilibrium shifts to relieve that stress. (⬤⬤, p. 203) In the case of a saturated solution of a gas in a liquid, an equilibrium exists whereby gas molecules enter and leave the solution at the same rate. When the system is stressed by increasing the pressure of the gas, more gas molecules go into solution to relieve that increase. Conversely, when the pressure of the gas is decreased, more gas molecules come out of solution to relieve the decrease.

$$[\text{Pressure} \longrightarrow]$$
$$\text{Gas} + \text{Solvent} \rightleftharpoons \text{Solution}$$

As an example of Henry's law in action, think about the fizzing that occurs when you open a bottle of soft drink or champagne. The bottle is sealed under greater than 1 atm of CO_2 pressure, causing some of the CO_2 to dissolve. When the bottle is opened, however, CO_2 pressure drops and gas comes fizzing out of solution.

Writing Henry's law in the form $P_{gas} = C/k$ shows that partial pressure can be used to express the concentration of a gas in a solution, a practice especially common in health-related sciences. Table 9.4 gives some typical values and illustrates the convenience of having the same unit for concentration of a gas in both air and blood.

TABLE 9.4 Partial Pressures and Normal Gas Concentrations in Body Fluids

SAMPLE	PARTIAL PRESSURE (mmHg)			
	P_{N_2}	P_{O_2}	P_{CO_2}	P_{H_2O}
Inspired air (dry)	597	159	0.3	3.7
Alveolar air (saturated)	573	100	40	47
Expired air (saturated)	569	116	28	47
Arterial blood	573	95	40	
Venous blood	573	40	45	
Peripheral tissues	573	40	45	

▲ The CO_2 gas dissolved under pressure comes out of solution when the bottle is opened and the pressure drops.

Compare the oxygen partial pressures in saturated alveolar air (air in the lungs) and in arterial blood, for instance. The values are almost the same because the gases dissolved in blood come to equilibrium with the same gases in the lungs.

If the partial pressure of a gas over a solution changes while the temperature is constant, the new solubility of the gas can be found easily. Because C/P is a constant value at constant temperature, Henry's law can be restated to show how one variable changes if the other changes:

$$\frac{C_1}{P_1} = \frac{C_2}{P_2} = k \quad \text{(Where } k \text{ is constant at a fixed temperature)}$$

Worked Example 9.3 gives an illustration of how to use this equation.

WORKED EXAMPLE **9.3** Solubility of Gases: Henry's Law

At a partial pressure of oxygen in the atmosphere of 159 mmHg, the solubility of oxygen in blood is 0.44 g/100 mL. What is the solubility of oxygen in blood at 11,000 ft, where the partial pressure of O_2 is 56 mmHg?

ANALYSIS According to Henry's law, the solubility of the gas divided by its pressure is constant:

$$\frac{C_1}{P_1} = \frac{C_2}{P_2}$$

Of the four variables in this equation, we know P_1, C_1, and P_2, and we need to find C_2.

BALLPARK ESTIMATE The pressure drops by a factor of about 3 (from 159 mmHg to 56 mmHg). Since the ratio of solubility to pressure is constant, the solubility must also drop by a factor of 3 (from 0.44 g/100 mL to about 0.15 g/100 mL).

SOLUTION

STEP 1: **Identify known information.** We have values for P_1, C_1, and P_2.

$P_1 = 159$ mmHg

$C_1 = 0.44$ g/100 mL

$P_2 = 56$ mmHg

STEP 2: **Identify answer and units.** We are looking for the solubility of O_2 (C_2) at a partial pressure P_2.

Solubility of O_2, C_2 = ?? g/100 mL

STEP 3: **Identify conversion factors or equations.** In this case, we restate Henry's law to solve for C_2.

$$\frac{C_1}{P_1} = \frac{C_2}{P_2} \Rightarrow C_2 = \frac{C_1 P_2}{P_1}$$

STEP 4: **Solve.** Substitute the known values into the equation and calculate C_2.

$$C_2 = \frac{C_1 P_2}{P_1} = \frac{(0.44 \text{ g}/100 \text{ mL})(56 \text{ mmHg})}{159 \text{ mmHg}} = 0.15 \text{ g}/100 \text{ mL}$$

BALLPARK CHECK: The calculated answer matches our estimate.

PROBLEM 9.6

At 20 °C and a partial pressure of 760 mmHg, the solubility of CO_2 in water is 0.169 g/100 mL. What is the solubility of CO_2 at 2.5×10^4 mmHg?

PROBLEM 9.7

At a total atmospheric pressure of 1.00 atm, the partial pressure of CO_2 in air is approximately 4.0×10^{-4} atm. Using the data in Problem 9.6, what is the solubility of CO_2 in an open bottle of seltzer water at 20 °C?

9.7 Units of Concentration

Although we speak casually of a solution of, say, orange juice as either "dilute" or "concentrated," laboratory work usually requires an exact knowledge of a solution's concentration. As indicated in Table 9.5, there are several common methods for expressing concentration. The units differ, but all the methods describe how much solute is present in a given quantity of solution.

TABLE 9.5 Some Units for Expressing Concentration

CONCENTRATION MEASURE	SOLUTE MEASURE	SOLUTION MEASURE
Molarity, M	Moles	Volume (L)
Weight/volume percent, (w/v)%	Weight (g)	Volume (mL)
Volume/volume percent, (v/v)%	Volume*	Volume*
Parts per million, ppm	Parts*	10^6 parts*

Any units can be used as long as they are the same for both solute and solution.

Let us look at each of the four concentration measures listed in Table 9.5 individually, beginning with *molarity*.

Mole/Volume Concentration: Molarity

We saw in Chapter 6 that the various relationships between amounts of reactants and products in chemical reactions are calculated in *moles* (Sections 6.4–6.6). Thus, the most generally useful means of expressing concentration in the laboratory is **molarity (M)**, the number of moles of solute dissolved per liter of solution. For example, a solution made by dissolving 1.00 mol (58.5 g) of NaCl in enough water to give 1.00 L of solution has a concentration of 1.00 mol/L, or 1.00 M. The molarity of any solution is found by dividing the number of moles of solute by the number of liters of solution (solute + solvent):

$$\text{Molarity (M)} = \frac{\text{Moles of solute}}{\text{Liters of solution}}$$

Note that a solution of a given molarity is prepared by dissolving the solute in enough solvent to give a *final* solution volume of 1.00 L, not by dissolving it in an *initial* volume of 1.00 L. If an initial volume of 1.00 L were used, the final solution volume might be a bit larger than 1.00 L because of the additional volume of the solute. In practice, the appropriate amount of solute is weighed and placed in a *volumetric flask*, as shown in Figure 9.6. Enough solvent is then added to dissolve the solute, and further solvent is added until an accurately calibrated final volume is reached. The solution is then shaken until it is uniformly mixed.

(a)

(b)

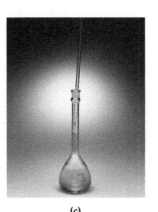
(c)

◀ **FIGURE 9.6 Preparing a solution of known molarity.** (a) A measured number of moles of solute is placed in a volumetric flask. (b) Enough solvent is added to dissolve the solute by swirling. (c) Further solvent is carefully added until the calibration mark on the neck of the flask is reached, and the solution is shaken until uniform.

APPLICATION ▶   Breathing and Oxygen Transport

Like all other animals, humans need oxygen. When we breathe, the freshly inspired air travels through the bronchial passages and into the lungs. The oxygen then diffuses through the delicate walls of the approximately 150 million alveolar sacs of the lungs and into arterial blood, which transports it to all body tissues.

Only about 3% of the oxygen in blood is dissolved; the rest is chemically bound to *hemoglobin* molecules, large proteins with *heme* groups embedded in them. Each hemoglobin molecule contains four heme groups, and each heme group contains an iron atom that is able to bind one O_2 molecule. Thus, a single hemoglobin molecule can bind up to four molecules of oxygen. The entire system of oxygen transport and delivery in the body depends on the pickup and release of O_2 by hemoglobin (Hb) according to the following series of equilibria:

$$O_2(\text{lungs}) \rightleftharpoons O_2(\text{blood}) \quad (\text{Henry's law})$$

$$Hb + 4\,O_2(\text{blood}) \rightleftharpoons Hb(O_2)_4$$

$$Hb(O_2)_4 \rightleftharpoons Hb + 4\,O_2 \quad (\text{cell})$$

The delivery of oxygen depends on the concentration of O_2 in the various tissues, as measured by partial pressure (P_{O_2}, Table 9.4). The amount of oxygen carried by hemoglobin at any given value of P_{O_2} is usually expressed as a percent saturation and can be found from the curve shown in the accompanying figure. When $P_{O_2} = 100$ mmHg, the saturation in the lungs is 97.5%, meaning that each hemoglobin is carrying close to its maximum of four O_2 molecules. When $P_{O_2} = 26$ mmHg, however, the saturation drops to 50%.

So, how does the body ensure that enough oxygen is available to the various tissues? When large amounts of oxygen are needed—during a strenuous workout, for example—oxygen is released from hemoglobin to the hardworking, oxygen-starved muscle cells, where P_{O_2} is low. Increasing the

▲ At high altitudes, the partial pressure of oxygen in the air is too low to saturate hemoglobin sufficiently. Additional oxygen is therefore needed.

supply of oxygen to the blood (by breathing harder and faster) shifts all the equilibria toward the right, according to Le Châtelier's principle (Section 7.9), to supply the additional O_2 needed by the muscles.

What about people living at high altitudes? In Leadville, CO, for example, where the altitude is 10,156 ft, the P_{O_2} in the lungs is only about 68 mmHg. Hemoglobin is only 90% saturated with O_2 at this pressure, meaning that less oxygen is available for delivery to the tissues. The body responds by producing erythropoietin (EPO), a hormone (Chapter 20) that stimulates the bone marrow to produce more red blood cells and hemoglobin molecules. The increase in Hb provides more capacity for O_2 transport and drives the Hb + O_2 equilibria to the right.

World-class athletes use the mechanisms of increased oxygen transport associated with higher levels of hemoglobin to enhance their performance. High-altitude training centers have sprung up, with living and training regimens designed to increase blood EPO levels. Unfortunately, some athletes have also tried to "cheat" by using injections of EPO and synthetic analogs, and "blood doping" to boost performance. This has led the governing bodies of many sports federations, including the Olympic Committee, to start testing for such abuse.

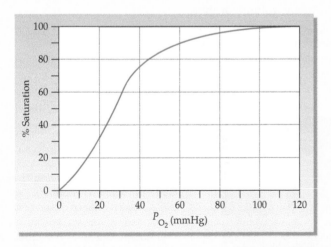

▲ An oxygen-carrying curve for hemoglobin. The percent saturation of the oxygen binding sites on hemoglobin depends on the partial pressure of oxygen (P_{O_2}).

See Additional Problem 9.92 at the end of the chapter.

Molarity can be used as a conversion factor to relate the volume of a solution to the number of moles of solute it contains. If we know the molarity and volume of a solution, we can calculate the number of moles of solute. If we know the number of moles of solute and the molarity of the solution, we can find the solution's volume.

$$\text{Molarity} = \frac{\text{Moles of solute}}{\text{Volume of solution (L)}}$$

$$\text{Moles of solute} = \text{Molarity} \times \text{Volume of solution}$$

$$\text{Volume of solution} = \frac{\text{Moles of solute}}{\text{Molarity}}$$

The flow diagram in Figure 9.7 shows how molarity is used in calculating the quantities of reactants or products in a chemical reaction, and Worked Examples 9.5 and 9.6 show how the calculations are done. Note that Problem 9.10 employs *millimolar* (mM) concentrations, which are useful in healthcare fields for expressing low concentrations such as are often found in body fluids (1 mM = 0.001 M).

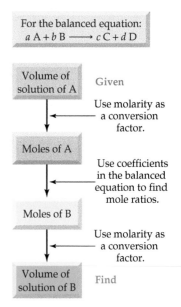

For the balanced equation:
$$a\,A + b\,B \longrightarrow c\,C + d\,D$$

Volume of solution of A — Given

Use molarity as a conversion factor.

Moles of A

Use coefficients in the balanced equation to find mole ratios.

Moles of B

Use molarity as a conversion factor.

Volume of solution of B — Find

▶ **FIGURE 9.7 Molarity and conversions.** A flow diagram summarizing the use of molarity for conversions between solution volume and moles to find quantities of reactants and products for chemical reactions in solution.

WORKED EXAMPLE **9.4** Solution Concentration: Molarity

What is the molarity of a solution made by dissolving 2.355 g of sulfuric acid (H_2SO_4) in water and diluting to a final volume of 50.0 mL? The molar mass of H_2SO_4 is 98.1 g/mol.

ANALYSIS Molarity is defined as moles of solute per liter of solution: M = mol/L. Thus, we must first find the number of moles of sulfuric acid by doing a mass to mole conversion, and then divide the number of moles by the volume of the solution.

BALLPARK ESTIMATE The molar mass of sulfuric acid is about 100 g/mol, so 2.355 g is roughly 0.025 mol. The volume of the solution is 50.0 mL, or 0.05 L, so we have about 0.025 mol of acid in 0.05 L of solution, which is a concentration of about 0.5 M.

SOLUTION

STEP 1: **Identify known information.** We know the mass of sulfuric acid and the final volume of solution.

Mass of H_2SO_4 = 2.355 g

Volume of solution = 50.0 mL

STEP 2: **Identify answer including units.** We need to find the molarity (M) in units of moles per liter.

STEP 3: **Identify conversion factors and equations.** We know both the amount of solute and the volume of solution, but first we must make two conversions: convert mass of H_2SO_4 to moles of H_2SO_4, using molar mass as a conversion factor, and convert volume from milliliters to liters:

$$\text{Molarity} = \frac{\text{Moles } H_2SO_4}{\text{Liters of solution}}$$

$$(2.355 \text{ g } H_2SO_4)\left(\frac{1 \text{ mol } H_2SO_4}{98.1 \text{ g } H_2SO_4}\right) = 0.0240 \text{ mol } H_2SO_4$$

$$(50.0 \text{ mL})\left(\frac{1 \text{ L}}{1000 \text{ mL}}\right) = 0.0500 \text{ L}$$

STEP 4: **Solve.** Substitute the moles of solute and volume of solution into the molarity expression.

$$\text{Molarity} = \frac{0.0240 \text{ mol } H_2SO_4}{0.0500 \text{ L}} = 0.480 \text{ M}$$

BALLPARK CHECK: The calculated answer is close to our estimate, which was 0.5 M.

WORKED EXAMPLE **9.5** Molarity as Conversion Factor: Molarity to Mass

A blood concentration of 0.065 M ethyl alcohol (EtOH) is sufficient to induce a coma. At this concentration, what is the total mass of alcohol (in grams) in an adult male whose total blood volume is 5.6 L? The molar mass of ethyl alcohol is 46.0 g/mol. (Refer to the flow diagram in Figure 9.7 to identify which conversions are needed.)

ANALYSIS We are given a molarity (0.065 M) and a volume (5.6 L), which allows us to calculate the number of moles of alcohol in the blood. A mole to mass conversion then gives the mass of alcohol.

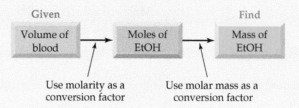

SOLUTION

$$(5.6 \text{ L blood})\left(\frac{0.065 \text{ mol EtOH}}{1 \text{ L blood}}\right) = 0.36 \text{ mol EtOH}$$

$$(0.36 \text{ mol EtOH})\left(\frac{46.0 \text{ g EtOH}}{1 \text{ mol EtOH}}\right) = 17 \text{ g EtOH}$$

WORKED EXAMPLE **9.6** Molarity as Conversion Factor: Molarity to Volume

In our stomachs, gastric juice that is about 0.1 M in HCl aids in digestion. How many milliliters of gastric juice will react completely with an antacid tablet that contains 500 mg of magnesium hydroxide? The molar mass of $Mg(OH)_2$ is 58.3 g/mol, and the balanced equation is

$$2 \text{ HCl}(aq) + \text{Mg(OH)}_2(aq) \longrightarrow \text{MgCl}_2(aq) + 2 \text{ H}_2\text{O}(l)$$

ANALYSIS We are given the molarity of HCl and need to find the volume. We first convert the mass of $Mg(OH)_2$ to moles and then use the coefficients in the balanced equation to find the moles of HCl that will react. Once we have the moles of HCl and the molarity in moles per liter, we can find the volume. These conversions are summarized in the following flow diagram.

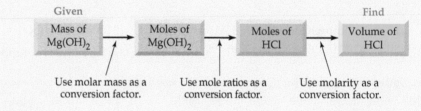

SOLUTION

$$[500 \text{ mg Mg(OH)}_2]\left(\frac{1 \text{ g}}{1000 \text{ mg}}\right)\left[\frac{1 \text{ mol Mg(OH)}_2}{58.3 \text{ g Mg(OH)}_2}\right] = 0.008\ 58 \text{ mol Mg(OH)}_2$$

$$[0.008\ 58 \text{ mol Mg(OH)}_2]\left[\frac{2 \text{ mol HCl}}{1 \text{ mol Mg(OH)}_2}\right]\left(\frac{1 \text{ L HCl}}{0.1 \text{ mol HCl}}\right) = 0.2 \text{ L (200 mL)}$$

PROBLEM 9.8

What is the molarity of a solution that contains 50.0 g of vitamin B_1 hydrochloride (molar mass = 337 g/mol) in 160 mL of solution?

PROBLEM 9.9

How many moles of solute are present in the following solutions?

(a) 175 mL of 0.35 M $NaNO_3$ **(b)** 480 mL of 1.4 M HNO_3

PROBLEM 9.10

The concentration of cholesterol ($C_{27}H_{46}O$) in blood is approximately 5.0 mM. How many grams of cholesterol are in 250 mL of blood?

PROBLEM 9.11

What mass (in grams) of calcium carbonate is needed to react completely with 65 mL of 0.12 M HCl according to the following equation?

$$2\,HCl(aq) + CaCO_3(aq) \longrightarrow CaCl_2(aq) + H_2O(l) + CO_2(g)$$

Weight/Volume Percent Concentration, (w/v)%

One of the most common methods for expressing percent concentration is to give the number of grams (weight) as a percentage of the number of milliliters (volume) of the final solution—called the **weight/volume percent concentration, (w/v)%.** Mathematically, (w/v)% concentration is found by taking the number of grams of solute per milliliter of solution and multiplying by 100%:

$$(w/v)\%\ \text{concentration} = \frac{\text{Mass of solute (g)}}{\text{Volume of solution (mL)}} \times 100\%$$

For example, if 15 g of glucose is dissolved in enough water to give 100 mL of solution, the glucose concentration is 15 g/100 mL or 15% (w/v):

$$\frac{15\ \text{g glucose}}{100\ \text{mL solution}} \times 100\% = 15\%\ (w/v)$$

To prepare 100 mL of a specific weight/volume solution, the weighed solute is dissolved in just enough solvent to give a final volume of 100 mL, not in an initial volume of 100 mL solvent. (If the solute is dissolved in 100 mL of *solvent*, the final volume of the *solution* will likely be a bit larger than 100 mL, since the volume of the solute is included.) In practice, solutions are prepared using a volumetric flask, as shown previously in Figure 9.5. Worked Example 9.7 illustrates how weight/volume percent concentration is found from a known mass and volume of solution.

> **WORKED EXAMPLE** **9.7** Solution Concentration: Weight/Volume Percent
>
> A solution of heparin sodium, an anticoagulant for blood, contains 1.8 g of heparin sodium dissolved to make a final volume of 15 mL of solution. What is the weight/volume percent concentration of this solution?
>
> ANALYSIS Weight/volume percent concentration is defined as the mass of the solute in grams divided by the volume of solution in milliliters and multiplied by 100%.
>
> BALLPARK ESTIMATE The mass of solute (1.8 g) is smaller than the volume of solvent (15 mL) by a little less than a factor of 10. The weight/volume percent should thus be a little greater than 10%.
>
> SOLUTION
>
> $$(w/v)\%\ \text{concentration} = \frac{1.8\ \text{g heparin sodium}}{15\ \text{mL}} \times 100\% = 12\%\ (w/v)$$
>
> BALLPARK CHECK: The calculated (w/v)% is reasonably close to our original estimate of 10%.

WORKED EXAMPLE **9.8** Weight/Volume Percent as Conversion Factor: Volume to Mass

How many grams of NaCl are needed to prepare 250 mL of a 1.5% (w/v) saline solution?

ANALYSIS We are given a concentration and a volume, and we need to find the mass of solute by rearranging the equation for (w/v)% concentration.

BALLPARK ESTIMATE The desired (w/v)% value, 1.5%, is between 1 and 2%. For a volume of 250 mL, we would need 2.5 g of solute for a 1% (w/v) solution and 5.0 g of solute for a 2% solution. Thus, for our 1.5% solution, we need a mass midway between 2.5 and 5.0 g, or about 3.8 g.

SOLUTION

$$\text{Since} \quad (w/v)\% = \frac{\text{Mass of solute in g}}{\text{Volume of solution in mL}} \times 100\%$$

$$\text{then} \quad \text{Mass of solute in g} = \frac{(\text{Volume of solution in mL})[(w/v)]\%}{100\%}$$

$$= \frac{(250)(1.5\%)}{100\%} = 3.75 \text{ g} = 3.8 \text{ g NaCl}$$

$$\text{(2 significant figures)}$$

BALLPARK CHECK: The calculated answer matches our estimate.

WORKED EXAMPLE **9.9** Weight/Volume Percent as Conversion Factor: Mass to Volume

How many milliliters of a 0.75% (w/v) solution of the food preservative sodium benzoate are needed to obtain 45 mg?

ANALYSIS We are given a concentration and a mass, and we need to find the volume of solution by rearranging the equation for (w/v)% concentration. Remember that 45 mg = 0.045 g.

BALLPARK ESTIMATE A 0.75% (w/v) solution contains 0.75 g (750 mg) for every 100 mL of solution, so 10 mL contains 75 mg. To obtain 45 mg, we need a little more than half this volume, or a little more than 5 mL.

SOLUTION

$$\text{Since} \quad (w/v)\% = \frac{\text{Mass of solute in g}}{\text{Volume of solution in mL}} \times 100\%$$

$$\text{then} \quad \text{Volume of solution in mL} = \frac{(\text{Mass of solute in g})(100\%)}{(w/v)\%}$$

$$= \frac{(0.045 \text{ g})(100\%)}{0.75\%} = 6.0 \text{ mL}$$

BALLPARK CHECK: The calculated answer is consistent with our estimate of a little more than 5 mL.

PROBLEM 9.12

In clinical lab reports, some concentrations are given in mg/dL. Convert a Ca^{2+} concentration of 8.6 mg/dL to weight/volume percent.

PROBLEM 9.13

What is the weight/volume percent concentration of a solution that contains 23 g of potassium iodide in 350 mL of aqueous solution?

PROBLEM 9.14

How many grams of solute are needed to prepare the following solutions?

(a) 125.0 mL of 16% (w/v) glucose ($C_6H_{12}O_6$)
(b) 65 mL of 1.8% (w/v) KCl

Volume/Volume Percent Concentration, (v/v)%

The concentration of a solution made by dissolving one liquid in another is often given by expressing the volume of solute as a percentage of the volume of final solution—the **volume/volume percent concentration, (v/v)%**. Mathematically, the volume of the solute (usually in milliliters) per milliliter of solution is multiplied by 100%:

$$(\text{v/v})\% \text{ concentration} = \frac{\text{Volume of solute (mL)}}{\text{Volume of solution (mL)}} \times 100\%$$

For example, if 10.0 mL of ethyl alcohol is dissolved in enough water to give 100.0 mL of solution, the ethyl alcohol concentration is (10.0 mL/100.0 mL) × 100% = 10.0% (v/v).

WORKED EXAMPLE   **9.10** Volume Percent: Volume of Solution to Volume of Solute

How many milliliters of methyl alcohol are needed to prepare 75 mL of a 5.0% (v/v) solution?

ANALYSIS We are given a solution volume (75 mL) and a concentration [5.0% (v/v), meaning 5.0 mL solute/100 mL solution]. The concentration acts as a conversion factor for finding the amount of methyl alcohol needed.

BALLPARK ESTIMATE A 5% (v/v) solution contains 5 mL of solute in 100 mL of solution, so the amount of solute in 75 mL of solution must be about three-fourths of 5 mL, which means between 3 and 4 mL.

SOLUTION

$$(75 \text{ mL solution})\left(\frac{5.0 \text{ mL methyl alcohol}}{100 \text{ mL solution}}\right) = 3.8 \text{ mL methyl alcohol}$$

BALLPARK CHECK: The calculated answer is consistent with our estimate of between 3 and 4 mL.

PROBLEM 9.15

How would you use a 500.0 mL volumetric flask to prepare a 7.5% (v/v) solution of acetic acid in water?

PROBLEM 9.16

What volume of solute (in milliliters) is needed to prepare the following solutions?

(a) 100 mL of 22% (v/v) ethyl alcohol   **(b)** 150 mL of 12% (v/v) acetic acid

Parts per Million (ppm)

The concentration units weight/volume percent, (w/v)%, and volume/volume percent, (v/v)%, can also be defined as *parts per hundred*(pph) since 1% means one item per 100 items. When concentrations are very small, as often occurs in dealing with trace amounts of pollutants or contaminants, it is more convenient to use **parts per million (ppm)** or **parts per billion (ppb)**. The "parts" can be in any unit of either mass or volume as long as the units of both solute and solvent are the same:

$$\text{ppm} = \frac{\text{Mass of solute (g)}}{\text{Mass of solution (g)}} \times 10^6 \quad \text{or} \quad \frac{\text{Volume of solute (mL)}}{\text{Volume of solution (mL)}} \times 10^6$$

$$\text{ppb} = \frac{\text{Mass of solute (g)}}{\text{Mass of solution (g)}} \times 10^9 \quad \text{or} \quad \frac{\text{Volume of solute (mL)}}{\text{Volume of solution (mL)}} \times 10^9$$

To take an example, the maximum allowable concentration in air of the organic solvent benzene (C_6H_6) is currently set by government regulation at 1 ppm. A concentration of 1 ppm means that if you take a million "parts" of air in any unit—say, mL—then 1 of those parts is benzene vapor and the other 999,999 parts are other gases:

$$1 \text{ ppm} = \frac{1 \text{ mL}}{1,000,000 \text{ mL}} \times 10^6$$

Because the density of water is approximately 1.0 g/mL at room temperature, 1.0 L (or 1000 mL) of an aqueous solution weighs 1000 g. Therefore, when dealing with very dilute concentrations of solutes dissolved in water, ppm is equivalent to mg solute/L solution, and ppb is equivalent to μg solute/L solution. To demonstrate that these units are equivalent, the conversion from ppm to mg/L is as follows:

$$1 \text{ ppm} = \left(\frac{1 \text{ g solute}}{10^6 \text{ g solution}}\right)\left(\frac{1 \text{ mg solute}}{10^{-3} \text{ g solute}}\right)\left(\frac{10^3 \text{ g solution}}{1 \text{ L solution}}\right) = \frac{1 \text{ mg solute}}{1 \text{ L solution}}$$

WORKED EXAMPLE **9.11** ppm as Conversion Factor: Mass of Solution to Mass of Solute

The maximum allowable concentration of chloroform, $CHCl_3$, in drinking water is 100 ppb. What is the maximum amount (in grams) of chloroform allowed in a glass containing 400 g (400 mL) of water?

ANALYSIS We are given a solution amount (400 g) and a concentration (100 ppb). This concentration of 100 ppb means

$$100 \text{ ppb} = \frac{\text{Mass of solute (g)}}{\text{Mass of solution (g)}} \times 10^9$$

This equation can be rearranged to find the mass of solute.

BALLPARK ESTIMATE A concentration of 100 ppb means there are 100×10^{-9} g (1×10^{-7} g) of solute in 1 g of solution. In 400 g of solution, we should have 400 times this amount, or $400 \times 10^{-7} = 4 \times 10^{-5}$ g.

SOLUTION

$$\text{Mass of solute (g)} = \frac{\text{Mass of solution (g)}}{10^9} \times 100 \text{ ppb}$$

$$= \frac{400 \text{ g}}{10^9} \times 100 \text{ ppb} = 4 \times 10^{-5} \text{ g (or 0.04 mg)}$$

BALLPARK CHECK: The calculated answer matches our estimate.

PROBLEM 9.17

What is the concentration in ppm of sodium fluoride in tap water that has been fluoridated by the addition of 32 mg of NaF for every 20 kg of solution?

PROBLEM 9.18

The maximum amounts of lead and copper allowed in drinking water are 0.015 mg/kg for lead and 1.3 mg/kg for copper. Express these values in parts per million, and tell the maximum amount of each (in grams) allowed in 100 g of water.

9.8 Dilution

Many solutions, from orange juice to chemical reagents, are stored in high concentrations and then prepared for use by *dilution*—that is, by adding additional solvent to lower the concentration. For example, you might make up 1/2 gal of orange juice by adding water to a canned concentrate. In the same way, you might buy a medicine or chemical reagent in concentrated solution and dilute it before use.

The key fact to remember about dilution is that the amount of *solute* remains constant; only the *volume* is changed by adding more solvent. If, for example, the initial and final concentrations are given in molarity, then we know that the number of moles of solute is the same both before and after dilution, and can be determined by multiplying molarity times volume:

$$\text{Number of moles} = \text{Molarity (mol/L)} \times \text{Volume (L)}$$

Because the number of moles remains constant, we can set up the following equation, where M_1 and V_1 refer to the solution before dilution, and M_2 and V_2 refer to the solution after dilution:

$$\text{Moles of solute} = M_1V_1 = M_2V_2$$

This equation can be rewritten to solve for M_2, the concentration of the solution after dilution:

$$M_2 = M_1 \times \frac{V_1}{V_2} \quad \text{where} \quad \frac{V_1}{V_2} \quad \text{is a } \textit{dilution factor}$$

The equation shows that the concentration after dilution (M_2) can be found by multiplying the initial concentration (M_1) by a **dilution factor**, which is simply the ratio of the initial and final solution volumes (V_1/V_2). If, for example, the solution volume *increases* by a factor of 5, from 10 mL to 50 mL, then the concentration must *decrease* to 1/5 its initial value because the dilution factor is 10 mL/50 mL, or 1/5. Worked Example 9.12 shows how to use this relationship for calculating dilutions.

The relationship between concentration and volume can also be used to find what volume of initial solution to start with to achieve a given dilution:

$$\text{Since} \quad M_1V_1 = M_2V_2$$
$$\text{then} \quad V_1 = V_2 \times \frac{M_2}{M_1}$$

In this case, V_1 is the initial volume that must be diluted to prepare a less concentrated solution with volume V_2. The initial volume is found by multiplying the final volume (V_2) by the ratio of the final and initial concentrations (M_2/M_1). For example, to decrease the concentration of a solution to 1/5 its initial value, the initial volume must be 1/5 the desired final volume. Worked Example 9.13 gives a sample calculation.

▲ Orange juice concentrate is diluted with water before drinking.

Dilution factor The ratio of the initial and final solution volumes (V_1/V_2).

Although the preceding equations and following examples deal with concentration units of molarity, it is worth noting that the dilution equation can be generalized to the other concentration units presented in this section, or

$$C_1V_1 = C_2V_2$$

WORKED EXAMPLE **9.12** Dilution of Solutions: Concentration

What is the final concentration if 75 mL of a 3.5 M glucose solution is diluted to a volume of 450 mL?

ANALYSIS The number of moles of solute is constant, so

$$M_1V_1 = M_2V_2$$

Of the four variables in this equation, we know the initial concentration M_1 (3.5 M), the initial volume V_1 (75 mL), and the final volume V_2 (450 mL), and we need to find the final concentration M_2.

BALLPARK ESTIMATE The volume increases by a factor of 6, from 75 mL to 450 mL, so the concentration must decrease by a factor of 6, from 3.5 M to about 0.6 M.

SOLUTION

Solving the above equation for M_2 and substituting in the known values gives

$$M_2 = \frac{M_1V_1}{V_2} = \frac{(3.5 \text{ M glucose})(75 \text{ mL})}{450 \text{ mL}} = 0.58 \text{ M glucose}$$

BALLPARK CHECK: The calculated answer is close to our estimate of 0.6 M.

WORKED EXAMPLE **9.13** Dilution of Solutions: Volume

Aqueous NaOH can be purchased at a concentration of 1.0 M. How would you use this concentrated solution to prepare 750 mL of 0.32 M NaOH?

ANALYSIS The number of moles of solute is constant, so

$$M_1V_1 = M_2V_2$$

Of the four variables in this equation, we know the initial concentration M_1 (1.0 M), the final volume V_2 (750 mL), and the final concentration M_2 (0.32 M), and we need to find the initial volume V_1.

BALLPARK ESTIMATE We want the solution concentration to decrease by a factor of about 3, from 1.0 M to 0.32 M, which means we need to dilute the 1.0 M solution by a factor of 3. This means the final volume must be about 3 times greater than the initial volume. Because our final volume is to be 750 mL, we must start with an initial volume of about 250 mL.

SOLUTION

Solving the above equation for V_1 and substituting in the known values gives

$$V_1 = \frac{V_2M_2}{M_1} = \frac{(750 \text{ mL})(0.32 \text{ M})}{1.0 \text{ M}} = 240 \text{ mL}$$

To prepare the desired solution, dilute 240 mL of 1.0 M NaOH with water to make a final volume of 750 mL.

BALLPARK CHECK: The calculated answer (240 mL) is reasonably close to our estimate of 250 mL.

PROBLEM 9.19

Hydrochloric acid is normally purchased at a concentration of 12.0 M. What is the final concentration if 100.0 mL of 12.0 M HCl is diluted to 500.0 mL?

PROBLEM 9.20

Aqueous ammonia is commercially available at a concentration of 16.0 M. How much of the concentrated solution would you use to prepare 500.0 mL of a 1.25 M solution?

PROBLEM 9.21

The Environmental Protection Agency has set the limit for arsenic in drinking water at 0.010 ppm. To what volume would you need to dilute 1.5 L of water containing 5.0 ppm arsenic to reach the acceptable limit?

9.9 Ions in Solution: Electrolytes

Look at Figure 9.8, which shows a light bulb connected to a power source through a circuit that is interrupted by two metal strips dipped into a beaker of liquid. When the strips are dipped into pure water, the bulb remains dark, but when they are dipped into an aqueous NaCl solution, the circuit is closed and the bulb lights. As mentioned previously in Section 4.1, this simple demonstration shows that ionic compounds in aqueous solution can conduct electricity. (⊂⊃, p. 79)

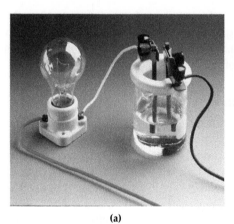

(a)   (b)

▲ **FIGURE 9.8** **A simple demonstration shows that electricity can flow through a solution of ions.** (a) With pure water in the beaker, the circuit is incomplete, no electricity flows, and the bulb does not light. (b) With a concentrated NaCl solution in the beaker, the circuit is complete, electricity flows, and the light bulb glows.

Substances like NaCl that conduct an electric current when dissolved in water are called **electrolytes**. Conduction occurs because negatively charged Cl^- anions migrate through the solution toward the metal strip connected to the positive terminal of the power source, whereas positively charged Na^+ cations migrate toward the strip connected to the negative terminal. As you might expect, the ability of a solution to conduct electricity depends on the concentration of ions in solution. Distilled water contains virtually no ions and is nonconducting; ordinary tap water contains low concentrations of dissolved ions (mostly Na^+, K^+, Mg^{2+}, Ca^{2+}, and Cl^-) and is weakly conducting; and a concentrated solution of NaCl is strongly conducting.

Electrolyte A substance that produces ions and therefore conducts electricity when dissolved in water.

Strong electrolyte A substance that ionizes completely when dissolved in water.

Weak electrolyte A substance that is only partly ionized in water.

Nonelectrolyte A substance that does not produce ions when dissolved in water.

Ionic substances like NaCl that ionize completely when dissolved in water are called **strong electrolytes**, and molecular substances like acetic acid (CH_3CO_2H) that are only partially ionized are **weak electrolytes**. Molecular substances like glucose that do not produce ions when dissolved in water are **nonelectrolytes**.

Strong electrolyte; completely ionized

$$NaCl(s) \xrightarrow[\text{in water}]{\text{Dissolve}} Na^+(aq) + Cl^-(aq)$$

Weak electrolyte; partly ionized

$$CH_3CO_2H(l) \underset{\text{in water}}{\overset{\text{Dissolve}}{\rightleftharpoons}} CH_3CO_2^-(aq) + H^+(aq)$$

Nonelectrolyte; not ionized

$$Glucose(s) \underset{\text{in water}}{\overset{\text{Dissolve}}{\rightleftharpoons}} Glucose(aq)$$

9.10 Electrolytes in Body Fluids: Equivalents and Milliequivalents

What happens if NaCl and KBr are dissolved in the same solution? Because the cations (K^+ and Na^+) and anions (Cl^- and Br^-) are all mixed together and no reactions occur between them, an identical solution could just as well be made from KCl and NaBr. Thus, we can no longer speak of having an NaCl + KBr solution; we can only speak of having a solution with four different ions in it.

A similar situation exists for blood and other body fluids, which contain many different anions and cations. Since they are all mixed together, it is difficult to "assign" specific cations to specific anions or to talk about specific ionic compounds. Instead, we are interested only in individual ions and in the total numbers of positive and negative charges. To discuss such mixtures, we use a new term—*equivalents* of ions.

Equivalent For ions, the amount equal to 1 mol of charge.

Gram-equivalent For ions, the molar mass of the ion divided by the ionic charge.

For ions, one **equivalent (Eq)** is equal to the number of ions that carry 1 mol of charge. Of more practical use is the unit **gram-equivalent**, which is the mass of the ion that contains one mole of charge. It can be calculated simply as the molar mass of the ion divided by the absolute value of its charge.

$$\text{One gram-equivalent of ion} = \frac{\text{Molar mass of ion (g)}}{\text{Charge on ion}}$$

If the ion has a charge of +1 or −1, 1 gram-equivalent of the ion is simply the molar mass of the ion in grams. Thus, 1 gram-equivalent of Na^+ is 23 g, and 1 gram-equivalent of Cl^- is 35.5 g. If the ion has a charge of +2 or −2, however, 1 gram-equivalent is equal to the ion's formula weight in grams divided by 2. Thus, 1 gram-equivalent of Mg^{2+} is (24.3 g)/2 = 12.2 g, and 1 gram-equivalent of CO_3^{2-} is [12.0 g + (3 × 16.0 g)]/2 = 30.0 g. The gram-equivalent is a useful conversion factor when converting from volume of solution to mass of ions, as seen in Worked Example 9.14.

The number of equivalents of a given ion per liter of solution can be found by multiplying the molarity of the ion (moles per liter) by the charge on the ion. Because ion concentrations in body fluids are often low, clinical chemists find it more convenient to talk about *milliequivalents* of ions rather than equivalents. One milliequivalent (mEq) of an ion is 1/1000 of an equivalent. For example, the normal concentration of Na^+ in blood is 0.14 Eq/L, or 140 mEq/L.

$$1 \text{ mEq} = 0.001 \text{ Eq} \qquad 1 \text{ Eq} = 1000 \text{ mEq}$$

Note that the gram-equivalent for an ion can now be expressed as grams per equivalent or as mg per mEq.

Average concentrations of the major electrolytes in blood plasma are given in Table 9.6. As you might expect, the total milliequivalents of positively and negatively charged electrolytes must be equal to maintain electrical neutrality. Adding

TABLE 9.6   Concentrations of Major Electrolytes in Blood Plasma

CATION	CONCENTRATION (mEq/L)
Na^+	136–145
Ca^{2+}	4.5–6.0
K^+	3.6–5.0
Mg^{2+}	3

ANION	CONCENTRATION (mEq/L)
Cl^-	98–106
HCO_3^-	25–29
SO_4^{2-} and HPO_4^{2-}	2

the milliequivalents of positive and negative ions in Table 9.6, however, shows a higher concentration of positive ions than negative ions. The difference, called the *anion gap*, is made up by the presence of negatively charged proteins and the anions of organic acids.

WORKED EXAMPLE   **9.14** Equivalents as Conversion Factors: Volume to Mass

The normal concentration of Ca^{2+} in blood is 5.0 mEq/L. How many milligrams of Ca^{2+} are in 1.00 L of blood?

ANALYSIS We are given a volume and a concentration in milliequivalents per liter, and we need to find an amount in milligrams. Thus, we need to calculate the gram-equivalent for Ca^{2+} and then use concentration as a conversion factor between volume and mass, as indicated in the following flow diagram:

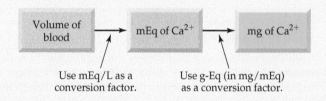

BALLPARK ESTIMATE The molar mass of calcium is 40.08 g/mol, and the calcium ion carries a charge of 2+. Thus, 1 g-Eq of Ca^{2+} equals about 20 g/Eq or 20 mg/mEq. This means that the 5.0 mEq of Ca^{2+} ions in 1.00 L of blood corresponds to a mass of 5.0 mEq Ca^{2+} × 20 mg/mEq = 100 mg Ca^{2+}.

SOLUTION

$$(1.00 \; \text{L blood})\left(\frac{5.0 \; \text{mEq } Ca^{2+}}{1.0 \; \text{L blood}}\right)\left(\frac{20.04 \; \text{mg } Ca^{2+}}{1 \; \text{mEq } Ca^{2+}}\right) = 100 \; \text{mg } Ca^{2+}$$

BALLPARK CHECK: The calculated answer (100 mg of Ca^{2+} in 1.00 L of blood) matches our estimate.

PROBLEM 9.22

How many grams are in 1 Eq of the following ions? How many grams in 1 mEq?

(a) K^+ **(b)** Br^- **(c)** Mg^{2+} **(d)** SO_4^{2-} **(e)** Al^{3+} **(f)** PO_4^{3-}

PROBLEM 9.23

Look at the data in Table 9.6, and calculate how many milligrams of Mg^{2+} are in 250 mL of blood.

9.11 Properties of Solutions

The properties of solutions are similar in many respects to those of pure solvents, but there are also some interesting and important differences. One such difference is that solutions have higher boiling points than the pure solvents; another is that solutions have lower freezing points. Pure water boils at 100.0 °C and freezes at 0.0 °C, for example, but a 1.0 M solution of NaCl in water boils at 101.0 °C and freezes at −3.7 °C.

Colligative property A property of a solution that depends only on the number of dissolved particles, not on their chemical identity.

The elevation of boiling point and the lowering of freezing point for a solution as compared with a pure solvent are examples of **colligative properties**—properties that depend on the *concentration* of a dissolved solute but not on its chemical identity. Other colligative properties are a lower vapor pressure for a solution compared with the pure solvent and *osmosis*, the migration of solvent molecules through a semipermeable membrane.

Colligative properties
- Vapor pressure is lower for a solution than for a pure solvent.
- Boiling point is higher for a solution than for a pure solvent.
- Freezing point is lower for a solution than for a pure solvent.
- Osmosis occurs when a solution is separated from a pure solvent by a semipermeable membrane.

Vapor Pressure Lowering in Solutions

We said in Section 8.12 that the vapor pressure of a liquid depends on the equilibrium between molecules entering and leaving the liquid surface. (⊂⊃, p. 241) Only those molecules at the surface of the liquid that are sufficiently energetic will evaporate. If, however, some of the liquid (solvent) molecules at the surface are replaced by other (solute) particles that do not evaporate, then the rate of evaporation of solvent molecules decreases and the vapor pressure of a solution is lower than that of the pure solvent (Figure 9.9). Note that the *identity* of the solute particles is irrelevant; only their concentration matters.

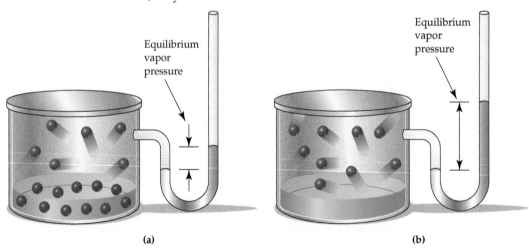

(a)   (b)

▲ **FIGURE 9.9 Vapor pressure lowering of solution.** (a) The vapor pressure of a solution is lower than (b) the vapor pressure of the pure solvent because fewer solvent molecules are able to escape from the surface of the solution.

APPLICATION ▶ Electrolytes, Fluid Replacement, and Sports Drinks

Athletes sweat. And the hotter the day, the more intense and longer lasting the activity, the more they sweat. Sweat loss during strenuous exercise on a hot day can amount to as much as 2 L/h, and the total sweat loss during a 24 h endurance run can exceed 16 L, or approximately 35 lb.

The composition of sweat is highly variable, not only with the individual but also with the time during the exercise and the athlete's overall conditioning. Typically, however, the Na^+ ion concentration in sweat is about 30–40 mEq/L, and that of K^+ ion is about 5–10 mEq/L. In addition, there are small amounts of other metal ions, such as Mg^{2+}, and there are sufficient Cl^- ions (35–50 mEq/L) to balance the positive charge of all these cations.

Obviously, all the water and dissolved electrolytes lost by an athlete through sweating must be replaced. Otherwise, dehydration, hyperthermia and heat stroke, dizziness, nausea, muscle cramps, impaired kidney function, and other difficulties ensue. As a rule of thumb, a sweat loss equal to 5% of body weight—about 3.5 L for a 150 lb person—is the maximum amount that can be safely allowed for a well-conditioned athlete.

Plain water works perfectly well to replace sweat lost during short bouts of activity up to a few hours in length, but a carbohydrate–electrolyte beverage, or "sports drink," is much superior for rehydrating during and after longer activity in which substantial amounts of electrolytes have been lost. Some of the better known sports drinks are little more than overpriced sugar–water solutions, but others are carefully formulated and highly effective for fluid replacement. Nutritional research has shown that a serious sports drink should meet the following criteria. There are several dry-powder mixes on the market to choose from.

- The drink should contain 6–8% of soluble complex carbohydrates (about 15 g per 8 oz serving) and only a small amount of simple sugar for taste. The complex carbohydrates, which usually go by the name "maltodextrin," provide a slow release of glucose into the bloodstream. Not only does the glucose provide a steady source of energy, it also enhances the absorption of water from the stomach.

- The drink should contain electrolytes to replenish those lost in sweat. Concentrations of approximately 20 mEq/L for Na^+ ions, 10 mEq/L for K^+ ion, and 4 mEq/L for Mg^{2+} ions are recommended. These amounts correspond to about 100 mg sodium, 100 mg potassium, and 25 mg magnesium per 8 oz serving.

- The drink should be noncarbonated because carbonation can cause gastrointestinal upset during exercise, and it should not contain caffeine, which acts as a diuretic.

- The drink should taste good so the athlete will want to drink it. Thirst is a poor indicator of fluid requirements, and most people will drink less than needed unless a beverage is flavored.

In addition to complex carbohydrates, electrolytes, and flavorings, some sports drinks also contain vitamin A (as beta-carotene), vitamin C (ascorbic acid), and selenium, which act as antioxidants to protect cells from damage. Some drinks also contain the amino acid glutamine, which appears to lessen lactic acid buildup in muscles and thus helps muscles bounce back more quickly after an intense workout.

▲ Endurance athletes avoid serious medical problems by drinking sports drinks to replace water and electrolytes.

See Additional Problems 9.93 and 9.94 at the end of the chapter.

Boiling Point Elevation of Solutions

One consequence of the vapor pressure lowering for a solution is that the boiling point of the solution is higher than that of the pure solvent. Recall from Section 8.12 that boiling occurs when the vapor pressure of a liquid reaches atmospheric pressure. (⊂⊃, p. 241) But because the vapor pressure of a solution is lower than that of the pure solvent at a given temperature, the solution must be heated to a higher temperature for its vapor pressure to reach atmospheric pressure. Figure 9.10 shows a close-up plot of vapor pressure versus temperature for pure water and for

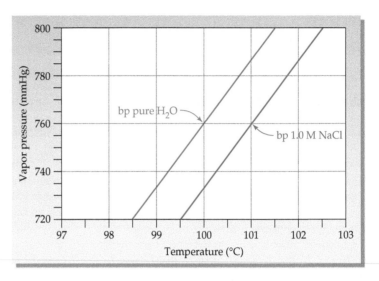

▲ **FIGURE 9.10 Vapor pressure and temperature.** A close-up plot of vapor pressure versus temperature for pure water (red curve) and for a 1.0 M NaCl solution (green curve). Pure water boils at 100.0 °C, but the solution does not boil until 101.0 °C.

a 1.0 M NaCl solution. The vapor pressure of pure water reaches atmospheric pressure (760 mmHg) at 100.0 °C, but the vapor pressure of the NaCl solution does not reach the same point until 101.0 °C.

For each mole of solute particles added, regardless of chemical identity, the boiling point of 1 kg of water is raised by 0.51 °C, or

$$\Delta T_{\text{boiling}} = \left(0.51\ ^\circ\text{C}\frac{\text{kg water}}{\text{mol particles}}\right)\left(\frac{\text{mol particles}}{\text{kg water}}\right)$$

The addition of 1 mol of a molecular substance like glucose to 1 kg of water therefore raises the boiling point from 100.0 °C to 100.51 °C. The addition of 1 mol of NaCl per kilogram of water, however, raises the boiling point by $2 \times 0.51\ ^\circ\text{C} = 1.02\ ^\circ\text{C}$ because the solution contains 2 mol of solute particles—Na^+ and Cl^- ions.

WORKED EXAMPLE   **9.15** Properties of Solutions: Boiling Point Elevation

What is the boiling point of a solution of 0.75 mol of KBr in 1.0 kg of water?

ANALYSIS The boiling point increases 0.51 °C for each mole of solute per kilogram of water. Since KBr is a strong electrolyte, there are 2 mol of ions (K^+ and Br^-) for every 1 mol of KBr that dissolves.

BALLPARK ESTIMATE The boiling point will increase about 0.5 °C for every 1 mol of ions in 1 kg of water. Since 0.75 mol of KBr produce 1.5 mol of ions, the boiling point should increase by (1.5 mol ions) × 0.5 °C/mol ions) = 0.75 °C

SOLUTION

$$\Delta T_{\text{boiling}} = \left(0.51\ ^\circ\text{C}\frac{\text{kg water}}{\text{mol ions}}\right)\left(\frac{2\ \text{mol ions}}{1\ \text{mol KBr}}\right)\left(\frac{0.75\ \text{mol KBr}}{1.0\ \text{kg water}}\right) = 0.77\ ^\circ\text{C}$$

The normal boiling point of pure water is 100 °C, so the boiling point of the solution increases to 100.77 °C.

BALLPARK CHECK: The 0.77 °C increase is consistent with our estimate of 0.75 °C.

PROBLEM 9.24

What is the boiling point of a solution of 0.67 mol of $MgCl_2$ in 0.50 kg of water?

PROBLEM 9.25

When 1.0 mol of HF is dissolved in 1.0 kg of water, the boiling point of the resulting solution is 100.5 °C. Is HF a strong or weak electrolyte? Explain.

●○ KEY CONCEPT PROBLEM 9.26

The following diagram shows plots of vapor pressure versus temperature for a solvent and a solution.

    (a) Which curve represents the pure solvent, and which the solution?

    (b) What are the approximate boiling points of the pure solvent and the solution?

    (c) What is the approximate concentration of the solution in mol/kg, if 1 mol of solute particles raises the boiling point of 1 kg of solvent by 3.63 °C?

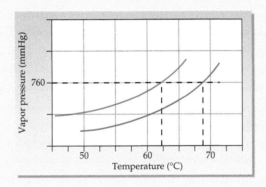

Freezing Point Depression of Solutions

Just as solutions have lower vapor pressure and consequently higher boiling points than pure solvents, they also have lower freezing points. Motorists in cold climates take advantage of this effect when they add "antifreeze" to the water in automobile cooling systems. Antifreeze is a nonvolatile solute, usually ethylene glycol ($HOCH_2CH_2OH$), that is added in sufficient concentration to lower the freezing point below the lowest expected outdoor temperature. In the same way, salt sprinkled on icy roads lowers the freezing point of ice below the road temperature and thus causes ice to melt.

Freezing point depression has much the same cause as vapor pressure lowering. Solute molecules are dispersed between solvent molecules throughout the solution, thereby making it more difficult for solvent molecules to come together and organize into ordered crystals.

For each mole of nonvolatile solute particles, the freezing point of 1 kg of water is lowered by 1.86 °C, or

$$\Delta T_{freezing} = \left(-1.86 \text{ °C} \frac{\text{kg water}}{\text{mol particles}}\right)\left(\frac{\text{mol particles}}{\text{kg water}}\right)$$

Thus, addition of 1 mol of antifreeze to 1 kg of water lowers the freezing point from 0.00 °C to −1.86 °C, and addition of 1 mol of NaCl (2 mol of particles) to 1 kg of water lowers the freezing point from 0.00 °C to −3.72 °C.

▲ A mixture of salt and ice is used to provide the low temperatures needed to make old-fashioned hand-cranked ice cream.

> **WORKED EXAMPLE**   **9.16** Properties of Solutions: Freezing Point Depression
>
> The cells of a tomato contain mostly an aqueous solution of sugar and other substances. If a typical tomato freezes at –2.5 °C, what is the concentration of dissolved particles in the tomato cells (in moles of particles per kg of water)?
>
> ANALYSIS The freezing point decreases by 1.86 °C for each mole of solute dissolved in 1 kg of water. We can use the decrease in freezing point (2.5 °C) to find the amount of solute per kg of water.
>
> BALLPARK ESTIMATE The freezing point will decrease by about 1.9 °C for every 1 mol of solute particles in 1 kg of water. To lower the freezing point by 2.5 °C therefore requires about 1.5 mol of particles per kg of water.
>
> SOLUTION
>
> $$\Delta T_{freezing} = -2.5\ °C$$
>
> $$= \left(-1.86\ °C\ \frac{kg\ water}{mol\ solute\ particles}\right)\left(\frac{??\ mol\ solute\ particles}{1.0\ kg\ water}\right)$$
>
> We can rearrange this expression to
>
> $$(-2.5\ °C)\left(\frac{1}{-1.86\ °C}\ \frac{mol\ solute\ particles}{kg\ water}\right) = 1.3\ \frac{mol\ solute\ particles}{kg\ water}$$
>
> BALLPARK CHECK: The calculated answer is relatively close to our estimate (1.5 mol/kg).

PROBLEM 9.27

What is the freezing point of a solution of 1.0 mol of glucose in 1.0 kg of water?

PROBLEM 9.28

When 0.5 mol of a certain ionic substance is dissolved in 1.0 kg of water, the freezing point of the resulting solution is −2.8 °C. How many ions does the substance give when it dissolves?

9.12 Osmosis and Osmotic Pressure

Certain materials, including those that make up the membranes around living cells, are *semipermeable*. They allow water and other small molecules to pass through, but they block the passage of large solute molecules or ions. When a solution and a pure solvent, or two solutions of different concentration, are separated by a semipermeable membrane, solvent molecules pass through the membrane in a process called **osmosis**. Although the passage of solvent through the membrane takes place in both directions, passage from the pure solvent side to the solution side is favored and occurs more often. As a result, the amount of liquid on the pure solvent side decreases, the amount of liquid on the solution side increases, and the concentration of the solution decreases.

Osmosis The passage of solvent through a semipermeable membrane separating two solutions of different concentration.

For the simplest explanation of osmosis, let us look at what happens on the molecular level. As shown in Figure 9.11, a solution inside a bulb is separated by a semipermeable membrane from pure solvent in the outer container. Solvent molecules in the outer container, because of their somewhat higher concentration, approach the membrane more frequently than do molecules in the bulb, thereby passing through more often and causing the liquid level in the attached tube to rise.

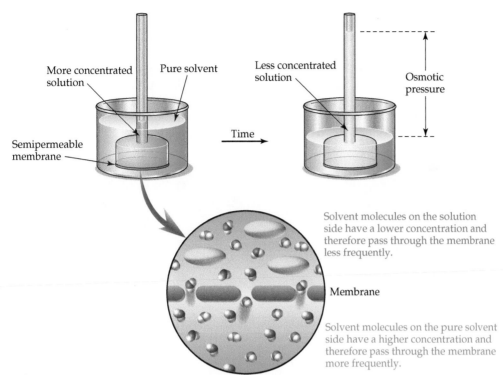

More concentrated solution
Pure solvent
Less concentrated solution
Osmotic pressure
Semipermeable membrane
Time

Solvent molecules on the solution side have a lower concentration and therefore pass through the membrane less frequently.

Membrane

Solvent molecules on the pure solvent side have a higher concentration and therefore pass through the membrane more frequently.

◀ **FIGURE 9.11 The phenomenon of osmosis.** A solution inside the bulb is separated from pure solvent in the outer container by a semipermeable membrane. Solvent molecules in the container have a slightly higher concentration than molecules in the bulb and therefore pass through the membrane more frequently. The liquid in the tube therefore rises until an equilibrium is reached. At equilibrium, the osmotic pressure exerted by the column of liquid in the tube is sufficient to prevent further net passage of solvent.

As the liquid in the tube rises, its increased weight creates an increased pressure that pushes solvent back through the membrane until the rates of forward and reverse passage become equal and the liquid level stops rising. The amount of pressure necessary to achieve this equilibrium is called the **osmotic pressure** (π) of the solution and can be determined from the expression

$$\pi = \left(\frac{n}{V}\right)RT$$

where n is the number of moles of particles in the solution, V is the solution volume, R is the gas constant (⚫⚫⚫, p. 231), and T is the absolute temperature of the solution. Note the similarity between this equation for the osmotic pressure of a solution and the equation for the pressure of an ideal gas, $P = (n/V)RT$. In both cases, the pressure has units of atmospheres.

Osmotic pressures can be extremely high, even for relatively dilute solutions. The osmotic pressure of a 0.15 M NaCl solution at 25 °C, for example, is 7.3 atm, a value that supports a difference in water level of approximately 250 ft!

As with other colligative properties, the amount of osmotic pressure depends only on the concentration of solute particles, not on their identity. Thus, it is convenient to use a new unit, *osmolarity* (osmol), to describe the concentration of particles in solution. The **osmolarity** of a solution is equal to the number of moles of dissolved particles (ions or molecules) per liter of solution. A 0.2 M glucose solution, for instance, has an osmolarity of 0.2 osmol, but a 0.2 M solution of NaCl has an osmolarity of 0.4 osmol because it contains 0.2 mol of Na$^+$ ions and 0.2 mol of Cl$^-$ ions.

Osmosis is particularly important in living organisms because the membranes around cells are semipermeable. The fluids both inside and outside cells must therefore have the same osmolarity to prevent buildup of osmotic pressure and consequent rupture of the cell membrane.

In blood, the plasma surrounding red blood cells has an osmolarity of approximately 0.30 osmol and is said to be **isotonic** with (that is, has the same osmolarity as) the cell contents. If the cells are removed from plasma and placed in 0.15 M NaCl (called *physiological saline solution*), they are unharmed because the osmolarity of the saline solution (0.30 osmol) is the same as that of plasma. If, however, red blood cells are placed in pure water or in any solution with an osmolarity much

Osmotic pressure The amount of external pressure applied to the more concentrated solution to halt the passage of solvent molecules across a semipermeable membrane.

Osmolarity (osmol) The sum of the molarities of all dissolved particles in a solution.

Isotonic Having the same osmolarity.

Hypotonic Having an osmolarity *less than* the surrounding blood plasma or cells.

Hypertonic Having an osmolarity *greater than* the surrounding blood plasma or cells.

lower than 0.30 osmol (a **hypotonic** solution), water passes through the membrane into the cell, causing the cell to swell up and burst, a process called *hemolysis*.

Finally, if red blood cells are placed in a solution having an osmolarity greater than the cell contents (a **hypertonic** solution), water passes out of the cells into the surrounding solution, causing the cells to shrivel, a process called *crenation*. Figure 9.12 shows red blood cells under all three conditions: isotonic, hypotonic, and hypertonic. Therefore, it is critical that any solution used intravenously be isotonic to prevent red blood cells from being destroyed.

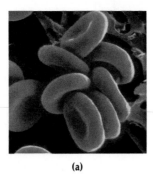 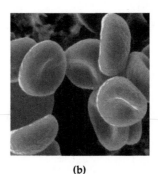 

(a) (b) (c)

► **FIGURE 9.12 Red blood cells.** In (a) an isotonic solution the blood cells are normal in appearance, but the cells in (b) a hypotonic solution are swollen because of water gain, and those in (c) a hypertonic solution are shriveled because of water loss.

WORKED EXAMPLE **9.17** Properties of Solutions: Osmolarity

The solution of glucose commonly used intravenously has a concentration of 5.0% (w/v) glucose. What is the osmolarity of this solution? The molecular weight of glucose is 180 amu.

ANALYSIS Since glucose is a molecular substance that does not give ions in solution, the osmolarity of the solution is the same as the molarity. Recall from Section 9.7 that a solution of 5.0% (w/v) glucose has a concentration of 5.0 g glucose per 100 mL of solution, which is equivalent to 50 g per liter of solution. Thus, finding the molar concentration of glucose requires a mass to mole conversion.

BALLPARK ESTIMATE One liter of solution contains 50 g of glucose (MW= 180 g/mol). Thus, 50 g of glucose is equal to a little more than 0.25 mol, so a solution concentration of 50 g/L is equal to about 0.25 osmol, or 0.25 M.

SOLUTION

STEP 1: Identify known information. We know the (w/v)% concentration of the glucose solution.

$$5.0\% \ (w/v) = \frac{5.0 \text{ g glucose}}{100 \text{ mL solution}} \times 100\%$$

STEP 2: Identify answer and units. We are looking for osmolarity, which in this case is equal to the molarity of the solution because glucose is a molecular substance and does not dissociate into ions.

$$\text{Osmolarity} = \text{Molarity} = \text{??} \ \text{mol/liter}$$

STEP 3: Identify conversion factors. The (w/v)% concentration is defined as grams of solute per 100 mL of solution, and molarity is defined as moles of solute per liter of solution. We will need to convert from milliliters to liters and then use molar mass to convert grams of glucose to moles of glucose.

$$\frac{\text{g glucose}}{100 \text{ mL}} \times \frac{1000 \text{ mL}}{\text{L}} = \frac{\text{g glucose}}{\text{L}}$$

$$\frac{\text{g glucose}}{\text{L}} \times \frac{1 \text{ mol glucose}}{180 \text{ g glucose}} = \frac{\text{moles glucose}}{\text{L}}$$

STEP 4: Solve. Starting with the (w/v)% glucose concentration, we first find the number of grams of glucose in 1 L of solution and then convert to moles of glucose per liter.

$$\left(\frac{5.0 \text{ g glucose}}{100 \text{ mL solution}}\right)\left(\frac{1000 \text{ mL}}{1 \text{ L}}\right) = 50 \frac{\text{g glucose}}{\text{L solution}}$$

$$\left(\frac{50 \text{ g glucose}}{1 \text{ L}}\right)\left(\frac{1 \text{ mol}}{180 \text{ g}}\right) = 0.28 \text{ M glucose} = 0.28 \text{ osmol}$$

BALLPARK CHECK: The calculated osmolarity is reasonably close to our estimate of 0.25 osmol

WORKED EXAMPLE **9.18** Properties of Solutions: Osmolarity

What mass of NaCl is needed to make 1.50 L of a 0.300 osmol solution? The molar mass of NaCl is 58.44 g/mol.

ANALYSIS Since NaCl is an ionic substance that produces 2 mol of ions (Na^+, Cl^-) when it dissociates, the osmolarity of the solution is twice the molarity. From the volume and the osmolarity we can determine the moles of NaCl needed and then perform a mole to mass converstion.

SOLUTION

STEP 1: **Identify known information.** We know the volume and the osmolarity of the final NaCl solution.

$$V = 1.50 \text{ L}$$
$$0.300 \text{ osmol} = \left(\frac{0.300 \text{ mol ions}}{L}\right)$$

STEP 2: **Identify answer and units.** We are looking for the mass of NaCl.

Mass of NaCl = ?? g

STEP 3: **Identify conversion factors.** Starting with osmolarity in the form (moles NaCl/L), we can use volume to determine the number of moles of solute. We can then use molar mass for the mole to mass conversion.

$$\left(\frac{\text{moles NaCl}}{\cancel{L}}\right) \times (\cancel{L}) = \text{moles NaCl}$$

$$(\cancel{\text{moles NaCl}}) \times \left(\frac{g \text{ NaCl}}{\cancel{\text{mole NaCl}}}\right) = g \text{ NaCl}$$

STEP 4: **Solve.** Use the appropriate conversions, remembering that NaCl produces two ions per formula unit, to find the mass of NaCl.

$$\left(\frac{0.300 \cancel{\text{ mol ions}}}{\cancel{L}}\right)\left(\frac{1 \text{ mol NaCl}}{2 \cancel{\text{ mol ions}}}\right)(1.50 \cancel{L}) = 0.225 \text{ mol NaCl}$$

$$(0.225 \cancel{\text{ mol NaCl}})\left(\frac{58.44 \text{ g NaCl}}{\cancel{\text{mol NaCl}}}\right) = 13.1 \text{ g NaCl}$$

PROBLEM 9.29

What is the osmolarity of the following solutions?

(a) 0.35 M KBr   (b) 0.15 M glucose + 0.05 M K_2SO_4

PROBLEM 9.30

What is the osmolarity of a typical oral rehydration solution (ORS) for infants that contains 90 mEq/L Na^+, 20 mEq/L K^+, 110 mEq/L Cl^-, and 2.0% glucose? The molecular weight of glucose is 180 amu.

9.13 Dialysis

Dialysis is similar to osmosis, except that the pores in a dialysis membrane are larger than those in an osmotic membrane so that both solvent molecules and small solute particles can pass through, but large colloidal particles such as proteins cannot pass. (The exact dividing line between a "small" molecule and a "large" one is imprecise, and dialysis membranes with a variety of pore sizes are available.) Dialysis membranes include animal bladders, parchment, and cellophane.

Perhaps the most important medical use of dialysis is in artificial kidney machines, where *hemodialysis* is used to cleanse the blood of patients whose kidneys malfunction (Figure 9.13). Blood is diverted from the body and pumped through a long cellophane dialysis tube suspended in an isotonic solution formulated to contain many of the same components as blood plasma. These substances—glucose, NaCl, $NaHCO_3$, and KCl—have the same concentrations in the dialysis solution as they do in blood so that they have no net passage through the membrane.

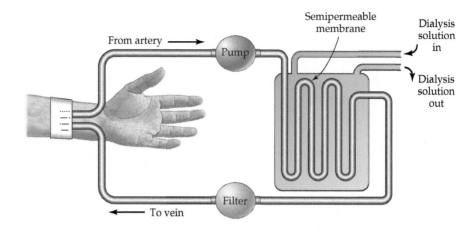

▶ **FIGURE 9.13 Operation of a hemodialysis unit used for purifying blood.** Blood is pumped from an artery through a coiled semipermeable membrane of cellophane. Small waste products pass through the membrane and are washed away by an isotonic dialysis solution.

APPLICATION ▶ Timed-Release Medications

There is much more in most medications than medicine. Even something as simple as a generic aspirin tablet contains a binder to keep it from crumbling, a filler to bring it to the right size and help it disintegrate in the stomach, and a lubricant to keep it from sticking to the manufacturing equipment. Timed-release medications are more complex still.

The widespread use of timed-release medication dates from the introduction of Contac decongestant in 1961. The original idea was simple: Tiny beads of medicine were encapsulated by coating them with varying thicknesses of a slow-dissolving polymer. Those beads with a thinner coat dissolve and release their medicine more rapidly; those with a thicker coat dissolve more slowly. Combining the right number of beads with the right thicknesses into a single capsule makes possible the gradual release of medication over a predictable time.

The technology of timed-release medications has become much more sophisticated in recent years, and the kinds of medications that can be delivered have become more numerous. Some medicines, for instance, either damage the stomach lining or are destroyed by the highly acidic environment in the stomach but can be delivered safely if given an *enteric coating*. The enteric coating is a polymeric material formulated so that it is stable in acid but reacts and is destroyed when it passes into the more basic environment of the intestines.

More recently, dermal patches have been developed to deliver drugs directly by diffusion through the skin. Patches are available to treat conditions from angina to motion sickness, as well as nicotine patches to help reduce cigarette cravings. One clever new device for timed release of medication through the skin uses the osmotic effect to force a drug from its reservoir. Useful only for drugs that do not dissolve in water, the device is divided into two compartments, one containing medication covered by a perforated membrane and the other containing a hygroscopic material (Section 9.3) covered by a semipermeable membrane. As moisture from the air diffuses through the membrane into the compartment with the hygroscopic material, the buildup of osmotic pressure squeezes the medication out of the other compartment through tiny holes.

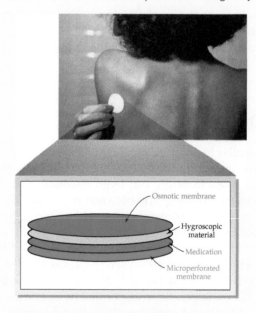

▲ The small beads of medicine are coated with different thicknesses of a slow-dissolving polymer so that they dissolve and release medicine at different times.

See Additional Problem 9.95 at the end of the chapter.

Small waste materials such as urea pass through the dialysis membrane from the blood to the solution side where they are washed away, but cells, proteins, and other important blood components are prevented by their size from passing through the membrane. In addition, the dialysis fluid concentration can be controlled so that imbalances in electrolytes are corrected. The wash solution is changed every 2 h, and a typical hemodialysis procedure lasts for 4–7 h.

As noted above, colloidal particles are too large to pass through a semipermeable membrane. Protein molecules, in particular, do not cross semipermeable membranes and thus play an essential role in determining the osmolarity of body fluids. The distribution of water and solutes across the capillary walls that separate blood plasma from the fluid surrounding cells is controlled by the balance between blood pressure and osmotic pressure. The pressure of blood inside the capillary tends to push water out of the plasma (filtration), but the osmotic pressure of colloidal protein molecules tends to draw water into the plasma (reabsorption). The balance between the two processes varies with location in the body. At the arterial end of a capillary, where blood pumped from the heart has a higher pressure, filtration is favored. At the venous end, where blood pressure is lower, reabsorption is favored, causing waste products from metabolism to enter the bloodstream.

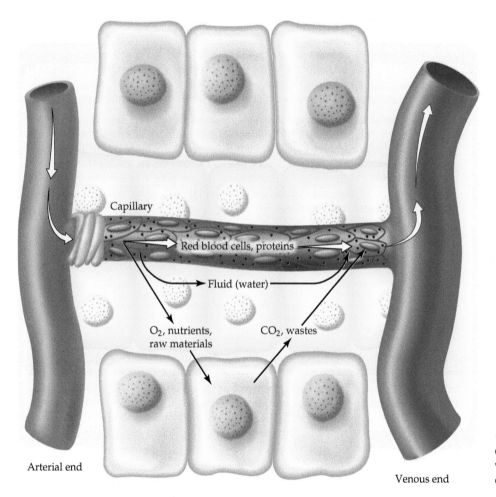

◄ The delivery of oxygen and nutrients to the cells and the removal of waste products are regulated by osmosis.

SUMMARY: REVISITING THE CHAPTER GOALS

1. What are solutions, and what factors affect solubility? Mixtures are classified as either *heterogeneous*, if the mixing is nonuniform, or *homogeneous*, if the mixing is uniform. *Solutions* are homogeneous mixtures that contain particles the size of ions and molecules (<2.0 nm diameter), whereas larger particles (2.0–500 nm diameter) are present in *colloids*.

KEY WORDS

Colligative property, *p. 278*
Colloid, *p. 256*
Dilution factor, *p. 273*

The maximum amount of one substance (the *solute*) that can be dissolved in another (the *solvent*) is called the substance's *solubility*. Substances tend to be mutually soluble when their intermolecular forces are similar. The solubility in water of a solid often increases with temperature, but the solubility of a gas decreases with temperature. Pressure significantly affects gas solubilities, which are directly proportional to their partial pressure over the solution (*Henry's law*).

2. **How is the concentration of a solution expressed?** The concentration of a solution can be expressed in several ways, including molarity, weight/weight percent composition, weight/volume percent composition, and parts per million. *Molarity*, which expresses concentration as the number of moles of solute per liter of solution, is the most useful method when calculating quantities of reactants or products for reactions in aqueous solution.

3. **How are dilutions carried out?** A dilution is carried out by adding more solvent to an existing solution. Only the amount of solvent changes; the amount of solute remains the same. Thus, the molarity times the volume of the dilute solution is equal to the molarity times the volume of the concentrated solution: $M_1V_1 = M_2V_2$.

4. **What is an electrolyte?** Substances that form ions when dissolved in water and whose water solutions therefore conduct an electric current are called *electrolytes*. Substances that ionize completely in water are *strong electrolytes*, those that ionize partially are *weak electrolytes*, and those that do not ionize are *nonelectrolytes*. Body fluids contain small amounts of many different electrolytes, whose concentrations are expressed as moles of ionic charge, or equivalents, per liter.

5. **How do solutions differ from pure solvents in their behavior?** In comparing a solution to a pure solvent, the solution has a lower vapor pressure at a given temperature, a higher boiling point, and a lower melting point. Called *colligative properties*, these effects depend only on the number of dissolved particles, not on their chemical identity.

6. **What is osmosis?** *Osmosis* occurs when solutions of different concentration are separated by a semipermeable membrane that allows solvent molecules to pass but blocks the passage of solute ions and molecules. Solvent flows from the more dilute side to the more concentrated side until sufficient *osmotic pressure* builds up and stops the flow. An effect similar to osmosis occurs when membranes of larger pore size are used. In *dialysis*, the membrane allows the passage of solvent and small dissolved molecules but prevents passage of proteins and larger particles.

UNDERSTANDING KEY CONCEPTS

9.31   Assume that two liquids are separated by a semipermeable membrane. Make a drawing that shows the situation after equilibrium is reached.

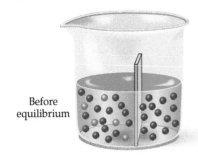

Before equilibrium

9.32   When 1 mol of HCl is added to 1 kg of water, the boiling point increases by 1.0 °C, but when 1 mol of acetic acid, CH_3CO_2H, is added to 1 kg of water, the boiling point increases by only 0.5 °C. Explain.

9.33   When 1 mol of HF is added to 1 kg of water, the freezing point decreases by 1.9 °C, but when 1 mol of HBr is added, the freezing point decreases by 3.7 °C. Which is more highly separated into ions, HF or HBr? Explain.

9.34   The graph at the top of page 289 shows the solubilities of two substances as a function of temperature. Which of the substances is a gas, and which is a liquid? Explain.

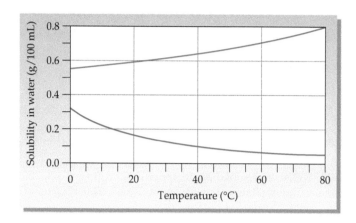

9.35 Assume that you have two full beakers, one containing pure water (blue) and the other containing an equal volume of a 10% (w/v) solution of glucose (green). Which of the drawings (a)–(c) best represents the two beakers after they have stood uncovered for several days and partial evaporation has occurred? Explain.

(a)   (b)   (c)

9.36 A beaker containing 150.0 mL of 0.1 M glucose is represented by (a). Which of the drawings (b)–(d) represents the solution that results when 50.0 mL is withdrawn from (a) and then diluted by a factor of 4?

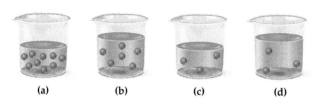

(a)   (b)   (c)   (d)

9.37 The following diagram shows parts of the vapor pressure curves for a solvent and a solution. Which curve is which?

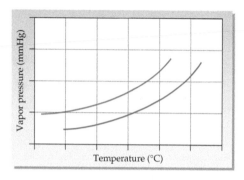

ADDITIONAL PROBLEMS

SOLUTIONS AND SOLUBILITY

9.38 What is the difference between a homogeneous mixture and a heterogeneous one?

9.39 How can you tell a solution from a colloid?

9.40 What characteristic of water allows it to dissolve ionic solids?

9.41 Why does water not dissolve motor oil?

9.42 Which of the following are solutions?

(a) Italian salad dressing
(b) Rubbing alcohol
(c) Algae in pond water
(d) Black coffee

9.43 Which of the following pairs of liquids are likely to be miscible?

(a) H_2SO_4 and H_2O
(b) C_8H_{18} and C_6H_6
(c) Na_3PO_4, and H_2O
(d) CS_2 and CCl_4

9.44 The solubility of NH_3 in water at an NH_3 pressure of 760.0 mmHg is 51.8 g/100 mL. What is the solubility of NH_3 if the partial pressure is reduced to 225.0 mmHg?

9.45 The solubility of CO_2 gas in water is 0.15 g/100 mL at a CO_2 pressure of 760 mmHg. What is the solubility of CO_2 in a soft drink (which is mainly water) that was bottled under a CO_2 pressure of 4.5 atm?

CONCENTRATION AND DILUTION OF SOLUTIONS

9.46 Is a solution highly concentrated if it is saturated? Is a solution saturated if it is highly concentrated?

9.47 How is weight/volume percent concentration defined?

9.48 How is molarity defined?

9.49 How is volume/volume percent concentration defined?

9.50 How would you prepare 750.0 mL of a 6.0% (v/v) ethyl alcohol solution?

9.51 A dilute solution of boric acid, H_3BO_3 is often used as an eyewash. How would you prepare 500.0 mL of a 0.50% (w/v) boric acid solution?

9.52 Describe how you would prepare 250 mL of a 0.10 M NaCl solution.

9.53 Describe how you would prepare 1.50 L of a 7.50% (w/v) $Mg(NO_3)_2$ solution.

9.54 What is the weight/volume percent concentration of the following solutions?

(a) 5.8 g KCl in 75 mL of solution
(b) 15 g sucrose in 380 mL of solution

9.55 The concentration of glucose in blood is approximately 90 mg/100 mL. What is the weight/volume percent concentration of glucose? What is the molarity of glucose?

9.56 How many grams of each substance are needed to prepare the following solutions?

(a) 50.0 mL of 8.0% (w/v) KCl
(b) 200.0 mL of 7.5% (w/v) acetic acid

9.57 Which of the following solutions is more concentrated?

(a) 0.50 M KCl or 5.0% (w/v) KCl
(b) 2.5% (w/v) $NaHSO_4$ or 0.025 M $NaHSO_4$

9.58 If you had only 23 g of KOH remaining in a bottle, how many milliliters of 10.0% (w/v) solution could you prepare? How many milliliters of 0.25 M solution?

9.59 Over-the-counter hydrogen peroxide solutions are 3% (w/v). What is this concentration in moles per liter?

9.60 The lethal dosage of potassium cyanide in rats is 10 mg KCN per kilogram of body weight. What is this concentration in parts per million?

9.61 The maximum concentration set by the U.S. Environmental Protection Agency for lead in drinking water is 15 ppb. What is this concentration in milligrams per liter? How many liters of water contaminated at this maximum level must you drink to consume 1.0 µg of lead?

9.62 What is the molarity of the following solutions?

(a) 12.5 g $NaHCO_3$ in 350.0 mL solution
(b) 45.0 g H_2SO_4 in 300.0 mL solution
(c) 30.0 g NaCl dissolved to make 500.0 mL solution

9.63 How many moles of solute are in the following solutions?

(a) 200 mL of 0.30 M acetic acid, CH_3CO_2H
(b) 1.50 L of 0.25 M NaOH
(c) 750 mL of 2.5 M nitric acid, HNO_3

9.64 How many milliliters of a 0.75 M HCl solution do you need to obtain 0.0040 mol of HCl?

9.65 Nalorphine, a relative of morphine, is used to combat withdrawal symptoms in heroin users. How many milliliters of a 0.40% (w/v) solution of nalorphine must be injected to obtain a dose of 1.5 mg?

9.66 A flask containing 450 mL of 0.50 M H_2SO_4 was accidentally knocked to the floor. How many grams of $NaHCO_3$ do you need to put on the spill to neutralize the acid according to the following equation?

$$H_2SO_4(aq) + 2\,NaHCO_3(aq) \longrightarrow$$
$$Na_2SO_4(aq) + 2\,H_2O(l) + 2\,CO_2(g)$$

9.67 How many milliliters of 0.0200 M $Na_2S_2O_3$ solution are needed to dissolve 0.450 g of AgBr?

$$AgBr(s) + 2\,Na_2S_2O_3(aq) \longrightarrow$$
$$Na_3Ag(S_2O_3)_2(aq) + NaBr(aq)$$

9.68 How much water must you add to 100.0 mL of orange juice concentrate if you want the final juice to be 20.0% of the strength of the original?

9.69 How much water would you add to 100.0 mL of 0.500 M NaOH if you wanted the final concentration to be 0.150 M?

9.70 An aqueous solution that contains 285 ppm of potassium nitrate (KNO_3) is being used to feed plants in a garden. What volume of this solution is needed to prepare 2.0 L of a solution that is 75 ppm in KNO_3?

9.71 What is the concentration of a NaCl solution, in (w/v)%, prepared by diluting 65 mL of a saturated solution, which has a concentration of 37 (w/v)%, to 480 mL?

9.72 Concentrated (12.0 M) hydrochloric acid is sold for household and industrial purposes under the name "muriatic acid." How many milliliters of 0.500 M HCl solution can be made from 25.0 mL of 12.0 M HCl solution?

9.73 Dilute solutions of $NaHCO_3$ are sometimes used in treating acid burns. How many milliliters of 0.100 M $NaHCO_3$ solution are needed to prepare 750.0 mL of 0.0500 M $NaHCO_3$ solution?

ELECTROLYTES

9.74 What is an electrolyte?

9.75 Give an example of a strong electrolyte and a nonelectrolyte.

9.76 What does it mean when we say that the concentration of Ca^{2+} in blood is 3.0 mEq/L?

9.77 What is the total anion concentration (in mEq/L) of a solution that contains 5.0 mEq/L Na^+, 12.0 mEq/L Ca^{2+}, and 2.0 mEq/L Li^+?

9.78 Kaochlor, a 10% (w/v) KCl solution, is an oral electrolyte supplement administered for potassium deficiency. How many milliequivalents of K^+ are in a 30 mL dose?

9.79 Calculate the gram-equivalent for each of the following ions:

(a) Ca^{2+} (b) K^+
(c) SO_4^{2-} (d) PO_4^{3-}

9.80 Look up the concentration of Cl^- ion in blood in Table 9.6. How many milliliters of blood would be needed to obtain 1.0 g of Cl^- ions?

9.81 Normal blood contains 3 mEq/L of Mg^{2+}. How many milligrams of Mg^{2+} are present in 150.0 mL of blood?

PROPERTIES OF SOLUTIONS

9.82 Which lowers the freezing point of 2.0 kg of water more, 0.20 mol NaOH or 0.20 mol $Ba(OH)_2$? Both compounds are strong electrolytes. Explain.

9.83 Which solution has the higher boiling point, 0.500 M glucose or 0.300 M KCl? Explain.

9.84 Methanol, CH_3OH, is sometimes used as an antifreeze for the water in automobile windshield washer fluids. How many grams of methanol must be added to 5.00 kg of water to lower its freezing point to −10.0 °C? For each mole of solute, the freezing point of 1 kg of water is lowered 1.86 °C.

9.85 Hard candy is prepared by dissolving pure sugar and flavoring in water and heating the solution to boiling. What is the boiling point of a solution produced by adding 650 g of cane sugar (molar mass 342.3 g/mol) to 1.5 kg of water? For each mole of nonvolatile solute, the boiling point of 1 kg of water is raised 0.51 °C.

OSMOSIS

9.86 Why do red blood cells swell up and burst when placed in pure water?

9.87 What does it mean when we say that a 0.15 M NaCl solution is isotonic with blood, whereas distilled water is hypotonic?

9.88 Which of the following solutions has the higher osmolarity?

(a) 0.25 M KBr or 0.20 M Na_2SO_4
(b) 0.30 M NaOH or 3.0% (w/v) NaOH

9.89 Which of the following solutions will give rise to a greater osmotic pressure at equilibrium: 5.00 g of NaCl in 350.0 mL water or 35.0 g of glucose in 400.0 mL water? For NaCl, MW = 58.5 amu; for glucose, MW = 180 amu.

9.90 A pickling solution is prepared by dissolving 270 g of NaCl in 3.8 L of water. Calculate the osmolarity of the solution.

9.91 An isotonic solution must be approximately 0.30 osmol. How much KCl is needed to prepare 175 mL of an isotonic solution?

Applications

9.92 How does the body increase oxygen availability at high altitude? [*Breathing and Oxygen Transport, p. 266*]

9.93 What are the major electrolytes in sweat, and what are their approximate concentrations in mEq/L? [*Electrolytes, Fluid Replacement, and Sports Drinks, p. 279*]

9.94 Why is a sports drink more effective than plain water for rehydration after extended exercise? [*Electrolytes, Fluid Replacement, and Sports Drinks, p. 279*]

9.95 How does an enteric coating on a medication work? [*Timed-Release Medications, p. 286*]

General Questions and Problems

9.96 Hyperbaric chambers, which provide high pressures (up to 6 atm) of either air or pure oxygen, are used to treat a variety of conditions, ranging from decompression sickness in deep-sea divers to carbon monoxide poisoning.

    (a) What is the partial pressure of O_2 (in millimeters of Hg) in a hyperbaric chamber pressurized to 5 atm with air that is 18% in O_2?

    (b) What is the solubility of O_2 (in grams per 100 mL) in the blood at this partial pressure? The solubility of O_2 is 2.1 g/100 mL for $P_{O_2} = 1$ atm.

9.97 Express the solubility of O_2 in Problem 9.96(b) in units of molarity.

9.98 Uric acid, the principal constituent of some kidney stones, has the formula $C_5H_4N_4O_3$. In aqueous solution, the solubility of uric acid is only 0.067 g/L. Express this concentration in (w/v)%, in parts per million, and in molarity.

9.99 Emergency treatment of cardiac arrest victims sometimes involves injection of a calcium chloride solution directly into the heart muscle. How many grams of $CaCl_2$ are administered in an injection of 5.0 mL of a 5.0% (w/v) solution? How many milliequivalents of Ca^{2+}?

9.100 Nitric acid, HNO_3, is available commercially at a concentration of 16 M. What volume would you use to prepare 750 mL of a 0.20 M solution?

9.101 One test for vitamin C (ascorbic acid, $C_6H_8O_6$) is based on the reaction of the vitamin with iodine:

$$C_6H_8O_6(aq) + I_2(aq) \longrightarrow C_6H_6O_6(aq) + 2\,HI(aq)$$

    (a) If 25.0 mL of a fruit juice requires 13.0 mL of 0.0100 M I_2 solution for reaction, what is the molarity of the ascorbic acid in the fruit juice?

    (b) The Food and Drug Administration recommends that 60 mg of ascorbic acid be consumed per day. How

many milliliters of the fruit juice in part (a) must a person drink to obtain the recommended dosage?

9.102 *Ringer's solution*, used in the treatment of burns and wounds, is prepared by dissolving 8.6 g of NaCl, 0.30 g of KCl, and 0.33 g of $CaCl_2$ in water and diluting to a volume of 1.00 L. What is the molarity of each component?

9.103 What is the osmolarity of Ringer's solution (see Problem 9.102)? Is it hypotonic, isotonic, or hypertonic with blood plasma (0.30 osmol)?

9.104 The typical dosage of statin drugs for the treatment of high cholesterol is 10 mg. Assuming a total blood volume of 5.0 L, calculate the concentration of drug in the blood in units of (w/v)%.

9.105 Assuming the density of blood in healthy individuals is approximately 1.05 g/mL, report the concentration of drug in Problem 9.104 in units of ppm.

9.106 In many states, a person with a blood alcohol concentration of 0.080% (v/v) is considered legally drunk. What volume of total alcohol does this concentration represent, assuming a blood volume of 5.0 L?

9.107 Ammonia is very soluble in water (51.8 g/L at 20 °C and 760 mmHg).

    (a) Show how NH_3 can hydrogen bond to water.

    (b) What is the solubility of ammonia in water in moles per liter?

9.108 Cobalt(II) chloride, a blue solid, can absorb water from the air to form cobalt(II) chloride hexahydrate, a pink solid. The equilibrium is so sensitive to moisture in the air that $CoCl_2$ is used as a humidity indicator.

    (a) Write a balanced equation for the equilibrium. Be sure to include water as a reactant to produce the hexahydrate.

    (b) How many grams of water are released by the decomposition of 2.50 g of cobalt(II) chloride hexahydrate?

9.109 How many milliliters of 0.150 M $BaCl_2$ are needed to react completely with 35.0 mL of 0.200 M Na_2SO_4? How many grams of $BaSO_4$ will be formed?

9.110 Many compounds are only partially dissociated into ions in aqueous solution. Trichloroacetic acid (CCl_3CO_2H), for instance, is partially dissociated in water according to the equation

$$CCl_3CO_2H(aq) \rightleftharpoons H^+(aq) + CCl_3CO_2^-(aq)$$

For a solution prepared by dissolving 1.00 mol of trichloroacetic acid in 1.00 kg of water, 36.0% of the trichloroacetic acid dissociates to form H^+ and $CCl_3CO_2^-$ ions.

    (a) What is the total concentration of dissolved ions and molecules in 1 kg of water?

    (b) What is the freezing point of this solution? (The freezing point of 1 kg of water is lowered 1.86 °C for each mole of solute particles.)

CHAPTER 10

Acids and Bases

CONCEPTS TO REVIEW

**Acids, Bases, and
Neutralization Reactions**
(Sections 4.11 and 6.10)

**Reversible Reactions and
Chemical Equilibrium**
(Section 7.7)

**Equilibrium Equations and
Equilibrium Constants**
(Section 7.8)

**Units of Concentration;
Molarity**
(Section 9.7)

Ion Equivalents
(Section 9.10)

▲ Acids are found in many of the foods we eat, including tomatoes, peppers, and these citrus fruits.

CONTENTS

CHAPTER GOALS

We have already touched on the subject of acids and bases on several occasions, but the time has come for a more detailed study that will answer the following questions:

1. What are acids and bases?

THE GOAL: Be able to recognize acids and bases and write equations for common acid–base reactions.

2. What effect does the strength of acids and bases have on their reactions?

THE GOAL: Be able to interpret acid strength using acid dissociation constants K_a and predict the favored direction of acid–base equilibria.

3. What is the ion-product constant for water?

THE GOAL: Be able to write the equation for this constant and use it to find the concentration of H_3O^+ or OH^-.

4. What is the pH scale for measuring acidity?

THE GOAL: Be able to explain the pH scale and find pH from the H_3O^+ concentration.

5. What is a buffer?

THE GOAL: Be able to explain how a buffer maintains pH and how the bicarbonate buffer functions in the body.

6. How is the acid or base concentration of a solution determined?

THE GOAL: Be able to explain how a titration procedure works and use the results of a titration to calculate acid or base concentration in a solution.

A cids! The word evokes images of dangerous, corrosive liquids that eat away everything they touch. Although a few well-known substances such as sulfuric acid (H_2SO_4) do indeed fit this description, most acids are relatively harmless. In fact, many acids, such as ascorbic acid (vitamin C), are necessary for life.

10.1 Acids and Bases in Aqueous Solution

Let us take a moment to review what we said about acids and bases in Sections 4.11 and 6.10 before going on to a more systematic study:

- An acid is a substance that produces hydrogen ions, H^+, when dissolved in water.
- A base is a substance that produces hydroxide ions, OH^-, when dissolved in water.
- The neutralization reaction of an acid with a base yields water plus a *salt*, an ionic compound composed of the cation from the base and the anion from the acid.

The above definitions of acids and bases were proposed in 1887 by the Swedish chemist Svante Arrhenius and are useful for many purposes. The definitions are limited, however, because they refer only to reactions that take place in aqueous solution. (We will see shortly how the definitions can be broadened.) Another issue is that the H^+ ion is so reactive it does not exist in water. Instead, H^+ reacts with H_2O to give the **hydronium ion**, H_3O^+, as mentioned in Section 4.11. When gaseous HCl dissolves in water, for instance, H_3O^+ and Cl^- are formed. As described in Section 5.8, electrostatic potential maps show that the hydrogen of HCl is positively polarized and electron-poor (blue), whereas the oxygen of water is negatively polarized and electron-rich (red):

Hydronium ion The H_3O^+ ion, formed when an acid reacts with water.

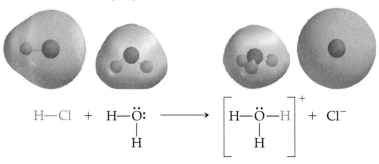

Thus, the Arrhenius definition is updated to acknowledge that an acid yields H_3O^+ in water rather than H^+. In practice, however, the notations H_3O^+ and $H^+(aq)$ are often used interchangeably.

The Arrhenius definition of a base is correct as far as it goes, but it is important to realize that the OH^- ions "produced" by the base can come from either of two sources. Metal hydroxides, such as NaOH, KOH, and $Ba(OH)_2$, are ionic compounds that already contain OH^- ions and merely release those ions when they dissolve in water. Ammonia, however, is not ionic and contains no OH^- ions in its structure. Nonetheless, ammonia is a base because it undergoes a reaction with water when it dissolves, producing NH_4^+ and OH^- ions:

$$NaOH(s) \xrightarrow[\text{in } H_2O]{\text{Dissolve}} Na^+(aq) + OH^-(aq)$$

> This OH^- ion comes from NaOH.

> This OH^- ion comes from H_2O.

$$H-\overset{..}{N}-H(g) + H_2O(l) \rightleftharpoons H-\overset{H}{\underset{H}{N^\pm}}-H(aq) + OH^-(aq)$$

The reaction of ammonia with water is a reversible process (Section 7.7) whose equilibrium strongly favors unreacted ammonia. (⫘, p. 198) Nevertheless, *some* OH^- ions are produced, so NH_3 is a base.

10.2 Some Common Acids and Bases

Acids and bases are present in a variety of foods and consumer products. Acids generally have a sour taste, and nearly every sour food contains an acid: Lemons, oranges, and grapefruit contain citric acid, for instance, and sour milk contains lactic acid. Bases are not so obvious in foods, but most of us have them stored under the kitchen or bathroom sink. Bases are present in many household cleaning agents, from perfumed toilet soap, to ammonia-based window cleaners, to the substance you put down the drain to dissolve hair, grease, and other materials that clog it.

Some of the most common acids and bases are listed below. It is a good idea at this point to learn their names and formulas, because we will refer to them often.

▲ Hydrochloric acid, also known as muriatic acid, has many industrial applications.

- **Sulfuric acid, H_2SO_4,** is probably the most important raw material in the chemical and pharmaceutical industries, and is manufactured in greater quantity worldwide than any other industrial chemical. Over 45 million tons are prepared in the United States annually for use in many hundreds of industrial processes, including the preparation of phosphate fertilizers. Its most common consumer use is as the acid found in automobile batteries. As anyone who has splashed battery acid on their skin or clothing knows, sulfuric acid is highly corrosive and can cause painful burns.

- **Hydrochloric acid, HCl,** or *muriatic acid* as it was historically known, has many industrial applications, including its use in metal cleaning and in the manufacture of high-fructose corn syrup. Aqueous HCl is also present as "stomach acid" in the digestive systems of most mammals.

- **Phosphoric acid, H_3PO_4,** is used in vast quantities in the manufacture of phosphate fertilizers. In addition, it is also used as an additive in foods and toothpastes. The tart taste of many soft drinks is due to the presence of phosphoric acid.

- **Nitric acid, HNO_3,** is a strong oxidizing agent that is used for many purposes, including the manufacture of ammonium nitrate fertilizer and military explosives. When spilled on the skin, it leaves a characteristic yellow coloration because of its reaction with skin proteins.

- **Acetic acid, CH_3CO_2H,** is the primary organic constituent of vinegar. It also occurs in all living cells and is used in many industrial processes such as the preparation of solvents, lacquers, and coatings.

- **Sodium hydroxide, NaOH,** also called *caustic soda* or *lye,* is the most commonly used of all bases. Industrially, it is used in the production of aluminum from its ore, in the production of glass, and in the manufacture of soap from animal fat. Concentrated solutions of NaOH can cause severe burns if allowed to sit on the skin for long. Drain cleaners often contain NaOH because it reacts with the fats and proteins found in grease and hair.

- **Calcium hydroxide, Ca(OH)₂,** or *slaked lime,* is made industrially by treating lime (CaO) with water. It has many applications, including its use in mortars and cements. An aqueous solution of Ca(OH)₂ is often called *limewater.*

- **Magnesium hydroxide, Mg(OH)₂,** or *milk of magnesia,* is an additive in foods, toothpaste, and many over-the-counter medications. Antacids such as Rolaids, Mylanta, and Maalox, for instance, all contain magnesium hydroxide.

- **Ammonia, NH₃,** is used primarily as a fertilizer, but it also has many other industrial applications including the manufacture of pharmaceuticals and explosives. A dilute solution of ammonia is frequently used around the house as a glass cleaner.

▲ Soap is manufactured by the reaction of vegetable oils and animal fats with the bases NaOH and KOH.

10.3 The Brønsted–Lowry Definition of Acids and Bases

The Arrhenius definition of acids and bases discussed in Section 10.1 applies only to reactions that take place in aqueous solution. A far more general definition was proposed in 1923 by the Danish chemist Johannes Brønsted and the English chemist Thomas Lowry. A **Brønsted–Lowry acid** is any substance that is able to give a hydrogen ion, H^+, to another molecule or ion. A hydrogen *atom* consists of a proton and an electron, so a hydrogen *ion,* H^+, is simply a proton. Thus, we often refer to acids as *proton donors.* The reaction need not occur in water, and a Brønsted–Lowry acid need not give appreciable concentrations of H_3O^+ ions in water.

Different acids can supply different numbers of H^+ ions, as we saw in Section 4.11. (, p. 98) Acids with one proton to donate, such as HCl and HNO₃, are called *monoprotic acids;* H₂SO₄ is a *diprotic acid* because it has two protons to donate, and H₃PO₄ is a *triprotic acid* because it has three protons to donate. Notice that the acidic H atoms (that is, the H atoms that are donated as protons) are bonded to electronegative atoms, such as chlorine or oxygen.

Brønsted–Lowry acid A substance that can donate a hydrogen ion, H^+, to another molecule or ion.

$$H—Cl$$

Hydrochloric acid
(monoprotic)

$$\underset{O}{\overset{O}{N}}—OH$$

Nitric acid
(monoprotic)

$$HO—\overset{O}{\underset{O}{S}}—OH$$

Sulfuric acid
(diprotic)

$$HO—\overset{O}{\underset{OH}{P}}—OH$$

Phosphoric acid
(triprotic)

Acetic acid (CH₃CO₂H), an example of an organic acid, actually has a total of 4 hydrogens, but only the one bonded to the electronegative oxygen is positively polarized and therefore acidic. The 3 hydrogens bonded to carbon are not acidic. Most organic acids are similar in that they contain many hydrogen atoms, but only the one in the —CO₂H group (blue in the electrostatic potential map) is acidic:

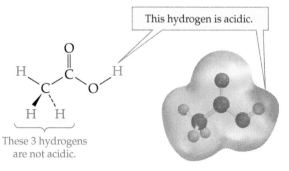

This hydrogen is acidic.

These 3 hydrogens are not acidic.

Brønsted–Lowry base A substance that can accept H^+ from an acid.

Whereas a Brønsted–Lowry acid is a substance that *donates* H^+ ions, a **Brønsted–Lowry base** is a substance that *accepts* H^+ from an acid. The reaction need not occur in water, and the Brønsted–Lowry base need not give appreciable concentrations of OH^- ions in water. Gaseous NH_3, for example, acts as a base to accept H^+ from gaseous HCl and yield the ionic solid $NH_4^+Cl^-$:

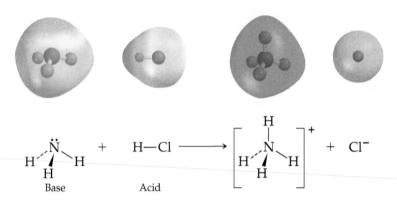

Base   Acid

Putting the acid and base definitions together, *an acid–base reaction is one in which a proton is transferred*. The general reaction between proton-donor acids and proton-acceptor bases can be represented as

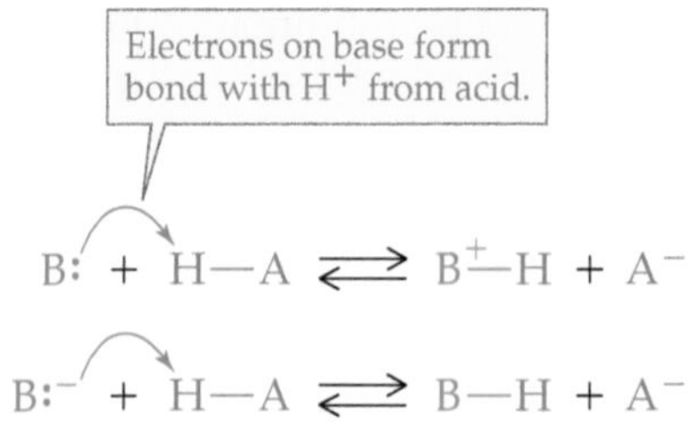

Electrons on base form bond with H^+ from acid.

$$B: + H-A \rightleftarrows B^+{-}H + A^-$$

$$B:^- + H-A \rightleftarrows B{-}H + A^-$$

where the abbreviation HA represents a Brønsted–Lowry acid and B: or B:$^-$ represents a Brønsted–Lowry base. Notice in these acid–base reactions that both electrons in the product B—H bond come from the base, as indicated by the curved arrow flowing from the electron pair of the base to the hydrogen atom of the acid. Thus, the B—H bond that forms is a coordinate covalent bond (Section 5.4). (⊂⊃⊃, p. 115) In fact, a Brønsted–Lowry base *must* have such a lone pair of electrons; without them, it could not accept H^+ from an acid.

A base can be either neutral (B:) or negatively charged (B:$^-$). If the base is neutral, then the product has a positive charge (BH^+) after H^+ has added. Ammonia is an example:

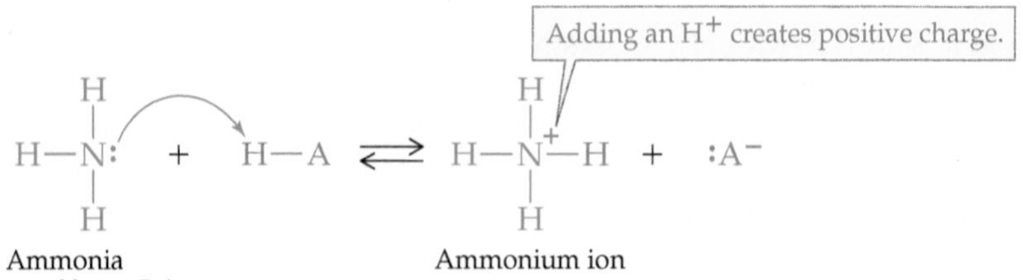

Adding an H^+ creates positive charge.

Ammonia
(a neutral base, B:)

Ammonium ion

If the base is negatively charged, then the product is neutral (BH). Hydroxide ion is an example:

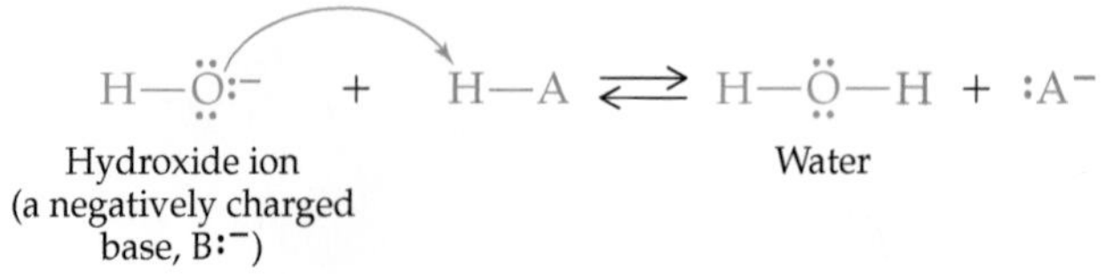

$$H-\ddot{O}:^- + H-A \rightleftarrows H-\ddot{O}-H + :A^-$$

Hydroxide ion
(a negatively charged
base, B:$^-$)

Water

An important consequence of the Brønsted–Lowry definitions is that the *products* of an acid–base reaction can also behave as acids and bases. Many acid–base reactions are reversible (Section 7.8), although in some cases the equilibrium constant for the reaction is quite large. (⬤⬤⬤, p. 200) For example, suppose we have as a forward reaction an acid HA donating a proton to a base B to produce A⁻. This product A⁻ is a base because it can act as a proton acceptor in the reverse reaction. At the same time, the product BH⁺ acts as an acid because it donates a proton in the reverse reaction:

Double arrow indicates reversible reaction.

$$B: \; + \; H{-}A \; \rightleftharpoons \; :A^- \; + \; \overset{+}{B}{-}H$$

Base   Acid   Base   Acid

Conjugate acid–base pair

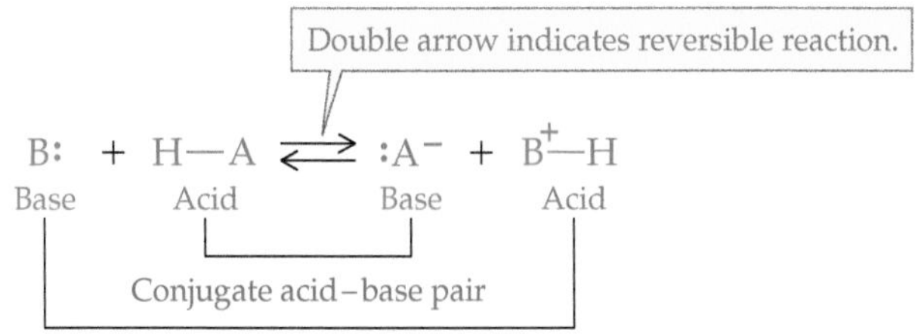

Pairs of chemical species such as B, BH⁺ and HA, A⁻ are called **conjugate acid–base pairs**. They are species that are found on opposite sides of a chemical reaction whose formulas differ by only one H⁺. Thus, the product anion A⁻ is the **conjugate base** of the reactant acid HA, and HA is the **conjugate acid** of the base A⁻. Similarly, the reactant B is the conjugate base of the product acid BH⁺, and BH⁺ is the conjugate acid of the base B. The number of protons in a conjugate acid–base pair is always one greater than the number of protons in the base of the pair. To give some examples, acetic acid and acetate ion, the hydronium ion and water, and the ammonium ion and ammonia all make conjugate acid–base pairs:

Conjugate acid–base pair Two substances whose formulas differ by only a hydrogen ion, H⁺.

Conjugate base The substance formed by loss of H⁺ from an acid.

Conjugate acid The substance formed by addition of H⁺ to a base.

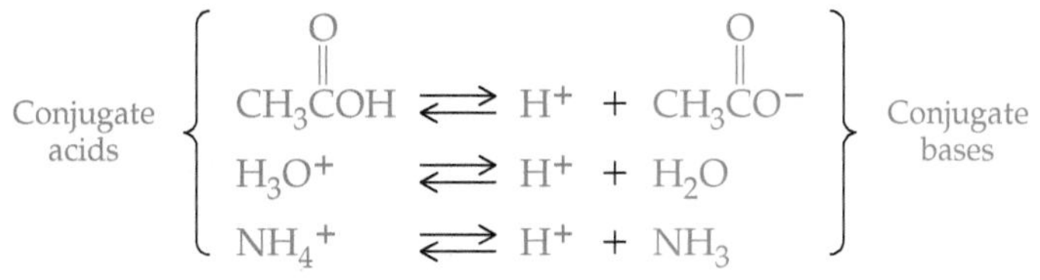

Conjugate acids

$$CH_3\overset{O}{\overset{\|}{C}}OH \; \rightleftharpoons \; H^+ \; + \; CH_3\overset{O}{\overset{\|}{C}}O^-$$

$$H_3O^+ \; \rightleftharpoons \; H^+ \; + \; H_2O$$

$$NH_4^+ \; \rightleftharpoons \; H^+ \; + \; NH_3$$

Conjugate bases

WORKED EXAMPLE   **10.1** Acids and Bases: Identifying Brønsted–Lowry Acids and Bases

Identify each of the following as a Brønsted–Lowry acid or base:

(a) $PO_4{}^{3-}$

(b) $HClO_4$

(c) CN^-

ANALYSIS A Brønsted–Lowry acid must have a hydrogen that it can donate as H⁺, and a Brønsted–Lowry base must have an atom with a lone pair of electrons that can bond to H⁺. Typically, a Brønsted–Lowry base is an anion derived by loss of H⁺ from an acid.

SOLUTION

(a) The phosphate anion ($PO_4{}^{3-}$) is a Brønsted–Lowry base derived by loss of 3 H⁺ ions from phosphoric acid, H_3PO_4.

(b) Perchloric acid ($HClO_4$) is a Brønsted–Lowry acid because it can donate an H⁺ ion.

(c) The cyanide ion (CN^-) is a Brønsted–Lowry base derived by removal of an H⁺ ion from hydrogen cyanide, HCN.

WORKED EXAMPLE **10.2** Acids and Bases: Identifying Conjugate
Acid–Base Pairs

Write formulas for

(a) The conjugate acid of the cyanide ion, CN^-
(b) The conjugate base of perchloric acid, $HClO_4$

ANALYSIS A conjugate acid is formed by adding H^+ to a base; a conjugate base is formed by removing H^+ from an acid.

SOLUTION

(a) HCN is the conjugate acid of CN^-.
(b) ClO_4^- is the conjugate base of $HClO_4$.

PROBLEM 10.1

Which of the following would you expect to be Brønsted–Lowry acids?

(a) HCO_2H (b) H_2S (c) $SnCl_2$

PROBLEM 10.2

Which of the following would you expect to be Brønsted–Lowry bases?

(a) SO_3^{2-} (b) Ag^+ (c) F^-

PROBLEM 10.3

Write formulas for:

(a) The conjugate acid of HS^- (b) The conjugate acid of PO_4^{3-}
(c) The conjugate base of H_2CO_3 (d) The conjugate base of NH_4^+

KEY CONCEPT PROBLEM 10.4

For the reaction shown here, identify the Brønsted–Lowry acids, bases, and conjugate acid–base pairs.

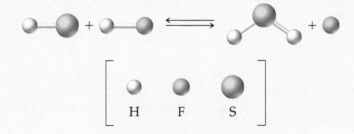

10.4 Water as Both an Acid and a Base

Water is neither an acid nor a base in the Arrhenius sense because it does not contain appreciable concentrations of either H_3O^+ or OH^-. In the Brønsted–Lowry sense, however, water can act as *both* an acid and a base. When in contact with a base, water reacts as a Brønsted–Lowry acid and *donates* a proton to the base. In its reaction with ammonia, for example, water donates H^+ to ammonia to form the ammonium ion:

$$NH_3 + H_2O \longrightarrow NH_4^+ + OH^-$$

| Ammonia | Water | Ammonium ion | Hydroxide ion |
| (base) | (acid) | (acid) | (base) |

When in contact with an acid, water reacts as a Brønsted–Lowry base and *accepts* H^+ from the acid. This, of course, is exactly what happens when an acid such as HCl dissolves in water, as discussed in Section 10.1.

Water uses two electrons to form a bond to H^+.

$$H-\ddot{O}: + H-Cl \longrightarrow H-\overset{+}{\underset{|}{\ddot{O}}}-H + Cl^-$$

Water   (An acid)   Hydronium ion
(A base)

Substances like water, which can react as either an acid or a base depending on the circumstances, are said to be **amphoteric** (am-pho-**tare**-ic). When water acts as an acid, it donates H^+ and becomes OH^-; when it acts as a base, it accepts H^+ and becomes H_3O^+.

Amphoteric Describing a substance that can react as either an acid or a base.

PROBLEM 10.5

Is water an acid or a base in the following reactions?

(a) $H_3PO_4(aq) + H_2O(l) \longrightarrow H_2PO_4^-(aq) + H_3O^+(aq)$

(b) $F^-(aq) + H_2O(l) \longrightarrow HF(aq) + OH^-(aq)$

(c) $NH_4^+(aq) + H_2O(aq) \longrightarrow NH_3(aq) + H_3O^+(aq)$

10.5 Acid and Base Strength

Some acids and bases, such as sulfuric acid (H_2SO_4), hydrochloric acid (HCl), or sodium hydroxide (NaOH), are highly corrosive. They react readily and, in contact with skin, can cause serious burns. Other acids and bases are not nearly as reactive. Acetic acid (CH_3COOH, the major component in vinegar) and phosphoric acid (H_3PO_4) are found in many food products. Why are some acids and bases relatively "safe," while others must be handled with extreme caution? The answer lies in how easily they produce the active ions for an acid (H^+) or a base (OH^-).

As indicated in Table 10.1, acids differ in their ability to give up a proton. The six acids at the top of the table are **strong acids**, meaning that they give up a proton easily and are essentially 100% **dissociated**, or split apart into ions, in water. Those remaining are **weak acids**, meaning that they give up a proton with difficulty and are substantially less than 100% dissociated in water. In a similar way, the bases at the top of the table are **weak bases** because they have little affinity for a proton, and the bases at the bottom of the table are **strong bases** because they grab and hold a proton tightly.

Note that diprotic acids, such as sulfuric acid, undergo two stepwise dissociations in water. The first dissociation yields HSO_4^- and occurs to the extent of nearly 100%, so H_2SO_4 is a strong acid. The second dissociation yields SO_4^{2-} and takes place to a much lesser extent because separation of a positively charged H^+ from the negatively charged HSO_4^- anion is difficult. Thus, HSO_4^- is a weak acid:

$$H_2SO_4(l) + H_2O(l) \longrightarrow H_3O^+(aq) + HSO_4^-(aq)$$

$$HSO_4^-(aq) + H_2O(l) \rightleftharpoons H_3O^+(aq) + SO_4^{2-}(aq)$$

Strong acid An acid that gives up H^+ easily and is essentially 100% dissociated in water.

Dissociation The splitting apart of an acid in water to give H^+ and an anion.

Weak acid An acid that gives up H^+ with difficulty and is less than 100% dissociated in water.

Weak base A base that has only a slight affinity for H^+ and holds it weakly.

Strong base A base that has a high affinity for H^+ and holds it tightly.

TABLE 10.1 Relative Strengths of Acids and Conjugate Bases

		ACID		CONJUGATE BASE			
Increasing acid strength	Strong acids: 100% dissociated	Perchloric acid	$HClO_4$	ClO_4^-	Perchlorate ion	Little or no reaction as bases	**Increasing base strength**
		Sulfuric acid	H_2SO_4	HSO_4^-	Hydrogen sulfate ion		
		Hydriodic acid	HI	I^-	Iodide ion		
		Hydrobromic acid	HBr	Br^-	Bromide ion		
		Hydrochloric acid	HCl	Cl^-	Chloride ion		
		Nitric acid	HNO_3	NO_3^-	Nitrate ion		
		Hydronium ion	H_3O^+	H_2O	**Water**		
	Weak acids	Hydrogen sulfate ion	HSO_4^-	SO_4^{2-}	Sulfate ion	Very weak bases	
		Phosphoric acid	H_3PO_4	$H_2PO_4^-$	Dihydrogen phosphate ion		
		Nitrous acid	HNO_2	NO_2^-	Nitrite ion		
		Hydrofluoric acid	HF	F^-	Fluoride ion		
		Acetic acid	CH_3COOH	CH_3COO^-	Acetate ion		
	Very weak acids	Carbonic acid	H_2CO_3	HCO_3^-	Bicarbonate ion	Weak bases	
		Dihydrogen phosphate ion	$H_2PO_4^-$	HPO_4^{2-}	Hydrogen phosphate ion		
		Ammonium ion	NH_4^+	NH_3	Ammonia		
		Hydrocyanic acid	HCN	CN^-	Cyanide ion		
		Bicarbonate ion	HCO_3^-	CO_3^{2-}	Carbonate ion		
		Hydrogen phosphate ion	HPO_4^{2-}	PO_4^{3-}	Phosphate ion		
		Water	H_2O	OH^-	**Hydroxide ion**	Strong base	

Perhaps the most striking feature of Table 10.1 is the inverse relationship between acid strength and base strength. *The stronger the acid, the weaker its conjugate base; the weaker the acid, the stronger its conjugate base.* HCl, for example, is a strong acid, so Cl^- is a very weak base. H_2O, however, is a very weak acid, so OH^- is a strong base.

Why is there an inverse relationship between acid strength and base strength? To answer this question, think about what it means for an acid or base to be strong or weak. A strong acid H—A is one that readily gives up a proton, meaning that its conjugate base A^- has little affinity for the proton. But this is exactly the definition of a weak base—a substance that has little affinity for a proton. As a result, the reverse reaction occurs to a lesser extent, as indicated by the size of the forward and reverse arrows in the reaction:

Larger arrow indicates forward reaction is stronger.

$$H—A + H_2O \rightleftharpoons H_3O^+ + A^-$$

If this is a strong acid because it gives up a proton readily . . .

. . . then this is a weak base because it has little affinity for a proton.

In the same way, a weak acid is one that gives up a proton with difficulty, meaning that its conjugate base has a high affinity for the proton. But this is just the definition of a strong base—a substance that has a high affinity for the proton. The reverse reaction now occurs more readily.

$$H\!-\!A \ + \ H_2O \ \rightleftarrows \ H_3O^+ \ + \ A^-$$

If this is a weak acid because it gives up a proton with difficulty . . .

Larger arrow indicates reverse reaction is stronger.

. . . then this is a strong base because it has a high affinity for a proton.

Knowing the relative strengths of different acids as shown in Table 10.1 makes it possible to predict the direction of proton-transfer reactions. *An acid–base proton-transfer equilibrium always favors reaction of the stronger acid with the stronger base, and formation of the weaker acid and base.* That is, the proton always leaves the stronger acid (whose weaker conjugate base cannot hold the proton) and always ends up in the weaker acid (whose stronger conjugate base holds the proton tightly). Put another way, in a contest for the proton, the stronger base always wins.

Stronger acid + Stronger base $\rightleftarrows$ Weaker base + Weaker acid

To try out this rule, compare the reactions of acetic acid with water and with hydroxide ion. The idea is to write the equation, identify the acid on each side of the arrow, and then decide which acid is stronger and which is weaker. For example, the reaction of acetic acid with water to give acetate ion and hydronium ion is favored in the reverse direction, because acetic acid is a weaker acid than H_3O^+:

$$\underset{\text{Weaker acid}}{CH_3\overset{\displaystyle O}{\overset{\displaystyle \|}{C}}OH} \ + \ H_2O \ \rightleftarrows \ CH_3\overset{\displaystyle O}{\overset{\displaystyle \|}{C}}O^- \ + \ \underset{\text{Stronger acid}}{H_3O^+}$$

Reverse reaction is favored.

This base holds the proton less tightly . . . . . . than this base does.

On the other hand, the reaction of acetic acid with hydroxide ion to give acetate ion and water is favored in the forward direction, because acetic acid is a stronger acid than H_2O:

$$\underset{\text{Stronger acid}}{CH_3\overset{\displaystyle O}{\overset{\displaystyle \|}{C}}OH} \ + \ OH^- \ \rightleftarrows \ CH_3\overset{\displaystyle O}{\overset{\displaystyle \|}{C}}O^- \ + \ \underset{\text{Weaker acid}}{H_2O}$$

Forward reaction is favored.

This base holds the proton more tightly . . . . . . than this base does.

WORKED EXAMPLE **10.3** Acid/Base Strength: Predicting Direction of H-transfer Reactions

Write a balanced equation for the proton-transfer reaction between phosphate ion ($PO_4{}^{3-}$) and water, and determine in which direction the equilibrium is favored.

ANALYSIS Look in Table 10.1 to see the relative acid and base strengths of the species involved in the reaction. The acid–base proton-transfer equilibrium will favor reaction of the stronger acid and formation of the weaker acid.

SOLUTION
Phosphate ion is the conjugate base of a weak acid ($HPO_4{}^{2-}$) and is therefore a relatively strong base. Table 10.1 shows that $HPO_4{}^{2-}$ is a stronger acid than H_2O, and OH^- is a stronger base than $PO_4{}^{3-}$, so the reaction is favored in the reverse direction:

$$\underset{\text{Weaker base}}{PO_4{}^{3-}(aq)} \ + \ \underset{\text{Weaker acid}}{H_2O(l)} \ \rightleftarrows \ \underset{\text{Stronger acid}}{HPO_4{}^{2-}(aq)} \ + \ \underset{\text{Stronger base}}{OH^-(aq)}$$

APPLICATION ▶ GERD—Too Much Acid or Not Enough?

Strong acids are very caustic substances that can dissolve even metals, and no one would think of ingesting them. However, the major component of the gastric juices secreted in the stomach is hydrochloric acid—a strong acid—and the acidic environment in the stomach is vital to good health and nutrition.

Stomach acid is essential for the digestion of proteins and for the absorption of certain micronutrients, such as calcium, magnesium, iron, and vitamin B_{12}. It also creates a sterile environment in the gut by killing yeast and bacteria that may be ingested. If these gastric juices leak up into the esophagus, the tube through which food and drink enter the stomach, they can cause the burning sensation in the chest or throat known as either heartburn or acid indigestion. Persistent irritation of the esophagus is known as gastroesophageal reflux disease (GERD) and, if untreated, can lead to more serious health problems.

Hydrogen ions and chloride ions are secreted separately from the cytoplasm of cells lining the stomach and then combine to form HCl that is usually close to 0.10 M. The HCl is then released into the stomach cavity, where the concentration is diluted to about 0.01–0.001 M. Unlike the esophagus, the stomach is coated by a thick mucus layer that protects the stomach wall from damage by this caustic solution.

Those who suffer from acid indigestion can obtain relief using over-the-counter antacids, such as Tums or Rolaids (see Section 10.14, p. 320). Chronic conditions such as GERD, however, are often treated with prescription medications. GERD can be treated by two classes of drugs. Proton-pump inhibitors (PPI), such as Prevacid and Prilosec, prevent the production the H^+ ions in the parietal cells, while H2-receptor blockers (Tagamet, Zantac, and Pepcid) prevent the release of stomach acid into the lumen. Both drugs effectively decrease the production of stomach acid to ease the symptoms of GERD.

Ironically, GERD can also be caused by not having enough stomach acid—a condition known as *hypochlorhydria*. The valve that controls the release of stomach contents to the small intestine is triggered by acidity. If this valve fails to open because the stomach is not acidic enough, the contents of the stomach can be churned up into the esophagus.

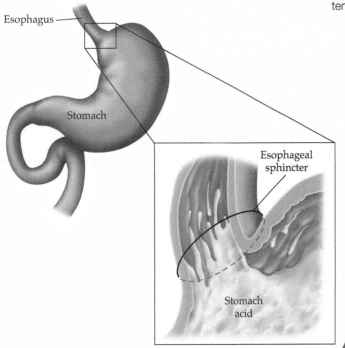

▲ The burning sensation and other symptoms associated with GERD are caused by the reflux of the acidic contents of the stomach into the esophagus.

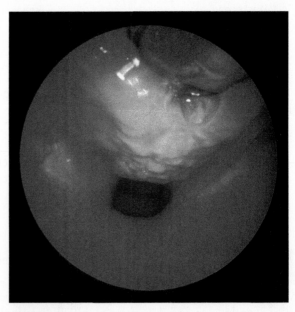

▲ If not treated, GERD can cause ulcers and scarring of esophageal tissue.

See Additional Problem 10.96 at the end of the chapter.

PROBLEM 10.6

Use Table 10.1 to identify the stronger acid in the following pairs:

(a) H_2O or NH_4^+
(b) H_2SO_4 or CH_3CO_2H
(c) HCN or H_2CO_3

PROBLEM 10.7

Use Table 10.1 to identify the stronger base in the following pairs:

(a) F^- or Br^- **(b)** OH^- or HCO_3^-

PROBLEM 10.8

Write a balanced equation for the proton-transfer reaction between a hydrogen phosphate ion and a hydroxide ion. Identify each acid–base pair, and determine in which direction the equilibrium is favored.

━◉ KEY CONCEPT PROBLEM 10.9

From this electrostatic potential map of the amino acid alanine, identify the most acidic hydrogens in the molecule:

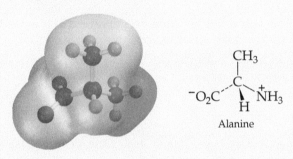

Alanine

10.6 Acid Dissociation Constants

The reaction of a weak acid with water, like any chemical equilibrium, can be described by an equilibrium equation (Section 7.8), where square brackets indicate the concentrations of the enclosed species in molarity (moles per liter). (⊂⊃, p. 200)

For the reaction $HA(aq) + H_2O(l) \rightleftharpoons H_3O^+(aq) + A^-(aq)$

We have $$K = \frac{[H_3O^+][A^-]}{[HA][H_2O]}$$

Because water is a solvent as well as a participant for the reaction, its concentration is essentially constant and has no effect on the equilibrium. Therefore, we usually put the equilibrium constant K and the water concentration $[H_2O]$ together to make a new constant called the **acid dissociation constant, K_a.** The acid dissociation constant is simply the hydronium ion concentration $[H_3O^+]$ times the conjugate base concentration $[A^-]$ divided by the undissociated acid concentration $[HA]$:

Acid dissociation constant $$K_a = K[H_2O] = \frac{[H_3O^+][A^-]}{[HA]}$$

For a strong acid, the H_3O^+ and A^- concentrations are much larger than the HA concentration, so K_a is very large. In fact, the K_a values for strong acids such as HCl are so large that it is difficult and not very useful to measure them. For a weak acid, however, the H_3O^+ and A^- concentrations are smaller than the HA concentration, so K_a is small. Table 10.2 gives K_a values for some common acids and illustrates several important points:

- Strong acids have K_a values much greater than 1 because dissociation is favored.
- Weak acids have K_a values much less than 1 because dissociation is not favored.

TABLE 10.2 Some Acid Dissociation Constants, K_a, at 25 °C

ACID	K_a	ACID	K_a
Hydrofluoric acid (HF)	3.5×10^{-4}	*Polyprotic acids*	
Hydrocyanic acid (HCN)	4.9×10^{-10}	Sulfuric acid	
Ammonium ion (NH_4^+)	5.6×10^{-10}	H_2SO_4	Large
		HSO_4^-	1.2×10^{-2}
Organic acids		Phosphoric acid	
Formic acid (HCOOH)	1.8×10^{-4}	H_3PO_4	7.5×10^{-3}
Acetic acid (CH_3COOH)	1.8×10^{-5}	$H_2PO_4^-$	6.2×10^{-8}
Propanoic acid	1.3×10^{-5}	HPO_4^{2-}	2.2×10^{-13}
(CH_3CH_2COOH)		Carbonic acid	
Ascorbic acid (vitamin C)	7.9×10^{-5}	H_2CO_3	4.3×10^{-7}
		HCO_3^-	5.6×10^{-11}

- Donation of each successive H^+ from a polyprotic acid is more difficult than the one before it, so K_a values become successively lower.
- Most organic acids, which contain the $-CO_2H$ group, have K_a values near 10^{-5}.

PROBLEM 10.10

Benzoic acid has $K_a = 6.5 \times 10^{-5}$, and citric acid has $K_a = 7.2 \times 10^{-4}$. Which of the two is the stronger acid?

10.7 Dissociation of Water

We saw previously that water is amphoteric – it can act as an acid when a base is present and as a base when an acid is present. What about when no other acids or bases are present, however? In this case, one water molecule acts as an acid while another water molecule acts as a base, reacting to form the hydronium and hydroxide ions:

$$H_2O(l) + H_2O(l) \rightleftharpoons H_3O^+(aq) + OH^-(aq)$$

Because each dissociation reaction yields one H_3O^+ ion and one OH^- ion, the concentrations of the two ions are identical. At 25 °C, the concentration of each is 1.00×10^{-7} M. We can write the equilibrium constant expression for the dissociation of water as

$$K = \frac{[H_3O^+][OH^-]}{[H_2O][H_2O]}$$

and $$K_a = K[H_2O] = \frac{[H_3O^+][OH^-]}{[H_2O]}$$

where $[H_3O^+] = [OH^-] = 1.00 \times 10^{-7}$ M   (at 25 °C)

As both a reactant and a solvent, the concentration of water is essentially constant. We can therefore put the acid dissociation constant K_a and the water concentration $[H_2O]$ together to make a new constant called the **ion-product constant for water (K_w)**, which is simply the H_3O^+ concentration times the OH^- concentration. At 25 °C, $K_w = 1.00 \times 10^{-14}$.

Ion-product constant for water $\quad K_w = K_a[H_2O] = [H_3O^+][OH^-]$

$$= (1.00 \times 10^{-7})(1.00 \times 10^{-7})$$

$$= 1.00 \times 10^{-14} \quad \text{(at 25 °C)}$$

The importance of the equation $K_w = [H_3O^+][OH^-]$ is that it applies to all aqueous solutions, not just to pure water. Since the product of $[H_3O^+]$ times $[OH^-]$ is always constant for any solution, we can determine the concentration of one species if we know the concentration of the other. If an acid is present in solution, for instance, so that $[H_3O^+]$ is large, then $[OH^-]$ must be small. If a base is present in solution so that $[OH^-]$ is large, then $[H_3O^+]$ must be small. For example, for a 0.10 M HCl solution, we know that $[H_3O^+] = 0.10$ M because HCl is 100% dissociated. Thus, we can calculate that $[OH^-] = 1.0 \times 10^{-13}$ M:

Since $\quad K_w \times [H_3O^+][OH^-] = 1.00 \times 10^{-14}$

we have $\quad [OH^-] = \dfrac{K_w}{[H_3O^+]} = \dfrac{1.00 \times 10^{-14}}{0.10} = 1.0 \times 10^{-13}$ M

Similarly, for a 0.10 M NaOH solution, we know that $[OH^-] = 0.10$ M, so $[H_3O^+] = 1.0 \times 10^{-13}$ M:

$$[H_3O^+] = \frac{K_w}{[OH^-]} = \frac{1.00 \times 10^{-14}}{0.10} = 1.0 \times 10^{-13} \text{ M}$$

Solutions are identified as acidic, neutral, or basic (*alkaline*) according to the value of their H_3O^+ and OH^- concentrations:

Acidic solution: $\quad [H_3O^+] > 10^{-7}$ M and $[OH^-] < 10^{-7}$ M

Neutral solution: $\quad [H_3O^+] = 10^{-7}$ M and $[OH^-] = 10^{-7}$ M

Basic solution: $\quad [H_3O^+] < 10^{-7}$ M and $[OH^-] > 10^{-7}$ M

WORKED EXAMPLE **10.4** Water Dissociation Constant: Using K_w to Calculate $[OH^-]$

Milk has an H_3O^+ concentration of 4.5×10^{-7} M. What is the value of $[OH^-]$? Is milk acidic, neutral, or basic?

ANALYSIS The OH^- concentration can be found by dividing K_w by $[H_3O^+]$. An acidic solution has $[H_3O^+] > 10^{-7}$ M, a neutral solution has $[H_3O^+] = 10^{-7}$ M, and a basic solution has $[H_3O^+] < 10^{-7}$ M.

BALLPARK ESTIMATE Since the H_3O^+ concentration is slightly *greater* than 10^{-7} M, the OH^- concentration must be slightly *less* than 10^{-7} M, on the order of 10^{-8}.

SOLUTION

$$[OH^-] = \frac{K_w}{[H_3O^+]} = \frac{1.00 \times 10^{-14}}{4.5 \times 10^{-7}} = 2.2 \times 10^{-8} \text{ M}$$

Milk is slightly acidic because its H_3O^+ concentration is slightly larger than 1×10^{-7} M.

BALLPARK CHECK The OH^- concentration is of the same order of magnitude as our estimate.

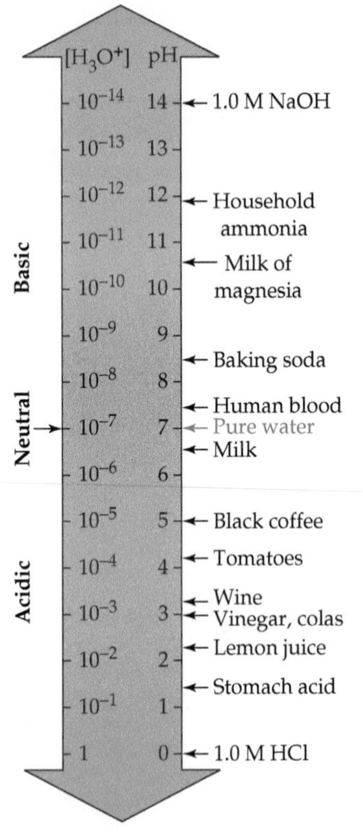

[H3O+] pH
10-14 14 1.0 M NaOH
10-13 13
10-12 12 Household ammonia
10-11 11
Milk of magnesia
10-10 10
10-9 9
Baking soda
10-8 8
Human blood
10-7 7 Pure water
Milk
10-6 6
10-5 5 Black coffee
10-4 4 Tomatoes
10-3 3 Wine
Vinegar, colas
10-2 2 Lemon juice
Stomach acid
10-1 1
1 0 1.0 M HCl
Basic
Neutral
Acidic

▲ **FIGURE 10.1 The pH scale and the pH values of some common substances.** A low pH corresponds to a strongly acidic solution, a high pH corresponds to a strongly basic solution, and a pH of 7 corresponds to a neutral solution.

p function The negative common logarithm of some variable, $pX = -\log(X)$.

pH A measure of the acid strength of a solution; the negative common logarithm of the H_3O^+ concentration.

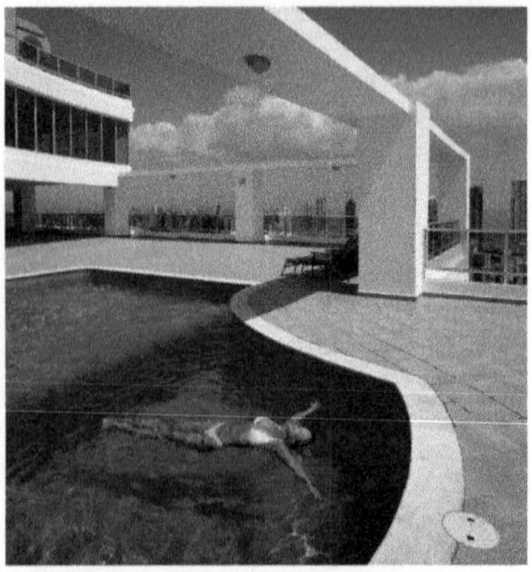

▲ Adding only a teaspoonful of concentrated (6 M) hydrochloric acid lowers the pH of this pool from 7 to 6. Lowering the pH from 7 to 1 would take 400 gallons.

PROBLEM 10.11

Identify the following solutions as either acidic or basic. What is the value of $[OH^-]$ in each?

(a) Beer, $[H_3O^+] = 3.2 \times 10^{-5}$ M

(b) Household ammonia, $[H_3O^+] = 3.1 \times 10^{-12}$ M

10.8 Measuring Acidity in Aqueous Solution: pH

In many fields, from medicine to chemistry to winemaking, it is necessary to know the exact concentration of H_3O^+ or OH^- in a solution. If, for example, the H_3O^+ concentration in blood varies only slightly from a value of 4.0×10^{-8} M, death can result.

Although correct, it is nevertheless awkward to refer to low concentrations of H_3O^+ using molarity. If you were asked which concentration is higher, 9.0×10^{-8} M or 3.5×10^{-7} M, you would probably have to stop and think for a moment before answering. Fortunately, there is an easier way to express and compare H_3O^+ concentrations—the *pH scale.*

The pH of an aqueous solution is a number, usually between 0 and 14, that indicates the H_3O^+ concentration of the solution. A pH smaller than 7 corresponds to an acidic solution, a pH larger than 7 corresponds to a basic solution, and a pH of exactly 7 corresponds to a neutral solution. The pH scale and pH values of some common substances are shown in Figure 10.1

Mathematically, a **p function** is defined as the negative common logarithm of some variable. The **pH** of a solution, therefore, is the negative common logarithm of the H_3O^+ concentration:

$$\mathbf{pH} = -\log[H^+] \text{ (or}[H_3O^+])$$

If you have studied logarithms, you may remember that the common logarithm of a number is the power to which 10 must be raised to equal the number. The pH definition can therefore be restated as

$$[H_3O^+] = 10^{-pH}$$

For example, in neutral water at 25 °C, where $[H_3O^+] = 1 \times 10^{-7}$ M, the pH is 7; in a strong acid solution where $[H_3O^+] = 1 \times 10^{-1}$ M, the pH is 1; and in a strong base solution where $[H_3O^+] = 1 \times 10^{-14}$ M, the pH is 14:

$$\textit{Acidic solution:}\quad pH < 7, \quad [H_3O^+] > 1 \times 10^{-7}\text{ M}$$
$$\textit{Neutral solution:}\quad pH = 7, \quad [H_3O^+] = 1 \times 10^{-7}\text{ M}$$
$$\textit{Basic solution:}\quad pH > 7, \quad [H_3O^+] < 1 \times 10^{-7}\text{ M}$$

Keep in mind that the pH scale covers an enormous range of acidities because it is a *logarithmic* scale, which involves powers of 10 (Figure 10.2). A change of only 1 pH unit means a tenfold change in $[H_3O^+]$, a change of 2 pH units means a hundredfold change in $[H_3O^+]$, and a change of 12 pH units means a change of 10^{12} (a million) in $[H_3O^+]$.

To get a feel for the size of the quantities involved, think of a typical backyard swimming pool, which contains about 100,000 L of water. You would have to add only 0.10 mol of HCl (3.7 g) to lower the pH of the pool from 7.0 (neutral) to 6.0, but you would have to add 10,000 mol of HCl (370 kg!) to lower the pH of the pool from 7.0 to 1.0.

The logarithmic pH scale is a convenient way of reporting the relative acidity of solutions, but using logarithms can also be useful when calculating H_3O^+ and

OH⁻ concentrations. Remember that the equilibrium between H_3O^+ and OH^- in aqueous solutions is expressed by K_w, where

$$K_w = [H_3O^+][OH^-] = 1 \times 10^{-14} \quad \text{(at 25 °C)}$$

If we convert this equation to its negative logarithmic form, we obtain

$$-\log(K_w) = -\log(H_3O^+) - \log(OH^-)$$

$$-\log(1 \times 10^{-14}) = -\log(H_3O^+) - \log(OH^-)$$

$$or \quad 14.00 = pH + pOH$$

The logarithmic form of the K_w equation can simplify the calculation of solution pH from OH⁻ concentration, as demonstrated in Worked Example 10.7.

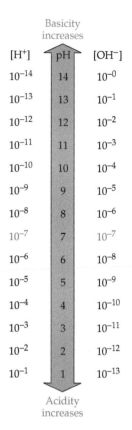

<table>
<tr><td></td><td>Basicity increases</td><td></td></tr>
</table>

$[H^+]$	pH	$[OH^-]$
10^{-14}	14	10^{-0}
10^{-13}	13	10^{-1}
10^{-12}	12	10^{-2}
10^{-11}	11	10^{-3}
10^{-10}	10	10^{-4}
10^{-9}	9	10^{-5}
10^{-8}	8	10^{-6}
10^{-7}	7	10^{-7}
10^{-6}	6	10^{-8}
10^{-5}	5	10^{-9}
10^{-4}	4	10^{-10}
10^{-3}	3	10^{-11}
10^{-2}	2	10^{-12}
10^{-1}	1	10^{-13}

Acidity increases

▲ **FIGURE 10.2 The relationship of the pH scale to H⁺ and OH⁻ concentrations.**

WORKED EXAMPLE   10.5 Measuring Acidity: Calculating pH from $[H_3O^+]$

The H_3O^+ concentration in coffee is about 1×10^{-5} M. What pH is this?

ANALYSIS The pH is the negative common logarithm of the H_3O^+ concentration: $pH = -\log[H_3O^+]$.

SOLUTION
Since the common logarithm of 1×10^{-5} M is −5, the pH is 5.0.

WORKED EXAMPLE   10.6 Measuring Acidity: Calculating $[H_3O^+]$ from pH

Lemon juice has a pH of about 2. What $[H_3O^+]$ is this?

ANALYSIS In this case, we are looking for the $[H_3O^+]$, where $[H_3O^+] = 10^{-pH}$.

SOLUTION
Since pH = 2.0, $[H_3O^+] = 10^{-2} = 1 \times 10^{-2}$ M.

WORKED EXAMPLE   10.7 Measuring Acidity: Using K_w to Calculate $[H_3O^+]$ and pH

A cleaning solution is found to have $[OH^-] = 1 \times 10^{-3}$ M. What is the pH?

ANALYSIS To find pH, we must first find the value of $[H_3O^+]$ by using the equation $[H_3O^+] = K_w/[OH^-]$. Alternatively, we can calculate the pOH of the solution and then use the logarithmic form of the K_w equation: pH = 14.00 − pOH.

SOLUTION
Rearranging the K_w equation, we have

$$[H_3O^+] = \frac{K_w}{[OH^-]} = \frac{1.00 \times 10^{-14}}{1 \times 10^{-3}} = 1 \times 10^{-11} \text{ M}$$

$$pH = -\log(1 \times 10^{-11}) = 11.0$$

Using the logarithmic form of the K_w equation, we have

$$pH = 14.0 - pOH = 14.0 - (-\log(OH^-))$$

$$pH = 14.0 - (-\log(1 \times 10^{-3}))$$

$$pH = 14.0 - 3.0 = 11.0$$

> **WORKED EXAMPLE** **10.8** Measuring Acidity: Calculating pH of Strong Acid Solutions
>
> What is the pH of a 0.01 M solution of HCl?
>
> ANALYSIS To find pH, we must first find the value of $[H_3O^+]$.
>
> SOLUTION
> Since HCl is a strong acid (Table 10.1), it is 100% dissociated, and the H_3O^+ concentration is the same as the HCl concentration: $[H_3O^+] = 0.01$ M, or 1×10^{-2} M, and pH = 2.0.

PROBLEM 10.12

Which solution has the higher H_3O^+ concentration, one with pH = 5 or one with pH = 9? Which has the higher OH^- concentration?

PROBLEM 10.13

Give the pH of solutions with the following concentrations:

(a) $[H_3O^+] = 1 \times 10^{-5}$ M

(b) $[OH^-] = 1 \times 10^{-9}$ M

PROBLEM 10.14

Give the hydronium ion concentrations of solutions with the following values of pH. Which of the solutions is most acidic? Which is most basic?

(a) pH 13.0   **(b)** pH 3.0   **(c)** pH 8.0

PROBLEM 10.15

What is the pH of a 1×10^{-4} M solution of HNO_3?

10.9 Working with pH

Converting between pH and H_3O^+ concentration is easy when the pH is a whole number, but how do you find the H_3O^+ concentration of blood, which has a pH of 7.4, or the pH of a solution with $[H_3O^+] = 4.6 \times 10^{-3}$ M? Sometimes it is sufficient to make an estimate. The pH of blood (7.4) is between 7 and 8, so the H_3O^+ concentration of blood must be between 1×10^{-7} and 1×10^{-8} M. To be exact about finding pH values, though, requires a calculator.

Converting from pH to $[H_3O^+]$ requires finding the *antilogarithm* of the negative pH, which is done on many calculators with an "INV" key and a "log" key. Converting from $[H_3O^+]$ to pH requires finding the logarithm, which is commonly done with a "log" key and an "expo" or "EE" key for entering exponents of 10. Consult your calculator instructions if you are not sure how to use these keys. Remember that the sign of the number given by the calculator must be changed from minus to plus to get the pH.

The H_3O^+ concentration in blood with pH = 7.4 is

$$[H_3O^+] = antilog(-7.4) = 4 \times 10^{-8} \text{ M}$$

The pH of a solution with $[H_3O^+] = 4.6 \times 10^{-3}$ M is

$$pH = -\log(4.6 \times 10^{-3}) = -(-2.34) = 2.34$$

A note about significant figures: An antilogarithm contains the same number of digits that the original number has to the right of the decimal point. A logarithm contains the same number of digits to the right of the decimal point that the original number has

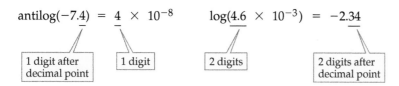

antilog(−7.4) = 4 × 10⁻⁸   log(4.6 × 10⁻³) = −2.34

| 1 digit after decimal point | 1 digit | 2 digits | 2 digits after decimal point |

WORKED EXAMPLE   10.9 Working with pH: Converting a pH to $[H_3O^+]$

Soft drinks usually have a pH of approximately 3.1. What is the $[H_3O^+]$ concentration in a soft drink?

ANALYSIS To convert from a pH value to an $[H_3O^+]$ concentration requires using the equation $[H_3O^+] = 10^{-pH}$, which requires finding an antilogarithm on a calculator.

BALLPARK ESTIMATE Because the pH is between 3.0 and 4.0, the $[H_3O^+]$ must be between 1×10^{-3} and 1×10^{-4}. A pH of 3.1 is very close to 3.0, so the $[H_3O^+]$ must be just slightly below 1×10^{-3} M.

SOLUTION
Entering the negative pH on a calculator (−3.1) and pressing the "INV" and "log" keys gives the answer 7.943×10^{-4}, which must be rounded off to 8×10^{-4} since the pH has only one digit to the right of the decimal point.

BALLPARK CHECK The calculated $[H_3O^+]$ of 8×10^{-4} M is between 1×10^{-3} M and 1×10^{-4} M and, as we estimated, just slightly below 1×10^{-3} M. (Remember, 8×10^{-4} is 0.8×10^{-3}.)

WORKED EXAMPLE   10.10 Working with pH: Calculating pH for Strong Acid Solutions

What is the pH of a 0.0045 M solution of $HClO_4$?

ANALYSIS Finding pH requires first finding $[H_3O^+]$ and then using the equation $pH = -\log[H_3O^+]$. Since $HClO_4$ is a strong acid (see Table 10.1), it is 100% dissociated, and so the H_3O^+ concentration is the same as the $HClO_4$ concentration.

BALLPARK ESTIMATE Because $[H^+] = 4.5 \times 10^{-3}$ M is close to midway between 1×10^{-2} M and 1×10^{-3} M, the pH must be close to the midway point between 2.0 and 3.0. (Unfortunately, because the logarithm scale is not linear, trying to estimate the midway point is not a simple process.)

SOLUTION
$[H_3O^+] = 0.0045$ M $= 4.5 \times 10^{-3}$ M. Taking the negative logarithm gives pH = 2.35.

BALLPARK CHECK The calculated pH is consistent with our estimate.

WORKED EXAMPLE   **10.11** Working with pH: Calculating pH for Strong Base Solutions

What is the pH of a 0.0032 M solution of NaOH?

ANALYSIS Since NaOH is a strong base, the OH^- concentration is the same as the NaOH concentration. Starting with the OH^- concentration, finding pH requires either using the K_w equation to find $[H_3O^+]$ or calculating pOH and then using the logarithmic form of the K_w equation.

BALLPARK ESTIMATE Because $[OH^-] = 3.2 \times 10^{-3}$ M is close to midway between 1×10^{-2} M and 1×10^{-3} M, the pOH must be close to the midway point between 2.0 and 3.0. Subtracting the pOH from 14 would therefore yield a pH between 11 and 12.

SOLUTION

$$[OH^-] = 0.0032 \text{ M} = 3.2 \times 10^{-3} \text{ M}$$

$$[H_3O^+] = \frac{K_w}{(3.2 \times 10^{-3})} = 3.1 \times 10^{-12} \text{ M}$$

Taking the negative logarithm gives pH $= -\log(3.1 \times 10^{-12}) = 11.51$. Alternatively, we can calculate pOH and subtract from 14.00 using the logarithmic form of the K_w equation. For $[OH^-] = 0.0032$ M,

$$\text{pOH} = -\log(3.2 \times 10^{-3}) = 2.49$$

$$\text{pH} = 14.00 - 2.49 = 11.51$$

Since the given OH^- concentration included two significant figures, the final pH includes two significant figures beyond the decimal point.

BALLPARK CHECK The calculated pH is consistent with our estimate.

PROBLEM 10.16

Identify the following solutions as acidic or basic, estimate $[H_3O^+]$ values for each, and rank them in order of increasing acidity:

(a) Saliva, pH = 6.5   (b) Pancreatic juice, pH = 7.9

(c) Orange juice, pH = 3.7   (d) Wine, pH = 3.5

PROBLEM 10.17

Find the pH of the following solutions:

(a) Seawater with $[H_3O^+] = 5.3 \times 10^{-9}$ M

(b) A urine sample with $[H_3O^+] = 8.9 \times 10^{-6}$ M

PROBLEM 10.18

What is the pH of a 0.0025 M solution of HCl?

10.10 Laboratory Determination of Acidity

Acid–base indicator A dye that changes color depending on the pH of a solution.

The pH of water is an important indicator of water quality in applications ranging from swimming pool and spa maintenance to municipal water treatment. There are several ways to measure the pH of a solution. The simplest but least accurate method is to use an **acid–base indicator**, a dye that changes color depending on

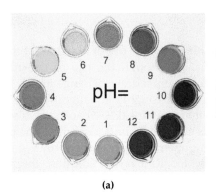

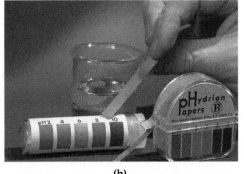

(a)   (b)

▲ **FIGURE 10.3 Finding pH.** (a) The color of universal indicator in solutions of known pH from 1 to 12. (b) Testing pH with a paper strip. Comparing the color of the strip with the code on the package gives the approximate pH.

the pH of the solution. For example, the well-known dye *litmus* is red below pH 4.8 but blue above pH 7.8 and the indicator *phenolphthalein* (fee-nol-**thay**-lean) is colorless below pH 8.2 but red above pH 10. To make pH determination particularly easy, test kits are available that contain a mixture of indicators known as *universal indicator* to give approximate pH measurements in the range 2–10 (Figure 10.3a). Also available are rolls of "pH paper," which make it possible to determine pH simply by putting a drop of solution on the paper and comparing the color that appears to the color on a calibration chart (Figure 10.3b).

A much more accurate way to determine pH uses an electronic pH meter like the one shown in Figure 10.4. Electrodes are dipped into the solution, and the pH is read from the meter.

▲ **FIGURE 10.4 Using a pH meter to obtain an accurate reading of pH.** Is milk of magnesia acidic or basic?

APPLICATION ▶ pH of Body Fluids

Each fluid in our bodies has a pH range suited to its function, as shown in the accompanying table. The stability of cell membranes, the shapes of huge protein molecules that must be folded in certain ways to function, and the activities of enzymes are all dependent on appropriate H_3O^+ concentrations.

pH of Body Fluids

FLUID	pH
Blood plasma	7.4
Interstitial fluid	7.4
Cytosol	7.0
Saliva	5.8–7.1
Gastric juice	1.6–1.8
Pancreatic juice	7.5–8.8
Intestinal juice	6.3–8.0
Urine	4.6–8.0
Sweat	4.0–6.8

Blood plasma and the interstitial fluid surrounding cells, which together comprise one-third of body water, have a slightly basic pH of 7.4. In fact, one of the functions of blood is to neutralize the acid by-products of cellular metabolism. The fluid within cells, called the *cytosol*, is slightly more acidic than the fluid outside, so a pH differential exists.

The strongly acidic gastric juice in the stomach has three important functions. First, gastric juice aids in the digestion of proteins by causing them to denature, or unfold. Second, it kills most of the bacteria we consume along with our food. Third, it converts the enzyme that breaks down proteins from an inactive form to the active form.

When the acidic mixture of partially digested food (*chyme*) leaves the stomach and enters the small intestine, it triggers secretion by the pancreas of an alkaline fluid containing bicarbonate ions, HCO_3^-. A principal function of this pancreatic juice and other intestinal fluids is to dilute and neutralize the hydrochloric acid carried along from the stomach.

Urine has a wide normal pH range, depending on the diet and recent activities. It is generally acidic, though, because one important function of urine is to eliminate a quantity of hydrogen ion equal to that produced by the body each day. Without this elimination, the body would soon be overwhelmed by acid.

See Additional Problem 10.97 at the end of the chapter.

10.11 Buffer Solutions

Buffer A combination of substances that act together to prevent a drastic change in pH; usually a weak acid and its conjugate base.

Much of the body's chemistry depends on maintaining the pH of blood and other fluids within narrow limits. This is accomplished through the use of **buffers**—combinations of substances that act together to prevent a drastic change in pH.

Most buffers are mixtures of a weak acid and a roughly equal concentration of its conjugate base—for example, a solution that contains 0.10 M acetic acid and 0.10 M acetate ion. If a small amount of OH^- is added to a buffer solution, the pH increases, but not by much because the acid component of the buffer neutralizes the added OH^-. If a small amount of H_3O^+ is added to a buffer solution, the pH decreases, but again not by much because the base component of the buffer neutralizes the added H_3O^+.

To see why buffer solutions work, look at the equation for the acid dissociation constant of an acid HA.

For the reaction: $\quad HA(aq) + H_2O(l) \rightleftharpoons A^-(aq) + H_3O^+(aq)$

we have $\qquad K_a = \dfrac{[H_3O^+][A^-]}{[HA]}$

Rearranging this equation shows that the value of $[H_3O^+]$, and thus the pH, depends on the ratio of the undissociated acid concentration to the conjugate base concentration, $[HA]/[A^-]$:

$$[H_3O^+] = K_a\dfrac{[HA]}{[A^-]}$$

In the case of the acetic acid–acetate ion buffer, for instance, we have

$$CH_3CO_2H(aq) + H_2O(l) \rightleftharpoons H_3O^+(aq) + CH_3CO_2^-(aq)$$
$$\text{(0.10 M)} \hspace{6cm} \text{(0.10 M)}$$

and $\quad [H_3O^+] = K_a\dfrac{[CH_3CO_2H]}{[CH_3CO_2^-]}$

Initially, the pH of the 0.10 M acetic acid–0.10 M acetate ion buffer solution is 4.74. When acid is added, most is removed by reaction with $CH_3CO_2^-$. The equilibrium reaction shifts to the left, and as a result the concentration of CH_3CO_2H increases and the concentration of $CH_3CO_2^-$ decreases. As long as the changes in $[CH_3CO_2H]$ and $[CH_3CO_2^-]$ are relatively small, however, the ratio of $[CH_3CO_2H]$ to $[CH_3CO_2^-]$ changes only slightly, and there is little change in the pH.

When base is added to the buffer, most is removed by reaction with CH_3CO_2H. The equilibrium shifts to the right, and so the concentration of CH_3CO_2H decreases and the concentration of $CH_3CO_2^-$ increases. Here too, though, as long as the concentration changes are relatively small, there is little change in the pH.

The ability of a buffer solution to resist changes in pH when acid or base is added is illustrated in Figure 10.5. Addition of 0.010 mol of H_3O^+ to 1.0 L of pure water changes the pH from 7 to 2, and addition of 0.010 mol of OH^- changes the pH from 7 to 12. A similar addition of acid to 1.0 L of a 0.10 M acetic acid–0.10 M acetate ion buffer, however, changes the pH only from 4.74 to 4.68, and addition of base changes the pH only from 4.74 to 4.85.

As we did with K_w, we can convert the rearranged K_a equation to its logarithmic form to obtain

$$pH = pK_a - \log\left(\dfrac{[HA]}{[A^-]}\right)$$

or $\quad pH = pK_a + \log\left(\dfrac{[A^-]}{[HA]}\right)$

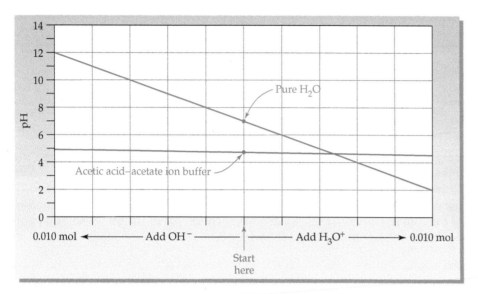

▲ **FIGURE 10.5 A comparison of the change in pH.** When 0.010 mol of acid and 0.010 mol of base are added to 1.0 L of pure water and to 1.0 L of a 0.10 M acetic acid–0.10 M acetate ion buffer, the pH of the water varies between 12 and 2, while the pH of the buffer varies only between 4.85 and 4.68.

This expression is known as the **Henderson–Hasselbalch equation** and is very useful in buffer applications, particularly in biology and biochemistry. Examination of the Henderson–Hasselbalch equation provides useful insights into how to prepare a buffer and into the factors that affect the pH of a buffer solution.

The effective pH range of a buffer will depend on the pK_a of the acid HA and on the relative concentrations of HA and conjugate base A^-. In general, the most effective buffers meet the following conditions:

- The pK_a for the weak acid should be close to the desired pH of the buffer solution.
- The ratio of [HA] to $[A^-]$ should be close to 1, so that neither additional acid nor additional base changes the pH of the solution dramatically.
- The molar amounts of HA and A^- in the buffer should be approximately 10 times greater than the molar amounts of either acid or base you expect to add so that the ratio $[A^-]/[HA]$ does not undergo a large change.

Henderson–Hasselbalch equation The logarithmic form of the K_a equation for a weak acid, used in applications involving buffer solutions.

| WORKED EXAMPLE | 10.12 Buffers: Selecting a Weak Acid for a Buffer Solution |

Which of the organic acids in Table 10.2 would be the most appropriate for preparing a pH 4.15 buffer solution?

ANALYSIS The pH of the buffer solution depends on the pK_a of the weak acid. Remember that $pK_a = -\log(K_a)$.

SOLUTION
The K_a and pK_a values for the four organic acids in Table 10.2 are tabulated below. The ascorbic acid ($pK_a = 4.10$) will produce a buffer solution closest to the desired pH of 4.15.

ORGANIC ACID	K_a	pK_a
Formic acid (HCOOH)	1.8×10^{-4}	3.74
Acetic acid (CH₃COOH)	1.8×10^{-5}	4.74
Propanoic acid (CH₃CH₂COOH)	1.3×10^{-5}	4.89
Ascorbic acid (vitamin C)	7.9×10^{-5}	4.10

WORKED EXAMPLE 10.13 Buffers: Calculating the pH of a Buffer Solution

What is the pH of a buffer solution that contains 0.100 M HF and 0.120 M NaF? The K_a of HF is 3.5×10^{-4}, and so $pK_a = 3.46$.

ANALYSIS The Henderson–Hasselbalch equation can be used to calculate the pH of a buffer solution: $pH = pK_a + \log\left(\dfrac{[F^-]}{[HF]}\right)$.

BALLPARK ESTIMATE If the concentrations of F^- and HF were equal, the log term in our equation would be zero, and the pH of the solution would be equal to the pK_a for HF, which means $pH = 3.46$. However, since the concentration of the conjugate base ($[F^-] = 0.120$ M) is slightly higher than the concentration of the conjugate acid ($[HF] = 0.100$ M), then the pH of the buffer solution will be slightly higher (more basic) than the pK_a.

SOLUTION

$$pH = pK_a + \log\left(\frac{[F^-]}{[HF]}\right)$$

$$pH = 3.46 + \log\left(\frac{(0.120)}{(0.100)}\right) = 3.46 + 0.08 = 3.54$$

BALLPARK CHECK The calculated pH of 3.54 is consistent with the prediction that the final pH will be slightly higher than the pK_a of 3.46.

WORKED EXAMPLE 10.14 Buffers: Measuring the Effect of Added Base on pH

What is the pH of 1.00 L of the 0.100 M hydrofluoric acid–0.120 M fluoride ion buffer system described in Worked Example 10.13 after 0.020 mol of NaOH is added?

ANALYSIS Initially, the 0.100 M HF–0.120 M NaF buffer has $pH = 3.54$, as calculated in Worked Example 10.13. The added base will react with the acid as indicated in the neutralization reaction,

$$HF(aq) + OH^-(aq) \longrightarrow H_2O(l) + F^-(aq)$$

which means $[HF]$ decreases and $[F^-]$ increases. With the pK_a and the concentrations of HF and F^- known, pH can be calculated using the Henderson–Hasselbalch equation.

BALLPARK ESTIMATE After the neutralization reaction, there is more conjugate base (F^-) and less conjugate acid (HF), and so we expect the pH to increase slightly from the initial value of 3.54.

SOLUTION
When 0.020 mol of NaOH is added to 1.00 L of the buffer, the HF concentration *decreases* from 0.100 M to 0.080 M as a result of an acid–base reaction. At the same time, the F^- concentration *increases* from 0.120 M to 0.140 M because additional F^- is produced by the neutralization. Using these new values gives

$$pH = 3.46 + \log\left(\frac{(0.140)}{(0.080)}\right) = 3.46 + 0.24 = 3.70$$

The addition of 0.020 mol of base causes the pH of the buffer to rise only from 3.54 to 3.70.

BALLPARK CHECK The final pH, 3.70, is slightly more basic than the initial pH of 3.54, consistent with our prediction.

PROBLEM 10.19

What is the pH of 1.00 L of the 0.100 M hydrofluoric acid–0.120 M fluoride ion buffer system described in Worked Example 10.13 after 0.020 mol of HNO_3 is added?

PROBLEM 10.20

The ammonia/ammonium buffer system is used to optimize polymerase chain reactions (PCR) used in DNA studies. The equilibrium for this buffer can be written as

$$NH_4^+(aq) \rightleftharpoons H^+(aq) + NH_3(aq)$$

Calculate the pH of a buffer that contains 0.050 M ammonium chloride and 0.080 M ammonia. The K_a of ammonium is 5.6×10^{-10}.

KEY CONCEPT PROBLEM 10.21

A buffer solution is prepared using CN^- (from NaCN salt) and HCN in the amounts indicated. The K_a for HCN is 4.9×10^{-10}. Calculate the pH of the buffer solution.

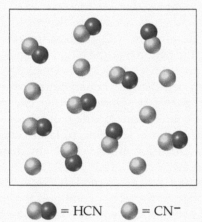

⬤⬤ = HCN　◯ = CN^-

10.12 Buffers in the Body

The pH of body fluids is maintained by three major buffer systems. Two of these buffers, the carbonic acid–bicarbonate (H_2CO_3–HCO_3^-) system and the dihydrogen phosphate–hydrogen phosphate system, depend on weak acid–conjugate base interactions exactly like those of the acetate buffer system described in the preceding section:

$$H_2CO_3(aq) + H_2O(l) \rightleftharpoons HCO_3^-(aq) + H_3O^+(aq) \qquad pK_a = 6.37$$
$$H_2PO_4^-(aq) + H_2O(l) \rightleftharpoons HPO_4^{2-}(aq) + H_3O^+(aq) \qquad pK_a = 7.21$$

The third buffer system depends on the ability of proteins to act as either proton acceptors or proton donors at different pH values.

To illustrate the action of buffers in the body, take a look at the carbonic acid–bicarbonate system, the principal buffer in blood serum and other extracellular fluids. (The hydrogen phosphate system is the major buffer within cells.) Because carbonic acid is unstable and therefore in equilibrium with CO_2 and water, there is an extra step in the bicarbonate buffer mechanism:

$$CO_2(aq) + H_2O(l) \rightleftharpoons H_2CO_3(aq) \rightleftharpoons HCO_3^-(aq) + H_3O^+(aq)$$

As a result, the bicarbonate buffer system is intimately related to the elimination of CO_2, which is continuously produced in cells and transported to the lungs to be exhaled.

Because most CO_2 is present simply as the dissolved gas rather than as H_2CO_3, the acid dissociation constant for carbonic acid in blood can be written using $[CO_2]$:

$$K_a = \frac{[H_3O^+][HCO_3^-]}{[CO_2]}$$

which can be rearranged to

An increase in $[CO_2]$ raises $[H_3O^+]$ and lowers pH.
A decrease in $[CO_2]$ lowers $[H_3O^+]$ and raises pH.

$$[H_3O^+] = K_a\frac{[CO_2]}{[HCO_3^-]}$$

Converting this rearranged equation to the logarithmic form of the Henderson–Hasselbalch equation yields

$$pH = pK_a + \log\left(\frac{[HCO_3^-]}{[CO_2]}\right)$$

This rearranged equation shows that an increase in $[CO_2]$ makes the ratio of $[HCO_3^-]$ to $[CO_2]$ smaller, thereby decreasing the pH; that is, the blood becomes more acidic. Similarly, a decrease in $[CO_2]$ makes the ratio of $[HCO_3^-]$ to $[CO_2]$ larger, thereby increasing the pH; that is, the blood becomes more basic. At the normal blood pH of 7.4, the ratio $[HCO_3^-]/[CO_2]$ is about 20 to 1.

The relationships between the bicarbonate buffer system, the lungs, and the kidneys are shown in Figure 10.6. Under normal circumstances, the reactions shown in the figure are at equilibrium. Addition of excess acid (red arrows) causes formation of H_2CO_3 and results in lowering of H_3O^+ concentration. Removal of acid (blue arrows) causes formation of more H_3O^+ by dissociation of H_2CO_3. The maintenance of pH by this mechanism is supported by a reserve of bicarbonate ions in body fluids. Such a buffer can accommodate large additions of H_3O^+ before there is a significant change in the pH, a condition that meets the body's needs because excessive production of acid is a more common body condition than excessive loss of acid.

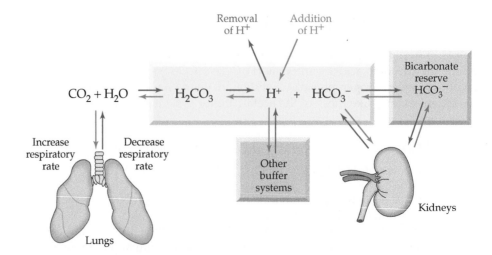

▶ **FIGURE 10.6 Relationships of the bicarbonate buffer system to the lungs and the kidneys.** The red and blue arrows show the responses to the stresses of increased or decreased respiratory rate and removal or addition of acid.

A change in the breathing rate provides a quick further adjustment in the bicarbonate buffer system. When the CO_2 concentration in the blood starts to rise, the breathing rate increases to remove CO_2, thereby decreasing the acid concentration (red arrows in Figure 10.6). When the CO_2 concentration in the blood starts to

APPLICATION ▶   Buffers in the Body: Acidosis and Alkalosis

A group of teenagers at a rock concert experience a collective fainting spell. A person taking high doses of aspirin for chronic pain appears disoriented and is having trouble breathing. An insulin-dependent diabetic patient complains of tiredness and stomach pains. An athlete who recently completed a highly strenuous workout suffers from muscle cramps and nausea. A patient on an HIV drug regimen experiences increasing weakness and numbness in the hands and feet. What do all these individuals have in common? They are all suffering from abnormal fluctuations in blood pH, resulting in conditions known as *acidosis* (pH < 7.35) or *alkalosis* (pH > 7.45).

The highly complex series of reactions and equilibria that take place throughout the body are very sensitive to pH—variations of even a few tenths of a pH unit can produce severe physiological symptoms. The carbonate–bicarbonate buffer system (Section 10.12) maintains the pH of blood serum at a fairly constant value of 7.4. The effective pH depends on the relative amounts of CO_2 and bicarbonate dissolved in the blood:

$$CO_2(aq) + H_2O(l)$$
$$\rightleftharpoons H_2CO_3(aq) \rightleftharpoons HCO_3^-(aq) + H_3O^+(aq)$$

Anything that significantly shifts the balance between dissolved CO_2 and HCO_3^- can raise or lower the pH. How does this happen, and how does the body compensate?

Respiratory acidosis can be caused by a decrease in respiration, which leads to a buildup of excess CO_2 in the blood and a corresponding decrease in pH. This could be caused by a blocked air passage due to inhaled food—removal of the blockage restores normal breathing and a return to the optimal pH. *Metabolic acidosis* results from an excess of other acids in the blood that reduce the bicarbonate concentration. High doses of aspirin (acetyl salicylic acid, Section 17.5), for example, increase the hydronium ion concentration and decrease the pH. Strenuous exercise generates excess lactate in the muscles, which is released into the bloodstream (Section 23.11). The liver converts lactate into glucose, which is the body's major source of energy; this process consumes bicarbonate ions, which decreases the pH. Some HIV drug therapies can damage cellular mitochondria (Section 21.3),

resulting in a buildup of lactic acid in the cells and blood stream. In the case of the diabetic patient, lack of insulin causes the body to start burning fat, which generates ketones and keto acids (Chapter 16), organic compounds that lower the blood pH.

The body attempts to correct acidosis by increasing the rate and depth of respiration—breathing faster "blows off" CO_2, shifting the CO_2–bicarbonate equilibrium to the left and lowering the pH. The net effect is rapid reversal of the acidosis. Although this may be sufficient for cases of respiratory acidosis, it provides only temporary relief for metabolic acidosis. A long-term solution depends on removal of excess acid by the kidneys, which can take several hours.

What about our teenage fans? In their excitement they have hyperventilated—their increased breathing rate has removed too much CO_2 from their blood and they are suffering from *respiratory alkalosis*. The body responds by "fainting" to decrease respiration and restore the CO_2 levels in the blood. When they regain consciousness, they will be ready to rock once again.

▲ Hyperventilation, the rapid breathing due to excitement or stress, removes CO_2 and increases blood pH resulting in respiratory alkalosis.

See Additional Problems 10.98 and 10.99 at the end of the chapter.

fall, the breathing rate decreases and acid concentration increases (blue arrows in Figure 10.6).

Additional backup to the bicarbonate buffer system is provided by the kidneys. Each day a quantity of acid equal to that produced in the body is excreted in the urine. In the process, the kidney returns HCO_3^- to the extracellular fluids, where it becomes part of the bicarbonate reserve.

🔗 Looking Ahead

In Chapter 29, we will see how the regulation of blood pH by the bicarbonate buffer system is particularly important in preventing *acidosis* and *alkalosis*.   🔗

10.13 Acid and Base Equivalents

We said in Section 9.10 that it is sometimes useful to think in terms of ion *equivalents* (Eq) and *gram-equivalents* (g-Eq) when we are primarily interested in an ion itself rather than the compound that produced the ion. (⬤⬤, p. 276) For similar reasons, it can also be useful to consider acid or base equivalents and gram-equivalents.

When dealing with ions, the property of interest was the charge on the ion. Therefore, 1 Eq of an ion was defined as the number of ions that carry 1 mol of charge, and 1 g-Eq of any ion was defined as the molar mass of the ion divided by the ionic charge. For acids and bases, the property of interest is the number of H^+ ions (for an acid) or the number of OH^- ions (for a base) per formula unit. Thus, 1 **equivalent of acid** contains 1 mol of H^+ ions, and 1 g-Eq of an acid is the mass in grams that contains 1 mol of H^+ ions. Similarly, 1 **equivalent of base** contains 1 mol of OH^- ions, and 1 g-Eq of a base is the mass in grams that contains 1 mol of OH^- ions:

Equivalent of acid Amount of an acid that contains 1 mole of H^+ ions.

Equivalent of base Amount of base that contains 1 mole of OH^- ions.

$$\text{One gram-equivalent of acid} = \frac{\text{Molar mass of acid (g)}}{\text{Number of } H^+ \text{ ions per formula unit}}$$

$$\text{One gram-equivalent of base} = \frac{\text{Molar mass of base (g)}}{\text{Number of } OH^- \text{ ions per formula unit}}$$

Thus 1 g-Eq of the monoprotic acid HCl is

$$\text{1 g-Eq HCl} = \frac{36.5 \text{ g}}{1 \, H^+ \text{ per HCl}} = 36.5 \text{ g}$$

which is the molar mass of the acid, but one gram-equivalent of the diprotic acid H_2SO_4 is

$$\text{1 g-Eq } H_2SO_4 = \frac{98.0 \text{ g}}{2 \, H^+ \text{ per } H_2SO_4} = 49.0 \text{ g}$$

which is the molar mass divided by 2 because 1 mol of H_2SO_4 contains 2 mol of H^+.

$$\text{One equivalent of } H_2SO_4 = \frac{\text{Molar mass of } H_2SO_4}{2} = \frac{98.0 \text{ g}}{2} = 49.0 \text{ g}$$

Divide by 2 because H_2SO_4 is diprotic.

Using acid–base equivalents has two practical advantages: First, they are convenient when only the acidity or basicity of a solution is of interest rather than the identity of the acid or base. Second, they show quantities that are chemically equivalent in their properties; 36.5 g of HCl and 49.0 g of H_2SO_4 are chemically equivalent quantities because each reacts with 1 Eq of base. *One equivalent of any acid neutralizes one equivalent of any base.*

Because acid–base equivalents are so useful, clinical chemists sometimes express acid and base concentrations in *normality* rather than molarity. The **normality (N)** of an acid or base solution is defined as the number of equivalents (or milliequivalents) of acid or base per liter of solution. For example, a solution made by dissolving 1.0 g-Eq (49.0 g) of H_2SO_4 in water to give 1.0 L of solution has a concentration of 1.0 Eq/L, which is 1.0 N. Similarly, a solution that contains 0.010 Eq/L of acid is 0.010 N and has an acid concentration of 10 mEq/L:

$$\text{Normality (N)} = \frac{\text{Equivalents of acid or base}}{\text{Liters of solution}}$$

The values of molarity (M) and normality (N) are the same for monoprotic acids, such as HCl, but are not the same for diprotic or triprotic acids. A solution made by diluting 1.0 g-Eq (49.0 g = 0.50 mol) of the diprotic acid H_2SO_4 to a volume of 1.0 L has a *normality* of 1.0 N but a *molarity* of 0.50 M. For any acid or base, normality is always equal to molarity times the number of H^+ or OH^- ions produced per formula unit:

Normality of acid = (Molarity of acid) × (Number of H^+ ions produced per formula unit)

Normality of base = (Molarity of base) × (Number of OH^- ions produced per formula unit)

WORKED EXAMPLE **10.15** Equivalents: Mass to Equivalent Conversion for Diprotic Acid

How many equivalents are in 3.1 g of the diprotic acid H_2S? The molar mass of H_2S is 34.0 g.

ANALYSIS The number of acid or base equivalents is calculated by doing a gram to mole conversion using molar mass as the conversion factor and then multiplying by the number of H^+ ions produced.

BALLPARK ESTIMATE The 3.1 g is a little less than 0.10 mol of H_2S. Since it is a diprotic acid, (two H^+ per mole), this represents a little less than 0.2 Eq of H_2S.

SOLUTION

$$(3.1 \text{ g } H_2S)\left(\frac{1 \text{ mol } H_2S}{34.0 \text{ g } H_2S}\right)\left(\frac{2 \text{ Eq } H_2S}{1 \text{ mol } H_2S}\right) = 0.18 \text{ Eq } H_2S$$

BALLPARK CHECK The calculated value of 0.18 is consistent with our prediction of a little less than 0.2 Eq of H_2S.

WORKED EXAMPLE **10.16** Equivalents: Calculating Equivalent Concentrations

What is the normality of a solution made by diluting 6.5 g of H_2SO_4 to a volume of 200 mL? What is the concentration of this solution in milliequivalents per liter? The molar mass of H_2SO_4 is 98.0 g.

ANALYSIS Calculate how many equivalents of H_2SO_4 are in 6.5 g by using the molar mass of the acid as a conversion factor and then determine the normality of the acid.

SOLUTION

STEP 1: **Identify known information.** We know the molar mass of H_2SO_4, the mass of H_2SO_4 to be dissolved, and the final volume of solution.

MW of H_2SO_4 = 98.0 g/mol
Mass of H_2SO_4 = 6.5 g
Volume of solution = 200 mL

STEP 2: **Identify answer including units.** We need to calculate the normality of the final solution.

Normality = ?? (equiv./L)

STEP 3: **Identify conversion factors.** We will need to convert the mass of H_2SO_4 to moles, and then to equivalents of H_2SO_4. We will then need to convert volume from mL to L.

$$(6.5 \text{ g } H_2SO_4)\left(\frac{1 \text{ mol } H_2SO_4}{98.0 \text{ g } H_2SO_4}\right)\left(\frac{2 \text{ Eq } H_2SO_4}{1 \text{ mol } H_2SO_4}\right)$$
$$= 0.132 \text{ Eq } H_2SO_4 \text{ (don't round yet!)}$$
$$(200 \text{ mL})\left(\frac{1 \text{ L}}{1000 \text{ mL}}\right) = 0.200 \text{ L}$$

STEP 4: **Solve.** Dividing the number of equivalents by the volume yields the Normality.

$$\frac{0.132 \text{ Eq } H_2SO_4}{0.200 \text{ L}} = 0.66 \text{ N}$$

The concentration of the sulfuric acid solution is 0.66 N, or 660 mEq/L.

10.14 Some Common Acid–Base Reactions

Among the most common of the many kinds of Brønsted–Lowry acid–base reactions are those of an acid with hydroxide ion, an acid with bicarbonate or carbonate ion, and an acid with ammonia or a related nitrogen-containing compound. Let us look briefly at each of the three types.

Reaction of Acids with Hydroxide Ion

One equivalent of an acid reacts with 1 Eq of a metal hydroxide to yield water and a salt in a neutralization reaction (Section 6.10): (⊂⊃, p. 165)

$$HCl(aq) + KOH(aq) \longrightarrow H_2O(l) + KCl(aq)$$

(An acid)   (A base)   (Water)   (A salt)

Such reactions are usually written with a single arrow because their equilibria lie far to the right and they have very large equilibrium constants ($K = 5 \times 10^{15}$; Section 7.8). The net ionic equation (Section 6.13) for all such reactions makes clear why acid-base equivalents are useful and why the properties of the acid and base disappear in neutralization reactions: The equivalent ions for the acid (H$^+$) and the base (OH$^-$) are used up in the formation of water.

$$H^+(aq) + OH^-(aq) \longrightarrow H_2O(l)$$

Reaction of Acids with Bicarbonate and Carbonate Ion

Bicarbonate ion reacts with acid by accepting H$^+$ to yield carbonic acid, H$_2$CO$_3$. Similarly, carbonate ion accepts two protons in its reaction with acid. As mentioned on p. 315, though, that H$_2$CO$_3$ is unstable, rapidly decomposing to carbon dioxide gas and water:

$$H^+(aq) + HCO_3^-(aq) \longrightarrow [H_2CO_3(aq)] \longrightarrow H_2O(l) + CO_2(g)$$
$$2\,H^+(aq) + CO_3^{2-}(aq) \longrightarrow [H_2CO_3(aq)] \longrightarrow H_2O(l) + CO_2(g)$$

Most metal carbonates are insoluble in water—marble, for example, is almost pure calcium carbonate, CaCO$_3$—but they nevertheless react easily with aqueous acid. In fact, geologists often test for carbonate-bearing rocks by putting a few drops of aqueous HCl on the rock and watching to see if bubbles of CO$_2$ form (Figure 10.7). This reaction is also responsible for the damage to marble and

▲ **FIGURE 10.7 Marble.** Marble, which is primarily CaCO$_3$, releases bubbles of CO$_2$ when treated with hydrochloric acid.

limestone artwork caused by acid rain (See Application, p. 324). The most common application involving carbonates and acid, however, is the use of antacids that contain carbonates, such as Tums or Rolaids, to neutralize excess stomach acid.

PROBLEM 10.25

Write a balanced equation for each of the following reactions:

(a) $KHCO_3(aq) + H_2SO_4(aq) \longrightarrow$?

(b) $MgCO_3(aq) + HNO_3(aq) \longrightarrow$?

Reaction of Acids with Ammonia

Acids react with ammonia to yield ammonium salts, such as ammonium chloride, NH_4Cl, most of which are water-soluble:

$$NH_3(aq) + HCl(aq) \longrightarrow NH_4Cl(aq)$$

Living organisms contain a group of compounds called *amines*, which contain nitrogen atoms bonded to carbon. Amines react with acids just as ammonia does, yielding water-soluble salts. Methylamine, for example, an organic compound found in rotting fish, reacts with HCl:

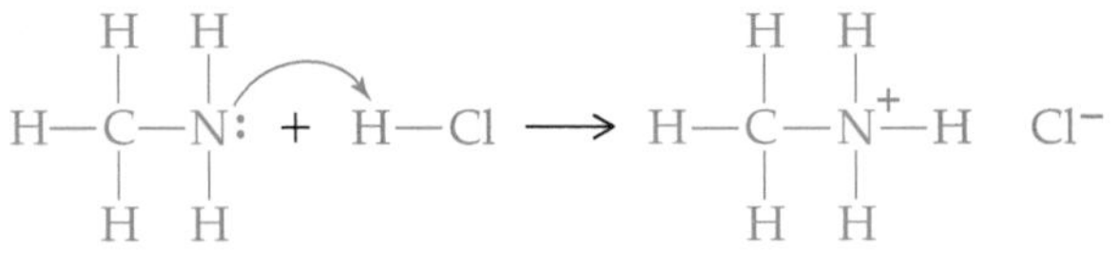

▲ This limestone statue adorning the Rheims Cathedral in France has been severely eroded by acid rain.

$$\begin{array}{ccc} & \underset{\text{Methylamine}}{\underset{\displaystyle |}{\overset{\displaystyle |}{H-C-N:}}} + H-Cl \longrightarrow & \underset{\text{Methylammonium chloride}}{\underset{\displaystyle |}{\overset{\displaystyle |}{H-C-\overset{+}{N}-H}}} \quad Cl^- \end{array}$$

⊂O⊃ Looking Ahead

In Chapter 15, we will see that amines occur in all living organisms, both plant and animal, as well as in many pharmaceutical agents. Amines called amino acids form the building blocks from which proteins are made, as we will see in Chapter 18. ⊂O⊃

PROBLEM 10.26

What products would you expect from the reaction of ammonia and sulfuric acid in aqueous solution?

$$NH_3(aq) + H_2SO_4(aq) \longrightarrow$$?

PROBLEM 10.27

Show how ethylamine ($C_2H_5NH_2$) reacts with hydrochloric acid to form an ethylammonium salt.

10.15 Titration

Determining the pH of a solution gives the solution's H_3O^+ concentration but not necessarily its total acid concentration. That is because the two are not the same thing. The H_3O^+ concentration gives only the amount of acid that has dissociated into ions, whereas total acid concentration gives the sum of dissociated plus undissociated acid. In a 0.10 M solution of acetic acid, for instance, the total acid concentration is 0.10 M, yet the H_3O^+ concentration is only 0.0013 M (pH = 2.89) because acetic acid is a weak acid that is only about 1% dissociated.

Titration A procedure for determining the total acid or base concentration of a solution.

The total acid or base concentration of a solution can be found by carrying out a **titration** procedure, as shown in Figure 10.8. Let us assume, for instance, that we want to find the acid concentration of an HCl solution. (We could equally well need to find the base concentration of an NaOH solution.) We begin by measuring out a known volume of the HCl solution and adding an acid–base indicator. Next, we fill a calibrated glass tube called a *buret* with an NaOH solution of known concentration, and we slowly add the NaOH to the HCl until neutralization is complete (the *end point*), identified by a color change in the indicator.

(a)   (b)

▲ **FIGURE 10.8   Titration of an acid solution of unknown concentration with a base solution of known concentration.**   (a) A measured volume of the acid solution is placed in the flask along with an indicator. (b) The base of known concentration is then added from a buret until the color change of the indicator shows that neutralization is complete (the *end point*).

Reading from the buret gives the volume of the NaOH solution that has reacted with the known volume of HCl. Knowing both the concentration and volume of the NaOH solution then allows us to calculate the molar amount of NaOH, and the coefficients in the balanced equation allow us to find the molar amount of HCl that has been neutralized. Dividing the molar amount of HCl by the volume of the HCl solution gives the concentration. The calculation thus involves mole–volume conversions just like those done in Section 9.7. (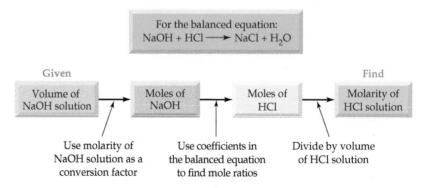, p. 265) Figure 10.9 shows a flow diagram of the strategy, and Worked Example 10.17 shows how to calculate total acid concentration.

For the balanced equation:
$$NaOH + HCl \longrightarrow NaCl + H_2O$$

Given

| Volume of NaOH solution | Moles of NaOH | Moles of HCl | Molarity of HCl solution |

Find

Use molarity of NaOH solution as a conversion factor

Use coefficients in the balanced equation to find mole ratios

Divide by volume of HCl solution

▲ **FIGURE 10.9   A flow diagram for an acid–base titration.**   This diagram summarizes the calculations needed to determine the concentration of an HCl solution by titration with an NaOH solution of known concentration. The steps are similar to those shown in Figure 9.7.

WORKED EXAMPLE **10.17** Titrations: Calculating Total Acid Concentration

When a 5.00 mL sample of household vinegar (dilute aqueous acetic acid) is titrated, 44.5 mL of 0.100 M NaOH solution is required to reach the end point. What is the acid concentration of the vinegar in moles per liter, equivalents per liter, and milliequivalents per liter? The neutralization reaction is

$$CH_3CO_2H(aq) + NaOH(aq) \longrightarrow CH_3CO_2^-Na^+(aq) + H_2O(l)$$

ANALYSIS To find the molarity of the vinegar, we need to know the number of moles of acetic acid dissolved in the 5.00 mL sample. Following a flow diagram similar to Figure 10.9, we use the volume and molarity of NaOH to find the number of moles. From the chemical equation, we use the mole ratio to find the number of moles of acid, and then divide by the volume of the acid solution. Because acetic acid is a monoprotic acid, the normality of the solution is numerically the same as its molarity.

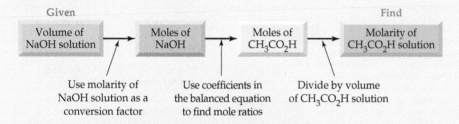

BALLPARK ESTIMATE The 5.00 mL of vinegar required nearly nine times as much NaOH solution (44.5 mL) for complete reaction. Since the neutralization stoichiometry is 1:1, the molarity of the acetic acid in the vinegar must be nine times greater than the molarity of NaOH, or 0.90 M.

SOLUTION
Substitute the known information and appropriate conversion factors into the flow diagram, and solve for the molarity of the acetic acid:

$$(44.5 \text{ mL NaOH})\left(\frac{0.100 \text{ mol NaOH}}{1000 \text{ mL}}\right)\left(\frac{1 \text{ mol CH}_3\text{CO}_2\text{H}}{1 \text{ mol NaOH}}\right)$$

$$\times \left(\frac{1}{0.005\ 00 \text{ L}}\right) = 0.890 \text{ M CH}_3\text{CO}_2\text{H}$$

$$= 0.890 \text{ N CH}_3\text{CO}_2\text{H}$$

Expressed in milliequivalents, this concentration is

$$\frac{0.890 \text{ Eq}}{L} \times \frac{1000 \text{ mEq}}{1 \text{ Eq}} = 890 \text{ mEq/L}$$

BALLPARK CHECK The calculated result (0.890 M) is very close to our estimate of 0.90 M.

PROBLEM 10.28

A titration is carried out to determine the concentration of the acid in an old bottle of aqueous HCl whose label has become unreadable. What is the HCl concentration if 58.4 mL of 0.250 M NaOH is required to titrate a 20.0 mL sample of the acid?

APPLICATION ▶ Acid Rain

A s the water that evaporates from oceans and lakes condenses into raindrops, it dissolves small quantities of gases from the atmosphere. Under normal conditions, rain is slightly acidic, with a pH close to 5.6, because of atmospheric CO_2 that dissolves to form carbonic acid:

$$CO_2(aq) + H_2O(l) \rightleftharpoons$$
$$H_2CO_3(aq) \rightleftharpoons HCO_3^-(aq) + H_3O^+(aq)$$

In recent decades, however, the acidity of rainwater in many industrialized areas of the world has increased by a factor of over 100, to a pH between 3 and 3.5.

The primary cause of this so-called *acid rain* is industrial and automotive pollution. Each year, large power plants and smelters pour millions of tons of sulfur dioxide (SO_2) gas into the atmosphere, where some is oxidized by air to produce sulfur trioxide (SO_3). Sulfur oxides then dissolve in rain to form dilute sulfurous acid (H_2SO_3) and sulfuric acid (H_2SO_4):

$$SO_2(g) + H_2O(l) \longrightarrow H_2SO_3(aq)$$
$$SO_3(g) + H_2O(l) \longrightarrow H_2SO_4(aq)$$

Nitrogen oxides produced by the high-temperature reaction of N_2 with O_2 in coal-burning plants and in automobile engines further contribute to the problem. Nitrogen dioxide (NO_2) dissolves in water to form dilute nitric acid (HNO_3) and nitric oxide (NO):

$$3\,NO_2(g) + H_2O(l) \longrightarrow 2\,HNO_3(aq) + NO(g)$$

Oxides of both sulfur and nitrogen have always been present in the atmosphere, produced by such natural sources as volcanoes and lightning bolts, but their amounts have increased dramatically over the last century because of industrialization. The result is a notable decrease in the pH of rainwater in more densely populated regions, including Europe and the eastern United States.

Many processes in nature require such a fine pH balance that they are dramatically upset by the shift that has occurred in the pH of rain. Some watersheds contain soils that have high "buffering capacity" and so are able to neutralize acidic compounds in acid rain (Section 10.11). Other areas, such as the northeastern United States and eastern Canada, where soil buffering capacity is poor, have experienced negative ecological effects. Acid rain releases aluminum salts from soil, and the ions then wash into streams. The low pH and increased aluminum levels are so toxic to fish and other organisms that many lakes and streams in these areas are devoid of aquatic life. Massive tree die-offs have occurred throughout central and eastern Europe as acid rain has lowered the pH of the soil and has leached nutrients from leaves.

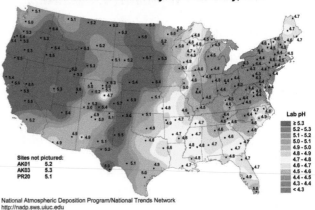

Hydrogen ion concentration as pH from measurements made at the Central Analytical Laboratory, 1996

Sites not pictured:
AK01   5.2
AK03   5.3
PR20   5.1

National Atmospheric Deposition Program/National Trends Network
http://nadp.sws.uiuc.edu

Lab pH
≥ 5.3
5.2 - 5.3
5.1 - 5.2
5.0 - 5.1
4.9 - 5.0
4.8 - 4.9
4.7 - 4.8
4.6 - 4.7
4.5 - 4.6
4.4 - 4.5
4.3 - 4.4
< 4.3

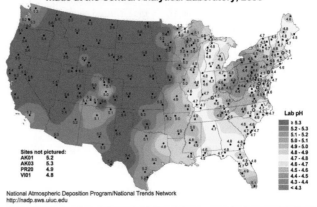

Hydrogen ion concentration as pH from measurements made at the Central Analytical Laboratory, 2006

Sites not pictured:
AK01   5.2
AK03   5.3
PR20   4.9
VI01   4.8

National Atmospheric Deposition Program/National Trends Network
http://nadp.sws.uiuc.edu

Lab pH
≥ 5.3
5.2 - 5.3
5.1 - 5.2
5.0 - 5.1
4.9 - 5.0
4.8 - 4.9
4.7 - 4.8
4.6 - 4.7
4.5 - 4.6
4.4 - 4.5
4.3 - 4.4
< 4.3

▲ These maps compare the average pH of precipitation in the United States in 1996 and in 2006. During this period, total acid deposition in much of the eastern United States decreased substantially.

Fortunately, acidic emissions in the United States have been greatly reduced in recent years as a result of the Clean Air Act Amendments of 1990. Industrial emissions of SO_2 and nitrogen oxides decreased by over 40% from 1990 to 2007, resulting in a decrease in acid rain depositions, particularly in the eastern United States and Canada (see accompanying figure). While significant reductions have been realized, most environmental scientists agree that additional reductions in these pollutant emissions are necessary to ensure the recovery of affected lakes and streams.

See Additional Problems 10.100 and 10.101 at the end of the chapter.

PROBLEM 10.29

How many milliliters of 0.150 M NaOH are required to neutralize 50.0 mL of 0.200 M H_2SO_4? The balanced neutralization reaction is:

$$H_2SO_4(aq) + 2\,NaOH(aq) \longrightarrow Na_2SO_4(aq) + 2\,H_2O(l).$$

PROBLEM 10.30

A 21.5 mL sample of a KOH solution of unknown concentration requires 16.1 mL of 0.150 M H_2SO_4 solution to reach the end point in a titration. What is the molarity of the KOH solution?

10.16 Acidity and Basicity of Salt Solutions

It is tempting to think of all salt solutions as neutral; after all, they come from the neutralization reaction between an acid and a base. In fact, salt solutions can be neutral, acidic, or basic, depending on the ions present, because some ions react with water to produce H_3O^+ and some ions react with water to produce OH^-. To predict the acidity of a salt solution, it is convenient to classify salts according to the acid and base from which they are formed in a neutralization reaction. The classification and some examples are given in Table 10.3.

TABLE 10.3 Acidity and Basicity of Salt Solutions

ANION DERIVED FROM ACID THAT IS:	CATION DERIVED FROM BASE THAT IS:	SOLUTION	EXAMPLE
Strong	Weak	Acidic	NH_4Cl, NH_4NO_3
Weak	Strong	Basic	$NaHCO_3$, KCH_3CO_2
Strong	Strong	Neutral	$NaCl$, KBr, $Ca(NO_3)_2$
Weak	Weak	More information needed	

The general rule for predicting the acidity or basicity of a salt solution is that the stronger partner from which the salt is formed dominates. That is, a salt formed from a strong acid and a weak base yields an acidic solution because the strong acid dominates; a salt formed from a weak acid and a strong base yields a basic solution because the base dominates; and a salt formed from a strong acid and a strong base yields a neutral solution because neither acid nor base dominates. Here are some examples.

Salt of Strong Acid + Weak Base ⟶ Acidic Solution

A salt such as NH_4Cl, which can be formed by reaction of a strong acid (HCl) with a weak base (NH_3), yields an acidic solution. The Cl^- ion does not react with water, but the NH_4^+ ion is a weak acid that gives H_3O^+ ions:

$$NH_4^+(aq) + H_2O(l) \rightleftharpoons NH_3(aq) + H_3O^+(aq)$$

Salt of Weak Acid + Strong Base ⟶ Basic Solution

A salt such as sodium bicarbonate, which can be formed by reaction of a weak acid (H_2CO_3) with a strong base (NaOH), yields a basic solution. The Na^+ ion does not react with water, but the HCO_3^- ion is a weak base that gives OH^- ions:

$$HCO_3^-(aq) + H_2O(l) \rightleftharpoons H_2CO_3(aq) + OH^-(aq)$$

Salt of Strong Acid + Strong Base ⟶ Neutral Solution

A salt such as NaCl, which can be formed by reaction of a strong acid (HCl) with a strong base (NaOH), yields a neutral solution. Neither the Cl^- ion nor the Na^+ ion reacts with water.

Salt of Weak Acid + Weak Base

Both cation and anion in this type of salt react with water, so we cannot predict whether the resulting solution will be acidic or basic without quantitative information. The ion that reacts to the greater extent with water will govern the pH—it may be either the cation or the anion.

WORKED EXAMPLE **10.18** Acidity and Basicity of Salt Solutions

Predict whether the following salts produce an acidic, basic, or neutral solution:

(a) $BaCl_2$ (b) NaCN   (c) NH_4NO_3

ANALYSIS Look in Table 10.1 (p. 300) to see the classification of acids and bases as strong or weak.

SOLUTION

(a) $BaCl_2$ gives a neutral solution because it is formed from a strong acid (HCl) and a strong base $[Ba(OH)_2]$.

(b) NaCN gives a basic solution because it is formed from a weak acid (HCN) and a strong base (NaOH).

(c) NH_4NO_3 gives an acidic solution because it is formed from a strong acid (HNO_3) and a weak base (NH_3).

PROBLEM 10.31

Predict whether the following salts produce an acidic, basic, or neutral solution:

(a) K_2SO_4 (b) Na_2HPO_4 (c) MgF_2 (d) NH_4Br

KEY WORDS

Acid dissociation constant (K_a), p. 303

Acid–base indicator, p. 310

Amphoteric, p. 299

Brønsted–Lowry acid, p. 295

Brønsted–Lowry base, p. 296

Buffer, p. 312

Conjugate acid, p. 297

Conjugate acid–base pair, p. 297

Conjugate base, p. 297

SUMMARY: REVISITING THE CHAPTER GOALS

1. **What are acids and bases?** According to the *Brønsted–Lowry definition,* an acid is a substance that donates a hydrogen ion (a proton, H^+) and a base is a substance that accepts a hydrogen ion. Thus, the generalized reaction of an acid with a base involves the reversible transfer of a proton:

$$B: + H—A \rightleftharpoons A:^- + H—B^+$$

In aqueous solution, water acts as a base and accepts a proton from an acid to yield a *hydronium ion,* H_3O^+. Reaction of an acid with a metal hydroxide, such as KOH, yields water and a salt; reaction with bicarbonate ion (HCO_3^-) or carbonate ion (CO_3^{2-}) yields water, a salt, and CO_2 gas; and reaction with ammonia yields an ammonium salt.

2. **What effect does the strength of acids and bases have on their reactions?** Different acids and bases differ in their ability to give up or accept a proton. A *strong acid* gives up a proton easily and is 100% *dissociated* in aqueous solution; a *weak acid* gives up a proton with difficulty, is only slightly dissociated in water, and establishes an equilibrium between dissociated and undissociated forms. Similarly, a *strong base* accepts and holds a proton

readily, whereas a *weak base* has a low affinity for a proton and establishes an equilibrium in aqueous solution. The two substances that are related by the gain or loss of a proton are called a *conjugate acid–base pair*. The exact strength of an acid is defined by an *acid dissociation constant*, K_a:

For the reaction $\quad HA + H_2O \rightleftharpoons H_3O^+ + A^-$

we have $\quad K_a = \dfrac{[H_3O^+][A^-]}{[HA]}$

A proton-transfer reaction always takes place in the direction that favors formation of the weaker acid.

3. **What is the ion-product constant for water?** Water is *amphoteric*; that is, it can act as either an acid or a base. Water also dissociates slightly into H_3O^+ ions and OH^- ions; the product of whose concentrations in any aqueous solution is the *ion-product constant for water*, $K_w = [H_3O^+][OH^-] = 1.00 \times 10^{-14}$ at 25 °C.

4. **What is the pH scale for measuring acidity?** The acidity or basicity of an aqueous solution is given by its *pH*, defined as the negative logarithm of the hydronium ion concentration, $[H_3O^+]$. A pH below 7 means an acidic solution; a pH equal to 7 means a neutral solution; and a pH above 7 means a basic solution.

5. **What is a buffer?** The pH of a solution can be controlled through the use of a *buffer* that acts to remove either added H^+ ions or added OH^- ions. Most buffer solutions consist of roughly equal amounts of a weak acid and its conjugate base. The bicarbonate buffer present in blood and the hydrogen phosphate buffer present in cells are particularly important examples.

6. **How is the acid or base concentration of a solution determined?** Acid (or base) concentrations are determined in the laboratory by *titration* of a solution of unknown concentration with a base (or acid) solution of known strength until an indicator signals that neutralization is complete.

UNDERSTANDING KEY CONCEPTS

10.32 Identify the Brønsted–Lowry acid and base in the following reactions:

= H $\quad$ ● = C $\quad$ ● = O $\quad$ ● = F

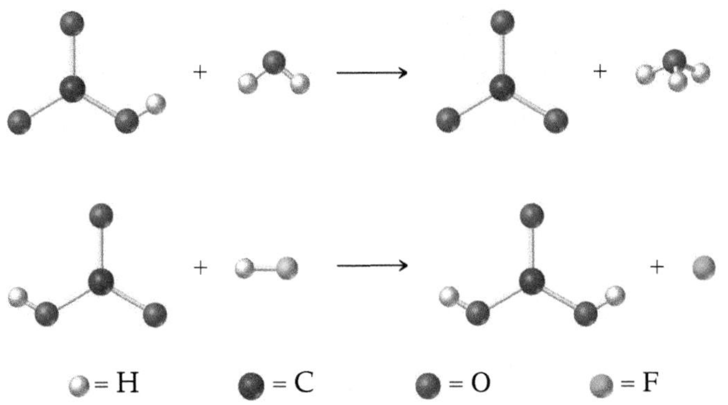

10.33 An aqueous solution of OH^-, represented as a blue sphere, is allowed to mix with a solution of an acid H_nA, represented as a red sphere. Three possible outcomes are depicted by boxes (1)–(3), where the green spheres represent A^{n-}, the anion of the acid:

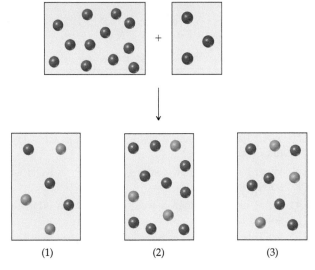

(1) $\qquad$ (2) $\qquad$ (3)

Which outcome corresponds to the following reactions?
(a) $HF + OH^- \longrightarrow H_2O + F^-$
(b) $H_2SO_3 + 2\,OH^- \longrightarrow 2\,H_2O + SO_3^{2-}$
(c) $H_3PO_4 + 3\,OH^- \longrightarrow 3\,H_2O + PO_4^{3-}$

10.34 Electrostatic potential maps of acetic acid (CH_3CO_2H) and ethyl alcohol (CH_3CH_2OH) are shown. Identify the most acidic hydrogen in each, and tell which of the two is likely to be the stronger acid.

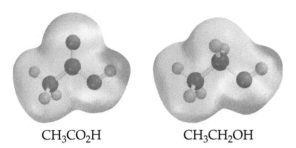

CH₃CO₂H   CH₃CH₂OH

10.35 The following pictures represent aqueous acid solutions. Water molecules are not shown.

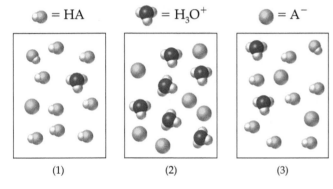

   (1)   (2)   (3)

(a) Which picture represents the weakest acid?
(b) Which picture represents the strongest acid?
(c) Which picture represents the acid with the smallest value of K_a?

10.36 The following pictures represent aqueous solutions of a diprotic acid H_2A. Water molecules are not shown.

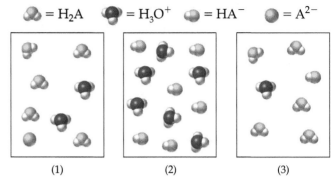

   (1)   (2)   (3)

(a) Which picture represents a solution of a weak diprotic acid?
(b) Which picture represents an impossible situation?

10.37 Assume that the red spheres in the buret represent H^+ ions, the blue spheres in the flask represent OH^- ions, and you are carrying out a titration of the base with the acid. If the volumes in the buret and the flask are identical and the concentration of the acid in the buret is 1.00 M, what is the concentration of the base in the flask?

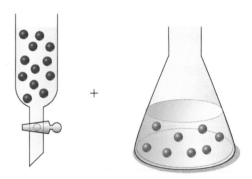

+

ADDITIONAL PROBLEMS

ACIDS AND BASES

10.38 What happens when a strong acid such as HBr is dissolved in water?

10.39 What happens when a weak acid such as CH_3CO_2H is dissolved in water?

10.40 What happens when a strong base such as KOH is dissolved in water?

10.41 What happens when a weak base such as NH_3 is dissolved in water?

10.42 What is the difference between a monoprotic acid and a diprotic acid? Give an example of each.

10.43 What is the difference between H^+ and H_3O^+?

10.44 Which of the following are strong acids? Look at Table 10.1 (*p. 300*) if necessary.
(a) $HClO_4$ **(b)** H_2CO_3
(c) H_3PO_4 **(d)** NH_4^+
(e) HI   **(f)** $H_2PO_4^-$

10.45 Which of the following are weak bases? Look at Table 10.1 (*p. 300*) if necessary.
(a) NH_3 **(b)** $Ca(OH)_2$
(c) HPO_4^{2-} **(d)** LiOH
(e) CN^- **(f)** NH_2^-

BRØNSTED–LOWRY ACIDS AND BASES

10.46 Identify the following substances as a Brønsted–Lowry base, a Brønsted–Lowry acid, or neither:
(a) HCN   **(b)** $CH_3CO_2^-$
(c) $AlCl_3$ **(d)** H_2CO_3
(e) Mg^{2+} **(f)** $CH_3NH_3^+$

10.47 Label the Brønsted–Lowry acids and bases in the following equations, and tell which substances are conjugate acid–base pairs.
(a) $CO_3^{2-}(aq) + HCl(aq) \longrightarrow HCO_3^-(aq) + Cl^-(aq)$
(b) $H_3PO_4(aq) + NH_3(aq) \longrightarrow H_2PO_4^-(aq) + NH_4^+(aq)$

(c) $NH_4^+(aq) + CN^-(aq) \rightleftharpoons NH_3(aq) + HCN(aq)$
(d) $HBr(aq) + OH^-(aq) \longrightarrow H_2O(l) + Br^-(aq)$
(e) $H_2PO_4^-(aq) + N_2H_4(aq)$

$$\rightleftharpoons HPO_4^{2-}(aq) + N_2H_5^+(aq)$$

10.48 Write the formulas of the conjugate acids of the following Brønsted–Lowry bases:

(a) $ClCH_2CO_2^-$
(b) C_5H_5N
(c) SeO_4^{2-}
(d) $(CH_3)_3N$

10.49 Write the formulas of the conjugate bases of the following Brønsted–Lowry acids:

(a) HCN
(b) $(CH_3)_2NH_2^+$
(c) H_3PO_4
(d) $HSeO_3^-$

10.50 The hydrogen-containing anions of many polyprotic acids are amphoteric. Write equations for HCO_3^- and $H_2PO_4^-$ acting as bases with the strong acid HCl and as acids with the strong base NaOH.

10.51 Write balanced equations for proton-transfer reactions between the listed pairs. Indicate the conjugate pairs, and determine the favored direction for each equilibrium.

(a) HCl and PO_4^{3-}
(b) HCN and SO_4^{2-}
(c) $HClO_4$ and NO_2^-
(d) CH_3O^- and HF

10.52 Tums, a drugstore remedy for acid indigestion, contains $CaCO_3$. Write an equation for the reaction of Tums with gastric juice (HCl).

10.53 Write balanced equations for the following acid–base reactions:

(a) $LiOH + HNO_3 \longrightarrow$
(b) $BaCO_3 + HI \longrightarrow$
(c) $H_3PO_4 + KOH \longrightarrow$
(d) $Ca(HCO_3)_2 + HCl \longrightarrow$
(e) $Ba(OH_2) + H_2SO_4 \longrightarrow$

ACID AND BASE STRENGTH: K_a AND pH

10.54 How is K_a defined? Write the equation for K_a for the generalized acid HA.

10.55 Rearrange the equation you wrote in Problem 10.54 to solve for $[H_3O^+]$ in terms of K_a.

10.56 How is K_w defined, and what is its numerical value at 25 °C?

10.57 How is pH defined?

10.58 A solution of 0.10 M HCl has a pH = 1.00, whereas a solution of 0.10 M CH_3COOH has a pH = 2.88. Explain.

10.59 Calculate $[H_3O^+]$ for the 0.10 M CH_3COOH solution in Problem 10.58. What percent of the weak acid is dissociated?

10.60 Write the expressions for the acid dissociation constants for the three successive dissociations of phosphoric acid, H_3PO_4, in water.

10.61 Find K_a values in Table 10.2, and decide which acid in the following pairs is stronger:

(a) HCO_3H or HF
(b) HSO_4^- or HCN
(c) $H_3PO_4^-$ or HPO_4^{2-}
(d) $CH_3CH_2CO_2H$ or CH_3CO_2H

10.62 Which substance in the following pairs is the stronger base? Look at Table 10.1 if necessary.

(a) OH^- or PO_4^{3-}
(b) Br^- or NO_2^-
(c) NH_3 or OH^-
(d) CN^- or H_2O
(e) I^- or HPO_4^{2-}

10.63 Based on the K_a values in Table 10.1, rank the following solutions in order of increasing pH: 0.10 M HCOOH, 0.10 M HF, 0.10 M H_2CO_3, 0.10 M HSO_4^-, 0.10 M NH_4^+.

10.64 The electrode of a pH meter is placed in a sample of urine, and a reading of 7.9 is obtained. Is the sample acidic, basic, or neutral? What is the concentration of H_3O^+ in the urine sample?

10.65 A 0.10 M solution of the deadly poison hydrogen cyanide, HCN, has a pH of 5.2. Is HCN acidic or basic? Is it strong or weak?

10.66 Normal gastric juice has a pH of about 2. Assuming that gastric juice is primarily aqueous HCl, what is the HCl concentration?

10.67 Human spinal fluid has a pH of 7.4. Approximately what is the H_3O^+ concentration of spinal fluid?

10.68 What is the approximate pH of a 0.10 M solution of a strong monoprotic acid? Of a 0.10 M solution of a strong base, such as KOH?

10.69 Calculate the pOH of each solution in Problems 10.64–10.67.

10.70 Approximately what pH do the following H_3O^+ concentrations correspond to?

(a) Fresh egg white: $[H_3O^+] = 2.5 \times 10^{-8}$ M
(b) Apple cider: $[H_3O^+] = 5.0 \times 10^{-4}$ M
(c) Household ammonia: $[H_3O^+] = 2.3 \times 10^{-12}$ M

10.71 What are the OH^- concentration and pOH for each solution in Problem 10.70? Rank the solutions according to increasing acidity.

10.72 What are the H_3O^+ and OH^- concentrations of solutions that have the following pH values?

(a) pH 4
(b) pH 11
(c) pH 0
(d) pH 1.38
(e) pH 7.96

10.73 About 12% of the acid in a 0.10 M solution of a weak acid dissociates to form ions. What are the H_3O^+ and OH^- concentrations? What is the pH of the solution?

BUFFERS

10.74 What are the two components of a buffer system? How does a buffer work to hold pH nearly constant?

10.75 Which system would you expect to be a better buffer: $HNO_3 + Na^+NO_3^-$, or $CH_3CO_2H + CH_3CO_2^-Na^+$? Explain.

10.76 The pH of a buffer solution containing 0.10 M acetic acid and 0.10 M sodium acetate is 4.74.

    (a) Write the Henderson–Hasselbalch equation for this buffer.

    (b) Write the equations for reaction of this buffer with a small amount of HNO_3 and with a small amount of NaOH.

10.77 Which of the following buffer systems would you use if you wanted to prepare a solution having a pH of approximately 9.5?

    (a) 0.08 M $H_2PO_4^-$/0.12 M HPO_4^{2-}

    (b) 0.08 M NH_4^+/0.12 M NH_3

10.78 What is the pH of a buffer system that contains 0.200 M hydrocyanic acid (HCN) and 0.150 M sodium cyanide (NaCN)? The pK_a of hydrocyanic acid is 9.31.

10.79 What is the pH of 1.00 L of the 0.200 M hydrocyanic acid–0.150 M cyanide ion buffer system described in Problem 10.78 after 0.020 mol of HCl is added? After 0.020 mol of NaOH is added?

10.80 What is the pH of a buffer system that contains 0.15 M NH_4^+ and 0.10 M NH_3? The pK_a of NH_4^+ is 9.25.

10.81 How many moles of NaOH must be added to 1.00 L of the solution described in Problem 10.80 to increase the pH to 9.25?

CONCENTRATIONS OF ACID AND BASE SOLUTIONS

10.82 What does it mean when we talk about acid *equivalents* and base *equivalents*?

10.83 How is normality defined as a means of expressing acid or base concentration?

10.84 Calculate the gram-equivalent for each of the following acids and bases.

    (a) HNO_3 **(b)** H_3PO_4

    (c) KOH   **(d)** $Mg(OH)_2$

10.85 What mass of each of the acids and bases in Problem 10.84 is needed to prepare 500 mL of 0.15 N solution?

10.86 How many milliliters of 0.0050 N KOH are required to neutralize 25 mL of 0.0050 N H_2SO_4? To neutralize 25 mL of 0.0050 N HCl?

10.87 What is the normality of a 0.12 M H_2SO_4 solution? Of a 0.12 M H_3PO_4 solution?

10.88 How many equivalents of an acid or base are in the following?

    (a) 0.25 mol $Mg(OH)_2$

    (b) 2.5 g $Mg(OH)_2$

    (c) 15 g CH_3CO_2H

10.89 What mass of citric acid (triprotic, $C_6H_5O_7H_3$) contains 152 mEq of citric acid?

10.90 What are the molarity and the normality of a solution made by dissolving 5.0 g of $Ca(OH)_2$ in enough water to make 500.0 mL of solution?

10.91 What are the molarity and the normality of a solution made by dissolving 25 g of citric acid (triprotic, $C_6H_5O_7H_3$) in enough water to make 800 mL of solution?

10.92 Titration of a 12.0 mL solution of HCl requires 22.4 mL of 0.12 M NaOH. What is the molarity of the HCl solution?

10.93 What volume of 0.085 M HNO_3 is required to titrate 15.0 mL of 0.12 M $Ba(OH)_2$ solution?

10.94 Titration of a 10.0 mL solution of KOH requires 15.0 mL of 0.0250 M H_2SO_4 solution. What is the molarity of the KOH solution?

10.95 If 35.0 mL of a 0.100 N acid solution is needed to reach the end point in titration of 21.5 mL of a base solution, what is the normality of the base solution?

Applications

10.96 The concentration of HCl when released to the stomach cavity is diluted to between 0.01 and 0.001 M [*GERD—Too Much Acid or Not Enough? p. 302*]

    (a) What is the pH range in the stomach cavity?

    (b) Write a balanced equation for the neutralization of stomach acid by $NaHCO_3$.

    (c) How many grams of $NaHCO_3$ are required to neutralize 15.0 mL of a solution having a pH of 1.8?

10.97 Which body fluid is most acidic? Which is most basic? [*pH of Body Fluids, p. 311*]

10.98 Metabolic acidosis is often treated by administering bicarbonate intravenously. Explain how this treatment can increase blood serum pH. [*Buffers in the Body: Acidosis and Alkalosis, p. 317*]

10.99 The normal $[HCO_3^-]/[CO_2]$ ratio in the blood is about 20 to 1 at a pH = 7.4. What is this ratio at pH = 7.3 (acidosis) and at pH = 7.5 (alkalosis)? [*Buffers in the Body: Acidosis and Alkalosis, p. 317*]

10.100 Rain typically has a pH of about 5.6. What is the H_3O^+ concentration in rain? [*Acid Rain, p. 324*]

10.101 Acid rain with a pH as low as 1.5 has been recorded in West Virginia. [*Acid Rain, p. 324*]

    (a) What is the H_3O^+ concentration in this acid rain?

    (b) How many grams of HNO_3 must be dissolved to make 25 L of solution that has a pH of 1.5?

General Questions and Problems

10.102 Alka-Seltzer, a drugstore antacid, contains a mixture of $NaHCO_3$, aspirin, and citric acid, $C_6H_5O_7H_3$. Why does Alka-Seltzer foam and bubble when dissolved in water? Which ingredient is the antacid?

10.103 How many milliliters of 0.50 M NaOH solution are required to titrate 40.0 mL of a 0.10 M H_2SO_4 solution to an end point?

10.104 Which solution contains more acid, 50 mL of a 0.20 N HCl solution or 50 mL of a 0.20 N acetic acid solution? Which has a higher hydronium ion concentration? Which has a lower pH?

10.105 One of the buffer systems used to control the pH of blood involves the equilibrium between $H_2PO_4^-$ and HPO_4^{2-}. The pK_a for $H_2PO_4^-$ is 7.21.

(a) Write the Henderson–Hasselbalch equation for this buffer system.

(b) What HPO_4^{2-} to $H_2PO_4^-$ ratio is needed to maintain the optimum blood pH of 7.40?

10.106 A 0.15 M solution of HCl is used to titrate 30.0 mL of a $Ca(OH)_2$ solution of unknown concentration. If 140 mL of HCl is required, what is the concentration (in molarity) of the $Ca(OH)_2$ solution?

10.107 Which of the following combinations produces an effective buffer solution? Assuming equal concentrations of each acid and its conjugate base, calculate the pH of each buffer solution.

(a) NaF and HF   (b) $HClO_4$ and $NaClO_4$

(c) NH_4Cl and NH_3 (d) KBr and HBr

10.108 One method of analyzing ammonium salts is to treat them with NaOH and then heat the solution to remove the NH_3 gas formed.

$$NH_4^+(aq) + OH^-(aq) \longrightarrow NH_3(g) + H_2O(l)$$

(a) Label the Brønsted–Lowry acid–base pairs.

(b) If 2.86 L of NH_3 at 60 °C and 755 mmHg is produced by the reaction of NH_4Cl, how many grams of NH_4Cl were in the original sample?

10.109 One method of reducing acid rain is *scrubbing* the combustion products before they are emitted from power plant smoke stacks. The process involves addition of an aqueous suspension of lime (CaO) to the combustion chamber and stack, where the lime reacts with SO_2 to give calcium sulfite ($CaSO_3$).

(a) Write the balanced chemical equation for this reaction.

(b) How much lime is needed to remove 1 kg of SO_2?

10.110 Sodium oxide, Na_2O, reacts with water to give NaOH.

(a) Write a balanced equation for the reaction.

(b) What is the pH of the solution prepared by allowing 1.55 g of Na_2O to react with 500.0 mL of water? Assume that there is no volume change.

(c) How many milliliters of 0.0100 M HCl are needed to neutralize the NaOH solution prepared in (b)?

CHAPTER 11

Nuclear Chemistry

CONCEPTS TO REVIEW

Atomic Theory
(Section 3.1)

Elements and Atomic Number
(Section 3.2)

Isotopes
(Section 3.3)

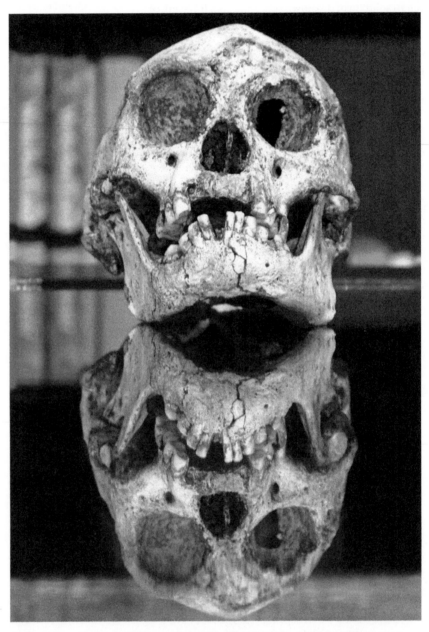

▲ The age of this skull, from a hominid discovered in 2004 in Indonesia, is estimated to be 18,000 years.

CONTENTS

CHAPTER GOALS

In this chapter we will answer the following questions about nuclear chemistry:

1. What is a nuclear reaction, and how are equations for nuclear reactions balanced?

THE GOAL: Be able to write and balance equations for nuclear reactions.

2. What are the different kinds of radioactivity?

THE GOAL: Be able to list the characteristics of three common kinds of radiation—α, β, and γ (alpha, beta, and gamma).

3. How are the rates of nuclear reactions expressed?

THE GOAL: Be able to explain half-life and calculate the quantity of a radioisotope remaining after a given number of half-lives.

4. What is ionizing radiation?

THE GOAL: Be able to describe the properties of the different types of ionizing radiation and their potential for harm to living tissue.

5. How is radioactivity measured?

THE GOAL: Be able to describe the common units for measuring radiation.

6. What is transmutation?

THE GOAL: Be able to explain nuclear bombardment and balance equations for nuclear bombardment reactions.

7. What are nuclear fission and nuclear fusion?

THE GOAL: Be able to explain nuclear fission and nuclear fusion.

I n all of the reactions we have discussed thus far, only the *bonds* between atoms have changed; the chemical identities of atoms themselves have remained unchanged. Anyone who reads the paper or watches television knows, however, that atoms *can* change, often resulting in the conversion of one element into another. Atomic weapons, nuclear energy, and radioactive radon gas in our homes are all topics of societal importance, and all involve *nuclear chemistry*—the study of the properties and reactions of atomic nuclei.

11.1 Nuclear Reactions

Recall from Section 3.2 that an atom is characterized by its *atomic number, Z,* and its *mass number, A.* (⬭, p. 53) The atomic number, written below and to the left of the element symbol, gives the number of protons in the nucleus and identifies the element. The mass number, written above and to the left of the element symbol, gives the total number of **nucleons**, a general term for both protons (p) and neutrons (n). The most common isotope of carbon, for example, has 12 nucleons: 6 protons and 6 neutrons: $^{12}_{6}C$.

Nucleon A general term for both protons and neutrons.

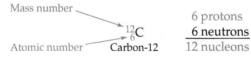

Atoms with identical atomic numbers but different mass numbers are called *isotopes* (Section 3.3), and the nucleus of a specific isotope is called a **nuclide**. (⬭, p. 54) Thirteen isotopes of carbon are known—two occur commonly (^{12}C and ^{13}C) and one (^{14}C) is produced in small amounts in the upper atmosphere by the action of neutrons from cosmic rays on ^{14}N. The remaining ten carbon isotopes have been produced artificially. Only the two commonly occurring isotopes are stable indefinitely. The others undergo spontaneous **nuclear reactions**, which change their nuclei. Carbon-14, for example, slowly decomposes to give nitrogen-14 plus an electron, a process we can write as

Nuclide The nucleus of a specific isotope of an element.

Nuclear reaction A reaction that changes an atomic nucleus, usually causing the change of one element into another.

$$^{14}_{6}C \longrightarrow {}^{14}_{7}N + {}^{0}_{-1}e$$

The electron is often written as $^{0}_{-1}e$, where the superscript 0 indicates that the mass of an electron is essentially zero when compared with that of a proton or neutron, and the subscript -1 indicates that the charge is -1. (The subscript in this instance is not a true atomic number.)

Nuclear reactions, such as the spontaneous decay of ^{14}C, are distinguished from chemical reactions in several ways:

- A *nuclear* reaction involves a change in an atom's nucleus, usually producing a different element. A *chemical* reaction, by contrast, involves only a change in distribution of the outer-shell electrons around the atom and never changes the nucleus itself or produces a different element.

- Different isotopes of an element have essentially the same behavior in chemical reactions but often have completely different behavior in nuclear reactions.

- The rate of a nuclear reaction is unaffected by a change in temperature or pressure or by the addition of a catalyst.

- The nuclear reaction of an atom is essentially the same whether it is in a chemical compound or in an uncombined, elemental form.

- The energy change accompanying a nuclear reaction can be up to several million times greater than that accompanying a chemical reaction. The nuclear transformation of 1.0 g of uranium-235 releases 3.4×10^8 kcal, for example, whereas the chemical combustion of 1.0 g of methane releases only 12 kcal.

11.2 The Discovery and Nature of Radioactivity

The discovery of *radioactivity* dates to the year 1896 when the French physicist Henri Becquerel made a remarkable observation. While investigating the nature of phosphorescence—the luminous glow of some minerals and other substances that remains when the light is suddenly turned off—Becquerel happened to place a sample of a uranium-containing mineral on top of a photographic plate that had been wrapped in black paper and put in a drawer to protect it from sunlight. On developing the plate, Becquerel was surprised to find a silhouette of the mineral. He concluded that the mineral was producing some kind of unknown radiation, which passed through the paper and exposed the photographic plate.

Radioactivity The spontaneous emission of radiation from a nucleus.

Marie Sklodowska Curie and her husband, Pierre, took up the challenge and began a series of investigations into this new phenomenon, which they termed **radioactivity**. They found that the source of the radioactivity was the element uranium (U) and that two previously unknown elements, which they named polonium (Po) and radium (Ra), were also radioactive. For these achievements, Becquerel and the Curies shared the 1903 Nobel Prize in physics.

Further work on radioactivity by the English scientist Ernest Rutherford established that there were at least two types of radiation, which he named *alpha* (α) and *beta* (β) after the first two letters of the Greek alphabet. Shortly thereafter, a third type of radiation was found and named for the third Greek letter, *gamma* (γ).

Subsequent studies showed that when the three kinds of radiation are passed between two plates with opposite electrical charges, each is affected differently. Alpha radiation bends toward the negative plate and must therefore have a positive charge. Beta radiation, by contrast, bends toward the positive plate and must have a negative charge, whereas gamma radiation does not bend toward either plate and has no charge (Figure 11.1).

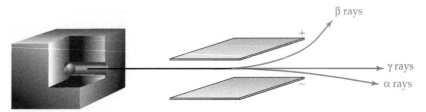

▲ **FIGURE 11.1 The effect of an electric field on α, β, and γ, radiation.** The radioactive source in the shielded box emits radiation, which passes between the two electrically charged plates. Alpha radiation is deflected toward the negative plate, β radiation is deflected toward the positive plate, and γ radiation is not deflected.

Another difference among the three kinds of radiation soon became apparent when it was discovered that alpha and beta radiations are composed of small particles with a measurable mass, whereas **gamma (γ) radiation** consists of high-energy electromagnetic waves and has no mass (see the Application "Atoms and Light" in Chapter 3). (⊂⊃, p. 72) Rutherford was able to show that a **beta (β) particle** is an electron (e⁻) and that an **alpha (α) particle** is simply a helium nucleus, He^{2+}. (Recall that a helium *atom* consists of two protons, two neutrons, and two electrons. When the two electrons are removed, the remaining helium nucleus, or α particle, has only the two protons and two neutrons.)

Yet a third difference among the three kinds of radiation is their penetrating power. Because of their relatively large mass, α particles move slowly (up to about one-tenth the speed of light) and can be stopped by a few sheets of paper or by the top layer of skin. Beta particles, because they are much lighter, move at up to nine-tenths the speed of light and have about 100 times the penetrating power of α particles. A block of wood or heavy protective clothing is necessary to stop β radiation, which can otherwise penetrate the skin and cause burns and other damage. Gamma rays move at the speed of light (3.00×10^8 m/s) and have about 1000 times the penetrating power of α particles. A lead block several inches thick is needed to stop γ radiation, which can otherwise penetrate and damage the body's internal organs.

The characteristics of the three kinds of radiation are summarized in Table 11.1. Note that an α particle, even though it is an ion with a 2+ charge, is usually written using the symbol ^4_2He without the charge. A β particle is usually written $^0_{-1}e$, as noted previously.

Gamma (γ) radiation Radioactivity consisting of high-energy light waves.

Beta (β) particle An electron (e⁻), emitted as radiation.

Alpha (α) particle A helium nucleus (He^{2+}), emitted as α radiation.

TABLE 11.1   Characteristics of α, β, and γ Radiation

TYPE OF RADIATION	SYMBOL	CHARGE	COMPOSITION	MASS (AMU)	VELOCITY	RELATIVE PENETRATING POWER
Alpha	α, ^4_2He	+2	Helium nucleus	4	Up to 10% speed of light	Low (1)
Beta	β, $^0_{-1}e$	−1	Electron	1/1823	Up to 90% speed of light	Medium (100)
Gamma	γ, $^0_0γ$	0	High-energy radiation	0	Speed of light (3.00×10^8 m/s)	High (1000)

11.3 Stable and Unstable Isotopes

Every element in the periodic table has at least one radioactive isotope, or **radioisotope**, and more than *3300* radioisotopes are known. Their radioactivity is the result of having unstable nuclei, although the exact causes of this instability are not fully understood. Radiation is emitted when an unstable radioactive nucleus, or **radionuclide**, spontaneously changes into a more stable one.

For elements in the first few rows of the periodic table, stability is associated with a roughly equal number of neutrons and protons (Figure 11.2). Hydrogen, for example, has stable ^1_1H (protium) and ^2_1H (deuterium) isotopes, but its ^3_1H isotope (tritium) is radioactive. As elements get heavier, the number of neutrons relative to protons in stable nuclei increases. Lead-208 ($^{208}_{82}Pb$), for example, the most abundant stable isotope of lead, has 126 neutrons and 82 protons in its nuclei. Nevertheless, of the 35 known isotopes of lead, only 3 are stable whereas 32 are radioactive. In fact, there are only 264 stable isotopes among all the elements. All isotopes of elements with atomic numbers higher than that of bismuth (83) are radioactive.

Most of the more than 3300 known radioisotopes have been made in high-energy particle accelerators by reactions that will be described in Section 11.10. Such isotopes are called *artificial radioisotopes* because they are not found in nature. All isotopes of the transuranium elements (those heavier than uranium) are artificial. The much smaller number of radioactive isotopes found in the earth's crust, such as $^{238}_{92}U$, are called *natural radioisotopes*.

Aside from their radioactivity, different radioisotopes of the same element have the same chemical properties as stable isotopes, which accounts for their great

Radioisotope A radioactive isotope.

Radionuclide The nucleus of a radioactive isotope.

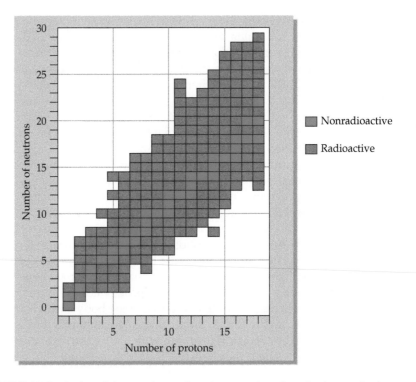

▲ **FIGURE 11.2 A plot of the numbers of neutrons and protons for known isotopes of the first 18 elements.** Stable (nonradioactive) isotopes of these elements have equal or nearly equal numbers of neutrons and protons.

usefulness as *tracers*. A chemical compound tagged with a radioactive atom undergoes exactly the same reactions as its nonradioactive counterpart. The difference is that the tagged compound can be located with a radiation detector and its whereabouts determined, as discussed in the Application "Body Imaging" on page 352.

11.4 Nuclear Decay

Think for a minute about the consequences of α and β radiation. If radioactivity involves the spontaneous emission of a small particle from an unstable atomic nucleus, then the nucleus itself must undergo a change. With that understanding of radioactivity came the startling discovery that atoms of one element can change into atoms of another element, something that had previously been thought impossible. The spontaneous emission of a particle from an unstable nucleus is called **nuclear decay**, or *radioactive decay*, and the resulting change of one element into another is called **transmutation**.

> **Nuclear decay:** Radioactive element $\longrightarrow$ New element + Emitted particle

We now look at what happens to a nucleus when nuclear decay occurs.

Nuclear decay The spontaneous emission of a particle from an unstable nucleus.

Transmutation The change of one element into another.

Alpha Emission

When an atom of uranium-238 ($^{238}_{92}$U) emits an α particle, the nucleus loses two protons and two neutrons. Because the number of protons in the nucleus has now changed from 92 to 90, the *identity* of the atom has changed from uranium to thorium. Furthermore, since the total number of nucleons has decreased by 4, uranium-238 has become thorium-234 ($^{234}_{90}$Th) (Figure 11.3).

Note that the equation for a nuclear reaction is not balanced in the usual chemical sense because the kinds of atoms are not the same on both sides of the arrow. Instead, we say that a nuclear equation is balanced when the number of nucleons is the same on both sides of the equation and when the sums of the charges on the nuclei plus any ejected subatomic particles (protons or electrons) are the same on

$$^{238}_{92}U \longrightarrow {}^{234}_{90}Th + {}^{4}_{2}He$$

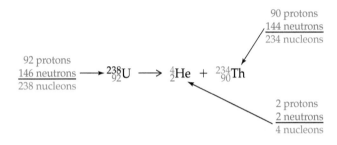

$^{238}_{92}U$	$^{234}_{90}Th$	$^{4}_{2}He$
92 protons ●	90 protons ●	2 protons ●
146 neutrons ●	144 neutrons ●	2 neutrons ●
238 total	234 total	4 total

◀ **FIGURE 11.3 Alpha emission.** Emission of an α particle from an atom of uranium-238 produces an atom of thorium-234.

both sides. In the decay of $^{238}_{92}U$ to give $^{4}_{2}He$ and $^{234}_{90}Th$, for example, there are 238 nucleons and 92 nuclear charges on both sides of the nuclear equation.

$$\underset{\substack{92\text{ protons}\\146\text{ neutrons}\\238\text{ nucleons}}}{\longrightarrow} {}^{238}_{92}U \longrightarrow {}^{4}_{2}He + {}^{234}_{90}Th$$

90 protons
144 neutrons
234 nucleons

2 protons
2 neutrons
4 nucleons

WORKED EXAMPLE   **11.1** Balancing Nuclear Reactions: Alpha Emission

Polonium-208 is one of the α emitters studied by Marie Curie. Write the equation for the α decay of polonium-208, and identify the element formed.

ANALYSIS Look up the atomic number of polonium (84) in the periodic table, and write the known part of the nuclear equation, using the standard symbol for polonium-208:

$$^{208}_{84}Po \longrightarrow {}^{4}_{2}He + ?$$

Then calculate the mass number and atomic number of the product element, and write the final equation.

SOLUTION
The mass number of the product is $208 - 4 = 204$, and the atomic number is $84 - 2 = 82$. A look at the periodic table identifies the element with atomic number 82 as lead (Pb).

$$^{208}_{84}Po \longrightarrow {}^{4}_{2}He + {}^{204}_{82}Pb$$

Check your answer by making sure that the mass numbers and atomic numbers on the two sides of the equation are balanced:

    Mass numbers: $208 = 4 + 204$ Atomic numbers: $84 = 2 + 82$

PROBLEM 11.1

High levels of radioactive radon-222 ($^{222}_{86}Rn$) have been found in many homes built on radium-containing rock, leading to the possibility of health hazards. What product results from α emission by radon-222?

PROBLEM 11.2

What isotope of radium (Ra) is converted into radon-222 by α emission?

Beta Emission

Whereas α emission leads to the loss of two protons and two neutrons from the nucleus, β emission involves the *decomposition* of a neutron to yield an electron and a proton. This process can be represented as

$$\,^1_0n \longrightarrow \,^1_1p + \,^0_{-1}e$$

where the electron ($\,^0_{-1}e$) is ejected as a β particle, and the proton is retained by the nucleus. Note that the electrons emitted during β radiation come from the *nucleus* and not from the occupied orbitals surrounding the nucleus.

The net result of β emission is that the atomic number of the atom increases by 1 because there is a new proton. The mass number of the atom remains the same, however, because a neutron has changed into a proton leaving the total number of nucleons unchanged. For example, iodine-131 ($\,^{131}_{53}I$), a radioisotope used in detecting thyroid problems, undergoes nuclear decay by β emission to yield xenon-131 ($\,^{131}_{54}Xe$):

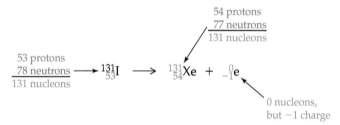

Note that the superscripts (mass numbers) are balanced in this equation because a β particle has a mass near zero, and the subscripts are balanced because a β particle has a charge of -1.

WORKED EXAMPLE **11.2** Balancing Nuclear Reactions: Beta Emission

Write a balanced nuclear equation for the β decay of chromium-55.

ANALYSIS Write the known part of the nuclear equation:

$$\,^{55}_{24}Cr \longrightarrow \,^0_{-1}e + ?$$

Then calculate the mass number and atomic number of the product element, and write the final equation.

SOLUTION
The mass number of the product stays at 55, and the atomic number increases by 1, 24 + 1 = 25, so the product is manganese-55.

$$\,^{55}_{24}Cr \longrightarrow \,^0_{-1}e + \,^{55}_{25}Mn$$

Check your answer by making sure that the mass numbers and atomic numbers on the two sides of the equation are balanced:

Mass numbers: $55 = 0 + 55$ Atomic numbers: $24 = -1 + 25$

PROBLEM 11.3

Carbon-14, a β emitter, is a rare isotope used in dating archaeological artifacts. Write a nuclear equation for the decay of carbon-14.

PROBLEM 11.4

Write nuclear equations for β emission from the following radioisotopes:

(a) ${}^{3}_{1}\mathrm{H}$ **(b)** ${}^{210}_{82}\mathrm{Pb}$ **(c)** ${}^{20}_{9}\mathrm{F}$

Gamma Emission

Emission of γ rays, unlike the emission of α and β particles, causes no change in mass or atomic number because γ rays are simply high-energy electromagnetic waves. Although γ emission can occur alone, it usually accompanies α or β emission as a mechanism for the new nucleus that results from a transmutation to get rid of some extra energy.

Since γ emission affects neither mass number nor atomic number, it is often omitted from nuclear equations. Nevertheless, γ rays are of great importance. Their penetrating power makes them by far the most dangerous kind of external radiation for humans and also makes them useful in numerous medical applications. Cobalt-60, for example, is used in cancer therapy as a source of penetrating γ rays that kill cancerous tissue.

$$ {}^{60}_{27}\mathrm{Co} \longrightarrow {}^{60}_{28}\mathrm{Ni} + {}^{0}_{-1}\mathrm{e} + {}^{0}_{0}\gamma $$

Positron Emission

In addition to α, β, and γ radiation, there is another common type of radioactive decay process called *positron emission*, which involves the conversion of a proton in the nucleus into a neutron plus an ejected **positron**, ${}^{0}_{1}\mathrm{e}$ or β^{+}. A positron, which can be thought of as a "positive electron," has the same mass as an electron but a positive charge. This process can be represented as

Positron A "positive electron," which has the same mass as an electron but a positive charge.

$$ {}^{1}_{1}\mathrm{p} \longrightarrow {}^{1}_{0}\mathrm{n} + {}^{0}_{1}\mathrm{e} $$

The result of positron emission is a decrease in the atomic number of the product nucleus because a proton has changed into a neutron, but no change in the mass number. Potassium-40, for example, undergoes positron emission to yield argon-40, a nuclear reaction important in geology for dating rocks. Note once again that the sum of the two subscripts on the right of the nuclear equation ($18 + 1 = 19$) is equal to the subscript in the ${}^{40}_{19}\mathrm{K}$ nucleus on the left.

19 protons
21 neutrons
40 nucleons

$$ {}^{40}_{19}\mathrm{K} \longrightarrow {}^{40}_{18}\mathrm{Ar} + {}^{0}_{1}\mathrm{e} $$

0 nucleons
but 1 charge

18 protons
22 neutrons
40 nucleons

Electron Capture

Electron capture, symbolized E.C., is a process in which the nucleus captures an inner-shell electron from the surrounding electron cloud, thereby converting a proton into a neutron. The mass number of the product nucleus is unchanged, but the atomic number decreases by 1, just as in positron emission. The conversion of mercury-197 into gold-197 is an example:

Electron capture (E.C.) A process in which the nucleus captures an inner-shell electron from the surrounding electron cloud, thereby converting a proton into a neutron.

80 protons
117 neutrons
197 nucleons

Inner-shell
electron

79 protons
118 neutrons
197 nucleons

$$ {}^{197}_{80}\mathrm{Hg} + {}^{0}_{-1}\mathrm{e} \longrightarrow {}^{197}_{79}\mathrm{Au} $$

Do not plan on using this reaction to get rich, however. Mercury-197 is not one of the naturally occurring isotopes of Hg and is typically produced by transmutation reactions as discussed in Section 11.10.

Characteristics of the five kinds of radioactive decay processes are summarized in Table 11.2.

TABLE 11.2   A Summary of Radioactive Decay Processes

PROCESS	SYMBOL	CHANGE IN ATOMIC NUMBER	CHANGE IN MASS NUMBER	CHANGE IN NUMBER OF NEUTRONS
α emission	$^4_2$He or α	-2	-4	-2
β emission	$^0_{-1}$e or β^{-*}	$+1$	0	-1
γ emission	$^0_0\gamma$ or γ	0	0	0
Positron emission	$^0_1$e or β^{+*}	-1	0	$+1$
Electron capture	E.C.	-1	0	$+1$

*Superscripts are used to indicate the charge associated with the two forms of beta decay; β^-, or a beta particle, carries a -1 charge, while β^+, or a positron, carries a $+1$ charge.

WORKED EXAMPLE   **11.3** Balancing Nuclear Reactions: Electron Capture, Positron Emission

Write balanced nuclear equations for the following processes:

(a) Electron capture by polonium-204: $^{204}_{84}$Po $+ \, ^0_{-1}$e $\longrightarrow$?

(b) Positron emission from xenon-118: $^{118}_{54}$Xe $\longrightarrow \, ^0_1$e + ?

ANALYSIS The key to writing nuclear equations is to make sure that the number of nucleons is the same on both sides of the equation and that the number of charges is the same.

SOLUTION

(a) In electron capture, the mass number is unchanged and the atomic number decreases by 1, giving bismuth-204: $^{204}_{84}$Po $+ \, ^0_{-1}$e $\longrightarrow \, ^{204}_{83}$Bi

Check your answer by making sure that the number of nucleons and the number of charges are the same on both sides of the equation:

Mass number: $204 + 0 = 204$ Atomic number: $84 + (-1) = 83$

(b) In positron emission, the mass number is unchanged and the atomic number decreases by 1, giving iodine-118: $^{118}_{54}$Xe $\longrightarrow \, ^0_1$e $+ \, ^{118}_{53}$I.

CHECK! Mass number: $118 = 0 + 118$ Atomic number: $54 = 1 + 53$

PROBLEM 11.5

Write nuclear equations for positron emission from the following radioisotopes:

(a) $^{38}_{20}$Ca   (b) $^{118}_{54}$Xe   (c) $^{79}_{37}$Rb

PROBLEM 11.6

Write nuclear equations for electron capture by the following radioisotopes:

(a) $^{62}_{30}$Zn   (b) $^{110}_{50}$Sn   (c) $^{81}_{36}$Kr

🔑 KEY CONCEPT PROBLEM 11.7

The red arrow in this graph indicates the changes that occur in the nucleus of an atom during a nuclear reaction. Identify the isotopes involved as product and reactant, and name the type of decay process.

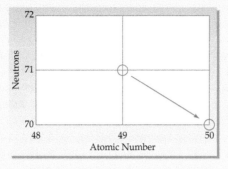

11.5 Radioactive Half-Life

The rate of radioactive decay varies greatly from one radioisotope to another. Some radioisotopes, such as uranium-238, decay at a barely perceptible rate over billions of years, but others, such as carbon-17, decay within thousandths of a second.

Rates of nuclear decay are measured in units of **half-life ($t_{1/2}$)**, defined as the amount of time required for one-half of a radioactive sample to decay. For example, the half-life of iodine-131 is 8.021 days. If today you have 1.000 g of $^{131}_{53}I$, then 8.021 days from now you will have only 50% of that amount (0.500 g) because one-half of the sample will have decayed into $^{131}_{54}Xe$. After 8.021 more days (16.063 days total), you will have only 25% (0.250 g) of your original $^{131}_{53}I$ sample; after another 8.021 days (24.084 days total), you will have only 12.5% (0.125 g); and so on. Each passage of a half-life causes the decay of one-half of whatever sample remains. The half-life is the same no matter what the size of the sample, the temperature, or any other external conditions. There is no known way to slow down, speed up, or otherwise change the characteristics of radioactive decay.

Half-life ($t_{1/2}$) The amount of time required for one-half of a radioactive sample to decay.

$$1.000 \text{ g } ^{131}_{53}I \xrightarrow[\text{days}]{8} \begin{array}{c} 0.500 \text{ g } ^{131}_{53}I \\ 0.500 \text{ g } ^{131}_{54}Xe \end{array} \xrightarrow[\text{days}]{8} \begin{array}{c} 0.250 \text{ g } ^{131}_{53}I \\ 0.750 \text{ g } ^{131}_{54}Xe \end{array} \xrightarrow[\text{days}]{8} \begin{array}{c} 0.125 \text{ g } ^{131}_{53}I \\ 0.875 \text{ g } ^{131}_{54}Xe \end{array} \longrightarrow$$

One half-life   Two half-lives   Three half-lives
                   (16 days total)   (24 days total)

The fraction of radioisotope remaining after the passage of each half-life is represented by the curve in Figure 11.4 and can be calculated as

$$\text{fraction remaining} = (0.5)^n$$

where n is the number of half-lives that have elapsed.

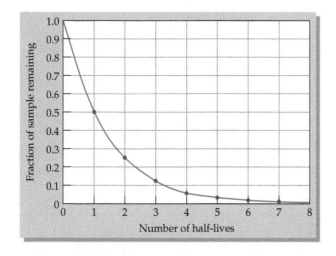

◀ **FIGURE 11.4 The decay of a radioactive nucleus over time.** All nuclear decays follow this curve, whether the half-lives are measured in years, days, minutes, or seconds. That is, the fraction of sample remaining after one half-life is 0.50, the fraction remaining after two half-lives is 0.25, the fraction remaining after three half-lives is 0.125, and so on.

APPLICATION ▶   Medical Uses of Radioactivity

The origins of nuclear medicine date from 1901 when the French physician Henri Danlos first used radium in the treatment of a tubercular skin lesion. Since that time, the use of radioactivity has become a crucial part of modern medical care, both diagnostic and therapeutic. Current nuclear techniques can be grouped into three classes: (1) in vivo procedures, (2) radiation therapy, and (3) imaging procedures. The first two are described here, and the third one is described on page 352 in the Application "Body Imaging."

In Vivo Procedures

In vivo studies—those that take place inside the body—are carried out to assess the functioning of a particular organ or body system. A *radiopharmaceutical* agent is administered, and its path in the body—whether absorbed, excreted, diluted, or concentrated—is determined by analysis of blood or urine samples.

Among the many in vivo procedures utilizing radioactive agents is a simple method for the determination of whole-blood volume by injecting a known quantity of red blood cells labeled with radioactive chromium-51. After a suitable interval to allow the labeled cells to be distributed evenly throughout the body, a blood sample is taken and blood volume is calculated by comparing the concentration of labeled cells in the blood with the quantity of labeled cells injected. This and similar procedures are known as *isotope dilution* and are described by

$$R_{sample} = R_{tracer}\left(\frac{W_{sample}}{W_{system} + W_{tracer}}\right)$$

where R_{sample} is the counting rate of the analyzed sample, R_{tracer} is the counting rate of the tracer added to the system, and W refers to either the mass or volume of the analyzed sample, added tracer, or total system as indicated.

Therapeutic Procedures

Therapeutic procedures—those in which radiation is purposely used as a weapon to kill diseased tissue—involve either external or internal sources of radiation. External radiation therapy for the treatment of cancer is often carried out with γ rays emanating from a cobalt-60 source. The highly radioactive source is shielded by a thick lead container and has a small opening directed toward the site of the tumor. By focusing the radiation beam on the tumor, the tumor receives the full exposure while exposure of surrounding parts of the body is minimized. Nevertheless, enough healthy tissue is affected so that most patients treated in this manner suffer the effects of radiation sickness.

Internal radiation therapy is a much more selective technique than external therapy. In the treatment of thyroid disease, for example, a radioactive substance such as iodine-131 is administered. This powerful β emitter is incorporated into the iodine-containing hormone thyroxine, which concentrates in the thyroid gland. Because β particles penetrate no farther than several millimeters, the localized ^{131}I produces

a high radiation dose that destroys only the surrounding diseased tissue. To treat some tumors, such as those in the female reproductive system, a radioactive source is placed physically close to the tumor for a specific amount of time.

Boron neutron-capture therapy (BNCT) is a relatively new technique in which boron-containing drugs are administered to a patient and concentrate in the tumor site. The tumor is then irradiated with a neutron beam from a nuclear reactor. The boron absorbs a neutron and undergoes transmutation to produce an alpha particle and a lithium nucleus. These highly energetic particles have very low penetrating power and can kill nearby tumor tissue while sparing the healthy surrounding tissue. Because one disadvantage of BNCT is the need for access to a nuclear reactor, this treatment is available only in limited locations.

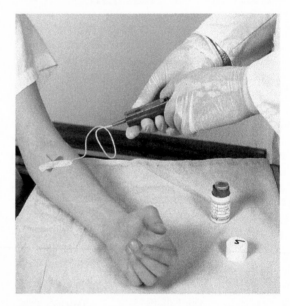

▲ A person's blood volume can be found by injecting a small amount of radioactive chromium-51 and measuring the dilution factor.

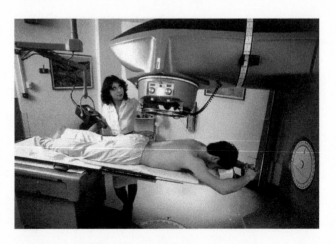

▲ T/B/W when new photo chosen.

See Additional Problems 11.70 and 11.71 at the end of the chapter.

The half-lives of some useful radioisotopes are given in Table 11.3. As you might expect, radioisotopes that are used internally for medical applications have fairly short half-lives so that they decay rapidly and do not remain in the body for prolonged periods.

TABLE 11.3   Half-Lives of Some Useful Radioisotopes

RADIOISOTOPE	SYMBOL	RADIATION	HALF-LIFE	USE
Tritium	$^{3}_{1}H$	β	12.33 years	Biochemical tracer
Carbon-14	$^{14}_{6}C$	β	5730 years	Archaeological dating
Sodium-24	$^{24}_{11}Na$	β	14.959 hours	Examining circulation
Phosphorus-32	$^{32}_{15}P$	β	14.262 days	Leukemia therapy
Potassium-40	$^{40}_{19}K$	β, β^{+}	1.277×10^{9} years	Geological dating
Cobalt-60	$^{60}_{27}Co$	β, γ	5.271 years	Cancer therapy
Arsenic-74	$^{74}_{33}As$	β^{+}	17.77 days	Locating brain tumors
Technetium-99m*	$^{99m}_{43}Tc$	γ	6.01 hours	Brain scans
Iodine-131	$^{131}_{53}I$	β	8.021 days	Thyroid therapy
Uranium-235	$^{235}_{92}U$	α, γ	7.038×10^{8} years	Nuclear reactors

*The m in technetium-99m stands for metastable, meaning that the nucleus undergoes γ emission but does not change its mass number or atomic number.

WORKED EXAMPLE   11.4 Nuclear Reactions: Half-Life

Phosphorus-32, a radioisotope used in leukemia therapy, has a half-life of about 14 days. Approximately what percent of a sample remains after 8 weeks?

ANALYSIS Determine how many half-lives have elapsed. For an integral number of half-lives, we can multiply the starting amount (100%) by 1/2 for each half-life that has elapsed.

SOLUTION
Since one half-life of $^{32}_{15}P$ is 14 days (2 weeks), 8 weeks represents four half-lives. The fraction that remains after 8 weeks is thus

Four half-lives

$$\text{Final Percentage} = 100\% \times (0.5)^{4} = 100\% \times \left(\tfrac{1}{2} \times \tfrac{1}{2} \times \tfrac{1}{2} \times \tfrac{1}{2} \right)$$

$$= 100\% \times \tfrac{1}{16} = 6.25\%$$

WORKED EXAMPLE   11.5 Nuclear Reactions: Half-Life

As noted on page 341 and in Table 11.3, iodine-131 has a half-life of about 8 days. Approximately what fraction of a sample remains after 20 days?

ANALYSIS Determine how many half-lives have elapsed. For a non-integral number (i.e., fraction) of half-lives, use the equation below to determine the fraction of radioisotope remaining.

$$\text{fraction remaining} = (0.5)^{n}$$

BALLPARK ESTIMATE Since the half-life of iodine-131 is 8 days, an elapsed time of 20 days is 2.5 half-lives. The fraction remaining should be between 0.25 (fraction remaining after two half-lives) and 0.125 (fraction remaining after three half-lives). Since the relationship between the number of half-lives and fraction remaining is not linear (see Figure 11.4), the fraction remaining will not be exactly halfway between these values but instead will be slightly closer to the lower fraction, say 0.17.

SOLUTION

$$\text{fraction remaining} = (0.5)^n = (0.5)^{2.5} = 0.177$$

BALLPARK CHECK: The fraction remaining is close to our estimate of 0.17.

PROBLEM 11.8

The half-life of carbon-14, an isotope used in archaeological dating, is 5730 years. What percentage of $^{14}_{6}C$ remains in a sample estimated to be 17,000 years old?

➡️ KEY CONCEPT PROBLEM 11.9

What is the half-life of the radionuclide that shows the following decay curve?

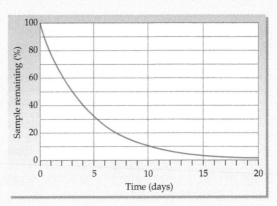

Decay series A sequential series of nuclear disintegrations leading from a heavy radioisotope to a non-radioactive product.

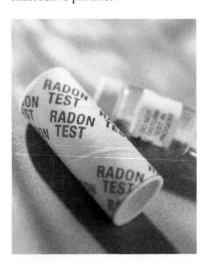

▲ Radon gas can be detected and measured by this home detection kit.

11.6 Radioactive Decay Series

When a radioactive isotope decays, nuclear change occurs and a different element is formed. Often, this newly formed nucleus is stable, but sometimes the product nucleus is itself radioactive and undergoes further decay. In fact, some radioactive nuclei undergo a whole **decay series** of nuclear disintegrations before they ultimately reach a nonradioactive product. This is particularly true for the isotopes of heavier elements. Uranium-238, for example, undergoes a series of 14 sequential nuclear reactions, ultimately stopping at lead-206 (Figure 11.5).

One of the intermediate radionuclides in the uranium-238 decay series is radium-226. Radium-226 has a half-life of 1600 years and undergoes α decay to produce radon-222, a gas. Rocks, soil, and building materials that contain radium are sources of radon-222, which can seep through cracks in basements and get into the air inside homes and other buildings. Radon itself is a gas that passes in and out of the lungs without being incorporated into body tissue. If, however, a radon-222 atom should happen to decay while in the lungs, the solid decay product polonium-218 results. Further decay of the ^{218}Po emits α particles, which can damage lung tissue.

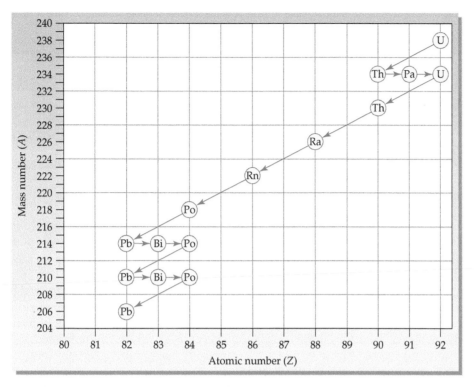

▲ **FIGURE 11.5** **The decay series from $^{238}_{92}$U to $^{206}_{82}$Pb.** Each isotope except for the last is radioactive and undergoes nuclear decay. The long slanted arrows represent α emissions, and the short horizontal arrows represent β emissions.

11.7 Ionizing Radiation

High-energy radiation of all kinds is often grouped together under the name **ionizing radiation**. This includes not only α particles, β particles, and γ rays, but also *X rays* and *cosmic rays*. **X rays** are like γ rays; they have no mass and consist of high-energy electromagnetic radiation. The only difference between them is that the energy of X rays is somewhat less than that of γ rays (see the Application "Atoms and Light" in Chapter 3). **Cosmic rays** are not rays at all but are a mixture of high-energy particles that shower the earth from outer space. They consist primarily of protons, along with some α and β particles.

The interaction of any kind of ionizing radiation with a molecule knocks out an electron, converting the atom or molecule into an extremely reactive ion:

$$\text{Molecule} \xrightarrow[\text{radiation}]{\text{ionizing}} \text{Ion} + e^-$$

The reactive ion can react with other molecules nearby, creating still other fragments that can in turn cause further reactions. In this manner, a large dose of ionizing radiation can destroy the delicate balance of chemical reactions in living cells, ultimately causing the death of an organism.

A small dose of ionizing radiation may not cause visible symptoms but can nevertheless be dangerous if it strikes a cell nucleus and damages the genetic machinery inside. The resultant changes might lead to a genetic mutation, to cancer, or to cell death. The nuclei of rapidly dividing cells, such as those in bone marrow, the lymph system, the lining of the intestinal tract, or an embryo, are the most readily damaged. Because cancer cells are also rapidly dividing they are highly susceptible to the effects of ionizing radiation, which is why radiation therapy is an effective treatment for many types of cancer (see Application on p. 342). Some properties of ionizing radiation are summarized in Table 11.4.

Ionizing radiation A general name for high-energy radiation of all kinds.

X rays Electromagnetic radiation with an energy somewhat less than that of γ rays.

Cosmic rays A mixture of high-energy particles—primarily of protons and various atomic nuclei—that shower the earth from outer space.

TABLE 11.4 Some Properties of Ionizing Radiation

TYPE OF RADIATION	ENERGY RANGE*	PENETRATING DISTANCE IN WATER**
α	3–9 MeV	0.02–0.04 mm
β	0–3 MeV	0–4 mm
X	100 eV–10 keV	0.01–1 cm
γ	10 keV–10 MeV	1–20 cm

*The energies of subatomic particles are often measured in electron volts (eV): $1\ eV = 6.703 \times 10^{-19}$ cal.
**Distance at which one-half of the radiation is stopped.

The effects of ionizing radiation on the human body vary with the energy of the radiation, its distance from the body, the length of exposure, and the location of the source outside or inside the body. When coming from outside the body, γ rays and X rays are potentially more harmful than α and β particles because they pass through clothing and skin and into the body's cells. Alpha particles are stopped by clothing and skin, and β particles are stopped by wood or several layers of clothing. These types of radiation are much more dangerous when emitted within the body, however, because all their radiation energy is given up to the immediately surrounding tissue. Alpha emitters are especially hazardous internally and are almost never used in medical applications.

Health professionals who work with X rays or other kinds of ionizing radiation protect themselves by surrounding the source with a thick layer of lead or other dense material. Protection from radiation is also afforded by controlling the distance between the worker and the radiation source because radiation intensity (I) decreases with the square of the distance from the source. The intensities of radiation at two different distances, 1 and 2, are given by the equation

$$\frac{I_1}{I_2} = \frac{d_2{}^2}{d_1{}^2}$$

For example, suppose a source delivers 16 units of radiation at a distance of 1.0 m. Doubling the distance to 2.0 m decreases the radiation intensity to one-fourth:

$$\frac{16\ \text{units}}{I_2} = \frac{(2\ \text{m})^2}{(1\ \text{m})^2}$$

$$I_2 = 16\ \text{units} \times \frac{1\ \text{m}^2}{4\ \text{m}^2} = 4\ \text{units}$$

WORKED EXAMPLE   **11.6** Ionizing Radiation: Intensity versus Distance from the Source

If a radiation source gives 75 units of radiation at a distance of 2.4 m, at what distance does the source give 25 units of radiation?

ANALYSIS Radiation intensity (I) decreases with the square of the distance (d) from the source according to the equation

$$\frac{I_1}{I_2} = \frac{d_2{}^2}{d_1{}^2}$$

We know three of the four variables in this equation (I_1, I_2, and d_1), and we need to find d_2.

BALLPARK ESTIMATE In order to decrease the radiation intensity from 75 units to 25 units (a factor of 3), the distance must *increase* by a factor of $\sqrt{3} = 1.7$. Thus, the distance should increase from 2.4 m to about 4 m.

SOLUTION

STEP 1: Identify known information. We know three of the four variables.

$I_1 = 75$ units

$I_2 = 25$ units

$d_1 = 2.4$ m

STEP 2: Identify answer and units.

$d_2 = ???$ m

STEP 3: Identify equation. Rearrange the equation relating intensity and distance to solve for d_2.

$$\frac{I_1}{I_2} = \frac{d_2^2}{d_1^2}$$

$$d_2^2 = \frac{I_1 d_1^2}{I_2} \implies d_2 = \sqrt{\frac{I_1 d_1^2}{I_2}}$$

STEP 4: Solve. Substitute in known values so that unwanted units cancel.

$$d_2 = \sqrt{\frac{(75 \text{ units})(2.4 \text{ m})^2}{(25 \text{ units})}} = 4.2 \text{ m}$$

BALLPARK CHECK The calculated result is consistent with our estimate of about 4 m.

PROBLEM 11.10

A β-emitting radiation source gives 250 units of radiation at a distance of 4.0 m. At what distance does the radiation drop to one-tenth its original value?

11.8 Detecting Radiation

Small amounts of naturally occurring radiation have always been present, but people have been aware of it only within the past 100 years. The problem is that radiation is invisible. We cannot see, hear, smell, touch, or taste radiation, no matter how high the dose. We can, however, detect radiation by taking advantage of its ionizing properties.

The simplest device for detecting exposure to radiation is the photographic film badge worn by people who routinely work with radioactive materials. The film is protected from exposure to light, but any other radiation striking the badge causes the film to fog (remember Becquerel's discovery). At regular intervals, the film is developed and compared with a standard to indicate the radiation exposure.

Perhaps the best-known method for detecting and measuring radiation is the *Geiger counter*, an argon-filled tube containing two electrodes (Figure 11.6). The inner walls of the tube are coated with an electrically conducting material and given a negative charge, and a wire in the center of the tube is given a positive charge. As radiation enters the tube through a thin window, it strikes and ionizes argon atoms, which briefly conduct a tiny electric current between the walls and the center electrode. The passage of the current is detected, amplified, and used to produce a clicking sound or to register on a meter. The more radiation that enters the tube, the more frequent the clicks. Geiger counters are useful for seeking out a radiation source in a large area and for gauging the intensity of emitted radiation.

The most versatile method for measuring radiation in the laboratory is the *scintillation counter*, a device in which a substance called a *phosphor* emits a flash of light when struck by radiation. The number of flashes are counted electronically and converted into an electrical signal.

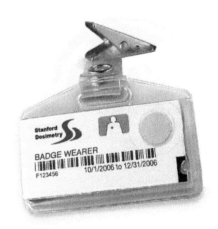

▲ This photographic film badge is a common device for monitoring radiation exposure.

▲ Radiation is conveniently detected and measured using this scintillation counter, which electronically counts the flashes produced when radiation strikes a phosphor.

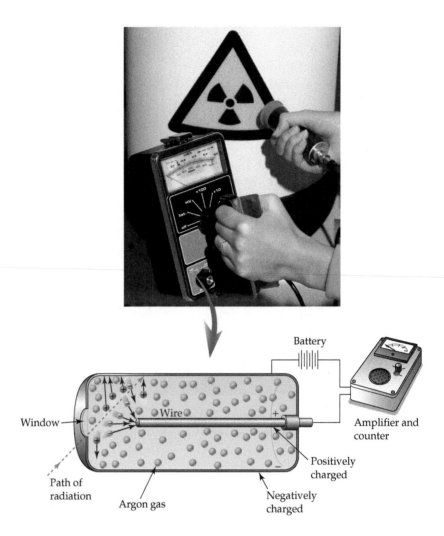

▶ **FIGURE 11.6 A Geiger counter for measuring radiation.** As radiation enters the tube through a thin window, it ionizes argon atoms and produces electrons that conduct a tiny electric current between the walls and the center electrode. The current flow then registers on the meter.

11.9 Measuring Radiation

Radiation intensity is expressed in different ways, depending on what characteristic of the radiation is measured (Table 11.5). Some units measure the number of nuclear decay events, while others measure exposure to radiation or the biological consequences of radiation.

TABLE 11.5 Common Units for Measuring Radiation

UNIT	QUANTITY MEASURED	DESCRIPTION
Curie (Ci)	Decay events	Amount of radiation equal to 3.7×10^{10} disintegrations per second
Roentgen (R)	Ionizing intensity	Amount of radiation producing 2.1×10^9 charges per cubic centimeter of dry air
Rad	Energy absorbed per gram of tissue	1 rad = 1 R
Rem	Tissue damage	Amount of radiation producing the same damage as 1 R of X rays
Sievert (Sv)	Tissue damage	1 Sv = 100 rem

The *curie* (Ci), the *millicurie* (mCi), and the *microcurie* (μCi) measure the number of radioactive disintegrations occurring each second in a sample. One curie is the decay rate of 1 g of radium, equal to 3.7×10^{10} disintegrations per second; 1 mCi = 0.001 Ci = 3.7×10^7 disintegrations per second; and 1 μCi = 0.000 001 Ci = 3.7×10^4 disintegrations per second.

APPLICATION ▶ Irradiated Food

The idea of irradiating food to kill harmful bacteria is not new; it goes back almost as far as the earliest studies on radiation. Not until the 1940s did serious work get under way, however, when U.S. Army scientists found that irradiation increased the shelf-life of ground beef. Nevertheless, widespread civilian use of the technique has been a long time in coming, spurred on in recent years by outbreaks of food poisoning that resulted in several deaths.

The principle of food irradiation is simple: Exposure of contaminated food to ionizing radiation—usually γ rays produced by cobalt-60 or cesium-137—destroys the genetic material of any bacteria or other organisms present, thereby killing them. Irradiation will not, however, kill viruses or prions (⬤⬤⬤, p. 584), the cause of mad-cow disease. The food itself undergoes little if any change when irradiated and does not itself become radioactive. The only real argument against food irradiation, in fact, is that it is *too* effective. Knowing that irradiation will kill nearly all harmful organisms, a food processor might be tempted to cut back on normal sanitary practices!

Food irradiation has been implemented to a much greater extent in Europe than in the United States. The largest marketers of irradiated food are Belgium, France, and the Netherlands, which irradiate between 10,000 and 20,000 tons of food per year. One of the major concerns in the United States is the possible generation of *radiolytic products*, compounds formed in food by exposure to ionizing radiation. The U.S. Food and Drug Administration, after studying the matter extensively, has declared that food irradiation is safe and that it does not appreciably alter the vitamin or other nutritional content of food. Spices, fruits, pork, and vegetables were

approved for irradiation in 1986, followed by poultry in 1990 and red meat, particularly ground beef, in 1997. In 2000, approval was extended to whole eggs and sprouting seeds. Should the food industry adopt irradiation of meat as its standard practice, such occurrences as the 1993 Seattle outbreak of *E. coli* poisoning caused by undercooked hamburgers will become a thing of the past.

NON · IRRADIATED ·

IRRADIATED · (0.2 M RAD)

STRAWBERRIES ·

15 DAYS STORAGE 38°F (4°C)

▲ Irradiating food kills bacteria and extends shelf-life. The strawberries in these two containers were picked at the same time, but only the batch on the right was irradiated.

See Additional Problems 11.72 and 11.73 at the end of the chapter.

The dosage of a radioactive substance administered orally or intravenously is usually given in millicuries. To calculate the size of a dose, it is necessary to determine the decay rate of the isotope solution per milliliter. Because the emitter concentration is constantly decreasing as it decays, the activity must be measured immediately before administration. Suppose, for example, that a solution containing iodine-131 for a thyroid function study is found to have a decay rate of 0.020 mCi/mL and the dose administered is to be 0.050 mCi. The amount of the solution administered must be

$$\frac{0.05 \text{ mCi}}{\text{Dose}} \times \frac{1 \text{ mL } {}^{131}\text{I solution}}{0.020 \text{ mCi}} = 2.5 \text{ mL } {}^{131}\text{I solution/dose}$$

- **Roentgen** The *roentgen* (R) is a unit for measuring the ionizing intensity of γ or X radiation. In other words, the roentgen measures the capacity of the radiation for affecting matter. One roentgen is the amount of radiation that produces 2.1×10^9 units of charge in 1 cm^3 of dry air at atmospheric pressure. Each collision of ionizing radiation with an atom produces one ion, or one unit of charge.

- **Rad** The *rad* (radiation absorbed dose) is a unit for measuring the energy absorbed per gram of material exposed to a radiation source and is defined as the absorption of 1×10^{-5} J of energy per gram. The energy absorbed varies with the type of material irradiated and the type of radiation. For most purposes, though, the roentgen and the rad are so close that they can be considered identical when used for X rays and γ rays: 1 R = 1 rad.

- **Rem** The *rem* (roentgen equivalent for man) measures the amount of tissue damage caused by radiation, taking into account the differences in energy of different types of radiation. One rem is the amount of radiation that produces the same effect as 1 R of X rays.

  Rems are the preferred units for medical purposes because they measure equivalent doses of different kinds of radiation. For example, 1 rad of α radiation causes 20 times more tissue damage than 1 rad of γ rays, but 1 rem of α radiation and 1 rem of γ rays cause the same amount of damage. Thus, the rem takes both ionizing intensity and biological effect into account, whereas the rad deals only with intensity.

- **SI Units** In the SI system, the *becquerel* (Bq) is defined as one disintegration per second. The SI unit for energy absorbed is the *gray* (Gy; 1 Gy = 100 rad). For radiation dose, the SI unit is the *sievert* (Sv), which is equal to 100 rem.

The biological consequences of different radiation doses are given in Table 11.6. Although the effects seem fearful, the average radiation dose received annually by most people is only about 0.27 rem. About 80% of this *background radiation* comes from natural sources (rocks and cosmic rays); the remaining 20% comes from medical procedures such as X rays and from consumer products. The amount due to emissions from nuclear power plants and to fallout from testing of nuclear weapons in the 1950s is barely detectable.

TABLE 11.6   Biological Effects of Short-Term Radiation on Humans

DOSE (REM)	BIOLOGICAL EFFECTS
0–25	No detectable effects
25–100	Temporary decrease in white blood cell count
100–200	Nausea, vomiting, longer-term decrease in white blood cells
200–300	Vomiting, diarrhea, loss of appetite, listlessness
300–600	Vomiting, diarrhea, hemorrhaging, eventual death in some cases
Above 600	Eventual death in nearly all cases

▲ After the 1986 nuclear-reactor disaster at Chernobyl, security police in Ukraine limited access to the area within 30 km of the site. (©Shirley Clive/Greenpeace International)

PROBLEM 11.11

Radiation released during the 1986 Chernobyl nuclear power plant disaster is expected to increase the background radiation level worldwide by about 5 mrem. By how much will this increase the annual dose of the average person. Express your answer as a percentage.

PROBLEM 11.12

A solution of selenium-75, a radioisotope used in the diagnosis of pancreatic disease, is found just prior to administration to have an activity of 44 μCi/mL. How many milliliters should be administered intravenously for a dose of 175 μCi?

11.10 Artificial Transmutation

Artificial transmutation The change of one atom into another brought about by a nuclear bombardment reaction.

Very few of the approximately 3300 known radioisotopes occur naturally. Most are made from stable isotopes by **artificial transmutation**, the change of one atom into another brought about by nuclear bombardment reactions.

When an atom is bombarded with a high-energy particle, such as a proton, neutron, α particle, or even the nucleus of another element, an unstable nucleus is created in the collision. A nuclear change then occurs, and a different element is produced. For example, transmutation of ^{14}N to ^{14}C occurs in the upper atmosphere when neutrons produced by cosmic rays collide with atmospheric nitrogen. In the collision, a neutron dislodges a proton (^{1}H) from the nitrogen nucleus as the neutron and nucleus fuse together:

$$^{14}_{7}N + ^{1}_{0}n \longrightarrow ^{14}_{6}C + ^{1}_{1}H$$

Artificial transmutation can lead to the synthesis of entirely new elements never before seen on earth. In fact, all the *transuranium elements*—those elements with atomic numbers greater than 92—have been produced by bombardment reactions. For example, plutonium-241 (^{241}Pu) can be made by bombardment of uranium-238 with α particles:

$$^{238}_{92}U + ^{4}_{2}He \longrightarrow ^{241}_{94}Pu + ^{1}_{0}n$$

Plutonium-241 is itself radioactive, with a half-life of 14.35 years, decaying by β emission to yield americium-241, which in turn decays by α emission with a half-life of 432.2 years. (If the name *americium* sounds vaguely familiar, it is because this radioisotope is used in smoke detectors.)

$$^{241}_{94}Pu \longrightarrow ^{241}_{95}Am + ^{0}_{-1}e$$

Note that all the equations just given for artificial transmutations are balanced. The sum of the mass numbers and the sum of the charges are the same on both sides of each equation.

▲ Smoke detectors contain a small amount of americium-241. The α particles emitted by this radioisotope ionize the air within the detector, causing it to conduct a tiny electric current. When smoke enters the chamber, conductivity drops and an alarm is triggered.

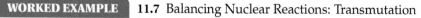

WORKED EXAMPLE **11.7** Balancing Nuclear Reactions: Transmutation

Californium-246 is formed by bombardment of uranium-238 atoms. If four neutrons are also formed, what particle is used for the bombardment?

ANALYSIS First write an incomplete nuclear equation incorporating the known information:

$$^{238}_{92}U + ? \longrightarrow ^{246}_{98}Cf + 4\,^{1}_{0}n$$

Then find the numbers of nucleons and charges necessary to balance the equation. In this instance, there are 238 nucleons on the left and $246 + 4 = 250$ nucleons on the right, so the bombarding particle must have $250 - 238 = 12$ nucleons. Furthermore, there are 92 nuclear charges on the left and 98 on the right, so the bombarding particle must have $98 - 92 = 6$ protons.

SOLUTION
The missing particle is $^{12}_{6}C$.

$$^{238}_{92}U + ^{12}_{6}C \longrightarrow ^{246}_{98}Cf + 4\,^{1}_{0}n$$

PROBLEM 11.13

What isotope results from α decay of the americium-241 in smoke detectors?

PROBLEM 11.14

The element berkelium, first prepared at the University of California at Berkeley in 1949, is made by α bombardment of $^{241}_{95}Am$. Two neutrons are also produced during the reaction. What isotope of berkelium results from this transmutation? Write a balanced nuclear equation.

APPLICATION ▶

We are all familiar with the appearance of a standard X-ray image, produced when X rays pass through the body and the intensity of the radiation that exits is recorded on film. X-ray imaging is, however, only one of a host of noninvasive imaging techniques that are now in common use.

Among the most widely used imaging techniques are those that give diagnostic information about the health of various parts of the body by analyzing the distribution pattern of a radioactively tagged substance in the body. A radiopharmaceutical agent that is known to concentrate in a specific organ or other body part is injected into the body, and its distribution pattern is monitored by an external radiation detector such as a γ-ray camera. Depending on the medical condition, a diseased part might concentrate more of the radiopharmaceutical than normal and thus show up on the film as a radioactive hot spot against a cold background. Alternatively, the diseased part might concentrate less of the radiopharmaceutical than normal and thus show up as a cold spot on a hot background.

Among the radioisotopes most widely used for diagnostic imaging is technetium-99*m*, whose short half-life of only six hours minimizes the patient's exposure to radioactivity. Bone scans using this nuclide, such as that shown in the accompanying photograph, are an important tool in the diagnosis of cancer and other conditions.

Several other techniques now used in medical diagnosis are made possible by *tomography*, a technique in which computer processing allows production of images through "slices" of the body. In X-ray tomography, commonly known as *CAT* or *CT* scanning (computerized tomography), the X-ray source and an array of detectors move rapidly in a circle around a patient's body, collecting up to 90,000 readings. CT scans can detect structural abnormalities such as tumors without the use of radioactive materials.

Combining tomography with radioisotope imaging gives cross-sectional views of regions that concentrate a radioactive substance. One such technique, *positron emission tomography* (PET), utilizes radioisotopes that emit positrons and ultimately yield γ rays. Oxygen-15, nitrogen-13, carbon-11, and

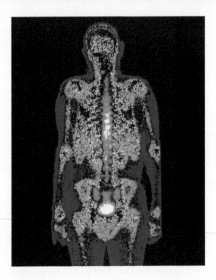

▲ A bone scan carried out with radioactive technetium-99*m*. Color has been added to help the visualization.

fluorine-18 are commonly used for PET because they can be readily incorporated into many physiologically active compounds. An ¹⁸F-labeled glucose derivative, for instance, is useful for imaging brain regions that respond to various stimuli. The disadvantage of PET scans is that the necessary radioisotopes are so short-lived that they must be produced on-site immediately before use. The cost of PET is therefore high, because a hospital must install and maintain the necessary nuclear facility.

Magnetic resonance imaging (MRI) is a medical imaging technique that uses powerful magnetic and radio-frequency fields to interact with specific nuclei in the body (usually the nuclei of hydrogen atoms) to generate images in which the contrast between soft tissues is much better than that seen with CT. The original name for this technique was *nuclear* magnetic resonance imaging, but the *nuclear* was eliminated because in the public mind this word conjured up negative images of ionizing radiation. Ironically, MRI does not involve any nuclear radiation at all.

See Additional Problems 11.74 and 11.75 at the end of the chapter.

PROBLEM 11.15

Write a balanced nuclear equation for the reaction of argon-40 with a proton:

$$^{40}_{18}\text{Ar} + ^{1}_{1}\text{H} \longrightarrow ? + ^{1}_{0}\text{n}$$

11.11 Nuclear Fission and Nuclear Fusion

In the preceding section, we saw that particle bombardment of various elements causes artificial transmutation and results in the formation of new, usually heavier elements. Under very special conditions with a very few isotopes, however, different kinds of nuclear events occur. Certain very heavy nuclei can split apart, and certain very light nuclei can fuse together. The two resultant processes—**nuclear fission** for the fragmenting of heavy nuclei and **nuclear fusion** for the joining together of light nuclei—have changed the world since their discovery in the late 1930s and early 1940s.

The huge amounts of energy that accompany these nuclear processes are the result of mass-to-energy conversions and are predicted by Einstein's equation

$$E = mc^2$$

where E = energy, m = mass change associated with the nuclear reaction, and c = the speed of light (3.0×10^8 m/s). Based on this relationship, a mass change as small as 1 µg results in a release of 2.15×10^4 kcal of energy!

Nuclear fission The fragmenting of heavy nuclei.

Nuclear fusion The joining together of light nuclei.

Nuclear Fission

Uranium-235 is the only naturally occurring isotope that undergoes nuclear fission. When this isotope is bombarded by a stream of relatively slow-moving neutrons, its nucleus splits to give isotopes of other elements. The split can take place in more than 400 ways, and more than 800 different fission products have been identified. One of the more frequently occurring pathways generates barium-142 and krypton-91, along with two additional neutrons plus the one neutron that initiated the fission:

$$^{1}_{0}\text{n} + ^{235}_{92}\text{U} \longrightarrow ^{142}_{56}\text{Ba} + ^{91}_{36}\text{Kr} + 3\,^{1}_{0}\text{n}$$

As indicated by the balanced nuclear equation above, *one* neutron is used to initiate fission of a ^{235}U nucleus, but *three* neutrons are released. Thus, a nuclear **chain reaction** can be started: 1 neutron initiates one fission that releases 3 neutrons. The 3 neutrons initiate three new fissions that release 9 neutrons. The 9 neutrons initiate nine fissions that release 27 neutrons, and so on at an ever faster pace (Figure 11.7). It is worth noting that the neutrons produced by fission reactions are highly energetic. They possess penetrating power greater than α and β particles, but less than γ rays. In a nuclear fission reactor, the neutrons must first be slowed down to allow them to react. If the sample size is small, many of the neutrons escape before initiating additional fission events, and the chain reaction stops. If a sufficient amount of ^{235}U is present, however—an amount called the **critical mass**—then the chain reaction becomes self-sustaining. Under high-pressure conditions that confine the ^{235}U to a small volume, the chain reaction occurs so rapidly that a nuclear explosion results. For ^{235}U, the critical mass is about 56 kg, although the amount can be reduced to approximately 15 kg by placing a coating of ^{238}U around the ^{235}U to reflect back some of the escaping neutrons.

An enormous quantity of heat is released during nuclear fission—the fission of just 1.0 g of uranium-235 produces 3.4×10^8 kcal, for instance. This heat can be used to convert water to steam, which can be harnessed to turn huge generators and produce electric power. The use of nuclear power is much more advanced in some countries than in others, with Lithuania and France leading the way by generating about 86% and 77%, respectively, of their electricity in nuclear plants. In the United States, only about 22% of the electricity is nuclear-generated.

Two major objections that have caused much public debate about nuclear power plants are safety and waste disposal. Although a nuclear explosion is not possible under the conditions that exist in a power plant, there is a serious potential radiation hazard should an accident rupture the containment vessel holding the nuclear fuel and release radioactive substances to the environment. Perhaps even more important is the problem posed by disposal of radioactive wastes from nuclear plants. Many of these wastes have such long half-lives that hundreds or even thousands of years must elapse before they will be safe for humans to approach. How to dispose of such hazardous materials safely is an unsolved problem.

Chain reaction A reaction that, once started, is self-sustaining.

Critical mass The minimum amount of radioactive material needed to sustain a nuclear chain reaction.

▲ Energy from the fission of uranium-235 is used to produce steam and generate electricity in this nuclear power plant.

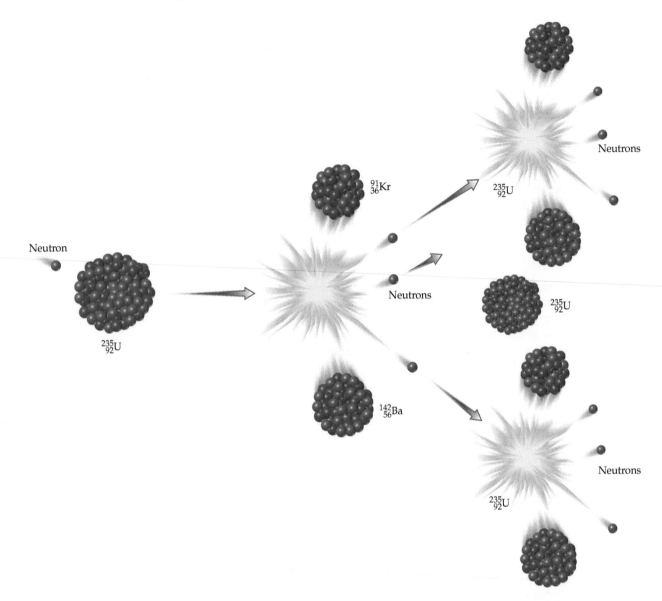

▲ **FIGURE 11.7 A chain reaction.** Each fission event produces additional neutrons that induce more fissions. The rate of the process increases at each stage. Such chain reactions usually lead to the formation of many different fission products in addition to the two indicated.

PROBLEM 11.16

What other isotope besides tellurium-137 is produced by nuclear fission of uranium-235?

$$^{235}_{92}\text{U} + {}^{1}_{0}\text{n} \longrightarrow {}^{137}_{52}\text{Te} + 2\,{}^{1}_{0}\text{n} + \text{?}$$

Nuclear Fusion

Just as heavy nuclei such as ^{235}U release energy when they undergo *fission*, very light nuclei such as the isotopes of hydrogen release enormous amounts of energy when they undergo *fusion*. In fact, it is just such a fusion reaction of hydrogen nuclei to produce helium that powers our sun and other stars. Among the processes thought to occur in the sun are those in the following sequence leading to helium-4:

$$^{1}_{1}\text{H} + {}^{2}_{1}\text{H} \longrightarrow {}^{3}_{2}\text{He}$$
$$^{3}_{2}\text{He} + {}^{3}_{2}\text{He} \longrightarrow {}^{4}_{2}\text{He} + 2\,{}^{1}_{1}\text{H}$$
$$^{3}_{2}\text{He} + {}^{1}_{1}\text{H} \longrightarrow {}^{4}_{2}\text{He} + {}^{0}_{1}\text{e}$$

APPLICATION ▶ Archaeological Radiocarbon Dating

Biblical scrolls are found in a cave near the Dead Sea. Are they authentic? A mummy is discovered in an Egyptian tomb. How old is it? The burned bones of a man are dug up near Lubbock, Texas. How long ago did humans live on the North American continent? Using a technique called *radiocarbon dating*, archaeologists can answer these and many other questions. (The Dead Sea Scrolls are 1900 years old and authentic, the mummy is 3100 years old, and the human remains found in Texas are 9900 years old.)

Radiocarbon dating depends on the slow and constant production of radioactive carbon-14 atoms in the upper atmosphere by bombardment of nitrogen atoms with neutrons from cosmic rays. Carbon-14 atoms combine with oxygen to yield $^{14}CO_2$, which slowly mixes with ordinary $^{12}CO_2$ and is then taken up by plants during photosynthesis. When these plants are eaten by animals, carbon-14 enters the food chain and is distributed evenly throughout all living organisms.

As long as a plant or animal is living, a dynamic equilibrium is established in which the organism excretes or exhales the same amount of ^{14}C that it takes in. As a result, the ratio of ^{14}C to ^{12}C in the living organism is the same as that in the atmosphere—about 1 part in 10^{12}. When the plant or animal dies, however, it no longer takes in more ^{14}C. Thus, the $^{14}C/^{12}C$ ratio in the organism slowly decreases as ^{14}C undergoes radioactive decay. At 5730 years (one ^{14}C half-life) after the death of the organism, the $^{14}C/^{12}C$ ratio has decreased by a factor of 2; at 11,460 years after death, the $^{14}C/^{12}C$ ratio has decreased by a factor of 4; and so on.

By measuring the amount of ^{14}C remaining in the traces of any once-living organism, archaeologists can determine how long ago the organism died. Human hair from well-preserved remains, charcoal or wood fragments from once-living trees, and cotton or linen from once-living plants are all useful sources for radiocarbon dating. The accuracy of the technique lessens as a sample gets older and the amount of ^{14}C it contains diminishes, but artifacts with an age of 1000–20,000 years can be dated with reasonable accuracy.

▲ Radiocarbon dating has determined that these charcoal paintings in the Lascaux cave in France are approximately 15,000 years old.

See Additional Problems 11.76 and 11.77 at the end of the chapter.

Under the conditions found in stars, where the temperature is on the order of 2×10^7 K and pressures approach 10^5 atmospheres, nuclei are stripped of all their electrons and have enough kinetic energy that nuclear fusion readily occurs. The energy of our sun, and all the stars, comes from thermonuclear fusion reactions in their core that fuse hydrogen and other light elements transmuting them into heavier elements. On earth, however, the necessary conditions for nuclear fusion are not easily created. For more than 50 years scientists have been trying to create the necessary conditions for fusion in laboratory reactors, including the Tokamak Fusion Test Reactor (TFTR) at Princeton, New Jersey, and the Joint European Torus (JET) at Culham, England. Recent advances in reactor design have raised hopes that a commercial fusion reactor will be realized within the next 20 years.

If the dream becomes reality, controlled nuclear fusion can provide the ultimate cheap, clean power source. The fuel is deuterium (^2H), available in the oceans in limitless amounts, and there are few radioactive by-products.

▲ A researcher stands inside the D3D Tokamak nuclear fusion reactor at the General Atomics facility in San Diego, California.

SUMMARY: REVISITING THE CHAPTER GOALS

1. **What is a nuclear reaction, and how are equations for nuclear reactions balanced?** A *nuclear reaction* is one that changes an atomic nucleus, causing the change of one element into another. Loss of an α particle leads to a new atom whose atomic number is 2 less than

KEY WORDS

Alpha (α) particle, *p. 335*

Artificial transmutation, *p. 350*

that of the starting atom. Loss of a β particle leads to an atom whose atomic number is 1 greater than that of the starting atom:

$$\alpha \text{ emission: } {}^{238}_{92}\text{U} \longrightarrow {}^{234}_{90}\text{Th} + {}^{4}_{2}\text{He}$$

$$\beta \text{ emission: } {}^{131}_{53}\text{I} \longrightarrow {}^{131}_{54}\text{Xe} + {}^{0}_{-1}\text{e}$$

A nuclear reaction is balanced when the sum of the *nucleons* (protons and neutrons) is the same on both sides of the reaction arrow and when the sum of the charges on the nuclei plus any ejected subatomic particles is the same.

2. **What are the different kinds of radioactivity?** *Radioactivity* is the spontaneous emission of radiation from the nucleus of an unstable atom. The three major kinds of radiation are called *alpha* (α), *beta* (β), and *gamma* (γ). Alpha radiation consists of helium nuclei, small particles containing two protons and two neutrons (${}^{4}_{2}\text{He}$); β radiation consists of electrons (${}^{0}_{-1}\text{e}$); and γ radiation consists of high-energy light waves. Every element in the periodic table has at least one radioactive isotope, or *radioisotope*.

3. **How are the rates of nuclear reactions expressed?** The rate of a nuclear reaction is expressed in units of *half-life* ($t_{1/2}$), where one half-life is the amount of time necessary for one half of the radioactive sample to decay.

4. **What is ionizing radiation?** High-energy radiation of all types—α particles, β particles, γ rays, and X rays—is called *ionizing radiation*. When any of these kinds of radiation strikes an atom, it dislodges an electron and gives a reactive ion that can be lethal to living cells. Gamma rays and X rays are the most penetrating and most harmful types of external radiation; α and β particles are the most dangerous types of internal radiation because of their high energy and the resulting damage to surrounding tissue.

5. **How is radioactivity measured?** Radiation intensity is expressed in different ways according to the property being measured. The *curie* (*Ci*) measures the number of radioactive disintegrations per second in a sample; the *roentgen* (*R*) measures the ionizing ability of radiation; the *rad* measures the amount of radiation energy absorbed per gram of tissue; and the *rem* measures the amount of tissue damage caused by radiation. Radiation effects become noticeable with a human exposure of 25 rem and become lethal at an exposure above 600 rem.

6. **What is transmutation?** *Transmutation* is the change of one element into another brought about by a nuclear reaction. Most known radioisotopes do not occur naturally but are made by bombardment of an atom with a high-energy particle. In the ensuing collision between particle and atom, a nuclear change occurs and a new element is produced by *artificial transmutation*.

7. **What are nuclear fission and nuclear fusion?** With a very few isotopes, including ${}^{235}_{92}\text{U}$, the nucleus is split apart by neutron bombardment to give smaller fragments. A large amount of energy is released during this *nuclear fission*, leading to use of the reaction for generating electric power. *Nuclear fusion* results when small nuclei such as those of tritium (${}^{3}_{1}\text{H}$) and deuterium (${}^{2}_{1}\text{H}$) combine to give a heavier nucleus.

UNDERSTANDING KEY CONCEPTS

11.17 Magnesium-28 decays by β emission to give aluminum-28. If yellow spheres represent ${}^{28}_{12}\text{Mg}$ atoms and blue spheres represent ${}^{28}_{13}\text{Al}$ atoms, how many half-lives have passed in the following sample?

11.18 Write a balanced nuclear equation to represent the decay reaction described in Problem 11.17.

11.19 Refer to Figure 11.4 and then make a drawing similar to those in Problem 11.17 representing the decay of a sample of ${}^{28}_{12}\text{Mg}$ after approximately four half-lives have passed.

11.20 Write the symbol of the isotope represented by the following drawing. Blue spheres represent neutrons and red spheres represent protons.

11.21 Shown below is a portion of the decay series for plutonium-241 (${}^{241}_{94}\text{Pu}$). The series has two kinds of arrows: shorter arrows pointing right and longer arrows pointing left. Which arrow corresponds to an α emission, and which to a β emission? Explain.

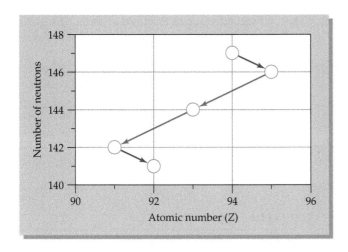

11.22 Identify and write the symbol for each nuclide in the decay series shown in Problem 11.21.

11.23 Identify the isotopes involved, and tell the type of decay process occurring in the following nuclear reaction:

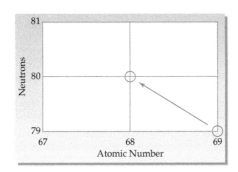

11.24 What is the half-life of the radionuclide that shows the following decay curve?

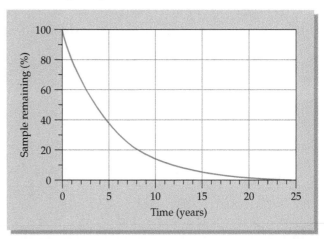

11.25 What is wrong with the following decay curve? Explain.

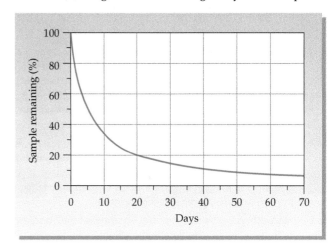

ADDITIONAL PROBLEMS

RADIOACTIVITY

11.26 What does it mean to say that a substance is radioactive?

11.27 Describe how α radiation, β radiation, γ radiation, positron emission, and electron capture differ.

11.28 List several ways in which a nuclear reaction differs from a chemical reaction.

11.29 What word is used to describe the change of one element into another?

11.30 What symbol is used for an α particle in a nuclear equation?

11.31 What symbol is used for a β particle in a nuclear equation? For a positron?

11.32 Which kind of radiation, α, β, or γ, has the highest penetrating power, and which has the lowest?

11.33 What happens when ionizing radiation strikes an atom in a chemical compound?

11.34 How does ionizing radiation lead to cell damage?

11.35 What are the main sources of background radiation?

11.36 How can a nucleus emit an electron during β decay when there are no electrons present in the nucleus to begin with?

11.37 What is the difference between an α particle and a helium atom?

NUCLEAR DECAY AND TRANSMUTATION

11.38 What does it mean to say that a nuclear equation is balanced?

11.39 What are transuranium elements, and how are they made?

11.40 What happens to the mass number and atomic number of an atom that emits an α particle? A β particle?

11.41 What happens to the mass number and atomic number of an atom that emits a γ ray? A positron?

11.42 How does nuclear fission differ from normal radioactive decay?

11.43 What characteristic of uranium-235 fission causes a chain reaction?

11.44 What products result from radioactive decay of the following β emitters?

(a) $^{35}_{16}S$ (b) $^{24}_{10}Ne$ (c) $^{90}_{38}Sr$

11.45 What products result from radioactive decay of the following α emitters?

(a) $^{190}_{78}Pt$ (b) $^{208}_{87}Fr$ (c) $^{245}_{96}Cm$

11.46 Identify the starting radioisotopes needed to balance each of these nuclear reactions:

(a) $? + {}^{4}_{2}He \rightarrow {}^{113}_{49}In$

(b) $? + {}^{4}_{2}He \rightarrow {}^{13}_{7}N + {}^{1}_{0}n$

11.47 Identify the product radioisotope needed to balance each of these nuclear reactions:

(a) $^{140}_{55}Cs \rightarrow ? + {}^{0}_{-1}e$

(b) $^{248}_{96}Cm \rightarrow ? + {}^{4}_{2}He$

11.48 Balance the following equations for the nuclear fission of $^{235}_{92}U$:

(a) $^{235}_{92}U + {}^{1}_{0}n \rightarrow {}^{160}_{62}Sm + {}^{72}_{30}Zn + ? \, {}^{1}_{0}n$

(b) $^{235}_{92}U + {}^{1}_{0}n \rightarrow {}^{87}_{35}Br + ? + 3 \, {}^{1}_{0}n$

11.49 Complete and balance the following nuclear equations:

(a) $^{126}_{50}Sn \rightarrow {}^{0}_{-1}e + ?$

(b) $^{210}_{88}Ra \rightarrow {}^{4}_{2}He + ?$

(c) $^{76}_{36}Kr + {}^{0}_{-1}e \rightarrow ?$

11.50 For centuries, alchemists dreamed of turning base metals into gold. The dream finally became reality when it was shown that mercury-198 can be converted into gold-198 on bombardment by neutrons. What small particle is produced in addition to gold-198? Write a balanced nuclear equation for the reaction.

11.51 Cobalt-60 (half-life = 5.3 years) is used to irradiate food, to treat cancer, and to disinfect surgical equipment. It is produced by irradiation of cobalt-59 in a nuclear reactor. It decays to nickel-60. Write nuclear equations for the formation and decay reactions of cobalt-60.

11.52 Bismuth-212 attaches readily to monoclonal antibodies and is used in the treatment of various cancers. It is formed after the parent isotope undergoes a decay series consisting of four α decays and one β decay. What is the parent isotope for this decay series?

11.53 Meitnerium-266 ($^{266}_{109}Mt$) was prepared in 1982 by bombardment of bismuth-209 atoms with iron-58. What other product must also have been formed? Write a balanced nuclear equation for the transformation.

HALF-LIFE

11.54 What does it mean when we say that strontium-90, a waste product of nuclear power plants, has a half-life of 28.8 years?

11.55 What percentage of the original mass remains in a radioactive sample after two half-lives have passed? After three half-lives? After 3.5 half-lives?

11.56 Selenium-75, a β emitter with a half-life of 120 days, is used medically for pancreas scans. Approximately how much selenium-75 would remain from a 0.050 g sample that has been stored for one year?

11.57 Approximately how long would it take a sample of selenium-75 to lose 99% of its radioactivity? (See Problem 11.56.)

11.58 The half-life of mercury-197 is 64.1 hours. If a patient undergoing a kidney scan is given 5.0 ng of mercury-197, how much will remain after 7 days? After 30 days?

11.59 Gold-198, a β emitter used to treat leukemia, has a half-life of 2.695 days. The standard dosage is about 1.0 mCi/kg body weight.

(a) What is the product of the β emission of gold-198?

(b) How long does it take a 30.0 mCi sample of gold-198 to decay so that only 3.75 mCi remains?

(c) How many millicuries are required in a single dosage administered to a 70.0 kg adult?

MEASURING RADIOACTIVITY

11.60 Describe how a Geiger counter works.

11.61 Describe how a film badge works.

11.62 Describe how a scintillation counter works.

11.63 Why are rems the preferred units for measuring the health effects of radiation?

11.64 Approximately what amount (in rems) of short-term exposure to radiation produces noticeable effects in humans?

11.65 Match each unit in the left column with the property being measured in the right column:

1. curie   (a) Ionizing intensity of radiation
2. rem   (b) Amount of tissue damage
3. rad   (c) Number of disintegrations per second
4. roentgen   (d) Amount of radiation per gram of tissue

11.66 Technetium-99m is used for radioisotope-guided surgical biopsies of certain bone cancers. A patient must receive an injection of 28 mCi of technetium-99m 6–12 hours before surgery. If the activity of the solution is 15 mCi, what volume should be injected?

11.67 Sodium-24 is used to study the circulatory system and to treat chronic leukemia. It is administered in the form of saline (NaCl) solution, with a therapeutic dosage of 180 μCi/kg body weight. How many milliliters of a 6.5 mCi/mL solution are needed to treat a 68 kg adult?

11.68 A selenium-75 source is producing 300 rem at a distance of 2.0 m. What is its intensity at 25 m?

11.69 If a radiation source has an intensity of 650 rem at 1.0 m, what distance is needed to decrease the intensity of exposure to below 25 rem, the level at which no effects are detectable?

Applications

11.70 What are the three main classes of techniques used in nuclear medicine? Give an example of each. [*Medical Uses of Radioactivity*, p. 342]

11.71 A 2 mL solution containing 1.25 μCi/mL is injected into the blood stream of a patient. After dilution, a 1.00 mL sample is withdrawn and found to have an activity of 2.6×10^{-4} μCi. Calculate total blood volume. [*Medical Uses of Radioactivity*, p. 342]

11.72 What is the purpose of food irradiation, and how does it work? [*Irradiated Food, p. 349*]

11.73 What kind of radiation is used to treat food? [*Irradiated Food, p. 349*]

11.74 What are the advantages of CT and PET relative to conventional X rays? [*Body Imaging, p. 352*]

11.75 What advantages does MRI have over CT and PET imaging? [*Body Imaging, p. 352*]

11.76 Why is ^{14}C dating useful only for samples that contain material from objects that were once alive? [*Archaeological Radiocarbon Dating, p. 355*]

11.77 Some dried beans with a ^{14}C/^{12}C ratio one-eighth of the current value are found in an old cave. How old are the beans? [*Archaeological Radiocarbon Dating, p. 355*]

General Questions and Problems

11.78 Harmful chemical spills can often be cleaned up by treatment with another chemical. For example, a spill of H_2SO_4 might be neutralized by addition of $NaHCO_3$. Why is it that the harmful radioactive wastes from nuclear power plants cannot be cleaned up just as easily?

11.79 Why is a scintillation counter or Geiger counter more useful for determining the existence and source of a new radiation leak than a film badge?

11.80 Technetium-99m, used for brain scans and to monitor heart function, is formed by decay of molybdenum-99.
(a) By what type of decay does ^{99}Mo produce ^{99m}Tc?
(b) Molybdenum-99 is formed by neutron bombardment of a natural isotope. If one neutron is absorbed and there are no other by-products of this process, from what isotope is ^{99}Mo formed?

11.81 The half-life of technetium-99m (Problem 11.80) is 6.01 hours. If a sample with an initial activity of 15 μCi is injected into a patient, what is the activity in 24 hours, assuming that none of the sample is excreted?

11.82 Plutonium-238 is an α emitter used to power batteries for heart pacemakers.
(a) Write the balanced nuclear equation for this emission.
(b) Why is a pacemaker battery enclosed in a metal case before being inserted into the chest cavity?

11.83 Sodium-24, a beta-emitter used in diagnosing circulation problems, has a half-life of 15 hours.
(a) Write the balanced nuclear equation for this emission.
(b) What fraction of sodium-24 remains after 50 hours?

11.84 High levels of radioactive fallout after the 1986 accident at the Chernobyl nuclear power plant in what is now Ukraine resulted in numerous miscarriages and many instances of farm animals born with severe defects. Why are embryos and fetuses particularly susceptible to the effects of radiation?

11.85 One way to demonstrate the dose factor of ionizing radiation (penetrating distance × ionizing energy) is to think of radiation as cookies. Imagine that you have four cookies—an α cookie, a β cookie, a γ cookie, and a neutron cookie. Which one would you eat, which would you hold in your hand, which would you put in your pocket, and which would you throw away?

11.86 What are the main advantages of fusion relative to fission as an energy source? What are the drawbacks?

11.87 Write a balanced nuclear equation for
(a) α emission of ^{162}Re and
(b) β emission of ^{188}W.

11.88 Balance the following transmutation reactions:
(a) $^{253}_{99}$Es + ? → $^{256}_{101}$Md + $^{1}_{0}$n
(b) $^{250}_{98}$Cf + $^{11}_{5}$B → ? + 4 $^{1}_{0}$n

11.89 The most abundant isotope of uranium, ^{238}U, does not undergo fission. In a *breeder reactor*, however, a ^{238}U atom captures a neutron and emits two beta particles to make a fissionable isotope of plutonium, which can then be used as fuel in a nuclear reactor. Write the balanced nuclear equation.

11.90 Boron is used in *control rods* for nuclear reactors because it can absorb neutrons and emit α particles. Balance the equation
$$^{10}_{5}B + ^{1}_{0}n \longrightarrow ? + ^{4}_{2}He$$

11.91 Thorium-232 decays by a ten-step series, ultimately yielding lead-208. How many α particles and how many β particles are emitted?

11.92 Californium-246 is formed by bombardment of uranium-238 atoms. If four neutrons are formed as by-products, what particle is used for the bombardment?

CHAPTER 12

Introduction to Organic Chemistry: Alkanes

CONCEPTS TO REVIEW

Covalent Bonds
(Sections 5.1 and 5.2)

Multiple Covalent Bonds
(Section 5.3)

Drawing Lewis Structures
(Section 5.6)

VSEPR and Molecular Shapes
(Section 5.7)

Polar Covalent Bonds
(Section 5.8)

▲ The gasoline, kerosene, and other products of this petroleum refinery are primarily mixtures of simple organic compounds called alkanes.

CONTENTS

CHAPTER GOALS

In this and the next five chapters, we will look at the chemistry of organic compounds, beginning with answers to the following questions:

1. What are the basic properties of organic compounds?

THE GOAL: Be able to identify organic compounds and the types of bonds contained in them.

2. What are functional groups, and how are they used to classify organic molecules?

THE GOAL: Be able to classify organic molecules into families by functional group.

3. What are isomers?

THE GOAL: Be able to recognize and draw constitutional isomers.

4. How are organic molecules drawn?

THE GOAL: Be able to convert between structural formulas and condensed or line structures.

5. What are alkanes and cycloalkanes, and how are they named?

THE GOAL: Be able to name an alkane or cycloalkane from its structure, or write the structure, given the name.

6. What are the general properties and chemical reactions of alkanes?

THE GOAL: Be able to describe the physical properties of alkanes and the products formed in the combustion and halogenation reactions of alkanes.

As knowledge of chemistry slowly grew in the 1700s, mysterious differences were noted between compounds obtained from living sources and those obtained from minerals. It was found, for instance, that chemicals from living sources were often liquids or low-melting solids, whereas chemicals from mineral sources were usually high-melting solids. Furthermore, chemicals from living sources were generally more difficult to purify and work with than those from minerals. To express these differences, the term *organic chemistry* was introduced to mean the study of compounds from living organisms, and *inorganic chemistry* was used to refer to the study of compounds from minerals.

Today we know that there are no fundamental differences between organic and inorganic compounds: The same scientific principles are applicable to both. The only common characteristic of compounds from living sources is that they contain the element carbon as their primary component. Thus, organic chemistry is now defined as the study of carbon-based compounds.

Why is carbon special? The answer derives from its position in the periodic table. As a group 4A nonmetal, carbon atoms have the unique ability to form four strong covalent bonds. Also, unlike atoms of other elements, carbon atoms can readily form strong bonds with other carbon atoms to produce long chains and rings. As a result, only carbon is able to form such an immense array of compounds, from methane with one carbon atom to DNA with billions of carbons.

12.1 The Nature of Organic Molecules

Let us begin a study of **organic chemistry**—the chemistry of carbon compounds—by reviewing what we have seen in earlier chapters about the structures of organic molecules:

Organic chemistry The study of carbon compounds.

- **Carbon is tetravalent; it always forms four bonds** (Section 5.2). In methane, for example, carbon is connected to four hydrogen atoms:

Methane, CH_4

- **Organic molecules have covalent bonds** (Section 5.2). In ethane, for example, the bonds result from the sharing of two electrons, either between two C atoms or a C and a H atom:

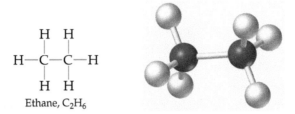

Ethane, C_2H_6

- **Organic molecules contain polar covalent bonds when carbon bonds to an electronegative element on the right side of the periodic table** (Section 5.8). In chloromethane, for example, the electronegative chlorine atom attracts electrons more strongly than carbon, resulting in polarization of the C—Cl bond so that carbon has a partial positive charge, $\delta+$, and chlorine has a partial negative charge, $\delta-$. In electrostatic potential maps (Section 5.8), the chlorine atom is therefore in the red region of the map and the carbon atom in the blue region:

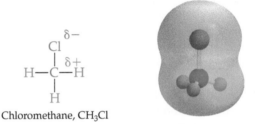

Chloromethane, CH_3Cl

- **Carbon forms multiple covalent bonds by sharing more than two electrons with a neighboring atom** (Section 5.3). In ethylene, for example, the two carbon atoms share four electrons in a double bond; in acetylene (also called ethyne), the two carbons share six electrons in a triple bond:

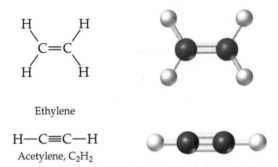

Ethylene

H—C≡C—H
Acetylene, C_2H_2

- **Organic molecules have specific three-dimensional shapes** (Section 5.7). When carbon is bonded to four atoms, as in methane, CH_4, the bonds are oriented toward the four corners of a regular tetrahedron with carbon in the center. Such three-dimensionality is commonly shown using normal lines for bonds in the plane of the page, dashed lines for bonds receding behind the page, and wedged lines for bonds coming out of the page:

- **Organic molecules often contain hydrogen, nitrogen, and oxygen, in addition to carbon** (Section 5.6). Nitrogen can form single, double, and triple bonds to carbon; oxygen can form single and double bonds:

$$C-N \quad C-O \quad C-H$$
$$C=N \quad C=O$$
$$C\equiv N$$

Covalent bonding makes organic compounds quite different from the inorganic compounds we have been concentrating on up to this point. For example, inorganic compounds such as NaCl have high melting points and high boiling points because they consist of large numbers of oppositely charged ions held together by strong electrical attractions (Section 4.4). (⊂⊃, p. 84) Organic compounds, by contrast, consist of atoms joined by covalent bonds into individual molecules. Because the molecules are attracted to one another only by weak non-ionic intermolecular forces (Section 8.11), organic compounds generally have lower melting and boiling points than inorganic salts. (⊂⊃, p. 235) Because of their relatively low melting and boiling points, simple organic compounds are usually liquids at room temperature, and a few are gases.

Other important differences between organic and inorganic compounds include solubility and electrical conductivity. Whereas many inorganic compounds dissolve in water to yield solutions of ions that conduct electricity (Section 9.9), most organic compounds are insoluble in water, and almost all of those that are soluble do not conduct electricity. (⊂⊃, p. 275) Only small polar organic molecules, such as glucose and ethyl alcohol, or large molecules with many polar groups, such as some proteins, dissolve in water. This lack of water solubility for organic compounds has important practical consequences, varying from the difficulty in removing greasy dirt and cleaning up environmental oil spills to drug delivery.

◀ Oil spills can be a serious environmental problem because oil is insoluble in water.

⊂⊃ **Looking Ahead**

The interior of a living cell is largely a water solution that contains many hundreds of different compounds. In later chapters, we will see how cells use membranes composed of water-insoluble organic molecules to enclose their watery interiors and to regulate the flow of substances across the cell boundary. ⊂⊃

12.2 Families of Organic Molecules: Functional Groups

More than 18 *million* organic compounds are described in the scientific literature. Each of these 18 million compounds has unique physical properties, such as a melting point and a boiling point, each has unique chemical properties, and many of them have unique biological properties (both desired and undesired). How can we ever understand them all?

Chemists have learned through experience that organic compounds can be classified into families according to their structural features and that the chemical

Functional group An atom or group of atoms within a molecule that has a characteristic physical and chemical behavior.

behavior of the members of a family is often predictable based on these specific grouping of atoms. Instead of 18 million compounds with seemingly random chemical reactivity, there are just a few general families of organic compounds whose chemistry falls into simple patterns.

The structural features that allow us to classify organic compounds into distinct chemical families are called **functional groups**. A functional group is an atom or group of atoms that has a characteristic physical and chemical behavior. Each functional group is always part of a larger molecule, and a molecule may have more than one class of functional group present, as we shall soon see. An important property of functional groups is that a given functional group *tends to undergo the same reactions in every molecule of which it is a part*. For example, the carbon–carbon double bond is a common functional group. Ethylene (C_2H_4), the simplest compound with a double bond, undergoes many chemical reactions similar to those of oleic acid ($C_{18}H_{34}O_2$), a much larger and more complex compound that also contains a double bond. Both, for example, react with hydrogen gas in the same manner, as shown in Figure 12.1. These identical reactions with hydrogen are typical: *The chemistry of an organic molecule is primarily determined by the functional groups it contains, not by its size and complexity.*

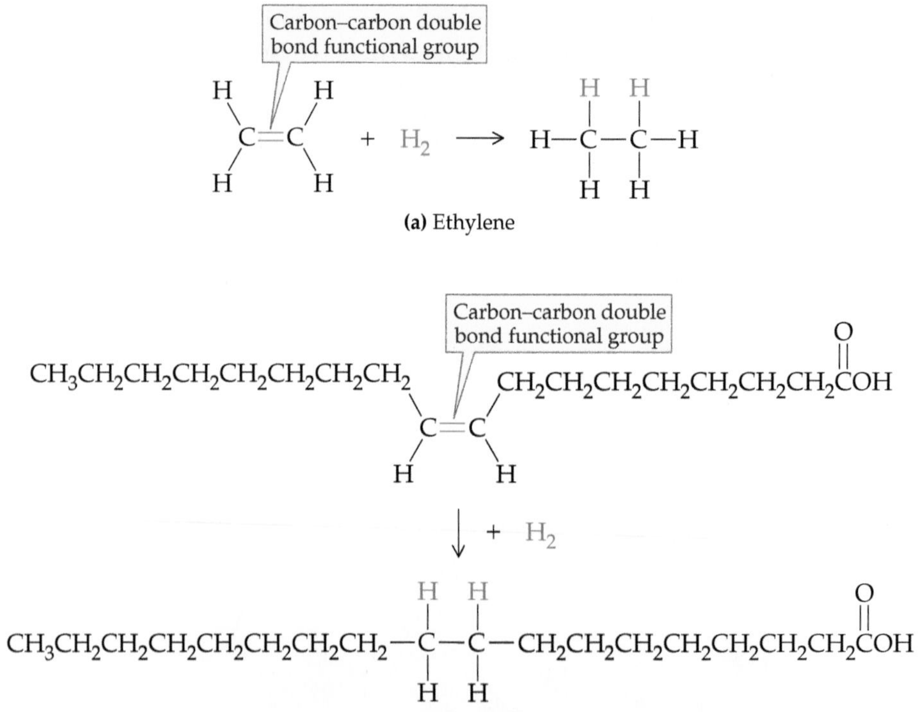

▶ **FIGURE 12.1 The reactions of (a) ethylene and (b) oleic acid with hydrogen.** The carbon–carbon double-bond functional group adds 2 hydrogen atoms in both cases, regardless of the complexity of the rest of the molecule.

Table 12.1 lists some of the most important families of organic molecules and their distinctive functional groups. Compounds that contain a $C=C$ double bond, for instance, are in the *alkene* family; compounds that have an —OH group bound to a tetravalent carbon are in the *alcohol* family; and so on.

Much of the chemistry discussed in this and the next five chapters is the chemistry of the families listed in Table 12.1, so it is best to memorize the names and become familiar with their structures now. Note that they fall into three groups:

Hydrocarbon An organic compound that contains only carbon and hydrogen.

- The first four families in Table 12.1 are **hydrocarbons**, organic compounds that contain only carbon and hydrogen. *Alkanes* have only single bonds and contain no functional groups. As we will see, the absence of functional groups makes alkanes relatively unreactive. *Alkenes* contain a carbon–carbon double-bond functional group; *alkynes* contain a carbon–carbon triple-bond functional group; and *aromatic* compounds contain a six-membered ring of carbon atoms with three alternating double bonds.

- The next four families in Table 12.1 have functional groups that contain only single bonds and have a carbon atom bonded to an electronegative atom.

TABLE 12.1 Some Important Families of Organic Molecules

FAMILY NAME	FUNCTIONAL GROUP STRUCTURE*	SIMPLE EXAMPLE	NAME ENDING
Alkane	Contains only C—H and C—C single bonds	CH_3CH_3 Ethane	-ane
Alkene	C=C	H_2C=CH_2 Ethylene	-ene
Alkyne	—C≡C—	H—C≡C—H Acetylene (Ethyne)	-yne
Aromatic	(benzene ring structure)	(benzene structure) Benzene	None
Alkyl halide	—C—X (X=F, Cl, Br, I)	CH_3—Cl Methyl chloride	None
Alcohol	—C—O—H	CH_3—OH Methyl alcohol (Methanol)	-ol
Ether	—C—O—C—	CH_3—O—CH_3 Dimethyl ether	None
Amine	—C—N	CH_3—NH_2 Methylamine	-amine
Aldehyde	—C—C—H (C=O)	CH_3—C—H (C=O) Acetaldehyde (Ethanal)	-al
Ketone	—C—C—C— (C=O)	CH_3—C—CH_3 (C=O) Acetone	-one
Carboxylic acid	—C—C—OH (C=O)	CH_3—C—OH (C=O) Acetic acid	-ic acid
Anhydride	—C—C—O—C—C— (C=O, C=O)	CH_3—C—O—C—CH_3 (C=O, C=O) Acetic anhydride	None
Ester	—C—C—O—C— (C=O)	CH_3—C—O—CH_3 (C=O) Methyl acetate	-ate
Amide	—C—C—NH_2, —C—C—N—H, (C=O) and —C—C—N— (C=O)	CH_3—C—NH_2 (C=O) Acetamide	-amide

*The bonds whose connections are not specified are assumed to be attached to carbon or hydrogen atoms in the rest of the molecule.

Alkyl halides have a carbon–halogen bond; *alcohols* have a carbon–oxygen bond; *ethers* have two carbons bonded to the same oxygen; and *amines* have a carbon–nitrogen bond.

- The remaining families in Table 12.1 have functional groups that contain a carbon–oxygen double bond: *aldehydes, ketones, carboxylic acids, anhydrides, esters,* and *amides.*

WORKED EXAMPLE 12.1 Molecular Structures: Identifying Functional Groups

To which family of organic compounds do the following compounds belong? Explain.

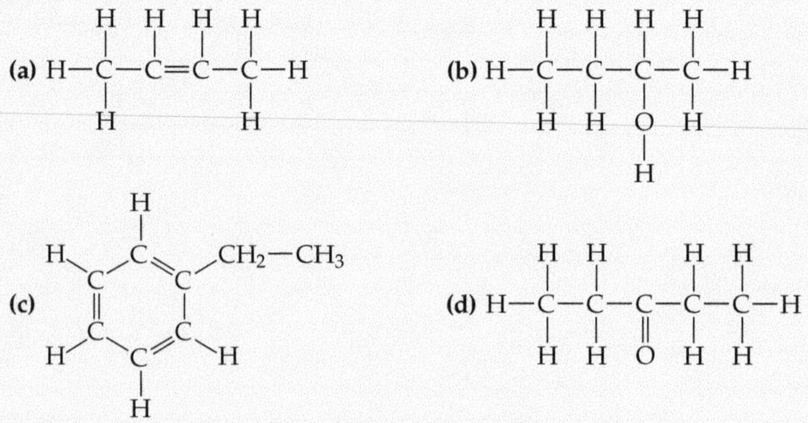

ANALYSIS Identify each functional group from the list in Table 12.1, and name the corresponding family to which the compound belongs.

SOLUTION

(a) This compound contains only carbon and hydrogen atoms, so it is a *hydrocarbon*. There is a carbon–carbon double bond, so it is an *alkene*.

(b) The O—H group bonded to tetravalent carbon identifies this compound as an *alcohol*.

(c) This compound also contains only carbon and hydrogen atoms, which identifies it as a *hydrocarbon*. The six-membered carbon ring with alternating double bonds also identifies this compound as an *aromatic* hydrocarbon compound.

(d) The carbon–oxygen double bond in the middle of the carbon chain (as opposed to at either end of the chain) identifies this compound as a *ketone*.

WORKED EXAMPLE 12.2 Molecular Structures: Drawing Functional Groups

Given the family of organic compounds to which the compound belongs, propose structures for compounds having the following chemical formulas.

(a) An amine having the formula C_2H_7N

(b) An alkyne having the formula C_3H_4

(c) An ether having the formula $C_4H_{10}O$

ANALYSIS Identify the functional group for each compound from Table 12.1. Once the atoms in this functional group are eliminated from the chemical formula, the remaining structure can be determined. (Remember that each carbon atom forms four bonds, nitrogen forms three bonds, oxygen forms two bonds, and hydrogen forms only one bond.)

SOLUTION

(a) Amines have a C—NH₂ group. Eliminating these atoms from the formula leaves 1 C atom and 5 H atoms. Since only the carbons are capable of forming more than one bond, the 2 C atoms must be bonded together. The remaining H atoms are then bonded to the carbons until each C has 4 bonds.

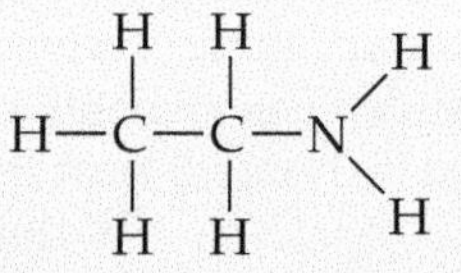

$$\begin{array}{c} \text{H}\ \ \text{H}\qquad \text{H} \\ |\ \ \ | \quad\ \ / \\ \text{H}-\text{C}-\text{C}-\text{N} \\ |\ \ \ | \quad\ \ \backslash \\ \text{H}\ \ \text{H}\qquad \text{H} \end{array}$$

(b) The alkynes contain a C≡C bond. This leaves 1 C atom and 4 H atoms. Attach this C to one of the carbons in the triple bond, and then distribute the H atoms until each carbon has a full complement of four bonds.

$$\begin{array}{c} \text{H} \\ | \\ \text{H}-\text{C}-\text{C}\equiv\text{C}-\text{H} \\ | \\ \text{H} \end{array}$$

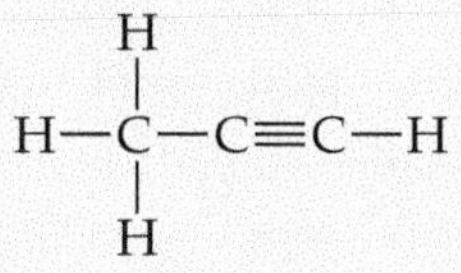

(c) The ethers contain a C—O—C group. Eliminating these atoms leaves 2 C atoms and 10 H atoms. The C atoms can be distributed on either end of the ether group, and the H atoms are then distributed until each carbon atom has a full complement of four bonds.

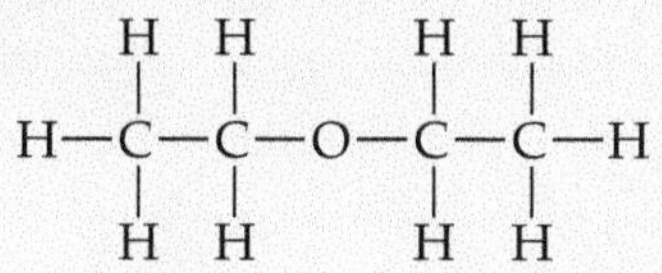

$$\begin{array}{c} \text{H}\ \ \text{H}\qquad \text{H}\ \ \text{H} \\ |\ \ \ |\qquad |\ \ \ | \\ \text{H}-\text{C}-\text{C}-\text{O}-\text{C}-\text{C}-\text{H} \\ |\ \ \ |\qquad |\ \ \ | \\ \text{H}\ \ \text{H}\qquad \text{H}\ \ \text{H} \end{array} \quad\text{or}\quad \begin{array}{c} \text{H}\ \ \text{H}\ \ \text{H}\qquad \text{H} \\ |\ \ \ |\ \ \ |\qquad | \\ \text{H}-\text{C}-\text{C}-\text{C}-\text{O}-\text{C}-\text{H} \\ |\ \ \ |\ \ \ |\qquad | \\ \text{H}\ \ \text{H}\ \ \text{H}\qquad \text{H} \end{array}$$

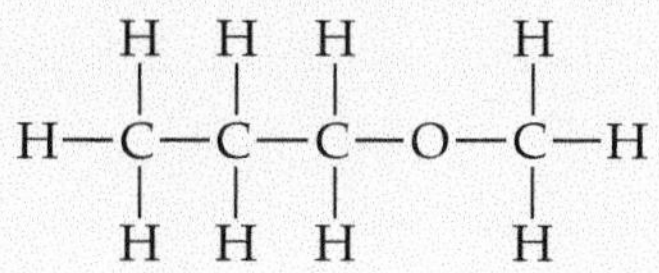

PROBLEM 12.1

Many organic compounds contain more than one functional group. Locate and identify the functional groups in (a) lactic acid, from sour milk; (b) methyl methacrylate, used in making Lucite and Plexiglas; and (c) phenylalanine, an amino acid found in proteins.

(a) 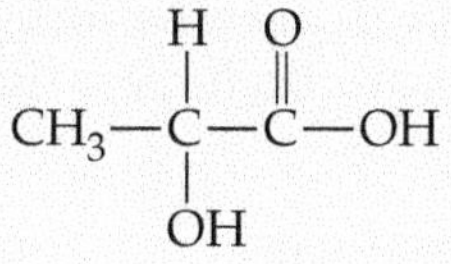 $\begin{array}{c} \text{H}\quad\text{O} \\ |\quad\ \ \| \\ \text{CH}_3-\text{C}-\text{C}-\text{OH} \\ | \\ \text{OH} \end{array}$

(b) $\begin{array}{c} \text{O} \\ \| \\ \text{CH}_2{=}\text{C}-\text{C}-\text{O}-\text{CH}_3 \\ | \\ \text{CH}_3 \end{array}$

(c) $\begin{array}{c} \text{H}\qquad\ \ \text{H} \\ \backslash\qquad\ / \\ \text{C}{=}\text{C}\qquad\qquad\quad \text{H}\quad\text{O} \\ /\qquad\ \ \backslash\qquad\quad |\quad\ \ \| \\ \text{H}-\text{C}\qquad\quad \text{C}-\text{CH}_2-\text{C}-\text{C}-\text{OH} \\ \|\qquad\quad /\qquad\qquad | \\ \text{C}-\text{C}\qquad\qquad \text{NH}_2 \\ /\qquad\ \ \backslash \\ \text{H}\qquad\ \ \text{H} \end{array}$

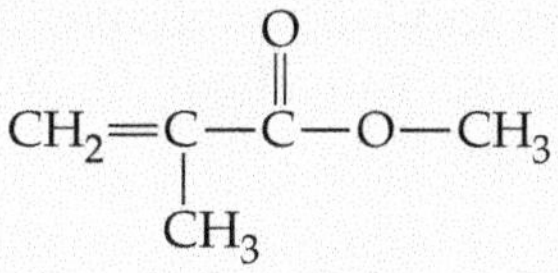

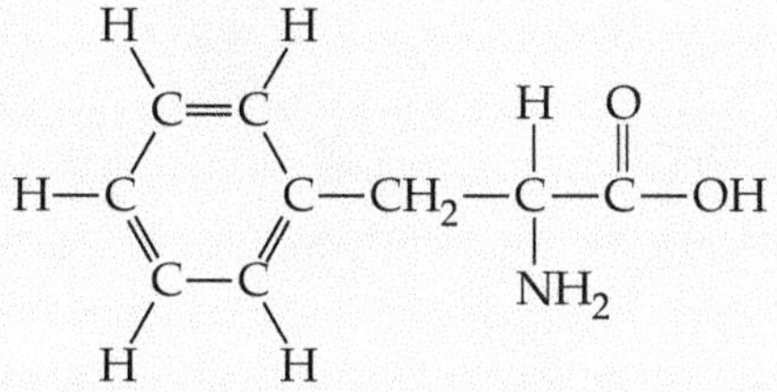

PROBLEM 12.2

Propose structures for molecules that fit the following descriptions:

(a) C_2H_4O containing an aldehyde functional group

(b) $C_3H_6O_2$ containing a carboxylic acid functional group

12.3 The Structure of Organic Molecules: Alkanes and Their Isomers

Alkane A hydrocarbon that has only single bonds.

Hydrocarbons that contain only single bonds belong to the family of organic molecules called **alkanes**. Imagine how one carbon and four hydrogens can combine, and you will realize there is only one possibility: methane, CH_4. Now imagine how two carbons and six hydrogens can combine—only ethane, CH_3CH_3, is possible. Likewise with the combination of three carbons with eight hydrogens—only propane, $CH_3CH_2CH_3$, is possible. The general rule for *all* hydrocarbons except methane is that each carbon *must* be bonded to at least one other carbon. The carbon atoms bond together to form the "backbone" of the compound, with the hydrogens on the periphery. The general formula for alkanes is C_nH_{2n+2}, where n is the number of carbons in the compound.

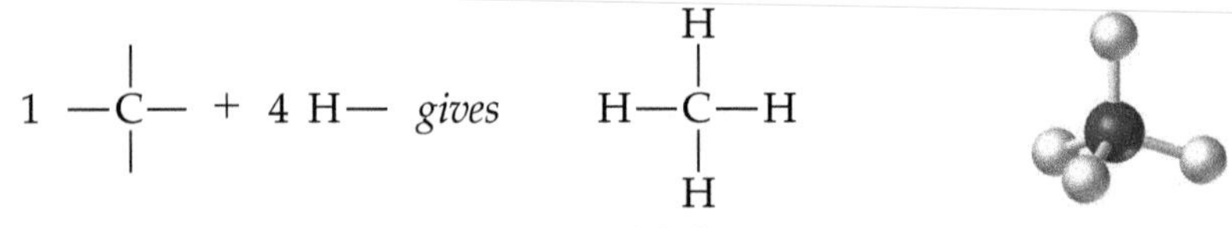

Methane

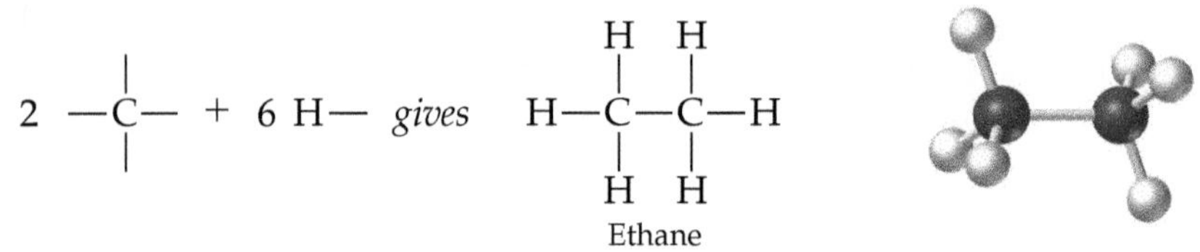

Ethane

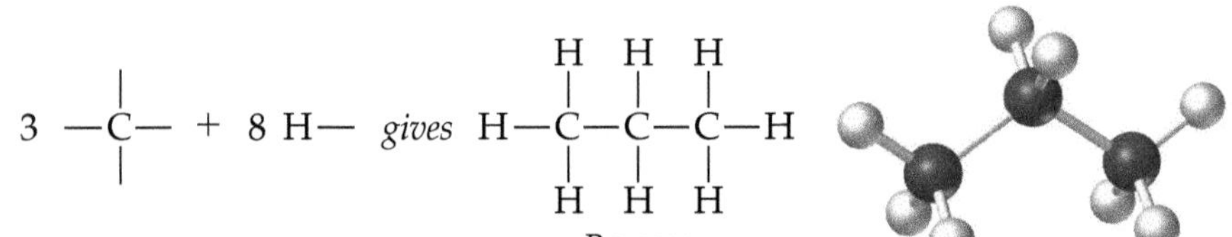

Propane

Isomers Compounds with the same molecular formula but different structures.

As larger numbers of carbons and hydrogens combine, the ability to form *isomers* arises. Compounds that have the same molecular formula but different structural formulas are called **isomers** of one another. For example, there are two ways in which molecules that have the formula C_4H_{10} can be formed: The four carbons can either be joined in a contiguous row or have a branched arrangement:

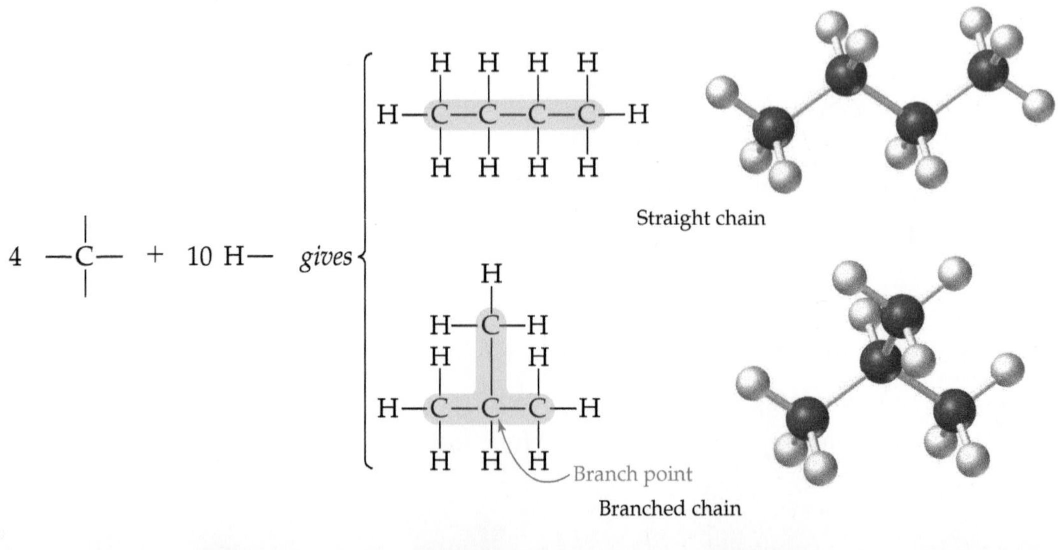

Straight chain

Branch point

Branched chain

The same is seen with the molecules that have the formula C_5H_{12}, for which three isomers are possible:

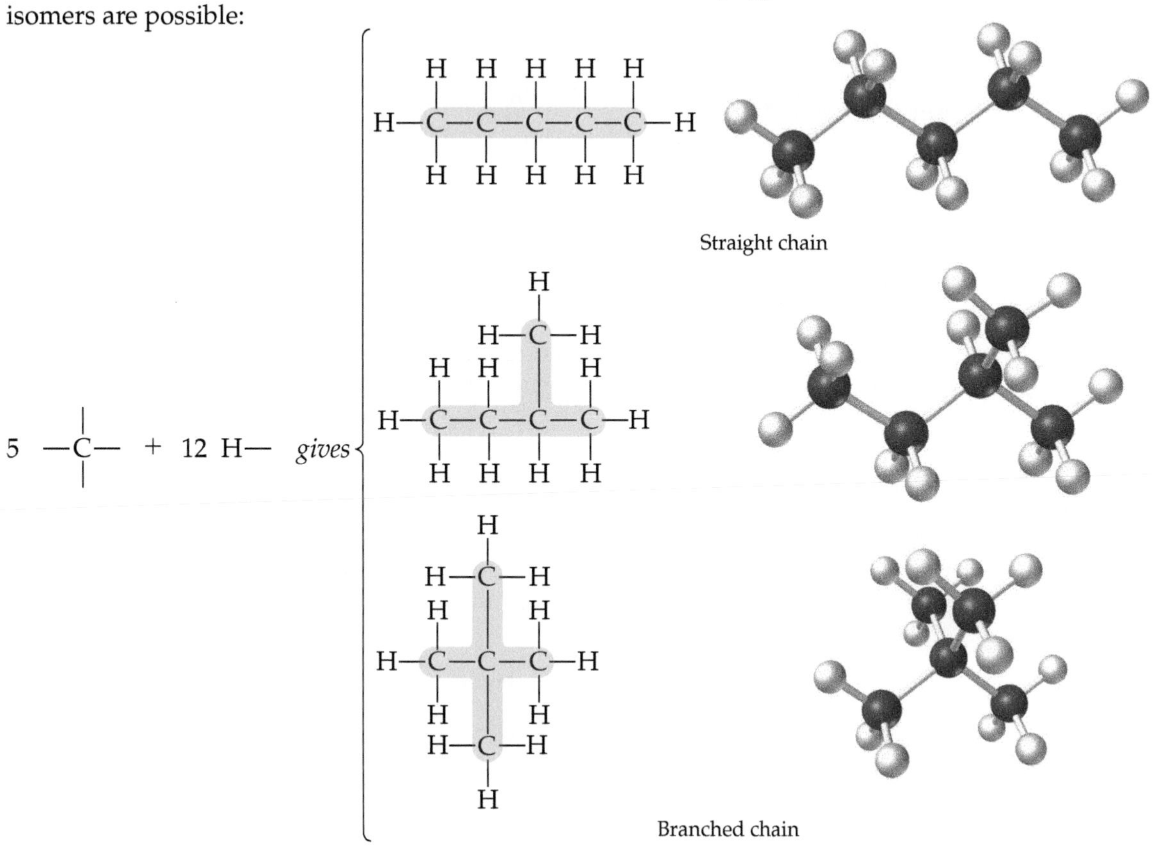

Straight chain

$$5 \ \ -\overset{|}{\underset{|}{C}}- \ \ + \ \ 12 \ H- \ \ gives$$

Branched chain

Compounds with all their carbons connected in a continuous chain are called **straight-chain alkanes**; those with a branching connection of carbons are called **branched-chain alkanes**. Note that in a straight-chain alkane, you can draw a line through all the carbon atoms without lifting your pencil from the paper. In a branched-chain alkane, however, you must either lift your pencil from the paper or retrace your steps to draw a line through all the carbons.

The two isomers of C_4H_{10} and the three isomers of C_5H_{12} shown above are **constitutional isomers**—compounds with the same molecular formula but with different connections among their constituent atoms. Needless to say, the number of possible alkane isomers grows rapidly as the number of carbon atoms increases.

Constitutional isomers of a given molecular formula are chemically completely different from one another. They have different structures, different physical properties such as melting and boiling points, and potentially different physiological properties. For example, ethyl alcohol and dimethyl ether both have the formula C_2H_6O, but ethyl alcohol is a liquid with a boiling point of 78.5 °C and dimethyl ether is a gas with a boiling point of −23 °C (Table 12.2). Clearly, molecular formulas by

Straight-chain alkane An alkane that has all its carbons connected in a row.

Branched-chain alkane An alkane that has a branching connection of carbons.

Constitutional isomers Compounds with the same molecular formula but different connections among their atoms.

TABLE 12.2   Some Properties of Ethyl Alcohol and Dimethyl Ether

NAME AND MOLECULAR FORMULA	STRUCTURE		BOILING POINT	MELTING POINT	PHYSIOLOGICAL ACTIVITY
Ethyl alcohol C_2H_6O			78.5 °C	− 117.3 °C	Central-nervous-system depressant
Dimethyl ether C_2H_6O			− 23 °C	− 138.5 °C	Nontoxic; anesthetic at high concentration

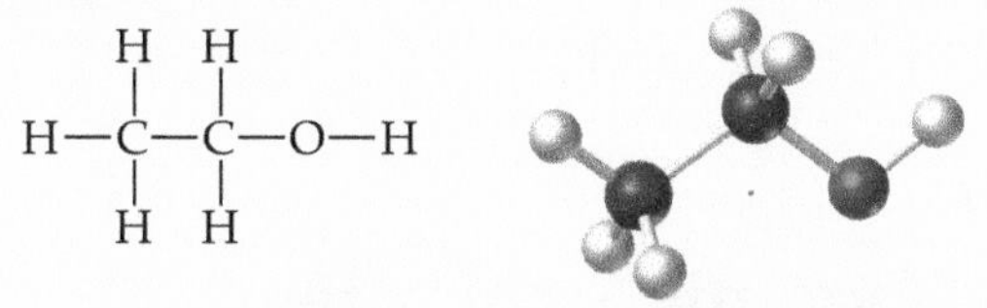

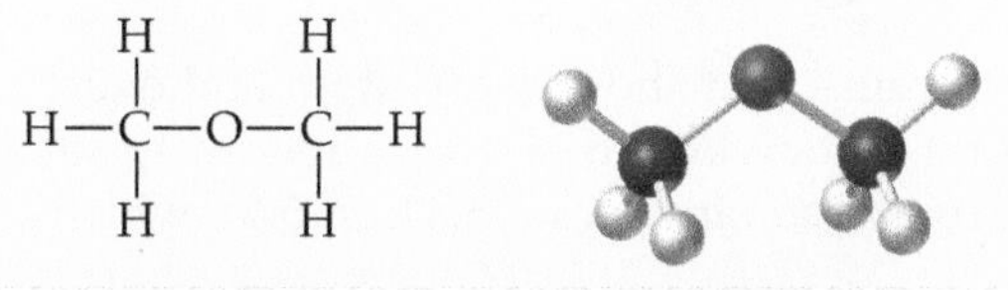

themselves are not very useful in organic chemistry; a knowledge of structure is also necessary.

> **WORKED EXAMPLE** **12.3** Molecular Structures: Drawing Isomers

Draw all isomers that have the formula C_6H_{14}.

ANALYSIS Knowing that all the carbons must be bonded together to form the molecule, find all possible arrangements of the 6 carbon atoms. Begin with the isomer that has all 6 carbons in a straight chain, then draw the isomer that has 5 carbons in a straight chain, using the remaining carbon to form a branch, then repeat for the isomer having 4 carbons in a straight chain and 2 carbons in branches. Once each carbon backbone is drawn, arrange the hydrogens around the carbons to complete the structure. (Remember that each carbon can only have *four* bonds.)

SOLUTION

The straight-chain isomer contains all 6 carbons bonded to form a chain with no branches. The branched isomers are drawn by starting with either a 5-carbon chain or a 4-carbon chain, and adding the extra carbons as branches in the middle of the chain. Hydrogens are added until each carbon has a full complement of 4 bonds.

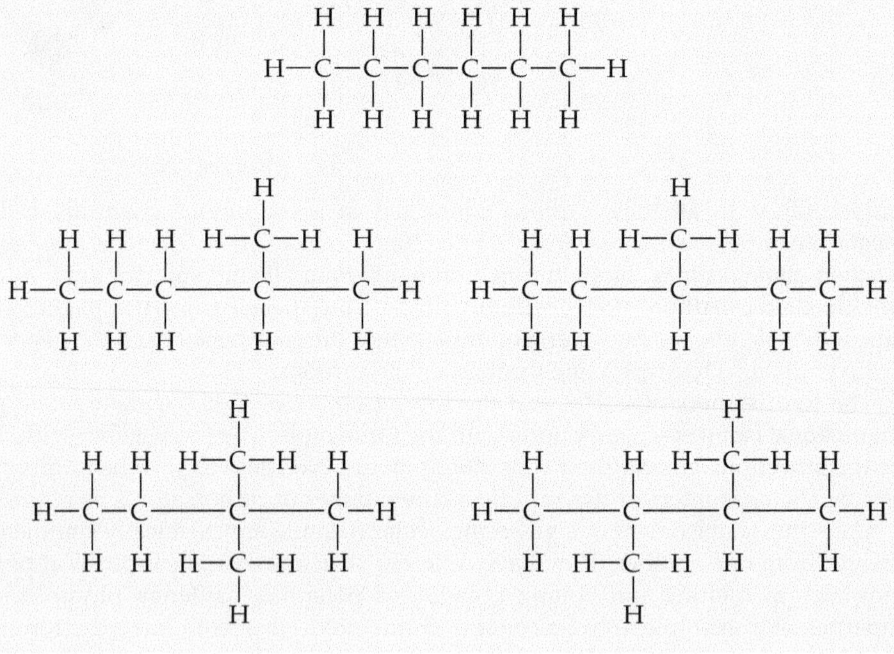

PROBLEM 12.3

Draw the straight-chain isomer with the formula C_7H_{16}.

PROBLEM 12.4

Draw any two of the seven branched-chain isomers with the formula C_7H_{16}.

12.4 Drawing Organic Structures

Condensed structure A shorthand way of drawing structures in which C—C and C—H bonds are understood rather than shown.

Drawing structural formulas that show every atom and every bond in a molecule is both time-consuming and awkward, even for relatively small molecules. Much easier is the use of **condensed structures** (Section 5.6), which are simpler but still show the essential information about which functional groups are present and how atoms are connected. (⬤, p. 118) In condensed structures, C—C and C—H single bonds are not shown; rather, they are "understood." If a carbon atom has 3 hydrogens bonded to it, we write CH_3; if the carbon has 2 hydrogens bonded to it, we write CH_2; and so on. For example, the 4-carbon, straight-chain alkane (butane) and its branched-chain isomer (2-methylpropane) can be written as the following condensed structures:

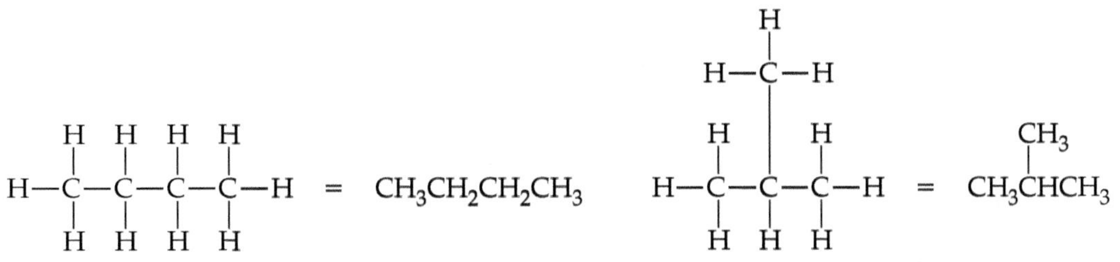

Butane — Structural formula — Condensed formula — 2-Methylpropane — Structural formula — Condensed formula

Note in these condensed structures for butane and 2-methylpropane that the horizontal bonds between carbons are not usually shown—the CH_3 and CH_2 units are simply placed next to one another—but that the vertical bond in 2-methyl-propane *is* shown for clarity.

Occasionally, as a further simplification, not all the CH_2 groups (called **methylenes**) are shown. Instead, CH_2 is shown once in parentheses, with a subscript to the right of the) indicating the number of methylene units strung together. For example, the 6-carbon straight-chain alkane (hexane) can be written as

Methylene Another name for a CH_2 unit.

$$CH_3CH_2CH_2CH_2CH_2CH_3 = CH_3(CH_2)_4CH_3$$

WORKED EXAMPLE **12.4** Molecular Structures: Writing Condensed Structures

Write condensed structures for the isomers from Worked Example 12.3.

ANALYSIS Eliminate all horizontal bonds, substituting reduced formula components (CH_3, CH_2, and so on) for each carbon in the compound. Show vertical bonds to branching carbons for clarity.

SOLUTION

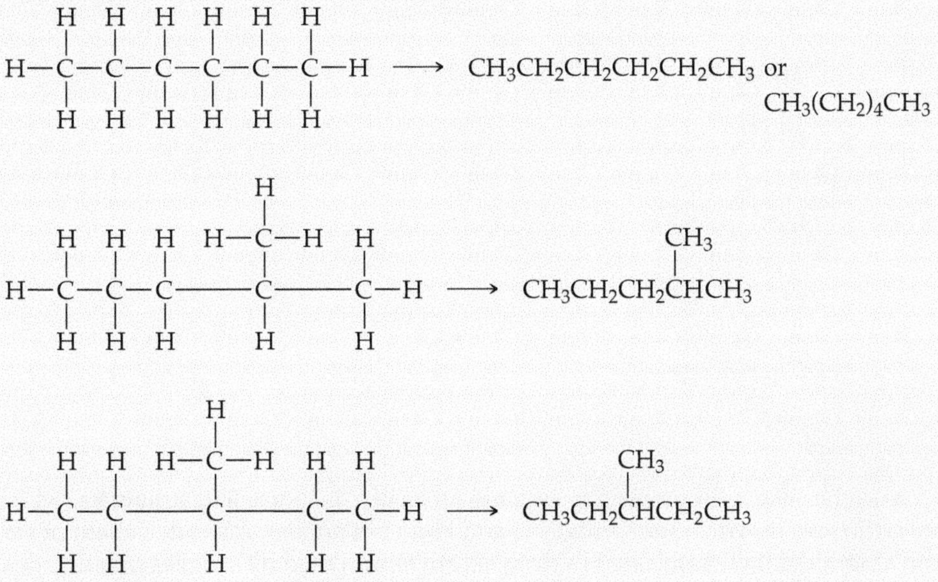

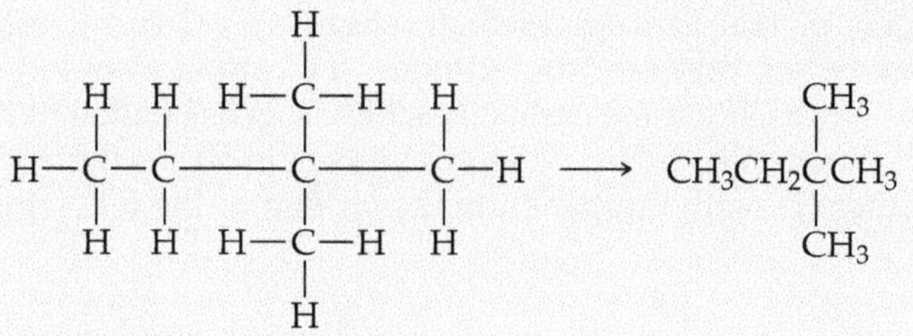

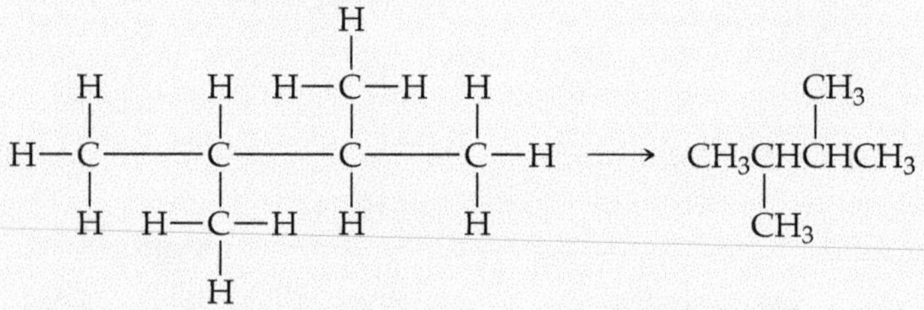

$$
\begin{array}{c}
\text{H} \\
| \\
\text{H} \quad \text{H} \quad \text{H}-\text{C}-\text{H} \quad \text{H} \\
| \quad\; | \qquad\quad | \qquad | \\
\text{H}-\text{C}-\text{C}\!\!-\!\!-\!\!-\!\!\text{C}\!\!-\!\!-\!\!-\!\!\text{C}-\text{H} \\
| \quad\; | \qquad\quad | \qquad | \\
\text{H} \quad \text{H} \quad \text{H}-\text{C}-\text{H} \quad \text{H} \\
| \\
\text{H}
\end{array}
\quad\longrightarrow\quad
\begin{array}{c}
\text{CH}_3 \\
| \\
\text{CH}_3\text{CH}_2\text{CCH}_3 \\
| \\
\text{CH}_3
\end{array}
$$

$$
\begin{array}{c}
\text{H} \\
| \\
\text{H} \qquad \text{H} \quad \text{H}-\text{C}-\text{H} \quad \text{H} \\
| \qquad\; | \qquad\quad | \qquad | \\
\text{H}-\text{C}\!\!-\!\!-\!\!-\!\!\text{C}\!\!-\!\!-\!\!-\!\!\text{C}\!\!-\!\!-\!\!\text{C}-\text{H} \\
| \qquad\; | \qquad\quad | \qquad | \\
\text{H} \quad \text{H}-\text{C}-\text{H} \quad \text{H} \qquad \text{H} \\
| \\
\text{H}
\end{array}
\quad\longrightarrow\quad
\begin{array}{c}
\text{CH}_3 \\
| \\
\text{CH}_3\text{CHCHCH}_3 \\
| \\
\text{CH}_3
\end{array}
$$

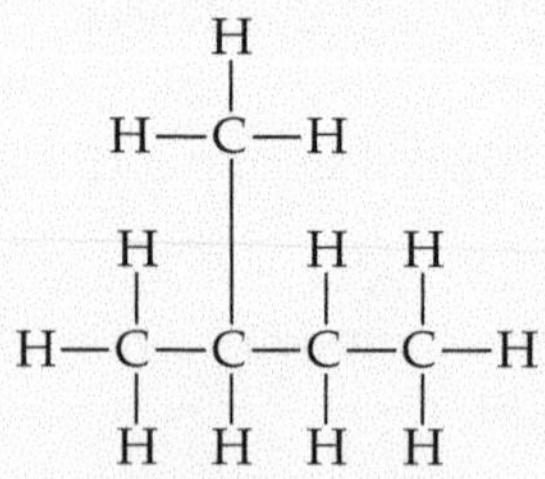

PROBLEM 12.5

Draw the following three isomers of C_5H_{12} as condensed structures:

$$
\textbf{(a)} \quad
\begin{array}{c}
\text{H} \quad \text{H} \quad \text{H} \quad \text{H} \quad \text{H} \\
| \qquad | \qquad | \qquad | \qquad | \\
\text{H}-\text{C}-\text{C}-\text{C}-\text{C}-\text{C}-\text{H} \\
| \qquad | \qquad | \qquad | \qquad | \\
\text{H} \quad \text{H} \quad \text{H} \quad \text{H} \quad \text{H}
\end{array}
$$
Pentane

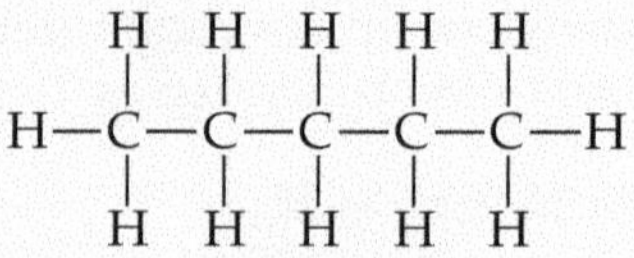

$$
\textbf{(b)} \quad
\begin{array}{c}
\text{H} \\
| \\
\text{H}-\text{C}-\text{H} \\
| \\
\text{H} \qquad\quad \text{H} \quad \text{H} \\
| \qquad\quad | \qquad | \\
\text{H}-\text{C}-\text{C}-\text{C}-\text{C}-\text{H} \\
| \qquad | \qquad | \qquad | \\
\text{H} \quad \text{H} \quad \text{H} \quad \text{H}
\end{array}
$$
2-Methylbutane

$$
\textbf{(c)} \quad
\begin{array}{c}
\text{H} \\
| \\
\text{H}-\text{C}-\text{H} \\
| \\
\text{H} \qquad\quad \text{H} \\
| \qquad\quad | \\
\text{H}-\text{C}-\text{C}-\text{C}-\text{H} \\
| \qquad | \qquad | \\
\text{H} \qquad \text{H} \\
| \\
\text{H}-\text{C}-\text{H} \\
| \\
\text{H}
\end{array}
$$
2,2-Dimethylpropane

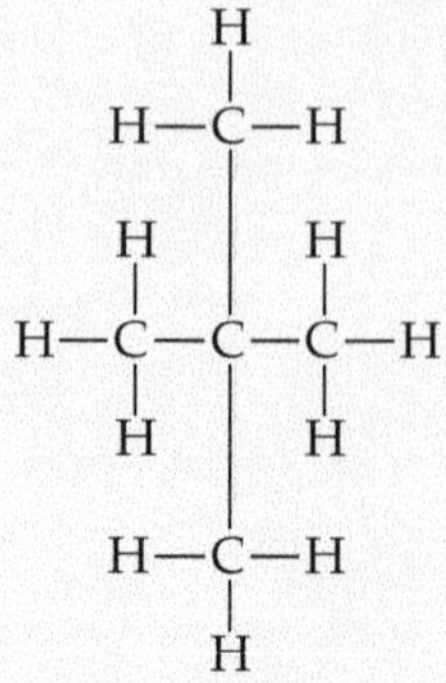

Line structure A shorthand way of drawing structures in which carbon and hydrogen atoms are not shown. Instead, a carbon atom is understood to be wherever a line begins or ends and at every intersection of two lines, and hydrogens are understood to be wherever they are needed to have each carbon form four bonds.

Another way of representing organic molecules is to use **line structures**, which are structures in which the symbols C and H do not appear. Instead, a chain of carbon atoms and their associated hydrogens are represented by a zigzag arrangement of short lines, with any branches off the main chain represented by additional lines. The line structure for 2-methylbutane, for instance, is

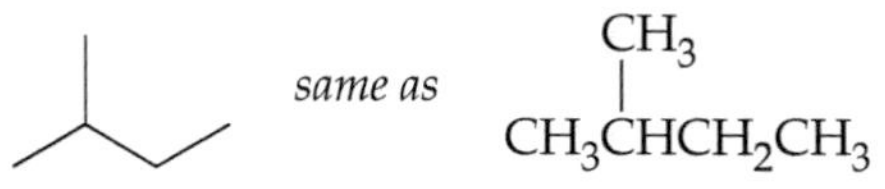

same as
CH3
CH3CHCH2CH3

Line structures are a simple and quick way to represent organic molecules without the clutter arising from showing all carbons and hydrogens present. Chemists, biologists, pharmacists, doctors, and nurses all use line structures to conveniently convey to one another very complex organic structures. Another advantage is that a line structure gives a more realistic depiction of the angles seen in a carbon chain.

Drawing a molecule in this way is simple, provided one follows these guidelines:

1. Each carbon-carbon bond is represented by a line.
2. Anywhere a line ends or begins, as well as any vertex where two lines meet, represents a carbon atom.
3. Any atom other than another carbon or a hydrogen attached to a carbon must be shown.
4. Since a neutral carbon atom forms four bonds, all bonds not shown for any carbon are understood to be the number of carbon-hydrogen bonds needed to have the carbon form four bonds.

CH3
CH2
CH3
CH3
CH
CH3
CH2
CH3
CH
CH3

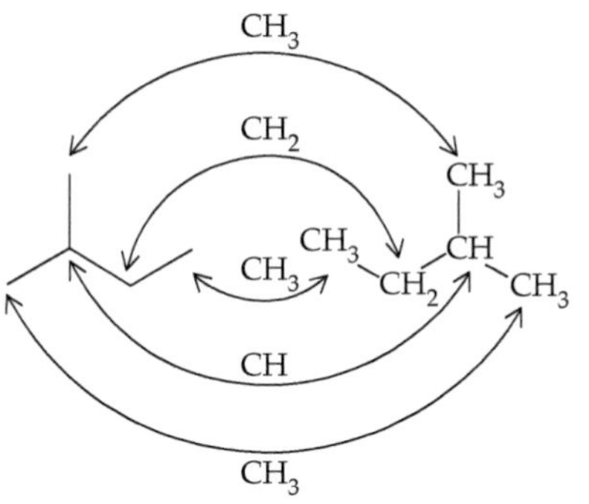

Converting line structures to structural formulas or to condensed structures is simply a matter of correctly interpreting each line ending and each intersection in a line structure. For example, the common pain reliever ibuprofen has the condensed and line structures

CH3
HC=CH
O
CH3CHCH2—C
C—CH—C—OH
CH—CH
CH3
OH
O

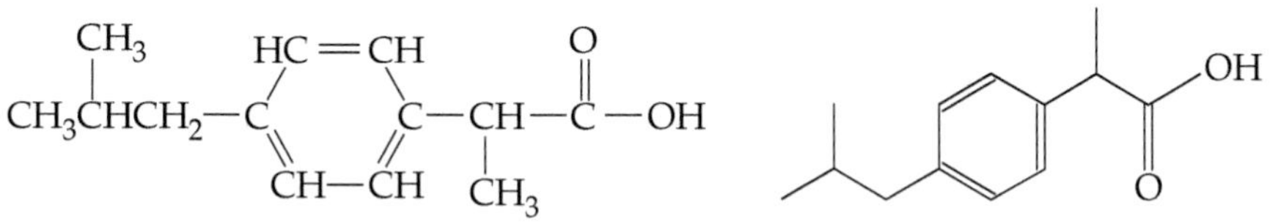

Finally, it is important to note that chemists and biochemists often use a mixture of structural formulas, condensed structures, and line structures to represent the molecules they study. As you progress through this textbook, you will see many complicated molecules represented in this way, so it is a good idea to get used to thinking interchangably in all three formats.

> **WORKED EXAMPLE** | **12.5** Molecular Structures: Converting Condensed Structures to Line Structures

Convert the following condensed structures to line structures:

$$
\text{(a)} \quad \underset{\underset{\textstyle CH_3}{|}}{\overset{\overset{\textstyle CH_3}{|}}{CH_3CH_2CHCHCH_2CH_3}}
\qquad
\text{(b)} \quad \underset{\underset{\textstyle CH_3}{|}\;\underset{\textstyle CH_3}{|}}{\overset{\overset{\textstyle OH}{|}\;\overset{\textstyle Cl}{|}}{CH_3CHCH-C\;CH_2CH_3}}
$$

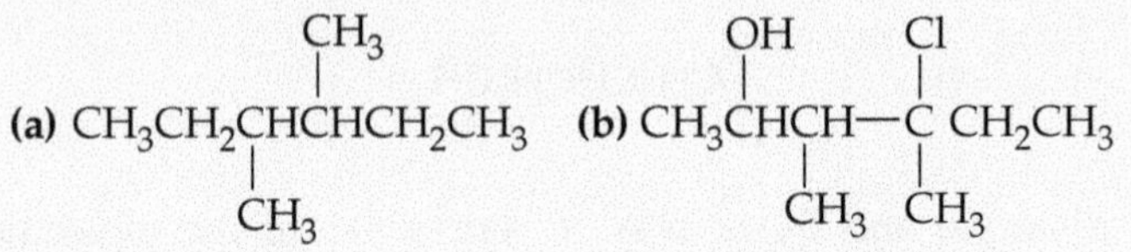

ANALYSIS Find the longest continuous chain of carbon atoms in the condensed structure. Begin the line structure by drawing a zigzag line in which the number of vertices plus line ends equals the number of carbon atoms in the chain. Show branches coming off the main chain by drawing vertical lines at the vertices as needed. Show all atoms that are not carbons or are not hydrogens attached to carbons.

SOLUTION

(a) Begin by drawing a zigzag line in which the total number of ends + vertices equals the number of carbons in the longest chain (here 6, with the carbons numbered for clarity):

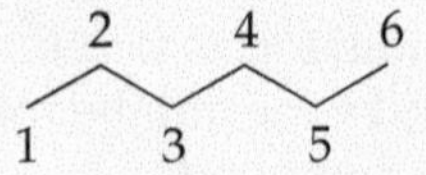

Looking at the condensed structure, you see CH_3 groups on carbons 3 and 4; these two methyl groups are represented by lines coming off those carbons in the line structure:

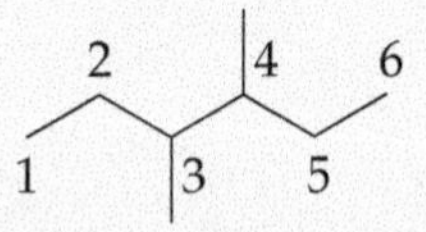

This is the complete line structure. Notice that the hydrogens are not shown, but understood. For example, carbon 4 has three bonds shown: one to carbon 3, one to carbon 5, and one to the branch methyl group; the fourth bond this carbon must have is understood to be to a hydrogen.

(b) Proceed as in (a), drawing a zigzag line for the longest chain of carbon atoms, which again contains 6 carbons. Next draw a line coming off each carbon bonded to a CH_3 group (carbons 3 and 4). Both the OH and the Cl groups must be shown to give the final structure:

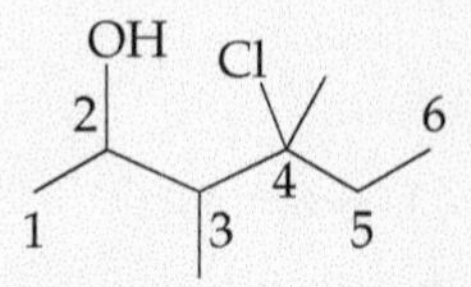

Note from this line structure than it does not matter in such a two-dimensional drawing what direction you show for a group that branches off the main chain, as long as it is attached to the correct carbon. This is true for condensed structures as well. Quite often the direction that a group is shown coming off a main chain of carbon atoms is chosen simply for aesthetic reasons.

WORKED EXAMPLE 12.6 Molecular Structures: Converting Line Structures to Condensed Structures

Convert the following line structures to condensed structures:

(a)

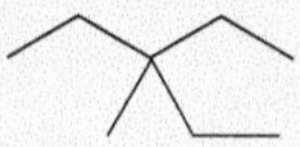

(b)

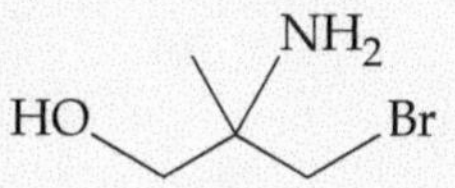

ANALYSIS Convert all vertices and line ends to carbons. Write in any noncarbon atoms and any hydrogens bonded to a noncarbon atom. Add hydrogens as needed so that each carbon has four groups attached. Remove lines connecting carbons except for branches.

SOLUTION

(a) Anywhere a line ends and anywhere two lines meet, write a C:

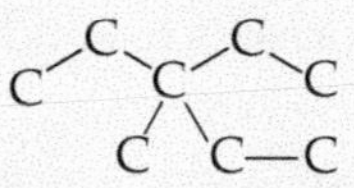

Because there are no atoms other than carbons and hydrogens in this molecule, the next step is to add hydrogens as needed to have four bonds for each carbon:

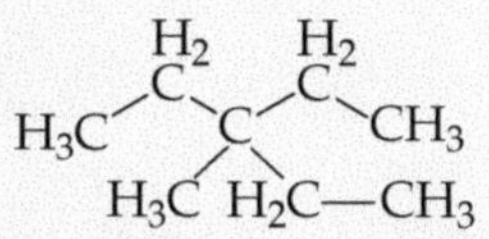

Finally, eliminate all lines except for branches to get the condensed structure:

$$CH_3CH_2 \overset{\overset{\displaystyle CH_3}{|}}{\underset{\underset{\displaystyle CH_2CH_3}{|}}{C}} CH_2CH_3$$

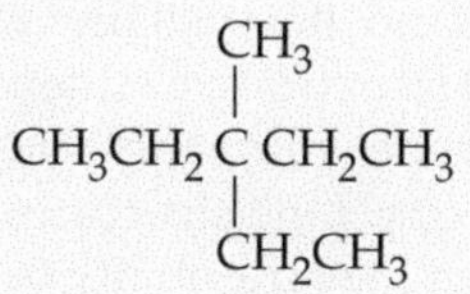

(b) Begin the condensed structure with a drawing showing a carbon at each line end and at each intersection of two lines:

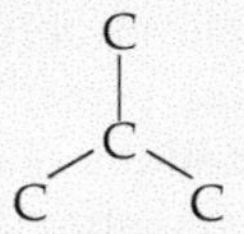

Next write in all the noncarbon atoms and the hydrogen bonded to the oxygen. Then add hydrogens so that each carbon forms four bonds:

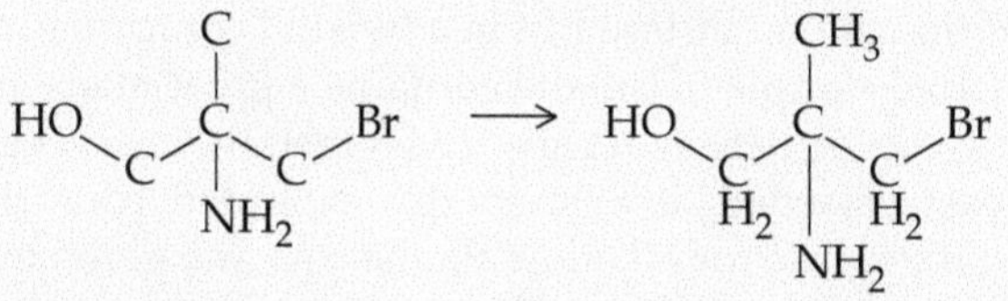

Eliminate all lines except for branches for the completed condensed structure:

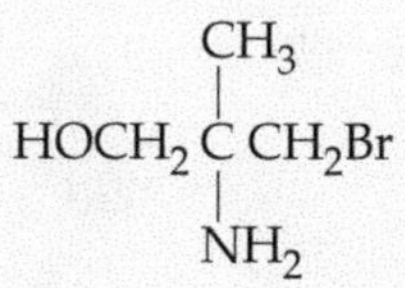

$$HOCH_2 \overset{\overset{\displaystyle CH_3}{|}}{\underset{\underset{\displaystyle NH_2}{|}}{C}} CH_2Br$$

PROBLEM 12.6

Convert the following condensed structures to line structures:

(a)
$$CH_3CH_2\overset{\overset{\displaystyle CH_2CH_3}{|}}{\underset{\underset{\displaystyle CH_2OH}{|}}{C}}—CH_2CH_2CH_3$$

(b)
$$CH_3\overset{\overset{\displaystyle CH_2CH_3}{|}}{\underset{\underset{\displaystyle CH_3CHCH_2CH_3}{|}}{CH}}CH\;CH_2\overset{\overset{\displaystyle CH_3}{|}}{CH}CH_3$$

(c)
$$CH_3\overset{\overset{\displaystyle Br}{|}}{\underset{\underset{\underset{\displaystyle CHCH_2CH_3}{|}}{\displaystyle CH_3}}{C}}—CHCH_2CH_2\overset{\overset{\displaystyle Cl}{|}}{CH}CH_2CH_3$$

PROBLEM 12.7

Convert the following line structures to condensed structures:

(a)

(b)

12.5 The Shapes of Organic Molecules

Every carbon atom in an alkane has its four bonds pointing toward the four corners of a tetrahedron, but chemists do not usually worry about three-dimensional shapes when writing condensed structures. Condensed structures do not imply any particular three-dimensional shape; they only indicate the connections between atoms without specifying geometry. Line structures do try to give some feeling for the shape of a molecule, but even here the ability to show three-dimensional shape is limited unless dashed and wedged lines are used for the bonds (page 125).

Butane, for example, has no one single shape because *rotation* takes place around carbon–carbon single bonds. The two parts of a molecule joined by a carbon–carbon single bond in a noncyclic structure are free to spin around the bond, giving rise to an infinite number of possible three-dimensional geometries, or **conformations**. The various conformations of a molecule such as butane are called **conformers** of one another. Conformers differ from one another as a result of rotation around carbon–carbon single bonds. Although the conformers of a given molecule have different three-dimensional shapes and different energies, the conformers cannot be separated from one another. A given butane molecule might be in its fully extended conformation at one instant but in a twisted conformation an instant later (Figure 12.2). An actual sample of butane contains a great many molecules that are constantly changing conformation. At any given instant, however, most of the molecules have the least crowded, lowest-energy extended conformation shown in Figure 12.2a. The same is true for all other alkanes: At any given instant, most molecules are in the least crowded conformation.

Conformation The specific three-dimensional arrangement of atoms in a molecule.

Conformer Molecular structures having identical connections between atoms; that is, they represent identical compounds.

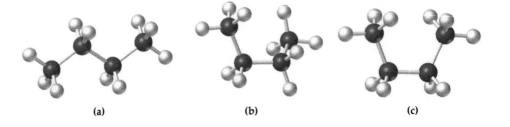

▶ **FIGURE 12.2 Some conformations of butane (there are many others as well).** The least crowded, extended conformation in (a) is the lowest-energy one.

(a)   (b)   (c)

As long as any two structures have identical connections between atoms, they are conformers of each other and represent the same compound, no matter how the structures are drawn. Sometimes you have to mentally rotate structures to see whether they are conformers or different molecules. To see that the following two structures represent conformers of the same compound rather than two isomers, picture one of them flipped right to left so that the red CH_3 groups are on the same side:

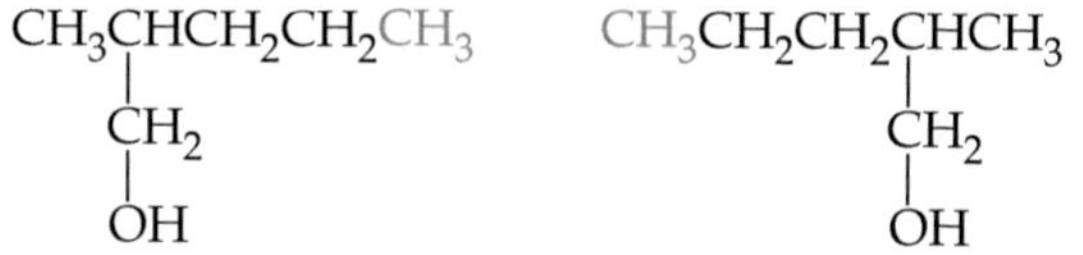

$$CH_3CHCH_2CH_2CH_3 \qquad CH_3CH_2CH_2CHCH_3$$
$$| \qquad\qquad\qquad\qquad |$$
$$CH_2 \qquad\qquad\qquad\qquad CH_2$$
$$| \qquad\qquad\qquad\qquad |$$
$$OH \qquad\qquad\qquad\qquad OH$$

Another way to determine whether two structures are conformers is to name each one using the IUPAC nomenclature rules (Section 12.6). If two structures have the same name, they are conformers of the same compound.

WORKED EXAMPLE **12.7** Molecular Structures: Identifying Conformers

The following structures all have the formula C_7H_{16}. Which of them represent the same molecule?

$$\qquad CH_3 \qquad\qquad\qquad\qquad\qquad\qquad CH_3$$
$$\qquad | \qquad\qquad\qquad\qquad\qquad\qquad |$$
(a) 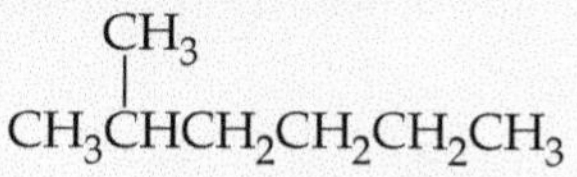 $CH_3CHCH_2CH_2CH_2CH_3$ (b) 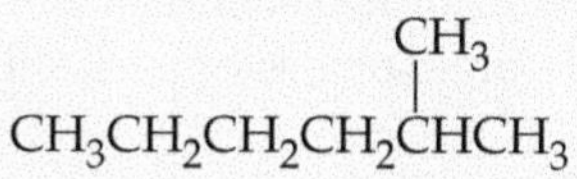 $CH_3CH_2CH_2CH_2CHCH_3$

$$\qquad CH_3$$
$$\qquad |$$
(c) 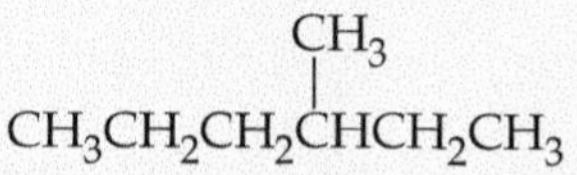 $CH_3CH_2CH_2CHCH_2CH_3$

ANALYSIS Pay attention to the *connections* between atoms. Do not get confused by the apparent differences caused by writing a structure right to left versus left to right. Begin by identifying the longest chain of carbon atoms in the molecule.

SOLUTION
Molecule (a) has a straight chain of 6 carbons with a $-CH_3$ branch on the second carbon from the end. Molecule (b) also has a straight chain of 6 carbons with a $-CH_3$ branch on the second carbon from the end and is therefore identical to (a). That is, (a) and (b) are conformers of the same molecule. The only difference between (a) and (b) is that one is written "forward" and one is written "backward." Molecule (c), by contrast, has a straight chain of 6 carbons with a $-CH_3$ branch on the *third* carbon from the end and is therefore an isomer of (a) and (b).

WORKED EXAMPLE **12.8** Molecular Structures: Identifying Conformers and Isomers

Are the following pairs of compounds the same (conformers), isomers, or unrelated?

$$\qquad\qquad CH_3 \qquad\quad CH_3$$
$$\qquad\qquad | \qquad\qquad |$$
(a) 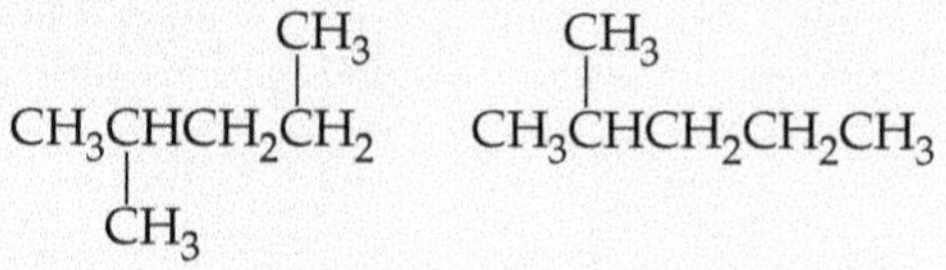 $CH_3CHCH_2CH_2 \qquad CH_3CHCH_2CH_2CH_3$
$$\qquad |$$
$$\qquad CH_3$$

$$\qquad\qquad\qquad\qquad\qquad\qquad CH_2CH_3$$
$$\qquad\qquad\qquad\qquad\qquad\qquad |$$
(b) 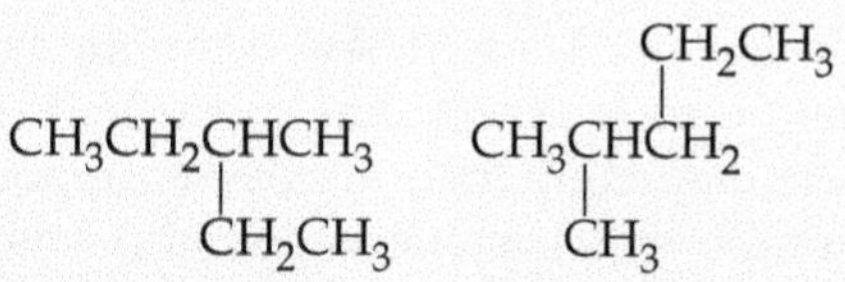 $CH_3CH_2CHCH_3 \qquad CH_3CHCH_2$
$$\qquad\qquad | \qquad\qquad\qquad |$$
$$\qquad\qquad CH_2CH_3 \qquad\qquad CH_3$$

$$\qquad\qquad\qquad\qquad\qquad\qquad\qquad O$$
$$\qquad\qquad\qquad\qquad\qquad\qquad\qquad ||$$
(c) 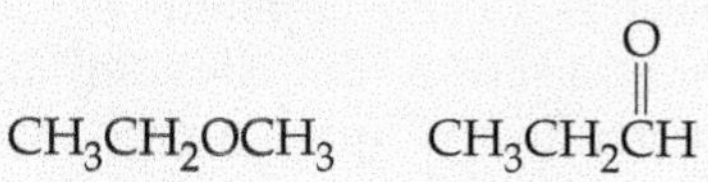 $CH_3CH_2OCH_3 \qquad CH_3CH_2CH$

ANALYSIS First compare molecular formulas to see if the compounds are related, and then look at the structures to see if they are the same compound or isomers. Find the longest continuous carbon chain in each, and then compare the locations of the substituents connected to the longest chain.

SOLUTION

(a) Both compounds have the same molecular formula (C_6H_{14}) so they are related. Since the —CH_3 group is on the second carbon from the end of a 5-carbon chain in both cases, these structures represent the same compound and are conformers of each other.

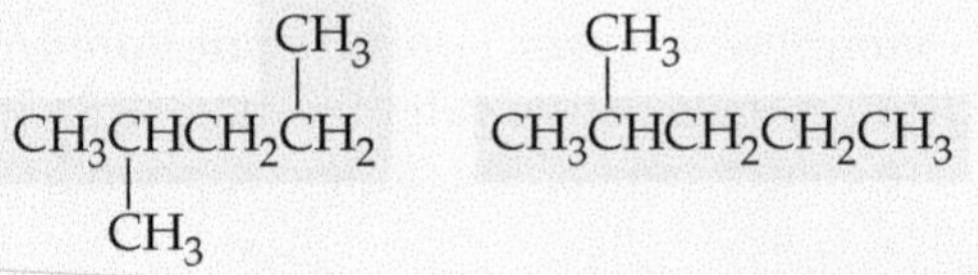

$$CH_3CHCH_2CH_2 \quad CH_3CHCH_2CH_2CH_3$$

(b) Both compounds have the same molecular formula (C_6H_{14}) and the longest chain in each is 5 carbon atoms. A comparison shows, however, that the —CH_3 group is on the middle carbon atom in one structure and on the second carbon atom in the other. These compounds are isomers of each other.

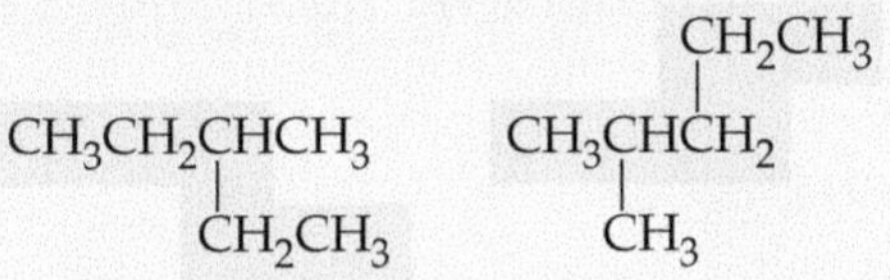

$$CH_3CH_2CHCH_3 \quad CH_3CHCH_2$$

(c) These compounds have different formulas (C_3H_8O and C_3H_6O), so they are unrelated; they are neither conformers nor isomers of each other.

PROBLEM 12.8

Which of the following structures are conformers?

(a) 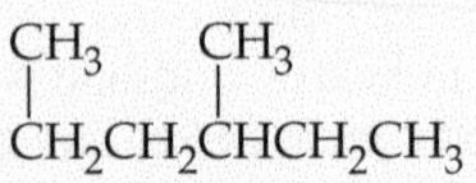 $CH_2CH_2CHCH_2CH_3$

(b) 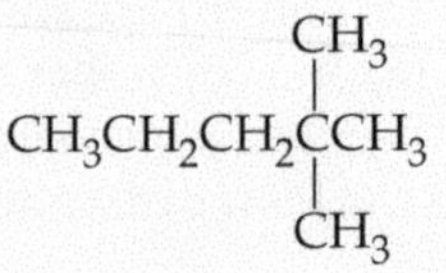 $CH_3CH_2CH_2CCH_3$

(c) 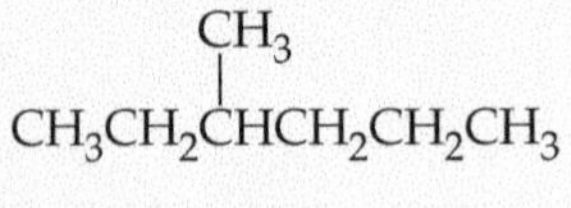 $CH_3CH_2CHCH_2CH_2CH_3$

PROBLEM 12.9

There are 18 isomers with the formula C_8H_{18}. Draw condensed structures for as many as you can and then convert those condensed structures to line structures.

12.6 Naming Alkanes

When relatively few pure organic chemicals were known, new compounds were named at the whim of their discoverer. Thus, urea is a crystalline substance first isolated from urine, and the barbiturates were named by their discoverer in honor of his friend Barbara. As more and more compounds became known, however, the need for a systematic method of naming compounds became apparent.

The system of naming (*nomenclature*) now used is one devised by the International Union of Pure and Applied Chemistry, IUPAC (pronounced **eye**-you-pack). In the IUPAC system for organic compounds, a chemical name has three

APPLICATION ▶ Displaying Molecular Shapes

Molecular shapes are critical to the proper functioning of biological molecules. The tiniest difference in shape can cause two compounds to behave differently or to have different physiological effects in the body. It is therefore critical that chemists be able both to determine molecular shapes with great precision and to visualize these shapes in useful ways.

Three-dimensional shapes of molecules can be determined by *X-ray crystallography*, a technique that allows us to "see" molecules in a crystal using X-ray waves rather than light waves. The molecular "picture" obtained by X-ray crystallography looks at first like a series of regularly spaced dark spots against a lighter background. After computerized manipulation of the data, however, recognizable molecules can be drawn. Relatively small molecules like morphine are usually displayed in either a ball-and-stick format (a), which emphasizes the connections among atoms, or in a space-filling format (b), which emphasizes the overall shape. Chemists find this useful in designing new organic molecules that have specific biological properties that make the molecules useful as therapeutic agents.

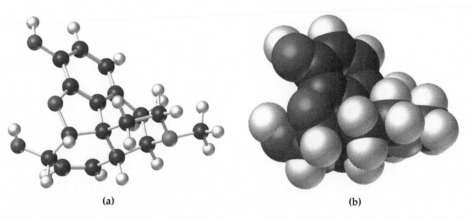

(a) (b)

▲ This computer-generated model of morphine is displayed in both (a) ball-and-stick format and (b) space-filling format.

Enormous biological molecules like enzymes and other proteins are best displayed on computer terminals where their structures can be enlarged, rotated, and otherwise manipulated for the best view. An immunoglobulin molecule, for instance, is so large that little detail can be seen in ball-and-stick or space-filling views. Nevertheless, a cleft inside the molecule is visible if the model is rotated in just the right way.

See Additional Problem 12.64 at the end of the chapter.

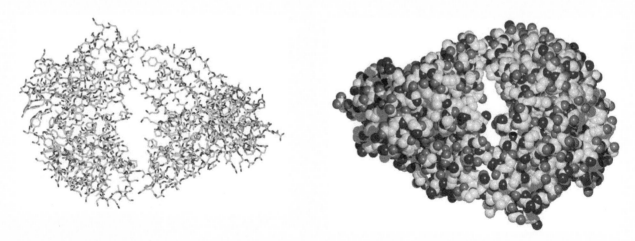

▲ Computer-generated models of an immunoglobulin, one of the antibodies in blood that protect us from harmful invaders such as bacteria and viruses.

Substituent An atom or group of atoms attached to a parent compound.

parts: *prefix*, *parent*, and *suffix*. The prefix specifies the location of functional groups and other **substituents** in the molecule; the parent tells how many carbon atoms are present in the longest continuous chain; and the suffix identifies what family the molecule belongs to:

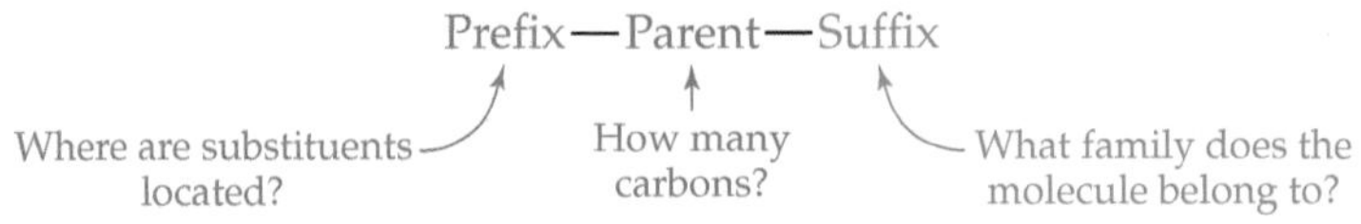

Prefix—Parent—Suffix

Where are substituents located?   How many carbons?   What family does the molecule belong to?

Straight-chain alkanes are named by counting the number of carbon atoms and adding the family suffix *-ane*. With the exception of the first four compounds—*meth*ane, *eth*ane, *prop*ane, and *but*ane—whose parent names have historical origins, the alkanes are named from Greek numbers according to the number of carbons present (Table 12.3). Thus, *pent*ane is the 5-carbon alkane, *hex*ane is the 6-carbon alkane, and so on. The first ten alkane names are so common that they should be memorized.

TABLE 12.3   Names of Straight-Chain Alkanes

NUMBER OF CARBONS	STRUCTURE	NAME
1	CH_4	*Meth*ane
2	CH_3CH_3	*Eth*ane
3	$CH_3CH_2CH_3$	*Prop*ane
4	$CH_3CH_2CH_2CH_3$	*But*ane
5	$CH_3CH_2CH_2CH_2CH_3$	*Pent*ane
6	$CH_3CH_2CH_2CH_2CH_2CH_3$	*Hex*ane
7	$CH_3CH_2CH_2CH_2CH_2CH_2CH_3$	*Hept*ane
8	$CH_3CH_2CH_2CH_2CH_2CH_2CH_2CH_3$	*Oct*ane
9	$CH_3CH_2CH_2CH_2CH_2CH_2CH_2CH_2CH_3$	*Non*ane
10	$CH_3CH_2CH_2CH_2CH_2CH_2CH_2CH_2CH_2CH_3$	*Dec*ane

Alkyl group The part of an alkane that remains when a hydrogen atom is removed.

Methyl group The $-CH_3$ alkyl group.

Ethyl group The $-CH_2CH_3$ alkyl group.

Substituents such as $-CH_3$ and $-CH_2CH_3$ that branch off the main chain are called **alkyl groups**. An alkyl group can be thought of as the part of an alkane that remains when 1 hydrogen atom is removed to create an available bonding site. For example, removal of a hydrogen from methane gives the **methyl group,** $-CH_3$, and removal of a hydrogen from ethane gives the **ethyl group,** $-CH_2CH_3$. Notice that these alkyl groups are named simply by replacing the *-ane* ending of the parent alkane with an *-yl* ending:

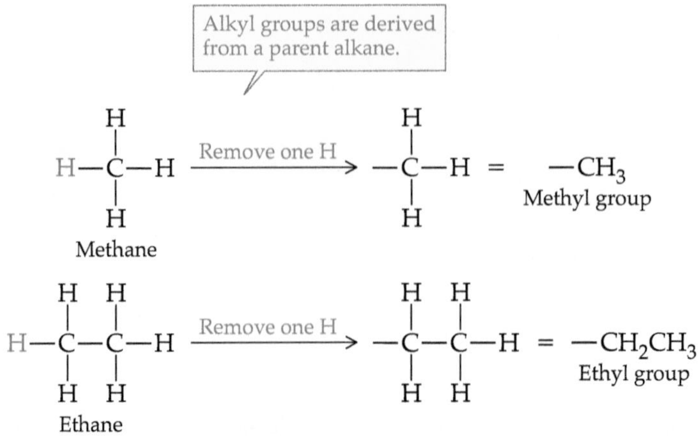

Both methane and ethane have only one "kind" of hydrogen. It does not matter which of the 4 methane hydrogens is removed, so there is only one possible methyl group. Similarly, it does not matter which of the 6 equivalent ethane hydrogens is removed, so only one ethyl group is possible.

The situation is more complex for larger alkanes, which contain more than one kind of hydrogen. Propane, for example, has two different kinds of hydrogens. Removal of any one of the 6 hydrogens attached to an end carbon yields a straight-chain alkyl group called **propyl**, whereas removal of either one of the 2 hydrogens attached to the central carbon yields a branched-chain alkyl group called **isopropyl**:

Propyl group The straight-chain alkyl group $—CH_2CH_2CH_3$.

Isopropyl group The branched-chain alkyl group $—CH(CH_3)_2$.

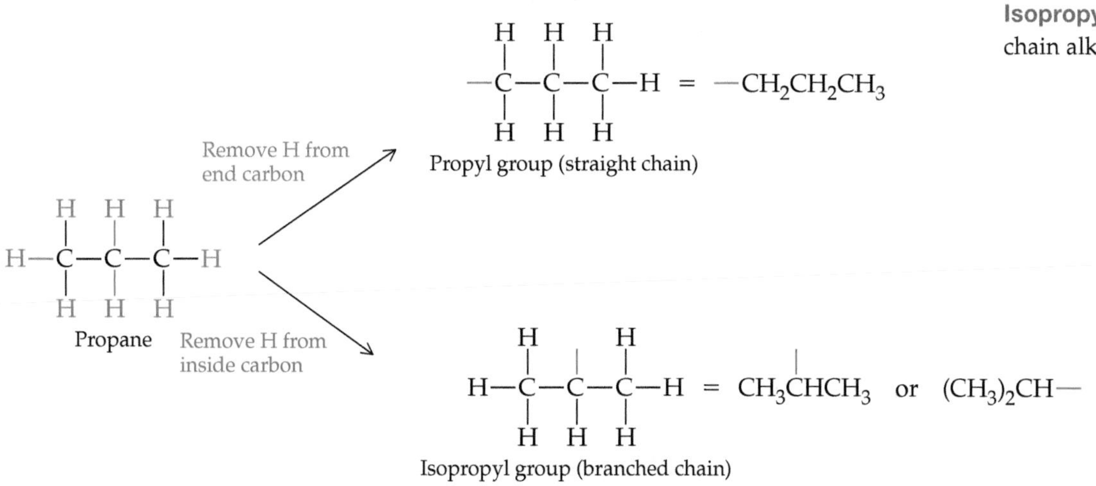

It is important to realize that alkyl groups are not compounds but rather are simply partial structures that help us name compounds. The names of some common alkyl groups are listed in Table 12.4; you will want to memorize them.

TABLE 12.4 Some Common Alkyl Groups*

$CH_3—$ Methyl	$CH_3CH_2—$ Ethyl	$CH_3CH_2CH_2—$ *n*-Propyl	CH_3 $CH_3CH—$ Isopropyl
$CH_3CH_2CH_2CH_2—$ *n*-Butyl	$CH_3CHCH_2CH_3$ *sec*-Butyl	CH_3 $CH_3CHCH_2—$ Isobutyl	CH_3CCH_3 CH_3 *tert*-Butyl

**The red bond shows the connection to the rest of the molecule.*

Notice that four butyl (four-carbon) groups are listed in Table 12.4: butyl, *sec*-butyl, isobutyl, and *tert*-butyl. The prefix *sec-* stands for *secondary*, and the prefix *tert-* stands for *tertiary*, referring to the number of other carbon atoms attached to the branch point. There are four possible substitution patterns, called *primary, secondary, tertiary,* and *quaternary*. A **primary (1°) carbon atom** has 1 other carbon attached to it (typically indicated as an —R group in the molecular structure), a **secondary (2°) carbon atom** has 2 other carbons attached, a **tertiary (3°) carbon atom** has 3 other carbons attached, and a **quaternary (4°) carbon atom** has 4 other carbons attached:

Primary (1°) carbon atom A carbon atom with 1 other carbon attached to it.

Secondary (2°) carbon atom A carbon atom with 2 other carbons attached to it.

Tertiary (3°) carbon atom A carbon atom with 3 other carbons attached to it.

Quaternary (4°) carbon atom A carbon atom with 4 other carbons attached to it.

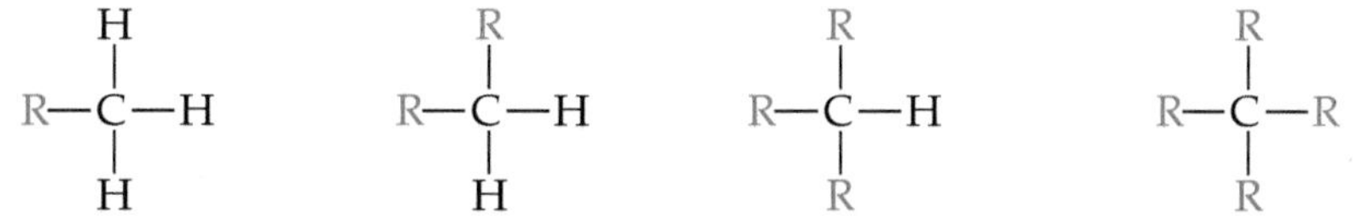

Primary carbon (1°) has one other carbon attached. *Secondary* carbon (2°) has two other carbons attached. *Tertiary* carbon (3°) has three other carbons attached. *Quaternary* carbon (4°) has four other carbons attached.

The symbol **R** *is used here and in later chapters as a general abbreviation for any organic substituent.* You should think of it as representing the **R**est of the molecule, which we are not bothering to specify. The R is used to allow you to focus on a particular structural feature of a molecule without the "clutter" of the other atoms in the molecule detracting from it. The R might represent a methyl, ethyl, or propyl group, or any of a vast number of other possibilities. For example, the generalized formula R—OH for an alcohol might refer to an alcohol as simple as CH_3OH or CH_3CH_2OH or one as complicated as cholesterol.

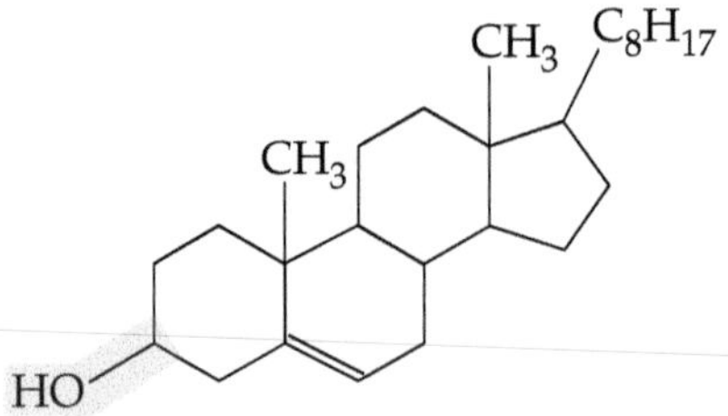

Branched-chain alkanes can be named by following four steps:

STEP 1: Name the main chain. Find the longest continuous chain of carbons, and name the chain according to the number of carbon atoms it contains. The longest chain may not be immediately obvious because it is not always written on one line; you may have to "turn corners" to find it.

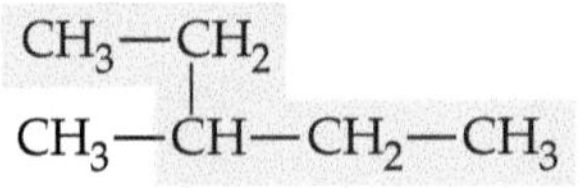

$$CH_3-CH_2$$
$$\quad\quad\quad |$$
$$CH_3-CH-CH_2-CH_3$$

Name as a substituted pentane, not as a substituted butane, because the *longest* chain has five carbons.

STEP 2: Number the carbon atoms in the main chain, beginning at the end nearer the first branch point:

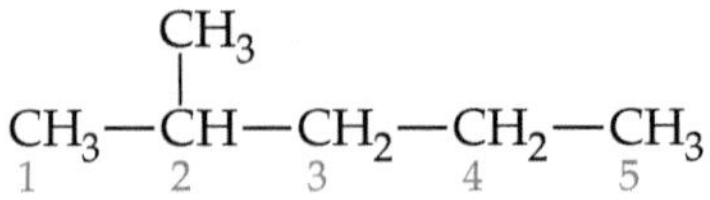

$$\quad\quad\; CH_3$$
$$\quad\quad\quad |$$
$$CH_3-CH-CH_2-CH_2-CH_3$$
$$\;\;1\quad\; 2\quad\;\; 3\quad\;\; 4\quad\;\; 5$$

The first (and only) branch occurs at C2 if we start numbering from the left, but would occur at C4 if we started from the right by mistake.

STEP 3: Identify the branching substituents, and number each according to its point of attachment to the main chain:

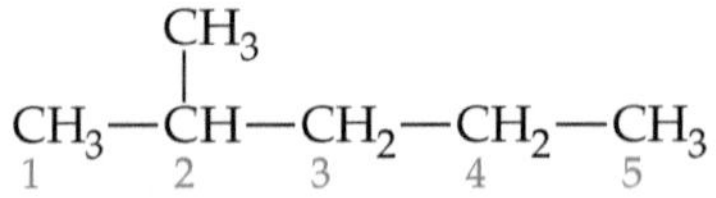

$$\quad\quad\; CH_3$$
$$\quad\quad\quad |$$
$$CH_3-CH-CH_2-CH_2-CH_3$$
$$\;\;1\quad\; 2\quad\;\; 3\quad\;\; 4\quad\;\; 5$$

The main chain is a pentane. There is one —CH_3 substituent group connected to C2 of the chain.

If there are two substituents on the same carbon, assign the same number to both. There must always be as many numbers in the name as there are substituents.

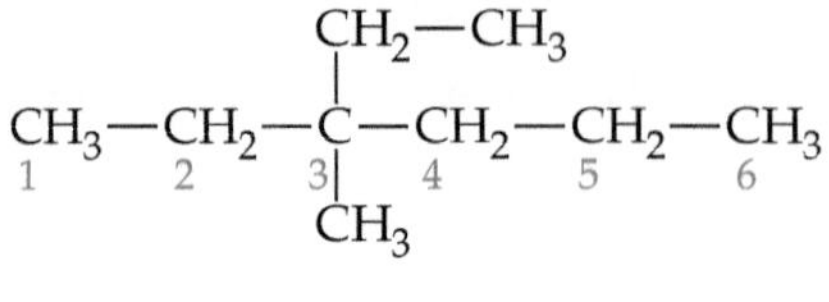

$$\quad\quad\quad\quad CH_2-CH_3$$
$$\quad\quad\quad\quad\quad\; |$$
$$CH_3-CH_2-C-CH_2-CH_2-CH_3$$
$$\;\;1\quad\;\; 2\quad\; 3|\;\; 4\quad\;\; 5\quad\;\; 6$$
$$\quad\quad\quad\quad\; CH_3$$

The main chain is a hexane. There are two substituents, a —CH_3 and a —CH_2CH_3, both connected to C3 of the chain.

STEP 4: Write the name as a single word, using hyphens to separate the numbers from the different prefixes and commas to separate numbers if necessary. If two or more different substituent groups are present, cite them in alphabetical order. If two or more identical substituents are present, use one of the prefixes *di-*, *tri-*, *tetra-*, and so forth, but do not use these prefixes for alphabetizing purposes.

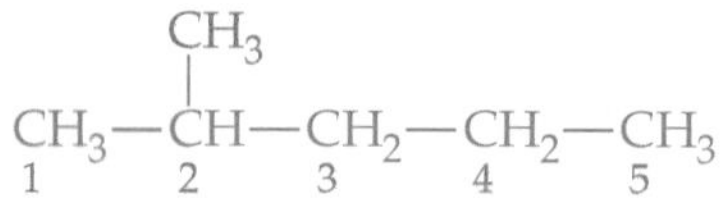

$$CH_3-\underset{\underset{1}{|}}{\overset{\overset{CH_3}{|}}{CH}}-\underset{3}{CH_2}-\underset{4}{CH_2}-\underset{5}{CH_3}$$

2-Methylpentane (a five-carbon main chain with a 2-methyl substituent)

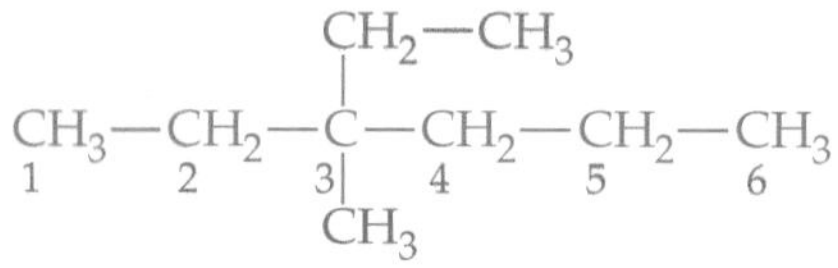

$$CH_3-\underset{1}{CH_2}-\underset{\underset{3}{\overset{\overset{CH_2-CH_3}{|}}{C}}}{\underset{CH_3}{|}}-\underset{4}{CH_2}-\underset{5}{CH_2}-\underset{6}{CH_3}$$

3-Ethyl-3-methylhexane (a six-carbon main chain with 3-ethyl and 3-methyl substituents cited alphabetically)

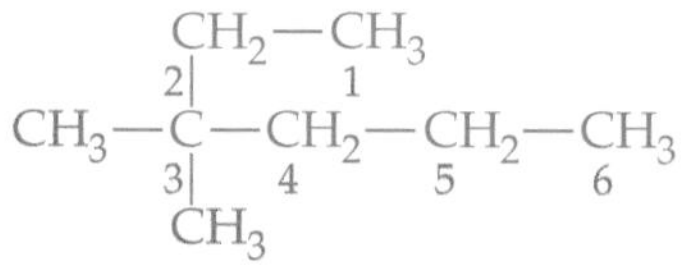

$$CH_3-\underset{\underset{3}{\overset{\overset{\overset{2}{|} \quad 1}{CH_2-CH_3}}{C}}}{\underset{CH_3}{|}}-\underset{4}{CH_2}-\underset{5}{CH_2}-\underset{6}{CH_3}$$

3,3-Dimethylhexane (a six-carbon main chain with two 3-methyl substitutents)

WORKED EXAMPLE   **12.9** Naming Organic Compounds: Alkanes

What is the IUPAC name of the following alkane?

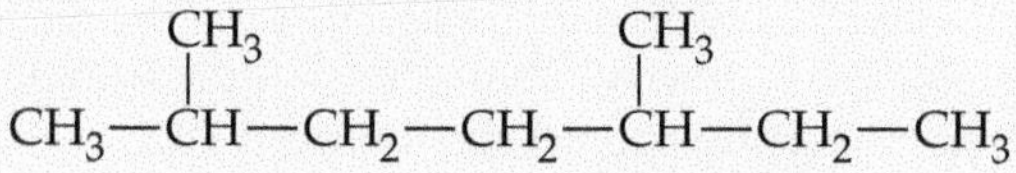

$$CH_3-\overset{\overset{CH_3}{|}}{CH}-CH_2-CH_2-\overset{\overset{CH_3}{|}}{CH}-CH_2-CH_3$$

ANALYSIS Follow the four steps outlined in the text.

SOLUTION

STEP 1: The longest continuous chain of carbon atoms is seven, so the main chain is a *hept*ane.

STEP 2: Number the main chain beginning at the end nearer the first branch:

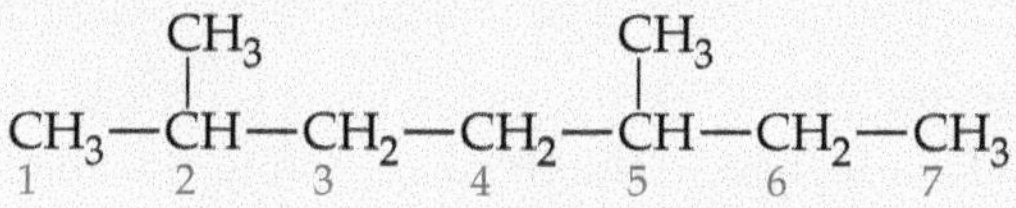

$$CH_3-\underset{2}{\overset{\overset{CH_3}{|}}{CH}}-\underset{3}{CH_2}-\underset{4}{CH_2}-\underset{5}{\overset{\overset{CH_3}{|}}{CH}}-\underset{6}{CH_2}-\underset{7}{CH_3}$$
$$\underset{1}{}$$

STEP 3: Identify and number the substituents (a 2-methyl and a 5-methyl in this case):

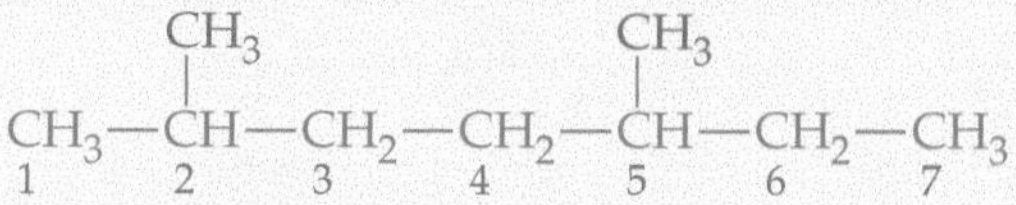

$$\underset{1}{CH_3}-\underset{2}{\overset{\overset{CH_3}{|}}{CH}}-\underset{3}{CH_2}-\underset{4}{CH_2}-\underset{5}{\overset{\overset{CH_3}{|}}{CH}}-\underset{6}{CH_2}-\underset{7}{CH_3}$$

Substituents: 2-methyl, 5-methyl

STEP 4: Write the name as one word, using the prefix *di-* because there are two methyl groups. Separate the two numbers by a comma, and use a hyphen between the numbers and the word.

Name: 2, 5-Dimethylheptane

WORKED EXAMPLE   **12.10** Molecular Structure: Identifying 1°, 2°, 3°, and 4° Carbons

Identify each carbon atom in the following molecule as primary, secondary, tertiary, or quaternary.

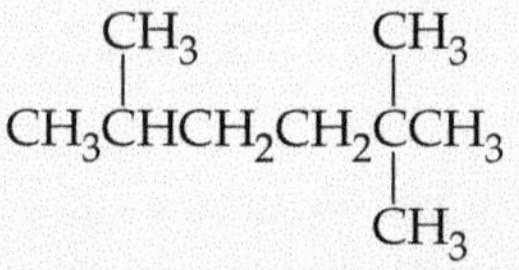

$$CH_3\overset{\overset{CH_3}{|}}{CH}CH_2CH_2\underset{\underset{CH_3}{|}}{\overset{\overset{CH_3}{|}}{C}}CH_3$$

ANALYSIS Look at each carbon atom in the molecule, count the number of other carbon atoms attached, and make the assignment accordingly: primary (1 carbon attached); secondary (2 carbons attached); tertiary (3 carbons attached); quaternary (4 carbons attached).

SOLUTION

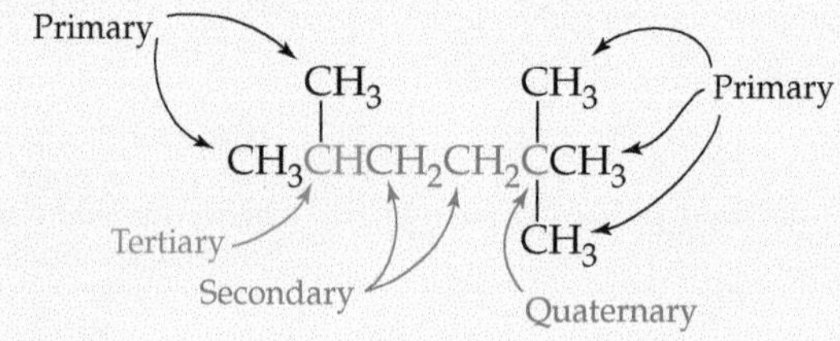

Primary CH$_3$ CH$_3$ Primary

CH$_3$CHCH$_2$CH$_2$CCH$_3$

Tertiary CH$_3$

Secondary Quaternary

WORKED EXAMPLE **12.11** Molecular Structures: Drawing Condensed Structures from Names

Draw condensed structures corresponding to the following IUPAC names:

(a) 2,3-Dimethylpentane

(b) 3-Ethylheptane

ANALYSIS Starting with the parent chain, add the named alkyl substituent groups to the appropriately numbered carbon atom(s).

SOLUTION

(a) The parent chain has 5 carbons (*pent*ane), with two methyl groups (—CH$_3$) attached to the second and third carbon in the chain:

CH$_3$CH$_3$

CH$_3$CH CH CH$_2$CH$_3$
1   2   3   4   5

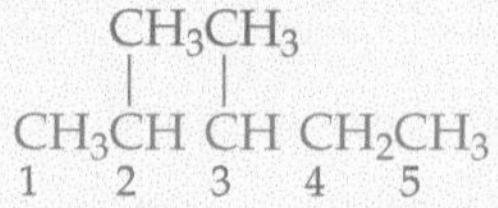

(b) The parent chain has 7 carbons (*hept*ane), with one ethyl group (—CH$_2$CH$_3$) attached to the third carbon in the chain:

CH$_2$CH$_3$

CH$_3$CH$_2$CH CH$_2$CH$_2$CH$_2$CH$_3$
1   2   3   4   5   6   7

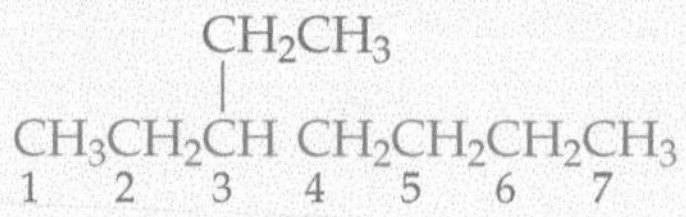

PROBLEM 12.10

What are the IUPAC names of the following alkanes?

CH$_2$—CH$_3$ CH$_3$

(a) 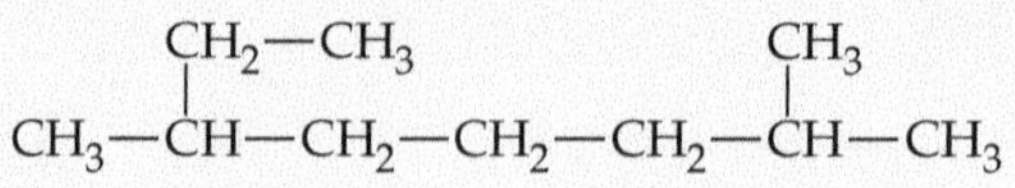 CH$_3$—CH—CH$_2$—CH$_2$—CH$_2$—CH—CH$_3$

CH$_2$—CH$_3$

(b) 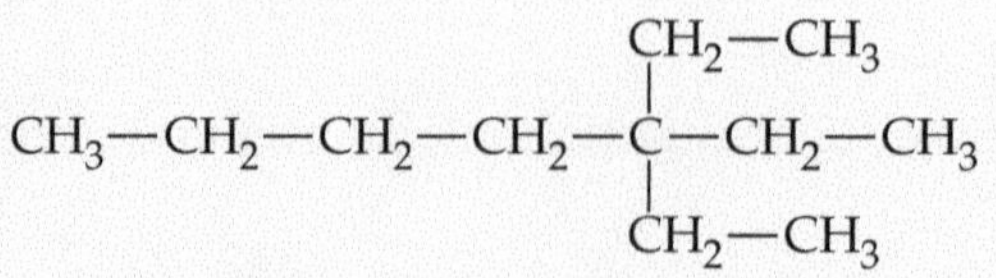 CH$_3$—CH$_2$—CH$_2$—CH$_2$—C—CH$_2$—CH$_3$

CH$_2$—CH$_3$

PROBLEM 12.11

Draw both condensed and line structures corresponding to the following IUPAC names and label each carbon as primary, secondary, tertiary, or quaternary:

(a) 3-Methylhexane   (b) 3,4-Dimethyloctane

(c) 2,2,4-Trimethylpentane

PROBLEM 12.12

Draw and name alkanes that meet the following descriptions:

(a) An alkane with a tertiary carbon atom

(b) An alkane that has both a tertiary and a quaternary carbon atom

KEY CONCEPT PROBLEM 12.13

What are the IUPAC names of the following alkanes?

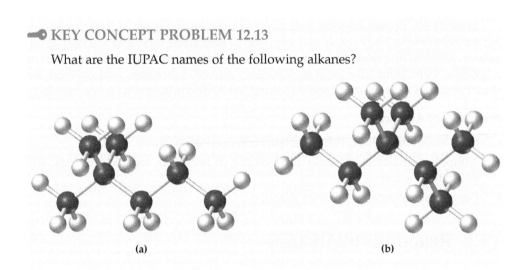

(a)   (b)

12.7 Properties of Alkanes

Alkanes contain only nonpolar C—C and C—H bonds, so the only intermolecular forces influencing them are weak London dispersion forces (Section 8.11). (●━━●, p. 235) The effect of these forces is shown in the regularity with which the melting and boiling points of straight-chain alkanes increase with molecular size (Figure 12.3). The first four alkanes—methane, ethane, propane, and butane—are gases at room temperature and pressure. Alkanes with 5–15 carbon atoms are liquids; those with 16 or more carbon atoms are generally low-melting, waxy solids.

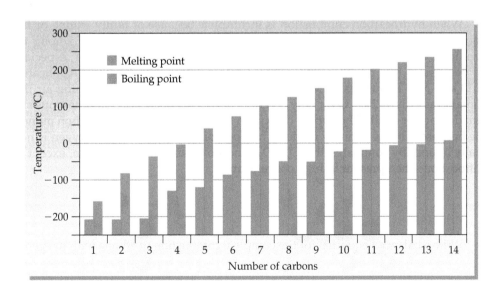

◄ **FIGURE 12.3** The boiling and melting points for the C_1–C_{14} straight-chain alkanes increase with molecular size.

In keeping with their low polarity, alkanes are insoluble in water but soluble in nonpolar organic solvents, including other alkanes (Section 9.2). (●━━●, p. 257) Because alkanes are generally less dense than water, they float on its surface.

Quaternary (4°) carbon atom, *p. 381*

Secondary (2°) carbon atom, *p. 381*

Straight-chain alkane, *p. 369*

Substituent, *p. 380*

Tertiary (3°) carbon atom, *p. 381*

6. **What are the general properties and chemical reactions of alkanes?** Alkanes are generally soluble only in nonpolar organic solvents, have weak intermolecular forces, and are nontoxic. Their principal chemical reactions are *combustion*, a reaction with oxygen that gives carbon dioxide and water, and *halogenation*, a reaction in which hydrogen atoms are replaced by chlorine or bromine.

SUMMARY OF REACTIONS

1. **Combustion of an alkane with oxygen (Section 12.8):**

$$CH_4 + 2\,O_2 \longrightarrow CO_2 + 2\,H_2O$$

2. **Halogenation of an alkane to yield an alkyl halide (Section 12.8):**

$$CH_4 + Cl_2 \longrightarrow CH_3Cl + HCl$$

UNDERSTANDING KEY CONCEPTS

12.19 How many hydrogen atoms are needed to complete the hydrocarbon formulas for the following carbon backbones?

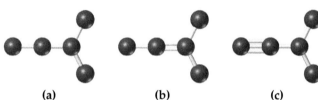

(a)　　　　　　(b)　　　　　　(c)

12.20 Convert the following models into condensed structures (gray = C; ivory = H; red = O):

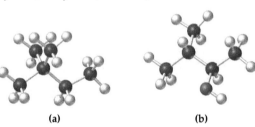

(a)　　　　　　　　(b)

12.21 Convert the following models into line drawings (gray = C; ivory = H; red = O; blue = N):

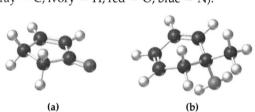

(a)　　　　　　　　(b)

12.22 Identify the functional groups in the following compounds:

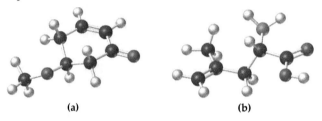

(a)　　　　　　　　(b)

12.23 Give systematic names for the following alkanes:

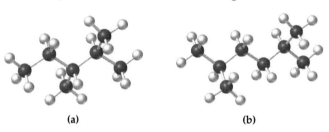

(a)　　　　　　　　(b)

12.24 Give systematic names for the following cycloalkanes:

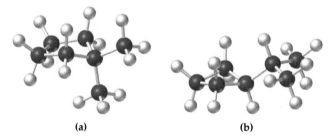

(a)　　　　　　　　(b)

12.25 The following two compounds are isomers, even though both can be named 1,3-dimethylcyclopentane. What is the difference between them?

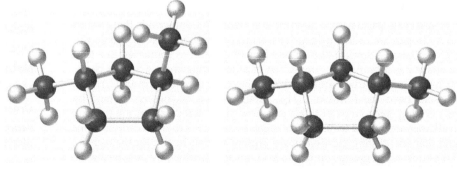

(a)　　　　　　　　　　　　　　　　　(b)

ADDITIONAL PROBLEMS

ORGANIC MOLECULES AND FUNCTIONAL GROUPS

12.26 What characteristics of carbon make possible the existence of so many different organic compounds?

12.27 What are functional groups, and why are they important?

12.28 Why are most organic compounds nonconducting and insoluble in water?

12.29 If you were given two unlabeled bottles, one containing hexane and one containing water, how could you tell them apart?

12.30 What is meant by the term *polar covalent bond*? Give an example of such a bond.

12.31 Give examples of compounds that are members of the following families:

(a) Alcohol (b) Amine
(c) Carboxylic acid (d) Ether

12.32 Locate and identify the functional groups in the following molecules ($-SO_2N-$ is a sulfanilamide):

(a)

Viagra

(b)

Aspirin

12.33 Identify the functional groups in the following molecules:

(a)

Vitamin A

(b)

Ambien

12.34 Propose structures for molecules that fit the following descriptions:

(a) A ketone with the formula $C_5H_{10}O$
(b) An ester with the formula $C_6H_{12}O_2$
(c) A compound with the formula $C_2H_5NO_2$ that is both an amine and a carboxylic acid

12.35 Propose structures for molecules that fit the following descriptions:

(a) An amide with the formula C_4H_9NO
(b) An aldehyde that has a ring of carbons, $C_6H_{10}O$
(c) An aromatic compound that is also an ether, $C_8H_{10}O$

ALKANES AND ISOMERS

12.36 What requirement must be met for two compounds to be isomers?

12.37 If one compound has the formula C_5H_{10} and another has the formula C_4H_{10}, are the two compounds isomers? Explain.

12.38 What is the difference between a secondary carbon and a tertiary carbon? Between a primary carbon and a quaternary carbon?

12.39 Why is it not possible for a compound to have a *quintary* carbon (five R groups attached to C)?

12.40 Give examples of compounds that meet the following descriptions:

(a) An alkane with two tertiary carbons
(b) A cycloalkane with only secondary carbons

12.41 Give examples of compounds that meet the following descriptions:

(a) A branched-chain alkane with only primary and quaternary carbons
(b) A cycloalkane with three substituents

12.42 There are three isomers with the formula C_3H_8O. Draw the condensed structure and the line structure for each isomer.

12.43 Write condensed structures for the following molecular formulas. (You may have to use rings and/or multiple bonds in some instances.)

(a) C_2H_7N
(b) C_4H_8 (Write the line structure as well.)
(c) C_2H_4O
(d) CH_2O_2 (Write the line structure as well.)

12.44 How many isomers can you write that fit the following descriptions?

(a) Alcohols with formula $C_4H_{10}O$
(b) Amines with formula C_3H_9N
(c) Ketones with formula $C_5H_{10}O$

12.45 How many isomers can you write that fit the following descriptions?

(a) Aldehydes with formula $C_5H_{10}O$
(b) Esters with formula $C_4H_8O_2$
(c) Carboxylic acids with formula $C_4H_8O_2$

12.46 Which of the following pairs of structures are identical, which are isomers, and which are unrelated?

(a) $CH_3CH_2CH_3$ and $CH_3CH_2CH_3$ with CH_2CH_3

(b) CH_3-N-CH_3 and CH_3CH_2-N-H with H, H

(c) $CH_3CH_2CH_2-O-CH_3$ and

$$CH_3CH_2CH_2-\overset{\overset{\displaystyle O}{\|}}{C}-CH_3$$

(d) $CH_3-\overset{\overset{\displaystyle O}{\|}}{C}-CH_2CH_2CH(CH_3)_2$ and

$$CH_3CH_2-\overset{\overset{\displaystyle O}{\|}}{C}-CH_2CH_2CH_2CH_3$$

(e) $CH_3CH=CHCH_2CH_2-O-H$ and

$$CH_3CH_2\overset{\displaystyle CH}{\underset{\displaystyle CH_3}{|}}-\overset{\overset{\displaystyle O}{\|}}{C}-H$$

12.47 Which structure(s) in each group represent the same compound, and which represent isomers?

(a)
$$H-\overset{\overset{\displaystyle H}{|}}{\underset{\displaystyle H}{C}}-\overset{\overset{\displaystyle H}{|}}{\underset{\displaystyle H}{C}}-\overset{\overset{\displaystyle H}{|}}{\underset{\displaystyle H}{C}}-\overset{\overset{\displaystyle H}{|}}{\underset{\displaystyle H}{C}}-H$$

$$H-\overset{\overset{\displaystyle H}{|}}{\underset{\displaystyle}{C}}-H$$
$$H-\overset{\overset{\displaystyle H}{|}}{\underset{\displaystyle H}{C}}-\overset{\overset{\displaystyle H}{|}}{\underset{\displaystyle H}{C}}-\overset{\overset{\displaystyle H}{|}}{\underset{\displaystyle H}{C}}-H$$
$$H-\overset{\overset{\displaystyle H}{|}}{\underset{\displaystyle H}{C}}-\overset{\overset{\displaystyle H}{|}}{\underset{\displaystyle H}{C}}-\overset{\overset{\displaystyle H}{|}}{\underset{\displaystyle}{C}}-H$$
$$\qquad\qquad H-\overset{\overset{\displaystyle H}{|}}{\underset{\displaystyle H}{C}}-H$$

(b) $CH_3\overset{\displaystyle CHCHCH_3}{\underset{\displaystyle Br}{|}}$ $CH_3\overset{\displaystyle CHCHCH_3}{\underset{\displaystyle Br}{|}}$

$$\overset{\displaystyle CH_3}{\underset{}{|}}$$
$$CH_2CHCH_2CH_3$$
$$\underset{\displaystyle Br}{|}$$

12.48 What is wrong with the following structures?

(a) $CH_3=CHCH_2CH_2OH$

(b) $CH_3CH_2CH=\overset{\overset{\displaystyle O}{\|}}{C}-CH_3$

(c) $CH_2CH_2CH_2C\equiv\overset{\displaystyle CCH_3}{\underset{}{|}}\overset{\displaystyle CH_3}{}$

12.49 There are two things wrong with the following structure. What are they?

ALKANE NOMENCLATURE

12.50 What are the IUPAC names of the following alkanes?

(a) $CH_3CH_2CH_2CH_2\overset{\displaystyle CHCHCH_2CH_3}{\underset{\displaystyle CH_3}{\overset{\displaystyle CH_2CH_3}{|}}}$

(b) $CH_3CH_2CH_2\overset{\displaystyle CHCH_2CHCH_3}{\underset{\displaystyle CH_2CH_3}{\overset{\displaystyle CH_3CHCH_3}{|}}}$

(c) $CH_3\overset{\displaystyle CCH_2CH_2CH_2CHCH_3}{\underset{\displaystyle CH_3}{\overset{\displaystyle CH_3 \qquad CH_3}{|\qquad\quad|}}}$

(d) $CH_3CH_2CH_2\overset{\displaystyle CCH_3}{\underset{\displaystyle CH_3CHCH_3}{\overset{\displaystyle CH_2CH_2CH_2CH_3}{|}}}$

(e) $CH_3\overset{\displaystyle CCH_2CCH_3}{\underset{\displaystyle CH_3 \quad CH_3}{\overset{\displaystyle CH_3 \quad CH_3}{|\qquad|}}}$

(f) $CH_3CH_2\overset{\displaystyle CCH_2CH}{\underset{\displaystyle CH_3CH_2 \quad CH_3}{\overset{\displaystyle CH_3CH_2 \quad CH_3}{|\qquad\quad|}}}$

(g) $CH_3(CH_2)_7\overset{\displaystyle C-CH_3}{\underset{\displaystyle CH_3}{\overset{\displaystyle CH_3}{|}}}$

12.51 Give IUPAC names for the five isomers with the formula C_6H_{14}.

12.52 Write condensed structures for the following compounds:

(a) 4-*tert*-Butyl-3,3,5-trimethylheptane
(b) 2,4-Dimethylpentane
(c) 4,4-Diethyl-3-methyloctane
(d) 3-Isopropyl-2,3,6,7-tetramethylnonane
(e) 3-Isobutyl-1-isopropyl-5-methylcycloheptane
(f) 1,1,3-Trimethylcyclopentane

12.53 Draw structures that correspond to the following IUPAC names:

(a) 1,1-Dimethylcyclopropane
(b) 1,2,3,4-Tetramethylcyclopentane
(c) 4-*tert*-Butyl-1,1-dimethylcyclohexane
(d) Cycloheptane
(e) 1,3,5-Triisopropylcyclohexane
(f) 1,3,5,7-Tetramethylcyclooctane

12.54 Name the following cycloalkanes:

(a)

(b)

(c)

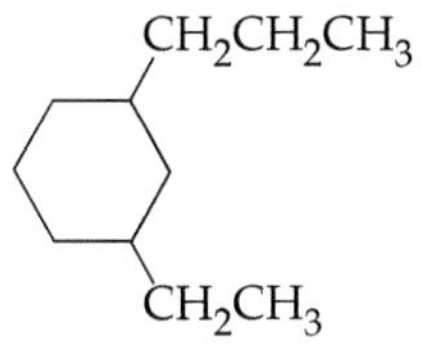

CH₂CH₂CH₃ / CH₂CH₃ on cyclohexane ring

$CH_2CH_2CH_3$

CH_2CH_3

(d)

CH_3

CH_3 — ... —$CH_2CH_2CH_2CH_3$

CH_3

CH_3

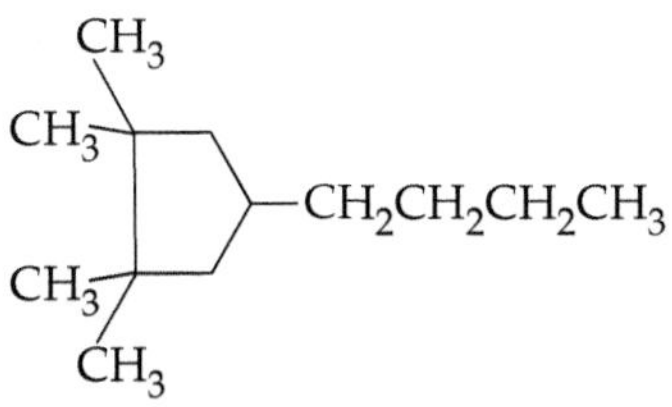

12.55 Name the following cycloalkanes:

(a)

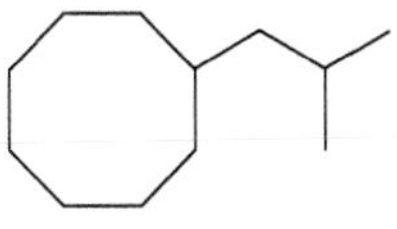

cyclooctane with isobutyl group

(b)

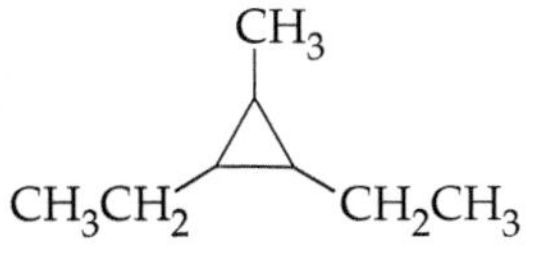

CH_3

CH_3CH_2 — cyclopropane — CH_2CH_3

(c)

CH_3

$CH_3CH_2CH_2$ — cyclopentane — CH_2CH_3

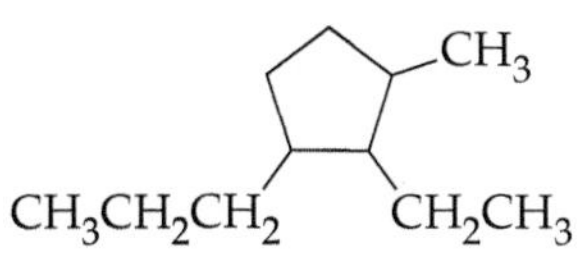

12.56 The following names are incorrect. Tell what is wrong with each, and provide the correct names.

(a)

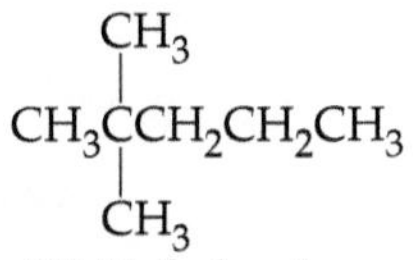

CH_3

$CH_3CCH_2CH_2CH_3$

CH_3

2,2-Methylpentane

(b)

CH_3 CH_3

CH—CH_2—CH

CH_3 CH_3

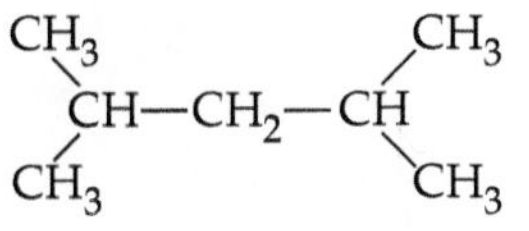

1,1-Diisopropylmethane

(c)

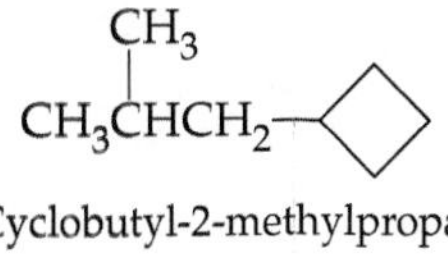

CH_3

CH_3CHCH_2— □

1-Cyclobutyl-2-methylpropane

12.57 The following names are incorrect. Write the structural formula that agrees with the apparent name, and then write the correct name of the compound.

(a) 2-Ethylbutane
(b) 2-Isopropyl-2-methylpentane
(c) 5-Ethyl-1,1-methylcyclopentane
(d) 3-Ethyl-3,5,5-trimethylhexane
(e) 1,2-Dimethyl-4-ethylcyclohexane
(f) 2,4-Diethylpentane
(g) 5,5,6,6-Methyl-7,7-ethyldecane

12.58 Draw structures and give IUPAC names for the nine isomers of C_7H_{16}.

12.59 Draw the structural formulas and name all cyclic isomers with the formula C_6H_{12}.

REACTIONS OF ALKANES

12.60 Propane, commonly known as LP gas, burns in air to yield CO_2 and H_2O. Write a balanced equation for the reaction.

12.61 Write a balanced equation for the combustion of isooctane, C_8H_{16}, a component of gasoline.

12.62 Write the formulas of the three singly chlorinated isomers formed when 2,2-dimethylbutane reacts with Cl_2 in the presence of light.

12.63 Write the formulas of the seven doubly brominated isomers formed when 2,2-dimethylbutane reacts with Br_2 in the presence of light.

Applications

12.64 Why is it important to know the shape of a molecule? [*Displaying Molecular Shapes, p. 379*]

12.65 How does petroleum differ from natural gas? [*Petroleum, p. 388*]

12.66 What types of hydrocarbons burn most efficiently in an automobile engine? [*Petroleum, p. 388*]

General Questions and Problems

12.67 Identify the functional groups in the following molecules:

(a) Testosterone, a male sex hormone

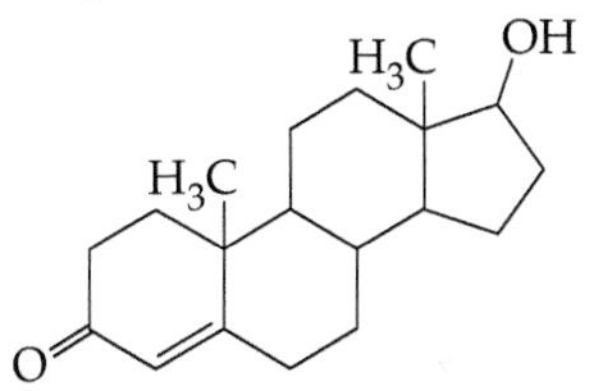

H_3C OH

H_3C

O

(b) Aspartame, an artificial sweetener

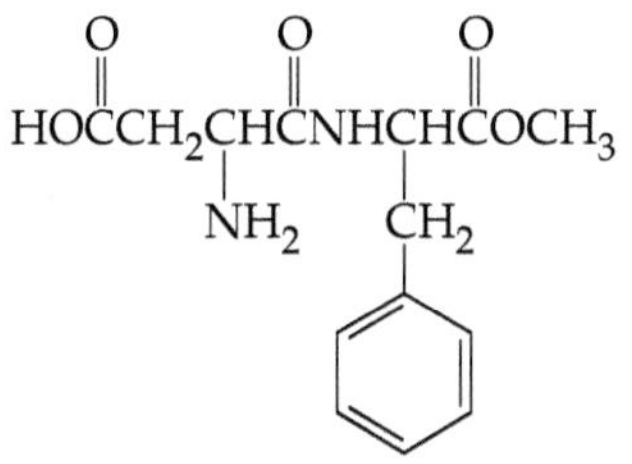

O   O   O

$HOCCH_2CHCNHCHCOCH_3$

NH_2 CH_2

benzene ring

12.68 Label each carbon in Problem 12.67 as primary, secondary, tertiary, or quaternary.

12.69 If someone reported the preparation of a compound with the formula C_3H_9 most chemists would be skeptical. Why?

12.70 Most lipsticks are about 70% castor oil and wax. Why is lipstick more easily removed with petroleum jelly than with water?

12.71 When cyclopentane is exposed to Br_2 in the presence of light, reaction occurs. Write the formulas of:

(a) All possible monobromination products
(b) All possible dibromination products

12.72 Which do you think has a higher boiling point, pentane or neopentane (2,2-dimethylpropane)? Why?

12.73 Propose structures for the following:

(a) An aldehyde, C_4H_8O
(b) An iodo-substituted alkene, C_5H_9I
(c) A cycloalkane, C_7H_{14}
(d) A diene (dialkene), C_5H_8

CHAPTER 18

Amino Acids and Proteins

CONCEPTS TO REVIEW

Acid–base properties
(Sections 6.10, 10.9, 17.3)

Hydrolysis reactions
(Section 17.6)

Intermolecular forces
(Section 8.11)

Polymers
*(Applications, p. 127, p. 420;
Sections 13.8, 17.7)*

▲ Meat, fish, dairy products, beans, and nuts are all high in protein content.

CHAPTER GOALS

In this chapter, we will look at the following questions about amino acids and proteins:

1. What are the structural features of amino acids?

THE GOAL: Be able to describe and recognize amino acid structures and illustrate how they are connected in proteins.

2. What are the properties of amino acids?

THE GOAL: Be able to describe how the properties of amino acids depend on their side chains and how their ionic charges vary with pH.

3. Why do amino acids have "handedness"?

THE GOAL: Be able to explain what is responsible for handedness and recognize simple molecules that display this property.

4. What is the primary structure of a protein and what conventions are used for drawing and naming primary structures?

THE GOAL: Be able to define protein primary structure, explain how primary structures are represented, and draw and name a simple protein structure, given its amino acid sequence.

5. What types of interactions determine the overall shapes of proteins?

THE GOAL: Be able to describe and recognize disulfide bonds, hydrogen bonding along the protein backbone, and noncovalent interactions between amino acid side chains in proteins.

6. What are the secondary and tertiary structures of proteins?

THE GOAL: Be able to define these structures and the attractive forces that determine their nature, describe the α-helix and β-sheet, and distinguish between fibrous and globular proteins.

7. What is quaternary protein structure?

THE GOAL: Be able to define quaternary structure, identify the forces responsible for quaternary structure, and give examples of proteins with quaternary structure.

8. What chemical properties do proteins have?

THE GOAL: Be able to describe protein hydrolysis and denaturation, and give some examples of agents that cause denaturation.

The word *protein* is a familiar one. Taken from the Greek *proteios*, meaning "primary," "protein" is an apt description for the biological molecules that are of primary importance to all living organisms. Approximately 50% of your body's dry weight is protein. Some proteins, such as the collagen in connective tissue, serve a structural purpose. Others direct responses to internal and external conditions. And still other proteins defend the body against foreign invaders. Most importantly, as enzymes, proteins catalyze almost every chemical reaction that occurs in your body. Because of their importance and the role they play in all biochemical functions, we have chosen to discuss proteins, which are polymers of amino acids, in this first chapter devoted to biochemistry.

18.1 An Introduction to Biochemistry

Biochemistry, the study of molecules, and their reactions in living organisms, is based on the inorganic and organic chemical principles outlined in the first chapters of this book. Now we are ready to investigate the chemical basis of life. Physicians are faced with biochemistry every day because all diseases are associated with abnormalities in biochemistry. Nutritionists evaluate our dietary needs based on our biochemistry. And the pharmaceutical industry designs molecules that mimic or alter the action of biomolecules. The ultimate goal of biochemistry is to understand the structures of biomolecules and the relationship between their structures and functions.

Biochemistry is the common ground for the life sciences. Microbiology, botany, zoology, immunology, pathology, physiology, toxicology, neuroscience, cell biology—in all these fields, answers to fundamental questions are being found at the molecular level.

The principal classes of biomolecules are *proteins, carbohydrates, lipids*, and *nucleic acids*. Some biomolecules are small and have only a few functional

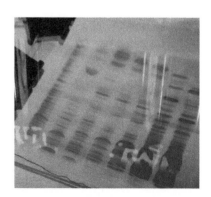

▲ **An electrophoretic gel.** Proteins have been separated by size and stained blue for viewing. Diseases can cause changes in the protein patterns seen.

groups. Others are huge and their biochemistry is governed by the interactions of large numbers of functional groups. Proteins, the subject of this chapter; nucleic acids (Chapters 26, 27); and large carbohydrates (Section 22.9) are all polymers, some containing hundreds, thousands, or even millions of repeating units.

Biochemical reactions must continuously break down food molecules, generate and store energy, build up new biomolecules, and eliminate waste. Each biomolecule has its own role to play in these processes. But despite the huge size of some biomolecules and the complexity of their interactions, their functional groups and chemical reactions are no different from those of simpler organic molecules. *All the principles of chemistry introduced thus far apply to biochemistry.* Of the functional groups introduced in previous chapters, those listed in Table 18.1 are of greatest importance in biomolecules.

TABLE 18.1 Functional Groups of Importance in Biochemical Molecules

FUNCTIONAL GROUP	STRUCTURE	TYPE OF BIOMOLECULE
Amino group	$-NH_3{}^+$, $-NH_2$	Amino acids and proteins (Sections 18.3, 18.7)
Hydroxyl group	$-OH$	Monosaccharides (carbohydrates) and glycerol: a component of triacylglycerols (lipids) (Sections 22.4, 24.2)
Carbonyl group	$\begin{matrix} O \\ \| \\ -C- \end{matrix}$	Monosaccharides (carbohydrates); in acetyl group (CH_3CO) used to transfer carbon atoms during catabolism (Sections 22.4, 21.4, 21.8)
Carboxyl group	$\begin{matrix} O & & O \\ \| & & \| \\ -C-OH, & -C-O^- \end{matrix}$	Amino acids, proteins, and fatty acids (lipids) (Sections 18.3, 18.7, 24.2)
Amide group	$\begin{matrix} O \\ \| \\ -C-N- \\ \| \end{matrix}$	Links amino acids in proteins; formed by reaction of amino group and carboxyl group (Section 18.7)
Carboxylic acid ester	$\begin{matrix} O \\ \| \\ -C-O-R \end{matrix}$	Triacylglycerols (and other lipids); formed by reaction of carboxyl group and hydroxyl group (Section 24.2)
Phosphates, mono-, di-, tri-	$\begin{matrix} & O \\ \| & \| \\ -C-O-P-O^- \\ \| & \| \\ & O^- \end{matrix}$ $\begin{matrix} & O & O \\ \| & \| & \| \\ -C-O-P-O-P-O^- \\ \| & \| & \| \\ & O^- & O^- \end{matrix}$ $\begin{matrix} & O & O & O \\ \| & \| & \| & \| \\ -C-O-P-O-P-O-P-O^- \\ \| & \| & \| & \| \\ & O^- & O^- & O^- \end{matrix}$	ATP and many metabolism intermediates (Sections 17.8, 21.5, and throughout metabolism sections)
Hemiacetal group	$\begin{matrix} \| \\ -C-OH \\ \| \\ OR \end{matrix}$	Cyclic forms of monosaccharides; formed by a reaction of carbonyl group with hydroxyl group (Sections 16.7, 22.4)
Acetal group	$\begin{matrix} \| \\ -C-OR \\ \| \\ OR \end{matrix}$	Connects monosaccharides in disaccharides and larger carbohydrates; formed by reaction of carbonyl group with hydroxyl group (Sections 16.7, 22.7, 22.9)

⊂◯⊃ **Looking Ahead**

The focus in the rest of this book is on human biochemistry and the essential structure–function relationships of biomolecules. In this and the next two chapters, we examine the structure of proteins and the roles of proteins and other molecules in controlling biochemical reactions. Next, we present an overview of metabolism and the production of energy (Chapter 21). Then we discuss the structure and function of carbohydrates (Chapters 22 and 23), the structure and function of lipids (Chapters 24 and 25), the role of nucleic acids in protein synthesis and heredity (Chapters 26 and 27), the metabolism of proteins (Chapter 28), and the chemistry of body fluids (Chapter 29). ⊂◯⊃

18.2 Protein Structure and Function: An Overview

Proteins are polymers of **amino acids**. Every amino acid in a protein contains an amine group a carboxyl group (COOH), and an R group called a **side chain**, all bonded to a central carbon atom known as the alpha (α) carbon. The amino acids in proteins are **alpha-amino (α-amino) acids**—the amine group in each is connected to the carbon atom "*alpha* to" (next to) the carboxylic acid group. The R groups may be hydrocarbons, or they may contain a functional group:

> The alpha carbon is the central carbon in an amino acid to which the amine, carboxyl and side chain R groups attach.

$$H_2N-\underset{\underset{R}{|}}{\overset{\overset{H}{|}}{C}}\overset{\alpha}{-}\overset{\overset{O}{\|}}{C}-OH$$

Side chain R group, different for each amino acid

An α-amino acid

Two or more amino acids can link together by forming amide bonds (⊂◯⊃, Section 17.4), which are known as **peptide bonds** when they occur in proteins. A *dipeptide* results from the formation of a peptide bond between the —NH$_2$ group of one amino acid and the —COOH group of a second amino acid. For example, valine and cysteine are connected in a dipeptide as follows:

Protein A large biological molecule made of many amino acids linked together through amide (peptide) bonds.

Amino acid A molecule that contains both an amino group and a carboxylic acid functional group.

Side chain (amino acid) The group bonded to the carbon next to the carboxyl group in an amino acid; different in different amino acids.

Alpha- ($\alpha-$) amino acid An amino acid in which the amino group is bonded to the carbon atom next to the —COOH group.

Peptide bond An amide bond that links two amino acids together.

$$\underset{\underset{\underset{CH_3}{\diagup}\,\underset{CH_3}{\diagdown}}{CH}}{H_2N-CH}-\overset{\overset{O}{\|}}{C}-OH \;+\; \underset{\underset{\underset{S-H}{|}}{CH_2}}{H_2N-CH}-\overset{\overset{O}{\|}}{C}-OH \;\longrightarrow\; \underset{\underset{\underset{CH_3}{\diagup}\,\underset{CH_3}{\diagdown}}{CH}}{H_2N-CH}-\overset{\overset{O}{\|}}{C}-\overset{\text{Peptide bond}}{NH}-\underset{\underset{\underset{S-H}{|}}{CH_2}}{CH}-\overset{\overset{O}{\|}}{C}-OH \;+\; H_2O$$

Valine   Cysteine   A dipeptide

Peptide bond

A *tripeptide* results from linkage of three amino acids via two peptide bonds, and so on. Any number of amino acids can link together to form a linear chainlike polymer—a *polypeptide*.

Proteins have four levels of structure, each of which is explored later in this chapter.

- *Primary structure* is the sequence of amino acids in a protein chain (Section 18.7).
- *Secondary structure* is the regular and repeating spatial organization of neighboring segments of single protein chains (Section 18.9).
- *Tertiary structure* is the overall shape of a protein molecule (Section 18.10) produced by regions of secondary structure combined with the overall bending and folding of the protein chain.
- *Quaternary structure* refers to the overall structure of proteins composed of more than one polypeptide chain (Section 18.11).

What roles do proteins play in living things? No doubt, you are aware that a hamburger is produced from muscle protein and that we depend on our own muscle proteins for every move we make. But this is only one of many essential roles of proteins. They provide *structure* and *support* to tissues and organs throughout our bodies. As *hormones* and *enzymes*, they control all aspects of metabolism. In body fluids, water-soluble proteins pick up other molecules for *storage* or *transport*. And the proteins of the immune system provide *protection* against invaders. To accomplish their biological functions, which are summarized in Table 18.2, some proteins must be tough and fibrous, whereas others must be globular and soluble in body fluids. The overall shape of a protein molecule, as you will see often in the following chapters, is essential to the role of that protein in our metabolism.

TABLE 18.2   Classification of Proteins by Function

TYPE	FUNCTION	EXAMPLE
Enzymes	Catalysts	*Amylase*—begins digestion of carbohydrates by hydrolysis
Hormones	Regulate body functions by carrying messages to receptors	*Insulin*—facilitates use of glucose for energy generation
Storage proteins	Make essential substances available when needed	*Myoglobin*—stores oxygen in muscles
Transport proteins	Carry substances through body fluids	*Serum albumin*—carries fatty acids in blood
Structural proteins	Provide mechanical shape and support	*Collagen*—provides structure to tendons and cartilage
Protective proteins	Defend the body against foreign matter	*Immunoglobulin*—aids in destruction of invading bacteria
Contractile proteins	Do mechanical work	*Myosin and actin*—govern muscle movement

18.3 Amino Acids

The proteins in all living organisms are built from the 20 α-amino acids listed in Table 18.3. For 19 of these amino acids, only the identity of the side chain attached to the α carbon differs. The remaining amino acid (proline) is a secondary amine whose nitrogen and α carbon atoms are joined in a five-membered ring. Each amino acid has a three-letter shorthand code that is included in the table—for example, Ala (alanine), Gly (glycine), and Pro (proline).

The 20 protein amino acids are classified as neutral, acidic, or basic, depending on the nature of their side chains. The 15 neutral amino acids are further divided into those with nonpolar side chains and those with polar functional groups such as amide or hydroxyl groups in their side chains. As we explore the structure and

TABLE 18.3 **The 20 Protein Amino Acids with Their Abbreviations and Isoelectric Points.** The structures are written here in their fully ionized forms. These ions and the isoelectric points given in parentheses are explained in Section 18.4.

Nonpolar Side Chains

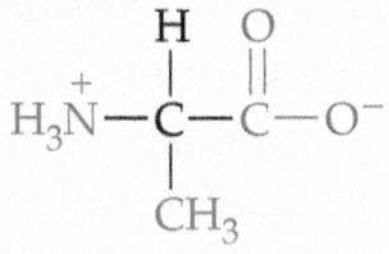

Alanine, Ala (6.0) 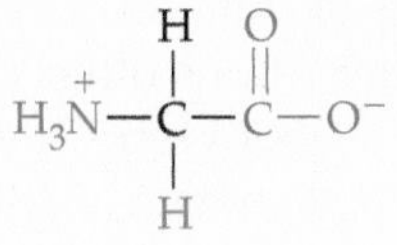 Glycine, Gly (6.0) 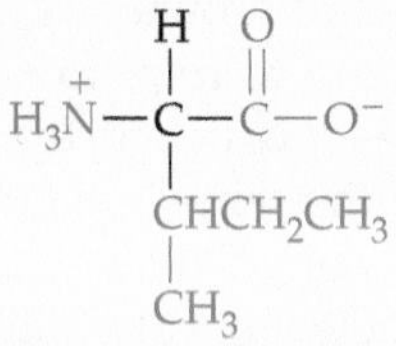 Isoleucine, Ile (6.0) 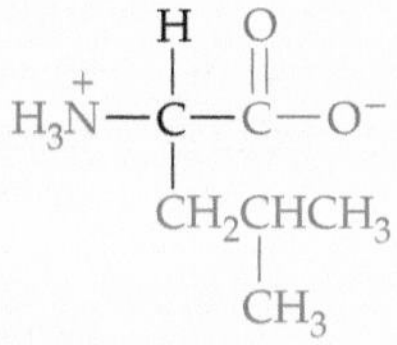 Leucine, Leu (6.0)

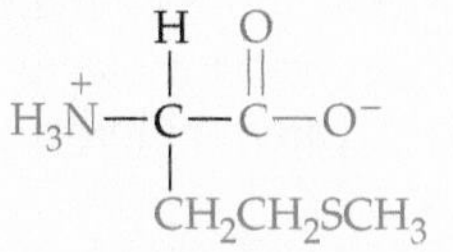

Methionine, Met (5.7) 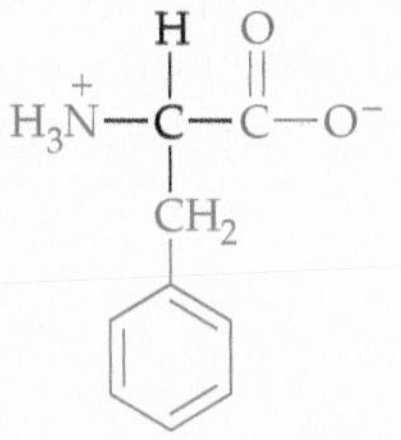 Phenylalanine, Phe (5.5) 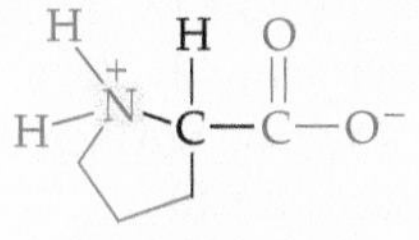 Proline, Pro (6.3) 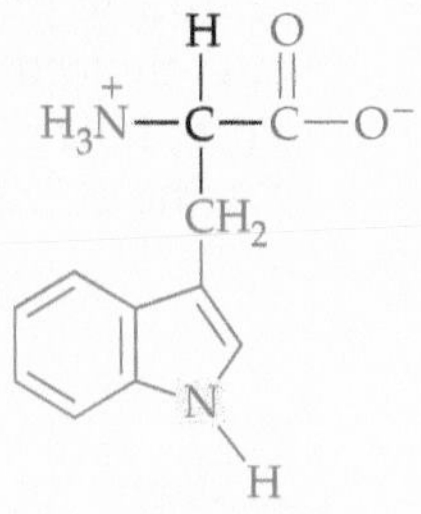 Tryptophan, Trp (5.9) 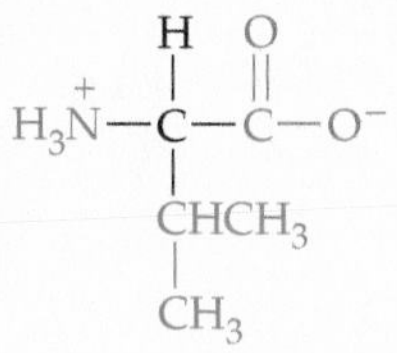 Valine, Val (6.0)

Polar, Neutral Side Chains

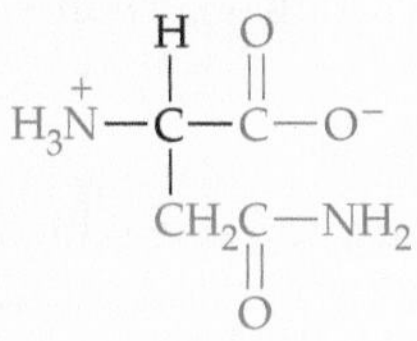

Asparagine, Asn (5.4) 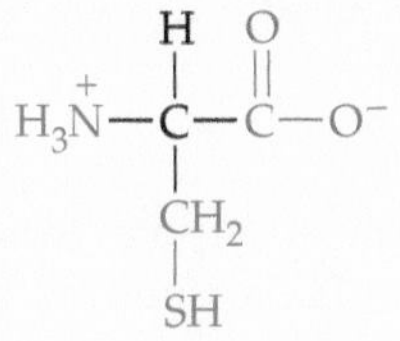 Cysteine, Cys (5.0) 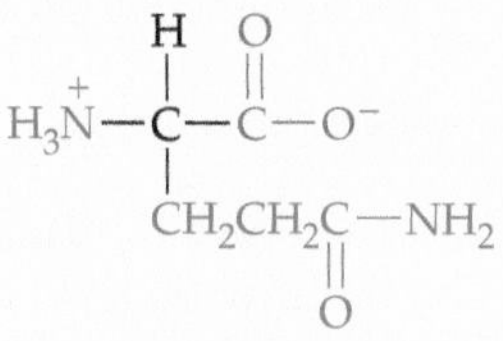 Glutamine, Gln (5.7) 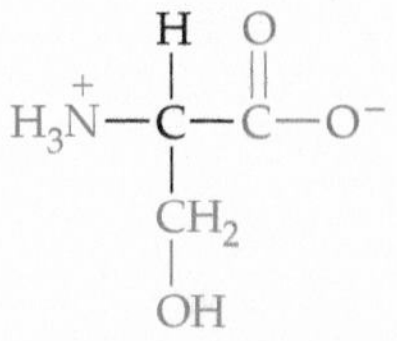 Serine, Ser (5.7)

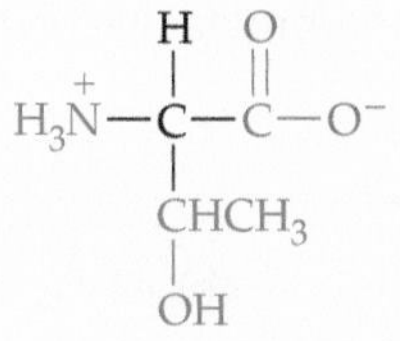

Threonine, Thr (5.6) 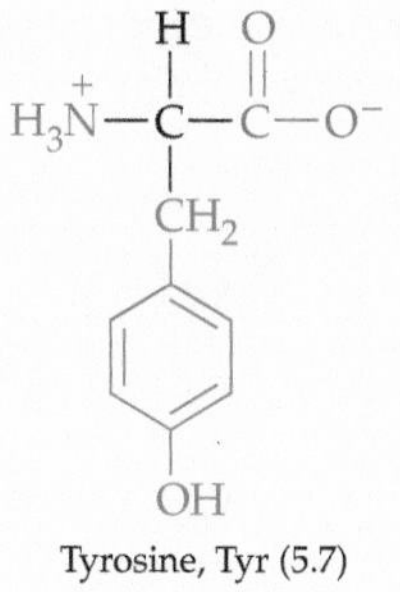 Tyrosine, Tyr (5.7)

Acidic Side Chains

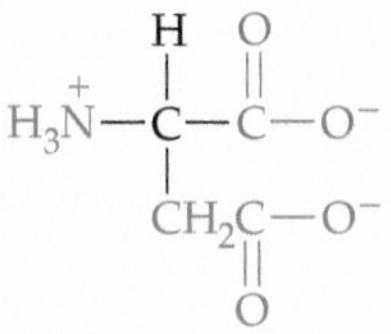

Aspartic acid, Asp (3.0)
(Aspartate)

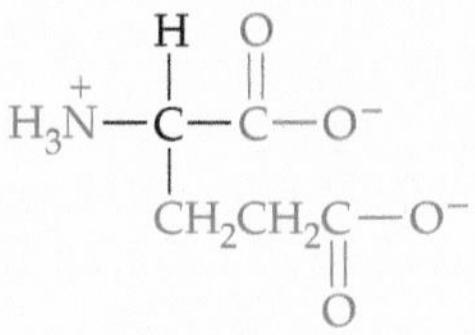

Glutamic acid, Glu (3.2)
(Glutamate)

Basic Side Chains

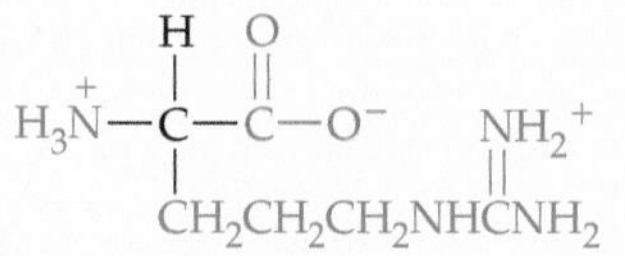

Arginine, Arg (10.8)

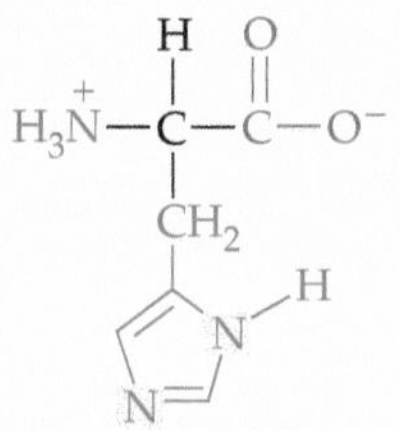

Histidine, His (7.6)

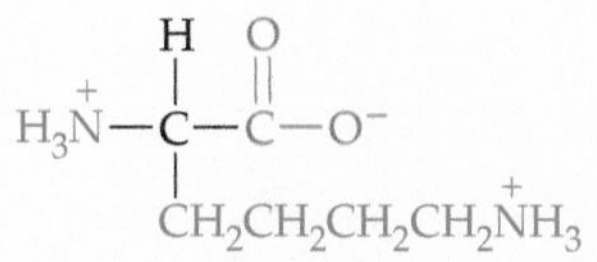

Lysine, Lys (9.7)

function of proteins, you will see that it is the sequence of amino acids in a protein and the chemical nature of their side chains that enable proteins to perform their varied functions.

Intermolecular forces are of central importance in determining the shapes and functions of proteins. (⊂⊃, Section 8.11) In the context of biochemistry it is more meaningful to refer to all interactions other than covalent bonding as **noncovalent forces**. Noncovalent forces act between different molecules or between different parts of the same large molecule, which is often the case in proteins (Section 18.8).

The nonpolar side chains are described as **hydrophobic** (water-fearing)—they are not attracted to water molecules. To avoid aqueous body fluids, they gather into clusters that provide a water-free environment, often a pocket within a large protein molecule. The polar, acidic, and basic side chains are **hydrophilic** (water-loving)—they *are* attracted to polar water molecules. They interact with water molecules much as water molecules interact with one another. Attractions between water molecules and hydrophilic groups on the surface of folded proteins impart water solubility to the proteins. (⊂⊃, Section 9.2)

Noncovalent forces Forces of attraction other than covalent bonds that can act between molecules or within molecules.

Hydrophobic Water-fearing; a hydrophobic substance does not dissolve in water.

Hydrophilic Water-loving; a hydrophilic substance dissolves in water.

PROBLEM 18.1

Name the common amino acids that contain an aromatic ring, contain sulfur, are alcohols, and have alkyl-group side chains.

PROBLEM 18.2

Draw alanine showing the tetrahedral geometry of its α carbon.

PROBLEM 18.3

Choose one amino acid with a nonpolar side chain and one with a polar side chain; draw the two dipeptides formed by these two amino acids.

PROBLEM 18.4

Indicate whether each of the molecules shown below is an α-amino acid or not and explain why.

(a) 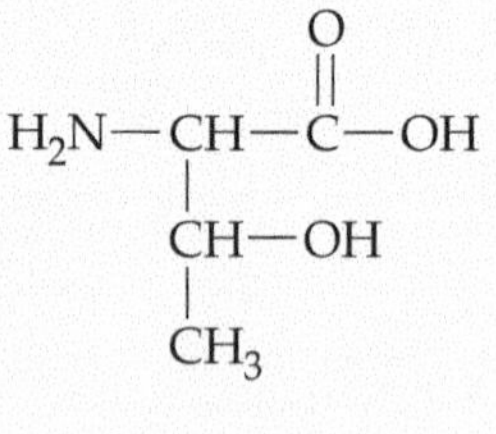 $H_2N-CH-C-OH$ with $\overset{O}{\overset{\|}{}}$ above the C, and below CH: $CH-OH$ then CH_3

(b) $H_2N-C-CH_2CH_2CH_3$ with $\overset{O}{\overset{\|}{}}$ above the C

(c) $CH_3CH_2CH-CH_2-NH_2$ with OH below the CH

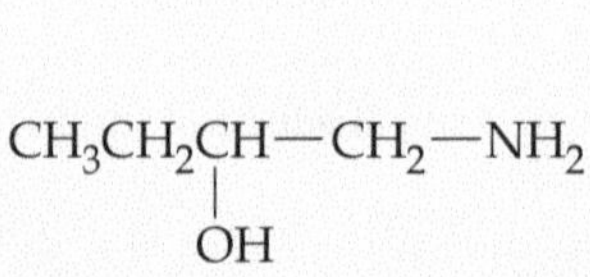

(d) 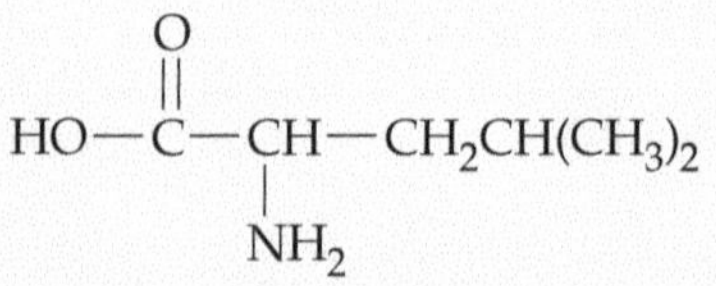 $HO-C-CH-CH_2CH(CH_3)_2$ with $\overset{O}{\overset{\|}{}}$ above the C and NH_2 below the CH

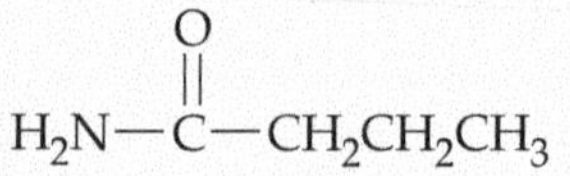

PROBLEM 18.5

Which of the following pairs of amino acids can form hydrogen bonds between their side-chain groups? Draw the pairs that can hydrogen-bond through their side chains and indicate the hydrogen bonds.

(a) Phe, Thr   (b) Asn, Ser   (c) Thr, Tyr   (d) Gly, Trp

PROBLEM 18.6

In the ball-and-stick model of valine near the beginning of Section 18.2, identify the carboxyl group, the amino group, and the R group.

18.4 Acid–Base Properties of Amino Acids

Amino acids contain both an acidic group, —COOH, and a basic group, —NH$_2$. As you might expect, these two groups can undergo an intramolecular acid–base reaction. The result is transfer of the hydrogen from the —COOH group to the —NH$_2$ group to form a *dipolar* ion, an ion that has one positive charge and one negative charge and is thus electrically neutral. Dipolar ions are known as **zwitterions** (from the German *zwitter*, "hybrid"). The zwitterion form of threonine is shown here, and those of the other amino acids commonly found in proteins in mammals are given in Table 18.3.

Zwitterion A neutral dipolar ion that has one + charge and one − charge.

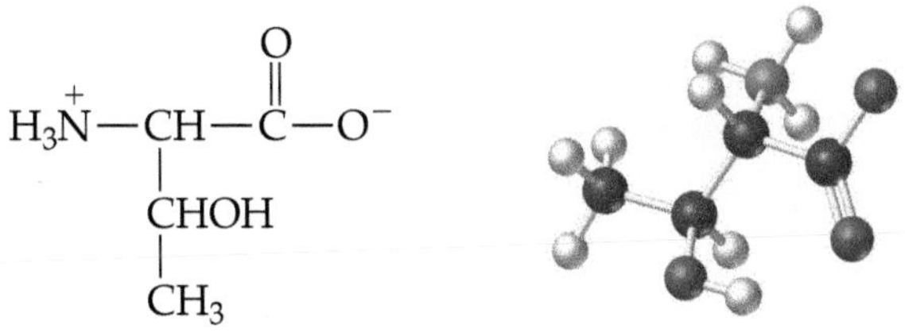

Threonine—zwitterion

Because they are zwitterions, amino acids have many of the physical properties we associate with salts. (⬤▭, Section 4.4) Pure amino acids can form crystals, have high melting points, and are soluble in water but not in hydrocarbon solvents.

In acidic solution (low pH), amino acid zwitterions accept protons on their basic —COO⁻ groups to leave only the positively charged —NH$_3^+$ groups. In basic solution (high pH), amino acid zwitterions *lose* protons from their acidic —NH$_3^+$ groups to leave only the negatively charged —COO⁻ groups:

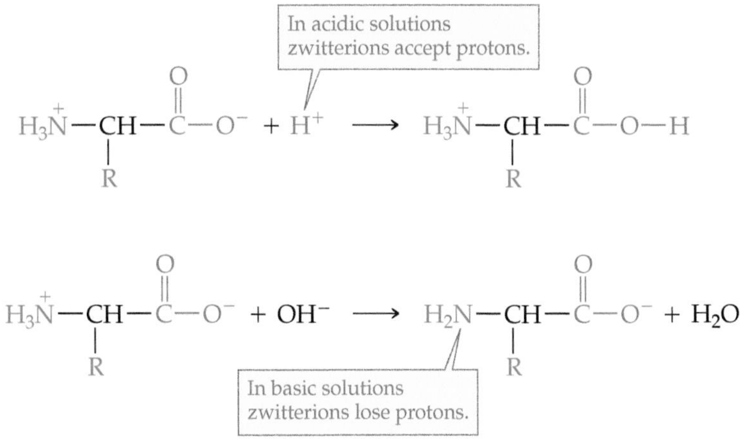

Amino acids are never present in the completely nonionized form in either the solid state or aqueous solution. The charge of an amino acid molecule at any given moment depends on the particular amino acid and the pH of the medium. The pH at which the net positive and negative charges are evenly balanced is the amino acid's **isoelectric point (pI)**. At this point, the net charge of all the amino acids in a sample is zero. (The mathematical relationship between isoelectric points and acid dissociation constants is discussed in Appendix C.)

Isoelectric point (pI) The pH at which a sample of an amino acid has equal numbers of + and − charges.

The two amino acids with acidic side chains, aspartic acid and glutamic acid, have isoelectric points at more acidic (lower) pH values than those with neutral side chains. Since the side-chain —COOH groups of these compounds are substantially ionized at physiological pH of 7.4, these amino acids are usually referred to as *aspartate* and *glutamate*, the names of the anions formed when the —COOH groups in the side chains are ionized. (Recall that the same convention is used, for example, for sulfate ion from sulfuric acid or nitrate ion from nitric acid.)

APPLICATION ▶ Nutrition in Health and Disease

To a professional, nutrition is more about the chemical components of what we eat than the flavor, form, and texture of our food. No matter what the recipe, once inside our bodies, it is only the quantity and fate of the proteins, carbohydrates, fats, minerals, and vitamins that matters.

A massive reevaluation of what we eat is occurring in the United States. Increasingly, fruits and vegetables are "in" and red meat is "out." The ongoing changes are in response to experimental evidence about the relationships between body chemistry and health. Fruits and vegetables contain a growing catalog of "phytochemicals" (which just means chemicals from plants) that appear to counteract cancer, heart disease, and a host of other conditions. And meat—especially the fat and cholesterol that naturally occur in meat—most certainly plays a role in the development of heart disease.

As a guide to a healthy diet, the U.S. Department of Agriculture, after lengthy study and consultation, remodeled the *Food Guide Pyramid* in 2005 into MyPyramid, Steps to a Healthier You. The dietary guidelines outlined in MyPyramid can be tailored to your own individual parameters such as weight, age, and activity level. MyPyramid emphasizes consumption of whole grains, fruits, and vegetables, represented by wide vertical stripes on the pyramid (see below), foods that should be eaten in larger amounts. Other foods, such as fats and oils, that should be used sparingly are represented by a narrow stripe. The principal sources of protein are in the milk and meat groups; these groups are represented by stripes of moderate widths. (In later chapters, we will return to the pyramid as we discuss the role of fats and carbohydrates in our diets.)

MyPyramid provides individualized guidelines for average healthy adults who eat a typical American diet. Guidelines for infants, the elderly, and persons with diseases must be tailored to specific needs. Designing a diet for such individuals depends on understanding body chemistry, food chemistry, and the distinctive characteristics of the individuals to be fed. In specifying diets for medical patients, nutritionists must know their patient's medical history, blood and urine levels of key chemicals, medications, physical dimensions (underweight or obese?), energy requirements, and allergies (if any). In the past decade, modified versions of the Food Guide Pyramid for various ethnic and cultural groups, for young children, for the elderly, for vegetarians, and individuals looking for "healthy weight" dietary guidelines have been developed. (One example of an alternative pyramid can be seen at www.usda.gov/kids/index.html; MyPyramid is found at www.mypyramid.gov.)

To give just one example of the implications of patient assessment, consider a person taking an amine antidepressant such as phenelzine (Nardil). Phenelzine acts by inhibiting the enzyme that removes amino groups from amino acids during their normal metabolism (Section 27.3). Some foods, especially those that are aged, fermented, or decayed, contain tyramine, an amine produced from the protein amino acid tyrosine. Notice the structural similarities among these compounds:

Phenelzine
(an antidepressant)

Tyramine
(a pressor)

Tyrosine
(α-amino acid)

Tyramine is a *pressor*—it constricts blood vessels and elevates blood pressure, which can cause irregular heartbeat, severe headache, and in serious cases, intracranial hemorrhage and cardiac failure. Ordinarily, tyramine is inactivated by removal of its amino group by the same enzymes that act on the protein amino acids. In the presence of phenelzine, however, this does not occur. A person taking phenelzine must avoid foods that contain high levels of tyramine. There is also some indication (though not proven) that tyramine in foods triggers migraine headaches.

Foods Containing Relatively High Levels of Tyramine

Cheese
Smoked fish
Chocolate
Pork products
Dry sausage
Sauerkraut
Peanuts
Beer, ale, and some wines
Bananas

▲ MyPyramid from the U.S. Department of Agriculture.

Grains	Vegetables	Fruits	Milk	Meat & Beans
Eat 6 oz. every day	Eat 2.5 cups every day	Eat 2 cups every day	Get 3 cups every day; for kids aged 2 to 8, it's 2	Eat 5.5 oz. every day

See Additional Problem 18.72 at the end of the chapter.

WORKED EXAMPLE 18.1 Determining Side-Chain Hydrophobicity/Hydrophilicity

Consider the structures of phenylalanine and serine in Table 18.3. Which of these two amino acids has a hydrophobic side chain and which has a hydrophilic side chain?

ANALYSIS Identify the side chains. The side chain in phenylalanine is an alkane. The side chain in serine contains a hydroxyl group.

SOLUTION
The hydrocarbon side chain in phenylalanine is an alkane, which is nonpolar and hydrophobic. The hydroxyl group in the side chain of serine is polar and is therefore hydrophilic.

WORKED EXAMPLE 18.2 Drawing Zwitterion Forms

Look up the zwitterion structure of valine in Table 18.3. Draw valine as it would be found (a) at low pH and (b) at high pH.

ANALYSIS At low pH, which is acidic, basic groups may gain H^+ and at high pH, which is basic, acidic groups may lose H^+. In the zwitterion form of an amino acid, the $-COO^-$ group is basic and the $-NH_3^+$ is acidic.

SOLUTION
Valine has an alkyl-group side chain that is unaffected by pH. At low pH, which is acidic, valine adds a hydrogen ion to its carboxyl group to give the structure on the left below. At high pH, which is basic, valine loses a hydrogen ion from its acidic $-NH_3^+$ group to give the structure on the right below.

$$
\begin{array}{cc}
\overset{+}{H_3N}-CH-\overset{\overset{O}{\|}}{C}-OH & H_2N-CH-\overset{\overset{O}{\|}}{C}-O^- \\
\quad\ | & \qquad | \\
\quad\ CHCH_3 & \qquad CHCH_3 \\
\quad\ | & \qquad | \\
\quad\ CH_3 & \qquad CH_3 \\
\text{Low pH} & \text{High pH}
\end{array}
$$

PROBLEM 18.7

Draw the structure of glutamic acid at low pH and at high pH.

PROBLEM 18.8

Use the definitions of acids and bases as proton donors and proton acceptors to explain which functional group in the zwitterion form of an amino acid is an acid and which is a base. (See zwitterion of threonine, p. 559.)

18.5 Handedness

Are you right-handed or left-handed? Although you may not think about it very often, handedness affects almost everything you do. It also affects the biochemical activity of molecules.

Anyone who plays softball knows that the last available glove always fits the wrong hand. This happens because your hands are not identical. Rather, they are mirror images. When you hold your left hand up to a mirror, the image you see looks like your right hand (Figure 18.1). Try it.

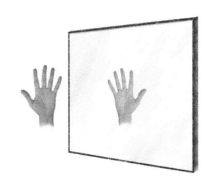

▲ FIGURE 18.1 **The meaning of** *mirror image.* If you hold your left hand up to a mirror, the image you see looks like your right hand.

Chiral Having right- or left-handedness with two *different* mirror-image forms.

Achiral The opposite of chiral; having superimposable mirror images and thus no right- or left-handedness.

▲ **FIGURE 18.2** **The meaning of superimposable.** It is easy to visualize the chair on top of its mirror image.

Additionally, note that the mirror images of your hand cannot be superimposed on each other; one does not completely fit on top of the other. Objects that have handedness in this manner are said to be **chiral** (pronounced **ky**-ral, from the Greek *cheir*, meaning "hand").

Not all objects are handed, of course. There is no such thing as a right-handed tennis ball or a left-handed coffee mug. When a tennis ball or a coffee mug is held up to a mirror, the image reflected is identical to the ball or mug itself. Objects like the coffee mug that lack handedness are said to be nonchiral, or **achiral**. Their mirror images are superimposable because they have a plane of symmetry. Take a minute to convince yourself of this by studying the chair in Figure 18.2.

PROBLEM 18.9

Which of the following objects are chiral?

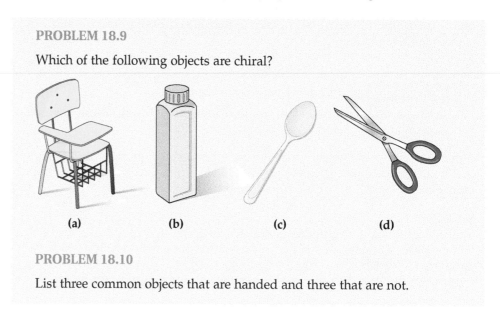

(a)   (b)   (c)   (d)

PROBLEM 18.10

List three common objects that are handed and three that are not.

18.6 Molecular Handedness and Amino Acids

Just as certain objects are chiral, certain molecules are also chiral. Alanine and propane provide a comparison between chiral and achiral molecules:

Alanine, a chiral molecule   *Propane, an achiral molecule*

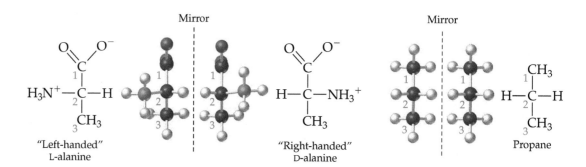

"Left-handed"
L-alanine

"Right-handed"
D-alanine

Propane

Alanine is a chiral molecule. Its mirror images cannot be superimposed. As a result, alanine exists in two forms that are mirror images of each other: a "right-handed" form known as D-alanine and a "left-handed" form known as L-alanine. (Note: The D and L designations are derived from the relationship of the structure of the amino acids to the structure of glyceraldehyde.) (⌐⊂⊃⌐, Section 22.2) Propane, by contrast, is an achiral molecule. The molecule and its mirror image are identical and it has no left- and right-handed isomers.

Why are some molecules chiral but others are not? Can we predict chirality from structural formulas? Recall from Section 5.7 that carbon forms four bonds oriented to the four corners of an imaginary tetrahedron. (⬤⬤, pp. 122–125) The formulas for alanine and propane are drawn below in a manner that emphasizes the four groups bonded to the central carbon atom. In alanine, this carbon is connected to *four different groups*: a —COO⁻ group, an —H atom, an —NH₃⁺ group, and a —CH₃ group:

$$\underset{\substack{\text{Alanine}\\\text{(chiral)}}}{H_3\overset{+}{N}-\underset{\underset{CH_3}{|}}{\overset{\overset{COO^-}{|}}{C}}-H}
\left.\begin{array}{l}1.-COO^-\\2.-H\\3.-NH_3^+\\4.-CH_3\end{array}\right\}\text{Different}
\qquad
\underset{\substack{\text{Propane}\\\text{(achiral)}}}{H-\underset{\underset{CH_3}{|}}{\overset{\overset{CH_3}{|}}{C}}-H}
\left.\begin{array}{l}1.-CH_3\\2.-CH_3\end{array}\right\}\text{Identical}
\left.\begin{array}{l}3.-H\\4.-H\end{array}\right\}\text{Identical}$$

Such a carbon atom is referred to as a **chiral carbon atom**. The presence of one chiral carbon atom always produces a chiral molecule that exists in mirror-image forms. Thus, alanine is chiral. In propane the central carbon atom is bonded to two pairs of identical groups, and the two other carbon atoms are each bonded to three hydrogen atoms. The propane molecule has no chiral carbon atoms and is therefore achiral. (If a molecule has two or more chiral carbon atoms, it may or may not be chiral, depending on its overall shape.)

The two mirror-image forms of a chiral molecule like alanine are called either **enantiomers** (pronounced **en-an-ti-o-mer**) or **optical isomers** ("optical" because of their effect on polarized light; we will discuss this in Section 22.2). The mirror-image relationship of the enantiomers of a compound with four different groups on one carbon atom is illustrated in Figure 18.3.

Like other isomers, enantiomers have the same formula but different arrangements of their atoms. More specifically, enantiomers are one kind of **stereoisomer**, compounds that have the same formula and atoms with the same connections but different spatial arrangements. (Cis–trans isomers are stereoisomers, too. ⬤⬤, Section 13.3) Pairs of enantiomers have many of the same physical properties. Both enantiomers of alanine, for example, have the same melting point, the same solubility in water, the same isoelectric point, and the same density. But pairs of enantiomers always differ in their effect on polarized light and in how they react with other molecules that are also chiral. Most importantly, pairs of enantiomers often differ in their biological activity, odors, tastes, or activity as drugs. For example, the very different natural flavors of spearmint and caraway seeds are attributed to these two enantiomers:

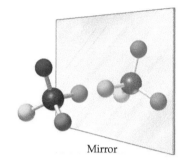

Chiral carbon atom A carbon atom bonded to four different groups.

▲ **FIGURE 18.3 A chiral molecule.** The central atom is bonded to four different groups; the molecule is therefore chiral.

Enantiomers (optical isomers) The two mirror-image forms of a chiral molecule.

Stereoisomers Isomers that have the same molecular and structural formulas but different spatial arrangements of their atoms.

L-carvone
(in spearmint)

D-carvone
(in caraway)

What about the amino acids listed in Table 18.3? Are any of them chiral? Of the 20 common amino acids, 19 are chiral because they have four different groups bonded to their α carbons, —H, —NH₂, —COOH, and —R (the side chain). Only glycine, H₂NCH₂COOH, is achiral; its α carbon is bonded to two hydrogen atoms. Even though the naturally occurring chiral α-amino acids have pairs of enantiomers, nature uses only a single isomer of each for making proteins. For historical reasons (as you will see in Section 22.2), the naturally occurring isomers are all classified as left-handed, or L-amino acids.

The artificial sweetener aspartame (sold as Equal or NutraSweet) provides another excellent illustration of the delicate nature of the structure–function relationship and its role in biochemistry. Aspartame is the methyl ester of a dipeptide

▲ Spearmint leaves and caraway seeds. The very different flavors of these food seasonings are imparted by a pair of enantiomers, which interact in different ways with our taste buds.

made from aspartate and phenylalanine in which both amino acids have the naturally occurring "left-handed" or L chirality. By contrast, the methyl esters of aspartate and phenylalanine dipeptides that have two D isomers or one D isomer combined with one L isomer are bitter.

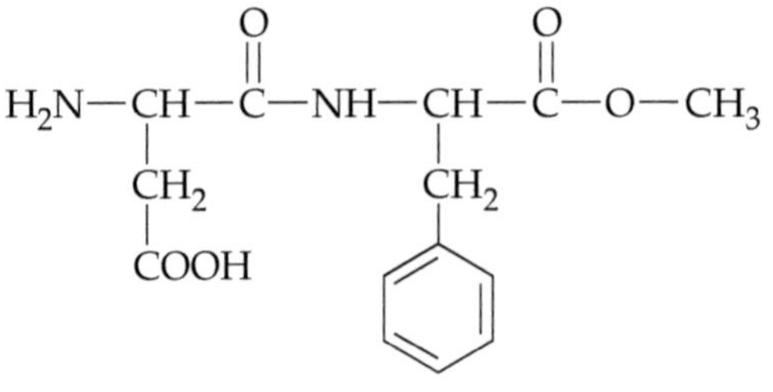

$$H_2N-CH-\overset{\overset{O}{\parallel}}{C}-NH-CH-\overset{\overset{O}{\parallel}}{C}-O-CH_3$$

Aspartame
(methyl ester of aspartylphenylalanine)

▲ This artificial sweetener would not taste sweet if either of the two amino acids in its molecular structure were D rather than L isomers.

Looking Ahead

Amino acids, as you have seen, are chiral. Chirality is an important property of another major class of biomolecules. The individual sugar units in all carbohydrates are chiral, a topic addressed in Sections 22.2 and 22.3.

WORKED EXAMPLE **18.3** Determining Chirality

Lactic acid can be isolated from sour milk. Is lactic acid chiral?

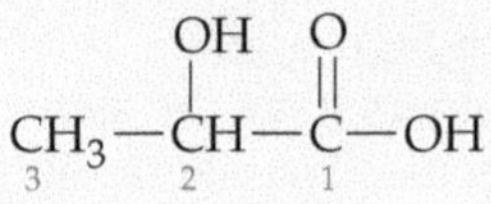

$$\underset{3}{CH_3}-\underset{2}{\overset{\overset{OH}{|}}{CH}}-\underset{1}{\overset{\overset{O}{\parallel}}{C}}-OH$$

Lactic acid

ANALYSIS A molecule is chiral if it contains one C atom bonded to four different groups. Identify any C atoms that meet this condition.

SOLUTION
To find out if lactic acid is chiral, list the groups attached to each carbon atom:

Groups on carbon 1	Groups on carbon 2	Groups on carbon 3
1. —OH	1. —COOH	1. —CH(OH)COOH
2. =O	2. —OH	2. —H
3. —CH(OH)CH₃	3. —H	3. —H
	4. —CH₃	4. —H

Next, look at the lists to see if any carbon atom is attached to four different groups. Of the three carbons, carbon 2 has four different groups, and lactic acid is therefore chiral.

PROBLEM 18.11

2-Aminopropane is an achiral molecule, but 2-aminobutane is chiral. Explain.

PROBLEM 18.12

Which of the following molecules are chiral?

(a) 3-Chloropentane

(b) 2-Chloropentane

(c) 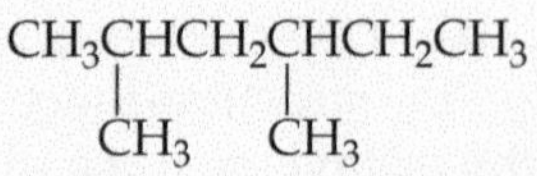 CH₃CHCH₂CHCH₂CH₃
       | |
      CH₃ CH₃

PROBLEM 18.13

Two of the 20 common amino acids have two chiral carbon atoms in their structures. Identify these amino acids and their chiral carbon atoms.

KEY CONCEPT PROBLEM 18.14

Two isomers have the formula C_2H_4BrCl. Draw them and identify any chiral carbon atoms.

18.7 Primary Protein Structure

The **primary structure** of a protein is the sequence in which its amino acids are lined up and connected by peptide bonds. Along the *backbone* of the protein is a chain of alternating peptide bonds and α carbons. The amino acid side chains (R_1, R_2, ...) are substituents along the backbone, where they are bonded to the α carbons:

Primary protein structure The sequence in which amino acids are linked by peptide bonds in a protein.

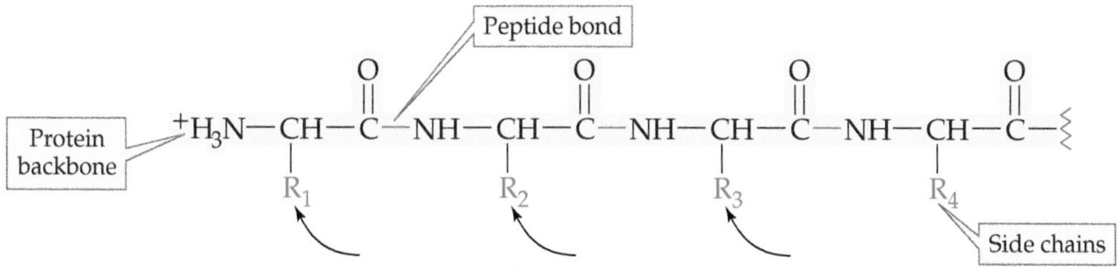

The carbon and nitrogen atoms along the backbone lie in a zigzag arrangement, with tetrahedral bonding around the α carbons. The electrons of each carbonyl-group double bond are shared to a considerable extent with the adjacent C—N bond. This sharing makes the C—N bond sufficiently like a double bond that there is no rotation around it. (Section 13.3) The result is that the carbonyl group, the —NH group bonded to it, and the two adjacent α carbons form a rigid, planar unit. The side-chain groups extend to opposite sides of the chain. Whether in a dipeptide or a huge polymer chain, these peptide units are planar:

Planar units along a protein chain

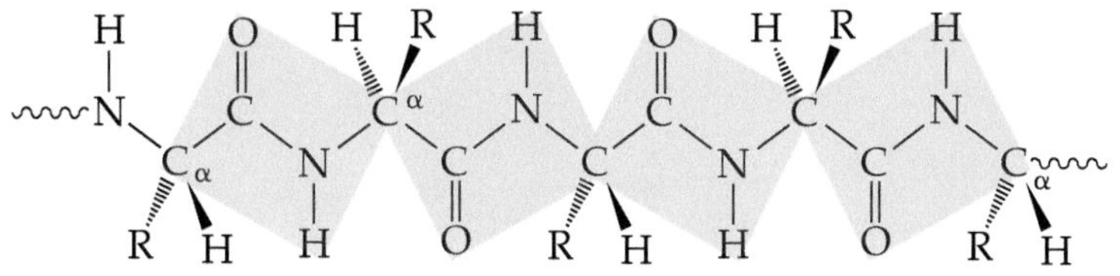

One planar unit

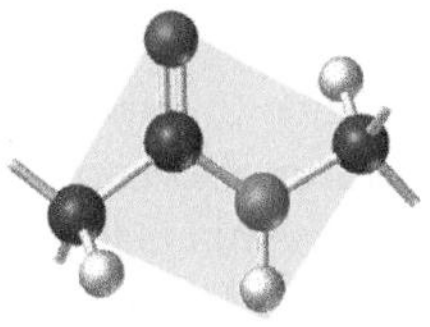

A pair of amino acids—for example, alanine and serine—can be combined to form two different dipeptides. The alanine $—COO^-$ can react with the serine $—NH_3^+$:

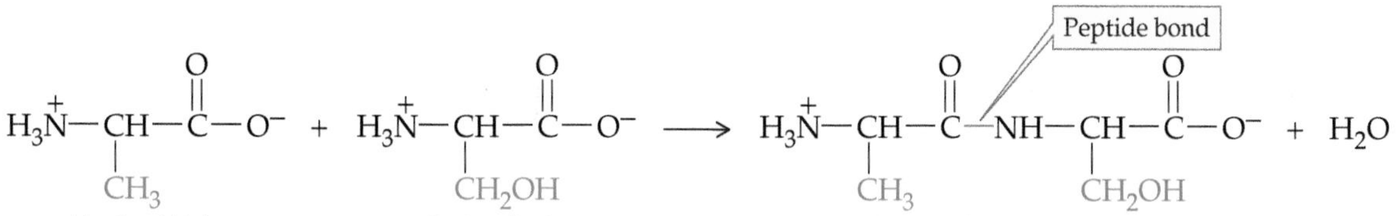

Alanine (Ala) Serine (Ser) Alanylserine (Ala-Ser)

Or the serine —COO⁻ can react with the alanine —NH₃⁺:

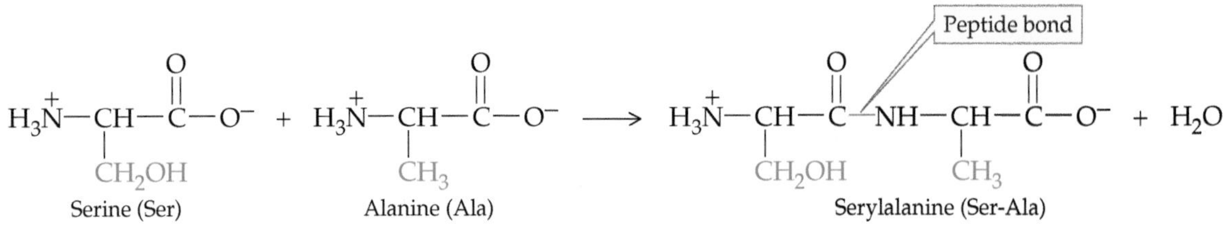

Serine (Ser) + Alanine (Ala) → Serylalanine (Ser-Ala) + H₂O

Amino-terminal (N-terminal) amino acid The amino acid with the free —NH₃⁺ group at the end of a protein.

Carboxyl-terminal (C-terminal) amino acid The amino acid with the free —COO⁻ group at the end of a protein.

Residue An amino acid unit in a polypeptide.

By convention, peptides and proteins are always written with the **amino-terminal amino acid** (also called N-terminal amino acid, the one with the free —NH₃⁺) on the left and the **carboxyl-terminal amino acid** (also called the C-terminal amino acid, the one with the free —COO⁻ group) on the right. The individual amino acids joined in the chain are referred to as **residues**.

A peptide is named by citing the amino acid residues in order, starting at the N-terminal acid and ending with the C-terminal acid. All residue names except the C-terminal one have the *-yl* ending instead of *-ine*, as in alanylserine (abbreviated Ala-Ser) or serylalanine (Ser-Ala).

The primary structure of a protein is the result of the amino acids being lined up one by one to form peptide bonds in precisely the correct order. Consider that there are six ways in which three different amino acids can be joined, more than 40,000 ways in which eight amino acids can be joined, and more than 360,000 ways in which ten amino acids can be joined. Despite the rapid increase in possible combinations with the number of amino acid residues present, only the one correct isomer can do the job. For example, human *angiotensin II* must have its eight amino acids arranged in exactly the correct order:

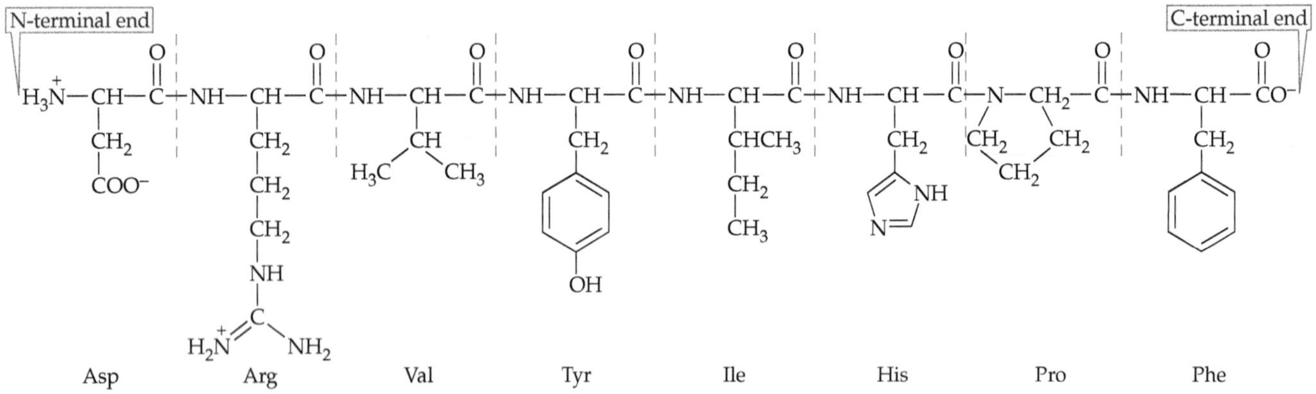

Asp — Arg — Val — Tyr — Ile — His — Pro — Phe

If not arranged properly, this hormone will not participate as it should in regulating blood pressure.

So crucial is primary structure to function—no matter how big the protein—that the change of only one amino acid can sometimes drastically alter a protein's biological properties. Sickle-cell anemia is the best-known example of the potentially devastating result of amino acid substitution. It is a hereditary disease caused by a genetic difference that replaces one amino acid (glutamate, Glu) in each of two polypeptide chains of the hemoglobin molecule with another (valine, Val).

Sickle-cell anemia is named for the "sickle" shape of affected red blood cells. (A sickle is a tool with a curved blade and short handle that is used to cut tall grass.) The sickling of the cells and the resultant painful, debilitating, and potentially fatal disease are entirely the result of the single amino acid substitution. The change replaces a hydrophilic, carboxylic acid–containing side chain (Glu) on hemoglobin with a hydrophobic, neutral hydrocarbon side chain (Val) and thus alters the shape of the hemoglobin molecule. (The effect of the change in charge on electrophoresis is illustrated in the Application, "Protein Analysis by Electrophoresis," p. 573.)

Hemoglobin, found solely inside red blood cells, is the molecule that carries oxygen in the blood and releases it where it is needed. Each red blood cell contains millions of hemoglobin molecules. Sickling takes place in red blood cells carrying the sickle-cell form of hemoglobin that has released oxygen. In this state, a hydrophobic pocket is exposed on the surface of the hemoglobin and the hydrophobic valine side chain on another hemoglobin molecule is drawn into this pocket. As this combining takes place in more and more hemoglobin molecules in a red blood cell, insoluble fibrous chains are formed. The stiff fibers force the cell into the sickled shape. Normal hemoglobin molecules that have released oxygen do not form such fibers because the —COO⁻ side chain in glutamate is too hydrophilic to enter the hydrophobic pocket on another hemoglobin molecule. Thus, each individual molecule of normal hemoglobin does not form part of any chain and no deformation of a normal red blood cell occurs. Furthermore, the hydrophobic pocket is not available in any oxygen-carrying hemoglobin molecule because of a change in shape that occurs when the molecule picks up oxygen.

Sickled red blood cells are fragile, and because they are inflexible, they tend to collect and block capillaries, causing inflammation and pain, and possibly blocking blood flow in a manner that damages major organs. Also, they have a short lifespan, which causes afflicted individuals to become severely anemic.

The percentage of individuals carrying the genetic trait for sickle-cell anemia is highest among people in ethnic groups with origins in tropical regions where malaria is prevalent. The ancestors of these individuals survived because if they were infected with malaria it was not fatal. Malaria-causing parasites enter red blood cells and reproduce there. In a person with the sickle-cell trait, the cells respond by sickling and the parasites cannot multiply. As a result, the genetic trait for sickle-cell anemia is carried forward in the surviving population.

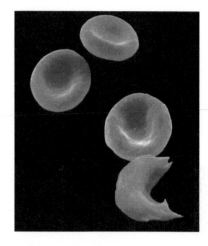

▲ Three normal (convex) and one sickled red blood cells. Because of their shape, sickled cells tend to clog vessels.

⬤ Looking Ahead

More than any other kind of biomolecule, proteins are in control of our biochemistry. Are you wondering how each of our thousands of proteins is produced with all their amino acids lined up in the correct order? The information necessary to do this is stored in DNA, and the remarkable machinery that does the job resides in the nuclei of our cells. Chapter 26 provides the details of how protein synthesis is accomplished.

WORKED EXAMPLE **18.4** Drawing Dipeptides

Draw the structure of the dipeptide Ala-Gly.

ANALYSIS You need the names and structures of the two amino acids. Since alanine is named first, it is amino-terminal and glycine is carboxyl-terminal. Ala-Gly must have a peptide bond between the alanine —COO⁻ and the glycine —NH₃⁺.

SOLUTION
The structures of alanine and glycine, and the structure of the Ala-Gly dipeptide are

$$H_3\overset{+}{N}-CH-\overset{\displaystyle O}{\overset{\|}{C}}-O^- \qquad H_3\overset{+}{N}-CH_2-\overset{\displaystyle O}{\overset{\|}{C}}-O^-$$

$$\underset{CH_3}{|}$$

Alanine (Ala)   Glycine (Gly)

and

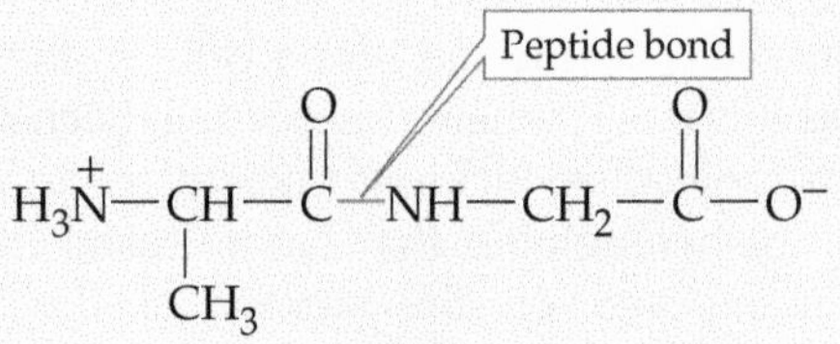

Ala-Gly

PROBLEM 18.15

(a) Use the three-letter shorthand notations to name all the isomeric tripeptides that can be made from serine, tyrosine, and glycine.

(b) Draw the complete structure of the tripeptides that have glycine as the amino-terminal amino acid.

PROBLEM 18.16

Using three-letter abbreviations, show the six tripeptides that contain leucine, tryptophan, and serine.

PROBLEM 18.17

Identify the amino acids in the following dipeptide and tripeptide, and write the abbreviated forms of the peptide names.

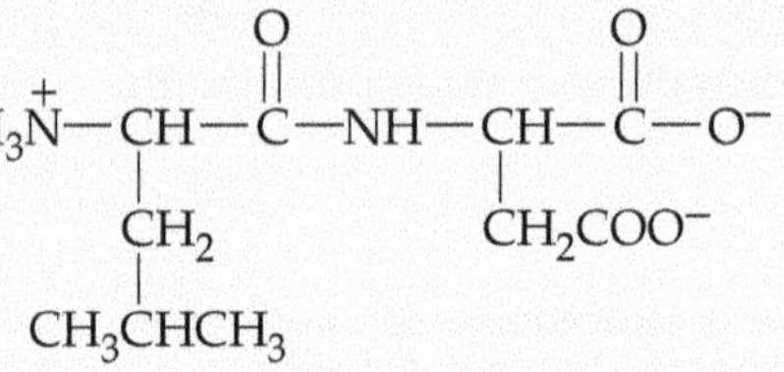

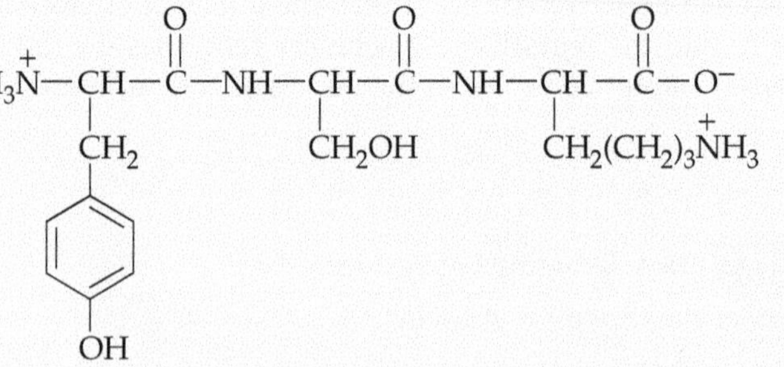

PROBLEM 18.18

Copy the structure of the tripeptide in Problem 18.17b and circle the two planar regions along the backbone.

◄● KEY CONCEPT PROBLEM 18.19

Endoproteases are enzymes that hydrolyze proteins at specific points within their sequences. Chymotrypsin is an endoprotease that cuts on the C-terminal side of aromatic amino acids. In Table 18.3 identify the three amino acids that have aromatic side chains. Now determine the number of fragments that result when chymotrypsin reacts with vasopressin, which has the structure

Asp-Tyr-Phe-Glu-Asn-Cys-Pro-Lys-Gly

and then write out the sequences of these fragments using the standard three-letter designator for each amino acid.

APPLICATION ▶ Proteins in the Diet

From a biochemical viewpoint, what are our protein requirements? Proteins are a necessary part of the daily diet because our bodies do not store proteins like they do carbohydrates and fats. Children need large amounts of protein for proper growth, and adults need protein to replace what is lost each day by normal biochemical reactions. Furthermore, 9 of the 20 amino acids are not synthesized by adult humans and must be obtained in the diet. These are known as the *essential amino acids* (histidine, isoleucine, leucine, lysine, methionine, phenylalanine, threonine, tryptophan, valine).

The total recommended daily amount of protein for an adult, which is the *minimum* required for good health, is 0.8 g per kilogram of body weight. For a 70 kg (154 lb) male, this is 56 g, and for a 55 kg (121 lb) female, it is 44 g. For reference, a McDonald's Big Mac contains 25 g of protein (along with 29 g of fat). The average protein intake in the United States is about 110 g/day, well above what most of us need.

Not all foods are equally good sources of protein. A *complete* protein source provides each of the nine essential amino acids in sufficient amounts to meet our minimum daily needs. Most meat and dairy products meet this requirement, but many vegetable sources such as wheat and corn do not.

Vegetarians must be careful to adopt a diet that includes all of the essential amino acids, which means consuming a variety of foods. In some regions, food combinations that automatically provide *complementary* proteins (proteins that together supply all of the essential amino acids) are traditional, for example, rice and lentils in India, corn tortillas and beans in Mexico, and rice and black-eyed peas in the southern United States. The grains are low in lysine and threonine, whereas the legumes (lentils, beans, and peas) supply these amino acids, but are low in methionine and tryptophan, which are present in grains.

Protein is the major source of nitrogen in the diet. A healthy adult is normally at nitrogen equilibrium, meaning that the amount of nitrogen taken in each day is equal to the amount excreted. Infants and children, pregnant women, those recovering from starvation, and those with healing wounds are usually in *positive nitrogen balance*—they are excreting less nitrogen than they consume, a condition to be expected when new tissue is growing. The reverse condition, *negative nitrogen balance*, occurs when more nitrogen is excreted than consumed. This happens when protein intake is inadequate, during starvation, and in a number of pathologic conditions including malignancies, malabsorption syndromes, and kidney disease.

▲ This typical Mexican meal contains a complementary protein food combination: beans and rice.

Health and nutrition professionals group all disorders caused by inadequate protein intake as *protein-energy malnutrition* (PEM). Children, because of their higher protein needs, suffer most from this kind of malnutrition. The problem is rampant where meat and milk are in short supply and where the dietary staples are vegetables or grains. An individual is malnourished to some degree if *any* of the essential amino acids are deficient in their diet.

Protein deficiency alone is rare, however, and its symptoms are usually accompanied by those of vitamin deficiencies, infectious diseases, and starvation. At one end of the spectrum is *kwashiorkor*, in which protein is deficient although caloric intake may be adequate. Children with kwashiorkor have edema (swelling due to water retention) and an enlarged liver, and are underdeveloped. The word "kwashiorkor" is from the language of Ghana and translates as "the sickness the older child gets when the next child is born." The onset of kwashiorkor comes when weaning from mother's milk results in conversion to a high-carbohydrate, low-protein diet consisting primarily of corn or cassava gruel. At the other end of the spectrum is *marasmus*, which is the result of starvation. As distinguished from kwashiorkor, marasmus in children is identified with severe muscle wasting, below-normal stature, and poor response to treatment.

See Additional Problems 18.73 through 18.76 and 18.84 at the end of the chapter.

18.8 Shape-Determining Interactions in Proteins

Without interactions between atoms in amino acid side chains or along the backbone, protein chains would twist about randomly in body fluids like spaghetti strands in boiling water. The essential structure–function relationship for each protein depends on the polypeptide chain being held in its necessary shape by these interactions. Before we look at the secondary, tertiary, and quaternary structures of proteins, it will be helpful to understand the kinds of interactions that determine the shapes of protein molecules.

Hydrogen Bonds along the Backbone

Hydrogen bonds form when a hydrogen atom bonded to a highly electronegative atom is attracted to another highly electronegative atom that has an unshared electron pair. The hydrogens in the —NH— groups and the oxygens in the —C=O groups along protein backbones meet these conditions:

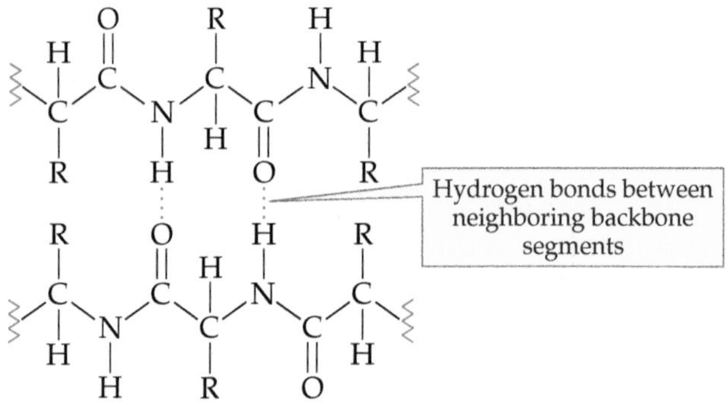

Hydrogen bonds between neighboring backbone segments

This type of hydrogen bonding creates pleated sheet and helical secondary structures, as described in Section 18.9 and as illustrated in the imaginary protein in Figure 18.4.

Hydrogen Bonds of R Groups with Each Other or with Backbone Atoms

Some amino acid side chains contain atoms that can form hydrogen bonds. Side-chain hydrogen bonds can connect different parts of a protein molecule, sometimes nearby and sometimes far apart along the chain. In the protein in Figure 18.4, hydrogen bonds between side chains have created folds in two places. Often hydrogen-bonding side chains are present on the surface of a folded protein, where they can hydrogen-bond with surrounding water molecules.

Ionic Attractions between R Groups (Salt Bridges)

Where there are ionized acidic and basic side chains, the attraction between their positive and negative charges creates what are sometimes known as *salt bridges*. A basic lysine side chain and an acidic aspartate side chain have formed a salt bridge in the middle of the protein shown in Figure 18.4.

Hydrophobic Interactions between R Groups

Hydrocarbon side chains are attracted to each other by the dispersion forces caused by the momentary uneven distribution of electrons. (⬤, Section 8.11) The result is that these groups cluster together in the same way that oil molecules cluster on the surface of water (⬤, Section 9.2), so that these interactions are often referred to as *hydrophobic*. By clustering in this manner, the hydrophobic groups shown in Figure 18.4 create a water-free pocket in the protein chain. Although the individual

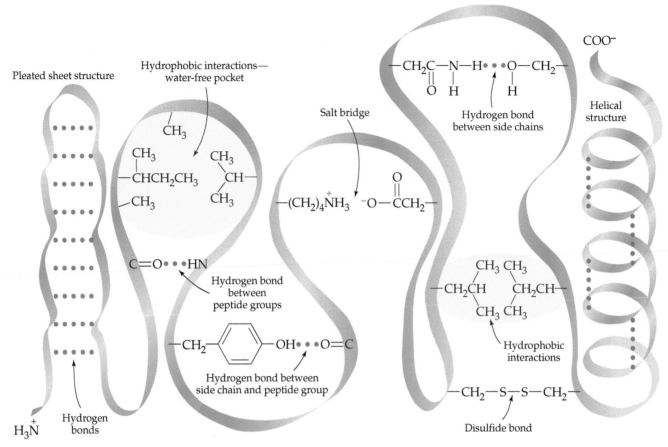

▲ **FIGURE 18.4** **Interactions that determine protein shape.** The regular pleated sheet (*left*) and helical structure (*right*) are created by hydrogen bonding between neighboring backbone atoms; the other interactions involve side-chain groups that can be nearby or quite far apart in the protein chain.

attractions are weak, their large number in proteins plays a major role in stabilizing the folded structures.

Covalent Sulfur–Sulfur Bonds

In addition to the noncovalent interactions, one type of covalent bond plays a role in determining protein shape. Cysteine amino acid residues have side chains containing thiol functional groups (—SH) that can react to form sulfur–sulfur bonds (—S—S—) (⊂⊃, Section 14.9):

If the cysteines are in different protein chains, the otherwise separate chains are linked together. If the cysteines are in the same chain, a loop is formed in the chain. Insulin provides a good example. It consists of two polypeptide chains connected by **disulfide bonds** in two places. One of the chains also has a loop caused by a third disulfide bond.

Disulfide bond An S—S bond formed between two cysteine side chains; can join two peptide chains together or cause a loop in a peptide chain.

Structure of insulin

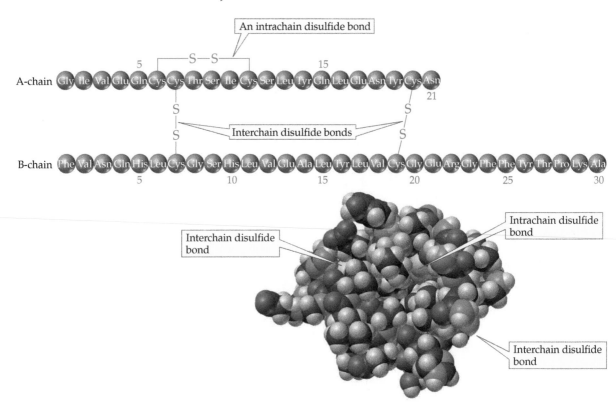

The structure and function of insulin are of intense interest because of its role in glucose metabolism and the need for supplementary insulin by individuals with diabetes (discussed in Section 23.9). Undoubtedly because of this need, studies of insulin have led the way in our still-developing ability to determine the structure of a biomolecule and prepare it synthetically.

In a historically important accomplishment, the amino acid sequence of insulin was determined in 1951—it was the *first* protein for which this was done. It took 15 years before the cross-linking and complete structure of the molecule were determined and a successful laboratory synthesis was carried out. With the advent of biotechnology in the 1980s, once again insulin was first. Until then, diabetic individuals relied on insulin extracted from the pancreas of cows, and because of differences in three amino acids from human insulin, allergic reactions occasionally resulted. In 1982, human insulin became the first commercial product of genetic engineering to be licensed by the U.S. government for clinical use.

⊂⊙⊃ Looking Ahead

Insulin and angiotensin II (p. 566) are representative of a class of small polypeptides that are hormones—they are released when a chemical message must be carried from one place to another. Hormones are discussed in Sections 20.2–20.5. ⊂⊙⊃

WORKED EXAMPLE   **18.5** Drawing Side-Chain Interactions

What type of noncovalent interaction occurs between the threonine and glutamine side chains? Draw the structures of these amino acids to show the interaction.

ANALYSIS The side chains of threonine and glutamine contain an amide group and a hydroxyl group, respectively. These groups do not form salt bridges because they do not ionize. They are polar and therefore not hydrophobic. They form a hydrogen bond between the oxygen of the amide carbonyl group and the hydrogen of the hydroxyl group.

SOLUTION

The noncovalent, hydrogen bond interaction between threonine and glutamine is as follows:

$$C=O \qquad\qquad\qquad C=O$$
$$CH-CH_2-CH_2-C=O\cdots H-O-CH-CH$$
$$NH \qquad\qquad NH_2 \qquad\qquad CH_3\ NH$$

PROBLEM 18.20

Look at Table 18.3 and identify the type of noncovalent interaction expected between the side chains of the following pairs of amino acids:

(a) Glutamine and tyrosine   **(b)** Leucine and proline

(c) Aspartate and arginine   **(d)** Isoleucine and phenylalanine

APPLICATION ▶ Protein Analysis by Electrophoresis

Protein molecules in solution can be separated from each other by taking advantage of their net charges. In the electric field between two electrodes, a positively charged particle moves toward the negative electrode and a negatively charged particle moves toward the positive electrode. This movement, known as *electrophoresis*, varies with the strength of the electric field, the charge of the particle, the size and shape of the particle, and the nature of the medium in which the protein is moving.

The net charge on a protein is determined by how many of the acidic or basic side-chain functional groups in the protein are ionized, and this, like the charge of an amino acid (Section 18.4), depends on the pH. Thus, the mobility of a protein during electrophoresis depends on the pH of the medium. If the medium is at a pH equal to the isoelectric point of the protein, the protein does not move.

By varying the nature of the medium between the electrodes and other conditions, proteins can be separated in a variety of ways, including by their molecular weight. Once the separation is complete, the various proteins are made visible by the addition of a dye.

Electrophoresis is routinely used in the clinical laboratory for determining which proteins are present in a blood sample. One application is in the diagnosis of sickle-cell anemia (p. 566). Normal adult hemoglobin (HbA) and hemoglobin showing the inherited sickle-cell trait (HbS) differ in their charges. Therefore, HbA and HbS move different distances during electrophoresis in a medium with constant pH. The accompanying diagram compares the results of electrophoresis of the hemoglobin extracted from red blood cells for a normal individual, one with sickle-cell anemia (two inherited sickle-cell genes), and one with sickle-cell trait (one normal and one inherited sickle-cell gene). With sickle-cell trait, an individual is likely to suffer symptoms of the disease only under conditions of severe oxygen deprivation.

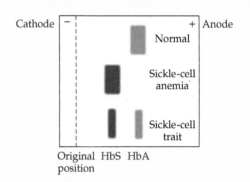

▲ **Gel electrophoresis of hemoglobin.** Hemoglobin in samples placed at the original position have moved left to right as shown. The normal individual has only HbA. The individual with sickle-cell anemia has no HbA, and the individual with sickle-cell trait has roughly equal amounts of HbA and HbS. HbA and HbS have negative charges of different magnitudes because HbS has two fewer Glu residues than HbA.

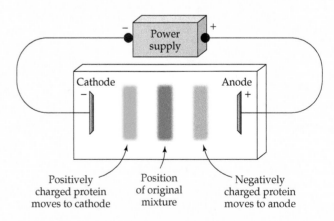

▲ Movement of charged molecules in electrophoresis.

See Additional Problems 18.77–18.78 and 18.83 at the end of the chapter.

PROBLEM 18.21

In Figure 18.4, identify the amino acids that have formed (a) hydrogen bonds from their side chains and (b) hydrophobic side-chain interactions.

18.9 Secondary Protein Structure

Secondary protein structure
Regular and repeating structural patterns (for example, α-helix, β-sheet) created by hydrogen bonding between backbone atoms in neighboring segments of protein chains.

Alpha- (α-) helix Secondary protein structure in which a protein chain forms a right-handed coil stabilized by hydrogen bonds between peptide groups along its backbone.

The spatial arrangement of the polypeptide backbones of proteins constitutes **secondary protein structure**. The secondary structure includes two kinds of repeating patterns known as the **alpha-helix** (α-helix), and the **beta-sheet** (β-sheet). In both, hydrogen bonding between *backbone* atoms holds the polypeptide chain in place. The hydrogen bonding connects the carbonyl oxygen atom of one peptide unit with the amide hydrogen atom of another peptide unit (—C=O· · ·H—N—). In large protein molecules, regions of α-helix and β-sheet structure are connected either by randomly arranged loops or coils that are a third type of secondary structure.

α-Helix

A single protein chain coiled in a spiral with a right-handed (clockwise) twist is known as an **alpha-helix (α-helix)** (Figure 18.5a). The helix, which resembles a coiled telephone cord, is stabilized by hydrogen bonds between each backbone carbonyl

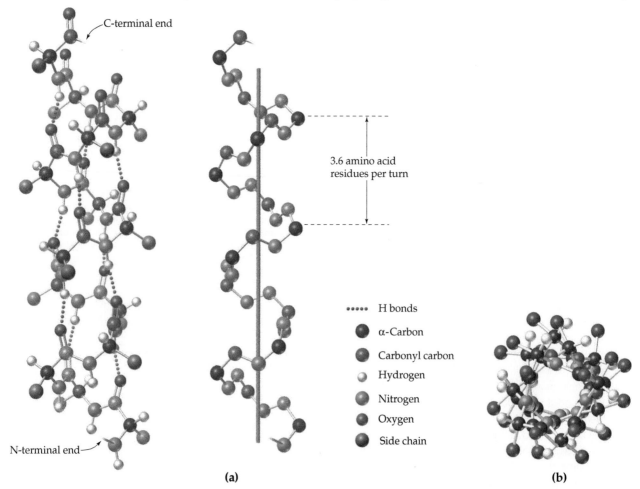

3.6 amino acid residues per turn

C-terminal end

N-terminal end

····· H bonds
● α-Carbon
● Carbonyl carbon
○ Hydrogen
● Nitrogen
● Oxygen
● Side chain

(a)　　　　　　　　　　　　　　(b)

▲ **FIGURE 18.5 Alpha-helix secondary structure.** (a) The coil is held in place by hydrogen bonds (dotted red lines) between each carbonyl oxygen and the amide hydrogen four amino acid residues above it. The chain is a right-handed coil (shown separately on the right), and the hydrogen bonds lie parallel to the vertical axis. (b) Viewed from the top into the center of the helix, the side chains point to the exterior of the helix.

oxygen and an amide hydrogen four amino acid residues farther along the backbone. The hydrogen bonds lie vertically along the helix, and the amino acid R groups extend to the outside of the coil. Although the strength of each individual hydrogen bond is small, the large number of bonds in the helix results in an extremely stable secondary structure. A view of the helix from the top (Figure 18.5b) clearly shows the side chains on the amino acids oriented to the exterior of the helix.

β-Sheet

In the **beta-sheet (β-sheet)** structure, the polypeptide chains are held in place by hydrogen bonds between pairs of peptide units along neighboring backbone segments. The protein chains, which are extended to their full length, bend at each α carbon so that the sheet has a pleated contour, with the R groups extending above and below the sheet (Figure 18.6).

Beta- (β-) sheet Secondary protein structure in which adjacent protein chains either in the same molecule or in different molecules are held in place by hydrogen bonds along the backbones.

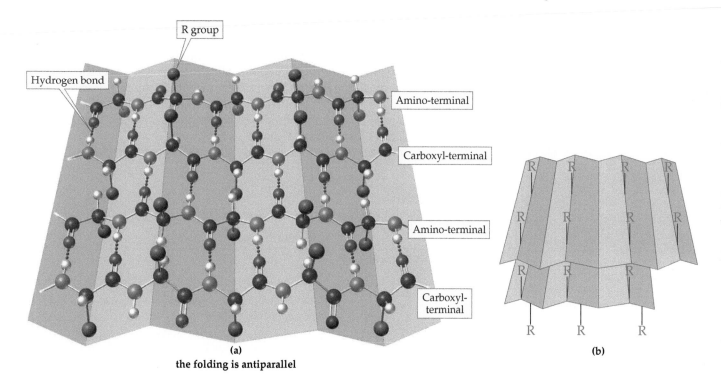

(a)
the folding is antiparallel

(b)

▲ **FIGURE 18.6 Beta-sheet secondary structure.** (a) The hydrogen bonds between neighboring protein chains. The protein chains usually lie side by side so that alternating chains run from the N-terminal end to the C-terminal end and from the C-terminal end to the N-terminal end (known as the *antiparallel* arrangement). (b) A pair of stacked pleated sheets illustrate how the R groups point above and below the sheets.

PROBLEM 18.22

Examine the α-helix in Figure 18.5 and determine how many backbone C and N atoms are included in the loop between an amide hydrogen atom and the carbonyl oxygen to which it is hydrogen-bonded.

Secondary Structure in Fibrous and Globular Proteins

Proteins are classified in several ways, one of which is to identify them as either *fibrous proteins* or *globular proteins*. In an example of the integration of molecular structure and function that is central to biochemistry, fibrous and globular proteins each have functions made possible by their distinctive structures.

Fibrous protein A tough, insoluble protein whose protein chains form fibers or sheets.

Globular protein A water-soluble protein whose chain is folded in a compact shape with hydrophilic groups on the outside.

▲ The proteins found in eggs, milk, and cheese are examples of globular proteins. A spider web is made from fibrous protein.

Secondary structure is primarily responsible for the nature of **fibrous proteins**—tough, insoluble proteins in which the chains form long fibers or sheets. Wool, hair, and fingernails are made of fibrous proteins known as *α-keratins*, which are composed almost completely of α-helixes. In α-keratins, pairs of α-helixes are twisted together into small fibrils that are in turn twisted into larger and larger bundles. The hardness, flexibility, and stretchiness of the material varies with the number of disulfide bonds. In fingernails, for example, large numbers of disulfide bonds hold the bundles in place.

Natural silk and spider webs are made of *fibroin*, a fibrous protein almost entirely composed of stacks of β-sheets. For such close stacking, the R groups must be relatively small (see Figure 18.6). Fibroin contains regions of alternating glycine (—H on α carbon) and alanine (—CH$_3$ on α carbon). The sheets stack so that sides with the smaller glycine hydrogens face each other and sides with the larger alanine methyl groups face each other.

Globular proteins are water-soluble proteins whose chains are folded into compact, globe-like shapes. Their structures, which vary widely with their functions, are not regular like those of fibrous proteins. Where the protein chain folds back on itself, sections of α-helix and β-sheet are usually present, as illustrated in Figure 18.4. The presence of hydrophilic side chains on the outer surfaces of globular proteins accounts for their water solubility, allowing them to travel through the blood and other body fluids to sites where their activity is needed. Furthermore, many globular proteins are enzymes that are dissolved in the intercellular fluids inside cells. The overall shapes of globular proteins represent another level of structure, tertiary structure, discussed in the next section.

Table 18.4 compares the occurrences and functions of some fibrous and globular proteins.

TABLE 18.4 Some Common Fibrous and Globular Proteins

NAME	OCCURRENCE AND FUNCTION
Fibrous proteins (insoluble)	
Keratins	Found in skin, wool, feathers, hooves, silk, fingernails
Collagens	Found in animal hide, tendons, bone, eye cornea, and other connective tissue
Elastins	Found in blood vessels and ligaments, where ability of the tissue to stretch is important
Myosins	Found in muscle tissue
Fibrin	Found in blood clots
Globular proteins (soluble)	
Insulin	Regulatory hormone for controlling glucose metabolism
Ribonuclease	Enzyme that catalyzes RNA hydrolysis
Immunoglobulins	Proteins involved in immune response
Hemoglobin	Protein involved in oxygen transport
Albumins	Proteins that perform many transport functions in blood; protein in egg white

18.10 Tertiary Protein Structure

Tertiary protein structure The way in which an entire protein chain is coiled and folded into its specific three-dimensional shape.

The overall three-dimensional shape that results from the folding of a protein chain is the protein's **tertiary structure**. In contrast to secondary structure, which depends mainly on attraction between backbone atoms, tertiary structure depends mainly on interactions of amino acid side chains that are far apart along the same backbone.

Although the bends and twists of the protein chain in a globular protein may appear irregular and the three-dimensional structure may appear random, this is not the case. Each protein molecule folds in a distinctive manner that is determined by its primary structure and results in its maximum stability. A protein with the shape in which it functions in living systems is known as a **native protein**.

The noncovalent interactions and disulfide covalent bonds described in Section 18.8 govern tertiary structure. The enzyme *ribonuclease*, shown here as an example, is drawn in a style that shows the combination of α-helix and β-sheet regions, the loops connecting them, and four disulfide bonds:

Native protein A protein with the shape (secondary, tertiary, and quaternary structure) in which it exists naturally in living organisms.

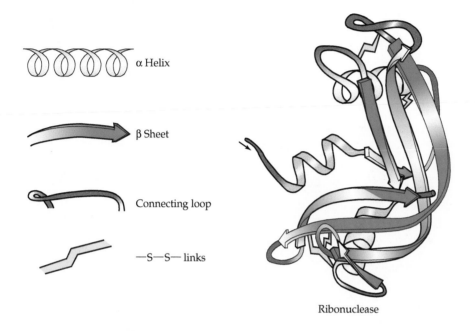

α Helix

β Sheet

Connecting loop

—S—S— links

Ribonuclease

The structure of ribonuclease is representative of the tertiary structure of globular, water-soluble proteins. The hydrophobic, nonpolar side chains congregate in a hydrocarbon-like interior, and the hydrophilic side chains, which provide water solubility, congregate on the outside. Ribonuclease is classified as a **simple protein** because it is composed only of amino acid residues (124 of them). The drawing shows ribonuclease in a style that clearly represents the combination of secondary structures in the overall tertiary structure of a globular protein.

Simple protein A protein composed of only amino acid residues.

Myoglobin is another example of a small globular protein. A relative of hemoglobin (described in the next section), myoglobin stores oxygen in skeletal muscles for use when there is an immediate need for energy. Structurally, the 153 amino acid residues of myoglobin are arranged in eight α-helical segments connected by short segments looped so that hydrophilic amino acid residues are on the exterior of the compact, spherical tertiary structure. Like many proteins, myoglobin is not a simple protein, but is a **conjugated protein**—a protein that is aided in its function by an associated non–amino acid nonprotein group. The oxygen-carrying portion of myoglobin has a heme group embedded within the polypeptide chain. In Figure 18.7 the myoglobin molecule is drawn in four different ways, each often used to illustrate the shapes of protein molecules. Some examples of other kinds of conjugated proteins are listed in Table 18.5.

Conjugated protein A protein that incorporates one or more non–amino acid units in its structure.

⚷ KEY CONCEPT PROBLEM 18.23

Hydrogen bonds are important in stabilizing both the secondary and tertiary structures of proteins. How do the groups that form hydrogen bonds in the secondary and tertiary structures differ?

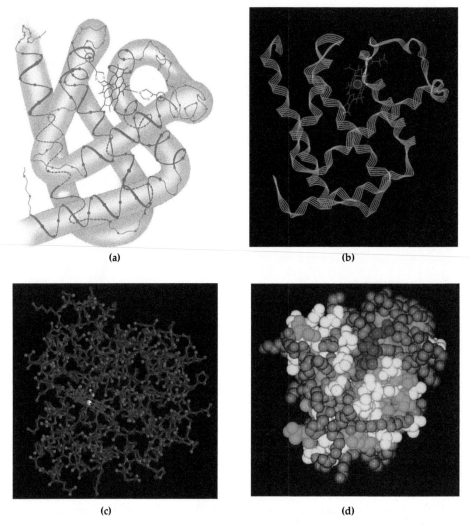

▲ **FIGURE 18.7**   **Myoglobin, drawn in four styles.**   In each panel the red structure embedded in the protein is a molecule of heme, to which O_2 binds. (a) The sausage-like shape is often used alone to represent the helical portions of a globular protein. (b) A protein *ribbon model* shows the helical portions as a ribbon. (c) A ball-and-stick molecular model of myoglobin. (d) A space-filling model of myoglobin in which the hydrophobic residues are blue and the hydrophilic residues are purple.

TABLE 18.5   Some Examples of Conjugated Proteins

CLASS OF PROTEIN	NONPROTEIN PART	EXAMPLES
Glycoproteins	Carbohydrates	Glycoproteins in cell membranes (Section 24.7)
Lipoproteins	Lipids	High- and low-density lipoproteins that transport cholesterol and other lipids through the body (Section 25.2)
Metalloproteins	Metal ions	The enzyme cytochrome oxidase, necessary for biological energy production, and many other enzymes
Phosphoproteins	Phosphate groups	Milk casein, which provides essential nutrients to infants
Hemoproteins	Heme	Hemoglobin (transplants oxygen) and myoglobin (stores oxygen)
Nucleoproteins	RNA (ribonucleic acid)	Found in cell ribosomes, where they take part in protein synthesis

18.11 Quaternary Protein Structure

The fourth and final level of protein structure, and the most complex, is **quaternary protein structure**—the way in which two or more polypeptide subunits associate to form a single three-dimensional protein unit. The individual polypeptides are held together by the same noncovalent forces responsible for tertiary structure. In some cases, there are also covalent bonds and the protein may incorporate a non–amino acid portion. *Hemoglobin* and *collagen* are both well-understood examples of proteins with quaternary structure essential to their function.

Quaternary protein structure The way in which two or more protein chains aggregate to form large, ordered structures.

Hemoglobin

Hemoglobin (Figure 18.8a) is a conjugated quaternary protein composed of four polypeptide chains (two α chains and two β chains) held together primarily by the interaction of hydrophobic groups, and four heme groups. The polypeptides are similar in composition and tertiary structure to myoglobin (Figure 18.7). The α chains have 141 amino acids, and the β chains have 146 amino acids.

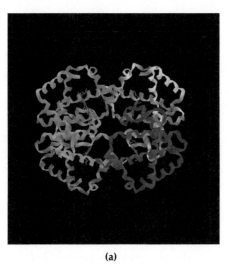

(a)

(b)

◀ **FIGURE 18.8 Heme and hemoglobin, a protein with quaternary structure.** (a) The polypeptides are shown in purple, green, blue, and yellow, with their heme units in red. Each polypeptide resembles myoglobin in structure. (b) A heme unit is present in each of the four polypeptides in hemoglobin.

The hemes (Figure 18.8b), one in each of the four polypeptides, each contain an iron atom that is essential to their function. Hemoglobin is the oxygen carrier in red blood cells. In the lungs, O_2 binds to the Fe^{2+}, so that each hemoglobin can carry a maximum of four O_2 molecules. In tissues in need of oxygen, the O_2 is released, and CO_2 (the product of respiration) is picked up and carried back to the lungs. (Oxygen transport is discussed further in Section 29.6.)

Collagen

Collagen is the most abundant of all proteins in mammals, making up 30% or more of the total. A fibrous protein, collagen is the major constituent of skin, tendons, bones, blood vessels, and other connective tissues. The basic structural unit of collagen (*tropocollagen*) consists of three intertwined chains of about 1000 amino acids each. Each stiff, rod-like chain is loosely coiled in a left-handed (counterclockwise) direction (Figure 18.9a). Three of these coiled chains wrap around one another (in a clockwise direction) to form a stiff, rod-like triple helix (Figure 18.9b) in which the chains are held together by hydrogen bonds.

The various kinds of collagen have in common a glycine residue at every third position. Only glycine residues (with —H as the side chain on the α carbon) can fit in the center of the tightly coiled triple helix. The larger side chains face the exterior of the helix. Proline is incorporated into the originally synthesized collagen molecules. A hydroxyl group is then added to some proline residues in a reaction that requires vitamin C (Section 19.10). Herein lies the explanation for the symptoms of scurvy, the disease that results from vitamin C deficiency. When vitamin C is in short supply, collagen is deficient in hydroxylated proline residues and, as a result,

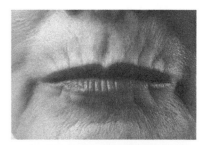

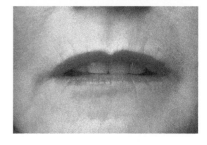

▲ Collagen injections are used to smooth away facial wrinkles, as seen in these before and after photos.

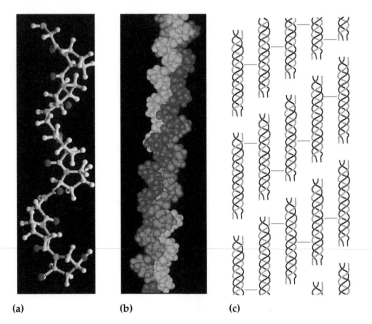

▶ **FIGURE 18.9 Collagen.** (a) A single collagen helix (carbon, green; hydrogen, light blue; nitrogen, dark blue; oxygen, red). (b) The triple helix of tropocollagen. (c) The quaternary structure of a cross-linked collagen, showing the assemblage of tropocollagen molecules.

(a)   (b)   (c)

forms fibers poorly. The results are the skin lesions and fragile blood vessels that accompany scurvy.

The tropocollagen triple helixes are assembled into collagen in a quaternary structure formed by a great many strands overlapping lengthwise (Figure 18.9c). Depending on the exact purpose collagen serves in the body, further structural modifications occur. In connective tissue like tendons, covalent bonds between strands give collagen fibers a rigid, cross-linked structure. In teeth and bones, calcium hydroxyapatite $[Ca_5(PO_4)_3OH]$ deposits in the gaps between chains to further harden the overall assembly.

Protein Structure Summary

- **Primary structure**—the sequence of amino acids connected by peptide bonds in the polypeptide chain; for example, Asp-Arg-Val-Tyr.

- **Secondary structure**—the arrangement in space of the polypeptide chain, which includes the regular patterns of the α-helix and the β-sheet (held together by hydrogen bonds between backbone carbonyl and amino groups in amino acid residues along adjacent chains segments) plus the loops and coils that connect these segments.

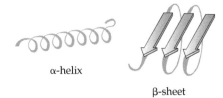

α-helix

β-sheet

- **Tertiary structure**—the folding of a protein molecule into a specific three-dimensional shape held together by noncovalent interactions primarily between amino acid side chains that can be quite far apart along the backbone and, in some cases, by disulfide bonds between side-chain thiol groups.

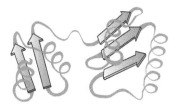

- **Quaternary structure**—two or more protein chains assembled in a larger three-dimensional structure held together by noncovalent interactions.

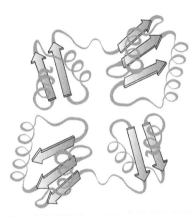

- **Classes of proteins**
- *Fibrous proteins* are tough, insoluble, and composed of fibers and sheets; *globular proteins* are water-soluble and have chains folded into compact shapes.
- *Simple proteins* contain only amino acid residues; *conjugated proteins* include one or more non–amino acid units.

KEY CONCEPT PROBLEM 18.24

Identify the following statements as descriptive of the secondary, tertiary, or quaternary structure of a protein. What type(s) of interaction(s) stabilize each type of structure?

(a) The polypeptide chain has a number of bends and twists resulting in a compact structure.

(b) The polypeptide backbone forms a right-handed coil.

(c) The four polypeptide chains are arranged in a spherical shape.

APPLICATION ▶ Collagen—A Tale of Two Diseases

Case 1: Aboard a British naval ship around 1740. Approximately half of the crew, able-bodied seamen and officers alike, cannot work due to illness. Symptoms include joint pain and swelling, blackened bruises on the skin, and swollen, bleeding gums accompanied by tooth loss. Several sailors have died after spontaneous bleeding from nasal mucous membranes.

Case 2: A hospital emergency room in 2008. A 4-month-old infant girl is brought to the emergency room by her parents. She is in pain and her left arm does not appear "normal." An X-ray establishes that she has a broken arm.

Both of these cases are the result of defects in collagen synthesis. The curable disease scurvy is responsible for the first; the infant in Case 2 suffers from osteogenesis imperfecta, also known as brittle bone disease, an incurable genetic disease.

The symptoms of scurvy have been recognized for centuries due to its prevalence; it is experienced whenever fresh fruits and vegetables are not available for long periods of time. Armies, navies, and medieval people in northern regions in late winter were particularly susceptible to scurvy due to lack of fresh produce. In modern times scurvy is rarely seen except in the elderly, those on highly unusual diets and sometimes in infants. It may also be seen on college campuses

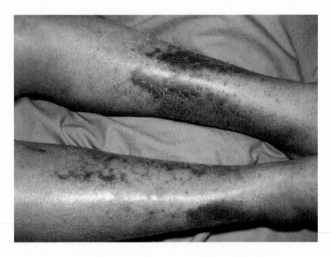

▲ Visible signs of scurvy. Note the swollen ankles and the bruising and lesions on the lower legs that are characteristic of scurvy.

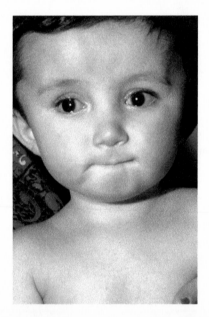

▲ Child with osteogenesis imperfecta. One characteristic of osteogenesis imperfecta is the blue color of the sclera (whites) of the eyes.

where students away from home forget why they should eat fresh fruits and vegetables.

We now know that scurvy results from the synthesis of defective collagen. Collagen is synthesized continuously by the body as old cells and tissues are remodeled and the process is dependent upon vitamin C. Humans neither produce nor store vitamin C in their bodies; it must be obtained daily from the diet. Vitamin C is necessary for the addition of hydroxyl groups to proline by the enzyme prolyhydroxylase after the synthesis of a collagen chain. Proline makes up

about one-third of the amino acids in collagen. About half of the proline residues are hydroxylated, resulting in stabilization of the helical structure of each individual collagen chain. This stabilization further enhances the formation of the triple helix of tropocollagen (Figure 18.9). Lack of vitamin C leads to the formation of weak collagen and tropocollagen. Since tropocollagen is part of capillary walls, it is not surprising that weak collagen leads to the spontaneous bruising, bleeding, and soft tissue swelling that are characteristic of scurvy.

Scurvy is both preventable and curable. Prior to the discovery of vitamin C and the recognition of its role at the molecular level in the prevention of scurvy, fresh food, which inevitably included fruits and vegetables, was recognized as a cure for the disease. The British naval surgeon James Lind is generally attributed with the definitive experiment (in 1747) showing that citrus fruit, in particular lemons and limes, cured scurvy developed during long sea voyages. Subsequently, the British Navy supplied its sailors with lemons and limes during voyages as a preventative treatment for scurvy. This simple move both improved the health and survival rate of the sailors and also resulted in British sailors being known as "limeys."

The disease of the infant in Case 2, osteogenesis imperfecta, is also a collagen disease. Unlike scurvy, which is a dietary disease, osteogenesis imperfecta is inherited. The genetic defect is dominant, meaning it can be inherited from only one parent. The primary symptom of this disease is spontaneous broken bones.

Collagen forms the scaffold for bone. Collagen fibers are the bone matrix, which is filled in with calcium containing crystals of hydroxyapatite ($Ca_5[PO_4]_3OH$). The combination of collagen and hydroxyapaptite makes strong bone tissue. In osteogenesis imperfecta, incorrectly synthesized collagen leads to weaker bone structures. Type I osteogenesis imperfecta is most common and fractures occur primarily before puberty. Other symptoms are grayness of the sclera (white part) of the eye, loose joints, low muscle tone, and brittle teeth. In more severe types of osteogenesis imperfecta, the child may have numerous, frequent fractures, even before birth, small stature, and respiratory problems. Treatment is supportive, aimed at preventing fractures and strengthening muscles. There is no cure for osteogenesis imperfecta, although current research is directed at understanding the underlying biochemical defect in hopes of designing better treatment.

It is difficult to distinguish osteogenesis imperfecta from child abuse. However, the types of spontaneous bone fractures seen in osteogenesis imperfecta are not the typical fractures seen in child abuse cases. A definitive diagnosis of osteogenesis imperfecta requires genetic testing of tissue from the child. Only a small amount of skin tissue is needed. (⊂⊃, See Chapter 27: Genomics for DNA testing.)

See Additional Problems 18.79 and 18.80 at the end of the chapter.

18.12 Chemical Properties of Proteins

Protein Hydrolysis

Just as a simple amide can be hydrolyzed to yield an amine and a carboxylic acid, a protein can be hydrolyzed. (⬭⬭⬭, Section 17.6) In protein hydrolysis, the reverse of protein formation, peptide bonds are hydrolyzed to yield amino acids. In fact, digestion of proteins in the diet involves nothing more than hydrolyzing peptide bonds. For example,

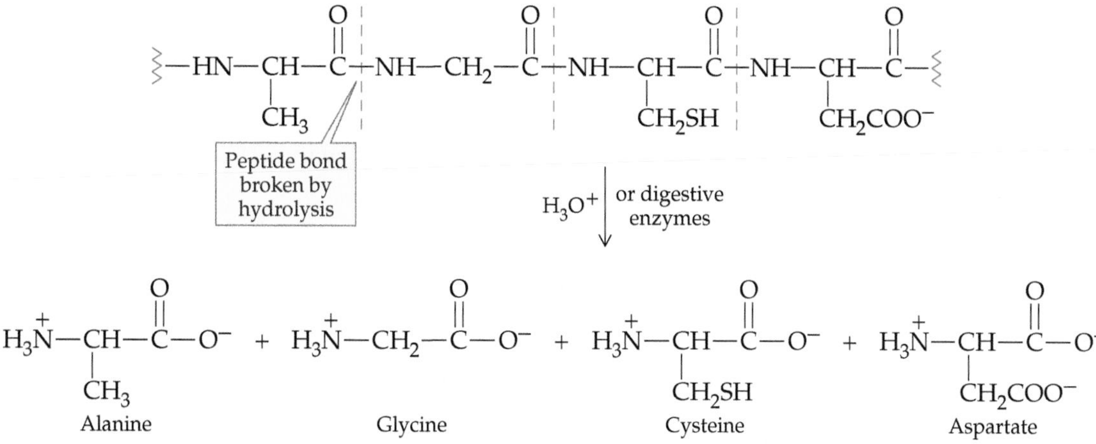

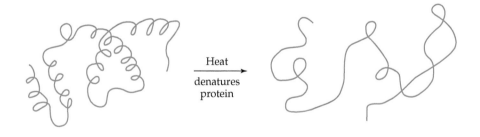

Alanine · Glycine · Cysteine · Aspartate

A chemist in the laboratory might choose to hydrolyze a protein by heating it with a solution of hydrochloric acid. Most digestion of proteins in the body takes place in the stomach and small intestine, where the process is catalyzed by enzymes (Section 28.1). Once formed, individual amino acids are absorbed through the wall of the intestine and transported in the bloodstream to wherever they are needed.

Protein Denaturation

Since the overall shape of a protein is determined by a delicate balance of noncovalent forces, it is not surprising that a change in protein shape often results when the balance is disturbed. Such a disruption in shape that does not affect the protein's primary structure is known as **denaturation**. When denaturation of a globular protein occurs, for example, the structure unfolds from a well-defined globular shape to a randomly looped chain:

Denaturation The loss of secondary, tertiary, or quaternary protein structure due to disruption of noncovalent interactions and/or disulfide bonds that leaves peptide bonds and primary structure intact.

▲ Protein denaturation in action: The egg white denatures as the egg fries.

Denaturation is accompanied by changes in physical, chemical, and biological properties. Solubility is often decreased by denaturation, as occurs when egg white is cooked and the albumins coagulate into an insoluble white mass. Enzymes lose their catalytic activity and other proteins are no longer able to carry out their biological functions when their shapes are altered by denaturation.

Agents that cause denaturation include heat, mechanical agitation, detergents, organic solvents, extremely acidic or basic pH, and inorganic salts.

- **Heat** The weak side-chain attractions in globular proteins are easily disrupted by heating, in many cases only to temperatures above 50 °C. Cooking meat converts some of the insoluble collagen into soluble gelatin, which can be used in glue and for thickening sauces.

- **Mechanical agitation** The most familiar example of denaturation by agitation is the foam produced by beating egg whites. Denaturation of proteins at the surface of the air bubbles stiffens the protein and causes the bubbles to be held in place.

- **Detergents** Even very low concentrations of detergents can cause denaturation by disrupting the association of hydrophobic side chains.

- **Organic compounds** Polar solvents such as acetone and ethanol interfere with hydrogen bonding by competing for bonding sites. The disinfectant action of ethanol, for example, results from its ability to denature bacterial protein.

- **pH change** Excess H^+ or OH^- ions react with the basic or acidic side chains in amino acid residues and disrupt salt bridges. One familiar example of denaturation by pH change is the protein coagulation that occurs when milk turns sour because it has become acidic.

- **Inorganic salts** Sufficiently high concentrations of ions can disturb salt bridges.

Most denaturation is irreversible: Hard-boiled eggs do not soften when their temperature is lowered. Many cases are known, however, in which unfolded proteins spontaneously undergo *renaturation*—a return to their native state when placed in a nondenaturing medium. Renaturation is accompanied by recovery of biological activity, indicating that the protein has completely refolded to its stable secondary and tertiary structure. By spontaneously refolding into their native shapes, proteins demonstrate that all the information needed to determine these shapes is present in the primary structure.

APPLICATION ▶ Prions: Proteins that Cause Disease

No one believed it at first. The existence of a protein that duplicates itself and causes disease seemed impossible. Only bacteria, viruses, and other microorganisms that have DNA are able to reproduce and cause disease. That had been believed for a long time.

Even more unbelievable was the proposal that a form of protein could be responsible for disease that can be inherited, that can be transmitted between individuals, and that can arise spontaneously in the absence of inheritance or transmission. Stanley B. Prusiner, a neurologist, received the Nobel Prize for Physiology and Medicine in 1997 for his research demonstrating that indeed such proteins exist and do cause disease in all of these ways.

Prusiner named these proteins *prions* (pronounced **pree-**ons), for "proteinaceous infectious particles." Dr. Prusiner began his prion research in 1974. Some are still skeptical and there is much to be learned, but accumulating evidence indicates that all of these unbelievable premises are correct.

Prion-caused disease leaped into worldwide notice in the 1990s when individuals in Great Britain began to die from Creutzfeldt–Jakob disease (CJD) and it became apparent that the cause was eating beef from cows infected with mad-cow disease, known technically as bovine spongiform encephalopathy (BSE). The BSE name summarizes a major symptom of these and other prion diseases in which open spaces develop in the brain tissue, thereby becoming sponge-like. Other diseases in the spongiform encephalopathy family include scrapie in sheep; a chronic wasting disease in elk and mule deer; and in humans, inherited CJD and kuru, which occurred among natives in New Guinea who honored their dead relatives by eating their brains but disappeared when the cannibalism ceased. There is no therapy for the spongiform encephalopathies. All types are fatal and are characterized by loss of muscular control and symptoms of dementia.

The following statements summarize some well-supported facts known about prion proteins:

- Humans and all animals tested thus far have a gene for making a normal prion protein that resides in the brain and does not cause disease.

- An inherited genetic defect can cause one amino acid (proline) in normal prion protein to be replaced by another (leucine), resulting in a prion that is responsible for one of the inherited human prion diseases.

- The difference between normal and disease-causing prions lies in their secondary structure. Alpha helixes in the normal prion are replaced by β-sheets, resulting in a prion with a different shape.

- A misfolded, disease-causing prion can induce a normal prion to flip from the normal shape to the disease-causing shape. It does not matter whether the disease-causing prion arises from a genetic defect, enters the body in food or in some other manner, or is formed randomly and spontaneously. Exactly how the change in shape occurs is not yet understood, but the result is an accelerating spread of the disease-causing form.

- The infectious nature of prions is not affected by either heat or UV radiation treatment, both of which destroy bacteria and viruses. Therefore, cooked beef from infected cows can contain infectious prions.

- Synthetic prions (made using recombinant DNA technology) cause neurological disease in mice similar to mad cow disease or CJD.

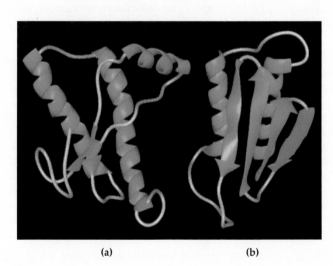

(a)　　　　　　　　(b)

▲ (a) A normal prion. (b) Proposed conformation for a disease-causing prion. (To interpret these drawings, see the picture of ribonuclease, p. 577.)

Many unanswered questions lie behind the ongoing efforts to understand prions and their disease-causing potential. Are some individuals more susceptible to prion-caused diseases than others? To what extent can the disease move from one species to another? Can a diagnostic test be developed to identify those who are susceptible or already exposed to abnormal prions? Looming over all is a most intriguing, major question: Could it be that other neurodegenerative diseases that create abnormal structures in the brain, including Alzheimer's disease and Parkinson's disease, are also prion diseases? Some of these questions may be answered soon because Dr. Prusiner and his colleagues reported the synthesis of infectious prions in bacteria in 2004. This ground-breaking work is leading to new approaches in studying diseases associated with amyloid plaque formation and/or brain structure degeneration.

Meanwhile, the epidemic of mad-cow disease in Great Britain was devastating. Millions of cattle with BSE were slaughtered, and more than 120 people in Great Britain have died from CJD since 1995.

An initial ban on the export of beef from Great Britain to other European countries was lifted in 1998, but their beef exports remain just a fraction of what they were and bans on import continue in some countries. BSE has, however, been identified in cattle in several other European countries and fears are growing that it can be transmitted by sheep and that it might spread outside of Europe.

In November, 2001, the U.S. Department of Agriculture released the results of a major scientific study that assessed the risk of mad cow disease in the United States. The principal conclusions of the study were that early actions prevented the disease from entering the United States, but that vigilance and testing must continue. Unfortunately, in December, 2003, a dairy cow in Washington State tested positive for mad cow disease after slaughter, resulting in temporary bans (since removed) on the importation of U.S. beef by several countries. This particular cow was born in Canada, and no other positive cases have been found in the United States. It is unlikely that humans will develop CJD from eating beef in the United States because all nerve and brain tissue as well as intestinal tissue are excluded from the food chain—both human and animal.

See Additional Problems 18.81 and 18.82 at the end of the chapter.

SUMMARY: REVISITING THE CHAPTER GOALS

KEY WORDS

1. **What are the structural features of amino acids?** *Amino acids* in body fluids have an ionized carboxylic acid group ($-COO^-$), an ionized amino group ($-NH_3^+$), and a side-chain R group bonded to a central carbon atom (the α carbon). Twenty different amino acids occur in *proteins* (Table 18.3), connected by *peptide bonds* (amide bonds) formed between the carboxyl group of one amino acid and the amino group of the next.

Achiral, *p. 562*

Alpha- (α-) amino acid, *p. 555*

Alpha- (α-) helix, *p. 574*

2. What are the properties of amino acids? Amino acid side chains have acidic or basic functional groups or neutral groups that are either polar or nonpolar. In glycine, the "side chain" is a hydrogen atom. The dipolar ion in which the amino and carboxylic acid groups are both ionized is known as a *zwitterion*. For each amino acid, there is a distinctive *isoelectric point*—the pH at which the numbers of positive and negative charges in a solution are equal. At more acidic pH, some carboxylic acid groups are not ionized; at more basic pH, some amino groups are not ionized.

3. Why do amino acids have "handedness"? An object, including a molecule, has "handedness"—is *chiral*—when it has no plane of symmetry and thus has mirror images that cannot be superimposed on each other. A simple molecule can be identified as chiral if it contains a carbon atom bonded to four different groups. All α-amino acids except glycine meet this condition by having four different groups bonded to the α carbon.

4. What is the primary structure of a protein and what conventions are used for drawing and naming primary structures? Proteins are polymers of amino acids (*polypeptides*). Their *primary structure* is the linear sequence in which the amino acids are connected by peptide bonds. Using formulas or amino acid abbreviations, the primary structures are written with the amino-terminal end on the left (^+H_3N—) and the carboxyl-terminal end on the right (—COO^-). To name a peptide, the names of the amino acids are combined, starting at the amino-terminal end, with the endings of all but the carboxyl-terminal amino acid changed to -*yl*. Primary structures are often represented by combining three-letter abbreviations for the amino acids.

5. What types of interactions determine the overall shapes of proteins? Protein chains are drawn into their distinctive and biochemically active shapes by attractions between atoms along their backbones and between atoms in side-chain groups. Hydrogen bonding can occur between the backbone carbonyl groups and amide hydrogens of adjacent protein chains. *Noncovalent interactions* between side chains include ionic bonding between acidic and basic groups (*salt bridges*), and *hydrophobic interactions* among nonpolar groups. Covalent sulfur–sulfur bonds (*disulfide bonds*) can form bridges between the side chains in cysteine.

6. What are the secondary and tertiary structures of proteins? *Secondary structures* include the regular, repeating three-dimensional structures held in place by hydrogen bonding between backbone atoms within a chain or in adjacent chains. The *α-helix* is a coil with hydrogen bonding between carbonyl oxygens and amide hydrogens four amino acid residues farther along the same chain. The *β-sheet* is a pleated sheet with adjacent protein-chain segments connected by hydrogen bonding between peptide groups. The adjacent chains in the β-sheet may be parts of the same protein chain or different protein chains. Secondary structure mainly determines the properties of *fibrous proteins*, which are tough and insoluble. *Tertiary structure* is the overall three-dimensional shape of a folded protein chain. Tertiary structure determines the properties of *globular proteins*, which are water-soluble, with hydrophilic groups on the outside and hydrophobic groups on the inside. Globular proteins often contain regions of α-helix and/or β-sheet secondary structures.

7. What is quaternary protein structure? Proteins that incorporate more than one peptide chain are said to have *quaternary structure*. In a quaternary structure, two or more folded protein subunits are united in a single structure by noncovalent interactions. Hemoglobin, for example, consists of two pairs of subunits, with a nonprotein heme molecule in each of the four subunits. Collagen is a fibrous protein composed of protein chains twisted together in triple helixes.

8. What chemical properties do proteins have? The peptide bonds are broken by *hydrolysis*, which may occur in acidic solution or during enzyme-catalyzed digestion of proteins in food. The end result of hydrolysis is production of the individual amino acids from the protein. *Denaturation* is the loss of overall structure by a protein while retaining its primary structure. Among the agents that cause denaturation are heat, mechanical agitation, pH change, and exposure to a variety of chemical agents, including detergents.

UNDERSTANDING KEY CONCEPTS

18.25 Draw the structure of the following tripeptides at low pH and high pH. At each pH, assume that all functional groups that might do so are ionized.

(a) Val-Gly-Leu   (b) Arg-Lys-His
(c) Tyr-Pro-Ser   (d) Glu-Asp-Phe
(e) Gln-Ala-Asn   (f) Met-Trp-Cys

18.26 Interactions of amino acids on the interior of proteins are key to the shapes of proteins. In group (a) below, which pairs of amino acids form hydrophobic interactions? In group (b), which pairs form ionic interactions? Which pairs in group (c) form hydrogen bonds?

(a) 1. Pro...Phe
     2. Lys...Ser
     3. Thr...Leu
     4. Ala...Gly

(b) 1. Val...Leu
     2. Glu...Lys
     3. Met...Cys
     4. Asp...His

(c) 1. Cys...Cys
     2. Asp...Ser
     3. Val...Gly
     4. Met...Cys

18.27 Draw the hexapeptide Asp-Gly-Phe-Leu-Glu-Ala in linear form showing all of the atoms, and show (using dotted lines) the hydrogen bonding that stabilizes this structure if it is part of an α-helix.

18.28 Compare and contrast the characteristics of fibrous and globular proteins. Consider biological function, water solubility, amino acid composition, secondary structure, and tertiary structure. Give examples of three fibrous and three globular proteins. (Hint: Make a table.)

18.29 Cell membranes are studded with proteins. Some of these proteins, involved in the transport of molecules across the membrane into the cell, span the entire membrane and are called trans-membrane proteins. The interior of the cell membrane is hydrophobic and nonpolar, whereas both the extracellular and intracellular fluid are water-based.

(a) List three amino acids you would expect to find in the trans-membrane protein in the part that lies within the cell membrane.
(b) List three amino acids you would expect to find in the trans-membrane protein in the part that lies outside the cell.
(c) List three amino acids you would expect to find in the trans-membrane protein in the part that lies inside the cell.

ADDITIONAL PROBLEMS

AMINO ACIDS

18.30 The amino acids in most biological systems are said to be α-L-acids. What does the prefix "α" mean?

18.31 What does the prefix "L" in α-L-acid mean?

18.32 What amino acids do the following abbreviations stand for? Draw the structure of each.

(a) Ala   (b) Cys   (c) Asp

18.33 What amino acids do the following abbreviations stand for? Draw the structure of each.

(a) Leu
(b) Tyr
(c) Asn

18.34 Name and draw the structures of the amino acids that fit these descriptions:

(a) Contains a thiol group
(b) Contains a phenol group

18.35 Name and draw the structures of the amino acids that fit these descriptions:

(a) Contains an isopropyl group
(b) Contains a secondary alcohol group

18.36 At neutral pH, which of the following amino acids has a net positive charge, which has a net negative charge, and which is neutral?

(a) Glutamine
(b) Histidine
(c) Methionine

18.37 At neutral pH, which of the following amino acids has a net positive charge, which has a net negative charge, and which is neutral?

(a) Glutamic acid   (b) Arginine   (c) Leucine

18.38 Which of the following forms of aspartic acid would you expect to predominate at low pH, neutral pH, and high pH?

(a) $\overset{O}{\overset{\|}{HOC}}-CH_2\overset{\underset{\displaystyle +NH_3}{|}}{CH}-\overset{O}{\overset{\|}{CO^-}}$

(b) $\overset{O}{\overset{\|}{{}^-OC}}-CH_2\overset{\underset{\displaystyle NH_2}{|}}{CH}-\overset{O}{\overset{\|}{CO^-}}$

(c) $\overset{O}{\overset{\|}{HOC}}-CH_2\overset{\underset{\displaystyle +NH_3}{|}}{CH}-\overset{O}{\overset{\|}{COH}}$

18.39 Which of the following forms of lysine would you expect to predominate at low pH, neutral pH, and high pH?

(a) $\overset{+}{NH_3}-\overset{\overset{\displaystyle H}{|}}{\underset{\underset{\displaystyle NH_3^+}{\underset{|}{(CH_2)_4}}}{\overset{|}{C}}}-\overset{O}{\overset{\|}{C}}-O^-$

(b) $NH_3^+-C-C-OH$

$\overset{H}{\underset{(CH_2)_4}{|}}$ $\overset{O}{\underset{}{||}}$

NH_3^+

(c) $NH_3^+-C-C-O^-$

$\overset{H}{\underset{(CH_2)_4}{|}}$ $\overset{O}{\underset{}{||}}$

NH_2

HANDEDNESS IN MOLECULES

18.40 What does the term *chiral* mean? Give two examples.

18.41 What does the term *achiral* mean? Give two examples.

18.42 Which of the following objects are chiral?

(a) A mayonnaise jar
(b) A rocking chair
(c) A coin

18.43 Which of the following objects are achiral?

(a) A pair of scissors
(b) A comb
(c) A vase

18.44 Draw the structures of the following compounds. Which of them is chiral? Mark each chiral carbon with an asterisk.

(a) 2-Bromo-2-chloropropane
(b) 2-Bromo-2-chlorobutane
(c) 2-Bromo-2-chloro-3-methylbutane

18.45 Draw the structures of the following compounds. Which of them is chiral? Mark each chiral carbon with an asterisk.

(a) 2-Chloropentane
(b) Cyclopentane
(c) 2-Methylpropanol

18.46 Which of the carbon atoms marked with arrows in the following compound are chiral?

$$CH_3CHCH_2CH_3$$
$$|$$
$$F$$

18.47 Which of the carbon atoms marked with arrows in the following compound are chiral?

PEPTIDES AND PROTEINS

18.48 What is the difference between a simple protein and a conjugated protein?

18.49 What kinds of molecules are found in the following classes of conjugated proteins in addition to the protein part?

(a) Metalloproteins
(b) Hemoproteins
(c) Lipoproteins
(d) Nucleoproteins

18.50 Name four biological functions of proteins in the human body, and give an example of a protein for each function.

18.51 What is meant by the following terms as they apply to proteins, and what primary interactions stabilize the structure?

(a) Primary structure
(b) Secondary structure
(c) Tertiary structure
(d) Quaternary structure

18.52 Why is cysteine such an important amino acid for defining the tertiary structure of some proteins?

18.53 What conditions are required for disulfide bonds to form between cysteine residues in a protein?

18.54 How do the following noncovalent interactions help to stabilize the tertiary and quaternary structure of a protein? Give an example of a pair of amino acids that could give rise to each interaction.

(a) Hydrophobic interactions
(b) Salt bridges (ionic interactions)

18.55 How do the following interactions help to stabilize the tertiary and quaternary structure of a protein? Give an example of a pair of amino acids that could give rise to each interaction.

(a) Side-chain hydrogen bonding
(b) Disulfide bonds

18.56 What kinds of changes take place in a protein when it is denatured?

18.57 Explain how a protein is denatured by the following:

(a) Heat
(b) Strong acids
(c) Organic solvents

18.58 Use the three-letter abbreviations to name all tripeptides that contain valine, methionine, and leucine.

18.59 Write structural formulas for the two dipeptides that contain leucine and aspartate.

18.60 Which of the following amino acids are most likely to be found on the outside of a globular protein, and which of them are more likely to be found on the inside? Explain each answer. (Hint: Consider the effect of the amino acid side chain in each case.)

(a) Valine
(b) Aspartate
(c) Histidine
(d) Alanine

18.61 Which of the following amino acids are most likely to be found on the outside of a globular protein? Which are more likely to be found on the inside? Explain each answer. (Hint: Consider the effect of the amino acid side chain in each case.)

(a) Leucine   (b) Glutamate
(c) Phenylalanine   (d) Glutamine

18.62 Why do you suppose diabetics must receive insulin sub-cutaneously by injection rather than orally?

18.63 Individuals with phenylketonuria (PKU) are sensitive to phenylalanine in their diet. Why is a warning on foods containing aspartame (L-aspartyL-L-phenylalanine methyl ester) of concern to PKU individuals?

18.64 The *endorphins* are a group of naturally occurring neuro-transmitters that act in a manner similar to morphine to control pain. Research has shown that the biologically active parts of the endorphin molecules are simple pen-tapeptides called *enkephalins*. Draw the structure of the methionine enkephalin with the sequence Tyr-Gly-Gly-Phe-Met. Identify the N-terminal and C-terminal amino acids.

18.65 Refer to Problem 18.64. Draw the structure of the leucine enkephalin with the sequence Tyr-Gly-Gly-Phe-Leu. Identify the N-terminal and C-terminal amino acids.

PROPERTIES AND REACTIONS OF AMINO ACIDS AND PROTEINS

18.66 Much of the chemistry of amino acids is the familiar chemistry of carboxylic acids and amine functional groups. What products would you expect to obtain from the following reactions of glycine?

(a) 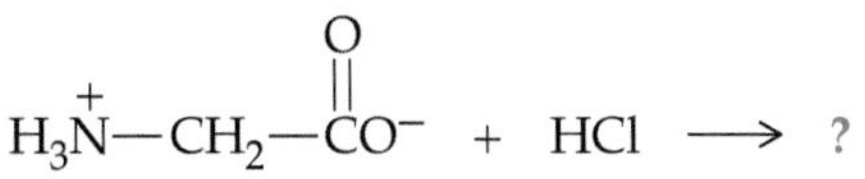 $H_3\overset{+}{N}-CH_2-\overset{\overset{\displaystyle O}{\|}}{C}O^- + HCl \longrightarrow$?

(b) 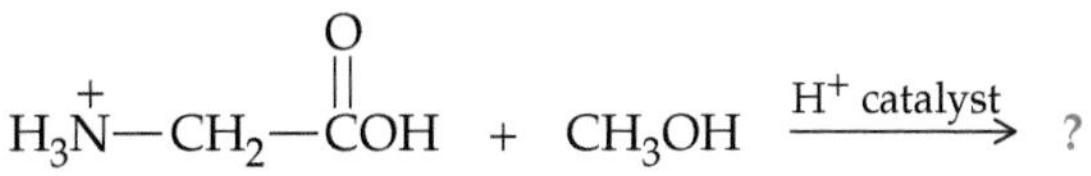 $H_3\overset{+}{N}-CH_2-\overset{\overset{\displaystyle O}{\|}}{C}OH + CH_3OH \xrightarrow{H^+ \text{ catalyst}}$?

18.67 A scientist tried to prepare the simple dipeptide glycyl-glycine by the following reaction:

$$2\,H_3\overset{+}{N}CH_2\overset{\overset{\displaystyle O}{\|}}{C}O^- \longrightarrow H_3\overset{+}{N}CH_2\overset{\overset{\displaystyle O}{\|}}{C}NHCH_2\overset{\overset{\displaystyle O}{\|}}{C}O^-$$

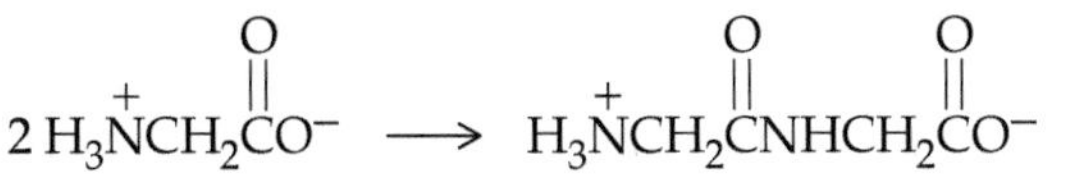

An unexpected product formed during the reaction. This product is found to have the molecular formula $C_4H_6N_2O_2$ and to contain two peptide bonds. What happened?

18.68 **(a)** Identify the amino acids present in the peptide shown below.
(b) Identify the N-terminal and C-terminal amino acids of the peptide.
(c) Show the structures of the products that are obtained on digestion of the peptide at physiological pH.

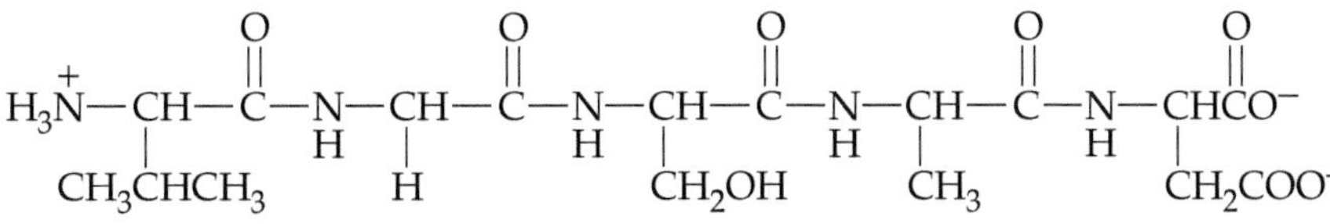

18.69 **(a)** Identify the amino acids present in the peptide shown below.
(b) Identify the N-terminal and C-terminal amino acids of the peptide.
(c) Show the structures of the products that are obtained on digestion of the peptide at physiological pH.

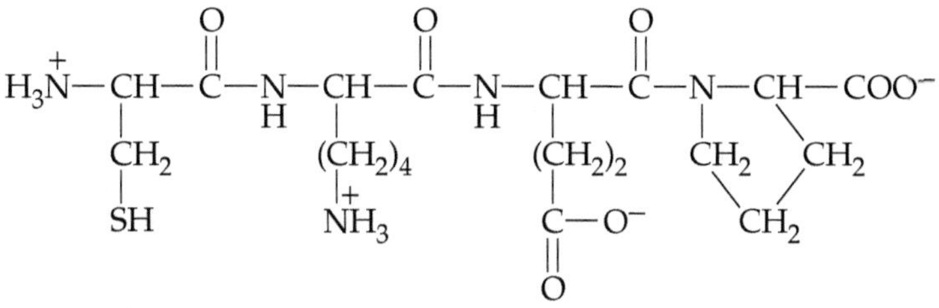

18.70 Which would you expect to be more soluble in water, a peptide rich in alanine and leucine, or a peptide rich in lysine and aspartate? Explain.

18.71 Proteins are usually less soluble in water at their isoelec-tric points. Explain.

Applications

18.72 **(a)** Tyramine is said to be the "decarboxylation" product of the amino acid tyrosine. Write the reaction and explain what is meant by "decarboxylation."
(b) Phenelzine inhibits the "deamination" of tyramine. What key characteristic of phenelzine makes it similar enough to tyramine that it is able to block deamination of tyramine? [*Nutrition in Health and Disease, p. 560*]

18.73 Why is it more important to have a daily source of protein than a daily source of fat or carbohydrates? [*Proteins in the Diet, p. 569*]

18.74 What is an incomplete protein? [*Proteins in the Diet, p. 569*]

18.75 In general, which is more likely to contain a complete (balanced) protein for human use—food from plant sources or food from animal sources? Explain. [*Proteins in the Diet, p. 569*]

18.76 Two of the most complete (balanced) proteins (that is, proteins that have the best ratio of the amino acids for humans) are cow's milk protein (casein) and egg white protein. Explain why (not surprisingly) these are very balanced proteins for human growth and development. [*Proteins in the Diet, p. 569*]

18.77 The proteins collagen, bovine insulin, and human hemo-globin have isoelectric points of 6.6, 5.4, and 7.1, respec-tively. Suppose a sample containing these proteins is applied to an electrophoresis strip in a buffer at pH 6.6. Describe the motion of each with respect to the positive and negative electrodes in the electrophoresis apparatus. [*Protein Analysis by Electrophoresis, p. 573*]

18.78 Three dipeptides are separated by electrophoresis at pH 5.8. If the dipeptides are Arg-Trp, Asp-Thr, and Val-Met, describe the motion of each with respect to the positive and negative electrodes in the electrophoresis apparatus. [*Protein Analysis by Electrophoresis, p. 573*]

18.79 In the middle ages both citizens of besieged cities and members of the armies laying siege would die of scurvy, a non-contagious disease, during long sieges. Explain why this would occur. [*Collagen—A Tale of Two Diseases, p. 581*]

18.80 Describe the cause and biochemical defect that results in osteogenesis imperfecta. [*Collagen—A Tale of Two Diseases, p. 581*]

18.81 The change from a normal to a disease-causing prion results in a change from α-helices to β-sheets. How might this change alter the overall structure and intermolecular forces in the prion? [*Prions: Proteins that Cause Disease, p. 584*]

18.82 List the properties of disease-causing prions that made their existence difficult to accept. [*Prions: Proteins that Cause Disease, p. 584*]

18.83 A family visits their physician with their sick child. The four-month-old baby is pale, has obvious episodes of pain, and is not thriving. The doctor orders a series of blood tests, including a test for hemoglobin types. The results show that the infant is not only anemic but that the anemia is due to sickle-cell anemia. The family wants to know if their other two children have sickle-cell anemia, sickle-cell trait, or no sickle-cell gene at all.

(a) What test will be used?

(b) Sketch the expected results if samples for each child are tested at the same time.

(c) What is the difference between sickle-cell anemia and sickle-cell trait?

[*Protein Analysis by Electrophoresis, p. 573*]

18.84 What could you prepare for dinner for a strict vegan that provides all of the essential amino acids in appropriate amounts? (Remember, strict vegans do not eat meat, eggs, milk, or products that contain those animal products.) [*Proteins in the Diet, p. 569*]

General Questions and Problems

18.85 What is the difference between protein digestion and protein denaturation? Both occur after a meal.

18.86 Fresh pineapple cannot be used in gelatin desserts because it contains an enzyme that hydrolyzes the proteins in gelatin, destroying the gelling action. Canned pineapple can be added to gelatin with no problem. Why?

18.87 Both α-keratin and tropocollagen have helical secondary structure. How do they differ?

18.88 Bradykinin, a peptide that helps to regulate blood pressure, has the primary structure Arg-Pro-Pro-Gly-Phe-Ser-Pro-Phe-Arg.

(a) Draw the complete structural formula of bradykinin.

(b) Bradykinin has a very kinked secondary structure. Why?

18.89 For each amino acid listed, tell whether its influence on tertiary structure is largely through hydrophobic interactions, hydrogen bonding, formation of salt bridges, covalent bonding, or some combination of these effects.

(a) Tyrosine

(b) Cysteine

(c) Asparagine

(d) Lysine

(e) Tryptophan

(f) Alanine

(g) Leucine

(h) Methionine

18.90 When subjected to oxidation, the chiral carbon in 2-pentanol becomes achiral. Why does this happen?

18.91 Why is hydrolysis of a protein not considered to be denaturation?

18.92 Oxytocin is a small peptide that is used to induce labor by causing contractions in uterine walls. It has the primary structure Cys-Tyr-Ile-Gln-Asn-Cys-Pro-Leu-Gln. This peptide is held in a cyclic configuration by a disulfide bridge. Draw a diagram of oxytocin, showing the disulfide bridge.

18.93 Methionine has a sulfur atom in its formula. Explain why methionine does not form disulfide bridges.

18.94 List the amino acids that are capable of hydrogen bonding if included in a peptide chain. Draw an example of two of these amino acids hydrogen-bonding to one another. For each one, draw a hydrogen bond to water in a separate sketch. Refer to Section 8.11 for help with drawing hydrogen bonds.

18.95 Four of the most abundant amino acids in proteins are leucine, alanine, glycine, and valine. What do these amino acids have in common? Would you expect these amino acids to be found on the interior or on the exterior of the protein?

18.96 Globular proteins are water-soluble, whereas fibrous proteins are insoluble in water. Indicate whether you expect the following amino acids to be on the surface of a globular protein or on the surface of a fibrous protein.

(a) Ala

(b) Glu

(c) Leu

(d) Phe

(e) Ser

(f) Val

18.97 In Figure 18.7, notice the small purple segment in each rendering of the molecule. These purple segments connecting adjacent regions of secondary structure are often referred to either as "reverse turns" or as "bends." The two most common amino acids in reverse turns are glycine and proline. Use your knowledge of the structures of these two amino acids to speculate on why they might be found in reverse turns.

18.98 During sickle-cell anemia research to determine the modification involved in sickling, sequencing of the affected person's hemoglobin β-subunit reveals that the sixth amino acid is valine rather than glutamate; thus, the replacement of glutamate by valine severely alters the three-dimensional structure of hemoglobin. Which amino acid, if it replaced the Glu, would cause the least disruption in hemoglobin structure? Why?

18.99 As a chef, you prepare a wide variety of foods daily. The following dishes all contain protein. What method (if any) has been used to denature the protein present in each food?

(a) Charcoal grilled steak
(b) Pickled pigs' feet
(c) Meringue
(d) Steak tartare (raw chopped beef)
(e) Salt pork

CHAPTER 22

Carbohydrates

CONCEPTS TO REVIEW

Molecular shape
(Section 5.7)

Chirality
(Section 18.5)

Oxidation–reduction reactions
(Sections 6.11, 6.12, 14.5, 16.5, 16.6)

▲ Corn stores glucose in the polysaccharides starch and cellulose.

CHAPTER GOALS

In this chapter, we will answer the following questions about carbohydrates:

1. What are the different kinds of carbohydrates?

THE GOAL: Be able to define monosaccharides, disaccharides, and polysaccharides, and recognize examples.

2. Why are monosaccharides chiral, and how does this influence the numbers and types of their isomers?

THE GOAL: Be able to identify the chiral carbon atoms in monosaccharides, predict the number of isomers for different monosaccharides, and identify pairs of enantiomers.

3. What are the structures of monosaccharides, and how are they represented in written formulas?

THE GOAL: Be able to explain relationships among open-chain and cyclic monosaccharide structures, describe the isomers of monosaccharides, and show how they are represented by Fischer projections and cyclic structural formulas.

4. How do monosaccharides react with oxidizing agents and alcohols?

THE GOAL: Be able to identify reducing sugars and the products of their oxidation, recognize acetals of monosaccharides, and describe glycosidic linkages in disaccharides.

5. What are the structures of some important disaccharides?

THE GOAL: Be able to identify the monosaccharides combined in maltose, lactose, and sucrose, and describe the types of linkages between the monosaccharides.

6. What are the functions of some important carbohydrates that contain modified monosaccharide structures?

THE GOAL: Be able to identify the functions of chitin, connective-tissue polysaccharides, heparin, and glycoproteins.

7. What are the structures and functions of cellulose, starch, and glycogen?

THE GOAL: Be able to describe the monosaccharides and linkages in these polysaccharides, their uses and fates in metabolism.

The word *carbohydrate* originally described glucose, the simplest and most readily available sugar. Because glucose has the formula $C_6H_{12}O_6$, it was once thought to be a "hydrate of carbon," $C_6(H_2O)_6$. Although this view has been abandoned, the name "carbohydrate" persisted, and we now use it to refer to a large class of biomolecules with similar structures. Carbohydrates have in common many hydroxyl groups on adjacent carbons together with either an aldehyde or ketone group. Glucose, for example, has five —OH groups and one —CHO group:

$$
\begin{array}{c}
\text{H} \quad \text{H} \quad \text{H} \quad \text{OH} \text{H} \quad \text{O} \\
| \quad\ | \quad\ | \quad\ | \quad\ | \quad\ \| \\
\text{HO}-\text{C}-\text{C}-\text{C}-\text{C}-\text{C}-\text{C}-\text{H} \\
| \quad\ | \quad\ | \quad\ | \quad\ | \\
\text{H} \quad \text{OH} \text{OH} \text{H} \quad \text{OH}
\end{array}
$$

Glucose

Carbohydrates are synthesized by plants and stored as starch, a polymer of glucose. When starch is eaten and digested, the freed glucose becomes a major source of the energy required by living organisms. Thus, carbohydrates are intermediaries by which energy from the sun is made available to animals.

22.1 An Introduction to Carbohydrates

Carbohydrates are a large class of naturally occurring polyhydroxy aldehydes and ketones. **Monosaccharides**, sometimes known as **simple sugars**, are the simplest carbohydrates. They have from three to seven carbon atoms, and each contains one aldehyde or one ketone functional group. If the sugar has an aldehyde group, it is classified as an **aldose**. If it has a ketone group, the sugar is classified as a **ketose**. The aldehyde group is always at the end of the carbon chain, and the ketone group is always on the second carbon of the chain. In either case, there is a —CH₂OH group at the other end of the chain.

Carbohydrate A member of a large class of naturally occurring polyhydroxy ketones and aldehydes.

Monosaccharide (simple sugar) A carbohydrate with three to seven carbon atoms.

Aldose A monosaccharide that contains an aldehyde carbonyl group.

Ketose A monosaccharide that contains a ketone carbonyl group.

693

Monosaccharides

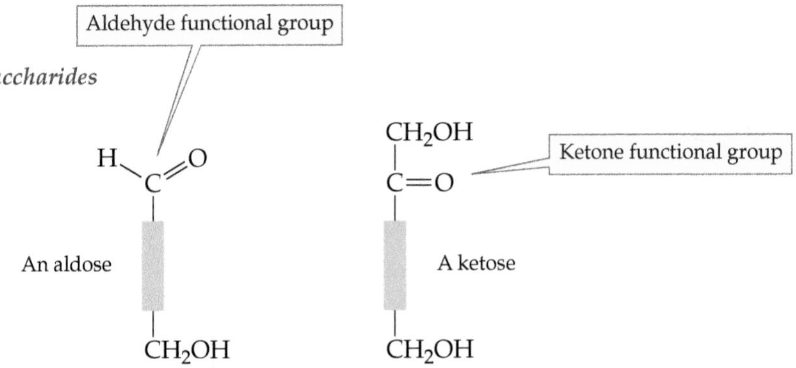

Aldehyde functional group

Ketone functional group

An aldose

A ketose

There are hydroxyl groups on all the carbon atoms between the carbonyl carbon atom and the —CH$_2$OH at the other end, and also on the end carbon next to a ketone group, as illustrated in the following three structures. The family-name ending -*ose* indicates a carbohydrate, and simple sugars are known by common names like *glucose, ribose,* and *fructose* rather than systematic names.

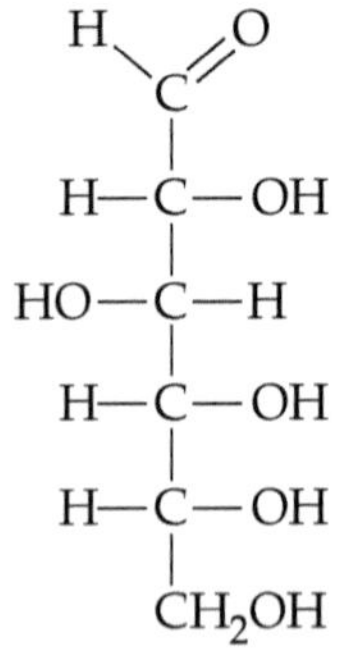

Glucose, an aldohexose
(monomer for starch and cellulose; major source of energy)

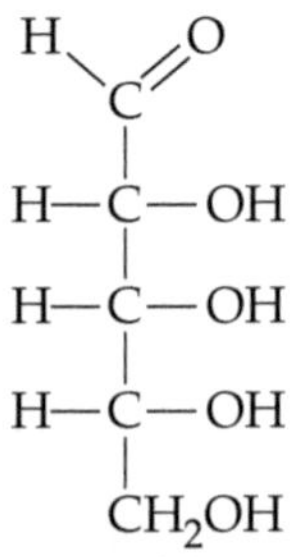

Ribose, an aldopentose
(a component of ATP, coenzymes, and RNA)

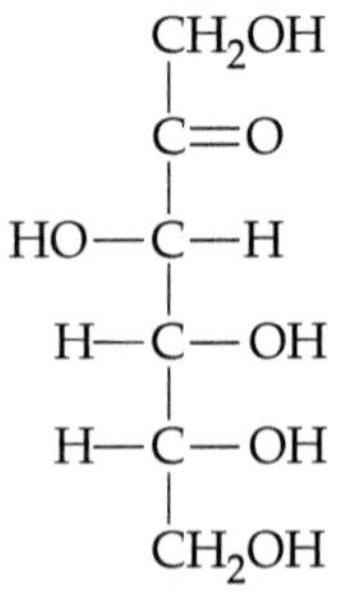

Fructose, a ketohexose
(present in corn syrup and fruit)

The number of carbon atoms in an aldose or ketose is specified by the prefixes *tri-, tetr-, pent-, hex-,* or *hept-*. Thus, glucose is an aldo*hex*ose (*aldo-* = aldehyde, *-hex* = 6 carbons; *-ose* = sugar); fructose is a keto*hex*ose (a 6-carbon ketone sugar); and ribose is an aldo*pent*ose (a 5-carbon aldehyde sugar). Most naturally occurring simple sugars are aldehydes with either 5 or 6 carbons.

Because of their many functional groups, monosaccharides undergo a variety of structural changes and chemical reactions. They react with each other to form **disaccharides** and **polysaccharides** (also known as **complex carbohydrates**), which are polymers of monosaccharides. Their functional groups are involved in reactions with alcohols, lipids or proteins to form biomolecules with specialized functions. These and other carbohydrates are introduced in later sections of this chapter. First, we are going to discuss two important aspects of carbohydrate structure:

Disaccharide A carbohydrate composed of two monosaccharides.

Polysaccharide (complex carbohydrate) A carbohydrate that is a polymer of monosaccharides.

- Monosaccharides are chiral molecules (Sections 22.2, 22.3).
- Monosaccharides exist mainly in cyclic forms rather than the straight-chain forms shown above (Section 22.4).

WORKED EXAMPLE 22.1 Classifying Monosaccharides

Classify the monosaccharide shown as an aldose or a ketose, and name it according to its number of carbon atoms.

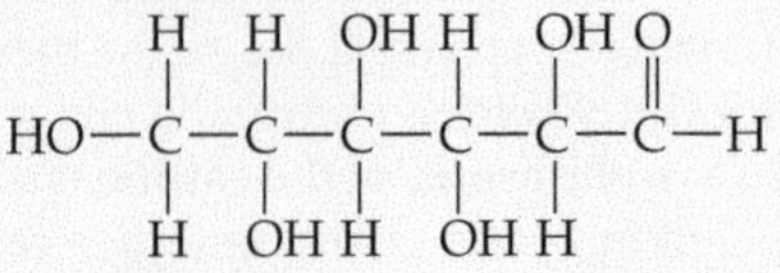

ANALYSIS First determine if the monosaccharide is an aldose or a ketose. Then determine the number of carbon atoms present. This monosaccharide is an aldose because an aldehyde group is present. It contains 6 carbon atoms.

SOLUTION
The monosaccharide is a 6-carbon aldose, so we refer to it as an aldohexose.

PROBLEM 22.1

Classify the following monosaccharides as an aldose or a ketose, and name each according its number of carbon atoms.

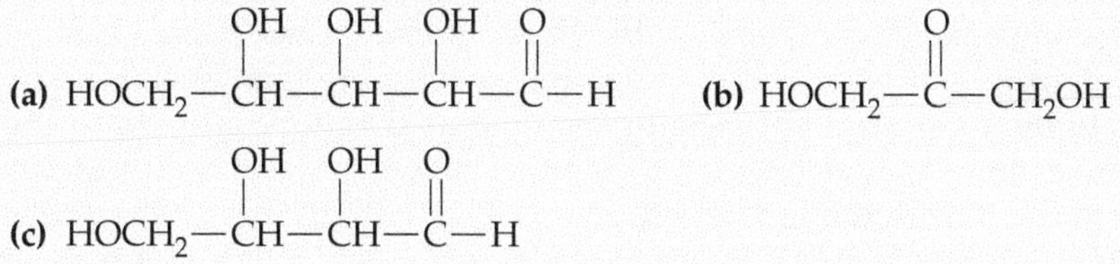

(a) $HOCH_2-\overset{\overset{\displaystyle OH}{|}}{CH}-\overset{\overset{\displaystyle OH}{|}}{CH}-\overset{\overset{\displaystyle OH}{|}}{CH}-\overset{\overset{\displaystyle O}{||}}{C}-H$ (b) $HOCH_2-\overset{\overset{\displaystyle O}{||}}{C}-CH_2OH$

(c) $HOCH_2-\overset{\overset{\displaystyle OH}{|}}{CH}-\overset{\overset{\displaystyle OH}{|}}{CH}-\overset{\overset{\displaystyle O}{||}}{C}-H$

PROBLEM 22.2

Draw the structures of an aldopentose and a ketohexose.

22.2 Handedness of Carbohydrates

You have seen that amino acids are chiral (that is, not superimposable on their mirror images) because they contain carbon atoms bonded to four different groups. Glyceraldehyde, an aldotriose and the simplest naturally occurring carbohydrate, has the structure shown below. Because four different groups are bonded to the number 2 carbon atom ($-CHO$, $-H$, $-OH$, and $-CH_2OH$), this molecule is also chiral. ($\color{gray}{\bowtie}$, Section 18.5)

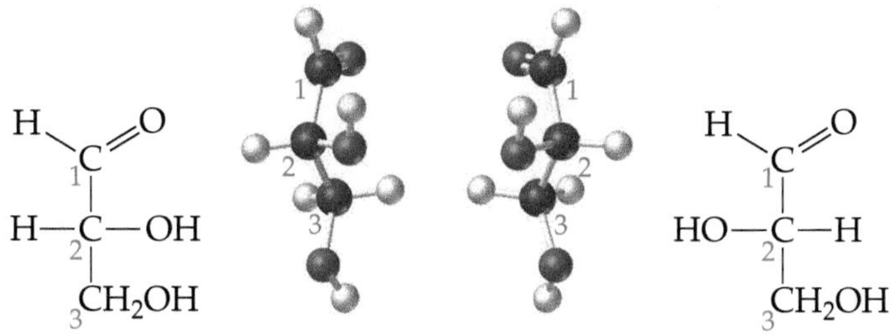

D-Glyceraldehyde
Right-handed

L-Glyceraldehyde
Left-handed

Chiral compounds lack a plane of symmetry and exist as a pair of enantiomers in either a "right-handed" D form or a "left-handed" L form. Like all enantiomers, the two forms of glyceraldehyde have the same physical properties except for the way in which they affect polarized light.

Light as we usually see it consists of electromagnetic waves oscillating in all planes at right angles to the direction of travel of the light beam. ($\color{gray}{\bowtie}$, p. 72) When ordinary light is passed through a polarizer, only waves in one plane get through, producing what is known as *plane-polarized light*. (Polaroid sunglasses work on a similar principle.) Solutions of *optically active* chemical compounds change the plane in which the light is polarized. The angle by which the plane is rotated can be measured in an instrument known as a *polarimeter*, which works on the principle diagrammed in Figure 22.1. Each enantiomer of a pair rotates the plane of the light

▶ **FIGURE 22.1 Principle of a polarimeter, used to determine optical activity.** A solution of an optically active isomer rotates the plane of the polarized light by a characteristic amount.

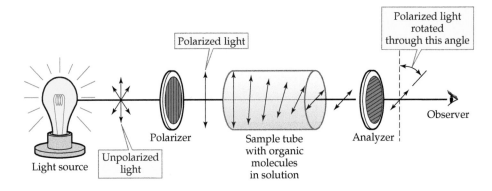

by the same amount, but the directions of rotation are *opposite*. If one enantiomer rotates the plane of the light to the left, the other rotates it to the right.

Compounds like glyceraldehyde that have *one* chiral carbon atom can exist as two enantiomers. But what about compounds with more than one chiral carbon atom? How many isomers are there of compounds that have two, three, four, or more chiral carbons? Aldotetroses, for example, have two chiral carbon atoms and can exist in the four isomeric forms shown in Figure 22.2. These four aldotetrose stereoisomers consist of two mirror-image pairs of enantiomers, one pair named *erythrose* and one pair named *threose*. Because erythrose and threose are stereoisomers but not mirror images of each other, they are described as **diastereomers**.

Diastereomers Stereoisomers that are not mirror images of each other.

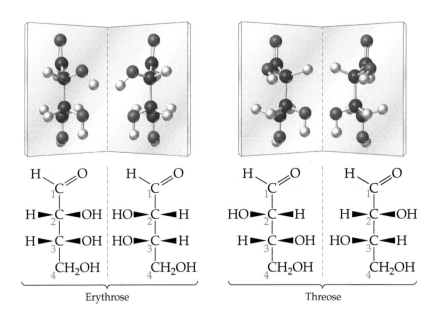

▶ **FIGURE 22.2 Two pairs of enantiomers: The four isomeric aldotetroses (2,3,4-trihydroxybutanals).** Carbon atoms 2 and 3 are chiral. Their —H atoms and —OH groups are written here to show their mirror-image relationship. Erythrose and threose exist as enantiomeric pairs.

In general, a compound with n chiral carbon atoms has a maximum of 2^n possible stereoisomers and half that many pairs of enantiomers. The aldotetroses, for example, have $n = 2$ so that $2^n = 2^2 = 4$, meaning that four stereoisomers are possible. Glucose, an aldohexose, has four chiral carbon atoms and a total of $2^4 = 16$ possible stereoisomers (8 pairs of isomers). All 16 stereoisomers of glucose are known. (In some cases, fewer than the maximum predicted number of stereoisomers exist because some of the molecules have symmetry planes that make them identical to their mirror images.)

PROBLEM 22.3

Aldopentoses have three chiral carbon atoms. What is the maximum possible number of aldopentose stereoisomers?

PROBLEM 22.4

From monosaccharides (a)–(d) in Problem 22.5, choose the one that is the enantiomer of the unlabeled monosaccharide shown.

PROBLEM 22.5

Notice in structures (a)–(d) below that the bottom carbon and its substituents are written as CH_2OH in every case. How does the C in this group differ in each case from the C atoms above it? Why must the locations of the H atoms and —OH groups attached to the carbons between this one and the carbonyl group be shown?

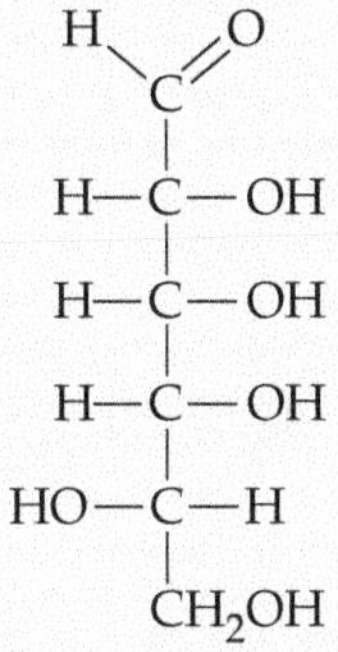

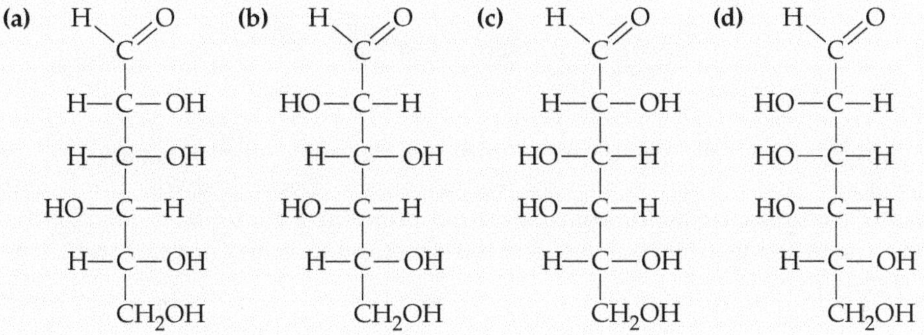

(a)

(b)

(c)

(d)

22.3 The D and L Families of Sugars: Drawing Sugar Molecules

A standard method of representation called a **Fischer projection** has been adopted for drawing stereoisomers on a flat page so that we can tell one from another. A chiral carbon atom is represented in a Fischer projection as the intersection of two crossed lines, and this carbon atom is considered to be on the printed page. Bonds that point up and out of the page are shown as horizontal lines, and bonds that point behind the page are shown as vertical lines. Until now, we have used solid wedges and dashed lines to represent bonds above and behind the printed page, respectively, with ordinary solid lines for bonds in the plane of the page. (⬤⬤, p. 124) The relationship between such a structure and a Fischer projection is as follows:

Fischer projection Structure that represents chiral carbon atoms as the intersections of two lines, with the horizontal lines representing bonds pointing out of the page and the vertical lines representing bonds pointing behind the page. For sugars, the aldehyde or ketone is at the top.

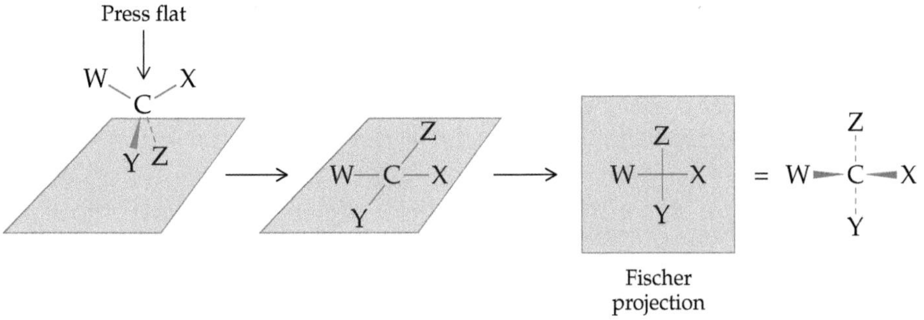

Fischer
projection

In a Fischer projection, the aldehyde or ketone carbonyl group of a monosaccharide is always placed at the top. The result is that —H and —OH groups projecting above the page are on the left and right of the chiral carbons, and groups projecting behind the page are above and below the chiral carbons. The Fischer projection of one of the enantiomers of glyceraldehyde is therefore interpreted as follows:

Fischer projection of a glyceraldehyde enantiomer

Bonds out of page
Bonds into page

$$CHO$$
$$HO\text{---}H$$
$$CH_2OH$$

Fischer projection

$$= \quad HO\text{---}C\text{---}H \atop \displaystyle CHO \atop CH_2OH \quad =$$

For comparison, the same glyceraldehyde enantiomer is represented below in the conventional manner, showing the tetrahedron of bonds to the chiral carbon.

$$CHO$$
$$HO \diagup C \diagdown CH_2OH$$
$$H$$
$$=$$

D Sugar Monosaccharide with the —OH group on the chiral carbon atom farthest from the carbonyl group pointing to the right in a Fischer projection.

L Sugar Monosaccharide with the —OH group on the chiral carbon atom farthest from the carbonyl group pointing to the left in a Fischer projection.

Monosaccharides are divided into two families—the **D sugars** and the **L sugars**—based on their structural relationships to glyceraldehyde. Consistently writing monosaccharide formulas as Fischer projections allows us to identify the D and L forms at a glance. Look again at the structural formulas of the D and L forms of glyceraldehyde.

Mirror

$$H\diagdown C\diagup O$$
$$H\text{---}\text{---}OH$$
$$CH_2OH$$
D-Glyceraldehyde

$$H\diagdown C\diagup O$$
$$HO\text{---}\text{---}H$$
$$CH_2OH$$
L-Glyceraldehyde

In the D form, the —OH group on carbon 2 comes out of the plane of the paper and points to the *right*; in the L form, the —OH group at carbon 2 comes out of the plane of the paper and points to the *left*. If you mentally place a mirror plane between these Fischer projections, you can see that they are mirror images.

Nature has a strong preference for one type of handedness in carbohydrates, just as it does in amino acids and in snail shells. It happens, however, that carbohydrates and amino acids have opposite handedness. Most naturally occurring α-amino acids belong to the L family, but most carbohydrates belong to the D family.

The designations D and L derive from the Latin *dextro* for "right" and *levo* for "left." *In all Fischer projections, the D form of a monosaccharide has the hydroxyl group on the chiral carbon atom farthest from the carbonyl group pointing toward the right, whereas the mirror-image L form has the hydroxyl group on this same carbon pointing toward the left.*

Fischer projections of molecules with more than one chiral carbon atom are written with the chiral carbons one above the other in a vertical line. To simplify visualizing the structures, we often include the C's for the chiral carbons in the

▲ Nature's preference. Snail shells have a preferred handedness, as do many molecules.

APPLICATION ▶ Chirality and Drugs

Nature is better at synthesizing single optical isomers than chemists are. Laboratory synthesis schemes that yield a mixture of optical isomers (a *racemic mixture*) are easy to develop. It is more difficult to devise synthetic schemes that yield a single isomer, but the goal of modern drug development is often creation of a drug molecule that binds with a specific hormone, enzyme, or cellular receptor. Because most biomolecules are chiral, a chiral drug molecule (single isomer) is likely to meet the need most effectively by fitting most closely with the target. Whether a pharmaceutical company decides to produce a racemic mixture of a particular drug molecule or a single isomer of the molecule is an issue of scientific, medical, and commercial importance in the drug industry.

The route to a chiral drug molecule might start with natural chiral reactants, with a natural enzyme, or with synthesis of a pair of enantiomers that are then separated from each other. It is often important to have the separate enantiomers available during the elaborate testing needed to prove a drug effective. Sometimes, marketing the mixture of isomers is the wrong thing to do. Naproxen, for example, the active ingredient in the pain killer and anti-inflammatory Aleve, is sold as a single enantiomer. The other enantiomer causes liver damage.

The size of the single-enantiomer drug market has increased every year since its inception about 15 years ago. With expanding research efforts, the ability to produce such drugs is growing easier. The top five classes of single-enantiomer drugs are cardiovascular drugs, antibiotics, hormones, cancer drugs, and those for central-nervous-system disorders.

See Additional Problems 22.77 and 22.78 at the end of the chapter.

plane of the page. Otherwise, the structures are interpreted like Fischer projections. Two pairs of aldohexose enantiomers are represented below in this manner. Given the Fischer projection of one enantiomer, you can draw the other by reversing the substituents on the left and right of each chiral atom. Note that each pair of enantiomers has a different name.

Two pairs of aldohexose enantiomers

It would be easy to assume that the use of D and L, because they stand for *dextro* and *levo*, carries some meaning about the direction of rotation of plane-polarized light. Logical as it seems, this is not the case. The D and L relate directly only to the position of that —OH group on the chiral carbon farthest from the carbonyl carbon in a Fischer projection. And the D and L isomers do indeed rotate plane-polarized light in opposite directions. But—and here is the point to remember—*the direction of rotation cannot be predicted*. There are D isomers that rotate polarized light to the left and L isomers that rotate it to the right.

WORKED EXAMPLE 22.2 Identifying D and L Isomers

Identify the following monosaccharides as (a) D-ribose or L-ribose, (b) D-mannose or L-mannose.

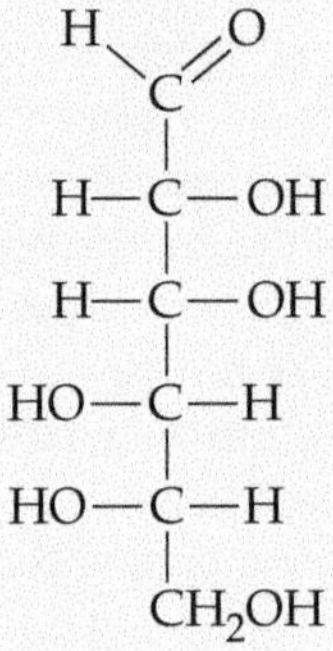

ANALYSIS To identify D or L isomers, you must check the location of the —OH group on the chiral carbon atom farthest from the carbonyl group. In a Fischer projection, this is the carbon atom above the bottom one. The —OH group points left in an L enantiomer and right in a D enantiomer.

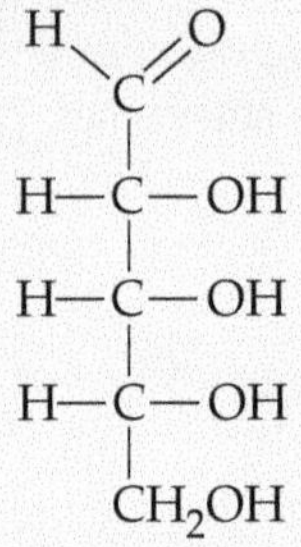

SOLUTION
In (a) the —OH group on the chiral carbon above the bottom of the structure points to the right, so this is D-ribose. In (b) this —OH group points to the left, so this is L-mannose.

PROBLEM 22.6

Draw the enantiomer of the following monosaccharides, and in each pair identify the D sugar and the L sugar.

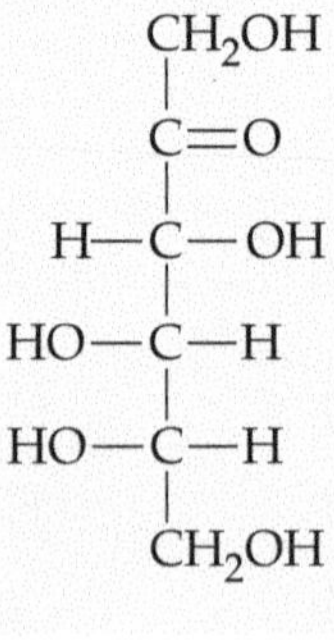

22.4 Structure of Glucose and Other Monosaccharides

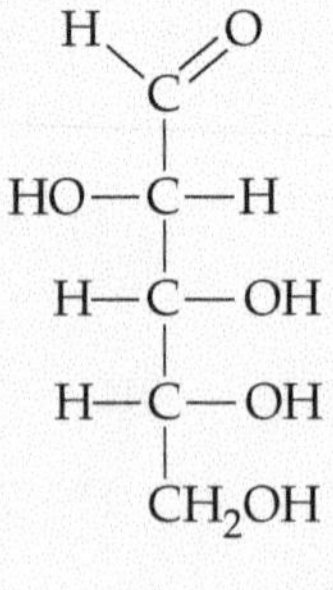

D-Glucose, also called *dextrose* or *blood sugar*, is the most widely occurring of all monosaccharides and has the most important function. In nearly all living organisms, D-glucose serves as a source of energy to fuel biochemical reactions. It is stored as starch in plants and glycogen in animals (Section 22.9). Our discussion here of the structure of D-glucose illustrates a major point about the structure of monosaccharides: Although they can be written with the carbon atoms in a straight chain, monosaccharides with five or six carbon atoms exist primarily in their cyclic forms.

Look at the Fischer projection of D-glucose at the top left-hand corner of Figure 22.3 (p. 701) and notice the locations of the aldehyde group and the hydroxyl groups. You have seen that aldehydes and ketones react reversibly with alcohols to

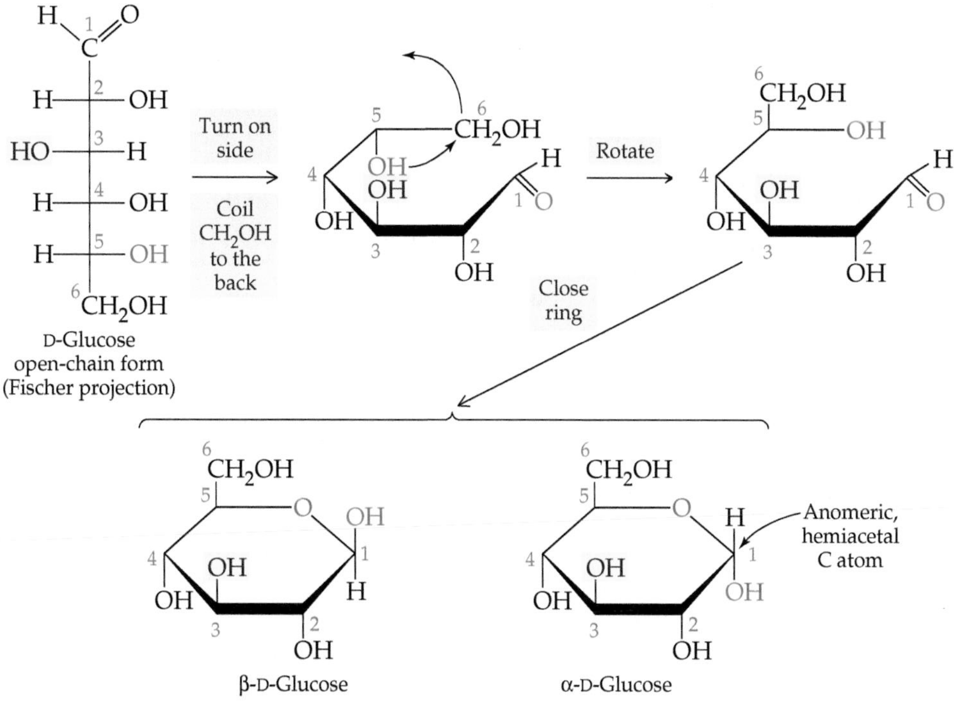

▲ **FIGURE 22.3 The structure of D-glucose.** D-Glucose can exist as an open-chain hydroxy aldehyde or as a pair of cyclic hemiacetals. The cyclic forms differ only at C1, where the —OH group is either on the opposite side of the six-membered ring from the CH_2OH (α) or on the same side (β). To convert the Fischer projection into the six-membered ring formula, the Fischer projection is laid down with C1 to the right and the other end curled around at the back. Then the single bond between C4 and C5 is rotated so that the —CH_2OH group is vertical. Finally, the hemiacetal O—R bond is formed by connecting oxygen from the —OH group on C5 to C1, and the hemiacetal O—H group is placed on C1. (H's on carbons 2–5 are omitted here for clarity.)

yield hemiacetals as shown below. (⬤▭, Section 16.7) (Remember that the key to recognizing the hemiacetal is a carbon atom bonded to both an —OH and an —OR group.)

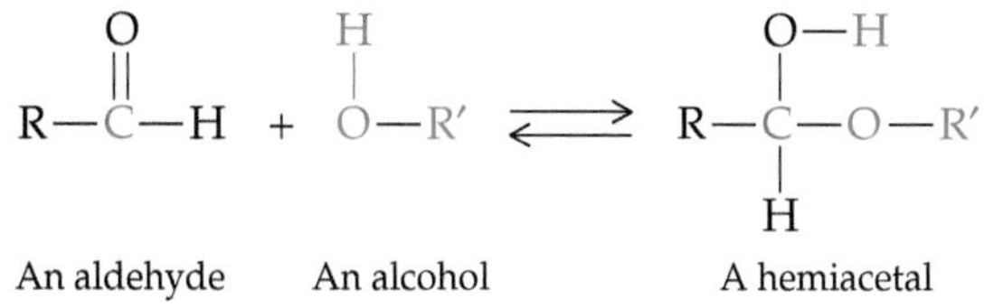

An aldehyde   An alcohol   A hemiacetal

Since glucose has alcohol hydroxyl groups and an aldehyde carbonyl group in the same molecule, *internal* hemiacetal formation is possible. The aldehyde carbonyl group at carbon 1 (C1) and the hydroxyl group at carbon 5 (C5) in glucose react to form a six-membered ring that is a hemiacetal. Monosaccharides with five or six carbon atoms form rings in this manner.

The three structures at the top in Figure 22.3 show how to picture the 5-hydroxyl and the aldehyde group approaching each other for hemiacetal formation. When visualized in this manner, Fischer projections are converted to cyclic structures that (like the Fischer projections) can be interpreted consistently because the same relative arrangements of the groups on the chiral carbon atoms are maintained.

In the cyclic structures at the bottom of Figure 22.3, note how the —OH group on carbon 3, which is on the left in the Fischer projection, points *up* in the cyclic structure, and —OH groups that were on the right on carbons 2 and 4 point *down*.

When cyclic structures (called *Haworth projections*) are drawn as shown in Figure 22.3, such relationships are always maintained. Note also that the —CH₂OH group in D sugars is always *above* the plane of the ring.

The hemiacetal carbon atom (C1) in the cyclic structures, like that in other hemiacetals, is bonded to two oxygen atoms (one in —OH and one in the ring). This carbon is chiral. As a result, there are two cyclic forms of glucose, known as the α and β forms. To see the difference, compare the locations of the hemiacetal —OH groups on C1 in the two bottom structures in Figure 22.3. In the β form, the hydroxyl at C1 points *up* and is on the same side of the ring as the —CH₂OH group at C5. In the α form, the hydroxyl at C1 points *down* and is on the opposite side of the ring from the —CH₂OH group. This relationship is maintained in cyclic monosaccharide structures drawn like those in Figure 22.3.

Cyclic monosaccharides that differ only in the positions of substituents at carbon 1 are known as **anomers**, and carbon 1 is said to be an **anomeric carbon atom**. It was the carbonyl carbon atom (C1 in an aldose and C2 in a hexose) that is now bonded to two O atoms. Note that the α and β anomers of a given sugar are not optical isomers because they are not mirror images.

Although the structural difference between anomers appears small, it has enormous biological consequences. For example, this one small change in structure accounts for the vast difference between the digestibility of starch, which we can digest, and that of cellulose, which we cannot digest (Section 22.9).

Ordinary crystalline glucose is entirely in the cyclic α form. Once dissolved in water, however, equilibrium is established among the open-chain form and the two anomers. The optical rotation of a freshly made solution of α-D-glucose gradually changes from its original value until it reaches a constant value that represents the optical activity of the equilibrium mixture. A solution of β-D-glucose or a mixture of the α and β forms also undergoes this gradual change in rotation, known as **mutarotation**, until the ring opening and closing reactions come to the following equilibrium:

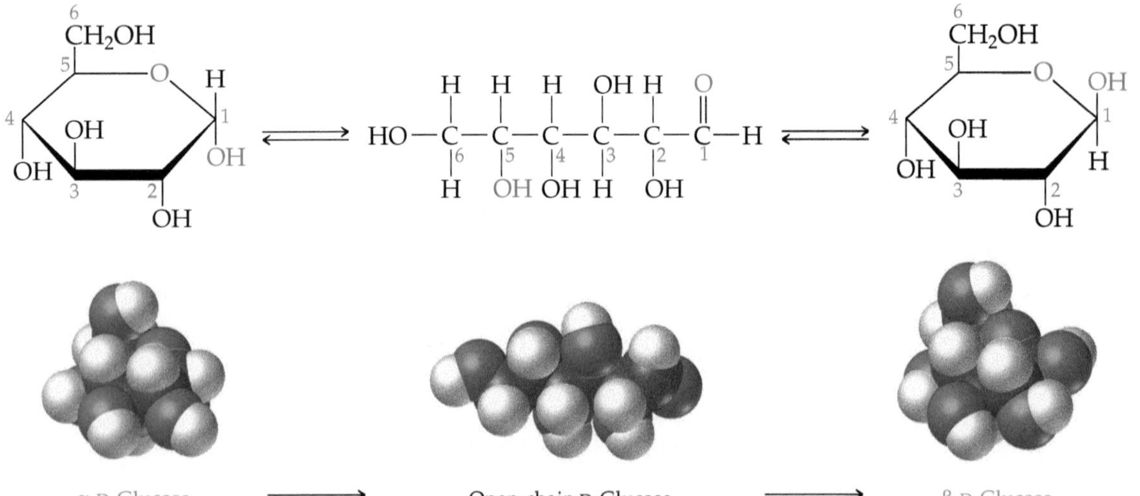

Anomers Cyclic sugars that differ only in positions of substituents at the hemiacetal carbon (the anomeric carbon); the α form has the —OH on the opposite side from the —CH₂OH; the β form has the —OH on the same side as the —CH₂OH.

Anomeric carbon atom The hemiacetal C atom in a cyclic sugar; the C atom bonded to an —OH group and an O in the ring.

Mutarotation Change in rotation of plane-polarized light resulting from the equilibrium between cyclic anomers and the open-chain form of a sugar.

α-D-Glucose		Open-chain D-Glucose		β-D-Glucose
(36%)		(0.02%)		(64%)

All monosaccharides with five or six carbon atoms establish similar equilibria, but with different percentages of the different forms present.

Monosaccharide Structures—Summary

- Monosaccharides are polyhydroxy aldehydes or ketones.
- Monosaccharides have three to seven carbon atoms, and a maximum of 2^n possible stereoisomers, where n is the number of chiral carbon atoms.
- D and L enantiomers differ in the orientation of the —OH group on the chiral carbon atom farthest from the carbonyl. In Fischer projections, D sugars have this —OH on the right and L sugars have this —OH on the left.

- D-Glucose (and other 6-carbon aldoses) forms cyclic hemiacetals conventionally represented (as in Figure 22.3) so that —OH groups on chiral carbons on the left in Fischer projections point up and those on the right in Fischer projections point down.

- In glucose, the hemiacetal carbon (*the anomeric carbon*) is chiral, and α and β anomers differ in the orientation of the —OH groups on this carbon. The α anomer has the —OH on the opposite side from the —CH$_2$OH, and the β anomer has the —OH on the same side as the —CH$_2$OH.

Enantioners

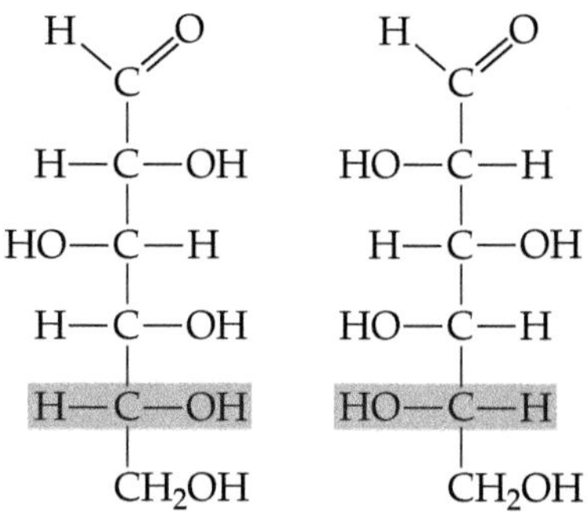

D-Glucose   L-Glucose

WORKED EXAMPLE **22.3** Converting Fisher Projections to Cyclic Hemiacetals

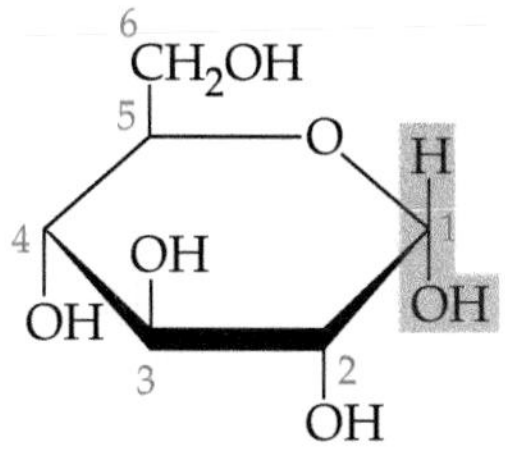

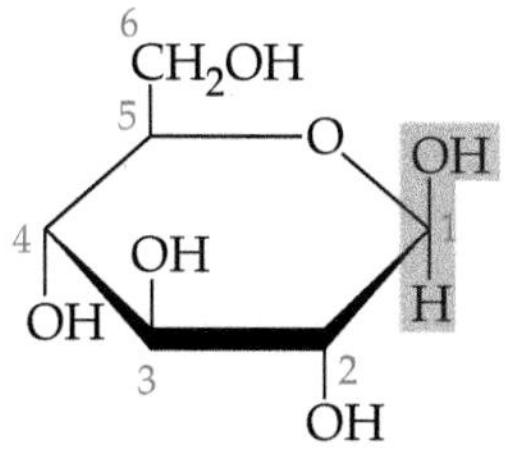

The open-chain form of D-altrose, an aldohexose isomer of glucose, has the following structure. Draw D-altrose in its cyclic hemiacetal form:

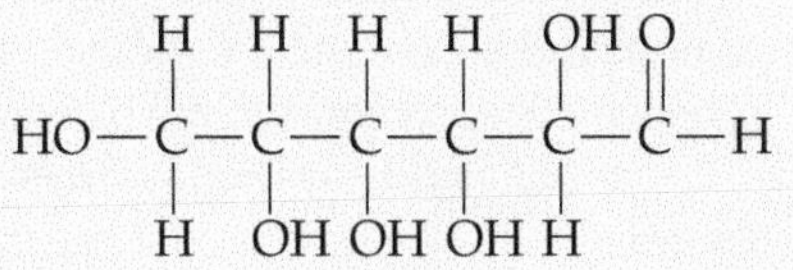

D-Altrose

SOLUTION
First, coil D-altrose into a circular shape by mentally grasping the end farthest from the carbonyl group and bending it backward into the plane of the paper:

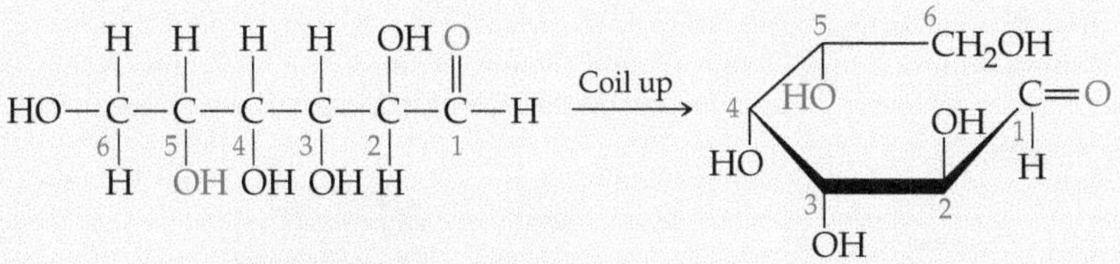

Anomers

α-D-Glucose

β-D-Glucose

Next, rotate the bottom of the structure around the single bond between C4 and C5 so that the —CH$_2$OH group at the end of the chain points up and the —OH group on C5 points toward the aldehyde carbonyl group on the right:

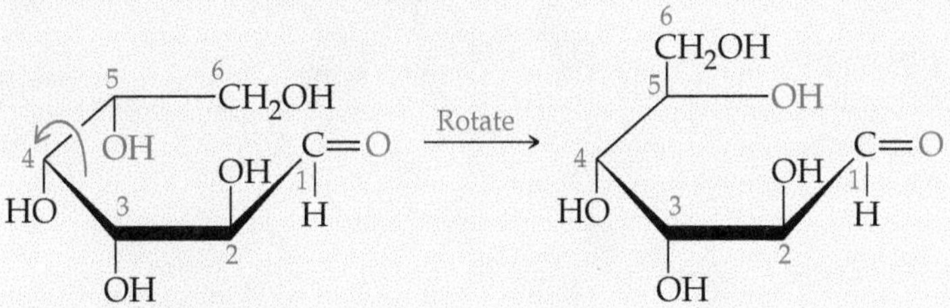

Finally, add the —OH group at C5 to the carbonyl C=O to form a hemiacetal ring. The new —OH group formed on C1 can be either up (β) or down (α):

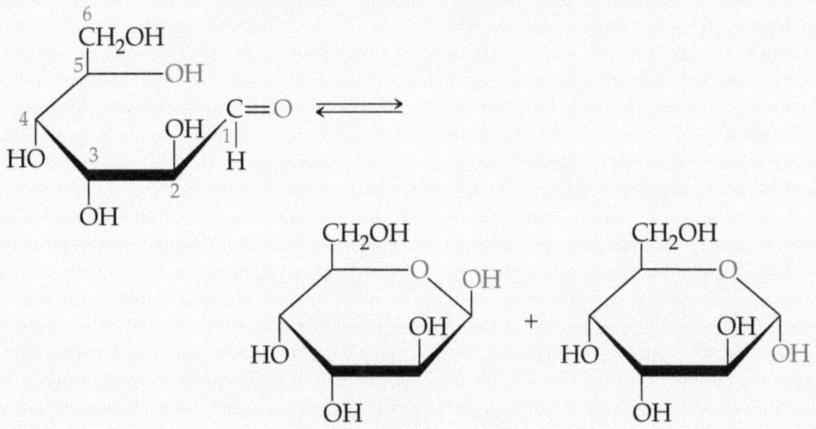

β α

APPLICATION ▶ Carbohydrates in the Diet

The major monosaccharides in our diets are fructose and glucose from fruits and honey. The major disaccharides are sucrose, commonly called table sugar and refined from both sugar cane and sugar beets, and lactose from milk. In addition, our diets contain large amounts of the digestible polysaccharide starch, present in grains such as wheat and rice, root vegetables such as potatoes, and legumes such as beans and peas. Nutritionists often refer to polysaccharides as *complex carbohydrates*.

How easily and how rapidly complex carbohydrates are digested and absorbed affects blood sugar levels. Consumption of the easily digested carbohydrates found in refined foods, such as white bread and rice, or in potatoes results in rapid elevation of blood glucose levels followed by lower-than-desired levels a few hours later. Carbohydrates that are digested and absorbed more slowly are associated with healthier blood sugar responses. The glycemic index is a scale that compares the blood sugar response to eating a complex carbohydrate with the response evoked by glucose. Foods with a low glycemic index release glucose slowly; foods with a high glycemic index release glucose rapidly during digestion and should be limited in the diet.

The body's major use of digestible carbohydrates is to provide energy, 4 kcal per gram of carbohydrate. A small amount of any excess carbohydrate is converted to glycogen for storage in the liver and muscles, but most dietary carbohydrate in excess of our immediate needs for energy is converted into fat.

The MyPyramid meal-planning tool (p. 560) reflects the emphasis on decreasing the amounts of meat and increasing the amounts of nonmeat products in our diet. The widest stripe of the pyramid is the recommendation for six 8-ounce equivalent servings per day of bread, cereal, rice, and pasta, all foods high in complex carbohydrates. Half of these servings should consist of whole grains. If your reaction is, I cannot possibly eat that much, you should know that a 1-ounce equivalent serving, as defined for the pyramid, is quite small: 1 slice of bread; 1/2 cup of cooked rice, pasta, or cereal; or 1 cup of cold cereal.

In terms of *total* carbohydrate, which includes both simple sugars and fiber, the *Nutrition Facts* labels on packaged foods (p. 621) give percentages based on a recommended 300 g per day of total carbohydrate and 25 g per day of dietary fiber (the nondigestible carbohydrates). These quantities provide 2000 Cal a day, with 60% of the calories from carbohydrates. The label also gives the total grams of sugars in the food, without a percentage because there is no recommended daily quantity of sugars. For purposes of the label, "sugars" are defined as all monosaccharides and disaccharides, whether naturally present or added.

As an option, the label may also include grams of *soluble fiber* and *insoluble fiber*. Taken together, these are the types of polysaccharides that are neither hydrolyzed to monosaccharides nor absorbed into the bloodstream.

The U.S. Food and Drug Administration is responsible for reviewing the scientific basis for health claims for foods. Two allowed claims relate to carbohydrates. The first states that a diet high in fiber may lower the risk of cancer and heart disease if the diet is also low in saturated fats and cholesterol. The second states that foods high in the soluble fiber from whole oats (oat bran) may also reduce the risk of heart disease, again when the diet is also low in saturated fats and cholesterol. (For further information, see the Application "Dietary Fiber" at the end of this chapter.)

▲ **Some healthy dietary carbohydrates.**

See Additional Problems 22.79 and 22.80 at the end of the chapter.

PROBLEM 22.7

D-Talose, a constituent of certain antibiotics, has the open-chain structure shown below. Draw D-talose in its cyclic hemiacetal form.

$$\begin{array}{c}
\text{H} \quad \text{H} \quad \text{OH} \; \text{OH} \; \text{OH} \; \text{O} \\
\text{HO}-\text{C}-\text{C}-\text{C}-\text{C}-\text{C}-\text{C}-\text{H} \\
\text{H} \quad \text{OH} \; \text{H} \quad \text{H} \quad \text{H} \quad \text{H}
\end{array}$$

D-Talose

PROBLEM 22.8

The cyclic structure of D-idose, an aldohexose, is shown below. Convert this to the straight-chain Fischer projection structure.

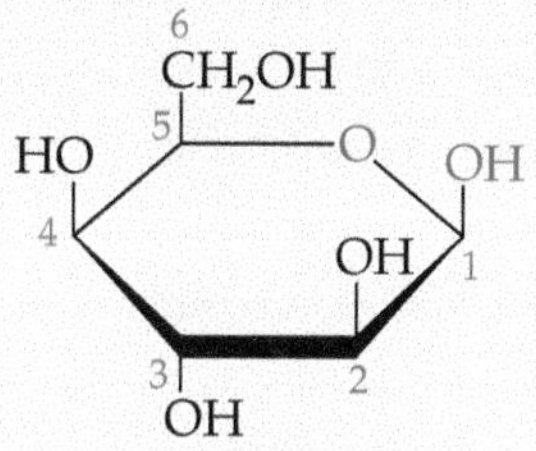

D-Idose

KEY CONCEPT PROBLEM 22.9

Ouabain is a potent poison derived from a plant and used as a dart poison.

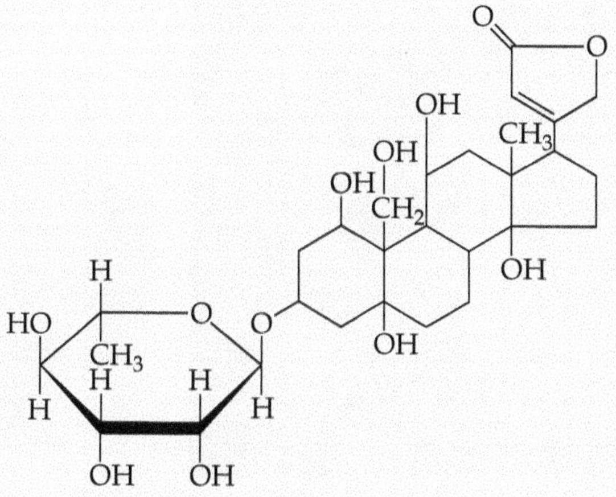

Ouabain

The structure can be roughly divided into three sections: a monosaccharide ring, a four-ring system, and an oxygen-containing ring known as a lactone. (a) Identify the monosaccharide ring according to the number of carbons in the ring. Based on the location of the linkage between the monosaccharide ring and the larger ring system, is the monosaccharide the α or the β form? (b) The large ring system is similar to that in a class of molecules that you encountered in an earlier chapter. Identify this class of molecule. (c) Look closely at the "lactone" ring. A lactone is a cyclic version of what common organic functional group?

22.5 Some Important Monosaccharides

The monosaccharides, with their many opportunities for hydrogen bonding through their hydroxyl groups, are generally high-melting, white, crystalline solids that are soluble in water and insoluble in nonpolar solvents. Most monosaccharides and disaccharides are sweet-tasting (Table 22.1), digestible, and nontoxic (Figure 22.4). Except for glyceraldehyde (an aldotriose) and fructose (a ketohexose), the carbohydrates of interest in human biochemistry are all aldohexoses or aldopentoses. Most are in the D family.

Glucose

Glucose is the most important simple carbohydrate in human metabolism. It is the final product of carbohydrate digestion and provides acetyl groups for entry into

TABLE 22.1 Relative Sweetness of Some Sugars and Sugar Substitutes

NAME	TYPE	SWEETNESS
Lactose	Disaccharide	16
Galactose	Monosaccharide	30
Maltose	Disaccharide	33
Glucose	Monosaccharide	75
Sucrose	Disaccharide	100
Fructose	Monosaccharide	175
Cyclamate	Artificial	3000
Aspartame	Artificial	15,000
Saccharin	Artificial	35,000
Sucralose	Artificial	60,000

(a)

(b)

(c)

▲ **FIGURE 22.4 Common sugars.** (a) Sucrose (glucose + fructose) is found in sugar cane and sugar beets. (b) Jam, with galactose in the pectin that stiffens it. (c) Honey, which is high in fructose.

the citric acid cycle as acetyl-SCoA. (⬭, Section 21.8) Maintenance of an appropriate blood glucose level is essential to human health. The hormones insulin and glucagon regulate blood glucose concentration. Because glucose is metabolized without further digestion, glucose solutions can be supplied intravenously to restore blood glucose levels.

⬭ Looking Ahead

In Chapter 23 we will describe the metabolic pathway (glycolysis) by which glucose is converted to pyruvate and then to acetyl-SCoA for entry into the citric acid cycle. The role of insulin in controlling blood glucose concentrations and the way in which those concentrations are affected by diabetes mellitus are also examined there. ⬭

Galactose

D-Galactose is widely distributed in plant gums and pectins, the sticky polysaccharides present in plant cells. It is also a component of the disaccharide lactose (milk sugar) and is produced from lactose during digestion. Like glucose, galactose is an aldohexose; it differs from glucose only in the spatial orientation of the —OH group at carbon 4. In the body, galactose is converted to glucose to provide energy and is synthesized from glucose to produce lactose for milk and compounds needed in brain tissue.

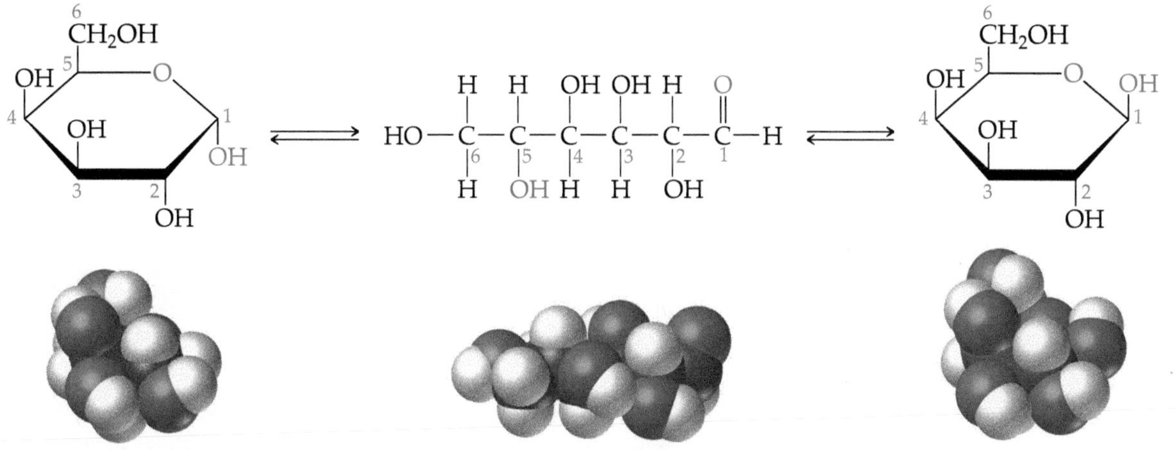

α-D-Galactose   Open-chain galactose   β-D-Galactose

A group of genetic disorders known as *galactosemias* result from an inherited deficiency of any of several enzymes needed to metabolize galactose. The result is a buildup of galactose or galactose 1-phosphate in blood and tissues. Early symptoms in infants include vomiting, an enlarged liver, and general failure to thrive. Other possible outcomes are liver failure, mental retardation, and development of cataracts when galactose in the eye is reduced to a polyhydroxy alcohol that accumulates. Treatment of galactosemia consists of a galactose-free diet for life.

Fructose

D-Fructose, often called *levulose* or *fruit sugar*, occurs in honey and many fruits. It is one of the two monosaccharides combined in the disaccharide sucrose. Fructose is produced commercially in large quantities by hydrolysis of cornstarch to make high fructose corn syrup. Like glucose and galactose, fructose is a 6-carbon sugar. However, it is a ketohexose rather than an aldohexose. In solution, fructose forms five-membered rings:

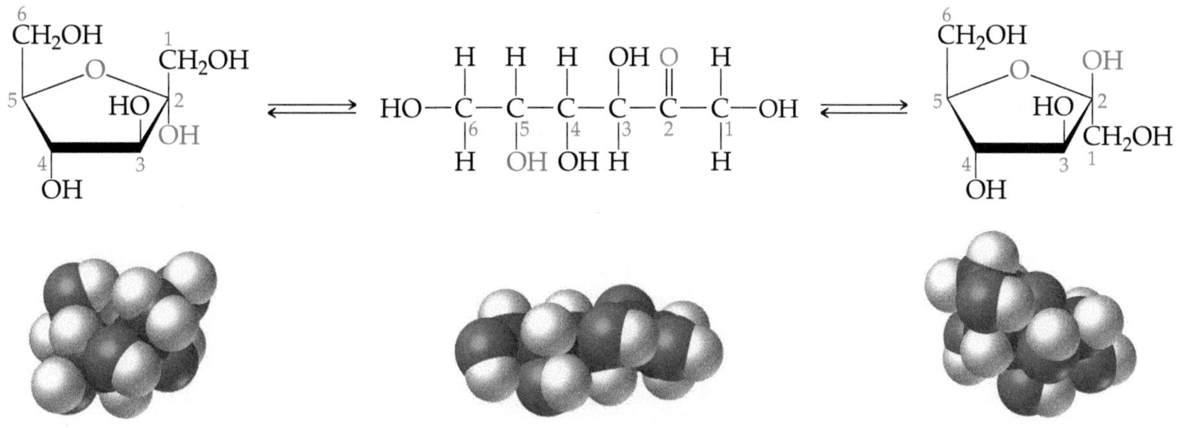

α-D-Fructose   Open-chain D-Fructose   β-D-Fructose

Fructose is sweeter than sucrose and is an ingredient in many sweetened beverages and prepared foods. As a phosphate, it is an intermediate in glucose metabolism.

Ribose and 2-Deoxyribose

Ribose and its relative 2-deoxyribose are both 5-carbon aldehyde sugars. These two sugars are most important as parts of larger biomolecules. You have already seen ribose as a constituent of coenzyme A (Figure 19.10), in ATP and the second messenger cyclic AMP (Figure 20.3) and in oxidizing and reducing agent coenzymes (p. 675).

As its name indicates, 2-*deoxy*ribose differs from ribose by the absence of one oxygen atom, that in the —OH group at C2. Both ribose and 2-deoxyribose exist in the usual mixture of open-chain and cyclic hemiacetal forms.

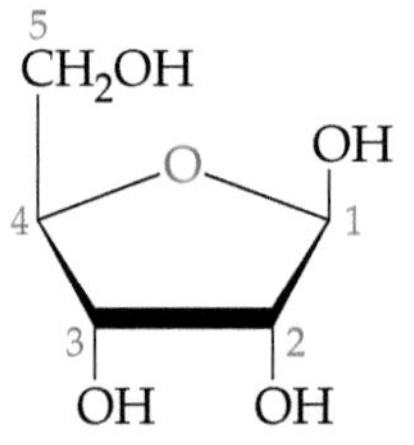

β-D-Ribose 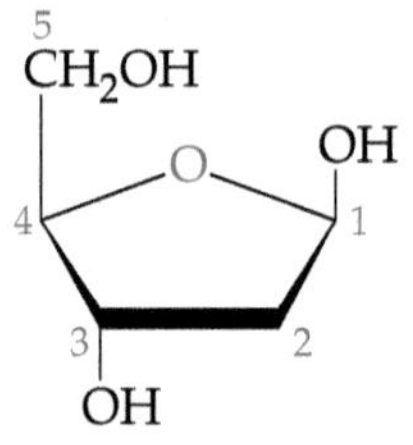 β-D-2-Deoxyribose

Looking Ahead

Ribose is part of RNA, ribonucleic acid, and deoxyribose is part of DNA, deoxyribonucleic acid. Chapter 26 is devoted to the roles of DNA in protein synthesis and heredity.

PROBLEM 22.10

In the following monosaccharide hemiacetal, identify the anomeric carbon atom, number all the carbon atoms, and identify it as the α or β anomer.

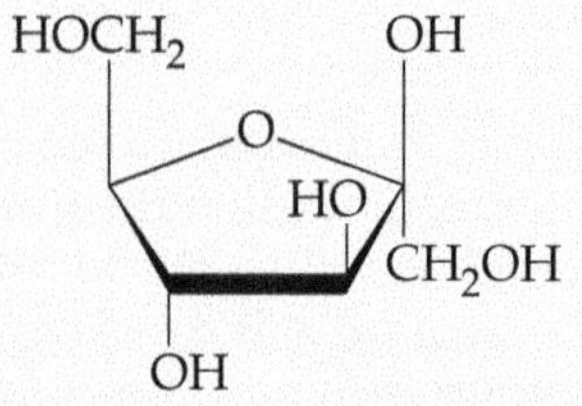

PROBLEM 22.11

Identify the chiral carbons in α-D-fructose, α-D-ribose, and β-D-2-deoxyribose.

PROBLEM 22.12

Draw the structures of cyclic AMP and ATP (Figure 20.3), and identify the portion of the molecule from ribose.

PROBLEM 22.13

L-Fucose is one of the naturally occurring L monosaccharides. It is present in the short chains of monosaccharides by which blood groups are classified (see the Application "Cell-Surface Carbohydrates and Blood Type," p. 720). Compare the structure of L-fucose given below with the structures of α- and β-D-galactose and answer the following questions.

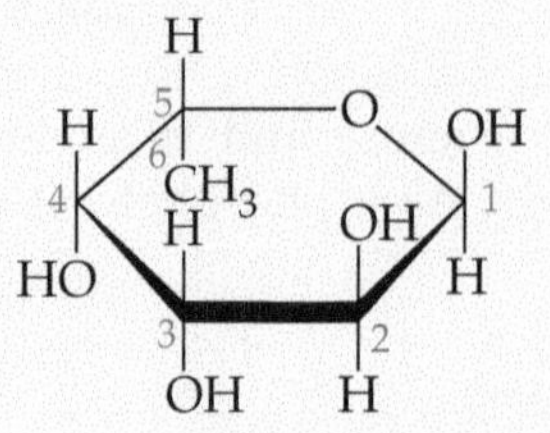

L-Fucose

(a) Is L-fucose an α or β anomer?

(b) Compared with galactose, on which carbon is L-fucose missing an oxygen?

(c) How do the positions of the —OH groups above and below the plane of the ring on carbons 2, 3, and 4 compare in D-galactose and L-fucose?

(d) "Fucose" is a common name. Is 6-deoxy-L-galactose a correct name for fucose?

22.6 Reactions of Monosaccharides

Reaction with Oxidizing Agents: Reducing Sugars

Aldehydes can be oxidized to carboxylic acids (RCHO → RCOOH), a reaction that applies to the open-chain form of aldose monosaccharides. (⊂⊃, Section 16.5) As the open-chain aldehyde is oxidized, its equilibrium with the cyclic form is displaced, in accord with Le Châtelier's principle, so that the open-chain form continues to be produced. (⊂⊃, p. 203) As a result, the aldehyde group of the monosaccharide is ultimately oxidized to a carboxylic acid group. For glucose, the reaction is

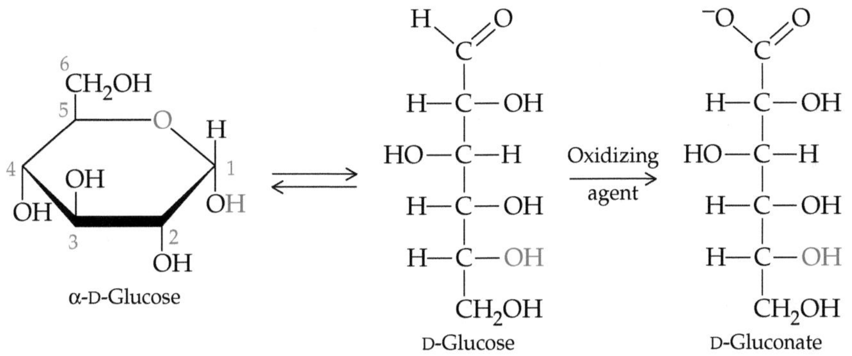

α-D-Glucose D-Glucose D-Gluconate

Carbohydrates that react with mild oxidizing agents are classified as **reducing sugars** (they reduce the oxidizing agent).

You probably would not predict it, but in basic solution, ketoses are also reducing sugars. The explanation is that, under these conditions, a ketone that has a hydrogen atom on the carbon adjacent to the carbonyl carbon undergoes a rearrangement. This hydrogen moves over to the carbonyl oxygen. The product is an *enediol*, "ene" for the double bond and "diol" for the two hydroxyl groups. The enediol rearranges to give an aldose, which is susceptible to oxidation.

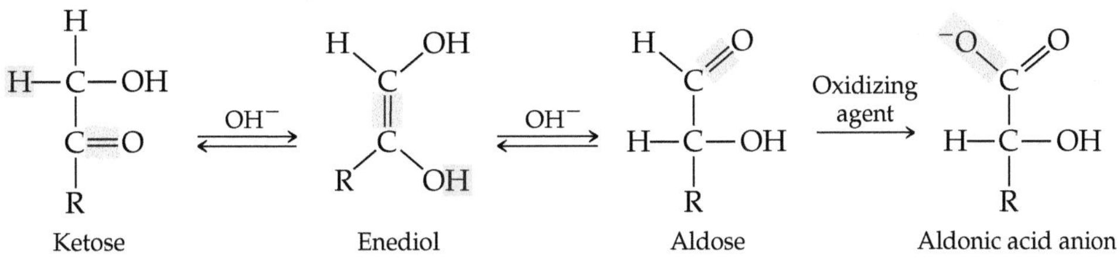

Reducing sugar A carbohydrate that reacts in basic solution with a mild oxidizing agent.

Ketose Enediol Aldose Aldonic acid anion

Here also, oxidation of the aldehyde to an acid drives the equilibria toward the right, and complete oxidation of the ketose occurs. Thus, *in basic solution, all monosaccharides, whether aldoses or ketoses, are reducing sugars.* This ability to act as reducing agents is the basis for most laboratory tests for the presence of monosaccharides.

The first equilibrium above—between the ketose and the enediol—is an example of *keto–enol tautomerism*, an equilibrium that results from a shift in position of a hydrogen atom and a double bond. Keto–enol tautomerism is possible whenever there is a hydrogen atom on a carbon adjacent to a carbonyl carbon.

Reaction with Alcohols: Glycoside and Disaccharide Formation

Hemiacetals react with alcohols with the loss of water to yield acetals, compounds with two —OR groups bonded to the same carbon. (⬤⬤, Section 16.7)

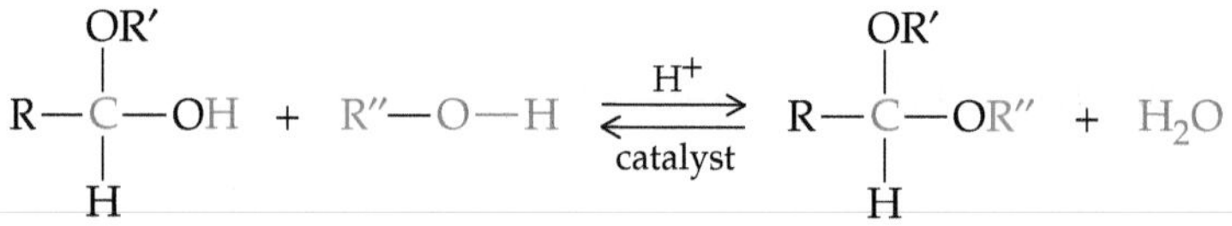

A hemiacetal   An alcohol   An acetal

Glycoside A cyclic acetal formed by reaction of a monosaccharide with an alcohol, accompanied by loss of H_2O.

Because glucose and other monosaccharides are cyclic hemiacetals, they also react with alcohols to form acetals, which are called **glycosides**. In a glycoside, the —OH group on the anomeric carbon atom is replaced by an —OR group. For example, glucose reacts with methanol to produce methyl glucoside. (Note that a *gluc*oside is a cyclic acetal formed by glucose. A cyclic acetal derived from *any* sugar is a *glyc*oside.)

Formation of a glycoside

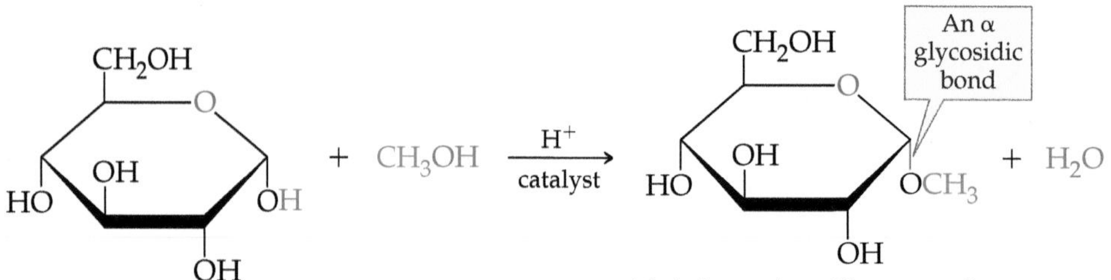

α-D-Glucose   Methyl α-D-glucoside, an acetal

Glycosidic bond Bond between the anomeric carbon atom of a monosaccharide and an —OR group.

The bond between the anomeric carbon atom of the monosaccharide and the oxygen atom of the —OR group is called a **glycosidic bond**. Since glycosides like the one shown above do not contain hemiacetal groups that establish equilibria with open-chain forms, they are *not* reducing sugars.

In larger molecules, including disaccharides and polysaccharides, monosaccharides are connected to each other by glycosidic bonds. For example, a disaccharide forms by reaction of the anomeric carbon of one monosaccharide with an —OH group of a second monosaccharide.

Formation of a glycosidic bond between two monosaccharides

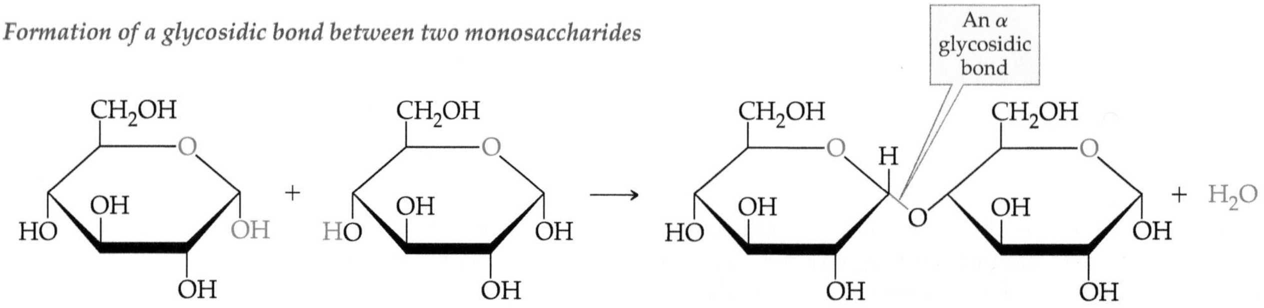

The reverse of this reaction is a *hydrolysis* and is the reaction that takes place during digestion of all carbohydrates.

Hydrolysis of a disaccharide

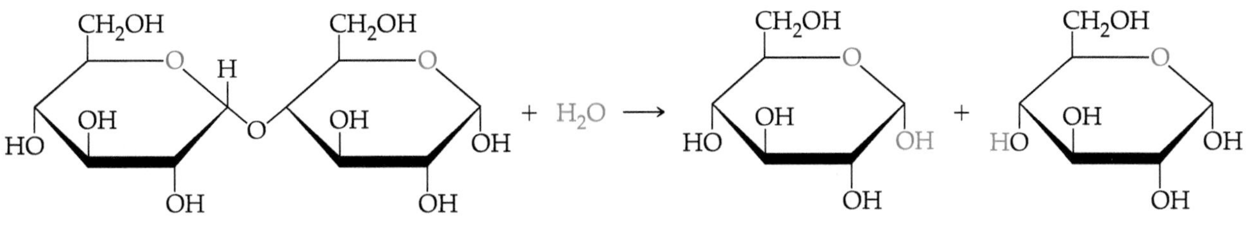

PROBLEM 22.14

Draw the structure of the α and β anomers that result from the reaction of methanol and ribose (see p. 710). Are these compounds acetals or hemiacetals?

Formation of Phosphate Esters of Alcohols

Phosphate esters of alcohols contain a $-PO_3^{2-}$ group bonded to the oxygen atom of an $-OH$ group. The $-OH$ groups of sugars can add $-PO_3^{2-}$ groups to form phosphate esters in the same manner. The resulting phosphate esters of monosaccharides appear as reactants and products throughout the metabolism of carbohydrates. Glucose phosphate is the first to be formed and sets the stage for subsequent reactions. It is produced by the transfer of a $-PO_3^{2-}$ group from ATP to glucose in the first step of glycolysis, the metabolic pathway followed by glucose and other sugars, which is described in Chapter 23. Glycolysis leads to the ultimate conversion of glucose to the acetyl groups that are carried into the citric acid cycle.

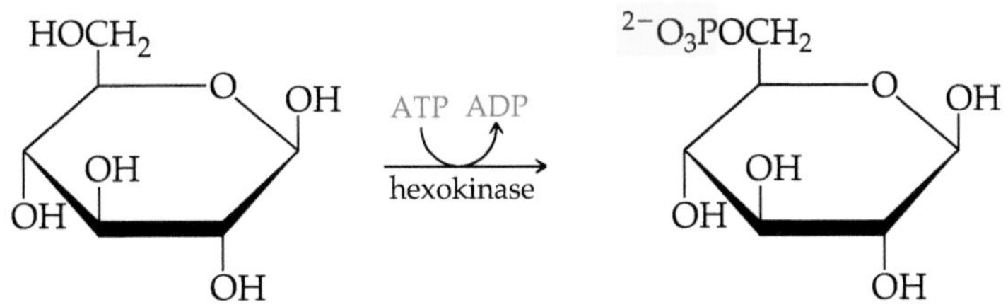

Glucose

Glucose
6-phosphate

22.7 Disaccharides

Every day, you eat a disaccharide—sucrose, common table sugar. Sucrose is made of two monosaccharides, one glucose and one fructose, covalently bonded to each other. Sucrose is present in modest amounts, along with other mono- and disaccharides, in most fresh fruits and many fresh vegetables. But most sucrose in our diets has been added to something. Perhaps you add it to your coffee or tea. Or it is there in a ready-to-eat food product that you buy, maybe breakfast cereal, ice cream, or a "super-sized" soda, or even bread. Excessive consumption of high-sucrose foods has been blamed for everything from criminal behavior to heart disease to hyperactivity in children, but without any widely accepted scientific proof. A proven connection with heart disease does exist, of course, but by way of the contribution of excess sugar calories to obesity.

Disaccharide Structure

The two monosaccharides in a disaccharide are connected by a glycosidic bond. The bond may be α or β as in cyclic monosaccharides: α points below the ring and β points above the ring (see Figure 22.3). The structures include glycosidic bonds that create a **1,4 link**, that is, a link between C1 of one monosaccharide and C4 of the second monosaccharide:

1,4 Link A glycosidic link between the hemiacetal hydroxyl group at C1 of one sugar and the hydroxyl group at C4 of another sugar.

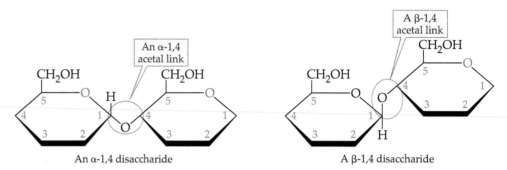

An α-1,4 disaccharide   A β-1,4 disaccharide

The three naturally occurring disaccharides discussed in the following sections are the most common ones. They illustrate the three different ways monosaccharides are linked: by a glycosidic bond in the α orientation (maltose), a glycosidic bond in the β orientation (lactose), or a bond that connects two anomeric carbon atoms (sucrose).

Maltose

Maltose, often called malt sugar, is present in fermenting grains and can be prepared by enzyme-catalyzed degradation of starch. It is used in prepared foods as a sweetener. In the body, it is produced during starch digestion by α-amylase in the small intestine and then hydrolyzed to glucose by a second enzyme, maltase.

Two α-D-glucose molecules are joined in maltose by an α-1,4 link. A careful look at maltose shows that it is both an acetal (at C1 in the glucose on the left below) and a hemiacetal (at C1 in the glucose on the right below). Since the acetal ring on the left does not open and close spontaneously, it cannot react with an oxidizing agent. The hemiacetal group on the right, however, establishes equilibrium with the aldehyde, making maltose a reducing sugar.

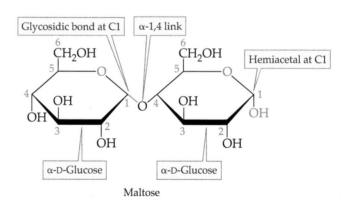

Maltose

Lactose

Lactose, or milk sugar, is the major carbohydrate in mammalian milk. Human milk, for example, is about 7% lactose. Structurally, lactose is a disaccharide composed of β-D-galactose and β-D-glucose. The two monosaccharides are connected by

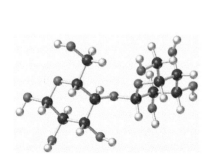

a β-1,4 link. Like maltose, lactose is a reducing sugar because the glucose ring (on the right in the following structure) is a hemiacetal at C1.

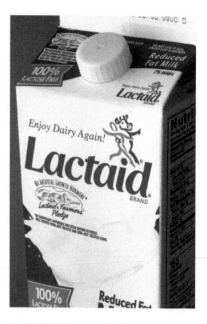

Lactose

▲ Milk for lactose-intolerant individuals. The lactose content of the milk has been decreased by treating it with lactase.

Lactose intolerance in adults is an unpleasant, though not life-threatening, condition that is prevalent in all populations. In fact, it has been suggested that the *absence* of this condition in adults rather than its presence is the deviation from the norm. The activity of lactase, the enzyme that allows lactose digestion by infants, apparently gradually diminishes over the years. Because lactose remains in the intestines rather than being absorbed, it raises the osmolarity there, which draws in excess water. (, Section 9.12) Bacteria in the intestine also ferment the lactose to produce lactate, carbon dioxide, hydrogen, and methane. The result is bloating, cramps, flatulence, and diarrhea. The condition may be treated by a lactose-free diet, which extends to limitations on taking the many medications and artificial sweeteners in which lactose is an inactive ingredient. An alternative is the use of commercial enzyme preparations taken before milk products are consumed and Lactaid, milk that has been treated with lactase to reduce its lactose content.

Sucrose

Sucrose—plain table sugar—is probably the most common highly purified organic chemical used in the world. Sugar beets and sugarcane are the most common sources of sucrose. Hydrolysis of sucrose yields one molecule of D-glucose and one molecule of D-fructose. The 50:50 mixture of glucose and fructose that results, often referred to as *invert sugar*, is commonly used as a food additive because it is sweeter than sucrose.

Sucrose differs from maltose and lactose in that it has no hemiacetal group because a 1,2 link joins *both* anomeric carbon atoms. The absence of a hemiacetal group means that sucrose is not a reducing sugar. Sucrose is the only common disaccharide that is not a reducing sugar.

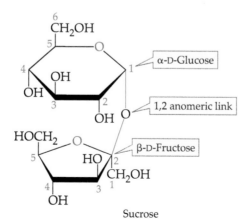

Sucrose

APPLICATION ▶ Cell Walls: Rigid Defense Systems

All cells are defined by the presence of a plasma membrane, which confines the cell's contents inside a lipid bilayer studded with proteins. (CO, Section 21.3) Bacteria and higher plants surround the plasma membrane with a rigid cell wall. Cell walls differ markedly in composition, but not in primary function between higher plants and bacteria. The primary function of a cell wall is to make the cell rigid. The rigidity of the wall prevents the cell from bursting due to osmotic pressure, because the dissolved metabolites and ions inside the cell are at a greater concentration than outside. In addition to its rigidity, the cell wall also gives shape to the cell and protects it from pathogens.

Plant cell walls are composed of fibrils of cellulose in a polymer matrix of pectins, lignin, and hemicellulose. Although you might think each cell is isolated from the others, plant cell walls contain small perforations that permit contact between adjacent cells. This allows for the transfer of nutrients and signals. Cellulose chains range from about 6000 to 16,000 glucose units in length. Neighboring chains of cellulose form hydrogen bonds between them, thereby strengthening the cell wall.

In addition to providing strength and shape, bacterial cell walls provide a rigid platform for the attachment of flagella and pilli. Furthermore, the composition of the cell wall provides attachment sites for bacteriophages (viruses that infect bacteria). Although bacterial cell walls do contain modified sugar polymers, they do not contain cellulose. Cell wall composition varies among bacterial species and is an important factor in distinguishing between some groups of bacteria. A majority of bacterial cell walls are composed of a polymer of *peptidoglycan*, an alternating sequence of the modified sugars *N*-acetylglucosamine (NAG) and *N*-acetylmuraminic acid (NAMA). Peptidoglycan strands are cross-linked to one another by short peptide bridges; these bridges are unique in that both D-alanine and L-alanine are present. The interlocked strands form a porous, multilayered grid over the bacterial plasma membrane.

Fortunately, animals have developed natural defenses that can control many bacteria. For example, lysozyme—an enzyme found naturally in tears, saliva, and egg white—hydrolyzes the peptidoglycan cell wall of pathogenic bacteria, thereby killing them. In the middle of the twentieth century the antibiotic penicillin was developed. The penicillin family members all contain a beta-lactam ring that allows these compounds to act as "suicide inhibitors" of the enzymes that synthesize the peptidoglycan cross-linking peptide chain. Penicillin and its relatives target only reproducing bacteria. Mammals do not contain the enzyme pathway that synthesizes peptidoglycans, and this is what allows us to kill the bacteria without harming ourselves.

Today we take the availability and effectiveness of antibiotics for granted. When penicillin was discovered, it was hailed as a "magic bullet" because it could cure bacterial infections that were often fatal. Unfortunately, bacteria have developed resistance to penicillin and its relatives; resistant bacteria have developed enzymes that destroy the beta-lactam ring, thereby destroying the effectiveness of penicillin. Other antibiotics have since been developed, but the spread of antibiotic-resistant bacterial strains is a public health concern due to the "bullet-proof vest" nature of the bacterial cell wall.

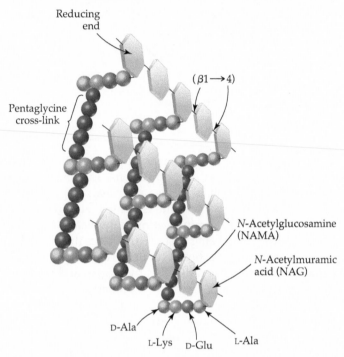

▲ **Peptidoglycan structure:** Strands of alternating NAG and NAMA connected by peptides form a mesh covering the bacterial cell membrane.

Penicillin

where R =

or

or

See Additional Problems 22.81 through 22.84 at the end of the chapter.

WORKED EXAMPLE **22.4** Identifying Reducing Sugars

The disaccharide cellobiose can be obtained by enzyme-catalyzed hydrolysis of cellulose. Do you expect cellobiose to be a reducing or a nonreducing sugar?

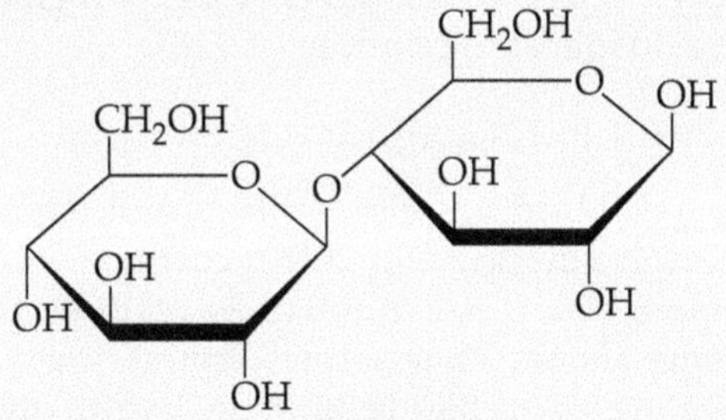

Cellobiose

ANALYSIS To be a reducing sugar, a disaccharide must contain a hemiacetal group, that is, a carbon bonded to one —OH group and one —OR group. The ring at the right in the structure above has such a group.

SOLUTION
Cellobiose is a reducing sugar.

PROBLEM 22.15

Refer to the cellobiose structure in Worked Example 22.4. How would you classify the link between the monosaccharides in cellobiose?

PROBLEM 22.16

Refer to the cellobiose structure in Worked Example 22.4. Show the structures of the two monosaccharides that are formed on hydrolysis of cellobiose. What are their names?

KEY CONCEPT PROBLEM 22.17

Identify the following disaccharides. (a) The disaccharide contains two glucose units joined by an α-glycosidic linkage. (b) The disaccharide contains fructose and glucose. (c) The disaccharide contains galactose and glucose.

22.8 Variations on the Carbohydrate Theme

Monosaccharides with modified functional groups are components of a wide variety of biomolecules. Also, short chains of monosaccharides (known as *oligosaccharides*) enhance the functions of proteins and lipids to which they are bonded.

In this section we mention a few of the more interesting and important variations on the carbohydrate theme, several of which incorporate the modified glucose molecules shown here. Their distinctive functional groups are highlighted in yellow:

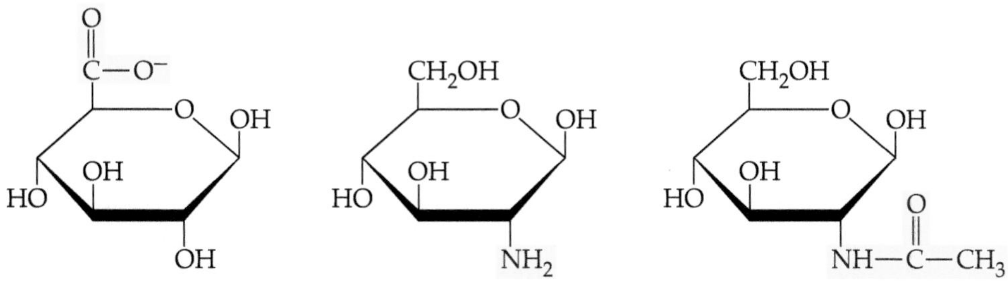

β-D-Glucuronate   β-D-Glucosamine   N-Acetyl-β-D-Glucosamine

▲ A fungus beetle from the Amazon rainforest in its purple-spotted exoskeleton made of chitin.

Chitin

The shells of lobsters, beetles, and spiders are made of chitin, the second most abundant polysaccharide in the natural world. (Cellulose is the most abundant.) Chitin is a hard, structural polymer. It is composed of *N*-acetyl-D-glucosamine rather than glucose but is otherwise identical to cellulose (p. 718).

Connective Tissue and Polysaccharides

Connective tissues such as blood vessels, cartilage, and tendons are composed of protein fibers embedded in a syrupy matrix that contains unbranched polysaccharides (*mucopolysaccharides*). The gel-like mixtures of these polysaccharides with water serve as lubricants and shock absorbers around joints and in extracellular spaces. Note the repeating disaccharide units in two of these polysaccharides, hyaluronate and chondroitin:

Hyaluronate repeating unit

Chondroitin 6-sulfate repeating unit

Hyaluronate molecules contain up to 25,000 disaccharide units and form a quite rigid, very viscous mixture with water molecules attracted to its negative charges. This mixture is the *synovial fluid* that lubricates joints. It is also present within the eye. *Chondroitin 6-sulfate* (also the 4-sulfate) is present in tendons and cartilage, where it is linked to proteins. It has been used in artificial skin. Chondroitin sulfates and glucosamine sulfate are available as dietary supplements in health food stores and are promoted as cures for osteoarthritis, in which cartilage at joints deteriorates. They are prescribed by veterinarians for arthritic dogs, and there is anecdotal evidence for benefits in humans.

Heparin

Another of the polysaccharides associated with connective tissue, heparin is valuable medically as an *anticoagulant* (an agent that prevents or retards the clotting of blood). Heparin is composed of a variety of different monosaccharides, many of them containing sulfate groups.

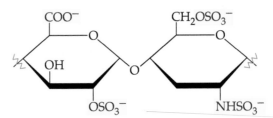

Example of repeating unit in heparin

▲ Blood on its way to the clinical lab. The vials with the lavender tops contain heparin and are used for blood destined for a routine hematology screen.

Notice the large number of negative charges in this heparin repeating unit. Heparin binds strongly to a blood-clotting factor and in this way prevents clot formation. It is used clinically to prevent clotting after surgery or serious injury. Also, a coating of heparin is applied to any surfaces that will come into contact with blood that must not clot, such as the interiors of test tubes used for blood samples collected for analysis or materials in prosthetic implants for the body.

Glycoproteins

Proteins that contain short carbohydrate chains (*oligosaccharide* chains) are known as **glycoproteins**. (The prefix *glyco-* always refers to carbohydrates.) The carbohydrate is connected to the protein by a glycosidic bond between an anomeric carbon and a side chain of the protein. The bond is either a C—N glycosidic bond or a C—O glycosidic bond:

Glycoprotein A protein that contains a short carbohydrate chain.

OUTSIDE OF CELL

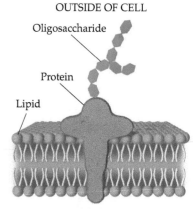

INSIDE OF CELL

Glycoproteins have important functions on the surfaces of all cells. (You might say our cells are sugar-coated.) The protein portion of the molecule lies within the cell membrane, and the hydrophilic carbohydrate portion extends into the surrounding fluid. There, the oligosaccharide chains function as receptors for molecular messengers, other cells, pathogenic microorganisms, or drugs. They are also responsible for the familiar A, B, O system of typing blood. (See the Application "Cell-Surface Carbohydrates and Blood Type," p. 720.)

One unusual glycoprotein, found in the bloodstream and other body fluids of some Antarctic fish species, functions as an antifreeze. This glycoprotein is a polymer with a repeating tripeptide (alanine-alanine-threonine) unit that has a disaccharide (galactosyl-*N*-acetylgalactosamine) bonded to every threonine. The polymer varies in length from 17 to 50 units. It does not protect against freezing by lowering the freezing point, as does the antifreeze used in car radiators; instead the polar groups on the glycoprotein bind with water molecules at the surface of tiny ice crystals, slowing the growth of the crystals. As the blood circulates through the liver, it warms enough for the ice crystals to melt before they harm the organism.

▲ Atlantic codfish, which can survive in frigid water.

⬡ Looking Ahead

The basic components of cell membranes are lipid molecules. The wonderfully complex structure and function of the membrane are explored in Sections 24.5 and 24.6. Glycolipids—carbohydrates bonded to lipids—are, like glycoproteins, essential in cell membranes and are also discussed in Section 24.5. ⬡

PROBLEM 22.18

In *N*-linked glycoproteins, the sugar is usually attached to the protein by a bond to the N atom in a side-chain amide. Which amino acids can form such a bond?

PROBLEM 22.19

Identify the type of glycosidic linkage in the repeating unit of heparin illustrated in this section.

22.9 Some Important Polysaccharides

Polysaccharides are polymers of tens, hundreds, or even many thousands of monosaccharides linked together through glycosidic bonds of the same type as in maltose and lactose. Three of the most important polysaccharides are *cellulose, starch,* and *glycogen*. The repeating units making up cellulose and starch are compared in the following structures:

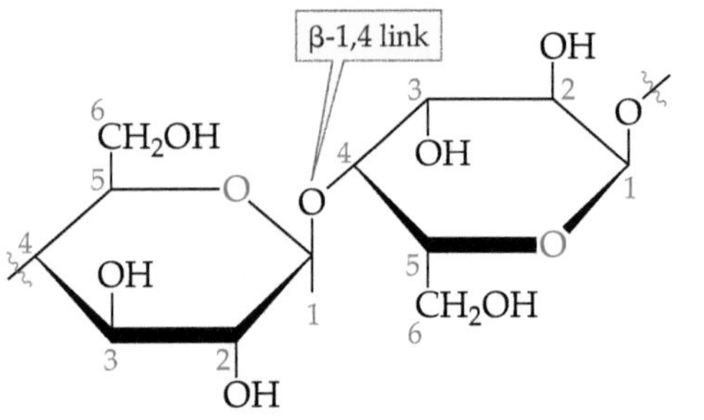

Cellulose repeating unit

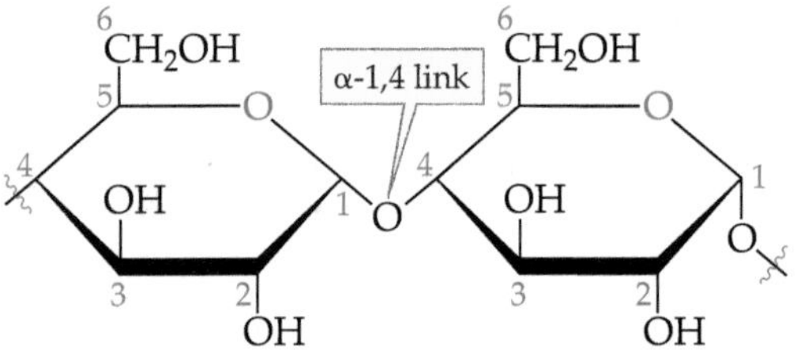

Starch and glycogen repeating unit

Cellulose

Cellulose is the fibrous substance that provides structure in plants. Each huge cellulose molecule consists of several thousand β-D-glucose units joined in a long, straight chain by β-1,4 links. The bonding in cellulose is illustrated above by the flat hexagons we have used so far for monosaccharides. In reality, because of the tetrahedral bonding at each carbon atom, the carbohydrate rings are not flat but are bent up at one end and down at the other in what is known as the *chair conformation*:

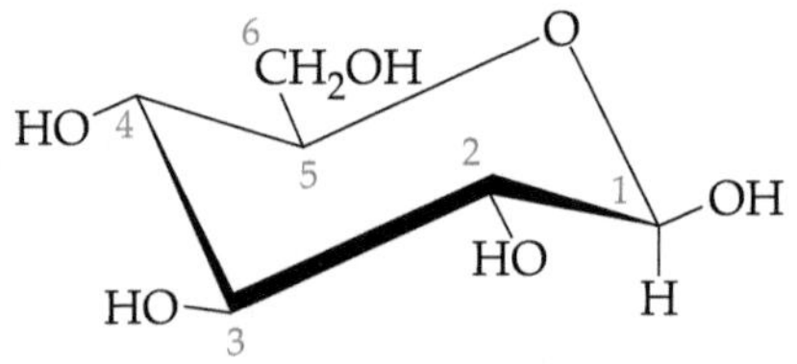

Chair conformation of β-D-glucose

Inspection of the chair conformation shows that the bulkier hydroxyl groups point toward the sides of the ring as does the —CH$_2$OH. This *equatorial* position minimizes interactions between these bulky substituents on the ring. The smaller substituents on the ring (the H atoms) extend either above or below the ring in the *axial* position. This axial/equatorial arrangement resulting from the chair conformation is the most energetically stable form of a six-membered carbohydrate ring.

When the cellulose structure is drawn with all the rings in the chair conformation it is much easier to see how each glucose ring is reversed relative to the next by comparing the locations of the ring O atoms:

Cellulose

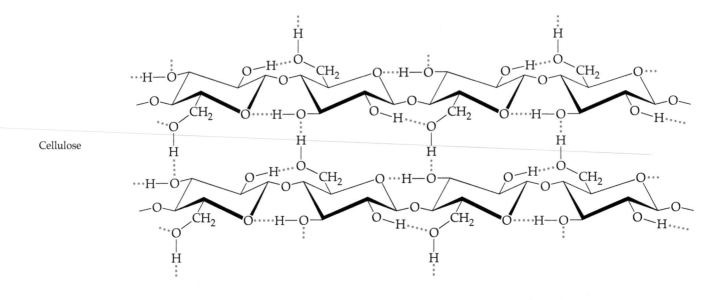

Note in this drawing how the ring O in the top left ring is at the bottom of the ring, the ring O in the ring to the right is at the top of the ring, and so on. The hydrogen bonds within chains and between chains (shown in red) contribute to the rigidity and toughness of cellulose fibers.

Earlier we noted that the seemingly minor distinction between the α and β forms of cyclic sugars accounts for a vast difference between cellulose and starch. Cows and other grazing animals, termites, and moths are able to digest cellulose because microorganisms colonizing their digestive tracts produce enzymes that hydrolyze its β glycosidic bonds. Humans neither produce such enzymes nor harbor such organisms, and therefore cannot hydrolyze cellulose, although some is broken down by bacteria in the large intestine. Cellulose is what grandma used to call "roughage," and we need it in our diets in addition to starch.

Starch

Starch, like cellulose, is a polymer of glucose. In starch, individual glucose units are joined by α-1,4 links rather than by the β-1,4 links of cellulose. Starch is fully digestible and is an essential part of the human diet. It is present only in plant material; our major sources are beans, the grains wheat and rice, and potatoes.

Unlike cellulose, which has only one form, there are two kinds of starch—amylose and amylopectin. *Amylose*, which accounts for about 20% of starch, is somewhat soluble in hot water and consists of several hundred to a thousand α-D-glucose units linked in long chains by the α-1,4 glycosidic bonds. Instead of lying side by side and flat as in cellulose, amylose tends to coil into helices (Figure 22.5). Dissolved amylose makes the cooking water cloudy when you boil potatoes.

▲ **FIGURE 22.5 Helical structure of amylose.**

Amylose

Amylopectin, which accounts for about 80% of starch, is similar to amylose but has much larger molecules (up to 100,000 glucose units per molecule) and has α-1,6 branches approximately every 25 units along its chain. A glucose molecule at one of these branch points (shaded below) is linked to three other sugars. Amylopectin is not water-soluble.

Branch point in amylopectin (also glycogen)

APPLICATION ▶ Cell-Surface Carbohydrates and Blood Type

Nearly 100 years ago, scientists discovered that human blood can be classified into four blood group types, called A, B, AB, and O. This classification results from the presence on red blood cell surfaces of three different oligosaccharide units, designated A, B, and O (see the diagram). Individuals with type AB blood have both A and B oligosaccharides displayed on the same cells.

Selecting a matching blood type is vitally important in choosing blood for transfusions because a major component of the body's immune system (⬭▭, Chapter 28) is a collection of proteins called *antibodies* that recognize and attack foreign substances, such as viruses, bacteria, potentially harmful macromolecules and foreign blood cells. Among the targets of these antibodies are cell-surface molecules that are not present on the individual's own cells and are thus "foreign blood cells." For example, if you have type A blood, your plasma (the liquid portion of the blood) contains antibodies to the type B oligosaccharide. Thus, if type B blood enters your body, its red blood cells will be recognized as foreign and your immune system will launch an attack on them. The result is clumping of the cells (agglutination), blockage of capillaries, and possibly death.

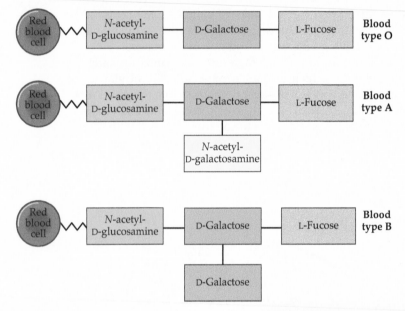

Because of the danger of such interactions, both the blood types that individuals can receive and the blood types of recipients to whom they can donate blood are limited, as indicated in the accompanying table. A few features of the table deserve special mention:

- Note in the diagram that type O cell-surface oligosaccharides are similar in composition to those of types A and B. Consequently, people with blood types A, B, and AB all lack antibodies to type O cells. Individuals with type O blood are therefore known as "universal donors"—in an emergency, their blood can safely be given to individuals of all blood types.

- Similarly, type AB individuals are known as "universal recipients." Because people with type AB blood have both A and B molecules on their red cells, their blood contains no antibodies to A, B, or O, and they can, if necessary, receive blood of all types.

- In theory, antibodies in the plasma of donated blood could also attack the red cells of the recipient. In practice, such reactions are unlikely to cause significant harm. Unless very large quantities of whole blood or

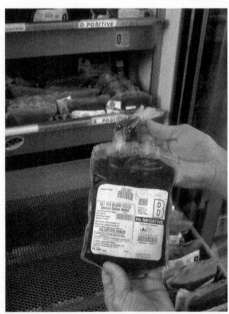

▲ A unit of packed blood cells stored in blood bank refrigeration until needed for transfusion.

plasma (the fluid portion of the blood) are transfused, the donor's blood is quickly diluted by mixing with the much larger volume of the recipient's blood. Moreover, many transfusions today consist of packed red cells, with a minimum of the antibody-containing

plasma. Nevertheless, exact matching of blood types is preferred whenever possible.

See Additional Problems 22.85 and 22.86 at the end of the chapter.

INDIVIDUALS WITH BLOOD TYPE . . .	. . . HAVE ANTIBODIES TO TYPE . . .,	. . . CAN RECEIVE FROM TYPE . . .,	. . . AND CAN DONATE TO TYPE
O	A and B	O	O, A, and B*
A	B	O and A	A and AB
B	A	O and B	B and AB
AB	None	O, A and B*	AB

*Red blood cells only

Starch molecules are digested mainly in the small intestine by α-amylase, which catalyzes hydrolysis of the α-1,4 links. As is usually the case in enzyme-catalyzed reactions, α-amylase is highly specific in its action. It hydrolyzes only α acetal links between glucose units (found in starch) and leaves β acetal links (found in cellulose) untouched.

PROBLEM 22.20

An individual starch molecule contains thousands of glucose units but has only a single hemiacetal group at the end of the long polymer chain. Would you expect starch to be a reducing carbohydrate? Explain.

Glycogen

Glycogen, sometimes called *animal starch*, serves the same energy storage role in animals that starch serves in plants. Some of the glucose from starches in our diet is used immediately as fuel, and some is stored as glycogen for later use. The largest amounts of glycogen are stored in the liver and muscles. In the liver, glycogen is a source of glucose, which is formed there when hormones signal a need for glucose in the blood. In muscles, glycogen is converted to glucose 6-phosphate for the synthesis of ATP.

Structurally, glycogen is similar to amylopectin in being a long polymer of α-D-glucose with the same type of branch points in its chain. Glycogen has many more branches than amylopectin, however, and is much larger—up to one million glucose units per molecule.

Comparison of branching in amylopectin and glycogen

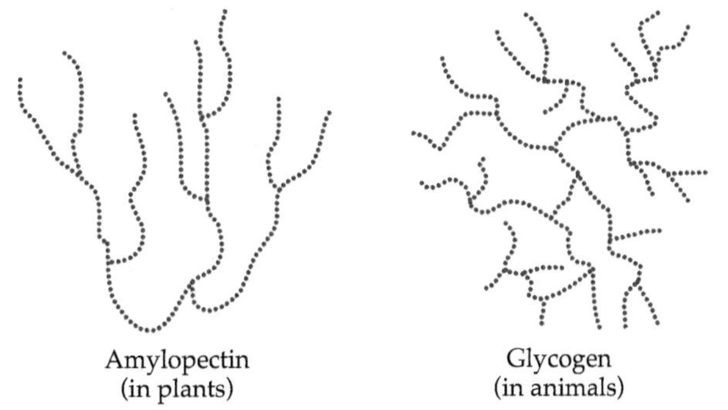

Amylopectin
(in plants)

Glycogen
(in animals)

APPLICATION ▶ Dietary Fiber

Dietary fiber includes cellulose and all other indigestible polysaccharides in vegetables, both soluble and insoluble. The major categories of noncellulose fiber are hemicellulose, pectins and gums, and lignins.

Hemicellulose is a collective term for insoluble plant polysaccharides other than cellulose. These polysaccharides are composed of xylose, mannose, galactose, and modifications of these monosaccharides.

Pectins and vegetables gums, which contain galactose modified by the addition of carboxylic acid and *N*-acetyl groups, comprise the "soluble" portion of dietary fiber. Their outstanding characteristic is solubility in water or the formation of sticky or gelatinous dispersions with water. Pectins, which are present in fruits, are responsible for the "gel" in jelly. Because this texture of their dispersions in water is a desirable characteristic, pectins are often added to prepared foods to retain moisture, thicken sauces, or give a creamier texture.

Lignin, which like cellulose provides rigid structure in plants and especially in trees, is an insoluble dietary fiber. It is not a polysaccharide, however, but a polymer of complex structure that contains phenyl groups connected by carbon–carbon and carbon–oxygen bonds.

Foods high in insoluble fiber include wheat, bran cereals, and brown rice. Beans, peas, and other legumes contain both soluble and insoluble fiber and are high in small polysaccharides that contain galactose bonded to glucose residues. These small polysaccharides are digested by bacteria in the gut, with the production of lactate, short-chain fatty acids, and gaseous by-products including hydrogen, carbon dioxide, and methane.

Fiber functions in the body to soften and add bulk to solid waste. Studies have shown that increased fiber in the diet may reduce the risk of colon and rectal cancer, hemorrhoids, diverticulosis, and cardiovascular disease. A reduction in the risk of developing colon and rectal cancer may also occur because potentially carcinogenic substances are absorbed on fiber surfaces and eliminated before doing any harm. Pectin may also absorb and carry away bile acids, causing an increase in their synthesis from cholesterol in the liver and a resulting decrease in blood cholesterol levels.

▲ Beano, a product that contains α-galactosidase. Beano promises to diminish the production of gas in the large intestine.

The U.S. Food and Drug Administration periodically reviews the MyPyramid meal-planning tool (p. 560) and the related Dietary Guidelines for Americans. In the sixth edition, released in 2005, the guidelines were described as providing "science-based advice to promote health and to reduce risk for chronic diseases through diet and physical activity." A significant change in the new edition is the recommendation "Choose fiber-rich fruits, vegetables and whole grains often." To accomplish this, you should choose foods with ingredients such as these whole grains listed *first* on the ingredients label: brown rice, oatmeal, graham flour, pearl barley, whole oats, whole wheat, or whole rye. (Note that ingredients listed as "wheat flour" and "enriched flour" are not whole grains.) Unlike refined grains, all of the recommended whole grains have a low glycemic index. The new guidelines emphasize eating two cups each of fiber-rich fruits and vegetables daily.

See Additional Problems 22.87 and 22.88 at the end of the chapter.

KEY WORDS

1,4 Link, *p. 712*

Aldose, *p. 693*

Anomeric carbon atom, *p. 702*

Anomers, *p. 702*

Carbohydrate, *p. 693*

D Sugar, *p. 698*

Diastereomers, *p. 696*

Disaccharide, *p. 694*

SUMMARY: REVISITING THE CHAPTER GOALS

1. **What are the different kinds of carbohydrates?** *Monosaccharides* are compounds with three to seven carbons, an aldehyde group on carbon 1 (an *aldose*) or a ketone group on carbon 2 (a *ketose*), and hydroxyl groups on all other carbons. *Disaccharides* consist of two monosaccharides; *polysaccharides* are polymers composed of up to thousands of monosaccharides.

2. **Why are monosaccharides chiral, and how does this influence the numbers and types of their isomers?** Monosaccharides can contain several chiral carbon atoms, each bonded to one —H, one —OH, and two other carbon atoms in the carbon chain. A monosaccharide with n chiral carbon atoms may have 2^n stereoisomers and half that number of pairs of enantiomers. The members of different enantiomeric pairs are *diastereomers*—they are *not* mirror images of each other.

3. What are the structures of monosaccharides, and how are they represented in written formulas? *Fischer projection formulas* represent the open-chain structures of monosaccharides. They are interpreted as shown below, with the D and L enantiomers in a pair identified by having the —OH group on the chiral carbon farthest from the carbonyl group on the right (the D isomer) or the left (the L isomer).

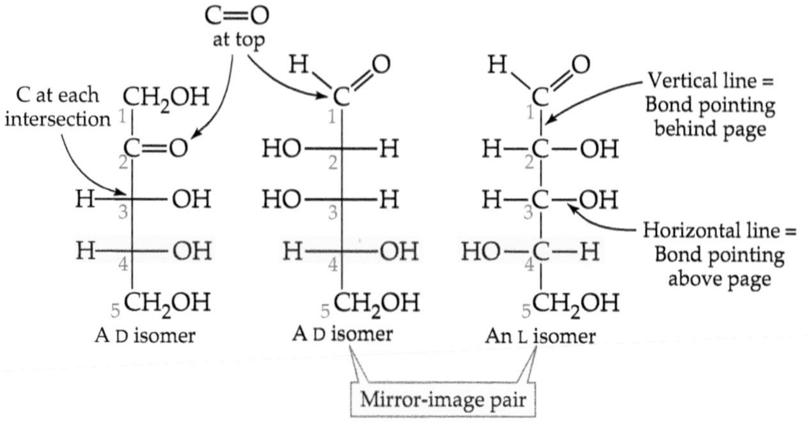

A D isomer   A D isomer   An L isomer

Mirror-image pair

In solution, open-chain monosaccharides with five or six carbons establish equilibria with cyclic forms that are hemiacetals. The hemiacetal carbon (bonded to two O atoms) is referred to as the *anomeric carbon*, and this carbon is chiral. Two isomers of the cyclic form of a D or L monosaccharide, known as *anomers*, are possible because the —OH on the anomeric carbon may lie above or below the plane of the ring.

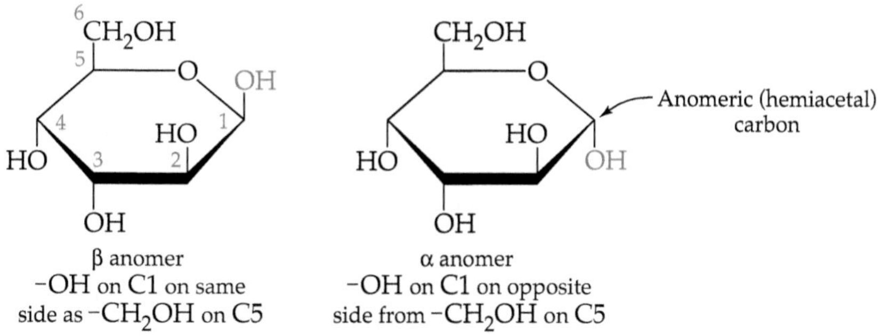

β anomer
−OH on C1 on same
side as −CH$_2$OH on C5

α anomer
−OH on C1 on opposite
side from −CH$_2$OH on C5

4. How do monosaccharides react with oxidizing agents and alcohols? Oxidation of a monosaccharide can result in a carboxyl group on the first carbon atom (C1 in the Fischer projection). Ketoses, as well as aldoses, are *reducing sugars* because the ketose is in equilibrium with an aldose form (via an enediol) that can be oxidized.

Reaction of a hemiacetal with an alcohol produces an acetal. For a cyclic monosaccharide, reaction with an alcohol converts the —OH group on the anomeric carbon to an —OR group. The bond to the —OR group, known as a *glycosidic bond*, is α or β to the ring as was the —OH group. Disaccharides result from glycosidic bond formation between two monosaccharides.

5. What are the structures of some important disaccharides? In *maltose*, two D-glucose molecules are joined by an α-glycosidic bond that connects C1 (the anomeric carbon) of one molecule to C4 of the other—an α-1,4 *link*. In *lactose*, D-galactose and D-glucose are joined by a β-1,4 link. In *sucrose*, D-fructose and D-glucose are joined by a glycosidic bond between the two anomeric carbons, a 1,2 link. Unlike maltose and lactose, sucrose is not a *reducing sugar* because it has no hemiacetal that can establish equilibrium with an aldehyde.

6. What are the functions of some important carbohydrates that contain modified monosaccharide structures? *Chitin* is a hard structural polysaccharide found in the shells of lobsters and insects. Joints and intracellular spaces are lubricated by polysaccharides like *hyaluronate* and *chondroitin 6-sulfate*, which have ionic functional groups and form gel-like mixtures with water. *Heparin*, a polysaccharide with many ionized sulfate groups, binds to a clotting factor and thus acts as an anticoagulant. *Glycoproteins* have short carbohydrate chains bonded to proteins; the carbohydrate segments (*oligosaccharides*) function as receptors at cell surfaces.

7. *What are the structures and functions of cellulose, starch, and glycogen?* *Cellulose* is a straight-chain polymer of β-D-glucose with β-1,4 links; it provides structure in plants. Cellulose is not digestible by humans, but is digestible by animals whose digestive tract contains bacteria that provide enzymes to hydrolyze the β-glycosidic bonds. *Starch* is a polymer of α-D-glucose connected by α-1,4 links in straight-chain (*amylose*) and branched-chain (*amylopectin*) forms. Starch is a storage form of glucose for plants and is digestible by humans. *Glycogen* is a storage form of glucose for animals, including humans. It is structurally similar to amylopectin, but is more highly branched. Glycogen from meat in the diet is also digestible.

UNDERSTANDING KEY CONCEPTS

22.21 During the digestion of starch from potatoes, the enzyme α-amylase catalyzes the hydrolysis of starch into maltose. Subsequently, the enzyme maltase catalyzes the hydrolysis of maltose into two glucose units. Write a word equation for the enzymatic conversion of starch to glucose. Classify each of the carbohydrates in the equation as a disaccharide, monosaccharide, or polysaccharide.

22.22 Identify the following as diastereomers, enantiomers, and/or anomers. (a) α-D-fructose and β-D-fructose (b) D-galactose and L-galactose (c) L-allose and D-glucose (both aldohexoses)

22.23 Consider the trisaccharide A, B, C at the bottom of this page.
  (a) Identify the hemiacetal and acetal linkages.
  (b) Identify the anomeric carbons, and indicate whether each is α or β.
  (c) State the numbers of the carbons that form glycosidic linkages between monosaccharide A and monosaccharide B.
  (d) State the numbers of the carbons that form glycosidic linkages between monosaccharide B and monosaccharide C.

22.24 Hydrolysis of both glycosidic bonds in the trisaccharide A, B, C at the bottom of this page yields three monosaccharides.
  (a) Are any two of these monosaccharides the same?
  (b) Are any two of these monosaccharides enantiomers?
  (c) Draw the Fischer projections for the three monosaccharides.
  (d) Assign a name to each monosaccharide.

22.25 The trisaccharide shown with Problem 22.24 has a specific sequence of monosaccharides. To determine this sequence, we could react the trisaccharide with an oxidizing agent. Since one of the monosaccharides in the trisaccharide is a reducing sugar, it would be oxidized from an aldehyde to a carboxylate. Which of the monosaccharides (A, B, or C) is oxidized? Write the structure of the oxidized monosaccharide that results after hydrolysis of the trisaccharide. How does this reaction assist in identifying the sequence of the trisaccharide?

22.26 Are one or more of the disaccharides maltose, lactose, cellobiose, and sucrose part of the trisaccharide in Problem 22.24? If so, identify which disaccharide and its location. (Hint: Look for an α-1,4 link, β-1,4 link, or 1,2 link, and then determine if the correct monosaccharides are present.)

22.27 Cellulose, amylose, amylopectin, and glycogen are the polysaccharides of glucose that we examined in this chapter. The major criteria that distinguish these four polysaccharides include α-glycosidic links or β-glycosidic links, 1,4 links or both 1,4 and 1,6 links, and the degree of branching. Describe each polysaccharide using these five criteria. (Hint: Make a table.)

22.28 In solution, glucose exists predominantly in the cyclic hemiacetal form, which does not contain an aldehyde group. How is it possible for mild oxidizing agents to oxidize glucose?

A   B   C

ADDITIONAL PROBLEMS

CLASSIFICATION AND STRUCTURE OF CARBOHYDRATES

22.29 What is a carbohydrate?

22.30 What is the family-name ending for a sugar?

22.31 What is the structural difference between an aldose and a ketose?

22.32 Classify the following carbohydrates by indicating the nature of the carbonyl group and the number of carbon atoms present. For example, glucose is an aldohexose.

(a)

```
      H    O
       \  //
        C
        |
   HO—C—H
        |
    H—C—OH
        |
      CH₂OH
```
Threose

(b)

```
      CH₂OH
        |
       C=O
        |
    H—C—OH
        |
    H—C—OH
        |
      CH₂OH
```
Ribulose

(c)

```
      H    O
       \  //
        C
        |
    H—C—OH
        |
   HO—C—H
        |
    H—C—OH
        |
      CH₂OH
```
Xylose

(d)

```
      CH₂OH
        |
       C=O
        |
   HO—C—H
        |
   HO—C—H
        |
    H—C—OH
        |
      CH₂OH
```
Tagatose

22.33 How many chiral carbon atoms are present in each of the molecules shown in Problem 22.32?

22.34 How many chiral carbon atoms are there in each of the two parts of the repeating unit in heparin (p. 716)? What is the total number of chiral carbon atoms in the repeating unit?

22.35 Draw the open-chain structure of a ketoheptose.

22.36 Draw the open-chain structure of a 4-carbon deoxy sugar.

22.37 Name four important monosaccharides and tell where each occurs in nature.

22.38 Name a common use for each monosaccharide listed in Problem 22.37.

HANDEDNESS IN CARBOHYDRATES

22.39 How are enantiomers related to each other?

22.40 What is the structural relationship between L-glucose and D-glucose?

22.41 Only three stereoisomers are possible for 2,3-dibromo-2,3-dichlorobutane. Draw them, indicating which pair are enantiomers (optical isomers). Why does the other isomer not have an enantiomer?

22.42 In Section 16.6 you saw that aldehydes react with reducing agents to yield primary alcohols (RCH=O → RCH₂OH). The structures of two D-aldotetroses are shown. One of them can be reduced to

yield a chiral product, but the other yields an achiral product. Explain.

```
      H    O                   H    O
       \  //                    \  //
        C                        C
        |                        |
    H—C—OH               HO—C—H
        |                        |
    H—C—OH                H—C—OH
        |                        |
      CH₂OH                   CH₂OH
   D-Erythrose              D-Threose
```

22.43 What is the definition of an optically active compound?

22.44 What does a polarimeter measure?

22.45 Sucrose and D-glucose rotate plane-polarized light to the right; D-fructose rotates light to the left. When sucrose is hydrolyzed, the glucose–fructose mixture rotates light to the left.

(a) What does this indicate about the relative degrees of rotation of light of glucose and fructose?

(b) Why do you think the mixture is called "invert sugar"?

22.46 What generalization can you make about the direction and degree of rotation of light by enantiomers?

REACTIONS OF CARBOHYDRATES

22.47 What does the term *reducing sugar* mean?

22.48 What structural property makes a sugar a reducing sugar?

22.49 What is mutarotation? Do all chiral molecules do this?

22.50 What are anomers, and how do the anomers of a given sugar differ from each other?

22.51 What is the structural difference between the α hemiacetal form of a carbohydrate and the β form?

22.52 D-Gulose, an aldohexose isomer of glucose, has the cyclic structure shown here. Which is shown, the α form or the β form?

```
          CH₂OH
   OH  _____  O
      /      \
         \
          _____ OH
      /    \
    OH      OH
```
D-Gulose

22.53 In its open-chain form, D-mannose, an aldohexose found in orange peels, has the structure shown here. Coil mannose around and draw it in the cyclic hemiacetal α and β forms.

```
            H   H   H   OH  OH  O
            |   |   |   |   |   ||
     HO—C — C — C — C — C — C—H
            |   |   |   |   |
            H   OH  OH  H   H
```
D-Mannose

22.54 In its open-chain form, D-altrose has the structure shown here. Coil altrose around and draw it in the cyclic hemiacetal α and β forms.

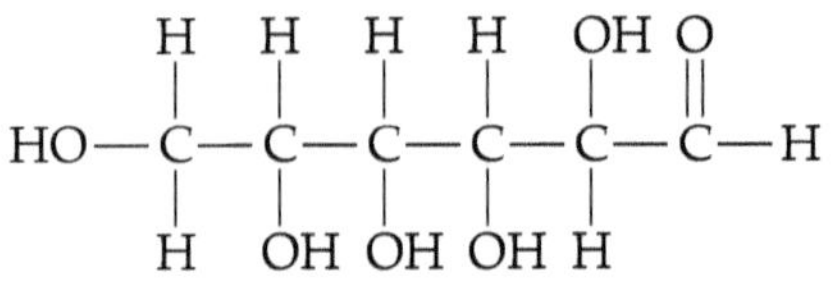

D-Altrose

22.55 Draw D-gulose (Problem 22.52) in its open-chain aldehyde form, both coiled and uncoiled.

22.56 D-Ribulose, a ketopentose related to ribose, has the following structure in open-chain form. Coil ribulose around and draw it in its five-membered cyclic β hemiacetal form.

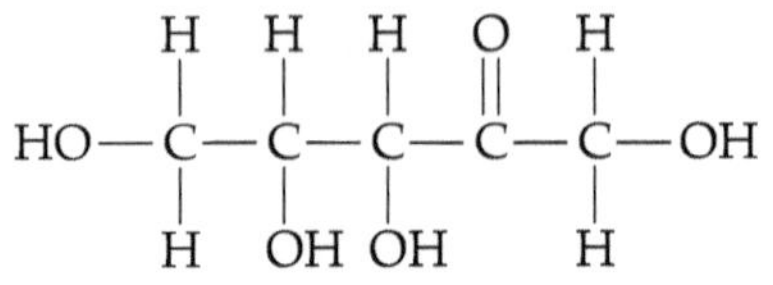

D-Ribulose

22.57 D-Allose, an aldohexose, is identical to D-glucose except that the hydroxyl group at C3 points down rather than up in the cyclic hemiacetal form. Draw the β form of this cyclic form of D-allose.

22.58 Draw D-allose (Problem 22.57) in its open-chain form.

22.59 Treatment of D-glucose with a reducing agent yields sorbitol, a substance used as a sugar substitute by diabetics. Draw the structure of sorbitol.

22.60 Reduction of D-fructose with a reducing agent yields a mixture of D-sorbitol along with a second, isomeric product. What is the structure of the second product?

22.61 Treatment of an aldose with an oxidizing agent such as Tollens' reagent (Section 16.5) yields a carboxylic acid. Gluconic acid, the product of glucose oxidation, is used as its magnesium salt for the treatment of magnesium deficiency. Draw the structure of gluconic acid.

22.62 Oxidation of the aldehyde group of ribose yields a carboxylic acid. Draw the structure of ribonic acid.

22.63 What is the structural difference between a hemiacetal and an acetal?

22.64 What are glycosides, and how can they be formed?

22.65 Look at the structure of D-mannose (Problem 22.53) and draw the two glycosidic products that you expect to obtain by reacting D-mannose with methanol.

22.66 Draw a disaccharide of two mannose molecules attached by an α-1,4 glycosidic linkage. Explain why the glycosidic products in Problem 22.65 are *not* reducing sugars, but the product in this problem *is* a reducing sugar.

DISACCHARIDES AND POLYSACCHARIDES

22.67 Give the names of three important disaccharides. Tell where each occurs in nature. From which two monosaccharides is each made?

22.68 Lactose and maltose are reducing disaccharides, but sucrose is a nonreducing disaccharide. Explain.

22.69 Amylose (a form of starch) and cellulose are both polymers of glucose. What is the main structural difference between them? What roles do these two polymers have in nature?

22.70 How are amylose and amylopectin similar to each other, and how are they different from each other?

22.71 *Gentiobiose*, a rare disaccharide found in saffron, has the following structure. What simple sugars do you obtain on hydrolysis of gentiobiose?

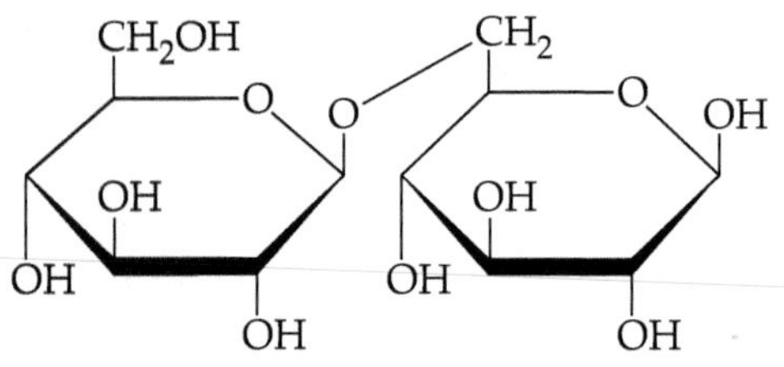

Gentiobiose

22.72 Does gentiobiose (Problem 22.71) have an acetal grouping? A hemiacetal grouping? Do you expect gentiobiose to be a reducing or nonreducing sugar? How would you classify the linkage (α or β and carbon numbers) between the two monosaccharides?

22.73 *Trehalose*, a disaccharide found in the blood of insects, has the following structure. What simple sugars would you obtain on hydrolysis of trehalose?

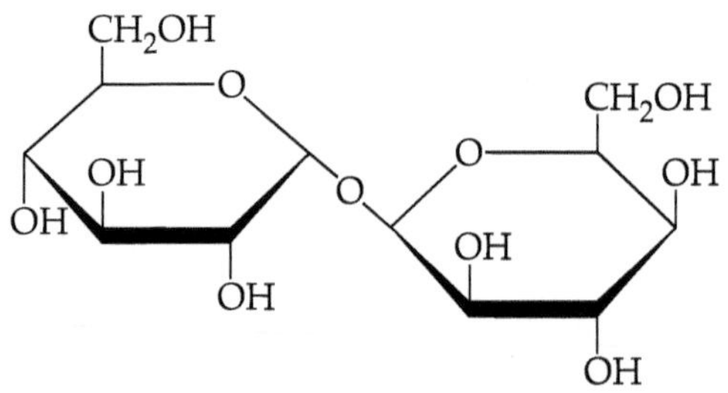

Trehalose

22.74 Does trehalose (Problem 22.73) have an acetal grouping? A hemiacetal grouping? Do you expect trehalose to be a reducing or nonreducing sugar? Classify the linkage between the two monosaccharides.

22.75 Amylopectin (a form of starch) and glycogen are both α-linked polymers of glucose. What is the structural difference between them? What roles do they serve in nature?

22.76 *Amygdalin* (Laetrile) is a glycoside isolated in 1830 from almond and apricot seeds. It is called a cyanogenic glycoside because hydrolysis with aqueous acid liberates hydrogen cyanide (HCN) along with benzaldehyde and two molecules of glucose. Structurally, amygdalin is a glycoside composed of gentiobiose (Problem 22.71) and an alcohol, mandelonitrile. Draw the structure of amygdalin.

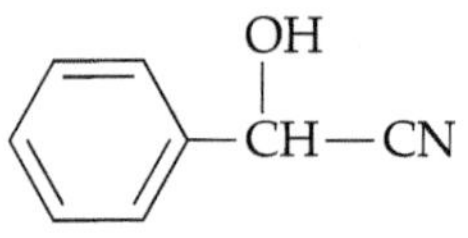

Mandelonitrile

Applications

22.77 Give some advantages and disadvantages of synthesizing and marketing a single-enantiomer drug. [*Chirality and Drugs, p. 699*]

22.78 What is the advantage of using enzymes in the synthesis of single-enantiomer drugs? [*Chirality and Drugs, p. 699*]

22.79 Carbohydrates provide 4 kcal per gram. If a person eats 200 g per day of digestible carbohydrates, what percentage of a 2000 kcal daily diet would be digestible carbohydrate? [*Carbohydrates in the Diet, p. 704*]

22.80 Give an example of a complex carbohydrate in the diet and a simple carbohydrate in the diet. Are soluble fiber and insoluble fiber complex or simple carbohydrates? [*Carbohydrates in the Diet, p. 704*]

22.81 List three functions of all cell walls. [*Cell Walls: Rigid Defense Systems, p. 714*]

22.82 Name the monomeric unit and the polymer that makes up most of a plant cell wall. [*Cell Walls: Rigid Defense Systems, p. 714*]

22.83 Name the individual units and the crosslink for the polymer that makes up most of a bacterial cell wall. [*Cell Walls: Rigid Defense Systems, p. 714*]

22.84 When you take the antibiotic penicillin when you are ill, why does the penicillin kill a bacterial cell but not your liver cells? [*Cell Walls: Rigid Defense Systems, p. 714*]

22.85 Look at the structures of the blood group determinants. What groups do all blood types have in common? [*Cell-Surface Carbohydrates and Blood Type, p. 720*]

22.86 People with type O blood can donate blood to anyone, but they cannot receive blood from everyone. From whom can they not receive blood? People with type AB blood can receive blood from anyone, but they cannot give blood to everyone. To whom can they give blood? Why? [*Cell-Surface Carbohydrates and Blood Type, p. 720*]

22.87 Our bodies do not have the enzymes required to digest cellulose, yet it is a necessary addition to a healthy diet. Why? [*Dietary Fiber, p. 722*]

22.88 Name two types of soluble fiber and their sources. [*Dietary Fiber, p. 722*]

General Questions and Problems

22.89 What is the relationship between D-ribose (p. 700) and D-xylose (Problem 22.32c)? What generalizations can you make about D-ribose and D-xylose with respect to the following?

(a) Melting point
(b) Rotation of plane-polarized light
(c) Density
(d) Solubility in water
(e) Chemical reactivity

22.90 What is the relationship between D-ribose and L-ribose? What generalizations can you make about D-ribose and L-ribose with respect to the following?

(a) Melting point
(b) Rotation of plane-polarized light
(c) Density
(d) Solubility in water
(e) Chemical reactivity

22.91 Are the α and β forms of monosaccharides enantiomers of each other? Why or why not?

22.92 Are the α and β forms of the disaccharide lactose enantiomers of each other? Why or why not?

22.93 L-Sorbose, which is used in the commercial production of vitamin C, differs from D-fructose only at carbon 5. Draw the open-chain structure of D-sorbose and the five-membered ring in the β form.

22.94 D-Fructose can form a six-membered cyclic hemiacetal as well as the more prevalent five-membered cyclic form. Draw the α isomer of D-fructose in the six-membered ring.

22.95 *Raffinose*, found in sugar beets, is the most prevalent trisaccharide. It is formed by an α-1,6 linkage of D-galactose to the glucose portion of sucrose. Draw the structure of raffinose.

22.96 Does raffinose (Problem 22.95) have a hemiacetal grouping? An acetal grouping? Is raffinose a reducing sugar?

22.97 When you chew a cracker for several minutes, it begins to taste sweet. What do you think the saliva in your mouth does to the starch in the cracker?

22.98 Write the open-chain structure of the only ketotriose. Name this compound and explain why it has no optical isomers.

22.99 Write the open-chain structure of the only ketotetrose. Name this compound. Does it have an optical isomer?

22.100 What is lactose intolerance, and what are its symptoms?

22.101 Many people who are lactose intolerant can eat yogurt, which is prepared from milk curdled by bacteria, with no problems. Give a reason why this is possible.

22.102 What is the group of disorders that result when the body lacks an enzyme necessary to digest galactose? What are the symptoms?

22.103 When a person cannot digest galactose, its reduced form, called dulcitol, often accumulates in the blood and tissues. Write the structure of the open-chain form of dulcitol. Does dulcitol have an enantiomer? Why or why not?

22.104 L-Fucose is also known as 6-deoxy-α-L-galactose. How many chiral carbons are present in L-fucose?

APPENDIX A
Scientific Notation

What Is Scientific Notation?

The numbers that you encounter in chemistry are often either very large or very small. For example, there are about 33,000,000,000,000,000,000,000 H_2O molecules in 1.0 mL of water, and the distance between the H and O atoms in an H_2O molecule is 0.000 000 000 095 7 m. These quantities are more conveniently written in *scientific notation* as 3.3×10^{22} molecules and 9.57×10^{-11} m, respectively. In scientific notation (also known as *exponential notation*), a quantity is represented as a number between 1 and 10 multiplied by a power of 10. In this kind of expression, the small raised number to the right of the 10 is the exponent.

NUMBER	EXPONENTIAL FORM	EXPONENT
1,000,000	1×10^6	6
100,000	1×10^5	5
10,000	1×10^4	4
1,000	1×10^3	3
100	1×10^2	2
10	1×10^1	1
1		
0.1	1×10^{-1}	−1
0.01	1×10^{-2}	−2
0.001	1×10^{-3}	−3
0.000 1	1×10^{-4}	−4
0.000 01	1×10^{-5}	−5
0.000 001	1×10^{-6}	−6
0.000 000 1	1×10^{-7}	−7

Numbers greater than 1 have *positive* exponents, which tell how many times a number must be *multiplied* by 10 to obtain the correct value. For example, the expression 5.2×10^3 means that 5.2 must be multiplied by 10 three times:

$$5.2 \times 10^3 = 5.2 \times 10 \times 10 \times 10 = 5.2 \times 1000 = 5200$$

Note that doing this means moving the decimal point three places to the right:

$$5200.$$
123

The value of a positive exponent indicates *how many places to the right the decimal point must be moved* to give the correct number in ordinary decimal notation.

Numbers less than 1 have *negative exponents*, which tell how many times a number must be *divided* by 10 (or multiplied by one-tenth) to obtain the correct value. Thus, the expression 3.7×10^{-2} means that 3.7 must be divided by 10 two times:

$$3.7 \times 10^{-2} = \frac{3.7}{10 \times 10} = \frac{3.7}{100} = 0.037$$

Note that doing this means moving the decimal point two places to the left:

$$0.037$$

The value of a negative exponent indicates *how may places to the left the decimal point must be moved* to give the correct number in ordinary decimal notation.

Representing Numbers in Scientific Notation

How do you convert a number from ordinary notation to scientific notation? If the number is greater than or equal to 10, shift the decimal point to the *left* by n places until you obtain a number between 1 and 10. Then, multiply the result by 10^n. For example, the number 8137.6 is written in scientific notation as 8.1376×10^3:

Number of places decimal point was shifted to the left

$$8137.6 = 8.1376 \times 10^3$$

Shift decimal point to the left by 3 places to get a number between 1 and 10

When you shift the decimal point to the left by three places, you are in effect dividing the number by $10 \times 10 \times 10 = 1000 = 10^3$. Therefore, you must multiply the result by 10^3 so that the value of the number is unchanged.

To convert a number less than 1 to scientific notation, shift the decimal point to the *right* by n places until you obtain a number between 1 and 10. Then, multiply the result by 10^{-n}. For example, the number 0.012 is written in scientific notation as 1.2×10^{-2}:

Number of places decimal point was shifted to the right

$$0.012 = 1.2 \times 10^{-2}$$

Shift decimal point to the right by 2 places to get a number between 1 and 10

When you shift the decimal point to the right by two places, you are in effect multiplying the number by $10 \times 10 = 100 = 10^2$. Therefore, you must multiply the result by 10^{-2} so that the value of the number is unchanged. ($10^2 \times 10^{-2} = 10^0 = 1$.)

The following table gives some additional examples. To convert from scientific notation to ordinary notation, simply reverse the preceding process. Thus, to write the number 5.84×10^4 in ordinary notation, drop the factor of 10^4 and move the decimal point 4 places to the *right* ($5.84 \times 10^4 = 58,400$). To write the number 3.5×10^{-1} in ordinary notation, drop the factor of 10^{-1} and move the decimal point 1 place to the *left* ($3.5 \times 10^{-1} = 0.35$). Note that you don't need scientific notation for numbers between 1 and 10 because $10^0 = 1$.

NUMBER	SCIENTIFIC NOTATION
58,400	5.84×10^4
0.35	3.5×10^{-1}
7.296	$7.296 \times 10^0 = 7.296 \times 1$

Mathematical Operations with Scientific Notation

Addition and Subtraction in Scientific Notation

To add or subtract two numbers expressed in scientific notation, both numbers must have the same exponent. Thus, to add 7.16×10^3 and 1.32×10^2, first write the latter number as 0.132×10^3 and then add:

$$
\begin{array}{r}
7.16 \times 10^3 \\
+0.132 \times 10^3 \\
\hline
7.29 \times 10^3
\end{array}
$$

The answer has three significant figures. (Significant figures are discussed in Section 2.4.) Alternatively, you can write the first number as 71.6×10^2 and then add:

$$
\begin{array}{r}
71.6 \times 10^2 \\
+\ 1.32 \times 10^2 \\
\hline
72.9 \times 10^2 = 7.29 \times 10^3
\end{array}
$$

Subtraction of these two numbers is carried out in the same manner.

$$
\begin{array}{r}
7.16 \times 10^3 \\
-0.132 \times 10^3 \\
\hline
7.03 \times 10^3
\end{array}
\quad \text{or} \quad
\begin{array}{r}
71.6 \times 10^2 \\
-\ 1.32 \times 10^2 \\
\hline
70.3 \times 10^2 = 7.03 \times 10^3
\end{array}
$$

Multiplication in Scientific Notation

To multiply two numbers expressed in scientific notation, multiply the factors in front of the powers of 10 and then add the exponents. For example,

$$(2.5 \times 10^4)(4.7 \times 10^7) = (2.5)(4.7) \times 10^{4+7} = 12 \times 10^{11} = 1.2 \times 10^{12}$$

$$(3.46 \times 10^5)(2.2 \times 10^{-2}) = (3.46)(2.2) \times 10^{5+(-2)} = 7.6 \times 10^3$$

Both answers have two significant figures.

Division in Scientific Notation

To divide two numbers expressed in scientific notation, divide the factors in front of the powers of 10 and then subtract the exponent in the denominator from the exponent in the numerator. For example,

$$\frac{3 \times 10^6}{7.2 \times 10^2} = \frac{3}{7.2} \times 10^{6-2} = 0.4 \times 10^4 = 4 \times 10^3 \quad \text{(1 significant figure)}$$

$$\frac{7.50 \times 10^{-5}}{2.5 \times 10^{-7}} = \frac{7.50}{2.5} \times 10^{-5-(-7)} = 3.0 \times 10^2 \quad \text{(2 significant figures)}$$

Scientific Notation and Electronic Calculators

With a scientific calculator you can carry out calculations in scientific notation. You should consult the instruction manual for your particular calculator to learn how to enter and manipulate numbers expressed in an exponential format. On most calculators, you enter the number $A \times 10^n$ by (i) entering the number A, (ii) pressing a key labeled EXP or EE, and (iii) entering the exponent n. If the exponent is negative, you press a key labeled $+/-$ before entering the value of n. (Note that you do not enter the number 10.) The calculator displays the number $A \times 10^n$ with the number A on the left followed by some space and then the exponent n. For example,

$$4.625 \times 10^2 \quad \text{is displayed as} \quad 4.625\ 02$$

To add, subtract, multiply, or divide exponential numbers, use the same sequence of keystrokes as you would in working with ordinary numbers. When you add or subtract on a calculator, the numbers need not have the same exponent; the calculator automatically takes account of the different exponents. Remember, though, that the calculator often gives more digits in the answer than the allowed number of significant figures. It's sometimes helpful to outline the calculation on paper, as in the preceding examples, to keep track of the number of significant figures.

PROBLEM A.1

Perform the following calculations, expressing the results in scientific notation with the correct number of significant figures. (You don't need a calculator for these.)

(a) $(1.50 \times 10^4) + (5.04 \times 10^3)$

(b) $(2.5 \times 10^{-2}) - (5.0 \times 10^{-3})$

(c) $(6.3 \times 10^{15}) \times (10.1 \times 10^3)$

(d) $(2.5 \times 10^{-3}) \times (3.2 \times 10^{-4})$

(e) $(8.4 \times 10^4) \div (3.0 \times 10^6)$

(f) $(5.530 \times 10^{-2}) \div (2.5 \times 10^{-5})$

ANSWERS

(a) 2.00×10^4 | **(b)** 2.0×10^{-2} | **(c)** 6.4×10^{19}

(d) 8.0×10^{-7} | **(e)** 2.8×10^{-2} | **(f)** 2.2×10^3

PROBLEM A.2

Perform the following calculations, expressing the results in scientific notation with the correct number of significant figures. (Use a calculator for these.)

(a) $(9.72 \times 10^{-1}) + (3.4823 \times 10^2)$

(b) $(3.772 \times 10^3) - (2.891 \times 10^4)$

(c) $(1.956 \times 10^3) \div (6.02 \times 10^{23})$

(d) $3.2811 \times (9.45 \times 10^{21})$

(e) $(1.0015 \times 10^3) \div (5.202 \times 10^{-9})$

(f) $(6.56 \times 10^{-6}) \times (9.238 \times 10^{-4})$

ANSWERS

(a) 3.4920×10^2 | **(b)** -2.514×10^4 | **(c)** 3.25×10^{-21}

(d) 3.10×10^{22} | **(e)** 1.925×10^{11} | **(f)** 6.06×10^{-9}

APPENDIX B
Conversion Factors

Length   SI Unit: Meter (m)

   1 meter = 0.001 kilometer (km)

           = 100 centimeters (cm)

           = 1.0936 yards (yd)

   1 centimeter = 10 millimeters (mm)

                = 0.3937 inch (in.)

   1 nanometer = 1×10^{-9} meter

   1 Angstrom (Å) = 1×10^{-10} meter

   1 inch = 2.54 centimeters

   1 mile = 1.6094 kilometers

Volume   SI Unit: Cubic meter (m^3)

   1 cubic meter = 1000 liters (L)

   1 liter = 1000 cubic centimeters (cm^3)

         = 1000 milliliters (mL)

         = 1.056710 quarts (qt)

   1 cubic inch = 16.4 cubic centimeters

Temperature   SI Unit: Kelvin (K)

  0 K = $-273.15\ °C$

      = $-459.67\ °F$

  $°F = (9/5)\ °C + 32°;\ °F = (1.8 \times °C) + 32°$

  $°C = (5/9)(°F - 32°);\ °C = \dfrac{(°F - 32°)}{1.8}$

  $K = °C + 273.15°$

Mass   SI Unit: Kilogram (kg)

   1 kilogram = 1000 grams (g)

           = 2.205 pounds (lb)

   1 gram = 1000 milligrams (mg)

         = 0.03527 ounce (oz)

   1 pound = 453.6 grams

   1 atomic mass unit = 1.66054×10^{-24} gram

Pressure   SI Unit: Pascal (Pa)

   1 pascal = 9.869×10^{-6} atmosphere

   1 atmosphere = 101,325 pascals

             = 760 mmHg (Torr)

             = 14.70 lb/in^2

Energy   SI Unit: Joule (J)

   1 joule = 0.23901 calorie (cal)

   1 calorie = 4.184 joules

   1 Calorie (nutritional unit) = 1000 calories

                      = 1 kcal

Glossary

1,4 Link A glycosidic link between the hemiacetal hydroxyl group at C1 of one sugar and the hydroxyl group at C4 of another sugar.

Acetal A compound that has two ether-like —OR groups bonded to the same carbon atom.

Acetyl coenzyme A (acetyl-SCoA) Acetyl-substituted coenzyme A—the common intermediate that carries acetyl groups into the citric acid cycle.

Acetyl group A $CH_3C=O$ group.

Achiral The opposite of chiral; having no right- or left-handedness and no nonsuperimposable mirror images.

Acid A substance that provides H^+ ions in water.

Acid dissociation constant (K_a) The equilibrium constant for the dissociation of an acid (HA), equal to $[H^+][A^-]/[HA]$

Acidosis The abnormal condition associated with a blood plasma pH below 7.35; may be respiratory or metabolic.

Acid–base indicator A dye that changes color depending on the pH of a solution.

Activation (of an enzyme) Any process that initiates or increases the action of an enzyme.

Activation energy (E_{act}) The amount of energy necessary for reactants to surmount the energy barrier to reaction; affects reaction rate.

Active site A pocket in an enzyme with the specific shape and chemical makeup necessary to bind a substrate.

Active transport Movement of substances across a cell membrane with the assistance of energy (for example, from ATP).

Actual Yield The amount of product actually formed in a reaction.

Acyl group An $RC=O$ group.

Addition reaction A general reaction type in which a substance X—Y adds to the multiple bond of an unsaturated reactant to yield a saturated product that has only single bonds.

Addition reaction, aldehydes and ketones Addition of an alcohol or other compound to the carbon–oxygen double bond to give a carbon–oxygen single bond.

Adenosine triphosphate (ATP) The principal energy-carrying molecule; removal of a phosphoryl group to give ADP releases free energy.

Aerobic In the presence of oxygen.

Agonist A substance that interacts with a receptor to cause or prolong the receptor's normal biochemical response.

Alcohol A compound that has an —OH group bonded to a saturated, alkane-like carbon atom, R—OH.

Alcoholic fermentation The anaerobic breakdown of glucose to ethanol plus carbon dioxide by the action of yeast enzymes.

Aldehyde A compound that has a carbonyl group bonded to one carbon and one hydrogen, RCHO.

Aldose A monosaccharide that contains an aldehyde carbonyl group.

Alkali metal An element in group 1A of the periodic table.

Alkaline earth metal An element in group 2A of the periodic table.

Alkaloid A naturally occurring nitrogen-containing compound isolated from a plant; usually basic, bitter, and poisonous.

Alkalosis The abnormal condition associated with a blood plasma pH above 7.45; may be respiratory or metabolic.

Alkane A hydrocarbon that has only single bonds.

Alkene A hydrocarbon that contains a carbon–carbon double bond.

Alkoxide ion The anion resulting from deprotonation of an alcohol, RO^-.

Alkoxy group An —OR group.

Alkyl group The part of an alkane that remains when a hydrogen atom is removed.

Alkyl halide A compound that has an alkyl group bonded to a halogen atom, R—X.

Alkyne A hydrocarbon that contains a carbon–carbon triple bond.

Allosteric control An interaction in which the binding of a regulator at one site on a protein affects the protein's ability to bind another molecule at a different site.

Allosteric enzyme An enzyme whose activity is controlled by the binding of an activator or inhibitor at a location other than the active site.

Alpha (α) particle A helium nucleus (He^{2+}), emitted as α-radiation.

Alpha- (α-) amino acid An amino acid in which the amino group is bonded to the carbon atom next to the —COOH group.

Alpha- (α-) helix Secondary protein structure in which a protein chain forms a right-handed coil stabilized by hydrogen bonds between peptide groups along its backbone.

Amide A compound that has a carbonyl group bonded to a carbon atom and a nitrogen atom group, $RCONR'_2$, where the R' groups may be alkyl groups or hydrogen atoms.

Amine A compound that has one or more organic groups bonded to nitrogen; primary, RNH_2; secondary, R_2NH; or tertiary, R_3N.

Amino acid A molecule that contains both an amino group and a carboxylic acid functional group.

Amino acid pool The entire collection of free amino acids in the body.

Amino group The —NH_2 functional group.

Amino-terminal (N-terminal) amino acid The amino acid with the free —NH_3^+ group at the end of a protein.

Ammonium ion A positive ion formed by addition of hydrogen to ammonia or an amine (may be primary, secondary, or tertiary).

Ammonium salt An ionic compound composed of an ammonium cation and an anion; an amine salt.

Amorphous solid A solid whose particles do not have an orderly arrangement.

Amphoteric Describing a substance that can react as either an acid or a base.

Anabolism Metabolic reactions that build larger biological molecules from smaller pieces.

Anaerobic In the absence of oxygen.

Anion A negatively charged ion.

Anomeric carbon atom The hemiacetal C atom in a cyclic sugar; the C atom bonded to an —OH group and an O in the ring.

Anomers Cyclic sugars that differ only in positions of substituents at the hemiacetal carbon (the anomeric carbon); the α form has the —OH on the opposite side from the —CH_2OH; the β form has the —OH on the same side as the —CH_2OH.

Antagonist A substance that blocks or inhibits the normal biochemical response of a receptor.

Antibody (immunoglobulin) Glycoprotein molecule that identifies antigens.

Anticodon A sequence of three ribonucleotides on tRNA that recognizes the complementary sequence (the codon) on mRNA.

Antigen A substance foreign to the body that triggers the immune response.

Antioxidant A substance that prevents oxidation by reacting with an oxidizing agent.

Aqueous solution A solution in which water is the solvent.

Aromatic The class of compounds containing benzene-like rings.

Artificial transmutation The change of one atom into another brought about by a nuclear bombardment reaction.

Atom The smallest and simplest particle of an element.

Atomic mass unit (amu) A convenient unit for describing the mass of an atom; 1 amu = 1/12 the mass of a carbon-12 atom.

Atomic number (Z) The number of protons in an atom.

Atomic theory A set of assumptions proposed by English scientist John Dalton to explain the chemical behavior of matter.

Atomic weight The weighted average mass of an element's atoms.

ATP synthase The enzyme complex in the inner mitochondrial membrane at which hydrogen ions cross the membrane and ATP is synthesized from ADP.

Autoimmune disease Disorder in which the immune system identifies normal body components as antigens and produces antibodies to them.

Avogadro's law Equal volumes of gases at the same temperature and pressure contain equal numbers of molecules (V/n = constant, or $V_1/n_1 = V_2/n_2$).

Avogadro's number (N_A) The number of units in 1 mole of anything; 6.02×10^{23}.

Balanced equation Describing a chemical equation in which the numbers and kinds of atoms are the same on both sides of the reaction arrow.

Base A substance that provides OH^- ions in water.

Base pairing The pairing of bases connected by hydrogen bonding (G-C and A-T), as in the DNA double helix.

Beta- (β-) Oxidation pathway A repetitive series of biochemical reactions that degrades fatty acids to acetyl-SCoA by removing carbon atoms two at a time.

Beta (β) particle An electron (e^-), emitted as β radiation.

Beta- (β-) Sheet Secondary protein structure in which adjacent protein chains either in the same molecule or in different molecules are held in place by hydrogen bonds along the backbones.

Bile acids Steroid acids derived from cholesterol that are secreted in bile.

Bile Fluid secreted by the liver and released into the small intestine from the gallbladder during digestion; contains bile acids, bicarbonate ion, and other electrolytes.

Binary compound A compound formed by combination of two different elements.

Blood clot A network of fibrin fibers and trapped blood cells that forms at the site of blood loss.

Blood plasma Liquid portion of the blood; an extracellular fluid.

Blood serum Fluid portion of blood remaining after clotting has occurred.

Boiling point (bp) The temperature at which liquid and gas are in equilibrium.

Bond angle The angle formed by three adjacent atoms in a molecule.

Bond dissociation energy The amount of energy that must be supplied to break a bond and separate the atoms in an isolated gaseous molecule.

Bond length The optimum distance between nuclei in a covalent bond.

Boyle's law The pressure of a gas at constant temperature is inversely proportional to its volume ($PV = $ constant, or $P_1V_1 = P_2V_2$).

Branched-chain alkane An alkane that has a branching connection of carbons.

Brønsted–Lowry acid A substance that can donate a hydrogen ion, H^+, to another molecule or ion.

Brønsted–Lowry base A substance that can accept H^+ from an acid.

Buffer A combination of substances that act together to prevent a drastic change in pH; usually a weak acid and its conjugate base.

Carbohydrate A member of a large class of naturally occurring polyhydroxy ketones and aldehydes.

Carbonyl compound Any compound that contains a carbonyl group $C=O$.

Carbonyl group A functional group that has a carbon atom joined to an oxygen atom by a double bond, $C=O$.

Carbonyl-group substitution reaction A reaction in which a new group replaces (substitutes for) a group attached to a carbonyl-group carbon in an acyl group.

Carboxyl group The $-COOH$ functional group.

Carboxyl-terminal (C-terminal) amino acid The amino acid with the free $-COO^-$ group at the end of a protein.

Carboxylate anion The anion that results from ionization of a carboxylic acid, $RCOO^-$.

Carboxylic acid A compound that has a carbonyl group bonded to a carbon atom and an $-OH$ group, $RCOOH$.

Carboxylic acid salt An ionic compound containing a carboxylic anion and a cation.

Catabolism Metabolic reaction pathways that break down food molecules and release biochemical energy.

Catalyst A substance that speeds up the rate of a chemical reaction but is itself unchanged.

Cation A positively charged ion.

Centromeres The central regions of chromosomes.

Chain reaction A reaction that, once started, is self-sustaining.

Change of state The conversion of a substance from one state to another—for example, from a liquid to a gas.

Charles's law The volume of a gas at constant pressure is directly proportional to its Kelvin temperature ($V/T = $ constant, or $V_1/T_1 = V_2/T_2$).

Chemical change A change in the chemical makeup of a substance.

Chemical compound A pure substance that can be broken down into simpler substances by chemical reactions.

Chemical equation An expression in which symbols and formulas are used to represent a chemical reaction.

Chemical equilibrium A state in which the rates of forward and reverse reactions are the same.

Chemical formula A notation for a chemical compound using element symbols and subscripts to show how many atoms of each element are present.

Chemical reaction A process in which the identity and composition of one or more substances are changed.

Chemistry The study of the nature, properties, and transformations of matter.

Chiral carbon atom (chirality center) A carbon atom bonded to four different groups.

Chiral Having right- or left-handedness; able to have two different mirror-image forms.

Chromosome A complex of proteins and DNA; visible during cell division.

Cis-trans isomers Alkenes that have the same connections between atoms but differ in their three-dimensional structures because of the way that groups are attached to different sides of the double bond. The cis isomer has hydrogen atoms on the same side of the double bond; the trans isomer has them on opposite sides.

Citric acid cycle The series of biochemical reactions that breaks down acetyl groups to produce energy carried by reduced coenzymes and carbon dioxide.

Clones Identical copies of organisms, cells, or DNA segments from a single ancestor.

Codon A sequence of three ribonucleotides in the messenger RNA chain that codes for a specific amino acid; also the three nucleotide sequence (a stop codon) that stops translation.

Coefficient A number placed in front of a formula to balance a chemical equation.

Coenzyme An organic molecule that acts as an enzyme cofactor.

Cofactor A nonprotein part of an enzyme that is essential to the enzyme's catalytic activity; a metal ion or a coenzyme.

Colligative property A property of a solution that depends only on the number of dissolved particles, not on their chemical identity.

Colloid A homogeneous mixture that contains particles that range in diameter from 2 to 500 nm.

Combined gas law The product of the pressure and volume of a gas is proportional to its temperature ($PV/T = $ constant, or $P_1V_1/T_1 = P_2V_2/T_2$).

Combustion A chemical reaction that produces a flame, usually because of burning with oxygen.

Competititve (enzyme) inhibition Enzyme regulation in which an inhibitor competes with a substrate for binding to the enzyme active site.

Concentration A measure of the amount of a given substance in a mixture.

Concentration gradient A difference in concentration within the same system.

Condensed structure A shorthand way of drawing structures in which $C-C$ and $C-H$ bonds are understood rather than shown.

Conformation The specific three-dimensional arrangement of atoms in a molecule at a given instant.

Conformers Molecular structures having identical connections between atoms.

Conjugate acid The substance formed by addition of H^+ to a base.

Conjugate acid–base pair Two substances whose formulas differ by only a hydrogen ion, H^+.

Conjugate base The substance formed by loss of H^+ from an acid.

Conjugated protein A protein that incorporates one or more non-amino acid units in its structure.

Constitutional isomers Compounds with the same molecular formula but different connections among their atoms.

Conversion factor An expression of the relationship between two units.

Coordinate covalent bond The covalent bond that forms when both electrons are donated by the same atom.

Cosmic rays A mixture of high-energy particles—primarily of protons and various atomic nuclei—that shower the earth from outer space.

Covalent bond A bond formed by sharing electrons between atoms.

Critical mass The minimum amount of radioactive material needed to sustain a nuclear chain reaction.

Crystalline solid A solid whose atoms, molecules, or ions are rigidly held in an ordered arrangement.

Cycloalkane An alkane that contains a ring of carbon atoms.

Cycloalkene A cyclic hydrocarbon that contains a double bond.

Cytoplasm The region between the cell membrane and the nuclear membrane in a eukaryotic cell.

Cytosol The fluid part of the cytoplasm surrounding the organelles within a cell.

d-Block element A transition metal element that results from the filling of d orbitals.

D-Sugar Monosaccharide with the $-OH$ group on the chiral carbon atom farthest from the carbonyl group pointing to the right in a Fischer projection.

Dalton's law The total pressure exerted by a mixture of gases is equal to the sum of the partial pressures exerted by each individual gas.

Decay series A sequential series of nuclear disintegrations leading from a heavy radioisotope to a nonradioactive product.

Degree of unsaturation The number of carbon–carbon double bonds in a molecule.

Dehydration The loss of water from an alcohol to yield an alkene.

Denaturation The loss of secondary, tertiary, or quaternary protein structure due to disruption of noncovalent interactions and/or disulfide bonds that leaves peptide bond and primary structure intact.

Density The physical property that relates the mass of an object to its volume; mass per unit volume.

Deoxyribonucleotide A nucleotide containing 2-deoxy-D-ribose.

Diabetes mellitus A chronic condition due to either insufficient insulin or failure of insulin to activate crossing of cell membranes by glucose.

Diastereomers Stereoisomers that are not mirror images of each other.

Digestion A general term for the breakdown of food into small molecules.

Dilution factor The ratio of the initial and final solution volumes (V_1/V_2).

Dipole–dipole force The attractive force between positive and negative ends of polar molecules.

Disaccharide A carbohydrate composed of two monosaccharides.

Dissociation The splitting apart of an acid in water to give H^+ and an anion.

Disulfide A compound that contains a sulfur–sulfur bond, RS–SR.

Disulfide bond (in protein) An S–S bond formed between two cysteine side chains; can join two peptide chains together or cause a loop in a peptide chain.

DNA (deoxyribonucleic acid) The nucleic acid that stores genetic information; a polymer of deoxyribonucleotides.

Double bond A covalent bond formed by sharing two electron pairs.

Double helix Two strands coiled around each other in a screwlike fashion; in most organisms the two polynucleotides of DNA form a double helix.

Drug Any substance that alters body function when it is introduced from an external source.

Eicosanoid A lipid derived from a 20-carbon unsaturated carboxylic acid.

Electrolyte A substance that produces ions and therefore conducts electricity when dissolved in water.

Electron A negatively charged subatomic particle.

Electron affinity The energy released on adding an electron to a single atom in the gaseous state.

Electron capture A process in which the nucleus captures an inner-shell electron from the surrounding electron cloud, thereby converting a proton into a neutron.

Electron configuration The specific arrangement of electrons in an atom's shells and subshells.

Electron shell A grouping of electrons in an atom according to energy.

Electron subshell A grouping of electrons in a shell according to the shape of the region of space they occupy.

Electron-dot symbol An atomic symbol with dots placed around it to indicate the number of valence electrons.

Electron-transport chain The series of biochemical reactions that passes electrons from reduced coenzymes to oxygen and is coupled to ATP formation.

Electronegativity The ability of an atom to attract electrons in a covalent bond.

Element A fundamental substance that can't be broken down chemically into any simpler substance.

Elimination reaction A general reaction type in which a saturated reactant yields an unsaturated product by losing groups from two adjacent carbon atoms.

Enantiomers, optical isomers The two mirror-image forms of a chiral molecule.

Endergonic A nonspontaneous reaction or process that absorbs free energy and has a positive ΔG.

Endocrine system A system of specialized cells, tissues, and ductless glands that excretes hormones and shares with the nervous system the responsibility for maintaining constant internal body conditions and responding to changes in the environment.

Endothermic A process or reaction that absorbs heat and has a positive ΔH.

Energy The capacity to do work or supply heat.

Enthalpy A measure of the amount of energy associated with substances involved in a reaction.

Enthalpy change (ΔH) An alternative name for heat of reaction.

Entropy (S) The amount of disorder in a system.

Enzyme A protein or other molecule that acts as a catalyst for a biological reaction.

Equilibrium constant (K) Value of the equilibrium constant expression for a given reaction.

Equivalent For ions, the amount equal to 1 mol of charge.

Equivalent of acid Amount of an acid that contains 1 mole of H^+ ions.

Equivalent of base Amount of base that contains 1 mole of OH^- ions.

Erythrocytes Red blood cells; transporters of blood gases.

Essential amino acid An amino acid that cannot be synthesized by the body and thus must be obtained in the diet.

Ester A compound that has a carbonyl group bonded to a carbon atom and an —OR′ group, RCOOR′.

Esterification The reaction between an alcohol and a carboxylic acid to yield an ester plus water.

Ether A compound that has an oxygen atom bonded to two organic groups, R—O—R.

Ethyl group The —CH_2CH_3 alkyl group.

Exergonic A spontaneous reaction or process that releases free energy and has a negative ΔG.

Exon A nucleotide sequence in DNA that is part of a gene and codes for part of a protein.

Exothermic A process or reaction that releases heat and has a negative ΔH.

Extracellular fluid Fluid outside cells.

f-Block element An inner transition metal element that results from the filling of f orbitals.

Facilitated diffusion Passive transport across a cell membrane with the assistance of a protein that changes shape.

Factor–label method A problem-solving procedure in which equations are set up so that unwanted units cancel and only the desired units remain.

Fat A mixture of triacylglycerols that is solid because it contains a high proportion of saturated fatty acids.

Fatty acid A long-chain carboxylic acid; those in animal fats and vegetable oils often have 12–22 carbon atoms.

Feedback control Regulation of an enzyme's activity by the product of a reaction later in a pathway.

Fermentation The production of energy under anaerobic conditions.

Fibrin Insoluble protein that forms the fiber framework of a blood clot.

Fibrous protein A tough, insoluble protein whose protein chains form fibers or sheets.

Filtration (kidney) Filtration of blood plasma through a glomerulus and into a kidney nephron.

Fischer projection Structure that represents chiral carbon atoms as the intersections of two lines, with the horizontal lines representing bonds pointing out of the page and the vertical lines representing bonds pointing behind the page. For sugars, the aldehyde or ketone is at the top.

Formula unit The formula that identifies the smallest neutral unit of a compound.

Formula weight The sum of the atomic weights of the atoms in one formula unit of any compound.

Free radical An atom or molecule with an unpaired electron.

Free-energy change (ΔG) The criterion for spontaneous change (negative ΔG; $\Delta G = \Delta H - T \Delta S$).

Functional group An atom or group of atoms within a molecule that has a characteristic structure and chemical behavior.

Gamma (γ) radiation Radioactivity consisting of high-energy light waves.

Gas A substance that has neither a definite volume nor a definite shape.

Gas constant (R) The constant R in the ideal gas law, $PV = nRT$.

Gas laws A series of laws that predict the influence of pressure (P), volume (V), and temperature (T) on any gas or mixture of gases.

Gay-Lussac's law For a fixed amount of gas at a constant voume, pressure is directly proportional to the Kelvin temperature (P/T = constant, or $P_1/T_1 = P_2/T_2$).

Gene Segment of DNA that directs the synthesis of a single polypeptide.

Genetic (enzyme) control Regulation of enzyme activity by control of the synthesis of enzymes.

Genetic code The sequence of nucleotides, coded in triplets (codons) in mRNA, that determines the sequence of amino acids in protein synthesis.

Genome All of the genetic material in the chromosomes of an organism; its size is given as the number of base pairs.

Genomics The study of whole sets of genes and their functions.

Globular protein A water–soluble protein whose chain is folded in a compact shape with hydrophilic groups on the outside.

Glomerular filtrate Fluid that enters the nephron from the glomerulus; filtered blood plasma.

Gluconeogenesis The biochemical pathway for the synthesis of glucose from non-carbohydrates, such as lactate, amino acids, or glycerol.

Glycerophospholipid (phosphoglyceride) A lipid in which glycerol is linked by ester bonds to two fatty acids and one phosphate, which is in turn linked by another ester bond to an amino alcohol (or other alcohol).

Glycogenesis The biochemical pathway for synthesis of glycogen.

Glycogenolysis The biochemical pathway for breakdown of glycogen to free glucose.

Glycol A dialcohol, or diol having the two –OH groups on adjacent carbons.

Glycolipid A lipid with a fatty acid bonded to the C2—NH_2 and a sugar bonded to the C1—OH group of sphingosine.

Glycolysis The biochemical pathway that breaks down a molecule of glucose into two molecules of pyruvate plus energy.

Glycoprotein A protein that contains a short carbohydrate chain.

Glycoside A cyclic acetal formed by reaction of a monosaccharide with an alcohol, accompanied by loss of H_2O.

Glycosidic bond Bond between the anomeric carbon atom of a monosaccharide and an —OR group.

Gram-equivalent For ions, the molar mass of the ion divided by the ionic charge.

Group One of the 18 vertical columns of elements in the periodic table.

Guanosine diphosphate (GDP) An energy-carrying molecule that can gain or lose a phosphoryl group to transfer energy.

Guanosine triphosphate (GTP) An energy-carrying molecule similar to ATP; removal of a phosphoryl group to give GDP releases free energy.

Half-life ($t_{1/2}$) The amount of time required for one-half of a radioactive sample to decay.

Halogen An element in group 7A of the periodic table.

Halogenation (alkene) The addition of Cl_2 or Br_2 to a multiple bond to give a 1,2-dihalide product.

Halogenation (aromatic) The substitution of a halogen group (—X) for a hydrogen on an aromatic ring.

Heat The kinetic energy transferred from a hotter object to a colder object when the two are in contact.

Heat of fusion The quantity of heat required to completely melt a substance once it has reached its melting point.

Heat of reaction (ΔH) The amount of heat absorbed or released in a reaction.

Heat of vaporization The quantity of heat needed to completely vaporize a liquid once it has reached its boiling point.

Hemiacetal A compound with both an alcohol-like —OH group and an ether-like —OR group bonded to the same carbon atom.

Hemostasis The stopping of bleeding.

Henderson-Hasselbalch equation The logarithmic form of the K_a equation for a weak acid, used in applications involving buffer solutions.

Henry's law The solubility of a gas in a liquid is directly proportional to its partial pressure over the liquid at constant temperature.

Heterocycle A ring that contains nitrogen or some other atom in addition to carbon.

Heterogeneous mixture A nonuniform mixture that has regions of different composition.

Heterogeneous nuclear RNA The initially synthesized mRNA strand containing both introns and exons.

Homogeneous mixture A uniform mixture that has the same composition throughout.

Hormone A chemical messenger secreted by cells of the endocrine system and transported through the bloodstream to target cells with appropriate receptors where it elicits a response.

Hydration The addition of water to a multiple bond to give an alcohol product.

Hydrocarbon An organic compound that contains only carbon and hydrogen.

Hydrogen bond The attraction between a hydrogen atom bonded to an electronegative O, N, or F atom and another nearby electronegative O, N, or F atom.

Hydrogenation The addition of H_2 to a multiple bond to give a saturated product.

Hydrohalogenation The addition of HCl or HBr to a multiple bond to give an alkyl halide product.

Hydrolysis A reaction in which a bond or bonds are broken and the H— and —OH of water add to the atoms of the broken bond or bonds.

Hydronium ion The H_3O^+ ion, formed when an acid reacts with water.

Hydrophilic Water-loving; a hydrophilic substance dissolves in water.

Hydrophobic Water-fearing; a hydrophobic substance does not dissolve in water.

Hygroscopic Having the ability to pull water molecules from the surrounding atmosphere.

Hyperglycemia Higher-than-normal blood glucose concentration.

Hypertonic Having an osmolarity greater than the surrounding blood plasma or cells.

Hypoglycemia Lower-than-normal blood glucose concentration.

Hypotonic Having an osmolarity less than the surrounding blood plasma or cells.

Ideal gas A gas that obeys all the assumptions of the kinetic–molecular theory.

Ideal gas law A general expression relating pressure, volume, temperature, and amount for an ideal gas: $PV = nRT$.

Immune response Defense mechanism of the immune system dependent on the recognition of specific antigens, including viruses, bacteria, toxic substances, and infected cells; either cell-mediated or antibody-mediated.

Induced-fit model A model of enzyme action in which the enzyme has a flexible active site that changes shape to best fit the substrate and catalyze the reaction.

Inflammation Result of the inflammatory response: includes swelling, redness, warmth, and pain.

Inflammatory response A nonspecific defense mechanism triggered by antigens or tissue damage.

Inhibition (of an enzyme) Any process that slows or stops the action of an enzyme.

Inner transition metal element An element in one of the 14 groups shown separately at the bottom of the periodic table.

Intermolecular force A force that acts between molecules and holds molecules close to one another in liquids and solids.

Interstitial fluid Fluid surrounding cells: an extracellular fluid.

Intracellular fluid Fluid inside cells.

Intron A portion of DNA between coding regions of a gene (exons); is transcribed and then removed from final messenger RNA.

Ion An electrically charged atom or group of atoms.

Ion-product constant for water (K_w) The product of the H_3O^+ and OH^- molar concentrations in water or any aqueous solution ($K_w = [H_3O^+][OH^-] = 1.00 \times 10^{-14}$).

Ionic bond The electrical attractions between ions of opposite charge in a crystal.

Ionic compound A compound that contains ionic bonds.

Ionic equation An equation in which ions are explicitly shown.

Ionic solid A crystalline solid held together by ionic bonds.

Ionization energy The energy required to remove one electron from a single atom in the gaseous state.

Ionizing radiation A general name for high-energy radiation of all kinds.

Irreversible (enzyme) inhibition Enzyme deactivation in which an inhibitor forms covalent bonds to the active site, permanently blocking it.

Isoelectric point (pI) The pH at which a sample of an amino acid has equal number of + and − charges.

Isomers Compounds with the same molecular formula but different structures.

Isopropyl group The branched-chain alkyl group —$CH(CH_3)_2$.

Isotonic Having the same osmolarity.

Isotopes Atoms with identical atomic numbers but different mass numbers.

Ketoacidosis Lowered blood pH due to accumulation of ketone bodies.

Ketogenesis The synthesis of ketone bodies from acetyl-SCoA.

Ketone A compound that has a carbonyl group bonded to two carbons in organic groups that can be the same or different, $R_2C\text{=}O$, RCOR'.

Ketone bodies Compounds produced in the liver that can be used as fuel by muscle and brain tissue; 3-hydroxybutyrate, acetoacetate, and acetone.

Ketose A monosaccharide that contains a ketone carbonyl group.

Kinetic energy The energy of an object in motion.

Kinetic–molecular theory (KMT) of gases A group of assumptions that explain the behavior of gases.

L-Sugar Monosaccharide with the —OH group on the chiral carbon atom farthest from the carbonyl group pointing to the left in a Fischer projection.

Law of conservation of energy Energy can be neither created nor destroyed in any physical or chemical change.

Law of conservation of mass Matter can be neither created nor destroyed in any physical or chemical change.

Le Châtelier's principle When a stress is applied to a system in equilibrium, the equilibrium shifts to relieve the stress.

Lewis base A compound containing an unshared pair of electrons.

Lewis structure A molecular representation that shows both the connections among atoms and the locations of lone-pair valence electrons.

Limiting reagent The reactant that runs out first in a chemical reaction.

Line structure A shorthand way of drawing structures in which atoms aren't shown; instead, a carbon atom is understood to be at every intersection of lines, and hydrogens are filled in mentally.

Lipid A naturally occurring molecule from a plant or animal that is soluble in nonpolar organic solvents.

Lipid bilayer The basic structural unit of cell membranes; composed of two parallel sheets of membrane lipid molecules arranged tail to tail.

Lipogenesis The biochemical pathway for synthesis of fatty acids from acetyl-SCoA.

Lipoprotein A lipid–protein complex that transports lipids.

Liposome A spherical structure in which a lipid bilayer surrounds a water droplet.

Liquid A substance that has a definite volume but that changes shape to fit its container.

London dispersion force The short-lived attractive force due to the constant motion of electrons within molecules.

Lone pair A pair of electrons that is not used for bonding.

Main group element An element in one of the two groups on the left or the six groups on the right of the periodic table.

Markovnikov's rule In the addition of HX to an alkene, the H becomes attached to the carbon that already has the most H's, and the X becomes attached to the carbon that has fewer H's.

Mass A measure of the amount of matter in an object.

Mass number (A) The total number of protons and neutrons in an atom.

Matter The physical material that makes up the universe; anything that has mass and occupies space.

Melting point (mp) The temperature at which solid and liquid are in equilibrium.

Messenger RNA (mRNA) The RNA that carries the code transcribed from DNA and directs protein synthesis.

Metal A malleable element with a lustrous appearance that is a good conductor of heat and electricity.

Metalloid An element whose properties are intermediate between those of a metal and a nonmetal.

Methyl group The $-CH_3$ alkyl group.

Methylene Another name for a CH_2 unit.

Micelle A spherical cluster formed by the aggregation of soap or detergent molecules so that their hydrophobic ends are in the center and their hydrophilic ends are on the surface.

Miscible Mutually soluble in all proportions.

Mitochondrial matrix The space surrounded by the inner membrane of a mitochondrion.

Mitochondrion (plural, mitochondria) An egg-shaped organelle where small molecules are broken down to provide the energy for an organism.

Mixture A blend of two or more substances, each of which retains its chemical identity.

Mobilization (of triacylglycerols) Hydrolysis of triacylglycerols in adipose

tissue and release of fatty acids into the bloodstream.

Molar mass The mass in grams of one mole of a substance, numerically equal to the molecular weight.

Molarity (M) Concentration expressed as the number of moles of solute per liter of solution.

Mole The amount of a substance corresponding to 6.02×10^{23} units.

Molecular compound A compound that consists of molecules rather than ions.

Molecular formula A formula that shows the numbers and kinds of atoms in one molecule of a compound.

Molecular weight The sum of the atomic weights of the atoms in a molecule.

Molecule A group of atoms held together by covalent bonds.

Monomer A small molecule that is used to prepare a polymer.

Monosaccharide (simple sugar) A carbohydrate with 3–7 carbon atoms.

Mutagen A substance that causes mutations.

Mutarotation Change in rotation of plane-polarized light resulting from the equilibrium between cyclic anomers and the open-chain form of a sugar.

Mutation An error in base sequence that is carried along in DNA replication.

n-propyl group The straight-chain alkyl group $-CH_2CH_2CH_3$.

Native protein A protein with the shape (secondary, tertiary, and quaternary structure) in which it exists naturally in living organisms.

Net ionic equation An equation that does not include spectator ions.

Neurotransmitter A chemical messenger that travels between a neuron and a neighboring neuron or other target cell to transmit a nerve impulse.

Neutralization reaction The reaction of an acid with a base.

Neutron An electrically neutral subatomic particle.

Nitration The substitution of a nitro group $(-NO_2)$ for a hydrogen on an aromatic ring.

Noble gas An element in group 8A of the periodic table.

Noncompetitive (enzyme) inhibition Enzyme regulation in which an inhibitor binds to an enzyme elsewhere than at the active site, thereby changing the shape of the enzyme's active site and reducing its efficiency.

Noncovalent forces Forces of attraction other than covalent bonds that can act between molecules or within molecules.

Nonelectrolyte A substance that does not produce ions when dissolved in water.

Nonessential amino acid One of eleven amino acids that are synthesized in the body and are therefore not necessary in the diet.

Nonmetal An element that is a poor conductor of heat and electricity.

Normal boiling point The boiling point at a pressure of exactly 1 atmosphere.

Normality (N) A measure of acid (or base) concentration expressed as the number of acid (or base) equivalents per liter of solution.

Nuclear decay The spontaneous emission of a particle from an unstable nucleus.

Nuclear fission The fragmenting of heavy nuclei.

Nuclear fusion The joining together of light nuclei.

Nuclear reaction A reaction that changes an atomic nucleus, usually causing the change of one element into another.

Nucleic acid A polymer of nucleotides.

Nucleon A general term for both protons and neutrons.

Nucleoside A five-carbon sugar bonded to a cyclic amine base; like a nucleotide but missing the phosphate group.

Nucleotide A five-carbon sugar bonded to a cyclic amine base and one phosphate group (a nucleoside monophosphate); monomer for nucleic acids.

Nucleus The dense, central core of an atom that contains protons and neutrons.

Nuclide The nucleus of a specific isotope of an element.

Octet rule Main-group elements tend to undergo reactions that leave them with 8 valence electrons.

Oil A mixture of triacylglycerols that is liquid because it contains a high proportion of unsaturated fatty acids.

Orbital A region of space within an atom where an electron in a given subshell can be found.

Organic chemistry The study of carbon compounds.

Osmolarity (osmol) The sum of the molarities of all dissolved particles in a solution.

Osmosis The passage of solvent through a semipermeable membrane separating two solutions of different concentration.

Osmotic pressure The amount of external pressure applied to the more concentrated solution to halt the passage of solvent molecules across a semipermeable membrane.

Oxidation The loss of one or more electrons by an atom.

Oxidation number A number that indicates whether an atom is neutral, electron-rich, or electron-poor.

Oxidation–Reduction, or Redox, reaction A reaction in which electrons are transferred from one atom to another.

Oxidative deamination Conversion of an amino acid $-NH_2$ group to an α-keto group, with removal of NH_4^+.

Oxidative phosphorylation The synthesis of ATP from ADP using energy released in the electron-transport chain.

Oxidizing agent A reactant that causes an oxidation by taking electrons from or increasing the oxidation number of another reactant.

p-Block element A main group element that results from the filling of p orbitals.

Partial pressure The pressure exerted by a gas in a mixture.

Parts per billion (ppb) Number of parts per one billion (10^9) parts.

Parts per million (ppm) Number of parts per one million (10^6) parts.

Passive transport Movement of a substance across a cell membrane without the use of energy, from a region of higher concentration to a region of lower concentration.

Pentose phosphate pathway The biochemical pathway that produces ribose (a pentose), NADPH, and other sugar phosphates from glucose; an alternative to glycolysis.

Peptide bond An amide bond that links two amino acids together.

Percent yield The percent of the theoretical yield actually obtained from a chemical reaction.

Period One of the 7 horizontal rows of elements in the periodic table.

Periodic table A table of the elements in order of increasing atomic number and grouped according to their chemical similarities.

pH A measure of the acid strength of a solution; the negative common logarithm of the H_3O^+ concentration.

Phenol A compound that has an —OH group bonded directly to an aromatic, benzene-like ring, Ar—OH.

Phenyl The C_6H_5— group.

Phosphate ester A compound formed by reaction of an alcohol with phosphoric acid; may be a monoester, $ROPO_3H_2$; a diester, $(RO)_2PO_3H$; or a triester, $(RO)_3PO$; also may be a di- or triphosphate.

Phospholipid A lipid that has an ester link between phosphoric acid and an alcohol (glycerol or sphingosine).

Phosphoryl group The —PO_3^{2-} group in organic phosphates.

Phosphorylation Transfer of a phosphoryl group, —PO_3^{2-}, between organic molecules.

Physical change A change that does not affect the chemical makeup of a substance or object.

Physical quantity A physical property that can be measured.

Polar covalent bond A bond in which the electrons are attracted more strongly by one atom than by the other.

Polyatomic ion An ion that is composed of more than one atom.

Polymer A large molecule formed by the repetitive bonding together of many smaller molecules.

Polymorphism A variation in DNA sequence within a population.

Polysaccharide (complex carbohydrate) A carbohydrate that is a polymer of monosaccharides.

Polyunsaturated fatty acid A long-chain fatty acid that has two or more carbon–carbon double bonds.

Positron A "positive electron," which has the same mass as an electron but a positive charge.

Potential energy Energy that is stored because of position, composition, or shape.

Precipitate An insoluble solid that forms in solution during a chemical reaction.

Pressure The force per unit area pushing against a surface.

Primary carbon atom A carbon atom with one other carbon attached to it.

Primary protein structure The sequence in which amino acids are linked by peptide bonds in a protein.

Product A substance that is formed in a chemical reaction and is written on the right side of the reaction arrow in a chemical equation.

Property A characteristic useful for identifying a substance or object.

Protein A large biological molecule made of many amino acids linked together through amide (peptide) bonds.

Proton A positively charged subatomic particle.

Pure substance A substance that has uniform chemical composition throughout.

Quaternary ammonium ion A positive ion with four organic groups bonded to the nitrogen atom.

Quaternary ammonium salt An ionic compound composed of a quaternary ammonium ion and an anion.

Quaternary carbon atom A carbon atom with four other carbons attached to it.

Quaternary protein structure The way in which two or more protein chains aggregate to form large, ordered structures.

Radioactivity The spontaneous emission of radiation from a nucleus.

Radioisotope A radioactive isotope.

Radionuclide The nucleus of a radioactive isotope.

Reabsorption (kidney) Movement of solutes out of filtrate in a kidney tubule.

Reactant A substance that undergoes change in a chemical reaction and is written on the left side of the reaction arrow in a chemical equation.

Reaction mechanism A description of the individual steps by which old bonds are broken and new bonds are formed in a reaction.

Reaction rate A measure of how rapidly a reaction occurs.

Rearrangement reaction A general reaction type in which a molecule undergoes bond reorganization to yield an isomer.

Receptor A molecule or portion of a molecule with which a hormone, neurotransmitter, or other biochemically active molecule interacts to initiate a response in a target cell.

Recombinant DNA DNA that contains segments from two different species.

Reducing agent A reactant that causes a reduction by giving up electrons or increasing the oxidation number of another reactant.

Reducing sugar A carbohydrate that reacts in basic solution with a mild oxidizing agent.

Reduction The gain of one or more electrons by an atom.

Reductive deamination Conversion of an α-keto acid to an amino acid by reaction with NH_4^+.

Regular tetrahedron A geometric figure with four identical triangular faces.

Replication The process by which copies of DNA are made when a cell divides.

Residue (amino acid) An amino acid unit in a polypeptide.

Resonance The phenomenon where the true structure of a molecule is an average among two or more conventional structures.

Reversible reaction A reaction that can go in either the forward direction or the reverse direction, from products to reactants or reactants to products.

Ribonucleotide A nucleotide containing D-ribose.

Ribosomal RNA (rRNA) The RNA that is complexed with proteins in ribosomes.

Ribosome The structure in the cell where protein synthesis occurs; composed of protein and rRNA.

RNA (ribonucleic acids) The nucleic acids (messenger, transfer, and ribosomal) responsible for putting the genetic information to use in protein synthesis; polymers of ribonucleotides.

Rounding off A procedure used for deleting nonsignificant figures.

s-Block element A main group element that results from the filling of an s orbital.

Salt An ionic compound formed from reaction of an acid with a base.

Saponification The reaction of an ester with aqueous hydroxide ion to yield an alcohol and the metal salt of a carboxylic acid.

Saturated A molecule whose carbon atoms bond to the maximum number of hydrogen atoms.

Saturated fatty acid A long-chain carboxylic acid containing only carbon–carbon single bonds.

Saturated solution A solution that contains the maximum amount of dissolved solute at equilibrium.

Scientific Method Systematic process of observation, hypothesis, and experimentation to expand and refine a body of knowledge.

Scientific notation A number expressed as the product of a number between 1 and 10, times the number 10 raised to a power.

Second messenger Chemical messenger released inside a cell when a hydrophilic hormone or neurotransmitter interacts with a receptor on the cell surface.

Secondary carbon atom A carbon atom with two other carbons attached to it.

Secondary protein structure Regular and repeating structural patterns (for example, α-helix, β-sheet) created by hydrogen bonding between backbone atoms in neighboring segments of protein chains.

Secretion (kidney) Movement of solutes into filtrate in a kidney tubule.

SI units Units of measurement defined by the International System of Units.

Side chain (amino acid) The group bonded to the carbon next to the carboxyl group in an amino acid; different in different amino acids.

Significant figures The number of meaningful digits used to express a value.

Simple diffusion Passive transport by the random motion of diffusion through the cell membrane.

Simple protein A protein composed of only amino acid residues.

Single bond A covalent bond formed by sharing one electron pair.

Single nucleotide polymorphism Common single-base-pair variation in DNA.

Soap The mixture of salts of fatty acids formed on saponification of animal fat.

Solid A substance that has a definite shape and volume.

Solubility The maximum amount of a substance that will dissolve in a given amount of solvent at a specified temperature.

Solute A substance dissolved in a liquid.

Solution A homogeneous mixture that contains particles the size of a typical ion or small molecule.

Solvation The clustering of solvent molecules around a dissolved solute molecule or ion.

Solvent The liquid in which another substance is dissolved.

Specific gravity The density of a substance divided by the density of water at the same temperature.

Specific heat The amount of heat that will raise the temperature of 1 g of a substance by 1 °C.

Specificity (enzyme) The limitation of the activity of an enzyme to a specific substrate, specific reaction, or specific type of reaction.

Spectator ion An ion that appears unchanged on both sides of a reaction arrow.

Sphingolipid A lipid derived from the amino alcohol sphingosine.

Spontaneous process A process or reaction that, once started, proceeds on its own without any external influence.

Standard molar volume The volume of one mole of a gas at standard temperature and pressure (22.4 L).

Standard temperature and pressure (STP) Standard conditions for a gas, defined as 0 °C (273 K) and 1 atm (760 mmHg) pressure.

State of matter The physical state of a substance as a solid, a liquid, or a gas.

Stereoisomers Isomers that have the same molecular and structural formulas, but different spatial arrangements of their atoms.

Steroid A lipid whose structure is based on the following tetracyclic (four-ring) carbon skeleton:

Straight-chain alkane An alkane that has all its carbons connected in a row.

Strong acid An acid that gives up H^+ easily and is essentially 100% dissociated in water.

Strong base A base that has a high affinity for H^+ and holds it tightly.

Strong electrolyte A substance that ionizes completely when dissolved in water.

Structural formula A molecular representation that shows the connections among atoms by using lines to represent covalent bonds.

Subatomic particles Three kinds of fundamental particles from which atoms are made: protons, neutrons, and electrons.

Substituent An atom or group of atoms attached to a parent compound.

Substitution reaction A general reaction type in which an atom or group of atoms in a molecule is replaced by another atom or group of atoms.

Substrate A reactant in an enzyme catalyzed reaction.

Sulfonation The substitution of a sulfonic acid group ($—SO_3H$) for a hydrogen on an aromatic ring.

Supersaturated solution A solution that contains more than the maximum amount of dissolved solute; a nonequilibrium situation.

Synapse The place where the tip of a neuron and its target cell lie adjacent to each other.

Telomeres The ends of chromosomes; in humans, contain long series of repeating groups of nucleotides.

Temperature The measure of how hot or cold an object is.

Tertiary carbon atom A carbon atom with three other carbons attached to it.

Tertiary protein structure The way in which an entire protein chain is coiled and folded into its specific three-dimensional shape.

Theoretical yield The amount of product formed assuming complete reaction of the limiting reagent.

Thiol A compound that contains an —SH group, R—SH.

Titration A procedure for determining the total acid or base concentration of a solution.

Transamination The interchange of the amino group of an amino acid and the keto group of an α-keto acid.

Transcription The process by which the information in DNA is read and used to synthesize RNA.

Transfer RNA (tRNA) The RNA that transports amino acids into position for protein synthesis.

Transition metal element An element in one of the 10 smaller groups near the middle of the periodic table.

Translation The process by which RNA directs protein synthesis.

Transmutation The change of one element into another.

Triacylglycerol (triglyceride) A triester of glycerol with three fatty acids.

Triple bond A covalent bond formed by sharing three electron pairs.

Turnover number The maximum number of substrate molecules acted upon by one molecule of enzyme per unit time.

Unit A defined quantity used as a standard of measurement.

Unsaturated A molecule that contains a carbon–carbon multiple bond, to which more hydrogen atoms can be added.

Unsaturated fatty acid A long-chain carboxylic acid containing one or more carbon–carbon double bonds.

Urea cycle The cyclic biochemical pathway that produces urea for excretion.

Valence electron An electron in the outermost, or valence, shell of an atom.

Valence shell The outermost electron shell of an atom.

Valence-shell electron-pair repulsion (VSEPR) model A method for predicting molecular shape by noting how many electron charge clouds surround atoms and assuming that the clouds orient as far away from one another as possible.

Vapor The gas molecules in equilibrium with a liquid.

Vapor pressure The partial pressure of gas molecules in equilibrium with a liquid.

Vitamin An organic molecule, essential in trace amounts that must be obtained in the diet because it is not synthesized in the body.

Volume/volume percent concentration [(v/v)%] Concentration expressed as the number of milliliters of solute dissolved in 100 mL of solution.

Wax A mixture of esters of long-chain carboxylic acids with long-chain alcohols.

Weak acid An acid that gives up H^+ with difficulty and is less than 100% dissociated in water.

Weak base A base that has only a slight affinity for H^+ and holds it weakly.

Weak electrolyte A substance that is only partly ionized in water.

Weight A measure of the gravitational force that the earth or other large body exerts on an object.

Weight/volume percent concentration [(w/v)%] Concentration expressed as the number of grams of solute per 100 mL of solution.

Whole blood Blood plasma plus blood cells.

X rays Electromagnetic radiation with an energy somewhat less than that of γ rays.

Zwitterion A neutral dipolar ion that has one + charge and one − charge.

Zymogen A compound that becomes an active enzyme after undergoing a chemical change.

Answers to Selected Problems

Short answers are given for in-chapter problems, *Understanding Key Concepts* problems, and even-numbered end-of-chapter problems. Explanations and full answers for all problems are provided in the accompanying *Study Guide and Solutions Manual*.

Chapter 1

1.1 all; natural: (a), (d); synthetic: (b), (c) **1.2** physical: (a), (d); chemical: (b), (c) **1.3** solid **1.4** mixture: (a), (d); pure: (b), (c) **1.5** physical: (a), (c); chemical: (b) **1.6** chemical change **1.7** (a) Na (b) Ti (c) Sr (d) Y (e) F (f) H **1.8** (a) uranium (b) calcium (c) neodymium (d) potassium (e) tungsten (f) tin **1.9** (a) 1 nitrogen atom, 3 hydrogen atoms (b) 1 sodium atom, 1 hydrogen atom, 1 carbon atom, 3 oxygen atoms (c) 8 carbon atoms, 18 hydrogen atoms (d) 6 carbon atoms, 8 hydrogen atoms, 6 oxygen atoms **1.10** (a) chromium (24) (b) potassium (19) (c) sulfur (16) (d) radon (86) **1.11** Metalloids are at the boundary between metals and nonmetals. **1.12** helium (He), neon (Ne), argon (Ar), krypton (Kr), xenon (Xe), radon (Rn) **1.13** copper (Cu), silver (Ag), gold (Au) **1.14** red: vanadium, metal; green: boron, metalloid; blue: bromine, nonmetal **1.15** Americium, a metal **1.16** Chemistry is the study of matter. **1.18** physical: (a), (c), (e); chemical: (b), (d) **1.20** A gas has no definite shape or volume; a liquid has no definite shape but has a definite volume; a solid has a definite volume and a definite shape. **1.22** gas **1.24** mixture: (a), (b), (d), (f); pure: (c), (e) **1.26** element: (a); compound: (b), (c); mixture: (d), (e), (f) **1.28** (a) reactant: hydrogen peroxide; products: water, oxygen (b) compounds: hydrogen peroxide, water; element: oxygen **1.30** 117 elements; 90 occur naturally **1.32** Metals: lustrous, malleable, conductors of heat and electricity; nonmetals: gases or brittle solids, nonconductors; metalloids: properties intermediate between metals and nonmetals. **1.34** (a) Gd (b) Ge (c) Tc (d) As (e) Cd **1.36** (a) nitrogen (b) potassium (c) chlorine (d) calcium (e) phosphorus (f) manganese **1.38** Only the first letter of a chemical symbol is capitalized. **1.40** (a) Br (b) Mn (c) C (d) K **1.42** (a) A mixture doesn't have a chemical formula. (b) The symbol for nitrogen is N. **1.44** (a) magnesium, sulfur, oxygen (b) iron, bromine (c) cobalt, phosphorus (d) arsenic, hydrogen (e) calcium, chromium, oxygen **1.46** Carbon, hydrogen, nitrogen, oxygen; ten atoms **1.48** $C_{13}H_{18}O_2$ **1.50** (a) metal (b) nonmetal **1.52** 9 carbons, 8 hydrogens, 4 oxygens; 21 atoms **1.54** (a) A physical change doesn't alter chemical makeup; a chemical change alters a substance's chemical makeup. (b) Melting point is the temperature at which a change of state from solid to liquid occurs; boiling point is the temperature at which a change of state from liquid to gas occurs. (c) A reactant is a substance that undergoes change in a chemical reaction; a product is a substance formed as a result of a chemical reaction. (d) A metal is a lustrous malleable element that is a good conductor of heat and electricity; a nonmetal is an element that is a poor conductor. **1.56** compounds: (a), (c), (e); elements: (b), (d) **1.58** mixture **1.60** (a) Fe (b) Cu (c) Co (d) Mo (e) Cr (f) F (g) S **1.62** Elements 115,119: metals Element 117: metal or metalloid

Chapter 2

2.1 (a) deciliter (b) milligram (c) nanosecond (d) kilometer (e) microgram **2.2** (a) L (b) kg (c) nm (d) Mm **2.3** (a) 0.000 000 001 m (b) 0.1 g (c) 1000 m (d) 0.000 001 s (e) 0.000 000 001 g **2.4** (a) 3 (b) 4 (c) 5 (d) exact **2.5** 32.3 °C; three significant figures **2.6** (a) 5.8×10^{-2} g (b) 4.6792×10^4 m (c) 6.072×10^{-3} cm (d) 3.453×10^2 kg **2.7** (a) 48,850 mg (b) 0.000 008 3 m (c) 0.0400 m **2.8** (a) 6.3000×10^5 (b) 1.30×10^3 (c) 7.942×10^{11} **2.9** 2.78×10^{-10} m = 2.78×10^2 pm **2.10** (a) 2.30 g (b) 188.38 mL (c) 0.009 L (d) 1.000 kg **2.11** (a) 50.9 mL (b) 0.078 g (c) 11.9 m (d) 51 mg (e) 103 **2.12** (a) 1 L = 1000 mL; 1 mL = 0.001 L (b) 1 g = 0.03527 oz; 1 oz = 28.35 g (c) 1 L = 1.057 qt; 1 qt = 0.9464 L **2.13** (a) 454 g (b) 2.5 L (c) 105 qt **2.14** 795 mL **2.15** 7.36 m/s **2.16** (a) 3.4 kg (b) 120 mL **2.17** (a) 10.6 mg/kg (b) 36 mg/kg **2.18** 57.8 °C **2.19** −38.0 °F; 234.3 K **2.20** 7,700 cal

2.21 0.21 cal/g °C **2.22** float: ice, human fat, cork, balsa wood; sink: gold, table sugar, earth **2.23** 8.392 mL **2.24** 2.21 g/cm³ **2.25** more dense **2.26** (a) 34 mL (b) 2.7 cm; two significant figures **2.27** (no answer) **2.28** (a) 0.977 (b) three (c) less dense **2.29** The smaller cylinder is more precise because the gradations are smaller. **2.30** 3 1/8 in.; 8.0 cm **2.31** start: 0.11 mL stop: 0.25 mL volume: 0.14 mL **2.32** (a) Both are equally precise. (b) 355 mL **2.33** higher in chloroform **2.34** A physical quantity consists of a number and a unit. **2.36** mass (kg); volume (m³); length (m); temperature (K) **2.38** They are the same. **2.40** (a) centiliter (b) decimeter (c) millimeter (d) nanoliter (e) milligram (f) cubic meter (g) cubic centimeter **2.42** 10^9 pg, 3.5×10^4 pg **2.44** (a) 9.457×10^3 (b) 7×10^{-5} (c) 2.000×10^{10} (d) 1.2345×10^{-2} (e) 6.5238×10^2 **2.46** (a) 6 (b) 3 (c) 3 (d) 4 (e) 1–5 (f) 2–3 **2.48** (a) 7,926 mi, 7,900 mi, 7,926.38 mi (b) $7.926\ 381 \times 10^3$ mi **2.50** (a) 12.1 g (b) 96.19 cm (c) 263 mL (d) 20.9 mg **2.52** (a) 0.3614 cg (b) 0.0120 ML (c) 0.0144 mm (d) 60.3 ng (e) 1.745 dL (f) 1.5×10^3 cm **2.54** (a) 97.8 kg (b) 0.133 mL (c) 0.46 ng (d) 2.99 Mm **2.56** (a) 62.1 mi/hr (b) 91.1 ft/s **2.58** 4×10^3 cells/in. **2.60** 10 g **2.62** 6×10^{10} cells **2.64** 37.0 °C, 310.2 K **2.66** 537 cal = 0.537 kcal **2.68** 0.092 cal/g·°C **2.70** Hg: 76 °C; Fe: 40.7 °C **2.72** 0.179 cm³ **2.74** 11.4 g/cm³ **2.76** 0.7856 g/mL; sp gr = 0.7856 **2.78** (a) 2.0×10^{-6} cm (b) 1.3×10^6 cells/in (c) 1 mL = 0.269 fluidram (1 mL = 16 minim (e) 1 minim = 2.08×10^{-3} fluid ounce **2.80** −2 °C; 271 K **2.82** (a) BMI = 29 (b) BMI = 23.7 (c) BMI = 24.4; individual (a) **2.84** 3.12 in; 7.92 cm Discrepancies are due to rounding errors and changes in significant figures. **2.86** 177 °C **2.88** 3.9×10^{-2} g/dL iron, 8.3×10^{-3} g/dL calcium, 2.24×10^{-1} g/dL cholesterol **2.90** 7.8×10^6 mL/day **2.92** 0.13 g **2.94** 4.4 g; 0.0097 lb **2.96** 2200 mL **2.98** 2.2 tablespoons **2.100** iron **2.102** 4.99×10^{10} L **2.104** (a) 2×10^3 mg/L (b) 2×10^3 μg/mL (c) 2 g/L (d) 2×10^3 ng/μL **2.106** 34.1 °C **2.108** float

Chapter 3

3.1 14.0 amu **3.2** 4.99×10^{-8} g **3.3** 6.02×10^{23} atoms in all cases **3.4** When the mass in grams is numerically equal to the mass in amu, there are 6.02×10^{23} atoms. **3.5** (a) Re (b) Ca (c) Te **3.6** 27 protons, 27 electrons, 33 neutrons **3.7** technetium **3.8** The answers agree **3.9** $^{79}_{35}Br$, $^{81}_{35}Br$ **3.10** (a) $^{11}_{5}B$ (b) $^{56}_{26}Fe$ (c) $^{37}_{17}Cl$ **3.11** group 3A, period 3 **3.12** silver, calcium **3.13** Nitrogen (1), phosphorus (2), arsenic (3), antimony (4), bismuth (5) **3.14** Metals: titanium, scandium; nonmetals: selenium, argon; metalloids: tellurium, astatine **3.15** (a) nonmetal, main group, noble gas (b) metal, main group (c) nonmetal, main group (d) metal, transition element **3.16** red = zinc, metal, period 4, group 2B; blue = oxygen, period 6, group 6A **3.17** 6, 2, 6 **3.18** 10, neon **3.19** 12, magnesium **3.20** (a) $1s^2 2s^2 2p^2$ (b) $1s^2 2s^2 2p^6 3s^2 3p^3$ (c) $1s^2 2s^2 2p^6 3s^2 3p^5$ (d) $1s^2 2s^2 2p^6 3s^2 3p^6 4s^1$ **3.21** $1s^2 2s^2 2p^6 3s^2 3p^2$; $1s^2 2s^2 2p^6 3s^2 3p^6 4s^2 3d^{10} 4p^6$ **3.22** $4p^3$, all are unpaired **3.23** gallium **3.24** (a) $1s^2 2s^2 2p^5$; [He] $2s^2 2p^5$ (b) $1s^2 2s^2 2p^6 3s^2 3p^1$; [Ne] $3s^2 3p^1$ (c) $1s^2 2s^2 2p^6 3s^2 3p^6 4s^2 3d^{10} 4p^3$; [Ne] $4s^2 3d^{10} 4p^6$ **3.25** group 2A **3.26** group 7A, $1s^2 2s^2 2p^6 3s^2 3p^5$ **3.27** group 6A, $ns^2 np^4$ **3.28** ·X· **3.29** :Rn: ·Pb· :Xe: ·Ra· **3.30** (a) p orbital (b) s orbital

3.31

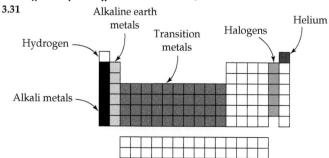

Alkaline earth metals
Transition metals
Halogens
Helium
Hydrogen
Alkali metals

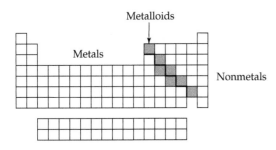

Metalloids

Metals

Nonmetals

3.32 red: gas (fluorine); blue: atomic number 79 (gold); green: (calcium); beryllium, magnesium, strontium, barium, and radium are similar. **3.33**

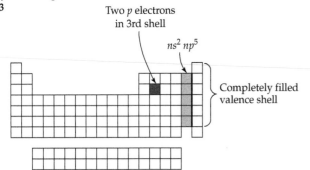

Two p electrons in 3rd shell

$ns^2 np^5$

Completely filled valence shell

3.34 selenium **3.35** $1s^2 2s^2 2p^6 3s^2 3p^6 4s^2 3d^{10} 4p^3$ **3.36** Matter is composed of atoms. Atoms of different elements differ. Compounds consist of different atoms combined in specific proportions. Atoms do not change in chemical reactions. **3.38 (a)** 3.4702×10^{-22} g **(b)** 2.1801×10^{-22} g **(c)** 6.6465×10^{-24} g **3.40** 14.01 g **3.42** 6.022×10^{23} atoms **3.44** protons (+ charge, 1 amu); neutrons (no charge, 1 amu); electrons (− charge, 0.0005 amu). **3.46 (a)** potassium **(b)** tin **(c)** zinc **3.48** 18, 20, 22 **3.50 (a)** and **(c)** **3.52 (a)** F-19 **(b)** Ne-19 **(c)** F-21 **(d)** Mg-21 **3.54 (a)** $^{14}_{6}$C **(b)** $^{39}_{19}$K **(c)** $^{20}_{10}$Ne **3.56** $^{12}_{6}$C—six neutrons $^{13}_{6}$C—seven neutrons $^{14}_{6}$C—eight neutrons **3.58** 63.55 amu **3.60** Eight electrons are needed to fill the 3s and 3p subshells. **3.62** Am, metal **3.64 (a, b)** transition metals **(c)** 3d **3.66 (a)** Rb: (i), (v), (vii) **(b)** W: (i), (iv) **(c)** Ge: (iii), (v) **(d)** Kr: (ii), (v), (vi) **3.68** selenium **3.70** sodium, potassium, rubidium, cesium, francium **3.72** 2 **3.74** 2, 8, 18 **3.76** 3, 4, 4 **3.78** 10, neon **3.80 (a)** two paired, two unpaired **(b)** four paired, one unpaired **(c)** two unpaired **3.82** 2, 1, 2, 0, 3, 4 **3.84** 2 **3.86** beryllium, 2s; arsenic, 4p **3.88 (a)** 8 **(b)** 4 **(c)** 2 **(d)** 1 **(e)** 3 **(f)** 7 **3.90** A scanning tunneling microscope has much higher resolution. **3.92** H, He **3.94 (a)** ultraviolet **(b)** gamma waves **(c)** X rays **3.96** He, Ne, Ar, Kr, Xe, Rn **3.98** Tellurium atoms have more neutrons than iodine atoms. **3.100** 1 (2 e), 2 (8 e), 3 (18 e), 4 (32 e), 5 (18 e), 6 (4 e) **3.102** 79.90 amu **3.104** carbon weighs more **3.106** 12 g **3.108** Sr, metal, group 2A, period 5, 38 protons **3.110** 2, 8, 18, 10, 2; metal **3.112 (a)** The 4s subshell fills before 3d. **(b)** The 2s subshell fills before 2p. **(c)** Silicon has 14 electrons: $1s^2 2s^2 2p^6 3s^2 3p^2$. **(d)** The 3s electrons have opposite spins. **3.114** An electron will fill or half-fill a d subshell instead of filling an s subshell of a higher shell.

Chapter 4

4.1 Mg^{2+} is a cation **4.2** S^{2-} is an anion **4.3** O^{2-} is an anion. **4.4** less than Kr, but higher than most other elements **4.5 (a)** B **(b)** Ca **(c)** Sc **4.6 (a)** H **(b)** S **(c)** Cr **4.7** Potassium ($1s^2 2s^2 2p^6 3s^2 3p^6 4s^1$) can gain the argon configuration by losing 1 electron. **4.8** Aluminum can lose 3 electrons to form Al^{3+}. **4.9** X: would be a 2A metal and would lose electrons; ·Ÿ· would be a 6A nonmetal and would gain electrons.

$$X\!:\; +\; \cdot\ddot{Y}\cdot\; \longrightarrow\; X^{2+}\; +\; :\ddot{Y}:^{2-}$$

4.10 cation **4.11 (b)**

4.12 (a) $Se + 2 e^- \rightarrow Se^{2-}$ **(b)** $Ba \rightarrow Ba^{2+} + 2 e^-$ **(c)** $Br + e^- \rightarrow Br^-$ **4.13 (a)** copper(II) ion **(b)** fluoride ion **(c)** magnesium ion **(d)** sulfide ion **4.14 (a)** Ag^+ **(b)** Fe^{2+} **(c)** Cu^+ **(d)** Te^{2-} **4.15** Na^+, sodium ion; K^+, potassium ion; Ca^{2+}, calcium ion; Cl^-, chloride ion **4.16 (a)** nitrate ion **(b)** cyanide ion **(c)** hydroxide ion **(d)** hydrogen phosphate ion **4.17 (a)** HCO_3^- **(b)** NH_4^+ **(c)** PO_4^{3-} **(d)** MnO_4^- **4.18 (a)** AgI **(b)** Ag_2O

(c) Ag_3PO_4 **4.19 (a)** Na_2SO_4 **(b)** $FeSO_4$ **(c)** $Cr_2(SO_4)_3$ **4.20** $(NH_4)_2CO_3$ **4.21** $Al_2(SO_4)_3$, $Al(CH_3CO_2)_3$ **4.22** blue: K_2S; red: $BaBr_2$ green: Al_2O_3 **4.23** Calcium ion = Ca^{2+}; nitride ion = N^{3-}; calcium nitride formula = Ca_3N_2 **4.24** $BaSO_4$ **4.25** silver(I) sulfide **4.26 (a)** tin(IV) oxide **(b)** calcium cyanide **(c)** sodium carbonate **(d)** copper(I) sulfate **(e)** barium hydroxide **(f)** iron(II) nitrate **4.27 (a)** Li_3PO_4 **(b)** $CuCO_3$ **(c)** $Al_2(SO_3)_3$ **(d)** CuF **(e)** $Fe_2(SO_4)_3$ **(f)** NH_4Cl **4.28** Cr_2O_3 chromium (III) oxide **4.29** Acids: (a), (d); bases (b), (c) **4.30 (a)** HCl **(b)** H_2SO_4 **4.31**

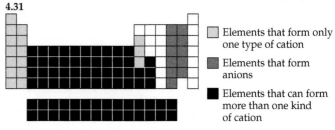

	Elements that form only one type of cation
	Elements that form anions
	Elements that can form more than one kind of cation

All of the other elements form neither anions nor cations readily.
4.32

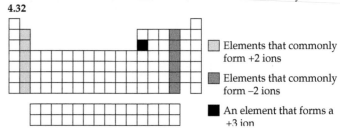

	Elements that commonly form +2 ions
	Elements that commonly form −2 ions
	An element that forms a +3 ion

4.33 (a) O^{2-} **(b)** Na^+ **(c)** Ca **4.34 (a)** sodium atom (larger) **(b)** Na^+ ion (smaller) **4.35 (a)** chlorine atom (smaller) **(b)** Cl^- anion (larger) **4.36** red: MgO; blue: LiCl; green: $AlBr_3$ **4.37 (a)** ZnS **(b)** $PbBr_2$ **(c)** CrF_3 **(d)** Al_2O_3 **4.38 (a)** ·Be· **(b)** :Ne: **(c)** ·Sr· **(d)** ·Al· **4.40 (a)** $Ca \rightarrow Ca^{2+} + 2 e^-$ **(b)** $Au \rightarrow Au^+ + e^-$ **(c)** $F + e^- \rightarrow F^-$ **(d)** $Cr \rightarrow Cr^{3+} + 3 e^-$ **4.42** true: (d); false: (a), (b), (c) **4.44** Main group atoms undergo reactions that leave them with a noble gas electron configuration. **4.46** −2 **4.48 (a)** Sr **(b)** Br **4.50 (a)** $1s^2 2s^2 2p^6 3s^2 3p^6 4s^2 3d^{10} 4p^6$ **(b)** $1s^2 2s^2 2p^6 3s^2 3p^6 4s^2 3d^{10} 4p^6$ **(c)** $1s^2 2s^2 2p^6 3s^2 3p^6$ **(d)** $1s^2 2s^2 2p^6 3s^2 3p^6 4s^2 3d^{10} 4p^6 5s^2 4d^{10} 5p^6$ **(e)** $1s^2 2s^2 2p^6$ **4.52 (a)** O **(b)** Li **(c)** Zn **(d)** N **4.54** none **4.56** Cr^{2+}: $1s^2 2s^2 2p^6 3s^2 3p^6 3d^4$; Cr^{3+}: $1s^2 2s^2 2p^6 3s^2 3p^6 3d^3$ **4.58** greater **4.60 (a)** sulfide ion **(b)** tin(II) ion **(c)** strontium ion **(d)** magnesium ion **(e)** gold(I) ion **4.62 (a)** Se^{2-} **(b)** O^{2-} **(c)** Ag^+ **4.64 (a)** OH^- **(b)** HSO_4^- **(c)** $CH_3CO_2^-$ **(d)** MnO_4^- **(e)** OCl^- **(f)** NO_3^- **(g)** CO_3^{2-} **(h)** $Cr_2CO_7^{2-}$ **4.66 (a)** $Al_2(SO_4)_3$ **(b)** Ag_2SO_4 **(c)** $ZnSO_4$ **(d)** $BaSO_4$ **4.68 (a)** $Al_2(SO_4)_3$ **(b)** Ag_2SO_4 **(c)** $ZnSO_4$ **(d)** $BaSO_4$
4.70

	S^{2-}	Cl^-	PO_4^{3-}	CO_3^{2-}
copper(II)	CuS	$CuCl_2$	$Cu_3(PO_4)_2$	$CuCO_3$
Ca^{2+}	CaS	$CaCl_2$	$Ca_3(PO_4)_2$	$CaCO_3$
NH_4^+	$(NH_4)_2S$	NH_4Cl	$(NH_4)_3PO_4$	$(NH_4)_2CO_3$
ferric ion	Fe_2S_3	$FeCl_3$	$FePO_4$	$Fe_2(CO_3)_3$

4.72 copper(II) sulfide, copper(II) chloride, copper(II) phosphate, copper(II) carbonate; calcium sulfide, calcium chloride, calcium phosphate, calcium carbonate; ammonium sulfide, ammonium chloride, ammonium phosphate, ammonium carbonate; iron(III) sulfide, iron(III) chloride, iron(III) phosphate, iron(III) carbonate **4.74 (a)** magnesium carbonate **(b)** calcium acetate **(c)** silver(I) cyanide **(d)** sodium dichromate **4.76** $Ca_3(PO_4)_2$ **4.78** An acid gives H^+ ions in water; a base gives OH^- ions. **4.80 (a)** $H_2CO_3 \rightarrow 2 H^+ + CO_3^{2-}$ **(b)** $HCN \rightarrow H^+ + CN^-$ **(c)** $Mg(OH)_2 \rightarrow Mg^{2+} + 2 OH^-$ **(d)** $KOH \rightarrow K^+ + OH^-$ **4.82** To a geologist, a mineral is a naturally occurring crystalline compound. To a nutritionist, a mineral is a metal ion essential for human health. **4.84** slight **4.86** Sodium protects against fluid loss and is necessary for muscle contraction and transmission of nerve impulses.

4.88 10 Ca^{2+}, 6 PO$_4$$^{3-}$, 2 OH$^-$ **4.90** H$^-$ has the helium configuration, 1s^2 **4.92 (a)** CrO$_3$ **(b)** VCl$_5$ **(c)** MnO$_2$ **(d)** MoS$_2$ **4.94 (a)** −1 **(b)** 3 gluconate ions per iron(III)   **4.96 (a)** Co(CN)$_2$ **(b)** UO$_3$ **(c)** SnSO$_4$ **(d)** MnO$_2$ **(e)** K$_3$PO$_4$ **(f)** Ca$_3$P$_2$ **(g)** LiHSO$_4$ **(h)** Al(OH)$_3$ **4.98 (a)** metal **(b)** nonmetal **(c)** X$_2$Y$_3$ **(d)** X: group 3A; Y: group 6A

Chapter 5

5.1 :I̤:I̤: ; xenon   **5.2 (a)** P 3, H 1 **(b)** Se 2, H 1 **(c)** H 1, Cl 1 **(d)** Si 4, F 1

5.3 PbCl$_4$ **5.4 (a)** CH$_2$Cl$_2$ **(b)** BH$_3$ **(c)** NI$_3$ **(d)** SiCl$_4$

5.5

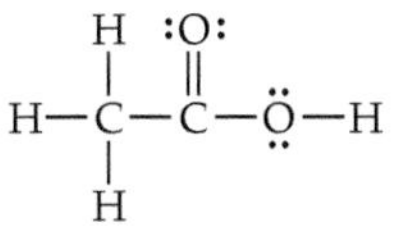

5.6

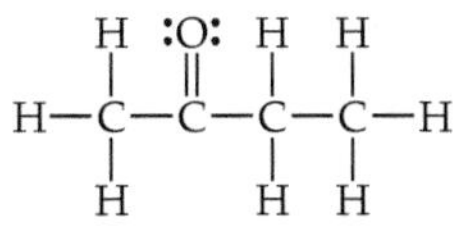

5.7

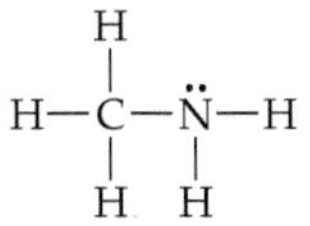

5.8 (a) **(b)** **(c)**

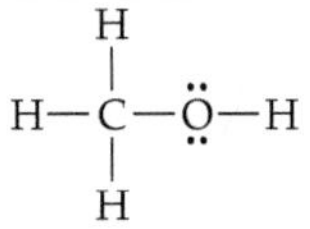

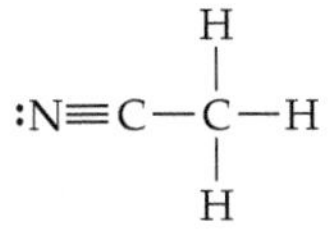

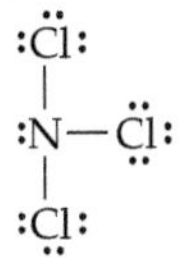

5.9 (a) **(b)** **(c)** **(d)**

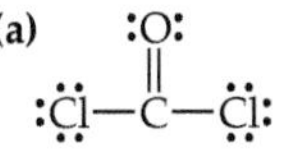

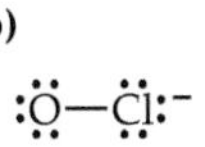

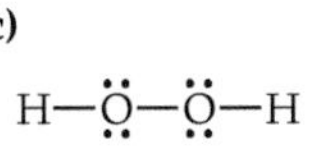

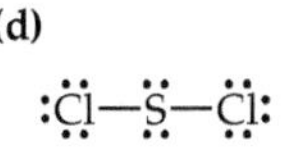

5.10

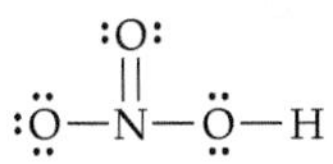

5.11 (a) C$_6$H$_{10}$O$_2$ **(b)**

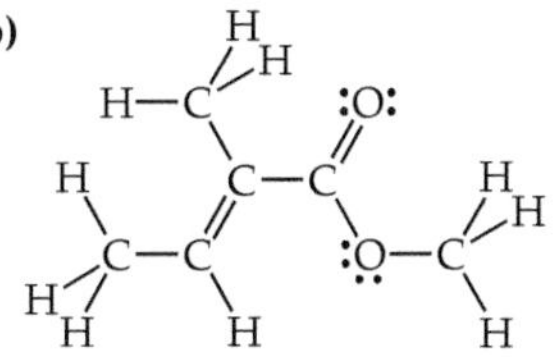

5.12 tetrahedral

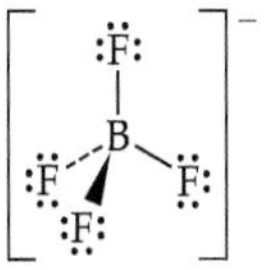

5.13 chloroform: tetrahedral; dichloroethylene: planar   **5.14** Both are tetrahedral.   **5.15** Both are bent.

5.16
(a) bent
(b) tetrahedral
(c) tetrahedral
(d) planar triangular
(e) pyramidal

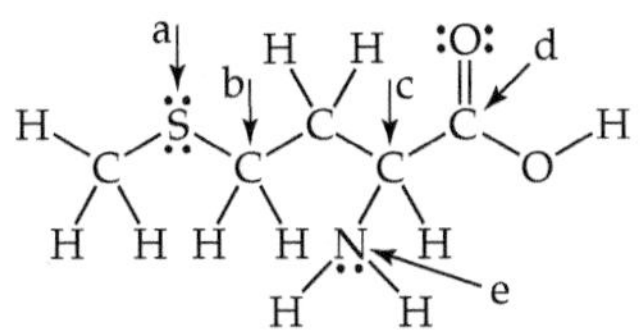

5.17 H < P < S < N < O   **5.18 (a)** polar covalent **(b)** ionic **(c)** covalent **(d)** polar covalent   **5.19 (a)** $^{\delta+}$S—F$^{\delta-}$ **(b)** $^{\delta+}$P—O$^{\delta-}$ **(c)** $^{\delta+}$As—Cl$^{\delta-}$

5.20

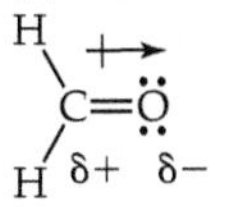

5.21 The carbons are tetrahedral; the oxygen is bent.

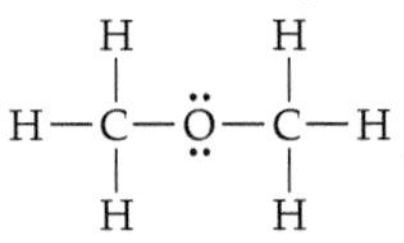

5.22

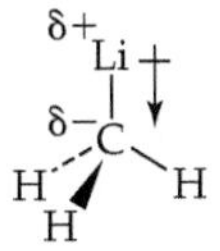

5.23 (a) disulfur dichloride **(b)** iodine chloride **(c)** iodine trichloride

5.24 (a) SeF$_4$ **(b)** P$_2$O$_5$ **(c)** BrF$_3$ **5.25** molecular solid   **5.26** AlCl$_3$ is a covalent compound, and Al$_2$O$_3$ is ionic   **5.27 (a)** ionic **(b)** covalent **5.28 (a)**   **5.29 (a)** tetrahedral **(b)** pyramidal **(c)** planar triangular **5.30 (c)** is square planar   **5.31 (a)** C$_8$H$_9$NO$_2$
(b)

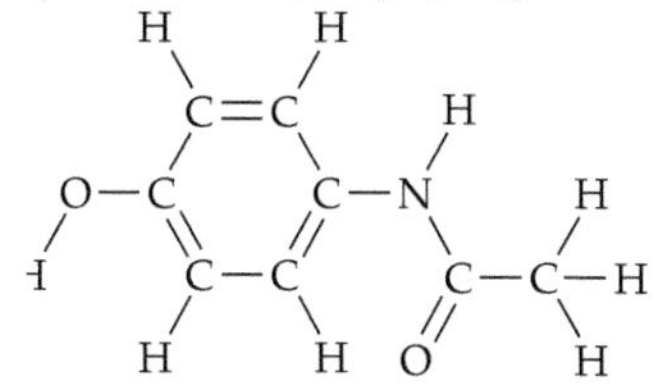

(c) All carbons are trigonal planar except the —CH$_3$ carbon. Nitrogen is pyramidal.   **5.32**

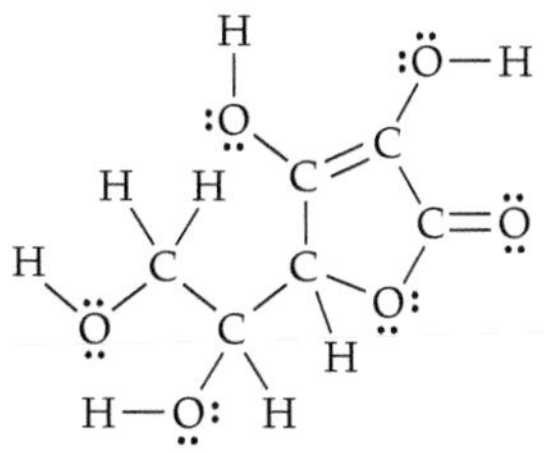

5.33 C$_{13}$H$_{10}$N$_2$O$_4$

5.34
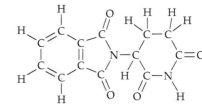
:O: ← electron-rich

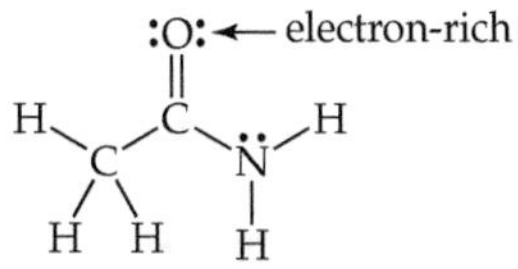

5.36 In a coordinate covalent bond, both electrons in the bond come from the same atom.   **5.38** covalent bonds: **(a) (b)**; ionic bonds: **(c) (d) (e)** **5.40** two covalent bonds   **5.42 (b), (c)**   **5.44** SnCl$_4$ **5.46** the N–O bond **5.48 (a)** A molecular formula shows the numbers and kinds of atoms; a structural formula shows how the atoms are bonded to one another. **(b)** A structural formula shows the bonds between atoms; a condensed structure shows atoms but not bonds.   **(c)** A lone pair of valence electrons is not shared in a bond; a shared pair of electrons is shared between two atoms.   **5.50 (a)** 10 **(b)** 10 **(c)** 24 **(d)** 20   **5.52** Too many hydrogens **5.54 (a)** **(b)** **(c)**

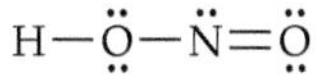

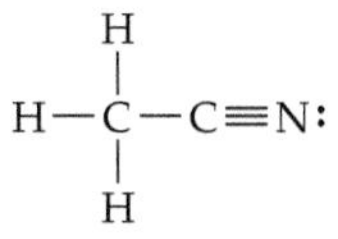

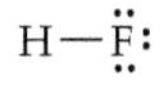

5.56 (a) CH$_3$CH$_2$CH$_3$ **(b)** H$_2$C=CHCH$_3$ **(c)** CH$_3$CH$_2$Cl **5.58** CH$_3$CO$_2$H
5.60
(a) **(b)** **(c)**

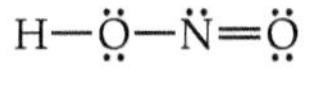

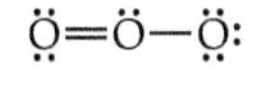

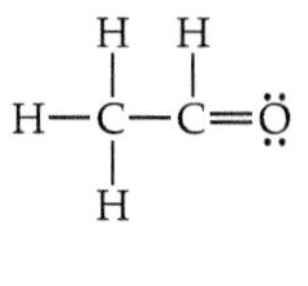

5.62 H—C—Ö—C—H   Dimethyl ether

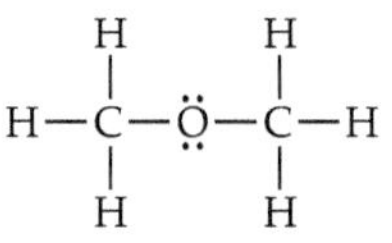

5.64 Tetrachloroethylene contains a double bond

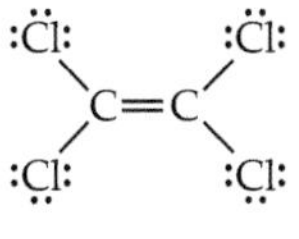

5.66

$$H-\overset{|}{\underset{H}{N}}-\overset{..}{O}-H$$

5.68 (a) $\left[H-\overset{:O:}{\underset{}{C}}-\overset{..}{O}:\right]^{-}$ (b) $\left[:\overset{:O:}{\underset{}{O}}-\overset{}{C}-\overset{..}{O}:\right]^{2-}$ (c) $\left[:\overset{..}{\underset{}{O}}-\overset{:O:}{\underset{}{S}}-\overset{..}{O}:\right]^{2-}$

(d) $\left[:\overset{..}{S}-C\equiv N:\right]^{-}$ (e) $\left[:\overset{..}{\underset{:O:}{O}}-\overset{:O:}{\underset{}{P}}-\overset{..}{O}:\right]^{3-}$ (f) $\left[:\overset{..}{O}-\overset{..}{\underset{..}{Cl}}-\overset{..}{O}:\right]^{-}$

5.70 tetrahedral; pyramidal; bent **5.72 (a), (b)** tetrahedral **(c), (d)** planar triangular **(e)** pyramidal **5.74** All are planar triangular, except for the $-CH_3$ carbon, which is tetrahedral. **5.76** It should have low electronegativity, like other alkali metals. **5.78** Cl > C > Cu > Ca > Cs

5.80
(a) $\overset{\delta-}{O}-\overset{\delta+}{Br}$ (b) $\overset{\delta-}{N}-\overset{\delta+}{H}$ (c) $\overset{\delta+}{P}-\overset{\delta-}{O}$

(d) nonpolar (e) $\overset{\delta-}{C}-\overset{\delta+}{Li}$

5.82 $PH_3 < HCl < H_2O < CF_4$

5.84 (a) $H-Cl$ (b) (c) (d) nonpolar

polar   polar   polar

5.86 S—H bonds are less polar because S is less electronegative than O.
5.88 (a) silicon tetrachloride **(b)** sodium hydride **(c)** antimony pentafluoride **(d)** osmium tetroxide **5.90 (a)** SeO_2 **(b)** XeO_4 **(c)** N_2S_5 **(d)** P_3Se_4
5.92 It relaxes arterial walls. **5.94** Carbohydrates, DNA, and proteins are all polymers that occur in nature. **5.96** no

5.98 (a)

(b) The C=O carbons are planar triangular; the other carbons are tetrahedral. **(c)** The C=O bonds are polar. **5.100 (a)** C forms 4 bonds **(b)** N forms 3 bonds **(c)** S forms 2 bonds **(d)** could be correct
5.102 (b) tetrahedral **(c)** contains a coordinate covalent bond **(d)** has 19 p and 18 e⁻

$$\left[H-\overset{H}{\underset{H}{P}}-H\right]^{+}$$

5.104 (a) calcium chloride **(b)** tellurium dichloride **(c)** boron trifluoride **(d)** magnesium sulfate **(e)** potassium oxide **(f)** iron(III) fluoride **(g)** phosphorus trifluoride
5.106   **5.108**

5.110 (a)   (b)

Chapter 6
6.1 (a) Solid cobalt(II) chloride plus gaseous hydrogen fluoride gives solid cobalt(II) fluoride plus gaseous hydrogen chloride. **(b)** Aqueous

lead(II) nitrate plus aqueous potassium iodide gives solid lead(II) iodide plus aqueous potassium nitrate. **6.2** balanced: **(a), (c) 6.3** $3 O_2 \rightarrow 2 O_3$
6.4 (a) $Ca(OH)_2 + 2 HCl \rightarrow CaCl_2 + 2 H_2O$ **(b)** $4 Al + 3 O_2 \rightarrow 2 Al_2O_3$
(c) $2 CH_3CH_3 + 7 O_2 \rightarrow 4 CO_2 + 6 H_2O$ **(d)** $2 AgNO_3 + MgCl_2 \rightarrow$
$2 AgCl + Mg(NO_3)_2$ **6.5** $2 A + B_2 \rightarrow A_2B_2$ **6.6 (a)** 206.0 amu
(b) 232.0 amu **6.7** 1.71×10^{21} molecules **6.8** 0.15 g **6.9** 111.0 amu
6.10 0.217 mol; 4.6 g **6.11** 5.00 g weighs more **6.12 (a)** $Ni + 2 HCl \rightarrow$
$NiCl_2 + H_2$; 4.90 mol **(b)** 6.00 mol **6.13** $6 CO_2 + 6 H_2O \rightarrow C_6H_{12}O_6 +$
$6 O_2$; 90.0 mol CO_2 **6.14 (a)** 39.6 mol **(b)** 13.8 g **6.15** 6.31 g WO_3;
0.165 g H_2 **6.16** 44.7 g; 57.0% **6.17** 49.3 g **6.18** A_2 **6.19 (a)** precipitation **(b)** redox **(c)** acid–base neutralization **6.20** Soluble: **(b), (d)**; insoluble: **(a), (c), (e) 6.21** precipitation: **(a), (b)**
6.22 (a) $2 CsOH(aq) + H_2SO_4(aq) \rightarrow Cs_2SO_4(aq) + 2 H_2O(l)$
(b) $Ca(OH)_2(aq) + 2 CH_3CO_2H(aq) \rightarrow Ca(CH_3CO_2)_2(aq) + 2 H_2O(l)$
(c) $NaHCO_3(aq) + HBr(aq) \rightarrow NaBr(aq) + CO_2(g) + H_2O(l)$
6.23 (a) oxidizing: Cu; reducing: Fe **(b)** oxidizing: Cl; reducing: Mg
(c) oxidizing: Cr_2O_3; reducing: Al **6.24** $2 K + Br_2 \rightarrow 2 KBr$; oxidizing: Br_2; reducing: K **6.25 (a)** V(III) **(b)** Sn(IV) **(c)** Cr(VI) **(d)** Cu(II) **(e)** Ni(II)
6.26 (a) not redox **(b)** Na oxidized from 0 to +1; H reduced from +1 to 0
(c) C oxidized from 0 to +4; O reduced from 0 to -2 **(d)** not redox
(e) S oxidized from +4 to +6; Mn reduced from +7 to +2
6.27 (a) $Zn(s) + Pb^{2+}(aq) \rightarrow Zn^{2+}(aq) + Pb(s)$
(b) $OH^-(aq) + H^+(aq) \rightarrow H_2O(l)$
(c) $2 Fe^{3+}(aq) + Sn^{2+}(aq) \rightarrow 2 Fe^{2+}(aq) + Sn^{4+}(aq)$
6.28 (d) 6.29 (c) 6.30 reactants: **(d)**; products: **(c)**
6.31 $C_5H_{11}NO_2S$; MW = 149.1 amu **6.32 (a)** $A_2 + 3 B \rightarrow 2 AB_3$
(b) 2 mol AB_3; 0.67 mol AB_3 **6.33 (a)** box 1 **(b)** box 2 **(c)** box 3
6.34 Ag_2CO_3 and $Ag_2Cr_2O_4$ are possible **6.35** 22 g, 31 g **6.36** In a balanced equation, the numbers and kinds of atoms are the same on both sides of the reaction arrow. **6.38 (a)** $SO_2(g) + H_2O(g) \rightarrow H_2SO_3(aq)$
(b) $2 K(s) + Br_2(l) \rightarrow 2 KBr(s)$
(c) $C_3H_8(g) + 5 O_2(g) \rightarrow 3 CO_2(g) + 4 H_2O(l)$
6.40 (a) $2 C_2H_6(g) + 7 O_2(g) \rightarrow 4 CO_2(g) + 6 H_2O(g)$
(b) balanced **(c)** $2 Mg(s) + O_2(g) \rightarrow 2 MgO(s)$
(d) $2 K(s) + 2 H_2O(l) \rightarrow 2 KOH(aq) + H_2(g)$
6.42 (a) $Hg(NO_3)_2(aq) + 2 LiI(aq) \rightarrow 2 LiNO_3(aq) + HgI_2(s)$
(b) $I_2(s) + 5 Cl_2(g) \rightarrow 2 ICl_5(s)$ **(c)** $4 Al(s) + 3 O_2(g) \rightarrow 2 Al_2O_3(s)$
(d) $CuSO_4(aq) + 2 AgNO_3(aq) \rightarrow Ag_2SO_4(s) + Cu(NO_3)_2(aq)$
(e) $2 Mn(NO_3)_3(aq) + 3 Na_2S(aq) \rightarrow Mn_2S_3(s) + 6 NaNO_3(aq)$
(f) $4 NO_2(g) + O_2(g) \rightarrow 2 N_2O_5(g)$
(g) $P_4O_{10}(s) + 6 H_2O(l) \rightarrow 4 H_3PO_4(aq)$
6.44 (a) $2 C_4H_{10}(g) + 13 O_2(g) \rightarrow 8 CO_2(g) + 10 H_2O(l)$
(b) $C_2H_6O(g) + 3 O_2(g) \rightarrow 2 CO_2(g) + 3 H_2O(l)$
(c) $2 C_8H_{18}(g) + 25 O_2(g) \rightarrow 16 CO_2(g) + 18 H_2O(l)$

6.46 molecular weight = sum of the weights of individual atoms in a molecule; formula weight = sum of weights of individual atoms in a formula unit; molar mass = mass in grams of 6.022×10^{23} molecules or formula units of any substance **6.48** 5.25 mol ions **6.50** 10.6 g uranium
6.52 (a) 1 mol **(b)** 1 mol **(c)** 2 mol **6.54** 6.44×10^{-4} mol **6.56** 284.5 g
6.58 (a) 0.0132 mol **(b)** 0.0536 mol **(c)** 0.0608 mol **(d)** 0.0129 mol
6.60 0.27 g; 9.0×10^{20} molecules **6.62** 1.4×10^{-3} mol; 0.18 g
6.64 (a) $C_4H_8O_2(l) + 2 H_2(g) \rightarrow 2 C_2H_6O(l)$ **(b)** 3.0 mol **(c)** 138 g **(d)** 12.5 g
(e) 0.55 g **6.66 (a)** $N_2(g) + 3 H_2(g) \rightarrow 2 NH_3(g)$ **(b)** 0.471 mol **(c)** 16.1 g
6.68 (a) $Fe_2O_3(s) + 3 CO(g) \rightarrow 2 Fe(s) + 3 CO_2(g)$ **(b)** 1.59 g **(c)** 141 g
6.70 158 kg **6.72 (a)** CO is limiting **(b)** 11.4 g **(c)** 83.8%
6.74 (a) $CH_4(g) + 2 Cl_2(g) \rightarrow CH_2Cl_2(l) + 2 HCl(g)$ **(b)** 444 g **(c)** 202 g
6.76 (a) redox **(b)** neutralization **(c)** precipitation **(d)** neutralization
6.78 (a) $Ba^{2+}(aq) + SO_4^{2-}(aq) \rightarrow BaSO_4(s)$
(b) $Zn(s) + 2 H^+(aq) \rightarrow Zn^{2+}(aq) + H_2(g)$ **6.80** $Ba(NO_3)_2$
6.82 (a) $2 NaBr(aq) + Hg_2(NO_3)_2(aq) \rightarrow Hg_2Br_2(s) + 2 NaNO_3(aq)$
(d) $(NH_4)_2CO_3(aq) + CaCl_2(aq) \rightarrow CaCO_3(s) + 2 NH_4Cl(aq)$
(e) $2 KOH(aq) + MnBr_2(aq) \rightarrow Mn(OH)_2(s) + 2 KBr(aq)$
(f) $3 Na_2S(aq) + 2 Al(NO_3)_3(aq) \rightarrow Al_2S_3(s) + 6 NaNO_3(aq)$
6.84 (a) $2 Au^{3+}(aq) + 3 Sn(s) \rightarrow 3 Sn^{2+}(aq) + 2 Au(s)$
(b) $2 I^-(aq) + Br_2(l) \rightarrow 2 Br^-(aq) + I_2(s)$
(c) $2 Ag^+(aq) + Fe(s) \rightarrow Fe^{2+}(aq) + 2 Ag(s)$
6.86 Most easily oxidized: metals on left side; most easily reduced: groups 6A and 7A **6.88** oxidation number increases: **(b), (c)** oxidation

number decreases (a), (d) **6.90** (a) Co: +3 (b) Fe: +2 (c) U: +6
(d) Cu: +2 (e) Ti: +4 (f) Sn: +2 **6.92** (a) oxidized: S; reduced: O (b) oxidized: Na; reduced: Cl (c) oxidized: Zn; reduced: Cu (d) oxidized: Cl; reduced: F **6.94** $FeSO_4$; 151.9 g/mol; 91.8 mg Fe **6.96** Zn is the reducing agent, and Mn^{2+} is the oxidizing agent. **6.98** 132 kg Li_2O; not a redox reaction **6.100** 6×10^{13} molecules
6.102 (a) $C_{12}H_{22}O_{11}(s) \rightarrow 12\ C(s) + 11\ H_2O(l)$ (b) 25.3 g C (c) 8.94 g H_2O
6.104 (a) 6.40 g (b) 104 g
6.106 (a) $Al(OH)_3(aq) + 3\ HNO_3(aq) \rightarrow Al(NO_3)_3(aq) + 3\ H_2O(l)$
(b) $3\ AgNO_3(aq) + FeCl_3(aq) \rightarrow 3\ AgCl(s) + Fe(NO_3)_3(aq)$
(c) $(NH_4)_2Cr_2O_7(s) \rightarrow Cr_2O_3(s) + 4\ H_2O(g) + N_2(g)$
(d) $Mn_2(CO_3)_3(s) \rightarrow Mn_2O_3(s) + 3\ CO_2(g)$
6.108 (a) $2\ SO_2(g) + O_2(g) \rightarrow 2\ SO_3(g)$
(b) $SO_3(g) + H_2O(g) \rightarrow H_2SO_4(l)$ (c) SO_2: +4; SO_3, H_2SO_4: +6

Chapter 7

7.1 (a) endothermic (b) $\Delta H = +678$ kcal
(c) $C_6H_{12}O_6(aq) + 6\ O_2(g) \rightarrow 6\ CO_2(g) + 6\ H_2O(l) + 678$ kcal
7.2 (a) endothermic (b) 200 kcal (c) 74.2 kcal **7.3** 91 kcal
7.4 (a) increase (b) increase (c) decrease **7.5** (a) no (b) increases (c) yes
7.6 (a) +0.06 kcal/mol; nonspontaneous (b) 0.00 kcal/mol; equilibrium
(c) −0.05 kcal/mol; spontaneous **7.7** (a) positive (b) spontaneous at all temperatures
7.8   **7.9**

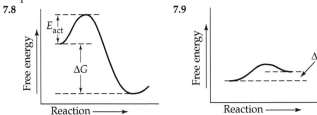

7.10 (a) rate increases (b) rate decreases (c) rate decreases

7.11 (a) $K = \dfrac{[NO_2]^2}{[N_2O_4]}$ (b) $K = \dfrac{[CH_3Cl][HCl]}{[CH_4][Cl_2]}$

(c) $K = \dfrac{[Br_2][F_2]^5}{[BrF_5]^2}$ **7.12** (a) products favored (b) reactants favored

(c) products favored **7.13** $K = 29.0$ **7.14** The reaction forming CD has larger K. **7.15** reaction favored by high pressure and low temperature
7.16 (a) favors reactants (b) favors product (c) favors product **7.17** ΔH is positive; ΔS is positive; ΔG is negative **7.18** ΔH is negative; ΔS is negative; ΔG is negative **7.19** (a) $2\ A_2 + B_2 \rightarrow 2\ A_2B$ (b) ΔH is negative; ΔS is negative; ΔG is negative **7.20** (a) blue curve represents faster reaction (b) red curve is spontaneous **7.21** red curve represents catalyzed reaction
7.22

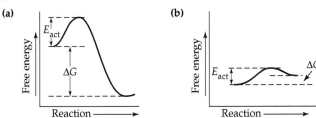

7.23 (a) positive (b) nonspontaneous at low temperature; spontaneous at high temperature **7.24** lower enthalpy for reactants
7.26 (a) positive (b) 43 kcal (c) 3.8 kcal
7.28 (a) $C_6H_{12}O_6 + 6\ O_2 \rightarrow 6\ CO_2 + 6\ H_2O$ (b) 1.0×10^3 kcal (c) 57 kcal
7.30 increased disorder: (a); decreased disorder: (b), (c)
7.32 A spontaneous process, once started, continues without external influence. **7.34** release or absorption of heat, and increase or decrease

in entropy **7.36** ΔH is usually larger than $T\Delta S$ **7.38** (a) endothermic (b) increases (c) $T\Delta S$ is larger than ΔH
7.40 (a) $H_2(g) + Br_2(l) \rightarrow 2\ HBr(g)$ (b) increases (c) yes, because ΔH is negative and ΔS is positive (d) $\Delta G = -25.6$ kcal/mol
7.42 the amount of energy needed for reactants to surmount the barrier to reaction
7.44

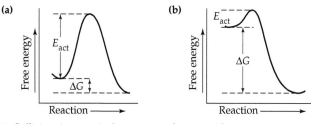

7.46 Collisions increase in frequency and occur with more energy.
7.48 A catalyst lowers the activation energy. **7.50** (a) yes (b) reaction rate is slow **7.52** At equilibrium, the rates of forward and reverse reactions are equal. Amounts of reactants and products need not be equal.

7.54 (a) $K = \dfrac{[CO_2]^2}{[CO]^2[O_2]}$ (b) $K = \dfrac{[HCl]^2[C_2H_4Cl_2]}{[Cl_2]^2[C_2H_6]}$

(c) $K = \dfrac{[H_3O^+][F^-]}{[HF][H_2O]}$ (d) $K = \dfrac{[O_3]^2}{[O_2]^3}$ **7.56** $K = 7.2 \times 10^{-3}$

7.58 (a) 0.087 mol/L (b) 0.023 mol/L **7.60** more reactant
7.62 (a) endothermic (b) reactants are favored (c) (1) favors ozone; (2) favors ozone; (3) favors O_2; (4) no effect; (5) favors ozone
7.64 (a) decrease (b) no effect (c) increase **7.66** increase
7.68 (a) increase (b) decrease (c) no effect (d) decrease **7.70** fat
7.72 thyroid, hypothalamus **7.74** conversion of N_2 into chemically useful compounds; microorganisms and lightning
7.76 (a) $2\ C_2H_3OH(l) + 3\ O_2(g) \rightarrow 2\ CO_2(g) + 2\ H_2O(g)$
(b) negative (c) 35.5 kcal (d) 5.63 g (e) 5.60 kcal/mL
7.78 (a) $Fe_3O_4(s) + 4\ H_2(g) \rightarrow 3\ Fe(s) + 4\ H_2O(g)$ $\Delta H = +36$ kcal/mol
(b) 12 kcal (c) 3.6 g H_2 (d) reactants **7.80** 450 g
7.82 (a) $4\ NH_3(g) + 5\ O_2(g) \rightarrow 4\ NO(g) + 6\ H_2O(g) + $ heat

(b) $K = \dfrac{[NO]^4[H_2O]^6}{[NH_3]^4[O_2]^5}$ (c) (1) favors reactants (2) favors reactants

(3) favors reactants (4) favors products **7.84** (a) exergonic
(b) $\Delta G = -10$ kcal/mol **7.86** 1.91 kcal; exothermic

Chapter 8

8.1 (a) disfavored by ΔH; favored by ΔS (b) +0.02 kcal/mol
(c) $\Delta H = -9.72$ kcal/mol; $\Delta S = -26.1$ cal/(mol·K) **8.2** 0.29 atm; 4.3 psi; 29,000 Pa **8.3** 1000 mmHg **8.4** 450 L **8.5** 1.3 atm, 64 atm
8.6 0.27 L; 0.88 L **8.7** 33 psi **8.8** 352 L **8.9** balloon (a)
8.10 4460 mol; 7.14×10^4 g CH_4; 1.96×10^5 g CO_2
8.11 5.0 atm **8.12** 1,100 mol; 4,400 g
8.13 (a)   (b)

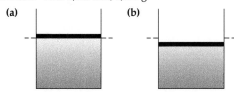

8.14 9.3 atm He; 0.19 atm O_2 **8.15** 75.4% N_2, 13.2% O_2, 5.3% CO_2, 6.2% H_2O **8.16** 35.0 mmHg **8.17** (c) **8.18** (a) decrease (b) increase
8.19 (a), (c) **8.20** (a) London forces (b) hydrogen bonds, dipole–dipole forces, London forces (c) dipole–dipole forces, London forces
8.21 1.93 kcal, 14.3 kcal

8.22

(a) 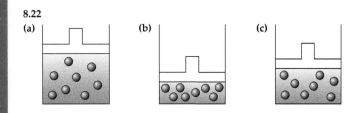 (b) (c)

(a) volume increases by 50% (b) volume decreases by 50% (c) volume unchanged **8.23 (c)**   **8.24 (c)**

8.25

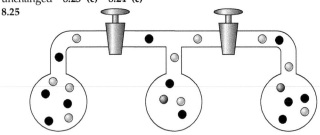

8.26

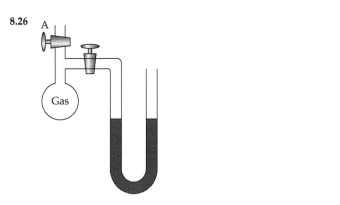

8.27 (a) 10 °C **(b)** 75 °C **(c)** 1.3 kcal/mol **(d)** 7.5 kcal/mol

8.28 (a) (b) (c)

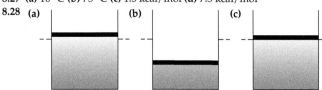

8.29 red = 300 mmHg; yellow = 100 mmHg; green = 200 mmHg
8.30 One atmosphere is equal to exactly 760 mmHg.   **8.32** (1) A gas consists of tiny particles moving at random with no forces between them. (2) The amount of space occupied by the gas particles is small. (3) The average kinetic energy of the gas particles is proportional to the Kelvin temperature. (4) Collisions between particles are elastic.
8.34 (a) 760 mmHg **(b)** 1310 mmHg **(c)** 5.7×10^3 mmHg **(d)** 711 mmHg **(e)** 0.314 mmHg   **8.36** 930 mmHg   **8.38** V varies inversely with P when n and T are constant.   **8.40** 101 mL   **8.42** 1.75 L   **8.44** V varies directly with T when n and P are constant.   **8.46** 364 K = 91 °C
8.48 220 mL   **8.50** P varies directly with T when n and V are constant.   **8.52** 1.2 atm   **8.54** 493 K = 220 °C   **8.56** 68.4 mL   **8.58 (a)** P increases by factor of 4 **(b)** P decreases by factor of 4   **8.60** 484 mL   **8.62** Because gas particles are so far apart and have no interactions, their chemical identity does not matter.   **8.64** 22.4 L   **8.66** the same number of molecules; the O_2 sample weighs more   **8.68** 11.8 g   **8.70** 15 kg   **8.72** $PV = nRT$
8.74 Cl_2 has fewer molecules but weighs more   **8.76** 370 atm $(3.7 \times 10^2$ atm)
8.78 2.2×10^4 mmHg   **8.80** 22.3 L   **8.82** the pressure contribution of one component in a mixture of gases   **8.84** 93 mmHg   **8.86** the partial pressure of the vapor above the liquid   **8.88** Increased pressure raises a liquid's boiling point; decreased pressure lowers it.   **8.90 (a)** all molecules **(b)** molecules with polar covalent bonds **(c)** molecules with —OH or —NH bonds   **8.92** Ethanol forms hydrogen bonds.   **8.94 (a)** 29.2 kcal **(b)** 173 kcal   **8.96** Atoms in a crystalline solid have a regular, orderly

arrangement.   **8.98** 4.82 kcal   **8.100** Systolic pressure is the maximum pressure just after contraction; diastolic pressure is the minimum pressure at the end of the heart cycle.   **8.102** Increase in atmospheric $[CO_2]$; increase in global temperatures   **8.104** The supercritical state is intermediate in properties between liquid and gas.   **8.106** As temperature increases, molecular collisions become more violent.   **8.108** 0.13 mol; 4.0 L   **8.110** 590 g/day   **8.112** 0.92 g/L; less dense than air at STP
8.114 (a) 0.714 g/L **(b)** 1.96 g/L **(c)** 1.43 g/L
8.116 (a) (b)

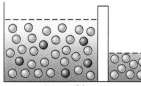

(c) Ethylene glycol forms hydrogen bonds.
8.118 (a) 492 °R **(b)** $R = 0.0455$ (L · atm)/(mol · °R)

Chapter 9
9.1 (a) heterogeneous mixture **(b)** homogeneous solution
(c) homogeneous colloid **(d)** homogeneous solution   **9.2 (c), (d)**
9.3 $Na_2SO_4 \cdot 10H_2O$ **9.4** 322 g   **9.5** 80 g/100 mL   **9.6** 5.6 g/100 mL
9.7 6.8×10^{-5} g/100 mL   **9.8** 0.925 M   **9.9 (a)** 0.061 mol **(b)** 0.67 mol
9.10 0.48 g   **9.11** 0.39 g   **9.12** 0.0086% (w/v)   **9.13** 6.6% (w/v)
9.14 (a) 20 g **(b)** 1.2 g   **9.15** Place 38 mL acetic acid in flask and dilute to 500.0 mL.   **9.16 (a)** 22 mL **(b)** 18 mL   **9.17** 1.6 ppm   **9.18** Pb: 0.015 ppm, 0.0015 mg; Cu: 1.3 ppm, 0.13 mg   **9.19** 2.40 M   **9.20** 39.1 mL
9.21 750 L   **9.22 (a)** 39.1 g; 39.1 mg **(b)** 79.9 g; 79.9 mg **(c)** 12.2 g; 12.2 mg
(d) 48.0 g; 48.0 mg **(e)** 9.0 g; 9.0 mg **(f)** 31.7 g; 31.7 mg   **9.23** 9.0 mg
9.24 102.0 °C   **9.25** weak electrolyte   **9.26 (a)** red curve is pure solvent; green curve is solution **(b)** solvent bp = 62 °C; solution bp = 69 °C **(c)** 2 M
9.27 –1.9 °C   **9.28** 3 ions/mol   **9.29 (a)** 0.70 osmol **(b)** 0.30 osmol
9.30 0.33 osmol
9.31

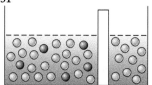

| Before equilibrium | At equilibrium |

9.32 HCl completely dissociates into ions; acetic acid dissociates only slightly.   **9.33** HBr is completely dissociated; HF is not.   **9.34** Upper red line: liquid; lower green line: gas   **9.35 (a)**   **9.36 (d)**   **9.37** green curve is solution; red curve is solvent   **9.38** homogeneous: mixing is uniform; heterogeneous: mixing is nonuniform   **9.40** polarity   **9.42 (b), (d)**
9.44 15.3 g/100 mL   **9.46** Concentrated solutions can be saturated or not; saturated solutions can be concentrated or not.   **9.48** Molarity is the number of moles of solute per liter of solution.   **9.50** Dissolve 45.0 mL of ethyl alcohol in water and dilute to 750.0 mL   **9.52** Dissolve 1.5 g NaCl in water to a final volume of 250 mL.   **9.54 (a)** 7.7% (w/v) **(b)** 3.9% (w/v)   **9.56 (a)** 4.0 g **(b)** 15 g   **9.58** 230 mL, 1600 mL   **9.60** 10 ppm
9.62 (a) 0.425 M   **(b)** 1.53 M   **(c)** 1.03 M   **9.64** 5.3 mL   **9.66** 37 g
9.68 400 mL   **9.70** 0.53 L   **9.72** 600 mL   **9.74** a substance that conducts electricity when dissolved in water   **9.76** Ca^{2+} concentration is 0.0015 M   **9.78** 40 mEq   **9.80** 0.28 L   **9.82** $Ba(OH)_2$ **9.84** 861 g
9.86 The inside of the cell has higher osmolarity than water, so water passes in and increases pressure.   **9.88 (a)** 0.20 M Na_2SO_4 **(b)** 3% (w/v) NaOH   **9.90** 2.4 osmol   **9.92** The body manufactures more hemoglobin.   **9.94** Sports drinks contain electrolytes, carbohydrate, and vitamins.   **9.96 (a)** 6.84 mmHg **(b)** 1.9 g/100 mL   **9.98 (a)** 0.0067% (w/v)
(b) 67 ppm **(c)** 0.000 40 M   **9.100** 9.4 mL   **9.102** NaCl: 0.147 M; KCl: 0.0040 M; $CaCl_2$: 0.0030 M   **9.104** 0.00020 % (w/v)   **9.106** 4.0 mL
9.108 (a) $CoCl_2 + 6 H_2O \rightarrow CoCl_2 \cdot 6H_2O$ **(b)** 1.13 g   **9.110 (a)** 1.36 mol particles **(b)** 2.53 °C

Chapter 10
10.1 (a), (b)   **10.2 (a), (c)**   **10.3 (a)** H_2S **(b)** HPO_4^{2-} **(c)** HCO_3^- **(d)** NH_3
10.4 acids: HF, H_2S; bases: HS^-, F^-; conjugate acid–base pairs: H_2S and

HS⁻, HF and F⁻ **10.5 (a)** base **(b)** acid **(c)** base **10.6 (a)** NH_4^+ **(b)** H_2SO_4 **(c)** H_2CO_3 **10.7 (a)** F⁻ **(b)** OH⁻ **10.8** $HPO_4^{2-} + OH^- \rightleftharpoons$ $PO_4^{3-} + H_2O$; favored in forward direction **10.9** The $-NH_3^+$ hydrogens are most acidic **10.10** citric acid **10.11 (a)** acidic, [OH⁻] = 3.1×10^{-10} M **(b)** basic, [OH⁻] = 3.2×10^{-3} M **10.12** pH = 5 has higher [H⁺]; pH 9 has higher [OH⁻] **10.13 (a)** 5 **(b)** 5 **10.14 (a)** 1×10^{-13} M **(b)** 1×10^{-3} M **(c)** 1×10^{-8} M; **(b)** is most acidic; **(a)** is most basic **10.15** pH = 4 **10.16 (a)** acidic, 3×10^{-7} M **(b)** most basic, 1×10^{-8} M **(c)** acidic 2×10^{-4} M **(d)** most acidic, 3×10^{-4} M **10.17 (a)** 8.28 **(b)** 5.05 **10.18** 2.60 **10.19** 3.38 **10.20** 9.45 **10.21** 9.13 **10.22 (a)** 0.079 Eq **(b)** 0.338 Eq **(c)** 0.14 Eq **10.23 (a)** 0.26 N **(b)** 1.13 N **(c)** 0.47 N

10.24 $Al(OH)_3 + 3 HCl \rightarrow AlCl_3 + 3 H_2O$; $Mg(OH)_2 + 2 HCl \rightarrow MgCl_2 + 2 H_2O$ **10.25 (a)** $2 KHCO_3 + H_2SO_4 \rightarrow 2 H_2O + 2 CO_2 + K_2SO_4$ **(b)** $MgCO_3 + 2 HNO_3 \rightarrow H_2O + CO_2 + Mg(NO_3)_2$ **10.26** $H_2SO_4 + 2 NH_3 \rightarrow (NH_4)_2SO_4$ **10.27** $CH_3CH_2NH_2 + HCl \rightarrow CH_3CH_2NH_3^+ Cl^-$ **10.28** 0.730 M **10.29** 133 mL **10.30** 0.225 M **10.31 (a)** neutral **(b)** basic **(c)** basic **(d)** acidic

10.32 (a)

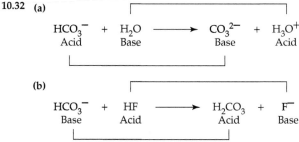

$$HCO_3^- + H_2O \longrightarrow CO_3^{2-} + H_3O^+$$

Acid   Base   Base   Acid

(b)

$$HCO_3^- + HF \longrightarrow H_2CO_3 + F^-$$

Base   Acid   Acid   Base

10.33 (a) box 2 **(b)** box 3 **(c)** box 1 **10.34** The O—H hydrogen in each is most acidic; acetic acid **10.35 (a)** box 1 **(b)** box 2 **(c)** box 1 **10.36 (a)** box 3 **(b)** box 1 **10.37** 0.67 M **10.38** HBr dissociates into ions **10.40** KOH dissociates into ions **10.42** A monoprotic acid can donate one proton; a diprotic acid can donate two. **10.44 (a), (e) 10.46 (a)** acid **(b)** base **(c)** neither **(d)** acid **(e)** neither **(f)** acid **10.48 (a)** CH_2ClCO_2H **(b)** $C_5H_5NH^+$ **(c)** $HSeO_4^-$ **(d)** $(CH_3)_3NH^+$ **10.50 (a)** $HCO_3^- + HCl \rightarrow H_2O + CO_2 + Cl^-$; $HCO_3^- + NaOH \rightarrow H_2O + Na^+ + CO_3^{2-}$ **(b)** $H_2PO_4^- + HCl \rightarrow H_3PO_4 + Cl^-$; $H_2PO_4^- + NaOH \rightarrow H_2O + Na^+ + HPO_4^{2-}$ **10.52** $2 HCl + CaCO_3 \rightarrow H_2O + CO_2 + CaCl_2$

10.54 $K_a = \dfrac{[H_3O^+][A^-]}{[HA]}$

10.56 $K_w = [H_3O^+][OH^-] = 1.0 \times 10^{-14}$
10.58 CH_3CO_2H is a weak acid and is only partially dissociated.

10.60
$$K_a = \frac{[H_2PO_4^{2-}][H_3O^+]}{[H_3PO_4]} \quad K_a = \frac{[HPO_4^{2-}][H_3O^+]}{[H_2PO_4^-]} \quad K_a = \frac{[PO_4^{3-}][H_3O^+]}{[HPO_4^{2-}]}$$

10.62 (a) OH⁻ **(b)** NO_2^- **(c)** OH⁻ **(d)** CN⁻ **(e)** HPO_4^{2-} **10.64** basic; 1.3×10^{-8} **10.66** 1×10^{-2} M **10.68** 1.0; 13.0 **10.70 (a)** 7.60 **(b)** 3.30 **(c)** 11.64 **10.72 (a)** 1×10^{-4} M; 1×10^{-10} M; **(b)** 1×10^{-11} M; 1×10^{-3} M **(c)** 1 M; 1×10^{-14} M **(d)** 4.2×10^{-2} M; 2.4×10^{-13} M **(e)** 1.1×10^{-8} M; 9.1×10^{-7} M **10.74** A buffer contains a weak acid and its anion. The acid neutralizes any added base, and the anion neutralizes any added acid.

10.76 (a) $pH = pK_a + \log\dfrac{[CH_3CO_2^-]}{[CH_3CO_2H]} = 4.74 + \log\dfrac{[0.100]}{[0.100]} = 4.74$

(b) $CH_3CO_2^- Na^+ + H^+ \rightarrow CH_3CO_2H + Na^+$; $CH_3CO_2H + OH^- \rightarrow CH_3CO_2^- + H_2O$ **10.78** 9.19 **10.80** 9.07 **10.82** An equivalent is the formula weight in grams divided by the number of H_3O^+ or OH⁻ ions produced. **10.84** 63.0 g; 32.7 g; 56.1 g; 29.3 g **10.86** 25 mL; 25 mL **10.88 (a)** 0.50 Eq **(b)** 0.084 Eq **(c)** 0.25 Eq **10.90** 0.13 M; 0.26 N **10.92** 0.22 M **10.94** 0.075 M **10.96 (a)** pH = 2 to 3 **(b)** $NaHCO_3 + HCl \rightarrow CO_2 + H_2O + NaCl^+$ **(c)** 20 mg

10.98 Intravenous bicarbonate neutralizes the hydrogen ions in the blood and restores pH. **10.100** 2×10^{-6} M **10.102** Citric acid reacts with sodium bicarbonate to release CO_2. **10.104** Both have the same amount of acid; HCl has higher [H_3O^+] and lower pH. **10.106** 0.35 M **10.108 (a)** NH_4^+, acid; OH⁻, base; NH_3, conjugate base; H_2O, conjugate acid **(b)** 5.56 g **10.110 (a)** $Na_2O(aq) + H_2O(l) \rightarrow 2 NaOH(aq)$ **(b)** 13.0 **(c)** 5000 mL

Chapter 11

11.1 $^{218}_{84}Po$ **11.2** $^{226}_{88}Ra$ **11.3** $^{14}_{6}C \rightarrow ^{0}_{-1}e + ^{14}_{7}N$ **11.4 (a)** $^{3}_{1}H \rightarrow ^{0}_{-1}e + ^{3}_{2}He$ **(b)** $^{210}_{82}Pb \rightarrow ^{0}_{-1}e + ^{210}_{83}Bi$ **(c)** $^{20}_{9}F \rightarrow ^{0}_{-1}e + ^{20}_{10}Ne$ **11.5 (a)** $^{38}_{20}Ca \rightarrow ^{0}_{1}e + ^{38}_{19}K$ **(b)** $^{118}_{54}Xe \rightarrow ^{0}_{1}e + ^{118}_{53}I$ **(c)** $^{79}_{37}Rb \rightarrow ^{0}_{1}e + ^{79}_{36}Kr$ **11.6 (a)** $^{62}_{30}Zn \rightarrow ^{0}_{-1}e + ^{62}_{29}Cu$ **(b)** $^{110}_{50}Sn + ^{0}_{-1}e \rightarrow ^{110}_{49}In$ **(c)** $^{81}_{36}Kr + ^{0}_{-1}e \rightarrow ^{81}_{35}Br$ **11.7** $^{120}_{49}In \rightarrow ^{0}_{-1}e + ^{120}_{50}Sn$ **11.8** 12% **11.9** 3 days **11.10** 13 m **11.11** 2% **11.12** 4.0 mL **11.13** $^{237}_{93}Np$ **11.14** $^{241}_{95}Am + ^{4}_{2}He \rightarrow 2 ^{1}_{0}n + ^{243}_{97}Bk$ **11.15** $^{40}_{18}Ar + ^{1}_{1}H \rightarrow ^{1}_{0}n + ^{40}_{19}K$ **11.16** $^{235}_{92}U + ^{1}_{0}n \rightarrow 2 ^{1}_{0}n + ^{137}_{52}Te + ^{97}_{40}Zr$ **11.17** 2 half-lives **11.18** $^{28}_{12}Mg \rightarrow ^{0}_{-1}e + ^{28}_{13}Al$ **11.19**

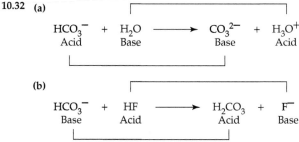

○ Aluminum—28
○ Magnesium—28

11.20 $^{14}_{6}C$ **11.21** The shorter arrows represent β emission; longer arrows represent α emission. **11.22** $^{241}_{94}Pu \rightarrow ^{241}_{95}Am \rightarrow ^{237}_{93}Np \rightarrow ^{233}_{91}Pa \rightarrow ^{233}_{92}U$ **11.23** $^{148}_{69}Tm \rightarrow ^{0}_{1}e + ^{148}_{68}Er$ or $^{148}_{69}Tm + ^{0}_{-1}e \rightarrow ^{148}_{68}Er$ **11.24** 3.5 years **11.25** The curve doesn't represent nuclear decay. **11.26** It emits radiation. **11.28** A nuclear reaction changes the identity of the atoms, is unaffected by temperature or catalysts, and often releases a large amount of energy. A chemical reaction does not change the identity of the atoms, is affected by temperature and catalysts, and involves relatively small energy changes. **11.30** $^{4}_{2}He$ **11.32** Gamma is highest and alpha is lowest. **11.34** by breaking bonds in DNA **11.36** A neutron decays to a proton and an electron. **11.38** The number of nucleons and the number of charges is the same on both sides. **11.40** α emission: Z decreases by 2 and A decreases by 4; β emission: Z increases by 1 and A is unchanged **11.42** In fission, a nucleus fragments to smaller pieces. **11.44 (a)** $^{35}_{17}Cl$ **(b)** $^{24}_{11}Na$ **(c)** $^{90}_{39}Y$ **11.46 (a)** $^{109}_{47}Ag$ **(b)** $^{10}_{5}B$ **11.48 (a)** $4 ^{1}_{0}n$ **(b)** $^{146}_{57}La$ **11.50** $^{198}_{80}Hg + ^{1}_{0}n \rightarrow ^{198}_{79}Au + ^{1}_{1}H$; a proton **11.52** $^{228}_{90}Th$ **11.54** Half of a sample decays in that time. **11.56** 0.006 g **11.58** 1 ng; 2×10^{-3} ng **11.60** The inside walls of a Geiger counter tube are negatively charged, and a wire in the center is positively charged. Radiation ionizes argon gas inside the tube, which creates a conducting path for current between the wall and the wire. **11.62** In a scintillation counter, a phosphor emits a flash of light when struck by radiation, and the flashes are counted. **11.64** more than 25 rems **11.66** 1.9 mL **11.68** 1.9 rem **11.70** *in vivo* procedures, therapeutic procedures, boron neutron capture **11.72** Irradiation kills harmful microorganisms by destroying their DNA. **11.74** They yield more data, including three-dimensional images. **11.76** Only living organisms incorporate C-14. After death, the ratio of C-14/C-12 decreases, and the ratio can be measured to determine age. **11.78** Nuclear decay is an intrinsic property of a nucleus and is not affected by external conditions. **11.80 (a)** β emission **(b)** Mo-98 **11.82 (a)** $^{238}_{94}Pu \rightarrow ^{4}_{2}He + ^{234}_{92}U$ **(b)** for radiation shielding **11.84** Their cells divide rapidly. **11.86** advantages: few harmful byproducts, fuel is inexpensive; disadvantage: needs a high temperature **11.88 (a)** $^{253}_{99}Es + ^{4}_{2}He \rightarrow ^{256}_{101}Md + ^{1}_{0}n$ **(b)** $^{250}_{98}Cf + ^{11}_{5}B \rightarrow ^{257}_{103}Lr + 4 ^{1}_{0}n$ **11.90** $^{10}_{5}B + ^{1}_{0}n \rightarrow ^{7}_{3}Li + ^{4}_{2}He$ **11.92** $^{238}_{92}U + 3 ^{4}_{2}He \rightarrow ^{246}_{98}Cf + 4 ^{1}_{0}n$

Chapter 12

12.1 (a) alcohol, carboxylic acid **(b)** double bond, ester **(c)** aromatic ring, amine, carboxylic acid **12.2 (a)** CH_3CHO **(b)** $CH_3CH_2CO_2H$ **12.3** $CH_3CH_2CH_2CH_2CH_2CH_2CH_3$

12.4

$$CH_3CH_2CH_2CH_2\overset{\overset{\displaystyle CH_3}{|}}{C}HCH_3 \qquad CH_3CH_2CH_2\overset{\overset{\displaystyle CH_3}{|}}{C}HCH_2CH_3$$

$$CH_3CH_2CH_2\overset{\overset{\displaystyle CH_3}{|}}{\underset{\underset{\displaystyle CH_3}{|}}{C}}CH_3 \qquad CH_3CH_2\overset{\overset{\displaystyle CH_3}{|}}{\underset{\underset{\displaystyle CH_3}{|}}{C}}HCHCH_3 \qquad CH_3CH_2\overset{\overset{\displaystyle CH_3}{|}}{\underset{\underset{\displaystyle CH_3}{|}}{C}}CH_2CH_3$$

$$CH_3\overset{\overset{\displaystyle CH_3}{|}}{C}HCH_2\overset{\overset{\displaystyle CH_3}{|}}{C}HCH_3 \qquad CH_3CH_2\overset{\overset{\displaystyle CH_2CH_3}{|}}{C}HCH_2CH_3 \qquad CH_3\overset{\overset{\displaystyle H_3C}{|}}{\underset{\underset{\displaystyle H_3C}{|}}{C}}{-}\overset{\overset{\displaystyle CH_3}{|}}{C}HCH_3$$

12.5 **(a)**

$$CH_3CH_2CH_2CH_2CH_3$$

Pentane

(b)

$$CH_3\overset{\overset{\displaystyle CH_3}{|}}{C}HCH_2CH_3$$

2-Methylbutane

(c)

$$CH_3\overset{\overset{\displaystyle CH_3}{|}}{\underset{\underset{\displaystyle CH_3}{|}}{C}}CH_3$$

2,2-Dimethylpropane

12.6 (a) **(b)** **(c)**

12.7 (a)

$$CH_3CH_2\overset{\overset{\displaystyle H_3C}{|}}{\underset{\underset{\displaystyle CH_2CHCH_3}{|}}{C}}{-}\overset{\overset{\displaystyle Cl}{|}}{C}HCH_2CH_3 \\ \qquad\qquad \underset{\underset{\displaystyle CH_3}{|}}{}$$

(b)

$$CH_3\overset{\overset{\displaystyle H_3C\;\;CH_3}{\diagdown\diagup}}{C}{-}\overset{\overset{\displaystyle }{|}}{\underset{\underset{\displaystyle CH_2CH_3}{|}}{C}}H{-}\overset{\overset{\displaystyle H_3C\;\;CH_3}{\diagdown\diagup}}{C}CH_3$$

12.8 Structures **(a)** and **(c)** are identical, and are isomers of **(b)**.

12.9

$$CH_3CH_2CH_2CH_2CH_2CH_2CH_2CH_3 \qquad CH_3CH_2CH_2CH_2CH_2\overset{\overset{\displaystyle CH_3}{|}}{C}HCH_3 \qquad CH_3CH_2CH_2CH_2\overset{\overset{\displaystyle CH_3}{|}}{C}HCH_2CH_3 \qquad CH_3CH_2CH_2\overset{\overset{\displaystyle CH_3}{|}}{C}HCH_2CH_2CH_3$$

$$CH_3CH_2CH_2CH_2\overset{\overset{\displaystyle CH_3}{|}}{\underset{\underset{\displaystyle CH_3}{|}}{C}}CH_3 \qquad CH_3CH_2CH_2\overset{\overset{\displaystyle CH_3}{|}}{\underset{\underset{\displaystyle CH_3}{|}}{C}}HCHCH_3 \qquad CH_3CH_2\overset{\overset{\displaystyle CH_3}{|}}{C}HCH_2\overset{\overset{\displaystyle CH_3}{|}}{C}HCH_3 \qquad CH_3\overset{\overset{\displaystyle CH_3}{|}}{C}HCH_2CH_2\overset{\overset{\displaystyle CH_3}{|}}{C}HCH_3$$

$$CH_3CH_2CH_2\overset{\overset{\displaystyle CH_3}{|}}{\underset{\underset{\displaystyle CH_3}{|}}{C}}CH_2CH_3 \qquad CH_3\overset{\overset{\displaystyle CH_3\;\;CH_3}{|\quad|}}{C}{-}\overset{}{\underset{\underset{\displaystyle CH_3\;\;CH_3}{|\quad|}}{C}}CH_3 \qquad CH_3CH_2\overset{\overset{\displaystyle CH_3}{|}}{C}HCHCH_2CH_3 \\ \qquad\qquad\qquad\qquad\qquad\qquad\qquad\qquad\qquad\qquad\qquad\qquad \underset{\underset{\displaystyle CH_3}{|}}{}$$

$$CH_3CH_2CH_2\overset{\overset{\displaystyle CH_2CH_3}{|}}{C}HCH_2CH_3 \qquad CH_3CH_2\overset{\overset{\displaystyle CH_3}{|}}{\underset{\underset{\displaystyle H_3C\;\;CH_3}{|}}{C}}HCCH_3$$

$$CH_3\overset{\overset{\displaystyle CH_3\;\;CH_3}{|\quad|}}{C}HCH_2\overset{}{C}CH_3 \qquad CH_3CH_2\overset{\overset{\displaystyle CH_3\;\;CH_3}{|\quad|}}{C}{-}CHCH_3 \qquad CH_3\overset{\overset{\displaystyle CH_3\;\;CH_3}{|\quad|}}{C}HCHCHCH_3 \qquad CH_3CH_2\overset{\overset{\displaystyle CH_2CH_3}{|}}{C}HCHCH_3 \qquad CH_3CH_2\overset{\overset{\displaystyle CH_2CH_3}{|}}{\underset{\underset{\displaystyle CH_3}{|}}{C}}CH_2CH_3$$

12.10 (a) 2,6-dimethyloctane **(b)** 3,3-diethylheptane

12.11 (a)

$$\underset{p}{CH_3}\underset{s}{CH_2}\underset{s}{CH_2}\overset{\overset{\displaystyle P\,CH_3}{|}}{\underset{t}{C}}H\underset{s}{CH_2}\underset{p}{CH_3}$$

(b)

$$\underset{p}{CH_3}\underset{s}{CH_2}\underset{s}{CH_2}\underset{s}{CH_2}\overset{\overset{\displaystyle P\,CH_3}{|}}{\underset{t}{C}}H\underset{s}{CH}\underset{s}{CH_2}\underset{p}{CH_3} \\ \qquad\qquad\qquad \underset{\underset{\displaystyle P\,CH_3}{|}}{}$$

(c)

$$\underset{p}{CH_3}\overset{\overset{\displaystyle P\,CH_3}{|}}{\underset{t}{C}}H\underset{s}{CH_2}\overset{\overset{\displaystyle P\,CH_3}{|}}{\underset{q}{C}}\underset{}{CH_3} \\ \qquad\qquad\qquad \underset{\underset{\displaystyle P\,CH_3}{|}}{}$$

12.12 There are many possible answers; for example:

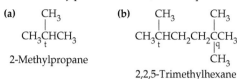

(a) CH₃CHCH₃ with CH₃ group
2-Methylpropane

(b) CH₃CHCH₂CH₂CCH₃ with CH₃ groups
2,2,5-Trimethylhexane

12.13 **(a)** 2,2-dimethylpentane **(b)** 2,3,3-trimethylpentane
12.14 2 C₂H₆ + 7 O₂ → 4 CO₂ + 6 H₂O
12.15

CH₃CH₂CH₂Cl + CH₃CHCH₃ (Cl) + CH₃CCH₃ (Cl, Cl) +

CH₃CH₂CHCl₂ + CH₃CHCH₂Cl (Cl) + CH₂CH₂CH₂ (Cl, Cl)

12.16 **(a)** 1-ethyl-4-methylcyclohexane **(b)** 1-ethyl-3-isopropylcyclopentane
12.17 **(a)** cyclohexane with CH₂CH₃, CH₂CH₃ groups **(b)** seven-membered ring with CH₃, H₃C, CH₃ groups

12.18 propylcyclohexane
12.19 **(a)** 12 hydrogens **(b)** 10 hydrogens **(c)** 8 hydrogens
12.20 **(a)** CH₃CCH₂CH₃ with CH₃ groups **(b)** CH₃CHCHCH₃ with CH₃ and OH

12.21 **(a)** cyclopentanone structure **(b)** cyclohexene with CH₃ and NH₂

12.22 **(a)** double bond, ketone, ether **(b)** double bond, amine, carboxylic acid **12.23** **(a)** 2,3-dimethylpentane **(b)** 2,5-dimethylhexane
12.24 **(a)** 1,1-dimethylcyclopentane **(b)** isopropylcyclobutane
12.25 The methyl groups are on the same side of the ring in one structure and on opposite sides in the other. **12.26** Carbon can form four strong bonds to itself and to many other elements. **12.28** Organic compounds are nonpolar. **12.30** A polar covalent bond is a bond in which electrons are shared unequally. **12.32** **(a)** amine, aromatic ring, ether, amide, sulfonamide double bond **(b)** aromatic ring, carboxylic acid, ester
12.34 **(a)** CH₃CH₂CH₂CCH₃ (O) Ketone **(b)** CH₃CH₂CH₂C—OCH₂CH₃ (O) Ester

(c) H₂N—CH₂C—OH (O)
Amine
carboxylic acid

12.36 They must have the same formula but different structures.
12.38 A primary carbon is bonded to one other carbon; a secondary carbon is bonded to two other carbons; a tertiary carbon is bonded to three other carbons; and a quaternary carbon is bonded to four other carbons.
12.40 **(a)** 2,3-dimethylbutane **(b)** cyclopentane
12.42 CH₃CH₂CH₂OH   CH₃CHCH₃ (OH)   CH₃CH₂—O—CH₃

propanol structure   isopropanol structure   ether structure

12.44
(a) CH₃CH₂CH₂CH₂OH   CH₃CH₂CHCH₃ (OH)   CH₃CHCH₂OH (CH₃)

CH₃CCH₃ (OH, CH₃)

(b) CH₃CH₂CH₂NH₂   CH₃CHCH₃ (NH₂)   CH₃CH₂NCH₃ (H)   CH₃NCH₃ (CH₃)

(c) CH₃CH₂CH₂CCH₃ (O)   CH₃CH₂CCH₂CH₃ (O)   CH₃CHCCH₃ (O, CH₃)

12.46 identical: **(a)**; isomers: **(b)**, **(d)**, **(e)**; unrelated: **(c)**   **12.48** All have a carbon with five bonds.   **12.50** **(a)** 4-ethyl-3-methyloctane **(b)** 5-isopropyl-3-methyloctane **(c)** 2,2,6-trimethylheptane **(d)** 4-isopropyl-4-methyloctane **(e)** 2,2,4,4-tetramethylpentane **(f)** 4,4-diethyl-2-methylhexane **(g)** 2,2-dimethyldecane
12.52
(a) H₃C C(CH₃)₃ ; CH₃CH₂C—CHCHCH₂CH₃ with CH₃, CH₃ **(b)** CH₃ CH₃ ; CH₃CHCH₂CHCH₃

(c) H₃C CH₂CH₃ ; CH₃CH₂CHCCH₂CH₂CH₂CH₃ with CH₂CH₃

(d) CH₃CHCH₃ CH₃ ; CH₃CHCCH₂CH₂CHCHCH₂CH₃ with H₃C CH₃ and CH₃

(e) CH₃CH (H₃C) seven-membered ring with CH₂CHCH₃ (CH₃), CH₃ **(f)** cyclopentane with CH₃, CH₃, H₃C

12.54 **(a)** 1-ethyl-3-methylcyclobutane **(b)** 1,1,3,3-tetramethylcyclopentane **(c)** 1-ethyl-3-propylcyclohexane **(d)** 4-butyl-1,1,2,2-tetramethylcyclopentane
12.56 **(a)** 2,2-dimethylpentane **(b)** 2,4-dimethylpentane **(c)** isobutylcyclobutane   **12.58** heptane, 2-methylhexane, 3-methylhexane, 2,2-dimethylpentane, 2,3-dimethylpentane, 2,4-dimethylpentane, 3,3-dimethylpentane, 3-ethylpentane, 2,2,3-trimethylbutane
12.60 C₃H₈ + 5 O₂ → 3 CO₂ + 4 H₂O
12.62
CH₃CH₂CCH₂Cl (CH₃) + CH₃CHCCH₃ (Cl, CH₃) + ClCH₂CH₂CCH₃ (CH₃)

12.64 Minor differences in shape cause differences in behavior.
12.66 Branched-chain hydrocarbons **12.68** **(a)** ketone, alcohol, double bond **(b)** carboxylic acid, amine, amide, ester, aromatic ring **12.70** nonpolar solvents dissolve nonpolar substances **12.72** pentane; more London forces

Chapter 13

13.1 (a) 2-methyl-3-heptene **(b)** 2-methyl-1,5-hexadiene **(c)** 3-methyl-3-hexene

13.2

(a)

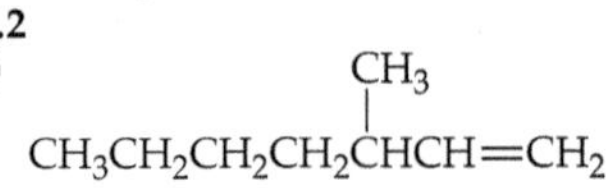

$$CH_3CH_2CH_2CH_2CHCH=CH_2$$
(with CH_3 substituent)

(b)

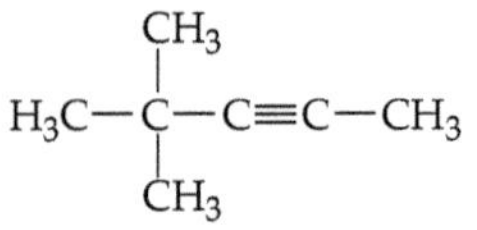

$$H_3C-\underset{CH_3}{\overset{CH_3}{C}}-C\equiv C-CH_3$$

(c)

$$CH_3CH_2CH_2CH=CHCHCH_3$$
(with CH_3 substituent)

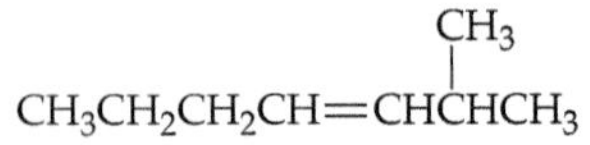

(d)

$$CH_3CH_2CH=C-\underset{CH_3}{\overset{CH_3\;CH_3}{C}}-CH_3$$

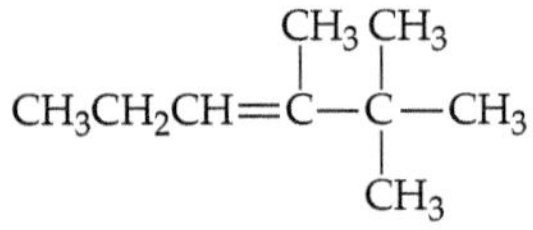

13.3 (a) 2,3-dimethyl-1-pentene **(b)** 2,3-dimethyl-2-hexene   **13.4 (a), (c)**

13.5

$$\underset{H_3C}{\overset{CH_3CH_2}{>}}C=C\underset{CH_3}{\overset{CH_2CH_3}{<}} \qquad \underset{H_3C}{\overset{CH_3CH_2}{>}}C=C\underset{CH_2CH_3}{\overset{CH_3}{<}}$$

cis-3,4-Dimethyl-3-hexene   trans-3,4-Dimethyl-3-hexene

13.6 (a) cis-4-methyl-2-hexene **(b)** trans-5,6-dimethyl-3-heptene
13.7 (a) substitution **(b)** addition **(c)** elimination   **13.8 (a), (b),**
(c) $CH_3CH_2CH_2CH_3$ **(d)** methylcyclohexane **13.9 (a)** 1,2-dibromo-2-methylpropane **(b)** 1,2-dichloropentane **(c)** 4,5-dichloro-2,4-dimethylheptane   **13.10 (a)** 1-chloro-1-methylcyclopentane **(b)** 2-bromobutane **(c)** 2-chloro-2-methylbutane **13.11 (a)** 3-ethyl-2-pentene **(b)** 2,3-dimethyl-1-butene or 2,3-dimethyl-2-butene
13.12 2-bromo-2,4-dimethylhexane
13.13 (a), (b) Same product is obtained.

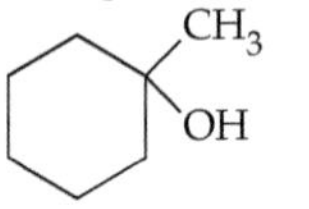

(structure: cyclohexane with CH_3 and OH on same carbon)

(c)

$$\underset{OH}{CH_3CHCH_2CH_2CH_3} \quad + \quad \underset{OH}{CH_3CH_2CHCH_2CH_3}$$

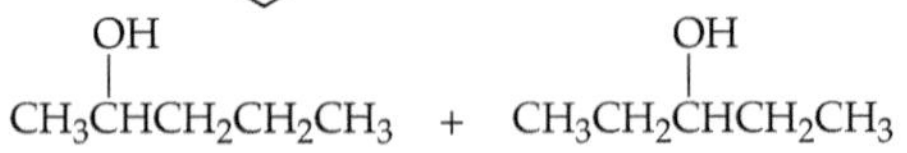

13.14 2-ethyl-1-butene or 3-methyl-2-pentene   **13.15** $(CH_3)_3C^+$
13.16

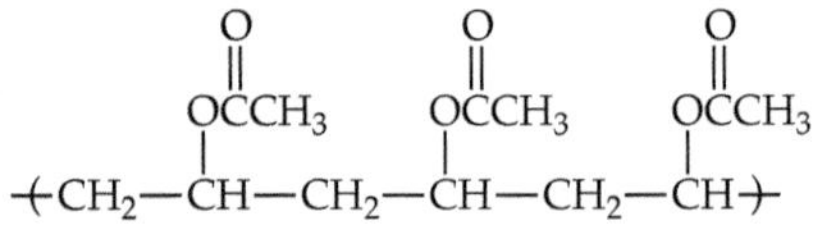

$$+CH_2-\underset{\underset{CH_3}{\overset{O}{C}}CH_3}{CH}-CH_2-\underset{\underset{CH_3}{\overset{O}{C}}CH_3}{CH}-CH_2-\underset{\underset{CH_3}{\overset{O}{C}}CH_3}{CH}+$$

13.17 (a)

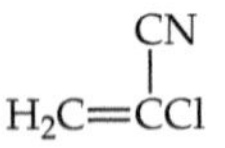

$$H_2C=\underset{CN}{CCl}$$

(b)

$$H_2C=\underset{CO_2CH_3}{CH}$$

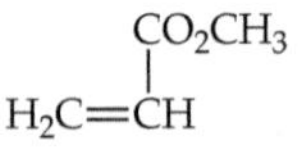

13.18 (a) m-ethylphenol **(b)** p-bromoaniline **(c)** 2-methyl-2-phenylbutane
13.19

(a) (benzene ring with Br and I ortho)
(b) (benzene ring with H_3C and NO_2)
(c) (benzene ring with CH_3CHCH_3 and CH_3CH–CH_3)

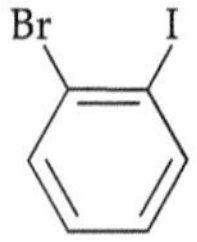

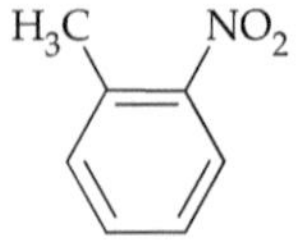

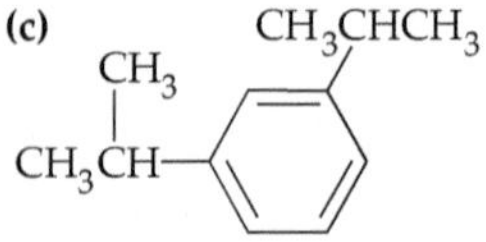

(d) (benzene ring with Cl and OH para)

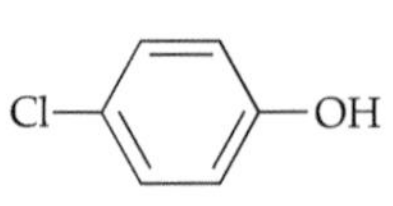

13.20 (a) o-isopropylphenol **(b)** p-bromoaniline
13.21 (a) (benzene ring with Br, H_3C, CH_3)
(b) (benzene ring with NO_2, H_3C, CH_3)
(c) (benzene ring with SO_3H, H_3C, CH_3)

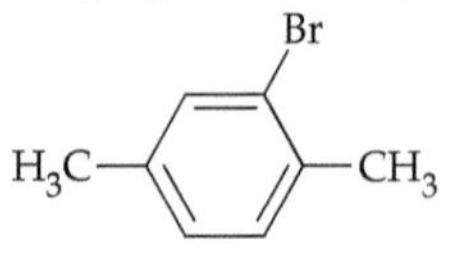

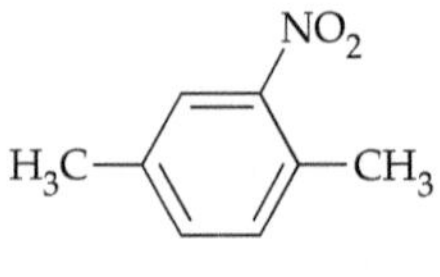

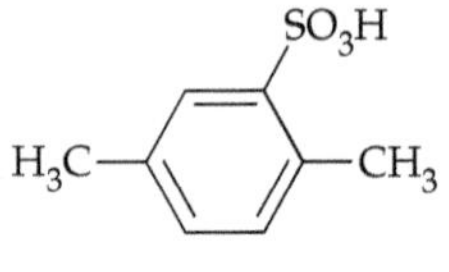

13.22 o-, m-, and p-bromotoluene
13.23

(a) 2,5-Dimethyl-2-heptene

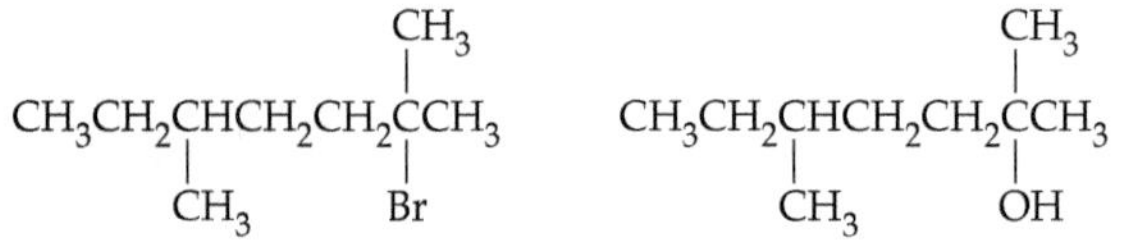

$$\underset{\underset{Br}{}}{CH_3CH_2CHCH_2CH_2CCH_3}\;(\text{with }CH_3) \qquad \underset{\underset{OH}{}}{CH_3CH_2CHCH_2CH_2CCH_3}\;(\text{with }CH_3)$$

(b) 3,3-Dimethylcyclopentene

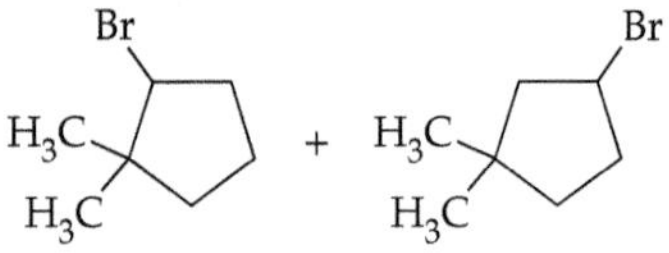

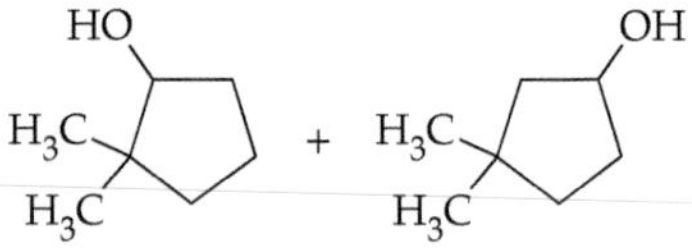

(cyclopentane with Br and two H_3C) + (cyclopentane with Br and two H_3C)

(cyclopentane with HO and two H_3C) + (cyclopentane with OH and two H_3C)

13.24 (a) 4,4-dimethyl-1-hexyne **(b)** 2,7-dimethyl-4-octyne
13.25 (a) m-isopropylphenol **(b)** o-bromobenzoic acid
13.26 (a)

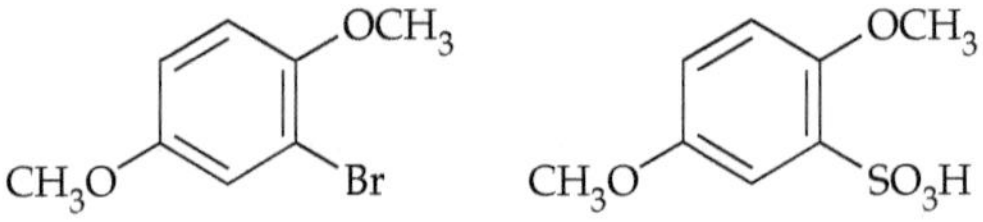

(benzene ring with OCH_3, CH_3O, Br) (benzene ring with OCH_3, CH_3O, SO_3H)

(b)

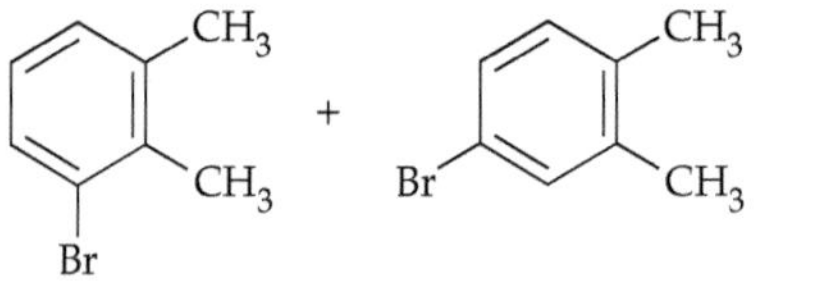

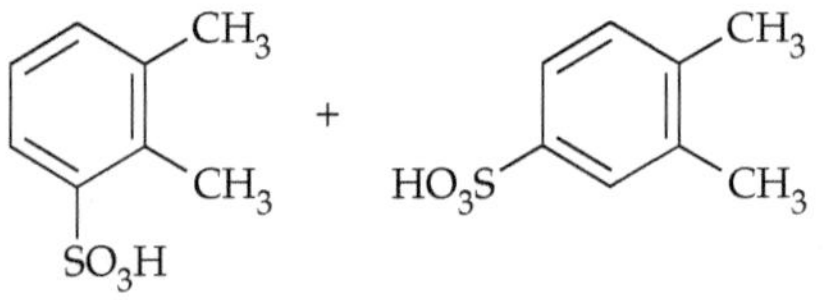

(benzene ring with CH_3, CH_3, Br) + (benzene ring with CH_3, Br, CH_3)

(benzene ring with CH_3, CH_3, SO_3H) + (benzene ring with CH_3, HO_3S, CH_3)

13.27

(a)

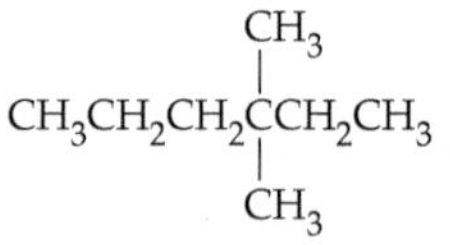

$$CH_3CH_2CH_2\underset{CH_3}{\overset{CH_3}{C}}CH_2CH_3$$
3,3-Dimethylhexane

(b)

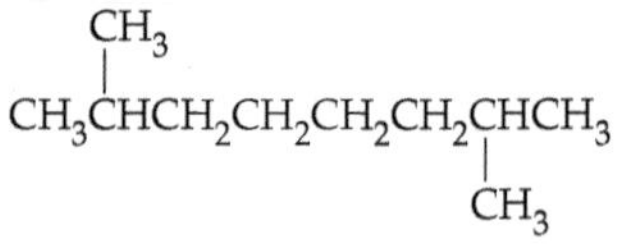

$$CH_3\underset{CH_3}{CH}CH_2CH_2CH_2CH_2\underset{CH_3}{CH}CH_3$$
2,7-Dimethyloctane

13.28

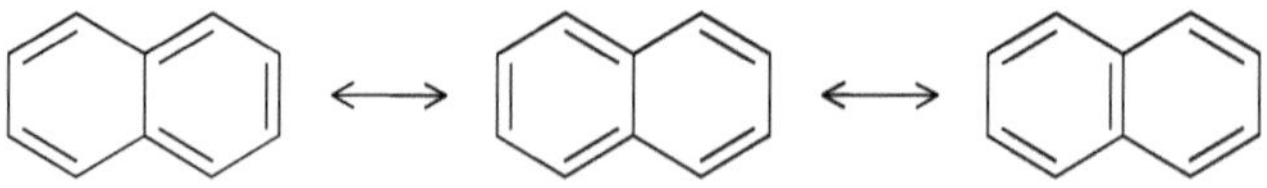

(naphthalene resonance structures) ⟷ (naphthalene) ⟷ (naphthalene)

13.29 2-methyl-2-pentene, 2-methyl-1-pentene   **13.30** They have C—C multiple bonds and can add hydrogen.   **13.32** alkene: –ene; alkyne: –yne; aromatic: –benzene
13.34

(a) $CH_3CH_2CH_2CH_2CH_2CH=CH_2$ **(b)** $CH_3CH_2CH_2C\equiv CH$

(c) (benzene ring with $-CH_2CH_3$)

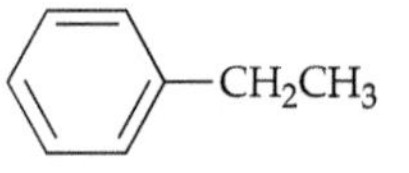

13.36 (a) 1-pentene **(b)** 2,5-dimethyl-3-hexyne **(c)** 2,3-dimethyl-2-butene **(d)** 2-ethyl-3-methyl-1,3-pentadiene **(e)** 2-ethyl-1.3-dimethylcyclohexene **(f)** 3-ethylisopropylcyclobutene

13.38 (a) CH_3CH_2 ... H / $C=C$ / H ... CH_2CH_3

(b) CH_3 / $CH_3CH_2CH=CHCHCH_3$

(c) CH_3 / $H_2C=CHC=CH_2$

(d) $CH_3CH_2CH_2$ ... CH_2CH_3 / $C=C$ / H ... H

(e) O_2N — (benzene ring) — CH_3

(f) Cl — (benzene ring) — OH

(g) $CH_3CH_2CH_2$ — (benzene ring) — $CH_2CH_2CH_3$

13.40 1-hexyne, 2-hexyne, 3-hexyne, 3-methyl-1-pentyne, 4-methyl-1-pentyne, 4-methyl-2-pentyne, 3,3-dimethyl-1-butyne **13.42** 1-pentene, 2-pentene, 2-methyl-1-butene, 3-methyl-1-butene, 2-methyl-2-butene **13.44** Each double bond carbon must be bonded to two different groups. **13.46** 2-pentene

13.48

(a) $CH_3CH_2CH_2$ ... CH_2CH_3 / $C=C$ / H ... H

(b) CH_3 / CH_3CH ... CH_3 / $C=C$ / H ... H

(c) CH_3 / H ... $CHCH_3$ / $C=C$ / CH_3CH ... H / CH_3

13.50 (a) identical **(b)** identical **13.52** substitution: two reactants exchange parts to give two products; addition: two reactants add to give one product **13.54** rearrangement **13.56 (a)** substitution **(b)** rearrangement

13.58

(a) H_3C, CH_3, H, H (cyclohexane) **(b)** H_3C, CH_3, Br, Br (cyclohexane) **(c)** H_3C, CH_3, H, Br (cyclohexane) **(d)** H_3C, CH_3, H, OH (cyclohexane)

13.60

(a) $CH_3CH=CHCCH_3$ with CH_3 + Cl_2 **(b)** $CH_3CH=CH_2$ + H_2

(c) $CH_3CH=CHCH_3$ or $H_2C=CHCH_2CH_3$ + HBr

(d) (cyclohexene) + HCl **(e)** (cyclohexane)$=CH_2$ + Cl_2

13.62 (benzene ring)$\overset{+}{C}HCH_3$

13.64

(three pyrrolidinone rings) $+H_2C-CH-H_2C-CH-H_2C-CH+$

13.66 (b) benzene + $Br_2 \rightarrow$ bromobenzene + HBr **13.68** methylcyclohexane **13.70** Rod cells are responsible for vision in dim light; cone cells are responsible for color vision.

13.72

$+CH_2-CH(CH_3)-CH_2-CH(CH_3)-CH_2-CH(CH_3)-CH_2-CH(CH_3)+_n$

$+CH_2-CH(CH_3)-CH_2-CH(CH_2CH_3)-CH_2-CH(CH_3)-CH_2-CH(CH_3)+_n$

13.74 The body converts it to a water-soluble diol epoxide that can react with DNA and lead to cancer. **13.76** yellow

13.78

(benzene ring with OH) $\overset{O}{C}-OH$ **Salicylic acid**

13.80 (a) 5-methyl-2-hexene **(b)** 4-methyl-2-heptyne **(c)** 2,3-dimethyl-1-butene **(d)** 1,2,4-trinitrobenzene **(e)** 3,4-dimethylcyclohexene **(f)** 3-methyl-1,3-pentadiene **13.82** Cyclohexene reacts with Br_2; benzene doesn't.

13.84

CH_3 / H_3C—(cyclohexene ring)—$CHCH_3$ **Menthene**

13.86

(a) CH_3 / $CH_3CH_2CH_2CH_2CHCH_3$ **(b)** Br—(benzene ring with NO_2)—Br **(c)** (cyclopentane)—OH

(d) CH_3CHCH_3 / $CH_3CHCH_2CHCH_3$ / OH **(e)** $CH_3CH_2CH_2CH_2CH_3$ **(f)** (benzene ring)—$CHCH_3$ / Cl

13.88 Naphthalene has a greater molar mass.

13.90

$CH_3CH=C-C(CH_3)(H_3C)-CH_3$ with CH_3 and H_3C or $CH_3CH_2C-C(CH_3)-CH_3$ with H_2C and CH_3 $\xrightarrow[H_2SO_4]{H_2O}$ catalyst

Chapter 14

14.1 (a) alcohol **(b)** alcohol **(c)** phenol **(d)** alcohol **(e)** ether **(f)** ether
14.2 A hydroxyl group is a part of a larger molecule.
14.3 (a) CH_3 OH / $CH_3CHCH_2CHCH_3$

secondary alcohol

(b) (cyclobutane)—OH

secondary alcohol

(c) OH CH_3 / $CH_3CH_2CH_2CH_2CHCH_2CHCH_3$

secondary alcohol

(d) OH / $CH_3CH_2CH_2CH_2CH_2CHCH_3$

secondary alcohol

(e) Cl / $ClCH_2CHCH_2OH$

primary alcohol

14.4 (a) 3-pentanol, secondary **(b)** 2-ethyl-1-pentanol, primary **(c)** 5,6-dichloro-2-ethyl-1-hexanol, primary **(d)** 2-isopropyl-4-methylcyclohexanol, secondary **14.5** See 14.3 and 14.4 **14.6 (a)** **14.7 (b)**
14.8 (a) propene **(b)** cyclohexene **(c)** 4-methyl-1-pentene (minor) and 4-methyl-2-pentene (major) **14.9 (a)** 2,3-dimethyl-2-butanol **(b)** 1-butanol or 2-butanol

14.10

14.11 (a)

(b)

(c)

14.12 (a) 2-propanol **(b)** cycloheptanol **(c)** 3-methyl-1-butanol

14.13 (a)

(b)

14.14 (a)

(b)

14.15 (a) p-chlorophenol **(b)** 4-bromo-2-methylphenol **14.16 (a)** methyl propyl ether **(b)** diisopropyl ether **(c)** methyl phenyl ether
14.17 (a) $CH_3CH_2CH_2S-SCH_2CH_2CH_3$
(b) $(CH_3)_2CHCH_2CH_2S-SCH_2CH_2CH(CH_3)_2$
14.18 (a) 1-chloro-1-ethylcyclopentane **(b)** 3-bromo-5-methylheptane
14.19 (a) 5-methyl-3-hexanol **(b)** m-methoxytoluene
(c) 3-methylcyclohexanol
14.20

14.21 $(CH_3)_2CHCH_2CH_2CHO$, $(CH_3)_2CHCH_2CH_2CO_2H$
14.22

14.23 (a)

(b)

(c)

14.24 Alcohols have an —OH group bonded to an alkane-like carbon atom; ethers have an oxygen atom bonded to two carbon atoms; and phenols have an —OH group bonded to a carbon of an aromatic ring.
14.26 Alcohols form hydrogen bonds. **14.28** ketone, carbon–carbon double bond, alcohol **14.30 (a)** 2-ethyl-1-pentanol **(b)** 3-methyl-1-butanol **(c)** 1,2,4-butanetriol **(d)** 2-methyl-2-phenyl-1-propanol **(e)** 2-ethyl-3-methylcyclohexanol **(f)** 3,3-dimethyl-2-hexanol

14.32 (a)

(b)

(c)

(d)

(e)

(f)

14.34 (a) primary **(b)** primary **(c)** primary, secondary **(d)** primary **(e)** secondary **(f)** secondary **14.36 (a)** < **(c)** < **(b)** **14.38** a ketone **14.40** aldehyde or carboxylic acid **14.42** Phenols dissolve in aqueous NaOH; alcohols don't.

14.44

(a)

(b)

(c)

(d)

(e)

$HOCH_2CH_2CH_2CH_2CH_2OH$

(f)

14.46

(a)

(b)

(c) NR **(d)**

(e) NR **(f)**

14.48 odor
14.50

14.52 Alcohols can form hydrogen bonds; thiols and alkyl chlorides cannot. **14.54** depressant **14.56** The liver is the site of alcohol metabolism. **14.58** a reactive species that contains an unpaired electron **14.60** diethyl ether **14.62** The ozone layer shields the earth from intense solar radiation. **14.64** alcohols: 1-butanol, 2-butanol, 2-methyl-1-propanol, 2-methyl-2-propanol; ethers: diethyl ether, methyl propyl ether, isopropyl methyl ether **14.66** Alcohols become less soluble as their nonpolar part becomes larger. **14.68** An antiseptic kills microorganisms on living tissue. **14.70 (a)** *p*-dibromobenzene **(b)** 1,2-dibromo-1-butene **(c)** *m*-propylanisole **(d)** 1,1-dibromocyclopentane **(e)** 6-chloro-2,4-dimethyl-2,4-hexanediol **(f)** 4-methyl-2,4,5-heptanetriol **(g)** 4-bromo-6,6-dimethyl-2-heptyne **(h)** 1-bromo-2-iodoocyclobutane

14.72 3,7-Dimethyl-2,6-octadiene-1-ol

$$CH_3\overset{CH_3}{\underset{}{C}}=CHCH_2CH_2\overset{CH_3}{\underset{}{C}}=CH\overset{O}{\underset{}{C}}-H$$

14.74 $C_2H_6O + 3\,O_2 \rightarrow 2\,CO_2 + 3\,H_2O$

Chapter 15

15.1 (a) primary **(b)** secondary **(c)** primary **(d)** secondary **(e)** tertiary

15.2 (a) Tetrabutylammonium hydroxide **(b)** Dimethylamine **(c)** *N*-Pentylaniline

15.3 (a)

$$CH_3CH_2CH_2CH_2CH_2CH_2NH_2$$

(b)

$$CH_3CH_2CH_2CH_2\overset{CH_3}{\underset{}{N}}H$$

(c)

a benzene ring with $-NH-$ and a CH_3 attached

(d)

$$\overset{NH_2}{\underset{}{CH_2}}CH_2\overset{OH}{\underset{}{C}}HCH_3$$

15.4 The ion has one less electron than the neutral atoms.

$$H_3C-\overset{CH_3}{\underset{CH_3}{\overset{|}{N^{\pm}}}}-CH_3$$

15.5 $CH_3CH_2CH_2CH_2NHCH_2CH_3$ *N*-Ethylbutylamine

15.6 Compound **(a)** is lowest boiling; **(b)** is highest boiling (strongest hydrogen bonds).

15.7 (a) structure showing hydrogen bonding of amine with water

(b) structure showing hydrogen bonding of trimethylamine with water

15.8 (a) Methylamine, Ethylamine, Dimethylamine, Trimethylamine **(b)** Pyridine **(c)** Aniline

15.9 (a) Piperidine: $C_5H_{11}N$ **(b)** Purine: $C_5H_4N_4$

15.10 (a) and **(d)**

15.11

reaction scheme: aniline $+\ H_2O \rightleftharpoons$ anilinium ion $+\ OH^-$; base, acid, base, acid labeled

15.12

(a) $CH_3CH_2\overset{}{\underset{CH_3}{C}}HNH_3^+\,Br^-(aq)$ **(b)** benzene ring with $-NH_3^+Cl^-(aq)$

(c) $CH_3CH_2NH_3^+CH_3COO^-(aq)$ **(d)** $CH_3NH_2 + H_2O(l) + NaCl(aq)$

15.13 (a) *sec*-Butylammonium bromide **(b)** Anilinium chloride **(c)** Ethylammonium acetate **(d)** Methylamine **15.14 (a)** Ethylamine **(b)** Triethylamine

15.15

(a) structure with HO, HO, OH, $-CHCH_2\overset{+}{N}H_2CH_3$

(b) benzene ring with $-CH_2\overset{CH_3}{\underset{}{C}}HNH_3^+$

15.16–15.17 (a)

$$CH_3CH_2CH_2CH_2CH_2CH_2\overset{CH_3}{\underset{CH_3}{\overset{|}{N}H}}^+Cl^-$$

Hexyldimethylammonium chloride
or N, N-Dimethylhexylammonium chloride
Salt of a tertiary amine

(b)

$$CH_3\overset{CH_3}{\underset{}{C}}HNH_3^+\,Br^-$$

Isopropylammonium bromide
Salt of a primary amine

15.18 $CH_3CH_2CH_2CH_2NH_3^+\ Cl^-(aq)\ +\ NaOH\,(aq) \rightarrow$
$CH_3CH_2CH_2NH_2 + H_2O(l) + NaCl(aq)$

15.19 Benadryl has the general structure. In Benadryl, R $=\ -CH_3$, and R' = R'' = C_6H_5-.

15.20

benzene ring with $-CH_2NH_3^+\ Cl^-$ benzene ring with $-CH_2NH_2\cdot HCl$

Benzylammonium chloride

15.21

structure: pyrrolidine ring with CH_3 and N^+ (labeled q), $CH_2CH_2NHCH_2$ (labeled s), connected to pyridine ring with N (labeled a) — "provides and accepts a hydrogen bond" and "accepts a hydrogen bond"

15.22 (a) All amine groups can participate in hydrogen bonding. **(b)** Histidine is water-soluble because it can form hydrogen bonds with water.

15.23

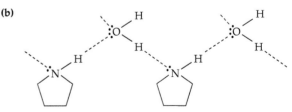

15.24

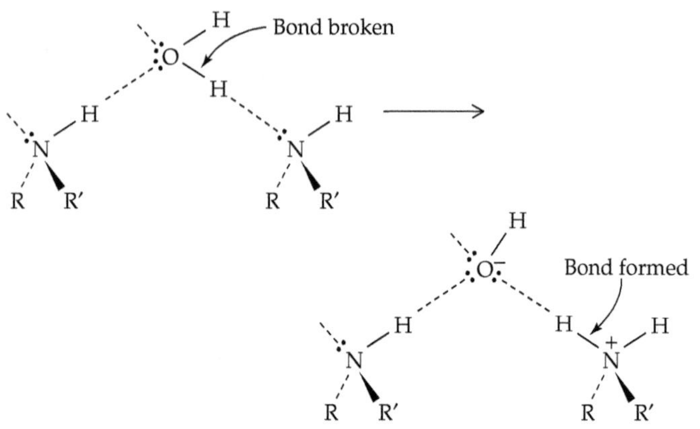

Bond broken

Bond formed

15.25 most basic: $(CH_3)_2NH$ least basic: $C_6H_5NH_2$

15.26

(a)

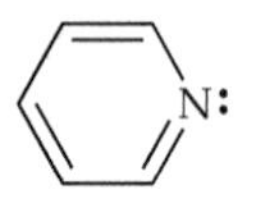

$+$ H_2O

(b) $CH_3\overset{+}{N}H_2CH(CH_3)_2$ $+$ OH^-

(c) No reaction

(d) $(CH_3)_3C NH_3{}^+Cl^-$

15.28 (a)

$$CH_3CH_2CH_2CH_2CH_2\overset{\overset{\displaystyle H}{|}}{N}CH_3$$

(b)

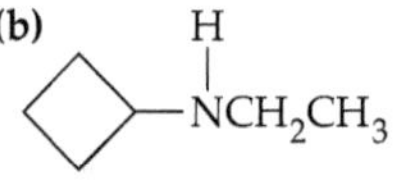

(c) $CH_3CH_2CH_2-$ $-NH_2$

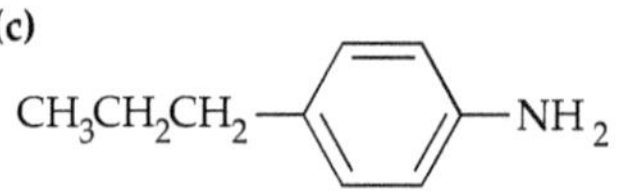

15.30 (a) Cyclobutylamine (primary) (b) Diphenylamine (secondary)
15.32 Diethylamine **15.34** (a) N-Methyl-2-butylammonium nitrate
(salt of a secondary amine).

(b)

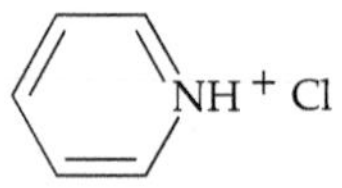

(salt of a tertiary amine)

(c)

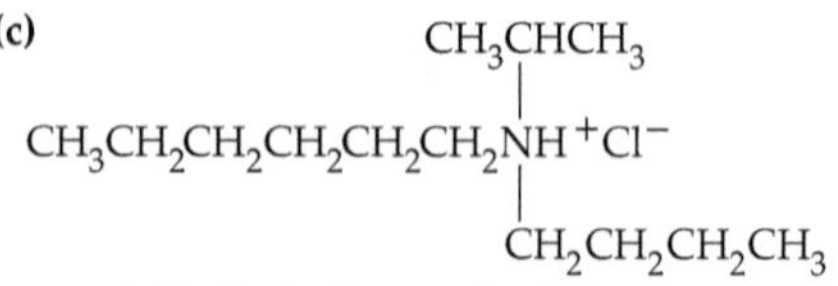

$$CH_3CH_2CH_2CH_2CH_2CH_2\overset{\overset{\displaystyle CH_3CHCH_3}{|}}{\underset{\underset{\displaystyle CH_2CH_2CH_2CH_3}{|}}{N}}H^+Cl^-$$

(salt of a tertiary amine)

15.36

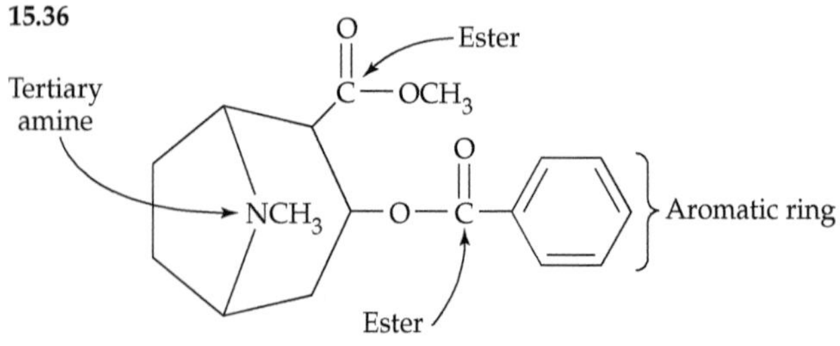

Tertiary amine

Ester

Aromatic ring

Ester

Cocaine

15.38

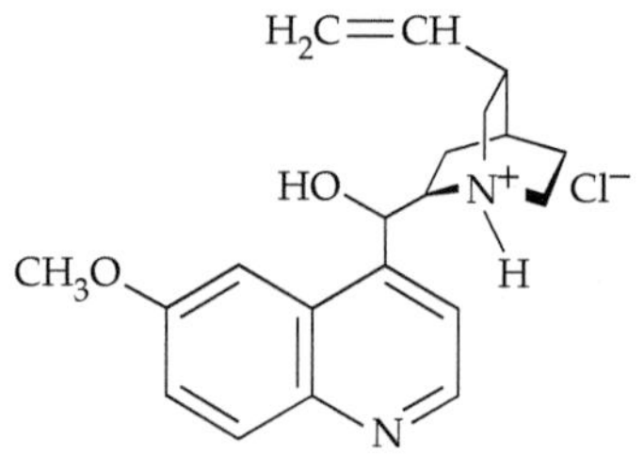

Quinine hydrochloride

15.40

(a)

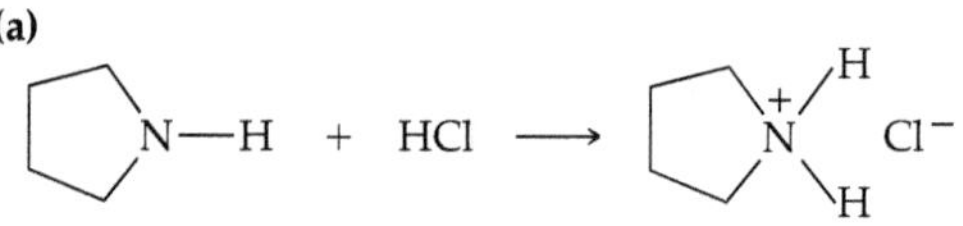

$N-H$ $+$ HCl $\longrightarrow$ Cl^-

(b)

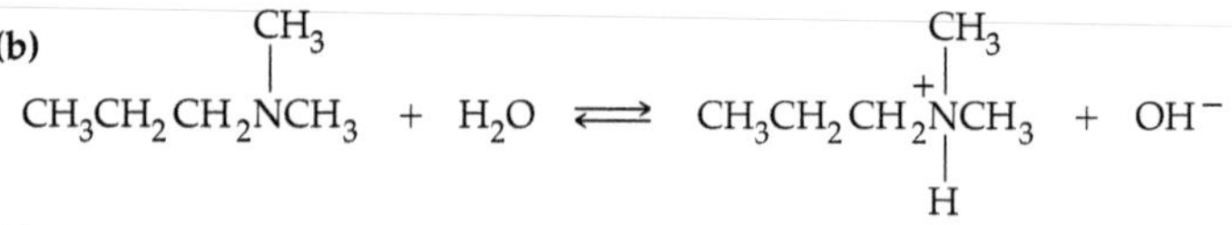

$$CH_3CH_2CH_2\overset{\overset{\displaystyle CH_3}{|}}{N}CH_3 + H_2O \rightleftharpoons CH_3CH_2CH_2\overset{\overset{\displaystyle CH_3}{|}}{\underset{\underset{\displaystyle H}{|}}{\overset{+}{N}}}CH_3 + OH^-$$

(c)

$NH_2{}^+\,Cl^-$ $+$ $NaOH$ $\longrightarrow$

$NH + H_2O + NaCl$

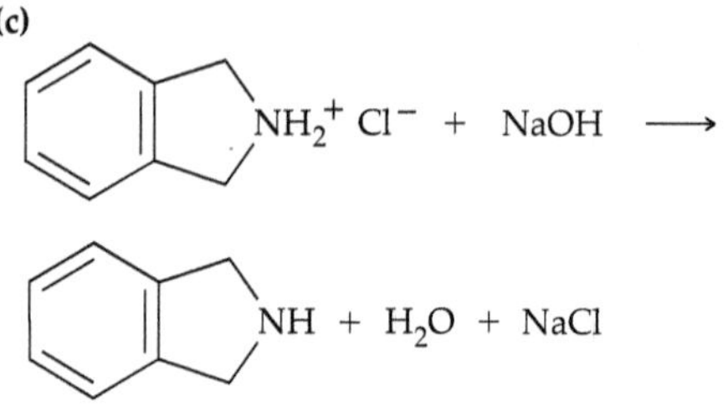

15.42 Choline doesn't react with HCl because its nitrogen isn't basic.
15.44 (1) lowering of blood pressure (2) memory enhancement (3) reduction of sickling in sickle-cell anemia (4) destruction of malaria parasites (5) destruction of the tuberculosis bacterium.
15.46

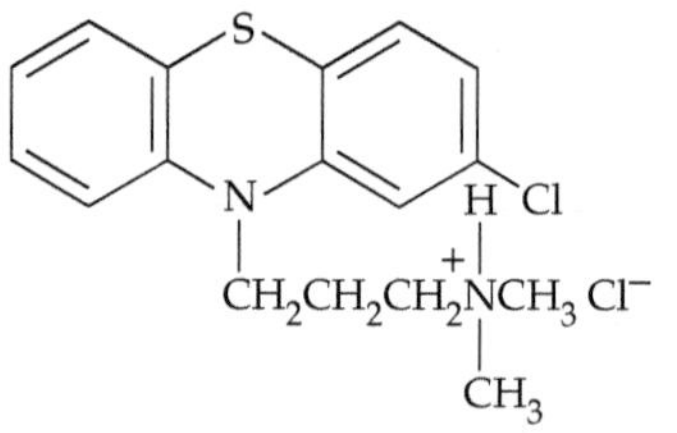

$$CH_2CH_2CH_2\overset{+}{N}CH_3\ Cl^-$$

15.48 (a) A forensic toxicologist deals with criminal cases involving drug abuse and poisoning (b) the structure of the toxin, its mode of action, a mechanism to reverse its effects
15.50 Its large hydrocarbon region is water-insoluble.
15.52

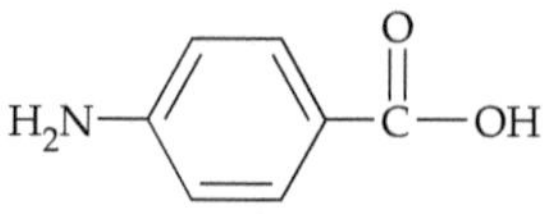

$$H_2N-\text{}-\overset{\overset{\displaystyle O}{\|}}{C}-OH$$

PABA

15.54 Amide

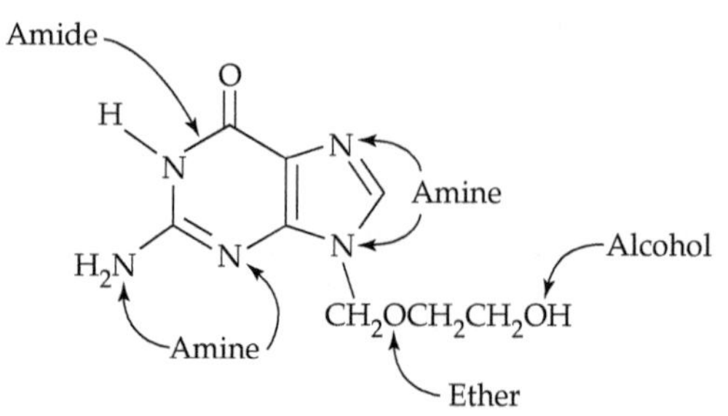

Acyclovir—related to purine

15.56 Amines: foul-smelling, somewhat basic, lower boiling (weaker hydrogen bonds); Alcohols: pleasant-smelling, not basic, higher boiling (stronger hydrogen bonds) **15.58 (a)** 6-Methyl-2-heptene **(b)** *p*-Isopropylphenol **(c)** Dibutylamine **15.60** Molecules of hexylamine can form hydrogen bonds to each other, but molecules of triethylamine can't. **15.62** Baeocystin is related to indole. **15.64** Pyridine forms H-bonds with water; benzene doesn't form H-bonds.

Chapter 16

16.1

(a)

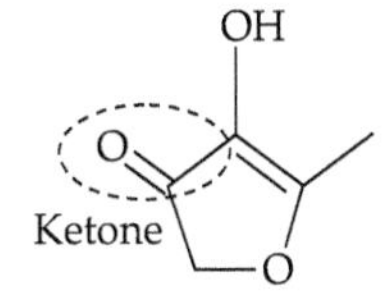
OH
O
Ketone
O

(b)

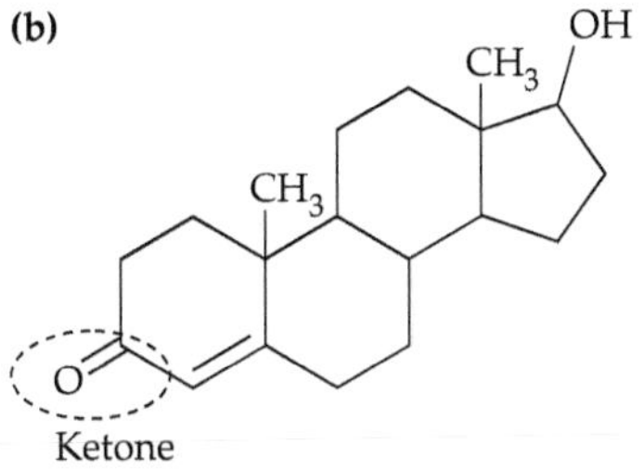
OH
CH3
CH3
O
Ketone

Testosterone

(c)

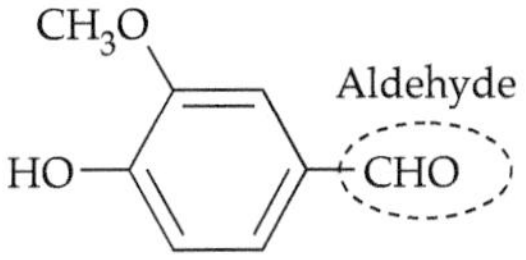
CH3O
Aldehyde
HO
CHO

Vanillin

(d) $C_4H_9COCH_3$ Ketone **(e)** C_4H_9CHO Aldehyde **(f)** $C_4H_9COOCH_3$ Ester

16.2 (d)

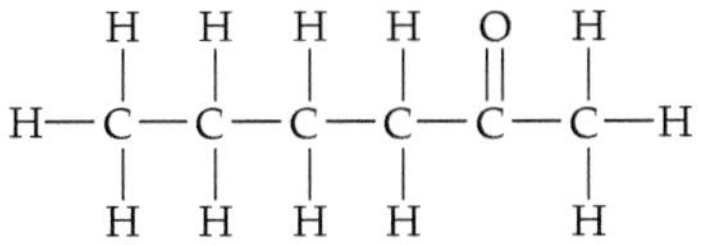

(e)

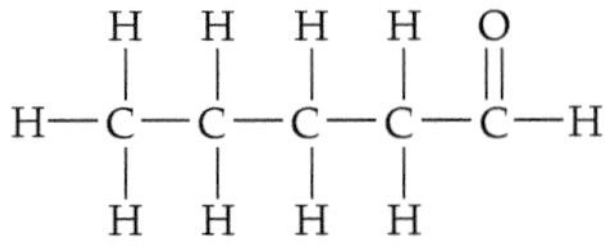

16.3 (a)

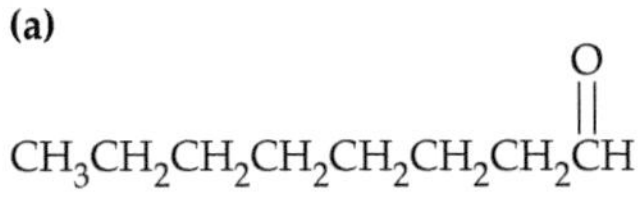
O
CH3CH2CH2CH2CH2CH2CH2CH

(b)

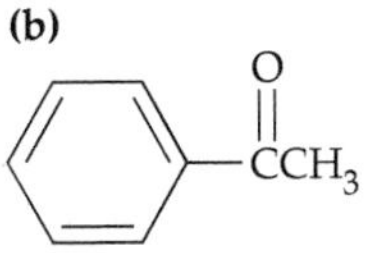
O
CCH3

(c)

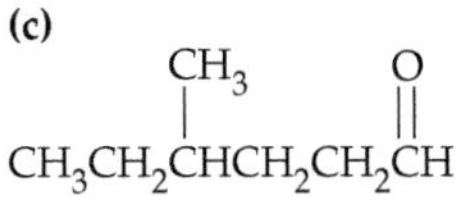
CH3 O
CH3CH2CHCH2CH2CH

(d)

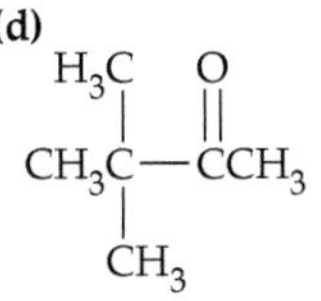
H3C O
CH3C—CCH3
CH3

16.4 (a) Pentanal **(b)** 3-Pentanone **(c)** 4-Methylhexanal **(d)** 4-Heptanone

16.5 (a)

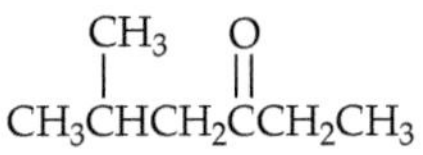
CH3 O
CH3CHCH2CCH2CH3

$C_7H_{14}O$
5-Methyl-3-hexanone
A ketone

(b)

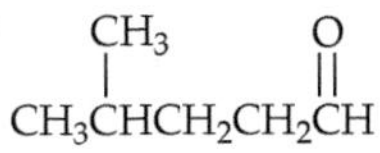
CH3 O
CH3CHCH2CH2CH

$C_6H_{12}O$
4-Methylpentanal
An aldehyde

16.6 (a) polar **(b)** flammable **(c)** liquid **(d)** bp of 100 °C

16.7 Alcohols form hydrogen bonds, which raise their boiling points. Aldehydes and ketones have higher boiling points than alkanes because they are polar.

16.8 (a)

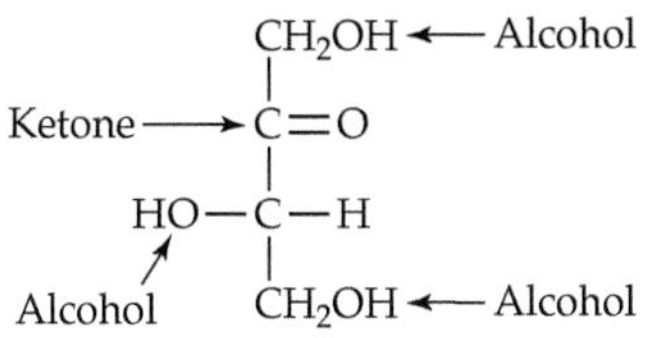
CH2OH ← Alcohol
Ketone → C=O
HO—C—H
Alcohol
CH2OH ← Alcohol

(b)

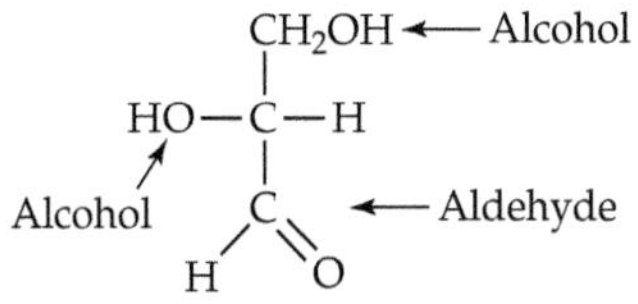
CH2OH ← Alcohol
HO—C—H
Alcohol
C ← Aldehyde
H O

(c)

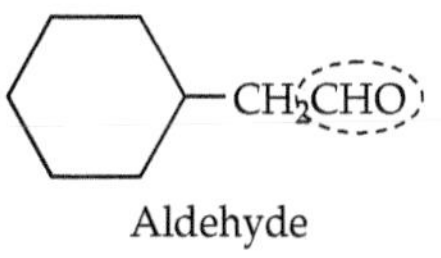
CH2CHO
Aldehyde

(d)

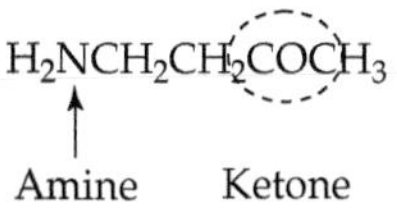
H2NCH2CH2COCH3
Amine
Ketone

16.9

(a)

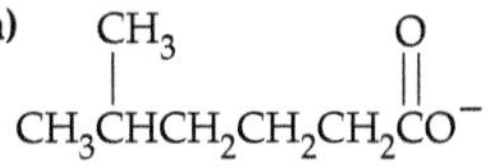
CH3 O
CH3CHCH2CH2CH2CO−

(b)

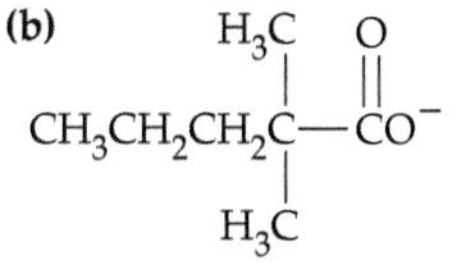
H3C O
CH3CH2CH2C—CO−
H3C

(c) NR

16.10

(a)

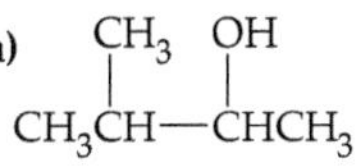
CH3 OH
CH3CH—CHCH3

(b)

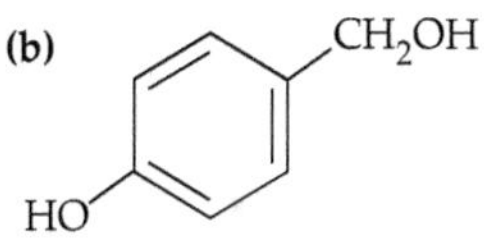
CH2OH
HO

(c)

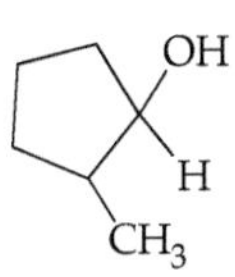
OH
H
CH3

16.11 (a)

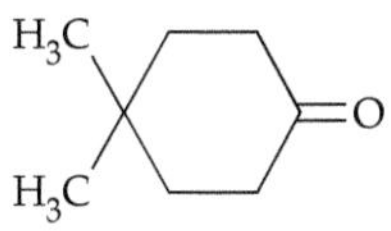
H3C
H3C
O

(b)

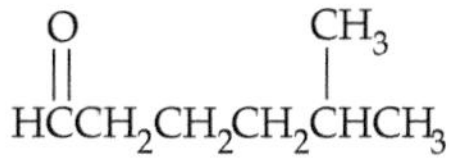
O CH3
HCCH2CH2CH2CHCH3

(c)

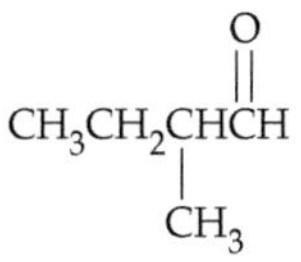
O
CH3CH2CHCH
CH3

16.12 Compound **(a)**

16.13

(a)

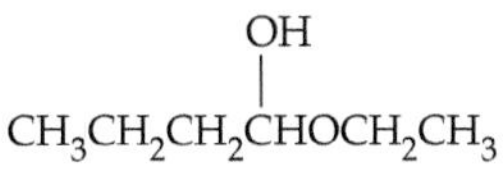
OH
CH3CH2CH2CHOCH2CH3

(b)

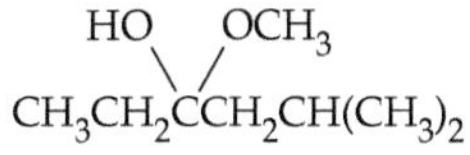
HO OCH3
CH3CH2CCH2CH(CH3)2

16.14

(a)

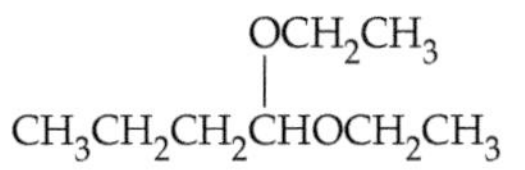
OCH2CH3
CH3CH2CH2CHOCH2CH3

(b)

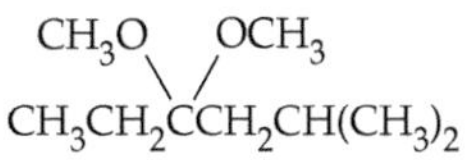
CH3O OCH3
CH3CH2CCH2CH(CH3)2

16.15 (a) neither **(b)** neither **(c)** acetal **(d)** hemiacetal **16.16** The acetal and the hemiacetal were both formed from ketones.

16.17 (a)

[benzene ring]—CH$_2$CCH$_2$CH$_3$ (C=O)   +   2 CH$_3$OH

(b)

CH$_3$CH$_2$CHO   +   2 CH$_3$CH$_2$CH$_2$OH

(c)

O
‖
HCH   +   2 CH$_3$CH$_2$CH$_2$OH

16.18 (a) Hydride adds to the carbonyl carbon. **(b)** The arrow to the right represents reduction, and the arrow to the left represents oxidation. **16.19** Aldehydes can be oxidized to carboxylic acids. Tollens' reagent differentiates an aldehyde from a ketone.

16.20

H   H   H   H
 \ | | |
  C=O:···H···O:···H   :O=C
 /   :   :   \
R   H   H   H   R
      \ | |
       :O:

16.21 (a) Under acidic conditions, an alcohol adds to the carbonyl group of an aldehyde to form a hemiacetal, which is unstable and further reacts to form an acetal.

(b)

O═H   O—H
| | --- Bonds broken
R—C═O—R'   ⟶   R—C—O—R'
| | — Bonds formed
H   H

16.22 In solution, glucose exists as a cyclic hemiacetal because this structure is more stable.   **16.23** One equivalent of an alcohol adds to the carbonyl group of an aldehyde or ketone to form a hemiacetal. Two equivalents of alcohol add to the carbonyl group to yield an acetal.

16.24 (a)   **(b)**   **(c)**

O   CH$_3$ O   O   O
‖ | ‖   ‖   ‖
CH$_3$CCH$_2$CH$_3$ CH$_3$CHCH$_2$CH   CH$_3$CCH$_2$CH$_2$CH

(d)

O
‖
HOCH$_2$CH$_2$CCH$_3$

16.26 Structure **(a)** is an aldehyde, and structure **(f)** is a ketone.

16.28

(a)   **(b)**   **(c)**

O   Cl   O   O
‖ | ‖   ‖
CH$_3$CHCHCH   CH$_3$CHCH$_2$CHCH   O$_2$N—[benzene ring]—CH
| |
CH$_3$ OH

(d)   **(e)**   **(f)**

O   O   O
‖   ‖   ‖
CH$_3$CH$_2$CH$_2$CH$_2$CH$_2$CH$_2$CCH$_3$ CH$_3$CHCCH$_3$H   [benzene ring]—CCH$_3$
                                | |
                                CH$_3$ CH$_3$

16.30 (a) 2,3-Dimethylbutanal **(b)** 4-Hydroxy-2-methylpentanal **(c)** 2,2-Dimethylpropanal **(d)** 2-Butanone **(e)** 5-Methyl-2-hexanone   **16.32** For **(a)**, a ketone can't occur at the end of a carbon chain. For **(b)**, the methyl group receives the lowest possible number. For **(c)**, numbering must start at the end of the carbon chain closer to the carbonyl group. **16.34** A hemiacetal is produced. **16.36 (a)** NR; cyclopentanol

(b)

O
‖
CH$_3$CH$_2$CH$_2$CH$_2$CH$_2$COH ;   CH$_3$CH$_2$CH$_2$CH$_2$CH$_2$CH$_2$OH

(c)

OH OH O   OH OH OH
 | | ‖ | | |
CH$_3$—C—C—C—OH   CH$_3$—C—C—C—H
 | | | | |
 H   H   H   H   H

16.38 (a)

H$_3$C—[benzene ring]—CHO   H$_3$C—[benzene ring]—CH$_2$OH

(b)   CHO   CH$_2$OH
                  | |
CH$_3$CH$_2$CHCH$_2$CHCH$_3$ CH$_3$CH$_2$CHCH$_2$CHCH$_3$
                  | |
                  CH$_3$ CH$_3$

(c) CH$_3$CH=CHCHO   CH$_3$CH=CHCH$_2$OH

16.40

(a)   OH   **(b)**   OH
                  | |
CH$_3$CH$_2$COCH$_2$CH$_2$CH$_3$ CH$_3$CH$_2$CH$_2$COCH(CH$_3$)$_2$
                  | |
                  CH$_3$ H

(c)

O
‖
CH$_3$CH$_2$CH$_2$CH   +   CH$_3$CH$_2$OH   +   CH$_3$OH

(d) H$_3$C
          \
           C=O   +   HOCH$_2$CH$_2$OH
          /
        H$_3$C

16.42   HO   CH$_3$
           [tetrahydrofuran ring with O]
                  CH$_3$

16.44 HOCH$_2$CH$_2$CH$_2$OH and CH$_2$O (formaldehyde).

16.46

Hemiacetal — OH   CH$_2$OH — Alcohol
                    \ /
                     C=O — Ketone
[steroid ring structure with CH$_3$ groups]
Ketone —
          —C—C double bond
          Aldosterone

16.48

HO—[benzene ring]—OH   +   H$_2$O$_2$ ⟶   O=[cyclohexadiene ring]=O

H$_2$O$_2$ is reduced

+   2 H$_2$O

16.50 Ethanol   **16.52 (a)** Advantages: inexpensive, no need to sacrifice animals. **(b)** Disadvantage: results of tests on cultured cells may not be reliable for more complex organisms.   **16.54** *p*-Methoxybenzaldehyde
16.56 Aldehydes are easily oxidized.
16.58

$$Cl_3CC(OH) \overset{OH}{\underset{H}{|}} OH$$

16.60 (a) *o*-Isopropylmethoxybenzene **(b)** 5,5-Diethyl-3-heptyne **(c)** *N*-Ethylcyclopentylammonium bromide **(d)** *N,N*-Diethylhexylamine
16.62

(a) CH_3CH_2CCHCH with I and O substituents (I, I)   **(b)** $BrCH_2CCHBr_2$ with O   **(c)** $CH_3CCH_2CH_2CCH_3$ with NH_2, O, CH_3

16.64 (a)

Benzene ring with CH_2CH—$OCH_2CH_2CH_3$ and $OCH_2CH_2CH_3$

(b)

$$CH_3CH_2CCH_2CH_2CH_3 \text{ with } CH_2CH_3$$

(c)

H_3C—(benzene ring)—$CH{=}CH_2$

16.66 Highest boiling = 1-butanol (strongest hydrogen bonds)

Chapter 17
17.1 carboxylic acid: **(c)**; amides: **(a) (f) (h)**; ester: **(d)**; none: **(b) (e) (g)**
17.2 (a)

$$\underset{6}{CH_3}\underset{5}{CH_2}\underset{4}{CH_2}\underset{3}{CH}\underset{2}{CH}\underset{1}{COH}$$ with OH, O, CH_2CH_3

(b) benzene ring with O_2N and COH (O)

17.3

$$H{-}O{-}\overset{O}{\underset{}{C}}{-}\overset{H}{\underset{H}{C}}{-}\overset{H}{\underset{H}{C}}{-}\overset{O}{\underset{}{C}}{-}O{-}H$$

$$HO{-}C({=}O){-}CH_2{-}CH_2{-}C({=}O){-}OH$$

17.4 2,3-Dibromopropanoic acid
17.5 (a)

benzene ring—$COCH(CH_3)_2$ (O)   **(b)** $CH_3CH_2CH_2CH_2COCH_2CH_3$ (O)

(c)

$$CH_3CH{=}CHCOCH(CH_3)_2 \text{ (O)}$$

17.6 CH_3COOH is highest boiling (most H-bonding). $CH_3CH_2CH_3$ is lowest boiling (nonpolar). **17.7 (a)** C_3H_7COOH is more soluble (smaller —R group). **(b)** $(CH_3)_2CHCOOH$ is more soluble (carboxylic acid).

17.8

$$CH_3CH_2COH \text{ (O)} \qquad CH_3CH_2COCH_3 \text{ (O)} \qquad CH_3CH_2CNH_2 \text{ (O)}$$
Propanoic acid   Methyl propanoate   Propanamide

$$CH_3CH_2CNHCH_3 \text{ (O)} \qquad CH_3CH_2CNCH_3 \text{ (O)} \text{ with } CH_3$$
N-Methylpropanamide   *N,N*-Dimethylpropanamide

17.9 (a) Propyl 3-hydroxypentanoate **(b)** *N*-Methyl-*p*-chlorobenzamide
17.10 (a)

$$CH_3CHCH_2CH_2CNH_2 \text{ with } CH_3, O$$

(b)

$$CH_3CH_2CNCH_2CH_3 \text{ with O, } CH_3$$

17.11 (a) (ii) **(b)** (i) **(c)** (iv) **(d)** (iii)   **17.12 (a)** (ii) **(b)** (i) **(c)** (iii) **(d)** (i) **(e)** (i) **(f)** (iii)
17.13 (a)

$$C_6H_5CNH_2 \text{ (O)}$$
Amide (C_7H_7NO)

(b)

$$CH_3CH_2COH \text{ (O)}$$
Carboxylic acid ($C_3H_6O_2$)

(c)

$$CH_3COCH_2CH_3 \text{ (O)}$$
Ester ($C_3H_6O_2$)

17.14 (a)

$$CH_3CHC{-}O^-\,Na^+ + H_2O \text{ with HO, O}$$

(b)

$$\left[CH_3CH_2CH_2C({-}C{=}O)({-}O^-) \text{ with } H_3C, CH_3 \right]_2 Ca^{2+}$$

17.15 (a)

$$\left[\text{benzene ring with } COO^- \text{ and OH} \right]_2 Ca^{2+}$$

(b)

$$H_2C{=}CHCOO^-\,Ca^+$$

17.16 $CH_3COO^-\ {}^-OOCCH_2CH_2CH_2COO^-\ Na^+\ K^+$
17.17 $HCOOCH_2CH(CH_3)_{2??}$
17.18 (a)

cyclohexane—OH + $HOCCH_2CH_2CH(CH_3)_2$ (O)

(b)

$$CH_3CH_2CH_2CH_2COH \text{ (O)} + HOCH(CH_3)_2$$

17.19
(a)

$$CH_3CHC{-}NHCH_3 \text{ with } CH_3, O$$

(b)

cyclopentane—$C({=}O){-}NH$—benzene ring

17.20

$$CH_3CH_2O{-}\text{(benzene ring)}{-}NH_2 + HOOCCH_3$$

17.21

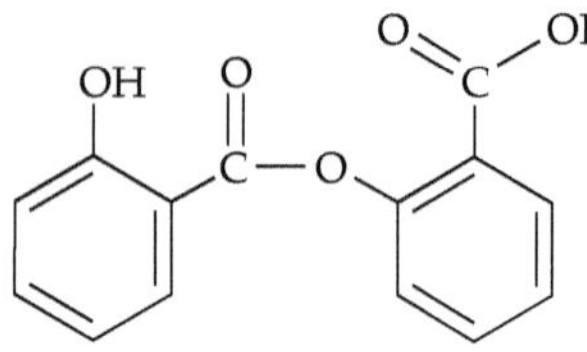

(d)

17.22 Aspirin is acidic (—COOH), lidocaine is basic (amine), benzocaine is weakly basic (aromatic amine), acetaminophen is weakly acidic (phenol).

17.23 Moisture in the air hydrolyzes the ester bond.

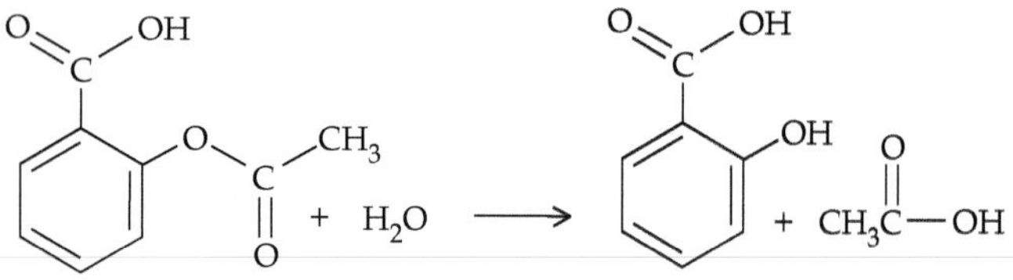

17.24 (a) *p*-Nitrobenzoic acid + 2-Propanol (b) Phenol + 2-Hydroxycyclopentanecarboxylic acid (c) Acrylic acid + Ethanol

17.25 (a) 2-Butenoic acid + Methylamine (b) *p*-Nitrobenzoic acid + Dimethylamine

17.26 (a)

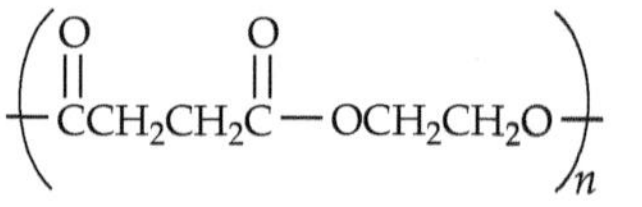

$$\left(\!\!-\overset{O}{\overset{\|}{C}}CH_2CH_2\overset{O}{\overset{\|}{C}}-OCH_2CH_2O\!-\!\right)_n$$

(b)

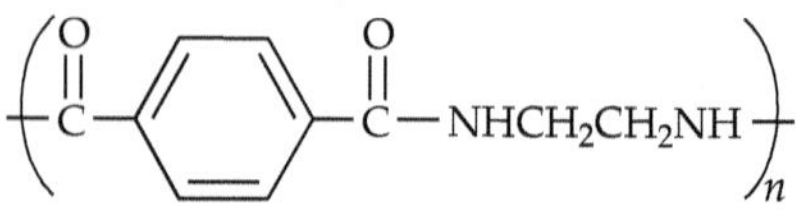

$$\left(\!\!-\overset{O}{\overset{\|}{C}}\!\!-\!\!\bigcirc\!\!-\!\!\overset{O}{\overset{\|}{C}}-NHCH_2CH_2NH\!-\!\right)_n$$

17.27

$$HO-\overset{O}{\overset{\|}{\underset{\underset{OH}{|}}{P}}}-O\overset{CH_3}{\overset{|}{C}}HCH_3 \qquad {}^-O-\overset{O}{\overset{\|}{\underset{\underset{O^-}{|}}{P}}}-O\overset{CH_3}{\overset{|}{C}}HCH_3$$

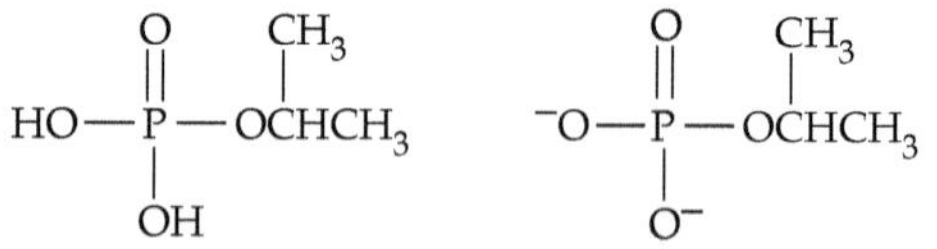

17.28 (a) amide + $H_2O \rightarrow CH_3COOH + NH_3$
(b) phosphate monoester + $H_2O \rightarrow CH_3CH_2OH + HOPO_3^{2-}$
(c) carboxylic acid ester + $H_2O \rightarrow CH_3CH_2COOH + HOCH_3$

17.29

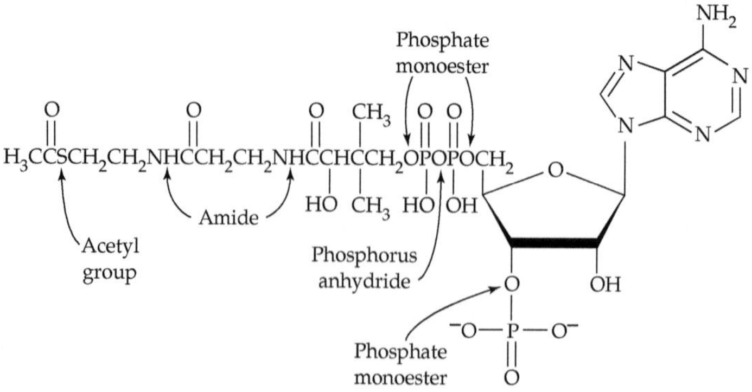

17.30 (a) At pH = 7.4, pyruvate and lactate are anions.
(b)

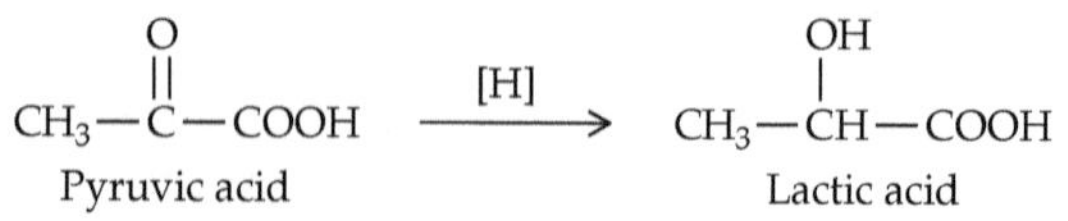

$$CH_3-\overset{O}{\overset{\|}{C}}-COOH \xrightarrow{[H]} CH_3-\overset{OH}{\overset{|}{C}}H-COOH$$

Pyruvic acid   Lactic acid

(c) Pyruvate and lactate have similar solubilities in water.

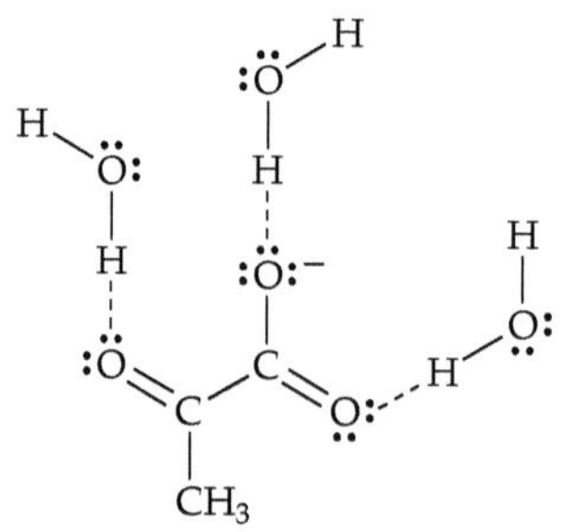

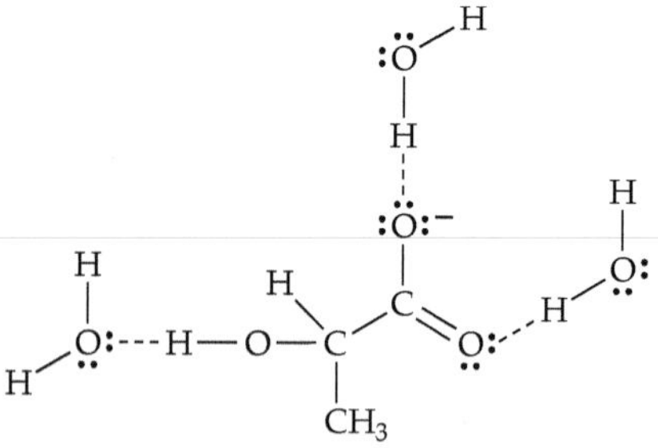

17.31 (a) H_2O + acid or base
(b)

$$+ \quad CH_3\overset{O}{\overset{\|}{C}}OH$$

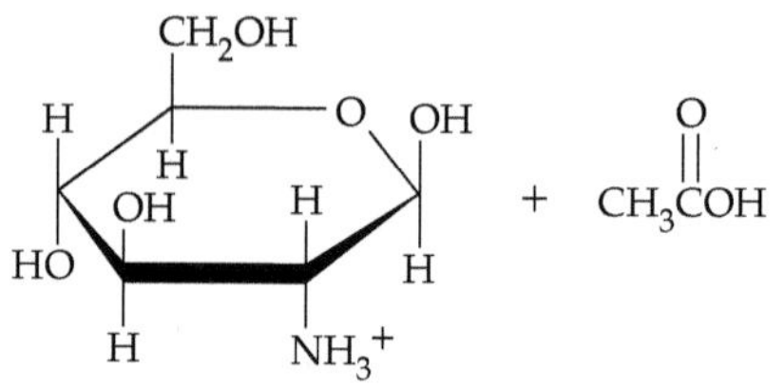

17.32 (a) a phosphate ester linkage
(b)

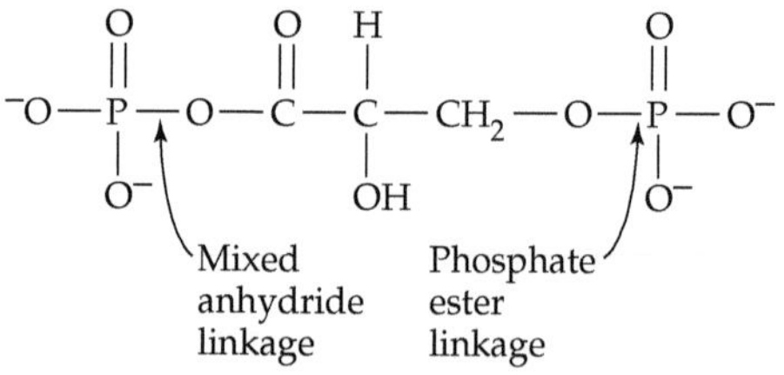

$${}^-O-\overset{O}{\overset{\|}{\underset{\underset{O^-}{|}}{P}}}-O-\overset{O}{\overset{\|}{C}}-\overset{H}{\overset{|}{\underset{\underset{OH}{|}}{C}}}-CH_2-O-\overset{O}{\overset{\|}{\underset{\underset{O^-}{|}}{P}}}-O^-$$

Mixed anhydride linkage   Phosphate ester linkage

17.33

$${}^-OOCCOO^- \qquad {}^-OOCCH_2COO^-$$
Oxalate   Malonate

$${}^-OOCCH_2CH_2COO^- \qquad {}^-OOCCH_2CH_2CH_2COO^-$$
Succinate   Glutarate

17.34
(a)

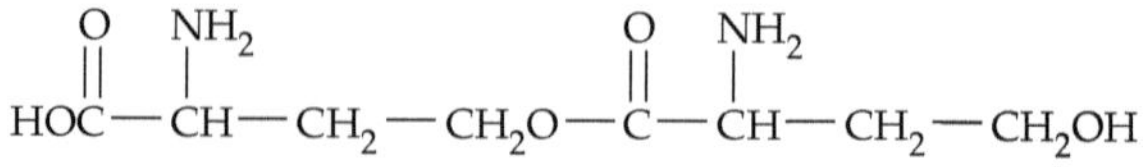

$$HO\overset{O}{\overset{\|}{C}}-\overset{NH_2}{\overset{|}{C}}H-CH_2-CH_2O-\overset{O}{\overset{\|}{C}}-\overset{NH_2}{\overset{|}{C}}H-CH_2-CH_2OH$$

(b)

$$HO\overset{O}{\overset{\|}{C}}-\overset{H}{\overset{|}{C}}-\overset{H}{\overset{|}{N}}-\overset{O}{\overset{\|}{C}}-\overset{NH_2}{\overset{|}{C}}H-CH_2-CH_2OH$$
$$\qquad\quad \underset{CH_2CH_2OH}{|}$$

(c)

H$_2$N
   CH—CH$_2$
O=C   CH$_2$
      O

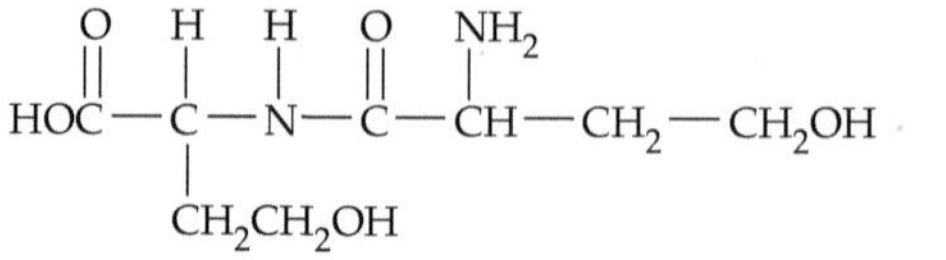

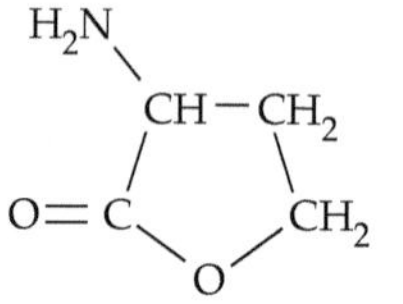

18.11 2-Aminobutane has a carbon with 4 different groups bonded to it.
18.12 chiral: **(b)**, **(c)**

18.13

Threonine   Isoleucine

18.14

18.15 (a)

| Gly–Ser–Tyr | Tyr–Ser–Gly | Ser–Tyr–Gly |
| Gly–Tyr–Ser | Tyr–Gly–Ser | Ser–Gly–Tyr |

(b)

Gly–Ser–Tyr

Gly–Tyr–Ser

18.16

| Leu–Trp–Ser | Trp–Leu–Ser | Ser–Trp–Leu |
| Leu–Ser–Trp | Trp–Ser–Leu | Ser–Leu–Trp |

18.17 (a) Leu–Asp **(b)** Tyr–Ser–Lys

18.18

Tyr–Ser–Lys

18.19 Asp–Tyr + Phe + Glu–Asn–Cys–Pro–Lys–Gly
18.20 (a) hydrogen bond **(b)** hydrophobic interaction **(c)** salt bridge **(d)** hydrophobic interaction **18.21 (a)** Tyr, Asp, Ser **(b)** Ala, Ile, Val, Leu
18.22 eleven backbone atoms **18.23** Secondary structure: stabilized by hydrogen bonds between amide nitrogens and carbonyl oxygens of polypeptide backbone. Tertiary structure: stabilized by hydrogen bonds between amino acid side-chain groups. **18.24 (a)** tertiary; **(b)** secondary; **(c)** quaternary **18.25** At low pH, the groups at the end of the polypeptide chain exist as $-NH_3^+$ and $-COOH$. At high pH, they exist as $-NH_2$ and $-COO^-$. In addition, side chain functional groups may be ionized as follows: **(a)** no change **(b)** Lys, His, Arg positively charged at low pH; Lys, His neutral at high pH: **(c)** Tyr neutral at low pH, negatively charged at high pH: **(d)** Glu, Asp neutral at low pH, negatively charged at high pH: **(e)** no change: **(f)** Cys neutral at low pH, negatively charged at high pH. **18.26 (a)** 1, 4 **(b)** 2, 4 **(c)** 2
18.27 *See below for answer.*
18.28 *Fibrous Proteins*: structural proteins, water-insoluble, contain many Gly and Pro residues, contain large regions of α-helix or β-sheet, few side-chain interactions. Examples: Collagen, α-Keratin, Fibroin. *Globular Proteins*: enzymes and hormones, usually water-soluble, contain most amino acids, contain smaller regions of α-helix and β-sheet, complex tertiary structure. Examples: Ribonuclease, hemoglobin, insulin.
18.29 (a) Leu, Phe, Ala or any other amino acid with a nonpolar side chain. **(b)** and **(c)** Asp, Lys, Thr or any other amino acid with a polar side chain. **18.30** The prefix "α" means that $-NH_2$ and $-COOH$ are bonded to the same carbon, the carbon atom in the alpha position (next to) the carbonyl carbon atom in the carboxyl group.

18.32 (a)   **(b)**

(c)

18.34 (a)   **(b)**

Cysteine (Cys)   Tyrosine (Tyr)

18.27

Asp–Gly–Phe–Leu–Glu–Ala

18.36 neutral: **(a) (c)** positive charge: **(b)** **18.38 (a), (c)** low pH **(b)** high pH **18.40** A chiral object is handed. Examples: glove, car. **18.42 (a)**
18.44

(a)

$$CH_3\overset{Cl}{\underset{Br}{\overset{|}{C}}}CH_3$$

Achiral

(b)

$$CH_3CH_2\overset{Cl}{\underset{Br}{\overset{|}{\overset{*}{C}}}}CH_3$$

Chiral

(c)

$$(CH_3)_2CH\overset{Cl}{\underset{Br}{\overset{|}{\overset{*}{C}}}}CH_3$$

Chiral

18.46

Chiral \ /Achiral

$$CH_3\overset{}{\underset{\underset{\text{Achiral}}{\overset{|}{F}}}{C}}HCH_2CH_3$$

18.48 A simple protein is composed only of amino acids. A conjugated protein consists of a protein associated with one or more nonprotein molecules.
18.50

TYPE OF PROTEIN	FUNCTION	EXAMPLE
Enzymes:	Catalyze biochemical reactions	Ribonuclease
Hormones:	Regulate body functions	Insulin
Storage proteins:	Store essential substances	Myoglobin
Transport proteins:	Transport substances through body fluids	Serum albumin
Structural proteins:	Provide shape and support	Collagen
Protective proteins:	Defend the body against foreign matter	Immunoglobulins
Contractile proteins:	Do mechanical work	Myosin and actin

18.52 Disulfide bonds stabilize tertiary structure. **18.54** In *hydrophobic interactions*, hydrocarbon side chains cluster in the center of proteins and make proteins spherical. Examples: Phe, Ile. *Salt bridges* bring together distant parts of a polypeptide chain. Examples: Lys, Asp. **18.56** When a protein is denatured, its nonprimary structure is disrupted, and it can no longer catalyze reactions. **18.58** Val–Met–Leu, Met–Val–Leu, Leu–Met–Val, Val–Leu–Met, Met–Leu–Val, Leu–Val–Met.
18.60 *Outside*: Asp, His (They can form H-bonds.) *Inside*: Val, Ala (They have hydrophobic interactions.) **18.62** Digestive enzymes would hydrolyze insulin if it were swallowed.

18.64

N-terminal ... C-terminal

18.66 (a) $H_3{}^+NCH_2COOH$ **(b)** $H_3{}^+NCH_2COOCH_3$
18.68 N-terminal: Val–Gly–Ser–Ala–Asp C-terminal
18.70 A peptide rich in Asp and Lys is more soluble, because its side chains are more polar and can form hydrogen bonds with water.
18.72

(a)

Tyrosine → Tyramine + CO_2

Decarboxylation is the loss of CO_2. **(b)** Phenelzine resembles tyramine (it has a phenyl group and an amino group) and blocks the enzyme that catalyzes deamination of tyramine. **18.74** An incomplete protein lacks one or more essential amino acids. **18.76** They must provide complete nutrition to developing organisms. **18.78** Arg–Trp moves to negative electrode, Val–Met doesn't move, Asp–Thr moves to positive electrode. **18.80** Osteogenesis imperfecta is a dominant genetic defect in which collagen is synthesized incorrectly, resulting in weak bones. **18.82** It was hard to accept that a protein might duplicate itself, cause disease, be responsible for inherited disease, be transmitted, and might arise spontaneously. **18.84** A combination of grains, legumes, and nuts in each meal provides all of the essential amino acids. **18.86** Canned pineapple has been heated to inactivate enzymes

18.88 (a)

Arg——Pro——Pro——Gly——Phe——Ser——Pro——Phe——Arg

(b) Proline rings introduce kinks and bends and prevent hydrogen bonds from forming.

18.90 Carbon is no longer bonded to four different groups.

18.92

Asn—Cys—Pro—Leu—Gln

Gln

Ile S

Tyr—Cys S

Oxytocin

18.94 Arg, Asp, Asn, Glu, Gln, His, Lys, Ser, Thr, Tyr

Asn O=C HC—CH₂C—N̈—H------:O—CH₂—CH Ser
NH O H C=O

Asn O=C HC—CH₂C—N—H------:O: :O------H—Ö—CH₂—CH Ser
NH O H C=O

18.96 On the outside of a globular protein: Glu, Ser. On the outside of a fibrous protein: Ala, Val. On the outside of neither: Leu, Phe.

18.98 Asp is similar in size and function to Glu.

Chapter 19

19.1 Kinases **19.2** (1) The enzyme might catalyze reactions within the eye. (2) Saline is sterile and isotonic. **19.3** iron, copper, manganese, molybdenum, vanadium, cobalt, nickel, chromium **19.4 (a)** NAD^+, coenzyme A, FAD; **(b)** They are minerals. **19.5 (a)** catalyzes the removal of two —H from glutamate. **(b)** catalyzes the transfer of an amino group from alanine to a second substrate. **(c)** catalyzes the formation of a bond between carbamoyl phosphate and another substrate. **(d)** catalyzes the isomerization of triose phosphate. **19.6 (a)** arginase **(b)** maltase **19.7** isomerase. It catalyzes the isomerization of glucose 6-phosphate. **19.8** Water adds to fumarate (substrate) to give L-malate (product). **19.9** Reaction **(a)** **19.10** Acidic, basic, and polar side chains take part in catalytic activity. All types of side chains hold the enzyme in the active site. **19.11** Substrate molecules are bound to all of the active sites. **(a)** no effect; **(b)** increases the rate. **19.12** higher at 30°; somewhat higher at 40°. **19.13** The rate is much greater at pH = 8. **19.14** molecule **(b)**, because it resembles the substrate. **19.15** a product that resembles the substrate. **19.16 (a)** competitive inhibition **(b)** covalent modification or feedback control **(c)** covalent modification **(d)** genetic control **19.17** Vitamin A—long hydrocarbon chain. Vitamin C—polar hydroxyl groups. **19.18** Retinal—aldehyde. Retinoic acid—carboxylic acid. Retinol—alcohol. Same functional group modified in each molecule. **19.19** enzyme cofactors; antioxidants; aid in absorption of calcium and phosphate ions; aid in synthesis of visual pigments and blood clotting factors.

19.20

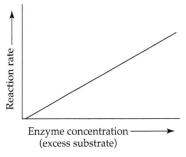

---- Hydrogen bonds

‖‖‖‖ Salt bridges

19.21 (a) oxidoreductase **(b)** dehydrogenase **(c)** L-lactate **(d)** pyruvate **(e)** L-lactate dehydrogenase

19.22 No. An enzyme usually catalyzes the reaction of only one isomer. D-Lactate might be a competitive inhibitor. **19.23** NAD^+ is an oxidizing agent and includes the vitamin niacin. **19.24 (a)** Rate increases when [substrate] is low, but max. rate is soon reached; max. rate is always lower than max. rate of uninhibited reaction. **(b)** Rate increases. **19.25 (a)** Addition or removal of a covalently bonded group changes the activity of an enzyme. **(b)** Hormones control the synthesis of enzymes. **(c)** Binding of the regulator at a site away from the catalytic site changes the shape of the enzyme. **(d)** Noncompetitive inhibition is a type of allosteric regulation (see part **(c)**). Competitive inhibition occurs when an inhibitor reversibly occupies an enzyme's active site. Irreversible inhibition results when an inhibitor covalently binds to an enzyme and destroys its ability to catalyze a reaction. **19.26 (a)** feedback inhibition **(b)** irreversible inhibition **(c)** genetic control **(d)** noncompetitive inhibition **19.27** From left to right: aspartate (acidic), serine, glutamine, arginine (basic), histidine (basic). **19.28 (a)** oxidation or reduction of a substrate; **(b)** addition of a small molecule to a double bond, or removal of a small molecule to form a double bond; **(c)** transfer of a functional group from one substrate to another **19.30 (a)** sucrase **(b)** fumarase **(c)** RNAse **19.32** An enzyme is a large three-dimensional molecule with a catalytic site into which a substrate can fit. Enzymes are specific in their action because only one or a few molecules have the appropriate shape and functional groups to fit into the catalytic site. **19.34 (a)** hydrolase **(b)** lyase **(c)** oxidoreductase **19.36 (a)** loss of CO_2 from a substrate; **(b)** transfer of a methyl group between substrates; **(c)** removal of two —H to form a double bond **19.38** hydrolase **19.40 (a)** riboflavin (B_2) **(b)** pantothenic acid (B_5) **(c)** pyridoxine (B_6) **19.42** Lock-and-key: An enzyme is rigid (lock) and only one specific substrate (key) can fit in the active site. Induced fit: An enzyme can change its shape to accommodate the substrate and to catalyze the reaction. **19.44** No. Protein folding can bring the residues close to each other. **19.46** In the stomach, an enzyme must be active at an acidic pH. In the intestine, an enzyme needs to be active at a higher pH and need not be active at pH = 1.5.

19.48

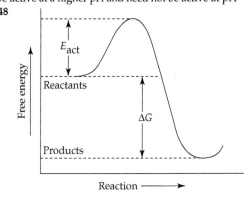

19.50 At a high substrate concentration relative to enzyme concentration, the rate of reaction increases as the enzyme concentration increases because more substrate can react if there are more active sites.

19.52 Increasing enzyme concentration increases the rate; increasing substrate concentration increases the rate until all active sites are filled, when the rate levels off. **19.54 (a) (b)** lowers rate; **(c)** denatures the enzyme and stops reaction **19.56** *Noncompetitive inhibition*: Inhibitor binds reversibly and noncovalently away from the active site and changes the shape of the site to make it difficult for the enzyme to

catalyze reactions. *Competitive inhibition*: Inhibitor binds reversibly and noncovalently at the active site and keeps the substrate from entering. *Irreversible inhibition*: Inhibitor irreversibly forms a covalent bond at the active site and destroys the catalytic ability of the enzyme. **19.58** diagram **(c)** **19.60** (1) displacing an essential metal from an active site; (2) bonding to a cysteine residue (irreversible) **19.62** Papain catalyzes the hydrolysis of peptide bonds and partially digests the proteins in meat. **19.64** One site is for catalysis, and one site is for regulation. **19.66** The end product of a reaction series is an inhibitor for an earlier step. **19.68** A zymogen is an enzyme synthesized in a form different from its active form because it might otherwise harm the organism. **19.70** Vitamins are small essential organic molecules that must be obtained from food. **19.72** Vitamin C is excreted, but vitamin A is stored in fatty tissue. **19.74** (1) Enzymes produce only one enantiomer of a product. (2) Enzymes allow difficult reactions to take place (3) Use of enzymes avoids reactions with hazardous byproducts. **19.76** Two strategies keep the enzyme active: (1) Use of chaperonins, enzymes that return a protein to its active form; (2) The protein itself is rigid and resists heat denaturation. **19.78** CPK, ALT, and LDH1 leak from damaged heart vessels. **19.80** A mild inhibitor allows closer control of blood pressure. A modification to pit viper protein might be to introduce a –SH residue near proline. **19.82** The body excretes excess water-soluble vitamins, but fat-soluble vitamins are stored in tissue. **19.84** They are the most important for maintaining good health.
19.86 *See below for answer.*
19.88 Blanching destroys enzymes that would cause deterioration in food quality. **19.90** Leu−Gly−Arg, Ile−Met−His, Tyr−Trp−Ala **19.92** Excess ethanol displaces methanol from the active site.

Chapter 20

20.1 (c) **20.2** The molecules resemble the heterocyclic part of cAMP, and they might act as inhibitors to the enzyme that inactivates cAMP. **20.3** Glu−His−Pro **20.4** The hydrophobic part of the structure is larger than the polar, hydrophilic part. **20.5** Testosterone has a —CH₃ group between the first two rings; nandrolone doesn't. Otherwise, their structures are identical. **20.6 (a)** 3 **(b)** 1 **(c)** 2 **20.7** Similarities: both structures have aromatic rings, secondary amine groups, alcohol groups. Differences: propranolol has an ether group and a naphthalene ring system; epinephrine has two phenol hydroxyl groups; the compounds have different side chain carbon skeletons. **20.8** Malathion: it's the least toxic. **20.9** An agonist (black widow spider venom) prolongs the biochemical response of a receptor. An antagonist (botulinus toxin) blocks or inhibits the normal response of a receptor. **20.10** phenol hydroxyl group, ether, carbon-carbon double bond, aromatic ring. THC is hydrophobic and is likely to accumulate in fatty tissue. **20.11 (a)** antihistamine **(b)** antidepressant **20.12 (a)** polypeptide hormone (produced in the anterior pituitary gland) **(b)** steroid hormone (produced in

ovaries) **(c)** Progesterone-producing cells have LH receptors. **(d)** Progesterone is lipid-soluble and can enter cells. **20.13** (1) Adenylate cyclase can produce a great many molecules of cAMP. (2) A large amount of glucose is released when glycogen phosphorylase is activated. **20.14 (a)** insulin (polypeptide hormone) **(b)** pancreas **(c)** in the bloodstream **(d)** Insulin doesn't enter cells directly because it can't pass through cell membranes. Instead, it binds with a cell surface receptor. **20.15** Neurotransmitters can act either by binding to receptors or by activating second messengers. **20.16** Enzymatic inactivation; reuptake of neurotransmitter molecules by presynaptic neuron. **20.17** These substances increase dopamine levels in the brain. The brain responds by decreasing the number and sensitivity of dopamine receptors. Thus more of the substance is needed to elevate dopamine levels, leading to addiction. **20.18** A hormone is a molecule that travels through the bloodstream to its target tissue, where it binds to a receptor and regulates biochemical reactions. **20.20** A hormone transmits a chemical message from an endocrine gland to a target tissue. A neurotransmitter carries an impulse between neighboring nerve cells. **20.22** Hormone binding is noncovalent and regulates a reaction, rather than catalyzing it. **20.24** The endocrine system manufactures and secretes hormones. **20.26** polypeptide hormones, steroid hormones, amino acid derivatives **20.28** Enzymes are proteins; hormones may be polypeptides, proteins, steroids, or amino acid derivatives. **20.30** Polypeptide hormones travel through the bloodstream and bind to cell receptors, which are on the outside of a cell. The receptors cause production within cells of "second messengers" that activate enzymes. **20.32** the adrenal medulla **20.34** through the bloodstream **20.36** In order of involvement; the hormone receptor, G protein, and adenylate cyclase. **20.38** It initiates reactions that release glucose from storage. Termination occurs when phosphodiesterase converts cAMP to AMP. **20.40** anaphylaxis **20.42** Insulin contains 51 amino acids, is released from the pancreas, and acts at cells, causing them to take up glucose. **20.44** mineralocorticoids (aldosterone), glucocorticoids (cortisone) sex hormones (testosterone, estrone). **20.46** estrone, estradiol, progesterone **20.48** epinephrine, norepinephrine, dopamine **20.50 (a)** amino acid derivative **(b)** polypeptide hormone **(c)** steroid hormone **20.52** A synapse is the gap between two nerve cells that neurotransmitters cross to transmit their message. **20.54** nerve cell, muscle cell, endocrine cell **20.56** A nerve impulse arrives at the presynaptic end of a neuron. The nerve impulse stimulates the movement of a vesicle, containing neurotransmitter molecules, to the cell membrane. The vesicle fuses with the cell membrane and releases the neurotransmitter, which crosses the synaptic cleft to a receptor site on the postsynaptic end of a second neuron. After reception, the cell transmits an electrical signal down its axon and passes on the impulse. Enzymes then deactivate the neurotransmitter so that the neuron can receive the next impulse. Alternatively, the neurotransmitter may be returned to the presynaptic neuron. **20.58** (1) Neurotransmitter

19.86

Vitamin E

molecules are released from a presynaptic neuron. (2) Neurotransmitter molecules bind to receptors on the target cell. (3) The neurotransmitter is deactivated   **20.60** They are secreted in the central nervous system and have receptors in brain tissue.   **20.62** Agonists prolong the response of a receptor. Antagonists block the response of a receptor.   **20.64** Antihistamines such as doxylamine counteract allergic responses caused by histamine by blocking histamine receptors in mucous membranes. Antihistamines such as cimetidine block receptors for histamine that stimulate production of stomach acid.   **20.66** Tricyclic antidepressant: Elavil   MAO inhibitor: Nardil   SSRI: Prozac   **20.68** Cocaine increases dopamine levels by blocking reuptake.   **20.70** Tetrahydrocannabinol (THC) increases dopamine levels in the same brain areas where dopamine levels increase after administration of heroin and cocaine.   **20.72** Endorphins are polypeptides with morphine-like activity. They are produced by the pituitary gland and have receptors in the brain.   **20.74** An ethnobotanist discovers what indigenous people have learned about the healing power of plants.   **20.76** Scientists who know about the exact size and shape of enzymes and receptors can design drugs that interact with the active sites of these biomolecules.   **20.78** Homeostasis is the maintenance of a constant internal environment.   **20.80** Plants don't have endocrine systems or a circulatory fluid like blood.   **20.82** Epibatidine acts as a painkiller at acetylcholine receptors in the central nervous system.   **20.84** The *hormone receptor* recognizes the hormone, sets in motion the stimulation process, and interacts with *G-protein*. This protein binds GTP and activates *adenylate cyclase*, which catalyzes the formation of cAMP.   **20.86** Signal amplification is the process by which a small signal induces a response much larger than the original signal. In the case of hormones, a small amount of hormone can bring about a very large response.   **20.88** Testosterone has an —OH group in the 5-membered ring; progesterone has an acetyl group in that position. Otherwise, the two molecules are identical. **20.90** Chocolate acts at dopamine receptors and produces feelings of satisfaction.   **20.92** Testosterone is converted to androsterone by reductions (C=O, C=C) in the first ring, and an oxidation of —OH in the five-membered ring.

Chapter 21

21.1 exergonic: **(a)**, **(c)**; endergonic: **(b)**; releases the most energy: **(a)**
21.2 Both pathways produce the same amount of energy.
21.3 **(a)** exergonic: oxidation of glucose; endergonic: photosynthesis **(b)** sunlight
21.4 **(a)**

Carbohydrates $\xrightarrow{\text{Digestion}}$ Glucose, sugars $\xrightarrow{\text{Glycolysis}}$

Pyruvate $\longrightarrow$ Acetyl-SCoA $\xrightarrow[\text{cycle}]{\text{Citric acid}}$

Reduced coenzymes $\xrightarrow[\text{transport}]{\text{Electron}}$ ATP

(b) pyruvate, acetyl-SCoA, citric acid cycle intermediates.
21.5

$$H_3C-\overset{\displaystyle O}{\overset{\|}{C}}-O-\overset{\displaystyle O}{\underset{\underset{O^-}{|}}{\overset{\|}{P}}}-O^- + H_2O \longrightarrow$$

$$H_3C-\overset{\displaystyle O}{\overset{\|}{C}}-O^- + {}^-O-\overset{\displaystyle O}{\underset{\underset{OH}{|}}{\overset{\|}{P}}}-O^- + H^+$$

21.6 Energy is produced only when it is needed.
21.7

$$\text{HOCH}_2\overset{\underset{OH}{|}}{C}\text{HCH}_2\text{OH} \xrightarrow[]{\text{ATP} \quad \text{ADP}} \text{HOCH}_2\overset{\underset{OH}{|}}{C}\text{HCH}_2\text{O}-\overset{\displaystyle O}{\underset{\underset{O^-}{|}}{\overset{\|}{P}}}-O^-$$

21.8 If a process is exergonic, its exact reverse is endergonic and can't occur unless it is coupled with an exergonic reaction in a different pathway.   **21.9** favorable ($\Delta G = -3.0$ kcal/mol).   **21.10** yes

21.11

$$^-OOC-\overset{\overset{\displaystyle \text{(H—O)} \quad COO^-}{|}}{\underset{\underset{\text{(H)}}{|}}{C}}-CH-CH_2COO^-$$

$$^-OOC-\overset{\overset{\text{(H)}}{|}}{C}H-\overset{\overset{\text{(H)}}{|}}{C}H-COO^-$$

$$^-OOC-CH_2-\overset{\overset{\displaystyle O-\text{(H)}}{|}}{\underset{\underset{\text{(H)}}{|}}{C}}-COO^-$$

21.12 Citric acid, isocitric acid.   **21.13** steps 3, 4, 6, 8.   **21.14** Succinic dehydrogenase catalyzes the removal of two hydrogens from succinate to yield fumarate.   **21.15** α-Ketoglutarate, oxaloacetate.   **21.16** isocitrate **21.17** Steps 1–4 correspond to the first stage, and steps 5–8 correspond to the second stage.   **21.18** Mitochondrial matrix   **21.19** O_2. Movement of H^+ from a region of high $[H^+]$ to a region of low $[H^+]$ releases energy that is used in ATP synthesis.
21.20 **(a)** Succinyl phosphate + $H_2O \rightarrow$ Succinate + $HOPO_3{}^{2-}$ + H^+
(b) ADP + $HOPO_3{}^{2-}$ + $H^+ \rightarrow$ ATP + H_2O $\Delta G = +7.3$ kcal/mol
21.21 **(a)** Stage 1 (digestion) **(b)** Stage 4 (ATP synthesis) **(c)** Stage 2 (glycolysis) **(d)** Stage 3 (citric acid cycle).   **21.22** Endergonic; coupled reactions   **21.23** NAD^+ accepts hydride ions; hydrogen ions are released to the mitochondrial matrix, and ultimately combine with reduced O_2 to form H_2O.   **21.24** **(a)** Step A (NAD^+) **(b)** Step B **(c)** product of A (in brackets)   **21.25** Step 1: lyase Step 2: isomerase Step 3: oxidoreductase Step 4: oxidoreductase, lyase Step 5: ligase Step 6: oxidoreductase Step 7: lyase Step 8: oxidoreductase   **21.26** Metals are better oxidizing and reducing agents. Also, they can accept and donate electrons in one-electron increments.   **21.28** An endergonic reaction requires energy, and an exergonic reaction releases energy. **21.30** Enzymes affect only the rate of a reaction, not the size or sign of ΔG.   **21.32** Exergonic: **(a)**, **(b)**; endergonic: **(c)**. Reaction **(a)** proceeds farthest toward products.
21.34

PROKARYOTIC CELLS	EUKARYOTIC CELLS
Quite small	Relatively large
No nucleus	Nucleus
Dispersed DNA	DNA in nucleus
No organelles	Organelles
Occur in single-celled organisms	Occur in single-celled and higher organisms

21.36 The cytoplasm consists of everything between the cell membrane and the nuclear membrane. The cytosol is the medium that fills the interior of the cell and contains electrolytes, nutrients, and many enzymes, in aqueous solution.   **21.38** A mitochondrion is egg-shaped and consists of a smooth, outer membrane and a folded inner membrane. The intermembrane space lies between the outer and inner membranes, and the space enclosed by the inner membrane is called the *mitochondrial matrix*.   **21.40** 90% of the body's ATP is synthesized in mitochondria. **21.42** Metabolism refers to all reactions that take place inside cells. Digestion is a part of metabolism in which food is broken down into small organic molecules.   **21.44** acetyl—ScoA   **21.46** Energy is released when ATP transfers a phosphoryl group.   **21.48** ATP has a triphosphate group bonded to C5 of ribose, and ADP has a diphosphate group in that position.   **21.50** $\Delta G = -4.5$ kcal/mol.
21.52

1,3-Bisphosphoglycerate $\xrightarrow[]{\text{ADP} \qquad \text{ATP}}$ 3-Phosphoglycerate

21.54 **(a)** NAD^+ is reduced. **(b)** NAD^+ is an oxidizing agent. **(c)** NAD^+ oxidizes secondary alcohol to a ketone. **(d)** $NADH/H^+$
(e)

$$H-\overset{|}{\underset{|}{C}}-OH \xrightarrow[]{NAD^+ \quad NADH/H^+} \overset{|}{\underset{|}{C}}=O$$

21.56 cellular mitochondria   **21.58** Both carbons are oxidized to CO_2. **21.60** 3 NADH, one $FADH_2$.   **21.62** Step 3 (isocitrate $\rightarrow \alpha$-ketoglutarate),

Step 4 (α-ketoglutarate → succinyl-SCoA) and Step 8 (malate → oxaloac-etate) store energy as NADH. **21.64** One complete citric acid cycle pro-duces four reduced coenzymes, which enter the electron transfer chain and ultimately generate ATP. **21.66** H_2O, ATP, oxidized coenzymes **21.68 (a)** FAD = flavin adenine dinucleotide; **(b)** CoQ = coenzyme Q; **(c)** NADH/H^+ = reduced nicotinamide adenine dinucleotide, plus hydrogen ion; **(d)** Cyt c = Cytochrome c **21.70** NADH, coenzyme Q, cytochrome c **21.72** The citric acid cycle would stop. **21.74** formation of ATP from the reactions of reduced coenzymes in the electron transport system **21.76 (a)** ATP **(b)** H_2O, oxidized coenzymes **20.78** Bacteria use H_2S because no light is available for the usual light-dependent reac-tion of H_2O that provides O_2 and electrons. **21.80** Answer based on reader's own weight and activity level **21.82** Daily activities such as walking use energy, and thus the body requires a larger caloric intake than that needed to maintain basal metabolism. **21.84** Oxygen con-sumption increases because the proton gradient from ATP production dissipates. **21.86** A seal has more brown fat because it needs to keep warm. **21.88** The light reaction produces O_2, NADPH, and ATP. The dark reaction produces carbohydrates from water and CO_2. **21.90** Refrigeration slows the breakdown of carbohydrates by decreasing the rate of respiration. Enzyme reactions are slower at low temperatures.

21.92

$$\text{CoAS}-\overset{\overset{\displaystyle O}{\|}}{\text{C}}-\text{CH}_3 \;+\; \begin{matrix}\text{COO}^- \\ | \\ \text{C}=\text{O} \\ | \\ \text{CH}_2 \\ | \\ \text{COO}^-\end{matrix} \xrightarrow{\text{condensation}} \text{CoAS}-\overset{\overset{\displaystyle O}{\|}}{\text{C}}-\text{CH}_2-\begin{matrix}\text{COO}^- \\ | \\ \text{C}-\text{OH} \\ | \\ \text{CH}_2 \\ | \\ \text{COO}^-\end{matrix}$$

21.94 oxidoreductases **21.96** FAD; oxidoreductases **21.98** isocitrate; malate **21.100** $O_2^-\cdot$, $OH^-\cdot$, and H_2O_2; superoxide dismutase, catalase, vitamins E, C, and A. **21.102** adipose tissue, skin cells, skeletal muscle, heart muscle.

Chapter 22

22.1 (a) aldopentose **(b)** ketotriose **(c)** aldotetrose

22.2

$$\text{HOCH}_2-\overset{\overset{\displaystyle OH}{|}}{\text{CH}}-\overset{\overset{\displaystyle OH}{|}}{\text{CH}}-\overset{\overset{\displaystyle OH}{|}}{\text{CH}}-\overset{\overset{\displaystyle O}{\|}}{\text{CH}}$$

An aldopentose

$$\text{HOCH}_2-\overset{\overset{\displaystyle OH}{|}}{\text{CH}}-\overset{\overset{\displaystyle OH}{|}}{\text{CH}}-\overset{\overset{\displaystyle OH}{|}}{\text{CH}}-\overset{\overset{\displaystyle O}{\|}}{\text{C}}-\text{CH}_2\text{OH}$$

A ketohexose

22.3 eight stereoisomers **22.4 (d)** **22.5** The bottom carbon is not chi-ral. The orientations of the hydroxyl groups bonded to the chiral carbons must be shown in order to indicate which stereoisomer is pictured.

22.6 (a)

$$\begin{matrix}\overset{\displaystyle H}{\searrow}\overset{\displaystyle C}{\diagup}^{\displaystyle O} \\ | \\ \text{HO}-\text{C}-\text{H} \\ | \\ \text{H}-\text{C}-\text{OH} \\ | \\ \boxed{\text{H}-\text{C}-\text{OH}} \\ | \\ \text{CH}_2\text{OH}\end{matrix} \qquad \begin{matrix}\overset{\displaystyle H}{\searrow}\overset{\displaystyle C}{\diagup}^{\displaystyle O} \\ | \\ \text{H}-\text{C}-\text{OH} \\ | \\ \text{HO}-\text{C}-\text{H} \\ | \\ \boxed{\text{HO}-\text{C}-\text{H}} \\ | \\ \text{CH}_2\text{OH}\end{matrix}$$

A D-aldopentose · · · · · · · An L-aldopentose

(b)

$$\begin{matrix}\text{CH}_2\text{OH} \\ | \\ \text{C}=\text{O} \\ | \\ \text{H}-\text{C}-\text{OH} \\ | \\ \text{HO}-\text{C}-\text{H} \\ | \\ \boxed{\text{HO}-\text{C}-\text{H}} \\ | \\ \text{CH}_2\text{OH}\end{matrix} \qquad \begin{matrix}\text{CH}_2\text{OH} \\ | \\ \text{C}=\text{O} \\ | \\ \text{HO}-\text{C}-\text{H} \\ | \\ \text{H}-\text{C}-\text{OH} \\ | \\ \boxed{\text{H}-\text{C}-\text{OH}} \\ | \\ \text{CH}_2\text{OH}\end{matrix}$$

An L-ketohexose · · · · · · · A D-ketohexose

22.7

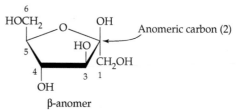

β-anomer · · · · · · · · · α-anomer

22.8

$$\begin{matrix}\overset{\displaystyle H}{\searrow}\overset{\displaystyle C}{\diagup}^{\displaystyle O} \\ | \\ \text{HO}-\text{C}-\text{H} \\ | \\ \text{H}-\text{C}-\text{OH} \\ | \\ \text{HO}-\text{C}-\text{H} \\ | \\ \text{H}-\text{C}-\text{OH} \\ | \\ \text{CH}_2\text{OH}\end{matrix}$$

D-Idose

22.9 (a) an α-hexose **(b)** a steroid **(c)** an ester

22.10

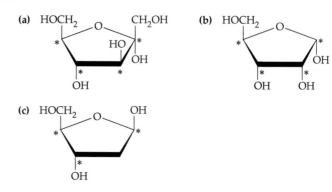

β-anomer

22.11

(a) HOCH$_2$ ... CH$_2$OH **(b)** HOCH$_2$ ... **(c)** HOCH$_2$ ...

22.12

Cyclic AMP   from ribose   ATP

22.13 (a) an α anomer **(b)** carbon 6 **(c)** Groups that are below the plane of the ring in D-galactose are above the plane of the ring in L-fucose. Groups that are above the plane of the ring in D-galactose are below the plane of the ring in L-fucose. **(d)** yes

22.14

Methyl α-D-riboside   Methyl β-D-riboside

22.15 a β-1,4 glycosidic link **22.16** β-D-Glucose + β-D-Glucose
22.17 (a) maltose **(b)** sucrose **(c)** lactose **22.18** glutamine, asparagine
22.19 an α-1,4 glycosidic link **22.20** No. There are too few hemiacetal units to give a detectable result.

22.21 Starch $\xrightarrow{\text{Amylase}}$ Maltose $\xrightarrow{\text{Maltase}}$ Glucose
    polysaccharide   disaccharide   monosaccharide

22.22 (a) diastereomers, anomers **(b)** enantiomers **(c)** diastereomers
22.23 (a) (b)

A   B   C
α-anomer β-anomer β-anomer

(c) α-1,4 linkage between C4 of B and C1 of A **(d)** β-1,4 linkage between C4 of C and C1 of B **22.24 (a) (b)** No monosaccharides are identical, and none are enantiomers.
(c) (d)

L-Fucose   D-Glucose   D-Galactose

22.25 Monosaccharide C is oxidized. Identification of the carboxylic acid also identifies the terminal monosaccharide.

22.26 No
22.27

POLYSACCHARIDE	LINKAGE	BRANCHING?
Cellulose	β-1,4	no
Amylose	α-1,4	no
Amylopectin	α-1,4	yes: α-1,6 branches occur ~ every 25 units
Glycogen	α-1,4	yes: even more α-1,6 branches than in amylopectin

22.28 Glucose is in equilibrium with its open-chain aldehyde form, which reacts with an oxidizing agent. **22.30** -ose **22.32 (a)** aldotetrose **(b)** ketopentose **(c)** aldopentose **(d)** ketohexose
22.34 right part = 4 chiral carbons; left part = 5 chiral carbons; total = 9 chiral carbons
22.36

Oxygen missing here

A four-carbon deoxy sugar

22.38 glucose – food, all living organisms; galactose – brain tissue, milk; fructose – fruit; ribose – nucleic acids **22.40** They are mirror images.
22.42 The reduction product of D-erythrose is achiral. **22.44** A polarimeter measures the degree of rotation of plane-polarized light by a solution of an optically active compound. **22.46** Equimolar solutions of enantiomers rotate light to the same degree but in opposite directions.
22.48 A reducing sugar contains an aldehyde or ketone group.
22.50 An anomer is one of a pair of hemiacetal stereoisomers formed when an open-chain sugar cyclizes. Anomers differ in the orientation of the hydroxyl group at the anomeric carbon. **22.52** the α form

22.54

$$HO-C-C-C-C-C-C-H$$ (open chain with H, H, H, H, OH, O; H, OH, OH, OH, H) = (pyranose ring with CH$_2$OH, OH, OH, C=O, H, OH)

β-D-Altrose

α-D-Altrose

22.56

22.58

$$HO-C-C-C-C-C-C-H$$ (H, H, H, H, H, O; H, OH, OH, OH, OH)

22.60

CH$_2$OH
HO—C—H
HO—C—H
H—C—OH
H—C—OH
CH$_2$OH

22.62

HO—C=O
H——OH
H——OH
H——OH
CH$_2$OH

22.64 A glycoside is an acetal that is formed when the hemiacetal —OH group of a carbohydrate reacts with an alcohol.

22.66

Hemiacetal carbon

The hemiacetal carbon in this problem is in equilibrium with an open-chain aldehyde that is a reducing sugar. **22.68** Sucrose has no hemiacetal group. **22.70** Amylose and amylopectin are both components of starch and both consist of long polymers of α-D-glucose linked by α-1,4 glycosidic bonds. Amylopectin is much larger and has α-1,6 branches every 25 units or so along the chain. **22.72** Gentiobiose contains both an acetal grouping and a hemiacetal grouping. Gentiobiose is a reducing sugar. A β-1,6 linkage connects the two monosaccharides. **22.74** Trehalose is a nonreducing sugar because it contains no hemiacetal linkages. The two D–glucose monosaccharides are connected by an α-1,1 acetal link.

22.76

22.78 Enzyme-catalyzed reactions usually produce only one enantiomer. **22.80** Starch is a complex carbohydrate. Glucose is a simple carbohydrate. Soluble and insoluble fiber are complex carbohydrates. **22.82** glucose, cellulose **22.84** Penicillin inhibits the enzyme that synthesizes bacterial cell walls. Mammals do not have this synthetic pathway. **22.86** People with type O blood can receive blood only from other donors that have type O blood. People with type AB blood can give blood only to other people with type AB blood. **22.88** pectin and vegetable gum: found in fruits, barley, oats, and beans. **22.90** D-Ribose and L-ribose are enantiomers that are identical in all properties (melting point, density, solubility, and chemical reactivity) except for the direction that they rotate plane-polarized light (b). **22.92** No, because they are not mirror images.

22.94

22.96 Raffinose is not a reducing sugar because it has no hemiacetal group. (It has acetal groups.)

22.98

$$HOCH_2CCH_2OH$$ (with C=O in middle)

1,3-Dihydroxyacetone has no optical isomers because it has no chiral carbons. **22.100** Lactose intolerance is an inability to digest lactose. Symptoms include bloating, cramps, and diarrhea. **22.102** Symptoms of galactosemia: vomiting, liver failure, mental retardation, cataracts. **22.104** 4 chiral carbons.

Chapter 23

23.1 (a) glycogenesis **(b)** glycogenolysis **(c)** gluconeogenesis **23.2** glycogenesis, pentose phosphate pathway, glycolysis **23.3 (a)** steps 6 and 7 **(b)** steps 9 and 10 **23.4** Isomerizations: steps 2, 5, 8

23.5

H—C=O
H—C—OH
HO—C—H
H—C—OH
H—C—OH
CH$_2$OPO$_3^{2-}$

⇌

CH$_2$OH
C=O
HO—C—H
H—C—OH
H—C—OH
CH$_2$OPO$_3^{2-}$

23.6 (a) pyruvate **(b)** Step 6: glyceraldehyde 3-phosphate is oxidized; NAD$^+$ is the oxidizing agent

23.7 Fructose 6-phosphate enters glycolysis at step 3.

23.8 Glucose and galactose differ in configuration at C4.   **23.9 (a)** The energy is lost as heat **(b)** The reverse of fermentation is very endothermic; loss of CO_2 drives the reaction to completion in the forward direction.   **23.10** Insulin decreases; blood glucose decreases, the level of glucagon increases. Glucagon causes the breakdown of liver glycogen and the release of glucose. As glycogen is used up, the level of free fatty acids and ketone bodies increases.
23.11 Sorbitol can't form a cyclic acetal because it doesn't have a carbonyl group.

Sorbitol

23.12 (a) The increase in $[H^+]$ drives the equilibrium shown in Section 23.9 to the right, causing the production of CO_2. **(b)** Le Châtelier's Principle. **23.13** phosphorylation, oxidation   **23.14** hydrolases   **23.15 (a)** when the supply of glucose is adequate and the body needs energy. **(b)** when the body needs free glucose. **(c)** when ribose 5-phosphate or NADPH are needed. **(d)** when glucose supply is adequate, and the body does not need to use glucose for energy production.   **23.16** Phosphorylations of glucose and fructose 6-phosphate produce important intermediates that repay the initial energy investment. Fructose 1,6-bisphosphate is cleaved into two three-carbon compounds, which are converted to pyruvate. **23.17 (a)** when the body needs energy, in mitochondria; **(b)** under anaerobic conditions, in yeast; **(c)** under anaerobic conditions, in muscle, red blood cells; **(d)** when the body needs free glucose, in the liver **23.18** Step 1: transferase Step 2: isomerase Step 3: transferase Step 4: lyase Step 5: isomerase Step 6: oxidoreductase, transferase Step 7: transferase Step 8: isomerase Step 9: lyase Step 10: transferase; transferases (because many reactions involve phosphate transfers). Ligases are associated with reactions that synthesize molecules, not with reactions that break down molecules. **23.19 (g)**, **(c)**, **(b)**, **(e)**, **(f)**, **(a)**, **(d)** **23.20** Sources of compounds for gluconeogenesis: pyruvate, lactate, citric acid cycle intermediates, many amino acids.   **23.21** Germinating seeds need to synthesize carbohydrates from fats; humans obtain carbohydrates from food.   **23.22 (a)** No **(b)** Molecular oxygen appears in the last step of the electron transport chain, where it combines with H^+ and electrons (from electron transport) to form H_2O.   **23.24** glucose + galactose; in the lining of the small intestine

23.26

TYPE OF FOOD MOLECULES	PRODUCTS OF DIGESTION
Proteins	Amino acids
Triacylglycerols	Glycerol and fatty acids
Sucrose	Glucose and fructose
Lactose	Glucose and galactose
Starch	Glucose

23.28 acetyl-SCoA; lactate; ethanol + CO_2 **23.30** glycogenolysis: breakdown of glycogen to form glucose glycogenesis: synthesis of glycogen from glucose **23.32** glycolysis: catabolism of glucose to pyruvate glycogenolysis: breakdown of glycogen to form glucose **23.34** ribose 5-phosphate, glycolysis intermediates **23.36 (a)** all organs; **(b)** liver; **(c) (d)** muscle, liver **23.38 (a)** pyruvate → lactate; **(b)** pyruvate → ethanol + CO_2 **23.40 (a)** Steps 1, 3, 4, 7, 10; **(b)** Step 6; **(c)** Step 9 **23.42** Direct (substrate level) phosphorylation: **(a)** 2 mol ATP **(b)** 0 **(c)** 1 mol ATP Oxidative phosphorylation (ideal): **(a)** 6 ATP **(b)** 3 ATP **(c)** 11 ATP Most of the ATP in the citric acid cycle is produced from reduced coenzymes in the electron transport chain.
23.44

23.46 4 mol acetyl-SCoA **23.48** Hypoglycemia: low blood sugar; weakness, sweating, rapid heartbeat, confusion, coma, death; Hyperglycemia: high blood sugar; increased urine flow, low blood pressure, coma, death **23.50** ketone bodies **23.52** In Type 2 diabetes, insulin is in good supply, but cell membrane receptors fail to recognize insulin. Individuals are often overweight.   **23.54** Excess glucose is converted to sorbitol, which can't be transported out of cells. This buildup changes osmolarity and causes cataracts and blindness. Excess glucose also causes neuropathy and poor circulation leading to limb amputation due to tissue death.   **23.56** *Type 1 diabetes* is caused by insufficient production of insulin in the pancreas. *Type 2 diabetes* is caused by the failure of cell membrane receptors to recognize insulin.   **23.58** muscle cells **23.60** The exact reverse of an energetically favorable pathway must occur by an alternate route in order to be favorable.   **23.62** pyruvate, lactate   **23.64** Several steps in the reverse of glycolysis are energetically unfavorable.   **23.66** Steps 1, 3, 10 of glycolysis; all involve phosphate transfers and require energy.   **23.68** when muscle glucose is depleted and oxygen is in short supply   **23.70** glycoproteins, bacteria, dextran, polysaccharide storage granules   **23.72** In an environment rich in sucrose, bacteria secrete an enzyme that transfers glucose units from digested sucrose to the dextran polymer. The residual fructose is metabolized to lactate, which lowers pH. The resulting acidic environment in the mouth dissolves minerals in teeth, leading to cavities.   **23.74** beer, wine, cheese, yogurt, sour cream, and buttermilk   **23.76** 140 g/dL (diabetic) vs 90 g/dL (normal)   **23.78** between the curve for a diabetic and a nondiabetic   **23.80** Creatine phosphate and glycogen are quickly used up.   **23.82** Cotton fabric, paper, and rayon. Cotton fabric and paper are made from unmodified cellulose. In rayon, the hydroxyl groups of cellulose are converted to acetate groups.   **23.84** Pyruvate is not phosphorylated.   **23.86** Yes. Fructose 6-phosphate enters glycolysis as a glycolysis intermediate.   **23.88** The body must avoid extreme fluctuations in glucose concentration.

Chapter 24

24.1 (a) eicosanoid (b) glycerophospholipid (c) wax

24.2

$$CH_3(CH_2)_{18}\overset{\overset{\displaystyle O}{\|}}{C}-OCH_2(CH_2)_{30}CH_3$$

24.3

$$CH_2O\overset{\overset{\displaystyle O}{\|}}{C}(CH_2)_7CH=CH(CH_2)_7CH_3$$
$$CHO\overset{\overset{\displaystyle O}{\|}}{C}(CH_2)_7CH=CH(CH_2)_7CH_3$$
$$CH_2O\overset{\overset{\displaystyle O}{\|}}{C}(CH_2)_7CH=CH(CH_2)_7CH_3$$

24.4 (a) butter (b) soybean oil (c) soybean oil **24.5** *See below for answer.*
24.6 When two different fatty acids are bonded to C1 and C3 of glycerol, C2 is chiral. **24.7** London forces; weak; hydrogen bonds between water molecules are stronger than London forces.
24.8 The acyl groups are from stearic acid.

$$CH_2O\overset{\overset{\displaystyle O}{\|}}{C}(CH_2)_7CH=CH(CH_2)_7CH_3$$
$$CHO\overset{\overset{\displaystyle O}{\|}}{C}(CH_2)_7CH=CH(CH_2)_7CH_3 \xrightarrow{3\,H_2}$$
$$CH_2O\overset{\overset{\displaystyle O}{\|}}{C}(CH_2)_7CH=CH(CH_2)_7CH_3$$

$$CH_2O\overset{\overset{\displaystyle O}{\|}}{C}(CH_2)_{16}CH_3$$
$$CHO\overset{\overset{\displaystyle O}{\|}}{C}(CH_2)_{16}CH_3$$
$$CH_2O\overset{\overset{\displaystyle O}{\|}}{C}(CH_2)_{16}CH_3$$

24.9

$$CH_2O\overset{\overset{\displaystyle O}{\|}}{C}(CH_2)_{16}CH_3$$
$$CHO\overset{\overset{\displaystyle O}{\|}}{C}(CH_2)_{16}CH_3 \xrightarrow{NaOH,\ H_2O}$$
$$CH_2O\overset{\overset{\displaystyle O}{\|}}{C}(CH_2)_7CH=CH(CH_2)_7CH_3$$

or the isomer

$$CH_2OH$$
$$CHOH \quad + \quad \begin{array}{l} 2\,CH_3(CH_2)_{16}COO^-Na^+ \\[6pt] CH_3(CH_2)_7CH=CH(CH_2)_7COO^-Na^+ \end{array}$$
$$CH_2OH$$

24.10 (a) glycerol, phosphate ion, choline, $RCOO^-Na^+$, $R'COO-Na^+$
(b) sphingosine, phosphate ion, choline, sodium palmitate

24.11

Choline Phosphate

Hydrophilic head

Myristic acid

Hydrophobic tail

Hydrophobic tail

24.12

Stearic acid acyl group

Oleic acid acyl group

Phosphate Ethanolamine

24.13 (a), (c), (e), (f) **24.14** They must be hydrophobic, contain many amino acids with nonpolar side chains, and must be folded so that the hydrophilic regions face outward. **24.15** yes; gasses diffuse through the cell membrane due to small size and no charge **24.16** Glucose 6-phosphate has a charged phosphate group and can't pass through the hydrophobic lipid bilayer. **24.17** The surfaces are in different environments and serve different functions. **24.18** carboxylic acid (most acidic), alcohol, C—C double bonds, ethers. The molecule has both polar and nonpolar regions. Form hydrogen bonds: —COOH, —OH.
24.19 A has the highest melting point. B and C are probably liquids at room temperature due to the high percentage of unsaturated fatty acids present. **24.20** B is 12.2% palmitic acid, 87.5% stearic acid after hydrogenation; C is 11.2% palmitic acid and 85.1% stearic acid after hydrogenation. These are very similar.
24.21

$$CH_2O\overset{\overset{\displaystyle O}{\|}}{C}(CH_2)_{14}CH_3$$
$$CHO\overset{\overset{\displaystyle O}{\|}}{C}(CH_2)_7CH=CH(CH_2)_7CH_3$$
$$CH_2O-\overset{\overset{\displaystyle O}{\|}}{P}-OCH_2CH_2$$

A glycerophospholipid

24.22 Because the membrane is fluid, it can flow together after an injury. **24.23** C_{16} saturated fatty acids. The polar head lies in lung tissue, and

---

24.5

the hydrocarbon tails protrude into the alveoli. **24.24** a naturally-occurring molecule that dissolves in nonpolar solvents **24.26** $CH_3(CH_2)_{16}COOH$; straight chain **24.28** *Saturated fatty acids* are long-chain carboxylic acids that contain no carbon–carbon double bonds. *Monounsaturated fatty acids* contain one carbon–carbon double bond. *Polyunsaturated fatty acids* contain two or more carbon–carbon double bonds. **24.30** An essential fatty acid can't be synthesized by the human body and must be part of the diet. **24.32** The double bonds in unsaturated fatty acids make it harder for them to be arranged in a crystal. **24.34** a triester of glycerol and 3 fatty acids **24.36** Fats: composed of TAGs containing saturated and unsaturated fatty acids, solids; Oils: composed of TAGs containing mostly unsaturated fatty acids, liquids.

24.38

$$CH_2-O-\overset{\overset{O}{\|}}{C}-CH_2(CH_2)_9CH_3$$
$$CH-O-\overset{\overset{O}{\|}}{C}-CH_2(CH_2)_9CH_3$$
$$CH_2-O-\overset{\overset{O}{\|}}{C}-CH_2(CH_2)_9CH_3$$

24.40 a protective coating

24.42

$$CH_3(CH_2)_{13}CH_2\overset{\overset{O}{\|}}{C}-OCH_2(CH_2)_{14}CH_3$$

24.44

$$CH_2-O-\overset{\overset{O}{\|}}{C}-(CH_2)_nCH_3$$
$$CH-O-\overset{\overset{O}{\|}}{C}-(CH_2)_nCH=CH(CH_2)_nCH_3$$
$$CH_2-O-\overset{\overset{O}{\|}}{P}-OCH_2CH_2CH_2\overset{+}{N}(CH_3)_3$$
$$\underset{O^-}{|}$$

24.46 hydrogenation **24.48** Hydrogenate some of the double bonds. **24.50** a product with cis and trans double bonds; "trans fatty acids" **24.52** glycerol, K^+ stearate, K^+ oleate, K^+ linolenate **24.54** The products have one or more of the double bonds hydrogenated. There could be up to 12 different products. **24.56** Glycerophospholipids have polar heads (point outward) and nonpolar tails that cluster to form the membrane. Triacylglycerols don't have polar heads. **24.58** sphingomyelins, glycolipids **24.60** Glycerophospholipids are components of cell membranes. Stored fats in the body are triacylglycerols. **24.62** Both liposomes and micelles are spherical clusters of lipids. A liposome resembles a spherical lipid bilayer, in which polar heads cluster both inside and outside of the sphere. A micelle has a single layer of lipid molecules. **24.64** Concentrations of all substances would be the same on both sides of the membrane.

24.66

$$CH_2-O-\overset{\overset{O}{\|}}{P}-OCH_2CH_2\overset{+}{N}(CH_3)_3$$
$$\underset{O^-}{|}$$
$$CH-NH-\overset{\overset{O}{\|}}{C}-(CH_2)_{16}CH_3$$
$$CHOH$$
$$CH=CH(CH_2)_{12}CH_3$$

24.68 3 glycerols, $RCOO^-\ Na^+$, $R'COO^-\ Na^+$, $R'COO^-\ Na^+$ $R'COO^-\ Na^+$, 2 phosphates **24.70** Facilitated diffusion requires carrier proteins. **24.72 (a)** facilitated diffusion **(b)** simple diffusion **(c)** active transport **24.74** A prostaglandin that stimulates uterine contractions.

24.76 an eicosanoid; Arachidonic acid is a precursor. **24.78** leukotrienes **24.80** prostaglandins **24.82** no more than 30% **24.84** fabric softeners, disinfecting soaps **24.86** cholesterol **24.88** glycolipids **24.90 (b) (c) (e) (f)** **24.92**

$$CH_2-O-\overset{\overset{O}{\|}}{C}-(CH_2)_{12}CH_3$$
$$CH-O-\overset{\overset{O}{\|}}{C}-(CH_2)_7CH=CHCH_2CH=CHCH_2CH_3$$
$$CH_2-O-\overset{\overset{O}{\|}}{C}-(CH_2)_{12}CH_3$$

or

$$CH_2-O-\overset{\overset{O}{\|}}{C}-(CH_2)_{12}CH_3$$
$$CH-O-\overset{\overset{O}{\|}}{C}-(CH_2)_{12}CH_3$$
$$CH_2-O-\overset{\overset{O}{\|}}{C}-(CH_2)_7CH=CHCH_2CH=CHCH_2CH_3$$

24.94 (a) beef fat **(b)** plant oil **(c)** pork fat **24.96** It is saponifiable. **24.98** sphingomyelins, cerebrosides, gangliosides **24.100** lower blood pressure, assist in blood clotting, stimulate uterine contractions, lower gastric secretions, cause swelling **24.102** 0.4g NaOH

Chapter 25

25.1 Cholate has 4 polar groups on its hydrophilic side that allow it to interact with an aqueous environment; its hydrophobic side interacts with TAGs. Cholate and cholesterol can't change roles. **25.2** Dihydroxyacetone phosphate is isomerized to glyceraldehyde 3-phosphate, which enters glycolysis. **25.3 (a), (b)** *Step 1*; a $C=C$ double bond is introduced; FAD is the oxidizing agent. *Step 3*; an alcohol is oxidized to a ketone; NAD^+ is the oxidizing agent. **(c)** *Step 2*; water is added to a carbon-carbon double bond. **(d)** *Step 4*; HSCoA displaces acetyl-SCoA, producing a chain-shortened acyl-SCoA fatty acid **25.4 (a)** 6 acetyl-SCoA, 5 β oxidations **(b)** 7 acetyl-SCoA, 6 β oxidations **25.5** Step 6, Step 7, Step 8 **25.6 (d)** **25.7 (a)** Acetyl-SCoA provides the acetyl groups used in synthesis of ketone bodies. **(b)** 3 **(c)** The body uses ketone bodies as an energy source during starvation. **25.8** Oxygen is needed to reoxidize reduced coenzymes, formed in β oxidation, that enter the electron transport chain. **25.9 (a)** chylomicrons; because they have the greatest ratio of lipid to protein **(b)** chylomicrons **(c)** HDL **(d)** LDL **(e)** HDL **(f)** VLDL; used for storage or energy production **(g)** LDL **25.10** high blood glucose → high insulin/low glucagon → fatty acid and TAG synthesis: low blood glucose → low insulin/high glucagon → TAG hydrolysis; fatty acid oxidation **25.11** Formation of a fatty acyl-SCoA is coupled with conversion of ATP to AMP and pyrophosphate. This energy expenditure is recaptured in β oxidation. **25.12** Less acetyl-SCoA can be catabolized in the citric acid cycle, and acetyl-SCoA is diverted to ketogenesis. **25.13** Catabolism of fat provides more calories/gram than does catabolism of glycogen, and, thus, fats are a more efficient way to store calories. **25.14** Ketone bodies can be metabolized to form acetyl-SCoA, which provides energy. **25.15** No. Although both these processes add or remove two carbon units, one is not the reverse of the other. The two processes involve different enzymes, coenzymes, and activation steps. **25.16** They slow the rate of movement of food through the stomach. **25.18** Bile emulsifies lipid droplets. **25.20** mono- and diacylglycerols, stearic acid, oleic acid, linoleic acid, glycerol **25.22** Acylglycerols, fatty acids, and protein are combined to form *chylomicrons*, which are lipoproteins used to transport lipids from the diet into the bloodstream. **25.24** by albumins **25.26** Steps 6–10 of the glycolysis pathway. **25.28** 9 molecules ATP;

21 molecules ATP **25.30** An adipocyte is a cell, almost entirely filled with fat globules, in which TAGs are stored and mobilized. **25.32** heart, liver, resting muscle cells **25.34** A fatty acid is converted to its fatty acyl-SCoA in order to activate it for catabolism. **25.36** The carbon β to the thioester group (two carbons away from the thioester group) is oxidized in the process. **25.38** 17 ATP **25.40** *Least* glucose, sucrose, capric acid, myristic acid *Most*

25.42

(a)

$$CH_3CH_2CH_2CH=CHCSCoA$$

(b)

$$CH_3CH_2CH_2CHCH_2CSCoA$$
(with OH and O substituents)

(c)

$$CH_3CH_2CH_2CCH_2CSCoA$$
(with two O substituents)

(d)

$$CH_3CH_2CH_2CSCoA \quad + \quad CH_3CSCoA$$

25.44 (a) 7 acetyl-SCoA, 6 cycles (b) 4 acetyl-SCoA, 3 cycles **25.46** lipogenesis **25.48** acetyl-SCoA **25.50** 7 cycles **25.52** Total cholesterol: 200 mg/dL or lower. LDL: 160 mg/dL or lower. HDL: 60 mg/dL or higher. **25.54** LDL carries cholesterol from the liver to tissues; HDL carries cholesterol from tissues to the liver, where it is converted to bile and excreted. **25.56** Type II diabetes, colon cancer, heart attacks, stroke **25.58** calorie-dense food, lack of exercise **25.60** The liver synthesizes many important biomolecules, it catabolizes glucose, fatty acids and amino acids, it stores many substances, and it inactivates toxic substances. **25.62** The excess acetyl-SCoA from catabolism of carbohydrates is stored as fat. The body can't resynthesize carbohydrate from acetyl-SCoA. **25.64** The alcohol intermediate is chiral. **25.66** Ketosis is a condition in which ketone bodies accumulate in the blood faster than they can be metabolized. Since two of the ketone bodies are carboxylic acids, they lower the pH of the blood, producing the condition known as ketoacidosis. Symptoms of ketoacidosis include dehydration, labored breathing, and depression; prolonged ketoacidosis may lead to coma and death. **25.68** Ketones have little effect on pH, but the two other ketone bodies are acidic, and they lower the pH of urine. **25.70** (a) endogenous (b) exogenous **25.72** $H_2C=CHC(CH_3)=CH_2$. Since cholesterol has 27 carbons, at least 6 2-methyl-1,3-butadiene molecules are needed.

Chapter 26

26.1

2'-Deoxythymidine

26.2 D-Ribose ($C_5H_{10}O_5$) has one more oxygen atom than 2-deoxy-D-ribose ($C_5H_{10}O_4$), and thus can form more hydrogen bonds.

26.3

2'-Deoxyadenosine 5'-monophosphate

26.4

Guanosine 5'-triphosphate (GTP)

26.5 dCMP—2'-Deoxycytidine 5'-monophosphate; CMP—Cytidine 5'-monophosphate; UDP—Uridine 5'-diphosphate; AMP—Adenosine 5'-monophosphate; ATP—Adenosine 5'-triphosphate **26.6** cytosine–guanine–adenine–uracil–adenine. The pentanucleotide comes from RNA because uracil is present.

26.7

26.8 (a) 3' C-G-G-A-T-C-A 5' (b) 3' T-T-A-C-C-G-A-G-T 5'

26.9

26.10 negatively charged (because of the phosphate groups)
26.11 (a) A longer strand has more hydrogen bonds. (b) A chain with a higher percent of G/C pairs has a higher melting point, because it has more hydrogen bonds. **26.12** (a) 3' G-U-C-U-G-A-C-A-U-G-U-G 5' (b) 5' A-U-C-A-U-A-C-G-U-C-G-C 3' **26.13** (a) GCU GCC GCA GCG (b) CCU CCC CCA CCG (c) UCU UCC UCA UCG AGU AGC (d) AAA AAG (e) UAU UAC **26.14** The sequence guanine-uracil-guanine codes for valine. **26.15** (a) Ile (b) Ala (c) Arg (d) Lys **26.16** Six mRNA triplets can code for Leu: CUU, CUC, CUA, CUG, UUA, and UUG Among the many possible combinations for Leu-Leu-Leu are:

5' UUAUUGCUU 3'   5' UUAUUGCUC 3'   5' UUAUUGCUA 3'
5' UUAUUGCUG 3'   5' UUACUUCUC 3'   5' UUACUUCUA 3'

26.17–26.18

mRNA sequence: 5' CAG—AUG—CCU—UGG—CCC—UUA 3'
Amino-acid sequence: Gln—Met——Pro——Trp——Pro——Leu
tRNA anticodons: 3' GUC—UAC—GGA—ACC—GGG—AAU 5'

26.19

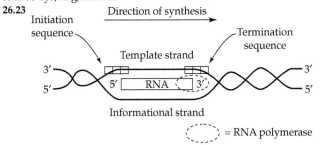

Guanosine 5'-monophosphate

26.20

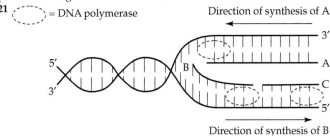

Sugar
Phosphate

Sequence of the left chain: 5' A-G-T-C 3'
Sequence of the right chain: 5' G-A-C-T 3'
26.21 ⟨ ⟩ = DNA polymerase

Direction of synthesis of A

Direction of synthesis of B

Segments B and C are joined by the action of a DNA ligase.
26.22 The sugar-phosphate backbone is found on the outside of the DNA double helix. Histones are positively charged; they contain groups such as Lys, Arg, and His.

26.23

Direction of synthesis
Initiation
sequence
Termination
sequence
Template strand
3' 3'
5' RNA 3'
5' 5'
Informational strand

⟨ ⟩ = RNA polymerase

26.24 More than one codon can code for each amino acid. Only one possibility is shown.

(a) 5' |C|A|A|C|A|C|C|C|C|G|G|G| 3' mRNA

(b) 3' |G|T|T|G|T|G|G|G|G|C|C|C| 5' DNA template strand

(c) 5' |C|A|A|C|A|C|C|C|C|G|G|G| 3' DNA informational strand

(d) 64 possible sequences

26.26 2-deoxyribose (DNA); ribose (RNA). 2-Deoxyribose is missing an —OH group at C2. **26.28** The purine bases (two fused heterocyclic rings) are adenine and guanine. The pyrimidine bases (one heterocyclic ring) are cytosine, thymine (in DNA), and uracil (in RNA). **26.30** DNA is largest; tRNA is smallest. **26.32** *Similarities*: All are polymerizations; all use a nucleic acid as a template; all use hydrogen bonding to bring the subunits into position. *Differences*: In replication, DNA makes a copy of itself. In transcription, DNA is used as a template for the synthesis of mRNA. In translation, mRNA is used as a template for the synthesis of proteins. Replication and transcription take place in the nucleus of cells, and translation takes place in ribosomes. **26.34** DNA, protein **26.36** 46 chromosomes (23 pairs) **26.38** They always occur in pairs: they always H-bond with each other. **26.40** 19% G, 19% C, 31% A, 31% T. (%G = %C; %A = %T: %T + %A + %C + %G = 100%) **26.42** 5' to 3'

26.44

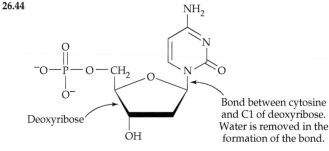

Deoxyribose

Bond between cytosine and C1 of deoxyribose. Water is removed in the formation of the bond.

26.46

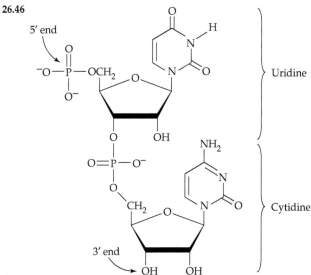

5' end

Uridine

Cytidine

3' end

26.48 the template strand **26.50** Each new DNA has one newly synthesized strand and one old strand. **26.52** An anticodon is a 3 nucleotide tRNA sequence that is complementary to an mRNA codon for a specific amino acid. **26.54** tRNAs for each amino acid differ in their anticodon sequences. **26.56** (a) GCU GCC GCA GCG (b) CAU CAC (c) CCU CCC CCA CCG **26.58** (3' → 5') (a) GGA (b) CGU (c) UAA **26.60** (3' → 5') TTGCCT **26.62** Asn-Gly **26.64** (5' → 3') UAU–GGU–GGU–UUU–AUG–UAA Other sequences are possible. **26.66** Viruses consist of a strand of nucleic acid wrapped in a protein coat; viruses can't replicate or manufacture protein independent of a host cell. **26.68** To be effective, a drug must be powerful enough to act on viruses within cells without damaging the cells and their genetic material. Vaccines prime the body to recognize viruses as foreign and to destroy them. **26.70** Ribozyme activity is common among the simplest and most primitive life forms, such as viroids, leading scientists to speculate that ribozyme catalysis might have preceded enzyme catalysis. **26.72** Influenza A viruses are described by a code that describes the hemagglutinins (H) and the neuraminidases (N) in the virus. The H1N1 virus was responsible for the 1918 influenza pandemic, and the H5N1 virus is present in avian flu. Since these viruses can undergo antigenic drift in host animals, there is concern when infected birds and animals harbor influenza viruses. **26.74** 249 bases **26.76** Met is removed after synthesis is complete.

Chapter 27

27.1 "once upon a time" **27.2** As a result of the SNP, the base sequence codes for Trp, instead of Cys. This change would probably affect the functioning of the protein. **27.3** 3′–T–C–T–A–G–//–A–5′ **27.4** (a) sticky (b) (c) not sticky **27.5** (a) comparative genomics (b) genetic engineering (c) pharmacogenetics (d) bioinformatics **27.6** (1) A genetic map, which shows the location of markers one million nucleotides apart, is created. (2) Next comes a physical map, which refines the distance between markers to 100,000 base pairs. (3) The chromosome is cleaved into large segments of overlapping clones. (4) The clones are fragmented into 500 base pieces, which are sequenced. **27.7** The variations are only a small part of the genome; the rest is identical among humans. A diverse group of individuals contributed DNA to the project. **27.8** *telomeres* (protect the chromosome from damage, involved with aging), *centromeres* (involved with cell division), *promoter sequences* (determine which genes will be replicated), *introns* (function unknown) **27.9** Similarities: both are variations in base sequences. Differences: A mutation is an error that is transferred during replication and affects only a few people; a polymorphism is a variation in sequence that is common within a population. **27.10** Recombinant DNA contains two or more DNA segments that do not occur together in nature. The DNA that codes for a specific human protein can be incorporated into a bacterial plasmid using recombinant DNA technology. The plasmid is then reinserted into a bacterial cell, where its protein-synthesizing machinery makes the desired protein. **27.11** Major benefits of genomics: creation of disease-resistant and nutrient-rich crops, gene therapy, genetic screening. Major negative outcomes: misuse of an individual's genetic information, prediction of a genetic disease for which there is no cure. **27.12** Celera broke the genome into many unidentified fragments. The fragments were multiplied and cut into 500 base pieces, which were sequenced. A supercomputer was used to determine the order of the bases. **27.14** 50% **27.16** (a) Approx. 200 genes are shared between bacteria and humans. (b) A single gene may produce several proteins. **27.18** The clones used in DNA mapping are identical copies of DNA segments from a single individual. In mapping, it is essential to have a sample large enough for experimental manipulation. **27.20** The youngest cells have long telomeres, and the oldest cells have short telomeres. **27.22** It is the constriction that determines the shape of a chromosome during cell division. **27.24** A silent mutation is a single base change that specifies the same amino acid. **27.26** random and spontaneous events, exposure to a mutagen **27.28** A SNP can result in the change in identity of an amino acid inserted into a protein a particular location in a polypeptide chain. The effect of a SNP depends on the function of the protein and the nature of the SNP. **27.30** A physician could predict the age at which inherited diseases might become active, their severity, and the response to various types of treatment. **27.32** a change in the type of side chain **27.34** (a) Substitution of Ala for Val may have minor effects (b) Substitution of His for Pro is more serious because the amino acids have very different side chains. **27.36** Proteins can be produced in large quantities. **27.38** Sticky ends are unpaired bases at the end of a DNA fragment. Recombinant DNA is formed when the sticky ends of the DNA of interest and of the DNA of the plasmid have complementary base pairs and can be joined by a DNA ligase. **27.40** (a) (b) not sticky **27.42** Proteomics, the study of the complete set

of proteins coded for by a genome or synthesized by a given type of cell, might provide information about the role of a protein in both healthy and diseased cells. **27.44** corn, soybeans **27.46** a DNA chip **27.48** a group of anonymous individuals **27.50** production of a large quantity of a specific segment of DNA **27.52** (1) digestion with a restriction endonuclease (2) separation of fragments by electrophoresis (3) fragments transferred to a nylon membrane (4) treatment of the blot with a radioactive DNA probe (5) identification of fragments by exposure to X-ray film. All samples must be analyzed under the same conditions in order to be compared. **27.54** A monogenic disease is caused by the variation in just one gene. **27.56** ATACTGA **27.58** A hereditary disease is caused by a mutation in the DNA of a germ cell and is passed from parent to offspring. The mutation affects the amino-acid sequence of an important protein and causes a change in the biological activity of the protein.

Chapter 28

28.1 (a) false (b) true (c) true (d) false (e) false **28.2** oxidoreductase; lyase

28.3

$$\underset{\text{4-Hydroxy-}\alpha\text{-ketopentanoate}}{CH_3\overset{\overset{\displaystyle OH}{|}}{C}H\,CH_2\overset{\overset{\displaystyle O}{\|}}{C}COO^-}$$

28.4

$$CH_3SCH_2CH_2\overset{\overset{\displaystyle O}{\|}}{C}HCOO^-$$

28.5 by the loss of two hydrogens to either NAD^+ or $NADP^+$
28.6 valine, leucine, isoleucine

$$\underset{\text{Valine}}{CH_3\overset{\overset{\displaystyle H_3C\ \ NH_3^+}{|\ \ \ |}}{CH}CHCOO^-} \ + \ \underset{\alpha\text{-Ketoglutarate}}{{}^-OOCCH_2CH_2\overset{\overset{\displaystyle O}{\|}}{C}COO^-}$$

$$\downarrow$$

$$\underset{\alpha\text{-Keto-3-methylbutanoate}}{CH_3\overset{\overset{\displaystyle H_3C\ \ O}{|\ \ \|}}{CH}CCOO^-} \ + \ \underset{\text{Glutamate}}{{}^-OOCCH_2CH_2\overset{\overset{\displaystyle NH_3^+}{|}}{CH}COO^-}$$

28.7 (a) 5 (b) 1 (c) 3
28.8

28.9 3-Phosphoglycerate → 3-Phosphohydroxypyruvate (oxidation) 3-Phosphohydroxypyruvate → 3-Phosphoserine (transamination) 3-Phosphoserine → Serine (hydrolysis)

28.10

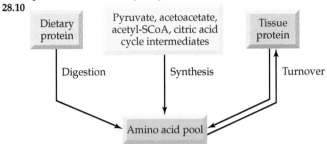

28.11 (1) Catabolism of an amino acid begins with a transamination reaction that removes the amino nitrogen (2) The resulting α-keto acid, which contains the carbon atoms, is converted to a common metabolic intermediate. (3) The amino group of glutamate (from the amino acid) is removed by oxidative deamination. (4) The amino nitrogen is transformed to urea in the urea cycle and is excreted. **28.12** glutamate dehydrogenase; alanine aminotransferase. Alanine is the product. **28.13** The carbon atoms from ketogenic amino acids can be converted to ketone bodies or to acetyl-SCoA. The carbon atoms from glucogenic amino acids can be converted to compounds that can enter gluconeogenesis and can form glucose, which can enter glycolysis and also yield acetyl-SCoA. **28.14** All amino acids are necessary for protein synthesis. The body can synthesize only some of them; the others must be provided by food and are thus essential in the diet. **28.15** to quickly remove ammonia from the body; buildup of urea and shortage of ornithine **28.16** throughout the body **28.18** pyruvate, 3-phosphoglycerate **28.20** In transamination, a keto group of an α-keto acid and an amino group of an amino acid change places.

28.22 (a)

(b)

28.24 An $-NH_3^+$ group of an amino acid is replaced by a carbonyl group, and ammonium ion is eliminated.

28.26

(a)   **(b)**

28.28 A ketogenic amino acid is catabolized to acetoacetyl-SCoA or acetyl-SCoA. Examples: leucine, isoleucine, lysine **28.30** Ammonia is toxic. **28.32** One nitrogen comes from carbamoyl phosphate, which is synthesized from ammonium ion by oxidative deamination. The other nitrogen comes from aspartate. **28.34** Nonessential amino acids are synthesized in humans in 1–3 steps. Essential amino acids are synthesized in microorganisms in 7–10 steps. **28.36** reductive amination; the reverse of oxidative deamination **28.38** phenylketonuria; mental retardation; restriction of phenylalanine in the diet **28.40 (b) (c) (d)** **28.42** Oxidized allopurinol inhibits the enzyme that converts xanthine to uric acid. The more soluble intermediates are excreted. The nitrogen at position 7 of hypoxanthine is at position 8 in allopurinol, where it blocks oxidation of xanthine. **28.44** tryptophan; emotional and behavioral problems **28.46** isoleucine + pyruvate → α-keto-3-methylpentanoate + alanine **28.48** Yes. Some amino acids yield two kinds of products—those that can enter the citric acid cycle and those that are intermediates of fatty acid metabolism. **28.50** Tissue is dynamic because its components are constantly being broken down and reformed.

28.52 (b) → **(e)** → **(d)** → **(f)** → **(a)** → **(c)** **28.54** An excess of one amino acid might overwhelm a transport system that other amino acids use, resulting in a deficiency of those amino acids. **28.56** The nitrogen may be converted to urea and excreted in the urine, or it may be used in the synthesis of a new nitrogen-containing compound.

Chapter 29

29.1 In the cell: the charged form. Outside the cell: the uncharged form. The uncharged form enters the cell more readily. **29.2 (a)** iii **(b)** ii **(c)** iv **(d)** v **(e)** i **29.3 (a)** pH goes down **(b)** $[O_2]$, $[CO_2]$, pH **29.4 (a)** respiratory acidosis **(b)** metabolic acidosis **(c)** metabolic alkalosis **(d)** respiratory alkalosis **(e)** respiratory acidosis **29.5 (a)** intracellular fluid **(b)** extracellular fluid **(c)** blood plasma, interstitial fluid **(d)** K^+, Mg^{2+}, HPO_4^{2-} **(e)** Na^+, Cl^-

29.6

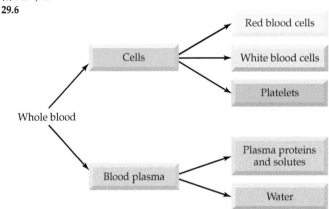

29.7 (a) O_2 **(b)** CO_2 **(c)** nutrients **(d)** waste products **(e)** hormones **(f)** white blood cells, platelets **29.8** swelling, redness, warmth, pain **29.9** enzymatic decarboxylation of histidine; Histamine dilates capillaries, increasing blood flow that reddens and warms the skin. Blood-clotting factors and defensive proteins cause pain and swelling. **29.10** *Cell-mediated immune response*: under control of T cells; arises when abnormal cells, bacteria, or viruses enter cells; invaders killed by T cells. *Antibody-mediated immune response*: under control of B cells, assisted by T cells; occurs when antigens enter cells; B cells divide to produce plasma cells, which form antibodies; an antibody-antigen complex inactivates the antigen. **29.11** Excess hydrogen ions are excreted by reaction with NH_3 or HPO_4^{2-}. H^+ ions also combine with bicarbonate, producing CO_2 that returns to the bloodstream. **29.12** intracellular fluid (64%), interstitial fluid (25%), plasma (8%) **29.14** Substances not soluble in blood, such as lipids, are transported by blood proteins. **29.16** Blood pressure in arterial capillaries is higher than interstitial fluid pressure, and blood pressure in venous capillaries is lower than interstitial fluid pressure. **29.18** the thoracic duct **29.20** it causes a decrease in the water content of the urine **29.22** seven percent **29.24** *Red blood cells* transport blood gases. *White blood cells* protect the body from foreign substances. *Platelets* assist in blood clotting. **29.26** *Inside cells:* K^+, Mg^{2+}, HPO_4^{2-}; *Outside cells:* Na^+, Cl^- **29.28** Antihistamines block attachment of the neurotransmitter histamine to its receptors. **29.30** immunoglobulins **29.32** Killer T cells destroy the invader; helper T cells enhance defenses; memory T cells can produce new killer T cells if needed. **29.34** Memory cells "remember" an antigen and are capable of producing antibodies to it for a long time. **29.36** Vitamin K, Ca^{2+} **29.38** They are released as zymogens in order to avoid undesirable clotting in noninjured tissues. **29.40** +2 **29.42** If pO_2 is below 10 mmHg, hemoglobin is unsaturated. If pO_2 is greater than 100 mmHg, hemoglobin is completely saturated. Between these pressures, hemoglobin is partially saturated. **29.44** a dissolved gas, bound to hemoglobin, bicarbonate ion

29.46

$$CO_2 + H_2O \underset{}{\overset{\text{Carbonic anhydrase}}{\rightleftharpoons}} HCO_3^- + H^+$$

29.48 7.35–7.45 below 7.35 = acidosis; above 7.35 = alkalosis

29.50 respiratory acidosis

29.52

$$H^+ + HCO_3^- \rightleftarrows CO_2 + H_2O$$

$$H^+ + HPO_4{}^{2-} \rightleftarrows H_2PO_4{}^-$$

29.54 Substances can either be transported into a cell or be transported out of a cell, but not both.   **29.56** The chemist might need to deliver a medication to brain cells of someone suffering from Parkinson's disease.

29.58 Automated analysis can reproducibly detect changes in enzyme levels that might indicate organ damage.   **29.60** It is a small, polar molecule.   **29.62** When $[Na^+]$ is high, secretion of ADH increases and causes the amount of water retained by the body to increase, causing swelling.   **29.64** Active transport is necessary when a cell needs a substance that has a higher concentration inside the cell than outside, or when a cell needs to secrete a substance that has a higher concentration outside the cell than inside.   **29.66** Hemostasis is the body's mechanism for preventing blood loss, and might be considered to be a part of homeostasis.

Photo Credits

Frontmatter: vii, Shutterstock; **viii,** Escher, M.C. (1898-1972), The M. C. Escher Company; **ix,** Corbis; **x,** iStockphoto.com; **xi,** Phil Degginger/Alamy; **xii,** Luca Bruno/AP; **xiii,** Shutterstock; **xiv,** Andrew Brookes/CORBIS.

Chapter 1: Opener, Bjanka Kadic/Alamy; **4** Richard Megna/Fundamental Photographs, NYC; **Fig. 1.2,** Eric Schrader/Pearson; **6,** Shutterstock; **7,** Richard Megna/Fundamental Photographs, NYC; **8,** iStockphoto; **9 (top),** Richard Megna/Fundamental Photographs, NYC; **9 (bottom),** Richard Megna/Fundamental Photographs, NYC; **12(a) (top left),** iStockphoto; **12(b) (top middle),** Wikipedia.org; **12(c) (top right),** Shutterstock; **12(a) (bottom left),** Shutterstock; **12(b) (bottom middle),** iStockphoto.com; **12(c) (bottom right),** Wikipedia.org; **13 (bottom left),** Lester V. Bergman/Corbis/Bettmann; **13 (bottom right),** Photo Courtesy of Texas Instruments Incorporated; **14,** Wikipedia.org.

Chapter 2: Opener, Pearson Asset Library/Pearson; **20,** CDC/C. Goldsmith, P. Feorino, E.L. Palmer, W.R. McManus; **Fig. 2.1(a),** Ohaus Corporation; **Fig 2.1(b),** Ohaus Corporation; **22 (bottom),** McCracken Photographers/Pearson Education/PH College; **24,** McCracken Photographers/Pearson Education/PH College; **25,** Corbis Royalty Free; **27,** Pearson Asset Library/Eric Schrader; **28(a) (left),** CDC/Dr. Thomas F. Sellers/Emory University; **28(b) (middle),** Eye of Science/Photo Researchers, Inc.; **28(c) (right),** Pearson Asset Library/Pearson; **29,** Frank LaBua/Pearson Education/PH College; **31,** Comstock Complete; **33,** Dennis Kunkel Phototake, NYC; **34,** Michal Heron/Pearson Education/PH College; **35,** iStockphoto.com; **36,** stockbyte/Photolibrary; **38,** Pearson Asset Library/Pearson; **39,** Richard Megna/Fundamental Photographs, NYC; **40,** Shutterstock; **41,** iStockphoto.com; **43,** Michael Wright; **44,** Eric Schrader/Pearson.

Chapter 3: Opener, Shutterstock; **49,** Paul Silverman/Fundamental Photographs, NYC; **50 (top),** Shutterstock; **50 (bottom),** AP Wide World Photos; **52,** Pearson Asset Library/Pearson; **57,** Richard Megna/Fundamental Photographs, NYC; **58,** Richard Megna/Fundamental Photographs, NYC; **60 (top),** Phillipe Plaily/Photo Researcher, Inc.; **60 (middle),** Pearson Asset Library/Pearson; **60 (bottom),** iStockphoto.com; **61,** NASA; **62,** iStockphoto.com; **73,** iStockphoto.com.

Chapter 4: Opener, Shutterstock; **79,** Richard Megna/Fundamental Photographs, NYC; **Fig. 4.2 (left and right),** Pearson Asset Library/Pearson; **Fig. 4.3 (bottom),** Ed Degginer/Color-Pic, Inc.; **84,** Richard Megna/Fundamental Photographs, NYC; **85(a) (left),** Chip Clark; **85(b) (middle)** and **85(c) (right),** Jeffrey A. Scovil; **89,** iStockphoto.com; **91,** Jeffrey A. Scovil; **97,** CNRI/Science Photo Library/Photo Researchers Inc.; **100,** Prof. P. Motta, Department of Anatomy, University "La Sapienza," Rome/Science Library/Photo Researchers, Inc.

Chapter 5: Opener, The M.C. Escher Company BV; **108,** Comstock Complete; **114,** Comstock Complete; **116,** iStockphoto.com; **117,** Farmland Industries, Inc.; **124,** Shutterstock; **127,** Courtesy of DuPont Nomex©; **135,** Shutterstock.

Chapter 6: Opener, Charles O'Rear/CORBIS/CORBIS-NY; **147,** David R. Frazier/Photo Researchers, Inc.; **148,** Richard Megna/Fundamental Photographs, NYC; **Fig. 6.1(a),** Phil Degginger/Color-Pic, Inc.; **149,** Tom Bochsler/Pearson Education/PH College; **153 (left),** Library of Congress; **153 (right),** Science Photo Library/Photo Researchers, Inc.; **158,** Richard Megna/Fundamental Photographs, NYC; **162 (top),** iStockphoto.com; **162 (bottom),** Richard Megna/Fundamental Photographs, NYC; **164,** Wikipedia.org; **167,** McCracken Photographers/Pearson Education/PH College; **168,** McCracken Photographers/Pearson Education/PH College; **171 (top),** iStockphoto.com; **171 (bottom),** Tony Freeman/PhotoEdit Inc.; **172,** Richard Megna/Fundamental Photographs, NYC.

Chapter 7: Opener, Getty Images, Inc.; **185,** Pearson Asset Library/Pearson; **186,** Shutterstock; **188,** Getty Images, Inc.—PhotoDisc; **189,** iStockphoto.com; **Fig. 7.1,** Tom Bochsler/Pearson Education/PH College; **193,** iStockphoto.com; **Fig. 7.5 (right),** AC/General Motors/Peter Arnold, Inc.; **198,** Reuters; **199,** IndexOpen; **201,** Richard Megna/Fundamental Photographs, NYC.

Chapter 8: Opener, Don King/Pacific Stock; **Fig. 8.3,** NASA Headquarters; **223,** iStockphoto.com; **224,** iStockphoto.com; **226,** iStockphoto.com; **227,** Pearson Asset Library/Pearson; **234,** ©John Van Hesselt/CORBIS All Rights Reserved; **241 (top),** Richard Megna/Fundamental Photographs, NYC; **241 (bottom),** iStockphoto.com; **242 (top),** iStockphoto.com; **Fig. 8.21 (middle),** Pearson Asset Library/Pearson; **242 (bottom),** AGE Fotostock America, Inc.; **243 (bottom left),** Jeffrey A. Scovil; **243 (bottom right),** iStickphoto.com; **244,** Shutterstock; **246,** Pearson Asset Library/Pearson; **248,** Shutterstock.

Chapter 9: Opener, Phil Schermeiser/National Geographic Imag Collection; **256 (left and middle),** iStockphoto.com; **256 (right),** Shutterstock; **258 (top),** Shutterstock; **258 (bottom)** Pearson Asset Library/Pearson; **259,** Jonathan Blair/Corbis/Bettmann; **262,** Richard Megna/Fundamental Photographs, NYC; **263,** Shutterstock; **Fig. 9.6,** Richard Megna/Fundamental Photographs, NYC; **266,** AP Wide World Photos; **273,** Pearson Asset Library/Tony Freeman/Photo Edit; **Fig.9.8,** Richard Megna/Fundamental Photographs, NYC; **279,** Gero Breloe/NewsCom; **280,** NewsCom; **Fig. 9.12 (a),** Pearson Asset Library/Dennis Kunkel/Phototake, **(b)** and **(c)** Dennis Kunkel/Phototake; **286 (left),** Martin Dohrn/Science Photo Library/Photo Researchers, Inc.; **286 (right),** Amet Jean Pierre/Corbis/Sygma.

Chapter 10: Opener, iStockphoto.com; **294,** Richard Megna/Fundamental Photographs, NYC; **295,** Eric Schrader/Pearson; **302,** ISM/PhototakeUSA.com; **306,** iStockphoto.com; **Fig. 10.4 (left),** Richard Megna/Fundamental Photographs, NYC; **Fig. 10.4 (right),** Tom Bochsler/Pearson Education/PH College; **Fig. 10.5,** Tom Bochsler/Pearson Education/PH College; **320,** Pearson Asset Library/Pearson; **321,** iStockphoto.com; **Fig. 10.8,** Ed Degginger/Color-Pic, Inc.; **324 (top and bottom),** National Atmospheric Deposition Program/National Trends Network.

Chapter 11: Opener, Corbis/Reuters America LLC; **342 (top),** Simon Fraser/Medical Physics, Royal Victoria Infirmar, Newcastle-upon-Tyne, England/Science Photo Library/Photo Researchers, Inc.; **342 (bottom),** Martin Dohrn/Science Photo Library/Photo Researchers, Inc.; **344,** Pearson Asset Library/Pearson; **347 (top),** Pearson Asset Library/Pearson; **347 (bottom),** Pearson Asset Library/Pearson; **Fig. 11.6 (top),** iStockphoto.com; **Fig. 11.6 (bottom),** Rennie Van Munchow/Phototake, NYC; **349** International Atomic Energy Agency; **350,** ©Shirley Clive/Greenpeace International; **351,** iStockphoto.com; **352,** Roger Tully/Getty Images Inc.—Stone Allstock; **353,** iStockphoto.com; **355 (top),** Colorfoto Hans Hinz, Basel, Switzerland; **355 (bottom),** Courtesy of General Atomics.

Chapter 12: Opener, Corbis Royalty Free; **363,** Andy Levin/Photo Researchers, Inc; **379,** John McMurry; **386,** iStockphoto.com; **388,** iStockphoto.com.

Chapter 13: Opener, iStockphoto.com; **397,** iStockphoto.com; **406,** Omikron/Photo Researchers, Inc.; **Fig. 13.1,** Richard Megna/Fundamental Photographs, NYC; **411 (left and right),** Richard Megna/Fundamental Photographs, NYC; **418 (left and right),** Eric Schrader/Pearson; **419,** Michal Heron/Pearson; **420 (top),** Museum of Applied Arts, Helsinki, Finland; **420 (bottom),** Mitch Kezar, Getty Images Inc.—Stone Allstock; **421,** iStockphoto.com; **423,** Shutterstock; **427,** Michael Holford/Michael Holford Photographs.

Chapter 14: Opener, iStockphoto.com; **437,** Pearson Asset Library/Pearson; **438,** Pearson Asset Library/Pearson; **447,** Advanced Safety Devices, Inc.; **448,** iStockphoto.com; **450,** Pearson Asset Library/Pearson; **452,** Rod Planck/Photo Researchers, Inc.; **453,** iStockphoto.com; **454,** Corbis/Bettmann; **456,** Photo Researchers, Inc.; **457,** NASA/Goddard Space Flight Center.

Chapter 15: Opener, iStockphoto.com; **472,** Olivier Matthys/Landov LLC; **475,** iStockphoto.com; **479,** Donald Clegg and Roxy Wilson/Pearson; **480,** SuperStock, Inc.; **481,** Pearson Asset Library/Pearson; **482,** Allan Rosenberg/Getty Images, Inc.—PhotoDisc; **483,** iStockphoto.com.

Chapter 16: Opener (main), Charles S. Lewallen; **Opener (inset),** Thomas Eisner and Daniel Aneshansley, Cornell University; **493 (photo),** Paul Marek, Department of Biology, East Carolina University; **493 (drawing),** Adapted from *Introduction to Ecoloical Biochemistry* 2/e by J.B. Harbone with permission of Academic Press, Inc., San Diego; **495,** ©Gail Mooney/CORBIS All Rights Reserved; **496,** iStockphoto.com; **497 (top),** iStockphoto.com; **497 (bottom),** iStockphoto.com; **Fig. 16.2 (a)** and **(b),** Richard Megna/Fundamental Photographs; **495,** iStockphoto.com; **503,** iStockphoto.com.

Chapter 17: Opener, Konrad Wothe/Minden Pictures; **522,** iStockphoto.com; **530,** Eric Schrader/Pearson; **531,** Pearson Asset Library/Pearson; **533,** Alan Levenson/Getty Images Inc.—Stone Allstock; **Fig. 17.1,** The Granger Collection; **537,** iStockPhoto.com; **541,** Pearson Asset Library/Pearson; **542,** Michael Temchine/NewsCom.

Chapter 18: Opener, Pixtal/AGE Fotostock; **553,** Peter Ginter/Science Faction; **553 (top),** iStockphoto.com; **553 (bottom),** iStockphoto.com; **564,** Pearson Asset Library/Pearson; **567,** Visuals Unlimited; **569,** iStockphoto.com; **576 (top),** Shutterstock; **576 (bottom),** Shutterstock; **Fig. 18.7(b),** Kim M. Gernert/Pearson Education/PH College; **Fig. 18.7(c),** Ken Eward/Photo

Researchers, Inc.; **Fig. 18.7(d)**, Kim M. Gernert/Pearson Education/PH College; **579 (top)** and **(bottom)**, Phototake NYC; **Fig. 18.9(a)**, Pearson Asset Library/Pearson; **582 (top)**, St. Mary's Hospital Medical School/Photo Researchers; **582 (bottom)**, NMSB/Custom Medical Stock Photo; **583**, iStockphoto.com.

Chapter 19: Opener, Phil Degginger/Alamy; **Fig. 19.1**, Richard Megna/Fundamental Photographs, NYC; **596**, Manuel C. Peitsch/Corbis/Bettmann; **597**, Manuel C. Peitsch/Corbis/Bettmann; **607**, iStockphoto; **613**, Abbott Laboratories; **614**, Ken Eward/Science Source/Photo Researchers; **615**, iStockphoto.com; **619**, iStockphoto.com.

Chapter 20: Opener, Luca Bruno/AP; **636**, Michal Heron/Pearson Education/PH College; **641**, Martin Shields/Alamy; **642**, Don W. Fawcett/Science Source/Photo Researchers, Inc.; **646**, Alan Sirulnikoff/Photo Researchers, Inc.; **647**, Shutterstock; **651**, Garden Raw Foods; **653**, Prasanna, M.D., Vondrasek, J., Wlodawer, A., Bhat, T.N., Application of InChI to curae, index and query 3-D structures. *PROTEINS. Structure, Function and Bioinformatics* 60, 1-4 (2005). (http://xpdb.nist.gov/hivsdb/hivsdb.html)

Chapter 21: Opener, Martin Harvey/Peter Arnold, Inc.; **659**, iStockphoto.com; **661**, iStockphoto.com; **663**, Al Giddings/Al Giddings Images, Inc.; **671**, iStockphoto.com; **673**, iStockphoto.com; **681 (a)** and **(b)**, Donald Clegg/Pearson Education/PH College; **Fig. 21.11(b)**, Manuel C. Peitsch/Corbis/Bettmann; **683**, Left-hand image: Clyde Gibbons, Martin C. Montgomery, Andrew G.W. Leslie & John E. Walker, The structure of the central stalk in bovine F1-ATPase at 2.4 × resolution in *Nature Structural Biology 7,* 1055-1061 (2000) Fig. 1a on page 1055. Right-hand image: Daniela Stock, Andrew G.W. Leslie, John E. Walker, Molecular Architecture of the Rotary Motor in AT Synthase, *Science* 26 November 1999: Vol. 286, no. 5445, pp. 1700-705 Fig. 2a (left) page 1702; **686**, iStockphoto.com.

Chapter 22: Opener, iStockphoto.com; **698**, iStockphoto.com; **704**, Shutterstock; **Fig. 22.4(a)**, Corbis Premium RF/Alamy; **Fig. 22.4(b)**, Eric Schrader/Pearson; **Fig. 22.4(c)**, iStockphoto.com; **713**, Eric Schrader/Pearson; **716 (top)**, Michael & Patricia Fogden/Minden Pictures; **716 (bottom)**, David Polack/Corbiss/Stock Market; **717**, Doug Allan/Oxford Scientific Films/Animals Animals/Earth Scenes; **720**, Larry Mulvehill/Science Source/Photo Researchers, Inc.; **722**, GlaxoSmithKline plc.

Chapter 23: Opener, Batista Moon/Shutterstock; **730**, Photo Lennart Nilsson/Albert Bonniers Forlag; **734**, Coordinates by T. Alber, G.A. Petsko and E. Lolis; image by Molecular Graphics and Modelling, Duke University. Simon & Schuster/PH College; **736 (left, middle, and right)**, iStockphoto.com; **Fig. 23.4**, Andrea Mattevi and Wim G.J. Hol/Pearson Education/PH College; **745**, iStockphoto.com; **748**, Winslow Townson/AP; **751**, Benelux/Photo Researchers, Inc.

Chapter 24: Opener, iStockphoto.com; **761**, Marcel Mochet/NewsCom; **763**, Eric Schrader/Pearson; **765**, Frank Lane Picture Agency/Corbis/Bettmann; **767**, iStockphoto.com; **759**, C Squared Studios/Getty Images, Inc.—Photodisc; **762**, Royalty Free/CORBIS All Rights Reserved; **777**, Kristen Brochmann/Fundamental Photographs, NYC.

Chapter 25: Opener, Art Wolfe/Getty Images Inc.—Stone Allstock; **791**, SPL/Photo Researchers, Inc.; **794**, John Sholtis/Amgen Inc.; **798**, iStockphoto.com.

Chapter 26: Opener, Javier Larea/SuperStock, Inc.; **809**, Micrograph by Conly L. Rieder, Division of Molecular Medicine, Wadsworth Center, Albany, New York 12201-0509; **813**, Prof. K. Seddon & Dr. T. Evans, Queen's University, Belfast/Photo Researchers, Inc.; **820**, Centers for Disease Control; **Fig. 26.4(b)**, reproduced by permission from H.J. Kreigstein and D.S. Hogness, *Proceedings of the National Academy of Sciences* 71:136 (1974), page 137, Fig. 2; **Fig. 26.7(b)**, Ken Eward/Science Source/Photo Researchers, Inc.; **834;** Centers for Disease Control; **822**, AP Wide World Photos.

Chapter 27: Opener, James King-Holmes/Photo Researchers, Inc.; **841**, BSIP/Ermakorr/Photo Researchers, Inc.; **843**, SPL/Photo Researchers, Inc.; **844 (right)**, Shutterstock; **844 (left, top)**, Dinodia/The Image Works; **844 (left, bottom)**, Biophoto Associates/Photo Researchers, Inc.; **834**, NewsCom; **849**, Dr. Gopal Murti/Photo Researchers, Inc.; **852**, Sinclair Stammers/Photo Researchers, Inc.; **854**, Courtesy Syngenta; **856**, Wong Maye-e/AP.

Chapter 28: Opener, Shutterstock; **862**, Eric Schrader/Pearson; **867**, iStockphoto.com; **869**, Dr. P. Marazzi/Photo Researchers, Inc.; **870**, Photo Researchers, Inc.; **874**, Staff Sgt. Eric T. Sheler/U.S. Air Force.

Chapter 29: Opener, ©Andrew Brookes/CORBIS All Rights Reserved; **884 (top)**, Bryan F. Peterson/Corbis/Stock Market; **884 (bottom)**, Mark Burnett/Photo Researchers, Inc.; **889 (left)**, Biology Media/Science Source/Photo Researchers, Inc.; **889 (right)**, Photo Lennart Nilsson/Albert Bonniers Forlag; **891**, Volker Steger/Peter Arnold, Inc.; **Fig. 29.10**, Michal Heron/Pearson Education/PH College; **893**, Bill Longcore/Photo Researchers, Inc.; **897**, Colin Cuthbert/Photo Researchers, Inc.

Index

Functional Groups of Importance in Biochemical Molecules

Functional Group	Structure	Type of Biomolecule
Amino group	$-NH_3^+$, $-NH_2$	Alkaloids and neurotransmitters; amino acids and proteins (Sections 15.1, 15.3, 15.6, 18.3, 18.7, 20.6)
Hydroxyl group	$-OH$	Monosaccharides (carbohydrates) and glycerol: a component of triacylglycerols (lipids) (Sections 17.4, 22.4, 24.2)
Carbonyl group	$$\overset{O}{\underset{\|}{\overset{\|\|}{-C-}}}$$	Monosaccharides (carbohydrates); in acetyl group (CH_3CO) used to transfer carbon atoms during catabolism (Sections 16.1, 17.4, 21.4, 21.8, 22.4)
Carboxyl group	$$-\overset{O}{\overset{\|\|}{C}}-OH, \quad -\overset{O}{\overset{\|\|}{C}}-O^-$$	Amino acids, proteins, and fatty acids (lipids) (Sections 17.1, 18.3, 18.7, 24.2)
Amide group	$$-\overset{O}{\overset{\|\|}{C}}-\underset{\|}{N}-$$	Links amino acids in proteins; formed by reaction of amino group and carboxyl group (Sections 17.1, 17.4, 18.7)
Carboxylic acid ester	$$-\overset{O}{\overset{\|\|}{C}}-O-R$$	Triacylglycerols (and other lipids); formed by reaction of carboxyl group and hydroxyl group (Sections 17.1, 17.4, 24.2)
Phosphates: mono-, di-, tri-	$$-\underset{\|}{\overset{\|}{C}}-O-\overset{O}{\underset{\underset{O^-}{\|}}{\overset{\|\|}{P}}}-O^-$$ $$-\underset{\|}{\overset{\|}{C}}-O-\overset{O}{\underset{\underset{O^-}{\|}}{\overset{\|\|}{P}}}-O-\overset{O}{\underset{\underset{O^-}{\|}}{\overset{\|\|}{P}}}-O^-$$ $$-\underset{\|}{\overset{\|}{C}}-O-\overset{O}{\underset{\underset{O^-}{\|}}{\overset{\|\|}{P}}}-O-\overset{O}{\underset{\underset{O^-}{\|}}{\overset{\|\|}{P}}}-O-\overset{O}{\underset{\underset{O^-}{\|}}{\overset{\|\|}{P}}}-O^-$$	ATP and many metabolism intermediates (Sections 17.8, 21.5, and throughout metabolism sections)
Hemiacetal group	$$-\underset{\underset{OR}{\|}}{\overset{\|}{C}}-OH$$	Cyclic forms of monosaccharides; formed by a reaction of carbonyl group with hydroxyl group (Sections 16.7, 22.4)
Acetal group	$$-\underset{\underset{OR}{\|}}{\overset{\|}{C}}-OR$$	Connects monosaccharides in disaccharides and larger carbohydrates; formed by reaction of carbonyl group with hydroxyl group (Sections 16.7, 22.7, 22.9)